D1542398

MANAGEMENT SCIENCE

MANAGEMENT SCIENCE

FOURTH EDITION

Laurence J. Moore
Virginia Polytechnic Institute and State University

Sang M. Lee
University of Nebraska

Bernard W. Taylor, III
Virginia Polytechnic Institute and State University

Allyn and Bacon   *Boston   London   Toronto   Sydney   Tokyo   Singapore*

Editor-in-Chief, Business and Economics: Rich Wohl
Editorial Assistant: Dominique Vachon
Cover Administrator: Linda Dickinson
Composition Buyer: Linda Cox
Manufacturing Buyer: Megan Cochran
Editorial-Production Service: Betty O'Bryant
Cover Designer: Susan Paradise

Library of Congress Cataloging-in-Publication Data
Moore, Laurence J.
    Management science / Laurence J. Moore, Sang M. Lee, Bernard W.
Taylor, III. — 4th ed.
        p.   cm.
    Includes bibliographical references and index.
    ISBN 0-205-15030-6
    1. Management science.   I. Lee, Sang M.   II. Taylor,
Bernard W. III. Title.
T56.L434   1992   92-20371
658.4'03—dc20   CIP

Text with AB:QM software
(5¼-inch and 3½-inch disks)   Text alone

9 780205 146376   9 780205 150304
ISBN 0-205-14637-6   ISBN 0-205-15030-6
H46378   H50305

We gratefully acknowledge the use in this text of LINDO, STORM, AB:QM, and GINO
management science software programs, which are referenced on page 847 and which constitute a continuation of this copyright page.

Printed in the United States of America
10 9 8 7 6 5 4   98 97 96

To my wife, Nancy
and my children, Becky, Andy, and Stefani

To my wife, Joyce
and my children Tosca and Amy

To my wife, Diane
and my children, Kathleen and Lindsey

Brief Contents

Contents

1

Introduction to Management Science

2

Introduction to Linear Programming

he Simplex Method

4

Duality and Sensitivity Analysis

5

Transportation and Assignment Problems

6

Network Models, Including CPM/PERT

7

Inventory Models

Decision Theory and Games

385

9

Markov Analysis

)

ueuing Theory   464

11

Simulation

14

Integer and Zero-One Programming   6

5

onlinear Programming   737

6

nplementation of Management Science   757

ntroduction to Matrix Methods   772

B

Calculus-Based (Classical) Optimization

7

C

Tables

8

D

AB:QM Tutorial

8

Preface

The field of management science encompasses a number of quantitative techniques and logical methodology for applying these techniques to decision-making problems. The purpose of this text is to provide the reader with a fundamental coverage of the techniques that comprise management science and to demonstrate their applications. This textbook intended primarily for graduate and upper-level undergraduate students in business administration.

Management science is a relatively new but increasingly accepted area of required curriculum in academic programs in business and administration. In the past, many of quantitative techniques that are now included in management science were taught almost exclusively in engineering, science, or doctoral-level business programs. The application these techniques to management decision-making problems was conducted primarily by specialists in the field with advanced technical degrees. The increased emphasis on the quantitative skills of undergraduate business students and the proliferation of the personal computer, however, have facilitated the inclusion of management science as an integral component of the business degree programs at most colleges and universities. Consequently more and more graduates are entering the professional business environment with management science skills. The successful application of management science techniques by the graduates has, in turn, increased the popular acceptance of the field.

As a result of the increasing popularity of the field, most business schools now of advanced courses (or sequences of courses) in management science at the undergraduate level required courses in management science at the master's (including the master of business administration) level, and doctoral programs in management science. It is for these courses and students that this text is intended.

Although this text was written for advanced undergraduate- and graduate-level courses in management science (or quantitative methods), we have attempted to maintain a basic straightforward presentation of the topics. The process of applying management science decision-making problems consists of identifying and analyzing the problem, building mathematical model of the problem, and then solving or testing the model using various quantitative techniques. Wherever possible, examples are employed to demonstrate this process and the various techniques in lieu of a proliferation of complex mathematical formulas. We have attempted to provide the student with conceptual knowledge of the properties, assumptions, and limitations of management science models and the realities of the decision environment. The advanced nature of the text derives from its detailed and in-depth coverage of each individual topic and the inclusion of all the topics most frequently associated with management science.

The degree of mathematical sophistication required of the business student using the text varies with the particular topic being covered. Chapters 1 through 5 require only college algebra as a prerequisite. Chapters 7 (Inventory Models), 11 (Simulation), and 15 (Nonlinear Programming) require some calculus. Chapters 6 (Network Models), 8 (Decision Theory and Games), 9 (Markov Analysis), 10 (Queuing Theory), and 11 (Simulation) also require some preliminary foundation in probability and statistics. Comprehensive appendices on linear algebra and matrices and calculus are provided, which can be used as either teaching or review aids for these fundamental prerequisites.

Because of the extensive and detailed coverage of topics, this text can be used in conjunction with a variety of course outlines. In general, it is not possible to cover all of the topics in this text in a one-quarter or one-semester course. Typically, an introductory M.B.A.-level course in management science will include the basic topics of linear programming contained in Chapters 2 through 5 plus one or more advanced topics in mathematical programming, such as goal programming (Chapter 13) or integer programming (Chapter 14), or several optimization topics, such as network models (Chapter 6), inventory (Chapter 7), or simulation (Chapter 11). A typical two-quarter sequence might cover linear programming topics and network and inventory models in the first quarter and dynamic programming in the second quarter. An academic-year sequence could cover all topics in the text.

Alternatively, selected portions of the text can be used for advanced undergraduate and graduate courses that are more specialized. For example, Chapters 12 through 15 exclusively could be used for a course in advanced topics in mathematical programming. Portions of the text can also be used for courses in such areas as linear programming and probabilistic models. The figure on page xxv shows the chapters grouped by major subject areas and their approximate relationships to the overall subject matter of management science.

Each chapter is accompanied by questions or problems that give the student practice in the solution techniques and demonstrate the applicability of management science to decision-making problems. The solution of these problems in conjunction with the textual material should provide the student with a thorough understanding of the individual quantitative techniques and an overall comprehension of the management science process.

We have revised the entire text to reflect the requests and recommendations for improvement received from numerous users and reviewers of the book. Our basic commitment to presenting the fundamental concepts in a straightforward and readable manner, however, remains unchanged.

For this fourth edition we have added a number of examples illustrating the use of personal computers to solve problems. A variety of different software packages has been employed for this purpose: AB:QM by Lee; LINDO and GINO by Schrage; and STORM by Emmons, Flowers, Khot, and Mathur. In each instance we have attempted to demonstrate software that has the required capability and is user friendly, inexpensive, and widely available. Also, we have included summaries of articles, which appeared in the *Interfaces* journal, reporting on real-world applications of management science techniques.

Management Science, fourth edition, is available in two forms: The text alone (ISBN 0-205-15030-6) and the text with the AB:QM software (ISBN 0-205-14637-6). The text with AB:QM version includes both 5¼-inch and 3½-inch disks. Supplements that accompany the text are *Solutions Manual, Test Bank,* and *Computerized Test Bank* (IBM: 5¼-inch disk).

Overall, we believe that the fourth edition of this text represents a significant improvement over the first three editions in terms of clarity of presentation of complex topics, illustrated applications of techniques presented, and exercises testing students' understanding of the topics included in each chapter.

Acknowledgments

We would like to acknowledge the assistance of numerous individuals who have provided comments and recommendations concerning the development of this text. Most especially, we would like to thank the following reviewers—Thomas E. Armstrong, The University of Maryland; Harvey J. Iglarsh, Georgetown University; James T. Lynch, Thunderbird School

of International Management; Yunus Kathawala, Eastern Illinois University; Danny Mye
Bowling Green University; and B. Madhu Rao, Bowling Green University—as well as o
colleagues at the University of Nebraska–Lincoln and at Virginia Tech. We very mu
appreciate the editorial assistance provided by Betty O'Bryant during the production pha
of the book and by Rich Wohl of Allyn and Bacon throughout the entire revision project

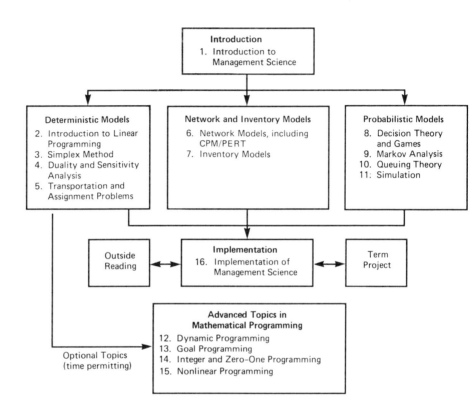

1

Introduction to Management Science

Management science is the application of the methods and techniques of modern science to today's problems of management decision making. The primary objective of management science is to help managers make better decisions by solving problems more effectively. In the interest of attaining this objective, a number of mathematical techniques and systematic procedures have been developed and adapted from other disciplines, such as the natural sciences, mathematics, and engineering, and applied to the problems of management.

At first glance, it may seem incongruous to combine the terms *management* and *science,* since management is often thought of as more of an art than a science. However, there has been an increasing effort during this century to apply scientific principles to the management process. At the turn of the century, early industrial engineers began to apply scientific techniques to industrial management. F. W. Taylor and Frank and Lillian Gilbreth were instrumental in the development and application of such scientific approaches to management as work standards, job design, and motion study. H. L. Gantt pioneered in scheduling with the Gantt chart, which serves as a foundation for some of the scheduling techniques most widely used today. Although these developments may seem simplistic to the sophisticated student and manager of today, at the time they represented significant "scientific" breakthroughs.

Interest in applying the methods of science to management problems has increased with the passage of time. It received a strong boost during World War II with the development of **operational research** in England. The British brought together groups of scientists from various disciplines to apply scientific methods to military problems—that is, to do "research" on military "operations." This approach was credited with the successful deployment of radar installations that were instrumental in the victory of the Battle of Britain. This same approach—bringing together scientists from different disciplines to apply various scientific techniques to logistical and operational problems—was later adopted successfully by the U.S. military forces.

It was only natural that a return to peacetime saw the development of an environment conducive to operations research in business and industry. The accelerated growth of the war economy, both in the United States and abroad, created a favorable environ ment for innovations in industry, new products and inventions, expanded industrial capacity, and increased consumer demand. This expansion, in turn, resulted in an increase in the number and complexity of management problems. It was in this environment that some managers and management analysts began to experiment with new problem-solving methods and techniques derived from the fundamentals of operations research. These managers were interested in solving problems and were receptive to new ways to do so.

One new problem-solving approach that encompassed the principles of operations research involved analyzing problems with the assistance of mathematical representations of problems, known as models. With the aid of various quantitative techniques, models were experimented on and manipulated to obtain solutions, which, in turn, assisted the manager in reaching better decisions. This general approach to problem solving also came to be known as *management science*. However, the applications of these techniques and models to decision making in general were limited by the capacity of people to solve them. The development of the electronic computer in the 1950s and 1960s provided the capacity to solve large and complex problems rapidly, eliminating a roadblock to the development and application of management science.

Today management science is a recognized and popular discipline in the field of business management. Applications of the quantitative techniques comprising management science are widespread, and they have been credited in numerous instances with increasing the efficiency and productivity of management. This increased popularity is reflected in the number of colleges and universities offering undergraduate and graduate management science courses and degree programs in management science (also called operations research, quantitative analysis, and decision science). Management science is now part of the fundamental curriculum of most programs in business administration.

Our purpose in this text is to provide an introduction to the more frequently used management science models and techniques. In conjunction with this objective, the methodology and logic behind mathematical model building will be discussed in each chapter. As we develop the mathematical models, it is important to keep in mind several basic facts about management science.

First, management science can be applied to a number of different types of organizations. It can be used to solve problems in such fields as government, military, business and industry, academia, and health care. Management science has evolved to the point where its application of scientific tools has become an invaluable aid in solving problems in a multitude of decision-making environments.

Second, although the mathematical techniques presented in this text emphasize manual solution, in every case programs or capabilities exist for computerized solutions. In all but the last chapter of this text, the computerized solution of problems is demonstrated and the computer program output shown.

Finally, although numerous quantitative techniques and examples of models and their applications are stressed in the text, it should be remembered that management science is more than just a collection of techniques. Management science involves a philosophy of approaching a problem in a logical manner, as does any science. An understanding of the logical, consistent, and systematic manner of problem solving employed by management science is even more basic to effective management than is a knowledge of the mechanics of the quantitative techniques themselves.

THE SCIENTIFIC METHOD

As noted in the previous section, management science encompasses the application of scientific approach to problem solving. The objective of scientific decision making is to make good choices from the existing alternatives by utilizing systematic means to generate information concerning the decision environment and evaluate the range of decision alternatives in a logical, precise manner. Thus, management science includes a carefully constructed methodology for analysis. This methodology, which has been adapted from the natural sciences, is termed the *scientific method*.

The scientific method consists of a generally recognized set of steps. Whether these steps are followed in precisely the order described often depends on the nature of the problem being studied and the individuals performing the analysis. However, a basic premise of scientific analysis is a rigorous and careful approach to all phases of the analysis.

Observation

This first step of the scientific method is the continuing study of the system (organization) in an attempt to identify problems. It is essential that the management scientists be always alert for operational problems. When a problem is indicated, the management scientist must analyze it carefully as a basis for subsequent steps in the scientific method.

Definition of the Problem

Before solutions to a problem can be considered, an accurate definition of the problem must be formulated. It has often been reported by organizations that failure in problem solving has resulted from an incorrect definition of the problem.

In addition to defining the problem, this step includes identifying the possible *alternatives* available to management. Also, the *objectives*, or *goals*, of the system under analysis must be clearly defined. The stated objectives help to focus the attention of the analyst on the problem and its effects on the total organization. Finally, in order to evaluate the performance of a proposed solution, *measurement criteria*, such as cost or profit, must be specified.

Model Construction

The classical description of the third step in the natural sciences is *formulation of the hypothesis*. For our purposes this step involves *formulation of a model* through which the system can be manipulated and experimented on. Models are abstractions of reality in which only those *components* relevant to the problem being analyzed are included. Thus a major portion of model construction involves identification of relevant components and description of the *relationships* among these components.

A model can take any of several alternative forms. It can be a graph, a flow chart, network, or a set of mathematical equations. This latter form is often referred to as symbolic model, and it is the type we will be most frequently concerned with in this text.

Model Validation

The fourth step requires that all assumptions employed in the construction of the model be identified and validated. In other words, the model must be checked to see if it correctly reflects the operation of the system it represents. The manager must operate and experiment with the model to make sure it reacts in the same way as the real system.

Problem Solution

Although the classical statement of the fifth step is *experimentation with the model,* in reality this step may involve solution or operation of the model in order to observe its performance under different conditions. Whether or not the problem reflected by the model is solved depends on the nature of the study and the objective of the analysis.

At this stage the various quantitative solution techniques and methods that are a major part of management science enter the process. Problem solving generally implies the application of one or more of these techniques to the model.

Implementation

The last step is the logical result of model development and problem solution. A scientific study is of little value unless it is ultimately put to use in some form. The true value of the process is in the impact that implementation has on the performance of the system studied. A critical aspect of this step is the interface between the management scientist (the model builder) and the management environment, not only at the end of the model development and solution but throughout the analysis procedure. To begin the scientific process, the model builder abstracts from reality; to complete the process, he or she must reestablish the model in reality.

Although the management science process includes all of the steps discussed above, the primary focus of this text is on two steps: model construction and solution. Therefore, a more careful delineation of model types and solution techniques will now be presented.

MODEL CLASSIFICATION

Models may be categorized into two groups: **deterministic models** and **probabilistic models.** Deterministic models are models developed under conditions of assumed certainty. They are necessarily simplifications of reality, since certainty is indeed rare. The advantage of such models is that they can generally be manipulated and solved with relative ease. Thus, complicated systems can often be modeled and analyzed if it can be assumed that all the numerical components of the system are known with certainty.

Probabilistic models are those in which uncertainty is assumed. Although incorporating uncertainty into a model may yield a more realistic representation of the situation, such a model is generally more difficult to analyze.

In this text, the first seven chapters deal predominantly with deterministic models. Chapters 2 through 5 deal exclusively with linear programming, one of the most familiar and frequently used management science techniques. Chapters 6 and 7 present the additional deterministic techniques of network and inventory models, although some aspects of these models are probabilistic. Chapters 8 through 11 present the probabilistic models and techniques of decision theory, game theory, Markov analysis, queueing, and simulation. Chapters 12 through 15 cover some of the more advanced topics in mathematical programming, including dynamic programming, goal programming, integer programming, and nonlinear programming.

ELEMENTS OF MODEL CONSTRUCTION

Management science models contain several elements that are combined in the construction of the model. These elements include **variables** and **parameters,** and their relationships. In this section these elements will be defined in greater detail. As an aid in presenting these elements and their relationships in model construction, a break-even model will be used as an example.

Break-even analysis is often referred to as cost-volume-profit analysis, because the purpose of the analysis is to study the relationship of cost, volume, and profit to determine the volume that equates revenue and cost. Break-even is defined as the volume (level of operation in terms of unit quantity, dollar volume, or percentage of capacity) required to arrive at the point where total revenue equals total costs.

For example, a book publisher is concerned with determining the quantity of book sales required to cover the fixed costs of publishing a new book. If the new book includes costly design and typesetting features, then fixed costs will be high and the resulting break-even volume will be higher than normal. If the book must compete with several similar books, forcing the publisher to offer the book at a competitive price, then the publisher can undertake the project only if projected sales volume at the competitive price exceeds the computed break-even point in revenue versus cost.

A manufacturing firm considering investment in automated equipment for production operations can make use of break-even analysis to determine the feasibility of doing so. Although investment in automated equipment may reduce the variable costs of production, the benefits of reduced variable costs may not offset the increase in the fixed cost required. Break-even analysis can assist management in determining the level of operation required to make such an investment beneficial.

Identification of Model Components

The first step of model construction is to abstract from the system of interest the elements that are essential to the problem analysis. The usual approach is to translate the essential elements and components into various symbols, to facilitate model construction and manipulation.

The major components of the break-even analysis model are total revenue, fixed costs, variable costs, and volume (or quantity).

Total Revenue

Total revenue reflects the sales forecast for the planning period and consists of the selling price multiplied by the quantity sold.

Fixed Costs

Fixed costs are costs not directly related to volume of production or sales. Fixed costs remain constant in dollar amount regardless of the level of output. Some examples of fixed cost are

> Depreciation on plant and equipment
> Executive and office staff salaries
> Property insurance and taxes
> Property rent
> Interest on investment
> Lump-sum advertising expenses

Variable Costs

Variable costs are often referred to as direct costs and are directly related to the volume of production or sales. Total variable costs are computed as the variable cost per unit multiplied by the level of operation (quantity). Some examples of variable costs are

> Direct materials
> Direct labor
> Sales commissions
> Packaging
> Freight out

Volume

The **volume** (quantity) of the operation is the level of operation, as specified in terms of (1) unit quantity, (2) dollar volume, or (3) percentage of capacity. Both total revenue and total variable costs are related to the level of operation (volume of production or sales).

ariables of the Model

The **variables** of a model are subdivided into at least three categories: (1) the solution, or decision, variable; (2) the criterion variable; and (3) exogenous variables.

Solution Variables

The first and most important type of variable that must be identified in any modeling process is the **solution (decision) variable.** A solution variable, which typically represents what the manager is making a decision about, is expressed as a mathematical symbol (as are all other variables). It is called a *variable* because the value it takes on can vary over a range of values as defined in the mathematical model. In the case of break-even analysis, the solution variable is the break-even volume, or quantity, that is to be solved for. In this model, Q will be designated as the symbol for quantity. Since the solution of this variable is often the basis for a decision, the solution variable is sometimes referred to as the decision variable. Alternatively, because the solution value of this variable results in a decision on the part of the manager, it may be said to be a controllable variable (the manager has control over decisions).

Criterion Variable

The **criterion variable** is the variable to be measured in order to evaluate various solutions. The criterion for evaluation of the example model is **profit,** where profit equal total revenue minus total cost. For example, at one level of output the profit might be negative, whereas at a higher level of output the profit might be positive. In the break even model, the objective is to solve for the quantity of output at which total revenue equals total cost—that is, profit equals zero. Thus, profit is designated as the criterion variable for our model and is denoted by the symbol Z.

Exogenous Variables

Exogenous variables are variables that derive their value from outside the system being modeled and, generally, cannot be controlled by the decision maker. The basic break even model assumes a perfectly competitive market such that price is determined by market forces and cannot be manipulated by the decision maker. Under such conditions the firm can produce and sell any quantity desired without affecting price. Thus, price $P,$ is an exogenous variable in the break-even model.

Parameters of the Model

The **parameters** of a model are the remaining elements of the model that complete the formulation of the relationships among the variables. Parameters are generally constant (numerical) values, which change only for different cases of the same problem.

In a model represented by a mathematical equation, the parameters of the model are the coefficients of the equation. The purpose of representing the parameters of the model as symbols is to obtain a solution to the model in a general form. A generalized mathematical model allows different cases of the same type of problem to be solved by substituting new values for the parameters into the general form. In this way, solutions can be obtained for specific problems without resolving the entire model.

The parameters of the break-even model are fixed cost and variable cost. Fixed cost will be denoted symbolically by FC and variable cost by VC.

It should be pointed out here that it is sometimes difficult to distinguish between exogenous variables and parameters. The given exogenous variable, price, might also be thought of as a model parameter, since it is assumed to be a given constant for the model Likewise, although a model component may be a parameter or exogenous variable in the model for one problem, it may be the decision variable for another problem. In the case of break-even analysis, both price and fixed cost can take on the role of decision variable under certain conditions.

Since the break-even model is concerned with the point at which total revenue equals total cost, we will assign each of these two model components a symbolic representation. Total revenue will be denoted by TR, and total cost will be denoted by TC.

Most management science models are composites of submodels. It is generally simplest to construct each of the submodels separately and then aggregate the submodels into the overall model as a last step. We will demonstrate this approach in construction of the break-even model by constructing the submodels for total revenue and total cost and then linking the two together into an overall model.

The model symbols are summarized as follows:

Q = quantity (solution variable)
Z = profit (criterion variable)
P = price (exogenous variable)
FC = fixed cost (parameter)
VC = variable cost (parameter)
TR = total revenue (submodel variable)
TC = total cost (submodel variable)

Model Relationships and Construction

The construction of the model consists of identifying the relationships among the system components. Where possible, the functional relationship among the variables and parameters is specified explicitly. This can be done in the case of the break-even analysis model, as the model is in fact a profit model (profit equals total revenue minus total cost).

In order to analyze any model and arrive at a decision, the relationship of the criterion variable to the solution variable must be specified. In break-even analysis, profit (Z) is the criterion variable, and quantity (Q) is the solution variable. Thus, the following relationship must be developed:

$$Z = f(Q)$$

(read as "Profit, Z, is functionally related to order size, Q").

We also know that the relationship of the criterion variable to the two submodels, TR and TC, is

$$Z = TR - TC$$

We will, therefore, develop each submodel separately and join the two as our last step.

Total Revenue

Total revenue is simply price multiplied by the quantity produced or sold. Therefore, our first submodel is

$$TR = P \cdot Q$$

Total Cost

Total variable cost is the unit variable cost multiplied by the quantity. Fixed cost is a constant dollar value, independent of volume. Thus, the second submodel is

$$TC = FC + VC \cdot Q$$

Profit Model

The profit model is given in terms of the criterion variable, solution variable, exogenous variable, and parameters as

$$Z = P \cdot Q - FC - VC \cdot Q$$

or

Profit = price $\cdot$ quantity $-$ fixed cost $-$ variable cost $\cdot$ quantity

Solution of the Model

We must now solve for the value of the solution variable (Q) in terms of the othe variables and parameters of the model. An objective in break-even analysis is to determin the value of Q for which profit (Z) equals zero. Therefore, the solution procedure to b employed here is to set the model for profit equal to zero and solve for Q. The solution procedure is as follows:

$$P \cdot Q - FC - VC \cdot Q = 0 \qquad \text{setting profit model equal to 0}$$
$$P \cdot Q - VC \cdot Q = FC \qquad \text{transposing FC}$$
$$Q(P - VC) = FC \qquad \text{collecting } Q \text{ separately}$$
$$Q_{BE} = \frac{FC}{P - VC} \qquad \text{dividing through by } P - VC$$

We identify Q_{BE} as the break-even point quantity. At the point where the volume of operation equals Q_{BE}, profit will equal zero (and total revenue will equal total cost) Note that $P - VC$ is the commonly known term **unit contribution**. Thus, the break even point is determined by dividing fixed cost by unit contribution.

The model solution illustrates the previously discussed general form of a solution that is, the break-even quantity can be determined by inserting the values for fixed cost price, and variable cost for the symbols FC, P, and VC in the Q_{BE} equation and obtaining a solution directly. Not all models can be solved in a general form, but whenever possible it is preferable to do so.

The Graphic Model and Solution

The preceding break-even model is displayed graphically in Figure 1.1. The graph illus trates that the break-even quantity, Q_{BE}, occurs at the point where profit, Z, equals zero (and where total revenue equals total cost). If we refer back to the model solution process

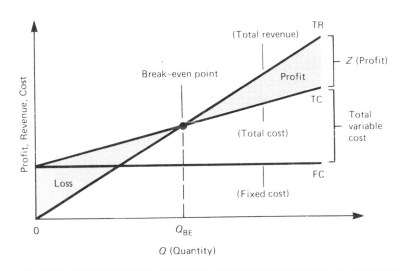

Figure 1.1 *Graphic Illustration of the Break-Even Model*

we see that the break-even point occurs where quantity multiplied by unit contribution is equal to fixed cost, or

$$Q(P - VC) = FC$$

Thus, as quantity is increased from zero to Q_{BE}, the total contribution toward fixed cost (quantity times unit contribution) is progressively covering a larger portion of fixed cost, and the loss is being reduced. As quantity is increased beyond Q_{BE}, the expression $Q(P - VC)$ exceeds fixed cost in the form of increasing profit.

Computerized Model Solution

In this text the various mathematical models that are presented in each chapter are solved manually, as in the case of the break-even model. However, the capability exists to solve these models using a computer, and so computerized solutions are also demonstrated throughout the text.

A number of different software packages are currently available for solving management science models on both mainframe and personal computers. In order to contrast varying solution capabilities, input requirements, and output formats, several different software packages will be employed in this text, including AB:QM by Lee and Shim;[1] LINDO by Schrage;[2] and STORM by Emmons, Flowers, Khot, and Mathur.[3]

LINDO is a widely available and powerful mathematical programming package with both mainframe and personal computer versions; the other two are general management science software packages for the personal computer. Although all of these packages have their unique characteristics and capabilities, they have one common attribute—they are very *user-friendly* and thus easy to use.

As a simple illustration of how these software packages will be employed in the text, we will demonstrate the computerized solution of the break-even model using the AB:QM package.

Recall that the break-even model includes the parameters FC and VC (fixed costs and variable costs) and the exogenous variable P (price), which form the model to determine the break-even quantity, Q_{BE}:

$$Q_{BE} = \frac{FC}{P - VC}$$

If we let FC = \$10,000, VC = \$10, and P = \$30, then we can manually solve the model as follows:

$$Q_{BE} = \frac{10,000}{30 - 10}$$
$$= 500 \text{ units}$$

---

[1] S. M. Lee, *AB:QM: Allyn & Bacon Quantitative Methods 3.0* (Boston: Allyn and Bacon, 1993).

[2] L. Schrage, *LINDO, Release 5.0* (Chicago: LINDO Systems, Inc.); and L. Schrage, *User's Manual for Linear, Integer, and Quadratic Programming with LINDO,* Release 5.0 (San Francisco: The Scientific Press, 1991).

[3] H. Emmons, A. D. Flowers, C. M. Khot, and K. Mathur, *STORM. Quantitative Modeling for Decision Support,* Version 3.0 (Englewood Cliffs, N.J.: Simon & Schuster, 1992).

This model can be solved using AB:QM as shown below.

```
Program: Break-Even Analysis

Problem Title : Example

***** Input Data *****

Total Fixed Cost     :     10000.00
Unit Variable Cost   :        10.00
Unit Selling Price   :        30.00
Expected Sales Units :         0.00

***** Program Output *****

-------------------------------------
Total Fixed Cost     :     10000.00
Unit Variable Cost   :        10.00
Unit Selling Price   :        30.00
Expected Sales Units :      Unknown
-------------------------------------

-------------------------------------
Break-Even Dollars   :     15000.00
Break-Even Quantity  :       500.00
-------------------------------------

***** End of Output *****
```

It can be readily observed that the dialogue between the computer and the user is very friendly: the input requirements are easily interpreted and the output format is straightforward. These are characteristics of all the software packages that will be employed in the text. However, as will be demonstrated, their solution capabilities, in terms of variety and breadth, vary. A tutorial on AB:QM is contained in Appendix D.

EXAMPLES OF MANAGEMENT SCIENCE MODELS

In this section some of the model types to be presented in this text will be reviewed briefly. These models will, by necessity, be somewhat simplified.

Example 1.1   Product Mix Decision

A wood products firm produces two kinds of paneling: colonial and western. The paneling is processed through two operations: pressing and finishing. The decision problem facing management is how many sheets of each type of paneling to produce in a month in order to gain the most profit.

The problem confronting management is that unlimited production of paneling is not possible—the firm is limited by the amount of resources available to produce the products. The problem then is to allocate the resources in the optimal manner in order to maximize profit.

The firm has resources in terms of pounds of wood product available, plant hours available for pressing, hours available for finishing, and a dollar budget. The resource requirements and availabilities for each type of paneling, which constitute the parameters of the model, are as follows:

Resource	Resource Requirement per 100-Sheet Lot		Total Resources Available per Month
	Colonial	Western	
Wood product	20 lb	40 lb	5000 lb
Pressing	4 hr	6 hr	400 hr
Finishing	3 hr	4 hr	500 hr
Cost (budget)	$40	$60	$7000

The firm receives $80 profit for every 100-sheet lot of colonial paneling and $100 profit for every 100-sheet lot of western paneling.

According to the management science process, now that the problem has been defined, the next step is to develop a model of the system. In other words, a mathematical formulation must be developed.

First, solution, or decision, variables must be defined. Since the decision in this problem concerns the amount of each type of paneling to produce, the two solution variables are defined as follows:

x_1 = the number of 100-sheet lots of colonial paneling to produce in one month

x_2 = the number of 100-sheet lots of western paneling to produce in one month

Next, the objective of the firm, to obtain the maximum possible profit, is transformed into a mathematical equation:

Maximize profit = $\$80x_1 + \$100x_2$

In management science terminology, this equation is referred to as the **objective function**. It is the amount of profit received for any values of x_1 and x_2. For example, if x_1 = 10 and x_2 = 20 (10 lots of colonial paneling and 20 lots of western paneling), the profit is $2800—an amount achieved by substituting the given values of x_1 and x_2 into the objective function. The objective is to maximize the value of the function by determining the best values for x_1 and x_2.

The firm's problem, however, is to maximize profit within the limitations of its available resources. The next step is to transform the resource requirements and availabilities into mathematical relationships. For example, there are 5000 pounds of wood product available to make paneling. Each lot of colonial requires 20 pounds, and each lot of western requires 40 pounds. Thus, the amount of wood product used for colonial paneling will be $20x_1$ (20 pounds per lot times the number of lots), and the amount of wood product used for western paneling will be $40x_2$. The total amount of wood product used will be $20x_1 + 40x_2$, which must be 5000 pounds or less. The other three constraints for pressing, finishing, and budget are developed in a similar manner.

Wood product: $20x_1 + 40x_2 \leqslant 5000$ lb
Pressing: $4x_1 + 6x_2 \leqslant 400$ hr
Finishing: $3x_1 + 4x_2 \leqslant 500$ hr
Cost (budget): $40x_1 + 60x_2 \leqslant \$7000$

These relationships are referred to as **constraints** because they specify that the utilization of each resource cannot exceed the total amount of the resource available. The $\leqslant$ inequality signs indicate the limitations of these relationships (i.e., the firm can use an amount equal to or less than, but not more than, these resource amounts).

The mathematical model formulation can now be summarized as

Maximize $Z = 80x_1 + 100x_2$
subject to
$$20x_1 + 40x_2 \leqslant 5000$$
$$4x_1 + 6x_2 \leqslant 400$$
$$3x_1 + 4x_2 \leqslant 500$$
$$40x_1 + 60x_2 \leqslant 7000$$

The next step would be to solve this set of mathematical relationships to determine values for x_1 and x_2 that both satisfy the constraints and achieve the objective. However this step will be explained later in the text. This is a linear programming model, a topic that will be covered in Chapters 2 through 4. It is an example of a deterministic model that *optimizes* the specified criterion, subject to limited resources. That is, uncertainty i not considered in the model, which is formulated to determine the one "best," or "optimal," solution.

Example 1.2 Transportation Problem

An asphalt company produces asphalt at three plants within a geographic region. The asphalt is then transported in trucks from the plants to construction sites where roads are being paved. Presently the company is under contract to supply asphalt to three road paving locations. The decision problem for the management of this company is to minimize the cost of transporting asphalt from plants to construction sites. More specifically management desires to know the number of truckloads to ship from each plant to each road-paving site in order to minimize cost, given the availability of asphalt at each plant and the requirement at each paving site. The transportation costs from each plant to each site are given below in tabular form.

Plant	Transportation Costs to Each Paving Site			Supply (in truckloads)
	1	2	3	
A	$40	$25	$30	120
B	75	50	60	80
C	15	45	50	80
Demand (in truckloads)	150	70	60	280

The constraints of this problem are the maximum amounts of asphalt that the company is able to supply from each of its three plants and the amounts demanded at each site for the planning period. This information is given in the column labeled *supply* and the row labeled *demand*.

This problem can be formulated mathematically as a linear programming model within the following general framework:

> Minimize total transportation cost
> subject to
> > Supply constraints
> > Demand constraints

Within this model, the decision variables are the amounts transported from each site to each destination.

The supply constraints represent the fact that only a limited amount can be supplied from each plant (120, 80, and 80 truckloads, respectively). Thus, regardless of which of the three sites the asphalt is shipped to, total shipments from plant A cannot exceed 120. Similarly, a limited amount is demanded at each site (150, 70, and 60 truckloads, respectively). So regardless of which plant(s) the asphalt comes from, the total delivered to site 1 should not exceed 150 truckloads. The objective function signifies that the truckloads should be allocated in a manner that will meet the demand at the sites, not exceed the supply at each plant, and do so at the lowest transportation cost. Since the actual model formulation is somewhat more complex than that of the linear programming problem discussed previously, we will refrain from presenting it here. This model type is a special case of linear programming that will be presented in detail in Chapter 5.

Example 1.3   Construction Scheduling Problem

A construction company has contracted to build a new office building. The company's management wants to develop a construction schedule that will allow them to finish within the allotted time. They have identified five major steps in the building's construction: finalizing the design, digging footings, building the foundation, transporting steel and other materials, and constructing the building. The objective of the company is to complete the project on time.

As an aid in planning and scheduling, a precedence diagram for the different construction activities has been developed (see Figure 1.2). By allocating time to each building activity, one can turn this precedence diagram into a CPM/PERT network, which can be used to determine overall project duration. This type of project network can also be used to determine the time at which each event should occur in order to maintain the project schedule. (The circles in the network in Figure 1.2 indicate the completion of an activity and the start of another.) CPM/PERT (which is presented in Chapter 6) is just one of the network model types that will be presented in the text.

Example 1.4   Inventory Control Problem

Consider a manager of a plant who is concerned about the costs of keeping material on hand to produce products. The manager desires to have this inventory cost be as low as

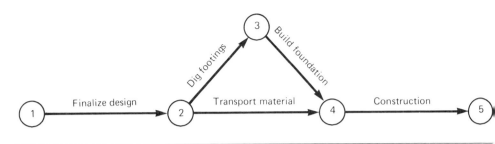

Figure 1.2 *A Precedence Diagram*

possible. The manager has determined that there are two primary costs associated with how much material is ordered and kept in inventory. First, there is the cost of ordering the material—that is, the costs involved in having the order processed, loaded on trucks, and delivered by the supplier. Second, there is the cost of carrying the material as inventory prior to its use. This cost includes the value of the storage space taken up by the material and the interest lost on money invested in inventory. The manager has determined that the sum of these two costs rises or falls depending on the amount of material ordered. Figure 1.3 is a graphic representation (a model) of these inventory costs for various order sizes, developed by the manager.

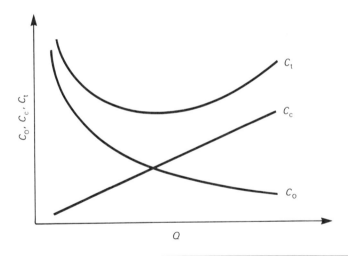

Figure 1.3 *Graphic Model of the Inventory Problem*

The graph in Figure 1.3 illustrates the relationship of three variables, C_o, C_c, and C_t, to a fourth variable, Q. The model is a simplified representation of inventory costs in which inventory carrying cost (C_c), ordering cost (C_o), and total inventory cost (C_t) are related to the quantity of material ordered (Q). For larger orders, the inventory carrying cost (C_c) is greater whereas the ordering cost (C_o) is lower, since fewer orders are required. For smaller orders, the carrying cost is lower but the ordering cost is greater, because of an increase in the number of orders. Total inventory cost (C_t) first decreases and then increases, as a function of order size. The objective is to determine the order size (Q) that minimizes the total of the two types of inventory costs ($C_o + C_c = C_t$). The mathematical

n Application of Management Science: Dispatching Trucks at Reynolds Metals Company

eynolds Metals Company is an international uminum company with sales (in 1989) of $6.2 llion, over half of which were in cans, flexible ackaging, and consumer products. Reynolds has 2 decentralized operating divisions, several ibsidiaries, and 60 domestic manufacturing icilities. Each division is a profit center sponsible for its own marketing, sales, ianufacturing, facilities, and operations. The ompany spends over $.25 billion annually on uck, rail, ship, and air transportation costs to eceive raw materials and ship its products from ver 120 locations, including plants, warehouses, ibsidiaries, and customers. Reynolds incurs nnual interstate truck freight bills in excess of 80 million.

Consistent with its decentralized operating hilosophy, the company's divisions and plants have traditionally been responsible for their own freight operations. Plants selected their own carriers, negotiated rates, and arranged shipments. However, because of variability in service and quality standards and concerns about costs, in 1987 Reynolds decided to centralize the management and operations of its interstate truck shipments. Using management science techniques and the leadership of management scientists, Reynolds was able to develop and introduce a Central Dispatch facility in Richmond, Virginia, that oversees the scheduling and servicing of truck shipments both internally and from suppliers. The company was also able to reduce the number of carriers it used from over 200 to 14 core carriers who were strong financially, had good drivers, were well-maintained, and had good and sufficient equipment.

determination of order sizes and costs for different inventory systems is the subject of Chapter 7.

xample 1.5   Feasibility Study for Facility Expansion

A bank's management is considering the installation of another drive-in window or windows to supplement the single drive-in window already in use. The bank operations officer has observed that on occasion the waiting line for the present drive-in window is so long that customers leave or become irate with the teller. The bank's management has requested the operations officer to analyze the teller system and determine how many additional windows would be required to achieve a reasonable waiting time for customers. The officer has also been instructed to compare the construction and operating costs for the window(s) with the estimated losses resulting from customer ill will when customers must wait for service.

This is a classic problem in queueing, or waiting line analysis. In Chapter 10, various queueing models will be presented that would enable the operations officer to perform the analysis requested by management. Information that can be obtained from these models includes the average time a customer must wait prior to service, the average number of customers waiting in line to be served, the average time a customer is at the bank (both in line and being served), the probability that a certain number of customers will be in line, and the percentage of time the teller is idle. This information can then be used to

The development of the Central Dispatch facility encompassed two management science modeling techniques—simulation and mixed integer programming. The simulation model was developed to provide on-time delivery service, which was the top priority of Central Dispatch. The service goal was set at 100% on-time delivery to customers. The mixed integer programming model was developed to select core carriers and deploy them in an optimal manner such that freight costs and truck shortages were minimized. The core carriers selected by the integer programming model were further evaluated by the simulation model. The simulation model replicated the daily shipping activities at the company's plants, warehouses, and suppliers. A typical day in the simulation includes identifying shipments, dispatching trucks, and shipping. A plant can request a truck for a shipment as much as four days in advance or as little as a few hours.

The simulation model was constructed using the SLAM simulation software and FORTRAN and was run on an IBM 3090 computer. The Central Dispatch model covers over 104 truck locations encompassing over 75,000 annual truck shipments.

The Central Dispatch management science models were developed at a cost of $618,000 for equipment, software, and programming. The Central Dispatch facility is saving Reynolds Metals over $7 million annually in freight costs. With the old, decentralized system, the on-time delivery (service) rate was approximately 80% and it is 95% with the new Central Dispatch system. The Central Dispatch system has given Reynolds a competitive advantage and has helped attract new customers. Management science was seen by Reynolds management to be essential to this project and was cited as the difference between success and failure.

Source: E. W. Moore, Jr., "The Indispensable Role of Management Science in Centralizing Freight Operations at Reynolds Metals Company," *Interfaces,* 21, no. 1 (January–February 1991): 107–129.

determine the cost trade-offs associated with building and operating new drive-in windows. Such information would allow the operations officer to determine the expected waiting time of customers at two windows instead of one and then to compare the construction and added operating costs with the decrease in losses resulting from dissatisfied customers. Note that the output generated from a queueing model is probabilistic and descriptive. In other words, queueing models are examples of models that do not optimize (do not seek a "best" solution), but provide operating statistics that describe the system being analyzed (e.g., average waiting time is a statistical descriptor).

In many cases queueing problems are so complex that they cannot be analyzed through traditional queueing models. In such cases simulation is a possible alternative modeling form. In a simulation a computerized description of the problem situation is constructed and used to generate the sort of operating statistics described previously. Simulation, which can be used as an alternative to many analytic models (i.e., models with a mathematical formulation and solution), is the topic of Chapter 11.

Example 1.6   Machine Acquisition Problem

A manufacturing firm is attempting to decide how many of three different types of new machines it must purchase to keep pace with normal plant growth and increasing product demand. The three machine types are small, medium, and heavy duty, and their costs are $1500, $3500, and $5000, respectively. The purchase of machines is constrained by space limitations, budget limitations, and maintenance capabilities. The firm's management staff has developed the following linear programming model for this decision problem:

Maximize sales $= \$2000x_1 + \$5000x_2 + \$8000x_3$
subject to
$$40x_1 + 70x_2 + 100x_3 \leqslant 750 \text{ ft}^2$$
$$\$1500x_1 + \$3500x_2 + \$5000x_3 \leqslant \$20,000$$
$$x_1 + x_2 + x_3 \leqslant 7$$

In this model, the values for x are nonnegative integers, which are the decision variables representing the number of machine purchases of each type. The objective function is the increase in dollar sales resulting from the new machines. The constraints reflect (1) the space limitations in the plant, (2) the budget limitation for the purchase of machinery, and (3) the total number of machines that can be purchased and maintained.

This model structure is similar to the model structure for the linear programming model in our first example. However, the crucial difference is that in this model the values of the decision variables that optimize the solution must be integers—it is not possible to purchase fractions of machines. This difference requires a substantial adjustment in the solution technique used in a normal linear programming model. Therefore, the topic of integer programming is presented as an advanced topic of mathematical programming in Chapter 14. Problems requiring integer solutions can sometimes also be solved by using dynamic programming, which is presented in Chapter 12.

SUMMARY

The examples presented in this chapter are only a sample of the many problems that may be attacked by management science modeling and solution techniques. Although at this point the examples have been necessarily brief and simplified, with actual solutions not discussed, in later chapters the construction of these model types and others will be presented in detail and illustrated with examples and their solutions. This method offers the reader a broad spectrum of knowledge of the mechanics of model building and problem solving. However, the ultimate test of the management scientist, or any person who applies the management science process and techniques, is the ability to transfer textbook knowledge to the real world. Thus there is an art to the application of management science, but it is an art predicated on both practical experience and a sound basic knowledge of the tools of management science. The first of these necessities is beyond the realm of textbooks; the second, however, is the purpose of this text.

REFERENCES

ACKOFF, R. L., and RIVETT, P. *A Manager's Guide to Operations Research*. New York: John Wiley & Sons, 1963.

ACKOFF, R. L., and SASIENI, M. W. *Fundamentals of Operations Research*. New York: John Wiley & Sons, 1968.

BAUMOL, W. J. *Economic Theory and Opera-*

tions Analysis. 4th ed. Englewood Cliffs, New Jersey: Prentice-Hall, 1977.

BEER, S. *Management Sciences: The Business Use of Operations Research*. Garden City, New York: Doubleday & Company, 1967.

BIERMAN, H.; BONINI, C. P.; and HAUS-

MAN, W. H. *Quantitative Analysis for Business Decisions.* 8th ed. Homewood, Illinois: Richard D. Irwin, 1991.

BUDNICK, F. S.; MOJENA, R.; and VOLLMAN, T. E. *Principles of Operations Research for Management.* Homewood, Illinois: Richard D. Irwin, 1988.

CHURCHMAN, C. W.; ACKOFF, R. L.; and ARNOFF, E. L. *Introduction to Operations Research.* New York: John Wiley & Sons, 1957.

HILLIER, F. S., and LIEBERMAN, G. J. *Introduction to Operations Research.* 4th ed. San Francisco: Holden-Day, 1986.

PHILLIPS, D. T.; RAVINDRAN, A.; SOLBERG, J. J. *Operations Research: Principles and Practice.* 2d ed. New York: John Wiley & Sons, 1987.

TAHA, HAMDY A. *Operations Research: A Introduction.* 5th ed. New York: Macmi lan, 1992.

TEICHROEW, P. *An Introduction to Manag ment Science.* New York: John Wiley Sons, 1964.

WAGNER, HARVEY M. *Principles of Opera tions Research.* 2d ed. Englewood Cliff New Jersey: Prentice-Hall, 1975.

WAGNER, HARVEY M. *Principles of Manag ment Science.* 2d ed. Englewood Cliff New Jersey: Prentice-Hall, 1975.

WINSTON, W. L. *Operations Research, Appl cations and Algorithms,* 2nd ed. Bosto PWS-Kent, 1991.

STUDY QUESTIONS

1. Define *management science* and the field of study it encompasses.

2. Discuss the history and development of management science.

3. List and discuss the steps of the scientific method.

4. Why has management science as an academic discipline increased in popularity du ing the past several decades?

5. Define the term *model* in relation to management science.

6. Distinguish between *probabilistic* and *deterministic* models. Classify the various top ics in this text according to these two categories.

7. Define the following model components and discuss their relationships: *decision var ables, criterion variable, exogenous variables,* and *parameters.*

8. Construct the break-even model from the model components Q (quantity), (profit), P (price), FC (fixed cost), VC (variable cost), TR (total revenue), and T (total cost).

9. Derive the formula for determining the break-even quantity from the break-eve model.

10. An electrical manufacturer produces radios. The fixed cost for producing radios eac day is $10,000, and the variable cost is $5 per radio. Each radio is sold for $2 Given this information, determine (a) the daily break-even quantity, (b) total breal even revenue, (c) total break-even cost, and (d) total break-even profit.

11. Develop a graphic model of the break-even analysis in problem 10.

12. Consider a product mix decision problem where an electrical manufacturer attempting to determine how many clocks and radios to produce. Verbally descril the possible objective(s) of the firm, the decision variables, the types of resourc constraints that could exist, and the possible model parameters.

13. Develop a mathematical model for the transportation problem in this chapter (Example 1.2), using the general model framework given in the problem explanation as a guideline.

14. Identify types of problems other than the construction scheduling problem (Example 1.3) for which a precedence diagram could be used.

15. In Figure 1.3, indicate how the value of Q that would result in the lowest cost would be determined. Based on this graphical analysis, explain how the lowest cost value of Q could be determined mathematically.

16. Describe several different examples of problems, like the bank facility expansion problem (Example 1.5), to which waiting line analysis could be applied.

17. Identify several examples of decision-making problems, like the machine acquisition problem (Example 1.6), that require integer solutions.

2

Introduction to Linear Programming

Linear programming is perhaps the best known and one of the most widely used techniques of management science. It is a mathematical method of allocating scarce resources to achieve an objective, such as maximizing profit. Linear programming has found wide application in business, as most managerial problems involve resource allocation. For example, management decision problems in the areas of production planning, capital budgeting, personnel allocation, advertising, and promotion planning are concerned with the achievement of a given objective (profit maximization or cost minimization) subject to limited resources (money, material, labor, time, etc.). Linear programming involves the description of a real-world decision situation as a mathematical model that consists of a linear objective function and linear resource constraints. In this chapter a brief history of linear programming will be presented, followed by several example problems demonstrating the mathematical model formulation process, a general linear programming model and its properties, and a graphical interpretation of linear programming.

HISTORY OF LINEAR PROGRAMMING

Although the origin of mathematical programming techniques dates back to the development of theories of linear and nonlinear equations, George B. Dantzig is generally recognized as the pioneer of linear programming. Dantzig did much of his work during World War II, when he was employed by the U.S. Air Force to search for mathematical techniques to solve military logistics problems. His research was encouraged by other scholars, such as J. Von Neumann, L. Hurwicz, and T. C. Koopmans, who were working on the same general subject. The original name given to the technique was *programming of interdependent activities in a linear structure*, later shortened to *linear programming*.

After the war, many scholars joined Dantzig in the further development of the concept of linear programming. The first paper on a workable solution method (now known as the *simplex method*) was published by Dantzig in 1947. Dantzig collaborated with Marshall Wood, Alex Orden, and their associates in developing the simplex method while working on research projects for the U.S. Air Force.

Early applications of linear programming were predominantly to military problems such as logistics, transportation, and procurement problems. Wassily Leontief's input-output analysis provided a base for the application of linear programming to interindustry economic analysis.

After 1947, researchers such as A. Charnes, W. W. Cooper, A. Henderson, and W. Orchard-Hays joined Dantzig in developing and exploring new applications for linear programming. Linear programming was soon being applied to a large number of public and private sector problems. Linear programming was found to be a powerful problem-solving approach for managerial decision analysis in business. The number of linear programming applications has increased in recent years with the development and sophistication of electronic computers.

MODEL FORMULATION AND EXAMPLES

Although linear programming has been successfully applied to a wide spectrum of problems across many different fields, business and industry, agriculture, and the military have made the most extensive use of linear programming. The typical decision problem confronted by management groups in various settings is the optimum allocation of scarce resources. Resources can be money, labor, material, machine capacity, time, space, or technology. Management's task is to achieve the best possible outcome with these limited resources. The desired outcome is expressed either as the maximization of some measure, such as profit, effectiveness, welfare, or return, or the minimization of such elements as cost, time, and distance.

Once the problem has been identified, the goals of management established, and the applicability of linear programming determined, the next step in solving an unstructured, real-world problem is the formulation of a mathematical model. This entails three major steps: (1) the identification of solution variables (the quantity of the activity in question), (2) the development of an objective function that is a linear relationship of the solution variables, and (3) the determination of system constraints, which are also linear relationships of the decision variables, that reflect the limited resources of the problem.

In this section, seven different examples are presented that demonstrate the steps in linear programming model formulation. These examples are typical of linear programming applications and have been widely used to demonstrate model formulation. Through careful analysis of each of these examples, the reader should be able to grasp the major characteristics of model formulation and the fundamentals of linear programming.

Example 2.1   Product Mix Problem

A manufacturing company wishes to determine how many of each of three different products it should produce, given limited resources, in order to maximize total profit. The labor and material requirements and the contribution to profit for each of the three products are as follows:

		Resource Requirements		
Resources	Product 1	Product 2	Product 3	Availability
Labor (hr/unit)	5	2	4	240 hr
Materials (lb/unit)	4	6	3	400 lb
Profit ($/unit)	3	5	2	

There are 240 hours of labor available daily for production. The supply of materia is limited to 400 pounds per day. The decision problem is to determine the quantity each product to produce in order to maximize total profit. This problem meets all tl requirements of a linear programming problem (requirements that will become appare as additional examples are studied). Now we shall formulate the problem as a line programming model.

Decision Variables

The three decision variables in the problem are the quantities of products 1, 2, and 3 be produced on a daily basis. These quantities can be represented symbolically as

x_1 = quantity of product 1
x_2 = quantity of product 2
x_3 = quantity of product 3

Objective Function

The objective of the product mix problem is to maximize total profit. It should be obv ous that total profit is the sum of profits gained from each individual product. Profit fro product 1 is determined by multiplying the unit profit, $3, by the number of units pr duced, x_1. Profits for products 2 and 3 are determined similarly. Thus, total profit, can be expressed as

Maximize $Z = 3x_1 + 5x_2 + 2x_3$
where
$3x_1$ = profit from product 1
$5x_2$ = profit from product 2
$2x_3$ = profit from product 3

System Constraints

In this problem the constraints are the limited amounts of labor and material availab for production. Production of each of the three products requires both labor and materi inputs. For product 1, the labor required to produce each unit is 5 hours. Thus, the lab requirement for product 1 is $5x_1$ hours. Similarly, product 2 requres $2x_2$ hours of labc and product 3 requires $4x_3$ hours. The total number of labor hours available for produ tion is 240. Thus, the *labor* constraint is

$5x_1 + 2x_2 + 4x_3 \leq 240$

The constraint for material requirements is formulated in the same manner. Product 1 (x_1) requires 4 pounds for every unit produced, product 2 (x_2) requires 6 pounds per unit, and product 3 (x_3) requires 3 pounds per unit. Since there are 400 pounds of *raw material* available, this constraint is expressed as

$$4x_1 + 6x_2 + 3x_3 \leqslant 400$$

We also restrict each decision variable to a positive value, since it would be illogical to produce negative quantities of a product. These restrictions are called **nonnegativity constraints** and are expressed mathematically as

$$x_1 \geqslant 0, \; x_2 \geqslant 0, \; x_3 \geqslant 0$$

Most linear programming applications have nonnegativity constraints. However, the linear programming solution procedure is capable of handling negative decision variable values if for some reason the problem requires them and the model is appropriately formulated. Negative values frequently occur when the decision variable defines a rate such as a growth or inflation rate, which can increase or decrease. Its decrease would be denoted by a negative value. Instances where this condition occurs and the procedure for handling it are discussed in Chapter 3.

One might question the expression of the constraints as inequalities ($\leqslant$) rather than as equalities ($=$). A strict equality would imply the total use of production capacity, whereas a $\leqslant$ inequality allows the use of full capacity only *if* that is what the optimal solution requires. A $\leqslant$ inequality allows for some unused capacity if that is what the optimal solution requires. In many cases a solution with some unused production capacity will result in a better outcome, or greater profit, than a solution requiring the use of all resources. The $\leqslant$ inequality simply provides the flexibility that allows either type of solution to occur.

Now the complete linear programming problem can be summarized as a mathematical model:

$$\text{Maximize } Z = 3x_1 + 5x_2 + 2x_3$$
subject to
$$5x_1 + 2x_2 + 4x_3 \leqslant 240$$
$$4x_1 + 6x_2 + 3x_3 \leqslant 400$$
$$x_1, x_2, x_3 \geqslant 0$$

Solving this model for the optimum values of the decision variables, x_1, x_2, and x_3, will maximize the total profit, Z.

Example 2.2   Diet Problem

The preceding product mix problem was an example of a maximization problem. The following diet problem is an example of a minimization problem.

A hospital dietician must prepare breakfast menus every morning for the hospital patients. Part of the dietician's responsibility is to make certain that minimum daily requirements for vitamins A and B are met. At the same time, the menus must be kept at the lowest possible cost to avoid waste. The main breakfast staples providing vitamins

A and B are eggs, bacon, and cereal. The vitamin requirements and vitamin contributions for each staple are as follows.

Vitamin	Vitamin Contributions			Minimum Daily Requirement (mg)
	mg/Egg	mg/Bacon Strip	mg/Cereal Cup	
A	2	4	1	16
B	3	2	1	12

The cost of an egg is four cents, the cost of a bacon strip is three cents, and a cup o cereal costs two cents. The dietician wants to know how much of each staple to serve in order to meet the minimum daily requirements while minimizing total cost.

Decision Variables

The diet problem contains three decision variables that reflect the number of units of each type of food placed on the menu.

x_1 = number of eggs served
x_2 = number of bacon strips served
x_3 = number of cups of cereal served

Objective Function

The objective of this problem is to minimize the total cost of each breakfast. The tota cost in this case is simply the sum of the per unit costs from each serving of eggs, bacon and cereal. Thus, the objective function is expressed as

Minimize $Z = 4x_1 + 3x_2 + 2x_3$
where
$4x_1$ = cost (cents) of eggs per serving
$3x_2$ = cost (cents) of bacon per serving
$2x_3$ = cost (cents) of cereal per serving

System Constraints

In the diet problem, the constraints reflect the minimum daily vitamin requiremen established by the dietician. Each type of breakfast food yields the previously specifie quantity of vitamins (in mg) per unit. The constraint for vitamin A is

$2x_1 + 4x_2 + 1x_3 \geq 16$
where
$2x_1$ = vitamin contribution of eggs (in mg) per serving
$4x_2$ = vitamin contribution of bacon (in mg) per serving
$1x_3$ = vitamin contribution of cereal (in mg) per serving

Unlike Example 2.1, this example uses $\geq$ inequalities, specifying the minimu amount of vitamins needed. In other words, *at least* 16 milligrams of vitamin A mu be achieved. In the simplest and most general form of linear programming, maximization problems employ $\leqslant$ inequalities, whereas minimization problems use $\geqslant$ inequalities. However, this is not an absolute rule, as more complex problems frequently have both $\leqslant$ and $\geqslant$ constraints as well as equalities.

The constraint for vitamin B is constructed similarly:

$$3x_1 + 2x_2 + 1x_3 \geqslant 12$$

The complete linear programming problem can now be summarized.

Minimize $Z = 4x_1 + 3x_2 + 2x_3$
subject to
$$2x_1 + 4x_2 + 1x_3 \geqslant 16$$
$$3x_1 + 2x_2 + 1x_3 \geqslant 12$$
$$x_1, x_2, x_3 \geqslant 0$$

By solving this model for the values of the decision variables, x_1, x_2, and x_3, the dietician will obtain the minimum total cost (minimum value of Z) possible, while at the same time meeting the minimum requirements for vitamins A and B.

Example 2.3 Transportation Problem

An appliance manufacturer ships refrigerators from three warehouses to three retail stores on a monthly basis. Each warehouse has the following number of refrigerators available for shipment each month:

Warehouse	Capacity
1. St. Louis	200
2. Philadelphia	150
3. Atlanta	300
	650

Each retail store has the following monthly demand for refrigerators:

Store	Demand
A. New York	100
B. Chicago	300
C. Houston	250
	650

The cost for shipping refrigerators from each warehouse to each store differs according to the mode of transportation and the distance. The shipping cost per refrigerator for each route is given as follows:

From Warehouse	To Store		
	A	B	C
1	$10	$5	$12
2	4	9	15
3	15	8	6

The appliance firm desires to know the number of refrigerators to ship from each warehouse to each store in order to meet the demand at each store at the total minimum shipping cost.

Decision Variables

(handwritten annotation: $x_{1A}, x_{1B}, x_{1C}, x_{2A}, x_{2B}, x_{3B}, x_{3A}, x_{3B}$)

This problem contains nine decision variables that reflect the number of refrigerators shipped from each of the three warehouses to each of the three stores. The variables are expressed algebraically as

x_{ij} = the number of refrigerators shipped from warehouse i to store j, where
$i = 1, 2, 3$ and $j = A, B, C$

For example, variable x_{2B} represents the number of refrigerators shipped from warehouse 2 in Philadelphia to store B in Chicago.

Objective Function

The objective of the appliance manufacturer is to minimize total shipping cost. Since each shipping route has an associated cost per refrigerator, the objective function reflects the total cost for shipping all units demanded.

$$\text{Minimize } Z = \$10x_{1A} + 5x_{1B} + 12x_{1C} + 4x_{2A} + 9x_{2B} + 15x_{2C}$$
$$+ 15x_{3A} + 8x_{3B} + 6x_{3C}$$

System Constraints

The system constraints in this problem represent the supply available at each warehouse and the demand at each store. Consider warehouse 1 in St. Louis. It is able to supply a total of 200 refrigerators to any of the three stores, A, B, and C. This constraint is written as

(handwritten: Supply) $x_{1A} + x_{1B} + x_{1C} = 200$

In other words, the sum of all refrigerators shipped from warehouse 1 to stores A, B, and C must equal 200, the available supply at warehouse 1. This constraint is an equality for two reasons. First, the number of refrigerators shipped from warehouse 1 cannot exceed the amount available, 200. Second, the number shipped cannot be less than 200, since the total number available, 650, equals the total number demanded, 650. There is demand at the stores for all refrigerators shipped; thus, all refrigerators at each warehouse will be shipped. The supply constraints for warehouses 2 and 3 are constructed similarly.

$$x_{2A} + x_{2B} + x_{2C} = 150$$
$$x_{3A} + x_{3B} + x_{3C} = 300$$

There are also three demand constraints, which are constructed in the same way as the supply constraints. For example, at store A, there are 100 refrigerators demanded from any of the three warehouses.

$$x_{1A} + x_{2A} + x_{3A} = 100$$

The demand constraints are also equalities, for the same reasons the supply constraints are. The remaining demand constraints for stores B and C are

$$x_{1B} + x_{2B} + x_{3B} = 300$$
$$x_{1C} + x_{2C} + x_{3C} = 250$$

The complete linear programming model for this problem is summarized as

Minimize $Z = 10x_{1A} + 5x_{1B} + 12x_{1C} + 4x_{2A} + 9x_{2B} + 15x_{2C}$
$$+ 15x_{3A} + 8x_{3B} + 6x_{3C}$$

subject to

$$x_{1A} + x_{1B} + x_{1C} = 200$$
$$x_{2A} + x_{2B} + x_{2C} = 150$$
$$x_{3A} + x_{3B} + x_{3C} = 300$$
$$x_{1A} + x_{2A} + x_{3A} = 100$$
$$x_{1B} + x_{2B} + x_{3B} = 300$$
$$x_{1C} + x_{2C} + x_{3C} = 250$$
$$x_{ij} \geq 0$$

Solution of the above linear programming model will yield the minimum cost pattern of shipments from warehouses to stores to meet prescribed demands.

Example 2.4   Production Scheduling Problem

A production manager is attempting to determine a production schedule for the next five months for a product. From past production records the manager knows that 2000 units can be produced per month. Also, an additional 600 units can be produced monthly on an overtime basis. The unit cost of items produced is $10 on a regular time basis and $15 on an overtime basis. Contracted sales per month are as follows:

Month	Contracted Sales
1	1200
2	2100
3	2400
4	3000
5	4000

Inventory carrying costs are $2 per unit per month. The manager does not want any inventory carried over past the fifth month. The manager wants to know the monthly production that will minimize total production and inventory costs.

Decision Variables

The decision variables in this problem reflect the regular production per month, the overtime production per month, and the end-of-month inventory for months 1 through 4 The variables are expressed algebraically as

x_i = regular production in month i, where i = 1, 2, 3, 4, 5
y_i = overtime production in month i, where i = 1, 2, 3, 4, 5
w_i = units in inventory at end of month i, where i = 1, 2, 3, 4

For example, variables x_2, y_2, and w_2 represent the units of regular and overtim production in month 2 and units in inventory at the end of month 2, respectively.

Objective Function

The objective of the production manager is to minimize total cost. The cost of producin one unit during regular production is $10, the overtime cost per unit is $15, and th carrying cost per unit of inventory is $2.

$$\text{Minimize } Z = \$10(x_1 + x_2 + x_3 + x_4 + x_5) + 15(y_1 + y_2 + y_3 + y_4 + y_5)$$
$$+ 2(w_1 + w_2 + w_3 + w_4)$$

System Constraints

The first group of constraints in this problem represents the available regular and overtin production capacity per month. The available regular production capacity of 2000 uni per month results in the following constraints:

$x_i \le 2000$, for all i

The available overtime capacity per month of 600 units is represented by the followir constraints:

$y_i \le 600$, for all i

The second group of constraints represents the monthly production schedules. F month 1, the regular and overtime production, minus any units to be held in invento at the end of month 1, must equal the demand of 1200 units.

$x_1 + y_1 - w_1 = 1200$

In the second month, the regular and overtime production plus the inventory carried ov from month 1, minus any units of inventory to be held over at the end of month 2, mu equal the second month demand of 2100 units.

$x_2 + y_2 + w_1 - w_2 = 2100$

beg inv – end inv

The production scheduling constraints for months 3 and 4 are constructed similarly.

$$x_3 + y_3 + w_2 - w_3 = 2400$$
$$x_4 + y_4 + w_3 - w_4 = 3000$$

The constraint for month 5 must reflect the condition that no inventory is to be carried over at the end of month 5.

$$x_5 + y_5 + w_4 = 4000$$

The complete linear programming model is

Minimize $Z = \$10(x_1 + x_2 + x_3 + x_4 + x_5) + 15(y_1 + y_2 + y_3 + y_4 + y_5)$
$$+ 2(w_1 + w_2 + w_3 + w_4)$$

subject to

$$\begin{aligned} x_i &\leq 2000 &&(i = 1, 2, 3, 4, 5) \\ y_i &\leq 600 &&(i = 1, 2, 3, 4, 5) \\ x_1 + y_1 - w_1 &= 1200 \\ x_2 + y_2 + w_1 - w_2 &= 2100 \\ x_3 + y_3 + w_2 - w_3 &= 2400 \\ x_4 + y_4 + w_3 - w_4 &= 3000 \\ x_5 + y_5 + w_4 &= 4000 \\ x_i, y_i, w_i &\geq 0 \end{aligned}$$

Solution of the above linear programming model will yield the optimum schedule of regular and overtime production, as well as inventory to carry, for the five-month planning period.

Example 2.5   Blend Problem

A refinery blends four petroleum components into three grades of gasoline—regular, premium, and low lead. Management wishes to determine the optimal mix of the four components that will maximize profit. The maximum quantities available of each component and the cost per barrel are as follows:

Component	Maximum Barrels Available/Day	Cost/Barrel
1	5000	$ 9
2	2400	7
3	4000	12
4	1500	6

In order to ensure the proper blend for each gasoline grade, limits on the percentages of the components in each blend have been determined. The blends as well as the selling price of each grade are given as follows:

Grade	Component Specifications	Selling Price/ Barrel
Regular	Not less than 40% of 1	$12
	Not more than 20% of 2	
	Not less than 30% of 3	
Premium	Not less than 40% of 3	18
Low lead	Not more than 50% of 2	10
	Not less than 10% of 1	

Decision Variables

The blend problem is somewhat more complex than the previous two examples and, a result, requires some additional thought in defining the decision variables. At f glance it is tempting to define three decision variables, x_1, x_2, and x_3, that would repres the quantities of regular, premium, and low-lead gasoline produced, respectively. Ho ever, these decision variables would not reflect the decision problem proposed by ma agement. They want to know not only the amount of each grade to produce, but also amount of each component to blend to produce each grade. In addition, managem desires to maximize profit. If three decision variables for gasoline grades were used, o information on selling price would be included in the mathematical model. Since pro is determined by subtracting cost from selling price and cost information is available o on the four petroleum components, it is necessary to include the quantity of compone used as well as the quality of grades produced.

Thus, in this problem the decision variables must reflect the quantity of each co ponent used in each grade. These quantities can be represented algebraically as

x_{ij} = barrels of component i used in gasoline grade j per day, where $i = 1$,
   2, 3, 4 and j = R (regular), P (premium), L (low lead)

This results in twelve decision variables. As an example, consider one decision va able x_{2P}. This variable represents the amount of component 2 used in the production premium grade gasoline per day. Thus, the amount of each grade of gasoline produc is actually made up of the sum of the four components used in each grade, as follows

Regular: $x_{1R} + x_{2R} + x_{3R} + x_{4R}$
Premium: $x_{1P} + x_{2P} + x_{3P} + x_{4P}$
Low lead: $x_{1L} + x_{2L} + x_{3L} + x_{4L}$

Objective Function

The objective of the blend problem is to maximize total profit. This requires that the c of each barrel be subtracted from the revenue obtained from each barrel. Revenue determined by multiplying selling price by the total amount of each grade of gasol produced. For example, the selling price of regular grade is $12 per barrel, which m be multiplied by the total quantity of regular grade gasoline produced from each of four components, $x_{1R} + x_{2R} + x_{3R} + x_{4R}$. On the other hand, the cost of componen is found by multiplying the cost per barrel, $9, by the total quantity of component 1 used for each grade of gasoline, $x_{1R} + x_{1P} + x_{1L}$. Computing the revenues and costs for the other grades and components in a similar manner results in an objective function that combines all costs and revenues.

$$\text{Maximize } Z = 12(x_{1R} + x_{2R} + x_{3R} + x_{4R}) + 18(x_{1P} + x_{2P} + x_{3P} + x_{4P})$$
$$+ 10(x_{1L} + x_{2L} + x_{3L} + x_{4L}) - 9(x_{1R} + x_{1P} + x_{1L})$$
$$- 7(x_{2R} + x_{2P} + x_{2L}) - 12(x_{3R} + x_{3P} + x_{3L})$$
$$- 6(x_{4R} + x_{4P} + x_{4L})$$

Combining terms yields the following simplified objective function:

$$\text{Maximize } Z = 3x_{1R} + 5x_{2R} + 6x_{4R} + 9x_{1P} + 11x_{2P} + 6x_{3P}$$
$$+ 12x_{4P} + 1x_{1L} + 3x_{2L} + 4x_{4L} - 2x_{3L}$$

The negative term, $-2x_{3L}$, in the objective function results from the fact that the cost of component 3 is greater than the selling price of low lead.

ystem Constraints

In this problem, the model constraints reflect the limited amounts of each component available and the blend requirements for each grade. The availability constraints show that the total quantity of each component used in all three grades of gasoline is limited to the barrels of component available per day.

$$x_{1R} + x_{1P} + x_{1L} \leqslant 5000$$
$$x_{2R} + x_{2P} + x_{2L} \leqslant 2400$$
$$x_{3R} + x_{3P} + x_{3L} \leqslant 4000$$
$$x_{4R} + x_{4P} + x_{4L} \leqslant 1500$$

The blend requirements are slightly more complicated. Looking at just the first requirement for regular grade gasoline, we see that component 1 must constitute at least 40% of the total amount of regular. This constraint is reflected as

$$\frac{x_{1R}}{x_{1R} + x_{2R} + x_{3R} + x_{4R}} \geqslant .40$$

where $x_{1R} + x_{2R} + x_{3R} + x_{4R}$ equals the total amount of regular gasoline.

This constraint can be rewritten in a form more consistent with linear programming constraint inequalities:

$$x_{1R} \geqslant .40(x_{1R} + x_{2R} + x_{3R} + x_{4R})$$

and finally

$$.6x_{1R} - .4x_{2R} - .4x_{3R} - .4x_{4R} \geqslant 0$$

This latter constraint reflects the linear form into which all linear programming constraints must be converted before eventual solution. All decision variables must be on the left-hand side of the inequality and all constants on the right-hand side. Also, all quantities on the right-hand side must be nonnegative values.

The other two blend requirements for regular grade gasoline can be transformed in constraints in a similar fashion.

$$-.2x_{1R} + .8x_{2R} - .2x_{3R} - .2x_{4R} \leq 0$$
$$-.3x_{1R} - .3x_{2R} + .7x_{3R} - .3x_{4R} \geq 0$$

The single blend requirement for premium grade gasoline is

$$\frac{x_{3P}}{x_{1P} + x_{2P} + x_{3P} + x_{4P}} \geq .40$$

which converted becomes

$$-.4x_{1P} - .4x_{2P} + .6x_{3P} - .4x_{4P} \geq 0$$

The two blend requirements for low lead gasoline are

$$-.50x_{1L} + .50x_{2L} - .50x_{3L} - .50x_{4L} \leq 0$$
$$.90x_{1L} - .10x_{2L} - .10x_{3L} - .10x_{4L} \geq 0$$

The complete linear programming formulation for the blend problem can be summarized as

$$\text{Maximize } Z = 3x_{1R} + 5x_{2R} + 6x_{4R} + 9x_{1P} + 11x_{2P} + 6x_{3P}$$
$$+ 12x_{4P} + 1x_{1L} + 3x_{2L} + 4x_{4L} - 2x_{3L}$$

subject to

$$x_{1R} + x_{1P} + x_{1L} \leq 5000$$
$$x_{2R} + x_{2P} + x_{2L} \leq 2400$$
$$x_{3R} + x_{3P} + x_{3L} \leq 4000$$
$$x_{4R} + x_{4P} + x_{4L} \leq 1500$$
$$.6x_{1R} - .4x_{2R} - .4x_{3R} - .4x_{4R} \geq 0$$
$$-.2x_{1R} + .8x_{2R} - .2x_{3R} - .2x_{4R} \leq 0$$
$$-.3x_{1R} - .3x_{2R} + .7x_{3R} - .3x_{4R} \geq 0$$
$$-.4x_{1P} - .4x_{2P} + .6x_{3P} - .4x_{4P} \geq 0$$
$$-.5x_{1L} + .5x_{2L} - .5x_{3L} - .5x_{4L} \leq 0$$
$$.9x_{1L} - .1x_{2L} - .1x_{3L} - .1x_{4L} \geq 0$$
$$\text{all } x_{ij} \geq 0$$

When the previous model is solved for all values of x_{ij}, the optimum quantities each grade of gasoline will be obtained as

Regular: $x_{1R} + x_{2R} + x_{3R} + x_{4R}$
Premium: $x_{1P} + x_{2P} + x_{3P} + x_{4P}$
Low lead: $x_{1L} + x_{2L} + x_{3L} + x_{4L}$

In addition, the optimum quantities of each component will be determined as

Component 1: $x_{1R} + x_{1P} + x_{1L}$
Component 2: $x_{2R} + x_{2P} + x_{2L}$
Component 3: $x_{3R} + x_{3P} + x_{3L}$
Component 4: $x_{4R} + x_{4P} + x_{4L}$

In this model, profit (Z) is maximized by simultaneously considering revenues gasoline grades and costs of components.

ample 2.6 Crop Mix Problem

A farm owner wants to know how many acres of three different crops to plant on three different plots in order to maximize profit.

The farmer's tract of land consists of 2000 acres. The farmer has subdivided the tract into three plots and has contracted with three local farm families to operate the plots. The farm owner has instructed each sharecropper to plant three crops: corn, peas, and soybeans. The size of each plot has been determined by the capabilities of each local farmer. Plot sizes, crop restrictions, and profit per acre are given in the following tables.

Plot	Acreage
1	500
2	800
3	700

Crop	Maximum Acreage	Profit/Acre
Corn	900	$600
Peas	700	450
Soybeans	1000	300

Any of the three crops may be planted on any of the plots; however, the farm owner has placed the following restrictions on the farming operation. At least 60% of each plot must be under cultivation. To ensure that each sharecropper works according to his or her potential and resources (which determined the acreage allocation), the owner wants the same proportion of each plot to be under cultivation. The owner's objective is to determine how much of each crop to plant on each plot in order to maximize profit.

cision Variables

The decision variables for this problem define the amount of each crop planted on each farm. These amounts are expressed symbolically as

x_{ij} = acres of crop i planted on plot j, where i = c (corn), p (peas),
s (soybeans) and j = 1, 2, 3

This results in nine decision variables.

bjective Function

The objective of the farm owner is to maximize profit. Profit is determined by computing the product of the profit per acre for each crop and the total number of acres of the crop planted on all three plots. Thus, the objective function reflects the profit gained from each crop.

$$\text{Maximize } Z = 600(x_{c1} + x_{c2} + x_{c3}) + 450(x_{p1} + x_{p2} + x_{p3})$$
$$+ 300(x_{s1} + x_{s2} + x_{s3})$$

System Constraints

The system constraints are constructed to reflect the limited resources of the farm and th operating restrictions established by the owner. The first set of constraints defines th upper and lower limits of cultivated acreage on each plot. The upper limit, naturally, the acreage allocation established by the owner, and the lower limit is the 60% of avai able acreage that must be planted. The result is the following constraints:

$$300 \leq x_{c1} + x_{p1} + x_{s1} \leq 500$$
$$480 \leq x_{c2} + x_{p2} + x_{s2} \leq 800$$
$$420 \leq x_{c3} + x_{p3} + x_{s3} \leq 700$$

However, since these constraints do not fit the normal linear programming format– all decision variables on the left side of the inequalities and quantities on the right side– they must be transformed. This can be achieved by transforming each constraint into tw constraints for maximum and minimum acreages. The result is the following si constraints:

$$x_{c1} + x_{p1} + x_{s1} \geq 300$$
$$x_{c1} + x_{p1} + x_{s1} \leq 500$$
$$x_{c2} + x_{p2} + x_{s2} \geq 480$$
$$x_{c2} + x_{p2} + x_{s2} \leq 800$$
$$x_{c3} + x_{p3} + x_{s3} \geq 420$$
$$x_{c3} + x_{p3} + x_{s3} \leq 700$$

Also, the previously stated restrictions on the total number of acres of each crop tha can be planted are shown by

$$x_{c1} + x_{c2} + x_{c3} \leq 900$$
$$x_{p1} + x_{p2} + x_{p3} \leq 700$$
$$x_{s1} + x_{s2} + x_{s3} \leq 1000$$

The final set of constraints reflects the owner's desire that an equal proportion of th total acreage of each of the three plots be cultivated. This has the effect of imposing equ work and output standards on all three sharecroppers. These constraints are computed ratios.

$$\frac{x_{c1} + x_{p1} + x_{s1}}{500} = \frac{x_{c2} + x_{p2} + x_{s2}}{800}$$

$$\frac{x_{c2} + x_{p2} + x_{s2}}{800} = \frac{x_{c3} + x_{p3} + x_{s3}}{700}$$

$$\frac{x_{c1} + x_{p1} + x_{s1}}{500} = \frac{x_{c3} + x_{p3} + x_{s3}}{700}$$

These three constraint ratios equate the proportion of cultivated land for all three cro to total acreage for each plot. However, these equations are not in the proper form for linear programming problem, so they must be transformed by cross multiplying, resultin in the following three constraints:

$$800(x_{c1} + x_{p1} + x_{s1}) - 500(x_{c2} + x_{p2} + x_{s2}) = 0$$
$$700(x_{c2} + x_{p2} + x_{s2}) - 800(x_{c3} + x_{p3} + x_{s3}) = 0$$
$$700(x_{c1} + x_{p1} + x_{s1}) - 500(x_{c3} + x_{p3} + x_{s3}) = 0$$

By carefully observing these three constraints, we can see that the third constraint is redundant. That is, if plot 1 is in proportion to plot 2 and plot 2 is proportional to plot 3, then plot 1 is automatically proportional to plot 3 and the equation reflecting this ratio can be eliminated.

The complete linear programming model is

$$\text{Maximize } Z = 600(x_{c1} + x_{c2} + x_{c3}) + 450(x_{p1} + x_{p2} + x_{p3})$$
$$+ 300(x_{s1} + x_{s2} + x_{s3})$$

subject to

$$x_{c1} + x_{p1} + x_{s1} \geqslant 300$$
$$x_{c1} + x_{p1} + x_{s1} \leqslant 500$$
$$x_{c2} + x_{p2} + x_{s2} \geqslant 480$$
$$x_{c2} + x_{p2} + x_{s2} \leqslant 800$$
$$x_{c3} + x_{p3} + x_{s3} \geqslant 420$$
$$x_{c3} + x_{p3} + x_{s3} \leqslant 700$$
$$x_{c1} + x_{c2} + x_{c3} \leqslant 900$$
$$x_{p1} + x_{p2} + x_{p3} \leqslant 700$$
$$x_{s1} + x_{s2} + x_{s3} \leqslant 1000$$
$$800(x_{c1} + x_{p1} + x_{s1}) - 500(x_{c2} + x_{p2} + x_{s2}) = 0$$
$$700(x_{c2} + x_{p2} + x_{s2}) - 800(x_{c3} + x_{p3} + x_{s3}) = 0$$
$$x_{ij} \text{ for all } i, j \geqslant 0$$

Example 2.7 Multiperiod Investment Problem

An investment firm has $1,000,000 to invest in four alternatives: stocks, bonds, certificates of saving, and real estate. The firm wishes to determine the mix of investments that will maximize the cash value at the end of six years.

Investment opportunities in stocks and bonds are available at the beginning of each of the next six years. Each dollar invested in stocks at the beginning of each year will return $1.20 (a profit of $.20) two years later and can be immediately reinvested in any alternative. Each dollar invested in bonds at the beginning of each year will return $1.40 three years later and can be reinvested immediately.

Investment opportunities in certificates of saving are available only once, at the beginning of the second year. Each dollar invested in certificates at the beginning of the second year will return $1.80 four years later.

Investment opportunities in real estate are available at the beginning of the fifth and sixth years. Each dollar invested in real estate will return $1.10 one year later.

In order to minimize risk, the firm has decided to diversify its investments. The total amount invested in stocks cannot exceed 30% of total investments, and at least 25% of total investments must be in certificates of saving.

Firm management wishes to determine the optimal mix of investments in the various alternatives that will maximize the amount of cash at the end of the sixth year.

Decision Variables

In order to fully comprehend the types of multiperiod investment decisions that must be made in this problem, it is helpful to employ a diagram of the investment process, as shown in Figure 2.1.

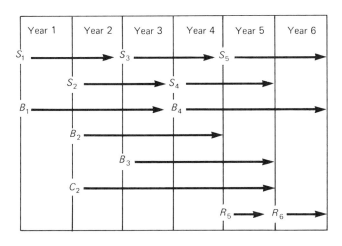

Figure 2.1 *Investment Scheme*

Figure 2.1 depicts each type of investment, the years in which it can be made, and time to maturity. For example, S_1 represents an investment in stocks at the beginning of year 1. The arrow leading from S_1 goes to the end of year 2, when the return is realized. Using the same notation as in Figure 2.1, we can define the decision variables as follows:

S_i = amount of money invested in stocks at the beginning of year i,
　　　where i = 1, 2, 3, 4, 5
B_i = amount of money invested in bonds at the beginning of year i,
　　　where i = 1, 2, 3, 4
C_2 = amount of money invested in certificates of saving in year 2
R_i = amount of money invested in real estate at the beginning of year i,
　　　where i = 5, 6
I_i = amount of money held idle and not invested at the beginning of year i

Objective Function

The objective of the investment firm is to maximize cash value at the end of the sixth year. From Figure 2.1 it can be seen that the amount of money at the end of the sixth year will be based on the values of S_5, B_4, and R_6. These amounts must be multiplied by their respective returns to yield their cash values at the end of the sixth year. In addition, the amount of money not invested at the beginning of the sixth year is included. This results in the objective function

Maximize Z = \$1.20S_5 + 1.40B_4 + 1.10R_6 + I_6

System Constraints

In this problem there are two types of constraints: equations that define the investment opportunities in a given year and inequalities that prescribe the investment policies established by management.

At the beginning of the first year, the only investments available are in stocks and bonds. There is a maximum amount of \$1 million available for these two investment alternatives. However, since the minimum length of maturity for the two alternatives is two years, if all the $1 million is invested in S_1 and B_1, there will be no funds available for investment at the beginning of the second year. If we signify the amount of money not invested at the beginning of year 1 as I_1, the investment opportunity constraint in the first year is

Year 1: $S_1 + B_1 + I_1 = 1,000,000$

In the second year, the investment opportunities will be S_2, B_2, and C_2. These opportunities plus the amount not invested (I_2) must equal the amount not invested in year 1 (I_1).

Year 2: $S_2 + B_2 + C_2 + I_2 = I_1$

For the remaining years the constraints are formulated in a manner similar to that used for years 1 and 2. The only difference is that the return and principal on the earlier investments will be available for reinvestment starting with year 3. For example, in year 3 the amount available for investment is I_2, the amount not invested the previous year, plus $1.20S_1$, the matured value of the stock investment at the beginning of period 1.

	Investment opportunities	*Amounts available*
Year 3:	$S_3 + B_3 + I_3 =$	$I_2 + 1.20S_1$
Year 4:	$S_4 + B_4 + I_4 =$	$I_3 + 1.20S_2 + 1.40B_1$
Year 5:	$S_5 + R_5 + I_5 =$	$I_4 + 1.20S_3 + 1.40B_2$
Year 6:	$R_6 + I_6 =$	$I_5 + 1.20S_4 + 1.40B_3 + 1.80C_2 + 1.10R_5$

These six constraints must be converted to the proper equation form. Two constraints must also be formulated for the firm's investment policies. First, it was determined that the total amount of investment in stocks, $\sum_{i=1}^{5} S_i$, should not exceed 30% of total investment in various alternatives,

$$\sum_{i=1}^{5} S_i + \sum_{i=1}^{4} B_i + C_2 + \sum_{i=5}^{6} R_i$$

which yields the following constraint:

$$\sum_{i=1}^{5} S_i \leq .30 \left(\sum_{i=1}^{5} S_i + \sum_{i=1}^{4} B_i + C_2 + \sum_{i=5}^{6} R_i \right)$$

Second, the amount invested in certificates of saving, C_2, must be at least 25% of the total investment.

$$C_2 \geq .25 \left(\sum_{i=1}^{5} S_i + \sum_{i=1}^{4} B_i + C_2 + \sum_{i=5}^{6} R_i \right)$$

Rearranging the preceding two constraints into the standard linear programming form results in the following two constraints:

$$.7 \sum_{i=1}^{5} S_i - .3 \sum_{i=1}^{4} B_i - .3C_2 - .3 \sum_{i=5}^{6} R_i \leq 0$$

$$- .25 \sum_{i=1}^{5} S_i - .25 \sum_{i=1}^{4} B_i + .75C_2 - .25 \sum_{i=5}^{6} R_i \geq 0$$

The complete linear programming formulation for the multiperiod investment problem can now be summarized.

Maximize $Z = 1.20S_5 + 1.40B_4 + 1.10R_6 + I_6$

subject to

$$S_1 + B_1 + I_1 = 1,000,000$$
$$S_2 + B_2 + C_2 - I_1 + I_2 = 0$$
$$-1.20S_1 + S_3 + B_3 - I_2 + I_3 = 0$$
$$-1.20S_2 + S_4 - 1.40B_1 + B_4 - I_3 + I_4 = 0$$
$$-1.20S_3 + S_5 - 1.40B_2 + R_5 - I_4 + I_5 = 0$$
$$-1.20S_4 - 1.40B_3 - 1.80C_2 - 1.10R_5 + R_6 - I_5 + I_6 = 0$$
$$.7 \sum_{i=1}^{5} S_i - .3 \sum_{i=1}^{4} B_i - .3C_2 - .3 \sum_{i=5}^{6} R_i \le 0$$
$$-.25 \sum_{i=1}^{5} S_i - .25 \sum_{i=1}^{4} B_i + .75C_2 - .25 \sum_{i=5}^{6} R_i \ge 0$$
$$S_i, B_i, C_i, R_i, I_i \ge 0$$

THE GENERALIZED LINEAR PROGRAMMING MODEL

From the detailed example problems just presented we are able to observe a distinct pattern for the general formulation of a linear programming problem. In each problem, decision variables, an objective function, and system constraints were defined, which together formed a mathematical model of a real-world-type situation. It would be wise for the reader to commit to memory the general model presented in this section, since the general symbolic notation will be referred to often in the discussion to follow.

Decision Variables

In each problem, decision variables, which denoted a level of activity or quantity produced, were defined. For our general model, n decision variables are defined as

x_1 = quantity of activity 1
x_2 = quantity of activity 2
.   .
.   .
x_j = quantity of activity j
.   .
.   .
x_n = quantity of activity n

or

x_j = quantity of activity j, where $j = 1, 2, \ldots, n$

Objective Function

The objective function represents the sum total of the contributions of each decision variable in the model toward an objective. It is represented as

Maximize $Z = c_1 x_1 + c_2 x_2 + \cdots + c_j x_j + \cdots + c_n x_n$

where

$Z = $ total value of the objective function

$c_j = $ contribution per unit of activity j $(1, 2, \ldots, n)$

The alternative form for the objective function is to *minimize* rather than maximize.

System Constraints

The constraints of a linear programming model represent the limited availability resources in the problem. We will let the amount of each of m resources available be defined as b_i (for $i = 1, 2, \ldots, m$). We will define a_{ij} as the amount of resource consumed per unit of activity j $(j = 1, 2, \ldots, n)$. Thus, constraint equations can be defined as

$$a_{11} x_1 + a_{12} x_2 + \cdots + a_{1j} x_j + \cdots + a_{1n} x_n \leq b_1$$
$$a_{21} x_1 + a_{22} x_2 + \cdots + a_{2j} x_j + \cdots + a_{2n} x_n \leq b_2$$

$$a_{i1} x_1 + a_{i2} x_2 + \cdots + a_{ij} x_j + \cdots + a_{in} x_n \leq b_i$$

$$a_{m1} x_1 + a_{m2} x_2 + \cdots + a_{mj} x_j + \cdots + a_{mn} x_n \leq b_m$$

$$x_1, x_2, \ldots, x_j, \ldots, x_n \geq 0$$

m = number of constraints

This general relationship shows all constraints as $\leq$ inequalities. Functional con straints can also be of the forms

$$a_{i1} x_1 + a_{i2} x_2 + \cdots + a_{ij} x_j + \cdots + a_{in} x_n \geq b_i$$

and

$$a_{i1} x_1 + a_{i2} x_2 + \cdots + a_{ij} x_j + \cdots + a_{in} x_n = b_i$$

The general form of the linear programming model can be summarized as

Maximize (or minimize) $Z = c_1 x_1 + c_2 x_2 + \cdots + c_j x_j + \cdots + c_n x_n$

subject to

$$a_{11} x_1 + a_{12} x_2 + \cdots + a_{1j} x_j + \cdots + a_{1n} x_n \quad (\leq, =, \geq)\ b_1$$
$$a_{21} x_1 + a_{22} x_2 + \cdots + a_{2j} x_j + \cdots + a_{2n} x_n \quad (\leq, =, \geq)\ b_2$$

$$a_{i1} x_1 + a_{i2} x_2 + \cdots + a_{ij} x_j + \cdots + a_{in} x_n \quad (\leq, =, \geq)\ b_i$$

$$a_{m1} x_1 + a_{m2} x_2 + \cdots + a_{mj} x_j + \cdots + a_{mn} x_n \quad (\leq, =, \geq)\ b_m$$

$$x_1, x_2, \ldots, x_j, \ldots, x_n \geq 0$$

To demonstrate this general notation, we will refer back to Example 2.1. The model formulation in that problem is

Maximize $Z = 3x_1 + 5x_2 + 2x_3$

subject to
$$5x_1 + 2x_2 + 4x_3 \leq 240$$
$$4x_1 + 6x_2 + 3x_3 \leq 400$$
$$x_1, x_2, x_3 \geq 0$$

Thus, in the general model notation, the problem is given as

Maximize $Z = c_1x_1 + c_2x_2 + c_3x_3$

subject to
$$a_{11}x_1 + a_{12}x_2 + a_{13}x_3 \leq b_1$$
$$a_{21}x_1 + a_{22}x_2 + a_{23}x_3 \leq b_2$$
$$x_1, x_2, x_3 \geq 0$$

where the model parameters are
$$c_1 = 3, c_2 = 5, c_3 = 2$$
$$a_{11} = 5, a_{12} = 2, a_{13} = 4, b_1 = 240$$
$$a_{21} = 4, a_{22} = 6, a_{23} = 3, b_2 = 400$$

Finally, making use of the concise algebraic form of the summation sign, we can express the generalized linear programming model as

Maximize (or minimize) $Z = \sum_{j=1}^{n} c_j x_j$

subject to

$$\sum_{j=1}^{n} a_{ij}x_j (\leq, =, \geq) b_i, \text{ for all } i \ (i = 1, 2, \ldots, m)$$

$$\text{all } x_j \geq 0$$

In this notation, the Example 2.1 problem is given as

Maximize $Z = \sum_{j=1}^{3} c_j x_j$

subject to

$$\sum_{j=1}^{3} a_{ij}x_j \leq b_i, \text{ for } i = 1, 2$$

$$x_j \geq 0, \text{ for } j = 1, 2, 3$$

The c_j, a_{ij}, and b_i values are the *parameters* of a linear programming problem that are assumed to be known constants.

PROPERTIES OF THE GENERAL LINEAR PROGRAMMING MODEL

The general linear programming model contains certain implicit properties that define what constitutes a valid linear programming problem. These properties require that the functional relationships in the problem be linear and additive, divisible, and deterministic. The reader may have already discovered these properties through the analysis of the example problems. In this section these properties will be explained in greater detail.

An Application of Linear Programming:
Optimizing Clerical Procurement at Canada Systems Group, Inc.

Canada's income tax laws permit individuals to make tax-deductible contributions to retirement funds called registered retirement savings plans (RRSP), similar to an IRA in the United States. Traditionally contributions to an RRSP are made during the last 60 days of the tax year during February and March. Investment Fund Services (IFS), part of the Financial Services Group, a division of Canada Systems Group, Inc., has been the only firm in the transaction processing business large enough to handle RRSP contributions. However, while the IFS division staff could handle the regular volume of RRSP transactions it processed each month, the incremental increase in RRSP contributions in

February and March created difficulties. In 1984 the volume of transactions unexpectedly grew by more than 100%, resulting in errors and delays in RRSP processing and additional labor costs of almost $500,000. In addition, several major clients threatened to not renew their contracts. To address the problem, a linear programming model was developed in order to plan the incremental staff requirements during the six-week period beginning February 1, 1985.

RRSP transactions arrive daily during the work week and processing by IFS required two sequential tasks: data preparation and data entry. The first activity included sorting and coding forms, checking for errors, making corrections,

Linearity

The primary requirement of linear programming is that the objective function and all related constraints must be **linear**. In other words, if a constraint involving two decision variables were graphed in two-dimensional space, it would form a straight line. Likewise, a constraint involving three decision variables would yield a plane (a flat surface), and, in general, a relationship of n decision variables would result in a hyperplane (a flat geometrical shape) in n-dimensional space.

Proportionality

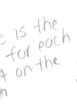

The term *linear* implies that relationships are directly proportional. **Proportionality** means that the rate of change, or slope, of the functional relationship is *constant*, and therefore changes of equal size in the value of a decision variable will result in exactly the same *relative* change in the functional value. For example, consider the case where a_{11} = 5 and x_1 = 2, in which case $a_{11}x_1$ = 10. If x_1 is increased by 5%, it becomes 2.1, and $a_{11}x_1$ then equals 10.5, which is also a 5% increase. In other words, the value of each term of a constraint $(a_{ij}x_j)$ is directly proportional to the level of the x_j variable, regardless of the values of any of the other decision variables in the problem. The same is true for the terms of the objective function.

Additivity

Linear programming also requires that the total measure of outcome (the objective function) and the total sum of resource usage (the constraints) be **additive**. For example, the total profit (Z) will equal the sum of profits earned from each individual activity, c_jx_j. Also, the sum total of a resource utilized must be exactly equal to the sum of the resources

grouping the forms according to specific
ds. The forms were then forwarded for data
ry into the computer system. A team of two
ff people with management science training
d one outside person was formed to address the
mplex manpower problem created by this
nsaction process during the 60-day RRSP
son. This task force focused on two items: the
rces of additional temporary manpower and
fining the decision variables. Following an
vestigation, two sources of temporary manpower
re determined, temporary outside personnel
red directly by Canada Systems Group and
rks obtained from an outside service bureau.
e model decisions were then defined as the
mber of clerks obtained from the two sources
e company's own personnel service and an

outside manpower service) for either the day,
afternoon, or night shifts and for either weekdays
or weekends. The objective of the model was to
minimize the wage cost (including benefits) of
this additional clerical staff. Constraints included
the number of available computer terminals,
office space limitations, available clerical personnel
from the two sources, and task demand. The
model consisted of 202 constraints and 226
variables.

Although RRSP volume increased by 25% in
1985 and wage rates increased, the cost of
managing the RRSP season was only $170,000, a
$320,000 decrease from the previous year. In
addition, IFS restored its reputation as a reliable
transaction processor.

rce: C. H. von Lanzenauer et al., "RRSP Flood: LP to the Rescue," *Interfaces,* 17, no. 4 (July–August 1987): 27–33.

used for each individual activity, $a_{ij}x_j$. This property is required for the model to be linear. The assumption that the terms of each relationship are additive implies that the activities are independent—that is, cross-product terms (such as $-x_1x_2$) do not arise because of interactions between some of the decision variables. Interactions, and resulting cross-product terms, might arise in a model of a problem where several products compete with one another in the marketplace.

x_j = quantity of each activity

Divisibility

The property of divisibility requires that the solution values obtained for the decision variables, x_j, not be restricted to integer values. This means that the x_j variables can take on any fractional solution value. Such variables are referred to as **continuous variables,** as opposed to **integer,** or **discrete, variables.** This condition is acceptable when the decision variables are naturally continuous. For example, if x_j equaled pounds of flour produced, a fractional value such as 3.4 pounds would be a logical solution.

In other words, linear programming solutions cannot be restricted to integer, or discrete, values for the solution variables. For example, although decision variables representing various types of aircraft to be produced should realistically have integer (whole number) solution values, linear programming solution will not necessarily yield a solution with integer values. In fact, the solution yielded by linear programming could, very likely, produce fractional values for the solution variables.

In many cases, nonfractional activities can simply and legitimately be rounded to the nearest integer values. This is most often the case when a large number of items, such as a thousand bolts, are being produced. Often rounding will result in an acceptable solution. However, rounding can affect optimality, especially when only a few large items are being produced, such as transformers or airplanes. Therefore, when integer values a strictly required, an alternative mathematical programming procedure, integer progran ming, can be used. This alternative method will be discussed in greater detail in Chapt 14. In the interim, the reader is asked to accept the assumption of divisibility and t sometimes inappropriate results it creates.

Certainty

[handwritten: C_j = cost of activity j contribution, a_{ij} = amt of resource i for activity j, b_i = total amt of resource i available for all cons]

In linear programming, the values of the model parameters (c_j, a_{ij}, and b_i) are assume to be known constants. Linear programming implicitly assumes a decision problem in static time frame in which all parameters are known with certainty. In real situation however, model parameters are rarely deterministic, since they reflect future as well present conditions, and future conditions are seldom known with certainty.

There are several ways to cope with parameter uncertainty in linear programmin models. Sensitivity analysis is a technique for testing solution values to see how sensitiv they are to parameter changes. Sensitivity analysis will be discussed in greater detail i Chapter 4.

GRAPHICAL INTERPRETATION OF LINEAR PROGRAMMING

Because of the property of linearity, linear programming problems can be illustrated and solved graphically if the problem is two-dimensional (i.e., there are two decision vari ables). Although problems in two dimensions are not commonplace in real-world situa tions, geometric interpretation of linear programming is quite useful. It provides a grea deal of insight into the modeling and solution of linear programming problems, which will be valuable in our solution of more complex problems in Chapter 3 via the simples algorithm. However, the reader should keep in mind the limitations of graphical analysis as a solution technique. Given the difficulty of drawing a multidimensional graph, the limitations of graphical analysis for problems involving more than two decision variables are obvious. *[handwritten: simplex method = for more than 2 dec. var.]*

Consider the following simple product mix problem. A manufacturing company produces two products, 1 and 2. Each product has resource requirements and profit contri- bution as follows:

Resource	Product 1	Product 2	Total Resources Available
Material (lb/unit)	1	2	10 lb
Labor (hr/unit)	6	6	36 hr
Profit ($/unit)	4	5	

In addition, because of demand forecasts, a maximum of 4 units of product 1 will be produced.

This problem is formulated as

Maximize $Z = 4x_1 + 5x_2$ (profit)
subject to
$$x_1 + 2x_2 \leq 10 \quad \text{(material)}$$
$$6x_1 + 6x_2 \leq 36 \quad \text{(labor)}$$
$$x_1 \leq 4 \quad \text{(product 1 restriction)}$$
$$x_1, x_2 \geq 0$$

The model formulation is represented graphically in Figure 2.2. In order to graph the three constraint inequalities, it is necessary to treat each as an equality. Then, by finding two points common to each linear equation, we can plot it on the graph. A simple way to plot each line is to let one variable in an equation equal zero and then solve for the remaining variable. For example, in the first constraint if $x_1 = 0$, then $2x_2 = 10$ and $x_2 = 5$. Similarly, if $x_2 = 0$, $x_1 = 10$. These points ($x_1 = 0$, $x_2 = 5$ and $x_1 = 10$, $x_2 = 0$) are then plotted on each axis and connected with a line, as in Figure 2.2.

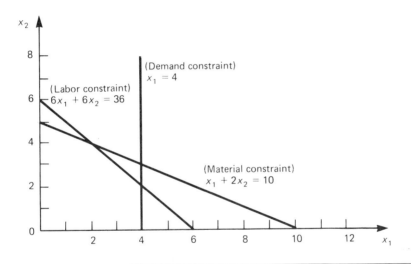

Figure 2.2 *Graphic Representation of the Product Mix Problem*

Reinserting the $\leq$ inequalities in each constraint forms a region that simultaneously satisfies all three constraint relationships. This region, the shaded area *ABCDE* in Figure 2.3, is defined as the feasible solution area, since it satisfies all system constraints. (The feasible solution area is restricted to the first quadrant because the variables x_1 and x_2 must be positive—x_1, $x_2 \geq 0$.) Any set of x_1, x_2 values outside this region is not a feasible solution, since it violates one or more of the constraints. For example, in Figure 2.3, points *R* (within the feasible region) and *S* (on the boundary of the feasible region) are two examples of feasible solutions, whereas points *P* and *Q* are examples of infeasible solutions.

Given the feasible solution space *ABCDE*, which contains all feasible solutions to the problem, we must now ascertain the point (x_1, x_2) that best fulfills the objective function. In this problem the objective is to maximize profit. In order to find the optimal solution, which maximizes Z (profit), the objective function must be plotted. However,

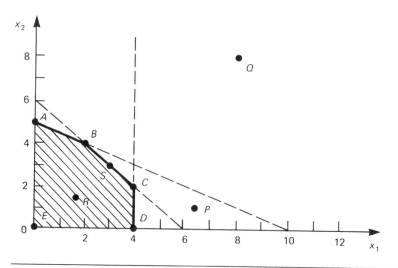

Figure 2.3 *Feasible and Infeasible Solutions*

Z is not the equation of a single line, but rather the equation of a multitude of lines depending on the value Z takes on.

Figure 2.4 shows the objective function plotted for several alternative values of Z. For example, $Z = 10 = 4x_1 + 5x_2$ results in the objective function line Z_1. By increasing the value of Z to 20, we can plot another objective function line, Z_2. Z_3, Z_4, and Z_5 are plots of alternative values for the objective function. Several properties relating to the objective function can be observed in Figure 2.4.

First, all Z_j values are parallel. This is because all levels of the objective function ($j = 1, 2, \ldots$), regardless of the value of Z, have the same slope. By solving the objective

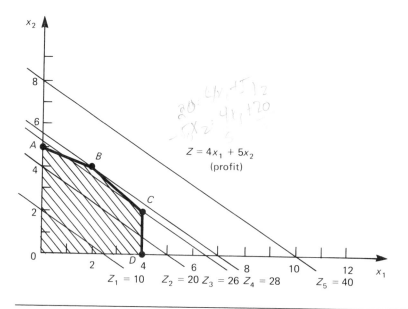

Figure 2.4 *Slope of the Objective Function*

function for x_2 in terms of Z and x_1, we arrive at the equation

$$x_2 = \tfrac{2}{5} - \tfrac{4}{5}x_1$$

[handwritten: x_2 becomes "y" for $y = mx + b$]

[handwritten: $y = b - mx$]

[handwritten in left margin: $= 4x_1 + 5x_2$ / $= 20 + 4x_1$ / $= +4 - \tfrac{4}{5}$ / 2]

which shows the slope of the objective function to be $-\tfrac{4}{5}$ for any value of Z. For example, if $Z = 10$ we have $x_2 = 2 - \tfrac{4}{5}x_1$, and for $Z = 20$ we have $x_2 = 4 - \tfrac{4}{5}x_1$. In general, the slope for all Z_j equations in this problem is $-\tfrac{4}{5}$.

Second, it is apparent that an infinite number of possible objective function lines exist. These lines begin at the origin and, as Z increases, move out into the solution space. As a result, the objective function in graphical analysis is often referred to as an iso-function line, reflecting the fact that Z is an infinite number of parallel lines.

Now, given that $Z_5 > Z_4 > Z_3 > Z_2 > Z_1$, it is clear that Z_1 is not the best value of Z, because the objective function can take on larger values. However, it is equally apparent that Z_5 is not optimal, because it contains no points (x_1, x_2) that satisfy the problem constraints (no point lies within the feasible solution space, *ABCDE*). Z_4 does have a point, *B* (where $x_1 = 2$ and $x_2 = 4$), in common with the feasible solution space and is larger than all other Z_j values within the region. Even the slightest increase in Z beyond the value of Z_4 would cause the objective function line to fall completely out of the solution space. On the other hand, if Z_4 were decreased by even a small amount, it would no longer include the best or optimal point. Thus, we have located the maximum value of Z at point *B*.

Since the optimal solution is found at a **corner point** formed by the intersection of two constraints, the values of x_1 and x_2 can be found by solving these two constraint equations (material and labor) simultaneously.

$$x_1 + 2x_2 = 10 \quad \text{(material)}$$
$$6x_1 + 6x_2 = 36 \quad \text{(labor)}$$

Thus,

$$x_1 + 2x_2 = 10$$
$$-(x_1 + x_2 = 6)$$
$$\overline{ x_2 = 4}$$

and

$$x_1 = 10 - 2(4)$$
$$= 2$$

Substituting $x_1 = 2$ and $x_2 = 4$ into the objective function results in the optimal value of Z.

$$Z = 4x_1 + 5x_2$$
$$= 4(2) + 5(4)$$
$$= 28$$

From this example, several important observations can be made. First, the optimal solution will always lie on the boundary of the feasible solution space. The feasible solution space forms a convex set of points. This means that the boundary of this region is made up of sets of straight lines (or flat planes) that converge at corners (often referred to as extreme points). As a result, there are no indentions in the boundary. (This definiti of **convexity** can be verified by observing that a line connecting any two points in th solution space is also in the solution space, as in Figure 2.5.) As a result of the proper of convexity, the boundary formed by the constraint equations must contain the set points that includes a unique maximum value for Z. Therefore, the boundary must con tain the optimal point.

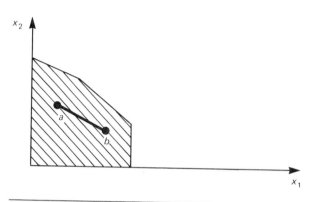

Figure 2.5 *A Convex Set*

Second, the optimal solution not only is on the boundary of the solution space bu more specifically is at a corner point formed by the intersection of two constraints. Thi is because the corner points are protrusions, or extremes, in the convex set and, thus, th outermost points on the boundary. For any linear programming problem, each extreme point feasible solution is at the intersection of n constraint equations, where n is the number of decision variables. Thus, the solution at any corner point can be found by solving n simultaneous equations. The exception to this property is a multiple optima solution that occurs when the objective function is parallel to a constraint line (i.e., the two functions have the same slope). This special case is discussed in greater detail later in this chapter.

Graphical Solution of a Minimization Problem

The graphical solution for a minimization problem is found in much the same way as that for a maximization problem, except for a few fundamental differences.

Consider the following problem:

Minimize $Z = 3x_1 + 3x_2$ (cost)
subject to
$$2x_1 + 4x_2 \geq 16 \quad \text{(required quantity of component mix)}$$
$$4x_1 + 3x_2 \leq 24 \quad \text{(resource use and availability)}$$
$$x_1 \geq 2 \quad \text{(minimum required quantity of component 1)}$$
$$x_1, x_2 \geq 0$$

The graphical representation of this problem, determined in a manner similar to that employed in the previous example, is shown in Figure 2.6. The feasible solution space in this problem is the shaded region, *ABC*. We have already determined that the optimal

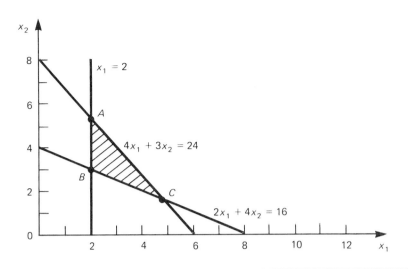

Figure 2.6 *Graphic Representation of the Minimization Problem*

solution will be found on the boundary of the feasible solution space at a corner point. However, whereas the optimal value in a maximization problem is at the corner point that maximizes the value of the objective function, the best solution in a minimization problem is at the point yielding the minimum value of Z. A series of iso-function lines is shown in Figure 2.7. Note that the values of Z decrease as the lines approach the origin. The iso-function line that has the lowest value and still remains in the feasible solution space is Z_3. This line corresponds to point B, the optimal corner point.

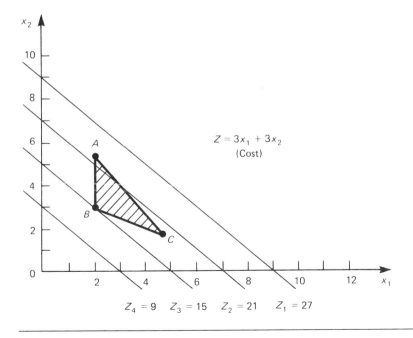

Figure 2.7 *Optimal Solution Point*

Solving the simultaneous equations that intersect at point B results in the optim solution.

$$x_1 = 2 \quad \text{(minimum required quantity of component 1)}$$
$$2x_1 + 4x_2 = 16 \quad \text{(component mix required)}$$

Thus,

$$x_2 = 4 - .5x_1$$
$$= 3$$

and

$$Z = 3(2) + 3(3)$$
$$= 15$$

SPECIAL CASES OF THE GENERAL LINEAR PROGRAMMING MODEL

Several exceptions exist to the general linear programming model. The complexities giv ing rise to these exceptions include the presence of multiple optimal solutions, infeasibl problems with no solution, and unbounded problems. These cases, like the general linea programming problem, can be illustrated via graphical analysis.

Multiple Optimal Solutions

Multiple optimal solutions exist in a linear programming problem when the objective function falls on more than one optimal point. Since the boundary of the solution space is a series of connected straight-line segments, the only time this situation can exist is when the slopes of the objective function and one of the constraint equations (straight-line segments) are the same. This results in the objective function's passing through two adjacent corner points (constraint intersections). The following problem is a modified version of the problem presented on page 45 and solved graphically in Figure 2.4. The only change is in the objective function, where the coefficient of x_2 has been changed from 5 to 4. This will result in multiple optimal solutions.

Maximize $Z = 4x_1 + 4x_2$
subject to
$$x_1 + 2x_2 \leqslant 10$$
$$6x_1 + 6x_2 \leqslant 36$$
$$x_1 \leqslant 4$$
$$x_1, x_2 \geqslant 0$$

The objective function Z in Figure 2.8 touches points B and C simultaneously as it reaches its maximum value on the boundary of the solution space (for Z_2). Thus, all points on the constraint line, between and including points B and C, represent optimal values. Typically, however, only points B and C are referred to as the alternative optimal solutions, with the realization that an infinite number of points in between are also optimal.

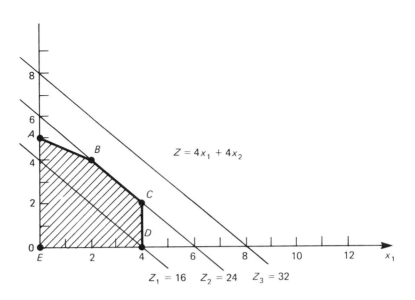

Figure 2.8 *Multiple Optimal Solutions*

In certain instances, the existence of multiple optimal solutions can benefit the decision maker, since the number of decision alternatives, or the range of decision options, i enlarged. Choosing among multiple optimal solutions allows the decision maker greate flexibility. For example, a manager would have greater choice as to product mix.

An Infeasible Problem

In some cases a linear programming problem has no feasible solution. In other word: there are no points that simultaneously satisfy all constraints in the problem. An exampl of an infeasible problem is depicted graphically in Figure 2.9.

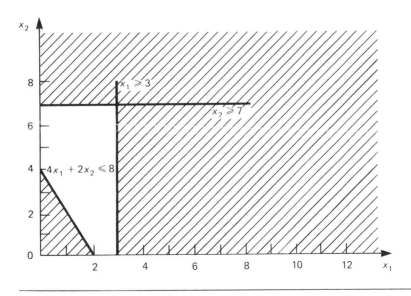

Figure 2.9 *No Feasible Solutions*

The example problem is formulated in the following model:

Maximize $Z = 5x_1 + 3x_2$

subject to

$$4x_1 + 2x_2 \leqslant 8$$
$$x_1 \geqslant 3$$
$$x_2 \geqslant 7$$
$$x_1, x_2 \geqslant 0$$

Since the three constraints do not overlap, there is no feasible solution space. Thus the objective function does not pass through any point that meets all three constraints at once. There are no values of the decision variables that satisfy all the requirements posec by the constraints.

An Unbounded Problem

In some problems the feasible solution space formed by the constraints is not confined within a closed boundary. In these cases, the objective function can sometimes increase indefinitely without ever reaching its maximum limit, since it never reaches a constraint boundary. The following is an example of this type of problem. (See Figure 2.10 for a graphical representation.)

Maximize $Z = 4x_1 + 2x_2$

subject to

$$-x_1 + 2x_2 \leqslant 6$$
$$-x_1 + x_2 \leqslant 2$$
$$x_1, x_2 \geqslant 0$$

Because this is a maximization problem, the optimal solution would normally be found on an outer boundary of the solution space. However, as can be seen in Figure 2.10, a boundary is never reached as the objective function increases. Therefore, Z, profit,

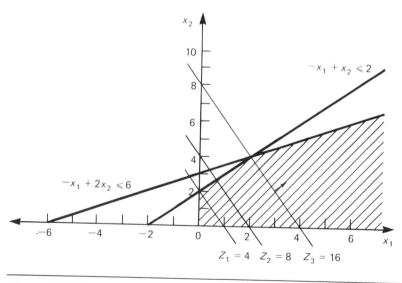

Figure 2.10 Unbounded Solution

increases infinitely without bound. Clearly this is not a realistic problem. Realistic maximization problems have limited resources that make infinitely large profits impossible. Thus, unbounded maximization problems arise only when a mistake has occurred in the linear programming formulation or when a constraint has been inadvertently omitted. Note, however, that in the case of a minimization problem, if all variables were restricted to nonnegative values, the solution would occur at the origin.

SUMMARY In this chapter we have studied the formulation of linear programming through several examples, examined its general properties, and presented a graphical interpretation of the model and its solution characteristics. In doing so, we identified the three main components of linear programming models: (1) decision variables, (2) objective function, and (3) system constraints. Properties of linear programming that were defined include (1) linearity and additivity, (2) divisibility, and (3) certainty. The graphical interpretation of linear programming pointed out the concept of convex solution spaces and the existence of optimal solutions at the intersection of constraint equations, which form the feasible region boundary.

This chapter has provided you with the necessary insight and background to confront the next important step in our presentation of linear programming: the solution process. As we have already noted, graphical solution is quite limited. In the next chapter we will present the simplex method for solving linear programming problems. This straightforward solution technique is one reason linear programming has become such a popular, widely applied technique in management science.

REFERENCES

BAZARAA, M. S., and JARVIS, J. J. *Linear Programming and Network Flows.* New York: John Wiley & Sons, 1977.

BRADLEY, S. P.; HAX, A. C.; and MAGNANTI, T. L. *Applied Mathematical Programming.* Reading, Massachusetts: Addison-Wesley Publishing Company, 1977.

CHARNES, A., and COOPER, W. W. *Management Models and Industrial Applications of Linear Programming.* New York: John Wiley & Sons, 1961.

COOPER, L., and STEINBERG, D. *Methods and Applications of Linear Programming.* Philadelphia: W. B. Saunders Company, 1974.

DANTZIG, G. B. *Linear Programming and Extensions.* Princeton, New Jersey: Princeton University Press, 1963.

GAVER, D. P., and THOMPSON, G. L. *Programming and Probability Models in Operations Research.* Belmont, California: Wadsworth Publishing Company, 1973.

HADLEY, G. *Linear Programming.* Reading, Massachusetts: Addison-Wesley Publishing Company, 1962.

HILLIER, F. S., and LIEBERMAN, G. J. *Introduction to Operations Research.* 4th ed. San Francisco: Holden-Day, 1986.

IGNIZIO, J. P. *Linear Programming in Single and Multiple Objective Systems.* Englewood Cliffs, New Jersey: Prentice-Hall, 1982.

KWAK, N. K. *Mathematical Programming with Business Applications.* New York: McGraw-Hill, 1973.

LLEWELLYN, R. W. *Linear Programming.* New York: Holt, Rinehart and Winston, 1964.

LOOMBA, N. P., and TURBAN, E. *Applied Programming for Management.* New York: Holt, Rinehart and Winston, 1974.

LUENBERGER, D. G. *Introduction to Linear and Non-Linear Programming.* Reading, Massachusetts: Addison-Wesley Publishing Company, 1973.

McMILLAN, C. *Mathematical Programming.* 2d ed. New York: John Wiley & Sons, 1975.

NAYLOR, T. H.; BYRNE, E. T.; and VERNON, J. M. *Introduction to Linear Programming: Methods and Cases.* Belmont, California: Wadsworth Publishing Company, 1971.

PFAFFENBERGER, R. C., and WALKER, D. A. *Mathematical Programming for Economics and Business.* Ames, Iowa: Iowa State University Press, 1976.

PHILLIPS, D. T.; RAVINDRAN, A.; and SOL-BERG, J. J. *Operations Research.* 2d e New York: John Wiley & Sons, 1987.

ROTHENBERG, R. I. *Linear Programming* New York: Elsevier North-Holland 1979.

SCHRAGE, L. *LINDO, An Optimization Mod eling System,* 4th. ed., San Francisco: Th Scientific Press, 1991.

SIMMONS, D. M. *Linear Programming fo Operations Research.* San Francisco Holden-Day, 1972.

TAHA, H. A. *Operations Research: An Introduction.* 5th ed. New York: Macmillan 1992.

WINSTON, W. L. *Introduction to Mathematical Programming, Applications and Algorithms,* Boston: PWS-Kent, 1991.

PROBLEMS

1. A company produces two products, A and B, which have gross profits of $400 and $350, respectively. Each unit of product must be processed on two assembly lines for a required production time as follows:

	Hr/Unit	
Product	Line 1	Line 2
A	12	4
B	4	8
Total Hours	60	40

The cost of the production capacity on assembly lines 1 and 2 is a sunk cost, that is, it has already been paid for and is incurred whether it is used or not.

Formulate a linear programming model to determine the optimal product mix that will maximize profit.

2. In problem 1, assume that the same assembly line capacities exist, however the company only has to pay for the hours used, that is, the hours on each production line are a variable cost rather than a sunk cost. The cost per hour for assembly line 1 is $20/hour, and the cost per hour for assembly line 2 is $30/hour. Given this information, reformulate the linear programming model to determine the optimal product mix to maximize profit.

3. A farmer makes a feed mix from two different ingredients, A and B. Each bag of ingredient A contributes 1 pound of required vitamins and 4 pounds of the required minerals to the feed mix. Each bag of ingredient B contributes 2 pounds of the required vitamins and 2 pounds of the required minerals to the feed mix. The feed

mix must contain at least 40 pounds of the required vitamins and 60 pounds of the required minerals. Because of additional nutrients in the ingredients, each batch of feed mix must contain at least 5 bags of each ingredient. A bag of ingredient A costs $8, and a bag of ingredient B costs $10. The farmer wants to know the number of bags of each ingredient to use in the mix that will minimize total cost.

Formulate a linear programming model for this problem.

4. A textile manufacturer produces two types of cotton cloth: denim and corduroy. Corduroy is a heavier grade of cotton cloth and, as such, requires 7.5 pounds of raw cotton to produce one yard, whereas denim requires 5 pounds of raw cotton per yard. A yard of corduroy requires 3.2 hours of processing time, and a yard of denim requires 3.0 hours. Although the demand for denim is practically unlimited, the maximum demand for corduroy is 510 yards per month. The textile manufacturer has 6500 pounds of cotton and 3000 hours of processing time available each month.

The processing time each month is a sunk cost. The cost of cotton is $.10 per pound, and it is considered a variable cost since any excess in a month is carried over to the next month's production. (A maximum of 6500 pounds of cotton is available each month due to limited storage capacity.) The manufacturer sells the cloth for $2.75 per yard for denim and $3.85 per yard for corduroy. The manufacturer wants to know how many yards of each type of cloth to produce to maximize profit.

Formulate a linear programming model for this problem.

5. An electrical manufacturer produces three products: clocks, radios, and toasters. These products have the following resource requirements:

	Cost/Unit($)	Labor/Unit(hr)
Clock	7	2
Radio	10	3
Toaster	5	1

Maximum daily demand for clocks, radios, and toasters is 200, 300, and 150 respectively. The manufacturer has a daily production budget of $2000 and at most 600 hours of labor. In-process inventory space is available for a combined total of 500 units. Selling prices are $15 for a clock, $20 for a radio, and $12 for a toaster. The manufacturer desires to know the optimal product mix that will maximize profit.

Formulate a linear programming model for this problem.

6. A farmer has 350 acres and plans to plant corn and soybeans. Each acre of corn costs $250 to plant, maintain, and harvest, whereas each acre of soybeans costs $140 to plant, maintain, and harvest. The farmer has a crop loan of $70,000 available to cover costs. Each acre of corn will yield 100 bushels of corn, and each acre of soybeans will yield 30 bushels of soybeans. The farmer has contracted to sell the corn and soybeans for $3.00 per bushel and $6.00 per bushel, respectively. However, the farmer must store both the corn and the soybeans for several months after harvest in a storage facility, which has a maximum capacity of 27,000 bushels. The farmer wants to know how many acres of each crop to plant to maximize profit. Let $x_1 =$

number of acres of corn to be planted and x_2 = number of acres of soybeans to be planted.

Formulate a linear programming model for this problem.

7. Refer to problem 6. Using the decision variables x_1 = number of bushels of corn to be produced and x_2 = number of bushels of soybeans to be produced, reformulate the linear programming model for the farmer in problem 6.

8. A local brewery produces three types of beer: premium, regular, and light. The brewery has enough vat capacity to produce 27,000 gallons of beer per month. A gallon of premium beer requires 4.3 pounds of grain, a gallon of regular requires 3.8 pounds of grain, and a gallon of light requires 3.5 pounds of grain. The brewery is able to acquire 45,000 pounds of grain every month. Although the brewery's largest seller is regular beer, it wants to have a competitive market mix of beer. Thus, the brewery wishes to produce at least 4000 gallons each of light beer and premium beer, but not more than 12,000 gallons of these two beers combined. The brewery makes a profit of $3.00 per gallon on premium beer, $2.40 per gallon on regular beer, and $2.80 per gallon on light beer. The brewery manager wants to know how much of each type of beer to produce to maximize profit.

Formulate a linear programming model for this problem.

9. A concrete company produces 40-pound bags of concrete mix. Each bag of concrete mix contains 5 pounds of cement plus two ingredients, A and B. The cement costs $.15 per pound. Each pound of ingredient A costs $.06 and contains 4 units of fine sand, 3 units of coarse sand, and 5 units of gravel. Each pound of B costs $.10 and contains 3 units of fine sand, 6 units of coarse sand, and 2 units of gravel. Each bag of concrete must contain at least 120 units of fine sand, 120 units of coarse sand, and 100 units of gravel. The company desires to know the best combination of ingredients A and B to minimize total cost.

Formulate a linear programming model for this problem.

10. An individual has received an inheritance of $950,000 and is planning to invest this cash in some mix of cattle, real estate, land, and antiques. The anticipated cash flows associated with these investment alternatives are shown below (where time 0 = present time; time 1 = end of one year from present, and so on.) The planning horizon is three years.

Investment Alternatives	Cash Flows at Time t ($)			
	0	1	2	3
Cattle	−1	+.4	+1.0	0
Real Estate	0	−1	+.3	+1.1
Land	−1	0	0	+1.7
Antiques	0	0	−1	+1.2

For example, $1 invested in cattle requires a $1.00 cash outflow at time 0 and yields $.40 at time 1 (after 1 year), and $1.00 at time 2 (after 2 years), and so forth, for each investment alternative. Any cash not invested in one of the four investment alternatives is put into the money market and earns 7% per year (that is, any funds not invested in cattle and land at time zero is put into the money market yielding $1.07 at time 1, and similarly for other periods). All positive cash flows in a period are received prior to investment decisions in that period. The individual wishes to know how much to invest in each alternative to maximize cash value at the end of 3 years.

Formulate a linear programming model for this problem.

11. A manufacturing company produces two products, A and B, at two different plants, 1 and 2. Plant 1 has resources available to produce 500 units of either product (or a combination of products) daily, and plant 2 has enough resources to produce 800 units. The cost for each product at each plant is as follows.

	Product A	Product B
Plant 1	$50	$45
Plant 2	60	30

Plant 1 has a daily budget of $20,000, and plant 2 has a budget of $30,000. Based on past sales, the company knows it cannot sell more than 600 units of product A and 800 units of product B. The selling price for product A is $80 and for product B is $70. The company wishes to know the number of units of A and B to produce at plants 1 and 2 to maximize profits.

Formulate a linear programming model for this problem.

12. A furniture manufacturer produces tables and chairs at two plants. The tables and chairs have the following resource requirements:

	Wood (lb)	Upholstery (yd)
Table	3	—
Chair	5	8

The two products require different production times (in hours) depending on the plant at which they are produced.

	Plant 1	Plant 2
Table	3.0	1.5
Chair	2.0	2.5

The standard costs of production for each product at each plant are as follows:

	Plant 1	Plant 2
Table	$200	$230
Chair	150	135

The firm has 1000 yards of upholstery available weekly. The firm has 200 pounds of wood available weekly at plant 1 and 240 pounds weekly at plant 2. The firm has 100 hours of production time available per week at plant 1 and 120 hours per week at plant 2. The company has a weekly budget of $11,000 for tables and $10,700 for chairs. The firm sells tables for $350 and chairs for $250. The manufacturer wants to know the number of tables and chairs to produce to maximize profit per week.

Formulate a linear programming model for this problem.

13. In problem 12, suppose the furniture manufacturer wants to eliminate the weekly budgets for tables and chairs as considerations in their weekly production planning. Also, sufficient upholstery is kept on hand such that it is never a constraint on production.

Formulate a linear programming model for this problem and comment on any unique features that may (or may not) exist.

14. The owner of a small machine shop has three employees and three machines: a grinder, a lathe, and a press. Each employee can operate each machine but with a different degree of expertise. The owner has work that requires the use of all three machines. The employees will take the following amounts of time (in minutes) to perform the job operations on each of the three machines.

	Grinder	Lathe	Press
Employee 1	25	32	19
Employee 2	41	50	38
Employee 3	17	23	21

The shop owner wants to know which employee to assign to each machine to minimize the time required to do the work operations.

Formulate a linear programming model for this problem.

15. A mining company owns two mines that can be operated seven days a week to produce ore. The mines have different locations and, thus, different production capacities. After crushing, the ore is graded and divided into three classes: high, medium, and low. The two mines are capable of the following daily production in tons:

	Mine 1	Mine 2
High Grade	6	2
Medium Grade	2	2
Low Grade	4	12

A contract with a smelting company calls for 41 tons of high grade ore, 25 tons of medium grade ore, and 77 tons of low grade ore per week. It costs the company $2000 per day to run the first mine and $1600 per day to run the second mine. The

mine owner wants to know the number of days to operate each mine in order to fil
the smelting company's order at minimum cost.

Formulate a linear programming model for this problem.

16. A manufacturer produces three types of plumbing equipment. Each type of equipment is produced on one of three assembly lines. The output on each line and time
available are   *like a batch you either make 15 on line 1 or you make none*

	Output (units/hr)	Time Available (hr/week)
Line 1	15	25
Line 2	10	40
Line 3	12	30

The primary raw materials used in producing these types of plumbing equip
ment are steel and copper tubing. The amount of raw material needed to produc
the equipment on each line is

	Steel (lb/unit)	Copper Tubing (ft/unit)
Line 1	50	15
Line 2	35	25
Line 3	40	20

At the present time, the company has available 40,000 pounds of steel an
20,000 feet of copper tubing each week. The company receives a profit margin c
$21 on each unit of the type of equipment produced on line 1, $28 on each unit c
the type produced on line 2, and $25 on each unit of the type produced on line 3
The manufacturer wants to know the number of hours that should be allocated o
each line for the production of the three types of equipment in order to maximiz
profit. Let the decision variables be x_i = number of hours on assembly line i (i =
1, 2, 3).

Formulate a linear programming model for this problem.

17. In problem 16, reformulate the problem as a linear programming model where th
decision variables are defined as: x_j = number of units of plumbing equipment typ
j (for j = 1, 2, 3).

18. Grain cooperatives in Kansas, Nebraska, and Iowa ship grain to three warehouses
Louisiana, Texas, and Georgia. The supply of grain per month at each source is

Source	Supply (tons)
Kansas	800
Nebraska	300
Iowa	600
	1700

The demand at each warehouse per month is

Destination	Demand (tons)
Louisiana	400
Texas	700
Georgia	500
	1600

The costs per ton for transporting grain from sources to destinations are

From	To		
	Louisiana	Texas	Georgia
Kansas	$20	$30	$50
Nebraska	25	15	30
Iowa	45	17	22

The firm wants to know the optimal amount to ship from each source to each destination in order to minimize cost.

Formulate a linear programming model for this problem.

19. A feed company produces a livestock feed mix from four ingredients: corn, peanuts, oats, and a vitamin supplement. The company produces the feed mix in various batch sizes (where the batch quantity in pounds = Q). The cost per pound of each ingredient used in the feed mix is

Ingredient	Cost/lb
Corn	$.10
Peanuts	.05
Oats	.15
Vitamins	.20

Each batch must be mixed according to the following specifications:

a. The mix must contain at least 30% peanuts.
b. The mix cannot contain more than 20% oats.
c. Each batch must contain at least 10% vitamin supplement.
d. The ratio of corn and oats to peanuts must be at least 3 to 2.

The feed company wants to have a model formulated and ready to solve each time they get ready to produce a batch of size Q. (That is, they want to be able to plug the value of Q, the batch size, into the model formulation, *in one and only one location*, and then solve for the optimum solution.)

Formulate a linear programming model for this problem.

20. A copy machine manufacturer produces two types of copy machines: basic and deluxe. Each basic machine produced contributes $700 to profit, and each deluxe

machine produced contributes $1000 to profit. Each copy machine is processed through an assembly operation and painting. If the assembly operation were completely devoted to basic machines, 550 machines per day could be assembled; and, if the assembly were completely devoted to deluxe machines, 300 machines per day could be assembled. If the painting were completely devoted to painting basic machines, 500 basic machines per day could be painted; and, if the painting were completely devoted to deluxe machines, 400 deluxe machines could be painted.

Formulate a linear programming model to maximize contribution to profit for the copy machine manufacturer.

21. A department store manager has four employees available to assign to three departments in the store: lamps, sporting goods, and linens. The manager desires that each of these departments have at least one, but not more than two, employees. In other words, two of the departments will have one employee, and one department will have two. Each employee has different areas of expertise that are reflected in the estimated daily sales each employee is expected to generate in each department, as shown below.

Employee	Department		
	Lamps	Sporting Goods	Linens
1	$130	$150	$ 90
2	275	300	100
3	180	225	140
4	200	120	160

The manager wishes to know which employee(s) to assign to each department to maximize expected sales.

Formulate a linear programming model for this problem.

22. In problem 21, suppose that the department store manager needs only one employee for each department and will lay off the extra employee. Formulate a new linear programming model that reflects this new condition.

23. Ace oil company produces and sells two grades of unleaded gasoline: high octane and low octane. It produces these two products by blending raw gasoline stock purchased on the open market. It currently has on hand two raw gasoline stocks as follows:

	Gallons	Octane Level
Raw Stock 1	80,000	70
Raw Stock 2	120,000	100

Demand for each of the two grades of unleaded gasoline is created by advertising. Each dollar spent on advertising creates 80 gallons of demand for high octane gas and 100 gallons of demand for low octane gas. The company advertises that the high octane gas will contain an average octane level of at least 95 and their low octane gas will contain an average octane level of at least 80. High octane gas is sold for $1.10 per gallon and low octane gas is sold for $.90 per gallon.

Formulate a linear programming model to maximize profits.

24. An auto parts manufacturer makes crankshafts that are sold to auto, truck, and tractor manufacturers. Each of the different vehicles requires a different crankshaft. The auto parts company is in the process of determining its production of each of the three types of crankshafts for the upcoming planning period. The marketing department has forecasted the following maximum demand for each of the crankshafts during the planning period:

Crankshafts	Maximum Demand
Autos	175
Trucks	65
Tractors	160

The parts company sells auto crankshafts for $27.75, truck crankshafts for $34.50, and tractor crankshafts for $30.00. As a matter of policy, it wants to produce no less than 50% of the forecasted demand for each product. It also wants to keep production of tractor crankshafts to a maximum of 40% of total crankshaft production.

The production department has estimated that the material costs for auto, truck, and tractor crankshafts will be $4.00, $6.00, and $5.50 per unit, respectively. The crankshafts are processed through forge, lathe, and grinding stations. In the upcoming planning period, there will be 600 hours available at the forge, where the direct labor cost is $2.25 per hour. The lathe station has 500 hours available, and the direct labor cost is $2.50 per hour. The grinding station has 480 hours available, and the direct labor cost is $2.75 per hour. The standard processing rate for auto crankshafts is 3 hours in forge, 2 hours in lathe, and 1 hour in grinding. Truck crankshafts require 4 hours in forge, 1 hour in lathe, and 3 hours in grinding, whereas tractor crankshafts require 2 hours at each station. The auto parts company wants to know the optimal plan for crankshaft production.

Formulate a linear programming model for this problem.

25. An apple products company purchases apples from local growers and makes applesauce and apple juice. It costs $.60 to produce a jar of applesauce and $.85 to produce a bottle of apple juice. To present a representative marketing mix to its customers, the company has made it a policy that at least 30%, but not more than 60%, of the items it produces be applesauce.

The company wants to produce up to, but not more than, the demand for each product. The company marketing manager estimates that the demand for applesauce is a maximum of 5,000 jars plus an additional 3 jars for each $1 spent on applesauce advertising. The maximum demand for apple juice is estimated to be 4,000 bottles plus an additional 5 bottles for every $1 spent to promote apple juice. The company has $16,000 to spend on producing and advertising applesauce and apple juice. Applesauce sells for $1.45 per jar, and apple juice sells for $1.75 per bottle. The company wants to know how many units of each apple product to produce and how much to spend on advertising for each product to maximize profit.

Formulate a linear programming model for this problem.

26. A firm is considering two investment opportunities with cash flows (in thousands of dollars) as shown below. Assume that at the current time (time zero), the firm has $100,000 to invest, and it will have another $80,000 to invest at time 1. The firm can invest any fractional amount in one or both investment opportunities up to the amounts shown below. Assuming that the firm's discount rate (r) is .10, formulate a linear programming model that will maximize the net present value of the firm's investment in the two opportunities.

	Cash Flows at Time t ($1,000)			
Opportunities	0	1	2	3
Investment 1	−70	−50	+70	+100
Investment 2	−80	−40	+90	+70

27. A distillery produces custom-blended whiskey. A particular blend consists of rye and bourbon whiskies. The company has received an order for a minimum of 400 gallons of this custom-blended whiskey.

The customer has specified that the order must contain at least 40% rye and no more than 250 gallons of bourbon. The customer has also specified that the blend should be mixed in the ratio of two parts rye to one part bourbon. The company can produce 500 gallons per week regardless of the blend, and it wants to complete this order in one week. The blend is sold for $5 per gallon. The brewing company' cost per gallon is $2 for rye and $1 for bourbon. The company wants to determine the blend mix that will meet customer requirements and maximize profits.

Formulate a linear programming model for this problem.

28. A manufacturer must meet the following contracted delivery schedule for a particular product over the next four months:

Month	Quantity Company Contracted to Deliver
1	5
2	6
3	8
4	9

The manufacturer has the option of producing more than is contracted for during any given month and storing the surplus product until needed. Storage cost is given as $1 per item per month.

Items can be produced in regular time or in overtime. The costs associated with each type of production are

Month	Regular Time	Overtime
1	$1	$2
2	4	6
3	2	4
4	4	6

The fluctuation in unit production costs is due to seasonal resource factors.

There is a capacity restriction as to regular and overtime production. The maximum number of units that may be produced during regular time in any month is 9 units. The maximum for overtime production is 3 units. There are no items available at the beginning of month 1, and the manufacturer does not want any surplus at the end of month 4. The manufacturer wants to know the optimum production schedule to minimize costs.

Formulate a linear programming model for this problem.

29. A transport company has expanded its shipping capacity by purchasing 90 trailer trucks from a competitor that went bankrupt. The company subsequently located 30 of the purchased trucks at each of its shipping warehouses in Charlotte, Memphis, and Louisville. The company makes shipments from each of these warehouses to terminals in St. Louis, Atlanta, and New York. Each truck is capable of making one shipment per week. The terminal managers have each indicated their capacity for extra shipments. The manager at St. Louis can accommodate 40 additional trucks per week, the manager at Atlanta can accommodate 60 additional trucks, and the manager at New York can accommodate 50 additional trucks. The company makes the following profit per truckload shipment from each warehouse to each terminal. The profits differ as a result of differences in products shipped, shipping costs, and transport rates.

	Terminal		
Warehouse	St. Louis	Atlanta	New York
Charlotte	$1800	$2100	$1600
Memphis	1000	700	900
Louisville	1400	800	2200

The company wants to know how many trucks to assign to each route (i.e., warehouse to terminal) to maximize profit.

Formulate a linear programming model for this problem.

30. A building supply company has received an order for boards in three lengths:

Length	Order Quantity
7 ft	700 boards
9 ft	1200 boards
10 ft	300 boards

The lumber the company has in stock is all standard-length 25-foot boards. There-fore, the company must cut the standard-length boards into the required lengths to meet the order requirements. Naturally, the company wishes to select cutting pat-terns that will minimize the number of standard-length boards used. The company wants to determine the optimal manner in which to cut up the 25-foot boards in order to meet the order requirements and minimize the number of standard-length boards used.

Formulate a linear programming model to determine the number of standard-length boards to cut.

31. In problem 30, when a board is cut according to a specific pattern, the amount of board left over is referred to as trim loss. Reformulate the linear programming model for problem 30 such that the objective is to minimize trim loss rather than to min-imize the total number of boards used.

32. A meat-processing firm produces wieners from four ingredients: chicken, beef, pork, and a cereal additive. The firm produces three types of wieners: regular, beef, and all meat. The company has the following amounts of each ingredient available on a daily basis:

	lb/Day	Cost/lb
Chicken	200	$.20
Beef	300	.30
Pork	150	.50
Cereal Additive	400	.05

Each type of wiener has certain ingredient specifications:

Wiener	Specifications	Selling Price/lb
Regular	Not more than 10% beef and pork combined; not less than 20% chicken	$ .90
Beef	Not less than 75% beef	1.25
All Meat	No cereal additive; not more than 50% beef and pork combined	1.75

The firm wants to know the amount of wieners of each type (in pounds) to produce in order to maximize profits.

Formulate a linear programming model for this problem.

33. A machine shop is planning next week's production. The shop makes cylinders, plates, and bushings. The selling prices are $25 per cylinder, $20 per plate, and $30 per bushing. There are three alternative production routes for each product. The following table gives the hours available, the operation times (in tenths of an hour) and the number of products required:

Routes	Cylinders			Plates			Bushings			Machine Hours Available
	1	2	3	1	2	3	1	2	3	
Lathes	.5	.7	1.1	.4	.2	0	.5	.2	0	800
Grinders	.5	0	.3	.5	.3	.3	.3	1.2	1.4	500
Welders	.5	.6	.3	.8	1.5	1.8	1.4	.7	.4	700
Minimum Product Requirements	100			200			300			

The machine shop wants to know the production schedule that will maximize total sales.

Formulate a linear programming model for this problem.

34. A commodities trading firm knows the prices at which it can buy and sell items of a certain commodity during the next four months. It is restricted from following the market trend by the limited capacity of its warehouse, which is 10,000 bushels. The buying price (c_i) and selling price (p_i) during each of the given months (i) are given as follows:

	Month i			
	1	2	3	4
c_i	$5	$6	$7	$8
p_i	4	8	6	7

No storage cost is assumed. Assume that sales are made at the beginning of the month, followed by purchases. At the beginning of the first month, there are 2000 bushels in the warehouse. The trading firm wants to know the amounts that should be bought and sold each month in order to maximize profit.

Formulate a linear programming model for this problem.

35. A young investor who has accumulated a large amount of money has sought advice from an investment counselor on how to invest some or all of the money. With the aid of the counselor, the investor has selected the following investment alternatives: common stock, treasury bills, AAA bonds, BBB bonds, income bonds, and negotiable certificates of deposit. After careful analysis, the counselor has determined the estimated yield for each investment alternative.

Investment Alternative	Estimated Annual Yield (%)
Common stock	12.00
Treasury bills	6.50
AAA bonds	8.00
BBB bonds	10.00
Income bonds	13.00
Negotiable certificates of deposit	7.00

The investor wants the investment in common stock to be no more than $50,000 and the investment in income bonds to be no more than 10% of the total invested in bonds (AAA, BBB, and income). The amount invested in negotiable certificates of deposit should be at least as much as the amount invested in treasury bills. In the interest of diversification, not more than 25% of the total investment should be invested in any one alternative. The investor wants to know the amount to invest in each alternative to maximize the expected return.

The investment counselor doesn't yet know the total amount to be invested, but he wants to go ahead and formulate a linear programming model now so that he can obtain a solution quickly once he learns the amount. Thus, he would like to have a linear programming model with the total amount given as Q just once in the model. When he learns the actual dollar amount, he will replace Q with the dollar amount and solve for the optimum solution.

Formulate a linear programming model for this problem.

36. A business firm that operates seven days a week requires different numbers of full-time employees on each day of the week as shown below. Each employee works five consecutive days each week and then has two days off. For example, an employee who works Sunday through Thursday, has Friday and Saturday off. The firm wishes to develop a schedule of employees that meets all their needs while minimizing the number of full-time employees.

Day	Number of Full-Time Employees Required
1. Sunday	30
2. Monday	45
3. Tuesday	43
4. Wednesday	40
5. Thursday	50
6. Friday	55
7. Saturday	60

Formulate a linear programming model to achieve the firm's goal.

37. A company that has a two-year contract to haul ore from an open-pit mine to loading docks for shipping needs 200 additional trucks. Purchased trucks have a useful life of two years and a purchase cost of $140,000 each. The company can lease trucks for $80,000 per year (paid at the beginning of the year). Purchased trucks will be purchased only at the beginning of the two-year period and have no salvage value at the end of two years. The mining company has $8 million cash available to lease and/or buy trucks at the beginning of year 1. In addition, the company can obtain a loan each year for as much as $20 million at 12% interest per year. The loan agreement requires that the company repay the borrowed amount plus interest at the end of each year. Each truck will earn $120,000 per year, which will become part of the cash flow of funds available to the company for truck leasing and loan repayment. The company wants to minimize the total cost of the trucks over a two-year period.

Formulate a linear programming model for this problem.

38. A shipping firm desires to know the maximum tonnage of goods it can transport

from city A to city F. The firm can contract for various transport carriers on different routes linking these cities via several intermediate stations as follows:

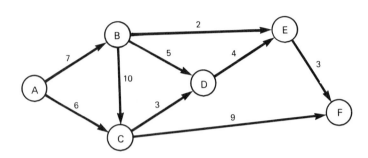

The firm can transport a maximum amount of goods from point to point, based on the maximum tonnage capacity available on each route segment, as shown on the diagram. The firm desires to determine the maximum tonnage that can be shipped from city A to city F.

Formulate a linear programming model for this problem.

39. An investor has $200,000 to invest in three alternatives—stocks, bonds, and certificates of saving—during the next four years. The investor wishes to cash in all investments at the end of four years and to receive as much cash as possible. The investor can invest in any of the three alternatives at the beginning of each year. Each dollar invested in stocks returns $1.15 at the end of a year. Each dollar invested in bonds returns $1.50 at the end of three years. Each dollar invested in savings certificates returns $1.25 at the end of two years. Bonds and savings certificates cannot be cashed in prior to their maturity date. To spread out the risk of the investments and have a balanced portfolio, the investor does not wish to invest more than 50% of the total investment in any single alternative. The investor wants to know how much to invest in each alternative during the next four years to maximize the amount of cash available at the end of the fourth year.

Formulate a linear programming model for this problem.

40. A large amusement theme park hires college students to work during the four summer months of May, June, July, and August. The park needs a total of 32,000 hours of this type of labor in May, 48,000 hours in June, 64,000 hours in July, and 48,000 hours in August. It takes one month of training before students can work regularly at a job, so they must be hired at least one month before they are needed. In addition, during training, each trainee requires 50 hours of supervision by an experienced employee. The experienced employee is not available for regular work during these 50 hours. Each experienced employee can work a maximum of 160 hours per month. If more employee hours are available than are required, the employees work less than 160 hours; no one is laid off. Fifteen percent of all experienced employees quit each month. Employees who quit agree to work out the month in which they quit. The salary of an experienced employee is $650 per month, and a trainee is paid $400 per month. Two hundred fifty experienced employees are available at the

beginning of May. The personnel director at the park wants to know how many employees to hire and train through July to minimize cost.

Formulate a linear programming model for this problem.

41. A firm sells four pieces of equipment, p_1, p_2, p_3, and p_4, which can be produced on five machines, m_1, m_2, m_3, m_4, and m_5, or purchased from an outside vendor. The time required (in hundredths of an hour) on each machine to produce each piece of equipment is

Equipment	Machine				
	m_1	m_2	m_3	m_4	m_5
p_1	.03	.00	.02	.04	.03
p_2	.00	.07	.06	.10	.07
p_3	.10	.15	.12	.12	.00
p_4	.04	.10	.06	.05	.06

Each machine is limited to 40 production hours per week. Demand for each piece of equipment is 700 units per week. The cost of producing each part on a machine and its price if purchased are

Equipment	Manufactured Cost/Unit	Purchase Price/Unit
p_1	$4.00	$5.25
p_2	6.00	9.00
p_3	3.75	5.20
p_4	2.80	3.00

The firm wants to know the combination of manufactured and purchased pieces of equipment that will minimize total cost.

Formulate a linear programming model for this problem.

42. A manufacturing firm produces a single product that consists of three components, in the following quantities.

Component	Required Quantity
C_1	2 units
C_2	4 units
C_3	3 units

The components are manufactured in three different plants and shipped to the central assembly location. Each plant produces all three components. However, the number of units of each component produced per production run differs at each plant because of the different types and ages of the machinery. The number of units of each component produced in each production run at each plant is given as follows:

	Production Rate (units per run)		
Component	Plant 1	Plant 2	Plant 3
C_1	5	7	4
C_2	7	6	8
C_3	10	8	5

The components are manufactured from two different raw materials. The rates which the raw materials are used per production run at each plant and the quantiti of raw materials available are given as follows:

	Raw Material Utilization per Run			Raw Material Available
Raw Material	Plant 1	Plant 2	Plant 3	
1	10	14	11	3000 units
2	18	12	13	3800 units

The firm wishes to determine the number of production runs to make at each plar to maximize the number of units of completed final product.

Formulate a linear programming model for this problem.

43. A manufacturing firm produces a single product consisting of three components tha are assembled together to form the product. The three components are manufacture in a production operation involving two lathes and three presses. The productio time (in minutes per unit) for each machine for the three components is as follows

	Production Times (min)		
Machine	Component 1	Component 2	Component 3
Lathe	10	8	6
Press	9	21	15

The firm splits the lathe workload evenly between the two lathes, and the press workload is split evenly among the three presses. Additionally, the firm wishes to produce quantities of components that will balance the daily loading among lathes and presses, so that, on the average, no machine is operated more than one hour per day longer than any other machine.

The firm also wishes to produce a quantity of components that will result in completely assembled products, without any partial assemblies. The objective of the firm is to maximize the number of units of assembled product produced per day.

Formulate a linear programming model for this problem.

44. A company produces six products in the following manner. Raw material is purchased and processed yielding three products (product 1, product 2, and product 3). The firm's production process is such that each unit of raw material purchased yields 2 units of product 1, 3 units of product 2, and 1 unit of product 3. The firm can

sell each of the three products or it can process them further. Further processing of product 1 yields .8 units of product 4; further processing of product 2 yields .5 units of product 3 yields .4 units of product 6. The selling prices, processing costs, and maximum forecasted demands for each product are given below. The cost of raw material per unit is $500 and a maximum of 400 units is available for the planning period.

Product	Sale Price ($)	Processing Cost ($)	Maximum Demand (units)
1	150	40	300
2	70	30	500
3	300	60	400
4	900	100	200
5	1200	150	300
6	600	120	100

Formulate a linear programming model for this problem.

45. Solve the following linear programming problem graphically.

Maximize $Z = 9x_1 + 12x_2$

subject to
$$4x_1 + 8x_2 \leq 64$$
$$5x_1 + 5x_2 \leq 50$$
$$15x_1 + 8x_2 \leq 120$$
$$x_1 \leq 7$$
$$x_2 \leq 7$$
$$x_1, x_2 \geq 0$$

46. Solve the following linear programming problem graphically.

Minimize $Z = 3x_1 + 6x_2$

subject to
$$3x_1 + 2x_2 \leq 18$$
$$x_1 + x_2 \geq 5$$
$$x_1 \leq 4$$
$$x_2 \leq 7$$
$$x_2/x_1 \leq 7/8$$
$$x_1, x_2 \geq 0$$

47. Solve the following linear programming problem graphically.

Minimize $Z = 8x_1 + 6x_2$

subject to
$$4x_1 + 2x_2 \geq 20$$
$$-6x_1 + 4x_2 \leq 12$$
$$x_1 + x_2 \geq 6$$
$$x_1, x_2 \geq 0$$

48. Solve the following linear programming problem graphically.

Maximize $Z = 8x_1 + 7x_2$
subject to
$$10x_1 + 8x_2 \geq 40$$
$$6x_1 + 16x_2 \leq 48$$
$$x_2 \geq 1$$
$$x_1, x_2 \geq 0$$

49. Solve the following linear programming problem graphically.

Minimize $Z = 4x_1 + 5x_2$
subject to
$$2x_1 + 2x_2 \geq 8$$
$$x_2 \leq 3$$
$$9x_1 + 3x_2 \leq 27$$
$$x_1, x_2 \geq 0$$

50. Solve the following linear programming problem graphically.

Maximize $Z = 3x_1 + 2x_2$
subject to
$$2x_1 + 4x_2 \leq 22$$
$$-x_1 + 4x_2 \leq 10$$
$$4x_1 - 2x_2 \leq 14$$
$$x_1 - 3x_2 \leq 1$$
$$x_1, x_2 \geq 0$$

51. Solve the following linear programming problem graphically.

Maximize $Z = 5x_1 + 2x_2$
subject to
$$3x_1 + 5x_2 \leq 15$$
$$10x_1 + 4x_2 \leq 20$$
$$x_1, x_2 \geq 0$$

52. Solve the following linear programming problem graphically.

Maximize $Z = 1.5x_1 + x_2$
subject to
$$x_1 \leq 4$$
$$x_1 - x_2 \leq 0$$
$$x, x_2 \geq 0$$

53. Solve the following linear programming problem graphically.

Maximize $Z = 3x_1 + 2x_2$
subject to
$$x_1 + x_2 \leq 1$$
$$x_1 + x_2 \geq 2$$
$$x_1, x_2 \geq 0$$

54. Solve the following linear programming problem graphically.

   Maximize $Z = x_1 + x_2$

   subject to
   $$x_1 - x_2 \geqslant -1$$
   $$-x_1 + 2x_2 \leqslant 4$$
   $$x_1, x_2 \geqslant 0$$

55. Solve the following linear programming problem graphically.

   Maximize $Z = 2x_1 + 3x_2$

   subject to
   $$x_1 + x_2 \leqslant 4$$
   $$3x_1 + x_2 \geqslant 4$$
   $$x_1 + 5x_2 \geqslant 4$$
   $$x_1 \leqslant 3$$
   $$x_2 \leqslant 3$$
   $$x_1, x_2 \geqslant 0$$

56. Solve the following linear programming problem graphically.

   Maximize $Z = 2x_1 + 2x_2$

   subject to
   $$x_1 - x_2 \geqslant 0$$
   $$-3x_1 + x_2 \geqslant 3$$
   $$x_1, x_2 \geqslant 0$$

57. Solve the following linear programming problem graphically.

   Maximize $Z = 5x_1 + x_2$

   subject to
   $$3x_1 + 4x_2 = 24$$
   $$x_1 \leqslant 6$$
   $$x_1 + 3x_2 \leqslant 12$$
   $$x_1, x_2 \geqslant 0$$

58. Solve the following linear programming problem graphically.

   Maximize $Z = 4x_1 + 6x_2$

   subject to
   $$2x_1 - 3x_2 \leqslant 12$$
   $$-x_1 + 2x_2 \leqslant 6$$
   $$x_1 \leqslant 6$$
   $$2x_1 + 5x_2 \leqslant 20$$
   $$x_1, x_2 \geqslant 0$$

59. Solve the following linear programming problem graphically.

   Minimize $Z = 8x_1 + 2x_2$

   subject to
   $$2x_1 - 6x_2 \leqslant 12$$
   $$5x_1 + 4x_2 \geqslant 40$$

$$x_1 + 2x_2 \geq 12$$
$$x_2 \leq 6$$
$$x_1, x_2 \geq 0$$

60. Solve problem 1 graphically.

61. Solve problem 3 graphically.

62. Solve problem 4 graphically.

63. Solve problem 6 graphically.

64. Solve problem 7 graphically.

65. Solve problem 9 graphically.

66. Solve problem 15 graphically.

67. Solve problem 20 graphically.

68. Solve problem 26 graphically.

69. Solve problem 27 graphically.

3

The Simplex Method

The **simplex method** of solving linear programming problems was first developed by George B. Dantzig in 1947 and has since been refined by numerous others. The simplex method is based on matrix algebra in that a set of simultaneous constraint equations is solved through the matrix inverse procedure. Although the simplex method may sound formidable, its basic steps are relatively simple. The mathematical procedure employs an iterative process of repeating a set of mathematical operations until the optimal solution is reached. In other words, in a profit maximization problem each successive operation yields a total profit greater than the profit resulting from the previous operation.

Quite simply, the simplex method is nothing more than a series of mathematical steps or, as some authors have noted, a mathematical "machine." Values from the formulated linear programming model are fed into the simplex machine, and a set of predefined mathematical operations is performed successively until the solution is generated. Thus, it would be possible for the reader to solve a linear programming problem by simply following the predefined simplex steps. However, in this chapter we will not only describe the simplex process but also offer the reader insight into the simplex mathematics that will further understanding of linear programming.

TRANSFORMATION OF THE GENERAL LINEAR PROGRAMMING MODEL TO THE STANDARD SIMPLEX FORM

In order to employ the simplex method for solving linear programming problems, it is first necessary to transform all inequality constraints in the model to equalities. The simplex method is a procedure based on the principles of matrix algebra. As such, it entails the solution of sets of simultaneous equations. However, the constraints of linear programming models are often in the form of inequalities, as shown in many of the examples in Chapter 2. Since inequalities are difficult to solve simultaneously, one of the primary requirements of the simplex method is that all constraint inequalities be transformed into equalities. (See Appendix A for the solution of linear programming problems via matrix algebra.) In order to demonstrate this transformation, an example linear programming model of a product mix problem will be used.

Example 3.1 Product Mix Problem

A manufacturing firm produces two products, 1 and 2. The requirements for labor a
materials for production of each product, as well as the resource availabilities, are
follows:

Resource	Resource Requirements		Total Available Resources
	Product 1	Product 2	
Labor	2 hr/unit	4 hr/unit	80 hr
Material	3 lb/unit	1 lb/unit	60 lb

The unit profit is \$100 for product 1 and \$80 for product 2. Management's proble
is to determine the optimal product mix that will maximize profit subject to availabil
of the limited resources. The linear programming model for this problem is formulat
as follows:

Maximize $Z = \$100x_1 + 80x_2$ (profit)
subject to
$$2x_1 + 4x_2 \leqslant 80 \qquad \text{(labor)}$$
$$3x_1 + x_2 \leqslant 60 \qquad \text{(material)}$$
$$x_1, x_2 \geqslant 0$$

where

x_1 = number of units of product 1
x_2 = number of units of product 2
Z = total profit (\$)

In this problem, the $\leqslant$ inequality constraints are converted into equations by inser
ing in each constraint a new variable called a **slack variable.** For this problem two slac
variables are needed, one for each of the two constraints. The addition of these slac
variables (denoted by s_i) results in the following converted constraint equations:

$$2x_1 + 4x_2 + s_1 = 80 \quad \text{(labor)}$$
$$3x_1 + x_2 + s_2 = 60 \quad \text{(material)}$$

where

s_1 = slack variable for labor constraint
s_2 = slack variable for material constraint

The addition of these slack variables has a specific function in the linear program
ming problem that can best be demonstrated via graphical analysis. The product mi
problem is shown graphically in Figure 3.1.

The feasible solution space is defined by the shaded area $OABC$. Every point in the
solution space can be defined in terms of the two decision variables, x_1 and x_2, and the
two slack variables, s_1 and s_2.

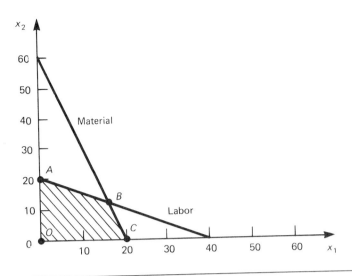

Figure 3.1 *Graphic Representation of the Product Mix Problem*

For example, at point C, $x_1 = 20$ and $x_2 = 0$. Substituting these values into both contraints results in the following values for s_1 and s_2:

Labor:
$$2x_1 + 4x_2 + s_1 = 80$$
$$2(20) + 4(0) + s_1 = 80$$
$$s_1 = 40$$

Material:
$$3x_1 + x_2 + s_2 = 60$$
$$3(20) + 1(0) + s_2 = 60$$
$$s_2 = 0$$

Slack, then, in reality is the amount of *unused* labor if 20 units of product 1 and zero units of product 2 are produced. Similar analyses can be performed at points A and B and for all points within the feasible solution space. For any point that is within the solution space but not on one of the constraint boundaries, slack will be present in both constraints, since all possible resources are not being employed. The most dramatic instance of unused resources is at the origin, O, where both $x_1 = 0$ and $x_2 = 0$. At the origin (which *is* a feasible solution point), $s_1 = 80$ and $s_2 = 60$. In other words, if there is no production, then all of the available resources are unused, or *slack*.

Table 3.1 gives the values for the decision variables, x_1 and x_2, and the associated values for the slack variables, s_1 and s_2, for each of the solution points shown in Figure 3.1.

In summary, the values of x_1 and x_2 represent the quantities of product 1 and product 2 to be produced, respectively, and the associated values of s_1 and s_2 represent the quantities of unused labor and material resources, respectively, when the associated quantities of products are produced. At point B, for example, all resources are used in

Table 3.1 *Variable Values for Various Solution Points*

Solution Point in Figure 3.1	Values of Decision Variables		Values of Slack Variables	
	x_1	x_2	s_1	s_2
A	0	20	0	40
B	16	12	0	0
C	20	0	40	0
O	0	0	80	60

the production of 16 units of product 1 and 12 units of product 2, since both slack variables (denoting unused resouces) are zero for that solution point.

From this analysis it can be ascertained that slack variables, which are defined as the amounts of unused resources, are introduced in order to convert inequality constraints into equalities.

We must now concern ourselves with the effect of the two additional variables on the objective function of the product mix problem. Recall that the original objective function represented the sum of the profits obtained from each product. Since slack variables are unused resources, it is obvious that they contribute nothing to the profit-maximizing objective of the problem. Thus, the objective function can be expressed as

$$\text{Maximize } Z = \$100x_1 + \$80x_2 + 0s_1 + 0s_2$$

THE SIMPLEX METHOD

The simplex method is a process that follows these general steps:

1. The process starts at the origin. (For Example 3.1, the initial solution is defined as $x_1 = 0$ and $x_2 = 0$.)

2. After the initial solution has been selected, the simplex process searches for a better solution, if one exists. (For Example 3.1, it searches for a solution with a higher profit, or Z value.) When a better solution is found, the simplex procedure automatically eliminates all the solutions that are not as good from further consideration.

3. This process is repeated until a better solution cannot be found. The simplex process then terminates and the optimal solution is indicated.

The General Simplex Tableau

One of the characteristics of the simplex method that contributes to its computational simplicity and ease of understanding is the conversion of the standard linear programming model into tableau form. Although several different formats of the simplex tableau have been described in different texts, the functions of these simplex tableaus are basically identical. We will employ the format shown in Table 3.2.

The symbols used in Table 3.2 are defined as follows:

c_j The profit or cost coefficients of the objective function; these are shown for each variable as c_1, c_2, c_3, c_4.

Table 3.2 *Simplex Tableau Format*

c_j c_b	basis	b_i^*	c_1 x_1	c_2 x_2	c_3 s_2	c_4 s_2
	z_j					
	$c_j - z_j$					

c_b	The profit or cost coefficients of the objective function for variables in the basis solution.
basis	The variables currently in the solution set—that is, the variables that have values at the solution point being analyzed. This combination of variables and associated values is referred to as a *basic feasible solution*.
b_i^* = cost of var. in basis	Initially, the values on the right-hand side of the problem constraints. As the simplex method iterates toward a solution, these values become the solution values for corresponding variables in the solution basis.

The row designations z_j and $c_j - z_j$ are computed values and, as such, will be defined as we proceed through the solution procedure.

All of these terms, c_j, c_b, *basis*, b_i^*, z_j, and $c_j - z_j$, are labels that appear in all subsequent tableaus. The blank areas (cells) and the variables, c_1, c_2, c_3, c_4, and so forth, will be replaced with values either provided directly from the model or computed.

he Initial Simplex Tableau

The tableau in Table 3.2 is set up for the four-variable, two-constraint product mix problem (Example 3.1) we have been using in this chapter. The formulation for this problem is given in equation form below and in tableau form in Table 3.3, with the parameters of the problem placed in the appropriate cells.

Maximize $Z = 100x_1 + 80x_2 + 0s_1 + 0s_2$ (profit)
subject to
$$2x_1 + 4x_2 + s_1 = 80 \qquad \text{(labor)}$$
$$3x_1 + x_2 + s_2 = 60 \qquad \text{(material)}$$
$$x_1, x_2, s_1, s_2 \geqslant 0$$

The sources of the values in the tableau become evident upon examination of Table 3.3 and the formulation of the product mix problem. However, to promote a better

Table 3.3 *Initial Simplex Tableau*

c_j c_b	basis	b_i^*	100 x_1	80 x_2	0 s_1	0 s_2
0	s_1	80	2	4	1	0
0	s_2	60	3	1	0	1
	z_j					
	$c_j - z_j$					

understanding of the simplex process, we will explain the origin of the tableau cell val
in greater detail.

The column with the heading *basis* contains the variables that are in the initial so
tion set. As we noted previously, the simplex method starts with an initial basic solut
at the origin and then proceeds to better solutions. Given a linear programming pr
lem with m constraint equations and n variables, there will always be m basic variab
and $n - m$ nonbasic variables. Basic variables are those variables in the solut
basis of the simplex tableau, with associated solution values; nonbasic variables
those variables that are not in the solution basis and, as such, are equal to zero. 1
the example problem, each iteration of the simplex solution process will contain t
basic variables corresponding to the two constraints ($m = 2$), and there will be two nonba
variables ($n - m = 2$).

We now know that a basic solution for our example problem consists of two ba
variables, while the other two variables equal zero. The initial basic solution is where
$= 80$ and $s_2 = 60$ (as shown in Table 3.3). Thus, the other two variables, x_1 and :
are nonbasic and are, by definition, equal to zero. Since $s_1 = 80$ denotes that all of t
labor resource is unused and $s_2 = 60$ denotes that all of the material resource is unuse
no productive activity is taking place, and x_1 and x_2 must equal zero. When x_1 and
are nonbasic (and, by definition, equal to zero), the associated solution on the Figure 3
graph is at point 0, the origin (where $x_1 = 0$, $x_2 = 0$). Therefore, the initial bas
solution is

$$2(0) + 4(0) + s_1 = 80$$
$$s_1 = 80$$
$$3(0) + 1(0) + s_2 = 60$$
$$s_2 = 60$$

This general property holds for all simplex problems of this type. The initial solutic
that begins the simplex process is always the solution at the origin. In Table 3.3, s_1 an
s_2 are the two variables forming the solution base. Note that the number of blank cel
(and empty rows) under the column entitled *basis* in Table 3.2 corresponds to the numbe
of constraint equations in the problem and, thus, the number of basic variables in th
solution. Thus, the total number of rows in the initial simplex tableau (two for th
problem) will remain constant for subsequent iterations. (Note that the nonnegativit
constraints, $x_1, x_2, s_1, s_2 \geq 0$, are not included in the tableau as constraint rows. Thi
is because the simplex process in its present form automatically excludes negative values
Conditions under which negative values may exist will be discussed later in this chapter.

The b_i^* column in Table 3.3 indicates the *right-hand-side* value of each constrain
equation. Thus, in the initial tableau, the b_i^* values are 80 for s_1 and 60 for s_2.

The x_j and s_i headings refer to the variables in the model. The tableau format call
for the decision variables (x_j) to be listed first, in order of magnitude of their subscrip
(j), followed by the slack variables, also listed from left to right in order of magnitude
of their subscript (i). Thus, in Table 3.3 the variables read, from left to right: x_1, x_2
s_1, and s_2.

The values within the tableau in the columns under each variable name (x_1, x_2, s_1
s_2) are the a_{ij} values (coefficients) in each constraint equation. Since the first row represents

i = constraint
j = activity
a_{11} - *amt of resource 1 used*
for activity 1

the first constraint, the a_{ij} values are

$$a_{11} = 2, a_{12} = 4, a_{13} = 1, a_{14} = 0$$

These values are shown in the row corresponding to s_1 in Table 3.3. The a_{ij} values for the second constraint are

$$a_{21} = 3, a_{22} = 1, a_{23} = 0, a_{24} = 1$$

The c_j values along the top row are the contributions per unit to the objective function of each variable. In the c_j row in Table 3.3, $c_1 = 100$, $c_2 = 80$, $c_3 = 0$, and $c_4 = 0$. The c_j values are also indicated along the left column of the initial simplex tableau for those variables in the solution basis (denoted by c_b). Since s_1 and s_2 are in the initial solution base, $c_3 = 0$ and $c_4 = 0$ are listed in this column.

This completes the process of filling in the cells in the initial simplex tableau. From this point on, the remaining cell values (z_j and $c_j - z_j$), as well as cell values in subsequent tableaus (i.e., iterations), are computed via the simplex algorithmic procedure.

IE SIMPLEX COMPUTATIONAL PROCESS

Let us review briefly the steps of the simplex method. The first step is to identify the initial basic feasible solution, and the next step is to proceed to better basic feasible solutions until the optimal solution is found. To complete the initial tableau, we need to evaluate the objective function value of the basic feasible solution. This is accomplished by computing the z_j row in the simplex tableau, as shown in Table 3.4. The values in the z_j row are determined by multiplying each a_{ij} value in the same column by its corresponding c_b value and then summing these products. For example, in the b_i^* column, the following computation is made:

$$
\begin{array}{cc}
c_b & b_i^* \\
0 \times 80 & = 0 \\
+ 0 \times 60 & = 0 \\
\hline
z_{b_i^*} & = 0
\end{array}
$$

Table 3.4 *The z Values of the Simplex Tableau*

c_b \ c_j	basis	b_i^*	100 x_1	80 x_2	0 s_1	0 s_2
0	s_1	80	2	4	1	0
0	s_2	60	3	1	0	1
	z_j	0	0	0	0	0
	$c_j - z_j$					

The z_j value in the b_i^* column is zero. This represents the total profit contribution of the basic solution. Since the solution base consists of only slack variables (s_1 and s_2), which contribute nothing to profit, the total value of the objective function is zero. The

z_j values are computed in a similar manner for the remaining columns. For example, computations for the z_j value in the x_1 column are shown in Table 3.5.

$$\begin{array}{c} c_b \quad x_1 \\ 0 \times 2 = 0 \\ + 0 \times 3 = 0 \\ \hline z_1 = 0 \end{array}$$

Similarly, all remaining z_j values (z_2, z_3, and z_4) are zero.

Table 3.5 The $c_j - z_j$ Values in the Simplex Tableau

c_b	c_j / basis	b_i^*	100 x_1	80 x_2	0 s_1	0 s_2
0	s_1	80	2	4	1	0
0	s_2	60	3	1	0	1
	z_j	0	0	0	0	0
	$c_j - z_j$		100	80	0	0

(handwritten margin notes):
← decrease in profit w/ prod. of 1 unit
← increase in profit w/ prod. of one unit

Now we must compute the bottom row of the simplex tableau, $c_j - z_j$. This is don by subtracting the z_j row values from the corresponding c_j values (shown at the top the tableau), as shown in Table 3.5. The $c_j - z_j$ row represents the net increase in prof associated with one additional unit of each variable. This property becomes more apparer if we look at a brief example.

The present simplex tableau is obviously not optimal, since the value of the objectiv function is zero. Thus, one of the nonbasic variables (x_1 or x_2) will become a bas variable. In other words, we will produce units of either product 1 or 2 in order to realiz some profit. Let us suppose that x_1 will become a basic variable. Since the contributio to profit (c_1) for x_1 is $100, we will increase the objective function value by that amour for every unit of product 1 produced. However, if we produce 1 unit of product 1 ($x = 1$), then the values of the slack variables must be decreased to reflect the quantities c labor and material resources used to produce 1 unit of product 1. Note from Table 3. that the labor and material utilization rates under x_1 are the values 2 and 3, respectively

In the variable columns, z_j represents the decrease in profit associated with the pro duction of 1 unit of each variable. In this case, since the decreases are in slack, there i no decrease in profit. Therefore, the total row value ($c_j - z_j$) is the per unit net increas in profit from entering a nonbasic variable into the solution basis. Note that for the basi variables $c_j - z_j$ is zero. Since these variables are already in the solution, they will neithe increase nor decrease the solution profit.

The Entering Nonbasic Variable

Now that the initial simplex tableau has been completed, the solution process can begin The first step is to determine the nonbasic variable that should enter the solution basis and become a basic variable. Observing Figure 3.2, we can see that a choice exists betweer the two variables x_1 and x_2. In other words, feasible solution points exist on both the x_1 and the x_2 axis.

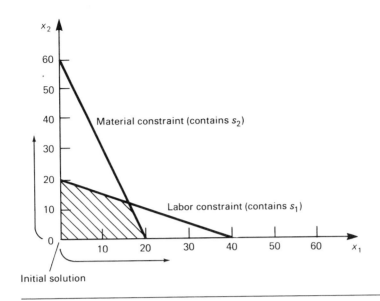

Figure 3.2 *Selection of the Entering Nonbasic Variable*

The **entering nonbasic variable** is the one that results in the largest increase in profit per unit. As noted earlier, the net increase (or decrease) in profit per unit is represented by $c_j - z_j$. The entering variable is x_1, since its $c_j - z_j$ value of 100 indicates that it provides the larger net increase of the two nonbasic variables. The x_1 column in Table 3.6 is referred to as the **pivot column** (the term *pivot* coming from the classical pivot operations in the solution of equivalent simultaneous equations). Referring again to Figure 3.2, note that the identification of x_1 as the entering nonbasic variable means that the solution point will be on the x_1 axis.

Table 3.6 *Determining the Pivot Column*

C_b	c_j / basis	b_i^*	100 x_1	80 x_2	0 s_1	0 s_2
0	s_1	80	2	4	1	0
0	s_2	60	3	1	0	1
	z_j	0	0	0	0	0
	$c_j - z_j$		100	80	0	0

Pivot column

The Leaving Basic Variable

Since it has been previously demonstrated that each basic solution contains only two (or m) variables, the next step in the solution process is the selection of the existing basic variable that must leave the basic solution and become zero if x_1 is to enter. Given that x_1 provides the greatest per unit increase in profit, it is desirable to produce as much x as possible. Looking at the labor constraint, we see that if all the labor resource is used to make product 1, s_1 is reduced to zero and x_1 becomes 40:

Labor:
$$2x_1 + 4x_2 + 1s_1 = 80$$
$$2x_1 + 4(0) + 1(0) = 80$$
$$2x_1 = 80$$
$$x_1 = 40$$

In other words, 80 hours of labor is enough to produce 40 units of product 1. Now, observing the material constraints and using all of the material slack (s_2) to produce product 1, we have

Material:
$$3x_1 + 1x_2 + 1s_2 = 60$$
$$3x_1 + 1(0) + 1(0) = 60$$
$$3x_1 = 60$$
$$x_1 = 20$$

The analysis of these two constraints indicates that there is enough labor to produce 40 units of product 1 and enough material to produce 20 units of product 1. This restricts the total value of x_1 to 20 units (see Figure 3.3). If 20 units of product 1 are produced, the total material resource will be consumed; thus, $s_2 = 0$. At the same time, when $x_1 = 20$, there is still some available labor left unused.

Labor:
$$2x_1 + 4x_2 + s_1 = 80$$
$$2(20) + 4(0) + s_1 = 80$$
$$s_1 = 40$$

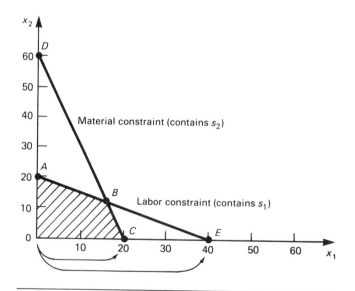

Figure 3.3 *Selection of the Leaving Basic Variable*

As a result, when x_1 enters the solution, s_2 is the leaving basic variable ($s_2 = 0$). This process is demonstrated graphically in Figure 3.3. As we move out on the x_1 axis, there are two alternative solution points to choose from, C and E. Point C corresponds to the material constraint, and point E corresponds to the labor constraint. Since point C ($x_1 = 20$) is the most constraining, point E ($x_1 = 40$) is infeasible (i.e., it is outside the feasible solution space). A unique and useful characteristic of the simplex method is that only feasible solution points are considered in the tableau basis. As can be deduced, this eliminates some of the solution points in the problem and contributes to the computational efficiency of the simplex method.

The general procedure for determining the leaving basic variable is to divide each b_i^* column value by its corresponding pivot column value. Select as the leaving basic variable the one that has the minimum nonnegative ratio.

$$
\begin{array}{ccl}
basis & b_i^* & x_1 \\
s_1 & 80 \div 2 & = 40 \\
s_2 & 60 \div 3 & = 20 \leftarrow \text{Minimum ratio}
\end{array}
$$

The leaving basic variable row is referred to as the **pivot row**. The value at the intersection of the pivot column and the pivot row is called the **pivot number**, or pivot point, and it is identified by a circle in Table 3.7.

Table 3.7 *Identification of Pivot Column, Pivot Row, and Pivot Number in the Initial Simplex Tableau*

C_b \ C_j	basis	b_i^*	100 x_1	80 x_2	0 s_1	0 s_2	
0	s_1	80	2	4	1	0	
0	s_2	60	③	1	0	1	Pivot row
	z_j	0	0	0	0	0	
	$c_j - z_j$		100	80	0	0	

Pivot column

The method for selecting the pivot row is more generally presented in terms of symbols, as follows. The pivot row is the row where we find the minimum ratio of

$$b_i^* / a_{ik} \geqslant 0, \text{ for } a_{ik} > 0$$

where

k = pivot column
i = row ($i = 1, 2, \ldots, m$) under consideration

In other words, the ratio must be nonnegative, and the divisor (in the pivot column) must be greater than zero. If either or both of these requirements are not met, the row under consideration is discarded as a candidate for the pivot row.

The Second Simplex Tableau

In the basis of the second simplex tableau, the variable x_1 has been substituted for s_2 which has left the basic solution. Table 3.8 shows the new basic solution, including the

Table 3.8 *Computation of the New Pivot Row Values in the Second Tableau*

c_b	c_j basis	b_i^*	100 x_1	80 x_2	0 s_1	0 s_2
0	s_1					
100	x_1	20	1	$\frac{1}{3}$	0	$\frac{1}{3}$
	z_j					
	$c_j - z_j$					
		$60 \div 3 = 20$	$3 \div 3 = 1$	$1 \div 3 = \frac{1}{3}$	$0 \div 3 = 0$	$1 \div 3 = \frac{1}{3}$

basis variables s_1 and x_1. The corresponding c_j value of 100 for x_1 is shown in the c_b column.

The second simplex tableau (following one iteration) is the new solution with the basic variables s_1 and x_1. In order to produce the cell values in the second simplex tableau, several mathematical operations, called pivot operations, must be performed.

First, the row values in the second tableau corresponding to the *pivot row in the initial tableau* are computed by dividing every cell value in the pivot row of the first tableau by the pivot number, 3. The new values, which are referred to as the new pivot row, are shown in Table 3.8. The computations that yield the new pivot row values are shown below Table 3.8. The general formula for this operation is

$$\text{New pivot row values} = \frac{\text{old pivot row values}}{\text{pivot number}}$$

These values represent the rate of substitution of the basis variable x_1 for every other variable shown at the top of each column. For example, the value $\frac{1}{3}$ at the intersection of the x_1 row and the s_2 column shows that every unit of x_1 produced requires 3 units of material slack (s_2). Thus, a 1 to 3 substitution ratio exists between x_1 and s_2. All other new pivot row values can be analyzed similarly.

The next operation is to compute all remaining cell values in the tableau. Since there are only two constraint rows in this problem, there is only one other row of values to be determined. However, if there were more than one remaining row, all these row values would be determined in the same way. These row values are computed using the following formula:

$$\text{New row value} = \text{old row value} - \left(\begin{array}{c} \text{corresponding} \\ \text{coefficient in} \\ \text{pivot column} \end{array} \times \begin{array}{c} \text{new pivot} \\ \text{row value} \end{array} \right)$$

Let us look at the cell value at the intersection of the s_1 row and the b_i^* column. Using the formula, we have

$$\text{New row value} = 80 - (2 \times 20) = 40$$

The computation of all cell values in the s_1 row is demonstrated in Table 3.9. These values are shown in tableau form in Table 3.10.[1]

---

[1] The reader may recognize this process as being analogous to the classical Gauss-Jordan process for solving linear equations. For a more detailed account of the latter process, see Appendix A.

Table 3.9 Computation of s_1 Row Values

Columns	Old Row Values	—	Coefficient in Pivot Column	×	New Pivot Row Value	=	New Row Value
b_i^*	80	—	(2	×	20)	=	40
x_1	2	—	(2	×	1)	=	0
x_2	4	—	(2	×	⅓)	=	$^{10}/_3$
s_1	1	—	(2	×	0)	=	1
s_2	0	—	(2	×	⅓)	=	$-^2/_3$

Table 3.10 New Row Values in the Second Simplex Tableau

c_b \ c_j	basis	b_i^*	100 x_1	80 x_2	0 s_1	0 s_2
0	s_1	40	0	$^{10}/_3$	1	$-^2/_3$
100	x_1	20	1	⅓	0	⅓
	z_j					
	$c_j - z_j$					

The basis value of s_1 in the new row, which is 40, represents the remaining slack in labor given the production of 20 units of product 1.

$$2x_1 + 4x_2 + s_1 = 80$$
$$2(20) + 4(0) + s_1 = 80$$
$$s_1 = 80 - 40$$
$$s_1 = 40 \text{ hr of unused labor}$$

Completing the Second Tableau

In order to complete the second simplex tableau, the z_j and $c_j - z_j$ row values must be determined in the same manner as in the initial tableau. To review briefly, the z_j row values are computed by multiplying the values in each column by the corresponding c_b values and summing the products. The $c_j - z_j$ values are found by subtracting each z_j value from the c_j value in the top row of the tableau. The cell values for the z_j row are found as follows:

$$Z_{bi} = (0)(40) + (100)(20) = 2000$$
$$z_1 = (0)(0) + (100)(1) = 100$$
$$z_2 = (0)(^{10}/_3) + (100)(^1/_3) = 33^1/_3$$
$$z_3 = (0)(1) + (100)(0) = 0$$
$$z_4 = (0)(-^2/_3) + (100)(^1/_3) = 33^1/_3$$

The z_j and $c_j - z_j$ row values are shown in tableau form in Table 3.11.

This completes the computation of the second simplex tableau. Note that the solution corresponds to point C in the graphical analysis in Figure 3.3. The value of th

Table 3.11 *Completed Second Simplex Tableau*

c_b	c_j basis	b_i^*	100 x_1	80 x_2	0 s_1	0 s_2
0	s_1	40	0	$^{10}/_3$	1	$-^{2}/_3$
100	x_1	20	1	$^{1}/_3$	0	$^{1}/_3$
	z_j	2000	100	$33^{1}/_3$	0	$33^{1}/_3$
	$c_j - z_j$		0	$46^{2}/_3$	0	$-33^{1}/_3$

objective function for this basic feasible solution is \$2000; this result can be verified by substituting the basic solution values into the original objective function.

he Third Simplex Tableau

Once the second tableau has been completed, the simplex process is repeated. Observing the second tableau, we can see that the $c_j - z_j$ value in column x_2, $46^{2}/_3$, is the largest positive value, indicating the greatest per unit net increase in profit. Thus, x_2 is the entering nonbasic variable, and the x_2 column is the pivot column. Dividing the two a_{ij} values in the x_2 column into their corresponding b_i^* column values results in the following:

$$
\begin{array}{lll}
basis & b_i^* & x_2 \\
s_1 & 40 \div ^{10}/_3 = 12 & \rightarrow \text{Minimum ratio} \\
x_1 & 20 \div ^{1}/_3 = 60 &
\end{array}
$$

Since 12 is the minimum nonnegative value, s_1 is the leaving basic variable and the s_1 row is the pivot row. The pivot row, pivot column, and pivot number are indicated in Table 3.12.

Table 3.12 *Pivot Column, Row, and Number for the Third Tableau*

c_b	c_j basis	b_i^*	100 x_1	80 x_2	0 s_1	0 s_2	
0	s_1	40	0	$(^{10}/_3)$	1	$-^{2}/_3$	Pivot row
100	x_1	20	1	$^{1}/_3$	0	$^{1}/_3$	
	z_j	2000	100	$33^{1}/_3$	0	$33^{1}/_3$	
	$c_j - z_j$		0	$46^{2}/_3$	0	$-33^{1}/_3$	

Pivot column

Dividing each cell value in the pivot row by $^{10}/_3$ results in the new pivot row values in the third tableau (see Table 3.14). The row values for the x_1 row are computed in Table 3.13 and shown in tableau form in Table 3.14.

The z_j and $c_j - z_j$ row values in the third tableau are determined in the same way as in the previous two tableaus. The simplex process now requires us to determine the new entering nonbasic variable and leaving basic variable (i.e., the pivot column and pivot row). However, observing the $c_j - z_j$ row, we see that there are no positive values.

Table 3.13 x_1 *Row Values for Third Simplex Tableau*

Column	Old Row Value	−	Coefficient in Pivot Column	×	New Pivot Row Value	=	New Row Value
b_i^*	20	−	($\frac{1}{3}$	×	12)	=	16
x_1	1	−	($\frac{1}{3}$	×	0)	=	1
x_2	$\frac{1}{3}$	−	($\frac{1}{3}$	×	1)	=	0
s_1	0	−	($\frac{1}{3}$	×	$\frac{3}{10}$)	=	$-\frac{1}{10}$
s_2	$\frac{1}{3}$	−	($\frac{1}{3}$	×	$-\frac{1}{5}$)	=	$\frac{2}{5}$

Table 3.14 *Completed Third Simplex Tableau*

c_b $\diagdown$ c_j	basis	b_i^*	100 x_1	80 x_2	0 s_1	0 s_2
80	x_2	12	0	1	$\frac{3}{10}$	$-\frac{1}{5}$
100	x_1	16	1	0	$-\frac{1}{10}$	$\frac{2}{5}$
	z_j	2560	100	80	14	24
	$c_j - z_j$		0	0	-14	-24

In the x_1 and x_2 columns, $c_j - z_j$ values are zero, since these are basic variables. In the s_1 and s_2 columns, $c_j - z_j$ values are negative. This means that if s_1 were chosen as the entering nonbasic variable, the objective function would *decrease* by \$14 per unit and if s_2 were selected, the objective function would *decrease* by \$24 per unit. The fact that there are no positive $c_j - z_j$ values indicates that there are no nonbasic variables that could be selected to enter the solution that would further *increase* profit. Therefore, the simplex process has ended, and an optimal solution has been reached. The optimal solution corresponds to point B in Figure 3.3.

$$x_1 = 16$$
$$x_2 = 12$$
$$Z = \$2560$$

In general, an optimal solution is identified in the simplex process when none of the values in the $c_j - z_j$ row is positive. Note that since s_1 and s_2 are not in the solution basis, they are, by definition, equal to zero. This means that there are no slack (unused) labor or material resources remaining. This is confirmed in Figure 3.3 by the fact that the point B solution is "on" the labor and material constraints, which means that the labor and material used are equal to the quantities available.

Summary of the Simplex Steps

The standard procedure for performing the simplex process for a maximization problem consists of the following steps:

1. Transform the problem into standard simplex form. This requires converting all constraint inequalities into equations by adding slack variables.

2. Set up the initial tableau. The initial basic feasible solution is at the origin. Thus, the solution base consists only of slack variables. z_j and $c_j - z_j$ row values must be computed.

3. Determine the entering nonbasic variable (i.e., the pivot column). The entering variable will be nonbasic. It is found by examining the $c_j - z_j$ row and selecting the largest positive value.

4. Determine the leaving basic variable (i.e., the pivot row). Divide each value in the b_i^* column by the corresponding pivot column value. Select as the leaving variable the one with the minimum nonnegative value (i.e., the most constraining one).

5. Compute the new tableau row values. The new row values corresponding to the old pivot row are computed using the following formula:

$$\text{New pivot row value} = \frac{\text{old pivot row value}}{\text{pivot number}}$$

All other row values are computed using the following formula:

$$\text{New row value} = \text{old row value} - \left(\begin{array}{c} \text{corresponding} \\ \text{coefficient in} \\ \text{pivot column} \end{array} \times \begin{array}{c} \text{new pivot} \\ \text{row value} \end{array} \right)$$

After all new tableau cell values have been computed, the z_j and $c_j - z_j$ rows are determined.

6. Ascertain if the new solution is optimal. The new basic solution is optimal if all values in the $c_j - z_j$ row are zero or negative. If a positive value exists, go to step 3 and repeat the simplex steps.

The steps of the simplex algorithm are illustrated in a flow diagram in Figure 3.4.

It was pointed out at the beginning of this chapter that the simplex method is based on matrix algebra. In fact, the simplex iterations yield the same results in tableau form as the Gauss-Jordan method for solving simultaneous equations yields in algebraic form. The algebraic approach to the example problem presented in this section is demonstrated in Appendix A. The interested reader is encouraged to review this supplementary material, as it lends further insight into the mathematics of the simplex process. Upon examination of the algebraic method, one characteristic that will become obvious is the existence of an **identity matrix** (a matrix with ones on the diagonal and zeroes elsewhere) at each iteration. The identity matrix can also be observed in the simplex tableaus in Tables 3.2 to 3.14 for the basic variables in each solution. Knowledge of this relationship will prove useful for certain aspects of sensitivity analysis to be presented in Chapter 4.

E MINIMIZATION PROBLEM

In the previous description of the simplex method, only one type of linear programming problem was considered—the maximization problem containing only $\leq$ constraints. In this section we will describe the simplex process for a minimization problem with $\geq$ constraints. A minimization problem is solved by means of the same basic steps as a maximization problem; however, there are several adjustments that must be made.

Since minimization problems typically involve $\geq$ constraints, the problem of converting $\geq$ constraints to equation form presents itself. Recall that for $\leq$ constraints a slack variable was added to form an equality. The interpretation of the slack variable was

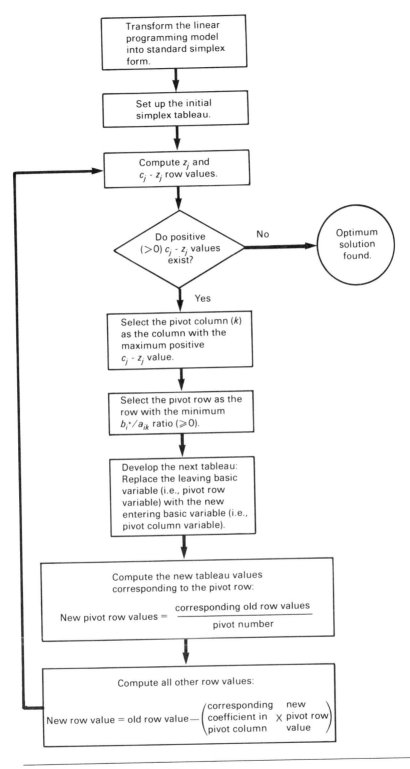

Figure 3.4 The Simplex Algorithm

that it represented the amount by which the quantity of resources available was not full utilized. However, this technique cannot be duplicated for $\geqslant$ constraints. In order to demonstrate the conversion technique for $\geqslant$ constraints, let us consider Example 3.2.

Example 3.2   Diet Problem

The example described here is a diet problem similar to the one in Example 2.2. The objective is to minimize the total cost per serving of breakfast while meeting minima. requirements for vitamins A and B. The vitamin contribution of each type of breakfast food, the unit costs, and minimum vitamin requirements are summarized in the following table.

Vitamin	Vitamin Contribution		Minimum Daily Requirements (mg)
	Egg (mg)	Bacon Strip (mg)	
A	2	4	16
B	3	2	12
Unit cost	4¢	3¢	

The diet problem is formulated as

Minimize $Z = 4x_1 + 3x_2$ (cost)

subject to

$$2x_1 + 4x_2 \geqslant 16 \qquad \text{(vitamin A)}$$
$$3x_1 + 2x_2 \geqslant 12 \qquad \text{(vitamin B)}$$
$$x_1, x_2 \geqslant 0$$

where

x_1 = number of eggs
x_2 = number of strips of bacon
Z = total cost (cents)

The first step in the simplex process for this problem is to convert the $\geqslant$ constraints to equation form. However, instead of adding a slack variable as for $\leqslant$ constraints, we "subtract" a **surplus variable.** The terms *slack* and *surplus* differ in that slack variables are added and reflect unused resources whereas surplus variables are subtracted and reflect an excess above a stated requirement. Both have identical notations, s_i.

Subtracting a surplus variable in the vitamin A constraint yields

$$2x_1 + 4x_2 - s_1 = 16$$

To test this equation, set $x_1 = 20$, $x_2 = 0$, and substitute these values into the equation.

$$2x_1 + 4x_2 - s_1 = 16$$
$$2(20) + 4(0) - s_1 = 16$$
$$40 - s_1 = 16$$
$$s_1 = 24 \quad \text{(excess above stated vitamin A requirement)}$$

Therefore, if we subtract the surplus variable (s_1) in the vitamin A constraint, the equality holds. However, consider the initial solution of the simplex tableau at the origin. At that point, $x_1 = 0$ and $x_2 = 0$, which, if substituted in the vitamin A equation, results in the following:

$$2(0) + 4(0) - s_1 = 16$$
$$s_1 = -16$$

A negative value for s_1 violates the nonnegativity restriction of linear programming and thus is inappropriate. This conflict can be observed graphically in Figure 3.5. The solution at the origin is outside the feasible solution space. To facilitate a solution outside the solution space, we introduce a temporary **artificial variable**. The artificial variable has no real meaning, but it allows the simplex process to begin with nonnegative values for the basic variables. This results in the needed initial basic feasible solution. In subsequent tableaus the simplex process will move toward a basic solution in the feasible solution space.

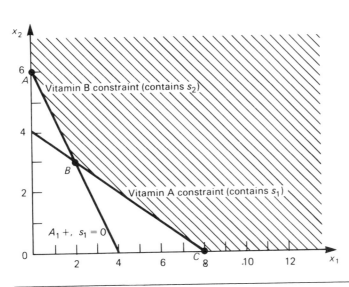

Figure 3.5 *Graphic Representation of the Diet Problem*

With an artificial variable (A_i) added, our vitamin A equation now becomes

$$2x_1 + 4x_2 - s_1 + A_1 = 16$$

To test the equality condition, let $x_1 = 20$, $x_2 = 0$, and $A_1 = 0$.

$$2(20) + 4(0) - s_1 + 1(0) = 16$$
$$s_1 = 24$$

Now let $x_1 = 0$, $x_2 = 0$, and $s_1 = 0$ (i.e., the origin).

$$2(0) + 4(0) - 1(0) + A_1 = 16$$
$$A_1 = 16$$

The constraint equation holds for either case. It can also be seen in Figure 3.5 that A_1 and s_1 are complementary. In other words, if A_1 is positive, s_1 is zero, and vice versa.

Converting each constraint to an equation by first subtracting a surplus variable and then adding an artificial variable results in the following equations in standard simplex form:

$$2x_1 + 4x_2 - s_1 + A_1 = 16 \quad \text{(vitamin A)}$$
$$3x_1 + 2x_2 - s_2 + A_2 = 12 \quad \text{(vitamin B)}$$

While adjusting the constraint equations to the proper form, we created two new variables, A_1 and A_2, which must be reflected in the objective function. Previously it was noted that the c_j value for a slack variable is zero, since it does not contribute to profit. Similarly, the c_j value for a *surplus* variable is zero, since it contributes nothing to cost. However, if a c_j value of zero is assigned to an *artificial* variable, it can end up in the final solution base as part of the optimal solution, just as a slack or surplus variable can end up in the solution. The artificial variable is added to the problem simply to aid in putting the constraint equations into proper form and setting up an initial basic solution. Therefore, a means must be devised for ensuring that artificial variables are not included in the optimal solution.

This can be accomplished by assigning a very large positive c_j (unit cost) value to the artificial variable in the objective function, making the artificial variable so costly that it never ends up in the final solution. This method is known as the **large M method,** since the c_j value assigned to the artificial variable is M, representing an extremely large positive value (for example, $1,000,000). This notation results in the following objective function for Example 3.2.

$$\text{Minimize } Z = 4x_1 + 3x_2 + 0s_1 + 0s_2 + MA_1 + MA_2$$

The simplex method will now drive the artificial variables out of the basic solution, since they cannot possibly lead to the objective of cost minimization.

inal Adjustments in the Minimization Problem

The final adjustment in the simplex method for a minimization problem is to reverse the final row designation from $c_j - z_j$ to $z_j - c_j$. In a minimization problem, the final row values represent the net unit decrease in cost for each variable. Thus, if we left the last row in the tableau as $c_j - z_j$, we would have to choose the largest negative value for the entering nonbasic variable. To be consistent with the previously defined decision rule, we use $z_j - c_j$ for the minimization problem, and we continue to use the largest positive value for the entering nonbasic variable.

The adjustments for the simplex solution to a minimization problem subject to $\geq$ constraints are summarized as follows:

1. Change all $\geq$ constraints to equation form by *subtracting* a surplus variable and *adding* an artificial variable.

2. In the objective function, assign a c_j value of M to each artificial variable.

3. In the simplex tableau, change the $c_j - z_j$ row to $z_j - c_j$.

Given these adjustments, Example 3.2 is converted to standard simplex form and solved (Tables 3.15–3.17) as follows:

Minimize $Z = 4x_1 + 3x_2 + 0s_1 + 0s_2 + MA_1 + MA_2$

subject to

$$2x_1 + 4x_2 - s_1 + A_1 = 16$$
$$3x_1 + 2x_2 - s_2 + A_2 = 12$$
$$x_1, x_2, s_1, s_2, A_1, A_2 \geqslant 0$$

Notice that A_1 and A_2 are in the initial solution base (Table 3.15). The pivot column, pivot row, and pivot number are all determined in the same manner as outlined for the maximization problem. Likewise, the second tableau (Table 3.16) is computed exactly the same way as in a maximization problem.

Table 3.15 *Initial Simplex Tableau*

c_b $\backslash$ c_j	basis	b_i^*	4 x_1	3 x_2	0 s_1	0 s_2	M A_1	M A_2	
M	A_1	16	2	④	-1	0	1	0	Pivot row
M	A_2	12	3	2	0	-1	0	1	
	z_j	28M	5M	6M	$-M$	$-M$	M	M	
	$z_j - c_j$		$5M - 4$	$6M - 3$	$-M$	$-M$	0	0	

Pivot column

Table 3.16 *Second Simplex Tableau*

c_b $\backslash$ c_j	basis	b_i^*	4 x_1	3 x_2	0 s_1	0 s_2	M A_2	
3	x_2	4	½	1	$-\frac{1}{4}$	0	0	
M	A_2	4	②	0	½	-1	1	Pivot row
	z_j	$4M + 12$	$2M + \frac{3}{2}$	3	$\frac{1}{2}M - \frac{3}{4}$	$-M$	M	
	$z_j - c_j$		$2M - \frac{5}{2}$	0	$\frac{1}{2}M - \frac{3}{4}$	$-M$	0	

Pivot column

In the second tableau, the A_1 column has been eliminated. This is a simple shortcut Once an artifical variable leaves the solution base, it will never return because of it extremely high c_j value, M. Thus, this column can be eliminated and the tableau reduced

The third simplex tableau results in the optimal solution (Table 3.17). All $z_j - c$ values are negative or zero, and the optimality test holds. Interpreting the simplex solu tion in terms of the original problem indicates that 2 eggs and 3 strips of bacon shoul be included in each serving. This solution will not only meet the daily vitamin require ments but also minimize the cost per serving at 17 cents. Since both surplus variables ar not in the solution basis, they are, by definition, equal to zero. Thus, the requirement for vitamins A and B were met exactly with no surplus in either case. This is furthe

An Application of Linear Programming: Scheduling Transit System Drivers in Montreal

The Société de Transport de la Communauté Urbaine de Montréal (Montreal Urban Community Transit Corporation or S.T.C.U.M.) is one of the largest public transit companies in North America. S.T.C.U.M. operates a fleet of buses, a subway system, a transit service for the handicapped, and two commuter rail lines, that altogether serve two million residents of the Montreal community. It has a staff of 8,000 and an annual budget of $577.5 million. The bus system includes 1,700 buses with 3,000 drivers that operate a system of 150 bus lines. The subway system includes 750 cars with 370 operators joined in a network of 65 underground stations. The handicapped transit system operates 50 special lift-equipped vehicles. The four transportation modes of the transit system, (bus, subway, handicapped transit, and commuter rail) provided over 340 million passenger trips in 1988.

One of the most difficult problems in managing a transit company of this size is the scheduling of vehicles and operating personnel. Scheduling is not only an important aspect of service but has a major impact on operating costs. The size of the system alone would make vehicle and crew scheduling a complex task; however the problem is exacerbated by a number of other factors including large variations in service levels during the day, seasonal demand changes, and complex work rules. Scheduling at S.T.C.U.M. is accomplished in two steps using a computerized system called HASTUS.

Vehicle scheduling is done first to determine the number of buses and subway trains necessary to meet demand on each route, while in the second scheduling phase drivers are assigned to vehicles. The HASTUS system contains three computer modules to accomplish these two steps in the scheduling process. HASTUS-Bus is used to schedule vehicles and then HASTUS-Macro is employed as the first step in assigning drivers to vehicles. The Macro module is also used for cost analysis in planning and union negotiations. The third module, HASTUS-Micro, uses the Macro solution as a guide to develop detailed driver schedules.

Table 3.17 Third Simplex Tableau (Optimal)

c_b	basis	b_i^*	4 x_1	3 x_2	0 s_1	0 s_2
3	x_2	3	0	1	$-3/8$	$1/4$
4	x_1	2	1	0	$1/4$	$-1/2$
	z_j	17	4	3	$-1/8$	$-5/4$
	$z_j - c_j$		0	0	$-1/8$	$-5/4$

illustrated by the fact that the solution is on point *B* in Figure 3.5, which is "on" each of the vitamin requirement constraints.

MIXED CONSTRAINT PROBLEM

The examples examined so far in this chapter have been of two types: a maximization problem with ≤ constraints and a minimization problem with ≥ constraints. Now let us consider Example 3.3, which includes mixed constraints.

The primary tool used in HASTUS-Macro is a linear programming model for crew scheduling. As input, it uses the output from HASTUS-Bus, which is a set of vehicle blocks. Four sets of blocks, for weekdays, holidays, Saturday, and Sunday, define the amount of work done by a bus from the time it leaves the garage until it returns. These blocks are partitioned into smaller, feasible work units for individual drivers. The linear programming module includes among its constraints a number of work rules derived through union negotiation. The first rule stipulates that all work pieces start and end at a point where driver changeovers occur (i.e., a relief point of which there are 75 in Montreal). Selecting the best relief times is a key factor in developing a cost effective crew schedule. A second rule stipulates that drivers are limited to 7.5-hour workdays over a 12.5-hour time span, while a third rule provides for a guaranteed 7.5 workday. Other linear programming model constraints ensure that the number of drivers during all time periods is greater than or equal to the number of vehicles, and define the block patterns.

The objective of the linear programming model is to determine the number of drivers assigned during a workday that will minimize the total workday cost (according to the union contract). The model includes approximately 3,000 variables. As noted, the solution generated by the linear programming model in HASTUS-Macro is used as input to develop a more detailed crew schedule in the Micro module.

The HASTUS system has resulted in direct savings of approximately $4 million annually through reduced manpower costs and vehicle requirements. It also is an effective tool for planning, budgeting, and union negotiations. It enables management to analyze "what-if?" situations, which previously took six weeks, in only a few minutes. Indirect savings from improved and more efficient managerial decision making is estimated to be in the millions of dollars. The HASTUS system was so successful in Montreal that it was subsequently adopted in 40 cities in 15 countries around the world.

Source: J-Y Blais et al., "The HASTUS Vehicle and Manpower Scheduling System at the Société de Transport de la Communauté Urbaine de Montréal," *Interfaces,* 20, no. 1 (January–February 1990): 26–42.

Example 3.3 Investment Problem

An individual desires to allocate $150 per month to a mix of investments in stocks and bonds. The estimated annual return on each dollar invested in stock is 20 cents, which includes dividends and an estimate of the appreciation in the price of the stock. The annual return on each dollar invested in a bond is 10 cents. Whereas the return on a bond is certain, the return on stock is an estimate subject to variability. Since the return on stock involves risk, the investor wants to limit the amount invested in stock to $40 a month. To ensure a minimum cash flow return, the investor will invest at least $20 a month in bonds. This example is formulated as a linear programming model as follows:

Maximize $Z = 20x_1 + 10x_2$

$X_1 + X_2 + A_1 = 150$

subject to

$$x_1 + x_2 = 150 \quad \text{(total monthly investment)}$$
$$x_1 \leq 40 \quad \text{(maximum investment in stock)}$$
$$x_2 \geq 20 \quad \text{(minimum investment in bonds)}$$
$$x_1, x_2 \geq 0$$

This problem differs from our previous examples in two ways. First, it is a maximization problem with a $\geq$ constraint. Second, it contains a constraint that is already in equation form. Before we solve this problem by the simplex method, adjustments must be made for these differences.

Converting an Equality Constraint

The equality constraint, $x_1 + x_2 = 150$, seems to be in the appropriate standard simplex form already. However, checking the solution at the origin ($x_1 = 0$, $x_2 = 0$), we find

$$x_1 + x_2 = 150$$
$$0 + 0 = 150$$
$$0 = 150$$

This is obviously an impossible outcome, since zero does not equal 150. The addition of a slack variable or the subtraction of a surplus variable would be inappropriate, however, because the equality itself indicates a strict condition where there are neither unused resources nor the possibility of overachieving a specified requirement. To begin the simplex solution process (with $x_1 = 0$ and $x_2 = 0$), we must temporarily violate the strict equality requirement; thus an artificial variable is added. The constraint becomes

$$x_1 + x_2 + A_1 = 150$$

Initially, the solution value of A_1 is 150, while $x_1 = 0$ and $x_2 = 0$.

Converting a $\geq$ Constraint in a Maximization Problem

In the case of the $\geq$ constraint, $x_2 \geq 20$ is converted to equation form in the same way as described previously for a minimization problem. A surplus variable is subtracted, and an artificial variable is added.

$$x_2 - s_2 + A_2 = 20$$

However, the c_j value assigned to the artificial variable (A_2) in the objective function is no longer a positive M. Since a positive M would represent a large profit in a maximization problem, the artificial variable would be assured of always being in the optimal solution base. Therefore, a negative M value ($-M$) must be employed for all artificial variable c_j values in the objective function. The same rule holds true for the artificial variable introduced in the equality constraint.

In standard simplex form, this problem becomes

Maximize $Z = 20x_1 + 10x_2 + 0s_1 + 0s_2 - MA_1 - MA_2$
subject to
$$x_1 + x_2 + A_1 = 150$$
$$x_1 + s_1 = 40$$
$$x_2 - s_2 + A_2 = 20$$
$$x_1, x_2, s_1, s_2, A_1, A_2 \geq 0$$

The simplex solution for this problem is presented in Tables 3.18–3.21.

Table 3.18 *Initial Simplex Tableau*

c_b \ c_j	basis	b_i^*	20 x_1	10 x_2	0 s_1	0 s_2	$-M$ A_1	$-M$ A_2	
$-M$	A_1	150	1	1	0	0	1	0	
0	s_1	40	1	0	1	0	0	0	
$-M$	A_2	20	0	①	0	-1	0	1	Pivot row
	z_j	$-170M$	$-M$	$-2M$	0	M	$-M$	$-M$	
	$c_j - z_j$		$20 + M$	$10 + 2M$	0	$-M$	0	0	

Pivot column

Table 3.19 *Second Simplex Tableau*

c_b \ c_j	basis	b_i^*	20 x_1	10 x_2	0 s_1	0 s_2	$-M$ A_1	
$-M$	A_1	130	1	0	0	1	1	
0	s_1	40	①	0	1	0	0	Pivot row
10	x_2	20	0	1	0	-1	0	
	z_j	$200 - 130M$	$-M$	10	0	$-10 - M$	$-M$	
	$c_j - z_j$		$20 + M$	0	0	$10 + M$	0	

Pivot column

Table 3.20 *Third Simplex Tableau*

c_b \ c_j	basis	b_i^*	20	10 x_2	0 s_1	0 s_2	$-M$ A_1	
$-M$	A_1	90	0	0	-1	①	1	Pivot row
20	x_1	40	1	0	1	0	0	
10	x_2	20	0	1	0	-1	0	
	z_j	$1000 - 90M$	20	10	$20 + M$	$-10 - M$	$-M$	
	$c_j - z_j$		0	0	$-20 - M$	$10 + M$	0	

Pivot column

Table 3.21 *Fourth Simplex Tableau*
(Optimal Solution)

c_b \ c_j	basis	b_i^*	20 x_1	10 x_2	0 s_1	0 s_2
0	s_2	90	0	0	-1	1
20	x_1	40	1	0	1	0
10	x_2	110	0	1	-1	0
	z_j	1900	20	10	10	0
	$c_j - z_j$		0	0	-10	0

The optimum solution for the investment example problem is

$x_1 = \$40$ (basic)

$x_2 = \$110$ (basic)

$s_1 = 0$ (nonbasic)

$s_2 = \$90$ (basic)

$Z = 1900$ cents $= \$19.00$

Thus, $40 is invested in stock and $110 is invested in bonds. The value of s_1 represents the slack in the $x_1 \leqslant 40$ constraint. Since s_1 is not in the basis, it has a value of zero. This means that the maximum allowable investment of $40 in stock was achieved. The value of s_2 represents the surplus in the $x_2 \geqslant 20$ constraint. Since s_2 equals $90, the investment of $110 in bonds exceeds the minimum required investment (of $20) by $90.

Table 3.22 is a brief review of the different simplex adjustments required for the alternative constraint forms.

Table 3.22 *Simplex Constraint Types and Their Resolutions*

| | | Objective Function Coefficient | |
| | | Maximization Problem | Minimization Problem |
Constraint	Adjustment in Constraint		
$\leqslant$	Add a slack variable	0	0
$=$	Add an artificial variable	$-M$	M
$\geqslant$	Subtract a surplus variable	0	0
	and add an artificial variable	$-M$	M

NEGATIVE VARIABLES

In the linear programming problems we have analyzed to this point, a nonnegativity restriction has been imposed on all model variables. Indeed, in most practical situations decision variables are naturally nonnegative. However, decision variables can, on occasion, define such concepts as production rates. In such a model a negative value for a decision variable would reflect a *decrease* in the rate of production, while a positive value would indicate an *increase* in the production rate.

In the simplex method, negative values are not allowed; thus, any problem with possible negative values must be converted to an equivalent problem with positive variables. There are two cases of negativity for which we will demonstrate the equivalency process: (1) variables that are totally unrestricted (unbounded) and (2) variables that are negative within a given bound.

Unrestricted Variables

If any or all of the decision variables in a problem can take on negative as well as positive values, they are said to be unrestricted. In order to solve the simplex problem, the variables that are unrestricted as to sign are converted to positive variables by using the following formula.[2]

$$x_j = \hat{x}_j - \hat{\hat{x}}$$

where

x_j = the unrestricted variable

$\hat{x}_j, \hat{\hat{x}} \geqslant 0$

The following example will demonstrate the need for and use of unrestricted variables in a linear programming problem.

Example 3.4   A Change in Inventory Capacity Problem

A company has obtained an additional 16 squares yards of inventory storage space. This extra space will enable the company to keep in storage increased quantities of either or both of the two products it produces, which in turn is expected to result in additional customer accounts and additional sales. The company estimates that for each additional case of product 1 stocked in inventory, 6 additional customer accounts will be obtained and an additional $9 per day in sales will result. Likewise, if the company were to decrease the quantity of product 1 stocked in inventory by 1 case, 6 current customers would be lost, and sales would go down by $9 per day. An increase of 1 in the number of cases of product 2 stocked in inventory will result in 3 additional customer accounts and an additional $18 per day in sales.

Two square yards of storage space are required to stock a case of either product. The company wishes to obtain no less than 18 additional customer accounts through use of the additional storage space. Managers have decided that they will accept either an increase or a decrease in the amount of product 1 presently stocked in inventory, but they will not accept any decrease in the quantity of product 2 stocked.

The company management wishes to know the amount of change in inventory of each product necessary to maximize the dollar increase in sales subject to the previous constraints. In order to determine the solution to this problem, the following linear programming model has been formulated.

Maximize $Z = 9x_1 + 18x_2$ ($ sales)

subject to

$6x_1 + 3x_2 \geqslant 18$ (new customer accounts)

$2x_1 + 2x_2 \leqslant 16$ (yd^2 additional storage space)

$x_1 \sim$ unrestricted

$x_2 \geqslant 0$

where

x_1 = number of additional cases of product 1 in stock
    (negative value denotes a decrease)

x_2 = number of additional cases of product 2 in stock

---

[2] $\hat{\hat{x}}$ is not subscripted, since it may be used for any number of unrestricted variables in a problem (e.g., $x_1 = \hat{x}_1 - \hat{\hat{x}}, x_2 = \hat{x}_2 - \hat{\hat{x}}$).

To convert this problem to the standard simplex form with all positive variables, w must substitute $\hat{x}_1 - \hat{\hat{x}}$ for x_1.

Maximize $Z = 9(\hat{x}_1 - \hat{\hat{x}}) + 18x_2$

subject to

$$6(\hat{x}_1 - \hat{\hat{x}}) + 3x_2 \geq 18$$
$$2(\hat{x}_1 - \hat{\hat{x}}) + 2x_2 \leq 16$$
$$\hat{x}_1, \hat{\hat{x}}, x_2 \geq 0$$

Expanding terms and converting all inequalities to equation form results in the fo lowing standard simplex form:

Maximize $Z = 9\hat{x}_1 - 9\hat{\hat{x}} + 18x_2 + 0s_1 + 0s_2 - MA_1$

subject to

$$6\hat{x}_1 - 6\hat{\hat{x}} + 3x_2 - s_1 + A_1 = 18$$
$$2\hat{x}_1 - 2\hat{\hat{x}} + 2x_2 + s_2 = 16$$
$$\hat{x}_1, \hat{\hat{x}}, x_2 \geq 0$$

The solution to this problem is shown in Tables 3.23–3.26. The last tableau yield the following optimal solution:

$$\hat{\hat{x}} = 2$$
$$x_2 = 10$$
$$Z = 162$$

remember order

Table 3.23 *Initial Simplex Tableau*

	c_j			9	−9	18	0	0	−M	
c_b	basis	b_i^*		$\hat{x}_1$	$\hat{\hat{x}}$	x_2	s_1	s_2	A_1	
−M	A_1	18		⑥	−6	3	−1	0	1	Pivot row
0	s_2	16		2	−2	2	0	1	0	
	z_j	−18M		−6M	6M	−3M	M	0	−M	
	$c_j - z_j$			9 + 6M	−9 − 6M	18 + 3M	−M	0	0	

Pivot column

Table 3.24 *Second Simplex Tableau*

	c_j		9	−9	18	0	0	
c_b	basis	b_i^*	$\hat{x}_1$	$\hat{\hat{x}}$	x_2	s_1	s_2	
9	x_1	3	1	−1	①	−⅙	0	Pivot row
0	s_2	10	0	0	1	⅓	1	
	z_j	27	9	−9	9/2	−3/2	0	
	$c_j - z_j$		0	0	27/2	3/2	0	

Pivot column

Table 3.25 *Third Simplex Tableau*

c_b	c_j basis	b_i^*	9 $\hat{x}_1$	-9 $\hat{\hat{x}}$	18 x_2	0 s_1	0 s_2	
18	x_2	6	2	-2	1	$-1/3$	0	
0	s_2	4	-2	②	0	$2/3$	1	Pivot row
	z_j	108	36	-36	18	-6	0	
	$c_j - z_j$		-27	27	0	6	0	

Pivot column

Table 3.26 *Fourth and Optimal Tableau*

c_b	c_j basis	b_i^*	9 $\hat{x}_2$	-9 $\hat{\hat{x}}$	18 x_2	0 s_1	0 s_2
18	x_2	10	0	0	1	$1/3$	1
-9	$\hat{\hat{x}}$	2	-1	1	0	$1/3$	$1/2$
	z_j	162	9	-9	18	3	$27/2$
	$c_j - z_j$		0	0	0	-3	$-27/2$

However, in order to determine the solution for the original problem variables, the variables must be reconverted to their original form.

$$x_1 = \hat{x}_1 - \hat{\hat{x}}$$
$$x_1 = 0 - 2$$
$$x_1 = -2$$

and

$$x_2 = 10$$
$$Z = 162$$

The solution to this problem does indeed have a negative value, $x_1 = -2$. Thus, the quantity of product 1 held in storage will be *reduced* by 2 cases, and the quantity of product 2 held in storage will be increased by 10 cases. The result is an increase in total dollar sales of $\$162$. The solution can be observed graphically in Figure 3.6.

Variables with a Negative Lower Bound

The other form that variables can take is to be negative but bounded. For example,

$$x_1 \geqslant -20$$

This case is actually the same as the previous unrestricted case except that the lower bound, 20, replaces the $\hat{\hat{x}}$ variable in the conversion of x,

$$x_1 = \hat{x}_1 - \hat{\hat{x}}$$
$$x_1 = \hat{x}_1 - 20$$

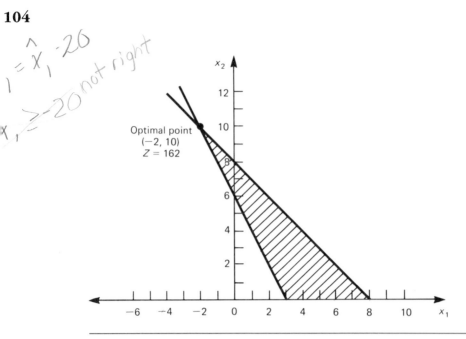

Handwritten annotations in left margin:
$= x_1 - 20$
$1 \geq -20$ not right
$x_1 \geq -20$ not right

Figure 3.6 *Graphic Analysis of an Unrestricted Variable Problem*

One might think that it would be possible to treat the inequality $x_1 \geq -20$ as another constraint by converting it to $-x_1 \leq 20$. However, this is not possible because the simplex method does not allow negative solution values for any variable in the basis.

Negative Right-Hand-Side Values

To see how a negative right-hand-side value is resolved, consider the following constraint:

$$-5x_1 + x_2 \leq -25$$

This constraint in its present form prohibits the solution of its accompanying problem by the simplex method. In the initial solution of the simplex model, $x_1 = 0$ and $x_2 = 0$. Therefore,

$$-5x_1 + x_2 + s_1 = -25$$
$$-5(0) + 0 + s_1 = -25$$
$$s_1 = -25$$

Clearly the nonnegativity restriction on s_1 has been violated. In order to resolve this discrepancy, the constraint must be adjusted by multiplying both sides of the original constraint by -1. This reverses the direction of the inequality, which now becomes

$$5x_1 - x_2 \geq 25$$

ADDITIONAL COMPLICATIONS AND THEIR RESOLUTIONS

Several additional complications that can occur in the solutions to linear programming problems include a tie for the pivot column, a tie for the pivot row, an infeasible problem, an unbounded problem, and multiple optimal solutions. These complications and their resolutions are discussed in the following sections.

Tie for the Pivot Column

The nonbasic variable that is selected to enter the solution (i.e., selection of the pivot column) is determined by the largest positive $c_j - z_j$ (or $z_j - c_j$) value. However, in any linear programming problem a tie can result from identical $c_j - z_j$ values. When a tie occurs, it can be broken by arbitrarily selecting one of the tied values. There is no wrong choice, although the selection of one variable may result in more iterations (i.e, more tableaus) than the selection of the other tied variable(s) would have. Regardless of which variable column is chosen, the optimal solution will eventually be found.

Tie for the Pivot Row and Degeneracy

Just as a tie can result for the pivot column, a tie can occur for the pivot row. Table 3.27 represents the initial tableau for a maximization problem.

Table 3.27 *Simplex Tableau with a Tie for the Pivot Row*

c_b	c_j basis	b_i^*	4 x_1	6 x_2	0 s_1	0 s_2	0 s_3	
0	s_1	40	6	4	1	0	0	$40 \div 4 = 10$
0	s_2	16	1	0	0	1	0	Tie
0	s_3	10	½	1	0	0	1	$10 \div 1 = 10$
	z_j	0	0	0	0	0	0	
	$c_j - z_j$		4	6	0	0	0	

Pivot column

After x_2 is selected as the entering variable in the initial tableau, it is determined that two rows, s_1 and s_3, are tied for the pivot row. If row s_3 is selected arbitrarily, the second tableau will be as shown in Table 3.28.

Table 3.28 *Second Simplex Tableau*

c_b	c_j basis	b_i^*	4 x_1	6 x_2	0 s_1	0 s_2	0 s_3	
0	s_1	0	4	0	1	0	-4	Pivot row
0	s_2	16	1	0	0	1	0	
6	x_2	10	½	1	0	0	1	
	z_j	60	3	6	0	0	6	
	$c_j - z_j$		1	0	0	0	-6	

Pivot column

In the second tableau we can see that a basic variable (s_1) has assumed a value of zero. This occurrence, which results from tied rows, is referred to as **degeneracy**. The zero b_i^* value can lead to a series of solutions that have the same z_j value—in this case

60. This situation is known as **cycling**, or **looping**, and can theoretically continue infinitely, with the simplex method never yielding an optimal solution. However, in practice, after a number of such loops, the simplex procedure will *usually* proceed normally and eventually reach an optimal solution. The main drawback to degeneracy is the increase in the number of tableaus that must be computed, which reduces the efficiency of the simplex method considerably.

As a general rule, the best way to break a tie between pivot rows is to simply select one arbitrarily. Tie-breaking methods have been developed to prevent infinite looping, but the extra simplex computations these methods require do not warrant their discussion here.

An Infeasible Problem

In Chapter 2, a problem with no feasible solution was illustrated graphically (Figure 2.9). This condition occurs when a problem has incompatible constraints and, as a result, there is no common feasible solution space. However, the existence of an infeasible solution may not always be apparent when the problem is formulated or during the simplex process. This is especially true for large linear programming problems that cannot be graphed.

The final simplex tableau shown in Table 3.29 demonstrates the identifying characteristics of an infeasible solution. All $c_j - z_j$ row values are negative or zero, indicating an optimal solution. However, observing the solution base, we see that there is an artificial variable in the final solution base and the z_j value is $90 - 2M$. Both of these values are totally meaningless, since the artificial variable has no meaning. Therefore, the existence of an artificial variable in the solution base of the final simplex tableau indicates that the problem is infeasible.

Table 3.29 *An Infeasible Problem*

c_b / c_j	basis	b_i^*	10 x_1	15 x_2	0 s_1	0 s_2	$-M$ A_1
10	x_1	9	1	3/2	1/2	0	0
—	A_1	2	0	-2	-1	-1	1
	z_j	$90 - 2M$	10	$15 + 2M$	$5 + M$	M	$-M$
	$c_j - z_j$		0	$-2M$	$-5 - M$	$-M$	0

An Unbounded Problem

Another difficulty that can occur in a linear programming problem is an unbounded solution, illustrated graphically in Figure 2.10. In this type of problem, the objective function can increase indefinitely without ever reaching a constraint boundary. Table 3.30 shows a tableau for a problem with an unbounded solution.

The entering variable in this tableau is indicated as x_2, because it has the maximum positive $c_j - z_j$ value. However, it is impossible to select a pivot row and a leaving variable, since both pivot column values are negative—there are no positive row ratios available to allow a pivot row selection. This tableau does not indicate an optimal solution, yet the simplex process is prohibited from continuing. In other words, as x_2 enters

Table 3.30 *An Unbounded Problem*

C_b	c_j basis	b_i^*	7 x_1	4 x_2	0 s_1	0 s_2	
0	s_1	6	0	−2	1	−1	$6 \div -2 = -3$
7	x_1	2	1	−1	0	1	$2 \div -1 = -2$
	z_j	14	7	−7	0	7	
	$c_j - z_j$		0	11	0	−7	

Pivot column

the solution, neither basic variable acts as a bound on the problem (i.e., both increase as x_2 increases). As a result, Z also increases indefinitely.

As a general rule, if a pivot row cannot be selected for lack of a positive ratio or if all a_{ij} values in the pivot column are negative or zero, the solution is unbounded.

Multiple Optimal Solutions

The final special case we will discuss is the existence of multiple optimal solutions. This type of problem is illustrated graphically in Chapter 2 (Figure 2.8). Consider the final simplex tableau for a maximization problem in Table 3.31.

Table 3.31 *Simplex Tableau with Multiple Optimal Solutions*

C_b	c_j basis	b_i^*	4 x_1	2 x_2	0 s_1	0 s_2
4	x_1	10	1	½	½	0
0	s_2	4	0	2	−1	1
	z_j	40	4	2	2	0
	$c_j - z_j$		0	0	−2	0

multiple optimal solutions

Examination of the $c_j - z_j$ row shows that all values are negative or zero; hence, the solution is optimal. However, x_2 is a *nonbasic* variable with a $c_j - z_j$ value that is neither positive nor negative but zero. Recalling that the $c_j - z_j$ value indicates the per unit net increase in profit that would be realized from entering a nonbasic variable, we can see that entering x_2 would neither decrease nor increase profit. It would result in a different solution mix. Selecting x_2 as an entering variable results in the tableau shown in Table 3.32.

Although Table 3.32 has a different solution mix, it has the same objective function value ($z_j = 40$) as Table 3.31. Thus, there are multiple optimal solutions. It should not be construed that these are the only two optimal solution points. A review of Figure 2.8 shows that in multiple optimal solutions all points on the constraint boundary between two adjacent corner-point optimal solutions are also optimal. Therefore, the tableaus in Tables 3.31 and 3.32 identify the adjacent corner-point solutions between which an infinite number of optimal solutions exist. In practice, however, the identifiable corner-point solutions are said to be *the* multiple optimal solutions.

Table 3.32 *Simplex Tableau with the Alternative Optimal Solution*

c_b	c_j basis	b_i^*	4 x_1	2 x_2	0 s_1	0 s_2
4	x_1	9	1	0	$3/4$	$-1/4$
2	x_2	2	0	1	$-1/2$	$1/2$
	z_j	40	4	2	2	0
	$c_j - z_j$		0	0	-2	0

As a general rule, when the $c_j - z_j$ row indicates an optimal solution, if the $c_j - z_j$ values of any *nonbasic* variables are zero, multiple optimal solutions exist. To find the alternative optimal solution(s), select the nonbasic variable with the $c_j - z_j$ value of zero as an entering variable and continue the simplex steps.

COMPUTERIZED SOLUTION OF LINEAR PROGRAMMING

If performed manually, the simplex method for solving linear programming problems described and demonstrated in this chapter is useful for solving only problems of a relatively small size. Linear programming problems of only four equations and three variables can result in as many as fourteen iterations (and occasionally even more). A linear programming problem with N constraints has been estimated to have an average of $2N$ iterations. Solving problems with only five constraints and an average of ten iterations can be so time consuming that the manual computation of the simplex method becomes impractical. Dr. George Dantzig, the developer of the simplex method, recalled the first large-scale application of the simplex method to a "diet" problem in 1947. The linear programming model, which included 9 equations and 77 variables, was solved using "hand-operated [mechanical] desk calculators" and required 120 man-days of labor.[3]

Today, a large number of software packages are available for solving linear programming problems on mainframe and personal computers. MPSIII and MPSX are widely used linear programming packages available for mainframe systems. These linear programming codes can solve problems with many thousands of variables and constraints. Here we will demonstrate the computerized solution of linear programming problems using both LINDO, an interactive linear programming package with mainframe and PC versions, and AB:QM, a general management science software package with linear programming capabilities.

Computerized Solution of a Maximization Problem

We will first apply LINDO to the linear programming problem presented in Example 3.1 at the beginning of this chapter. Recall the model formulation of this product mix problem:

Maximize $Z = \$100x_1 + 80x_2$ (profit)

---

[3] G. Dantzig, "Reminiscences About the Origins of Linear Programming," *Operations Research Letters* 1, no. 2 (April 1982): 43–48.

subject to

$$2x_1 + 4x_2 \leq 80 \text{ hr} \qquad \text{(labor)}$$
$$3x_1 + x_2 \leq 60 \text{ lb} \qquad \text{(material)}$$
$$x_1, x_2 \geq 0$$

where

x_1 = number of units of product 1
x_2 = number of units of product 2
Z = total profit ($)

The LINDO input instructions are straightforward, requiring that the objective function and constraints be typed in, just as they are shown in the model formulation.

```
: MAX 100X1 + 80X2
? ST
? 2X1 + 4X2 < 80
? 3X1 + X2 < 60
? END
: LOOK ALL
```

The command LOOK ALL instructs the package to display the complete model formulation on the terminal.

```
MAX      100 X1 + 80 X2
SUBJECT TO
         2)    2 X1 + 4 X2 <=    80
         3)    3 X1 + X2 <=    60
END

:
```

The LINDO linear programming package always considers the objective function to be the first function; thus, all constraints are numbered sequentially, beginning with the first constraint identified as function number 2.

Given that the user does not find any errors in this model formulation, the program is commanded to proceed to a solution. The series of tableaus and the solution as they appear on the terminal are shown below.

```
: TABL

THE TABLEAU
     ROW  (BASIS)          X1         X2  SLK    2  SLK    3
       1 ART          -100.000    -80.000   .000      .000      .000
       2 SLK   2          2.000      4.000  1.000      .000    80.000
       3 SLK   3          3.000      1.000   .000     1.000    60.000
```

```
: PIVOT
      X1 ENTERS AT VALUE    20.000        IN ROW    3 OBJ. VALUE=  2000.0

: TABL

THE TABLEAU
      ROW  (BASIS)          X1         X2   SLK   2   SLK   3
        1  ART              .000   -46.667        .000     33.333   2000.000
        2  SLK    2         .000     3.333       1.000      -.667     40.000
        3        X1        1.000      .333        .000       .333     20.000
: PIV
      X2 ENTERS AT VALUE    12.000        IN ROW    2 OBJ. VALUE=  2560.0

: TABL

THE TABLEAU
      ROW  (BASIS)          X1         X2   SLK   2   SLK   3
        1  ART              .000       .000      14.000     24.000   2560.000
        2        X2         .000      1.000        .300      -.200     12.000
        3        X1        1.000       .000       -.100       .400     16.000
: PIV
LP OPTIMUM FOUND   AT STEP       2

            OBJECTIVE FUNCTION VALUE

  1)          2560.00000

  VARIABLE           VALUE           REDUCED COST
        X1         16.000000            .000000
        X2         12.000000            .000000
      ROW     SLACK OR SURPLUS      DUAL PRICES
        2)            .000000        14.000000
        3)            .000000        24.000000

NO. ITERATIONS=         2
```

The computerized solution of the problem in Example 3.1 mirrors the simplex solution steps shown earlier in this chapter: three tableaus are required, and the optimal solution is the same as the one given previously. However, notice that the format of the computerized tableaus differs somewhat from the simplex format described in this chapter. For example, the b_i^* column is the third column from the left in the simplex tableaus presented previously, but these same values are on the far right of the computerized tableau. The z_j row does not exist in the computerized tableau, and instead of having a $c_j - z_j$ row as the bottom row of the tableaus, the computerized tableau has a $z_j - c_j$ row at the top. Notice that for each tableau the computerized solution describes the pivot operation that takes place, including the entering and leaving variables.

LINDO is a powerful software package that solves linear programming problems exclusively. AB:QM is a general management science software package for the personal computer that has the capacity to solve linear programming problems, although its capabilities are more limited than those of LINDO. Here we will use AB:QM to solve the same product mix example (Example 3.1) we previously solved with LINDO.

The model input is requested in the following format.

```
Linear Programming
┌──────────────────────────────────────────────────────────────────────────┐
│ Problem Title :   Example 3.1                                             │
│ Type of Problem (Max=1/Min=2) 1          Tableau(All=1/Final=2/No=3)1     │
│ Number of Constraints         2          Number of Variables        2     │
└──────────────────────────────────────────────────────────────────────────┘
┌──────────────────────────────────────────────────────────────────────────┐
│          X1          X2 T         Rhs                                     │
│ Obj.     100         80 x xxxxxxxxxx                                      │
│ C1         2          4 <          80                                     │
│ C2         3          1 <          60                                     │
│                                                                          │
│                                                                          │
│                                                                          │
│                                                                          │
│                                                                          │
└──────────────────────────────────────────────────────────────────────────┘
┌──────────────────────────────────────────────────────────────────────────┐
│ Home  End  Esc                                                           │
└──────────────────────────────────────────────────────────────────────────┘
```

The solution output is displayed in the following format, beginning with a summary of the model followed by the simplex tableaus and a summary of the solution.

```
Program: Linear Programming

Problem Title : Example 3.1

***** Input Data *****

Max.   Z =  100x1 + 80x2

Subject to

C1    2x1 + 4x2 <= 80
C2    3x1 + 1x2 <= 60

***** Program Output *****

Simplex Tableau :  0
```

\Cj			100.000	80.000	0.000	0.000
Cb \	Basis	Bi	x 1	x 2	s 1	s 2
0.000	s 1	80.000	2.000	4.000	1.000	0.000
0.000	s 2	60.000	3.000	1.000	0.000	1.000
	Zj	0.000	0.000	0.000	0.000	0.000
	Cj-Zj		100.000	80.000	0.000	0.000

```
Simplex Tableau :  1

        \Cj                          100.000      80.000      0.000       0.000
     Cb \    Basis         Bi          x  1        x  2        s  1        s  2
     -----------------------------------------------------------------------------
      0.000    s  1      40.000        0.000       3.333       1.000      -0.667
    100.000    x  1      20.000        1.000       0.333       0.000       0.333
     -----------------------------------------------------------------------------
             Zj          2000.000      100.000     33.333      0.000      33.333
             Cj-Zj                     0.000       46.667      0.000     -33.333


Simplex Tableau :  2

        \Cj                          100.000      80.000      0.000       0.000
     Cb \    Basis         Bi          x  1        x  2        s  1        s  2
     -----------------------------------------------------------------------------
     80.000    x  2      12.000        0.000       1.000       0.300      -0.200
    100.000    x  1      16.000        1.000       0.000      -0.100       0.400
     -----------------------------------------------------------------------------
             Zj          2560.000      100.000     80.000     14.000      24.000
             Cj-Zj                     0.000       0.000     -14.000     -24.000


             Final Optimal Solution

             Z =    2560.000


             ----------------------------------------------------
             Variable              Value         Reduced Cost
             ----------------------------------------------------
                x 1              16.000            0.000
                x 2              12.000            0.000
             ----------------------------------------------------
             Constraint   Slack/Surplus     Shadow Price
             ----------------------------------------------------
                C 1              0.000            14.000
                C 2              0.000            24.000
             ----------------------------------------------------
```

The simplex iterations provided in this output are similar to the corresponding tab leaus shown in Tables 3.5, 3.11, and 3.14. A tutorial on how to use AB:QM is contained in Appendix D.

Computerized Solution of a Minimization Problem

Next we will solve Example 3.2, the diet problem, using the AB:QM package. You wil recall that Example 3.2 is a minimization problem formulated as follows:

Minimize $Z = 4x_1 + 3x_2$ (cost)
subject to
$2x_1 + 4x_2 \geqslant 16$ mg   (vitamin A)
$3x_1 + 2x_2 \geqslant 12$ mg   (vitamin B)
$x_1, x_2 \geqslant 0$

where
x_1 = number of eggs
x_2 = number of strips of bacon
Z = total cost (cents)

The model input is entered in a manner similar to that shown for the product mix (maximization) problem. Thus we will show only the program's output.

```
Program: Linear Programming

Problem Title : Example 3.2

***** Input Data *****

Min.  Z =  4x1 + 3x2

Subject to

C1    2x1 + 4x2 >= 16
C2    3x1 + 2x2 >= 12

***** Program Output *****
```

Simplex Tableau : 0

\Cj Cb \ Basis	Bi	4.000 x 1	3.000 x 2	0.000 S 1	0.000 S 2
M A 1	16.000	2.000	4.000	-1.000	0.000
M A 2	12.000	3.000	2.000	0.000	-1.000
Zj	*+M*	M	M	-M	-M
Zj-Cj		M	M	-M	-M

\Cj Cb \ Basis	Bi	M A 1	M A 2
M A 1	16.000	1.000	0.000
M A 2	12.000	0.000	1.000
Zj	*+M*	M	M
Zj-Cj		0.000	0.000

Simplex Tableau : 1

\Cj Cb \ Basis	Bi	4.000 x 1	3.000 x 2	0.000 S 1	0.000 S 2
3.000 x 2	4.000	0.500	1.000	-0.250	0.000
M A 2	4.000	2.000	0.000	0.500	-1.000
Zj	*+M*	M	3.000	M	-M
Zj-Cj		M	0.000	M	-M

\Cj Cb \ Basis	Bi	M A 1	M A 2
3.000 x 2	4.000	0.250	0.000
M A 2	4.000	-0.500	1.000
Zj	*+M*	-M	M
Zj-Cj		-M	0.000

```
Simplex Tableau :   2
            \Cj                      4.000       3.000       0.000       0.000
       Cb \    Basis      Bi        x  1        x  2        S  1        S  2
----------------------------------------------------------------------------------
      3.000    x  2      3.000      0.000       1.000      -0.375       0.250
      4.000    x  1      2.000      1.000       0.000       0.250      -0.500
----------------------------------------------------------------------------------
              Zj        17.000      4.000       3.000      -0.125      -1.250
              Zj-Cj                 0.000       0.000      -0.125      -1.250

            \Cj                        M           M
       Cb \    Basis      Bi        A  1        A  2
----------------------------------------------------------------------------------
      3.000    x  2      3.000      0.375      -0.250
      4.000    x  1      2.000     -0.250       0.500
----------------------------------------------------------------------------------
              Zj        17.000      0.125       1.250
              Zj-Cj                   -M          -M

Final Optimal Solution

Z =      17.000

------------------------------------------------------
Variable           Value        Reduced Cost
------------------------------------------------------
   x 1             2.000           0.000
   x 2             3.000           0.000
------------------------------------------------------
Constraint   Slack/Surplus    Shadow Price
------------------------------------------------------
   C 1             0.000          -0.125
   C 2             0.000          -1.250
------------------------------------------------------
```

Although these computer-generated tableaus are similar to the tableaus shown in Tables 3.15, 3.16, and 3.17, there are a few differences among the minimization problem tableaus. You will notice that the simplex tableau in the computer output wraps around due to page width limitations. Another difference among the tableaus is that the computer-generated solution does not eliminate artificial variables as they are removed from the basis; they are retained in the tableaus.

Computerized Solution of the Mixed Constraint Problem

Next we will solve Example 3.3, the investment problem, using the STORM package. You will recall that Example 3.3 is a mixed constraint problem formulated as follows:

Maximize $Z = 20x_1 + 10x_2$

subject to

$$x_1 + x_2 = 150 \quad \text{(total monthly investment)}$$
$$x_1 \leqslant 40 \quad \text{(maximum investment in stock)}$$
$$x_2 \geqslant 20 \quad \text{(minimum investment in bonds)}$$
$$x_1, x_2 \geqslant 0$$

where

x_1 = investment stock

x_2 = investment in bonds

The model input is entered in the manner shown below.

```
                    STORM DATA SET LISTING
                DETAILED PROBLEM DATA LISTING FOR
                 Example 3.3  Investment Problem
ROW LABEL        STOCK      BONDS CONST TYPE      R H S       RANGE

OBJ COEFF        20.        10.        XXXX       XXXX        XXXX
TOTAL INV.       1.         1.          =         150.          .
MAX STOCK        1.         0.         <=         40.           .
MIN BONDS        0.         1.         >=         20.           .
VARBL TYPE       POS        POS        XXXX       XXXX        XXXX
LOWR BOUND        .          .         XXXX       XXXX        XXXX
UPPR BOUND        .          .         XXXX       XXXX        XXXX
INIT SOLN        0.         0.         XXXX       XXXX        XXXX
```

The model is printed out in standard linear programming format below.

```
              Example 3.3  Investment Problem
              PROBLEM DATA IN EQUATION STYLE

Maximize
     + 20 STOCK + 10 BONDS

Subject to

   TOTAL INV.
      + 1 STOCK + 1 BONDS =  150

   MAX STOCK
      + 1 STOCK <= 40

   MIN BONDS
      + 1 BONDS >= 20

              0 <= STOCK
              0 <= BONDS
```

The solution is given below.

```
               Example 3.3  Investment Problem
    OPTIMAL SOLUTION - SUMMARY REPORT (NONZERO VARIABLES)
              Variable          Value            Cost

        1      STOCK          40.0000         20.0000
        2      BONDS         110.0000         10.0000

        Slack Variables
        5    MIN BONDS        90.0000          0.0000

Objective Function Value = 1900
```

As can be seen from these examples, if one has access to a mainframe or person computer, it is quite easy and efficient to solve linear programming problems by usin software packages. The question that is often posed then is "Why learn the simple method when computer programs to solve linear programming problems are so readi available—especially in the business community?" There are several answers to this que tion. The most prominent is that learning the simplex process dramatically increases one understanding of linear programming. In this same vein, learning the simplex proce aids one in interpreting and implementing the solutions. Just because an unstructure problem has been modeled and solved does not automatically mean that the solutior are correct. Unless one knows the fundamentals of linear programming solutions, it difficult to adjust even a computer program. Thus, although the computer is an obviou aid in solving linear programming problems, in-depth knowledge of the simplex metho is a necessity for real expertise in the formulation and subsequent interpretation of th solution of linear programming problems.

An additional reason for studying the manual simplex procedure is that it is ver useful in understanding the principles and applications of sensitivity analysis and duality topics to be presented in Chapter 4.

SUMMARY

In this chapter, the simplex method for solving linear programming problems has beer presented, along with examples of both maximization and minimization problems and a discussion of the various complications that can occur and their resolution. In future chapters, variations of the linear programming problem that require special solution techniques will be discussed. However, all of these variations in linear programming are primarily alterations of the basic model presented in Chapters 2 and 3, and the alternative solution techniques are predominantly variations of the simplex method. Chapters 2 and 3 have laid the foundation of mathematical programming on which all special variations are based.

REFERENCES

BAZARAA, M. S., and JARVIS, J. J. *Linear Programming and Network Flows*. New York: John Wiley & Sons, 1977.

BRADLEY, S. P.; HAX, A. C.; and MAGNANTI, T. L. *Applied Mathematical Programming*. Reading, Massachusetts: Addison-Wesley Publishing Company, 1977.

CHARNES, A., and COOPER, W. W. *Management Models and Industrial Applications of Linear Programming*. New York: John Wiley & Sons, 1961.

COOPER. L., and STEINBERG, D. *Methods and Applications of Linear Programming*. Philadelphia: W. B. Saunders Company, 1974.

DANTZIG, G. B. *Linear Programming and Extensions*. Princeton, New Jersey: Princeton University Press, 1963.

GASS, S. *Linear Programming*. 4th ed. New York: McGraw-Hill, 1975.

GAVER, D. P., and THOMPSON, G. L. *Programming and Probability Models in Operations Research*. Belmont, California: Wadsworth Publishing Company, 1973.

HADLEY, G. *Linear Programming*. Reading, Massachusetts: Addison-Wesley Publishing Company, 1962.

HILLIER, F. S., and LIEBERMAN, G. J. *Introduction to Operations Research*. 4th ed. San Francisco: Holden-Day, 1986.

IGNIZIO, J. P. *Linear Programming in Single and Multiple Objective Systems.* Englewood Cliffs, New Jersey: Prentice-Hall, 1982.

LOOMBA, N. P., and TURBAN, E. *Applied Programming for Management.* New York: Holt, Rinehart and Winston, 1974.

LUENBERGER, D. G. *Introduction to Linear and Non-Linear Programming.* Reading, Massachusetts: Addison-Wesley Publishing Company, 1973.

McMILLAN, C. *Mathematical Programming.* 2d ed. New York: John Wiley & Sons, 1975.

NAYLOR, T. H.; BYRNE, E. T.; and VERNON, J. M. *Introduction to Linear Programming: Methods and Cases.* Belmont, California: Wadsworth Publishing Company, 1971.

ROTHENBERG, R. I. *Linear Programming.* New York: Elsevier North-Holland, 1979.

SCHRAGE, L. *LINDO, An Optimization Modeling System,* 4th. ed., San Francisco: The Scientific Press, 1991.

SIMMONS, D. M. *Linear Programming for Operations Research.* San Francisco: Holden-Day, 1972.

WAGNER, H. M. *Principles of Operations Research.* 2d ed. Englewood Cliffs, New Jersey: Prentice-Hall, 1975.

WINSTON, W. L. *Introduction to Mathematical Programming, Applications and Algorithms,* Boston: PWS-Kent Publishing Co., 1991.

PROBLEMS

1. A company produces two products, 1 and 2. The company has 12 employees; it takes 2 employees working all day to make a unit of product 1, and 1 employee working all day to produce a unit of product 2. The company wants to know how many units of products 1 and 2 (x_1 and x_2) to produce to maximize profit. The following linear programming model has been formulated for this problem

Maximize $Z = 100x_1 + 80x_2$ (profit, \$)
subject to
$$2x_1 + x_2 \leq 12 \qquad \text{(employees)}$$
$$x_2 \leq 8 \qquad \text{(demand, units)}$$
$$x_1, x_2 \geq 0$$

Solve this model using the simplex method.

2. A farmer grows corn and tobacco on a farm of 40 acres. The farmer has 120 hours of labor available for planting. The farmer wants to know how many acres of corn and tobacco (x_1 and x_2) to plant to maximize profit. The following linear programming model has been formulated for this problem.

Maximize $Z = 50x_1 + 30x_2$ (profit, \$)
subject to
$$2x_1 + 4x_2 \leq 120 \qquad \text{(labor, hr)}$$
$$x_1 + x_2 \leq 40 \qquad \text{(land, acres)}$$
$$x_1, x_2 \geq 0$$

Solve this model using the simplex method.

3. A jeweler makes bracelets and necklaces from silver and a base metal. The jeweler has 18 ounces of silver and 24 ounces of the base metal available. The jeweler wants to know how many bracelets and necklaces (x_1 and x_2) to make to maximize profit.

The following linear programming model has been formulated for this problem.

Maximize $Z = 40x_1 + 20x_2$ (profit, $)
subject to

$$3x_1 + 2x_2 \leqslant 18 \quad \text{(silver, oz)}$$
$$2x_1 + 4x_2 \leqslant 24 \quad \text{(base metal, oz)}$$
$$x_1 \leqslant 4 \quad \text{(demand, bracelets)}$$
$$x_1, x_2 \geqslant 0$$

Solve this model using the simplex method.

4. A bakery makes cakes, doughnuts, and cookies in batches. The bakery's constrainin resources are oven capacity and labor. Only one oven is available, and only one batcl of any item can be baked in it at a time. It is in use 24 hours a day. The bakery ha 30 labor hours available each day. The company wants to know how many batche of cakes, doughnuts, and cookies (x_1, x_2, x_3) to bake each day to maximize profit The following linear programming model has been formulated for this problem.

Maximize $Z = 6x_1 + 2x_2 + 12x_3$ (profit, $)
subject to

$$4x_1 + x_2 + 3x_3 \leqslant 24 \quad \text{(oven capacity, hr)}$$
$$2x_1 + 6x_2 + 3x_3 \leqslant 30 \quad \text{(labor, hr)}$$
$$x_1, x_2, x_3 \geqslant 0$$

Solve this model using the simplex method.

5. A marketing company is performing a survey by telephone and door-to-door. A telephone interviewer can conduct 10 interviews an hour, and a door-to-door inter- viewer can conduct 6 an hour. The survey requires at least 60 interviews an hour. The company already has 4 door-to-door interviewers it must use. The company wants to know how many telephone and door-to-door interviewers (x_1 and x_2) to use to minimize the cost per hour. The following linear programming model has been formulated for this problem.

Minimize $Z = 3x_1 + 5x_2$ (cost, $)
subject to

$$10x_1 + 6x_2 \geqslant 60 \quad \text{(interviews)}$$
$$x_2 \geqslant 4 \quad \text{(door-to-door interviewers)}$$
$$x_1, x_2 \geqslant 0$$

Solve this model using the simplex method.

6. A company makes an instant hot cereal that contains apples and raisins. Both of these ingredients contribute vitamin B and vitamin C to the cereal. The company wants to know how many ounces of apples and raisins (x_1 and x_2) must be in each package of cereal to meet minimum requirements for vitamin B and vitamin C and minimize cost. The following linear programming model has been formulated for this problem.

Minimize $Z = 4x_1 + 6x_2$ (cost, cents)
subject to

$$x_1 + x_2 \geqslant 8 \quad \text{(vitamin B, mg)}$$

$$2x_1 + x_2 \geqslant 12 \qquad \text{(vitamin C, mg)}$$
$$x_1, x_2 \geqslant 0$$

Solve this model using the simplex method.

7. A health foods company produces a health drink from three ingredients, A, B, and C. The health drink must contain at least 40 milligrams of vitamin C and 24 milligrams of vitamin D per bottle. The company wants to know how many ounces of each ingredient (x_1, x_2, and x_3) to put into a bottle of the drink to minimize cost. The following linear programming model has been formulated for this problem.

$$\text{Minimize } Z = 2x_1 + 4x_2 + x_3 \quad \text{(cost, cents)}$$
subject to
$$4x_1 + 8x_2 + 2x_3 \geqslant 40 \qquad \text{(vitamin C, mg)}$$
$$x_1 + 2x_2 + x_3 \geqslant 24 \qquad \text{(vitamin D, mg)}$$
$$x_1, x_2, x_3 \geqslant 0$$

Solve this model using the simplex method.

8. Solve the following linear programming problem using the simplex method.

$$\text{Maximize } Z = 9x_1 + 12x_2$$
subject to
$$4x_1 + 8x_2 \leqslant 64$$
$$5x_1 + 5x_2 \leqslant 50$$
$$15x_1 + 8x_2 \leqslant 120$$
$$x_1 \leqslant 7$$
$$x_2 \leqslant 7$$
$$x_1, x_2 \geqslant 0$$

9. Solve the following linear programming problem using the simplex method.

$$\text{Maximize } Z = 100x_1 + 75x_2 + 90x_3 + 95x_4$$
subject to
$$3x_1 + 2x_2 \leqslant 40$$
$$4x_3 + x_4 \leqslant 25$$
$$200x_1 + 250x_3 \leqslant 2000$$
$$100x_2 + 200x_4 \leqslant 2200$$
$$x_1, x_2, x_3, x_4 \geqslant 0$$

10. Solve the following linear programming problem using the simplex method.

$$\text{Maximize } Z = 60x_1 + 50x_2 + 45x_3 + 50x_4$$
subject to
$$x_2 \leqslant 20$$
$$x_4 \leqslant 15$$
$$10x_1 + 5x_2 \leqslant 120$$
$$8x_3 + 6x_4 \leqslant 135$$
$$x_1, x_2, x_3, x_4 \geqslant 0$$

11. Solve the following linear programming problem using the simplex method.

   Minimize $Z = 20x_1 + 16x_2$

   subject to

   $$3x_1 + x_2 \geqslant 6$$
   $$x_1 + x_2 \geqslant 4$$
   $$2x_1 + 6x_2 \geqslant 12$$
   $$x_1, x_2 \geqslant 0$$

12. Solve the following linear programming problem using the simplex method.

   Minimize $Z = 3x_1 + 5x_2 + 2x_3$

   subject to

   $$x_1 + x_2 - 3x_3 \geqslant 35$$
   $$x_1 + 2x_2 \geqslant 50$$
   $$-x_1 + x_2 + x_3 \geqslant 25$$
   $$x_1, x_2, x_3 \geqslant 0$$

13. A seamstress makes two clothing items, A and B. The seamstress can make 5 of each item in an hour and wishes to produce at least 25 items. The seamstress has 16 square feet of material to produce the items. The seamstress wants to know how many hours to spend making each item (x_1 and x_2) in order to maximize profit. The following linear programming model has been formulated for this problem.

   Maximize $Z = x_1 + 5x_2$ (profit, $)

   subject to

   $$5x_1 + 5x_2 \geqslant 25 \qquad \text{(items)}$$
   $$2x_1 + 4x_2 \leqslant 16 \qquad \text{(material, ft}^2\text{)}$$
   $$x_1 \leqslant 5 \qquad \text{(item A, hr)}$$
   $$x_1, x_2 \geqslant 0$$

   Solve using the simplex method.

14. Solve the following linear programming problem using the simplex method.

   Minimize $Z = 10x_1 + 6x_2 + 8x_3$

   subject to

   $$x_1 + 2x_2 + 4x_3 \geqslant 24$$
   $$2x_1 + 4x_2 = 40$$
   $$x_1, x_2, x_3 \geqslant 0$$

15. Solve the following linear programming problem using the simplex method.

   Maximize $Z = 10x_1 + 5x_2$

   subject to

   $$2x_1 + x_2 \geqslant 10$$
   $$x_1 = 4$$
   $$x_1 + 4x_2 \leqslant 20$$
   $$x_1, x_2 \geqslant 0$$

16. Solve the following linear programming problem using the simplex method.

Minimize $Z = 4x_1 + 3x_2$

subject to

$$2x_1 + x_2 \geq 10$$
$$-3x_1 + 2x_2 \leq 6$$
$$x_1 + x_2 \geq 6$$
$$x_1, x_2 \geq 0$$

17. Solve the following linear programming problem using the simplex method.

Maximize $Z = 30x_1 + 40x_2 + 20x_3$

subject to

$$100x_1 + 120x_2 + 70x_3 \leq 100,000$$
$$7x_1 + 10x_2 + 8x_3 \leq 8000$$
$$x_1 + x_2 + x_3 = 1000$$
$$x_1, x_2, x_3 \geq 0$$

18. Solve the following linear programming problem using the simplex method.

Maximize $Z = 4x_1 + 5x_2$

subject to

$$2x_1 + 2x_2 \geq 8 \quad b_2$$
$$x_2 = 3 \quad b_3$$
$$9x_1 + 3x_2 \leq 27 \quad b_1$$
$$x_1, x_2 \geq 0$$

19. Solve the following linear programming problem using the simplex method.

Minimize $Z = 2x_1 + x_2 + 2x_3 + 1.2x_4$

subject to

$$x_1 + x_3 \geq 300$$
$$x_3 + x_4 \geq 500$$
$$.6x_1 - .4x_2 \leq 0$$
$$x_1 + x_2 + x_3 + x_4 \geq 1000$$
$$x_1, x_2, x_3, x_4 \geq 0$$

20. Solve the following linear programming problem using the simplex method.

Maximize $Z = 10x_1 + 5x_2$

subject to

$$3x_1 + 9x_2 \geq 27$$
$$8x_1 + 6x_2 \geq 48$$
$$-4x_1 + 6x_2 \leq -12$$
$$8x_1 + 12x_2 = 24$$
$$x_1, x_2 \geq 0$$

21. Solve the following linear programming problem using the simplex method.

Minimize $Z = 3x_1 + 6x_2$

subject to
$$3x_1 + 2x_2 \leqslant 18$$
$$x_1 + x_2 \geqslant 5$$
$$x_1 \leqslant 4$$
$$x_2 \leqslant 7$$
$$x_1, x_2 \geqslant 0$$

22. Solve the following linear programming problem using the simplex method.

Maximize $Z = 40x_1 + 60x_2$
subject to
$$x_1 + 2x_2 \leqslant 30$$
$$4x_1 + 4x_2 \leqslant 72$$
$$x_1 \geqslant 5$$
$$x_2 \geqslant 12$$
$$x_1, x_2 \geqslant 0$$

23. Solve the following linear programming problem using the simplex method.

Minimize $Z = 6x_1 + 4x_2$
subject to
$$3x_1 + 2x_2 \geqslant 18$$
$$2x_1 + 4x_2 = 20$$
$$2x_2 \leqslant 8$$
$$x_1, x_2 \geqslant 0$$

24. Solve the following linear programming problem using the simplex method.

Maximize $Z = .7x_1 + 1.2x_2 + .9x_3$
subject to
$$x_1 + x_2 + x_3 = 2000$$
$$x_1 \leqslant 1500$$
$$x_2 \leqslant 400$$
$$x_3 \leqslant 700$$
$$.5x_1 + .8x_2 + .6x_3 \geqslant 750$$
$$x_1, x_2, x_3 \geqslant 0$$

25. Solve the following linear programming problem using the simplex method.

Maximize $Z = 600x_1 + 540x_2 + 375x_3$
subject to
$$x_1 + x_2 + x_3 \leqslant 12$$
$$x_1 \leqslant 5$$
$$80x_1 + 70x_2 + 50x_3 \leqslant 750$$
$$x_1, x_2, x_3 \geqslant 0$$

26. Solve the following linear programming problem using the simplex method.

Maximize $Z = 40x_1 + 35x_2 + 45x_3$

subject to
$$2x_1 + 3x_2 + 2x_3 \leqslant 120$$
$$4x_1 + 3x_2 + x_3 \leqslant 160$$
$$3x_1 + 2x_2 + 4x_3 \leqslant 100$$
$$x_1 + x_2 + x_3 \leqslant 40$$
$$x_1, x_2, x_3 \geqslant 0$$

27. Solve the following linear programming problem using the simplex method.

Maximize $Z = 5x_1 + 7x_2 + 8x_3$

subject to
$$x_1 + x_2 + x_3 \leqslant 32$$
$$x_1 \leqslant 20$$
$$x_2 \leqslant 15$$
$$x_3 \leqslant 18$$
$$x_1, x_2, x_3 \geqslant 0$$

28. Solve the following linear programming problem using the simplex method.

Maximize $Z = 7x_1 + 5x_2 + 5x_3$

subject to
$$x_1 + x_2 + x_3 \leqslant 25$$
$$2x_1 + x_2 + x_3 \leqslant 40$$
$$x_1 + x_2 \leqslant 25$$
$$x_3 \leqslant 60$$
$$x_1, x_2, x_3 \geqslant 0$$

29. Solve the following linear programming problem using the simplex method.

Minimize $Z = 15x_1 + 25x_2$

subject to
$$3x_1 + 4x_2 \geqslant 12$$
$$2x_1 + x_2 \geqslant 6$$
$$3x_1 + 2x_2 \leqslant 9$$
$$x_1, x_2 \geqslant 0$$

30. Solve the following linear programming problem using the simplex method.

Maximize $Z = x_1 + 2x_2 - x_3$

subject to
$$4x_2 + x_3 \leqslant 40$$
$$x_1 - x_2 \leqslant 20$$
$$2x_1 + 4x_2 + 3x_3 \leqslant 60$$
$$x_1, x_2, x_3 \geqslant 0$$

31. Solve the following linear programming problem using the simplex method.

Maximize $Z = 5x_1 + 2x_2 + 10x_3 + 8x_4$

subject to
$$2x_1 - 3x_2 + x_3 + 7x_4 \leqslant 32$$

(continued)

$$4x_1 + 6x_2 - 2x_3 - 2x_4 \leqslant 24$$
$$2x_1 - 4x_2 + x_3 + 2x_4 \leqslant 12$$
$$x_1, x_2, x_3, x_4 \geqslant 0$$

32. Solve the following linear programming problem using the simplex method.

Maximize $Z = 12x_1 + 4x_2$

subject to
$$5x_1 + 3x_2 \leqslant 30$$
$$x_1 - 3x_2 \leqslant 12$$
$$x_1 \geqslant 0$$
$$x_2 \approx \text{unrestricted}$$

33. Solve the following linear programming problem using the simplex method.

Minimize $Z = x_1 + x_2 + 2x_3$

subject to
$$2x_1 - x_2 - x_3 \geqslant 28$$
$$-x_1 - 4x_2 + 2x_3 \geqslant 40$$
$$x_1, x_3 \geqslant 0$$
$$x_2 \sim \text{unrestricted}$$

34. Solve the following linear programming problem using the simplex method.

Maximize $Z = -2x_1 + 8x_2$

subject to
$$-2x_1 + x_2 \leqslant 4$$
$$x_1 + 2x_2 \leqslant 4$$
$$x_1 \sim \text{unrestricted}$$
$$x_2 \geqslant -2$$

35. Solve the following linear programming problem using the simplex method.

Maximize $Z = 2x_1 + 4x_2 - 2x_3$

subject to
$$2x_1 + x_2 - 4x_3 \leqslant 6$$
$$-4x_1 - 2x_2 + x_3 \leqslant 5$$
$$2x_1 + 6x_2 = 10$$
$$x_1, x_2, x_3 \geqslant 0$$

36. Solve the following linear programming problem using the simplex method.

Minimize $Z = 2x_1 - x_2 + 3x_3$

subject to
$$x_1 + 2x_2 + x_3 \geqslant 12$$
$$x_2 - 2x_3 \geqslant -6$$
$$6 \leqslant x_1 + 2x_2 + 4x_3 \leqslant 24$$
$$x_1, x_2 \geqslant 0$$
$$x_3 \sim \text{unrestricted}$$

37. Solve the following linear programming problem using the simplex method.

Maximize $Z = 5x_1 + 7x_2 + 6x_3$

subject to
$$4x_1 + 2x_2 + x_3 \leqslant 8$$
$$-2x_1 + 4x_2 + 12x_3 \leqslant 24$$
$$x_1 + 2x_2 + x_3 \geqslant 6$$
$$x_1, x_2, x_3 \geqslant 0$$

38. Solve the following linear programming problem using the simplex method.

Maximize $Z = 4x_1 + 2x_2$

subject to
$$-2x_1 - x_2 \geqslant 30$$
$$x_1 - 2x_2 \geqslant 8$$
$$3x_1 - 2x_2 \leqslant 12$$
$$x_1, x_2 \sim \text{unrestricted}$$

39. Solve the following linear programming problem using the simplex method.

Maximize $Z = 10x_1 + 8x_2$

subject to
$$-6x_1 + 2x_2 \geqslant 12$$
$$x_1 - x_2 \geqslant -2$$
$$x_1, x_2 \sim \text{unrestricted}$$

40. Solve the following linear programming problem using the simplex method.

Minimize $Z = 2x_1 + 4x_2 + x_3$

subject to
$$2x_1 - 3x_2 + x_3 = 4$$
$$3x_1 - 4x_2 - x_3 \geqslant 1$$
$$x_1, x_2 \geqslant 0$$
$$x_3 \sim \text{unrestricted}$$

41. Solve the following linear programming problem using the simplex method.

Maximize $Z = 3x_1 - x_2 + 2x_3$

subject to
$$3x_1 + 2x_2 + 2x_3 = 0$$
$$2x_2 + x_3 \leqslant 400$$
$$6x_1 + x_2 \geqslant 600$$
$$x_1, x_2 \geqslant 0$$
$$x_3 \approx \text{unrestricted}$$

42. Solve the following linear programming problem using the simplex method.

Maximize $Z = 2x_1 + x_2 - x_3$

subject to
$$15 \leqslant x_1 \leqslant 25$$

(continued)

$$x_1 + 2x_2 - x_3 = 12$$
$$x_1, x_2 \geq 0$$
$$x_3 \sim \text{unrestricted}$$

43. Solve the following linear programming problem using the simplex method.

Minimize $Z = x_1 - 2x_2 + 4x_3$
subject to
$$-2x_1 + x_2 + 3x_3 = 3$$
$$2x_1 + x_2 + x_3 \geq 1$$
$$x_1, x_3 \geq 0$$
$$x_2 \sim \text{unrestricted}$$

44. Solve the following linear programming problem using the simplex method.

Maximize $Z = x_1 + 2x_2 + 2x_3$
subject to
$$x_1 + x_2 + 2x_3 \leq 12$$
$$2x_1 + x_2 + 5x_3 = 20$$
$$x_1 + x_2 - x_3 \geq 8$$
$$x_1, x_2, x_3 \geq 0$$

45. Solve the following linear programming problem using the simplex method.

Maximize $Z = 2x_1 - x_2$
subject to
$$-x_1 + x_2 \leq 1$$
$$-x_1 + 2x_2 \leq 4$$
$$x_1, x_2 \geq 0$$

46. Solve the following linear programming problem using the simplex method.

Maximize $Z = 4x_1 + 2x_2$
subject to
$$x_1 + x_2 \geq 1$$
$$-4x_1 + x_2 \leq 0$$
$$-x_1 + 4x_2 \geq 0$$
$$-x_1 + x_2 \leq 1$$
$$x_1 + x_2 \leq 6$$
$$x_1 \leq 3$$
$$x_1, x_2 \geq 0$$

47. Solve the following linear programming problem using the simplex method.

Maximize $Z = 9x_1 + 18x_2$
subject to
$$6x_1 + 3x_2 \geq 1800$$
$$2x_1 + 2x_2 \leq 1600$$
$$x_2 \geq 0$$
$$x_1 \sim \text{unrestricted}$$

48. Solve the following linear programming problem using the simplex method.

Maximize $Z = 4x_1 + 8x_2$

subject to

$$x_2 \leqslant 6$$
$$x_1 \leqslant 4$$
$$2x_1 + 3x_2 \leqslant 12$$
$$x_2 \geqslant 0$$
$$x_1 \geqslant -4$$

All the remaining problems refer to problems in Chapter 2. Solve the problems in Chapter 2 listed below using the simplex method.

49. Solve problem 1

50. Solve problem 2

51. Solve problem 3

52. Solve problem 4

53. Solve problem 6

54. Solve problem 7

55. Solve problem 13

56. Solve problem 15

57. Solve problem 20

58. Solve problem 26

59. Solve problem 27

60. Solve problem 5

61. Solve problem 8

62. Solve problem 9

63. Solve problem 10

64. Solve problem 11

65. Solve problem 17

Solve the problems in Chapter 2 listed below using a computer program such as AB:QM, STORM, LINDO, or others. Submit a report including: (a) a printout of the linear programming model or the linear programming model data input entered; (b) a printout of the solution generated by the computer program; and (c) a brief summary report giving the solution values for the decision variables and the criterion variable (objective function). Include with the solution values for the decision variables the units of measure used (e.g., gallons, pounds, units, square feet, etc.) and the real-world definitions of the decision variables (e.g., jet fuel, kerosene, cars, bolts, screws, etc.); and, include with the solution value for the criterion variable the units of measure used (e.g., dollars, hours, miles, etc.) and the definition of the variable (e.g., profit, cost, time, distance, etc.).

66. Solve problem 12

67. Solve problem 14

68. Solve problem 16

69. Solve problem 18

70. Solve problem 19 (Set $Q = 100$)

71. Solve problem 21

72. Solve problem 22

73. Solve problem 23

74. Solve problem 24

75. Solve problem 25

76. Solve problem 28

77. Solve problem 29

78. Solve problem 30

79. Solve problem 31

80. Solve problem 32

81. Solve problem 33

82. Solve problem 34
83. Solve problem 35 (Set $Q = 100,000$)
84. Solve problem 36
85. Solve problem 37
86. Solve problem 38
87. Solve problem 39
88. Solve problem 40
89. Solve problem 41
90. Solve problem 42
91. Solve problem 43
92. Solve problem 44

4

Duality and
Sensitivity Analysis

Identifying the optimal basic solution of a problem as outlined in the previous two chapters is not always the ultimate objective of linear programming. Quite often the final simplex tableau provides additional economic information that is even more important than the basic solution to the problem. The importance and depth of the additional information obtained from analyzing optimal simplex tableaus has generated a great deal of interest in this area of analysis. The two major topics of interest related to the study of optimal solutions are **duality** and **sensitivity analysis.** Duality is a unique property of linear programming that allows the economic valuation of constraint resources. Sensitivity analysis is the study of changes in the model parameters and the effects these changes have on the problem solution.

DUALITY

The term *duality* refers to the fact that every linear programming problem consists of two forms. The first, or original, form of the problem is called the **primal,** and the second form of the problem is called the **dual.** For every **primal solution** there exists a corresponding **dual solution.** As might be expected, the properties of one problem form are closely related to the properties of the other. As a result, the optimal solution to the primal form yields complete information about the solution to the dual form.

The dual solution provides significant information concerning the economic interpretation of the resource parameters of a linear programming problem. Hence, the dual can provide information to the manager regarding the value of resources, thereby aiding the manager in making decisions with respect to the acquisition of additional resources.

Example 4.1   Economic Interpretation of the Optimal Simplex Solution

Consider the following profit maximization problem for a manufacturing firm. The firm produces two products, 1 and 2. The production of products 1 and 2 is subject to the following resource requirements and availabilities of labor, material, and storage space:

	Resource Requirements		
Resource	Product 1	Product 2	Total Resources
Labor (hr/unit)	1	2	10 hr
Material (lb/unit)	6	6	36 lb
Storage (ft^2/unit)	8	4	40 ft^2

Given that profit per unit is $4 for product 1 and $5 for product 2, this problem is formulated as

Maximize $Z = \$4x_1 + 5x_2$ (profit)

subject to

$x_1 + 2x_2 \leqslant 10$ hr   (labor)
$6x_1 + 6x_2 \leqslant 36$ lb   (material)
$8x_1 + 4x_2 \leqslant 40$ ft^2 (storage)
$x_1, x_2 \geqslant 0$

[handwritten: – adding more of scarce resources increases profit, if labor is $6 an hr, if you pay more than $6+$1 for an extra labor hr, you will decrease profit; if you can pay $6.50 for that hr, you can increase profit]

Solving this problem via the simplex method results in the optimal simplex solution in Table 4.1.

Table 4.1 Optimal Simplex Solution   *[handwritten: score resource]*

c_j c_b	basis	b_i^*	4 x_1	5 x_2	0 s_1	0 s_2	0 s_3
5	x_2	4	0	1	1	$-\frac{1}{6}$	0
4	x_1	2	1	0	-1	$\frac{1}{3}$	0
0	s_3	8	0	0	4	-2	1
	z_j	28	4	5	1	$\frac{1}{2}$	0
	$c_j - z_j$		0	0	-1	$-\frac{1}{2}$	0

[handwritten left margin: ...nal value of ...one unit of ...would be $1. ...would go out and ...could go out and ...the more labor hr, ...profit would ...se by $1.]

[handwritten: if add one unit of s_1 resource (new) Z would decrease by $1]

[handwritten: marginal increase in Z value of $1]

[handwritten: shadow prices]

[handwritten: if s_1 enters basis, would decrease profit by $1 for every unit]

The model results that are most obvious, given your present knowledge of linear programming, are the optimal basic solution ($x_1 = 2$, $x_2 = 4$, $s_3 = 8$) and the maximum profit ($z_j = \$28$). However, there is additional information in the final tableau, related to the constraint resources (labor, material, and space), that has yet to be analyzed. This information is contained in the $c_j - z_j$ row of the final tableau. As previously noted, the $c_j - z_j$ row cell values indicate the per unit increase (or decrease) in profit that would be realized if the corresponding variable entered the solution base.

Observing the $c_j - z_j$ values under the s_1 and s_2 columns, we can see that if either of these variables entered the solution, profit would decline by $1 or $.50 per unit, respectively. Recall that s_1 represents unused labor resources and s_2 represents unused material resources. Since they are not in the basic solution, both s_1 and s_2 (in Table 4.1) are by definition equal to zero, which means that all labor and materials are being used. Therefore, entry of 1 unit of s_1 into the basic solution is analogous to reduction in the *use of labor* by 1 unit (i.e., if s_1 moves into the basis and equals 1, it represents 1 hour of labor not being used). Likewise, entry of 1 unit of s_2 results in reduction in the *use of material* by 1 unit.

Now, if entry of 1 unit of s_1 (reducing labor usage by 1 unit) would reduce profit by \$1, then the reverse process would increase profit by \$1. The same holds true for s_2, except that the marginal rate at which profit changes as s_2 (the quantity of material resource) changes is \$.50. It can therefore be logically deduced that \$1 and \$.50 represent the marginal values of these resources. In other words, we could expect profit to increase by \$1 or \$.50 if another unit of labor or material, respectively, could be obtained at the original price. The $c_j - z_j$ values under the slack variables are often referred to as **shadow prices,** since they are, in effect, the maximum additional prices the manager would be willing to pay to obtain more of the resources to maximize profit subject to the resource constraints. It is important to realize that these shadow prices, or marginal values, for resources are amounts in addition to the original prices paid for the resources. For example, if the original price paid per hour for labor was \$6, then, according to our analysis of the shadow prices, the firm would be willing to pay a maximum of \$7 for an additional hour of labor.   *shadow prices are marginal values*

Assume for a moment that the manager of the manufacturing firm wishes to place a value on the worth of the resources. Looking at the original model formulation, the manager sees only how much of each resource is required to produce each unit of product, how much of each resource is available, and the profit to be garnered from units produced. There is no indication of the worth (or cost) of those resources. Observing the maximum profit of \$28, the manager ascertains that the values of the resources must be defined in terms of their contributions to profit. Thus, the manager must distribute the profit among all employed resources in order to determine the implicit values of those resources in gaining that profit. These resource values are what is shown by the $c_j - z_j$ values under the slack variables in the final simplex tableau. Going one step further, we can see that the value of each resource corresponds to the slack variable for each resource constraint. Thus, the $c_j - z_j$ value for s_1 is the marginal value of labor, $c_j - z_j$ for s_2 is the marginal value of material, and $c_j - z_j$ for s_3 is the marginal value of storage space.

The question might now be asked, "What is the value of s_3, storage space?" The answer is that on a *marginal* basis storage space has no value, since storage is not a binding constraint ($s_3 = 8$ means that 8 square feet are left unused). An extra square foot of storage space has no value to the manager, since extra unused storage space already exists.

Thus, the resources of the linear programming problem have value, in the sense in which it is discussed here, only if they represent binding constraints on the problem. That is, the value is in terms of what it would be worth to have available additional units of the resources that are limiting possible production (and profit). The key to understanding the implicit value of resources, as given in the $c_j - z_j$ row in the optimal solution tableau, is to recognize that these are *marginal* values for the optimal solution, which is located on the solution space boundary created by those constraints that reflect resources that have value to the manager.

A unique characteristic of linear programming models is that the economic properties previously mentioned can be expressed within the dual form. In fact, a completely symmetrical model form can be developed from the original problem (primal form) in which the decision variables represent the values of the constraint resources.

The Dual Form of the Problem

If a linear programming maximization problem is defined as the primal, the corresponding dual is a minimization problem. Conversely, a primal minimization problem has a corresponding dual maximization form. The dual form of our previously discussed problem (Example 4.1) is a minimization problem, which is formulated as follows:

Minimize $Z = 10y_1 + 36y_2 + 40y_3$

subject to

$$y_1 + 6y_2 + 8y_3 \geq 4$$
$$2y_1 + 6y_2 + 4y_3 \geq 5$$
$$y_1, y_2, y_3 \geq 0$$

where

y_1 = marginal value of 1 hr of labor
y_2 = marginal value of 1 lb of material
y_3 = marginal value of 1 ft^2 of storage space

The relationship between the primal and dual formulations can be summarized as follows:

1. The maximization of a primal becomes a dual minimization.

2. The dual variables, y_1, y_2, and y_3, correspond to the resource constraints in the primal problem. Since there are $m = 3$ constraints in the primal, there are $m = 3$ variables in the dual.

3. The right-hand-side elements (b_i) in the primal correspond to the coefficients of the objective function in the dual. The values $b_1 = 10$, $b_2 = 36$, and $b_3 = 40$ form the objective function of the dual, $z_d = 10y_1 + 36y_2 + 40y_3$.

4. The a_{ij} constraint coefficients in the primal are the a_{ji} values in the dual:

Primal (a_{ij})				Dual (a_{ji})
a_{11}	=	1	=	a_{11}
a_{12}	=	2	=	a_{21}
a_{21}	=	6	=	a_{12}
a_{22}	=	6	=	a_{22}
a_{31}	=	8	=	a_{13}
a_{32}	=	4	=	a_{23}

5. The c_j values in the primal are right-hand-side values in the dual ($c_1 = 4$ and $c_2 = 5$).

6. All constraints in the maximization primal are $\leq$, and all constraints in the corresponding minimization dual are $\geq$.

The primal-dual relationship for the example production problem can be observed in Figure 4.1.

The Primal-Dual Relationship in General Form

An important format for expressing a linear programming problem that will be of benefit in the following discussion of the dual is the general form of a linear programming problem. Recall the general linear programming model for a maximization problem, originally shown in Chapter 2:

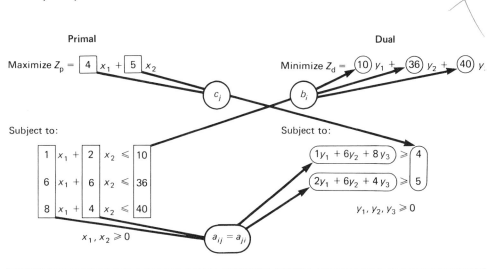

Figure 4.1 The Primal-Dual Relationship

$$\text{Maximize } Z_p = \sum_{j=1}^{n} c_j x_j$$

subject to

$$\sum_{j=1}^{n} a_{ij} x_j \leq b_i, \ i = 1, 2, \ldots, m$$

$$x_j \geq 0, j = 1, 2, \ldots, n$$

Applying the basic primal-dual conversions previously noted to the primal in general form results in the following general form for the dual:

$$\text{Minimize } Z_d = \sum_{i=1}^{m} b_i y_i$$

subject to

$$\sum_{i=1}^{m} a_{ij} y_i \geq c_j, j = 1, 2, \ldots, n$$

$$y_i \geq 0, i = 1, 2, \ldots, m$$

Analysis of the Dual Form

Now let us analyze the primal-dual relationships that were alluded to in our prior discussion of the primal. Tables 4.2 and 4.3 show the final optimal simplex solutions for the primal and dual forms of our example.

Primal
Maximize $Z_p = 4x_1 + 5x_2$
subject to
$$x_1 + 2x_2 \leq 10$$
$$6x_1 + 6x_2 \leq 36$$
$$8x_1 + 4x_2 \leq 40$$
$$x_1, x_2 \geq 0$$

Dual
Minimize $Z_d = 10y_1 + 36y_2 + 40y_3$
subject to
$$y_1 + 6y_2 + 8y_3 \geq 4$$
$$2y_1 + 6y_2 + 4y_3 \geq 5$$
$$y_1, y_2, y_3 \geq 0$$

Table 4.2 *Optimal Simplex Tableau for the Primal Form*

c_b	c_j basis	b_i^*	4 x_1	5 x_2	0 s_1	0 s_2	0 s_3
5	x_2	4	0	1	1	$-\frac{1}{6}$	0
4	x_1	2	1	0	-1	$\frac{1}{3}$	0
0	s_3	8	0	0	4	-2	1
	z_j	28	4	5	1	$\frac{1}{2}$	0
	$c_j - z_j$		0	0	-1	$-\frac{1}{2}$	0

Table 4.3 *Optimal Simplex Tableau for the Dual Form*

c_b	c_j basis	b_i^*	10 y_1	36 y_2	40 y_3	0 s'_1	0 s'_2
36	y_2	$\frac{1}{2}$	0	1	2	$-\frac{1}{3}$	$\frac{1}{6}$
10	y_1	1	1	1	0	-4	1	-1
	z_j	28	10	36	32	-2	-4
	$z_j - c_j$		0	0	-8	-2	-4

The relationship between the primal and dual solutions can be ascertained by observing the two simplex tableaus in Tables 4.2 and 4.3. Note that the negative $c_j - z_j$ row values under s_1 and s_2 of the primal tableau correspond to the solution values of y_1 and y_2 of the dual. Considering all $c_j - z_j$ values in the primal solution tableau, we have

Primal Tableau Column Headings	$c_j - z_j$ Values in Primal	Dual Tableau Basic (b_i^*) Solution
x_1	0	s'_1 (not in basis, therefore zero by definition)
x_2	0	s'_2 (not in basis, therefore zero by definition)
s_1	1	y_1
s_2	$\frac{1}{2}$	y_2
s_3	0	y_3 (not in basis, therefore zero by definition)

As noted previously, the dual variables, y_i, represent the marginal value of a unit of each resource, i. Thus, y_1, the marginal value of labor, equals \$1, and y_2, the marginal value of material, equals \$.50, as shown in Table 4.3.

Next, let us consider the fact that the optimal z_j values in Tables 4.2 and 4.3 both equal \$28. In other words,

$$\text{Maximize } Z_p = \$28 = \text{Minimize } Z_d$$

The economic interpretation of this property is one of the most ambiguous and difficult to explain concepts in linear programming. This property can best be observed analytically, employing the general form of the model. Let us begin by recalling the constraints of the general model of the primal.

$$\sum_{j=1}^{n} a_{ij} x_j \leq b_i, \, i = 1, 2, \ldots, m$$

Multiply both sides of this inequality by y_i and sum over i.

$$\sum_{i=1}^{m} y_i \left(\sum_{j=1}^{n} a_{ij} x_j \right) \leq \sum_{i=1}^{m} b_i y_i$$

Notice that the term $\sum_{i=1}^{m} b_i y_i$ is also the general form of the dual objective function, Z_d. Next, recall that the general form of the dual constraints is

$$\sum_{i=1}^{m} a_{ij} y_i \geq c_j, \, j = 1, 2, \ldots, n$$

If both sides of this inequality are multiplied by x_j and summed over j, then

$$\sum_{j=1}^{n} x_j \left(\sum_{i=1}^{m} a_{ij} y_i \right) \geq \sum_{j=1}^{n} c_j x_j$$

Notice that the term $\sum_{j=1}^{n} c_j x_j$ in this formulation is also the general form of the primal objective function, Z_p. Examining these several manipulations, we can further observe that the terms $\sum_{j=1}^{n} x_j (\sum_{i=1}^{m} a_{ij} y_i)$ and $\sum_{i=1}^{m} y_i (\sum_{j=1}^{n} a_{ij} x_j)$ are equal.

Thus, by combining these terms, we can determine the following relationship:

$$Z_p = \sum_{j=1}^{n} c_j x_j \leq \left[\sum_{j=1}^{n} x_j \left(\sum_{j=1}^{m} a_{ij} y_i \right) = \sum_{i=1}^{m} y_i \left(\sum_{j=1}^{n} a_{ij} x_j \right) \right] \leq \sum_{i=1}^{m} b_i y_i = Z_d$$

and

$$Z_p = Z_d$$

This analytical result is known as the **fundamental primal-dual relationship**. The literal interpretation of this relationship is that the value of the primal objective function is bounded by the corresponding value of the dual objective function. Carrying this relationship a step further, we find that if the optimal solution values (x_j) are feasible and the optimal dual solution values (y_i) are feasible, then

$$\text{Max } Z_p = \text{Min } Z_d$$

which corresponds to the primal-dual relationship previously noted.

Implicit in the fundamental primal-dual relationship is the property of **complementary slackness**. This property holds that for a positive basic variable in the primal,

the corresponding dual variable will equal zero. Alternatively, for a nonbasic variable
the primal (which is thus zero), the corresponding dual variable will be basic and positi
As an example, consider the primal and dual solutions of the production probl
illustrated in Tables 4.2 and 4.3. Observe that the basic variables in the primal (x_2, .
and s_3) have corresponding dual variables (s_2', s_1', and y_3) that are nonbasic and, th
equal to zero. Similarly, the nonbasic primal variables s_1 and s_2 equal zero, while in t
dual the corresponding variables y_1 and y_2 are basic and positive.

Exceptions to the Primal-Dual Relationship

The primal-dual transformation illustrated in this chapter is based on a maximizati
problem with all $\leqslant$ constraints. As prior illustrations in Chapters 2 and 3 have show
this linear programming form does not always exist. The rules for transforming the prim
form of a problem into the dual form are altered when the linear programming proble
contains mixed constraints (i.e., a combination of $\leqslant$, $=$, $\geqslant$ constraints) and/or unr
stricted variables. Each of the possible alternative cases will be considered separately.

An Equality Constraint

The following problem in primal form contains an equality constraint.

Maximize $Z_p = c_1 x_1 + c_2 x_2$
subject to
$$a_{11} x_1 + a_{12} x_2 = b_1$$
$$a_{21} x_1 + a_{22} x_2 \leqslant b_2$$
$$x_1, x_2 \geqslant 0$$

The equality constraint can also be expressed by the following two inequalit
constraints:

$$a_{11} x_1 + a_{12} x_2 \leqslant b_1$$
$$a_{11} x_1 + a_{12} x_2 \geqslant b_1$$

The second of these inequalities ($\geqslant$) can be transformed into a $\leqslant$ constraint by multi
plying through by -1:

$$-a_{11} x_1 - a_{12} x_2 \leqslant -b_1$$

The original problem can now be formulated with all $\leqslant$ constraints.

Maximize $Z_p = c_1 x_1 + c_2 x_2$
subject to
$$a_{11} x_1 + a_{12} x_2 \leqslant b_1$$
$$-a_{11} x_1 - a_{12} x_2 \leqslant -b_1$$
$$a_{21} x_1 + a_{22} x_2 \leqslant b_2$$
$$x_1, x_2 \geqslant 0$$

The problem is now in the proper form to construct the dual, with all $\leqslant$ constraints.
(Note that, in this and the following dual formulations, the constraint coefficients in the
dual are expressed in the a_{ij} subscript notation of the primal, in order to show where in
the primal the dual constraint coefficients come from.)

$$\text{Minimize } Z_d = b_1 y_1 - b_1 y_2 + b_2 y_3$$

subject to

$$a_{11}y_1 - a_{11}y_2 + a_{21}y_3 \geq c_1$$
$$a_{12}y_1 - a_{12}y_2 + a_{22}y_3 \geq c_2$$
$$y_1, y_2, y_3 \geq 0$$

This form of the dual of a primal problem is quite acceptable; however, with a few simple manipulations, an additional property of the dual of a problem with an equality constraint can be identified. First, all similar terms in the objective function and constraints are combined.

$$\text{Minimize } Z_d = b_1(y_1 - y_2) + b_2 y_3$$

subject to

$$a_{11}(y_1 - y_2) + a_{21}y_3 \geq c_1$$
$$a_{12}(y_1 - y_2) + a_{22}y_3 \geq c_2$$
$$y_1, y_2, y_3 \geq 0$$

It can now be seen that the term $y_1 - y_2$ in the preceding model is in the same form as it would be if y_1 were an unrestricted variable. Recall from Chapter 3 that if a variable x_j is unrestricted in sign, then the problem can be transformed into proper simplex form by letting

$$x_j = \hat{x}_j - \hat{\hat{x}}$$

which corresponds with the form of the term $y_1 - y_2$. This property enables us to develop the dual from the original primal problem, without transforming the original equality constraint. Thus, the dual of the original primal problem is formulated by treating the primal equality constraint as a $\leq$ constraint and letting y_1 be an unrestricted variable

$$\text{Minimize } Z_d = b_1 y_1 + b_2 y_2$$

subject to

$$a_{11}y_1 + a_{21}y_2 \geq c_1$$
$$a_{12}y_1 + a_{22}y_2 \geq c_2$$
$$y_1 \sim \text{unrestricted}$$
$$y_2 \geq 0$$
$$y_1 = \hat{y}_1 - \hat{\hat{y}}$$

In general, any equality constraint i in the primal results in an unrestricted variable y_i in the dual. The following example demonstrates the primal-dual transformation when there is an equality constraint.

Primal
$$\text{Maximize } Z_p = 3x_1 + 7x_2$$
subject to
$$4x_1 + 2x_2 \leq 24$$
$$x_1 + 7x_2 = 28$$
$$2x_1 + 3x_2 \leq 18$$
$$x_1, x_2 \geq 0$$

Dual
$$\text{Minimize } Z_d = 24y_1 + 28y_2 + 18y_3$$
subject to
$$4y_1 + y_2 + 2y_3 \geq 3$$
$$2y_1 + 7y_2 + 3y_3 \geq 7$$
$$y_1, y_3 \geq 0$$
$$y_2 \sim \text{unrestricted}$$

The opposite condition holds when the primal contains an unrestricted variable (x_j). In this case, the dual constraint (j) is an equality.

A $\geqslant$ Constraint

The other constraint possibility that alters the standard primal-dual transformation is the existence of a $\geqslant$ constraint. In this case, the direction of the inequality is reversed by multiplying the constraint by -1. For example,

$$a_{11}x_1 + a_{12}x_2 \geqslant b_1$$

becomes

$$-a_{11}x_1 - a_{12}x_2 \leqslant -b_1$$

The following example problem demonstrates the primal-dual transformation with all three constraint possibilities ($\leqslant$, $=$, $\geqslant$) plus an unrestricted variable:

Primal	*Dual*
Maximize $Z_p = 10x_1 + 3x_2 + 8x_3$	Minimize $Z_d = 16y_1 + 10y_2 - 20y_3$
subject to	subject to
$x_1 + 4x_2 + 2x_3 \leqslant 16$	$y_1 - 6y_3 \geqslant 10$
$3x_2 + x_3 = 10$	$4y_1 + 3y_2 - 2y_3 \geqslant 3$
$6x_1 + 2x_2 \geqslant 20$	$2y_1 + y_2 = 8$
$x_1, x_2 \geqslant 0$	$y_1, y_3 \geqslant 0$
$x_3 \sim$ unrestricted	$y_2 \sim$ unrestricted

The Dual Form of a Minimization Problem

A minimization problem can also be transformed into its dual form (a maximization problem). However, in the case of a minimization problem, the proper constraint form consists of all $\geqslant$ constraints. Thus, any mixed constraints must be converted to $\geqslant$ form. The following example model demonstrates the primal minimization problem and its dual form:

Primal	*Dual*
Minimize $Z_p = 3x_1 + 6x_2$	Maximize $Z_d = 16y_1 - 10y_2 + 20y_3$
subject to	subject to
$2x_1 + 7x_2 \geqslant 16$	$2y_1 - y_2 + 4y_3 \leqslant 3$
$x_1 \leqslant 10$	$7y_1 + 2y_3 \leqslant 6$
$4x_1 + 2x_2 = 20$	$y_1, y_2 \geqslant 0$
$x_1, x_2 \geqslant 0$	$y_3 \sim$ unrestricted

The dual variables (y_1, y_2, and y_3) represent the marginal value of relaxing the constraints of the primal problem in which the objective is to minimize total cost.

Summary of the Primal-Dual Relationships

The various primal-dual relationships are summarized in Table 4.4.

Table 4.4 Primal-Dual Relationships

Primal	Dual
$\text{Min } Z_p = \sum_{j=1}^{n} c_j x_j$	$\text{Min } Z_d = \sum_{i=1}^{m} b_i y_i$
Constraint i	Variable y_i
Variable x_j	Constraint j
$\leqslant$ constraints	$\geqslant$ constraints
constraint i, $=$	$y_i \sim$ unrestricted
$x_j \sim$ unrestricted	constraint j, $=$

Computerized Duality Analysis

Computer software packages that have the capability to solve linear programming problems also provide information regarding the dual solution. Both AB:QM and LINDO, which were used in Chapter 3 to solve linear programming problems, provide the dual solution as part of the solution output. For Example 4.1, which was introduced at the beginning of this chapter, LINDO provides the following solution output.

```
: look all

MAX       4 X1 + 5 X2
SUBJECT TO
        2)    X1 + 2 X2 <=    10
        3)    6 X1 + 6 X2 <=    36
        4)    8 X1 + 4 X2 <=    40
END

: go
LP OPTIMUM FOUND  AT STEP     2

            OBJECTIVE FUNCTION VALUE

    1)        28.0000000

    VARIABLE          VALUE           REDUCED COST
        X1          2.000000            .000000
        X2          4.000000            .000000


        ROW     SLACK OR SURPLUS      DUAL PRICES
        2)            .000000          1.000000
        3)            .000000           .500000
        4)           8.000000           .000000

    NO. ITERATIONS=        2
```

Notice that in the presentation of the final solution, the dual values (called *dual prices*) are given as part of the regular computer output: 1.00, .50, and .00. Recall from our discussion of LINDO in Chapter 3 that the LINDO linear programming package

always considers the objective function to be the first function; thus, all constraints
numbered sequentially, beginning with the first constraint, identified by LINDO as fu
tion number 2. Therefore, "row 2" in the LINDO output is the equivalent of s_1 in Ta
4.2. Although the format is somewhat different in the computerized output, the d
values are the same, as we determined earlier.

The AB:QM package provides the dual solution output in a more familiar form
shown below for the same example problem.

```
Program: Linear Programming

Problem Title : Example 4.1

***** Input Data *****

Max.  Z =  4x1 + 5x2

Subject to

C1    1x1 + 2x2 <= 10
C2    6x1 + 6x2 <= 36
C3    8x1 + 4x2 <= 40

***** Program Output *****

Final Optimal Solution At Simplex Tableau : 2

Z =      28.000

- - - - - - - - - - - - - - - - - - - - - - - - - - - - - -
Variable          Value          Reduced Cost
- - - - - - - - - - - - - - - - - - - - - - - - - - - - - -
   x 1            2.000             0.000
   x 2            4.000             0.000
- - - - - - - - - - - - - - - - - - - - - - - - - - - - - -
Constraint  Slack/Surplus      Shadow Price
- - - - - - - - - - - - - - - - - - - - - - - - - - - - - -
   C 1            0.000             1.000
   C 2            0.000             0.500
   C 3            8.000             0.000
- - - - - - - - - - - - - - - - - - - - - - - - - - - - - -
```

SENSITIVITY ANALYSIS

It is rare that a manager can determine the model parameters of a linear programming
problem (c_j, b_i, a_{ij}) with absolute certainty. In reality the model parameters are usuall
simply estimates and, as such, subject to some uncertainty. As a result, it may often b
desirable for a manager/decision maker to observe the effects of parameter changes (which
would reflect uncertainty) on the optimal solution of the problem. The analysis of param
eter changes and their effects on linear programming solutions is referred to as **sensitiv
ity, or postoptimality, analysis.** In other words, sensitivity analysis is the study o
parameter changes and the sensitivity of the optimal solution to these changes.

The most obvious means for analyzing parameter changes is to make the change in the original problem formulation, solve the problem again via the simplex method, and compare the new solution with the old. However, this process is both time consuming and computationally inefficient. Alternatively, it is generally possible to perform sensitivity analysis by manipulating the final simplex tableau.

The different categories of parameter changes that will be the subjects of this section include

1. Changes in right-hand-side values, b_i
2. Changes in the objective function coefficients, c_j
3. Changes in the constraint coefficients, a_{ij}
4. Addition of a new constraint
5. Addition of a new decision variable

anges in Right-Hand-Side Values, b_i

Recall the production Example, 4.1, from the previous section on duality.

Maximize $Z = 4x_1 + 5x_2$ (profit)
subject to
$$\begin{aligned} x_1 + 2x_2 &\leq 10 \text{ hr} \qquad \text{(labor)} \\ 6x_1 + 6x_2 &\leq 36 \text{ lb} \qquad \text{(material)} \\ 8x_1 + 4x_2 &\leq 40 \text{ ft}^2 \qquad \text{(space)} \\ x_1, x_2 &\geq 0 \end{aligned}$$

Now consider the effect of increasing one of the b_i values ($b_1 = 10$, $b_2 = 36$, $b_3 = 40$) by an amount Δ. For example, observe how a change in the labor constraint from 10 hours to 12 hours ($\Delta = 2$) is represented graphically in Figure 4.2. Increasing b_1 by

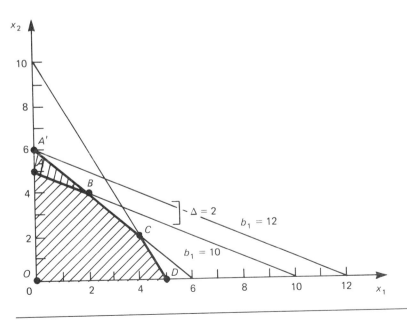

Figure 4.2 Change in the b_1 Parameter

2 hours (from 10 to 12) has the effect of moving the constraint equation, $x_1 + 2x_2 = b_1$, out from the origin to a new position parallel to the old constraint. This is an obviou result, since the slope of the constraint line has not changed but the axis intercepts have Note that this change redefines the feasible solution space from area $OABCD$ to area OA CD. This example demonstrates that a change in a b_i value can affect the final solution In other words, the feasible solution space may change to the point where the optima solution basis also changes.

It is possible to develop a general approach for determining a range for b_i over which the variables in the solution basis will remain optimal. In order to demonstrate thi approach, our production example will again be employed. Consider a general increas in the labor constraint of Δ hours. The problem constraints become

$$x_1 + 2x_2 \leq 10 + 1\Delta \text{ hr}$$
$$6x_1 + 6x_2 \leq 36 + 0\Delta \text{ lb}$$
$$8x_1 + 4x_2 \leq 40 + 0\Delta \text{ ft}^2$$

Substituting these constraints into the simplex process results in the initial tableau i Table 4.5.

Table 4.5 Initial Simplex Tableau

c_j c_b	basis	b_i^*	4 x_1	5 x_2	0 s_1	0 s_2	0 s_3
0	s_1	$10 + 1\Delta$	1	2	1	0	0
0	s_2	$36 + 0\Delta$	6	6	0	1	0
0	s_3	$40 + 0\Delta$	8	4	0	0	1
	z_j	0	0	0	0	0	0
	$c_j - z_j$		4	5	0	0	0

Observe that in Table 4.5 the *coefficients of* Δ in the b_i^* column are the same as the values in the s_1 column. The effect of this similarity becomes apparent in the final optima tableau (Table 4.6).

Table 4.6 Optimal Simplex Tableau

c_j c_b	basis	b_i^*	4 x_1	5 x_2	0 s_1	0 s_2	0 s_3
5	x_2	$4 + 1\Delta$	0	1	1	$-\frac{1}{6}$	0
4	x_1	$2 - 1\Delta$	1	0	-1	$\frac{1}{3}$	0
0	s_3	$8 + 4\Delta$	0	0	4	-2	1
	z_j	$28 + \Delta$	4	5	1	$\frac{1}{2}$	0
	$c_j - z_j$		0	0	-1	$-\frac{1}{2}$	0

The final optimal tableau shows that the coefficients of Δ in the b_i^* column have remained the same as the s_1 column values. In effect, the Δ coefficients can be considered an additional tableau column exactly like the s_1 column. Thus, the Δ coefficients in the

b_i^* column in the final tableau will always be the same as the values in the s_1 column. This means that it is unnecessary to go through all the simplex tableaus to determine the general effects of Δ on the final solution. As a general rule, it is only necessary to increase (or decrease) the final b_i^* values by a multiple of Δ, where the multiple is given by the column coefficients of the slack variable (s_i) for b_i. Thus, for this example, if the final tableau b_i^* values are

$$\frac{b_i^*}{\begin{matrix} 4 \\ 2 \\ 8 \end{matrix}}$$

and if a change in b_1 is prescribed, then the s_1 column values

$$\frac{s_1}{\begin{matrix} 1 \\ -1 \\ 4 \end{matrix}}$$

are added to the b_i^* values as Δ multiples, as follows:

$$x_2 = 4 + 1\Delta$$
$$x_1 = 2 - 1\Delta$$
$$s_3 = 8 + 4\Delta$$

From the prior discussion of the simplex method we know that these solution values will remain feasible as long as they are nonnegative. Thus, in order to determine the range of feasibility for b_1, the following inequalities are solved for Δ:

First basic variable, x_2: $\qquad 4 + \Delta \geqslant 0$
$$\Delta \geqslant -4$$
Second basic variable, x_1: $\qquad 2 - \Delta \geqslant 0$
$$-\Delta \geqslant -2$$
$$\Delta \leqslant 2$$
Third basic variable, s_3: $\qquad 8 + 4\Delta \geqslant 0$
$$4\Delta \geqslant -8$$
$$\Delta \geqslant -2$$

It can now be stated that the solution basis will remain nonnegative and, thus, feasible as long as

$$-4 \leqslant -2 \leqslant \Delta \leqslant 2$$

Since -2 is more constraining than -4, the latter value is discarded. (If -4 were used, then s_3 could become negative, but if -2 is used as the endpoint, then neither x_2 nor s_3 will become negative.) The range for Δ is, therefore,

$$-2 \leqslant \Delta \leqslant 2$$

Recalling that $b_1 = 10 + \Delta$ (or $\Delta = b_1 - 10$), we substitute this amount into the Δ range inequality to yield

$$-2 \leqslant b_1 - 10 \leqslant 2 \quad \text{or} \quad 8 \leqslant b_1 \leqslant 12$$

This range means that the *variables* in the optimal solution basis will remain feasible as long as b_1 is between 8 and 12 hours. However, it does not mean that the solution *values* will remain the same. For example, suppose $\Delta = 2$ and, thus, $b_1 = 12$. This results in the following solution values for x_2, x_1, and s_3:

$$x_2 = 4 + \Delta \qquad x_1 = 2 - \Delta \qquad s_3 = 8 + 4\Delta$$
$$x_2 = 6 \qquad\quad x_1 = 0 \qquad\quad s_3 = 16$$

To check the general approach and the range values, let $\Delta = 4$ and $b_1 = 14$. In this case, $x_1 = -2$, which renders the solution basis infeasible.

An additional property, which can be examined within the framework of a b change, relates to the value of model resources and, thus, the dual form of the problem. Consider the case where the manager desires to increase the available resources (b_i values). Which resources should be increased in order to realize the best marginal increase in the value of the objective function? To answer this question, observe the dual solution to the example previously highlighted in Tables 4.2 and 4.3:

$$Z_d = 28$$
$$y_1 = 1$$
$$y_2 = \tfrac{1}{2}$$
$$y_3 = 0$$

Labor hours should be increased, since they contribute the greatest amount ($y_1 = 1$) to the value of the objective function. Resource b_1 (labor hours) should be increased if possible, up to the maximum amount—12 hours. To increase b_1 beyond this amount would render the current solution basis infeasible.

Changes in b_i Values for $\geq$ Type Constraints

Thus far, we have considered only $\leq$ type constraints in determining the sensitivity ranges for b_i values. Recall that with a $\geq$ type constraint, we *subtract* a surplus variable rather than add a slack variable to form an equality. Thus, for a $\geq$ type constraint, we consider a $b_i - \Delta$ range rather than the $b_i + \Delta$ range used for a $\leq$ type constraint. This different specification of the right-hand-side range allows us to use the coefficients in the *surplus variable* columns in the optimal simplex tableau as our Δ multiples, whereas we previously used the coefficients in the slack variable columns.

Consider the minimization problem Example, 3.2, from Chapter 3:

Minimize $Z = 4x_1 + 3x_2$ (cost)
subject to
$$\begin{aligned} 2x_1 + 4x_2 &\geq 16 \qquad \text{(vitamin A)} \\ 3x_1 + 2x_2 &\geq 12 \qquad \text{(vitamin B)} \\ x_1, x_2 &\geq 0 \end{aligned}$$

The optimal simplex tableau for this problem is given in Table 4.7.

To determine the sensitivity range for b_1, we use $b_1 - \Delta$; thus, $b_1 = 16 - \Delta$. Note that we *subtract* Δ from the right-hand-side value (16) to reflect the fact that we subtract a surplus variable from the first constraint rather than add a slack variable.

Next, we identify the Δ multiples that are added to the b_i^* values in the optimal

Table 4.7 *Optimal Simplex Tableau*

c_b	c_j / basis	b_i^*	4 x_1	3 x_2	0 s_1	0 s_2
3	x_2	3	0	1	$-\frac{3}{8}$	$\frac{1}{4}$
4	x_1	2	1	0	$\frac{1}{4}$	$-\frac{1}{2}$
	z_j	17	4	3	$-\frac{1}{8}$	$-\frac{5}{4}$
	$z_j - c_j$		0	0	$-\frac{1}{8}$	$-\frac{5}{4}$

tableau. These values are in the s_1 column, as shown in the shaded section of Table 4.7.

$$x_2 = 3 - \tfrac{3}{8}\Delta$$
$$x_1 = 2 + \tfrac{1}{4}\Delta$$

Thus, in order to determine the range of feasibility for b_1, the following inequalities are solved for Δ:

First basic variable, x_2: $\quad 3 - \tfrac{3}{8}\Delta \geqslant 0$
$$-\tfrac{3}{8}\Delta \geqslant -3$$
$$\tfrac{3}{8}\Delta \leqslant 3$$
$$\Delta \leqslant 8$$

Second basic variable, x_1: $\quad 2 + \tfrac{1}{4}\Delta \geqslant 0$
$$\tfrac{1}{4}\Delta \geqslant -2$$
$$\Delta \geqslant -8$$

Therefore, the range for Δ is

$$-8 \leqslant \Delta \leqslant 8$$

Recalling that b_1 is equal to $16 - \Delta$ (or $\Delta = 16 - b_1$), we substitute this amount in the Δ range inequality, to yield

$$-8 \leqslant 16 - b_1 \leqslant 8$$

or

$$8 \leqslant b_1 \leqslant 24$$

In summary, when performing a sensitivity range analysis of right-hand-side values, for a $\leqslant$ type constraint, we use $b_i + \Delta$ to describe the range; but for a $\geqslant$ type constraint, we use $b_i - \Delta$ to describe the range. All other computations for the sensitivity analysis of b_i values are the same in either case.

Computer Determination of b_i Ranges

As was the case with duality analysis, computer software packages with linear programming capabilities also provide sensitivity analysis. For Example 4.1, for which we previously determined the b_i ranges, the AB:QM package provides the following sensitivity analysis.

```
Program: Linear Programming

Problem Title : Example 4.1

***** Input Data *****

Max.  Z =  4x1 + 5x2

Subject to

C1    1x1 + 2x2 <= 10
C2    6x1 + 6x2 <= 36
C3    8x1 + 4x2 <= 40

***** Program Output *****

Final Optimal Solution At Simplex Tableau : 2

Z =      28.000

------------------------------------------
Variable           Value        Reduced Cost
------------------------------------------
   x 1            2.000           0.000
   x 2            4.000           0.000
------------------------------------------
Constraint  Slack/Surplus   Shadow Price
------------------------------------------
   C 1            0.000           1.000
   C 2            0.000           0.500
   C 3            8.000           0.000
------------------------------------------
```

Right Hand Side Ranges

Constraints	Lower Limit	Current Values	Upper Limit	Allowable Increase	Allowable Decrease
C 1	8.000	10.000	12.000	2.000	2.000
C 2	30.000	36.000	40.000	4.000	6.000
C 3	32.000	40.000	No limit	No limit	8.000

```
***** End of Output *****
```

Changes in Objective Function Coefficients, c_j

Changes in the profit or cost contributions (c_j) in the objective function can occur for a basic or a nonbasic variable. The sensitivity ranges for each are determined differently thus, these two distinct cases will be studied separately.

Changes in c_j When x_j Is a Nonbasic Variable

To demonstrate sensitivity analysis for c_j parameters for nonbasic variables, we will employ the production example formulated below, which consists of two products, x and x_2, and two constraint equations. The first constraint is for labor and reflects the hour of labor required per unit for each product and the total hours available (12). The second constraint is for material and shows the pounds required per unit for each product and total pounds available (16).

Maximize $Z = \$6x_1 + 4x_2$ (profit)
subject to
$$2x_1 + 6x_2 \leq 12 \text{ hr} \qquad \text{(labor)}$$
$$4x_1 + 4x_2 \leq 16 \text{ lb} \qquad \text{(material)}$$
$$x_1, x_2 \geq 0$$

This problem is demonstrated graphically in Figure 4.3. The objective function indi cated by the dashed line Z has as its optimal point C. At this point, $x_1 = 4$, $x_2 = 0$ and $s_1 = 4$. However, if we increase c_2 from 4 to 8, the slope of the objective function becomes less steep, as shown by the dashed line Z. This reduction in slope results in a new optimal solution point, B, at which $x_1 = 3$ and $x_2 = 1$. This demonstrates the effect of a change in c_j: the slope of the objective function changes, which in turn can affect the optimality of the original solution. Hence, in performing sensitivity analysis on a c_j parameter, we are interested in determining a range for c_j over which the present solution will remain optimal.

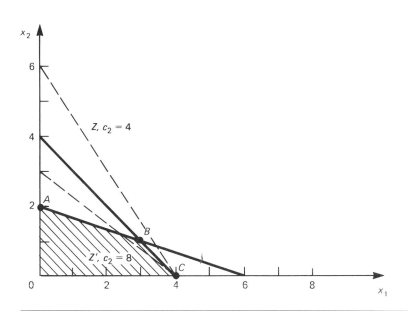

Figure 4.3 *Change in c_2 Causes Change in Slope of Objective Function*

When x_j is a nonbasic variable, it is necessary to observe only the final simplex tableau to determine the range values for c_j. Table 4.8 is the optimal solution tableau for the example problem.

Now consider the effect of a Δ change in c_2, the objective function contribution coefficient for the *nonbasic* variable x_2. Since x_2 is nonbasic and therefore c_2 is not included

Table 4.8 *Final Optimal Solution*

c_b	c_j basis	b_i^*	6 x_1	4 x_2	0 s_1	0 s_2
0	s_1	4	0	4	1	$-\frac{1}{2}$
6	x_1	4	1	1	0	$\frac{1}{4}$
	z_j	24	6	6	0	$\frac{3}{2}$
	$c_j - z_j$		0	-2	0	$-\frac{3}{2}$

in the c_b column, the only rows affected by a change in c_2 are the c_j and $c_j - z_j$ rows. Thus, a Δ change in c_2 results in the modified tableau in Table 4.9.

Table 4.9 *Final Tableau with a Δ Change in c_2*

c_b	c_j basis	b_i^*	6 x_1	4 + Δ x_2	0 s_1	0 s_2
0	s_1	4	0	4	1	$-\frac{1}{2}$
6	x_1.	4	1	1	0	$\frac{1}{4}$
	z_j	24	6	6	0	$\frac{3}{2}$
	$c_j - z_j$		0	$-2 + \Delta$	0	$-\frac{3}{2}$

The $c_j - z_j$ row value in the x_2 column is computed by subtracting 6 from $4 + \Delta$, which yields $-2 + \Delta$. This solution will remain optimal only if $c_j - z_j$ remains negative. Thus, to determine Δ, we make the following computation:

$$-2 + \Delta \leq 0$$
$$\Delta \leq 2$$

Recalling that $c_2 = 4 + \Delta$, or $\Delta = c_2 - 4$, we substitute this amount into the Δ inequality, to yield

$$c_2 - 4 \leq 2$$
$$c_2 \leq 6$$

As long as c_2 is less than 6, the present basic solution will remain optimal. This means not only that the variables x_1 and s_1 will remain in the solution basis, but also that the values for these variables ($x_1 = 4$, $s_1 = 4$) and the Z value ($z_j = 24$) will remain the same.

The fact that c_2 has a single-ended range can be seen in Figure 4.3. As c_2 increases (becomes ≥ 4), the objective function line becomes "flatter." As c_2 gets larger and the slope changes, the optimal solution changes from point C to point B (when $c_2 > 6$), thus changing the optimal solution. On the other hand, if c_2 gets smaller, the slope of the objective function will get steeper and steeper but the solution at point C will remain optimal, since the objective function will not pass through any other feasible solution point.

Changes in c_j When x_j Is a Basic Variable

The determination of a range for c_j over which the basic simplex solution remains optimal is somewhat more complex when x_j is a basic variable than when x_j is nonbasic. The primary difficulty results from the fact that, since x_j is a basic variable and therefore c_j is included in the c_b column, the z_j row values will be multiples of c_j. We will again consider the example employed in the previous section, except that now the Δ change will be for c_1 (Table 4.10).

Table 4.10 *Initial Simplex Tableau*

c_j	basis	b_i^*	$6 + \Delta$ x_1	4 x_2	0 s_1	0 s_2
c_b						
0	s_1	12	2	6	1	0
0	s_2	16	4	4	0	1
	z_j	0	0	0	0	0
	$c_j - z_j$		$6 + \Delta$	4	0	0

Performing the simplex operations results in the final simplex tableau (Table 4.11).

Table 4.11 *Final Simplex Tableau*

c_j	basis	b_i^*	$6 + \Delta$ x_1	4 x_2	0 s_1	0 s_2
c_b						
0	s_1	4	0	4	1	$-\frac{1}{2}$
$6 + \Delta$	x_1	4	1	1	0	$\frac{1}{4}$
	z_j	$24 + 4\Delta$	$6 + \Delta$	$6 + \Delta$	0	$\frac{3}{2} + \Delta/4$
	$c_j - z_j$		0	$-2 - \Delta$	0	$-\frac{3}{2} - \Delta/4$

In the final simplex tableau, notice that, since x_1 is a basic variable, the c_1 value ($6 + \Delta$) is included in the c_b column. As a result, $c_1 = 6 + \Delta$ becomes a multiple of the z_j row values. Therefore, the effect of the Δ change in the final tableau can be determined (without including the Δ change in all simplex iterations) simply by inserting $c_j + \Delta$ in place of c_j in the c_b column in the final tableau and calculating the $c_j - z_j$ values normally. This results in $c_j - z_j$ row values for both nonbasic variables, which include Δ values. If one of these variables enters the solution, then the present solution is no longer optimal. In order for the present basic solution to remain optimal, these $c_j - z_j$ values must remain negative or zero. Thus, we solve the following inequalities for the x_2 and s_2 column $c_j - z_j$ values.

For x_2 column:
$$-2 - \Delta \leq 0$$
$$-\Delta \leq 2$$
$$\Delta \geq -2$$
$$-{}^3\!/_2 - {}^1\!/_4\,\Delta \leq 0$$
$$-{}^1\!/_4\,\Delta \leq {}^3\!/_2$$

For s_2 column:
$$\Delta \geq -6$$

Since $c_1 = 6 + \Delta$, or $\Delta = c_1 - 6$, we substitute this amount into the Δ inequalit which yields

$$\Delta \geqslant -2$$
$$c_1 - 6 \geqslant -2$$
$$c_1 \geqslant 4$$

and

$$\Delta \geqslant -6$$
$$c_1 - 6 \geqslant -6$$
$$c_1 \geqslant 0$$

The range $c_1 \geqslant 0$, which was derived from the calculations for the s_2 column, indi cates that s_2 will not enter the basis as long as c_1 is positive. However, the range calculate from the x_2 column indicates that x_2 would enter the solution if c_1 fell to \$4 or less Thus, by process of elimination, we know that the present basic solution will remai optimal only as long as $c_1 \geqslant 4$.

Now let us observe the development of the range of sensitivity for c_j when *bot* decision variables are basic. Our example can be adjusted to yield such a solution by changing the objective function to $Z = 4x_1 + 6x_2$. A Δ change in the c_1 coefficien results in the following final optimal solution (Table 4.12).

Table 4.12 Final Simplex Tableau

c_j c_b	basis	b_i^*	$4 + \Delta$ x_1	6 x_2	0 s_1	0 s_2
6	x_2	1	0	1	$\frac{1}{4}$	$-\frac{1}{8}$
$4 + \Delta$	x_1	3	1	0	$-\frac{1}{4}$	$\frac{3}{8}$
	z_j	$18 + 3\Delta$	$4 + \Delta$	6	$\frac{1}{2} - \frac{1}{4}\Delta$	$\frac{3}{4} + \frac{3}{8}\Delta$
	$c_j - z_j$		0	0	$-\frac{1}{2} + \frac{1}{4}\Delta$	$-\frac{3}{4} - \frac{3}{8}\Delta$

For the two nonbasic variables (s_1 and s_2), the $c_j - z_j$ row values must remain neg- ative for the basic solution to remain optimal. Thus,

For s_1 column: $\quad -\frac{1}{2} + \frac{1}{4}\Delta \leqslant 0$
$$\frac{1}{4}\Delta \leqslant \frac{1}{2}$$
$$\Delta \leqslant 2$$

For s_2 column: $\quad -\frac{3}{4} - \frac{3}{8}\Delta \leqslant 0$
$$-\frac{3}{8} \leqslant \frac{3}{4}$$
$$\Delta \geqslant -2$$

Again, recalling that $c_1 = 4 + \Delta$, and therefore $\Delta = c_1 - 4$, we substitute this amount into the Δ inequality, to yield

$$\Delta \leqslant 2$$
$$c_1 - 4 \leqslant 2$$
$$c_1 \leqslant 6$$

and

$$\Delta \geqslant -2$$
$$c_1 - 4 \geqslant -2$$
$$c_1 \geqslant 2$$

or

$$2 \leqslant c_1 \leqslant 6$$

Figure 4.4 reflects this example and the c_1 range, which is bounded on both ends. Notice that the objective function will encounter a new feasible solution point, A or C, as it becomes flatter or steeper, respectively.

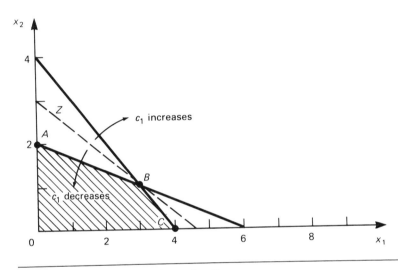

Figure 4.4 Graphic Analysis of c_1 Range

Computer Determination of c_j Ranges

The c_j ranges for our example, encompassed in Tables 4.8 through 4.11, are provided by the AB:QM package as follows:

```
Program: Linear Programming

Problem Title : Production Example

***** Input Data *****

Max.   Z =   6x1 + 4x2

Subject to

C1    2x1 + 6x2 <= 12
C2    4x1 + 4x2 <= 16
```

```
***** Program Output *****

Final Optimal Solution At Simplex Tableau : 1

Z =      24.000

------------------------------------------------
Variable          Value        Reduced Cost
------------------------------------------------
   x 1            4.000            0.000
   x 2            0.000            2.000
------------------------------------------------
Constraint   Slack/Surplus    Shadow Price
------------------------------------------------
   C 1            4.000            0.000
   C 2            0.000            1.500
------------------------------------------------

Objective Coefficient Ranges
-------------------------------------------------------------------------
              Lower      Current        Upper      Allowable    Allowable
Variables     Limit      Values         Limit      Increase     Decrease
-------------------------------------------------------------------------
   x 1         4.000      6.000       No limit     No limit      2.000
   x 2      No limit      4.000          6.000        2.000   No limit

Right Hand Side Ranges
-------------------------------------------------------------------------
              Lower      Current        Upper      Allowable    Allowable
Constraints   Limit      Values         Limit      Increase     Decrease
-------------------------------------------------------------------------
   C 1         8.000     12.000       No limit     No limit      4.000
   C 2         0.000     16.000         24.000        8.000     16.000

***** End of Output *****
```

The c_j ranges for the example when both decision variables are basic, as shown in Table 4.12, are provided by the STORM package as follows:

```
                    STORM DATA SET LISTING
                 DETAILED PROBLEM DATA LISTING FOR
                 Changes in Cj When Both Xj Are Basic
ROW LABEL    PRODUCT 1   PRODUCT 2 CONST TYPE      R H S        RANGE

OBJ COEFF        4.          6.        XXXX         XXXX        XXXX
LABOR            2.          6.         <=           12.           .
MATERIAL         4.          4.         <=           16.           .
VARBL TYPE      POS         POS        XXXX         XXXX        XXXX
LOWR BOUND       .           .         XXXX         XXXX        XXXX
UPPR BOUND       .           .         XXXX         XXXX        XXXX
INIT SOLN        0.          0.        XXXX         XXXX        XXXX

                 Changes in Cj When Both Xj Are Basic
                 PROBLEM DATA IN EQUATION STYLE

     Maximize
        + 4 PRODUCT 1 + 6 PRODUCT 2
```

```
    Subject to

      LABOR
         + 2 PRODUCT 1 + 6 PRODUCT 2 <= 12

      MATERIAL
         + 4 PRODUCT 1 + 4 PRODUCT 2 <= 16

                  0 <= PRODUCT 1
               -  0 <= PRODUCT 2
```

```
                        Changes in Cj When Both Xj Are Basic
      OPTIMAL SOLUTION - SUMMARY REPORT (NONZERO VARIABLES)
                 Variable              Value              Cost

          1      PRODUCT 1            3.0000            4.0000
          2      PRODUCT 2            1.0000            6.0000

    Objective Function Value = 18
```

```
                        Changes in Cj When Both Xj Are Basic
         SENSITIVITY ANALYSIS OF COST COEFFICIENTS
                             Current      Allowable      Allowable
                 Variable    Coeff.       Minimum        Maximum

          1      PRODUCT 1    4.0000       2.0000         6.0000
          2      PRODUCT 2    6.0000       4.0000        12.0000
```

Changes in Constraint Coefficients, a_{ij}

As with the b_i and c_j parameters, the sensitivity of solution optimality to changes in a_i parameters must be considered for *nonbasic* and *basic* variables separately.

Changes in a_{ij} When x_j Is a Nonbasic Variable

Following the solution of a linear programming problem, it may become necessary to change the unit resource requirements for a particular product (i.e., the a_{ij} coefficients). To determine the range of a_{ij} over which the optimality of the basic solution will not be affected when the a_{ij} coefficient of a nonbasic variable is changed, we follow a procedure similar to that used to determine the b_i range. Again the following production example will be employed:

Maximize $Z = \$6x_1 + 4x_2$ (profit)

subject to
$$2x_1 + 6x_2 \leq 12 \text{ hr} \qquad \text{(labor)}$$
$$4x_1 + 4x_2 \leq 16 \text{ lb} \qquad \text{(material)}$$
$$x_1, x_2 \geq 0$$

From previous analysis of this problem we know that x_2 is a nonbasic variable (see Table 4.8). Thus, we will first consider a Δ change in the labor requirement for product 2 (a_{12}). This results in the following new labor constraint:

$$2x_1 + (6 + \Delta)x_2 \leq 12$$

Substituting this new constraint equation into the initial simplex tableau yields Table 4.13.

Table 4.13 Initial Simplex Tableau

c_b	c_j basis	b_i^*	6 x_1	4 x_2	0 s_1	0 s_2
0	s_1	12	2	$6 + 1\Delta$	1	0
0	s_2	16	4	$4 + 0\Delta$	0	1
	z_j	0	0	0	0	0
	$c_j - z_j$		6	4	0	0

The Δ coefficients in the x_2 column and the coefficients in the s_1 column are identical. As a result, in the final tableau the Δ coefficients in the x_2 column will be the same as the s_1 column values (Table 4.14).

Table 4.14 Final Simplex Tableau

c_b	c_j basis	b_i^*	6 x_1	4 x_2	0 s_1	0 s_2
0	s_1	4	0	$4 + \Delta$	1	0
6	x_1	4	1	1	0	$\frac{1}{4}$
	z_j	24	6	6	0	$\frac{3}{2}$
	$c_j - z_j$		0	-2	0	$-\frac{3}{2}$

In the final tableau, it can be seen that a change in a_{12} has no effect on the final basic solution, since Δ is not present in the $c_j - z_j$ row. This is due to the fact that labor is not a binding constraint in the optimal solution. However, now consider a change in a_{22}, the material requirement for product 2.

$$4x_1 + (4 + \Delta)x_2 \leq 16$$

This will result in the optimal tableau in Table 4.15.

Table 4.15 Final Simplex Tableau

c_b	c_j basis	b_i^*	6 x_1	4 x_2	0 s_1	0 s_2
0	s_1	4	0	$4 + 0\Delta$	1	0
6	x_1	4	1	$1 + \frac{1}{4}\Delta$	0	$\frac{1}{4}$
	z_j	24	6	$6 + \frac{3}{2}\Delta$	0	$\frac{3}{2}$
	$c_j - z_j$		0	$-2 - \frac{3}{2}\Delta$	0	$-\frac{3}{2}$

Note that the Δ coefficients in the final tableau correspond to the appropriate slack column coefficients—in this case, s_2. It is clear from an examination of Table 4.15 that a change in a_{22} can affect the optimality of the final solution. To determine the a_{22} range over which the present basic solution will remain optimal, we solve the following $c_j - z_j \leqslant 0$ inequality:

$$-2 - \tfrac{3}{2}\Delta \leqslant 0$$
$$-\tfrac{3}{2}\Delta \leqslant 2$$
$$\Delta \geqslant -\tfrac{4}{3}$$

Since $a_{22} = \Delta + 4$, or $\Delta = a_{22} - 4$, we substitute this amount into the Δ inequality, yielding

$$a_{22} - 4 \geqslant -\tfrac{4}{3}$$
$$a_{22} \geqslant \tfrac{8}{3}$$

This range is interpreted as follows. If a_{22} becomes less than $\tfrac{8}{3}$, the present solution will no longer be optimal. In other words, a new variable will enter the solution basis. If a_{22} remains greater than $\tfrac{8}{3}$, the present basis will remain optimal and the solution values will remain the same.

The following computer output using AB:QM demonstrates the effect of changing the a_{22} value from a value of 4 to 2, which is less than $\tfrac{8}{3}$. Notice that a new solution variable, x_2, does, in fact, enter the solution and the solution values change.

```
Program: Linear Programming

Problem Title : Production Example

***** Input Data *****

Max.  Z =  6x1 + 4x2

Subject to

C1   2x1 + 6x2 <= 12
C2   4x1 + 2x2 <= 16

***** Program Output *****

Final Optimal Solution At Simplex Tableau : 2

Z =      24.800

-------------------------------------------
Variable            Value        Reduced Cost
-------------------------------------------
   x 1              3.600           0.000
   x 2              0.800           0.000
-------------------------------------------
Constraint   Slack/Surplus    Shadow Price
-------------------------------------------
   C 1              0.000           0.200
   C 2              0.000           1.400
-------------------------------------------
```

An Application of Linear Programming and Postoptimality Analysis: Optimal Wood Procurement for Cabinet Making

Wellborn Cabinet Inc., located in Alabama, is a cabinet manufacturing facility that includes a sawmill, four dry kilns, and a wood cabinet assembly plant. A major concern for cabinet makers like Wellborn is maintaining consistency in product quality, and since cabinet making is essentially an assembly operation in which parts are made from different materials from different sources, an effective raw material procurement policy is necessary to control costs and quality. A linear programming model was developed of the blank (i.e., cabinet components) production system that would determine the optimal wood procurement policy at Wellborn. To produce blanks, the company had been purchasing #1

and #2 grade logs of different diameter and length, and #1 and #2 grade lumber. The company used approximately 3.7 million board feet of lumber per year and about 73% of this came from logs processed at the company's sawmill, the remaining 23% coming from outside sources. Approximately 130 different sizes of blanks were produced for use in cabinet assembly.

The objective of the linear programming model was to minimize the total cost of producing blanks for a 5-day week of operation. Constraints included the sawmill and kiln capacities, demand for blanks at the assembly plant, and the available supply of raw materials (logs and lumber). The decision variables were

Changes in a_{ij} When x_j Is a Basic Variable

Changes in the a_{ij} coefficient of a basic variable can result in numerous changes in the final simplex tableau. This should be apparent, since the initial tableau pivot number could contain a Δ value and, as a result, could transmit multiples of Δ throughout the tableau in subsequent iterations. Therefore, it is possible for the final tableau to become infeasible as well as nonoptimal. Because of the profound effects caused by an a_{ij} change when x_j is a basic variable, it is difficult to prescribe a systematic means for sensitivity analysis. Methods have been developed to determine the sensitivity of the optimal solution to a_{ij} changes for basic variables. However, these methods are applicable only to special cases and even then the results cannot be obtained directly from the final tableau. Subsequent tableau iterations are generally required. Given these conditions, the best way to perform sensitivity analysis on a_{ij} parameter changes is simply to solve the problem again with the a_{ij} changes included.

The following computer output using AB:QM demonstrates the effect of changing a_{21} from 4 to 7. Notice that the basic variables change from Table 4.14.

```
Program: Linear Programming

Problem Title : Production Example

***** Input Data *****

Max.  Z =  6x1 + 4x2
```

the volume of different grade and size diameter logs and different grades of lumber required each week. The model results indicated the company could minimize total cost by purchasing only #2 grade logs of a certain dimension and #2 grade lumber of a certain type. Such a policy would save the company approximately $412,000 annually in raw material costs. In addition, analysis of the shadow prices of the different log types indicated the company would be better off purchasing smaller diameter logs. For example, the cost of producing blanks would be reduced by $37.08 (the shadow price) per 100 cubic feet with 9-inch diameter logs as opposed to a similar cost reduction of only $0.42 with 15-inch diameter logs. Sensitivity analysis was also used to determine the price ranges for logs for which the purchase policy indicated by the optimal solution should remain the same.

The linear programming model provided management at Wellborn Cabinet with the ability to address a number of important aspects of their operation quickly and inexpensively. These included the least-cost combination of raw materials; the desired mix of grades, sizes, and quantity of logs to be purchased; the size log to purchase in each grade classification; the maximum amount to pay for logs or lumber; whether or not lumber drying capacity should be increased, and if so, by how much; and the effect of changes in log and lumber prices on the raw material mix and the cost of producing blanks.

Source: H. F. Carino and C. H. LeNoir, Jr., "Optimizing Wood Procurement in Cabinet Manufacturing," *Interfaces*, 18, no. 2 (March–April 1988): 10–19.

```
Subject to

C1    2x1 + 6x2 <= 12
C2    7x1 + 4x2 <= 16

***** Program Output *****

Final Optimal Solution At Simplex Tableau : 2

Z =      14.588

-----------------------------------------------
Variable            Value         Reduced Cost
-----------------------------------------------
   x 1              1.412            0.000
   x 2              1.529            0.000
-----------------------------------------------
Constraint   Slack/Surplus    Shadow Price
-----------------------------------------------
   C 1             0.000            0.118
   C 2             0.000            0.824
-----------------------------------------------
```

Addition of a New Constraint

After solution of a linear programming problem, it may occur to the manager that a particular resource constraint was overlooked in the model formulation, or perhaps the manager may want to know the effect of adding a new resource to enhance a product. If the new constraint is added to the problem, the original solution can become infeasible. This will be true, though, only if the constraint is actively involved in the basic solution. Thus, the new constraint should first be tested to see if it does indeed affect the solution. To accomplish this, the manager tests original optimal solution values in the new constraint to see if the constraint is satisfied.

Consider the previous production problem with the following additional constraint for storage space:

$$4x_1 + 2x_2 \leq 20 \text{ ft}^2$$

The solution values indicated in Table 4.8 (for the two-constraint problems) are $x_1 = 4$, $x_2 = 0$, and $s_1 = 4$. Substituting these values into the new constraint, we find that this constraint is not violated: $4(4) + 2(0) \leq 20$. Since the optimal solution does not change, nothing additional needs to be done in terms of sensitivity analysis. However, consider the following new constraint:

$$4x_1 + 2x_2 \leq 12 \text{ ft}^2$$

The optimal solution values *do not* satisfy this constraint.

Although manual procedures (involving complex manipulations of the final simplex tableau) are available for determining the sensitivity of the optimal solution to a new constraint, the most efficient means is simply to solve the revised model using a computer software package. Most software packages enable the user to alter the model by adding a new constraint to the initial model.

The following computer output illustrates the LINDO procedure for adding a new constraint. It includes an explanation of the extend (ext) command, which permits the addition of a model constraint. Following this explanation and a presentation of the original model (per user request), the user enters the extend command, LINDO assigns a new row number (4), and then the user enters the new constraint. The revised model is presented (per user request), and then the solution is provided.

```
: help ext

EXTEND COMMAND:

PERMITS  YOU  TO ADD CONSTRAINT ROWS TO A PREVIOUSLY DEFINED
MODEL.  ENTER NEW ROWS AS YOU WOULD FOR "MAX" OR "MIN".   DO
NOT  TYPE  THE  KEYWORDS "MAX", "MIN", OR "SUBJECT TO".  NEW
ROWS WILL BE APPENDED TO THE END OF THE MODEL.  INDICATE END
OF EXTENSIONS BY TYPING "END".

: look all

MAX       6 X1 + 4 X2
SUBJECT TO
        2)    2 X1 + 6 X2 <=    12
        3)    4 X1 + 4 X2 <=    16
END
: ext
BEGIN EXTEND WITH ROW    4
? 4x1 + 2x2 < 12
? end
: look all
```

```
    MAX      6 X1 + 4 X2
    SUBJECT TO
          2)    2 X1 + 6 X2 <=    12
          3)    4 X1 + 4 X2 <=    16
          4)    4 X1 + 2 X2 <=    12
    END



    : go
    LP OPTIMUM FOUND  AT STEP      2

               OBJECTIVE FUNCTION VALUE

       1)          19.2000000

       VARIABLE         VALUE        REDUCED COST
          X1          2.400000          .000000
          X2          1.200000          .000000


          ROW    SLACK OR SURPLUS     DUAL PRICES
          2)          .000000           .200000
          3)         1.600000           .000000
          4)          .000000          1.400000

    NO. ITERATIONS=          2
```

Alternatively, with AB:QM, a new constraint can be added to the model by using the F7 key on the data input screen, and a constraint can be eliminated using the F9 key.

Addition of a New Decision Variable

The addition of a new model variable can be handled in much the same way as the addition of a new constraint, using the LINDO software package to revise the model. Consider the addition of a new variable x_3 (representing the introduction of a new third product) to the previous example, with corresponding c_j and a_{ij} coefficients.

Maximize $Z_p = \$6x_1 + 4x_2 + 3x_3$

subject to
$$2x_1 + 6x_2 + x_3 \leq 12 \text{ hr}$$
$$4x_1 + 4x_2 + 2x_3 \leq 16 \text{ lb}$$
$$x_1, x_2, x_3 \geq 0$$

The addition of a new variable to a model is accomplished by using the append (appc) command. The LINDO output on page 160 shows the procedure for applying the append command and adding the third variable to the model. Included is a description of the command and a summary of the original model (per user request). (Note that the entries following "appc x3" give the row number followed by the variable and its coefficient, where row 1 is the objective function.)

Alternatively, with AB:QM, a new decision variable can be added to the model by using the F8 key on the data input screen, and a variable can be eliminated using the F10 key.

```
: help appc

APPEND COLUMN COMMAND:

TYPE "APPC var-id" TO APPEND A NEW COLUMN TO THE MODEL WITH
NAME "var-id". FOLLOW THIS WITH THE ROW/VALUE PAIRS FOR THE
COLUMN. ONE PAIR PER LINE; ROW AND VALUE SEPARATED BY A
SPACE. END BY ENTERING A 0 FOR THE ROW. A COLUMN NAME OF
"RHS" WILL CAUSE THE INPUT TO BE INTERPRETED AS A NEW RHS.

: look all

MAX      6 X1 + 4 X2
SUBJECT TO
        2)    2 X1 + 6 X2 <=   12
        3)    4 X1 + 4 X2 <=   16
END

: appc x3
? 1 3x3
? 2 1x3
? 3 2x3
? 0

: look all

MAX      6 X1 + 4 X2 + 3 X3
SUBJECT TO
        2)    2 X1 + 6 X2 + X3 <=   12
        3)    4 X1 + 4 X2 + 2 X3 <=   16
END

: go
LP OPTIMUM FOUND  AT STEP     1

            OBJECTIVE FUNCTION VALUE

   1)      24.0000000

   VARIABLE       VALUE          REDUCED COST
        X1       4.000000          .000000
        X2        .000000         2.000000
        X3        .000000          .000000


      ROW    SLACK OR SURPLUS    DUAL PRICES
        2)       4.000000          .000000
        3)        .000000         1.500000

NO. ITERATIONS=          1
```

SUMMARY In this chapter, two of the most important concepts in linear programming, duality and sensitivity analysis, have been presented. The economic information provided by these two forms of analysis is often more useful and important to a manager or firm than the original problem and solution. In addition, the study of duality and sensitivity analysis engenders a thorough and complete understanding of linear programming in general. Therefore, the reader should not treat these topics lightly.

In the chapters that follow on mathematical programming, the topics will basically be variations of the general linear programming model discussed in Chapters 2, 3, and 4. As a result, the reader who has thoroughly studied these three chapters should be well prepared for these advanced topics.

REFERENCES

BAUMOL, W. J. *Economic Theory and Operations Analysis.* 4th ed. Englewood Cliffs, New Jersey: Prentice-Hall, 1977.

BAZARAA, M. S., and JARVIS, J. J. *Linear Programming and Network Flows.* New York: John Wiley & Sons, 1977.

BRADLEY, S. P.; HAX, A. C.; and MAGNANTI, T. L. *Applied Mathematical Programming.* Reading, Massachusetts: Addison-Wesley Publishing Company, 1977.

COOPER, L., and STEINBERG, D. *Methods and Applications of Linear Programming.* Philadelphia: W. B. Saunders Company, 1974.

DANTZIG, G. B. *Linear Programming and Extensions.* Princeton, New Jersey: Princeton University Press, 1963.

GAVER, D. P., and THOMPSON, G. L. *Programming and Probability Models in Operations Research.* Belmont, California: Wadsworth Publishing Company, 1973.

HADLEY, G. *Linear Programming.* Reading, Massachusetts: Addison-Wesley Publishing Company, 1962.

IGNIZIO, J. P. *Linear Programming in Single and Multiple Objective Systems.* Englewood Cliffs, New Jersey: Prentice-Hall, 1982.

LOOMBA, N. P. *Linear Programming: A Managerial Perspective.* 2d ed. New York: Macmillan, 1976.

LOOMBA, N. P., and TURBAN, E. *Applied Programming for Management.* New York: Holt, Rinehart and Winston, 1974.

LUENBERGER, D. G. *Introduction to Linear and Non-Linear Programming.* Reading, Massachusetts: Addison-Wesley Publishing Company, 1973.

MCMILLAN, C. *Mathematical Programming.* 2d ed. New York: John Wiley & Sons, 1975.

NAYLOR, T. H.; BYRNE, E. T.; and VERNON, J. M. *Introduction to Linear Programming: Methods and Cases.* Belmont, California: Wadsworth Publishing Company, 1971.

PFAFFENBERGER, R. C., and WALKER, D. A. *Mathematical Programming for Economics and Business.* Ames, Iowa: Iowa State University Press, 1976.

PHILLIPS, D. T.; RAVINDRAN, A.; and SOLBERG, J. J. *Operations Research: Principles and Practice.* 2d ed. New York: John Wiley & Sons, 1987.

ROTHENBERG, R. I. *Linear Programming.* New York: Elsevier North-Holland, 1979.

SCHRAGE, L. *LINDO, An Optimization Modeling System,* 4th ed. San Francisco: The Scientific Press, 1991.

SHOGAN, A. W. *Management Science.* Englewood Cliffs, New Jersey: Prentice-Hall, 1988.

SIMMONS, D. M. *Linear Programming for Operations Research.* San Francisco: Holden-Day, 1972.

SPIVEY, W. A., and THRALL, R. M. *Linear Optimization.* New York: Holt, Rinehart and Winston, 1970.

TAHA, H. A. *Operations Research: An Introduction.* 4th ed. New York: Macmillan, 1987.

WINSTON, W. L. *Introduction to Mathematical Programming, Applications and Algorithms,* Boston: PWS-Kent, 1991.

PROBLEMS

1. Recall problem 1 from Chapter 3. A company produces two products, 1 and 2. The company has 12 employees; it takes 2 employees working all day to make a unit of product 1, and 1 employee working all day to produce a unit of product 2. The maximum demand for product 2 is 8 units. The company wants to know how many

units of products 1 and 2 (x_1 and x_2) to produce to maximize profit. The following linear programming model has been formulated for this problem.

Maximize $Z = 100x_1 + 80x_2$ (profit, $)

subject to

$$2x_1 + x_2 \leqslant 12 \qquad \text{(employees)}$$
$$x_2 \leqslant 8 \qquad \text{(demand, units)}$$
$$x_1, x_2 \geqslant 0$$

Formulate the dual for this problem and define the dual variables.

2. Recall problem 2 from Chapter 3. A farmer grows corn and tobacco on a farm of 40 acres. The farmer has 120 hours of labor available for planting. The farmer wants to know how many acres of corn and tobacco (x_1 and x_2) to plant to maximize profit. The following linear programming model has been formulated for this problem.

Maximize $Z = 50x_1 + 30x_2$ (profit, $)

subject to

$$2x_1 + 4x_2 \leqslant 120 \qquad \text{(labor, hr)}$$
$$x_1 + x_2 \leqslant 40 \qquad \text{(land, acres)}$$
$$x_1, x_2 \geqslant 0$$

Formulate the dual for this problem and define the dual variables.

3. Recall problem 3 from Chapter 3. A jeweler makes bracelets and necklaces from silver and a base metal. The jeweler has 18 ounces of silver and 24 ounces of the base metal available. The jeweler wants to know how many bracelets and necklaces (x_1 and x_2) to make to maximize profit. The following linear programming model has been formulated for this problem.

Maximize $Z = 40x_1 + 20x_2$ (profit, $)

subject to

$$3x_1 + 2x_2 \leqslant 18 \qquad \text{(silver, oz)}$$
$$2x_1 + 4x_2 \leqslant 24 \qquad \text{(base metal, oz)}$$
$$x_1 \leqslant 4 \qquad \text{(demand, bracelets)}$$
$$x_1, x_2 \geqslant 0$$

Formulate the dual for this problem and define the dual variables.

4. Recall problem 4 from Chapter 3. A bakery makes cakes, doughnuts, and cookies in batches. The bakery's constraining resources are oven capacity and labor. Only one oven is available, and only one batch of any item can be baked in it at a time. It is in use 24 hours a day. The bakery has 30 labor hours available each day. The company wants to know how many batches of cakes, doughnuts, and cookies (x_1, x_2, and x_3) to bake each day to maximize profit. The following linear programming model has been formulated for this problem.

Maximize $Z = 6x_1 + 2x_2 + 12x_3$ (profit, $)

subject to

$$4x_1 + x_2 + 3x_3 \leqslant 24 \qquad \text{(oven capacity, hr)}$$
$$2x_1 + 6x_2 + 3x_3 \leqslant 30 \qquad \text{(labor, hr)}$$
$$x_1, x_2, x_3 \geqslant 0$$

Formulate the dual for this problem and define the dual variables.

5. A manufacturer produces two products, x_1 and x_2, from which the profits are $9

and $12, respectively. Each product must go through two production processes for which there are labor constraints. There is also a material constraint and a storage limitation. The problem is formulated as a linear programming model as follows:

Maximize $Z = 9x_1 + 12x_2$ (profit, $)

subject to

$$4x_1 + 8x_2 \leq 64 \qquad \text{(process 1, labor hr)}$$
$$5x_1 + 5x_2 \leq 50 \qquad \text{(process 2, labor hr)}$$
$$15x_1 + 8x_2 \leq 120 \qquad \text{(material, lb)}$$
$$x_1 \leq 7 \qquad \text{(storage space, units)}$$
$$x_2 \leq 7 \qquad \text{(storage space, units)}$$
$$x_1, x_2 \geq 0$$

The final optimal simplex tableau for this problem is

c_j c_b	basis	b_i^*	9 x_1	12 x_2	0 s_1	0 s_2	0 s_3	0 s_4	0 s_5
9	x_1	4	1	0	$-\frac{1}{4}$	$\frac{2}{5}$	0	0	0
0	s_5	1	0	0	$-\frac{1}{4}$	$\frac{1}{5}$	0	0	1
0	s_3	12	0	0	$\frac{7}{4}$	$-\frac{22}{5}$	1	0	0
0	s_4	3	0	0	$\frac{1}{4}$	$-\frac{2}{5}$	0	1	0
12	x_2	6	0	1	$\frac{1}{4}$	$-\frac{1}{5}$	0	0	0
	z_j	108	9	12	$\frac{3}{4}$	$\frac{6}{5}$	0	0	0
	$c_j - z_j$		0	0	$-\frac{3}{4}$	$-\frac{6}{5}$	0	0	0

a. Interpret the shadow prices in the $c_j - z_j$ row for this tableau.
b. Formulate the dual to this problem.
c. Define the dual variables.

6. A fertilizer company produces two kinds of fertilizer spreaders: regular and cyclone. Each spreader must go through two processes in which parts are made and then assembled. With x_1 = the quantity of regular spreaders produced and x_2 = the quantity of cyclone spreaders produced, the problem is formulated as

Maximize $Z = 9x_1 + 7x_2$ (profit, $)

subject to

$$12x_1 + 4x_2 \leq 60 \qquad \text{(process 1, production hr)}$$
$$4x_1 + 8x_2 \leq 40 \qquad \text{(process 2, production hr)}$$
$$x_1, x_2 \geq 0$$

The final optimal simplex tableau for this problem is

c_j c_b	basis	b_i^*	9 x_1	7 x_2	0 s_1	0 s_2
9	x_1	4	1	0	$\frac{1}{10}$	$-\frac{1}{20}$
7	x_2	3	0	1	$-\frac{1}{20}$	$\frac{3}{20}$
	z_j	57	9	7	$\frac{11}{20}$	$\frac{12}{20}$
	$c_j - z_j$		0	0	$-\frac{11}{20}$	$-\frac{12}{20}$

a. Interpret the shadow prices in the $c_j - z_j$ row for this tableau.
b. Formulate the dual to this problem.
c. Define the dual variables.

7. A furniture manufacturer makes two kinds of tables: end tables (x_1) and coffee tab (x_2). The manufacturer is restricted by material and labor constraints. The lin programming formulation of the manufacturer's problem is

Maximize $Z = 200x_1 + 300x_2$ (profit, \$)
subject to
$$2x_1 + 5x_2 \leqslant 180 \qquad \text{(labor, hr)}$$
$$3x_1 + 3x_2 \leqslant 135 \qquad \text{(wood, lb)}$$
$$x_1, x_2 \geqslant 0$$

The final optimal simplex tableau for this problem is

c_j c_b	basis	b_i^*	200 x_1	300 x_2	0 s_1	0 s_2
300	x_2	30	0	1	$1/3$	$-2/9$
200	x_1	15	1	0	$-1/3$	$5/9$
	z_j	12,000	200	300	$100/3$	$400/9$
	$c_j - z_j$		0	0	$-100/3$	$-400/9$

a. Interpret the shadow prices in the $c_j - z_j$ row for this tableau.
b. Formulate the dual to this problem.
c. Define the dual variables.

8. A chemical company makes bags of insecticide from two compounds, x_1 and x. Each pound of x_1 costs \$.06, and each pound of x_2 costs \$.10. Each compoun contains ingredients A, B, and C, and each bag of insecticide must contain at leas minimum amounts of these ingredients. The linear programming formulation of thi problem is

Minimize $Z = .06x_1 + .10x_2$ (cost, \$)
subject to
$$4x_1 + 3x_2 \geqslant 12 \qquad \text{(ingredient A, units)}$$
$$3x_1 + 6x_2 \geqslant 12 \qquad \text{(ingredient B, units)}$$
$$5x_1 + 2x_2 \geqslant 10 \qquad \text{(ingredient C, units)}$$
$$x_1, x_2 \geqslant 0$$

The final optimal simplex tableau for this problem is

c_b c_j	basis	b_i^*	.06 x_1	.10 x_2	0 s_1	0 s_2	0 s_3
0	s_3	3.6	0	0	$-8/5$	$7/15$	1
.10	x_2	0.8	0	1	$1/5$	$-4/15$	0
.06	x_1	2.4	1	0	$-2/5$	$1/5$	0
	z_j	.22	.06	.10	$-.004$	$-.014$	0
	$z_j - c_j$		0	0	$-.004$	$-.014$	0

a. Interpret the shadow prices in the $z_j - c_j$ row.
b. Formulate the dual to this problem.
c. Define the dual variables.

9. An electronics firm produces electric motors for washing machines (x_1) and dryers (x_2). The firm has resource constraints for production time, steel, and wire. The linear programming model has been formulated as

Maximize $Z = 70x_1 + 80x_2$ (profit, $)
subject to
$$2x_1 + x_2 \leqslant 19 \qquad \text{(production, hr)}$$
$$x_1 + x_2 \leqslant 14 \qquad \text{(steel, lb)}$$
$$x_1 + 2x_2 \leqslant 20 \qquad \text{(wire, ft)}$$
$$x_1, x_2 \geqslant 0$$

The final optimal simplex tableau for this problem is

c_b $\diagdown$ c_j	basis	b_i^*	70 x_1	80 x_2	0 s_1	0 s_2	0 s_3
70	x_1	6	1	0	2/3	0	−1/3
0	s_2	1	0	0	−1/3	1	−1/3
80	x_2	7	0	1	−1/3	0	2/3
	z_j	980	70	80	20	0	30
	$c_j - z_j$		0	0	−20	0	−30

a. Interpret the shadow prices in the $c_j - z_j$ row for this tableau.
b. Formulate the dual to this problem.
c. Define the dual variables.

10. A school dietician is attempting to determine a lunch menu that will minimize cost and meet certain minimum dietary requirements. The two main staples in the meal are meat and potatoes, which provide protein, iron, and carbohydrates. The problem has been formulated as follows:

$x_1 = $ oz of meat
$x_2 = $ oz of potatoes

Minimize $Z = .03x_1 + .02x_2$ (cost, $)
subject to
$$4x_1 + 5x_2 \geqslant 20 \qquad \text{(protein, mg)}$$
$$12x_1 + 3x_2 \geqslant 30 \qquad \text{(iron, mg)}$$
$$3x_1 + 2x_2 \geqslant 12 \qquad \text{(carbohydrates, mg)}$$
$$x_1, x_2 \geqslant 0$$

The final optimal simplex tableau for this problem is shown on page 166.
a. Interpret the shadow prices in the $c_j - z_j$ row for this tableau.
b. Formulate the dual to this problem.
c. Define the dual variables.

	c_j			.03	.02	0	0	0
c_b		basis	b_i^*	x_1	x_2	s_1	s_2	s_3
.02		x_2	3.6	0	1	0	.20	−.80
.03		x_1	1.6	1	0	0	−.133	.20
0		s_1	4.4	0	0	1	.47	−3.20
		z_j	.120	.03	.02	0	0	−.010
		$z_j − c_j$		0	0	0	0	−.010

11. A manufacturer produces three products daily, x_1, x_2, and x_3. The three products are each processed through three production operations with time constraints and then stored. The problem has been formulated as

$$\text{Maximize } Z = 40x_1 + 35x_2 + 45x_3 \quad \text{(profit, \$)}$$

subject to

$$
\begin{aligned}
2x_1 + 3x_2 + 2x_3 &\leq 120 && \text{(operation 1, hr)} \\
4x_1 + 3x_2 + x_3 &\leq 160 && \text{(operation 2, hr)} \\
3x_1 + 2x_2 + 4x_3 &\leq 100 && \text{(operation 3, hr)} \\
x_1 + x_2 + x_3 &\leq 40 && \text{(storage, ft}^2\text{)} \\
x_1, x_2, x_3 &\geq 0
\end{aligned}
$$

The final optimal simplex tableau for this problem is

	c_j			40	35	45	0	0	0	0
c_b		basis	b_i^*	x_1	x_2	x_3	s_1	s_2	s_3	s_4
0		s_1	10	−½	0	0	1	0	½	−4
0		s_2	60	2	0	0	0	1	1	−5
45		x_3	10	½	0	1	0	0	½	−1
35		x_2	30	½	1	0	0	0	−½	2
		z_j	1500	40	35	45	0	0	5	25
		$c_j − z_j$		0	0	0	0	0	−5	−25

a. Interpret the shadow prices in the $c_j − z_j$ row for this tableau.
b. Formulate the dual to this problem.
c. Define the dual variables.
d. How does the fact that this is a multiple optimal solution affect the interpretation of the dual values?

12. a. Formulate the dual to the following linear programming problem:

$$\text{Maximize } Z = 9x_1 + 12x_2$$

subject to

$$
\begin{aligned}
4x_1 + 8x_2 &\leq 64 \\
5x_1 + 5x_2 &\leq 50 \\
15x_1 + 8x_2 &\leq 120 \\
x_1 &\leq 7
\end{aligned}
$$

$$x_2 \leqslant 7$$
$$x_1, x_2 \geqslant 0$$

   b. Solve the dual problem using the simplex method.

13. a. Formulate the dual to the following linear programming problem:

$$\text{Minimize } Z = 20x_1 + 16x_2$$

subject to
$$3x_1 + x_2 \geqslant 6$$
$$x_1 + x_2 \geqslant 4$$
$$2x_1 + 6x_2 \geqslant 12$$
$$x_1, x_2 \geqslant 0$$

   b. Solve the dual problem using the simplex method.

14. Formulate the dual to the following linear programming problem:

$$\text{Maximize } Z = 25x_1 + 20x_2 + 10x_3 + 30x_4$$

subject to
$$x_1 + x_2 \leqslant 400$$
$$x_3 + x_4 \leqslant 600$$
$$50x_1 + 45x_2 \leqslant 16{,}000$$
$$40x_3 + 30x_4 \leqslant 25{,}000$$
$$2x_1 + 3x_3 \leqslant 800$$
$$4x_2 + x_4 \leqslant 900$$
$$x_1, x_2, x_3, x_4 \geqslant 0$$

15. Formulate the dual to the following linear programming problem:

$$\text{Maximize } Z = 2x_1 + 2x_2 - x_3$$

subject to
$$x_1 + x_2 - 2x_3 \leqslant 6$$
$$-2x_1 - x_2 + x_3 \leqslant 5$$
$$2x_1 + 6x_2 = 10$$
$$x_1, x_2, x_3 \geqslant 0$$

16. Formulate the dual to the following linear programming problem:

$$\text{Minimize } Z = x_1 + 2x_2 + x_3$$

subject to
$$2x_1 - 3x_2 + x_3 = 6$$
$$2x_1 - 3x_2 - x_3 \geqslant 1$$
$$x_1, x_2 \geqslant 0$$
$$x_3 \sim \text{unrestricted}$$

17. Formulate the dual to the following linear programming problem:

$$\text{Maximize } Z = 4x_1 + 10x_2 + 6x_3$$

subject to
$$x_1 + 3x_2 + 4x_3 \leqslant 40$$
$$2x_2 + x_3 \leqslant 20$$

(continued)

$$10x_1 + 6x_2 + 20x_3 = 100$$
$$x_1 + 2x_2 = 60$$
$$x_1, x_2, x_3 \geqslant 0$$

18. Formulate the dual to the following linear programming problem:

Minimize $Z = 2x_1 + 4x_2 + 3x_3$

subject to

$$x_1 + 2x_2 - 3x_3 \geqslant 30$$
$$x_1 + 2x_2 \geqslant 40$$
$$-x_1 + x_2 + x_3 \geqslant 30$$
$$x_1, x_2 \geqslant 0$$
$$x_3 \sim \text{unrestricted}$$

19. Formulate the dual to the following linear programming problem:

Maximize $Z = x_1 + 2x_2 + 2x_3$

subject to

$$x_1 + x_2 + 2x_3 \leqslant 12$$
$$2x_1 + x_2 + 5x_3 = 20$$
$$x_1 + x_2 - x_3 \geqslant 8$$
$$x_1, x_2, x_3 \geqslant 0$$

20. Using graphical analysis for problem 1 in this chapter, show graphically what would be the effect on the optimal solution if the profit for product 1 increased from $100 to $120. To $200.

21. Using graphical analysis for problem 2 in this chapter, show graphically what would be the effect on the optimal solution if an additional 10 acres of land is acquired by the farmer.

22. In problem 3 in this chapter, using graphical analysis, what profit for a necklace would result in no bracelets being produced, and what would be the optimal solution for this profit?

23. Using graphical analysis for problem 6 in this chapter, show graphically what would be the effect if the process 2 production hours required for product 2 were reduced from 8 hours to 5 hours. To 4 hours.

24. For problem 5 in this chapter, perform the following sensitivity analyses.
    a. Find the ranges for the b_1 and b_2 (labor hours) values for which the solution will remain feasible.
    b. Find the ranges for the c_1 and c_2 values for which the solution will remain optimal.

25. For problem 6 in this chapter, perform the following sensitivity analyses.
    a. Find the ranges for all b_i values for which the solution will remain feasible.
    b. Find the ranges for all c_j values for which the solution will remain optimal.

26. For problem 7 in this chapter, perform the following sensitivity analyses.
    a. Find the ranges for all b_i values for which the solution will remain feasible.
    b. Find the ranges for all c_j values for which the solution will remain optimal.

27. For problem 8 in this chapter, perform the following sensitivity analyses.
    a. Find the ranges for all b_i values for which the solution will remain feasible.
    b. Find the ranges for all c_j values for which the solution will remain optimal.

28. For problem 9 in this chapter, perform the following sensitivity analyses.
    a. Find the ranges for all b_i values for which the solution will remain feasible.
    b. Find the ranges for all c_j values for which the solution will remain optimal.

29. For problem 10 in this chapter, perform the following sensitivity analyses.
    a. Find the ranges for all b_i values for which the solution will remain feasible.
    b. Find the ranges for all c_j values for which the solution will remain optimal.

30. For problem 11 in this chapter, perform the following sensitivity analyses.
    a. Find the ranges for all b_i values for which the solution will remain feasible.
    b. Find the ranges for all c_j values for which the solution will remain optimal.

31. For the linear programming problem

    Maximize $Z = 6x_1 + 2x_2 + 12x_3$

    subject to
    $$4x_1 + x_2 + 3x_3 \leqslant 24$$
    $$2x_1 + 6x_2 + 3x_3 \leqslant 30$$
    $$x_1, x_2, x_3 \geqslant 0$$

    the optimal simplex tableau is

	c_j			6	2	12	0	0
c_b		basis	b_i^*	x_1	x_2	x_3	s_1	s_2
12		x_3	8	4/3	1/3	1	1/3	0
0		s_2	6	-2	5	0	-1	1
		z_j	96	16	4	12	4	0
		$c_j - z_j$		-10	-2	0	-4	0

    a. Find the ranges for all b_i values for which the solution will remain feasible.
    b. Find the ranges for all c_j values for which the solution will remain optimal.
    c. Find the range for a_{11} for which the solution will remain optimal.
    d. What effect will the addition of the following constraint have on the solution?

    $$x_1 + 2x_2 + 2x_3 \leqslant 12$$

32. For the linear programming problem

    Maximize $Z = 10x_1 + 8x_2$

    subject to
    $$x_1 + 3x_2 \leqslant 30$$
    $$6x_1 + 3x_2 \leqslant 120$$
    $$x_1, x_2 \geqslant 0$$

    the optimal simplex tableau is

C_b	c_j / basis	b_i^*	10 x_1	8 x_2	0 s_1	0 s_2
8	x_2	4	0	1	$2/5$	$-1/15$
10	x_1	18	1	0	$-1/5$	$1/5$
	z_j	212	10	8	$6/5$	$22/15$
	$c_j - z_j$		0	0	$-6/5$	$-22/15$

a. Find the feasible ranges for all b_i values.

b. Find the optimal ranges for all c_j values.

c. What effect will the addition of the following constraint have on the solution

$$2x_1 + x_2 \leqslant 40$$

d. What effect will the addition of the following constraint have on the solution

$$x_1 + x_2 \leqslant 20$$

e. What effect will the addition of a decision variable (x_3) to the model have
the solution?

Maximize $Z = 10x_1 + 8x_2 + 6x_3$

subject to

$$x_1 + 3x_2 + 2x_3 \leqslant 30$$
$$6x_1 + 3x_2 + 4x_3 \leqslant 120$$
$$x_1, x_2, x_3 \geqslant 0$$

33. For the linear programming problem

Minimize $Z = 3x_1 + 5x_2 + 2x_3$

subject to

$$x_1 + x_2 - 3x_3 \geqslant 35$$
$$x_1 + 2x_2 \geqslant 50$$
$$-x_1 + x_2 + x_3 \geqslant 25$$
$$x_1, x_2, x_3 \geqslant 0$$

the optimal simplex tableau is

C_b	c_j / basis	b_i^*	3 x_1	5 x_2	2 x_3	0 s_1	0 s_2	0 s_3
0	s_2	15	0	0	-4	$-3/2$	1	$-1/2$
3	x_1	5	1	0	-2	$-1/2$	0	$1/2$
5	x_2	30	0	1	-1	$-1/2$	0	$-1/2$
	z_j	165	3	5	-11	-4	0	-1
	$z_j - c_j$		0	0	-13	-4	0	-1

a. Explain how the feasible ranges for all b_i values would be determined.

b. Find the optimal ranges for all c_j values.

c. Explain the requirements for a change in a_{32}.

d. What effect will the addition of the following constraint have on the solution?

$$2x_1 + x_2 + x_3 \geqslant 30$$

e. What effect will the addition of the following constraint have on the solution?

$$x_2 + x_3 \geqslant 40$$

f. What effect will the addition of a fourth decision variable (x_4) to the model have on the solution?

Minimize $Z = 3x_1 + 5x_2 + 2x_3 + 3x_4$

subject to
$$x_1 + x_2 - 3x_3 + 2x_4 \geqslant 35$$
$$x_1 + 2x_2 + x_4 \geqslant 50$$
$$-x_1 + x_2 + x_3 + 2x_4 \geqslant 25$$
$$x_1, x_2, x_3, x_4 \geqslant 0$$

34. For the linear programming problem

Maximize $Z = 5x_1 + 7x_2 + 8x_3$

subject to
$$x_1 + x_2 + x_3 \leqslant 32$$
$$x_1 \leqslant 20$$
$$x_2 \leqslant 15$$
$$x_3 \leqslant 18$$
$$x_1, x_2, x_3 \geqslant 0$$

the optimal simplex tableau is

c_b $\diagdown$ c_j	basis	b_i^*	5 x_1	7 x_2	8 x_3	0 s_1	0 s_2	0 s_3	0 s_4
7	x_2	14	1	1	0	1	0	0	-1
0	s_2	20	1	0	0	0	1	0	0
0	s_3	1	-1	0	0	-1	0	1	1
8	x_3	18	0	0	1	0	0	0	1
	z_j	242	7	7	8	7	0	0	1
	$c_j - z_j$		-2	0	0	-7	0	0	-1

a. Find the feasible ranges for all b_i values.

b. Find the optimal ranges for all c_j values.

c. Find the optimal ranges for a_{11}.

d. What effect will the addition of the following constraint have on the solution?

$$2x_1 + 3x_2 + x_3 \leqslant 30$$

e. What effect will the addition of a fourth decision variable have on the solution?

Maximize $Z = 5x_1 + 7x_2 + 8x_3 + 6x_4$

subject to
$$x_1 + x_2 + x_3 + x_4 \leq 32$$
$$x_1 \leq 20$$
$$x_2 \leq 15$$
$$x_3 \leq 18$$
$$x_1, x_2, x_3, x_4 \geq 0$$

35. A food processing company produces three canned fruit products: mixed fruit, fruit cocktail, and fruit delight. The main ingredients in each product are pears and peaches. Each product is produced in lots and must go through three processes: mixing, canning, and packaging. The resource requirements for each product and each process are shown in the following linear programming formulation:

Maximize $Z = 10x_1 + 6x_2 + 8x_3$ (profit, $)
subject to
$$20x_1 + 10x_2 + 16x_3 \leq 320 \quad \text{(pears, lb)}$$
$$10x_1 + 20x_2 + 16x_3 \leq 400 \quad \text{(peaches, lb)}$$
$$x_1 + 2x_2 + 2x_3 \leq 43 \quad \text{(mixing, hr)}$$
$$x_1 + x_2 + x_3 \leq 60 \quad \text{(canning, hr)}$$
$$2x_1 + x_2 + x_3 \leq 40 \quad \text{(packaging, hr)}$$
$$x_1, x_2, x_3 \geq 0$$

The optimal simplex tableau is

c_b	c_j basis	b_i^*	10 x_1	6 x_2	8 x_3	0 s_1	0 s_2	0 s_3	0 s_4	0 s_5
10	x_1	8	1	0	$8/15$	$1/15$	$-1/30$	0	0	0
6	x_2	16	0	1	$8/15$	$-1/30$	$1/15$	0	0	0
0	s_3	3	0	0	$2/5$	0	$-1/10$	1	0	0
0	s_4	36	0	0	$-1/15$	$-1/30$	$-1/30$	0	1	0
0	s_5	8	0	0	$-3/5$	$-1/10$	0	0	0	1
	z_j	176	10	6	$128/15$	$7/15$	$7/15$	0	0	0
	$c_j - z_j$		0	0	$-8/15$	$-7/15$	$-1/15$	0	0	0

a. What is the maximum price the company would be willing to pay for additional pears? How much would be purchased at that price?

b. What is the marginal value of peaches? Over what range of peaches is this price valid?

c. The company can purchase a new machine for mixing that would increase the hours available for mixing from 43 to 60. Would this affect the optimal solution?

d. The company can also purchase a new machine for packaging that would increase the hours available for packaging from 40 to 50. Would this affect the optimal solution?

e. If the manager should attempt to secure additional units of only one of the resources, which should it be and how much should be secured?

(handwritten annotations: substitute values into ... from opt. constraint - refer new constraint ... sol. to notes)

f. The company is considering adding a third fruit, oranges, to the mix, to increase demand. The requirements for oranges and their availability are given by $2x_1 + 3x_2 + 2x_3 \leq 100$ oranges. What effect would this have on the solution?

g. The company is considering a new product, fancy fruit. Profit is $6 per lot. Each lot will contain 12 pounds of pears and 14 pounds of peaches and will require 2 hours to mix, 1 hour to can, and 2 hours to package. How would this affect the product mix given in the solution? *add new dec. var = rework pr*

36. A lumber products firm produces three types of pressed paneling from pine and spruce. The three types of paneling are Western, Old English, and Colonial (defined as x_1, x_2, and x_3, respectively). Each sheet must be cut and pressed. The resource requirements are given in the following linear programming formulation:

Maximize $Z = 4x_1 + 10x_2 + 8x_3$ (profit, $)
subject to

$$5x_1 + 4x_2 + 4x_3 \leq 200 \quad \text{(pine, lb)}$$
$$2x_1 + 5x_2 + 2x_3 \leq 160 \quad \text{(spruce, lb)}$$
$$x_1 + x_2 + 2x_3 \leq 50 \quad \text{(cutting, hr)}$$
$$2x_1 + 4x_2 + 2x_3 \leq 80 \quad \text{(pressing, hr)}$$
$$x_1, x_2, x_3 \geq 0$$

The optimal simplex tableau is

			4	10	8	0	0	0	0
c_b	basis	b_i^*	x_1	x_2	x_3	s_1	s_2	s_3	s_4
0	s_1	80	7/3	0	0	1	0	−4/3	−2/3
0	s_2	70	−1/3	0	0	0	1	1/3	−4/3
8	x_3	20	1/3	0	1	0	0	2/3	−1/6
10	x_2	10	1/3	1	0	0	0	−1/3	1/3
	z_j	260	6	10	8	0	0	2	2
	$c_j - z_j$		−2	0	0	0	0	−2	−2

a. What is the marginal value of an additional pound of spruce? Over what range of available spruce is this value valid?

b. What is the marginal value of an additional hour of cutting? Over what range is this value valid?

c. Given a choice between securing more cutting hours and more pressing hours, which should management select? Why?

d. If the amount of spruce available to the firm decreases from 160 to 100 pounds, will the solution be affected?

e. What unit profit would have to be made from Western paneling before management would consider producing it?

f. Management is considering changing the profit on Colonial paneling from $8 to $13. Would this affect the solution?

g. The firm is considering production of a new type of paneling, Mediterranean. It would yield a profit of $6, require 3 pounds of pine and 4 pounds of spruce, and take 1 hour to cut and 4 hours to press. Would the production of this new paneling affect the present solution?

37. A manufacturing firm produces four products, x_1, x_2, x_3, and x_4. Each product requires material and machine processing. The linear programming model is formulated as

$$\text{Maximize } Z = 2x_1 + 8x_2 + 10x_3 + 6x_4 \quad \text{(profit, \$)}$$

subject to

$$2x_1 + x_2 + 4x_3 + 2x_4 \leq 200 \quad \text{(material, lb)}$$
$$x_1 + 2x_2 + 2x_3 + x_4 \leq 160 \quad \text{(machine processing, hr)}$$
$$x_1, x_2, x_3, x_4 \geq 0$$

The optimal simplex tableau is

c_b	c_j basis	b_i^*	2 x_1	8 x_2	10 x_3	6 x_4	0 s_1	0 s_2
6	x_4	80	1	0	2	1	$\frac{2}{3}$	$-\frac{1}{3}$
8	x_2	40	0	1	0	0	$-\frac{1}{3}$	$\frac{2}{3}$
	z_j	800	6	8	12	6	$\frac{4}{3}$	$\frac{10}{3}$
	$c_j - z_j$		-4	0	-2	0	$-\frac{4}{3}$	$-\frac{10}{3}$

a. What is the marginal value of an additional pound of material? Over what range of material is this value valid?

b. What is the marginal value of additional hours of processing time? Over what range of hours is this value valid?

c. How much would the contribution to profit of x_1 have to increase before x_1 would be produced? Before x_4 would be produced?

d. Suppose new consumer standards require additional processing. The new processing requires 2 hours for x_1 and x_4 and 4 hours for x_2 and x_3. A total of 200 hours are available. Does this affect the solution?

38. In problem 14 in Chapter 2, using AB:QM, LINDO, STORM, or some other comparable software package, determine the effect on the optimal solution if employee 2 is given additional training such that his time required to operate the lathe is reduced to 45 minutes. If subsequently employee 1 also receives additional training to reduce the time required for her to operate the lathe to 30 minutes, will this alter the solution?

39. In problem 18 in Chapter 2, using AB:QM, LINDO, STORM, or some other comparable software package, determine that if supply could be increased at any of the three grain cooperatives, which should it be? How much can the supply be increased at this cooperative and still retain the current optimal shipping routes?

40. In problem 21 in Chapter 2, use the linear programming capabilities of the AB:QM, LINDO, STORM, or some comparable software package, to determine if an increase in the profit employee 1 generates in sporting goods from $150 to $160 would effect the optimal work assignment.

41. In problem 29 in Chapter 2, the terminal manager in Atlanta has determined that she can accommodate 70 trucks per week instead of 60. Using the sensitivity analysis feature of the AB:QM, LINDO, STORM, or some comparable software package, see if this change will result in a new optimal solution point. The company has also determined that it can increase its profit for its Memphis to New York route from $900 to $1,700. Will this change the optimal solution mix?

42. In problem 32 in Chapter 2, using AB:QM, LINDO, STORM, or some other comparable software package, determine which of the four ingredients the firm should seek a greater supply of and how much of that ingredient could be added while maintaining the current optimal wiener mixture.

43. In problem 34, in Chapter 2, use AB:QM, LINDO, STORM, or some other comparable software package. Assuming that the storage capacity can be increased from the 10,000 bushel capacity, in which month should it be increased? If the buying price in month 1 fell from $5 to $3 would the optimal monthly buying and selling pattern be altered? What would be the effect on the original solution if the selling price in month 4 increased from $7 to $8?

44. In problem 40 in Chapter 2, use AB:QM, LINDO, STORM, or some other software package to determine the effect on the optimal solution if only 10% of experienced employees quit each month instead of 15%.

5

Transportation and Assignment Problems

This chapter is concerned with two special types of linear programming applications, transportation and assignment problems. Although all linear programming problems can be solved by the simplex method, these special cases can be solved by special techniques (algorithms) that are generally more efficient than the simplex method. Many of the modeling concepts and solution procedures for these models are actually extensions of the linear programming concepts and procedures presented in the previous chapters.

THE TRANSPORTATION PROBLEM

In general, the transportation problem deals with the transportation of a product from a number of sources, with limited supplies, to a number of destinations, with specified demands, at the minimum total transportation cost. For example, a product produced at three factories (sources) must be distributed to three stores (destinations), as shown in Figure 5.1.

Each factory has a specified weekly production capacity, and each store has a specified weekly demand for the product. Given a unique unit cost of transporting the product from each factory to each store, the problem is to determine the number of units to ship from each factory to each store, with the objective of minimizing total transportation costs. The requirements (or constraints) of the problem are that demand at each store must be met without exceeding production capacity at each factory. The problem is illustrated as a generalized transportation network model in Figure 5.2.

The Balanced Transportation Problem

To illustrate the transportation problem, we will present an example in which total supply from all sources exactly equals total demand at all destinations. This type of problem is referred to as a **balanced transportation problem**.

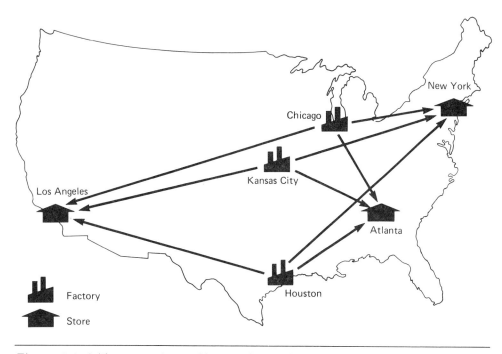

Figure 5.1 *A Transportation Problem Involving Three Factories and Three Stores*

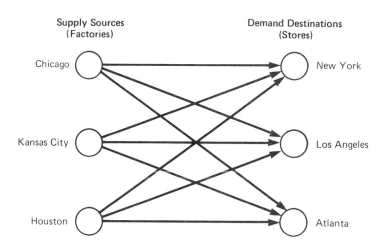

Figure 5.2 *Transportation Network Model for Three Factories and Three Stores*

Example 5.1 A Concrete Shipping Problem

A concrete company transports concrete from three plants to three construction sites. The supply capacities of the three plants, the demand requirements at the three sites, and the transportation costs ($/ton) are as follows:

From Plant	To Construction Site			Supply (tons)
	1	2	3	
1	$8	$5	$6	120
2	15	10	12	80
3	3	9	10	80
Demand (tons)	150	70	60	280

This transportation problem is illustrated as a network model in Figure 5.3. Each of the three plants ($i = 1, 2, 3$) can supply concrete to each of the three construction sites ($j = 1, 2, 3$). The problem is "balanced," since the total concrete demanded is equal to the total supply, 280 tons of concrete. It is rare to observe a balanced transportation problem in reality; however, the analysis of a balanced problem is a good starting point for understanding the transportation solution processes to be presented.

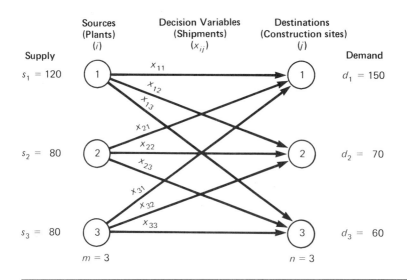

Figure 5.3 *Network Model for Concrete Transportation Problem*

This example problem can be formulated as a linear programming problem as follows:

Let x_{ij} = the number of tons of concrete shipped from plant i
($i = 1, 2, 3$) to site $j (j = 1, 2, 3$)

$$\text{Minimize } Z = \$8x_{11} + 5x_{12} + 6x_{13} + 15x_{21} + 10x_{22} + 12x_{23} + 3x_{31}$$
$$+ 9x_{32} + 10x_{33}$$

subject to

$$x_{11} + x_{12} + x_{13} = 120 \quad \text{(supply, plant 1)}$$
$$x_{21} + x_{22} + x_{23} = 80 \quad \text{(supply, plant 2)}$$
$$x_{31} + x_{32} + x_{33} = 80 \quad \text{(supply, plant 3)}$$
$$x_{11} + x_{21} + x_{31} = 150 \quad \text{(demand, site 1)}$$
$$x_{12} + x_{22} + x_{32} = 70 \quad \text{(demand, site 2)}$$
$$x_{13} + x_{23} + x_{33} = 60 \quad \text{(demand, site 3)}$$
$$\text{all } x_{ij} \geq 0$$

The model constraints represent the total amount that can be supplied by each plant and the total amount demanded at each construction site as sums of the individual shipping alternatives (i.e., routes). The constraints are represented as equalities because the problem is balanced (all units supplied will be distributed and all demand will be met). The objective function represents the total cost where each c_{ij} value is the per ton transportation cost from plant i to site j.

The general formulation of a transportation problem with m sources and n destinations is

$$\text{Minimize } Z = \sum_{i=1}^{m} \sum_{j=1}^{n} c_{ij} x_{ij}$$

subject to

$$\sum_{j=1}^{n} x_{ij} = s_i \quad \text{(supply, } s_i\text{, at source } i, i = 1, 2, \ldots, m)$$

$$\sum_{i=1}^{m} x_{ij} = d_j \quad \text{(demand, } d_j\text{, at destination } j, j = 1, 2, \ldots, n)$$

$$\text{all } x_{ij} \geq 0$$

The balanced condition of the transportation problem is expressed as

$$\sum_{i=1}^{m} s_i = \sum_{i=1}^{m} \left(\sum_{j=1}^{n} x_{ij} \right) = \sum_{j=1}^{n} \left(\sum_{i=1}^{m} x_{ij} \right) = \sum_{j=1}^{n} d_j$$

This problem could be solved using the simplex method, as were the linear programming problems in previous chapters; however, even a relatively small problem, such as our example with three sources and three destinations, can mushroom into a rather large simplex tableau with six constraints, nine decision variables, and six artificial variables. Inspection of the transportation problem reveals, however, that all the coefficients, a_{ij}, in the constraint equations are ones. This model feature leads to the use of special solution methods that are computationally more efficient than the simplex method.

The Transportation Tableau

Because of the special structure of the transportation problem, it can be put in a unique tabular form called the **transportation tableau**. This tableau has the general form shown in Table 5.1.

Table 5.1 General Transportation Tableau

From \ To	1	2	...	j	...	n	Supply
							Destinations
1	c_{11} x_{11}	c_{12} x_{12}	...	c_{1j} x_{1j}	...	c_{1n} x_{1n}	s_1
2	c_{21} x_{21}	c_{22} x_{22}	...	c_{2j} x_{2j}	...	c_{2n} x_{2n}	s_2
.	.	.		.		.	.
i	c_{i1} x_{i1}	c_{i2} x_{i2}	...	c_{ij} x_{ij}	...	c_{in} x_{in}	s_i
.	.	.		.		.	.
m	c_{m1} x_{m1}	c_{m2} x_{m2}	...	c_{mj} x_{mj}	...	c_{mn} x_{mn}	s_m
Demand	d_1	d_2	...	d_j	...	d_n	$\Sigma s_i = \Sigma d_j$

Sources are listed along the rows.

The sources are listed as rows and the destinations as columns. The tableau has $m \times n$ cells. The unit transportation cost (c_{ij}) is recorded in the small box in the upper-right-hand corner of each cell. The demand at each destination is recorded in the bottom row, and the supply from each source is listed in the right-hand column. The lower-right-hand corner box reflects the fact that supply and demand are equal. The x_{ij} variable in each cell represents the number of units transported from source i to destination j (which is to be solved for).

The transportation tableau for Example 5.1, the concrete transportation problem, is shown in Table 5.2.

Given in tableau form, the problem can now be solved via one of several transportation solution techniques. In order to begin the solution process, an initial basic feasible solution must be determined.

The Initial Solution

Referring to the general formulation of the transportation problem, we can see that there are m supply constraints and n demand constraints, which translates into $m + n$ total constraints. In a typical linear programming problem, the number of basic variables in the simplex tableau (b_i^*) is equal to the number of constraints. In a transportation problem, however, one of the constraints is redundant. The balance conditions

$$\sum_{i=1}^{m} s_i = \sum_{j=1}^{n} d_j$$

Table 5.2 *Transportation Tableau for Concrete Transportation Problem*

To From	1	2	3	Supply
1	8	5	6	120
2	15	10	12	80
3	3	9	10	80
Demand	150	70	60	280

ensure that if $m + n - 1$ constraints are met, then the $m + n$ equation will also be met. Since only $m + n - 1$ *independent* equations exist, the initial solution will have only $m + n - 1$ basic variables.

There are several methods available to develop an initial basic feasible solution. Three of the more popular methods for developing an initial solution will be examined: the **northwest corner method**, the **least-cost method**, and **Vogel's approxima-tion method (VAM)**.

Northwest Corner Method

The northwest corner method is the simplest of the three methods to develop an initial solution. The northwest corner method can be summarized as follows:

1. Start at the northwest corner (upper-left-hand corner) of the tableau and allocate as much as possible to x_{11} without violating the supply or demand constraints (i.e., x_{11} is set equal to the minimum of the values of s_1 or d_1).

2. This will exhaust the supply at source 1 and/or the demand for destination 1. Because no more units can be allocated to the exhausted row or column, it is eliminated. Next allocate as much as possible to the adjacent cell in the row or column that has not been eliminated. If both row and column are exhausted, move diagonally to the next cell.

3. Continue in the same manner until all supply has been exhausted and demand require-ments have been met.

For the transportation example in which tons of concrete are transported, the initial solution by the northwest corner method is shown in Table 5.3.

The initial solution is obtained as follows: (1) As many tons as possible are allocated to x_{11} according to x_{11} = min (120, 150) = 120. This exhausts the supply for plant 1, and row 1 is eliminated from further consideration. (2) Since x_{11} = 120, all but 30 tons demanded at site 1 have been supplied. The next adjacent cell, x_{21}, is allocated as much as possible according to x_{21} = min (80, 30) = 30. This eliminates column 1 from further consideration and reduces the supply at plant 2 to 50 tons. (3) Next, x_{22} = min

Table 5.3 *Initial Solution by the Northwest Corner Method*

To From	1	2	3	Supply
1	8 120	5	6	120
2	15 30	10 50	12	80
3	3	9 20	10 60	80
Demand	150	70	60	280

$(50, 70) = 50$, which eliminates row 2. (4) $x_{32} = \min (80, 20) = 20$. (5) $x_{33} = \min (60, 60) = 60$.

Notice that this stair-step process results in an initial solution with 5 ($m + n - 1$) basic variables and 4 nonbasic variables (i.e., zero allocation). For this solution, total cost is

$$Z = (\$8 \times 120) + (\$15 \times 30) + (\$10 \times 50) + (\$9 \times 20) + (\$10 \times 60)$$
$$= \$2690$$

Remember that this is only an *initial* solution and, thus, not necessarily optimal. In fact, of the three methods for obtaining an initial solution, the northwest corner is the least efficient, since it does not consider the unit transportation costs in making allocations. As a result, it is likely that several additional solution iterations will be required before the optimal solution is obtained.

Least-Cost Method

The least-cost method attempts to reflect the objective of cost minimization by systematically allocating to cells according to the magnitude of their unit costs. The general procedure for the least-cost method can be summarized as follows:

1. Select the x_{ij} variable (cell) with the minimum unit transportation cost (c_{ij}) and allocate as much as possible. For the minimum c_{ij}, $x_{ij} = \min (s_i, d_j)$. This will exhaust either row i or column j.

2. From the remaining cells that are feasible (i.e., have not been filled or had their row or column eliminated), select the minimum c_{ij} value and allocate as much as possible.

3. Continue this process until all supply and demand requirements have been satisfied.

Again consider Example 5.1, the concrete transportation example. Table 5.4 gives the initial cell allocation by the least-cost method.

The first step in the least-cost method results in an allocation to x_{31}, since $c_{31} = \$3$ is the minimum cell cost. The amount allocated is $x_{31} = \min (80, 150) = 80$. Since this allocation exhausts source 3 supply, row 3 is eliminated, and x_{32} and x_{33} are no

Table 5.4 *Initial Allocation by the Least-Cost Method*

To From	1		2		3		Supply
1		8		5		6	120
2		15		10		12	80
3	80	3		9		10	80
Demand	150		70		60		280

longer feasible. Also, the demand for 150 tons at site 1 is reduced by the 80 allocated tons, so the demand now equals 70 tons.

The next cell allocation is selected from the remaining six cells in Table 5.4. The minimum c_{ij} is $c_{12} = \$5$, and $x_{12} = \min(120, 70) = 70$. This allocation, shown in Table 5.5, fully satisfies the demand at site 2. Thus, x_{22} is eliminated as infeasible, and the remaining supply at plant 1 is reduced to 50 tons.

Table 5.5 *Second Allocation by the Least-Cost Method*

To From	1		2		3		Supply
1		8	70	5		6	120
2		15		10		12	80
3	80	3		9		10	80
Demand	150		70		60		280

The remaining cell allocations are made in the same manner. The initial solution by the least-cost method is shown in Table 5.6.

In the case of ties between the minimum c_{ij} values, simply select between the tied cells arbitrarily. Because this is only an initial solution, it has no effect on the eventual optimal solution, except possibly to increase the number of iterations required to obtain it.

The initial solution by the least-cost method as shown in Table 5.6 ($x_{12} = 70$, $x_{13} = 50$, $x_{21} = 70$, $x_{23} = 10$, and $x_{31} = 80$) results in the following total transportation cost:

Table 5.6 *Initial Solution by the Least-Cost Method*

To From	1	2	3	Supply
1	8	5 70	6 50	120
2	15 70	10	12 10	80
3	3 80	9	10.	80
Demand	150	70	60	280

$$Z = (\$5 \times 70) + (6 \times 50) + (15 \times 70) + (12 \times 10) + (3 \times 80)$$
$$= \$2060$$

A comparison of the total initial cost derived from the least-cost method with that derived from the northwest corner method shows a reduction of $630 with the least-cost method. In general, the least-cost method will usually result in a better (lower cost) initial solution than the northwest corner method. Since the least-cost method employs cost as a criterion for allocation and the northwest corner method does not, the former will usually require fewer additional iterations to find an optimal solution. However, cases can infrequently occur in which the same or a better initial solution is achieved using the northwest corner method.

Vogel's Approximation Method

Vogel's approximation method (VAM) typically provides a better initial solution than the northwest corner method does and often provides a better initial solution than the least-cost method does. In fact, in many cases the initial solution obtained by VAM will be optimal. VAM consists of making allocations in a manner that will minimize the penalty (i.e., regret or opportunity) cost for selecting the wrong cell for an allocation. The general procedure for the VAM can be summarized as follows:

1. Calculate the **penalty cost** for each row and column. The penalty cost for each row i is computed by subtracting the smallest c_{ij} value in the row from the next smallest c_{ij} value in the same row. Column penalty costs are obtained in the same way, by subtracting the smallest c_{ij} value in each column from the next smallest column c_{ij} value. These costs are the penalties for not selecting the minimum cell cost.

2. Select the row or column with the greatest penalty cost (breaking any ties arbitrarily). Allocate as much as possible to the cell with the minimum c_{ij} value in the selected row or column; that is, for minimum c_{ij}, $x_{ij} = \min(s_i, d_j)$. As a result, the largest penalties are avoided.

3. Adjust the supply and demand requirements to reflect the allocation(s) already made. Eliminate any rows and columns in which supply and demand have been exhausted.

4. If all supply and demand requirements have not been satisfied, go to the first step and recalculate new penalty costs. If all row and column values have been satisfied, the initial solution has been obtained.

Applying these steps to our example results in an initial VAM allocation in the transportation tableau as shown in Table 5.7.

Table 5.7 Initial VAM Allocation

From \ To	1	2	3	Supply	Row Penalty Costs
1	8	5	6	120	1
2	15	10	12	80	2
3	3 / 80	9	10	80	6
Demand	150	70	60	280	
Column Penalty Costs	5	4	4		

As an example of the calculation of penalty costs, consider the first row. The smallest c_{ij} value is 5 for c_{12}. The next smallest is $c_{13} = 6$. Thus, the penalty cost is the difference between these two values, $6 - 5 = \$1$. All remaining row and column penalty costs are computed in the same way.

The greatest penalty cost for this tableau is $6 for row 3. The allocation in this row is made to the cell with the minimum c_{ij} value—in this case, x_{31}. The amount allocated to x_{31} is min (80, 150) = 80. Now the tableau must be adjusted to reflect the exhaustion of source 3 supply and the elimination of row 3. In addition, the remaining demand at site 1 now becomes 70 tons rather than 150. The adjusted tableau with the newly calculated penalty costs and the second allocation is shown in Table 5.8.

Table 5.8 Transportation Tableau Adjusted for the Second VAM Allocation

From \ To	1	2	3	Supply	Row Penalty Costs
1	8 / 70	5	6	120	1
2	15	10	12	80	2
3	3 / 80	9	10	80	—
Demand	150	70	60	280	
Column Penalty Costs	7	5	6		

Column 1 is selected for the second allocation, since it has the greatest revised pen alty cost, $7. The allocation in this column is made to cell x_{11}, since it has the minimum c_{ij} value of $8. The amount allocated to x_{11} is min (120, 70) = 70. This allocation results in the elimination of column 1 and the reduction of row 1 supply to 50 tons. The process of allocation and recomputing penalty costs continues until all supply and demand requirements have been met. The initial solution for this example obtained by VAM is shown in Table 5.9.

Table 5.9 VAM Solution

To From	1	2	3	Supply
1	8 70	5	6 50	120
2	15	10 70	12 10	80
3	3 80	9	10	80
Demand	150	70	60	280

The total cost of this solution is

$$Z = (\$8 \times 70) + (6 \times 50) + (10 \times 70) + (12 \times 10) + (3 \times 80)$$
$$= \$1920$$

The total cost for this initial solution, $1920, is the lowest initial cost obtained from all three of the initial solution methods. In fact, this solution is also optimal, a condition that will be shown in the following discussion of solution methods. In general, VAM reduces the subsequent number of iterations required to reach the optimal solution, since it usually provides a better initial solution than the other two methods.

Determining an Optimal Solution

Two methods are presented for determining an optimal solution once an initial basic feasible solution has been obtained. These methods are the **stepping-stone method** and the **modified distribution method**.

Stepping-Stone Method

Once an initial basic feasible solution has been obtained for a transportation problem, the next step is to determine if the total transportation cost can be further reduced by entering a nonbasic variable into the solution (i.e., allocating units to an empty cell). The process of evaluating the nonbasic variables to determine if improvement is possible and then reallocating units is called the **stepping-stone method**.

The stepping-stone method derives its name from the fact that a closed loop of occupied cells is used to evaluate each empty cell (nonbasic variable). These occupied cells are thought of as stepping stones in a pond—the pond being the entire tableau.

Employing the initial solution obtained by the northwest corner method (Table 5.10), which we know is not optimal, we will demonstrate the evaluation of each non-basic variable via the stepping-stone method.

Table 5.10 Initial Northwest Corner Solution

To From	1	2	3	Supply
1	8 120	5	6	120
2	15 30	10 50	12	80
3	3	9 20	10 60	80
Demand	150	70	60	280

Each empty cell represents a nonbasic variable. For a nonbasic variable to enter the solution, it must contribute to a reduction in the value of the objective function. The variable x_{12} is arbitrarily considered as a possible entering variable. Suppose that we decide to allocate 1 unit to that cell. We then have 71 units in the second column of Table 5.10, which is a violation of the demand constraint. As a result, 1 unit must be subtracted from either 50 (x_{22}) or 20 (x_{32}) in column 2. We subtract 1 unit from x_{22}, yielding 49, and therefore column 2 has 70 units again. But row 2 now has 79 units, which violates the supply requirement. As a result, 1 unit must be added to x_{21}, which again conforms row 2 to the supply requirement of 80 units. However, column 1 now has 151 allocated units. Thus, 1 unit must be subtracted from x_{11} so that column 1 meets the demand constraint of 150 units. Row 1 is now completely satisfied even though 1 unit was subtracted from x_{11}, because originally 1 unit was added to x_{12}, the empty cell. This closed path process is the stepping-stone procedure. This path for x_{12} is shown in Table 5.11.

Table 5.11 Evaluation of Cell x_{12} According to the Stepping-Stone Method

To From	1	2	3	Supply
1	−1 — 8 → +1 120	5	6	120
2	+1 ← 15 — −1 30	10 50	12	80
3	3	9 20	10 60	80
Demand	150	70	60	280

Empty cell   *Closed loop*

$$x_{12} \qquad x_{12} \rightarrow x_{22} \rightarrow x_{21} \rightarrow x_{11} \rightarrow x_{12}$$
$$(+1) \quad (-1) \quad (+1) \quad (-1)$$

Several important conditions regarding the construction of stepping-stone paths should be mentioned at this point.

1. The direction taken, either clockwise or counterclockwise, is immaterial in determining the closed path. The same path will result regardless of direction.

2. There is only one unique closed path for each empty cell.

3. The path must follow (change direction at) only occupied cells, the exception being the nonbasic variable being evaluated.

4. Both empty and occupied cells can be skipped over in the construction of a closed path. Consider the following arbitrarily constructed example, which illustrates a closed path that skips over one allocated cell and several empty cells.

5. A path can cross over itself. Consider the following arbitrarily constructed example, where the nonbasic variable at the intersection of row 3 and column 1 is being evaluated.

6. Exactly one addition and one subtraction must appear in each row and column on the path.

The purpose of the path is to maintain the supply and demand constraints while reallocating units to an empty cell.

Now we must consider the cost of this reallocation. This is done by evaluating the costs along the closed path. If 1 unit is added to x_{12} in Table 5.11, a cost of \$5 (the unit transportation cost for x_{12}) will be incurred. However, the subsequent subtraction of 1 unit from x_{22} will reduce cost by \$10. Similarly, the addition of 1 unit to x_{21} will increase cost by \$15 while the subtraction of 1 unit from x_{11} will reduce cost by \$8. These cost additions and reductions are summarized as follows (where c_{ij}^* is the net cost change for allocating 1 unit of x_{ij}):

$$c_{12}^* = + c_{12} - c_{22} + c_{21} - c_{11}$$
$$= \$5 - 10 + 15 - 8$$
$$= +\$2$$

Thus, if 1 unit were reallocated to x_{12}, a net increase of \$2 in total transportation cost would result. Therefore, x_{12} should not be chosen as an entering variable, since it increases cost rather than reducing it.

All nonbasic variables (empty cells) are evaluated in the same manner to determine if any of them result in a net cost decrease and would therefore be candidates for the entering nonbasic variable. If no candidate exists (if all empty cells have positive c_{ij}^* values), then the solution is optimal. This is not the case for this example. Table 5.12 summarizes the various stepping-stone paths for all empty cells, and Table 5.13 summarizes the corresponding net cost changes resulting from each path.

Table 5.12 *Stepping-Stone Paths for All Nonbasic Variables*

Empty Cell	Closed Path
x_{12}	$x_{12} \rightarrow x_{22} \rightarrow x_{21} \rightarrow x_{11} \rightarrow x_{12}$
x_{13}	$x_{13} \rightarrow x_{33} \rightarrow x_{32} \rightarrow x_{22} \rightarrow x_{21} \rightarrow x_{11} \rightarrow x_{13}$
x_{23}	$x_{23} \rightarrow x_{33} \rightarrow x_{32} \rightarrow x_{22} \rightarrow x_{23}$
x_{31}	$x_{31} \rightarrow x_{21} \rightarrow x_{22} \rightarrow x_{32} \rightarrow x_{31}$

Table 5.13 *Cell Cost Summary for All Nonbasic Variables*

c_{ij}^*	Path Cost Reductions and Additions		Net Cost Change
c_{12}^*	\$ 5 − 10 + 15 − 8	=	+\$2
c_{13}^*	\$ 6 − 10 + 9 − 10 + 15 − 8	=	+\$2
c_{23}^*	\$12 − 10 + 9 − 10	=	+\$1
c_{31}^*	\$ 3 − 15 + 10 − 9	=	−\$11

From the cost analysis of all nonbasic variable stepping-stone paths in the example, it is evident that only x_{31} has a negative net cost change ($c_{31}^* = \$11$). Thus, x_{31} is the only nonbasic variable that, if entered into the solution basis, will reduce cost. If there were two or more nonbasic variables with negative c_{ij}^* values, then the one with the greatest net cost decrease would be selected. In the case of a tie, selection of the entering nonbasic variable is arbitrary.

Once it has been determined that x_{31} is the entering nonbasic variable, it must be decided how much will be allocated to the x_{31} cell. Given that each unit allocated to x_{31} will decrease cost by \$11, we naturally desire to allocate as many units as possible to x_{31}.

However, each unit allocated is taken from other occupied cells in the tableau. Thus, in order to maintain the supply and demand constraints, the allocation must be made according to the already determined stepping-stone path for x_{31} (see Tables 5.12 and 5.14).

Table 5.14 *Stepping-Stone Path for the Entering Nonbasic Variable, x_{31}*

From \ To	1	2	3	Supply
1	8 — 120	5	6	120
2	15 — 30	10 — 50	12	80
3	3	9 — 20	10 — 60	80
Demand	150	70	60	280

The amount allocated to x_{31} is restricted by the amount that can feasibly be transferred along the closed path. Notice that for every unit allocated to x_{31}, a unit is subtracted from x_{21} and x_{32}.

If more than 20 units are allocated to x_{31}, then x_{32} will become negative, resulting in an infeasible condition. Thus, the amount allocated to the nonbasic entering variable is restricted to the minimum amount in a cell to be subtracted from (x_{ij}^-) in the closed path. For this example,

$$x_{31} = \min (x_{21}^-, x_{32}^-)$$

and, in general,

$$\text{reallocated } x_{ij} = \min (x_{ij}^- \text{ on the closed path})$$

A reallocation of 20 units to x_{31}, the entering nonbasic variable, results in the following new tableau, with x_{32} as the leaving variable (Table 5.15).

The same stepping-stone process of evaluating each empty cell must be repeated for Table 5.15 to determine if the solution is optimal or if there is a new candidate for the entering nonbasic variable. This process results in two more iterations of the stepping-stone method before the optimal solution is achieved (Tables 5.16 and 5.17).

The optimal solution, shown in Table 5.17, is indicated by the fact that all empty cells have positive c_{ij}^* values. Thus, the solution can no longer be improved. The value of the objective function for the optimal solution is

$$Z = (\$8 \times 70) + (\$6 \times 50) + (\$10 \times 70) + (\$12 \times 10) + (\$3 \times 80)$$
$$= \$1920$$

Table 5.15 *Transportation Tableau with Initial Reallocation*

To From	1	2	3	Supply
1	8 120	5	6	120
2	15 10	10 70	12	80
3	3 20	9	10 60	80
Demand	150	70	60	280

Table 5.16 *Second Iteration:* x_{23} *Enters,* x_{21} *Leaves*

To From	1	2	3	Supply
1	8 120	5	6	120
2	15	10 70	12 10	80
3	3 30	9	10 50	80
Demand	150	70	60	280

Table 5.17 *Third Iteration (Optimal);* x_{13} *Enters,* x_{33} *Leaves*

To From	1	2	3	Supply
1	8 70	5	6 50	120
2	15	10 70	12 10	80
3	3 80	9	10	80
Demand	150	70	60	280

It should be noted that this solution is the same as the initial solution obtained by VAM (Table 5.9). The minimum cost shipping network for the concrete transportation problem is illustrated in Figure 5.4.

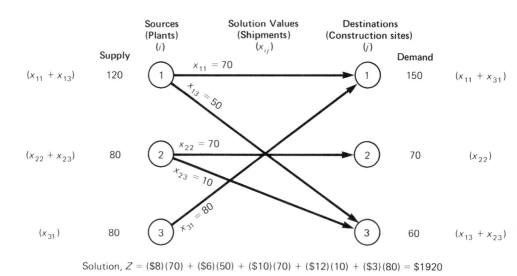

Solution, $Z = (\$8)(70) + (\$6)(50) + (\$10)(70) + (\$12)(10) + (\$3)(80) = \$1920$

Figure 5.4 *Minimum Cost Shipping Network for Concrete Transportation Problem*

Modified Distribution Method

The modified distribution (MODI) method of solution is a variation of the stepping-stone method based on the dual formulation. It differs from the stepping-stone method in that with MODI it is unnecessary to determine all the closed paths for nonbasic variables. Instead, the c^*_{ij} values are determined simultaneously, and the closed path is identified only for the entering nonbasic variable. This eliminates the cumbersome task of identifying all the stepping-stone paths.

In the MODI method, a value, u_i, is defined for each row (i) and a value, v_j, is defined for each column (j) in the transportation tableau. For each basic variable (occupied cell), x_{ij}, the following relationship exists:

$$u_i + v_j = c_{ij}$$

where

c_{ij} = unit cost of transportation

To demonstrate the MODI technique, we will refer back to the northwest corner initial solution of the concrete transportation example, which is shown again in Table 5.18 on page 200. Table 5.18 shows the u_i and v_j designations for each row and column.

Applying the relationship $u_i + v_j = c_{ij}$ for each basic variable results in the following equations:

$$x_{11}: \quad u_1 + v_1 = c_{11} = 8$$
$$x_{21}: \quad u_2 + v_1 = c_{21} = 15$$

Table 5.18 *Initial Northwest Corner Solution*

From \ To	1	2	3	Supply
$u_1 = 0$	8 **120**	5	6	120
$u_2 = 7$	15 —**30**	10 +**50**	12	80
$u_3 = 6$	3 +**20**	9 —**20**	10 **60**	80
Demand	150	70	60	280

with column headers $v_1 = 8$, $v_2 = 3$, $v_3 = 4$.

$$x_{22}: \quad u_2 + v_2 = c_{22} = 10$$
$$x_{32}: \quad u_3 + v_2 = c_{32} = 9$$
$$x_{33}: \quad u_3 + v_3 = c_{33} = 10$$

As can be observed, five equations ($m + n - 1$) with six unknowns ($m + n$) now exist. In order to solve this set of equations, it is necessary only to assign any of the unknowns (u_i or v_j) an arbitrary value. Usually, u_1 is assigned a value of zero. With $u_1 = 0$, it is an easy task to determine the values of the remaining variables as follows:

$$u_1 = 0$$
$$0 + v_1 = 8, \quad v_1 = 8$$
$$u_2 + 8 = 15, \quad u_2 = 7$$
$$7 + v_2 = 10, \quad v_2 = 3$$
$$u_3 + 3 = 9, \quad u_3 = 6$$
$$6 + v_3 = 10, \quad v_3 = 4$$

All the u_i and v_j values have now been determined (note that it is possible to have negative u_i and v_j values). The value of each nonbasic variable net cost change, c^*_{ij}, is now determined by the following relationship:

$$c^*_{ij} = c_{ij} - u_i - v_j$$

This formula for nonbasic variables results in c^*_{ij} values identical to those determined by the stepping-stone method.

$$c^*_{12} = c_{12} - u_1 - v_2 = 5 - 0 - 3 = +2$$
$$c^*_{13} = c_{13} - u_1 - v_3 = 6 - 0 - 4 = +2$$
$$c^*_{23} = c_{23} - u_2 - v_3 = 12 - 7 - 4 = +1$$
$$c^*_{31} = c_{31} - u_3 - v_1 = 3 - 6 - 8 = -11$$

As in the stepping-stone method, the negative value for c_{31} ($-\$11$) indicates that the present solution is not optimal and that x_{31} is the entering nonbasic variable. The amount allocated to x_{31} must now be determined *according to the stepping-stone procedure.* Thus, 20 units are allocated to x_{31}, resulting in the new tableau in Table 5.19.

Table 5.19 *First Iteration Determined by MODI*

	To				
	From	$v_1 = 8$ 1	$v_2 = 3$ 2	$v_3 = 15$ 3	Supply
$u_1 = 0$	1	8 120	5	6	120
$u_2 = 7$	2	15 10	10 70	12	80
$u_3 = -5$	3	3 20	9	10 60	80
	Demand	150	70	60	280

At this stage, the u_i, v_j, and c_{ij}^* values must be recomputed for this new tableau to test for optimality and determine the entering nonbasic variable (see Table 5.19). Next, the value for each nonbasic variable net cost change, c_{ij}^*, is determined by using the relationship $c_{ij}^* = c_{ij} - u_i - v_j$:

$$c_{12}^* = c_{12} - u_1 - v_2 = 5 - 0 - 3 = 2$$
$$c_{13}^* = c_{13} - u_1 - v_3 = 6 - 0 - 15 = -9$$
$$c_{23}^* = c_{23} - u_2 - v_3 = 12 - 7 - 15 = -10$$
$$c_{32}^* = c_{32} - u_3 - v_2 = 9 - (-5) - 3 = 11$$

The negative c_{ij}^* values indicate that the solution shown in Table 5.19 is not optimal. When two negative c_{ij}^* values exist, the "most negative" c_{ij}^* value determines the entering nonbasic variable. Thus, $c_{23}^* = -10$ designates x_{23} as the entering nonbasic variable. The amount allocated to x_{23} is determined according to the stepping-stone procedure. Thus, 10 units are allocated to x_{23}, resulting in the tableau in Table 5.20.

Table 5.20 *Second Iteration Determined by MODI*

	To				
	From	$v_1 = 8$ 1	$v_2 = 13$ 2	$v_3 = 15$ 3	Supply
$u_1 = 0$	1	8 120	5	6	120
$u_2 = -3$	2	15	10 70	12 10	80
$u_3 = -5$	3	3 30	9	10 50	80
	Demand	150	70	60	280

The u_i and v_j values for this iteration are shown in Table 5.20. Next, the computation of the c_{ij}^* values must again be repeated, which yields x_{13} as the entering nonbasic variable. The resulting optimal tableau is shown in Table 5.21. A comparison of Table 5.21 with Table 5.17, the optimal solution using the stepping-stone procedure, shows the two tableaus to be identical.

Table 5.21 Optimal Tableau by MODI

To From	1	2	3	Supply
1	8 70	5	6 50	120
2	15	10 70	12 10	80
3	3 80	9	10	80
Demand	150	70	60	280

The MODI method can be summarized in the following steps:

1. Determine u_i values for each row and v_j values for each column by using the relationship $c_{ij} = u_i + v_j$ for all basic variables, beginning with an assignment of zero to u_1.

2. Compute the net cost change, c_{ij}^*, for each nonbasic variable using the formula

$$c_{ij}^* = c_{ij} - u_i - v_j$$

3. If a negative c_{ij}^* value exists, the solution is not optimal. Select the x_{ij} variable with the greatest negative c_{ij}^* value as the entering nonbasic variable.

4. Allocate units to the entering nonbasic variable, x_{ij}, according to the stepping-stone process. Return to step 1.

Derivation of MODI from the Dual

The MODI method of evaluating nonbasic variables in the transportation tableau is directly related to the dual of the transportation primal. Consider the general formulation of a transportation problem with $m = 3$ rows and $n = 3$ columns:

Minimize $Z_p = c_{11}x_{11} + c_{12}x_{12} + c_{13}x_{13} + c_{21}x_{21} + c_{22}x_{22} + c_{23}x_{23}$
$$+ c_{31}x_{31} + c_{32}x_{32} + c_{33}x_{33}$$

subject to
$$x_{11} + x_{12} + x_{13} = s_1$$
$$x_{21} + x_{22} + x_{23} = s_2$$
$$x_{31} + x_{32} + x_{33} = s_3$$
$$x_{11} + x_{21} + x_{31} = d_1$$
$$x_{12} + x_{22} + x_{32} = d_2$$
$$x_{13} + x_{23} + x_{33} = d_3$$
$$x_{ij} \geq 0$$

where

s_i = supply requirements

d_j = demand requirements

Defining u_i as the dual variable for the source (supply) constraints and v_j as the dual variable for the destination (demand) constraints results in the following dual formulation:

Maximize $Z_d = (s_1u_1 + s_2u_2 + s_3u_3) + (d_1v_1 + d_2v_2 + d_3v_3)$

subject to

$$u_1 + v_1 \leqslant c_{11}$$
$$u_1 + v_2 \leqslant c_{12}$$
$$u_1 + v_3 \leqslant c_{13}$$
$$u_2 + v_1 \leqslant c_{21}$$
$$u_2 + v_2 \leqslant c_{22}$$
$$u_2 + v_3 \leqslant c_{23}$$
$$u_3 + v_1 \leqslant c_{31}$$
$$u_3 + v_2 \leqslant c_{32}$$
$$u_3 + v_3 \leqslant c_{33}$$
$$u_i, v_j \sim \text{unrestricted}$$

A property of duality is that each dual constraint representing a primal basic variable must exactly equal the contribution to profit c_{ij}. This means that the dual constraints for primal basic variables are equations,

$u_i + v_j = c_{ij}$, for all basic variables x_{ij} (i.e., for each occupied cell)

This results in $m + n - 1$ equations with $m + n$ unknowns, the same condition obtained in the MODI method.

Next we consider the dual constraints corresponding to the nonbasic primal variables. In each case, these constraints are of the form

$u_i + v_j \leqslant c_{ij}$ (i.e., for each unoccupied cell)

This is equivalent to $u_i + v_j - c_{ij} \leqslant 0$. Note at this point that the term $u_i + v_j$ is equivalent to the z_j in the simplex method, except that here it is denoted by the double subscript, z_{ij}, where i corresponds to the source, i, and j corresponds to the destination, j. Therefore, we have the equality

$z_{ij} = u_i + v_j$

Recall that in the simplex solution of a minimization problem, optimality is denoted by $z_j - c_j \leqslant 0$, which is equivalent to $z_{ij} - c_{ij} \leqslant 0$ for a transportation problem.

Therefore, if $z_{ij} - c_{ij} \geqslant 0$ for a nonbasic variable (i.e., an unoccupied cell), the solution is not optimal. The value of $z_{ij} - c_{ij}$ represents the amount by which the objective function would change for each unit of the nonbasic variable, x_{ij}, entered into the solution. Since, as previously indicated, $z_{ij} = u_i + v_j$, we can state our relationship as

$u_i + v_j - c_{ij} \geqslant 0$ (for nonbasic variables in a nonoptimal solution)

Multiplying this relationship by -1 yields

$$c_{ij} - u_i - v_j \leqslant 0$$

You will recognize this as the relationship used in the MODI method to determine the nonbasic variable net cost change, c_{ij}^*. Thus,

$$c_{ij}^* = c_{ij} - u_i - v_j$$

and when $c_{ij}^* \leqslant 0$, it indicates a nonoptimal solution and a candidate for the entering nonbasic variable.

The Unbalanced Transportation Problem

Thus far only a balanced transportation problem, where supply equals demand, has been considered. In most realistic situations, however, balanced cases are the exception. In general, **transportation** problems are **unbalanced problems**—supply exceeds demand, or vice versa. In the case of an unbalanced problem, the transportation solution method requires a slight modification.

The first case to be considered occurs when demand exceeds supply. To demonstrate this unbalanced condition, we will consider a modified version of the concrete transportation example used in the previous section. Assume that demand at site 3 has been increased from 60 tons to 90 tons. Total demand is now 310 tons, and total supply remains 280 tons. The problem is now reformulated as a linear programming model as follows:

$$\text{Minimize } Z = 8x_{11} + 5x_{12} + 6x_{13} + 15x_{21} + 10x_{22} + 12x_{23}$$
$$+ 3x_{31} + 9x_{32} + 10x_{33}$$

subject to
$$x_{11} + x_{12} + x_{13} = 120$$
$$x_{21} + x_{22} + x_{23} = 80$$
$$x_{31} + x_{32} + x_{33} = 80$$
$$x_{11} + x_{21} + x_{31} \leqslant 150$$
$$x_{12} + x_{22} + x_{23} \leqslant 70$$
$$x_{13} + x_{23} + x_{33} \leqslant 90$$
$$x_{ij} \geqslant 0$$

The $\leqslant$ demand constraints indicate that all units available will be supplied; however, one or more of the demand constraints will not be met, since total demand exceeds total supply by 30 tons. To reflect this condition in the transportation tableau, we add a "dummy" row to which all the units demanded, for which supply is not available, will be allocated. The modified tableau is shown in Table 5.22.

In effect, an imaginary source (a fictitious plant) has been added that balances supply and demand. The unit transportation costs of the three new dummy row cells are zero, since allocations to those cells do not affect the solution. These dummy cells are analogous to slack variables, which, you will recall, have c_{ij} values of zero in the objective function.

The 30 units of fictitious supply in the dummy row represent 30 units of demand that will not be met at one or more of the destinations. Thus, in the final solution, the amount shown to be transported from a dummy plant to a destination will represent the

Table 5.22 *Unbalanced Transportation Tableau with a Dummy Row Added (Demand > Supply)*

To From	1	2	3	Supply
1	8	5	6	120
2	15	10	12	80
3	3	9	10	80
Dummy	0	0	0	30
Demand	150	70	90	310

shortage, or unmet demand, for that destination. If a penalty cost is incurred for eac unit of unmet demand, the transportation costs for the dummy cells should be the penal cost amounts.

The addition of the dummy source does not affect the methods for obtaining a initial solution or stepping-stone and MODI methods for determining an optimal solu tion. The normal procedure should be followed in each case. The northwest corne method retains its same form. In the least-cost method, the dummy cells with c_{ij} value equal to zero are all tied for the minimum cost; thus, one of the cells can be selecte arbitrarily. Alternatively, the dummy row can be ignored initially and allocations mad to the cell with the minimum positive cell cost. Then, after all allocations have bee made, the excess is allocated to the appropriate feasible dummy cell. In the VAM, th dummy c_{ij} values are used as the lowest column cost values when penalty costs are com puted. In the stepping-stone and MODI methods, the dummy cells are treated exactl the same way as regular cells.

In the case where supply exceeds demand, the opposite modification of the tableau is required—a dummy *column* is added (see Table 5.23). For example, in our original concrete transportation problem, if demand at destination 1 is 100 tons instead of the original 150, total demand becomes 230 and total supply remains at 280 units. Again, the methods of solution remain unchanged.

The 50 units of fictitious demand in the dummy column represent 50 units of supply that will not be shipped from one or more sources. Thus, in the final solution, the amount shown to be transported from a plant to the dummy destination will represent the excess to be held at the plant. If a storage cost is incurred for each unit of unshipped product, the transportation cost for the dummy cells should be the storage cost amounts.

Degeneracy

In order to evaluate all empty cells in determining the entering nonbasic variable, the number of occupied cells (i.e., basic variables) must be equal to $m + n - 1$. If a trans-

Table 5.23 *Unbalanced Problem, Supply Exceeds Demand*

To From	1	2	3	Dummy	Supply
1	8	5	6	0	120
2	15	10	12	0	80
3	3	9	10	0	80
Demand	100	70	60	50	280

portation tableau has less than $m + n - 1$ occupied cells, it is degenerate. Degeneracy can occur either at the initial solution or during subsequent iterations.

Application of the stepping-stone or MODI solution method is prohibited if degeneracy exists. Without $m + n - 1$ basic variables, it is impossible to determine all the closed paths or to solve the $m + n - 1$ MODI equations ($u_i + v_j = c_{ij}$).

Consider the sample transportation tableau in Table 5.24 and the initial solution obtained by the northwest corner method. Because the demand at destination 1 is identical to the supply at source 1 (100 units), the chain of adjacent occupied cells is broken. As a result, there are only four basic variables when there should be five ($m + n - 1 = 5$). Thus, a degenerate solution exists.

Table 5.24 *A Degenerate Case Initial Solution*

To From	1	2	3	Supply
1	8 100	5	6	100
2	15	10 100	12 20	120
3	3	9	10 80	80
Demand	100	100	100	300

In order to compensate for this deficiency, a fictitious allocation must be made to one of the empty cells to reestablish the $m + n - 1$ condition. Thus, a 0 is allocated to one of several candidates. The allocation of 0 indicates that there are no actual units in that cell, but that it will be treated as an occupied cell for solution purposes. It is, in effect, a dummy allocation that enables the identification of all closed paths. Two of the possible candidates for the 0 allocation are x_{12} and x_{21}, since one of these two variables normally would have had an allocation in the northwest corner method if the initial allocation of 100 units to cell x_{11} had not completely satisfied both column 1 and row 1. (However, there are several other possible dummy candidates.) Unfortunately, there is no direct rule or methodology for determining the location for the dummy cell in the initial solution.

Selecting x_{12} as the dummy basic variable results in the tableau in Table 5.25, which can be evaluated in the usual manner.

Table 5.25 *Tableau with x_{12} as a Dummy Basic Variable*

From \ To	1	2	3	Supply
1	8 / 100	5 / 0	6	100
2	15	10 / 100	12 / 20	120
3	3	9	10 / 80	80
Demand	100	100	100	300

Now consider the case where the solution becomes degenerate during one of the iterations of the solution process. Table 5.26 is an initial solution obtained via the northwest corner method. Evaluation of the nonbasic variables for this tableau indicates that x_{31} should enter the solution basis. Allocating the maximum feasible amount of 30 units results in the tableau shown in Table 5.27.

Table 5.26 *Initial Solution via the Northwest Corner Method*

From \ To	1	2	3	Supply
1	8 / 120	5	6	120
2	15 / 30	10 / 50	12	80
3	3	9 / 30	10 / 50	80
Demand	150	80	50	280

Table 5.27 *First Iteration of the Tableau*

From \ To	1	2	3	Supply
1	8 120	5	6	120
2	15	10 80	12	80
3	3 30	9	10 50	80
Demand	150	80	50	280

When the allocation of 30 units is made to x_{31}, the solution becomes degenerate, since both x_{21} and x_{32} equal 30 units in Table 5.26. In other words, two variables left the basis when x_{31} entered, rather than the normal one variable. This occurrence is due to a tie between two leaving basic variables, which, you will recall from Chapter 3, is the condition in the simplex method that results in degeneracy in a simplex tableau. To proceed to the solution of this problem, we must allocate 0 to one of the two variables that were tied for the leaving basic variable, x_{21} or x_{32}. Doing so enables the further evaluation of the solution. Consider the example in Table 5.28, with the 0 allocation made to x_{32}.

Table 5.28 *Tableau with x_{32} as a Dummy Basic Variable*

From \ To	1	2	3	Supply
1	8 120	5	6	120
2	15	10 80	12	80
3	3 30	9	10 50	80
Demand	150	80	50	280

Evaluation of this tableau by the stepping-stone process identifies x_{12} as the entering nonbasic variable ($c_{12}^* = -\$9$). However, the stepping-stone path for this cell ($x_{12} \rightarrow x_{32} \rightarrow x_{31} \rightarrow x_{11}$) contains the 0 in x_{32} as the minimum amount to be subtracted. Hence, the stepping-stone process results only in a transfer of the 0 from x_{32} to x_{12} (Table 5.29). The solution process then continues in the normal manner.

Table 5.29 *Transfer of Dummy Basic Variable from* x_{32} *to* x_{12}

To From	1	2	3	Supply
1	8 120	5 0	6	120
2	15	10 80	12	80
3	3 30	9	10 50	80
Demand	150	80	50	280

Multiple Optimal Solutions

The optimal solution to a transportation problem exists when the net cost change, c_{ij}^*, for all nonbasic variables is positive. However, as in the simplex tableau, when a nonbasic variable has a net cost change of zero ($c_{ij}^* = 0$), an alternative optimal solution is implied. The total cost value remains the same, but a different solution mix (i.e., an alternative allocation pattern) exists.

Consider the optimal solution to the concrete transportation example shown again in Table 5.30. Evaluation of the nonbasic variables in this tableau shows that the solution is optimal, with a minimum total cost of $1920. However, the nonbasic variable x_{21} has a net cost change, c_{21}^*, of zero. Thus, a multiple optimal solution exists that can be identified by allocating as much as feasible to x_{21} according to the stepping-stone path—in this case, 10 units. This results in a different allocation pattern (Table 5.31) with a total cost of $1920.

Prohibited Routes

In many real-world problems, it is not possible to transport units over certain routes. A transportation problem with prohibited routes can be represented by assigning a large c_{ij}

Table 5.30 *Optimal Transportation Tableau*

To From	1	2	3	Supply
1	8 70	5	6 50	120
2	14	10 70	12 10	80
3	3 80	9	10	80
Demand	150	70	60	280

Table 5.31 *Alternative Optimal Solution*

To From	1	2	3	Supply
1	8 60	5	6 60	120
2	14 10	10 70	12	80
3	3 80	9	10	80
Demand	150	70	60	280

value, M, to the x_{ij} that is prohibited. The normal solution process is then conducted, with the M value treated as any other c_{ij} value. As in a simplex tableau, the variable with $c_{ij} = M$ will eventually be forced out of the solution. (The same result can be obtained by blocking out the prohibited cell and ignoring it in the solution process.)

Production and Inventory Scheduling Application

The transportation model is most frequently applied to distribution problems, as illustrated in Example 5.1. However, the transportation model can be applied to several other interesting problems. One of the more interesting applications of the transportation model is for production and inventory scheduling. The following example will demonstrate this unique application.

Example 5.2   A Manufacturing Company Production Schedule

A manufacturing company desires to develop a production schedule for the following year, by quarters. The production capacity, the product demand, the unit production cost for each period, and the per unit cost of holding excess units in inventory are as follows:

Quarter	Production Capacity (in units)	Product Demand (in units)	Unit Production Cost	Holding Cost per Unit (20% production cost)
1	650	400	$5.00	$1.00
2	650	600	$6.50	$1.30
3	650	500	$7.25	$1.45
4	650	750	$9.00	N/A

Note that whereas the production capacity for the firm is constant at 650 units per quarter, the units demanded per quarter reflect fluctuations in the amounts contracted for from quarter to quarter. The increasing unit production costs reflect inflation and union-negotiated wage costs. The holding cost is estimated to be a standard 20% of the cost of producing the product. The problem is further characterized by insufficient production

capacity to meet demand in the fourth quarter. The company desires to develop a
duction schedule to meet demand with existing production capacity at minimum
duction and inventory holding costs.

The transportation tableau, including the optimal solution for this problem
shown in Table 5.32.

Table 5.32 *Transportation Tableau and Optimal Solution for a Production and Inventory Problem*

From \ To	1	2	3	4	Dummy	Supply
1	5 400	6	7	8 250	0	650
2	M	6.5 600	7.8	9.1	0 50	650
3	M	M	7.25 500	8.7 150	0	650
4	M	M	M	9.0 350	0 300	650
Demand	400	600	500	750	350	2600

The sources given along the left side of the transportation tableau represent the qua
ters in which the product is produced, and the destinations given across the top of th
tableau represent the quarters in which the product is demanded. Notice that the tablea
is unbalanced, and therefore a dummy column has been added to reflect the fact tha
total production capacity (2600 units) exceeds the total demand of 2250 units by 35
units.

The cell-cost values along the diagonal from the upper left to the lower right of th
tableau represent the unit production costs. The cell-cost values to the right of the diag
onal (excluding the dummy column) include the production cost plus the per unit cos
of holding inventory for the indicated number of periods. For example, the cell cost fo
x_{13} of $7 includes the production cost of $5 plus the inventory holding cost of $1 pe
period ($2 total holding cost). The dummy column cell-cost values are all zeros, a
explained previously in this chapter. The cell-cost values to the left of the diagonal are
all M, since it is not considered possible to produce products in one period to mee
demand in a prior period. For example, it is not possible to meet the demand of perioc
1 with production in period 3; therefore, $c_{31} = M$. (The student may observe that all of
the cells to the left of the diagonal could represent a problem with backordering allowed.)

Interpreting the solution given in Table 5.32, we find that 650 units will be produced in the first quarter, of which 400 units will be used to meet demand in quarter 1
and 250 units will be held in inventory to meet demand in the fourth quarter. In the
second quarter, 600 units will be produced to meet demand in the second quarter; the

50 units in the dummy column denote that the production capacity will be underutilized by 50 units. The remainder of the solution can be interpreted similarly.

Maximization Transportation Problem

Thus far we have considered only transportation problems in which the objective function represents cost and therefore is minimized. However, problems in which an objective function is maximized can be classified as transportation problems (i.e., they have the general transportation formulation). For example, consider a distribution network where the sources are warehouses and the destinations are retail outlets. If management desired to consider the profit associated with each combination of warehouse and retail outlet, profit would be maximized rather than cost minimized.

The solution procedure for a maximization transportation problem requires that the largest cell value (i.e., profit coefficient) in the tableau be selected and all other tableau cell values be subtracted from it. This creates a new tableau of relative "cost" values, so the problem can then be solved according to the normal transportation methods previously presented.

An alternative method is to retain the profit coefficients in the transportation tableau and reverse the decision rules for obtaining initial and optimal solutions. To determine the initial solution according to the least-cost method (i.e., the greatest-profit method), allocate to cells based on the largest c_{ij} values instead of the smallest. In the VAM, from the greatest c_{ij} value in a row or column subtract the next greatest. In the stepping-stone and MODI solution methods, allocate to cells that have the maximum positive c_{ij}^* values rather than those with the greatest negative c_{ij}^* values. Optimality is achieved in either method when all c_{ij}^* values are negative or zero.

Computer Solution of the Transportation Problem

Most management science software packages have the capability to solve transportation problems. Transportation problems can also be solved as linear programming models using software packages. We will demonstrate the solution of a transportation problem formulated as a linear programming model in the following section on sensitivity analysis.

The transportation programs included in management science software packages for the personal computer have the advantage of being in the familiar transportation model format, and their input requirements are frequently simpler than those of linear programming programs (which require inputting an entire linear programming model). However, the ability of these packages to display the solution in transportation tableaus is limited to models of small size (typically 6 sources and 6 destinations). For models of greater dimensions, the solution is displayed in a format similar to that of linear programming output.

Following is the program for Example 5.1 obtained using the AB:QM software package. The initial solution was obtained using VAM, and the model was solved with MODI. The output includes the model input data and solution results obtained by VAM and MODI.

```
Program: Transportation

Problem Title : Example 5.1

***** Input Data *****

Minimization Problem :

         |       1          2         3|    Supply
   ------------------------------------------------
    1    |     8.0        5.0       6.0|    120.0
    2    |    15.0       10.0      12.0|     80.0
    3    |     3.0        9.0      10.0|     80.0
   ------------------------------------------------
   Demand|   150.0       70.0      60.0|


***** Program Output *****


Initial Solution by VAM
         |       1          2         3|    Supply
   ------------------------------------------------
    1    |    70.0        0.0      50.0|    120.0
    2    |     0.0       70.0      10.0|     80.0
    3    |    80.0        0.0       0.0|     80.0
   ------------------------------------------------
   Demand|   150.0       70.0      60.0|    280.0

Initial Solution    :              1920.0


Optimal Solution by MODI
         |       1          2         3|    Supply
   ------------------------------------------------
    1    |    70.0        0.0      50.0|    120.0
    2    |     0.0       70.0      10.0|     80.0
    3    |    80.0        0.0       0.0|     80.0
   ------------------------------------------------
   Demand|   150.0       70.0      60.0|    280.0

Optimal Solution    :              1920.0

< Initial solution is the Optimal solution >


***** End of Output *****
```

Sensitivity Analysis for Transportation Problems

The same type of sensitivity analysis performed on linear programming models in Chapter 4 to determine b_i and c_j ranges can be accomplished for a transportation problem when it is in a linear programming format. The output on page 207 is the linear programming solution for Example 5.1, including postoptimality analysis, using AB:QM.

Notice that variable names are denoted consecutively from x_1 to x_9, which is slightly different than the double subscripted variables shown on page 179 in the linear program-

```
Program: Linear Programming

Problem Title : Example 5.1

***** Input Data *****

Min.  Z =  8x1 + 5x2 + 6x3 + 15x4 + 10x5 + 12x6 + 3x7 + 9x8 + 10x9


Subject to

C1    1x1 + 1x2 + 1x3 = 120
C2    1x4 + 1x5 + 1x6 = 80
C3    1x7 + 1x8 + 1x9 = 80
C4    1x1 + 1x4 + 1x7 = 150
C5    1x2 + 1x5 + 1x8 = 70
C6    1x3 + 1x6 + 1x9 = 60

***** Program Output *****

Final Optimal Solution At Simplex Tableau : 6

Z =    1920.000

-------------------------------------------------
Variable         Value        Reduced Cost
-------------------------------------------------
   x 1           70.000           0.000
   x 2            0.000           1.000
   x 3           50.000           0.000
   x 4            0.000           1.000
   x 5           70.000           0.000
   x 6           10.000           0.000
   x 7           80.000           0.000
   x 8            0.000          10.000
   x 9            0.000           9.000
-------------------------------------------------
```

Objective Coefficient Ranges

Variables	Lower Limit	Current Values	Upper Limit	Allowable Increase	Allowable Decrease
x 1	-1.000	8.000	9.000	1.000	9.000
x 2	4.000	5.000	No limit	No limit	1.000
x 3	5.000	6.000	7.000	1.000	1.000
x 4	14.000	15.000	No limit	No limit	1.000
x 5	No limit	10.000	11.000	1.000	No limit
x 6	11.000	12.000	13.000	1.000	1.000
x 7	No limit	3.000	12.000	9.000	No limit
x 8	-1.000	9.000	No limit	No limit	10.000
x 9	1.000	10.000	No limit	No limit	9.000

Right Hand Side Ranges

Constraints	Lower Limit	Current Values	Upper Limit	Allowable Increase	Allowable Decrease
C 1	50.000	120.000	120.000	0.000	70.000
C 2	70.000	80.000	80.000	0.000	10.000
C 3	0.000	80.000	80.000	0.000	80.000
C 4	150.000	150.000	No limit	No limit	0.000
C 5	70.000	70.000	80.000	10.000	0.000
C 6	60.000	60.000	130.000	70.000	0.000

ming formulation of this model; otherwise the model is the same. The sensitivity analysis ranges are interpreted the same as was the case in Chapter 4. For example, the range for the fifth constraint (i.e., demand at construction site 2) is shown to be between 70 and 80. If demand at destination 2 was increased to 90 truckloads (requiring that the demand constraints be changed to $\leq$ since the problem is now unbalanced), the optimal solution basis would change as follows:

```
Program: Linear Programming

Problem Title : Example 5.1

***** Input Data *****

Min.  Z =  8x1 + 5x2 + 6x3 + 15x4 + 10x5 + 12x6 + 3x7 + 9x8 + 10x9


Subject to

C1    1x1 + 1x2 + 1x3 = 120
C2    1x4 + 1x5 + 1x6 = 80
C3    1x7 + 1x8 + 1x9 = 80
C4    1x1 + 1x4 + 1x7 <= 150
C5    1x2 + 1x5 + 1x8 <= 90
C6    1x3 + 1x6 + 1x9 <= 60

***** Program Output *****

Final Optimal Solution At Simplex Tableau : 5

Z =    1850.000


----------------------------------------------------
Variable         Value         Reduced Cost
----------------------------------------------------
   x 1          50.000            0.000
   x 2          10.000            0.000
   x 3          60.000            0.000
   x 4           0.000            2.000
   x 5          80.000            0.000
   x 6           0.000            1.000
   x 7          80.000            0.000
   x 8           0.000            9.000
   x 9           0.000            9.000
----------------------------------------------------
Constraint  Slack/Surplus   Shadow Price
----------------------------------------------------
   C 4          20.000            0.000
   C 5           0.000            3.000
   C 6           0.000            2.000
----------------------------------------------------
```

Likewise, consider a case where the firm might locate an alternative mode of transport, or route, from plant 1 to site 2, which would reduce the transportation cost from $5 per unit to $3 per unit. This change falls outside the limits of the sensitivity range for c_{12}, which is between $4 and ∞ as shown above, and as such, will result in a new solution basis, as follows:

```
***** Program Output *****

Final Optimal Solution At Simplex Tableau : 6

Z =    1870.000

-----------------------------------------------
Variable          Value          Reduced Cost
-----------------------------------------------
  x 1            50.000            0.000
  x 2            70.000            0.000
  x 3             0.000            1.000
  x 4            20.000            0.000
  x 5             0.000            0.000
  x 6            60.000            0.000
  x 7            80.000            0.000
  x 8             0.000           11.000
  x 9             0.000           10.000
-----------------------------------------------
```

Specific changes in the transportation model parameters can also be affected by using the editing commands of AB:QM. The existing cost, supply, and demand parameters can be changed by editing the model. Also, by using the F7 (InsRow), F8 (InsCol), F9 (DelRow) and F10 (DelCol) keys, new destinations and sources can be added or deleted to the original model.

THE TRANSSHIPMENT PROBLEM

An important extension of the transportation model formulation is the **transshipment problem,** in which items are shipped from sources to intermediate "transshipment" points and then are shipped on to their ultimate destinations. For example, items could be shipped from several factories to one or more warehouses and subsequently transshipped to several retail locations. The most general case would be one in which sources and destinations could be intermediate points of shipment between other sources and destinations. The transshipment problem can be solved via the transportation solution methods, with a few minor adjustments to the problem formulation.

Example 5.3   Transportation Model of a Transshipment Problem

Consider the basic transportation problem example in tableau form in Table 5.33.

Suppose each of the i sources and j destinations can also be an intermediate point of transshipment between another source and destination, yielding the modified tableau in Table 5.34, which shows all transshipment costs.

The c_{ij} values for the new cells are the transshipment costs as determined by management. The costs are often different for shipment in opposite directions because of alternative modes of transportation and route conditions. For example, the cost for the route from $i = 1$ to $j = 3$ is \$7 per unit, whereas the cost of going in the opposite direction,

An Application of the Transportation Model: Routing Naval Military Inductees in Thailand

Thailand inducts men into its compulsory military service four times per year. Men living in the coastal provinces are inducted into the Navy. When men are initially called into the Navy they report to a local drafting center and then are transported to the main naval base near Bangkok. If a man is from a northern province he is transported directly to the main naval base, while if a draftee is from a southern province, he is sent overland from one of 36 drafting centers to one of four branch bases, and, then transported by ship to the main naval base.

The assignment and transportation of draftees between these various facilities resulted several problems. First, it was desired to know how many men should be assigned and transported to each branch base, and second, given a solution to the first problem, which shi should be used to transport the men to the ma naval base. The solution to the first problem provided the transportation requirements for th more complex second problem.

The first problem was a standard transportation problem for which the following data was available: the number of men to be transported from each of the 36 drafting centers

Table 5.33 Basic Transportation Tableau

From (i) \ To (j)	1	2	3	Supply
1	12	11	7	70
2	8	6	14	80
3	9	10	12	50
Demand	60	100	40	200

from $j = 3$ to $i = 1$, is $10 per unit. The c_{ij} values are zero on the diagonal from the upper left to the lower right, since there is no shipping from a source to itself ($i = i$) o from a destination to itself ($j = j$).

The original problem is located in the upper-right-hand quadrant of Table 5.34 The new cells represent the possibility of intermediate transshipments. For example, cell $i = 1$ to cell $i = 3$ indicates that units can be shipped from source 1 to source 3 at a cost of $8 per unit before being shipped to a final destination, j. However, the transshipment tableau is incomplete in its present form.

The supply and demand "rim values" for the expanded tableau must reflect the fact that each source and destination could serve as a transshipment point for all units transported (total demand, which equals total supply), which is 200 units in this example. Thus, the rim values for demand at sources and supply at destinations are set at 200 units

e capacity at each branch base, and, the nsportation cost per draftee from each center to ch branch base. The problem was solved using standard transportation software package.

The original manual procedure for ansporting men to branch bases was to send ch man to the nearest base. This occasionally sulted in base capacities being exceeded, which quired that men be sent from these bases to ases with excess capacity. The solution of the ansportation model for the first problem educed the cost and time delays resulting from he extra trips required to redistribute the draftees. The solution also provided the input for the

second problem of deploying the men from the branch bases to the main naval base. This type of problem is known more commonly as a vehicle routing problem. The approach was to first develop a list of routes that nine ships might take and then develop a model to determine the number of times each route is used. The objective function was unique in that it was not to minimize distance or cost but to minimize the number of ships required for transporting draftees (leaving the maximum number of ships available for naval defense). An integer programming model was developed for the second problem and was solved using LINDO.

ource: P. Choypeng et al., "Optimal Ship Routing and Personnel Assignment for Naval Recruitment in Thailand," *Interfaces,* 6, no. 4 (July–August 1986): 47–52.

each, to establish upper limits on transshipments through those locations. Also, 200 must be added to the original supply values at sources, to reflect the fact that the total quantity potentially available equals the original amount available plus the maximum possible amount that could be transshipped through that location. Finally, 200 must also be

Table 5.34 *Transshipment Problem in Expanded Tableau Format*

From \ To		Sources			Destinations			Supply
		$i = 1$	$i = 2$	$i = 3$	$j = 1$	$j = 2$	$j = 3$	
Sources	$i = 1$	0	14	8	12	11	7	70
	$i = 2$	3	0	5	8	6	14	80
	$i = 3$	7	10	0	9	10	12	50
Destinations	$j = 1$	2	1	11	0	8	3	
	$j = 2$	6	5	3	1	0	2	
	$j = 3$	10	9	11	7	2	0	
	Demand				60	100	40	200

added to the original demand values at the destinations, to reflect the fact that the upper limit on demand is the quantity to be retained at each location plus the quantity to be transshipped through the location. The resulting modified supply and demand values are given in Table 5.35.

Table 5.35 *Complete Transshipment Tableau*

To \\ From	D1 $i = 1$	D2 $i = 2$	D3 $i = 3$	D4 $j = 1$	D5 $j = 2$	D6 $j = 3$	Supply
S1: $i = 1$	0	14	8	12	11	7	270
S2: $i = 2$	3	0	5	8	6	14	280
S3: $i = 3$	7	10	0	9	10	12	250
S4: $j = 1$	2	1	11	0	8	3	200
S5: $j = 2$	6	5	3	1	0	2	200
S6: $j = 3$	10	9	11	7	2	0	200
Demand	200	200	200	260	300	240	1400

Computer Solution of the Transshipment Problem

Table 5.35 is now in the form of a regular transportation model and can be solved as such. The problem was solved using AB:QM as shown on page 213.

Examining the program output, we see that all the values on the zero-cost diagonal can be ignored, since they represent items that are not transshipped. The remaining values represent the optimal solution. The transshipment network given by the optimal solution is presented in Figure 5.5.

Figure 5.5 illustrates the intermediate-point shipping of the transshipment problem. It shows that 70 units are shipped directly from source 1 (S1, $i = 1$) to destination 3 (D6, $j = 3$). However, 30 of those units are subsequently transshipped from destination 3 (S6, $j = 3$) to destination 2 (D5, $j = 2$), leaving a net total of 40 units, the amount demanded, at destination 3. The 30 units transshipped from destination 3 to destination 2 are combined with 80 units shipped directly from source 2 (S2, $i = 2$) to destination 2 (D5, $j = 2$), for a total of 110 units. However, 10 of these units are transshipped from destination 2 to destination 1, leaving a net total of the 100 units demanded at destination 2. The 10 units transshipped from destination 2 are combined with 50 units shipped from source 3, resulting in 60 total units at destination 1. The total minimum cost of the transshipment problem is $1490.

Program: Transportation

Problem Title : Transshipment Example

***** Input Data *****

Minimization Problem :

	1	2	3	4	5	6|	Supply
1	0.0	14.0	8.0	12.0	11.0	7.0|	270.0
2	3.0	0.0	5.0	8.0	6.0	14.0|	280.0
3	7.0	10.0	0.0	9.0	10.0	12.0|	250.0
4	2.0	1.0	11.0	0.0	8.0	3.0|	200.0
5	6.0	5.0	3.0	1.0	0.0	2.0|	200.0
6	10.0	9.0	11.0	7.0	2.0	0.0|	200.0
Demand|	200.0	200.0	200.0	260.0	300.0	240.0|	

***** Program Output *****

Initial Solution by VAM

	1	2	3	4	5	6|	Supply
1	200.0	0.0	0.0	0.0	0.0	70.0|	270.0
2	0.0	200.0	0.0	0.0	80.0	0.0|	280.0
3	0.0	0.0	200.0	0.0	50.0	0.0|	250.0
4	0.0	0.0	0.0	200.0	0.0	0.0|	200.0
5	0.0	0.0	0.0	60.0	140.0	0.0|	200.0
6	0.0	0.0	0.0	0.0	30.0	170.0|	200.0
Demand|	200.0	200.0	200.0	260.0	300.0	240.0|	1400.0

Initial Solution   :   1590.0

Optimal Solution by MODI

	1	2	3	4	5	6|	Supply
1	200.0	0.0	0.0	0.0	0.0	70.0|	270.0
2	0.0	200.0	0.0	0.0	80.0	0.0|	280.0
3	0.0	0.0	200.0	50.0	0.0	0.0|	250.0
4	0.0	0.0	0.0	200.0	0.0	0.0|	200.0
5	0.0	0.0	0.0	10.0	190.0	0.0|	200.0
6	0.0	0.0	0.0	0.0	30.0	170.0|	200.0
Demand|	200.0	200.0	200.0	260.0	300.0	240.0|	1400.0

Optimal Solution   :   1490.0

***** End of Output *****

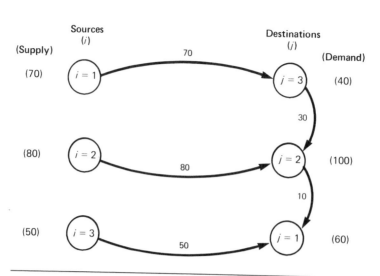

Figure 5.5 Transshipment Solution

THE ASSIGNMENT PROBLEM

An important variation of the transportation problem is the assignment problem, where there are equal numbers of sources and destinations and each source supply and destination demand equals *one*. Consequently, the quantity allocated, or assigned, must be either zero or one. The general linear programming formulation of an assignment problem with m sources and n destinations is

$$\text{Minimize } Z = \sum_{i=1}^{m} \sum_{j=1}^{n} c_{ij} x_{ij}$$

subject to

$$\sum_{j=1}^{n} x_{ij} = 1$$

$$\sum_{i=1}^{m} x_{ij} = 1$$

$$x_{ij} \geqslant 0$$

Because of its simple structure, the assignment problem can be solved most efficiently by its own unique method rather than by the previously described transportation methods. The assignment method is based on a theorem first proved by a Hungarian mathematician, Dr. Konig, and is, therefore, sometimes referred to as the **Hungarian method of assignment.**

Example 5.4   A Machine Operator Assignment Problem

The following example will be employed to demonstrate the assignment problem and its solution. Three operators are available to be assigned to work on three machines. Each operator is able to produce an item on a particular machine at a different per unit cost. For example, operator 1 can produce an item on machine 1 at a cost of $7, whereas it costs $8 to have operator 2 produce the same item on machine 1. The differing costs are a result of the different training and experience of the operators. The cost of each operator, i, working on each machine, j, is given as follows:

Operator i	Machine j 1	2	3	Supply
1	$7	$3	$5	1
2	8	9	2	1
3	9	6	8	1
Demand	1	1	1	3

The objective is to assign the operators to machines so that the minimum total cost is achieved.

If this problem is solved using standard transportation solution methods, the initial solution will be degenerate. (This can be easily verified by setting up the problem in the transportation tableau and determining the initial solution by any of the three methods.) However, the special characteristics of the assignment problem enable it to be solved in a more efficient manner.

The Assignment Method

The first step in the assignment method of solution is to develop an **opportunity cost table.** An opportunity cost is analogous to the penalty cost discussed in the VAM. In other words, if the wrong course of action is taken, a lost opportunity (or cost) results. This table is constructed by first subtracting the minimum value in each row from all other values in the same row. This action is referred to as a **row reduction.** For example, in row 1, the best course of action is to assign operator 1 to machine 2, since this results in the minimum cost of $3. If operator 1 were assigned to machine 1 instead, an opportunity cost (i.e., a penalty) of $4 would result, the difference in cost between the best course of action and the next best alternative.

The assignment tableau for the example problem, with row reductions made by subtracting 3 in row 1, 2 in row 2, and 6 in row 3, is shown in Table 5.36. (Note that since supply and demand are always one, the demand row and the supply column are deleted from assignment tableaus.) The fact that constant values are subtracted from each row has no effect on the optimal solution. Since the whole row is reduced by the same amount, the relationship between variables (i.e., their relative magnitude) is not changed.

Table 5.36 *Assignment Tableau with Row Reductions*

Operator \ Machine	1	2	3
1	4	0	2
2	6	7	0
3	3	0	2

Thus, the derivation of a zero in a row or column cell signifies the best course of action relative to other cells.

Referring to Table 5.36, notice that operator 1 can be assigned to machine 1 at a revised penalty cost of $4. However, this is not the lowest penalty cost assignment to machine 1, since operator 3 can be assigned to machine 1 at the lower penalty cost of $3. Therefore, an erroneous decision to assign operator 1 to machine 1 would result in a column opportunity cost of $1 ($4 − 3). The procedure for making row reductions is repeated for each column, resulting in a series of column reductions. Subtracting 3 from column 1, 0 from column 2, and 0 from column 3 results in the completed opportunity cost table (Table 5.37), with both row and column reductions.

Table 5.37 *Completed Opportunity Cost Table*

Machine Operator	1	2	3
1	1·	0	2
2	3	7	0
3	0	0	2

Although the values in the completed opportunity cost table are not the same as those in the original tableau (i.e., the original c_{ij} values), the relative magnitude between the cell values remains the same, since we subtracted constants from the rows and columns. The purpose of developing the opportunity cost table is to obtain at least one zero in each row and column, so that an assignment can be made with no opportunity cost resulting. In order to minimize the cost, assignments are made to those cells with zero values. Therefore, the optimal assignment is

Operator	Machine	Cost
1	2	$3
2	3	2
3	1	9
		$14

This problem was constructed so that the optimal solution was achieved upon completion of the opportunity cost table—three unique assignments could be made. Next we will consider the test for optimality and a solution procedure for the case in which an assignment tableau is not optimal. When this situation arises, an iterative solution process must be employed.

Solution Procedure for Nonoptimal Tableaus

Consider the example cost table in Table 5.38 for the assignment of four operators to four machines.

Table 5.38 *Initial Assignment Tableau*

Operator \ Machine	1	2	3	4
1	10	15	16	18
2	14	13	16	10
3	11	9	8	18
4	13	13	11	9

Row and column reductions for this cost schedule result in the opportunity cost table in Table 5.39.

Table 5.39 *Assignment Tableau with Row and Column Reductions*

Operator \ Machine	1	2	3	4
1	0	4	6	8
2	4	2	6	0
3	3	0	0	10
4	4	3	2	0

For an optimal assignment to exist, Table 5.39 must result in four unique assignments. Upon inspection it can be seen that this is not the case. Both operators 2 and 4 have an assignment to machine 4 *only;* thus, there is only one unique assignment for these two operators. A convenient way of determining whether the appropriate number of unique assignments exists is to draw, horizontally and/or vertically, the minimum number of lines required to cross out all zeros. If the minimum number of lines drawn is equal to the number of rows (m) or columns (n), then an optimal assignment is present. Performing this operation on the opportunity cost table (Table 5.39) results in Table 5.40.

Table 5.40 *Assignment Tableau with Line Tests for Independent Zeros*

Operator \ Machine	1	2	3	4
1	0	4	6	8
2	4	2	6	0
3	3	0	0	10
4	4	3	2	0

m = n = 4, but have 3 lines

go to step 4

As can be seen, only three lines are required to cross out all zeros (although these three lines could have been drawn in different positions); thus, the required four unique assignments do not exist. In order to progress toward optimality, the next step is to subtract the smallest uncrossed cell value from all other uncrossed cell values. This same minimum value is added to every value at the intersection of two lines. Thus, 2 is subtracted from the first three values in rows 2 and 4, and is added to 8 at the intersection of row 1 and column 4, and to 10 at the intersection of row 3 and column 4, as shown in Table 5.41.

Table 5.41 *Adjusted Assignment Tableau*

Operator \ Machine	1	2	3	4
1	0	4	6	10
2	2	0	4	0
3	3	0	0	12
4	2	1	0	0

The procedure of crossing out all zeros with the minimum number of lines serves to protect the existing optimal assignments from further alteration in the subsequent steps required to attain an optimal solution. The next step of subtracting the minimum uncrossed cell value from all other uncrossed cell values and then adding this value to each cell value where two lines intersect is actually a shortcut derivative of a more detailed procedure for revising the nonoptimal opportunity cost table. The more detailed procedure requires that *all* cell values in the tableau be reduced by the minimum uncrossed value, which is 2 in Table 5.40. This would result in a negative value of -2 in the cells where 2 was subtracted from zero, such as in the cell at the intersection of column 1 and row 1. In order to restore all positive or zero values to the tableau, a value of 2 would subsequently have to be added to all rows and columns in which a negative value of two was located. This would result in the same tableau as shown in Table 5.41.

The test for four unique assignments must be repeated. In this case, it now requires a minimum of four lines to cross out all zeros, regardless of how they are drawn. Analyzing Table 5.41, we find that the optimal assignments are as follows:

Operator	Machine	Cost
1	1	$10
2	4	10
3	2	9
4	3	11
		$40

However, there is also a second feasible optimal assignment for this problem (i.e., there are multiple optimal solutions):

Operator	Machine	Cost
1	1	$10
2	2	13
3	3	8
4	4	9
		$40

The solution procedure for the assignment method can be summarized as follows:

1. Develop the opportunity cost table through row and column reductions.

2. Draw the minimum number of horizontal and/or vertical lines necessary to cross out all zeros. If the number of lines satisfies the condition $m = n$, the optimal assignment has been determined. If not, perform step 3.

3. Subtract the minimum uncrossed value from all uncrossed cell values and add this same amount to all values at the intersection of lines.

4. Repeat the test for $m = n$ unique assignments.

Prohibited Assignments

It may occur that an assignment of an operator to a facility is prohibited—perhaps because of a physical impairment. In such cases, a value of M should be assigned to the cell representing the prohibited assignment and the solution method continued normally.

Unequal Supply and Demand

An important requirement of the assignment problem is that the number of rows, m, equal the number of columns, n. In realistic situations, however, this condition may not occur naturally. Often the number of available operators will exceed the number of machines, or vice versa. In such cases, a dummy row or column is added to balance the requirements. The procedure is the same as that utilized for the unbalanced transportation problem. The unit assignment costs for the dummy row or column will all be zero.

The cost table in Table 5.42 represents a situation where there are 4 operators and 3 machines. In the optimal solution, one of the operators will be assigned to the dummy machine.

Table 5.42 *An Unbalanced Assignment Tableau (Supply > Demand)*

Operator \ Machine	1	2	3	Dummy
1	7	10	4	0
2	9	8	6	0
3	11	3	2	0
4	7	6	3	0

A Maximization Assignment Problem

Thus far we have considered only assignment problems in which the objective function represents cost and, therefore, is minimized. However, problems in which an objective function is maximized can be classified as assignment problems (i.e., they have the general assignment formulation). For example, consider a problem in which operators are assigned to machines based on their differing productivity rates (i.e., units produced per time period). In this case, the objective would be to maximize the total productivity for all operators, rather than minimize total cost.

The solution procedure for a maximization assignment problem requires that the largest cell value (profit coefficient) in the tableau be selected, and all other tableau cell values be subtracted from it. This creates a new tableau of relative "cost" values, so that the problem can then be solved according to the normal assignment solution method.

Computer Solution of the Assignment Problem

We will employ the AB:QM package in conjunction with the example shown in Table 5.38, wherein four operators are assigned to four machines. The AB:QM input data and program output is shown below.

```
Program: Assignment

Problem Title : Operator/Machine Example

***** Input Data *****

Minimization Problem :

    |     1       2       3       4
  --------------------------------------
  1 |   10.0    15.0    16.0    18.0
  2 |   14.0    13.0    16.0    10.0
  3 |   11.0     9.0     8.0    18.0
  4 |   13.0    13.0    11.0     9.0
  --------------------------------------



***** Program Output *****

Final Revised Cost Table

    |     1       2       3       4
  --------------------------------------
  1 |    0.0     2.0     4.0     8.0
  2 |    4.0     0.0     4.0     0.0
  3 |    5.0     0.0     0.0    12.0
  4 |    4.0     1.0     0.0     0.0
  --------------------------------------
```

```
Optimum Solution :          40.0

        |  1   2   3   4
        -------------------
    1 |  1   0   0   0
    2 |  0   1   0   0
    3 |  0   0   1   0
    4 |  0   0   0   1
        -------------------


***** End of Output *****
```

SUMMARY
In this chapter, some of the more interesting and useful variations of the general linear programming problem were analyzed: the transportation, transshipment, and assignment problems. Although these variations were discussed in connection with a limited range of examples, they have many useful applications in the real world.

This chapter completes the presentation and analysis of *linear* programming; however, the field of mathematical programming contains several more advanced and useful techniques, some of which will be discussed in subsequent chapters.

REFERENCES

ACKOFF, R. L., and SASIENI, M. W. *Fundamentals of Operations Research*. New York: John Wiley & Sons, 1968.

BAZARAA, M. S., and JARVIS, J. J. *Linear Programming and Network Flows*. New York: John Wiley & Sons, 1977.

BRADLEY, S. P.; HAX, A. C.; and MAGNANTI, T. L. *Applied Mathematical Programming*. Reading, Massachusetts: Addison-Wesley Publishing Company, 1977.

CHARNES, A., and COOPER, W. W. *Management Models and Industrial Applications of Linear Programming*. New York: John Wiley & Sons, 1961.

CHURCHMAN, C. W.; ACKOFF, R. L.; and ARNOFF, E. L. *Introduction to Operations Research*. New York: John Wiley & Sons, 1957.

COOPER, L., and STEINBERG, D. *Methods and Applications of Linear Programming*. Philadelphia: W. B. Saunders Company, 1974.

DANTZIG, G. B. *Linear Programming and Extensions*. Princeton, New Jersey: Princeton University Press, 1963.

GAVER, D. P., and THOMPSON, G. L. *Programming and Probability Models in Operations Research*. Belmont, California: Wadsworth Publishing Company, 1973.

HILLIER, F. S., and LIEBERMAN, G. J. *Introduction to Operations Research*. 4th ed. San Francisco: Holden-Day, 1986.

HITCHCOCK, F. L. "The Distribution of a Product from Several Sources to Numerous Localities." *Journal of Mathematics and Physics* 20 (1941): 224–30.

HOFFMANN, T. R. *Production: Management and Manufacturing Systems*. Belmont, California: Wadsworth Publishing Company, 1967.

KOOPMANS, T. C., ed. *Activity Analysis of Production and Allocation*. Cowles Commission Monograph No. 13. New York: John Wiley & Sons, 1951.

KWAK, N. K. *Mathematical Programming with Business Applications*. New York: McGraw-Hill, 1973.

LEVIN, R. I., and LAMONE, R. *Linear Programming for Management Decisions*. Homewood, Illinois: Richard D. Irwin, 1969.

LLEWELLYN, R. W. *Linear Programming*. New York: Holt, Rinehart and Winston, 1964.

LOOMBA, N. P., and TURBAN, E. *Applied Programming for Management*. New York: Holt, Rinehart and Winston, 1974.

LUENBERGER, D. G. *Introduction to Linear and Non-Linear Programming*. Reading, Massachusetts: Addison-Wesley Publishing Company, 1973.

MCMILLAN, C. *Mathematical Programming*. 2d ed. New York: John Wiley & Sons, 1975.

NAYLOR, T. H.; BYRNE, E. T.; and VERNON, J. M. *Introduction to Linear Programming: Methods and Cases*. Belmont, California: Wadsworth Publishing Company, 1971.

ORCHARD-HAYS, W. *Advanced Linear Programming Computing Techniques*. New York: McGraw-Hill, 1968.

ROTHENBERG, R. I. *Linear Programming*. New York: Elsevier North-Holland, 1979.

SIMMONS, D. M. *Linear Programming for Operations Research*. San Francisco: Holden-Day, 1972.

TAHA, H. A. *Operations Research: An Introduction*. 5th ed. New York: Macmillan, 1992.

PROBLEMS

1. Example 2.3 in Chapter 2 is a transportation problem in which an appliance manufacturer ships refrigerators from warehouses to retail stores. Solve this problem, using the least-cost method to determine the initial solution and then the stepping-stone solution method. Compute total minimum cost.

2. A given transportation problem has the following costs and supply and demand requirements.

From \ To	1	2	3	4	Supply
1	$ 7	$ 6	$ 2	$12	70
2	3	9	8	7	40
3	10	4	11	5	100
Demand	30	60	90	30	210

    a. Find the initial solution using the northwest corner method, the least-cost method, and Vogel's approximation method. Compute total cost for each.

    b. Using the VAM initial solution, find the optimal solution using the stepping-stone method. Compute total minimum cost for the solution.

3. Solve the following transportation cost problem, using VAM to determine the initial solution and then the MODI solution method. Compute total minimum cost.

To From	1	2	3	4	Supply
1	20	17	16	21	150
2	15	10	18	12	90
3	12	22	14	15	210
Demand	125	100	120	105	450

4. A truck rental firm has accumulated excess trucks at three of its truck-leasing outlets as follows:

Leasing Outlet	Excess Trucks
1. Atlanta	70
2. St. Louis	115
3. Greensboro	60
	245

The firm has four outlets that have a shortage of rental trucks as follows:

Leasing Outlet	Truck Shortage
A. New Orleans	80
B. Cincinnati	50
C. Louisville	90
D. Pittsburgh	25
	245

The firm desires to transfer trucks from those outlets with excess trucks to those with a shortage at the minimum total cost. The following costs of transporting the trucks from city to city have been determined.

To From	A	B	C	D
1	$ 70	$80	$45	$90
2	120	40	30	75
3	110	60	70	80

Solve this problem, using the least-cost method to determine the initial solution and then the stepping-stone solution method. Compute total minimum cost.

5. In problem 4, what would be the effect on the optimal solution if there was no shortage of rental trucks at the New Orleans outlet?

6. Solve the following transportation problem:

To From	1	2	3	Supply
1	$40	$10	$20	800
2	15	20	10	500
3	20	25	30	600
Demand	1050	500	650	

7. A given transportation problem has the following costs and supply and demand requirements:

To From	1	2	3	Supply
A	$6	$7	$4	100
B	5	3	6	180
C	8	5	7	200
Demand	135	175	170	

Find the initial solution using the least-cost method and Vogel's approximation method. Is the VAM solution optimal? Explain.

8. a. Solve the following transportation problem, using VAM to find the initial solution and then the stepping-stone method.

To From	1	2	3	Supply
A	$ 6	$9	$M	130
B	12	3	5	70
C	4	8	11	100
Demand	80	110	60	

b. Formulate this problem as a general linear programming model.

9. Problem 18 at the end of Chapter 2 is a transportation problem in which grain cooperatives in Kansas, Nebraska, and Iowa ship grain to warehouses in Louisiana, Texas, and Georgia. Solve this problem, using VAM to determine the initial solution and then the MODI solution method. Compute total minimum cost.

10. Solve the following linear programming problem:

$$\text{Minimize } Z = 3x_{11} + 12x_{12} + 8x_{13} + 10x_{21} + 5x_{22} + 6x_{23} + 6x_{31} + 7x_{32}$$
$$+ 10x_{33}$$

subject to

$$x_{11} + x_{12} + x_{13} = 90$$
$$x_{21} + x_{22} + x_{23} = 30$$
$$x_{31} + x_{32} + x_{33} = 100$$
$$x_{11} + x_{21} + x_{31} \leq 70$$
$$x_{12} + x_{22} + x_{32} \leq 110$$
$$x_{13} + x_{23} + x_{33} \leq 80$$
$$x_{ij} \geq 0$$

11. A national beer company has breweries in two cities that can supply the following quantities of draft beer to its distributors each month:

Brewery	Monthly Supply (barrels)
A. Tampa	3500
B. St. Louis	5000
	8500

These breweries supply draft beer to distributors in six states, which have the following monthly demand:

Distributor	Monthly Demand (barrels)
1. Tennessee	1600
2. Georgia	1800
3. North Carolina	1500
4. South Carolina	950
5. Kentucky	1250
6. Virginia	1400
	8500

The following shipping costs per barrel have been determined:

To From	1	2	3	4	5	6
A	$.50	$.35	$.60	$.45	$.80	$.75
B	.25	.65	.40	.55	.20	.65

Solve this problem, using VAM to determine the initial solution and then the stepping-stone solution method. Compute total minimum cost.

12. In problem 11 in this chapter, the beer company has negotiated a new shipping contract with a trucking firm between its Tampa brewery and its distributor in Kentucky that reduces the shipping cost from $.80 per barrel to $.65 per barrel. How does this cost change affect the optimal solution?

13. a. Find the initial solution to the following transportation problem, using the least-cost method.

To From	1	2	3	Supply
A	$ 6	$9	$ 7	130
B	12	3	5	70
C	4	8	11	100
Demand	80	110	60	

b. Solve using the stepping-stone method.

14. Steel is produced and then stored in warehouses in three cities.

Warehouse Location	Weekly Production (tons)
A. Pittsburgh	150
B. Birmingham	210
C. Gary	320
	680

These plants supply steel to markets in four cities, which have the following demand:

Market Location	Weekly Demand (tons)
1. Detroit	130
2. St. Louis	70
3. Chicago	180
4. Norfolk	240
	620

The following shipping costs per ton have been determined:

To From	1	2	3	4
A	$14	$ 9	$16	$18
B	11	8	7	16
C	16	12	10	22

However, because of a truckers' strike, shipments are presently prohibited from Birmingham to Chicago.

a. Set up a transportation tableau for this problem and determine the initial solution. Identify the method used to find the initial solution.

b. Solve this problem using MODI.

c. Are there multiple optimal solutions? Explain. If there are alternative solutions, identify them.

d. Formulate this problem as a general linear programming model.

15. In problem 14 in this chapter, what would be the effect of a reduction in production capacity at the Gary location from 320 tons to 290 tons per week?

16. a. Set up the transportation tableau for the following linear programming problem, and determine the initial solution. Identify the method used to find the initial solution.

$$\text{Minimize } Z = 24x_{11} + 9x_{12} + 6x_{13} + 18x_{14} + 10x_{21} + 18x_{22}$$
$$+ 14x_{23} + 12x_{24} + 17x_{31} + 21x_{32} + 20x_{33} + Mx_{34}$$

subject to

$$x_{11} + x_{12} + x_{13} + x_{14} \leqslant 100$$
$$x_{21} + x_{22} + x_{23} + x_{24} \leqslant 180$$
$$x_{31} + x_{32} + x_{33} + x_{34} \leqslant 200$$
$$x_{11} + x_{21} + x_{31} = 120$$
$$x_{12} + x_{22} + x_{32} = 100$$
$$x_{13} + x_{23} + x_{33} = 90$$
$$x_{14} + x_{24} + x_{34} = 140$$
$$x_{ij} \geqslant 0$$

b. Solve this problem using MODI. Compute total minimum cost.

c. Are there multiple optimal solutions? Explain. If there are alternative solutions, identify them.

17. Tobacco is purchased and stored in warehouses in four cities at the end of each growing season.

Location	Capacity (tons)
A. Charlotte	90
B. Raleigh	50
C. Lexington	80
D. Danville	60
	280

These warehouses supply tobacco to companies in three cities, which have the following demand:

Plant	Demand (tons)
1. Richmond	120
2. Winston-Salem	100
3. Durham	110
	330

The following railroad shipping costs per ton have been determined:

To From	1	2	3
A	$ 7	$10	$ 5
B	12	9	4
C	7	3	11
D	9	5	7

However, because of railroad construction, shipments are presently prohibited from Charlotte to Richmond.

a. Set up the transportation tableau for this problem and determine the initial solution using VAM. Compute total cost.

b. Solve using MODI.

c. Are there multiple optimal solutions? Explain. If there are alternative solutions, identify them.

d. Formulate this problem as a linear programming model.

18. In problem 17, once the railroad construction is completed what will be the effect on the optimal shipping routes?

19. A national electronics firm sells microcomputers to universities and colleges on the east coast from three distribution warehouses. The firm is able to supply the following numbers of microcomputers to the universities by the beginning of the academic year:

Distribution Warehouse	Supply (microcomputers)
1. Richmond	420
2. Atlanta	610
3. Washington, D.C.	340
	1370

Four universities have the following demand for microcomputers that must be delivered and installed by the beginning of the academic year:

University	Demand (microcomputers)
A. Tech	520
B. A and M	250
C. State	400
D. Central	380
	1550

The shipping and installation costs per microcomputer from each distributor to each university are as follows:

To From	A	B	C	D
1	$22	$17	$30	$18
2	15	35	20	25
3	28	21	16	14

a. Set up the transportation tableau for this problem. Find the initial solution using VAM.

b. Solve for the optimal solution using MODI. Compute total minimum cost.

20. In problem 19, the electronics firm wants to better meet demand at the four universities it supplies. It is considering two alternatives: (1) expand its warehouse at Richmond to a capacity of 600 and contract with a new, larger shipping firm that will add $6 in handling and shipping cost per unit, or (2) leasing a new warehouse in Charlotte that can supply 300 units with shipping costs of $19 to Tech, $26 to A&M, $22 to State and $16 to Central. Ignoring capital costs (which are assumed to be approximately equal for both alternatives), which alternative should the firm select based solely on transportation costs?

21. The electronics firm in problem 19 has determined that when it is unable to meet the demand for microcomputers at the universities it supplies, the universities tend to purchase microcomputers elsewhere in the future. Thus, the firm has estimated a shortage cost for each microcomputer demanded but not supplied that reflects the loss of future sales and goodwill. These costs for each university are as follows:

University	Cost/Microcomputer
A. Tech	$40
B. A and M	65
C. State	25
D. Central	50

[handwritten annotation: "Instead of a "0"'s in the dummy cell's use these costs; use penalty cost."]

Solve problem 19 with these shortage costs included. Compute the total transportation cost and the total shortage cost.

22. a. Set up the transportation tableau for the following linear programming problem, and determine the initial solution using VAM.

Minimize $Z = 17x_{11} + 10x_{12} + 15x_{13} + 11x_{21} + 14x_{22} + 10x_{23} + 9x_{31}$
$+ 13x_{32} + 11x_{33} + 19x_{41} + 8x_{42} + 12x_{43}$

subject to

$x_{11} + x_{12} + x_{13} = 120$

$x_{21} + x_{22} + x_{23} = 70$ (continued)

$$x_{31} + x_{32} + x_{33} = 180$$
$$x_{41} + x_{42} + x_{43} = 30$$
$$x_{11} + x_{21} + x_{31} + x_{41} = 200$$
$$x_{12} + x_{22} + x_{32} + x_{42} = 120$$
$$x_{13} + x_{23} + x_{33} + x_{43} = 80$$

b. Solve using the stepping-stone method.

23. Oranges are grown, picked, and then stored in warehouses in Tampa, Miami, and Fresno. These warehouses supply oranges to markets in New York, Philadelphia, Chicago, and Boston. Following are the shipping costs per ton and the supply and demand requirements:

To From	New York	Philadelphia	Chicago	Boston	Supply
Tampa	$ 9	$14	$12	$17	200
Miami	11	10	6	10	200
Fresno	12	8	15	7	200
Demand	130	170	100	150	

Because of a distributors' agreement, shipments are prohibited from Miami to Chicago.

a. Set up the transportation tableau for this problem and determine the initial solution using the least-cost method.
b. Solve using MODI.
c. Are there multiple optimal solutions? Explain. If there are alternative solutions, identify them.
d. Formulate this problem as a linear programming model.

24. a. Set up the transportation tableau for the following transportation problem, and find the initial solution by the northwest corner method, least-cost method, and VAM. Compute the cost for each method.

To From	A	B	C	Supply
1	$7	$10	$6	300
2	4	9	8	150
3	5	7	15	400
Demand	200	400	350	

b. Using the VAM initial solution, solve the problem using the stepping-stone method.

25. A manufacturing firm produces diesel engines in four cities: Phoenix, Seattle,

Omaha, and St. Paul. The company is able to produce the following numbers of engines per month:

Plant	Production
1. Phoenix	5
2. Seattle	25
3. Omaha	20
4. St. Paul	25
	75

Three trucking firms that purchase the engines have the following demand in their plants in three cities:

Firm	Demand
A. Greensboro	10
B. Columbus	20
C. Louisville	15
	45

The transportation costs from source to destination per engine are given below in hundreds of dollars.

From \ To	A	B	C
1	$ 7	$ 8	$ 5
2	6	10	6
3	10	4	5
4	3	9	11

However, the Columbus firm will not accept engines made in Seattle and the Louisville firm will not accept engines from St. Paul; therefore, these routes are prohibited.

a. Set up the transportation tableau for this problem. Find the initial solution using VAM.

b. Solve for the optimal solution using the stepping-stone method. Compute the total minimum cost.

c. Formulate this problem as a linear programming model.

26. A rental car agency has six lots and they want to have a certain number of cars available at each lot at the beginning of each day for local rental. The agency would like a model they could quickly solve at the end of each day that would tell them how to redistribute the cars among the six lots at the minimum total mileage. The distances in miles between the six lots are

From \ To	1	2	3	4	5	6
1	—	12	17	18	10	20
2	14	—	10	19	16	15
3	14	10	—	12	8	9
4	8	16	14	—	12	15
5	11	21	16	18	—	10
6	24	12	9	17	15	—

The agency would like the following number of cars at each lot at the end of the day. Also shown is the number of available cars at each lot at the end of a particular day.

			Lot			
	1	2	3	4	5	6
Available	37	20	14	26	40	28
Desired	30	25	20	40	30	20

Determine the optimal reallocation of rental cars using any initial solution approach and any solution method.

27. a. Find the initial solution for the following transportation problem, using VAM.

From \ To	A	B	C	D	E	Supply
1	$21	$12	$28	$17	$ 9	50
2	15	13	20	50	12	60
3	18	17	22	10	8	40
4	M	2	10	5	1	70
5	33	29	35	27	23	30
Demand	40	30	50	60	50	

b. Solve using MODI.

28. a. Find the initial solution for the following transportation problem, using VAM.

From \ To	A	B	C	D	Supply
1	$20	$M	$17	$19	60
2	15	M	10	14	10
3	8	11	M	9	30
4	12	17	20	16	20
Demand	30	20	40	50	

b. Solve using the stepping-stone method.

29. Suppose in problem 14 in this chapter that all steel that is not shipped and remains in the warehouse incurs inventory carrying costs as follows:

Warehouse Location	Carrying Cost/Ton ($)
A. Pittsburgh	7
B. Birmingham	5
C. Gary	4

Solve this problem with the inventory carrying costs incorporated into the model in problem 16. Determine the initial solution by using VAM, and solve the problem by using MODI. Compute total minimum cost.

30. Solve problem 3 in this chapter, except now assume that the cell values in the transportation tableau represent per unit profit values rather than cost values. Use VAM to determine the initial solution method and then the stepping-stone solution method. Compute total maximum profit.

31. Problem 29 at the end of Chapter 2 is a transportation problem in which trailer trucks are allocated to the shipping warehouses of a transport company. Solve this problem, using the greatest-profit method to determine the initial solution and then the stepping-stone solution method. Compute total maximum profit.

32. A large manufacturing company is closing three of its existing plants and intends to transfer some of its more skilled employees to three of its plants that will remain open. The number of employees available to be transferred from each closing plant is as follows:

Closing Plant	Transferable Employees
1	60
2	105
3	70
	235

The following numbers of employees can be accommodated at the three plants remaining open:

Open Plants	Employees Demanded
A	45
B	90
C	35
	170

Each transferred employee will be able to increase product output per day at each plant as follows:

To From	A	B	C
1	5	8	6
2	10	9	12
3	7	6	8

The company desires to transfer employees from closing plants to open plants so that the increase in product output will be maximized.

Solve this transportation problem, using VAM to determine the initial solution and then the MODI solution method. Compute the total maximum increase in output.

33. The Export Corporation supplies their product to three foreign customers, each located in a different country. All of their product is supplied from two warehouses located on the East and the West coasts of the United States. For the coming planning period (a month), the Export Corporation has 5000 units of their product available at warehouse 1 and 6000 units available at warehouse 2. The demand for the product for the coming month is 4000 for each customer. The shipping costs (per unit) for the Export Corporation to supply its customers are as follows:

To From	Customer 1	Customer 2	Customer 3
Warehouse 1	$30	15	25
Warehouse 2	45	20	40

There is a penalty for unmet demand. For each unit of unmet demand for customer 1, the Export Corporation incurs a penalty cost of $100. For each unit of unmet demand for Customer 2, a penalty cost of $80 is incurred. For each unit of unmet demand for customer 3, the Export Corporation incurs a penalty for $120.

Formulate a balanced transportation model to minimize the total shipping and penalty costs for the Export Corporation for the coming planning period.

34. A company has eight salespeople it desires to allocate to three sales territories. Territory 1 requires three salespeople, and territories 2 and 3 require two salespeople each. It is estimated that each salesperson will be able to generate the amounts of dollar sales per day in each of the three territories shown in the table on page 235. The company desires to allocate the salespeople to the three territories so that sales will be maximized. Solve this transportation problem, using the greatest-profit method to determine the initial solution and then the stepping-stone solution method. Compute the maximum total sales per day.

	Territory			
Salesperson		1	2	3
A		$110	$150	$130
B		90	120	80
C		205	160	175
D		125	100	115
E		140	105	150
F		100	140	120
G		180	210	160
H		110	120	70

35. A manufacturing firm is planning a six-month production schedule for a new product. The production capacity is 800 units per month, and the quantity demanded fluctuates from month to month based on orders taken. The unit production cost first declines gradually because of the learning curve effect; then it increases abruptly because of a renegotiated union contract. Holding costs are 10% of the production cost per unit per month for items held in inventory. Given the summary information below, formulate the production and inventory problem as a transportation model in tableau format, and determine the initial solution by using the least-cost method.

Month	Production Capacity	Quantity of Product Demanded	Production Cost per Unit	Holding Cost per Unit
1	800	700	$10.00	$1.00
2	800	650	9.00	.90
3	800	750	8.00	.80
4	800	850	12.50	1.30
5	800	600	11.50	1.20
6	800	900	10.50	1.10

36. A firm produces several products at the same production facilities. The company is currently developing the production plan for one of its products for a four-month period. The monthly demand for the product is satisfied (a) from the current month's production, (b) from inventory of the product held from prior months' production, or (c) by backordering the product (i.e., filling the demand from production in a later month). The production cost per unit is $4. The holding cost is $.50 per unit per month for items held in inventory. The penalty cost incurred for back-ordered items is estimated at $2 per unit per month. The production capacity available for this particular product over the next four months is 50, 180, 280, and 270 units, respectively. The demand for the product over the four-month time period is 100, 200, 180, and 300 units, respectively.

   Formulate the transportation tableau for this problem and solve it, using the northwest corner method to determine the initial solution and the MODI method to determine the optimal solution.

37. Refer to Example 5.2, the production and inventory scheduling example presen
in this chapter. Assume that the firm has a production capacity of only 350 ur
per period instead of the 650 units previously given, but the firm can prode
another 350 units each period on a second shift. The production costs are, howev
50% higher for the second shift. Inventory holding costs in dollars per unit ;
period are the same as given previously, regardless of the shift during which ;
items are produced. Formulate this problem as a transportation model in table
format, and determine the initial solution using the least-cost method.

38. A distribution firm has three sources of supply, A, B, and C, and three destination
1, 2 and 3, that demand units. The shipping costs per unit as well as supply ai
demand are given as follows:

From \ To	1	2	3	Supply
A	$5	$4	$4	600
B	7	5	2	300
C	3	4	6	500
Demand	200	800	400	1400

In addition to being shipped directly from source to destination, units can be shippe
between sources, between destinations, and from destinations to sources. The un
shipping costs for these routes are

From \ To	A	B	C
A	$0	$8	$7
B	9	0	4
C	8	3	0

From \ To	1	2	3
1	$0	$6	$8
2	7	0	5
3	6	7	0

From \ To	A	B	C
1	$6	$5	$4
2	6	3	5
3	7	4	5

a. Formulate this problem as a transshipment model and solve.
b. Diagram the solution in network form.

39. A company produces units in three cities for outlets in three other cities. The shipping costs per unit as well as supply and demand are

To From	Atlanta	Richmond	Newark	Supply
Dallas	$4	$6	$10	1000
St. Louis	7	5	4	300
Chicago	8	7	6	100
Demand	200	400	800	

The company will also ship between sources and between destinations if such routing provides cheaper transportation. The unit shipping costs for these routes are

To From	Dallas	St. Louis	Chicago
Dallas	$0	$5	$7
St. Louis	4	0	3
Chicago	6	2	0

To From	Atlanta	Richmond	Newark
Atlanta	$0	$3	$5
Richmond	2	0	4
Newark	6	6	0

Shipping costs from the original destinations to the original sources are the same as shipping costs from sources to destinations.

a. Solve this problem as a transshipment model.
b. Diagram the solution in network form.

40. A manufacturing firm produces a product, which it stores in three different warehouses. The firm supplies its product to four retailers. Units can be shipped between warehouses and between retailers as well as from warehouses to retailers; however, units cannot be shipped from retailers back to warehouses. The amount supplied by each warehouse, the amount demanded by each retailer, and shipping costs per unit are shown in the tables on page 238.
a. Formulate this problem as a transshipment model and solve.
b. Diagram this solution in network form.

To From	R_1	R_2	R_3	R_4	Supply
W_1	$10	$14	$10	$ 5	80
W_2	12	9	6	7	120
W_3	7	11	8	13	110
Demand	50	100	100	60	

To From	W_1	W_2	W_3
W_1	$0	$4	$10
W_2	5	0	9
W_3	7	3	0

To From	R_1	R_2	R_3	R_4
R_1	$0	$7	$5	$8
R_2	7	0	6	5
R_3	4	5	0	7
R_4	9	6	4	0

41. In the following transshipment network, the values on the arrows are unit shipping costs. Nodes 1 and 2 represent sources that supply 20 units each; nodes 6 and 7 represent destinations where 10 and 30 units are demanded, respectively.

Formulate this network as a transportation problem, and solve to determine the optimal shipping routes that will minimize total cost.

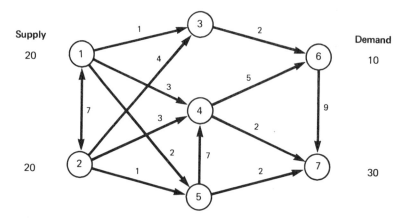

42. A firm produces a product at three factories and sells the product at three retail stores. The firm has four warehouses to which all products are shipped for distribution to retail stores. Units are never shipped directly from one factory to another, nor are units shipped from one retail outlet to another. Likewise, units are never

shipped directly from the factory to the retail store. However, units can be shipped from one warehouse to another. The firm wants to determine the shipping pattern from factories to warehouses to retail stores that will minimize cost. The various unit shipping costs are

To From	W_1	W_2	W_3	W_4
F_1	$ 5	$ 8	$4	$7
F_2	3	12	6	2
F_3	10	4	9	5

To From	R_1	R_2	R_3
W_1	$ 7	$12	$ 6
W_2	13	8	2
W_3	5	3	11
W_4	9	10	4

To From	W_1	W_2	W_3	W_4
W_1	$ 0	$ 4	$8	$ 3
W_2	9	0	7	10
W_3	6	2	0	5
W_4	12	11	4	0

The production capacities at the factories and the demand at the retail stores are

Factory	Retail Store
F_1: 1400	R_1: 1100
F_2: 1000	R_2: 2200
F_3: 1200	R_3: 500

a. Formulate this problem as a transshipment model and solve.

b. Diagram the shipping pattern in network form.

43. Problem 14 at the end of Chapter 2 is an assignment problem in which employees are assigned to machines in a machine shop. Solve this problem to determine which employee should be assigned to each machine in order to minimize the total time required to perform the work operations. Identify the optimal assignments and compute the total minimum time.

44. A small commuter airline in North Carolina has six flight attendants that it wants to assign to six monthly flight schedules in a way that will minimize the number of

nights they will be away from their homes. The nights each attendant must be av
from their home with each schedule are as follows:

Attendant \ Schedule	A	B	C	D	E	F
1	7	4	6	10	5	8
2	4	5	5	12	7	6
3	9	9	11	7	10	8
4	11	6	8	5	9	10
5	5	8	6	10	7	6
6	10	12	11	9	9	10

Identify the optimal assignments that will minimize the total number of nigh
the attendants will be away from home.

45. A job shop has four machinists to be assigned to four machines. The hourly cost
having each machine operated by each machinist is

Machinist \ Machine	A	B	C	D
1	$12	$11	$ 8	$14
2	10	9	10	8
3	14	8	7	11
4	6	8	10	9

However, because of a lack of experience, machinist 3 cannot operate machine B.

a. Determine the optimal assignment and compute total minimum cost.
b. Formulate this problem as a general linear programming model.

46. A pharmaceutical firm has five salespersons that the firm wants to assign to five sale
regions. Because of previously acquired contacts, the salespersons are able to cove
the regions in different amounts of time. The amount of time (in days) required b
each salesperson to cover each region is

Salesperson \ Region	A	B	C	D	E
1	17	10	15	16	20
2	12	9	16	9	14
3	11	16	14	15	12
4	14	10	10	18	17
5	13	12	9	15	11

Which salesperson should be assigned to each region in order to minimize total
time? Identify the optimal assignments and compute total minimum time.

47. A manufacturing firm has five employees and six machines. The firm desires to assign

the employees to the machines in a manner that will minimize cost. Following is a cost table showing the cost incurred by each employee on each machine:

Employee \ Machine	A	B	C	D	E	F
1	$12	$ 7	$20	$14	$ 8	$10
2	10	14	13	20	9	11
3	5	3	6	9	7	10
4	9	11	7	16	9	10
5	10	6	14	8	10	12

However, because of union rules regarding departmental transfers, employee 3 cannot be assigned to machine E and employee 4 cannot be assigned to machine B.

a. Solve this problem, indicating the optimal assignment and computing total minimum cost.

b. Formulate this problem as a general linear programming model.

48. Given the following cost table for an assignment problem, determine the optimal assignment for this problem, and compute total minimum cost. Identify all alternative solutions if multiple optimal solutions exist.

Worker \ Machine	A	B	C	D
1	$10	$2	$ 8	$ 6
2	9	5	11	9
3	12	7	14	14
4	3	1	4	2

49. An electronics firm produces electronic components that it supplies to various electrical manufacturers. Past quality-control records indicate that the number of defective items produced is different for each employee. The average number of defects produced by each employee per month for each of six components is given in the following table:

Employee \ Component	A	B	C	D	E	F
1	30	24	16	26	30	22
2	22	28	14	30	20	13
3	18	16	25	14	12	22
4	14	22	18	23	21	30
5	25	18	14	16	16	28
6	32	14	10	14	18	20

Determine the optimal assignment that will minimize the total average monthly defects.

50. A dispatcher presently has six taxicabs at different locations and five customers who have called for service. The mileage from each taxi's present location to each customer is

Cab \ Customer	1	2	3	4	5
A	7	2	4	10	7
B	5	1	5	6	6
C	8	7	6	5	5
D	2	5	2	4	5
E	3	3	5	8	4
F	6	2	4	3	4

Determine the optimal assignment(s) that will minimize the total mileage traveled.

51. A college athletic conference has six basketball officials it must assign to three conference games. Two officials must be assigned to each game. The conference office desires to assign the officials such that the total distance traveled by all six officials will be minimized. The distance each official would have to travel to each game is given in the following table:

Official \ Game	A	B	C
1	20	45	10
2	40	90	70
3	60	70	30
4	30	60	40
5	70	15	50
6	80	25	35

However, the conference office has decided not to assign official 4 to game A because of previous conflicts with one of the coaches.

a. Should this problem be solved by the transportation method or the assignment method? Explain.

b. Determine the optimal assignment(s) for this problem that will minimize the total distance traveled by the officials.

52. In problem 51, if the conflict between official 4 and the coach at game A was ignored by the conference office, determine if the assignment of officials should be altered and which officials would be affected.

53. A university department head has five instructors to be assigned to four different courses. In the past, all of the instructors have taught the courses and have been evaluated by the students. The rating for each instructor for each course is given in the following table (a perfect score is 100):

Course Instructor	A	B	C	D
1	80	75	90	85
2	95	90	90	97
3	85	95	88	91
4	93	91	80	84
5	91	92	93	88

The department head wants to know the optimal assignment of instructors to courses that will maximize the overall average evaluation. The instructor not assigned will be made a grader.

Solve this problem using the assignment method.

54. Solve the following linear programming problem:

$$\text{Minimize } Z = 18x_{11} + 30x_{12} + 20x_{13} + 18x_{14} + 25x_{21} + 27x_{22} + 22x_{23}$$
$$+ 16x_{24} + 30x_{31} + 26x_{32} + 19x_{33} + 32x_{34} + 40x_{41} + 36x_{42}$$
$$+ 27x_{43} + 29x_{44} + 30x_{51} + 26x_{52} + 18x_{53} + 24x_{54}$$

subject to

$$x_{11} + x_{12} + x_{13} + x_{14} \leq 1$$
$$x_{21} + x_{22} + x_{23} + x_{24} \leq 1$$
$$x_{31} + x_{32} + x_{33} + x_{34} \leq 1$$
$$x_{41} + x_{42} + x_{43} + x_{44} \leq 1$$
$$x_{51} + x_{52} + x_{53} + x_{54} \leq 1$$
$$x_{11} + x_{21} + x_{31} + x_{41} + x_{51} = 1$$
$$x_{12} + x_{22} + x_{32} + x_{42} + x_{52} = 1$$
$$x_{13} + x_{23} + x_{33} + x_{43} + x_{53} = 1$$
$$x_{14} + x_{24} + x_{34} + x_{44} + x_{54} = 1$$
$$x_{ij} \geq 0$$

55. Problem 22 at the end of Chapter 2 is an assignment problem in which employees are assigned to departments in a department store. Solve this problem to determine which employee should be assigned to each department in order to maximize expected sales. Identify the optimal assignments and compute the total maximum sales.

56. A manufacturing firm has five employees and five machines. The firm desires to assign the employees to the machines in a manner that will maximize total productivity. Following is a table that indicates the product output per day that each employee can generate on each machine:

Machine Employee	A	B	C	D	E
1	50	65	53	47	61
2	61	68	65	58	63
3	55	50	48	53	45
4	47	52	35	42	50
5	51	64	58	48	56

-6-

Network Models, Including CPM/PERT

Network models have played an increasingly important role in management science for at least two major reasons. First, models of real-world systems are relatively easy to conceive and construct in network form. Second, network models can be communicated effectively to management as visual facsimiles of the real-world systems under consideration. Therefore, the concepts of network analysis, commonly referred to as network flow theory, represent important topics in the study of management science.

Applications of network analysis have been made in areas such as information and product flows; cybernetics; transportation, distribution, and travel systems; and planning and control of one-time projects. The transportation and assignment models in Chapter 5, which were solved by special modifications of the linear programming solution algorithm, also represent network-oriented problems.

The network topics to be presented in this chapter are the shortest-route problem, the minimal spanning-tree problem, the maximal flow problem, and CPM/PERT for project planning and control.

The **shortest-route problem** involves finding the shortest route from an origin to a destination through a network of alternative routes. For example, this model can be used to determine the travel route from one city to another, over a network of possible roads, that will minimize total travel distance, time, and cost.

The **minimal spanning-tree problem** involves determining the route of connections between *all points* of a network, with the objective of minimizing the total length of these connections. For example, this model can be used to determine the routes for cable connections from a central point to all other points, which are defined as cable television customers, while minimizing the amount of cable used.

The **maximal flow problem** involves allocation of flows in a capacitated network in order to maximize the total flow through the network, from a specified source to a destination. For example, this model can be used to determine the maximum flow of oil from a refinery to a tank farm through a pipeline network with various flow capacities specified for each connecting pipeline.

The last network problem presented involves the analysis of one-time projects for planning and control purposes. The project activities are analyzed with respect to time, which results in time-dimensional networks. Project planning and control problems are usually modeled and analyzed by the well-known network techniques **CPM** (Critical Path Method) and **PERT** (Program Evaluation and Review Technique). One of the most important functions of these techniques is to determine the longest time path through the network. This path is referred to as the **critical path** because it includes the project activities that require the most careful control in order to complete the project on time.

NETWORK TERMINOLOGY AND NOTATION

Network models in management science have evolved from the more general **theory of graphs.** A graph model consists of two main components: nodes and branches. A **node** is one of a set of junction points, commonly denoted by a circle; certain pairs of the nodes are joined by connecting lines called **branches** (or arcs, links, or edges). When the branches of a graph are assumed to represent a flow of some sort, the graph is referred to as a *network*.

Figure 6.1 shows a network model consisting of six nodes and nine branches. Nodes are typically identified by numbers or letters within circles. Branches, the connecting lines (or arrows) between nodes, establish the model relationships. Figure 6.1 shows, for example, that since there is no connecting branch, there cannot be any flow or travel between nodes 2 and 3.

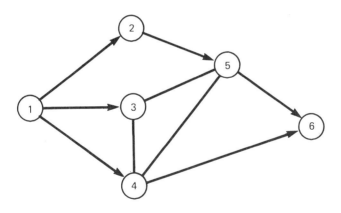

Figure 6.1 A Sample Network Model

Nodes typically represent locations, such as cities, pumping stations, switching centers, and air terminals. Branches can represent connecting roads, pipelines, cables, air travel routes, and so forth, with associated quantities, such as distance, time, costs, and capacity.

Given that any pair of nodes may be referred to, in general, as i and j, a branch may be identified as branch (i, j) or branch (j, i). For example, the network in Figure 6.1 consists of branches including (1, 3), (3, 4), and (4, 6) but does not include branches (2, 3) and (3, 2). Note that the (i, j) branch identification does not *necessarily* imply flow direction; that is, branch (3, 4) is the same as branch (4, 3), as flow may go in either direction between nodes 3 and 4.

A branch with a specified direction is referred to as a **directed branch,** which i oftentimes indicated graphically by a connecting line with an arrow showing the directio of required flow, such as branches (1, 2), (1, 3), and (1, 4) in Figure 6.1.

The flow times for an undirected branch may be different depending on the directio of flow; that is, flow may go in the two directions at different rates. In such a case, flow values are indicated separately for the flow from i to j (i, j) and from j to i (j, i).

When the flow direction has been determined for a particular branch, it will b denoted in the branch identification by ($i \rightarrow j$), showing that the flow is from node i t node j. For example, if the flow from node 1 to node 6 is determined to be from 1 to to 5 to 4 to 6, the undirected branches (3, 5) and (4, 5) will then be given as ($3 \rightarrow 5$) an ($5 \rightarrow 4$). Of course, branches (1, 3) and (4, 6) are *directed* and must flow as indicated from 1 to 3 and from 4 to 6.

A sequence of connecting branches between any two nodes i and j is referred to as a **chain** from i to j. For example, in Figure 6.1, the sequence of branches including (1, 3), (3, 4), and (4, 6) is one possible chain between nodes 1 and 6. If direction is specified along the chain, the chain is called a **path.** For example, if the flow between nodes 3 and 4 is from 3 to 4, then ($1 \rightarrow 3$), ($3 \rightarrow 4$), ($4 \rightarrow 6$) is also a path (which can be stated as $1 \rightarrow 3 \rightarrow 4 \rightarrow 6$). A **cycle** is a chain connecting a node to itself—(3, 4), (4, 5), (5, 3) is a cycle.

The origin in a network is usually referred to as the **source node,** and the desti-nation is frequently called the **sink node.** Thus, flow or travel in a network is usually from the source to the sink node. In the Figure 6.1 network, node 1 is the source and node 6 is the sink.

SHORTEST-ROUTE PROBLEM

The shortest-route problem is concerned with determining the shortest route from an origin to a destination through a connected network, given the distances associated with each branch of the network. For example, the nodes of the network may represent cities considered for travel from an origin city to a destination city, and the network branches may represent the roads with associated distances from one city to another. The problem is to determine the route to follow through the network of cities and connecting roads (nodes and connecting branches) in order to minimize total travel distance. Note that the objective could also be to minimize the total travel time or total travel cost. Also, the branches could be directed or undirected.

Various solution procedures have been proposed for the shortest-route problem, including linear programming. However, the following procedure is generally considered to be the simplest and quickest. The essence of the procedure is that it fans out from the origin node, successively identifying the next node that has the shortest distance route from the origin. Thus, the procedure not only finds the shortest route from the origin to the specified destination, but also, as a by-product, finds the shortest route from the origin to every other node in the network.

Example 6.1   A Shortest Delivery Route Problem

A trucking firm has a delivery it must make from its central distribution terminal to a factory in another city. The various routes a truck can take from the distribution terminal to the factory are shown in the Figure 6.2 network. The nodes represent cities, and the branches represent highways with associated travel distances in hundreds of miles. Node 1 represents the central distribution terminal, and node 8 represents the city in which the factory is located. The trucking firm desires to determine the shortest delivery route from the central distribution terminal, node 1, to the factory, node 8.

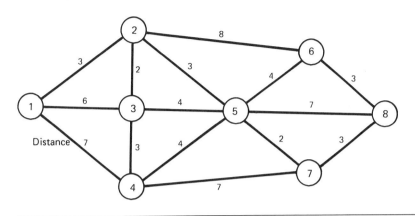

Figure 6.2 *Shortest-Route Network*

Note that all branches are *undirected,* so travel may occur in either direction, from node *i* to *j* or *j* to *i*, and the travel distance is the same in either case. However, there is a restriction in that travel cannot return from node 2, 3, or 4 to the origin node, 1, and it cannot return from the destination node, 8, to node 5, 6, or 7.

Solution Approach

The basic approach is to identify two sets of nodes, the **permanent set** and the **adjacent set.** Initially, only node 1, the origin, is placed in the permanent set. The nodes in the adjacent set are the nodes directly connected to the permanent set by connecting branches. Initially, in the Figure 6.2 network, only node 1 is in the permanent set, and the adjacent set includes nodes 2, 3, and 4, which are connected to node 1 by branches (1, 2), (1, 3), and (1, 4).

The basic steps of the procedure are as follows:

1. Designate the origin as the permanent set, and identify the adjacent set of nodes.

2. Identify the node in the adjacent set with the shortest distance from the origin.

3. *Store* the connecting branch (and its associated direction), which leads to the selected adjacent node. *Delete* from further consideration any other branches that lead from the permanent set to the selected adjacent set node.

4. Add the selected adjacent node to the permanent set.

5. Identify the new adjacent set of nodes, and repeat from step 2.

For example, *first* start with node 1 in the permanent set and nodes 2, 3, and 4 in the adjacent set (Figure 6.3). *Second,* select node 2 in the adjacent set as the node with the shortest distance from the origin. *Third,* store branch (1→2). *Fourth,* add node 2 to the permanent set, resulting in a permanent set consisting of nodes 1 and 2. *Fifth,* identify the new adjacent set consisting of nodes 3, 4, 5, and 6.

The initial case (A) and the first iteration (B) of the shortest-route solution procedure are shown in Figure 6.3. Shown are the nodes in the permanent set (indicated by dashed lines) and the nodes in the connecting adjacent set. Only the branches connecting the nodes in the permanent set to those in the adjacent set are shown. Note that after one iteration, node 3 is connected to the permanent set (nodes 1 and 2) by both the branches (1, 3) and (2, 3). Note also that the *stored* branch (1→2) is denoted by the bold line from node 1 to 2.

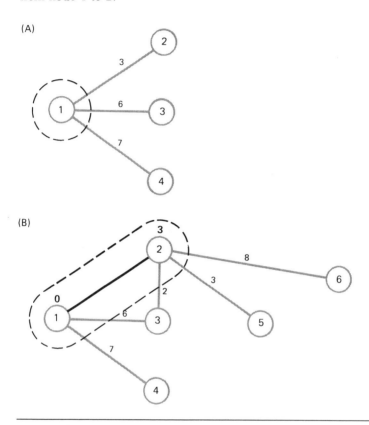

Figure 6.3 *(A) The Initial Permanent Set; (B) Permanent Set After One Iteration*

In order to select the next node for entry into the permanent set, return to step 2, which requires that the node in the newly defined adjacent set with the shortest route to the origin be identified. The computational procedure for this step is facilitated by assigning **labels** to nodes as they are put into the permanent set. The label value assigned to a node in the permanent set is defined as the shortest distance from that node to the origin (thus, the origin node, 1, has a label value of zero). In Figure 6.3(B), the label value of zero for node 1 and the label value of 3 for node 2 are shown in boldface above the permanent set nodes.

To determine which node from the connecting adjacent set to enter into the permanent set (i.e., which node has the shortest route to the origin), simply compute the sum of the label value (for the node in the permanent set) and the connecting branch distance for each connecting node, and select the node that results in the minimum value.

The second iteration of the procedure for the selection of one of the nodes from the adjacent set is described in Table 6.1. [Also refer to Figure 6.3(B).]

Table 6.1 Second Iteration for Selection of Adjacent Set Node

Permanent Set Node	Adjacent Set Node	Label Value	+	Connecting Branch Distance	=	Total Distance to Source
1	3	0	+	6	=	6
1	4	0	+	7	=	7
2	6	3	+	8	=	11
2	5	3	+	3	=	6
2	3	3	+	2	=	5 (minimum)

Thus, the node in the adjacent set with the shortest route to the origin is node 3, with a distance of 5 and with connecting branch (2→3). According to procedure, store branch (2→3) along with its associated flow direction. Note that branch (1, 3) must be deleted from further consideration, since we cannot have two optimal routes from the source to node 3. The new permanent set consists of nodes 1, 2, and 3, and a new adjacent set may now be identified.

Figure 6.4 shows the permanent set and the adjacent set after the second iteration. The adjacent set consists of nodes 4, 5, and 6. Note that the only differences between Figure 6.3(B) and Figure 6.4 are that the connecting branches (3, 4) and (3, 5) have been added because of the redefinition of the permanent set (addition of node 3) and branch (1, 3) has been deleted (shown as a dotted line) since branch (2→3) has been identified as part of the shortest route from node 1 to node 3.

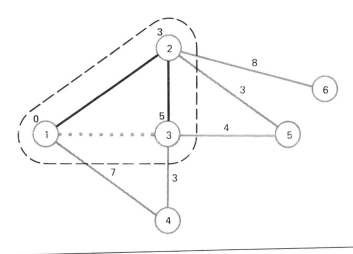

Figure 6.4 Permanent Set After Two Iterations

We are now ready to proceed with the third iteration in the solution procedure. The first three iterations are summarized in Table 6.2. Note that the adjacent set node with

the minimum total distance to the source is identified for each iteration. The branch t
be stored is indicated, and any branches to be deleted are denoted by an X to the righ
of the connecting branch (i, j) identification. Table 6.2 also shows the action taken afte
each iteration.

Table 6.2 Iterations 1, 2, and 3 of Shortest-Route Problem Solution Procedure

	Nodes					
Iteration	Permanent Set	Adjacent Set	Connecting Branch	Permanent Set Label	Connecting Branch Distance	Total Distance to Source
1	{1}	{2, 3, 4}	(1, 2)	0 +	3	= 3 (minimum
			(1, 3)	0 +	6	= 6
			(1, 4)	0 +	7	= 7

Action:
Store branch (1 → 2)
Add node 2 to permanent set

2	{1, 2}	{3, 4, 5, 6}	(1, 3)X	0 +	6	= 6
			(1, 4)	0 +	7	= 7
			(2, 6)	3 +	8	= 11
			(2, 5)	3 +	3	= 6
			(2, 3)	3 +	2	= 5 (minimum)

Action:
Store branch (2 → 3)
Delete branch (1, 3)
Add node 3 to permanent set

3	{1, 2, 3}	{4, 5, 6}	(1, 4)	0 +	7	= 7
			(2, 6)	3 +	8	= 11
			(2, 5)	3 +	3	= 6 (minimum)
			(3, 5)X	5 +	4	= 9
			(3, 4)	5 +	3	= 8

Action:
Store branch (2 → 5)
Delete branch (3, 5)
Add node 5 to permanent set

After the third iteration, the permanent set consists of nodes 1, 2, 3, and 5, as shown
in Figure 6.5. The connecting branch (2→5) has been stored, and the connecting branch
(3, 5) has been deleted.

To summarize the first three iterations: nodes 2, 3, and 5 have been added to the
permanent set (with node 1 initialized in the permanent set). Branches (1→2), (2→3),
and (2→5) have been stored, showing the shortest route from the source node to nodes
2, 3, and 5 in the permanent set. Branches (1, 3) and (3, 5) have been deleted from
further consideration (as shown by the dotted lines in Figure 6.5).

The permanent set now has one or more connecting branches to every other node in
the network (Figure 6.5). Thus, the adjacent set consists of nodes 4, 6, 7, and 8. Note
that node 4 now has three connecting branches from the permanent set, (1, 4), (3, 4),
and (5, 4), and node 6 has two connecting branches, (2, 6) and (5, 6). The label values

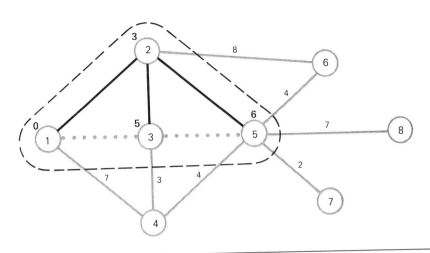

Figure 6.5 *Permanent Set After Three Iterations*

are shown above each node in the permanent set, indicating the shortest route distance from that node to the source.

The remaining iterations are constructed similarly. Figure 6.6 shows the permanent and adjacent sets, with connecting branches, after iteration 4. Table 6.3 summarizes the iterations required to obtain the shortest route from the source to the destination, node 8. Figure 6.7 shows iterations 5, 6, and 7, where part C is the final solution. This figure shows all network branches, with bold optimal route branches indicating the shortest route from the source to every other network node. The label values give the shortest distance from the origin to each node.

The shortest route from the source to the destination is given by branches $(1{\to}2)$, $(2{\to}5)$, $(5{\to}7)$, and $(7{\to}8)$, or path $1{\to}2{\to}5{\to}7{\to}8$. Thus, the optimal delivery route for a truck from the central distribution terminal to the factory is through the cities denoted by nodes 2, 5, and 7. The total travel distance is 1100 miles, which is the shortest of all alternative routes available.

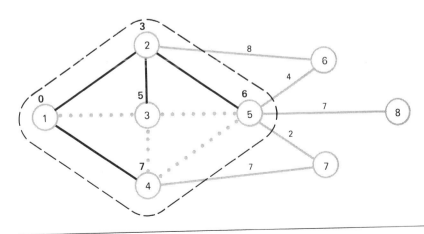

Figure 6.6 *Permanent Set After Four Iterations*

Table 6.3 *Iterations 4–7 of Shortest-Route Problem Solution Procedure*

	Nodes					Connecting	Total
Iteration	Permanent Set	Adjacent Set	Connecting Branch	Permanent Set Label		Branch Distance	Distance to Source
4	{1, 2, 3, 5}	{4, 6, 7, 8}	(1, 4)	0	+	7	= 7 (minimum)
			(2, 6)	3	+	8	= 11
			(3, 4)X	5	+	3	= 8
			(5, 6)	6	+	4	= 10
			(5, 8)	6	+	7	= 13
			(5, 7)	6	+	2	= 8
			(5, 4)X	6	+	4	= 10

Action:
Store branch (1 → 4)
Delete branches (3, 4) and (5, 4)
Add node 4 to permanent set

	Nodes					Connecting	Total
Iteration	Permanent Set	Adjacent Set	Connecting Branch	Permanent Set Label		Branch Distance	Distance to Source
5	{1, 2, 3, 4, 5}	{6, 7, 8}	(2, 6)	3	+	8	= 11
			(5, 6)	6	+	4	= 10
			(5, 8)	6	+	7	= 13
			(5, 7)	6	+	2	= 8 (minimum)
			(4, 7)X	7	+	7	= 14

Action:
Store branch (5 → 7)
Delete branch (4, 7)
Add node 7 to permanent set

	Nodes					Connecting	Total
Iteration	Permanent Set	Adjacent Set	Connecting Branch	Permanent Set Label		Branch Distance	Distance to Source
6	{1, 2, 3, 4, 5, 7}	{6, 8}	(2, 6)X	3	+	8	= 11
			(5, 6)	6	+	4	= 10 (minimum)
			(5, 8)X	6	+	7	= 13
			(7, 8)	8	+	3	= 11

Action:
Store branch (5 → 6)
Delete branch (2, 6)
Add node 6 to permanent set

	Nodes					Connecting	Total
Iteration	Permanent Set	Adjacent Set	Connecting Branch	Permanent Set Label		Branch Distance	Distance to Source
7	{1, 2, 3, 4, 5, 6, 7}	{8}	(5, 8)X	6	+	7	= 13
			(7, 8)	8	+	3	= 11 (minimum)
			(6, 8)X	10	+	3	= 13

Action:
Store branch (7 → 8)
Delete branches (5, 8) and (6, 8)
Add node 8 to permanent set
(Since node 8 is the destination, stop; optimal solution obtained)

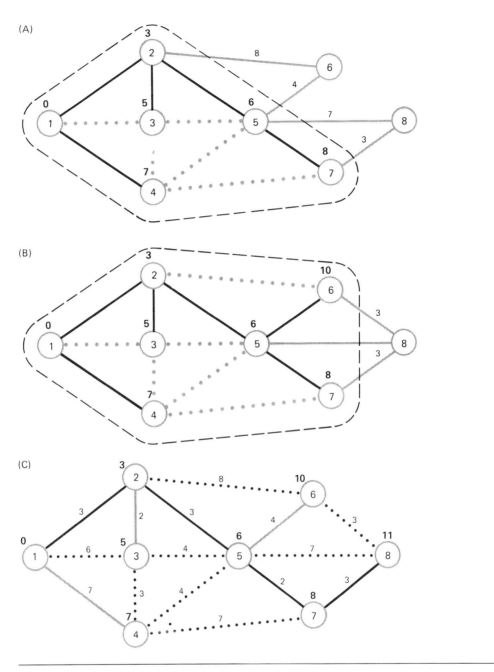

Figure 6.7 (A) Permanent Set After Five Iterations; (B)
Permanent Set After Six Iterations; (C) Final Solution After
Seven Iterations

An Application of the Shortest Route Problem: Ambulance Location at the State University of New York at Buffalo

On many university campuses the ambulance service is operated by student volunteers, which was the case on the Amherst Campus of the State University of New York (SUNY) at Buffalo. The ambulance service housed the ambulance at a single location in the student dormitory complex. However, since the campus population shifts from the dormitories at night to the offices, classrooms, and recreational facilities during the day, it was speculated that by moving the ambulance location around during the day to the various population centers, the response time for calls could be reduced. It has been shown in various studies that the time it takes for an ambulance to respond to a call has a significant effect on mortality rates of victims. As such, the objective of this project was to divide each 24-hour day into several time periods and locate the ambulance at an optimal site to minimize response time during each of the periods.

A network of the Amherst campus was constructed with 311 nodes and 340 branches. The nodes represent locations from which ambulance calls were made in the past and from which calls might originate in the future. They include 124 intersections, 2 ramps, 76 buildings, 10 playing fields, stadiums, or tennis courts, 44 pseudobuilding locations (not one around), 25 parking lots, 23 roadway turning points or connections, and 7 road entrances and exits. The network contains 263 nondirected branches and 77 directed branches. The branch lengths were

Computer Solution of the Shortest-Route Problem

We will demonstrate the AB:QM program for solving the shortest-route problem using Example 6.1. The program input and output follow.

```
Program: Network Models / Shortest Route

Problem Title : Example 6.1

***** Input Data *****

------------------------------
   SN          EN        Value
------------------------------
   1    <--->   2         3.00
   1    <--->   3         6.00
   1    <--->   4         7.00
   2    <--->   3         2.00
   2    <--->   5         3.00
   2    <--->   6         8.00
   3    <--->   4         3.00
   3    <--->   5         4.00
   4    <--->   5         4.00
   4    <--->   7         7.00
   5    <--->   6         4.00
   5    <--->   7         2.00
   5    <--->   8         7.00
   6    <--->   8         3.00
   7    <--->   8         3.00
------------------------------
```

determined using a campus survey. The shortest route algorithm was used to determine the shortest paths between all nodes in the network. These results formed the basis of the location model that was subsequently developed.

The number of time periods that were established in which to locate the ambulance is a trade-off between response time and the cost and inconvenience of relocating the ambulance. The more time periods that are established during the day (of smaller durations) the lower the response time. Four periods were ultimately determined; 7AM–10AM, 10AM–4PM, 4PM–7PM, and 7PM–7AM. Also different average ambulance travel speeds were selected from each period and location. During each time period the ambulance was moved to a location where the majority of past calls had derived during that period. The network model results showed the average response time would be reduced by 30%, from 3.38 minutes to 2.28 minutes.

However, when the location system was implemented, the average response time showed only a 6% reduction. Further investigation showed that the model assumed a constant ambulance speed that did not take into account the time to prepare the ambulance for starting and acceleration and deceleration times. In fact, it was discovered upon reading other research studies that because of the acceleration and deceleration times of emergency vehicles, travel time for distances between 0 and 2.5 miles (which is typically the case for a campus) differs very little.

Source: Y. M. Carson and R. Butta, "Locating an Ambulance on the Amherst Campus of the State University of New York at Buffalo," *Interfaces,* 20, no. 5 (September–October 1990): 43–49.

```
***** Program Output *****

---------------------------------
  SN        EN           Value
---------------------------------
  1 <---> 2              3.000
  2 <---> 5              3.000
  5 <---> 7              2.000
  7 <---> 8              3.000
---------------------------------

Shortest Path is  :

  1 <---> 2 <---> 5 <---> 7 <---> 8

Total Shortest Distance  :      11.000

***** End of Output *****
```

You will note that the AB:QM output includes only the shortest route from the start node (1) to the destination node (8). Alternatively, some other management science software packages generate the shortest routes from the start node to all other nodes in the network. For example, the following is the computer solution output for STORM showing the shortest paths to all network nodes as previously shown in Figures 6.3 to 6.7.

```
                    Example 6.1 - Shortest Route Problem
                       SHORTEST PATHS FROM NODE 1

      Destination      Distance      Path

      NODE 2            3.0000       NODE 2

      NODE 3            5.0000       NODE 2--NODE 3

      NODE 4            7.0000       NODE 4

      NODE 5            6.0000       NODE 2--NODE 5

      NODE 6           10.0000       NODE 2--NODE 5--NODE 6

      NODE 7            8.0000       NODE 2--NODE 5--NODE 7

      NODE 8           11.0000       NODE 2--NODE 5--NODE 7--NODE 8
```

MINIMAL SPANNING-TREE PROBLEM

The minimal spanning-tree problem is a variation of the shortest-route problem. However, the minimal spanning-tree problem is easier to solve, and the interpretation of the problem objective is different. Whereas the objective of the shortest-route problem is to determine the minimum distance (time or cost) *route* from a specified origin to a specified destination, the objective of the minimal spanning-tree problem is to *connect* all the network nodes such that the total branch lengths required are minimal (distance, time, or cost). The resulting solution forms a *tree* that "spans" (connects) all designated points (e.g., cities, terminals, street intersections, retail outlets).

There are numerous practical applications of the minimal spanning-tree problem—for example, determination of the minimum length of cable needed to connect a given set of homes to cable television; transmission wire to connect a given set of cities to electricity, pipeline to connect a given set of terminals, track to connect rail service to a set of on/off loading stations, bus routes to connect to specified stops. In general, it is applicable to transportation, distribution, and communication networks where all specified nodes (intersections, terminals, etc.) must be connected.

Solution Approach

The minimal spanning-tree problem can be solved rather easily by arbitrarily selecting any node and connecting it to the closest node, then selecting the node closest to *either* of the two nodes already connected and connecting this third node to the closest node in the initial set. This process is repeated until all nodes have been connected. The procedure is summarized as follows:

1. Arbitrarily select any node of the network and connect it to the nearest node (in terms of a specified measurement, such as distance, time, or cost).

2. Identify the unconnected node that is nearest to a connected node, and connect these two nodes. If there is a tie, arbitrarily choose one node.

3. Repeat step 2 until all nodes have been connected. The resulting spanning tree of connected nodes results in minimum total branch length.

xample 6.2   A Computer Network Spanning Problem

A large manufacturing plant desires to connect computer terminals at seven locations across the plant site to the computer at its computing center. The terminals will be connected with coaxial cable that must be laid through the existing network of steam tunnels. The network of steam tunnels is represented by the network in Figure 6.8. The values given along the branches represent the distances (in hundreds of feet) between the terminal locations, which are denoted by nodes 2 through 8 in Figure 6.8.

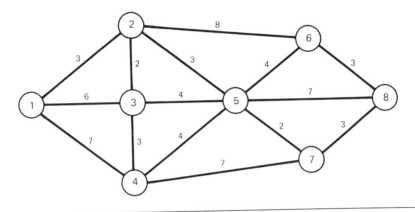

Figure 6.8 Minimal Spanning-Tree Network

The plant manager wishes to determine how to connect all seven terminals with the computer center so that the minimum amount of cable is required. Note that the network in Figure 6.8 is the same as the network in Figure 6.2, which was used to demonstrate the shortest-route problem. The same network is being employed for the minimal spanning-tree problem to distinguish between the two types of problems and solutions.

We could begin with *any* node in the network. However, node 1 will be selected to facilitate comparison with the previous shortest-route example problem. The unconnected node closest to node 1 is node 2, with a distance of 3 (hundred feet). Therefore, node 2 is connected to node 1 (as shown by the bold line in Figure 6.9, p. 258).

The unconnected node closest to either node 1 or node 2 is node 3, via branch (2, 3) with a distance of 2. Thus, node 3 is connected to node 2, as shown by the bold line in Figure 6.10, page 258.

There is a tie for closest unconnected node to any of the connected nodes 1, 2, or 3. Node 4 is a distance of 3 from node 3, and node 5 is also a distance of 3 from node 2. We can, therefore, arbitrarily select either candidate. Node 4 is selected to be connected to node 3, as shown in Figure 6.11, page 258.

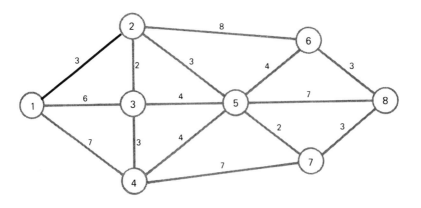

Figure 6.9 *Connection of Node 1 and Node 2*

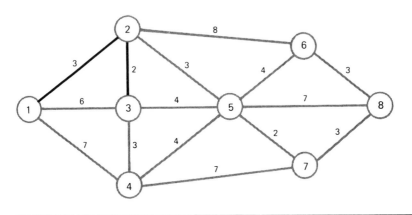

Figure 6.10 *Selection of Node 3 as Closest Unconnected Node*

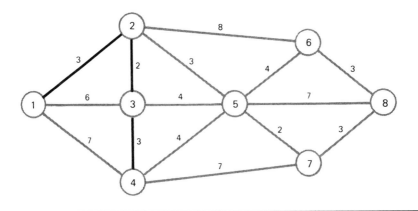

Figure 6.11 *Arbitrary Selection of Node 4 as Closest Unconnected Node*

Node 5 is now the closest unconnected node, with a distance of 3 from node 2. According to procedure, node 5 is connected to node 2, as shown by the bold line in Figure 6.12.

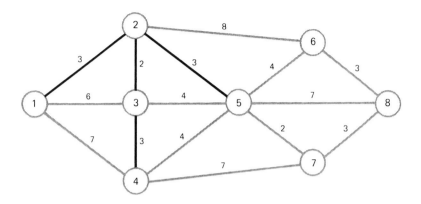

Figure 6.12 *Selection of Node 5 as Closest Unconnected Node*

Node 7 is now the closest unconnected node, with a distance of 2 to node 5. It is connected as shown in Figure 6.13.

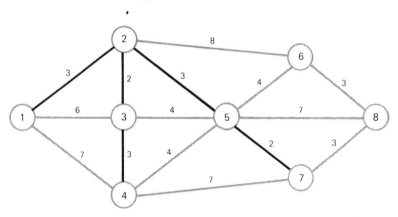

Figure 6.13 *Selection of Node 7 as Closest Unconnected Node*

The unconnected node closest to any connected node is now node 8, at a distance of 3 from node 7. Node 8 is connected to node 7 (Figure 6.14, p. 260).

Finally, the only unconnected node remaining is 6, and it is closest to node 8. Node 6 is connected to node 8 as shown in Figure 6.15, page 260.

All nodes are now connected, resulting in the minimal spanning tree of connections and a total length of 1900 feet of underground cable. As stated earlier, any node may be selected initially to begin the solution process without affecting the final results. This can be verified by choosing a node other than node 1 and repeating the solution procedure for this example.

Finally, the solution for the minimal spanning-tree problem, shown in Figure 6.15, may be contrasted to the solution for the shortest-route problem, which was shown in

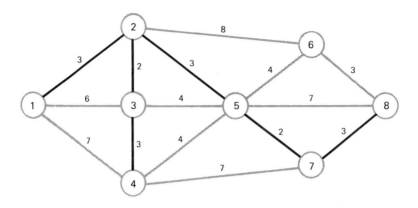

Figure 6.14 *Selection of Node 8 as Closest Unconnected Node*

Figure 6.7. Note that different solutions have been obtained for the two different problem definitions.

Figure 6.15 shows the minimum length of cable required to connect all terminal locations (nodes) in the network. On the other hand, Figure 6.7 shows the shortest travel route from the node 1 origin to a *specified* destination, where designation of different nodes in the network as the destination represents, in effect, *different trips.*

As a concluding note, it should be pointed out that neither the shortest-route problem nor the minimal spanning-tree problem addresses the problem of routing a traveler through a sequence of cities (nodes), where all cities must be visited at least once. In the so-called **traveling salesman problem,** the objective is to determine the sequence in which the cities should be visited in order to minimize the total distance traveled. The traveling salesman problem represents a class of problems known as combinatorial problems, which usually require solution by the **branch-and-bound method** presented in Chapter 14.

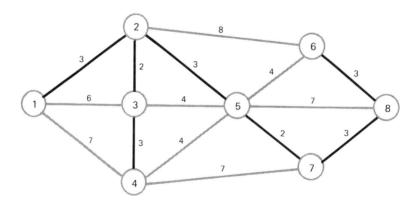

Figure 6.15 *Final Solution; Selection of Node 6 as Closest Unconnected Node*

ımputer Solution of the Minimal Spanning-Tree Problem

Following is the AB:QM program output for the computer-generated minimal spanning-tree solution of Example 6.2. The data input requirements are identical to those for the shortest-route problem presented in conjunction with the solution of Example 6.1

```
Program: Network Models / Minimum Spanning Tree

Problem Title : Example 6.2

***** Input Data *****

-----------------------------
  SN        EN        Value
-----------------------------
  1  <--->  2         3.00
  1  <--->  3         6.00
  1  <--->  4         7.00
  2  <--->  3         2.00
  2  <--->  5         3.00
  2  <--->  6         8.00
  3  <--->  4         3.00
  3  <--->  5         4.00
  4  <--->  5         4.00
  4  <--->  7         7.00
  5  <--->  6         4.00
  5  <--->  7         2.00
  5  <--->  8         7.00
  6  <--->  8         3.00
  7  <--->  8         3.00
-----------------------------

***** Program Output *****

-----------------------------
  SN        EN        Value
-----------------------------
  1  <--->  2         3.000
  2  <--->  5         3.000
  2  <--->  3         2.000
  3  <--->  4         3.000
  5  <--->  7         2.000
  6  <--->  8         3.000
  7  <--->  8         3.000
-----------------------------

Total Minimum Spanning Tree Lengths  :      19.000

***** End of Output *****
```

MAXIMAL FLOW PROBLEM

The maximal flow problem involves routing flows through a network in order to maximize the total flow from a specified source to a specified destination. Examples include product flow through a network of pipelines, message flow through a communication network, and vehicle flow over a network of roads.

The flow network consists of nodes connected by branches, where nodes might represent street intersections and branches represent the streets. In the case of a pipeline network, the nodes might represent junction points at valves or pumping stations, and the branches the connecting pipelines. The objective is to determine the maximum achievable flow from the source or origin of the network to the sink or destination, where each branch has a specified capacity restriction associated with it (e.g., street vehicle-flow capacity, pipeline product-flow capacity, or transmission wire message-flow capacity).

Prior to presentation of the solution procedure for the maximal flow problem, several key concepts will be presented.

Concepts and Assumptions of the Maximal Flow Problem

An essential assumption of the maximal flow problem is **conservation of flow.** This assumption states that total flow into a node must be exactly equal to the total flow out of the node. Figure 6.16 illustrates this concept, where the values along the arrows represent the flow quantities into and out of node i. Note that the total flow of 14 into node i is equal to the total flow out of node i.

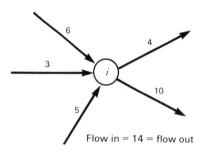

Figure 6.16 *Conservation of Flow at Node i*

The maximal flow problem may be applied to networks consisting of directed or undirected branches. Generally, the physical interpretation of directed versus undirected branches is relatively straightforward. For example, a network of natural gas pipelines, connecting at valves, represents a network of *undirected* branches—gas may flow in either direction through a pipeline of specified capacity. An example of a network of *directed* branches is an irrigation canal network where flow is controlled by gravity—the water must flow one direction only, downhill, along a canal of specified capacity. Another example of a directed branch is a one-way street in a traffic network with an associated one-way vehicle flow capacity.

It is apparent that when the flow is directed, or restricted, to one direction, the only meaningful capacity restriction is in the flow direction. However, in the case of undirected branches where flow may go in either direction, it is not necessarily true that the branch is also *capacity undirected*. The natural gas pipeline has an undirected capacity; the capacity of each pipeline remains the same regardless of the direction of gas flow. On the other hand, although a two-way street represents an undirected flow branch (flow can go in both directions), it may be *capacity directed* if it has one lane in one direction and three lanes in the opposite direction.

When a real-world maximal flow problem involves a possible *simultaneous* two-way flow with directed capacities, it is usually most convenient to treat the branch as two separate directed branches with associated capacities.

The final topic of interest in maximal flow problems is the concept of **net flow** along a branch. This concept is of special interest since the solution method of the maximal flow problem requires that we temporarily allow flows in *either direction* along a directed branch during the process of determining the solution, and then calculate the net flow (in the restricted direction) at the end of the solution procedure.

This particular feature of the maximal flow problem solution procedure is illustrated in Figure 6.17. Represented is a network of five natural gas pipelines, connected at points identified as junctions C and D. There are two input valves, A and B, and two output valves, E and F. The natural gas can flow through the pipelines under pressure at the capacity rates shown.

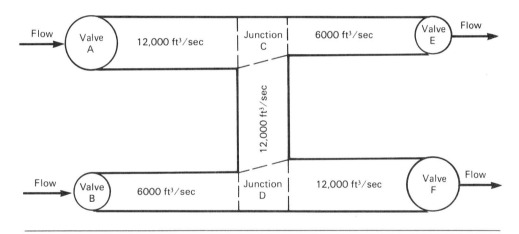

Figure 6.17 *Natural Gas Pipeline Diagram*

In network terminology, the nodes are identified as A, B, C, D, E, and F. The branches (pipelines) are denoted as (A, C), (B, D), (C, D), (C, E), and (D, F). Note that natural gas flows in at valves A and B, and out at valves E and F. The pipeline capacities are given as 12,000 cubic feet per second for branches (A, C), (C, D), and (D, F), and as 6000 cubic feet per second for branches (B, D) and (C, E). Junctions C and D represent interconnecting points of the pipelines, but not valves.

Suppose that initially only valves A and F are opened (valves B and E remain closed). Natural gas will flow at the rate of 12,000 cubic feet per second along the path A→C→ D→F, as soon as pipes (C, E) and (B, D) have filled. Note especially that the flow from node C to D is 12,000 cubic feet per second. Now, suppose that valves B and E are also opened. Almost instantaneously, the gas flow becomes as follows:

Branch (pipe)	Flow (ft³/sec)
(A→C)	12,000
(C→E)	6000
(B→D)	6000
(D→F)	12,000
(C→D)	6000

The net flow from node C to D is now reduced from 12,000 cubic feet per second to 6000 cubic feet per second. The change that has taken place is that 6000 of the 12,000 cubic feet per second of gas that had been flowing along the path A→C→D→F has been diverted (redirected) to (C→E). The 12,000 cubic feet per second of gas now flowing through (D→F) is made up of 6000 cubic feet per second from (B→D), the newly opened valve, and 6000 cubic feet per second still coming from A→C→D.

It is interesting to note that if we had simply retained the initial flow of 12,000 cubic feet per second along the path A→C→D→F, we could think of the new 6000 cubic feet per second flow as following path B→D→C→E. This would yield a fictitious two-way flow for (C, D) of

Branch (pipe)	Flow (ft³/sec)
(C→D)	12,000
(D→C)	6000

By subtracting the smaller flow from the larger, we obtain the direction and quantity of the actual net flow through (C→D) of 6000 cubic feet per second.

The solution method for the maximal flow problem employs the approach of temporarily assigning fictional flows in the wrong direction along a branch—in this instance, the assignment of a flow of 6000 cubic feet per second along (D→C)—in order to represent the real effect of redirecting part of the previously assigned flow—redirection of 6000 cubic feet per second from (C→D) to (C→E).

Solution Approach

For each *iteration* of the solution procedure for the maximal flow method, perform the following steps:

1. Find any path through the network, from the source node to the sink node, with *some* available flow capacity on each branch of the selected path. (If no such path exists, the optimal solution has been reached.)

2. Determine, on the path selected, the branch with the smallest flow capacity currently available. Call this capacity C, and allocate a *flow* of C to each branch on the selected path.

3. *Decrease* the currently available flow capacity of each branch on the selected path by amount C.

4. *Increase* by amount C the flow capacity *in the reverse direction* for each branch of the selected path. (Note: This step is performed in order to keep track of the potential flow redirection possible

for each branch on the selected path, as was described for the natural gas example.) Return to step 1.

The solution procedure will first be applied to the very simple network shown in Figure 6.18. The flow direction is from left to right, from source node 1 to sink node 4. The branch flow capacities are given by the numbers just above or to the right of each branch—next to the node from which the flow emanates. For example, the flow capacity for branch (1, 2) is 12 in the direction from node 1 to node 2. The flow capacity for that same branch in the reverse direction, from node 2 to node 1, is zero. Branch (1, 2) is a directed branch, in the direction from node 1 to node 2.

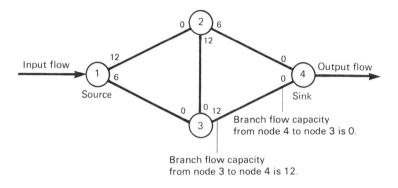

Figure 6.18 *Maximal Flow Network*

Inspection of the specified capacities for all the branches of the network reveals that all branches are directed, as indicated by positive flow capacities at one end of the branch (next to the node from which the flow emanates) and zero flow capacities at the other end of the branch.

It is apparent that this network is quite similar to the natural gas example, except that we now have a single source and a single sink. It is also apparent by inspection that the optimal solution will be flows of 12 for $(1 \rightarrow 2)$, 6 for $(1 \rightarrow 3)$, 6 for $(2 \rightarrow 3)$, 6 for $(2 \rightarrow 4)$, and 12 for $(3 \rightarrow 4)$. However, in order to illustrate the concept of temporary assignment of a fictional flow in the wrong direction along a branch, we will go through the steps of the solution procedure as follows.

1. Find any path through the network with positive flow capacity on each branch. Assume that path $1 \rightarrow 2 \rightarrow 3 \rightarrow 4$ is selected because we can see that this will allow us to assign the maximum flow of 12 on the first try.

2. Determine, on the path selected, the branch with the smallest flow capacity. Call this capacity C and allocate a flow of C to each branch selected. Allocate a flow of $C = 12$ to each of the branches $(1 \rightarrow 2)$, $(2 \rightarrow 3)$, and $(3 \rightarrow 4)$.

3. Decrease the currently available flow capacity of each branch on the selected path by amount C. Decrease each flow capacity number shown on the $1 \rightarrow 2 \rightarrow 3 \rightarrow 4$ path branches by crossing out the current capacity (12 in each case) and replacing it with the remaining capacity (zero in each case). This step is shown in Figure 6.19. It shows that there are no remaining flow capacities on those branches.

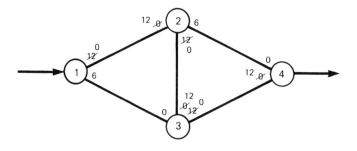

Figure 6.19 *Revised Flow Capacities Following the First Iteration of the Solution Procedure*

4. Increase by amount C the flow capacity in the reverse direction for each branch of the selected path. Increase each flow capacity number along the path $4\rightarrow3\rightarrow2\rightarrow1$ by crossing out the current capacity (zero in each case) and replacing it with the value added (12). This step is also shown in Figure 6.19.

Note that the network in Figure 6.19, with revised flow capacities, now shows possible flows of 6 from $(1\rightarrow3)$ and $(2\rightarrow4)$ and a possible flow of 12 from $(3\rightarrow2)$, even though branch $(2, 3)$ was originally defined as a directed branch in the direction of $(2\rightarrow3)$. Thus, we are going to allow a temporary assignment of flow in the wrong direction in order to redirect a portion of the current flow from node 2 to node 3 to a different path. If we did not do this, we would have to stop at this point, because there is no place for flow from $(1\rightarrow3)$ to go, since the capacity along $(3\rightarrow4)$ is used up.

Therefore, return to step 1 of the solution procedure and identify path $1\rightarrow3\rightarrow2\rightarrow4$ in Figure 6.19 with a potential maximal flow capacity of 6 units, as dictated by the flow capacities on branches $(1\rightarrow3)$ and $(2\rightarrow4)$. Allocate a flow of 6 branches $(1\rightarrow3)$, $(3\rightarrow2)$, and $(2\rightarrow4)$.

Next, reduce the branch flow capacities by the amount of assigned flow on the $1\rightarrow3\rightarrow2\rightarrow4$ path and *increase* the reverse-direction capacities for the same branches—the $4\rightarrow2\rightarrow3\rightarrow1$ path. This procedure is shown in Figure 6.20, where the old numbers have been crossed out and replaced by the new values. Note that branch $(2, 3)$ has now had its capacities revised twice. The 6 on branch $(2, 3)$ next to node 2 indicates that the actual

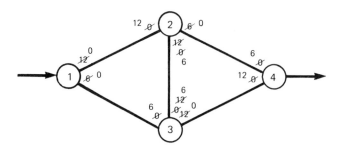

Figure 6.20 *Revised Flow Capacities Following Two Iterations of the Solution Procedure*

remaining capacity for branch (2→3) is 6 units. The 6 next to node 3 indicates a flow of 6 units from node 2 to node 3, which leaves us with a remaining flow of 6 that could potentially be redirected and thought of as a potential flow of 6 from node 3 to node 2.

Since there are no remaining positive capacity paths from the source to the sink, the optimal solution has been obtained. The solution is as follows:

Iteration	Path	Assigned Flow
Iteration 1	1→2→3→4	12
Iteration 2	1→3→2→4	6

As a final step, inspect each branch assignment to identify any flow allocations in both directions. Branch (2, 3) has the following two-way flow assignments:

Branch	Flow Assignment
(2→3)	12
(3→2)	6

Therefore, simply deduct the smaller flow assignment from the larger, which yields the true net flow assignment of 6 for branch (2→3). Thus, the maximum flow for the network is 18 units, summarized as follows:

	Branch		Flow	
Flow in	$\left\{\begin{array}{l}(1\rightarrow2)\\(1\rightarrow3)\end{array}\right.$		$\left.\begin{array}{l}12\\6\end{array}\right\}$	18
	(2→3)		6	
	$\left.\begin{array}{l}(2\rightarrow4)\\(3\rightarrow4)\end{array}\right\}$	Flow out	$\left.\begin{array}{l}6\\12\end{array}\right\}$	18

Example 6.3   A Rail Shipment Problem

A coal company desires to transport coal from its coal mines to an overseas shipping port on the east coast. The company transports coal from its mines to the port via a network of rail lines as shown in Figure 6.21. Node 1 in Figure 6.21 represents the railhead at the coal mines, and node 8 represents the port facility. The remaining nodes represent railroad junctions. The flow capacities shown along the branches emanating from each node are the maximum numbers of railroad coal cars (in hundreds) that can be included in a train scheduled from that junction for the planning period.

The coal company wishes to determine the maximum number of coal cars that can be transported from the mines to the shipping port during the planning period.

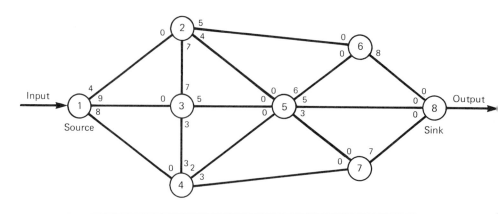

Figure 6.21 *Maximal Flow Network*

Recall that paths with positive flow capacities may be chosen arbitrarily, so the number of iterations required to reach a solution can vary depending on the order of the selection of paths.

Iteration 1 Path $1 \rightarrow 2 \rightarrow 6 \rightarrow 8$ is arbitrarily selected, and a maximum possible flow allocation of 4 units is assigned. The maximum flow for this path is due to the capacity of branch (1, 2). Figure 6.22 shows the revision of flow capacities on the selected path for iteration 1.

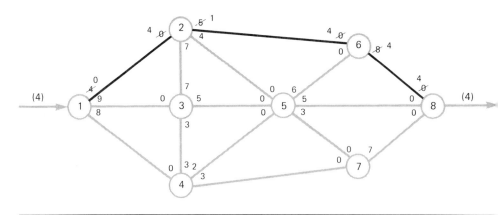

Figure 6.22 *Flow Capacities After One Iteration*

Iteration 2 Path $1 \rightarrow 3 \rightarrow 5 \rightarrow 8$ is arbitrarily selected, with a flow allocation of 5 units. Figure 6.23 shows the branch capacity revisions for this iteration.

Iteration 3 Path $1 \rightarrow 4 \rightarrow 7 \rightarrow 8$ is arbitrarily selected, with a flow allocation of 3 units. The maximum flow for this path is determined by the capacity of branch (4, 7). Figure 6.24 shows this iteration.

Iteration 4 Path $1 \rightarrow 3 \rightarrow 2 \rightarrow 5 \rightarrow 6 \rightarrow 8$ is next selected as a path with remaining available flow capacity. The maximum possible flow allocation of 4 units is assigned to this path (see Figure 6.25).

Iteration 5 Path $1 \rightarrow 4 \rightarrow 5 \rightarrow 7 \rightarrow 8$ is selected, with a flow allocation of 2 units. Figure 6.26 (p. 270) shows this iteration.

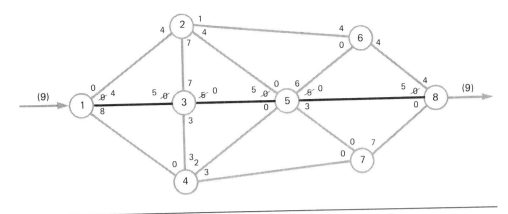

Figure 6.23 *Flow Capacities After Two Iterations*

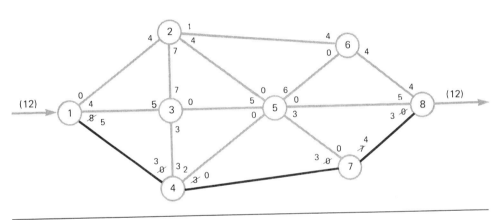

Figure 6.24 *Flow Capacities After Three Iterations*

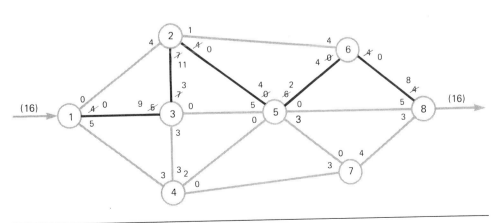

Figure 6.25 *Flow Capacities After Four Iterations*

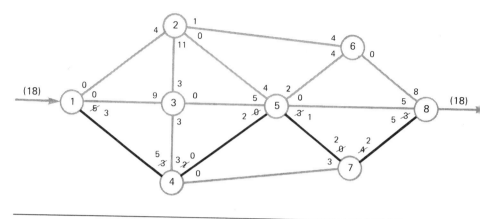

Figure 6.26 *Flow Capacities After Five Iterations*

Iteration 6 Path $1 \to 4 \to 3 \to 2 \to 6 \to 5 \to 7 \to 8$ is selected as the only remaining path with positi flow capacity. A maximum flow allocation of 1 is assigned. Figure 6.27 shows this iteration.

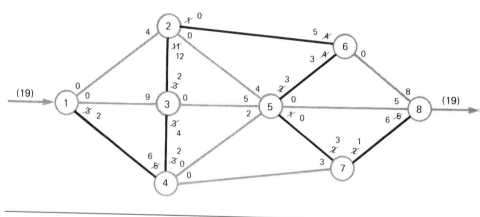

Figure 6.27 *Flow Capacities After Six Iterations*

Note that in iteration 6 an allocation of 1 was assigned to branch (5, 6) in the "wrong" direction (since this branch was shown in Fig. 6.21 to be directed from node 5 to node 6). The net flow for branch (5, 6) may now be determined as

Iteration	Flow Allocation	
	Branch	Flow
Iteration 4	(5→6)	4
Iteration 6	(6→5)	1

Therefore, the actual net flow for branch (5→6) will be 3 units. The effect will be to reroute 1 unit of the 4-unit flow that had been assigned to (5→6) to (5→7) instead.

Likewise, the 1 unit of flow rerouted away from (5→6) will be replaced at node 6 with the last unit of flow coming from (2→6), and it will, in turn, be sent to (6→8). The final network after all iterations is shown in Figure 6.28. The assigned flow amount is shown in parentheses for each branch, along with the direction of flow, which is indicated by arrows.

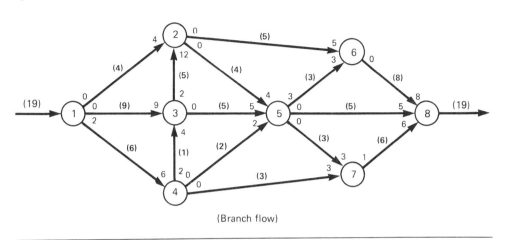

(Branch flow)

Figure 6.28 *Final Solution After All Iterations*

The allocated flow for each branch is summarized in Table 6.4. The individual allocations to each branch are shown for each iteration, and the total branch allocations are given at the bottom. Also shown is the branch capacity and the remaining branch capacity after the last iteration. These values may be verified by comparing them to Figure 6.28. Note that the reverse direction flow allocation for branch (5→6) is given as −1 in Table 6.4, yielding the net flow allocation in the total allocation row. Thus, the coal company can ship 1900 carloads of coal from the mines' railhead to the overseas loading port during the period in question.

Table 6.4 *Iterations and Allocated Flows of Maximal Flow Problem Solution Procedure*

Iteration	1→2	1→3	1→4	2→3	2→5	2→6	3→2	3→4	3→5	4→3	4→5	4→7	5→6	5→7	5→8	6→8	7→8
1	4					4										4	
2		5							5						5		
3			3									3					3
4		4			4		4						4			4	
5			2								2			2			2
6			1			1	1			1			−1	1			1
Total allocation	4	9	6	0	4	5	5	0	5	1	2	3	3	3	5	8	6
Capacity	4	9	8	7	4	5	7	3	5	3	2	3	6	3	5	8	7
Unused capacity	0	0	2	7	0	0	2	3	0	2	0	0	3	0	0	0	1

Computer Solution of the Maximal Flow Problem

In this section the maximal flow problem in Example 6.3 is solved using the STORM package, employed previously to solve the shortest-route problem. The following program output shows the data input (after the number of nodes and rows have been input) and the final solution. The number of rows is equal to the number of branches, in both directions (in this case 30), plus one row each for the start and end nodes. These rows are labeled as arcs on the summary of the data input and solution output, but can be identified by the start and end node numbers, which correspond to Figure 6.21.

```
                    STORM DATA SET LISTING
                    FLOW NETWORKS DATA SET


        Problem Description Parameters

        Title : Example 6.3 - Maximal Flow Network

        Number of nodes   :        8

        Number of rows    :        32
```

```
                    STORM DATA SET LISTING
                 DETAILED PROBLEM DATA LISTING FOR
                  Example 6.3 - Maximal Flow Network
```

ROW LABEL	FROM NODE	TO NODE	UNIT COST	LOWR BOUND	UPPR BOUND
ARC 1	1	2	0	0	4
ARC 2	2	1	0	0	0
ARC 3	1	3	0	0	9
ARC 4	3	1	0	0	0
ARC 5	1	4	0	0	8
ARC 6	4	1	0	0	0
ARC 7	2	3	0	0	7
ARC 8	3	2	0	0	7
ARC 9	2	5	0	0	4
ARC 10	5	2	0	0	0
ARC 11	2	6	0	0	5
ARC 12	6	2	0	0	0
ARC 13	3	5	0	0	5
ARC 14	5	3	0	0	0
ARC 15	3	4	0	0	3
ARC 16	4	3	0	0	3
ARC 17	4	5	0	0	2
ARC 18	5	4	0	0	0
ARC 19	4	7	0	0	3
ARC 20	7	4	0	0	0
ARC 21	5	6	0	0	6
ARC 22	6	5	0	0	0
ARC 23	5	7	0	0	3

```
ARC   24              7           5           0           0           0
ARC   25              5           8           0           0           5
ARC   26              8           5           0           0           0
ARC   27              6           8           0           0           8
ARC   28              8           6           0           0           0
ARC   29              7           8           0           0           7
ARC   30              8           7           0           0           0
ARC   31              .           1           0           0          50
ARC   32              8           .           0           0          50
```

```
          Example 6.3 - Maximal Flow Network
             MAXIMAL FLOW - SUMMARY REPORT

          Arc           From   To        Flow

          ARC  31        .      1         19
          ARC   1        1      2          4
          ARC   3        1      3          9
          ARC   5        1      4          6
          ARC   9        2      5          4
          ARC  11        2      6          5
          ARC   8        3      2          5
          ARC  13        3      5          5
          ARC  16        4      3          1
          ARC  17        4      5          2
          ARC  19        4      7          3
          ARC  21        5      6          3
          ARC  23        5      7          3
          ARC  25        5      8          5
          ARC  27        6      8          8
          ARC  29        7      8          6
          ARC  32        8      .         19

          Maximal Flow = 19
```

CPM/PERT FOR PROJECT PLANNING, SCHEDULING, AND CONTROL

CPM and PERT are two of the best-known network modeling techniques of management science. CPM (Critical Path Method) and PERT (Program Evaluation and Review Technique) were each developed to aid in the planning, scheduling, and control of large, complex projects.

PERT was developed in 1958 to aid in the planning and scheduling of the U.S. Navy's Polaris missile project, which involved over three thousand different contracting organizations. The outstanding success of the Polaris project is largely responsible for the popular acceptance of PERT as a planning and control device by government and business. CPM was developed independently and simultaneously by the DuPont Company to provide a technique for control of the maintenance of DuPont chemical plants.

The two techniques are almost identical with regard to their basic concepts, which focus on activities, events, predecessors, and a critical path. Thus, they are frequently referred to jointly as CPM/PERT. Both techniques are used as tools in the planning, scheduling, and control of projects that consist of numerous activities, which, although independent of one another, must be completed in a prescribed order or sequence.

Historically, the PERT technique emphasized the uncertainties associated with activity completion times, and fundamental to PERT is the concept of an event, or the reaching of a certain milestone in the completion of a project. CPM, on the other hand, has historically assumed certainty with regard to activity time estimates, and more emphasis has been placed on the trade-off between project cost and completion time. PERT has been widely used as a tool for planning and control of research and development projects, whereas CPM has been more frequently used in large construction projects. CPM/PERT analysis has been applied to numerous projects, including shipbuilding, highway construction, oil refinery maintenance, major building construction. missile countdown procedures, and auditing projects.

CPM/PERT Network Components and Precedence Relationships

CPM/PERT networks consist of two major components, activities and events. **Activities** of the network represent the project operations or tasks to be conducted. As such, activities consume time and resources and incur costs. **Events** of the network represent project milestones, such as the start or the completion of an activity, and occur at points in time. Prerequisites for CPM/PERT network modeling include breaking down the project to be analyzed into independent jobs, or activities, and specifying the precedence relationships for the activities.

CPM/PERT activities are commonly represented graphically by arrows (directed branches), and events are represented by circles (nodes) of the network. Figure 6.29, for example, illustrates the network activities, events, and precedence relationship for the construction of a new sidewalk, which includes (a) construction of concrete forms followed by (b) pouring of the concrete. The sidewalk construction project is summarized as follows:

Activity Identification	Activity Start and Finish Nodes (i, j)	Activity Description	Activity Predecessor	Activity Duration Estimate
a	(1, 2)	Construct	—	5 hr
b	(2, 3)	Pour concrete	a	1 hr

The network diagram in Figure 6.29 illustrates the precedence relationship of the two project activities—activity b (pouring of concrete) cannot begin until activity a (construction of forms) has been completed. Specification of the precedence relationships

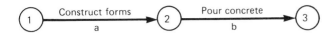

Figure 6.29 CPM/PERT *Network for Sidewalk Construction*

among project activities is a fundamental requirement of CPM/PERT modeling and analysis.

Node 1 in the network diagram is the event (starting construction of concrete forms) that represents the start of the project. Node 2 represents two events: completion of forms construction and starting the pouring of the concrete. Node 3 represents the completion of the pouring of the concrete, as well as the completion of the project.

A project node is said to have *occurred* (or to have been *realized*) when all activities terminating at the node have been completed. Only upon realization of a node can the activity or activities emanating from the node be started. For example, node 2 in Figure 6.29 is realized upon completion of activity a, the only activity terminating at node 2. Node 2 is realized at the end of 5 hours, the time required to construct the concrete forms. At this point in time, activity b (starting the pouring of concrete) emanating from node 2 may begin. The project is completed upon realization of code 3, completion of the pouring of the concrete. For the example shown, project completion will occur at the end of 6 hours.

Concurrent and Dummy Activities

The sidewalk construction example will be expanded slightly to demonstrate a case in which two activities are conducted concurrently. In this example, the activities include (a) construction of concrete forms and (a′) preparation of the concrete (mixing of the cement, gravel, and water to yield concrete ready for pouring). Both activities a and a′ are predecessors to activity b (pouring of the concrete). The redefined sidewalk construction project is shown graphically as a network in Figure 6.30(A) and is summarized as follows:

Activity Identification	Activity Start and Finish Nodes (i, j)	Activity Description	Activity Predecessor	Activity Duration Estimate
a′	(1, 2)	Prepare concrete	—	2 hr
a	(1, 2)	Construct forms	—	5 hr
b	(2, 3)	Pour concrete	a, a′	1 hr

The Figure 6.30(A) network, however, represents an incorrect modeling procedure for CPM/PERT networks. This network violates a basic rule of CPM/PERT modeling: *two or more network activities cannot simultaneously share the same start and finish nodes.* This rule has been violated in Figure 6.30(A), since both activities a and a′ emanate from node 1 and end at node 2.

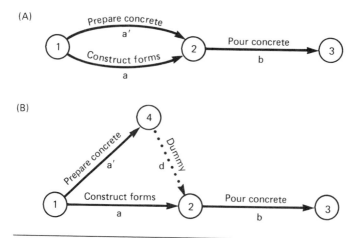

Figure 6.30 *Refined Network Models: (A) Incorrect Network Representation; (B) Correct Network Representation*

This problem is resolved with the introduction of a **dummy activity**. The correc network model for the redefined example is shown in Figure 6.30(B) and is summarize as follows:

Activity Identification	Activity Start and Finish Nodes (i, j)	Activity Description	Activity Predecessor	Activity Duration Estimate
a'	(1, 4)	Prepare concrete	—	2 hr
a	(1, 2)	Construct forms	—	5 hr
d	(4, 2)	Dummy activity	a'	0 hr
b	(2, 3)	Pour concrete	a, d	1 hr

The network has been correctly revised to include a new node, 4, and a new dummy activity, d, that emanates from node 4 and ends at node 2.[1] A dummy activity is illus- trated graphically by a dashed line and an arrowhead to indicate direction. A dummy activity does not consume time or resources, but it does preserve the required precedence relationship among project activities. Thus, the time duration associated with dummy activity d is zero.

Note that the numbers assigned to network nodes have no meaning in regard to activity precedence relationships. Rather, the precedence relationships are shown by the *arrangement* of the network of connected arrows and nodes. The predecessor for activity d is activity a', and the predecessors for activity b are activity a and activity d, which ensures the completion of activity a' prior to the start of activity b.

[1] It would have been equally correct to reverse the arrangement of activities a and a' in Figure 6.30(B)— to represent activity a by branch (1, 4) and a' by branch (1, 2). Either approach would correct the problem of having both activities a and a' emanating from node 1 and ending at node 2.

Project Critical Path

After a project has been decomposed (broken down) into its activities and events and estimates of the activity durations have been obtained, a primary objective of CPM/PERT analysis is to determine the minimum time required for completion of the entire project. The minimum time required for project completion is equal to the **longest time path,** or sequence of connected activities, through the network, which describes the precedence relationships of all project activities. The longest time path is also referred to as the **critical path.**

To illustrate the concept of the critical path, we will return to the sidewalk construction example, shown again in Figure 6.31. The estimated activity time durations are shown above each network activity.

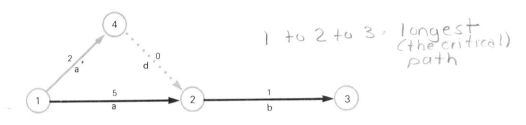

Figure shows: 1 to 2 to 3 = longest (the critical) path

Figure 6.31 *Project Network Critical Path*

Since activity a′ (preparation of concrete) is completed at the end of 2 hours, node 4 is *realized* at that point in time. The dummy activity, d, is then simultaneously started and completed within this same amount of time (2 hours), since it consumes zero time. However, node 2 is not yet realized at time 2 (at the end of 2 hours), since activity b (pouring of concrete) cannot begin until *both* its predecessors, a and d, have been completed. Activity a (construction of forms) is not completed until time 5—at the end of 5 hours. Thus, node 2 is said to be realized at time 5, which is equal to *the later of the completion times* for the two activities terminating at node 2, a and d.

Upon the completion of both predecessors to activity b (realization of node 2), activity b is started at time 5. Since the duration of activity b is 1 hour, it will be completed at time 6, event 3 will be realized, and the project will be completed.

The project is not considered complete until activity b is finished. Since activity b is the only activity following node 2, it obviously belongs to the critical path for determining project duration. However, from node 1 to node 2 there are two paths that are candidates for the critical path: path 1→4→2 and path 1→2. The path from node 1 to node 2 has been determined to be the longest duration path. Thus, the project critical path is 1→2→3, which yields a minimum possible project duration of 6 hours. Activities a and b are defined as **critical activities,** which determine overall project duration. The critical path is shown on the Figure 6.31 network by bold arrows.

In summary, the critical path is the longest path, or sequence of connected activities, through the network, which determines the minimum time required to complete the project. Activities on the critical path are referred to as **critical activities.** These activities, or jobs, are critical in determining the project's duration. In order to shorten the project completion time, it is necessary to shorten one or more of the activities on the critical path.

As a final point regarding Figure 6.31, note that activity a' (preparation of concrete) is completed after 2 hours, whereas activity b (pouring of the concrete) cannot begin until after the 5 hours required to complete activity a (construction of concrete forms) have passed. Thus, a **slack,** or **float,** period of 3 hours is associated with activity a'. This means that the preparation of the concrete may be delayed by up to 3 hours without delaying the overall project. On the other hand, activities a and b have zero slack; these activities cannot be delayed without delaying the entire project. Further computational methods for determining the project critical path and computing activity slacks will be presented in the following section on activity scheduling.

Activity Scheduling

A primary objective of CPM/PERT analysis is the determination of an **activity schedule,** which gives the start and finish times for each project activity. Preparation of such a schedule also provides a rigorous framework for determining the project critical path (and simultaneously the project duration) and computing the slack associated with each project activity.

Example 6.4   Installation of a Check-Processing System

The preparation of an activity schedule will be presented within the context of the following project example. The B & B National Bank wishes to plan and schedule the development and installation of a new computerized check-processing system. The changeover in check-processing procedures requires employment of additional personnel to operate the new system, development of new systems (computer software), and modification of existing check-sorting equipment. The activities required to complete the project and the precedence relationships among the activities have been determined by bank management and are given in the following table.

Activity	Description	Activity Predecessor
a	Position recruiting	—
b	System development	—
c	System training	a
d	Equipment training	a
e	Manual system test	b, c
f	Preliminary system changeover	b, c
g	Computer-personnel interface	d, e
h	Equipment modification	d, e
i	Equipment testing	h
j	System debugging and installation	f, g
k	Equipment changeover	g, i

The next step is to obtain estimates of the project activity times and construct the network diagram for the project. The following table gives a summary of the project

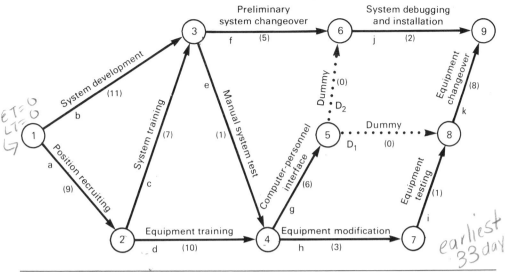

Figure 6.32 *Project Network for New Check-Processing System*

activities, showing the activity time (duration) estimates. Also shown are the start and end nodes (*i, j*) for each activity of the project network, which is illustrated in Figure 6.32. Note that it is necessary to include two dummy activities in the table and in Figure 6.32, since activity g, in conjunction with activity i, is a predecessor to activity k; and activity g, in conjunction with activity f, is a predecessor to activity j. Examination of the project network reveals that the activity precedence relationships can be achieved only by the inclusion of the dummy activities D_1 and D_2. Inclusion of the two dummy activities satisfies the additional CPM/PERT rule that a single activity cannot be shown as two different branches of the network. Without dummy activities D_1 and D_2, it would be necessary to show activity g as both the branches (4, 8) and (4, 6) in order to preserve the required precedence relationship. This problem is resolved by showing activity g as branch (4, 5) and connecting node 5 to nodes 6 and 8 with dummy activities.

Activity	Activity Start and End Nodes (*i, j*)	Activity Predecessor	Activity Duration (in days)
a	(1, 2)	—	9
b	(1, 3)	—	11
c	(2, 3)	a	7
d	(2, 4)	a	10
e	(3, 4)	b, c	1
f	(3, 6)	b, c	5
g	(4, 5)	d, e	6
h	(4, 7)	d, e	3
i	(7, 8)	h	1
D_1	(5, 8)	g	0
D_2	(5, 6)	g	0
j	(6, 9)	f, D_2	2
k	(8, 9)	i, D_1	8

The following discussion will present the CPM/PERT concepts of **earliest time** and **latest time.** In this discussion, network activities will be referred to by their star and end nodes, using the (i, j) notation given in the previous table. The terms *event* anc *node* will be used interchangeably throughout the discussion.

Earliest Time

The earliest time (ET) is the point in time at which *all* activities leading to a node have been completed. In other words, the earliest time is the time of node realization. ET for a node is determined as the *latest* activity completion time for all activities ending at the node. ET_i (where i denotes node i) is, therefore, the earliest starting time for all activities emanating from node i.

ET values for each event are calculated by means of a *forward* pass through the network, progressing from the project start node to the project completion node. Since node 1 is the initial project event in Figure 6.32, it follows that $ET_i = 0$. The earliest time for event 2 is equal to the completion time for activity $(1, 2)$, since this activity is the only activity terminating at event 2. Thus, $ET_2 = 9$, or the end of 9 days.

The earliest time for node 3 is determined as the latest activity completion time for either activity $(1, 3)$ or $(2, 3)$. The completion time for activity $(1, 3)$ is 11 days. Activity $(2, 3)$ is started at the end of 9 days (ET_2), conducted for a period of 7 days, and completed at the end of 16 days $(9 + 7 = 16)$. Since the activity completion time of 16 days for $(2, 3)$ is later than the completion time of 11 days for $(1, 3)$, the earliest time for node 3 is at the end of 16 days $(ET_3 = 16)$. Also, activities $(3, 4)$ and $(3, 6)$ emanating from node 3 cannot be started until the occurrence or realization of node 3 at time 16. This requirement preserves the stipulated precedence relationship of project activity starts given initially for this example.

The calculation procedure for determining the earliest time for each network node, j, is given as

Determine $ET_j = \max \{ET_i + t_{ij}\}$, for all activities (i, j) ending at node j
where

t_{ij} = estimated time duration for activity (i, j)
ET_i = earliest time that activity (i, j) can be started

For example, the earliest time for node 3 is computed as

$$
\begin{aligned}
ET_3 &= \max \{ET_1 + t_{13}, ET_2 + t_{23}\} \\
&= \max \{0 + 11, 9 + 7\} \\
&= \max \{11, 16\} \\
&= 16
\end{aligned}
$$

Calculations of the earliest times for all network nodes are summarized in Table 6.5. Notice that node 9, the project completion node, is realized at time 33 (at the end of 33 days). Therefore, the project duration is 33 days.

Latest Time

The next step in completing the activity-scheduling analysis and determining the project critical path is to compute the event latest times. The event latest time (LT) is the latest

Table 6.5 *Calculation of Earliest Times (Forward Pass)*

Activity Ending Node (j)	Activity Start Node (i)	Earliest Time + Activity Time ($ET_i + t_{ij}$)	Maximum* = Earliest Time at Node j (ET_j)
1	—	—	0*
2	1	0 + 9	9*
3	1	0 + 11	11
	2	9 + 7	16*
4	2	9 + 10	19*
	3	16 + 1	17
5	4	19 + 6	25*
6	3	16 + 5	21
	5	25 + 0	25*
7	4	19 + 3	22*
8	5	25 + 0	25*
	7	22 + 1	23
9	6	25 + 2	27
	8	25 + 8	33*

time an event can occur without delaying completion of the project beyond the time frame established in the forward pass. Recall that the forward pass determined the earliest project completion time to be 33 days. The objective of the latest time calculations is to determine to what extent each project activity can be delayed and the project still completed within 33 days.

LT values for each event are calculated by means of a *backward* pass through the network, starting at node 9 and ending at node 1. Since the objective is to complete the project by the earliest time ($ET_9 = 33$), it follows that LT_9 also equals 33. The latest time for event 6 is equal to $33 - 2 = 31$, or $LT_9 - t_{69} = LT_6$. Since the time required to complete activity (6, 9) is 2 days, node 6 must be realized by no later than time 31 in order to complete the project at time 33. The latest time for node 8 is given as $LT_9 - t_{89} = 33 - 8 = 25$.

Since activity (4, 5) precedes both activities (6, 9) and (8, 9), the dummy activities (5, 6) and (5, 8) have been included in the network to preserve this relationship. The duration for a dummy activity is always zero. The latest *allowable* time for realization of node 5 is calculated as the *earlier* of the times $LT_6 - t_{56}$ and $LT_8 - t_{58}$. Since both t_{56} and t_{58} equal zero, we have $31 - 0$ versus $25 - 0$. Thus, LT_5 must equal 25, the earlier time, in order to complete the project by time 33.

In general, the calculation procedure for determining the latest time for each network node, i, is given by the following:

Determine $LT_i = \min \{LT_j - t_{ij}\}$, for all activities ($i, j$) emanating from node i

For example, the latest time at node 5 is computed as

$$LT_5 = \min \{LT_6 - t_{56}, LT_8 - t_{58}\}$$
$$= \min \{31 - 0, 25 - 0\}$$
$$= \min \{31, 25\}$$
$$= 25$$

Calculations of the latest times for all network nodes are summarized in Table 6.6. By definition, $LT_n = ET_n$, where n is the project termination (or sink) node, and $LT_1 = ET_1 = 0$ for the project start (or source) node.

Table 6.6 Calculation of Latest Times (Backward Pass)

Activity Start Node (i)	Activity End Node (j)	Latest Activity Time Time ($LT_j - t_{ij}$)	Minimum* = Latest Time at Node i (LT_i)
9	—	—	33*
8	9	33 − 8	25*
7	8	25 − 1	24*
6	9	33 − 2	31*
5	6	31 − 0	31
	8	25 − 0	25*
4	5	25 − 6	19*
	7	24 − 3	21
3	4	19 − 1	18*
	6	31 − 5	26
2	3	18 − 7	11
	4	19 − 10	9*
1	2	9 − 9	0*
	3	18 − 11	7

The project network is shown in Figure 6.33, which gives the values for ET and LT alongside each network node. (The reader may ignore, for the time being, the TS and FS values alongside each network activity.) Note that the earliest times and latest times are equal for nodes along the path 1→2→4→5→8→9. Since the latest *allowable* node realization times, in order to complete the project at time 33, are exactly equal to the earliest *possible* node realization times, the sequence of connected activities along the 1→2→4→5→8→9 path constitutes the critical path. The bold arrows along this path denote critical activities. No activity along the critical path may be delayed if the project is to be completed at the end of 33 days. Thus, the schedule for these activities is rigid, without any allowance for variation.

Activity Slack

Activities not on the critical path may be delayed to some extent without delaying completion of the project beyond the 33-day time period. Activity slack computations provide

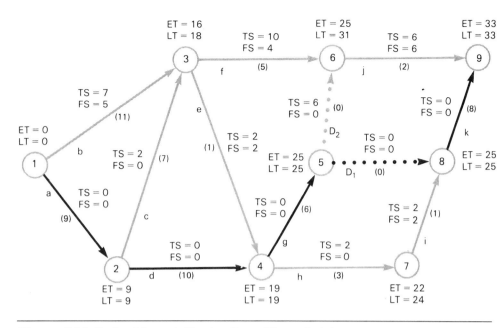

Figure 6.33 *Project Network Showing Event Times, Activity Slacks, and Critical Path*

a measure of the extent to which noncritical activities may be extended or delayed. These are the TS and FS values shown next to each activity in Figure 6.33, defined as total slack and free slack, respectively.

Two types of slack are defined for each activity of the project. **Total slack** (TS_{ij}) for activity (i, j) is the maximum time period available to schedule the activity minus the estimated duration of the activity. The times within which an activity must be scheduled are computed from the ET and LT values for each activity's start node and end node. Thus, the allowable scheduling time for activity (i, j) is determined from the computed values of ET_i and LT_j. For example, activity $(3, 6)$ must be scheduled to begin no earlier than time 16 ($ET_3 = 16$) and to end no later than time 31 ($LT_6 = 31$). The maximum time period available for completion of activity $(3, 6)$ is $LT_6 - ET_3 = 31 - 16 = 15$ days. Since activity $(3, 6)$ requires only 5 days for completion, it may be delayed or extended by as much as 10 days without delaying completion of the project.

Total slack values for each network activity are computed as follows:

$$TS_{ij} = LT_j - ET_i - t_{ij}$$
$$= \text{latest time at } j - \text{earliest time at } i - \text{activity } (i, j) \text{ duration}$$

For example, the total slack values for activities $(3, 6)$ and $(6, 9)$ are

$$TS_{36} = LT_6 - ET_3 - t_{36}$$
$$= 31 - 16 - 5$$
$$= 10$$
$$TS_{69} = LT_9 - ET_6 - t_{69}$$
$$= 33 - 25 - 2$$
$$= 6$$

The total slack values for each network activity are shown alongside each activity in Figure 6.33.

The total slack computation for each activity assumes that the activity (i, j) can begin at the earliest possible time (ET_i) and that it does not have to be completed until the latest allowable time (LT_j). Such a completion time for activity (i, j) would, of course, delay the start time for any immediate successor activities (at node j) until the completion of activity (i, j). Note that the total slack computation for activity $(3, 6)$ assumes that node 6 will not be realized until time $LT_6 = 31$. Thus, activity $(6, 9)$ could not begin until time 31. However, the total slack computation for activity $(6, 9)$ assumes that node 6 will be realized by time $ET_6 = 25$.

This leads to the concept of **shared slack** among activities in a given sequence. If activity $(3, 6)$ is delayed by only 4 days (with a completion time of $ET_6 = 25$), then activity $(6, 9)$ can start at $ET_6 = 25$ and will have a total slack time of 6 days, as previously computed. If, however, activity $(3, 6)$ is delayed by the total slack value of 10 days (with a completion time of $LT_6 = 31$), then activity $(6, 9)$ will have zero slack available.

Any delay in activity $(3, 6)$ beyond 4 days will reduce the slack for activity $(6, 9)$. Thus, both activities $(3, 6)$ and $(6, 9)$ jointly share 6 days' slack. That is, activity $(3, 6)$ may be delayed by 4 days, and, in addition, the *sequence of activities* on the path $3 \rightarrow 6 \rightarrow 9$ may be delayed by up to a total of 6 days without delaying the project.

In summary, activity $(3, 6)$ has a total slack of 10 days. It can be delayed by 4 days without any delay in the start time for activity $(6, 9)$. Activity $(6, 9)$ has a total slack of 6 days. For every day that activity $(3, 6)$ is delayed beyond 4 days, the slack time for activity $(6, 9)$ is reduced by a like amount. Thus, 6 days of slack are shared by activities $(3, 6)$ and $(6, 9)$, and activity $(3, 6)$ also has 4 days of **free slack**, referred to as FS_{ij}.

In general, free slack for an activity is defined as the amount by which an activity may be delayed without causing *any* delay in its *immediate successor* activities. The computation procedure for free slack for activity (i, j) is given as follows:

$$FS_{ij} = ET_j - ET_i - t_{ij}$$
$$= \text{earliest time at } j - \text{earliest time at } i - \text{activity } (i, j) \text{ duration}$$

For example, the free slack values for activities $(3, 6)$ and $(6, 9)$ are

$$FS_{36} = ET_6 - ET_3 - t_{36}$$
$$= 25 - 16 - 5$$
$$= 4$$
$$FS_{69} = ET_9 - ET_6 - t_{69}$$
$$= 33 - 25 - 2$$
$$= 6$$

The values for free slack are shown alongside each activity in Figure 6.33, and the entire project including all previously computed values is summarized in Table 6.7. The values of both total slack and free slack always equal zero for each activity on the critical path. In some cases, total activity slack is positive while free slack is equal to zero, since any delay in the activity would delay its successor activity(s) beyond its earliest start date. Also, in several cases, free slack equals total slack. This is because the activity does not share any slack with its successor activity(s). In all cases, FS ≤ TS.

Table 6.7 *Time Values for the Bank Check-Processing Project*

Activity	Alternate Activity Designation (i, j)	Activity Duration (t_{ij})	Earliest Time at Node i ET_i	Latest Time at Node j LT_j	For Activity (i, j) Total Slack TS_{ij}	For Activity (i, j) Free Slack FS_{ij}
a*	(1, 2)	9	0	9	0	0
b	(1, 3)	11	0	18	7	5
c	(2, 3)	7	9	18	2	0
d*	(2, 4)	10	9	19	0	0
e	(3, 4)	1	16	19	2	2
f	(3, 6)	5	16	31	10	4
g*	(4, 5)	6	19	25	0	0
h	(4, 7)	3	19	24	2	0
i	(7, 8)	1	22	25	2	2
D_1^*	(5, 8)	0	25	25	0	0
D_2	(5, 6)	0	25	31	6	0
j	(6, 9)	2	25	33	6	6
k*	(8, 9)	8	25	33	0	0

*Critical path activities

Computerized CPM/PERT Analysis

The capability to perform CPM/PERT network analysis is generally available in most management science software packages. In order to demonstrate these capabilities, we will use the AB:QM package. Following is the computer-generated analysis of the CPM network for the check-processing system installation in Example 6.4. The program output includes the input data requirements and a determination of earliest and latest times and slack for the network.

```
Program: CPM/PERT / CPM

Problem Title : Example 6.4

***** Input Data *****

---------------------------------------------
Activity    Start     End         Time
---------------------------------------------
    1         1         2        9.000
    2         1         3       11.000
    3         2         3        7.000
    4         2         4       10.000
    5         3         4        1.000
    6         3         6        5.000
    7         4         5        6.000
    8         4         7        3.000
    9         7         8        1.000
   10         5         8        0.000
   11         5         6        0.000
   12         6         9        2.000
   13         8         9        8.000
---------------------------------------------
```

```
***** Program Output *****

---------------------------------------------------------------------------
            Earliest      Earliest      Latest       Latest        Slack
Activity    Start(ES)     Finish(EF)    Start(LS)    Finish(LF)
---------------------------------------------------------------------------
    1 *        0.000         9.000         0.000         9.000        0.000
    2           0.000        11.000         7.000        18.000        7.000
    3           9.000        16.000        11.000        18.000        2.000
    4 *        9.000        19.000         9.000        19.000        0.000
    5          16.000        17.000        18.000        19.000        2.000
    6          16.000        21.000        26.000        31.000       10.000
    7 *       19.000        25.000        19.000        25.000        0.000
    8          19.000        22.000        21.000        24.000        2.000
    9          22.000        23.000        24.000        25.000        2.000
   10 *       25.000        25.000        25.000        25.000        0.000
   11          25.000        25.000        31.000        31.000        6.000
   12          25.000        27.000        31.000        33.000        6.000
   13 *       25.000        33.000        25.000        33.000        0.000
---------------------------------------------------------------------------
(* : Critical Path Activities)

Expected Completion Time :       33.000

***** End of Output *****
```

Notice that the times for earliest start (ES) and earliest finish (EF) and latest start (LS) and latest finish (LF) in this program-output table relate to the network activities, whereas the ET and LT values shown in Figure 6.33 and Table 6.7 relate to the network nodes. For example, at node 3 in Figure 6.33, ET = 16 and LT = 18, whereas the corresponding values in the program-output table for activity (1, 3) are EF = 11 and LF = 18. The reason for these differences is that there are two conventions for determining earliest and latest times. The convention employed in this text is to determine these times *at the node;* hence, they are *event* times. In other words, the earliest time node 3 can be realized is at 16 days, and the latest it can be realized is at 18 days. Alternatively, the convention used by many software packages is to determine earliest and latest times *on the activity;* hence, they are *activity* times. Thus, in the program output there is no single set of earliest and latest times associated with node 3. Instead, activity (1, 3) has one set of earliest and latest finish times (i.e., EF = 11 and LF = 18), and activity (2, 3) has another set (i.e., EF = 16 and LF = 18). The second set of times associated with activity (2, 3) corresponds to the nodal event times in Figure 6.33, because activity (2, 3) has no *free* slack whereas activity (1, 3) has free slack of 5 days.

The reason event scheduling is employed in this text (and in many other texts) is because it is computationally easier to demonstrate than activity scheduling. With event scheduling, we are able to use direct formulas to compute earliest and latest times; the process is not as simple with activity scheduling.

Probabilistic Activity Times

Up to this point, activity times have been presented as constant values. This treatment of time estimates as known constants, which yields a deterministic model, assumes certainty in specifying activity times. It is reasonable to expect that considerable uncertainty will often be associated with the estimation of project activity times.

The original version of PERT assumed that project activity times were random variables (probabilistic). It further assumed that the random variable, activity duration, could be associated with the beta distribution, which is a versatile probability distribution that can assume a variety of shapes.

The PERT method for project analysis assumes that three estimates of the activity duration will be obtained for each project activity. The activity duration estimates required are as follows:

1. *Optimistic time* (a_{ij}): the shortest possible time required for the completion of activity (i, j). The probability that the activity could be completed in a shorter time period is extremely small (approximately .01).

2. *Most likely time* (m_{ij}): the most likely (modal) time required to complete activity (i, j). If the activity were repeated many times, this is the duration that would occur most frequently.

3. *Pessimistic time* (b_{ij}): the longest possible time required for completion of activity (i, j). The probability that completion of the activity would take longer than this time estimate is extremely small (approximately .01).

Given the a_{ij}, m_{ij}, b_{ij} time estimates for each project activity and the assumption that the activity time follows a beta distribution, formulas have been derived for calculating the mean $(\hat{t}_{ij})$ and variance (v_{ij}) for each activity time distribution. These formulas are assumed to provide reasonable approximations of the parameters for the beta-distributed activity times. The formulas are given as follows:

Mean, or average, time: $\quad \hat{t}_{ij} = \dfrac{a_{ij} + 4m_{ij} + b_{ij}}{6}$

Variance: $\quad v_{ij} = \left(\dfrac{b_{ij} - a_{ij}}{6}\right)^2$

Three examples of the beta distribution, showing the relative locations of a_{ij}, m_{ij}, b_{ij}, and $\hat{t}_{ij}$, are illustrated in Figure 6.34. It is shown that the distribution is unimodal (has only one highest point) and continuous and has finite limits. The distribution may be symmetrical [Figure 6.34(C)] or skewed in either direction [Figure 6.34(A) and (B)].

Example 6.5   Check-Processing System with Probabilistic Activity Times

The project network is analyzed after the three time estimates obtained for each activity have been converted to the two parameter values, $\hat{t}_{ij}$ and v_{ij}. Table 6.8 gives the time estimates for the previous check-processing changeover problem (Example 6.4). The values provided for the three time estimates have been contrived to facilitate easy verification of the beta formula calculations and to yield mean activity times equal to the single-value estimates originally provided for the example. This way, network analysis in which mean activity times $(\hat{t}_{ij})$ are used to determine ET, LT, TS, FS, and the critical path will yield the same results as were obtained previously using the single-value estimates (t_{ij}) for activity times (shown in Figure 6.33).

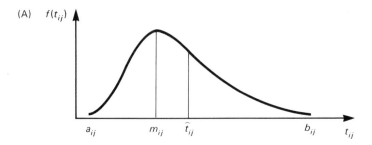

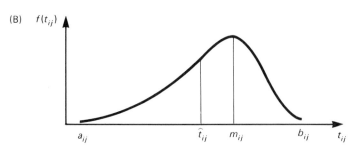

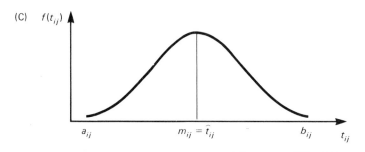

Figure 6.34 *Beta Distributions for Activity Times: (A) Skewed to Right; (B) Skewed to Left; (C) Symmetrical*

Table 6.8 *Probabilistic Time Estimates for Exampe 6.5*

Activity	Activity Nodes (i, j)	Time Estimates for Check-Processing Changeover			Beta Distribution Parameters	
		Optimistic a_{ij}	Most Likely m_{ij}	Pessimistic b_{ij}	Mean $\hat{t}_{ij}$	Variance v_{ij}
a*	(1, 2)	5	8	17	9	4
b	(1, 3)	3	12	15	11	4
c	(2, 3)	4	7	10	7	1
d*	(2, 4)	5	8	23	10	9
e	(3, 4)	1	1	1	1	0
f	(3, 6)	1	4	13	5	4
g*	(4, 5)	3	6	9	6	1
h	(4, 7)	1	2.5	7	3	1
i	(7, 8)	1	1	1	1	0
j	(6, 9)	2	2	2	2	0
k*	(8, 9)	5	8	11	8	1

*Critical path activities
Note: Dummy activities are excluded, since they have zero times.

The AB:QM output for this example is

```
Program: CPM/PERT / PERT

Problem Title : Example 6.5

***** Input Data *****

--------------------------------------------------------------------
Activity  Start    End    Optimistic     Likely     Pessimistic
--------------------------------------------------------------------
    1        1       2       5.000        8.000        17.000
    2        1       3       3.000       12.000        15.000
    3        2       3       4.000        7.000        10.000
    4        2       4       5.000        8.000        23.000
    5        3       4       1.000        1.000         1.000
    6        3       6       1.000        4.000        13.000
    7        4       5       3.000        6.000         9.000
    8        4       7       1.000        2.500         7.000
    9        5       6       0.000        0.000         0.000
   10        5       8       0.000        0.000         0.000
   11        7       8       1.000        1.000         1.000
   12        6       9       2.000        2.000         2.000
   13        8       9       5.000        8.000        11.000
--------------------------------------------------------------------

***** Program Output *****

--------------------------------------------------------------------
Activity          Activity Nodes      Mean      S.D.     Variance
--------------------------------------------------------------------
   1 *              1 --> 2           9.000     2.000     4.000
   2                1 --> 3          11.000     2.000     4.000
   3                2 --> 3           7.000     1.000     1.000
   4 *              2 --> 4          10.000     3.000     9.000
   5                3 --> 4           1.000     0.000     0.000
   6                3 --> 6           5.000     2.000     4.000
   7 *              4 --> 5           6.000     1.000     1.000
   8                4 --> 7           3.000     1.000     1.000
   9                5 --> 6           0.000     0.000     0.000
  10 *              5 --> 8           0.000     0.000     0.000
  11                7 --> 8           1.000     0.000     0.000
  12                6 --> 9           2.000     0.000     0.000
  13 *              8 --> 9           8.000     1.000     1.000
--------------------------------------------------------------------
(* : Critical Path Activities)

Expected Completion Time :      33.000

***** End of Output *****
```

Probability Statements About Project Completion Times

The PERT method assumes that activity times are statistically independent and identically distributed (beta); therefore, the means and variances for activity times may be added to yield total project mean time and variance along a network path. The PERT method further assumes that there will be sufficient activities involved such that the summed totals will be *normally distributed,* according to the **central limit theorem** of probability theory.

If the preceding assumptions are met, it is then possible to make probability statements about the expected (average) completion time for the project. Likewise, it should also be possible to make probability statements about the time required to reach various milestones within the project.

The probability statements in PERT are based on the earliest times (ET) for reaching various events in the network. Therefore, the sums of the activity mean and variance times always refer to the activities on the *longest (time) path* to the node for which probability statements are to be made.

In the bank check-processing example, the sum of the mean activity times on the critical path is 33 days. This is the expected, or mean, project time, which is assumed to be normally distributed. The sum of the variances for activity times on the critical path is 15 days. The calculations for determining the mean and variance of project time are summarized as follows:

$$\text{Mean project time:} \quad E(t) = \hat{t}_{12} + \hat{t}_{24} + \hat{t}_{45} + \hat{t}_{89}$$
$$= 9 + 10 + 6 + 8$$
$$= 33 \text{ days}$$
$$\text{Variance, project time:} \quad V(t) = v_{12} + v_{24} + v_{45} + v_{89}$$
$$= 4 + 9 + 1 + 1$$
$$= 15 \text{ days}$$

Given the mean and variance for the total project time and the assumption of normality, probability statements about project completion time can be made. In order to read probability values from a table for the normal curve, the value of the **standardized random variate** (Z) must first be determined. For the example project, it is calculated as follows:

$$Z = \frac{t' - E(t)}{\sqrt{V(t)}}$$

where
$E(t)$ = mean of normal distribution (mean project time)
$V(t)$ = variance of normal distribution (variance, project time)
t' = project completion time for which a probability statement is to be made

For example, suppose the bank wishes to know the probability of completing the project within 40 days or less ($t' = 40$). The computation is summarized as follows:

$$P(t \leqslant t') = P(t \leqslant 40) = P\left(Z \leqslant \frac{40 - 33}{\sqrt{15}}\right)$$
$$= P\left(Z \leqslant \frac{7}{3.873}\right)$$
$$= P(Z \leqslant 1.8)$$
$$= .9641$$

In other words, the probability value found in a normal distribution table (see Appendix C, Table C.3) for a Z value of 1.8 is .9641. This is illustrated in Figure 6.35, with the area under the curve to the left of 40 shown as .9641. Thus, there is a 96% chance of completion within 40 days and a 4% chance that project completion will require more than 40 days.

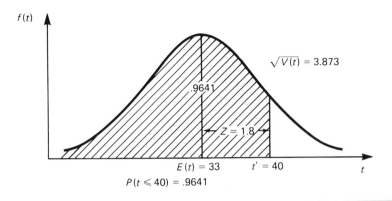

Figure 6.35 *Probability of Project Completion in 40 Days or Less*

In a similar manner, probability statements can be made about earliest completion times at each node of the project network by summing the $\hat{t}_{ij}$ and v_{ij} values for activities on the longest path to each node. This procedure provided by PERT for assessing project completion uncertainties is often attacked as not being rigorous in a probabilistic sense; however, it is often used in actual practice as a workable approach.[2]

Activity Costs and Project Crashing

Extensions of project time analysis are project **time/cost analysis** and project **crashing**. The term *crashing* refers to the shortening of project duration by rushing, or "crashing," one or more of the critical project activities to completion in less than normal time. This is achieved by devoting more resources (i.e., material, equipment, or labor) to the activity to be crashed. One example is working overtime on a project, which speeds up the completion of the activity but also adds to the cost in the form of overtime wages.

Network cost analysis has historically been associated with CPM; however, it can be applied to either PERT or CPM networks. The purpose of project cost analysis is to determine which activities in the network to crash and by how much.

In network cost analysis, the two types of costs associated with each activity are estimated: **normal-time cost** and **crash-time cost**. These costs are associated with two time estimates for each activity: **normal time** and **crash time**. In the case of CPM networks, this requires that a crash-time estimate be provided in addition to the normal expected time previously described. For PERT networks, the crash-time estimate is usually the most optimistic time estimate, a_{ij}. The normal-time estimate for PERT networks can be either the estimated most likely time, m_{ij}, or the computed expected time, $\hat{t}_{ij}$.

---

[2] For further discussion, see J. W. Pocock, "PERT as an Analytical Aid for Program Planning—Its Payoff and Problems," *Operations Research* 10 (1962): 893–903.

For purposes of simplicity, the relationship between normal-time cost and crash-time cost for an activity is generally assumed to be linear. (Such a relationship for one activity is illustrated in Figure 6.36.) Thus, the crash cost per unit of time can be estimated by computing the relative change in cost per unit change in time. For the example illustrated in Figure 6.36, the crash cost is $100 per week, computed as follows:

$$\frac{\text{Crash cost} - \text{normal cost}}{\text{Normal time} - \text{crash time}} = \frac{400 - 100}{5 - 2} = \frac{300}{3} = \$100$$

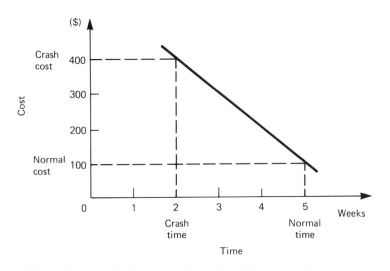

Figure 6.36 *Activity Time/Cost Relationship*

The objective of crash-cost analysis is to reduce the total project completion time while minimizing the cost of crashing. Since the project completion time can be shortened only by crashing critical activities, it follows that not all project activities should be crashed. However, as activities are crashed, the critical path may change, requiring further crashing of previously noncritical activities in order to further reduce the project completion time.

The general procedure for crashing project activities while minimizing cost is given as follows:

Step 0 Determine the minimum project time and associated critical path for the following two cases: (1) if all activities are completed in normal time and (2) if all activities are crashed. The normal-time critical path is the point of departure for the crashing analysis. Determination of the minimum project time when all activities are crashed provides the stopping point for the crashing analysis. Begin with the normal-time critical path.

Step 1 Identify and crash the activity on the critical path with the minimum crash cost per unit of time. If there is more than one critical path, identify and crash the activity(s) on the critical path(s) with the minimum joint crash cost per unit of time. Crash the minimum cost activity down to the point where (1) another path in the network becomes critical or (2) the activity has been crashed to its lowest possible value. This step is summarized in Figure 6.37.

Step 2 Revise the network, adjusting for the time and cost assigned to the crashed activity(s). Determine the critical path(s), using normal activity times for noncrashed activities and crash times

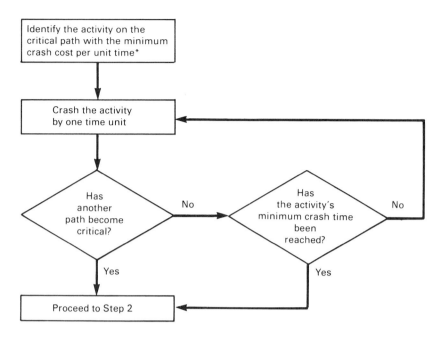

*If there is more than one critical path, identify and crash
the activity(s) on the critical path(s) with the minimum joint crash
cost per unit time.

Figure 6.37 *Step 1: Crashing the Minimum Cost Critical
Activity*

for crashed activities. If the project time equals the crashing time computed in step 0, stop; otherwise, return to step 1.

Example 6.6 Project Crashing

The following example illustrates an application of these steps to a specific project. The example project is described in the following table, which gives normal and crash times and normal and crash costs for each activity. The computed values of crash cost per week are also given. The total project cost if all activities are completed in normal time is $6400. If all activities are crashed, the total cost is $9800.

Activity	(i, j)	Time (Weeks)		Cost ($)		
		Normal	Crashed	Normal	Crashed	Crash Cost per Week
a	(1, 2)	14	6	1400	2200	100
b	(1, 3)	12	8	1000	1800	200
c	(2, 5)	18	14	1600	2000	100
d	(2, 4)	6	4	800	1200	200
e	(3, 4)	4	2	400	800	200
f	(4, 5)	8	6	400	600	100
g	(5, 6)	12	8	800	1200	100
				6400	9800	

The project network is illustrated in Figure 6.38. Activity crash costs per week are shown alongside each activity, and under each cost value are the values for normal time and crash time (in parentheses). For example, the normal time for activity (1, 2) is 14, the crash time is 6, and the cost per week of crashing is $100.

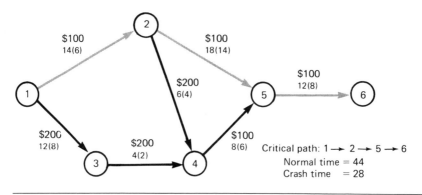

Figure 6.38 *Project Network*

Figure 6.38 shows that in step 0 the critical path is 1→2→5→6 for both normal and crash activity times. The project time, assuming normal activity times, is 44 weeks, at a total cost of $6400. If all activities are crashed, the project time is 28 weeks, at a total cost of $9800.

The normal-time critical path is the point of departure for the next step, and 28 weeks is the stopping point for the crashing analysis (the objective is to complete the project within 28 weeks at the least cost beyond $6400).

ITERATION 1
Step 1 Identify the activity on the critical path with the minimum crash cost per week. Since it is the same for each activity on the critical path, arbitrarily select activity (1, 2) to crash. It is crashed by 8 weeks to its lower limit, 6 weeks. The associated crashing cost is $800 ($100 × 8), yielding a total project cost of $7200 (6400 + 800).

Step 2 Revise the network, adjusting for the time and cost assigned to activity (1, 2), as shown in Figure 6.39. There are now two critical paths, 1→2→5→6 and 1→3→4→5→6. Note that the activity times used for the computation are the time values *not* in parentheses. Return to step 1.

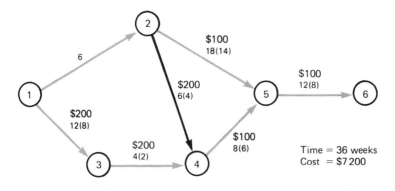

Figure 6.39 *Project Network with Activity (1, 2) Crashed*

ITERATION 2

Step 1 Select the activity(s) on the critical path(s) with the minimum crashing cost(s) that will reduce the total project time. Only by crashing activity (5, 6) can project time be reduced without crashing more than one activity. If project time could be reduced at less cost by crashing two activities (in one or both of the two critical paths), this would be done. However, in this case, the least-cost option is to crash activity (5, 6). Activity (5, 6) is crashed by 4 weeks to its lower limit of 8 weeks. The associated crashing cost is $400, resulting in a total project cost of $7600.

Step 2 Revise the network, adjusting for crashed activity (5, 6), as shown by the network in Figure 6.40(A). Project time has been reduced to 32 weeks; however, the critical paths remain 1→2→ 5→6 and 1→3→4→5→6. Return to step 1.

(A)

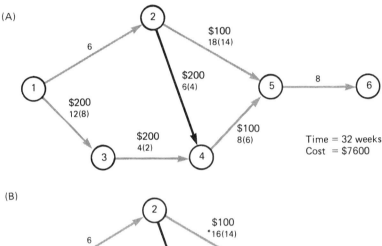

(B)

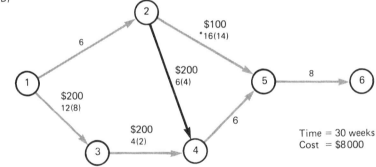

*Activity (2, 5) partially crashed by two time units

(C)

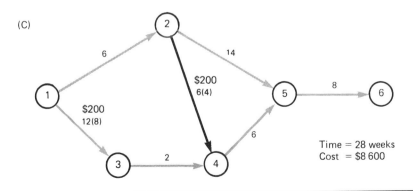

Figure 6.40 *Project Network with (A) Activities (1, 2) and (5, 6) Crashed; (B) Activities (1, 2), (5, 6), (2, 5), and (4, 5) Crashed; (C) Activities (1, 2), (5, 6), (2, 5), (4, 5), and (3, 4) Crashed*

ITERATION 3

Step 1 Select the activity(s) that can be crashed at minimum crashing cost and result in a reduction in project time. Since there is no single activity shared by both critical paths that has not been crashed, select two activities (one from each critical path) to be crashed at minimum crashing cost. If only a single activity is crashed on one of the critical paths, the other critical path will remain critical (unshortened), and the total project time will remain unchanged. Therefore, select two activities (one from each critical path) that result in the minimum *aggregate* weekly crashing cost.

Activity (2, 5) must be selected from path 1→2→5→6, as it is the only remaining activity not crashed. Select activity (4, 5) on path 1→3→4→5→6, since it has the least weekly crashing cost. Determine which of the two activities selected for crashing can be crashed by the least amount, and crash each activity by that amount. Although activity (2, 5) can be crashed by 4 weeks, activity (4, 5) can be crashed by only 2 weeks. Therefore, activity (4, 5) is crashed by 2 weeks to its lower limit of 6 weeks, and activity (2, 5) is crashed by 2 weeks to a duration of 16 weeks. Note that it makes no sense to crash (2, 5) further, since it would not shorten the overall project time, because of critical path 1→3→4→5→6. The cost of crashing activities (2, 5) and (4, 5) is $200 each, yielding a total crashing cost of $400 and a total project cost of $8000.

Step 2 Revise the network, reflecting crashed activities, as shown by the network in Figure 6.40(B). Total project time has been reduced to 30 weeks, and the same two critical paths exist. Return to step 1.

ITERATION 4

Step 1 Two weeks' crashing capability remains for activity (2, 5), since it was crashed by only 2 weeks in iteration 3. On the other critical path (1→3→4→5→6), activities (1, 3) and (3, 4) both have the same crashing cost, and both activities can be crashed by 2 weeks. Therefore, arbitrarily select activity (3, 4) to crash by 2 weeks to its lower limit of 2 weeks. Crash activity (2, 5) by its remaining 2 weeks' capability, to its lower limit of 14 weeks. The cost of crashing activity (2, 5) is $200, and the cost of crashing activity (3, 4) is $400, yielding a total crashing cost of $600 and a project cost of $8600.

Step 2 Revise the network, reflecting crashed activities, as shown by the network in Figure 6.40(C). Total project time has been reduced to 28 weeks, which is equal to the minimum time if all activities were crashed. Also, one of the critical paths consists entirely of crashed activities; therefore, no further reduction in project duration can be achieved.

The minimum possible project time has been obtained without crashing all project activities. The following table provides a summary of the solution results. Five of the seven project activities were crashed, with the resulting activity times shown. Total activity cost is shown to be $8600, including $6400 normal costs and $2200 crashing costs.

Activity	(i, j)	Decision	Crashing Cost ($)	Activity Time (weeks)	Activity Cost ($)
a	(1, 2)	Crash by 8	800	6	2200
b	(1, 3)	Normal	—	12	1000
c	(2, 5)	Crash by 4	400	14	2000
d	(2, 4)	Normal	—	6	800
e	(3, 4)	Crash by 2	400	2	800
f	(4, 5)	Crash by 2	200	6	600
g	(5, 6)	Crash by 4	400	8	1200
			2200		8600

The **trade-off** between project time and cost is summarized in the following table and illustrated in Figure 6.41. Shown are the total project times and costs, beginning with normal activity completion times and ranging through the successive steps of the crashing procedure.

Iteration	Result	Project Time (weeks)	Project Cost ($)
0	No crashings	44	6400
1	Activity (1, 2) crashed by 8 weeks	36	7200
2	Activity (5, 6) crashed by 4 weeks	32	7600
3	Activity (2, 5) initially crashed by 2 weeks and activity (4, 5) crashed by 2 weeks	30	8000
4	Activity (2, 5) further crashed by 2 weeks and activity (3, 4) crashed by 2 weeks	28	8600

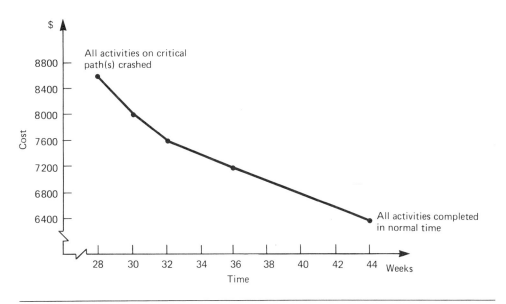

Figure 6.41 Time/Cost Trade-off Relationship

If the project must be completed within a less-than-normal time, Figure 6.41 shows the associated project direct costs within the feasible range of 44 weeks to 28 weeks. However, the appropriate decision structure for the crashing decision should include not only the direct costs considered thus far (such as direct materials, equipment, and labor costs) but also indirect costs (such as salaried personnel, facilities, interest, utilities, and other overhead costs), as well as any contractual penalties associated with project completion time.

Whereas direct costs are greatest when the project is crashed to the least possible time, indirect costs and penalties increase as a function of project time. Figure 6.42 is a hypothetical example, showing both direct and indirect project cost curves, as well as the total cost curve, as functions of different project completion times. The optimal project duration is the time associated with the minimum point on the total cost curve, as shown in Figure 6.42.

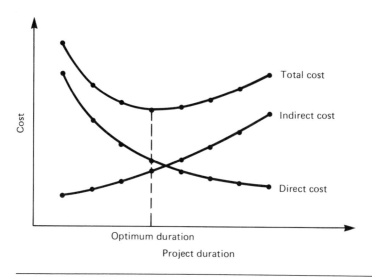

Figure 6.42 *Direct, Indirect, and Total Cost Curves*

Computerized Project Crashing

The AB:QM software package used to solve the network flow problems in the first part of this chapter also has a CPM/PERT component program and the capability to perform project crashing. Following is the AB:QM program output for our project crashing example, Example 6.6. The input data are identical to those contained in Example 6.6.

```
Program: CPM/PERT / CPM With Crashing

Problem Title : Example 6.6

***** Input Data *****

--------------------------------------------------------------------
                                TIME                    COST
                         -------------------   -------------------
Activity  Start   End    Normal     Crash      Normal      Crash
--------------------------------------------------------------------
    1       1      2     14.000     6.000     1400.000    2200.000
    2       1      3     12.000     8.000     1000.000    1800.000
    3       2      5     18.000    14.000     1600.000    2000.000
    4       2      4      6.000     4.000      800.000    1200.000
    5       3      4      4.000     2.000      400.000     800.000
    6       4      5      8.000     6.000      400.000     600.000
    7       5      6     12.000     8.000      800.000    1200.000
--------------------------------------------------------------------
```

```
***** Program Output *****
-------------------------------------------------------------------
                                   Crashing   Activity  Activity
Activity  Activity Nodes  Crash by   Cost       Time      Cost
-------------------------------------------------------------------
   1 *        1 --> 2      8.000     800.000    6.000   2200.000
   2 *        1 --> 3      2.000     400.000   10.000   1400.000
   3 *        2 --> 5      4.000     400.000   14.000   2000.000
   4          2 --> 4      0.000       0.000    6.000    800.000
   5 *        3 --> 4      0.000       0.000    4.000    400.000
   6 *        4 --> 5      2.000     200.000    6.000    600.000
   7 *        5 --> 6      4.000     400.000    8.000   1200.000
-------------------------------------------------------------------
(* : Critical Path Activities)      2200.000            8600.000

Expected Normal Completion Time  :   44.000
Expected Crashed Completion Time :   28.000

***** End of Output *****
```

Linear Programming Formulation of a CPM/PERT Network

As is the case with many types of network models, a linear programming model can be formulated for a CPM/PERT network. The following general linear programming model, when solved, will yield the earliest event times at each node, the earliest project completion time, and (on inspection of the dual solution) the critical path. The value of formulating a CPM/PERT network as a linear programming model is somewhat limited; however, it does provide the basis for a linear programming formulation of a project crashing analysis, which is very useful, as shown in the following section.

$$\text{Minimize } Z = \sum_{i=1}^{N} T_i$$

subject to
$$T_j - T_i \geq t_{ij}, \text{ for all } i \text{ and } j \text{ where } j > i$$
$$t_{ij} \geq 0$$

where
T_i = earliest event time for node i
T_j = earliest event time for node j
t_{ij} = activity time for activity (i, j)
N = number of the project completion node

As an example, consider the CPM/PERT network in Example 6.4, shown in Figure 6.32. The linear programming model of this network is formulated, using the LINDO software package, as follows:

```
: look all
MIN      T1 + T2 + T3 + T4 + T5 + T6 + T7 + T8 + T9
SUBJECT TO
        2) - T1 + T2 >=    9
        3) - T1 + T3 >=   11
        4) - T2 + T3 >=    7
        5) - T2 + T4 >=   10
        6) - T3 + T4 >=    1
        7) - T4 + T5 >=    6
        8) - T3 + T6 >=    5
        9) - T5 + T6 >=    0
       10) - T4 + T7 >=    3
       11) - T7 + T8 >=    1
       12) - T5 + T8 >=    0
       13) - T6 + T9 >=    2
       14) - T8 + T9 >=    8
END
:
```

Note that there is one constraint inequality in this model corresponding to each activity in the network (including dummy activities).

Solving this linear programming model with the LINDO package results in the following solution:

```
            OBJECTIVE FUNCTION VALUE
  1)        174.000000
  VARIABLE          VALUE         REDUCED COST
      T1           .000000          9.000000
      T2          9.000000          .000000
      T3         16.000000          .000000
      T4         19.000000          .000000
      T5         25.000000          .000000
      T6         25.000000          .000000
      T7         22.000000          .000000
      T8         25.000000          .000000
      T9         33.000000          .000000

      ROW    SLACK OR SURPLUS      DUAL PRICES
      2)           .000000         -8.000000
      3)          5.000000          .000000
      4)           .000000         -1.000000
      5)           .000000         -6.000000
      6)          2.000000          .000000
      7)           .000000         -4.000000
      8)          4.000000          .000000
      9)           .000000         -1.000000
     10)           .000000         -1.000000
     11)          2.000000          .000000
     12)           .000000         -2.000000
     13)          6.000000          .000000
     14)           .000000         -1.000000

  NO. ITERATIONS=     16
```

This solution is identical to the earliest time solution obtained by making a forward pass through the network, as shown in Table 6.5 and Figure 6.33. The Z value of 174 actually has no significance in the interpretation of the event solution times; it does, however, serve to force all event times to be as small as possible (earliest times).

Since each constraint in the linear programming model corresponds to a network activity, there will be a dual variable corresponding to each activity constraint. The dual variables that correspond to the critical path activities will always have dual solution values (shadow prices) greater than zero, since these are the activities that constrain the solution. Thus, to determine the critical path from the LINDO output, it is necessary only to observe which model constraints have dual shadow prices other than zero. For our example, the LINDO output identifies the constraints for activities $(1, 2)$, $(2, 4)$, $(4, 5)$, $(5, 8)$, and $(8, 9)$ as having dual prices greater than zero, thus indicating the critical path as $1 \rightarrow 2 \rightarrow 4 \rightarrow 5 \rightarrow 8 \rightarrow 9$.

Linear Programming Model for Project Crashing and the Computerized Solution

The objective of crashing analysis is to minimize the cost of crashing a project given the prescribed project completion time and the established limits on how much each project activity can be crashed. The general linear programming model to accomplish project crashing at minimum cost is

$$\text{Minimize } Z = \sum_{(i,j)} c_{ij} x_{ij}$$

subject to

$$x_{ij} \leq CL_{ij} \quad \text{(all } i, j)$$
$$T_i + t_{ij} - x_{ij} \leq T_j \quad \text{(all } i, j)$$
$$T_N \leq PCT$$
$$T_i, T_j, t_{ij}, x_{ij} \geq 0$$

where

x_{ij} = amount of time activity (i, j) is crashed (i.e., reduced)

t_{ij} = regular activity time for activity (i, j)

T_i = earliest event time for node i

T_j = earliest event time for node j

c_{ij} = cost per unit time of crashing activity (i, j)

CL_{ij} = crash limit, maximum number of time units activity (i, j) can be crashed

T_N = project completion (sink) node

PCT = Prescribed Completion Time for the project

As an example, consider the project crashing model in Example 6.6, illustrated in Figure 6.38 and its accompanying table. The complete linear programming model to crash this network to 28 weeks is formulated and solved using LINDO as follows:

$$\text{Minimize } Z = 100x_{12} + 200x_{13} + 200x_{24} + 100x_{25} + 200x_{34} + 100x_{45} + 100x_{56}$$

subject to

$$x_{12} \leq 8$$
$$x_{13} \leq 4$$

$$x_{24} \leq 2$$
$$x_{25} \leq 4$$
$$x_{34} \leq 2$$
$$x_{45} \leq 2$$
$$x_{56} \leq 4$$
$$T_1 + t_{12} - x_{12} - T_2 \leq 0$$
$$T_1 + t_{13} - x_{13} - T_3 \leq 0$$
$$T_2 + t_{24} - x_{24} - T_4 \leq 0$$
$$T_2 + t_{25} - x_{25} - T_5 \leq 0$$
$$T_3 + t_{34} - x_{34} - T_4 \leq 0$$
$$T_4 + t_{45} - x_{45} - T_5 \leq 0$$
$$T_5 + t_{56} - x_{56} - T_6 \leq 0$$
$$T_6 \leq 28 \text{ weeks}$$
$$T_i, T_j, t_{ij}, x_{ij} \geq 0$$

Note that in the printout of the LINDO LP model (p. 303), the normal activity times have been substituted for the t_{ij} variables, and the constraints rearranged so that the constant normal activity times are the right-hand-side values. The Z value of $2,200 is the sum of the crashing costs. Since the total normal time cost for the project is $6,400, this results in a total crashed project cost of $8,600. Note that the solution values for x_{ij} are the amount by which each activity will be crashed, that is, activity (1, 2) will be crashed by 8 weeks, from a normal time of 14 weeks down to 6 weeks, and so on for each activity.

Also, note that the LP model solution results in activity (1, 3) being crashed by 2 weeks and activity (3, 4) not being crashed at all. This is the opposite of the previously obtained result where activity (3, 4) was crashed by 2 weeks and activity (1, 3) was not crashed at all. This is because there is an alternate optimal solution, as indicated by the fact that there is a reduced cost of zero for the variable, x_{34}, in the LINDO solution printout. Recall that a variable with a zero solution value *and* a zero reduced cost indicates that an alternate optimal solution exists. This was also alluded to in the previous crashing analysis (in iteration 4, step 7) where we arbitrarily selected activity (3, 4) to crash rather than activity (1, 3) since they both had the same crashing costs.

Project Management Software for the Personal Computer

In a recent article by Wasil and Assad,[3] it was reported that during the period from 1985 to 1988 the number of commercially available project management software packages for personal computers increased from a few to over a hundred, and the cost of these packages ranges from several hundred to several thousand dollars. Total sales of these packages have been estimated at $51 million for 1987 alone. These figures indicate that project management has become one of the most visible and widely used management science techniques. One point emphasized was that an important role of project management programs is to aid in communications and information sharing among interested parties. Some of the more popular packages include Harvard Project Manager, Microsoft Project,

---

[3]E. Wasil and A. Assad, "Project Management on the PC: Software, Applications, and Trends," *Interfaces* 18, no. 2 (March-April 1988): 75–84.

```
TITLE    LP MODEL FOR PROJECT CRASHING (EXAMPLE 6.6)

MIN     100 X12 + 200 X13 + 200 X24 + 100 X25 + 200 X34 + 100 X45
     + 100 X56
SUBJECT TO
        2)    X12 <=    8
        3)    X13 <=    4
        4)    X24 <=    2
        5)    X25 <=    4
        6)    X34 <=    2
        7)    X45 <=    2
        8)    X56 <=    4
        9)    X12 - T1 + T2 >=    14
       10)    X13 - T1 + T3 >=    12
       11)    X24 - T2 + T4 >=    6
       12)    X25 - T2 + T5 >=    18
       13)    X34 - T3 + T4 >=    4
       14)    X45 - T4 + T5 >=    8
       15)    X56 - T5 + T6 >=    12
       16)    T6 <=    28
END

LP OPTIMUM FOUND AT STEP      14

        OBJECTIVE FUNCTION VALUE

        1)      2200.0000

VARIABLE          VALUE            REDUCED COST
     X12          8.000000             .000000
     X13          2.000000             .000000
     X24           .000000          200.000000
     X25          4.000000             .000000
     X34           .000000             .000000
     X45          2.000000             .000000
     X56          4.000000             .000000
      T1           .000000          300.000000
      T2          6.000000             .000000
      T3         10.000000             .000000
      T4         14.000000             .000000
      T5         20.000000             .000000
      T6         28.000000             .000000


     ROW    SLACK OR SURPLUS        DUAL PRICES
      2)           .000000             .000000
      3)          2.000000             .000000
      4)          2.000000             .000000
      5)           .000000             .000000
      6)          2.000000             .000000
      7)           .000000          100.000000
      8)           .000000          200.000000
      9)           .000000         -100.000000
     10)           .000000         -200.000000
     11)          2.000000             .000000
     12)           .000000         -100.000000
     13)           .000000         -200.000000
     14)           .000000         -200.000000
     15)           .000000         -300.000000
     16)           .000000          300.000000
```

Super Project Plus, Time Line, MacProject, Project Manager Workbench, OPEN PLA and PROMIS. Examples of the types of projects that such software packages have be applied to include the construction of a sawmill, installation of software systems at ho pitals, departmental reorganizations, development of a communications satellite, milita projects, facility and employee relocation, and highway construction. In addition, a nur ber of applications incorporate the use of project management within a management info mation system. The availability of powerful, user friendly project management softwa packages for the personal computer will only serve to increase the frequency of use of th technique.

SUMMARY

In this chapter several of the more important topics in network modeling were presente including the shortest-route problem, the minimal spanning-tree problem, the maxim flow problem, and the CPM/PERT technique for project planning and control. Networ modeling has become increasingly popular as a management science technique becau: of the communication value of visual network models to managers. This has been esp cially true of the last topic in this chapter, CPM/PERT, which has become one of th most frequently employed management planning tools. In fact, management scientis frequently use CPM/PERT for planning management science model development an implementation.

REFERENCES

BATTERSBY, A. *Network Analysis for Planning and Scheduling.* New York: John Wiley & Sons, 1970.

CONWAY, R. W.; MAXWELL, W. L.; and MILLER, L. W. *Theory of Scheduling.* Reading, Massachusetts: Addison-Wesley Publishing Company, 1967.

ELMAGHRABY, S. E. *Some Network Models in Management Science.* New York: Springer-Verlag, 1970.

EVARTS, H. F. *Introduction to PERT.* Boston: Allyn and Bacon, 1964.

FORD, L. R., JR., and FULKERSON, D. R. *Flows in Networks.* Princeton, New Jersey: Princeton University Press, 1962.

FRANK, H., and FRISCH, I. T. *Communication, Transmission and Transportation Networks.* Reading, Massachusetts: Addison-Wesley Publishing Company, 1971.

HILLIER, F. S., and LIEBERMAN, G. J. *Operations Research.* 4th ed. San Francisco: Holden-Day, 1986.

MARTINO, R. L. *Critical Path Networks.* Nev York: McGraw-Hill Book Company 1970.

MILLER, R. W. *Schedule, Cost and Profit Con trol with PERT: A Comprehensive Guide fo Program Management.* New York McGraw-Hill Book Company, 1963.

MODER, J.; PHILLIPS, C. R.; and DAVIS, E. W *Project Management with CPM and PERT and Precedence Diagramming.* 3d ed. Nev York: Van Nostrand Reinhold Company 1983.

RIGGS, J. L., and HEATH, C. O. *Guide to Cos Reduction Through Critical Path Scheduling.* Englewood Cliffs, New Jersey: Prentice-Hall, 1966.

WIEST, J. D., and LEVY, F. K. *A Management Guide to PERT/CPM.* 2d ed. Englewood Cliffs, New Jersey: Prentice-Hall, 1977.

1. The following figure represents a highway network, where distances are shown in hundreds of miles along each branch of the network. A trucking company wishes to know the shortest route from location 1 to location 7 (node 1 to node 7). Determine the shortest-route solution.

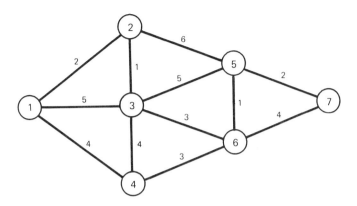

2. Assume that node 3 in the problem 2 network represents a central storage facility from which truckloads of materials are transported to each of the various endpoint locations denoted by nodes 1, 2, 4, 5, 6, and 7.

    a. Each individual shipment from the central storage facility is transported to only one of the alternative endpoint destinations. Determine the shortest routes from the central storage facility to each of the delivery endpoints.

    b. In which cases could fractional truckload deliveries be made (i.e., a portion of a truckload delivered to one location and the remainder to another location) without altering the shortest-route solutions obtained in part a? Provide a detailed statement.

3. For the problem 2 network, assume that a trucking company wishes to know the route requiring the least *time* to travel from node 1 to node 7. Trucks can average 50 miles per hour over each branch of the highway network with the following exceptions. The subroutes from nodes 2 to 3 and 6 to 5 are steep upgrades. Trucks can average speeds of only 25 miles per hour from 2 to 3 and from 6 to 5. On the other hand, trucks can average the normal 50 miles per hour on the downgrades, from 3 to 2 and from 5 to 6.

    a. Illustrate the network with the appropriate *directed* branches and associated values for evaluation of the minimum time route.

    b. Determine the shortest time route from node 1 to node 7.

    c. Assume that the destination is redefined as node 6 rather than node 7. Identify the alternative optimal routes from node 1.

    d. Given that a truck is at the node 7 destination, determine the shortest time route(s) for the return trip to node 1.

4. A clothing company produces denim jeans at one of its plants and then loads the
   into piggyback trailers, which are transported by truck to an east coast seaport f
   shipment overseas. There are several different routes the trucks can take from t
   plant to the seaport, as shown in the following network. In this network, node
   denotes the plant, node 8 denotes the seaport, and all remaining nodes denote inte
   mediate cities. Each branch represents an intra-city highway, and the values accom
   panying the branches are the travel times (in hours) between cities. Determine t
   shortest route between the plant and the seaport that the trucks should follow, ar
   give the total hours required for this route.

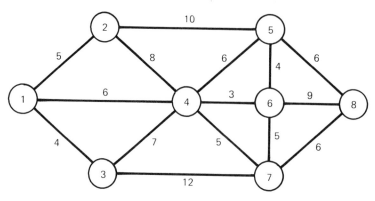

5. The administration of a university wants to connect eight buildings containing computer facilities (terminals, printers, etc.) on its campus to its central computer center
   via a coaxial-cable system. A separate cable must be laid to each different building
   The following network indicates the different paths the cable can follow from the
   computer center at node 1 to the eight buildings (nodes 2 through 9). The values
   accompanying each branch in the network are the distances (in hundreds of feet)
   between the various buildings and the computer center and the other buildings.
   Determine the shortest cable path between the computer center and each of the eight
   buildings, and indicate the length of each of these paths.

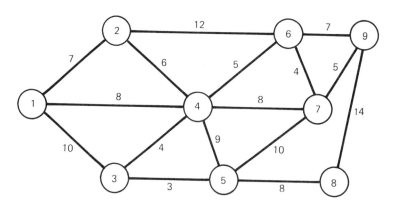

6. Determine the shortest route from origin to destination for the following transportation network. Distances are given along the network branches in hundreds of miles.

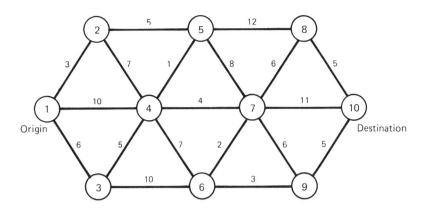

7. An operator of an aircraft charter service must determine in advance what route will be taken from origin to destination. The aircraft normally navigates from one VOR (very-high-frequency omnirange) station to another during the flight from the home field to another airport. The following network represents the possible flight paths considered. The intermediate nodes represent VOR stations, and the values along the network branches represent flight hours. Determine the shortest route (in flight hours) for the charter service from the origin to destination.

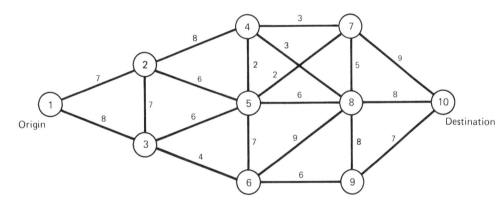

8. Determine the shortest route from the origin (node 1) to the destination (node 11) for the network given below, where distances are given along the network branches.

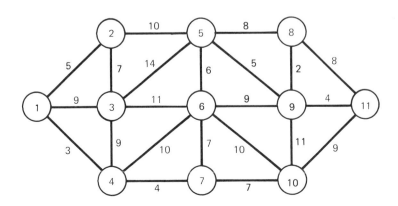

9. Determine the shortest route from node 1 (origin) to node 12 (destination) for the network given below, where distances are given along the network branches.

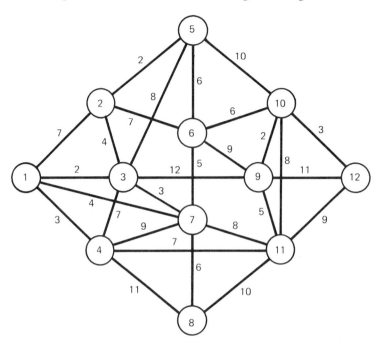

10. Assume that the values along the directed branches of the following network represent the *costs* associated with beginning at node i and ending at node j. The costs in hundreds of dollars are summarized as follows:

Beginning	Ending at Node j			
at Node i	$j = 1$	2	3	4
$i = 0$	$4	5	9	11
1	—	2	5	7
2	—	—	3	5
3	—	—	—	4

Determine the minimum-cost route from node 0 to node 4.

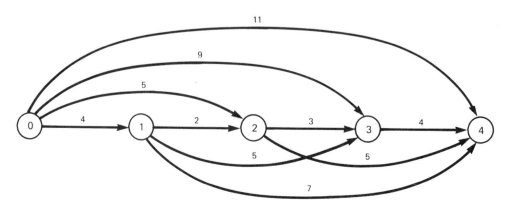

11. A railroad company is purchasing a new diesel unit to be used in the company's switching yard operations of coal cars. At the end of five years, the company is planning to replace all current coal cars with new, larger cars, so the diesel unit will have to be replaced with a new, larger unit at that time. However, the current diesel switching unit receives heavy use, resulting in rapidly increasing operating and maintenance costs as it ages. Therefore, it may be economical to replace it one or more times during the coming five-year planning period. The following table summarizes the company's estimated total net discounted costs associated with operation and replacement of the diesel unit (purchase price for new unit minus sale price for old unit, plus operating and maintenance costs of owned unit), assuming purchase at the end of year i and sale at the end of year j. Year 0 represents the current point in time, year 1 represents the end of year 1, and so on. Dollar values are given in hundreds of thousands.

Total Net Disounted Costs

Year Purchased (i)	Year Sold (j)				
	1	2	3	4	5
0	$5	6	8	14	20
1	—	5	7	11	15
2	—	—	5	9	13
3	—	—	—	5	11
4	—	—	—	—	5

Formulate and solve the problem as a shortest-route network problem. Determine at what times the diesel unit should be replaced during the five-year planning period in order to minimize total net discounted costs. (Hint: Examine the problem 10 network structure.)

12. Assume that each node in the following network represents a telephone location, and the objective is to connect all telephone locations using the minimum amount of telephone line. Determine the minimal spanning-tree solution.

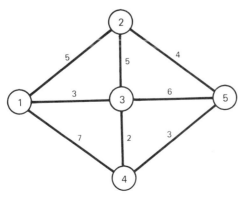

13. Assume that the network in problem 1 represents potential water main routes to connect homes in a new subdivision (where nodes represent home locations and

branch values represent distances in hundreds of yards). Determine the minima spanning-tree solution for the minimum pipeline required to connect all new homes

14. Assume that the network in problem 6 represents potential electrical transmissio line routes to connect all cities (nodes) in the network. Determine the minimal span ning-tree solution to minimize the transmission line required.

15. Assume that the network nodes in problem 7 represent homes to which undergrounc television cable is to be connected. The network branches represent streets along which the cable may be buried, and the values shown along the network branches represent distances in hundreds of feet. Determine the minimal spanning-tree solu tion to connect all homes to the television cable while minimizing the total length of television cable used.

16. One of the opposing forces in a simulated army battle wishes to set up a commu nications system that will connect the ten camps of its total command. The following network indicates the distances (in hundreds of yards) between the camps and the different paths over which a communications line can be constructed. Determine the minimal spanning tree that will result in the minimum distance communication system that will connect all ten camps.

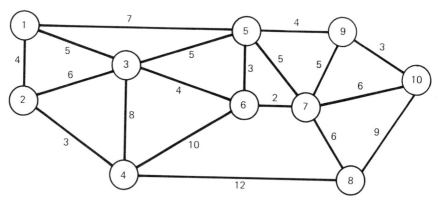

17. The management of a large manufacturing plant desires to connect the eleven major manufacturing areas of its plant (shown below) with a forklift truck route. Since the construction of such a route will require the absorption of a considerable amount of

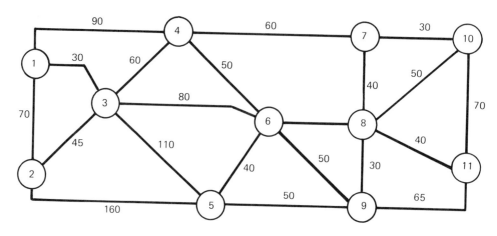

plant space and disrupt normal activities, management desires to minimize the total length of the forklift truck route. The network shows the distance in yards between the manufacturing areas (denoted by nodes 1 through 11). Determine the minimal spanning-tree forklift truck route for the plant, and indicate the total yards the route will require.

18. Determine the minimal spanning-tree solution for the network given below, where distances are given along the network branches.

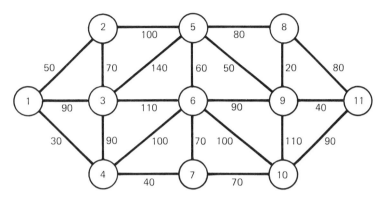

19. Determine the minimal spanning-tree solution for the network given below, where distances are given along the network branches.

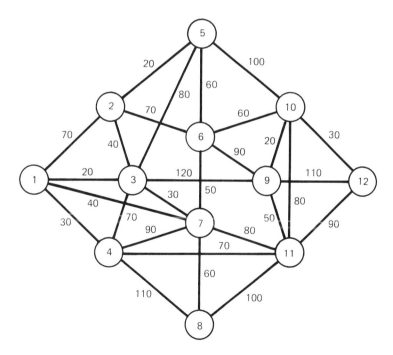

20. Given the following message transmission network, determine the maximum flow of messages from the input source to the output sink. The message flow capacity from node i to node j (in messages per minute) is given along branch (i, j) nearest

node i. Specify the solution quantity and direction of message flow for each branch of the network.

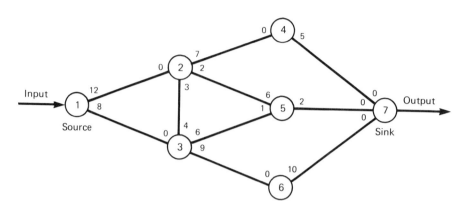

21. Given the following oil pipeline network, determine the maximim flow of oil from the input source to the output sink. The oil flow capacity from node i to node j (in barrels per minute) is given along branch (i, j) nearest node i. Specify the solution quantity and direction of flow for each branch of the pipeline network.

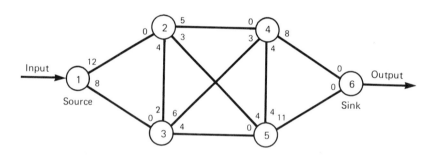

22. Given the following shipping network for a national parcel service, determine the maximum parcel flow from the source to the sink. The flow capacity from node i to node j (in 1,000s of parcels per day) is given along branch (i, j) nearest node i. Specify the solution quantity and flow for each branch of the shipping network.

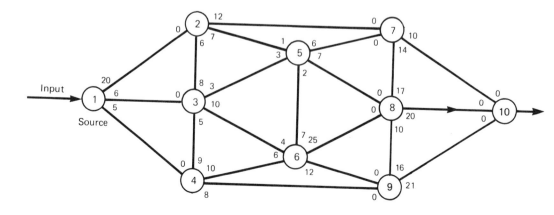

23. Given the following natural gas pipeline network, determine the maximum gas flow from the source to the sink. The flow capacity from node i to node j (in hundreds of cubic feet per second) is given along branch (i, j) nearest node i. Specify the solution quantity and direction of flow for each branch of the pipeline network.

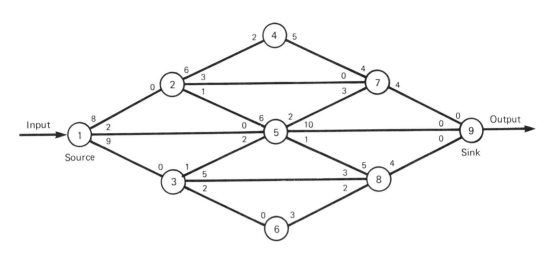

24. The traffic management office in a large urban area is attempting to analyze the potential traffic flow from a new office complex under construction to an interstate highway interchange during the evening rush period. Cars leave the office complex via one of three different exits, and then they travel through the city streets until they arrive at the interstate interchange. The following network shows the various street routes (branches) from the office complex (denoted by node 1) to the interstate interchange (node 9). All intermediate nodes represent street intersections, and the values accompanying the branches emanating from the nodes are the traffic capacities (expressed in thousands of cars per hour) along the streets. Determine the maximum flow of cars that the street system can absorb during the evening rush hour.

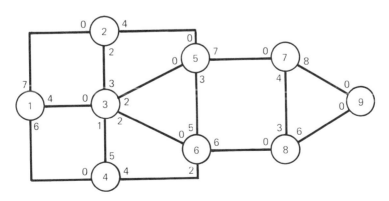

25. A large manufacturing company produces a product in five stages. Each stage of the manufacturing process is conducted at different plants. The following network shows the five different stages and the routes over which the partially completed product is shipped to the various plants at the different stages. Each node represents a differ-

ent plant; however, plants at the same stage perform the same operation. For exam
ple, at stage 2 of the manufacturing process, plants 2, 3, and 4 all perform the sam
stage 2 manufacturing operation. The values accompanying the branches emanatin
from each node indicate the maximum number of units (in thousands) that a par
ticular plant can produce and ship to another plant at the next stage. For example
plant 3 has the capacity to process and ship 7000 units of the product to plant 5
Determine the maximum number of units that can be processed through the five
stage manufacturing process and the number of units processed at each plant.

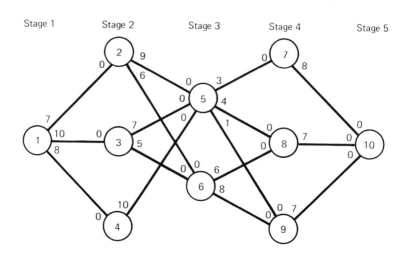

26. Formulate a linear programming model for the maximal flow network in problem
    25 and solve using a linear programming computer software package.

27. Determine the maximum flow capability for the network shown below, with flow
    capacities given along each branch. Specify the solution quantity and direction of
    flow for each branch of the network.

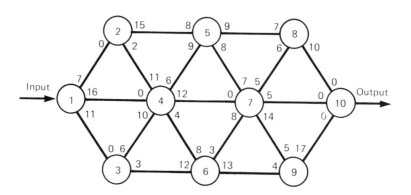

28. Determine the maximum flow capability for the following network, with flow capac-
    ities given along each branch. Specify the solution quantity and direction of flow for
    each branch of the network.

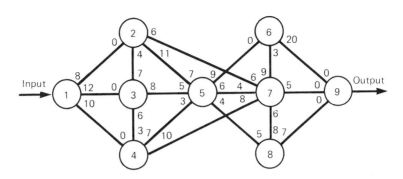

29. For the following project network, with activity times in months given along each network arrow, determine the ET and LT for each network node, the TS and FS for each project activity, and the critical path.

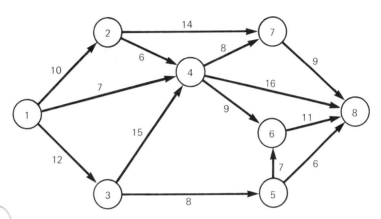

30. An equipment maintenance building is to be erected near a large construction site. An electric generator and a large water storage tank are to be installed a short distance away and connected to the building. The activity descriptions and estimated durations for the project are given in the following table, along with the required activity precedence relationships.

Activity	Activity Description	Activity Predecessor	Activity Duration (weeks)
a	Clear and level site	—	2
b	Erect building	a	6
c	Install generator	a	4
d	Install water tank	a	2
e	Install maintenance equipment	b	4
f	Connect generator and tank to building	b, c, d	5
g	Paint and finish work on building	b	3
h	Facility test and checkout	e, f	2

a. Construct the network figure for the project.
b. Determine the earliest time (ET) and latest time (LT) for each network node.

    c. Determine total slack (TS) and free slack (FS) for each project activity.

    d. Identify the project critical path and interpret its meaning.

    e. Prepare a table summarizing the project activity schedule.

31. Given the project in problem 30, assume that management has decided that activity h (test and checkout) requires only the completion of activity e (installation of maintenance equipment).

    a. Construct the project network.

    b. Determine the ET and LT values for each network node.

    c. Determine the TS and FS values for each project activity.

    d. Identify the critical path.

    e. Prepare a summary activity schedule for the project.

32. Given the following project network, where activity durations (in days) are shown alongside each network arrow, complete the following:

    a. Determine the ET and LT values for each node.

    b. Determine the TS and FS values for each activity.

    c. Identify the project critical path.

    d. Excluding dummy activities, identify those activities that share slack with another activity. Also identify which activity the slack is shared with and by what amount.

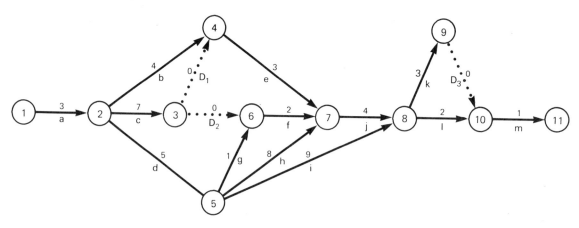

33. Assume that an additional activity, n, must be added to the project network in problem 32. Its predecessors are activities b and c, and its only successor is activity m. The estimated duration for activity n is 14 days.

    a. Determine ET and LT for each network node.

    b. Determine TS and FS for each project activity.

    c. Identify the project critical path.

    d. Identify the network path (sequence of activities) that determines the earliest time for each project node.

34. Assume that three time estimates, shown in the following table, are obtained for each activity in the project in problem 30.

    a. Compute the mean ($\hat{t}_{ij}$) and variance (v_{ij}) times for each activity.

	Time Estimates (weeks)		
	a	*m*	*b*
Activity	Optimistic	Most Likely	Pessimistic
a	1	2	3
b	4	6	14
c	2	4	6
d	1	2	5
e	3	4	11
f	1	5	6
g	1	3	5
h	2	2	2

b. Using the computed $\hat{t}_{ij}$ values, determine the earliest time and latest time for each network node.

c. Determine the TS and FS values for each project activity.

d. Identify the project critical path.

e. Compare the results for parts a, b, and c to results obtained in problem 30. Has the critical path changed? If so, what caused the change in the critical path? Has the project completion time changed? If so, what caused the change?

f. What is the probability the project will be completed in 16 weeks or less?

g. Determine the probability that the project will be completed in 19 weeks or less.

h. Determine the probability that the project will require 15 or more weeks for completion.

35. Assume that three time estimates are obtained for each activity in the project network in problem 32, as follows:

	Time Estimates (days)		
	a	*m*	*b*
Activity	Optimistic	Most Likely	Pessimistic
a	1	3	5
b	3	4	5
c	4	6	10
d	3	5	7
e	1	2	5
f	2	2	2
g	1	1	1
h	4	7	16
i	6	8	16
j	1	4	7
k	2	3	4
l	1	2	3
m	1	1	1

a. Compute the values of the mean and variance for each activity time.

b. Using the values computed in a, determine the values of ET and LT for each network node.

c. Determine the TS and FS values for each project activity.

d. Identify the project critical path.

e. Compare the results to the results for problem 32. Has the critical path changed?

f. Which project activities have the greatest amount of uncertainty with regard to duration? Are any of these activities on the critical path? What are the implications of this uncertainty with regard to project critical path?

g. Illustrate graphically the distribution of project completion time with associated mean and variance.

h. Determine the 95% confidence interval estimate of project completion time.

i. Determine the probability of project completion within 27 or less days.

36. Because of a cancellation of a prior engagement, a famous Nobel laureate has notified the student union of a university that he will be able to speak at their university next month. Because of the short planning period available, the student union would like to develop a CPM/PERT network to plan the laureate's visit to their campus and the speech. The activities of the network include renting an auditorium, printing tickets, arranging for ushers, issuing press releases, and finding accommodations for the laureate. The student union has made the following activity precedence relationships and time estimates for each activity.

Activity	Activity Predecessor	Time Estimates (days)		
		a Optimistic	m Most Likely	b Pessimistic
a	—	2	4	7
b	—	4	5	8
c	a	3	5	10
d	a	6	8	16
e	a	5	10	15
f	b,c	6	14	16
g	b,c	1	5	12
h	d	2	4	7
i	d	2	3	6
j	d	2	6	12
k	e,h	1	2	6
l	g	2	4	12
m	k,i	3	6	15

a. Determine the ET and LT values for each node.

b. Determine the TS and FS values for each activity.

c. Identify the project critical path.

d. Compute the probability that the student union can complete the arrangements within 30 days.

37. A project description provides estimates of both activity durations and associated direct costs. Two estimates are provided for each activity—estimated normal time (and associated cost) and estimated crash time (and associated cost):

Activity	(i, j)	Predecessor	Time Estimates (weeks)		Direct Cost Estimates ($1000s)	
			Normal	Crash	Normal	Crash
a	(1, 2)	—	20	8	100	148
b	(1, 4)	—	24	20	120	140
c	(1, 3)	—	14	7	70	119
d	(2, 4)	a	10	6	50	82
e	(3, 4)	c	11	5	55	73

    a. Determine the crashing cost per week for each activity.
    b. Determine the minimum cost project-crashing solution.
    c. How much can be saved by implementing the part b solution rather than crashing all project activities?
    d. Identify the project critical path(s) for the crashing solution.
    e. Illustrate with a table and a graph the time/cost trade-off for the problem.

38. A project description provides estimates of normal activity times (and associated costs) and crash activity times (and associated costs) as follows:

Activity	(i, j)	Predecessor	Time Estimates (days)		Direct Cost Estimates ($1000s)	
			Normal	Crash	Normal	Crash
a	(1, 2)	—	16	8	200	440
b	(1, 3)	—	14	9	100	180
c	(2, 4)	a	8	6	50	70
d	(2, 5)	a	5	4	60	130
e	(3, 5)	b	4	2	150	300
f	(3, 6)	b	6	4	80	160
g	(4 ,6)	c	10	7	300	450
h	(5, 6)	d, e	15	10	500	800

    a. Determine the crashing cost per day for each activity.
    b. Determine the minimum cost project-crashing solution.
    c. How much can be saved by implementing the part b solution rather than crashing all project activities?
    d. Identify the project critical path(s) for the crashing solution.
    e. Illustrate with a table and a graph the time/cost trade-off curve for the problem.

39. Formulate the linear programming model for the CPM/PERT network in problem 29.

40. Formulate the linear programming crashing model for problem 37.

41. Formulate the linear programming crashing model for problem 38.

42. The CPM network in problem 29 has normal and crash activity times and normal and crash activity costs as follows:

	Time Estimates (months)		Cost Estimates ($1000s)	
Activity	Normal	Crash	Normal	Crash
1–2	10	8	300	420
1–3	12	9	280	400
1–4	7	6	90	120
2–4	6	5	80	100
2–7	14	12	400	600
3–4	15	11	480	700
3–5	8	7	120	160
4–6	9	7	180	240
4–7	8	7	160	200
4–8	16	12	520	760
5–6	9	8	90	150
5–8	6	5	70	110
6–8	11	9	180	260
7–8	9	8	160	300

Using a management science computer software package with crashing capabilities

a. Determine the minimum cost project-crashing solution.
b. Identify the project critical path(s) for the crashing solution.
c. What would be the project cost and critical path(s) if the network is crashed to 40 months?

43. For problem 30 assume that the normal and crash activity times are the most likely and optimistic times provided in problem 34. The normal and crash activity costs are as follows:

Activity	Normal Cost	Crash Cost
a	$3,000	$5,000
b	9,000	14,000
c	1,500	4,000
d	2,000	3,000
e	1,800	2,600
f	6,000	15,000
g	2,400	6,000
h	900	900

Using a management science computer software package with crashing capabilities:

a. Determine the minimum cost project-crashing solution.
b. Identify the project critical path(s) for the crashing solution.
c. What would be the project cost and critical path(s) if the network is crashed to 12 weeks?

7

Inventory Models

Inventory analysis was one of the initial areas of application of quantitative methods and techniques first studied as early as 1915. Since then it has become one of the most popular areas of analysis, appearing in the majority of management science texts as well as accounting for a substantial portion of the literature in operations research and production management. It is not surprising that inventory analysis has held such a position of prominence in all forms of quantitative business methods, since inventory often represents as much as 40% of the total invested capital of industrial organizations. In addition to being a major portion of the total current assets of many businesses, inventory represents an important decision variable at all stages of product manufacturing, distribution, and sales. Thus, changes in inventory policy can have a significant effect throughout an organization.

Beyond these "practical" business reasons, inventory analysis is also an excellent vehicle for exposing the student of management science to the general classic modeling concepts. The methodology and logic employed in developing and analyzing inventory models provide a basic groundwork for management science modeling that can be transferred to other areas of application. In fact, the fundamental classic inventory model is so widely reproduced as an example of quantitative methods in business that the reader may already be familiar with basic inventory modeling.

The study of inventory in this chapter concentrates on the presentation of several of the more popular inventory models. These inventory models can be subdivided into two fundamental forms. The first form is the classic **deterministic EOQ model** and its several variations. The analysis of the classic model will provide the groundwork for the introduction of the second model form, the **stochastic inventory model.**

INVENTORY FUNCTIONS

Inventory is broadly defined as any stock of economic resources that are idle at a given point in time. This can include raw materials awaiting use in manufacturing operations, semifinished goods temporarily stored during the manufacturing process, finished goods awaiting distribution, and finished goods awaiting sale in wholesale or retail outlets. Inventory may also include nonphysical assets such as cash, accounts receivable, and human resources.

Although inventory is generally considered to be a nonearning asset, the optimal managerial decision is not simply to reduce inventory to the lowest possible level. Inventories are necessary to achieve workable systems of production, distribution, and marketing of physical goods. For example, raw materials must be accumulated in inventory for further processing into finished goods. Also, raw material inventories are often accumulated as a hedge against price inflation or labor strikes in industries supplying or using these materials. During the process of production, inventory serves the function of decoupling successive stages of manufacturing. This allows the various production departments to operate more independently, without direct reliance on the schedule of ouput of prior departments in the production process. The distribution of finished goods almost always requires certain quantities of inventory in transit and accumulations at intermediate delivery points.

It may also be more economical to carry a certain amount of inventory in order to produce or purchase in large lots so as to achieve reduced production setup costs or quantity discounts on items purchased. Inventories may be accumulated in order to smooth out the level of production operations so that employees do not have to be temporarily laid off and later rehired and retrained.

The most visible function of inventory is at the retail store level, where inventory is carried to absorb random fluctuations in demand. The objective of inventory at the retail level is to meet demand as it occurs and avoid out-of-stock situations, which can result in lost sales. Additionally, inventory on display serves as a promotional device.

Thus, although inventories are nonearning assets, it is apparent that inventories serve many functions that are vital to the overall production-distribution-marketing system. Since inventories are found throughout the system and constitute a major segment of total investment, it is crucial that good inventory management be practiced.

Basic Inventory Decisions

The basic inventory decisions concern what quantity to order and when to order. Thus, in attempts to model inventory systems, these are the important decision variables. Throughout the chapter it will be shown that in many cases it is possible to consider each of these decisions separately. However, in some cases the two decisions are interdependent, and the optimal values for the two decision variables must be obtained simultaneously. The rationale for considering these variables separately or jointly depends on the individual models, which will be discussed later in this chapter.

Evaluation Criteria—Inventory Costs

The most common criteria considered in inventory analysis are inventory-related costs, which can be categorized as (1) ordering costs, (2) carrying costs, and (3) shortage costs. Each of these will be discussed separately.

Ordering Costs

Ordering costs are those costs associated with replenishing the stock of inventory on hand. These costs vary with the number of orders made and are expressed in terms of dollar cost per order. The following are examples of costs incurred each time an order is made:

Requisitioning
Purchase order
Transportation

Receiving
Inspection
Placing in storage
Accounting and auditing
Payment to supplier

Carrying Costs

Carrying costs are those costs associated with holding a certain stock of inventory on hand. Carrying costs are often referred to as holding costs. These costs vary with the level of inventory held and sometimes with the time the item is held, as in the case of perishable goods. The longer goods are held in inventory, the longer money is tied up in those goods and the higher the inventory costs. In recent years, abnormally high inflation and interest rates have resulted in correspondingly high inventory carrying costs and thus focused increased management attention to inventory control. There are several components of carrying cost, and the relative impact of each depends on the type of inventory goods considered. The following are commonly considered components of carrying cost:

Forgone profit on investment tied up in inventory
Direct storage costs (rent, heat, lights, refrigeration, record keeping, security, etc.)
Product obsolescence or deterioration
Depreciation, taxes, and insurance
Interest charges on loans to purchase inventory

Carrying costs may be specified in several ways. The most general form is the dollar cost of carrying one unit in inventory per unit time. The time horizon commonly considered is one year; that is, the carrying cost is the cost of carrying one unit in inventory for one year. Another common approach is to specify carrying cost per year as a percentage of average inventory value; for example, carrying cost may equal 15% to 20% of average inventory value.

Shortage Costs

Shortage costs are often referred to as stockout costs. Inventory shortages occur when demand exceeds the supply of inventory on hand. Shortages may be either accidental or a planned policy of the company.

If inventory shortages result in the permanent loss of sales for items demanded but not filled, the shortage cost then includes profits lost because of unsatisfied demand. Additionally, shortages can result in an "ill-will" cost due to permanently lost customers and the associated long-term loss of future sales.

On the other hand, the firm may simply back order demands not filled when shortages occur. This is common practice in most mail-order houses. The relevant shortage costs then become the clerical and paperwork costs associated with back orders. However, back-ordered shortages may also result in some lost customers, creating some ill-will costs.

DETERMINISTIC INVENTORY MODELS

The classic model, often referred to as the EOQ (economic order quantity) model, is the simplest of the inventory models. Although it is too simplified to reflect most real-world situations, it is nevertheless a good base from which to launch a study of inventory models. The presentation of the classic EOQ model is organized into a series of steps, each describing a different model form. The first step describes the basic, or classic, inventory model, and succeeding steps reflect one or more changes in the basic assumptions of the initial model. The set of models represents a logical development of deterministic inventory models, from the simplest case to the more complex cases.

Assumptions of the Classic EOQ Model

The objective of the classic EOQ model is the minimization of total inventory costs, typically achieved by the determination of an optimal order quantity (Q). Additional assumptions of the deterministic EOQ model are as follows:

1. Inventory usage rate (demand) is constant over time.

2. Inventory demand is known with certainty.

3. The entire order quantity is received at one point in time.

4. Inventory is replenished when it is exactly zero (no excess stock is carried and no shortages are allowed).

5. Reorder lead time is zero (an order is received at the same instant it is placed).

The last assumption is unnecessary, since we could assume a constant, known reorder lead time without affecting our model results; however, in order to simplify the initial presentation, we will include this assumption.

The assumptions of the classic inventory model are illustrated graphically in Figure 7.1, which shows the inventory level over time.

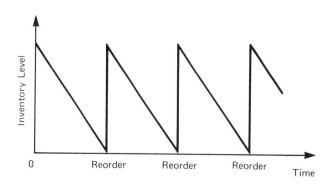

Figure 7.1 Inventory Level for Classic Inventory Model

Note in Figure 7.1 that the downward sloping line shows the level of inventory being reduced at a constant rate over time (constant and known demand). Also, since demand is constant and known and since receipt of goods ordered is instantaneous, the reorder point occurs when the inventory level falls to exactly zero.

Estimation of Demand

The assumptions of the classical EOQ model are generally unrealistic, although they do enable us to construct a rather simple, straightforward method for determining the amount of inventory to order. Specifically, demand for a product held in inventory is rarely, if ever, known with certainty or constant over time. A retailer can never be certain how much of a particular product will be demanded on a given day or that the same amount will be demanded each day during a week. (Instances where demand is known with certainty and is constant over time typically involve previously contracted sales.) In fact, demand is a particularly difficult item to predict, and, as a result, a number of different "forecasting" techniques have been developed in an attempt to forecast demand. People who use these techniques generally accept the premise that the results will not yield a completely accurate demand forecast. Rather, they provide a good estimate of what demand will be, or they provide a value that is close to what demand may be. In many cases, the forecast is viewed as successful if it simply predicts when demand will increase or decrease.

Forecast techniques range from the very simple (such as simple averages of previous demand) to very complex, computerized mathematical models. Many of the more popular forecasting methods are based on statistical regression techniques (i.e., simple and multiple regression). Forecasting methods such as exponential smoothing attempt to eliminate or smooth out the random dips and jumps in demand over time to establish a long-term pattern of demand. However, these techniques, as well as most other forecasting methods, employ previous demand data as the essential component in predicting future demand. Hence, forecasting techniques rarely reflect the unique or unexpected circumstance that will send demand plummeting or skyrocketing.

We will not explore the various available and widely applied forecasting techniques in this presentation of inventory control models. A number of excellent texts exist that are devoted entirely to forecasting methods. Several of the references cited at the end of this chapter contain complete sections on forecasting in a production environment.

In our presentation of the EOQ model and its several variations in this chapter, the assumption of certain, constant demand will be maintained. However, in the section on probabilistic inventory models, presented later in the chapter, we will explore several ways of compensating for the uncertainty of demand in the determination of a realistic inventory policy.

Formulation of the Classic EOQ Model

The objective of inventory analysis is to determine the optimal order quantity that will minimize total inventory costs. The two classes of costs included in the inventory model are ordering costs and carrying costs, and the objective is to minimize the sum of these two costs. Since it is assumed at this point that shortages never occur, shortage costs are not considered.

Figure 7.2 illustrates inventory costs graphically. Note that as the quantity per order increases, fewer orders are necessary and, therefore, ordering costs decrease. However, as order sizes increase, there will be more time between orders and inventory carried will increase, resulting in increased carrying costs. Total inventory costs first decrease as the order size increases but begin to rise again after a point. The objective of inventory analysis is to solve for the optimal value of order quantity that corresponds to minimum total inventory costs. This point, labeled Q_{opt}, is shown graphically in Figure 7.2

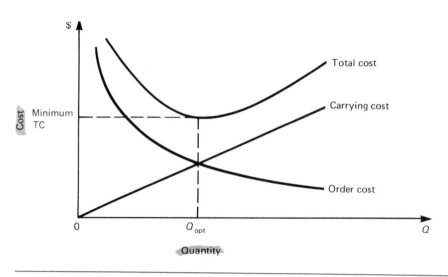

Figure 7.2 Classic Inventory Model

Model Symbols

The first step in constructing the inventory model is to define the variables and parameters (generally constants) of the model. Initially, the parameters of the model are given as symbols. The approach of inventory analysis is to define model parameters as symbols, when possible, and solve for the general case. Thus, one can substitute the values of the parameters into the solution for the general case model and obtain an optimal solution for a specific problem, without having to solve the entire model for each new set of parameter values. The model symbols are defined as follows:

TC = total annual inventory cost
C_o = ordering costs per order
C_c = carrying cost per unit per year
Q = quantity ordered, per order
D = demand (usage) for goods in inventory, expressed on an annual basis

Now that we have developed the inventory model components, the next step is to mold them into a mathematical model, which describes the behavior of cost as a function of order quantity. However, prior to construction of the mathematical model, the concept of **average inventory** will be examined. Note that the usage rate (demand) for goods in inventory is assumed to be constant; thus, the average inventory held will be $Q/2$, where Q (quantity ordered) is the maximum level of inventory held at the time of each order receipt. The average inventory level is illustrated graphically in Figure 7.3.

The EOQ Model

The inventory model is constructed by analyzing each of the cost categories separately. (A time period of one year will always be assumed; however, any time frame could be used.)

Total ordering cost per year is simply the cost per order. C_o, multiplied by the number of orders per year. Since total usage or demand is known to be D, the number of orders per year will be D/Q. Thus, we have

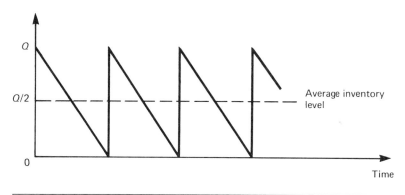

Figure 7.3 *Average Inventory Level*

$$\text{Total ordering cost} = C_o \cdot \frac{D}{Q}$$

Total carrying cost is the carrying cost per unit held per year, C_c, times the average number of units held ($Q/2$ from Figure 7.3). This yields

$$\text{Total carrying cost} = C_c \cdot \frac{Q}{2}$$

Total inventory cost is the sum of ordering and carrying costs as follows:

$$\text{Total annual cost} = \text{total ordering cost} + \text{total carrying cost}$$

or

$$TC = C_o \cdot \frac{D}{Q} + C_c \cdot \frac{Q}{2}$$

Note that a third cost component in the total inventory cost equation, total purchase cost, is not considered here. This cost, represented as $P \cdot D$ (where P is the purchase price per unit), is not included in the EOQ model, since purchase cost is not a decision variable and therefore does not enter into the determination of an optimal order quantity, Q. (An exception is the quantity discount model presented later in this chapter.) Thus, in a strict technical sense, total annual inventory cost can be written as

$$TC = C_o \cdot \frac{D}{Q} + C_c \cdot \frac{Q}{2} + P \cdot D$$

The model can now be solved for the optimal order quantity. For the above model, this can be accomplished by equating total carrying cost to total ordering cost and solving for Q. This corresponds to the point in Figure 7.2 where the curves for carrying cost and ordering cost intersect. (This approach will not work for all types of inventory models but, in general, holds true for equations of the form $y = ax^{-1} + bx$.) Thus, total ordering cost is set equal to total carrying cost.

$$C_o \frac{D}{Q} = C_c \frac{Q}{2}$$

Solving this equation for Q yields

$$Q^2 = \frac{2C_oD}{C_c}$$

and

$$Q_{opt} = \sqrt{\frac{2C_oD}{C_c}}$$

The optimal value of Q can also be determined as the lowest point on the total cost curve in Figure 7.2. This approach requires that the derivative of the total cost equation with respect to Q be computed.

$$TC = C_o\frac{D}{Q} + C_c\frac{Q}{2}$$

$$\frac{dTC}{dQ} = \frac{-C_oD}{Q^2} + \frac{C_c}{2}$$

Since this derivative represents the slope of the total cost curve, by setting the equation equal to zero and solving for Q, we will be solving for Q at the minimum cost point of the curve (i.e., where slope $= 0$). Thus,

$$0 = \frac{-C_oD}{Q^2} + \frac{C_c}{2}$$

$$Q_{opt} = \sqrt{\frac{2C_oD}{C_c}}$$

As has been demonstrated, for this simple EOQ model the algebraic approach will suffice; however, for more complex models it will be necessary to employ differential calculus.

Example 7.1   A Furniture Store Inventory Problem

A large furniture store, which sells furniture to businesses as well as homeowners, stocks a particular type of large table that sells very well. Handling and shipping costs the store $50 each time it orders these tables from the furniture manufacturer. The furniture store manager has determined that because of the interest on investment in the tables in stock, the physical handling cost, and the large amount of space these tables absorb in the warehouse, it costs $100 per year to hold a table in inventory. The manager has estimated (based on past sales records) that annual demand for the tables is 4900 units. The store manager wishes to know the optimal order size that will minimize the store's total inventory cost for tables.

The various parameters of the inventory model can be summarized as follows:

$C_o = \$50$ (cost per order)
$C_c = \$100$ (cost per unit held in inventory on an annual basis)
$D = 4900$ (demand for goods in inventory on an annual basis)

The solution for the optimal order quantity, then, is

$$Q_{opt} = \sqrt{\frac{2C_oD}{C_c}}$$

$$= \sqrt{\frac{(2)(50)(4900)}{100}}$$

$$= \sqrt{4900}$$

$$Q_{opt} = 70$$

The quantity that minimizes total inventory cost is 70 tables per order.

Several additional types of information may be desired regarding the inventory model, including the value of the minimum total inventory cost, how often to order per year, and the length of time between orders. The nature of the classic inventory model is such that once the value of Q has been determined, these other values can be computed directly. These values are defined as

N = number of orders per year
T_b = time between orders
T = total time (in this case, one year)

In the development of the EOQ model, it was shown that the number of orders per year equals annual demand divided by order size, or $N = D/Q$. Thus, for our example, the solution value for number of orders per year, N_{opt}, is

$$N_{opt} = \frac{D}{Q_{opt}} = \frac{4900}{70} = 70 \text{ orders per year}$$

Also, the solution value for time between orders is simply the total time horizon divided by the number of orders, or $T_b = T/N$. Thus,

$$(T_b)_{opt} = \frac{T}{N_{opt}} = \frac{365}{70} = 5.214 \cong 5 \text{ days between orders}$$

The value used for T may be 1 for one year, or it could be in months, weeks, or days, depending on the form of solution desired.

Finally, the minimum total inventory cost for the optimal value of Q may be derived by referring to the original model.

$$TC_{opt} = C_o \frac{D}{Q_{opt}} + C_c \frac{Q_{opt}}{2}$$

$$= 50 \cdot \frac{4900}{70} + 100 \cdot \frac{70}{2}$$

$$= \$7000$$

It is interesting to note that the formula for the determination of TC is analogous to the general form of the solution for Q, as follows:

$$TC_{opt} = C_o \frac{D}{Q_{opt}} + C_c \frac{Q_{opt}}{2}$$

Substituting for Q, the optimal solution in terms of model parameters, we have

$$TC_{opt} = \frac{C_o D}{\sqrt{\dfrac{2C_o D}{C_c}}} + \frac{C_c \sqrt{\dfrac{2C_o D}{C_c}}}{2}$$

Combining terms and performing several mathematical manipulations yields

$$TC_{opt} = \sqrt{2C_o C_c D}$$

Thus, we can simply substitute the parameter values for the model into this equation to obtain the minimum total inventory cost. For the example solution, this would yield

$$TC = \sqrt{(2)(50)(100)(4900)}$$
$$= \$7000$$

Computerized EOQ Analysis

The capability to perform EOQ analysis is a feature of most general management science software packages. Following is the program output for Example 7.1 using the AB:QM package. It includes the input data and the EOQ results.

```
Program: Inventory Models / EOQ

Problem Title : Example 7.1

***** Input Data *****

Annual demand    (units/year)        4900.00
Business days    (days/year)          365.00
Lead time        (days)                 0.00
Ordering cost    ($/order)             50.00
Holding cost     ($/unit/year)        100.00

***** Program Output *****

Optimal order quantity   (units/order)    :     70.000
Number of orders         (orders/year)    :     70.000
Inventory cycle          (days)           :      5.214
Maximum inventory level  (units)          :     70.000
Average inventory level  (units)          :     35.000
Reorder point            (units)          :      0.000
Demand rate              (units/day)      :     13.425
Total holding cost       ($/year)         :   3500.000
Total ordering cost      ($/year)         :   3500.000
Total inventory cost     ($/year)         :   7000.000

***** End of Output *****
```

order Point

The second step in our discussion of inventory models does not involve a new model at all. One assumption of the previous model is modified, and a new assumption is added. The assumption that goods ordered are received at the instant they are ordered (assumption 5) is now discarded. The other assumptions of the initial model remain the same, and it is now assumed that the time between placing and receiving an order is known and constant.

Modifying the last assumption of the initial model introduces the concept of reorder lead time. Thus, an additional consideration is added for model analysis, but the basic cost model previously presented is unchanged.

The inventory level is illustrated graphically in Figure 7.4. In this case it is assumed that there is some lag from the time the goods are ordered to the time the order is received. This lag is generally called **lead time.** Figure 7.4 illustrates the lead time for each order. Note that goods are now ordered before the level of inventory falls to zero. The inventory level at which an order is placed is termed the **reorder point.**

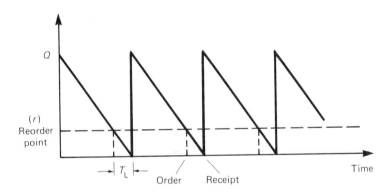

Figure 7.4 *Inventory Level with Reorder Point*

With the assumptions of this model—constant and known demand and constant and known lead time—the reorder point, r, can be determined independently of the order quantity, Q. The reorder point, lead time, number of working days in the year, annual demand, and demand during lead time are represented as follows:

$$r = \text{reorder point (inventory level in units)}$$
$$T_L = \text{lead time, in days}$$
$$T = \text{working days per year}$$
$$D = \text{annual demand, in units}$$
$$\text{DDLT} = \text{demand during lead time, in units}$$

First, the demand during lead time (DDLT) is computed as

$$\text{DDLT} = T_L \frac{D}{T} \qquad \text{(lead time in days} \times \text{daily demand)}$$

If the demand during lead time is less than or equal to the reorder quantity, that is, DDLT $\leq Q$, then the reorder point is

$r = $ DDLT

If the demand during lead time is greater than the reorder quantity, that is, if DDLT $\colon$ Q, then the reorder point is

$r = $ DDLT modulo Q

which means that r equals the remainder after dividing DDLT by Q an even number $\colon$ times. For example, if DDLT $= 550$ and $Q = 200$; then $r = 150 (550/200 = 2$ wit remainder of 150). This indicates that there are already two orders (for 200 each) tha have been placed but not yet delivered, and another order is to be placed when the inver tory level falls to 150.

Recall from Example 7.1 that the annual demand for tables was 4900, the lead tim to receive an order was 4 days, and the order quantity was 70. Thus, the reorder point determined as follows:

$$DDLT = 4 \left(\frac{4900}{365} \right) = 53.7 \cong 54$$

Since the DDLT is less than Q, the reorder point is

$r = $ DDLT $= 54$ units

Suppose, instead, that the lead time is 8 days. Then computing the DDLT yields

$$DDLT = 8 \left(\frac{4900}{365} \right) = 107.4 \cong 107$$

Since DDLT is greater than Q, (70), we must compute

$$DDLT \text{ modulo } Q = \frac{107}{70} = 1 \text{ with remainder of } 37$$

Therefore, $r = 37$ (reorder when inventory falls to 37 tables). This means that when the order is placed, another order has already been previously placed and will arrive before the order currently being placed. The order being placed will be received 8 days from the date of placement.

It is important to point out that the solution value for Q (the optimal order quantity) is not affected by the assumption that there is lead time involved in the receipt of goods. Therefore, the classic model may include the requirement that Q be computed by the method illustrated initially and also that r be determined separately.

Variations in the Classic EOQ Model

Two modifications in the EOQ model that result in different inventory model forms will now be discussed: carrying cost as a percentage and time as a model variable.

Carrying cost may be expressed as a percentage of average dollar value of inventory held rather than a dollar carrying cost per unit held. If the percentage approach is used, the unit price (or value) of the inventory in stock must also be specified in order to determine the average value of inventory held.

The variables for the carrying-cost portion of the model are now as follows:

K_c = carrying cost as a percentage of the average dollar value of inventory on an annual basis

P = price (or value) per unit of inventory held in inventory

The average value of inventory is given by $P(Q/2)$, and the equation for total annual carrying cost may now be expressed as

$$\text{Total carrying cost} = K_c P \frac{Q}{2}$$

That is, the annual carrying cost equals the percentage carrying cost times the average inventory value.

The total cost function now becomes

$$TC = C_o \frac{D}{Q} + K_c P \frac{Q}{2}$$

The same solution procedure is used for this modified model as was followed for the initial model; that is, equate the two types of inventory cost and solve for Q. Thus, we obtain

$$C_o \cdot \frac{D}{Q} = K_c \cdot P \cdot \frac{Q}{2}$$

and

$$Q_{opt} = \sqrt{\frac{2C_o D}{K_c P}}$$

The resulting model approach introduces a new parameter, P, price of goods in stock, and changes the definition of carrying cost from the dollar value of the initial model to a percentage value, K_c.

Suppose, for example, that the values of the model parameters were found to be the following:

C_o = \$50 (cost per order)

K_c = 20% (carrying cost as a percent of average inventory value on an annual basis)

D = 4900 (annual demand for goods in inventory)

P = \$500 (price or value per unit of goods in inventory)

The solution value for Q would be

$$Q = \sqrt{\frac{2C_o D}{K_c P}}$$

$$= \sqrt{\frac{(2)(50)(4900)}{(0.20)(500)}}$$

$$Q_{opt} = 70$$

Another fairly common practice in inventory models is to include the time horizon over which the inventory analysis is to apply as a variable. The symbol commonly used to denote the time horizon is T. In this case, the demand for goods in inventory is often specified as demand during time T. Also, the holding or carrying cost is often specified as the cost of holding one unit in inventory "per unit time" (such as days). For this case, it is necessary to include the variable T in the construction of the inventory model.

The inventory model will now be specified, where the total time horizon is simply identified as T and the following definitions apply:

D = demand during T (e.g., time horizon in days)
C_c = carrying cost per unit of inventory per unit time (e.g., per day)

Thus, the model is as follows:

$$\text{Ordering cost} = C_o \cdot \frac{D}{Q}$$

$$\text{Carrying cost} = C_c \cdot \frac{Q}{2} \cdot T$$

$$\text{TC} = C_o \frac{D}{Q} + C_c \frac{Q}{2} T$$

The solution to the preceding model is determined in a manner similar to that used for the initial model, yielding

$$C_o \frac{D}{Q} = C_c \frac{Q}{2} T$$

and

$$Q_{opt} = \sqrt{\frac{2C_o D}{C_c T}}$$

Q_{opt} is the optimal inventory order quantity for the system evaluated over the time horizon T (where C_c is specified in terms of the same time units as T).

Suppose we modify the previous example so that the time horizon is 6 months (or 182.5 days). For this example, the demand over that period would be 2450 units. The cost of carrying inventory, per day, would be 27.4¢ per unit day. Recall that ordering cost equals $50. Thus, the model solution would yield

$$Q = \sqrt{\frac{2C_o D}{C_c T}}$$

$$= \sqrt{\frac{(2)(50)(2,450)}{(0.274)(182.5)}}$$

$$Q_{opt} = 70$$

As expected, we obtain the same solution as was previously obtained.

Noninstantaneous Receipt Model

The next step in the development of inventory models is the case in which goods are received in a constant stream over time, rather than at one point in time. This would occur in a situation where items were produced for inventory and simultaneously used internally but not at the same rate. All other assumptions of the initial model (given on p. 324) remain unchanged—only assumption 3 is changed.

The parameters unique to this model are defined as follows:

R = rate at which goods are received over time on an annual basis; also known as the manufacturing rate or production rate

D = rate at which goods are demanded over time on an annual basis

All other model symbols (given on p. 326) are unchanged from the original model.

Attention must first be given to the average inventory for this model. Recall that in the initial EOQ model average inventory was half the maximum inventory level, which was Q, the reorder quantity. In this model, the maximum inventory level must be adjusted for the fact that the goods are received steadily and used over time. This is achieved as follows:

$$\frac{Q}{R} = \text{period required to receive, or produce, one entire order (order receipt period), expressed as a proportion of a year}$$

$$\frac{Q}{R} \cdot D = \text{number of units in inventory demanded (usage rate) during order receipt period}$$

$$Q - \left(\frac{Q}{R} \cdot D\right) = \text{maximum level of inventory for any given order}$$

$$\frac{1}{2}\left[Q - \left(\frac{Q}{R} \cdot D\right)\right] = \text{average inventory level}$$

This expression for average inventory can be modified to read

$$\frac{Q}{2}\left(1 - \frac{D}{R}\right)$$

Note that in this relationship the ratio D/R represents the proportion of production that goes to meet demand and $1 - (D/R)$ reflects the proportion of production allocated to inventory.

The inventory level for this case is illustrated graphically in Figure 7.5. Note that it is assumed that the rate at which an order is received is greater than its usage rate ($R > D$). Thus, immediately after an order is placed, the inventory level rises at a constant rate, $R - D$, up to the point $Q - (Q/R) \cdot D$, and then it falls at the constant demand rate, D.

The inventory model is now developed as follows:

$$\text{Ordering cost} = C_o \cdot \frac{D}{Q}$$

$$\text{Carrying cost} = C_c \cdot \frac{Q}{2}\left(1 - \frac{D}{R}\right)$$

$$TC = C_o \frac{D}{Q} + C_c \frac{Q}{2}\left(1 - \frac{D}{R}\right)$$

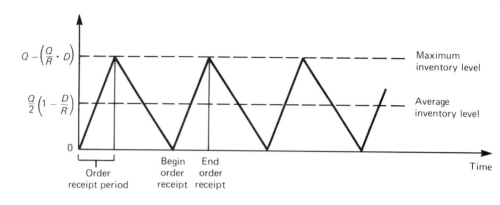

Figure 7.5 *Inventory Level for Noninstantaneous Receipt*

The solution is obtained in a manner similar to that used for the initial model.

$$C_o \frac{D}{Q} = C_c \frac{Q}{2}\left(1 - \frac{D}{R}\right)$$

Solving for Q, we have

$$Q^2 = \frac{2C_o D}{C_c\left(1 - \dfrac{D}{R}\right)}$$

and

$$Q_{opt} = \sqrt{\frac{2C_o D}{C_c\left(1 - \dfrac{D}{R}\right)}}$$

The solution is the same as that obtained for the classic EOQ model (page 344) except that C_c must be multiplied by the factor $1 - (D/R)$ to include the fact that goods are received over time, rather than at a single point in time.

Example 7.2   A Production Lot Size Problem

Recall that in Example 7.1 the furniture store ordered its tables from a manufacturer. Now, however, assume that the furniture store is an outlet for its own manufacturing facility on the premises. Therefore, the store manufactures its own items for inventory rather than ordering elsewhere. In this scenario we refer to the order quantity as the *production lot size*.

The order cost of $50 in Example 7.1 now becomes the set-up cost for each production run. The production rate is assumed to be 9800 tables per year. The carrying cost, C_c, of $100 and the annual demand, D, of 4900 tables remain the same as in Example 7.1. To summarize the parameters of this problem,

$C_o = \$50$ (set-up cost per production run)

$C_c = \$100$ (carrying cost per unit inventory per year)

$$D = 4900 \text{ units} \qquad \text{(annual demand)}$$
$$R = 9800 \text{ units} \qquad \text{(annual production rate)}$$

Thus, the solution yielded by the preceding model is

$$Q = \sqrt{\frac{2C_oD}{C_c\left(1 - \dfrac{D}{R}\right)}}$$

$$= \sqrt{\frac{(2)(50)(4900)}{100\left(1 - \dfrac{4900}{9800}\right)}}$$

$$Q_{opt} = \sqrt{9800} \cong 99 \text{ tables per production run}$$

Note that since the tables are produced over a time, there will be no carrying cost associated with the tables produced and sold immediately during the production run period. In the case of the example, exactly half of the tables are sold during the production period. Thus, the total carrying costs will be reduced for this case. Therefore, it is more economical to produce in large quantities in this case than in the case in which tables were purchased from another manufacturer.

The optimal number of production runs may be determined as follows:

$$N = \frac{D}{Q_{opt}}$$

$$= \frac{4900}{99} = 49.5$$

$$N_{opt} \cong 50 \text{ production runs per year}$$

The length (in days) between the starts of production runs will be

$$T_b = \frac{T}{N_{opt}}, \text{ where } T = 365$$

$$= \frac{365}{50} = 7.3$$

$$(T_b)_{opt} \cong 7 \text{ days between production run starts}$$

Thus, the optimal solution to this production-inventory problem is to produce 99 units per production run, with 50 production runs per year, starting every 7 working days. Note that since the production rate is 26.8 units per day, it will take $99/26.8 = 3.7$, or approximately 4 days, to complete a run. Thus, 3 days will remain before the start of the next production run for this product. During this time other goods can be produced. Also, the maximum inventory level reached will be

$$Q\left(1 - \frac{D}{R}\right) = 99\left(1 - \frac{4900}{9800}\right) = 49.5$$

or approximately 50 tables.

By using the same approach used in the initial model to develop the general model for total cost, we can see that the minimum total production-inventory cost will be

$$TC = \sqrt{2C_oC_cD\left(1 - \frac{D}{R}\right)}$$

$$= \sqrt{2(50)(100)(4900)(.5)}$$

$$TC_{opt} \cong \$4950$$

Computerized Analysis of the Production Lot Size Model

The AB:QM software package has the capability to analyze the EOQ model with non-instantaneous receipt and, specifically, the production lot size problem. Following is the computer-generated solution output for Example 7.2, including a summary of the input data.

```
Program: Inventory Models / Economic Lot Size

Problem Title : Example 7.2

***** Input Data *****

Annual demand     (units/year)          4900.00
Demand rate       (units/day)             13.42
Lead time         (days)                   0.00
Setup cost        ($/setup)               50.00
Holding cost      ($/unit/year)          100.00
Production rate   (units/day)             26.85

***** Program Output *****

Optimal order quantity    (units/order)   :     98.994
Number of orders          (orders/year)   :     49.498
Production cycle          (days)          :      3.687
Maximum inventory level   (units)         :     49.498
Average inventory level   (units)         :     24.749
Reorder point             (units)         :      0.000
Demand rate               (units/day)     :     13.425
Total holding cost        ($/year)        :   2474.905
Total setup cost          ($/setup)       :   2474.905
Total inventory cost      ($/year)        :   4949.810

***** End of Output *****
```

Inventory Model with Shortages

It was assumed in all previous model variations that an order was received (or that production began) at the precise instant the level of inventory reached zero. Thus, shortages were not allowed to occur, and shortage cost was ignored in the inventory analysis.

We will now modify this assumption by allowing inventory shortages to occur. However, it will be assumed that all demand not met because of an inventory shortage will be back ordered. Thus, all demand will eventually be met.

The assumptions of the original classic inventory model are retained here except for assumption 4, which precluded shortages (see p. 324). We continue to assume constant and known demand, instantaneous replenishment (the entire order is received simultaneously), and zero reorder lead time (receipt of goods the instant an order is placed).

The inventory level with shortages is illustrated in Figure 7.6. Since back-ordered demands (shortages) are filled when inventory is replenished, the maximum inventory level does not reach the level of Q (the order quantity). Rather, shortages (S) are filled immediately upon receipt of an order, and the inventory level returns to a level of V, which is equal to $Q - S$. Since the maximum inventory level is lowered, the inventory carrying cost is reduced. An extreme example of this case would occur if the entire demand for products were back ordered, resulting in no inventory and carrying costs of zero. However, the reduction of carrying costs must be balanced against the shortage costs associated with back orders.

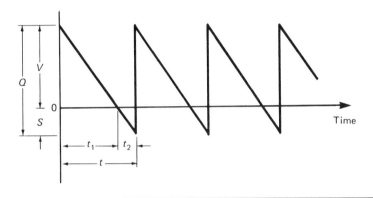

Figure 7.6 *Inventory Level with Shortages*

The same descriptions will be used for the previously defined model variables, with some additions, as follows:

TC = total annual inventory cost
C_o = ordering cost per order
C_c = carrying cost per unit of inventory per year
C_s = shortage cost per unit of shortage per year
Q = quantity ordered per order
D = demand, on an annual basis
N = number of orders per year
S = back-order quantity (shortages) per order
V = maximum inventory volume ($Q - S$)
t_1 = time period during which inventory is on hand in an order cycle
t_2 = time period during which there is a shortage in an order cycle
t = order cycle time—time between receipt of order ($t_1 + t_2$)

The time units used for t, t_1, and t_2 are fractions of a year. For example, if the order cycle time were 73 days, t would be .20 year (73 days $\div$ 365 days = .20 year).

The overall cost function for the inventory model with shortages, which is illustrated in Figure 7.7, is

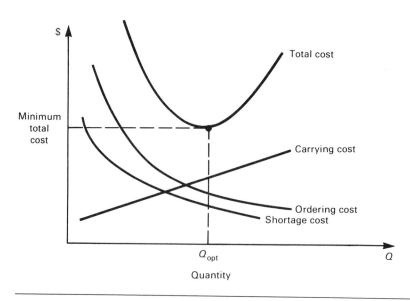

Figure 7.7 *Inventory Model with Shortages*

Total cost = ordering cost + carrying cost + shortage cost

The various components of this total cost model can be derived from inspection of the geometric properties of Figure 7.6. Carrying cost is computed as follows. Since the maximum inventory level is given as V, the average inventory level during the period inventory is available (i.e., during t_1) is $V/2$. Thus, the carrying cost during the period from the receipt of one order to the receipt of the next (t) is

$$C_c \cdot t_1 \cdot \frac{V}{2}$$

(Also note that this quantity is the area of the triangle in Figure 7.6 formed by these values, multiplied by C_c. Thus, the area reflects the amount of inventory on hand.)

The key to converting this carrying cost relationship to an annual basis is to recognize that the geometrical relationship of t_1 to V is equal to that of t to Q (i.e., similar triangles). Given that $t_1/V = t/Q$,

$$t_1 = t \cdot \frac{V}{Q}$$

Substituting this term into the previously defined carrying cost relationship yields

$$\text{Carrying cost per period} = \frac{C_c t V^2}{2Q}$$

Because $tN = 1$ year, which can be restated as $N = 1/t$, we can multiply the carrying cost equation by $1/t$ and obtain the annual carrying cost as follows:

$$\text{Annual carrying cost} = \frac{C_c V^2}{2Q}$$

The shortage cost is determined in a similar manner. Since S is the maximum level of shortages, the average shortage level during the period t_2 is $S/2$. Thus, the shortage cost during one order cycle (t) is

$$C_s \cdot t_2 \cdot \frac{S}{2}$$

The geometrical relationship of t_2 to S is equal to that of t to Q. Thus, $t_2/S = t/Q$ can be converted to

$$t_2 = t \cdot \frac{S}{Q}$$

By substituting this term into the previously defined shortage cost equation, we obtain

$$\text{Shortage cost per order period} = \frac{C_s t S^2}{2Q}$$

Multiplying this equation by $1/t$ results in the annual shortage cost,

$$\text{Annual shortage cost} = \frac{C_s S^2}{2Q}$$

Since $S = Q - V$, shortage cost can also be defined as

$$\frac{C_s(Q - V)^2}{2Q}$$

Ordering cost is unaffected by the allowance of shortages.

$$\text{Annual order cost} = \frac{C_o D}{Q}$$

The total cost model can now be written as

$$\text{TC} = \frac{C_o D}{Q} + \frac{C_c V^2}{2Q} + \frac{C_s(Q - V)^2}{2Q}$$

In order to determine the optimal values for Q and V, the total cost equation (TC) is differentiated with respect to Q and V, respectively. Each partial derivative is then set equal to zero and solved simultaneously for Q_{opt} and V_{opt}. To elaborate, the minimum point on the total cost curve has a slope of zero; thus, by determining the derivative, which defines the slope, and setting it equal to zero, we can determine the value of Q corresponding to the minimum cost:

$$\frac{\partial \text{TC}}{\partial Q} = 0 = -\frac{C_o D}{Q^2} + \frac{C_s}{2} - \frac{V^2}{2Q^2}(C_c + C_s)$$

$$\frac{\partial \text{TC}}{\partial V} = 0 = -C_s + \frac{C_c V}{Q} + \frac{C_s V}{Q}$$

Solving simultaneously yields

$$Q_{opt} = \sqrt{\frac{2C_oD}{C_c}} \cdot \sqrt{\frac{C_c + C_s}{C_s}}$$

$$V_{opt} = \sqrt{\frac{2C_oD}{C_c}} \cdot \sqrt{\frac{C_s}{C_c + C_s}}$$

$$S_{opt} = Q_{opt} - V_{opt}$$

The optimal solutions for t and TC are

$$t_{opt} = \sqrt{\frac{2C_o}{C_cD}} \cdot \sqrt{\frac{C_c + C_s}{C_s}}$$

$$TC_{opt} = \sqrt{2C_oC_cD} \cdot \sqrt{\frac{C_s}{C_c + C_s}}$$

Example 7.3   The Furniture Store Inventory Problem with Shortages

In Example 7.1 the furniture store did not allow shortages of tables to occur, and there was no back ordering of tables demanded that were not available. Now we will consider the same example except that shortages and back ordering will be allowed. The same order cost ($50), carrying cost ($100 per table), and annual demand (4900 tables) will be employed. In addition, an annual shortage cost of $200 per unit for each table unavailable when demanded will be assumed.

To summarize, the model parameters are given as

$C_o = \$50$ (order cost per order)
$C_c = \$100$ (carrying cost per unit per year)
$C_s = \$200$ (shortage cost per unit per year)
$D = 4900$ (annual demand)

The optimal solution for the problem is

$$Q = \sqrt{\frac{2C_oD}{C_c}} \cdot \sqrt{\frac{C_c + C_s}{C_s}}$$

$$= \sqrt{\frac{(2)(50)(4900)}{(100)}} \cdot \sqrt{\frac{100 + 200}{200}}$$

$Q_{opt} \cong 85$ tables

Note that the solution for Q in the shortage model is simply the classic EOQ solution multiplied by $\sqrt{(C_c + C_s)/C_s}$. Further solution results are as follows:

$$V = \sqrt{\frac{2C_oD}{C_c}} \cdot \sqrt{\frac{C_s}{C_c + C_s}}$$

$$= 70(0.82) = 57.4$$

$V_{opt} \cong 57$ tables

and

$$S_{opt} = Q_{opt} - V_{opt} = 85 - 57$$

$$S_{opt} \cong 28 \text{ tables}$$

Thus, the optimal decision is to allow a shortage of 28 tables to accumulate before ordering 85 tables, raising the inventory level to 57 tables. The optimal time, in years, between orders is

$$t = \sqrt{\frac{2C_o}{C_c D}} \cdot \sqrt{\frac{C_c + C_s}{C_s}} = \sqrt{\frac{(2)(50)}{(100)(4900)}} \cdot (122)$$

$$= \sqrt{\frac{1}{4900}} \cdot (1.22) = (.014)(1.22)$$

$$t_{opt} = .017 \text{ year}$$

By multiplying .017 by 365, we find that the optimal time between order receipts is approximately 6 days. The optimal total inventory cost associated with the preceding solution values is

$$TC = \sqrt{2C_o C_c D} \cdot \sqrt{\frac{C_s}{C_c + C_s}}$$

$$= \sqrt{(2)(50)(100)(4900)} \cdot \sqrt{\frac{200}{100 + 200}}$$

$$TC_{opt} \cong \$5715$$

The total cost is given, by category, as follows:

$$\text{Ordering cost} = \frac{C_o D}{Q} = \frac{50(4900)}{85} \cong \$2882$$

$$\text{Carrying cost} = \frac{C_c V^2}{2Q} = \frac{100(57)^2}{170} \cong \$1911$$

$$\text{Shortage cost} = \frac{C_s(Q - V)^2}{2Q} = \frac{200(28)^2}{170} \cong \$922$$

The following table compares the results of the original classic EOQ model in which shortages were not allowed with those of the same model where shortages are allowed.

	Classic EOQ Model No Shortages	Shortage Model
Q (order quantity)	70 units	85 units
V (maximum inventory volume)	70 units	57 units
S (shortage back orders)	0	28 units
TC (total inventory cost)	$7000	$5715
t (time between orders)	5 days	6 days

It is apparent that under certain circumstances it is economical to allow shortages. It should be pointed out that if shortage cost (C_s) were assigned the value of infinity in the shortage model, the solution results would be identical to those of the original classic EOQ model.

Computerized Analysis of Inventory Model with Shortages

Following is the computer-generated solution output for Example 7.3 using the AB:QM software package.

```
Program: Inventory Models / Planned Shortage

Problem Title : Example 7.3

***** Input Data *****

Annual demand    (units/year)        4900.00
Business days    (days/year)          365.00
Lead time        (days)                 0.00
Ordering cost    ($/order)             50.00
Holding cost     ($/unit/year)        100.00
Stockout cost    ($/unit/year)        200.00

***** Program Output *****

Optimal order quantity    (units/order)    :      85.732
Number of orders          (orders/year)    :      57.155
Inventory cycle           (days)           :       6.386
Maximum inventory level   (units)          :      57.155
Average inventory level   (units)          :      28.577
Reorder point             (units)          :       0.000
Demand rate               (units/day)      :      13.425
Total holding cost        ($/year)         :    1905.159
Total ordering cost       ($/year)         :    2857.738
Total inventory cost      ($/year)         :    5715.476
Total shortage cost       ($/year)         :     952.579
Shortage backordered      (units)          :      28.577

***** End of Output *****
```

Noninstantaneous Receipt Model with Shortages

The variation of the EOQ model that will be discussed next is the most general and complex of the deterministic EOQ models. This model expands on the noninstantaneous receipt model in that shortages are allowed. All other assumptions of the previous model remain the same. Figure 7.8 graphically illustrates the conditions surrounding this inventory model. Variables and parameters are defined the same way as in previous model cases with the following exceptions:

t_1 = time period during which inventory increases in an order cycle

t_2 = time period during which inventory is reduced in an order cycle

t_3 = time period during which the shortage increases in an order cycle

t_4 = time period during which the shortage is reduced in an order cycle

t = order cycle time ($t_1 + t_2 + t_3 + t_4$)

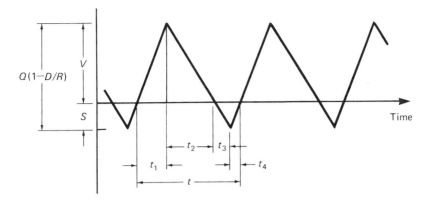

Figure 7.8 *Inventory Level with Shortages and Noninstantaneous Receipt*

Note that all times are on a yearly basis (i.e., fractions of a year).

Total annual cost for this model is

TC = ordering cost + carrying cost + shortage cost

In variable terms,

$$TC = \frac{D}{Q} \cdot \left(C_o + C_c \cdot (t_1 + t_2) \cdot \frac{V}{2} + C_s \cdot (t_3 + t_4) \cdot \frac{S}{2} \right)$$

The individual cost components comprising this equation are derived analytically from Figure 7.8. Notice that the carrying cost and the shortage cost terms are both derived in the same manner as in the previous shortage model. That is, carrying cost per cycle is the average inventory ($V/2$) during the period in which inventory exists ($t_1 + t_2$), multiplied by the carrying cost per unit (C_c). Shortage cost is developed similarly.

The total cost equation must now be modified such that the values of t_1, t_2, t_3, t_4, and V are expressed in terms of Q and S, the solution variables. By again observing Figure 7.8, we can identify relationships between these values and Q and S as follows. The various time values (t_1, t_2, t_3, and t_4) can be defined as

$$t_1 = \frac{V}{R - D} \qquad t_3 = \frac{S}{D}$$

$$t_2 = \frac{V}{D} \qquad t_4 = \frac{S}{R - D}$$

(Note that these four relationships are formulated by applying the simple formula rise ÷ run = slope to Figure 7.8.)

The terms ($t_1 + t_2$) and ($t_3 + t_4$) in the total cost equation can be redefined as

$$t_1 + t_2 = \frac{V}{R - D} + \frac{V}{D}$$

$$t_3 + t_4 = \frac{S}{D} + \frac{S}{R - D}$$

The term V in the $t_1 + t_2$ equation remains to be expressed in terms of Q and Recall from the derivation of the noninstantaneous receipt model that the maximum amount of inventory for any period is $Q[1 - (D/R)]$. However, it can be seen from Figure 7.8 that in this model the corresponding change in inventory level, from lowe level to highest level, is equal to $V + S$.

$$V + S = Q\left(1 - \frac{D}{R}\right)$$

and

$$V = Q\left(1 - \frac{D}{R}\right) - S$$

Since it has been determined that

$$t_1 + t_2 = V\left(\frac{1}{R - D} + \frac{1}{D}\right)$$

the value for V can be substituted in this equation to yield

$$t_1 + t_2 = \left[Q\left(1 - \frac{D}{R}\right) - S\right]\left(\frac{1}{R - D} + \frac{1}{D}\right)$$

Also, recall that

$$t_3 + t_4 = S\left(\frac{1}{R - D} + \frac{1}{D}\right)$$

Substituting these quantities for $t_1 + t_2$ and $t_3 + t_4$ plus the formulated value for V into the total cost equation presented on page 345 results in the following:

$$TC = \frac{D}{Q}\left[C_o + C_c\left[Q\left(1 - \frac{D}{R}\right) - S\right]\left(\frac{1}{R - D} + \frac{1}{D}\right)\left(\frac{Q\left(1 - \frac{D}{R}\right) - S}{2}\right)\right.$$
$$\left. + C_s\left[S\left(\frac{1}{R - D} + \frac{1}{D}\right)\right]\frac{S}{2}\right]$$

Simplifying, we have

$$TC = \frac{D}{Q}\left(C_o + \frac{C_c\left[Q\left(1 - \frac{D}{R}\right) - S\right]^2}{2D\left(1 - \frac{D}{R}\right)} + \frac{C_s S^2}{2D\left(1 - \frac{D}{R}\right)}\right)$$

and

$$TC = \frac{C_o D}{Q} + \frac{C_c\left[Q\left(1 - \frac{D}{R}\right) - S\right]^2}{2Q\left(1 - \frac{D}{R}\right)} + \frac{C_s S^2}{2Q\left(1 - \frac{D}{R}\right)}$$

In order to determine the optimal values of Q and S, this equation must be differentiated with respect to Q and S and equated to zero, shown as follows:

$$\frac{\partial TC}{\partial Q} = 0$$

$$= -\frac{C_o D}{Q^2} + \frac{C_c\left(1 - \frac{D}{R}\right)}{2} - \frac{C_c S^2}{2Q^2\left(1 - \frac{D}{R}\right)} - \frac{C_s S^2}{2Q^2\left(1 - \frac{D}{R}\right)}$$

and

$$\frac{\partial TC}{\partial S} = 0 = -C_c + \frac{C_c S}{Q\left(1 - \frac{D}{R}\right)} + \frac{C_s S}{Q\left(1 - \frac{D}{R}\right)}$$

The two resulting equations must be solved simultaneously for the optimal values of Q and S. Performing these mathematical operations yields

$$Q_{opt} = \sqrt{\frac{2C_o D}{C_c\left(1 - \frac{D}{R}\right)}} \cdot \sqrt{\frac{C_c + C_s}{C_s}}$$

$$S_{opt} = \sqrt{\frac{2C_o D}{C_s}} \cdot \sqrt{1 - \frac{D}{R}} \cdot \sqrt{\frac{C_c}{C_c + C_s}}$$

and

$$TC_{opt} = \sqrt{2C_o C_c D} \cdot \sqrt{1 - \frac{D}{R}} \cdot \sqrt{\frac{C_s}{C_c + C_s}}$$

Example 7.4   The Production Lot Size Model with Shortages

In Example 7.2, it was assumed that the furniture store employed as an example in this chapter was an outlet that manufactured its own inventory on the premises. We referred to the order quantity in this problem as the *production lot size*. In this example, we will expand Example 7.2 by assuming that shortages are possible. A shortage cost of $200 per unit is specified for each table unavailable when demanded. This shortage cost as well as all other model costs (from Example 7.2) are summarized as follows:

$C_o = \$50$ (ordering cost per order)
$C_c = \$100$ (carrying cost per unit of inventory per year)
$C_s = \$200$ (shortage cost per unit of shortage per year)
$D = 4900$ (annual demand)
$R = 9800$ (annual production rate)

The optimal values of Q and S, according to the previously developed formulas, are

$$Q = \sqrt{\frac{2C_oD}{C_c\left(1 - \dfrac{D}{R}\right)}} \cdot \sqrt{\frac{C_c + C_s}{C_s}}$$

$$= \sqrt{\frac{(2)(50)(4900)}{100\left(1 - \dfrac{4900}{9800}\right)}} \cdot \sqrt{\frac{100 + 200}{200}}$$

$$= 121.25$$

$$Q_{opt} \cong 121 \text{ tables}$$

and

$$S = \sqrt{\frac{2C_oD}{C_s}} \cdot \sqrt{1 - \frac{D}{R}} \cdot \sqrt{\frac{C_c}{C_c + C_s}}$$

$$= \sqrt{\frac{(2)(50)(4900)}{200}} \cdot \sqrt{1 - \frac{4900}{9800}} \cdot \sqrt{\frac{100}{100 + 200}}$$

$$= 20.21$$

$$S_{opt} \cong 20 \text{ tables}$$

Given these optimal values for Q and S, total cost is computed as follows:

$$TC = \sqrt{2C_oC_cD} \cdot \sqrt{1 - \frac{D}{R}} \cdot \sqrt{\frac{C_s}{C_c + C_s}}$$

$$= (7000)(.8165)(.7071)$$

$$TC = 4041.43 \cong \$4041$$

Also, the total cost is given by category as follows:

$$\text{Ordering cost} = \frac{C_oD}{Q} = \frac{50(4900)}{121} \cong \$2025$$

$$\text{Carrying cost} = \frac{C_c\left[Q\left(1 - \dfrac{D}{R}\right) - S\right]^2}{2Q\left(1 - \dfrac{D}{R}\right)} - \frac{100[121(.5) - 20]^2}{242(.5)} \cong \$1356$$

$$\text{Shortage cost} = \frac{C_sS^2}{2Q\left(1 - \dfrac{D}{R}\right)} = \frac{200(20)^2}{242(.5)} \cong \$661$$

The maximum inventory level, V, is

$$V = Q\left(1 - \frac{D}{R}\right) - S$$

$$= 121\left(1 - \frac{4900}{9800}\right) - 20 \cong 40 \text{ tables}$$

Thus, the optimal decision is to allow a shortage of 20 tables to accumulate before beginning production of 121 tables, raising the inventory level to a maximum level of 40 tables. The optimal time between production run starts is

$$t = t_1 + t_2 + t_3 + t_4 = \frac{Q}{D}$$

$$= \frac{121}{4900}$$

$$t_{opt} = .0247 \text{ yr} \cong 9 \text{ days}$$

Quantity Discount Model

The next stage in the development of inventory models is the case in which there is a price discount for goods purchased to replenish inventory if they are purchased in sufficient quantity. For example, the normal price for goods is $50; however, if they are purchased in an order size of at least 100 units, the quantity discount price becomes $48. This model is formulated in the same manner as the modified classic model in which carrying cost (K_c) was specified as a percentage of average dollar value of inventory held (p. 333). Thus, the price is also included in the carrying cost equation in order to yield the dollar value of inventory. If price breaks are allowed for large-quantity orders, the inventory model must consider not only ordering cost and carrying cost but also the cost of goods purchased.

Therefore, the model for the quantity discount case is

TC = total ordering cost + total carrying cost + total cost of goods

$$TC = C_o \frac{D}{Q} + K_c P \frac{Q}{2} + PD$$

Note that there are no variables introduced in this model. However, the definition of TC now includes the total value of goods purchased per year, which is indicated in the model by the term PD.

The model is solved in the following manner. First, TC is computed with a quantity discount, then without the discount. Next, the two total cost cases are compared, and the order quantity, Q, is the one that results in the minimum total cost.

This modeling situation is illustrated graphically in Figure 7.9. The TC curve is higher for the nondiscount case than for the discount case, since a higher product price is included if no discount is assumed. The minimum order quantity required to receive the price discount is indicated by the solid vertical line.

Note that only the darkened portions of the two curves are relevant to the analysis of the quantity discount model. That is, if Q is less than the discount quantity, the higher price is charged and the upper cost curve is relevant. If Q is equal to or greater than the discount quantity, the lower price is charged and the lower cost curve is relevant.

The objective is to determine whether the lowest point on the upper curve is less than the lowest *allowable* point on the lower curve. Since point *b* is lower than point *a* in Figure 7.9, taking advantage of the quantity discount results in the minimum total cost.

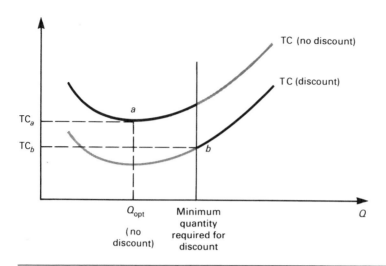

Figure 7.9 Inventory Model with Quantity Discount

Example 7.5   Ordering Chairs with a Quantity Discount

Suppose that the furniture store we have referred to in previous examples is now confronted with a decision regarding the ordering of lawn chairs from the manufacturer. The
price of a lawn chair to the store is $50, the cost of placing an order for chairs is $20,
and the carrying cost as a percent of average annual inventory is 20% of the price. The
store's annual demand is 300 lawn chairs. The manufacturer has offered the store a discount price of $48 a chair if the store will order 50 or more chairs per order. The store
must decide whether it is more economical to order the number of chairs specified in the
EOQ model or to order a minimum of 50 chairs and receive the discount. The various
parameters of this problem are summarized as follows:

$C_o = \$20$	(order cost per order)
$K_c = 20\%$	(carrying cost as a percentage of average inventory value per year)
$D = 300$ chairs	(total annual demand for lawn chairs)
$P = \$50$	(price per chair without a quantity discount)
$P' = \$48$	(price per chair with a quantity discount)

In order to receive the quantity discount price, order sizes must equal or exceed 50 units.
First determine Q_{opt} with the discount received.

$$Q_{opt} = \sqrt{\frac{2C_o D}{K_c P'}}$$

$$= \sqrt{\frac{(2)(20)(300)}{(0.20)(48)}}$$

$$= \sqrt{1250} \cong 35 \text{ chairs}$$

If the value of Q_{opt} is less than the minimum quantity required to receive the discount price, we must set Q equal to the required order quantity to receive the discount; thus, we set Q equal to 50. Computing the value of TC for $Q = 50$ and $P' = 48$, we have

$$TC = C_o \frac{D}{Q} + K_c P' \frac{Q}{2} + P'D$$

$$= (20)\left(\frac{300}{50}\right) + (.20)(48)\left(\frac{50}{2}\right) + (48)(300)$$

$$= \$14,760$$

Now, determine Q_{opt} without the quantity discount.

$$Q_{opt} = \sqrt{\frac{2C_o D}{K_c P}}$$

$$= \sqrt{\frac{(2)(20)(300)}{(.20)(50)}}$$

$$= \sqrt{1200} \cong 35 \text{ chairs}$$

Computing the value of TC for $Q = 35$ and $P = 50$ yields

$$TC = C_o \frac{D}{Q} + K_c P \frac{Q}{2} + PD$$

$$= (20)\left(\frac{300}{35}\right) + (.20)\left(\frac{35}{2}\right) + (50)(300)$$

$$\cong \$15,346$$

The results are summarized as follows:

	Order Size = 50 Discount	Order Size = 35 No Discount
Ordering cost	$ 120	$ 171
Carrying cost	240	175
Cost of goods	14,400	15,000
Total cost	$14,760	$15,346

With the discount the order size is larger, so fewer orders are placed and the ordering costs are less. Also, since the price is lower for the quantity discount case, the cost of goods is less. Carrying costs are more, since fewer orders mean that the average level of inventory is higher. This increase is somewhat offset by the lower price, which tends to reduce the average value of inventory held. The total inventory and goods cost is less when the discount is taken; therefore, the order quantity decided upon is 50.

Computerized Analysis of the Quantity Discount Model

The AB:QM software package has the capability to perform EOQ analysis with a quantity discount in a manner similar to that shown in this section. Following is the computer-generated output analysis from this package, including the input dialogue, a summary of the model, and the solution.

```
Program: Inventory Models / Quantity Discount

Problem Title : Example 7.5

***** Input Data *****

Method type :                                         All unit discount

Annual demand     (units/year)                                300.00
Business days     (days/year)                                 365.00
Lead time         (days)                                        0.00
Ordering cost     ($/order)                                    20.00
Holding cost as a fraction                                     0.200

------------------------------------------------------------------------
                   Lower Quantity  Upper Quantity  Unit Price
------------------------------------------------------------------------
Price break   1         0.00          49.00          50.00
Price break   2        50.00                         48.00
------------------------------------------------------------------------

***** Program Output *****

ALL UNIT DISCOUNT
-----------------


Optimal order price    :       48.000
Optimal order quantity :       50.000
Total inventory cost   :    14760.000
Reorder point          :        0.000

***** End of Output *****
```

Transportation Model of a Production-Inventory Problem

Chapter 5 (Transportation and Assignment Problems) included an example of a production and inventory scheduling problem formulated as a transportation model (in tableau format). The formulation of a production-inventory problem as a transportation model is summarized as follows:

Transportation Problem	Production-Inventory Problem
1. Source i	1. Production period i
2. Destination j	2. Demand period j
3. Supply at source i	3. Production capacity for period i
4. Demand at destination j	4. Demand for period j
5. Transportation cost from source i to destination j	5. Production and inventory cost for production in period i to supply demand in period j

The unit cost described above in item 5 under production-inventory problem is determined as follows:

$$c_{ij} = \begin{cases} \text{production cost in period } i, \text{ if } i = j \\ \text{production cost in period } i + \text{ inventory holding cost} \\ \text{from period } i \text{ to period } j, \text{ if } i < j \end{cases}$$

If back ordering is allowable, the following additional case exists:

$$c_{ij} = \text{production cost in period } i + \text{ back order penalty cost} \\ \text{from period } i \text{ to period } j, \text{ if } i > j$$

Table 7.1 illustrates a general case formulation of a production-inventory problem in a transportation model. Note that the source numbers are now production periods, and the destination numbers are now demand periods. The value of c_{11} is the unit cost of production in period 1 to supply demand in period 1. The value of c_{12} is the unit cost of production in period 1 plus the unit cost of carrying the item in inventory for one period, to supply demand in period 2. On the other hand, c_{21} is the unit cost of production in period 2 plus the unit penalty cost of using this production to supply demand of period 1 (i.e., the item is back ordered, and period 1 demand is supplied from period 2 production). The remaining c_{ij} values are computed in a similar manner. The remainder of the transportation tableau is interpreted as previously described in Chapter 5.

Table 7.1 *Formulation of a Production-Inventory Problem as a Transportation Model*

From i \ To j	Demand in Period j				Production capacity
	1	2	3	4	
1	c_{11} x_{11}	c_{12} x_{12}	c_{13} x_{13}	c_{14} x_{14}	s_1
2	c_{21} x_{21}	c_{22} x_{22}	c_{23} x_{23}	c_{24} x_{24}	s_2
3	c_{31} x_{31}	c_{32} x_{32}	c_{33} x_{33}	c_{34} x_{34}	s_3
4	c_{41} x_{41}	c_{42} x_{42}	c_{43} x_{43}	c_{44} x_{44}	s_4
Demand	d_1	d_2	d_3	d_4	

(Row label: Production in Period i)

Dynamic Programming Analysis of Production and Inventory Planning Problems

Chapter 12, Dynamic Programming, presents an example of an application of dynamic programming to production and inventory scheduling (Example 12.5). Dynamic programming is best suited for problems that involve a sequence of interrelated decisions. It requires that an appropriate recursive relationship be formulated for the individual problem. For the case in which demand fluctuates from period to period and inventory may be carried from one period to the next, dynamic programming can provide an efficient solution procedure.

The example of a production and inventory planning problem given in Chapter 12 is characterized by fluctuating demand and limited production capacity and inventory storage capacity. The production cost is defined as $50 to set up for production in a given period, plus $20 per unit. Inventory may be held, up to a maximum of 4 items. Dynamic programming is used to solve this production-inventory problem.

ABC Analysis

ABC analysis is a method for classifying inventory according to its dollar value to the firm. Typically thousands of items are held in inventory by a company, especially in manufacturing, but only a small percentage is of such a high dollar value to warrant close inventory control. In general, about 20% of the inventory items will account for 80% of the total dollar value of inventory. These are classified as "A" or "class A" items. "B" items represent another 30% of total inventory units, but only 15% of total inventory dollar value. The last class of items, "C," generally represents about 50% all of inventory units, but represents only a modest 5% of total dollar value.

An underlying principle of ABC analysis is that each class of inventory requires different levels of inventory control; that is, the higher the value of the inventory, the tighter the control. Thus, class A items should experience tight inventory control, while B and C require more relaxed (and perhaps minimal) attention.

The first step in applying ABC analysis is to classify all inventory items as either A, B, or C. This requires that each item in inventory be assigned a dollar value, which is computed by multiplying the dollar cost of one unit by the annual demand for that item. All items are then ranked according to their dollar value and the top 20% are classified as A items, the next 30% as B items, and the last 50% as C items. These classifications will not be exact, but they have been found to be close to the actual occurrence in firms with remarkable frequency.

The next step in ABC analysis is to determine the level of inventory control for each classification. Class A items require very tight inventory control because they represent such a large percentage of the total dollar value of inventory. Efforts should be made to keep inventory levels as low as possible and safety stocks should be minimized. This typically requires accurate demand forecasts and more detailed record keeping. The appropriate EOQ analysis or other inventory modelling procedures should be applied. In addition, close attention should be given to purchasing policies and procedures if the inventory items are acquired outside the firm.

B and C items typically require less stringent inventory control. Since carrying costs are usually lower for C items, higher inventory levels can sometimes be maintained with larger safety stocks. It may not even be necessary to apply sophisticated inventory analysis or models for controlling C items; simple manual observation may be sufficient.

The AB:QM software package used previously in this chapter has limited capability to perform ABC analysis. Given a list of inventory items, the per unit cost of each and the annual demand for each item, the ABC module will rank the items in order of their dollar value and compute the cumulative percentage for all items, thus enabling the user to manually construct ABC classifications. This is essentially the first step in ABC analysis described above.

INVENTORY MODELS WITH UNCERTAIN PARAMETER VALUES: STOCHASTIC MODELS

In the previous models many of the model components were treated as constants that were known with certainty; however, in real-world situations these parameter values are often uncertain. One of the inventory elements that is most commonly a random variable is demand. In most cases, the firm is uncertain about when demand for an item will occur and the amount that will be demanded. In such cases, demand is typically defined by a probability distribution.

Other elements subject to uncertainty include reorder lead time and customer back ordering. Often the firm does not know with certainty how long it will take to receive an order from a supplier and if the quantity ordered will be received. Thus, lead time can be considered a random variable. If enough inventory is not on hand, the firm cannot always be sure that a customer will back order, and if the customer does back order, that the same amount will be requested.

Many of the costs associated with inventory models can also be subject to uncertainty. Carrying costs and ordering costs can both be random variables in cases where the firm has no control over them. If customer back ordering is subject to uncertainty, then shortage costs to the firm are also subject to uncertainty.

There are a variety of models and techniques available to reflect conditions of uncertainty in inventory analysis, ranging from analytical approaches to such techniques as simulation. Some of these approaches are relatively simple and straightforward, whereas others are highly sophisticated and quite complex. In this section, several of the more straightforward approaches to reflecting uncertainty in inventory models will be presented. For a more in-depth study of probabilistic inventory models, the interested reader is directed to any of the numerous excellent texts listed in the references.

EOQ Sensitivity to Uncertain Parameters

One reason why the EOQ model is very popular and widely applied is that it tends to give reasonably good results even when the parameters, such as demand and the various inventory costs, are uncertain. The optimal order quantity value, Q_{opt}, determined by the EOQ model is, in general, not very sensitive to errors in parameter estimates. We will illustrate this characteristic of the EOQ model within the context of Example 7.1. Recall that in the furniture company example the following parameter values were given:

$$C_o = \$50 \qquad \text{(ordering cost per order)}$$
$$C_c = \$100 \qquad \text{(carrying cost per unit held in inventory per year)}$$
$$D = 4900 \qquad \text{(tables demanded per year)}$$

An Application of Inventory Management and Control: Parts Inventory Management at IBM

The computer industry has expanded dramatically in the last decade with enhanced technology resulting in many new products. This trend has also led to the necessity of maintaining service systems to support these products. For IBM the number of machines and computing equipment has increased, and this has in turn created a need for more extensive service and more spare parts. Approximately 1,000 IBM products are currently in service with installed units numbering in excess of tens of millions, and IBM has over 200,000 part numbers to support these products. For IBM to effectively compete in the information processing industry it is essential that they maintain a service parts logistics system to support the products they sell and install.

IBM's National Service Division (NSD) has developed an extensive and sophisticated parts inventory management system (PIMS) to provide prompt and reliable customer service. This system manages a parts distribution network consisting of 2 central warehouses, 21 field distribution centers located in metropolitan areas, 64 parts stations and 15,000 outside locations. NSD employs over 15,000 customer engineers to repair and maintain its installed products. The parts inventory maintained in this system is valued in the billions of dollars. PIMS employed EOQ formulas to determine parts replenishment batch sizes and set service priority goals.

Recently IBM made dramatic improvements to its parts inventory management system

The optimal order size with these parameters was previously determined to be

$$Q_{opt} = \sqrt{\frac{2C_oD}{C_c}}$$

$$= \sqrt{\frac{(2)(50)(4900)}{100}}$$

$$= 70 \text{ tables per order}$$

Now, however, let us assume that a 50% error was originally made in estimating demand. In other words, actual demand is really 7350 tables instead of 4900 tables (i.e., a 50% greater quantity). Recomputing the optimal order quantity with the actual demand value of 7350 tables, we have

$$Q_{opt} = \sqrt{\frac{(2)(50)(7350)}{100}}$$

$$= 85.7 \cong 86 \text{ tables per order}$$

A comparison of this new value of Q_{opt} with the previously computed optimal order size of 70 tables indicates that the 50% error in demand produced only a 22% error in the optimal order size. The effect of the square root in the EOQ formula was to "dampen" the impact of the error in demand.

A comparison of the minimum total cost computed using $Q_{opt} = 86$ tables and $D = 7350$ tables with the original minimum total cost value computed in Example 7.1 has a similar result. An error of 22% in total cost ($8750 versus $7000) resulted from a

bodied in a modelling framework called ptimizer. This system contained four basic odules: a forecasting system that estimates part ilure rates, a system to provide inventory data, a cision model that determined a stock control licy at each location and each part in the stem that minimizes the expected costs and tisfies service constraints, and, a system that terfaces the output of the decision module and MS. The new system resulted in a reduction in ventory investment, improved service, greater exibility in responding to changes in service quirements, planning capabilities, and better nderstanding of the impact of parts operations n customer service.

The Optimizer system recommended a reduction in the time-averaged value of inventory by approximately 25%; over a half billion dollars in inventory investment. However, some of the proposed inventory reduction was reallocated to improve service levels resulting in an annual total inventory reduction of one quarter billion dollars. Using the new system, IBM also made several strategic changes in its inventory network, including decreasing the number of field distribution centers and increasing parts stations and the replenishment rate at these stations. These changes resulted in a 10% improvement in parts availability and a $20 million annual savings in operating efficiency.

ource: M. Cohen, "Optimizer: IMB's Multi-Echelon Inventory System for Managing Service Logistics," *Interfaces,* 20, no. 1 anuary–February 1990): 65–82.

50% error in demand. Errors resulting from uncertain estimates of ordering, carrying, and shortage costs produce results of a like nature—errors in model cost estimates are dampened in the optimal order and total cost values.

This brief analysis indicates that the EOQ model can be employed with some degree of confidence even if one does not have total confidence in the estimates of the model parameters. To a certain extent, this lack of sensitivity to errors in parameter estimates accounts for the popularity of EOQ analysis.

Uncertain Demand Without Reordering

Frequently a firm is faced with making a one-time decision concerning how much to purchase or produce and store in inventory. This is particularly true with regard to highly perishable goods that may have a shelf life of one or two days, such as doughnuts at a drive-in bakery, or products that become obsolete very quickly, such as daily newspapers. This sort of situation represents a unique inventory problem in which a single order is placed (or a single production run is made) to achieve the stock of goods needed for the brief upcoming planning period. Typically, the problem is characterized by uncertain demand, such as a day's demand for doughnuts or newspapers. Thus, this type of inventory problem is categorized as uncertain demand without reordering. The following example is a classic illustration of this type of inventory problem.

Example 7.6   The Newsboy Problem

At 2:00 A.M. each day, a newsboy in a large city must decide how many bundles of the daily newspaper to stock for the upcoming day's sales. The newsboy must pay for the newspapers out of his own pocket at the time of delivery each morning. Any newspape that remain unsold at the end of the day can be sold to a scrap company, which shred the paper and sells it for packing material. If the newsboy runs out of newspapers and unable to meet all demand for his papers, no significant customer ill will is experience

The fluctuation in the daily demand for newspapers is indicated by the historic record given below:

Daily Demand for Newspapers	Number of Days Demand Recorded	Relative Frequency (probability)
21 bundles	60	.2
22 bundles	120	.4
23 bundles	90	.3
24 bundles	30	.1
	300	1.0

The newsboy must pay $3 a bundle (there are 20 papers in each bundle) for th newspapers, and he sells the newspapers for $5 a bundle. Any unsold papers are sold t the scrap company for $1 a bundle.

The table below summarizes the range of decision alternatives, possible event out comes, and associated dollar returns facing the newsboy.

	Possible Actions			
Event (demand)	Stock 21	Stock 22	Stock 23	Stock 24
21 bundles	$42	$40	$38	$36
22 bundles	42	44	42	40
23 bundles	42	44	46	44
24 bundles	42	44	46	48

This problem represents the type of problem presented in Chapter 8 in the section on decision theory models. Briefly, the solution procedure includes the computation of the expected return associated with each possible stocking action. For a particular stocking action, the expected return is determined by multiplying the probabilities for each demand level times the associated dollar return and summing these values to yield a weighted average return for each stocking action (where the weights are the demand probabilities). The unexpected return for stocking 23 bundles is found as follows:

(1) Event (demand)	(2) Probability	(3) Stock 23	(4) Col. (2) × Col. (3)
21 bundles	.2	$38	7.60
22 bundles	.4	42	16.80
23 bundles	.3	46	13.80
24 bundles	.1	46	4.60
			$42.80

Thus, the expected dollar return associated with stocking 23 bundles of newspaper is $42.80. The table below summarizes the expected return associated with each action.

Action	Expected Dollar Return
Stock 21 bundles	$42.00
Stock 22 bundles	$43.20 (maximum)
Stock 23 bundles	$42.80
Stock 24 bundles	$41.20

The optimum decision based on maximum expected return is to stock 22 bundles of newspapers. Of course, since demand for the newspapers is random, the day's dollar return will be $38, $42, or $46, depending on actual demand. Over the long run, however, by ordering 22 bundles each day the newboy should maximize the dollar returns. The interested reader should refer to Chapter 8 (Decision Theory and Games) for a more detailed presentation of expected values in decision theory.

Computerized Analysis of the Newsboy Problem

Most management science software packages for the personal computer have the capability to perform decision analysis. The newsboy problem is a specific type of decision theory (also referred to as decision analysis) problem and, as such, can be solved using the decision analysis program of most software packages. Following is the computer-generated output for Example 7.6 obtained by using the AB:QM software package. Note that the terminology and solution format are consistent with those in decision theory. For example, the term "Event" refers to the "demand" in Example 7.6, and the term "alternative" refers to the possible "stock actions" in our example. The input data are summarized in a tabular form, called a payoff table, that is a reversed version of our example table showing the event outcomes.

```
Program: Decision Theory / Decision Making Under Risk

Problem Title : Example 7.6

***** Input Data *****

Type of Problem  : Profit  Problem

--------------------------------------------------------------
                    Event  1   Event  2   Event  3   Event  4
--------------------------------------------------------------
Probability          0.200      0.400      0.300      0.100
--------------------------------------------------------------
Alternative   1     42.000     42.000     42.000     42.000
Alternative   2     40.000     44.000     44.000     44.000
Alternative   3     38.000     42.000     46.000     46.000
Alternative   4     36.000     40.000     44.000     48.000
--------------------------------------------------------------
```

```
***** Program Output *****

Expected Profit Table
-------------------------------------------
Alternative              Expected Profit
-------------------------------------------
       1                      42.000
       2                      43.200  <=
       3                      42.800
       4                      41.200
-------------------------------------------

  <=   indicate(s) the best alternative(s)

***** End of Output *****
```

Uncertain Demand with Reordering

All variations of the classic EOQ inventory model presented so far have been based on the assumption that demand is constant and known with certainty (assumptions 1 and 2 on p. 324). The alternative is for the demand rate to be stochastic, or probabilistic. If we maintain the assumption that lead time is constant and known with certainty, the order quantity can still be computed according to the classic EOQ formula, either by assuming that demand is constant and that no stockouts will occur or by using average demand $(\overline{D})$. In either case, the order quantity is not optimal but only an *approximated* optimal solution.

Since demand is actually a random variable, however, the computation of the *reorder point* is not so simple. One approach is to determine the *expected* (average) demand during lead time and reorder when that inventory level is reached. This is analogous to assuming that demand during lead time is also known and constant. This approach invariably leads to stockouts (shortages) at various intervals of time.

Alternatively, firms often maintain **safety stocks,** or buffers, of inventory to avoid inventory shortages when the demand during order lead time is not known with certainty. The problem then becomes the determination of the optimal safety stock to hold in order to avoid inventory stockouts.

Inventory Model with Safety Stocks

An illustration of the inventory level with safety stock is shown in Figure 7.10. In the third cycle of the model, inventory shortages would have occurred if no safety stock had been carried. In the first and second cycles of the model, a surplus of inventory would have occurred even without a safety stock. An implicit assumption of this model is that these surpluses and deficits balance out over a year, so on the average the excess inventory held is represented by the shaded area (safety-stock level).

Most often inventory safety stocks are never entirely depleted; therefore, the unit carrying cost for safety stock is multiplied by the entire safety-stock level. If the safety-stock inventory level is denoted by I_s and carrying cost per unit held per year is given by C_c, the annual safety-stock carrying costs are determined as $C_c I_s$.

The safety-stock costs must be balanced against the stockout costs, which are a func-

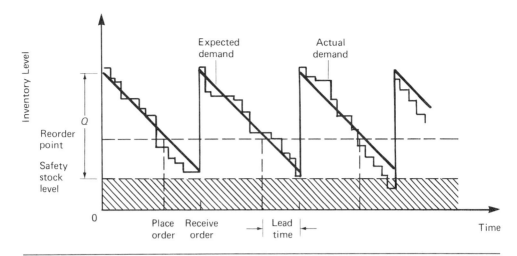

Figure 7.10 Inventory Level with Safety Stock

tion of the probabilistic demand and the safety stock held. In other words, a trade-off between carrying costs for inventory safety stocks and inventory stockout costs must be considered.

It is assumed that, although the demand during reorder lead time is not known with certainty, it can be described by a probability distribution. As an example, consider a firm that has kept records of the relative frequency of the levels of demand during lead time and developed the following probability distribution of demand during lead time:

Demand During Lead Time	Probability (relative frequency)
80	0.10
90	0.20
100	0.40
110	0.20
120	0.10
	1.00

From this probability distribution of demand during lead time it can be seen that if a reorder point of 120 units were used, the firm would never expect a stockout. Thus, stockout costs would be zero for this case. However, if 110 units were used as the reorder point, a demand of 120 units would be expected 10% of the time, resulting in stockouts 10% of the time. If 100 units were specified as the reorder point, stockouts of 10 units could be expected 20% of the time and stockouts of 20 units 10% of the time.

The expected average demand during lead time is computed as follows:[1]

$$E(\text{demand}) = .10(80) + .20(90) + .40(100) + .20(110) + .10(120)$$
$$= 100 \text{ units}$$

[1] Refer to Chapter 8 (Decision Theory and Games), in which the concept of expected value is discussed in detail.

If a reorder point of over 100 units is selected, the excess is considered the safety stock. The expected numbers of shortages for reorder points of 100, 110, and 120 (and associated safety stocks of 0, 10, and 20) are summarized as follows:

(1) Reorder Point	(2) Safety Stock	(3) Actual Lead Time Demand	(4) Resulting Shortage	(5) Probability of Demand and Resulting Shortage	(6) Col. 4 Times Col. 5	(7) Expected Shortage ($E[x]$)
100	0	100	0	0.4	0	
		110	10	0.2	2	4
		120	20	0.1	2	
110	10	110	0	0.2	0	
		120	10	0.1	1	1
120	20	120	0	0.1	0	0

Thus, the expected number of shortages incurred when no safety stock is allowed is 4. If a safety stock of 10 units is provided, the expected shortage is 1. Of course, if the reorder point is set at 120, providing a safety stock of 20 units, no shortages are incurred.

Since these computations yield the expected shortages per inventory order, the total expected shortages per year would simply be that figure multiplied by the number of orders.

We saw previously that when Q_{opt} is determined by the classic EOQ formula, we also can determine N, the optimal number of orders as D/Q_{opt}. Thus, we can obtain the total expected shortage costs.

$$\text{TSC} = C_s \cdot N \cdot E[x]$$

where

  TSC = total annual expected shortage cost
  C_s = cost per unit shortage
  N = number of orders per year
  $E[x]$ = expected number of shortages per order

As an example, assume that the inventory carrying cost has been determined to be $10 per unit per year ($C_c = 10$). Further assume that shortage costs have been estimated at $3 per unit shortage ($C_s = 3$). The classic EOQ model is used to determine Q_{opt} using *expected* annual demand. Using the formula $D/Q = N$, we can determine the number of orders per year. For this example, assume that $N = 12$ (orders per year).

Safety-stock inventory carrying cost is computed by simply multiplying the safety-stock level times the unit carrying cost ($10). Assuming that the previously given probability distribution of demand is appropriate, the cost analysis is as follows:

Safety Stock (I_s)	Inventory Level Carrying Cost (C_c)	Total Annual Safety Stock Carrying Cost ($C_c I_s$)
0	$10	$ 0
10	10	100
20	10	200

Expected shortage costs are computed as the combined product of the cost per unit shortage, the number of orders per year, and the expected shortage per order period.

Safety Stock Level	Cost per Unit Shortage (C_s)	Number of Orders per year (N)	Expected Shortages per Order Period $(E[x])$	Expected Annual Shortage Cost $(C_sNE[x])$
0	$3	12	4	$144
10	3	12	1	36
20	3	12	0	0

The appropriate safety-stock level is determined by comparing the various safety-stock levels and associated total carrying and shortage costs, summarized as follows:

Safety Stock Level (I_s)	Safety Stock Inventory Carrying Cost (C_cI_s)	Expected Shortage Cost $(C_sNE[x])$	Total Expected Costs
0	$ 0	$144	$144
10	100	36	136
20	200	0	200

Thus, total expected safety-stock carrying and inventory shortage costs are minimized when a safety stock of 10 units is carried (reorder point of 110 units). It should be pointed out that the optimal solution is now based on an *expected* cost value. This requires that the policy be carried out over a long period of time in order to balance out variations in actual costs.

Determining Safety Stocks According to Service Levels

A somewhat different approach to the determination of safety stocks is to use customer service levels. In this case, the goal is to satisfy some specified percentage of total customers on a regular basis. In order to achieve this prescribed service level, a safety stock is added to the average maximum inventory level. In this approach, the reorder point, r, is defined as

$$r = \overline{D}_L + Z\sigma_{D_L}$$

where

$\overline{D}_L$ = average demand during lead time

Z = number of standard deviations required for a specified service level (using a normal distribution)

σ_{D_L} = standard deviation of demand during lead time

The safety stock, SS, for this approach is $Z\sigma_{D_L}$.

This approach is analogous to developing the upper limit of a confidence interval.

The following example will demonstrate the approach. A firm desires to establish an inventory policy (i.e., an order quantity, reorder point, and safety stock) that will maintain a 95% service level. That is, 95% of all customers demanding the product during the lead time will be serviced. The daily demand for the product is normally distributed with a mean of 50 units and a standard deviation of 6 units. Lead time is constant and equals 5 days. Thus, average demand during lead time, $\overline{D}_L$, is 250 units (i.e., 50 units/day · 5 days) with a standard deviation, σ_{D_L}, of 13.4 units. (Since demand is independent, the variance of demand during lead time is equal to the sum of the variances of demand; that is, $\sigma^2_{D_L} = 5 \times 36 = 180$, so $\sigma_{D_L} = \sqrt{180} = 13.4$.) Order cost, C_o, equals \$20, and carrying cost, C_c, equals \$.20 per unit.

The optimal order quantity, Q, is computed by using the classic EOQ formula except that average annual demand is used in place of constant demand (i.e., $\overline{D} = 50 \times 365$).

$$Q_{opt} = \sqrt{\frac{2C_o\overline{D}}{C_c}}$$

$$= \sqrt{\frac{2(20)(50)(365)}{.20}}$$

$$\cong 1910$$

The reorder point is calculated separately and reflects the desired service level.

$$r = \overline{D}_L + Z\sigma_{D_L}$$

Since a 95% service level corresponds to a Z value of 1.645 standard deviations,

$$r = 250 + (1.645)(13.4)$$
$$= 250 + 22$$
$$= 272 \text{ units}$$

These computations indicate that the firm's inventory policy should be to order a quantity of 1910 units every time inventory falls to 272 units. This includes a safety stock of 22 units. The preceding example is illustrated graphically in Figure 7.11.

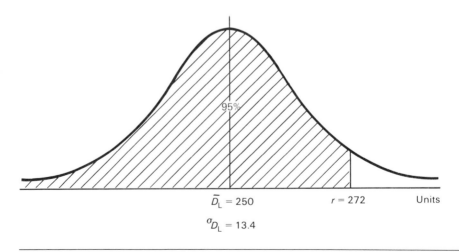

$\overline{D}_L = 250$ $r = 272$ Units

$\sigma_{D_L} = 13.4$

Figure 7.11 *Distribution of Daily Demand with Reorder Point*

nulation of Inventory Models

The examples of probabilistic inventory models presented in this section are somewhat simplified. Oftentimes in reality, such model parameters as order quantity, orders per year, reorder point, and safety stock are *interdependent* as well as uncertain. In such cases, alternative approaches are required.

The most powerful tool for dealing with uncertain inventory model parameters is *computer simulation.* With simulation, a complex inventory environment, in which several model parameters are subject to uncertainty, can be modeled and an inventory policy developed, which could not be accomplished analytically. Since simulation is the subject of Chapter 11, an in-depth presentation of this topic will not be presented here. However, we will illustrate via an example the general logic behind using simulation for inventory modeling.

Example 7.7 Simulating Inventory Demand

As an example of inventory simulation, we will consider a problem in which two model parameters, demand and reorder lead time, are uncertain. In this problem an appliance dealer is attempting to determine the optimal quantity and time for reordering refrigerators, given that the demand for refrigerators and the reorder lead time are uncertain. Based on an analysis of past sales records for 100 weeks, the appliance dealer has determined the following probability distribution for the weekly demand of refrigerators.

Refrigerators Demanded per Week	Frequency Distribution	Probability
5	20	.20
6	40	.40
7	30	.30
8	10	.10
	100	1.00

We must now develop a means to re-create, or *simulate,* weekly demand based on this probability distribution. This simulation can be accomplished by using the *Monte Carlo process* for selecting numbers randomly from a probability distribution (a process more fully discussed in Chapter 11). In the Monte Carlo process, the probability distribution must first be partitioned into ranges of values corresponding to the probabilities for each demand value, as follows:

Refrigerators Demanded per Week	Probability	Cumulative Probability	Random Number Range
5	.20	.20	0–19
6	.40	.60	20–59
7	.30	.90	60–89
8	.10	1.00	90–99
	1.00		

Note that the probability distribution has been converted into ranges between the numbers 0 and 99, or 100 total numbers. First observe the range corresponding to 5 un demanded; note that there are 20 numbers in the range 0–19, or 20 percent of the 1 numbers between 0 and 99. Likewise, the range of numbers for 6 units demanded, 20 59, contains 40 numbers, or 40 percent of the total 100 numbers. Thus, using this p cedure, we are able to partition the demand probabilities into ranges of numbers.

To simulate demand, we first generate a random number from a computer progra specifically designed for such a purpose or from a table of random numbers develop from a computer program. Table C.5 in Appendix C is such a random number table. an example, select the first number, 39, in the first column of Table C.5. Observing t ranges of random numbers developed from the probability distribution above, we s that 39 is in the range 20–59, which corresponds to a demand of 6 refrigerators. T probability of selecting a random number in this range is .40. In this manner, week demand can be re-created mathematically—that is, simulated.

The lead time for receiving refrigerators from the refrigerator manufacturer to replen ish inventory is also uncertain, so a second set of ranges of random numbers is constructe similarly, as follows:

Lead Time (weeks)	Probability Distribution	Cumulative Probability	Random Number Range
1	.30	.30	0–29
2	.40	.70	30–69
3	.30	1.00	70–99

Now we are prepared to develop a simulation model by simulating both demand and lead time.

The appliance dealer has determined the following cost parameters: $C_o = \$50$ per order, $C_c = \$1$ per refrigerator per week, and $C_s = \$120$ per refrigerator per shortage. Recall that the objective of the simulation is to help the appliance dealer determine the optimal order size and reorder point. Thus, several order sizes must be tested within the context of the simulation experiment to see which results in the minimum total inventory cost. We will begin the simulation by first testing an order size of 20 refrigerators. In addition, a reorder point must also be specified, to indicate when an order is placed. In this initial experiment, we will use a reorder point of 6 refrigerators. Back ordering will not be allowed when shortages exist. When an order is made in week n, it will arrive in week $n + LT$ (where LT = lead time).

The simulation experiment can be conducted by hand in tabular form, as shown in Table 7.2.

The simulation experiment conducted in Table 7.2 will be briefly described to illustrate the steps of the simulation process. First, notice that the simulation has been conducted for a period of 10 weeks, and that the initial starting conditions in week 1 show a beginning inventory balance of 10 units and no order received in week 1. Thus, as shown in the fourth column, the experiment begins with an inventory level of 10 units. The following steps occur in the simulation process.

ble 7.2 *Simulation Experiment for Example 7.7 with* $Q = 20$ *and* $r = 6$

ek	Beginning Inventory	Order Receipt	Inventory Level	R_1: D	Demand	Ending Inventory	R_2: LT	Lead Time	C_o +	C_c +	C_s =	TC
1	10	0	10	19	5	5	65	2	$50	$ 5	$ 0	$ 55
2	5	0	5	51	6	0	17	1	50	0	120	170
3	0	40	40	63	7	33			0	33	0	33
4	33	0	33	85	7	26			0	26	0	26
5	26	0	26	37	6	20			0	20	0	20
6	20	0	20	89	7	13			0	13	0	13
7	13	0	13	76	7	6	71	3	50	6	0	56
8	6	0	6	34	6	0	11	1	50	0	0	50
9	0	20	20	27	6	14			0	14	0	14
0	14	20	34	10	5	29			0	29	0	29

Average weekly inventory cost = $46.60

1. A random number, R_1, is selected from column 6 of Table C.5 in Appendix C. This value is 19. By observing the previously constructed ranges of random numbers for demand, we see that 19 corresponds to a demand of 5 units.

2. We subtract the demanded 5 units from the inventory level value of 10 units, yielding an ending inventory of 5 units. This is below the reorder point of 6 units, so a new order must be made.

3. A random number, R_2, is selected from Table C.5. This value is the second number in the sixth column, 65. This number corresponds to a lead time of 2 weeks. Thus, the order will be received in week 3 (week $n + LT = 1 + 2 = 3$).

4. Since an order was made, there is an order cost of $50; the 5 units of ending inventory results in a carrying cost of $5; and since there were no shortages, there is no shortage cost. Summing these costs yields a total inventory cost for week 1 of $55.

This step-by-step process is repeated for the remaining 9 weeks of the simulation experiment. At the completion of the experiment, an average weekly total cost of $46.60 is computed.

Although this brief experiment illustrates how an inventory system is simulated, it is incomplete. Normally a 10-period simulation is too short to yield a true "steady state" result. A 100- or even 1000-period simulation would be more appropriate. Further, this particular simulation experiment would represent only one part of a complete experiment. This simulation was conducted for one particular order size of 20 units and one reorder point of 6 units. In order to complete the simulation experiment, multiple simulation runs would have to be made with various combinations of Q and r. The combination of Q and r that yields the minimum total cost will indicate the optimal inventory policy. The fact that Q and r are interrelated, so each must be solved for simultaneously to obtain an optimum solution for the inventory problem in question, and the fact that both demand and reorder lead time are random variables result in a problem that is virtually impossible to analyze by any means other than simulation.

Finally, a true simulation model would be conducted on a computer rather than in a table by hand. It is readily apparent that performing the experiment in Table 7.2 for 1000 weeks by hand and then repeating this table for several hundred combinations of

Q and r would take several days, whereas these same steps can be done on a computer in several seconds. In an actual computer simulation, a computer language would be used to construct from the steps in Table 7.2 a simulation model that would subsequently be run on the computer. Model building and computer languages are discussed in greater detail in Chapter 11, Simulation.

Although brief and incomplete, the simulation example presented in this section nevertheless illustrates the potential of simulation for solving complex inventory problems with uncertain parameters. As the number of model parameters that are probabilistic increases, increasing the complexity of the inventory model, an analytic solution becomes impossible, and simulation provides the only viable alternative.

RECENT ADVANCES IN INVENTORY MANAGEMENT AND CONTROL

In recent years two important and popular advances in inventory management and control have evolved: materials requirement planning (MRP) and the Japanese just-in-time technique, also referred to as a kanban system. The evolution and popularity of the MRP system has closely paralleled advancements in computer technology since the mid-1960s. The Japanese just-in-time technique with kanbans, on the other hand, is relatively new to Americans, who have become seriously aware of this method for inventory control only during the past six or seven years.

Material Requirements Planning

Material requirements planning (MRP) is a computer-based production and inventory planning and control system employed primarily for products, or end items, that are assemblies of component parts. There are three objectives of an MRP system: (1) to ensure the availability of materials and components for assembly of the end item, (2) to minimize the level of inventory, and (3) to plan manufacturing activities, delivery schedules, and purchasing activities.

The basic logic of an MRP system is first to analyze an end item (finished product) and break it down into its various component parts, a procedure referred to as "exploding" the product. A schedule is then mapped out such that at a particular level of production the demand and lead time for a component can be employed to determine the demand and lead time for a subsequent component. In this manner, an MRP system determines how much of each component should be ordered and when the component should be ordered. Hence, the demand for a component at each level of production is dependent on the demand for that component at the next succeeding level of production.

The three major inputs to an MRP system are the *master production schedule,* the *product structure records,* and the *inventory status records.* The master production schedule outlines the production plans for all end items. The computerized MRP system then explodes this master schedule into individual time-phased component requirements. The product structure records, also called bills of materials, contain information on all raw materials, components, and subassemblies required for each end item. The bill of materials informs the MRP system of each item's part number, description, and quantity of components demanded per end item. Finally, the inventory status records contain the on-hand status and on-order status for all items in inventory, plus information on lead times and order sizes for all components.

The MRP system determines a component's gross requirements by exploding the bill of materials according to the master production schedule. The exploding process is simply a multiplication of the number of end items by the number of each component necessary to produce an end item. The net requirements are determined by subtracting the available inventory (indicated by the inventory status reports) from the gross requirements. The timing of orders is then determined by offsetting the order receipts by their lead time. In this manner, an MRP system indicates what to order, how much to order, and when to order.

The basic computer output of the MRP system is planned order releases, which can be in the form of purchase orders to vendors or work orders to the internal production operations, or shops. These releases indicate the timing and quantity of the orders.

As indicated previously, materials requirement planning has become a very popular and widely applied means for managing inventory. However, it does not necessarily supersede the EOQ models presented earlier in this chapter. The EOQ models are most applicable for inventory control of single products (not assembled end items) and of products with independent demand (not component-dependent demand). Thus, MRP systems tend to be an alternative to EOQ models for assembly-type manufacturing operations. In addition, MRP systems require order size determination, and EOQ models provide one of the several alternatives for determining order sizes within the MRP framework.

The Japanese Just-in-Time Technique with Kanbans

A more recent development in the area of inventory management and control has been the discovery on the part of U.S. firms of the Japanese **just-in-time technique with kanbans.** This Japanese system of inventory control is based on the premise that inventory is the root of all evil and should be kept at an absolute minimum level.

Multistage production processes can be classified into two types: push systems and pull systems. Most U.S. production operations are push systems, whereas the Japanese just-in-time operations are pull systems. The primary difference between the two systems is that in the pull system the succeeding stage demands and withdraws in-process units from the preceding stage only at the rate and time the succeeding stage consumes the items. In the push system, a forecast of demand, which includes allowances for lead times, is determined for each stage. The push process is controlled through inventory levels set at each stage in the system. In order to protect against an incorrect forecast, in-process inventory levels are often inflated to include safety stocks, which can result in unnecessarily high carrying costs.

From the Japanese perspective, push systems have several serious drawbacks. Pull systems are designed to obviate these drawbacks. Thus, the basic objectives of a pull system are (1) to minimize in-process inventory, (2) to minimize fluctuations of in-process inventory that simplify inventory controls, (3) to prevent amplified transmission of demand fluctuations from stage to stage, (4) to raise the level of shop control through decentralization, and (5) to reduce defects.

In the ideal pull system, inventory at each stage is one unit. When demand for a preceding stage's output is generated by the succeeding stage, the preceding stage's unit of inventory is transferred to the succeeding stage, where it is processed. The removal of inventory at the preceding stage authorizes the manufacture of an additional unit to replace the one just taken. No manufacturing can occur without such an authorization. As a result, each stage produces *just in time* to meet the demand of succeeding stages, which ultimately is controlled by demand for the final product. Actually, the ideal inventory of one unit is rarely achieved—units are produced in small lots or containers. The efficiency of the pull system is often measured in terms of the number of containers of goods produced and stored at each stage; the more the inventory, the lower the efficiency. Figure 7.12 presents a diagram of this just-in-time process between successive stages in a simple production system.[2]

The Japanese control the stage-to-stage authorization of container production with two kanbans. "Kanban" (pronounced kahn bahn) is the Japanese word for card. In fact, kanbans are just that—cards. One kanban, called a production kanban, accompanies the containers as they are being produced, as shown in Figure 7.12. Looking specifically at stage N in Figure 7.12, we see that when the production of a container is completed and demand from the succeeding stage ($N - 1$) occurs (as indicated by a withdrawal kanban from stage $N - 1$), the production kanban is removed from the container and is returned to the production-ordering kanban post at the same stage (N). The withdrawal kanban from stage $N - 1$ replaces the production kanban on the container, and it accompanies the container to stage $N - 1$.

For production activity to take place at stage N, both a production kanban and a container of the required parts accompanied by a withdrawal kanban must be present at that stage. The production kanban subsequently replaces the withdrawal kanban, and the withdrawal kanban is sent back to stage $N + 1$, where it authorizes stage $N + 1$ (the preceding stage) to produce another container, now required at stage N. This creates a continuous cycle of container movement among the stages.

In effect, the kanbans pull containers through the system, *just in time* to meet demand at each production stage, thus minimizing in-process inventories. In this process, two kanban swaps are made. One is made immediately prior to the production activity, and one is made immediately following the production activity at each stage. The production kanban never leaves its home stage, but the withdrawal kanban moves between stages. In other words, the production kanban acts as an intraprocess control apparatus, and the withdrawal kanban serves as the interprocess control apparatus.

Although the just-in-time technique with its use of kanbans has proved to be extremely successful in Japan, it is not certain that similar successes could be obtained if it were applied to U.S. production systems. The primary reasons for this uncertainty relate to behavioral, philosophical, and cultural aspects of the Japanese labor force and management.

The worker in Japan is highly trained and has a strong, positive philosophical view of the job. This tends to result in very little variability in job processing times. In fact, processing times often come close to being constant. In addition, the Japanese worker

---

[2] Figure 7.12 and the ensuing description are from P. Y. Huang, L. P. Rees, and B. W. Taylor, III, "A Simulation Analysis of the Japanese Just-In-Time Technique (with Kanbans) for a Multiline, Multistage Production System," *Decision Sciences* 14, no. 3 (July 1983): 326–344.

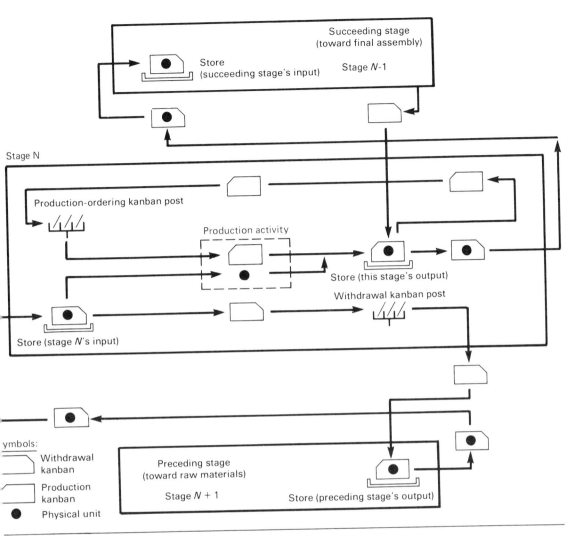

Figure 7.12 The Kanban System

does not tend to "call it a day" until the job is finished. The Japanese worker will frequently work past normal quitting time, if necessary, to meet that day's demand.

In Japan the scheduling system is rigorous to the point of being frozen. Japanese management, in general, is unlikely to change a production schedule over the short term (i.e., one to three months) for a preferred customer or a rush order, as a U.S. company might do. This acts to reduce further the variability in work load at work stations. Also, in Japan most companies operate with similar scheduling systems and similar philosophies regarding scheduling. Thus, Japanese companies are able to operate with the knowledge that their suppliers complement their own scheduling systems and will meet their scheduling needs. For example, there is extremely close coordination between Japanese auto assembly plants and parts suppliers. To meet the parts demand of the assembly operation, the supplier might make multiple deliveries in a day, an occurrence very unlikely among U.S. suppliers, who usually deliver once during a lengthy period of time.

Although a few U.S. companies have adopted the kanban system, almost all are still operating in an environment where suppliers and customers use their old systems.

SUMMARY

In this chapter, one of the more popular and traditional areas of management science, inventory modeling, was presented. Inventory modeling is one of the oldest examples of the application of mathematical modeling to a business function. As inventory is a concern of almost every type of organization, it provides an area of application and study for the student of management science that he or she is usually familiar with at least in general terms. Thus, it is an excellent vehicle for demonstrating basic concepts of model building that can be applied to other management science model forms. In addition, inventory is a potentially lucrative area for management science application, since it often represents a substantial portion of the total costs of a firm. In numerous instances, substantial reductions in total costs have been realized by developing more efficient inventory policies. Because of the pervasive nature of inventory in organizations, many of the models and techniques presented in other chapters in this text, such as simulation, mathematical programming, and dynamic programming, are often applied to the problems of inventory.

REFERENCES

BROWN, R. G. *Decision Rules for Inventory Management.* New York: Holt, Rinehart and Winston, 1967.

BUCHAN, J., and KOENIGSBERG, E. *Scientific Inventory Management.* Englewood Cliffs, New Jersey: Prentice-Hall, 1963.

BUFFA, E. S., and MILLER, JEFFREY. *Production-Inventory Systems: Planning and Control.* Rev. ed. Homewood, Illinois: Richard D. Irwin, 1979.

CHURCHMAN, C. W.; ACKOFF, R. L.; and ARNOFF, E. L. *Introduction to Operations Research.* New York: John Wiley & Sons, 1957.

FETTER, R. B., and DALLECK, W. C. *Decision Models for Inventory Management.* Homewood, Illinois: Richard D. Irwin, 1961.

HADLEY, G., and WHITIN, T. M. *Analysis of Inventory Systems.* Englewood Cliffs, New Jersey: Prentice-Hall, 1963.

MAGEE, J. F., and BOODMAN, D. M. *Production Planning and Inventory Control.* 2d ed. New York: McGraw-Hill, 1967.

MONDEN, Y. *Toyota Production System.* Nor-cross, Georgia: Industrial Engineering and Management Press, 1983.

ORLICKY, J. A. *Material Requirements Planning.* New York: McGraw-Hill Book Company, 1975.

STARR, M. K., and MILLER, D. W. *Inventory Control: Theory and Practice.* Englewood Cliffs, New Jersey: Prentice-Hall, 1962.

TERSINE, R. J. *Material Management and Inventory Systems.* New York: Elsevier North-Holland, 1979.

————. *Principles of Inventory and Materials Management.* 2d ed. New York: Elsevier North-Holland, 1982.

————. *Production/Operations Management: Concepts, Structure and Analysis.* 2d ed. New York: Elsevier North-Holland, 1984.

WAGNER, H. M. *Statistical Management of Inventory Systems.* New York: John Wiley & Sons, 1962.

WHITIN, T. M. *The Theory of Inventory Management.* Princeton, New Jersey: Princeton University Press, 1957.

PROBLEMS

1. Assume an inventory problem with the following conditions: inventory usage rate is constant over time and known with certainty; entire order is received at one point in time; inventory is replenished when it is exactly at zero (no excess stock carried and no shortages); and the order is received instantaneously (zero lead time to receive an order). Parameter values are

   Ordering cost = $70 per order
   Carrying cost = $3 per unit per year
   Demand = 5000 units per year

   Determine the following:

   a. Optimal order quantity per order
   b. Minimum total annual inventory costs
   c. The optimum number of orders per year
   d. The optimum time between orders (assuming a 365-day year)
   e. Illustrate the inventory model for this problem graphically. Show the answers to parts a and b on the graph.

2. An electronics store stocks and sells a particular brand of personal computer. It costs the firm $450 each time it places an order with the manufacturer for personal computers. The cost of carrying one personal computer in inventory for a year is $170. The store manager estimates that total annual demand for the personal computers will be 1,200 units, with a constant demand rate throughout the year. Orders are received within minutes after placement from a local warehouse maintained by the manufacturer. The store policy is to never have stockouts of the personal computers. The store is open for business every day of the year except Christmas Day. Determine the following:

   a. Optimal order quantity per order
   b. Minimum total annual inventory costs
   c. The optimum number of orders per year
   d. The optimum time between orders (in working days)
   e. Illustrate the inventory model for this problem graphically. Show the answers to parts a and b on the graph.

3. A firm is faced with the attractive situation in which it can obtain immediate delivery of an item it stocks for retail sale. The firm has, therefore, not bothered to order the item in any systematic way. However, recently profits have been squeezed due to increasing competitive pressures, and the firm has retained a management consultant to study its inventory management. The consultant has determined that the various costs associated with making an order for the item stocked are approximately $30 per order. She has also determined that the costs of carrying the item in inventory amount to approximately $20 per unit per year (primarily direct storage costs and foregone profit on investment in inventory). Demand for the item is reasonably constant over time and the forecast is for 19,200 units per year. When an order is placed

for the item, the entire order is immediately delivered to the firm by the supplier. The firm operates 6 days a week plus a few Sundays, or approximately 320 days per year. Determine the following:

a. Optimal order quantity per order
b. Total annual inventory ordering costs, carrying costs, and total costs associated with the optimal order size policy
c. Optimal number of orders to place per year
d. Number of operating days between orders, based on the optimal ordering policy
e. Illustrate the inventory level over time for this problem. Show the answers to parts a and d on the graph.

4. Refer to problem 3. Assume that the consultant hired by the firm in problem 3 wishes to illustrate to the firm's management the nature of the cost trade-off analysis employed to determine the inventory ordering policy. Illustrate the inventory model graphically by including along the horizontal axis order quantities of 50, 100, 150, 200, 250, 300, 350, and 400. Plot the associated ordering costs, carrying costs, and total costs (costs along the vertical axis). Show graphically that the optimal order quantity and the minimum total inventory cost are the values computed in problem 3.

5. A company dealing in a highly toxic chemical product must have the product delivered by special cargo trucks designed for safe shipment of chemicals. As such, ordering (and delivery) costs are relatively high at $1200 per order. The chemical product is produced in 1-gallon plastic containers. The cost of holding the chemical in storage is $50 per gallon per year. The annual demand for the chemical, which is constant over time, is 2000 gallons per year. The lead time from time of order placement until receipt is 10 days. The company operates 310 working days per year. Compute the following:

a. The optimal order quantity per order
b. The reorder point
c. The time between orders (in working days)
d. Illustrate the inventory level over time for this problem. Show the answers to parts a, b, and c on the graph.

6. Refer to problem 2. Assume now that orders are not received instantaneously but rather are received 20 working days after order placement. Determine the following:

a. The reorder point
b. The optimal number of orders per year
c. Describe the dependent relationship, if any, that exists between parts a and b.
d. How many working days after receipt of an order will the next order be placed?
e. Suppose the lead time to receive an order is 29 working days. What is the reorder point for this case?

7. Refer to problem 3. Assume that rather than receiving immediate delivery of an order, the firm must wait 2 working days for the order to arrive.

a. At what inventory level (reorder point) should the firm reorder?
b. Since the firm has to wait 2 working days for the order to arrive, should it recalculate the optimal order quantity? If so, what should that quantity be?

c. Illustrate the inventory level over time and show on the graph the point in time and the inventory level point at which an order would be placed.

8. Refer to problems 3 and 7. Suppose the lead time to receive an order is 12 working days.

   a. How many orders will the firm have outstanding at any given point in time?
   b. Shouldn't the firm simply lump these outstanding orders together and receive them all at once? Why or why not? Explain your answer.

9. Refer to problem 3. Complete a table showing the following: the order quantity, the number of orders per year, the annual ordering costs, the annual carrying costs, and the total inventory costs for the following two cases: (1) ordering every 12 days, and (2) ordering at the interval determined in the solution to problem 3. Which is the better alternative? Why is one alternative better than the other? Explain in terms of ordering costs and carrying costs.

10. The purchasing manager for a large steel firm must determine the ordering policy for coal to operate 12 converters. Each converter requires exactly 5 tons of coal per day to operate, and the firm operates 360 days per year. The purchasing manager has determined that the ordering cost is $80 per order, and the holding cost is 20% of the average value of coal on hand. The purchasing manager has negotiated a contract to obtain the coal for $12 per ton for the coming year. The lead time to receive an order of coal is 5 days.

   a. Determine the optimal quantity of coal to receive in each order.
   b. Determine the total inventory related costs associated with the optimal ordering policy. (Do not include the cost of the coal.)
   c. Determine the optimal number of coal orders for the coming year.
   d. Determine the optimal time between orders for the coming year.
   e. How much coal should be on hand when an order is placed?

11. A local independent gas station dealer owns five retail outlets that pump (sell) a total of 250,000 gallons per month. The owner buys her gasoline from a major oil company, adds various additives, and resells it at her gas stations. All gasoline purchased from the major oil company is delivered to a single bulk tank storage facility, from which the independent dealer then distributes gasoline to her five stations with a small tank truck. The major oil company charges the independent dealer $150 for each delivery of gasoline to the bulk tank, plus $.85 per gallon for the gasoline. The dealer has estimated her cost of holding gasoline in storage to be $.36 per gallon on an annual basis.

   a. Determine the optimum quantity of gasoline the dealer should order each time she orders.
   b. Determine the optimum number of orders per year the dealer should place for gasoline.
   c. Determine the time between orders, in days, for the optimum order policy, assuming a 365-day year.
   d. Assuming the lead time to receive an order is 3 days, what should the reorder level be?

    e. Assuming the lead time to receive an order is 7 days, what should the reorder level be?

    f. Determine the total cost associated with the optimal ordering decision: (1) excluding the cost of the gasoline, (2) including the cost of the gasoline.

12. Refer to problem 2. The electronics store in problem 2 assumed with certainty that the ordering cost is $450 per order and the inventory carrying cost is $170 per unit per year. However, the inventory model parameters are frequently only estimates that are subject to some degree of uncertainty. Consider four cases of variation in the model parameters as follows: (1) both ordering cost and carrying cost are 10% less than originally estimated, (2) both ordering cost and carrying cost are 10% higher than originally estimated, (3) ordering cost is 10% higher and carrying cost is 10% lower than originally estimated, and (4) ordering cost is 10% lower and carrying cost is 10% higher than originally estimated. Determine the optimal order quantity and associated total inventory cost for each of the four cases, and also compute the total cost for each of the four cases using the order quantity obtained in the problem 2 solution. Prepare a table with column headings for C_o, C_c, Q_{opt}, TC_{opt}, the problem 2 solution value for Q, and TC using the problem 2 solution value for Q, and the percentage difference in TC for the two TC values for each case (1, 2, 3, and 4) described above. Describe the sensitivity of the model solution to changes in parameter values.

13. An office supply company operates by stocking a large volume of items in its warehouses and then supplying customer orders. It maintains its inventory levels by borrowing cash from a local bank. The company estimates that its demand for borrowed cash is $17,000 per day and there are 305 working days per year. Any money borrowed during the fiscal year must be repaid with interest by the end of the current year. The annual interest rate charged by the bank is currently 9%. Any time a loan is obtained from the bank it charges the company a loan-origination fee of $1,200 plus 2¼ points (i.e., 2.25% of the amount borrowed). Determine the optimal amount of a loan for the company, the total annual cost of the company's borrowing policy, and the number of loans the company will obtain during the year. Also, determine the level of cash on hand at which the company should apply for a new loan given that it takes 15 days for a loan to be processed by the bank.

14. Assume an inventory problem with the following conditions: inventory usage rate is constant over time and known with certainty; the goods ordered are received at a constant rate over time; inventory replenishment is begun when the inventory level drops to exactly zero (no excess stock is carried and no shortages are allowed); and the order replenishment is begun immediately when ordered (zero lead time to begin receiving an order); a 365-day year. Parameter values are

    Ordering cost = $200 per order
    Carrying cost = $8 per unit per year
    Demand = 10,000 units per year
    Goods receipt rate (on an annualized basis) = 15,000 units/year

    Determine the following:

    a. Optimal order quantity per order

    b. Total annual inventory costs associated with the optimal ordering policy

c. The optimum number of orders per year

d. The quantity of goods used during each order receipt period

15. Refer to problem 14. Determine the following:

   a. The time between orders associated with the optimum ordering policy
   b. The maximum inventory level during each cycle
   c. The inventory receipt period for each order (in days)
   d. Illustrate the inventory level over time for this problem graphically. Show the answers to parts a, b, and c on the graph.

16. A local bakery produces fruit pies for freezing and subsequent sale. The bakery, which operates 5 days a week, 52 weeks a year, can produce pies at the rate of 64 pies per day. The bakery sets up the pie production operation and produces until a predetermined number (Q) have been produced. When not producing pies, the bakery uses its personnel and facilities for producing other bakery items. The setup cost for a production run of fruit pies is $500. The cost of holding frozen pies in storage is $5 per pie per year. The annual demand for frozen fruit pies, which is constant over time, is 5,000 pies. Determine the following:

   a. The optimum production run quantity (Q)
   b. The optimum number of production runs per year
   c. The optimum cycle time (time between run starts)
   d. The run length in working days
   e. The number of days per year producing fruit pies
   f. The costs associated with this analysis

17. A mail-order and general retail store in Vermont operates 365 days a year producing maple syrup to sell in its store on the premises and to ship. The cost of setting up the syrup-making equipment to produce a batch of syrup is $230. The cost of carrying a gallon of maple syrup in a temperature-controlled storeroom is $15 per gallon on an annual basis. Demand for maple syrup has been estimated to be 7500 gallons per year. The store is able to produce 9000 gallons per year. Shortages are not allowed. Determine the optimal number of gallons to produce during each production run and the total minimum annual inventory cost for maple syrup.

18. Assume that the store in problem 17 starts its new year on January 1, and that the store and the maple syrup production facilities are open 365 days per year. The store begins the new year with no inventory, and thus immediately begins a production run for maple syrup. Set up an approximate production schedule (rounding off fractional days to the nearest whole day) for the next six months, based on the optimal production order size determined in problem 17.

19. A lumber mill processes 10,000 logs annually, operating 250 days per year. Immediately upon receiving an order, the logging company supplier begins delivery to the lumber mill at the rate of 60 logs per day. The lumber mill has determined that the ordering cost per order is $62.50 and the cost of carrying logs in inventory, awaiting processing, is $15 per log on an annual basis. Determine the following:

   a. The optimal number of log orders
   b. The total inventory cost associated with the optimal order quantity
   c. The number of lumber mill operating days between orders
   d. The number of lumber mill operating days required to receive an order

e. Illustrate the inventory level model graphically. Show the answers to parts c and d and the maximum inventory level.

20. An aluminum company has predicted the demand for aluminum rivets for the coming year to be 20,000 cases. Past data show that the average demand rate is reasonably constant. The company produces at the rate of 160 cases of rivets per day, operating 250 working days annually. The production setup cost for each production run is $144. The annual carrying cost of rivets produced for inventory is $32 per case. Determine the following:

   a. Optimal quantity to produce for each production run
   b. Length (in working days) of each production run
   c. Time (in days) between production run start-ups
   d. Total production setup and inventory carrying costs
   e. Days per year that are used for production of rivets

21. The firm in problem 3 is considering reducing its inventory level further by allowing some shortages to occur. It would back order demand not met and fill the demand when the stock was replenished. It is estimated that the cost of shortages is $30 per unit on an annual basis. All other relevant data are given in problem 3. Determine the following:

   a. The new optimal order quantity
   b. The total inventory ordering, carrying, and shortage costs associated with the optimal order quantity
   c. The back-order quantity per order
   d. Perform a comparative analysis of the solution to problem 3 and the current solution, showing all the various costs involved.

22. The local bicycle dealer operates 7 days a week, closing only on Christmas day. The dealer pays $300 for each bicycle purchased from the manufacturer. The annual holding cost per bicycle is estimated to be 25% of the dollar value of inventory. The bicycle dealer sells an average of 25 bikes per week. Frequently, the dealer does not have a bike in stock when a customer purchases it and the bike is backordered. The dealer estimates his shortage cost per unit backordered, on an annual basis, to be $250 due to lost future sales (and profits). The ordering cost for each order is $100. Determine the following:

   a. The optimum order quantity for the bicycle dealer
   b. The optimum number of orders per year
   c. The optimum time between orders
   d. The maximum inventory level
   e. The maximum quantity backordered
   f. The maximum time a customer would have to wait for a backordered bicycle
   g. Prepare a table summarizing all costs, including ordering costs, carrying costs, shortage costs, product costs, and total cost.

23. In problem 2, an electronics store stocks and sells personal computers. The inventory order cost is $450, the carrying cost per year is $170 per unit, and the annual demand for personal computers is 1200 units. In the original problem description, the assumption was made that orders were received instantaneously, and no shortages

were allowed. However, now let us assume that shortages are allowed, and that the shortage cost is $600 per unit per year. Compute the optimal order quantity and minimum total annual inventory cost, and compare these results with those from problem 2.

24. For problem 23, determine the maximum inventory volume (V), the optimal shortage level (S), the time during which inventory is on hand (t_1), the time during which there is a shortage (t_2), and the time between order receipts (t). Illustrate these values graphically, as shown in Figure 7.6 in this chapter.

25. A firm produces its own inventory from its manufacturing facility and maintains an inventory policy that allows for shortages. Annual demand is 8000 units, and annual production is 10,000 units. The cost of ordering is $200 per order, and the cost of holding one item in storage is $5. The firm has estimated that each unit it is unable to supply and must back order costs it $15. Develop an inventory policy for the firm that contains the following:

    a. Optimal order size, Q
    b. Optimal shortage, S
    c. Total minimum cost
    d. Maximum inventory level, V
    e. t_1, t_2, t_3, t_4, and t (Explain each of these times.)
    f. Develop a graphical analysis of this policy (similar to Figure 7.8) that includes these values.

26. In problem 17, a mail-order and general retail store in Vermont produced maple syrup to sell at its store and to ship. Since the store produced its own inventory stock of syrup, a noninstantaneous receipt inventory model was required to determine the optimal production run quantity. Recall that the setup cost was $230, the annual carrying cost was $15 per gallon, annual demand was 7500 gallons, and the annual production capacity was 9000 gallons. Now assume that shortages are allowed, and that the annual shortage cost is $4 per gallon. Determine the optimal size of a production run of syrup and the minimum annual total cost.

27. For problem 26, determine the maximum inventory volume (V), the maximum shortage level (S), the time during which inventory increases (t_1), the time during which inventory is reduced (t_2), the time during which the shortage increases (t_3), the time during which the shortage is reduced (t_4), and the total order cycle time (t). Illustrate these values graphically as shown in Figure 7.8 in this chapter.

28. Solve problem 20, assuming that the aluminum company allows shortages to exist and that the shortage cost is $20 per unit. Compare the results of this model with the results for problem 20. Which policy results in the lower inventory cost?

29. A large grocery chain is faced with the following decision. The cost of ordering a particular item is $40 per order. The carrying cost is 25% of the average dollar value of inventory held on an annual basis. Yearly demand for the item is 20,000 cases at a constant rate. The grocery firm currently pays $40 per case for the item. However, it has been offered a $1-per-case discount if it orders in minimum lots of 1000 cases. Should the firm take the discount? Show a comparative analysis of all costs involved for the two alternatives.

30. Refer to problem 11. The major oil company that supplies the local independent gas dealer in problem 11 has offered to reduce the price it charges for gas by .25% if the dealer will take deliveries in quantities of 100,000 gallons. Should the dealer accept the offer? Prepare a cost analysis showing ordering costs, carrying costs, product costs, and total costs, and differences, for the two options available to the dealer. Discuss your conclusion.

31. Refer to problem 13. The local bank has offered the office supply company in problem 13 a discount where for any loan amount equal to or greater than $500,000 the bank will lower the number of points charged on the loan origination fee from 2.25% to 2%. What should the company's optimal loan amount be? Prepare a table giving a summary of all the various costs considered for each of the two alternatives.

32. The bookstore at a university purchases sweatshirts emblazoned with the school name and logo from a vendor. The vendor sells the sweatshirts to the store for $38 apiece. The cost to the bookstore for placing an order is $120 and the carrying cost is 25% of the average annual inventory value. The bookstore manager estimates that 1,700 sweatshirts will be sold during the year. The vendor has offered the bookstore the following volume discount schedule:

Order Size	Discount
$Q < 300$	0%
$300 \le Q < 500$	2%
$500 \le Q < 800$	4%
$800 \le Q$	5%

The bookstore manager wishes to determine the bookstore's optimal order quantity given the above quantity discount information. Prepare a table summarizing the values for price, order quantity, total ordering cost, total inventory carrying cost, total cost of goods purchased, and the total cost for each of the four alternatives available.

33. A manufacturing firm produces large electric magnets in two plants, one in Chicago and one in St. Louis. The firm has contracted with the federal government to produce and deliver the electric magnets to the Houston Space Center according to the following delivery schedule.

Month	No. of Electric Magnets
1	14
2	23
3	19
4	30

The firm is capable of producing a maximum of 13 magnets per month at the Chicago plant and 10 magnets per month at the St. Louis plant. The projected costs per unit of producing the magnets over the 4-month time horizon (including the effects of inflation), by plant, are as follows:

Month	Chicago Plant	St. Louis Plant
1	$14,000	$16,000
2	14,100	16,100
3	14,200	16,200
4	14,300	16,300

The firm can produce excess magnets in any given month and hold them in inventory for delivery according to the contracted delivery schedule. The estimated cost per unit of holding inventory at the end of a specified month is given below, by month and by plant.

End of Month	Chicago Plant	St. Louis Plant
1	$1000	$500
2	1100	600
3	1200	700
4	N/A*	N/A*

*There is no inventory holding cost given for month 4, since no inventory would be held at the end of month 4.

The contract requires that the firm deliver the magnets from its plants in Chicago and St. Louis to the Houston Space Center. The costs of shipping the magnets from each of the plants to Houston are given below (including estimated inflation):

Month	Chicago Plant	St. Louis Plant
1	$3000	$2000
2	3100	2100
3	3200	2200
4	3300	2300

Formulate the preceding production, inventory, and shipping problem as a transportation model in transportation tableau format.

34. The owner of a fresh fruit and vegetable stand in a farmers' market in the city purchases fresh cantaloupes each day from local farmers. The stand owner pays farmers $.50 each for the cantaloupes and prices them at $1 each. Any cantaloupes remaining unsold at the end of a day are given to the local mission for the poor. The daily

demand (to the nearest 10) for cantaloupes varies according to the following distribution.

Daily Demand for Cantaloupes	Probability
80	.10
90	.25
100	.40
110	.20
120	.05

Determine the optimum number of cantaloupes for the stand owner to stock. Use the maximum expected profit as the basis for reaching a decision.

35. Referring to problem 34, assume that the probability distribution for demand is instead the following:

Daily Demand for Cantaloupes	Probability
80	.10
90	.15
100	.20
110	.30
120	.25

Determine the optimum number of cantaloupes for the stand owner to stock. Use the maximum expected profit as the basis for reaching a decision.

36. A firm has developed a probability distribution of demand during lead time as follows:

Demand During Lead Time	Probability
500	.10
600	.20
700	.40
800	.20
900	.10
	1.00

Inventory carrying costs equal $.75 per unit per year, the cost per order is $150, the shortage cost has been estimated as $2 per unit, and the optimal number of orders per year is 10.

Determine the appropriate safety-stock level that will minimize safety-stock carrying and shortage costs.

37. The production foreman for a large mill has been having a problem with stockouts. On the other hand, he is under pressure from top management to keep the level of inventory down. He faces the difficult problem of fluctuating demand for the product in inventory. The foreman knows that he must keep some safety stock on hand to guard against higher than average demands, but he is unable to determine the optimal level to hold. Assume that you have been employed as a consultant to analyze the problem. The firm has contracted for 20 orders of 300 units per order. The inventory carrying cost is $5 per unit per year, and the estimated shortage cost is $4 per unit shortage. Past records show that the relative frequencies of various demand levels during the lead time to receive an order are as follows:

Demand During Lead Time (units)	Relative Frequency
240	0.05
260	0.10
280	0.20
300	0.30
320	0.20
340	0.10
360	0.05

Determine the following for the production foreman:

a. The optimal reorder level
b. The optimal safety stock to hold
c. The total safety-stock inventory carrying and shortage cost associated with the optimal reorder policy
d. The inventory carrying cost for the safety stock alone

Illustrate the decision model for this problem graphically.

38. Assume that the classic EOQ model was used to determine the order sizes in problem 37. What was the assumed ordering cost per order?

39. A lawn products store has determined the following regarding its demand for fertilizer:

$$\text{Average daily product demand} = 120 \text{ lb (normally distributed)}$$
$$\text{Standard deviation} = 30 \text{ lb}$$
$$\text{Lead time} = 10 \text{ days}$$
$$C_o = \$300 \text{ per order}$$
$$C_c = \$.08 \text{ per lb}$$

a. Compute the optimal order quantity.
b. Determine the safety stock and reorder point that will maintain a 95% service level.

40. A company desires to establish an inventory policy that will maintain a 90% service level. The daily demand for the company's product is normally distributed with a mean of 120 units and a standard deviation of 20 units. Lead time is constant and equals 7 days. Ordering costs equal $60, and carrying costs equal $.40 per unit.

   a. Determine the average demand during lead time and the standard deviation.
   b. Compute the optimal order quantity.
   c. Determine the reorder point that will reflect the desired service level.

41. A firm has established an inventory reorder point of 520 units under conditions of uncertain demand. Average demand during lead time is 400 units with a standard deviation of 80 and a safety stock of 120 units. What service level will be maintained by this reorder point?

42. In Example 7.7 in this chapter, a simulation model was illustrated in tabular form to show how an optimal inventory policy is developed given uncertain estimates of demand and lead time. In Table 7.2 a simulation experiment was conducted in which Q was 20 units and the reorder point, r, was 6 units. Repeat the simulation experiment in Table 7.2, but with $Q = 15$ units and $r = 4$ units. Use the same stream (i.e., column) of random numbers from Table C.5 in Appendix C that was used in Table 7.2.

Solve the following problems using a computer package such as AB:QM or STORM.

43. Solve problem 1	53. Solve problem 17
44. Solve problem 2	54. Solve problem 19
45. Solve problem 3	55. Solve problem 20
46. Solve problem 5	56. Solve problem 21
47. Solve problem 7	57. Solve problem 22
48. Solve problem 10	58. Solve problem 23
49. Solve problem 11	59. Solve problem 25
50. Solve problem 13	60. Solve problem 26
51. Solve problem 14	61. Solve problem 28
52. Solve problem 16	62. Solve problem 29

8

Decision Theory and Games

The environment within which decisions are made is often categorized into four states: **certainty, risk, uncertainty,** and **conflict.** Decision theory is primarily concerned with decision making under the conditions of risk and uncertainty. The theory of games is concerned with decision making under conflict. Both decision theory and game theory assist the decision maker in analyzing problems with numerous alternative courses of action and consequences. A basic objective of decision and game theories is to provide a structure wherein information concerning the relative likelihood of different occurrences may be evaluated to enable the decision maker to identify the best course of action.

A state of *certainty* exists when all the information required to make a decision is known and available—**perfect information**. In many of the previous chapters in this text, models were formulated and solved under conditions of assumed certainty. For example, in the analysis of linear programming problems in Chapter 2, the exact amount of resources required to produce a product, the available resources, and the unit profit were all assumed to be known with certainty. A similar condition of certainty was assumed in the presentation of transportation, assignment, and most of the network and inventory models. Assuming certainty for a problem where information is not known with certainty often provides a reasonable approximation of the optimal solution.

The condition of *risk* exists when perfect information is not available, but the probabilities that certain outcomes will occur can be estimated. Thus, for decision problems under risk, probability theory is an important component. Various stochastic methods such as chance-constrained programming, queuing theory, Markov analysis, simulation, and probabilistic inventory control have been developed for decision analysis under risk.

A state of *uncertainty* refers to a condition in which the probabilities of occurrences in a decision situation are not known. Under risk, the outcomes of a decision situation are defined by a probability distribution, whereas under uncertainty, no probability function can be determined. Therefore, *certainty* and *uncertainty* are the two extremes of a continuum representing available information, and *risk* is a point in between.

The fourth decision state, *conflict,* exists when the interests of two or more decision makers are in competition. In other words, if decision maker A benefits from a selected course of action, it is only because decision maker B has also taken a certain course of action. Hence, decision makers are interested not only in their own courses of action but also in the actions of others in the decision situation.

DECISION MAKING UNDER RISK

For decision making under risk, the various *courses of action* that are available and feasible must be identified first. Next, the *possible events* and their *associated probabilities* of occurrence must be estimated. (Events are also referred to as *states of nature*.) Thirdly, the *conditional payoff* for a given course of action under a given event is determined. It is not always a simple matter to identify the exact monetary payoffs for the action-event combinations. However, accumulated experiences and/or past records often provide relatively accurate estimated payoffs for many decisions. To demonstrate these steps in decision making under risk, several examples will be considered.

Example 8.1 Concession Problem

A concessions firm handles all the concessions for a professional football team. The manager of the firm is attempting to ascertain whether to stock the concession stands with cola or coffee. A local agreement among beverage dealers prohibits any one concessionaire from selling more than one beverage at a game. The payoff is primarily dependent on the weather conditions. If the weather is cold, selling coffee results in a greater payoff. On the other hand, if the weather is relatively warm, cola brings in a greater payoff. The courses of action, states of nature (events), probabilities of occurrence of the alternative states of nature, and payoffs associated with the different combinations of actions and states of nature are given in the following table:

Alternatives	States of Nature	
	$p_1 = .3$	$p_2 = .7$
Action (a_i)	Cold Weather	Warm Weather
Sell cola (a_1)	$1500	$5000
Sell coffee (a_2)	$4000	$1000

The conditions necessary for a decision problem under risk exist in this example. First, alternative courses of action are available and a choice must be made between them. Second, although occurrences of the states of nature (events) are not known with certainty, the probabilities of the occurrences can be determined from historical experience.

The most widely used criterion for decision making under risk is the **expected value,** which is discussed in detail in Appendix C. The expected value for a given course of action is simply the weighted average payoff, which is the sum of the payoffs for each action multiplied by the probabilities associated with each state of nature. For this example, the expected value for a_1, denoted by $E(a_1)$, is

$$E(a_1) = 1500(.3) + 5000(.7) = \$3950$$

The expected value for a_2 is

$$E(a_2) = 4000(.3) + 1000(.7) = \$1900$$

Comparing the expected values associated with each course of action indicates that a_1 (selling cola) is the logical alternative, since it has the higher expected payoff—$3950 compared to an expected payoff of $1900 for a_2 (selling coffee).

Now consider the condition in which the probability distribution of events is not known. In the previous example, this would mean that the probabilities for cold and warm weather were not available. Given this situation, the decision maker might desire to know the probability that would equalize the effects of the two courses of action. In order for the decision maker to be indifferent toward the two courses of action, the expected values must be identical. Since p_1 is defined as the probability of cold weather, p_2, the probability of warm weather, is defined as $1 - p_1$.

The expected values of a_1 and a_2 are now

$$E(a_1) = 1500p_1 + 5000(1 - p_1)$$
$$E(a_2) = 4000p_1 + 1000(1 - p_1)$$

Since indifference requires that the expected values be equal,

$$E(a_1) = E(a_2)$$
$$1500p_1 + 5000(1 - p_1) = 4000p_1 + 1000(1 - p_1)$$

Solving this equation, we find that $p_1 = .615$. If the probability of cold weather is .615 (and, thus, the probability of warm weather is .385), the decision maker will be indifferent about selling cola or coffee. However, if the probability of cold weather is greater than .615, the concessionaire should sell coffee since the expected value of selling coffee would be greater.

Although the expected value is employed as the decision criterion in this problem, this does not mean that a payoff of exactly \$3950 will result if a_1 is chosen. On the contrary, the eventual payoff of an action is rarely equal to the expected value. For example, if cola is sold and the weather is warm, \$5000 will be made. The expected value is used in problems involving risk because it maximizes the payoff over a given period of time. If the decision problem is repetitive, this same situation will occur a large number of times. Because the expected value is the same as the average payoff when the decision problem is repeated a number of times, it is a valid criterion for decision making.

When a decision problem under conditions of risk is not repetitive, the expected value may be inappropriate as a decision criterion. In real-world situations, a decision maker may avoid a course of action that has a very large conditional loss, or negative payoff, even when its expected value is greater than those of the alternative courses of action. This type of situation is considered in the following example.

Example 8.2 Investment Problem

A firm is contemplating two investment alternatives, A and B, involving two different financial conditions. Each condition has an equal probability of occurrence (i.e., $p_1 = .5$, $p_2 = .5$). The payoff matrix for this problem is shown in the following table:

Alternatives	States of Nature	
	$p_1 = .5$ Condition 1	$p_2 = .5$ Condition 2
Investment		
A	−\$1,000,000	\$1,060,000
B	\$ 20,000	\$ 30,000

The expected values for the two plans are

$$E(A) = -1,000,000(.5) + 1,060,000(.5) = \$30,000$$
$$E(B) = 20,000(.5) + 30,000(.5) = \$25,000$$

Although the expected value of plan A is \$5000 greater than that of plan B, the decision maker is unlikely to choose A over B. In this case, the decision maker might put a higher priority on avoiding the potential loss associated with condition 1 and investment A than on the long-run average payoff. If, however, the firm involved has sufficient liquid assets to absorb a large negative payoff, the expected value may well be justified as the decision criterion. (This concept of risk avoidance will be discussed in greater detail in the section on utility, page 392.)

Computerized Expected Value Analysis

General management science software packages for the personal computer have varying degrees of capability to solve decision theory problems. However, nearly all such software packages have program components for determining expected value. In this section we will employ the AB:QM software package to solve Example 8.1. Following are the program input data, a summary of the data entries, and the problem solution.

```
Program: Decision Theory / Decision Making Under Risk

Problem Title : Example 8.1

***** Input Data *****

Type of Problem   : Profit  Problem

-----------------------------------------------
                        Event  1    Event  2
-----------------------------------------------
Probability             0.300       0.700
-----------------------------------------------
Alternative  1         1500.000    5000.000
Alternative  2         4000.000    1000.000
-----------------------------------------------

***** Program Output *****

Expected Profit Table
-----------------------------------------------
Alternative             Expected Profit
-----------------------------------------------
    1                      3950.000 <=
    2                      1900.000
-----------------------------------------------

  <=  indicate(s) the best alternative(s)

***** End of Output *****
```

Expected Opportunity Loss

An alternative criterion for evaluating decisions under risk is known as the **expected opportunity loss (EOL)**. The fundamental principle behind EOL is the minimization of *expected regret* experienced because of the selection of a particular decision alternative. The concept of expected opportunity loss is demonstrated in the following example.

Consider a firm that has three investment alternatives, A, B, C, and two states of nature reflecting varying market conditions. The basic components of this decision are given in the following table:

Alternatives	States of Nature	
	$p_1 = .4$	$p_2 = .6$
Investment	Market Condition 1	Market Condition 2
A	$ 50,000	−$10,000
B	$ 15,000	$60,000
C	$100,000	$10,000

The opportunity losses (or regrets) are computed for each state of nature by first identifying the best course of action for each state of nature. For market condition 1, investment C is the best decision. The opportunity loss realized by selecting either investment A or B is computed by subtracting its payoff from the investment C payoff. Thus, the regret (opportunity loss) for investment A is $100,000 − 50,000 = \$50,000$, and for investment B, $100,000 − 15,000 = \$85,000$. The regret for each alternative action if market condition 2 is said to be known with certainty can be computed in the same manner as for market condition 1. In this case, investment B is the best alternative. The opportunity losses for all investment alternatives, given the states of nature, are summarized in the following table:

Alternatives	States of Nature	
	$p_1 = .4$	$p_2 = .6$
Investment	Market Condition 1	Market Condition 2
A	$50,000	$70,000
B	$85,000	0
C	0	$50,000

The expected opportunity loss, which includes the probability of each market condition, is computed by determining the expected value for each action. Thus,

$EOL_A = .4(50,000) + .6(70,000) = \$62,000$
$EOL_B = .4(85,000) + .6(0) = \$34,000$
$EOL_C = .4(0) + .6(50,000) = \$30,000$ least amt of loss

It can be seen that the best alternative is investment C, because it *minimizes* the expected regret, or opportunity loss, that can be suffered by the decision maker. Although

EOL is an alternative decision criterion for decision making under conditions of risk, th results will always be the same as those obtained by the expected value criterion previ ously presented. Thus, only one of the two methods need be applied to reach a decision

Expected Value of Perfect Information

An extension of the criteria of expected value and expected opportunity loss is th expected value of perfect information. When making a decision under condition of risk, we have less information available than under conditions of certainty. Within the context of decision theory, this situation is interpreted as having stated outcomes with associated probabilities (i.e., risk) rather than knowing with certainty which outcome wil occur. Information that, if it could be acquired, would change the decision condition from risk to certainty is said to be perfect information. Again, consider the investment example used in the previous EOL analysis.

The expected values for each investment alternative are computed as

$$E(A) = .4(50,000) + .6(-10,000) = \$14,000$$
$$E(B) = .4(15,000) + .6(60,000) = \$42,000$$
$$E(C) = .4(100,000) + .6(10,000) = \$46,000$$

These amounts represent the payoffs that could be expected by the investor given imperfect (partial) information. The best decision is investment C, based on its higher expected value of $46,000. If conditions of certainty existed, the decision maker would know in advance which event would occur (either market condition 1 or 2) and what action should be taken. If market condition 1 existed with certainty, then investment C should be made, with a return of $100,000. If condition 2 existed, then investment B should be selected, with a $60,000 return. Since the first condition occurs 40% of the time and the second occurs 60% of the time, the expected value under conditions of certainty would be

$$EV = .4(100,000) + .6(60,000) = \$76,000$$

Comparing the expected investment return with perfect information ($76,000) to the expected return without it ($46,000) yields the expected value of perfect information.

$$EVPI = 76,000 - 46,000 = \$30,000$$

The EVPI, $30,000, is the maximum amount the decision maker might pay (possibly to an investment counseling service or a research firm) to obtain perfect information. Perfect information, in this case, translates into knowing with certainty what state of nature will occur in the future. It should be noted that the EVPI is equal to the EOL of the best alternative, C. This is always the case, since the EOL is a measure of the difference between the expected values of decisions under conditions of risk and certainty.

Bayesian Analysis

If perfect information about which states of nature will occur in the future could be obtained, the decision maker could obviously make better decisions. However perfect information about the future is rare, although it is occasionally possible to gather some additional, imperfect information about the future that might improve decisions. In this section a process for using additional information by applying a probabilistic technique called **Bayesian analysis** will be demonstrated.

Bayesian analysis is a technique named after Thomas Bayes, an eighteenth-century clergyman who pioneered this area of analysis. The basic principle of Bayesian analysis is that additional information (if available) can sometimes enable one to alter or improve the marginal probabilities of the occurrence of an event. The altered probabilities are referred to as **revised, or posterior, probabilities**. Once the initial marginal and conditional probabilities are known, the posterior probability can be computed using Bayes's rule.

In general, Bayes's rule, or law, is formulated as

$$P(A_i \mid O) = \frac{P(O \mid A_i)P(A_i)}{\sum_{i=1}^{n} P(O \mid A_i)P(A_i)}$$

where

$$A_i = \text{a set of } n \text{ mutually exclusive and exhaustive events}$$
$$O = \text{an outcome of an experiment}$$
$$P(A_i) = \text{the marginal (or prior) probability for event } i$$
$$P(O \mid A_i) = \text{the conditional probability of outcome, } O, \text{ given the occurrence of } A_i$$
$$P(O) = \sum_{i=1}^{n} P(O \mid A_i)P(A_i)$$

For example, consider two events, A and B, and a third event C, that is conditionally dependent on A and B. Given the marginal probabilities of A and B, $P(A)$ and $P(B)$, and the conditional probabilities of C given A and B, $P(C \mid A)$ and $P(C \mid B)$, Bayes's law can be applied to determine the revised probability of A given event C, as follows:

$$P(A \mid C) = \frac{P(C \mid A)P(A)}{P(C \mid A)P(A) + P(C \mid B)P(B)}$$

Notice that the denominator in this relationship also equals $P(C)$.

Consider the investment example used in the previous section for the expected value of perfect information. Recall that using expected value, the best decision was determined to be investment C with an expected payoff of $46,000. The expected value of perfect information was computed to be $30,000. Therefore, the firm would likely be willing to pay up to $30,000 for information about the future states of nature, depending on how close to perfection the information was.

Suppose that the firm decided to hire a professional economic analyst to provide additional information about future economic conditions. The analyst constantly researches the state of the economy and economic trends, and the results of this research are what the firm will be purchasing.

The economic analyst will provide the firm with a report predicting which market condition, 1 or 2, will prevail. These report outcomes will be defined as I for market condition 1 and II for market condition 2. Based on the analyst's records in forecasting future economic conditions, the firm has determined conditional probabilities of the different report outcomes given the occurrence of each state of nature. The conditional probabilities of each report outcome, I and II, given the occurrence of each state of nature, 1 and 2, are

$$P(I \mid 1) = .80$$
$$P(II \mid 1) = .20$$
$$P(I \mid 2) = .10$$
$$P(II \mid 2) = .90$$

For example, if market condition 1 prevails in the future, the probability that the analys issued a report I predicting market condition 1 is .80. The other three conditional prob abilities can be interpreted similarly. Notice that these probabilities reflect the firm' belief that the analyst is a relatively accurate forecaster of future marketing conditions.

The firm not only has the conditional probabilities for the report, but also the mar ginal (or prior) probabilities that market conditions 1 or 2 will occur in the future

$$P(1) = .40$$
$$P(2) = .60$$

Using Bayes's law these prior probabilities can be revised to form posterior proba bilities. If the conditional probability that a report predicting market conditions 1 was presented given that those conditions actually prevail, $P(I \mid 1)$, the posterior probability of market conditions 1 occurring given a report indicating such is

$$P(1 \mid I) = \frac{P(I \mid 1)P(1)}{P(I \mid 1)\,P(1) + P(I \mid 2)P(2)}$$
$$= \frac{(.80)(.40)}{(.80)(.40) + (.10)(.60)}$$
$$= .842$$

The probability that market conditions 1 will occur in the future was originally deter mined by the firm to be .40. However, by obtaining the additional information in the analyst's report, the firm can revise this probability to be .842 that market conditions 1 will occur. The remaining posterior probabilities are

$$P(1 \mid II) = .129$$
$$P(2 \mid I) = .158$$
$$P(2 \mid II) = .871$$

The AB:QM software package can also provide Bayesian analysis. The program input and solution output for the investment example are as follows:

```
Program: Decision Theory / Bayes' Decision Rule

Problem Title : Investment Example

***** Input Data *****

---------------------------------------------
   Alternative          Prior Probability
---------------------------------------------
       1                    0.400
       2                    0.600
---------------------------------------------
```

```
-----------------------------------------
                    Conditional Probability
-----------------------------------------
Alternative         Event 1      Event 2
-----------------------------------------
     1               0.800        0.200
     2               0.100        0.900
-----------------------------------------


***** Program Output *****

Bayes' Decision Rule
-----------------------------------------
                    Posterior Probability
-----------------------------------------
Alternative         Event 1      Event 2
-----------------------------------------
     1               0.842        0.129
     2               0.158        0.871
-----------------------------------------


***** End of Output *****
```

Utility

Decision makers do not always select alternatives that maximize expected value (i.e., dollars) in a decision situation. This occurs for several reasons. First, people are not always willing to accept potential losses in the present in order to realize potential gains in the long run. These people can be described as *risk avoiders*. On the other hand, there are *risk takers* who are willing to gamble greater amounts of money than the current expected return would warrant. The following brief examples demonstrate the human tendency of risk aversion.

Consider a decision situation with two alternatives: (1) Flip a coin—if it comes up heads you receive $100,000, but if it comes up tails you receive nothing; or (2) receive a gift of $20,000 with certainty. The expected value of the first alternative is $50,000; thus the first alternative would be selected over the second alternative under the previously discussed decision criterion. However, rarely would a decision maker choose the first alternative over the second. In other words, the risk of receiving nothing (versus the certainty of receiving $20,000) offsets the potential large gain of $100,000 with a probability of .5. Most decision makers would opt for the security of the second alternative rather than gamble on the risk inherent in the first alternative.

A second example concerns the common practice of purchasing insurance. Almost everyone buys insurance coverage for his or her home, car, and/or life. The fact is the expected value of a return is negative, since insurance companies set rates that ensure them a profit. People buy insurance to avoid the possibility of a large potential loss.

Both of these examples indicate that people often make decisions that result in less expected payoff with less risk rather than decisions that result in greater payoff with increased risk. Every individual's attitude toward risk is heavily influenced by the magnitude of the potential payoffs (or losses) relative to personal wealth.

An Application of Decision Analysis:
Drug Testing of Athletes at Santa Clara University

The athletic board of governance at Santa Clara University was considering a proposal from the athletic director to implement a drug testing program for the university's athletes. A faculty member of Santa Clara and member of the board of governance, Charles D. Feinstein, developed a decision analysis model to analyze the ramifications of the proposal.

By developing this model he hoped to demonstrate to the board that the two essential issues relative to drug testing were the reliability of the testing procedure and the benefits of

identifying a drug user compared with the cost of a false identification, i.e., an error.

The model had two main decision alternatives, "test" or "don't test." The outcomes of the "don't test" decision were that the athlete "uses drugs" or "does not use drugs." The prior probability of the outcome "uses drugs" is the fraction of the population using drugs. The outcomes of the "test" decision were a "positive" or "negative" lab result. If a positive result is indicated, action is taken; and if the tested athlete actually uses drugs no cost results. However, if

This behavior can be explained by the concept of **utility,** which is defined as a measure of an individual decision maker's preference for monetary return (as opposed to avoiding risk). Von Neumann and Morgenstern developed a decision criterion whereby utility can be measured. According to their theory of utility, in a decision situation, a person will choose the alternative that maximizes his or her expected utility.

The Von Neumann and Morgenstern concept of utility is measured on a cardinal scale in units referred to as **utiles.** Utility is measured by observing a decision maker's pattern of decisions in risk situations.

For example, consider a homeowner who is attempting to decide whether or not to insure her house, which is valued at $50,000. The annual insurance premium is $300. There is a .0002 probability that the house will be destroyed by fire in the upcoming year. What should this individual do? The following payoff matrix for the *cost* of insurance can be developed:

	States of Nature	
Alternatives	$p_1 = .0002$ Fire	$p_2 = .9998$ No Fire
Insurance (a_1)	$ 300	$300
No insurance (a_2)	$50,000	0

The expected costs for the alternatives are

$E(a_1) = \$300$

$E(a_2) = .0002(50,000) + .9998(0) = \$10$

The obvious choice according to the expected value criterion would be to select alternative 2, no insurance, since it has a much lower expected cost. However, if the decision

the athlete does not use drugs (the test is wrong), there is a cost associated with a false accusation. If the test result is negative, some drug users are not identified, which has a cost, or some nonusers have had their privacy violated, also resulting in a cost.

The model demonstrated, for example, that if the drug test was 95% reliable, for a 5% probability that the athlete is a drug user, the probability was only 50% that those who test positively would actually be drug users. The expected cost criterion was used to compare the alternative decisions. The author was able to clearly show the board of governance that only

under very limited conditions would testing be preferred to nontesting.

It was concluded that the cost of falsely identifying a non-drug user was so large relative to the cost of not identifying a drug user, that a drug test that is only 95% reliable is not accurate enough to justify the risk of testing. Sir William Blackstone's quote that, "It is better that 10 guilty persons escape than one innocent suffer," was cited.

This decision analysis was decisive in convincing the board to unanimously vote to recommend against drug testing, which the president of the university concurred with.

Source: C. Feinstein, "Deciding Whether to Test Student Athletes for Drug Use," *Interfaces,* 20, no. 3 (May–June 1990): 80–87.

situation is reformulated in terms of utility, a different outcome occurs. If the insurance premium of $300 is valued at only -1 utile in relationship to the disastrous loss of $50,000, which is valued at $-100,000$ utiles, the utility matrix is presented as follows:

	States of Nature	
Alternatives	$p_1 = .0002$ Fire	$p_2 = .9998$ No Fire
Insurance (u_1)	-1	-1
No insurance (u_2)	$-100,000$	0

The expected utility for each alternative is given as follows:

$$E(u_1) = -1$$
$$E(u_2) = -100,000(.0002) = -20$$

In this case, the expected utility is higher (less negative) for alternative 1 than for alternative 2, indicating that insurance should be purchased, the logical choice of most homeowners.

The difficulty with employing utility as a decision criterion is the determination of utility values. The mechanics of determining utility are similar to those involved in determining expected value. Typically, a **utility curve** that relates utility values to dollar values is constructed. Such a curve usually is obtained by placing the decision maker in various hypothetical decision situations and plotting the decision maker's pattern of choices in terms of risk and utility. Figure 8.1 shows several utility curves and the risk preference associated with each.

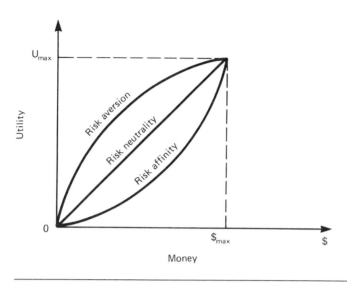

Figure 8.1 *Utility Curves and Associated Risk Preferences*

DECISION MAKING UNDER UNCERTAINTY

Decision making under uncertainty refers to decision situations in which the probabilities of potential outcomes are not known (or estimated). In a situation of uncertainty, the decision maker is cognizant of the alternative outcomes under varying states of nature, as in the decision situation under risk. However, the decision maker is unable to assign probabilities to the states of nature.

Example 8.3 Alternative Investments Under Uncertainty

Consider a decision maker who has $100,000 to invest in one of three alternative investment plans, involving, respectively, stocks, bonds, or a savings account. It is assumed that the decision maker wishes to invest all of the funds in one plan. The conditional payoffs of the investments are based on three potential economic conditions: accelerated, normal, or slow growth. The payoff matrix for this decision situation is constructed the same way as the one for a risk situation.

Alternatives	Economic Conditions		
Investment	Accelerated Growth	Normal Growth	Slow Growth
Stocks	$10,000	$6500	−$4000
Bonds	8000	6000	1000
Savings	5000	5000	5000

The payoff matrix reflects the fact that an investment in stocks or bonds will yield different returns, depending on the economic conditions. Investment in the savings plan guarantees a $5000 return, regardless of the economic conditions. Since a condition of uncertainty exists, there are no probabilities associated with the alternative states of nature (economic conditions). There are several criteria available for decision making under uncertainty. Some of the more prominent of these criteria will be examined via this investment example.

Laplace Criterion

The **Laplace criterion** suggests that since the probabilities of future states of nature are unknown, it should be assumed that all states of nature are equally likely to occur. In other words, each state of nature is assigned the same probability. Thus, in the investment example, a probability of ⅓ is assigned to each of the three economic conditions. Therefore, the expected values for the three investment alternatives are

$$E(\text{stocks}) = \tfrac{1}{3}(10{,}000) + \tfrac{1}{3}(6500) + \tfrac{1}{3}(-4000) = \$4167$$
$$E(\text{bonds}) = \tfrac{1}{3}(8000) + \tfrac{1}{3}(6000) + \tfrac{1}{3}(1000) = \$5000$$
$$E(\text{savings}) = \$5000$$

Using normal decision-making criteria, the decision maker would exclude stocks and be indifferent to the selection of either the savings plan or the bond plan.

Maximin Criterion

The **maximin criterion,** which is sometimes referred to as the Wald criterion after its originator, Abraham Wald, is based on the assumption that the decision maker is pessimistic, or conservative, about the future. With this criterion, the minimum returns for each alternative are compared and the alternative that yields the maximum of the minimum returns is selected. In our investment example, the minimum payoffs for each investment alternative are as follows:

Investment	Minimum Payoff
Stocks	−$4000
Bonds	1000
Savings	5000

Employing the maximin criterion, the decision maker would select the savings plan because it results in the maximum of the minimum returns, $5000.

The maximin criterion is obviously designed for the decision maker who is conservative about the future (i.e., a risk avoider). One flaw in this criterion is the exclusion of a large portion of the information available, since only the minimum returns for each alternative are used. Typically, in real-world situations, all available information is employed.

Maximax Criterion

The reverse approach to the maximin criterion is the **maximax criterion.** The maximax criterion is based on the assumption of an optimistic decision maker. With this criterion, the decision maker selects the alternative that represents the maximum of the maximum payoffs.

For our investment example, the maximum payoff for each of the three investment plans is as follows:

Investment	Maximum Payoff
Stocks	$10,000
Bonds	8000
Savings	5000

Employing the maximax criteria, the decision maker would select the stock plan because it results in the maximum of the maximum payoffs, $10,000.

The maximax criterion is an appropriate criterion for the decision maker who is optimistic about the future (i.e., a risk taker). However, like the maximin criterion, this method ignores much of the available information, an atypical occurrence in most realistic situations.

Hurwicz Criterion

The criterion suggested by Leonid Hurwicz represents a compromise between the maximin and maximax criteria. Decision makers in reality are rarely completely pessimistic or completely optimistic. In fact, the most accurate decision makers usually display a mixture of pessimism and optimism. As a result, Hurwicz devised a **coefficient of optimism** to measure the decision maker's degree of optimism. The scale of the coefficient of optimism, α, is from 0 to 1, where 0 reflects complete pessimism and 1 reflects complete optimism. (If $\alpha = 0$, the decision maker is said to have zero optimism, and if $\alpha = 1$, the decision maker is totally optimistic.) Since the coefficient of optimism is α, the coefficient of pessimism can be defined as $1 - \alpha$.

The Hurwicz approach requires that for each alternative, the maximum payoff should be multiplied by α and the minimum payoff multiplied by $1 - \alpha$. This results in weighted values, the highest of which represents the best alternative.

In our investment example, the maximum and minimum payoffs are

Investment	Maximum Payoff	Minimum Payoff
Stocks	$10,000	−$4000
Bonds	8000	1000
Savings	5000	5000

If the coefficient of optimism is $\alpha = .6$, the weighted value for each alternative is

Stocks:
$$10,000(.6) + [-4000(.4)] = \$4400$$

Bonds:
    $8000(.6) + 1000(.4) = \$5200$

Savings:
    $5000(.6) + 5000(.4) = \$5000$

Since the bond plan has the highest weighted value, it is selected as the best alternative. When $\alpha = 0$, the Hurwicz criterion becomes the maximin criterion, and when $\alpha = 1$, it becomes the maximax criterion.

A fundamental problem with the Hurwicz criterion is the determination of α. Often several α values have to be experimented with before a realistic estimation of the decision maker's degree of optimism can be determined. A further problem with this decision criterion is that it also excludes some available information (in this case, the economic condition of normal growth).

Regret Criterion

The **regret**, or **minimax, criterion** originated by L. J. Savage is based on the concept of opportunity loss introduced in the previous section on decision making under risk. The basic principle underlying this approach is that the decision maker experiences regret when a state of nature occurs that causes the selected alternative to realize less than the maximum payoff. The amount of regret, or opportunity loss, is determined by subtracting the alternative payoffs for each state of nature from the maximum payoff for that state. The regret criterion requires that the minimum of the maximum regrets be selected (i.e., it is a minimax criterion).

For our investment example, the following regret matrix can be developed:

Alternatives	Economic Conditions		
Investment	Accelerated Growth	Normal Growth	Slow Growth
Stocks	$ 0	$ 0	$9000
Bonds	2000	500	4000
Savings	5000	1500	0

In order to demonstrate the computation of the values in this table, we will consider the first state of nature, accelerated growth. Within this state of nature the stock plan is the best; thus, the opportunity loss resulting from the selection of the bond plan is $10,000 - 8000 = \$2000$, and from the selection of the savings plan, $10,000 - 5000 = \$5000$.

The maximum regret for each alternative is

Investment	Maximum Regret
Stocks	$9000
Bonds	4000
Savings	5000

Since the regret criterion requires the selection of the alternative that is the minimum of maximum regrets, the bond plan ($4000) is selected.

Summary of Decision Criteria

The decisions made in the example for each decision criterion are summarized as follows

Criterion	Decision (investment selected)
Laplace	Savings or bonds
Maximin	Savings
Maximax	Stocks
Hurwicz (α = .6)	Bonds
Regret	Bonds

This summary does not indicate a consensus decision. What results is a mix of possible decisions. The criterion and decision that are finally selected depends on the characteristics and philosophy of the decision maker. For example, the extremely optimistic decision maker might ignore the fact that only one criterion recommends the stock decision and select this investment simply because the maximax criterion most closely reflects this decision maker's view of the decision situation.

Computerized Decision Analysis Under Uncertainty

The AB:QM package, used previously in this chapter to determine the expected value of decision alternatives, also has the capability to perform decision analysis under conditions of uncertainty. Following are the input data for our investment example, a summary of the payoff table, and the recommended decision according to each of our decision-making criteria.

```
Program: Decision Theory / Decision Making Under Uncertainty

Problem Title : Example 8.3

***** Input Data *****

Type of Problem  : Profit  Problem

Hurwicz Alpha Coefficient:        0.600

----------------------------------------------------------
                        Event  1    Event  2    Event  3
----------------------------------------------------------
Alternative   1     10000.000    6500.000   -4000.000
Alternative   2      8000.000    6000.000    1000.000
Alternative   3      5000.000    5000.000    5000.000
----------------------------------------------------------
```

```
***** Program Output *****

Laplace
----------------------------------------
Alternative              Expected Value
----------------------------------------
    1                        4166.667
    2                        5000.000 <=
    3                        5000.000 <=
----------------------------------------


Maximin
----------------------------------------
Alternative              Expected Value
----------------------------------------
    1                       -4000.000
    2                        1000.000
    3                        5000.000 <=
----------------------------------------


Maximax
----------------------------------------
Alternative              Maximax Payoff
----------------------------------------
    1                       10000.000 <=
    2                        8000.000
    3                        5000.000
----------------------------------------


Hurwicz
----------------------------------------
Alternative              Hurwicz Payoff
----------------------------------------
    1                        4400.000
    2                        5200.000 <=
    3                        5000.000
----------------------------------------


Minimax
----------------------------------------
Alternative              Maximum Regret
----------------------------------------
    1                        9000.000
    2                        4000.000 <=
    3                        5000.000
----------------------------------------

  <=  indicate(s) the best alternative(s)

***** End of Output *****
```

DECISION TREES

The decision criteria that have been presented are applicable to situations within a static framework, such as a single time period. If the decision problem requires a series of related decisions, a decision tree can be useful. A **decision tree** is a schematic diagram of a sequence of alternative decisions and the results of those decisions. A decision tree is beneficial for several reasons. First, it provides a pictorial representation of the sequential decision process, which facilitates understanding of the process. Second, it makes the expected value computations easier, as they can be performed directly on the tree diagram. Third, the actions of more than one decision maker can be considered.

Example 8.4   New Product Promotion

Consider the following example, which demonstrates the use of a decision tree. A firm is attempting to decide whether or not to introduce a new product. Profit from the new product depends on three things:

1. Whether the competitive firm introduces a similar product;
2. The type of promotional campaign the firm launches;
3. The type of promotional campaign the competitor develops.

If the competitor does not introduce a similar product, the firm can launch a major promotional campaign and maximize profit. If the competitor introduces a product, the profit will depend on the promotional campaigns of both the firm and the competitor. There are three basic types of promotional campaigns based on cost: major, normal, and minor. The sequence of decisions and their consequences are shown as a decision tree in Figure 8.2.

At the first decision point, the firm has two alternatives: to introduce the product or not to introduce the product. If the firm does not introduce the product, the conditional profit will be, of course, zero. If the firm introduces the product, the competitor has two alternatives: to introduce or not to introduce a similar product. The probability of the competitor's introducing a product is .6 and not introducing a product is .4. At the second decision point, the firm has three promotional strategies: a major, normal, or minor campaign. If the competitor does not introduce a similar product, the firm's promotional effort will not bring any response from the competitor. However, if the competitor introduces a similar product, the response to the firm's promotional campaign will be one of the three types of promotional strategies. For example, if the firm employs a major promotional campaign, the probabilities for the competitor's responses are .5 for a major campaign, .4 for a normal campaign, and .1 for a minor campaign. If the response to the firm's major campaign is a major campaign from the competitor, the conditional profit will be $40,000. The major campaign–normal campaign combination results in $60,000, and the major-minor combination brings $120,000 conditional profit to the firm. These profit figures do not include the research and development costs of $70,000. Other combinations of campaigns, probabilities, and conditional profits are also shown in Figure 8.2.

The best way to analyze this kind of sequential decision problem is to work from the end of the decision tree and calculate the expected profit for each sequence of decisions. For example, the expected profit for the combination of decisions of the firm's introducing the product, the competitor's introducing a similar product, and the firm's using a major promotional campaign is

$$40,000(.5) + 60,000(.4) + 120,000(.1) = \$56,000$$

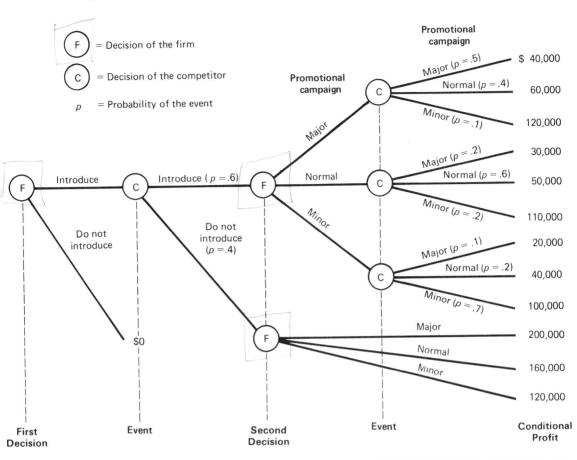

Figure 8.2 *Decision Tree for Promotion of New Product*

Figure 8.3 presents the decision tree with the expected profits for various decision points and events. The expected profits are shown in the rectangular boxes.

When the competitor introduces a similar product, the three promotional strategies result in the following expected profits: major campaign, $56,000; normal campaign, $58,000; minor campaign, $80,000. Since the greatest expected profit is associated with the minor campaign, we can eliminate the other two strategies (as indicated by the sign ‖). Thus, when the competitor introduces a similar product and the firm uses a minor promotional strategy, the optimal expected profit is $80,000.

If the competitor does not introduce a similar product, the highest conditional profit is $200,000 when the firm adopts a major campaign strategy. Therefore, we can eliminate the other two strategies (indicated by ‖ again). Now the expected profit of the firm's introduction of a new product can be calculated. This expected profit is the sum of the expected profit for the event that the competitor introduces a similar product ($80,000), multiplied by its probability (.6), plus the expected profit of the event that the competitor does not introduce a similar product ($200,000), multiplied by its probability (.4). Thus,

Expected profit = 80,000(.6) + 200,000(.4) = $128,000

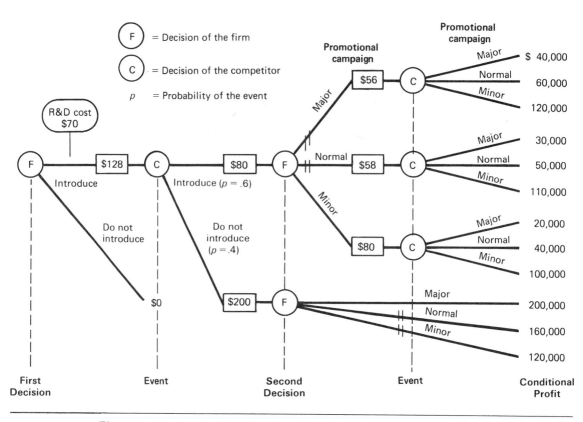

Figure 8.3 *Decision Tree with Expected Values*

The research and development cost for the new product is $70,000. Since the expected net profit of introducing the new product is $58,000, the decision to introduce the product should be made.

Computerized Analysis of Decision Trees

The AB:QM package used previously in this chapter also has the capability to perform decision tree analysis. The input data for our new product promotion example (8.4), the program output, and the recommended decision choices are shown on page 405.

GAME THEORY

The fundamental characteristic of game theory that differentiates it from decsion theory is the assumption that the decision maker is competing with other rational, intelligent, goal-seeking opponents. In decision theory, passive opponents exist, such as the states of nature. Thus, the word *game* is used to denote decisions under conditions of conflict or competition.

Game theory was introduced in 1944 by Von Neumann and Morgenstern in their classic work, *Theory of Games and Economic Behavior*. Although the book received praise as a landmark in decision theory, practical application of game theory to decisions involving conflict has been limited.

```
Program: Decision Theory / Decision Tree

Problem Title : Example 8.4

***** Input Data *****

Type of Problem  : Profit  Problem

------------------------------------------------
   Nodes        Type    Probability    Payoff
------------------------------------------------
  1 ->   2    Decision    None        0.000
  1 ->   3    Decision    None    -70000.000
  3 ->   4    Event      0.400        0.000
  3 ->   5    Event      0.600        0.000
  4 ->  18    Decision    None    200000.000
  4 ->  19    Decision    None    160000.000
  4 ->  20    Decision    None    120000.000
  5 ->   6    Decision    None        0.000
  5 ->   7    Decision    None        0.000
  5 ->   8    Decision    None        0.000
  6 ->   9    Event      0.500    40000.000
  6 ->  10    Event      0.400    60000.000
  6 ->  11    Event      0.100   120000.000
  7 ->  12    Event      0.200    30000.000
  7 ->  13    Event      0.600    50000.000
  7 ->  14    Event      0.200   110000.000
  8 ->  15    Event      0.100    20000.000
  8 ->  16    Event      0.200    40000.000
  8 ->  17    Event      0.700   100000.000
------------------------------------------------


***** Program Output *****

---------------------------------------------------------
   Nodes        Type    Probability   Payoff   Decision
---------------------------------------------------------
  1 ->   2    Decision    None        0.000
  1 ->   3    Decision    None    58000.000 <=  choice
  3 ->   4    Event      0.400    80000.000
  3 ->   5    Event      0.600    48000.000
  4 ->  18    Decision    None   200000.000 <=  choice
  4 ->  19    Decision    None   160000.000
  4 ->  20    Decision    None   120000.000
  5 ->   6    Decision    None    56000.000
  5 ->   7    Decision    None    58000.000
  5 ->   8    Decision    None    80000.000 <=  choice
  6 ->   9    Event      0.500    20000.000
  6 ->  10    Event      0.400    24000.000
  6 ->  11    Event      0.100    12000.000
  7 ->  12    Event      0.200     6000.000
  7 ->  13    Event      0.600    30000.000
  7 ->  14    Event      0.200    22000.000
  8 ->  15    Event      0.100     2000.000
  8 ->  16    Event      0.200     8000.000
  8 ->  17    Event      0.700    70000.000
---------------------------------------------------------

The conditional payoff of solution :   58000.000

***** End of Output *****
```

For our purposes, the most important contribution of game theory is its conceptual framework, which proves useful in understanding general decision problems. Game theory provides a framework for analyzing competitive situations in which the competitors (players) make use of logical thought processes and mathematical techniques to determine optimal strategies for winning. Thus, by studying game theory, the decision maker may ultimately learn to make more intelligent decisions.

Two-Person, Zero-Sum Games

Game theory is generally classified according to the number of opponents (or players). The usual distinction is between two-person games and games involving three or more persons. Game theory is largely undeveloped for games involving three or more persons, and it is this limitation that has restricted its applicability to real-world situations. However, the study of two-person games has enough theoretical merit to warrant its presentation.

Game theory is also categorized according to the total payoff available to the players, with zero-sum and constant-sum games distinguished from nonzero-sum and nonconstant-sum games. The theory of nonzero-sum games is also relatively undeveloped. Therefore, the presentation in this section will be limited to two-person, zero-sum games.

Formulation of the Two-Person, Zero-Sum Game

Consider a game situation in which there are two opponents, identified as player A and player B. Player A must select from alternative strategies while considering the concurrent strategy selections of player B. The conditions are analogous to those of decision theory except that states of nature are replaced by the various strategies available to the opponent.

The combined payoff to both players is a constant sum. In other words, the portion obtained by player A is lost by player B, who receives the remaining portion of the constant sum. For example, if two firms are competing for 100% of the market, the portion obtained by firm A is exactly the portion lost by firm B. Since no more than 100% of the market can be obtained, the constant sum is 100. The term zero-sum refers to the fact that the sum of A's positive payoff (gain) and B's negative payoff (loss) is zero.

Payoff Matrix

It is assumed that each player knows the exact payoffs for every possible combination of strategies available to each player. Also, the payoffs are in a form that is transferable to either player with the same value to each; that is, the players' utilities regarding payoff are the same.

The following table is a sample payoff matrix showing the payoffs for player A that result from all combinations of strategies for each player. The payoff matrix represents only the gains of player A. However, any gain by player A is a loss for player B, and the sum of the two is zero. For example, if A selects strategy 1 and B selects strategy x, then A wins 80% of the market and B loses 80% of the market, yielding a sum of zero. In terms of a constant sum, if A gains 80%, then player B receives 20%, which results in the constant sum of 100%. It is traditional to express the payoff matrix in terms of gains for the player on the side and losses for the player on top.

	Player B strategies		
	x	y	z
Player A strategies 1	80	40	75
2	70	35	30

By evaluating the alternative strategies of player B, we can see that if player A selects strategy 1 and B selects strategy x, player B will lose 80% of the market; if B selects y, 40% will be lost; and if B selects z, 75% will be lost. If player B is a cautious decision maker, strategy y will be selected in order to restrict the possible loss to 40%. This selection is shown in the following table. The value 40 is referred to as the **value of the game**.

	Player B strategies			
	x	y	z	
Player A strategies 1	80	(40)	75	← Player A selection
2	70	35	30	

↑
Player B
selection

Maximin and Minimax Principles

The maximin principle for gains and the minimax principle for losses are basically the same as the criteria presented in the discussion of decision theory. According to the maximin principle, decision maker A is pessimistic and thus selects the strategy that maximizes gains from among the minimum possible outcomes. At the same time, player B attempts to minimize losses from among the maximum anticipated losses (minimax).

For example, player A identifies the minimum gain from both available strategies (1 and 2) and selects the strategy that will return the maximum gain from among these minimum values. It can be seen in the following table that 40 is the minimum gain for strategy 1, and 30 is the minimum gain for strategy 2. Since the maximum of these two values is 40, strategy 1 is selected by player A. For player B, 80 is the maximum loss for strategy x. The maximum loss for y is 40, and the maximum loss for z is 75. The minimum of these losses is 40; thus, strategy y is selected by player B.

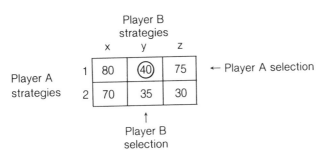

		Player B strategies			Minimum of A's row gains	
		x	y	z		
Player A strategies	1	80	(40)	75	(40)	(max)
	2	70	35	30	30	
Maximum of B's column losses		80	(40) (min)	75		

This analysis of strategy selection by players A and B results in a solution that satisfies both players. In other words, if A assumes that B is attempting to minimize A's gains and if B assumes that A is attempting to maximize B's losses, then the players have no incentive to change their strategy selections.

Since neither player would risk changing his or her strategy from the one selected, this type of result is referred to as a **pure strategy.** Pure strategies exist only when the solution has reached a point of equilibrium or steady state, which is referred to in game theory as a **saddle point.** A saddle point exists when neither player desires to change strategies, based on observation of the opponent's selection of a strategy. If A knows that B has selected strategy y, A's maximum gain is obtained by selecting strategy 1. Likewise, if B knows that A has selected strategy 1, B's losses can be minimized by selecting strategy y. Thus, neither player has any incentive to move to a different strategy.

It is important to note that, in general, the maximin (minimax) principle leads to the optimal solution for each player as long as each opponent follows this principle. However, if one of the players does not use this principle, the solution will not be optimal.

Role of Dominance

Referring again to the previous example, we can see that strategy 1 results in the maximum gain for player A, regardless of which strategy B selects. Thus, strategy 1 is said to **dominate** strategy 2. When a particular strategy is completely dominated by another strategy, the dominated strategy can be removed from the payoff matrix, since the player would never consider selecting it.

For player B, strategy x is dominated by strategy y, since the loss for strategy x is always greater than the loss for y regardless of which strategy player A selects. (For that matter, strategy x is also dominated by strategy z.) Therefore, strategy x can be removed from consideration.

The following table illustrates the resulting payoff matrix with the dominated strategies shaded. The resulting payoff matrix is easily evaluated. Player A can select only strategy 1, which means that player B will select y in order to restrict losses to 40 rather than 75. Note that the solution is the same as that previously obtained.

		Player B strategies		
		x	y	z
Player A strategies	1	80	40	75
	2	70	35	30

The concept of dominance is useful for a payoff matrix of large size. The rule of dominance can be employed to reduce the size of the matrix considerably prior to final analysis for determining optimal solution. Consider the example given in the following table, in which each player has four strategies. For player A, strategies 1 and 4 are dominated by strategy 2; therefore, they can be removed from the payoff matrix.

Player B
strategies

		w	x	y	z
	1	40	80	35	60
Player A strategies	2	65	90	55	70
	3	55	40	45	75
	4	45	25	50	50

Examining the remaining rows, 2 and 3, we can see that for player B, strategies w and z are dominated by y. Therefore, these columns can be removed, as shown in the following table:

Player B
strategies

		w	x	y	z
Player A strategies	2	65	90	55	70
	3	55	40	45	75

Finally, by examining the remaining 2-by-2 payoff matrix, we can see that row 2 now dominates row 3. Thus, the final payoff matrix consists of a single strategy for A and two strategies for B, as shown in the following table. To minimize loss, player B will select strategy y. Thus, the saddle point solution yields pure strategy 2 for A and pure strategy y for B, with the value of the game at 55.

Player B
strategies

		x	y
Player A strategy	2	90	⑤⑤

Two-Person, Zero-Sum Games with Mixed Strategies

Many times a two-person, zero-sum game will not result in the selection of pure strategies. This is because no point of equilibrium can be reached. For this type of game situation, it is possible to obtain a steady-state solution by assuming that the players will select mixed strategies.

Example 8.5   Union Contract Negotiations

As an example of a mixed strategy situation, consider a firm whose management and employees' union are engaged in contract negotiations. The payoff matrix for the two groups is shown in the following table. The payoffs are in cents per hour and represent the overall value of the salary and benefits increases per employee. The matrix represents gains to the union and losses to management.

	Management strategies			
	w	x	y	z
1	75	105	65	45
2	70	60	55	40
3	80	90	35	50
4	95	100	50	55

(Union strategies)

The union obviously wishes to maximize the employees' gains, while management desires to minimize its losses. Assuming both groups are prudent, the maximin (minimax) principle can be used to analyze the game. The maximin game results are shown in the following table:

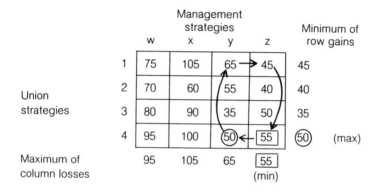

The selected strategies indicated in this table reflect the fact that there is no saddle point (i.e., common payoff value). Assuming that the union selected strategy 4, management would quickly switch its strategy from z to y in order to reduce its losses. Once management moved to strategy y, the union would select strategy 1, resulting in a gain of 65. This move by the union would be followed by a change in strategy by management to z in order to again reduce losses. The union would then move to strategy 4, and the process would begin again. Thus the game would end up in an infinite loop, as shown by the arrows. The maximin (minimax) approach results in an indeterminable solution where one of the players will always be dissatisfied.

Mixed Strategies

From the loop created in the previous table, it is apparent that only strategies 1 and 4 for the union and y and z for management are relevant. (This can be verified by reducing the payoff matrix by the dominance rule.) The following table reflects the reduced payoff matrix:

	Management strategies	
	y	z
Union strategies 1	65	45
4	50	55

The method of mixed strategies assumes that since neither player knows what strategy the other will select, each player will attempt to formulate a strategy that is indifferent to the opponent's strategy selection. This can be accomplished by randomly selecting among several strategies according to a predefined plan. The random selection plan involves selecting each strategy a certain percent of the time such that the player's gains (or losses) are equal regardless of the opponent's selection of strategies. Selection of a strategy a given percent of the time is analogous to selecting a strategy with a given probability on a one-time basis.

These probabilities (percentages) can be found for the union by determining the probabilities with which it must select strategies 1 and 4 in order for the expected gains to be the same, regardless of management's selection of strategy y or z.

If management selects strategy y, the possible payoffs to the union are 65 and 50. If the union selects strategy 1 with a probability of p [and therefore selects strategy 4 with a probability of $(1 - p)$], the union's expected gains are

$$(p)(65) + (1 - p)(50)$$

On the other hand, if management selects z, then the union's expected gains are

$$(p)(45) + (1 - p)(55)$$

Now, in order for the union to be indifferent to the strategy management selects, the expected gains of the union for each of management's possible selections must be equal. Thus, setting the two equations for the union's expected gains equal yields p as follows:

$$(p)(65) + (1 - p)(50) = (p)(45) + (1 - p)(55)$$
$$25p = 5$$
$$p = \tfrac{1}{5} = .2$$
$$1 - p = 1 - .2 = .8$$

Therefore, the union would select strategy 1 20% of the time and strategy 4 80% of the time, which results in the expected gains' being equal regardless of management's strategies.

Management would likewise determine probabilities for strategies y and z by equating expected losses if the union selects 1 to expected losses if the union selects 4:

$$(p)(65) + (1 - p)(45) = (p)(50) + (1 - p)(55)$$
$$25p = 10$$
$$p = \tfrac{2}{5} = .4$$
$$1 - p = 1 - .4 = .6$$

Therefore, management would select strategy y with a probability of .4 and z with a probability of .6.

It now becomes apparent that a common value in terms of *expected value* exists:

Union's Expected Gains:
    If management selects y, $(.2)(65) + (.8)(50) = 53.0$
    If management selects z, $(.2)(45) + (.8)(55) = 53.0$

Management's Expected Losses:
    If the union selects 1, $(.4)(65) + (.6)(45) = 53.0$
    If the union selects 4, $(.4)(50) + (.6)(55) = 53.0$

Thus, an equilibrium of sorts has been reached. The mixed strategy solution results in an expected game value of 53. It should be noted that if the negotiation process were repeated many times, the average would tend toward the expected value of 53. However, if there was only a single negotiation session, the actual result would be a single pure strategy for each player. Thus, one of the players, union or management, would be dissatisfied.

Computerized Game Theory

In order to demonstrate the analysis of a game theory problem using the AB:QM computer package, we will employ the "union versus management" mixed strategy game solved in Example 8.5. Following is a summary of the input data and the solution values for each player (player A refers to the union, and player B is the management designation). Note that the program requires that all dominated strategies be eliminated prior to model input.

```
Program: Game Theory

Problem Title : Example 8.5

***** Input Data *****

------------------------------------------------------------------------
    A \ B      Strategy  1  Strategy  2  Strategy  3  Strategy  4
------------------------------------------------------------------------
Strategy  1         75           105           65           45
Strategy  2         70            60           55           40
Strategy  3         80            90           35           50
Strategy  4         95           100           50           55
------------------------------------------------------------------------

***** Program Output *****

---------------
Mixed Strategy
---------------

For Player A:

Probabilty of Strategy   1          0.200
Probabilty of Strategy   2          0.000
Probabilty of Strategy   3          0.000
Probabilty of Strategy   4          0.800
```

```
For Player B:

Probabilty of Strategy    1        0.000
Probabilty of Strategy    2        0.000
Probabilty of Strategy    3        0.400
Probabilty of Strategy    4        0.600

Value for this game is         53.00

***** End of Output *****
```

LINEAR PROGRAMMING AND GAME THEORY

Linear programming can be applied to the two-person, zero-sum game to solve for the probabilities associated with mixed strategies. The major advantage of linear programming is that it can be applied to games with more than two strategies per player (e.g., 2-by-4, 3-by-3).

To illustrate the linear programming formulation of a game situation, we will consider the sample payoff matrix for a 2-by-4 game in the following table:

		Player B strategies			
		w	x	y	z
Player A strategies	1	80	35	55	50
	2	20	70	40	60

First, the game for player A will be formulated. The probabilities of selecting strategies 1 and 2 for player A are indicated by p_1 and p_2, respectively. If player B selects strategy w, then the expected mixed-strategy payoff to player A is $80p_1 + 20p_2$. Player A desires to select a mix of strategies 1 and 2 such that the expected payoff is the same regardless of B's action. In addition, player A's objective is to select the mixed strategy in such a way as to maximize the minimum expected payoffs.

The value of the game to A is determined by the strategy selected, regardless of whether the selection is optimal. Since A will attempt to maximize the expected payoff for the strategies B might select, the payoffs must be equal to or greater than the value of the game. (Then by maximizing the value of the game, A will maximize expected payoffs.)

If the value of the game is denoted by V, then the expected payoffs to A for different strategies of B can be written as

$$80p_1 + 20p_2 \geqslant V \quad \text{Player B selects strategy w}$$
$$35p_1 + 70p_2 \geqslant V \quad \text{Player B selects strategy x}$$
$$55p_1 + 40p_2 \geqslant V \quad \text{Player B selects strategy y}$$
$$50p_1 + 60p_2 \geqslant V \quad \text{Player B selects strategy z}$$

where

p_1 = probability that A will select strategy 1
p_2 = probability that A will select strategy 2

Since p_1 and p_2 are the probabilities with which A will select strategies 1 and 2, respectively, their sum must equal 1.0.

$$p_1 + p_2 = 1.0$$

Player A's objective is to maximize expected payoffs that can be achieved by maximizing the value of the game (V). Note that V has been defined as the criterion variable and p_1 and p_2 as the decision variables.

The desired linear programming form can be obtained by dividing the preceding constraints by V:

$$\frac{80p_1}{V} + \frac{20p_2}{V} \geqslant 1$$

$$\frac{35p_1}{V} + \frac{70p_2}{V} \geqslant 1$$

$$\frac{55p_1}{V} + \frac{40p_2}{V} \geqslant 1$$

$$\frac{50p_1}{V} + \frac{60p_2}{V} \geqslant 1$$

$$\frac{p_1}{V} + \frac{p_2}{V} = \frac{1}{V}$$

In order to simplify the model, let $p_1/V = p_1'$ and $p_2/V = p_2'$. The objective of player A is to maximize V, which can be achieved by minimizing $1/V$ (since as V becomes larger, $1/V$ becomes smaller). To simplify, let $1/V = V'$. The resulting linear programming model is now stated as

Minimize $V' = p_1' + p_2'$
subject to
$$80p_1' + 20p_2' \geqslant 1$$
$$35p_1' + 70p_2' \geqslant 1$$
$$55p_1' + 40p_2' \geqslant 1$$
$$50p_1' + 60p_2' \geqslant 1$$
$$p_1', p_2' \geqslant 0$$

The simplex solution to this model yields the following solution:

$$p_1' = \frac{3}{245}, p_2' = \frac{2}{245}, \text{ and } V' = \frac{1}{49}$$

Substituting p_1', p_2', and V' into the original variable relationships (i.e., $p_1' = p_1/V$, $p_2' = p_2/V$, $V' = 1/V$) yields the following:

$$p_1 = .6, p_2 = .4, \text{ and } V = 49$$

The value of the game applies only to strategies x and y for player B, which can be verified by applying the minimax principle to the payoff table (p. 428).

The linear programming formulation for player B is developed in a similar manner. Let the probabilities of selecting strategies w, x, y, and z be p_w, p_x, p_y, and p_z, respectively.

Player B wishes to minimize the maximum expected losses while facing the possibility that A might select strategy 1 or 2. The expected losses to B, for each of A's alternatives, are

$$80p_w + 35p_x + 55p_y + 50p_z$$
$$20p_w + 70p_x + 40p_y + 60p_z$$

If the value of the game is again denoted by V, B's objective will be to minimize V such that

$$80p_w + 35p_x + 55p_y + 50p_z \leqslant V$$
$$20p_w + 70p_x + 40p_y + 60p_z \leqslant V$$

Also,

$$p_w + p_x + p_y + p_z = 1$$

Dividing each constraint by V yields

$$\frac{80p_w}{V} + \frac{35p_x}{V} + \frac{55p_y}{V} + \frac{50p_z}{V} \leqslant 1$$
$$\frac{20p_w}{V} + \frac{70p_x}{V} + \frac{55p_y}{V} + \frac{60p_z}{V} \leqslant 1$$
$$\frac{p_w}{V} + \frac{p_x}{V} + \frac{p_y}{V} + \frac{p_z}{V} = \frac{1}{V}$$

To simplify the model, we will substitute the following new variables:

$$p'_w = \frac{p_w}{V}, \; p'_x = \frac{p_x}{V}, \; p'_y = \frac{p_y}{V}, \text{ and } p'_z = \frac{p_z}{V}$$

Player B desires to minimize V and maximize $1/V$, which is again denoted by V'. Thus, the following linear programming formulation for B results:

Maximize $V' = p'_w + p'_x + p'_y + p'_z$

subject to
$$80p'_w + 35p'_x + 55p'_y + 50p'_z \leqslant 1$$
$$20p'_w + 70p'_x + 40p'_y = 60p'_z \leqslant 1$$
$$p'_w, p'_x, p'_y, p'_z \geqslant 0$$

The simplex solution is

$$p'_x = \frac{3}{490}, \; p'_y = \frac{1}{70}, \text{ and } V' = \frac{1}{49}$$

Thus,

$$p_x = .3, \; p_y = .7, \text{ and } V = 49$$

p_w and p_z will have solution values of zero; therefore, strategies w and z will not be employed by player B in the mixed-strategy solution.

An additional point of interest regarding the simplex solution to the game problem is the fact that the dual solution for player A is player B's solution. In other words, the linear programming formulation for B is the dual of the formulation for A. Thus, it is only necessary to formulate and solve the linear programming problem for one of the players to yield the solutions for both.

This is illustrated in the LINDO computer solution for the primal problem (player A), shown below. The basic variables in the optimal solution are the same as previously stated:

$$p_1' = .012245 = \frac{3}{245}$$

$$p_2' = .008163 = \frac{2}{245}$$

and the value of the objective function is

$$V' = .020408 = \frac{1}{49}$$

The values of the dual solution variables are equal to the solution values found previously for the player B problem:

$$p_w' = 0$$

$$p_x' = .006122 = \frac{3}{490}$$

$$p_y' = .014286 = \frac{1}{70}$$

$$p_z' = 0$$

Following is the LINDO solution for the primal problem (player A).

```
: min p1 + p2
? st
? 80p1 + 20p2 > 1
? 35p1 + 70p2 > 1
? 55p1 + 40p2 > 1
? 50p1 + 60p2 > 1
? end
: look all

MIN       P1 + P2
SUBJECT TO
          2)      80 P1 + 20 P2 >=   1
          3)      35 P1 + 70 P2 >=   1
          4)      55 P1 + 40 P2 >=   1
          5)      50 P1 + 60 P2 >=   1
END

:
```

```
: go
LP OPTIMUM FOUND  AT STEP      4

              OBJECTIVE FUNCTION VALUE

    1)          .204081600E-01

    VARIABLE          VALUE          REDUCED COST
         P1          .012245            .000000
         P2          .008163            .000000

         ROW    SLACK OR SURPLUS     DUAL PRICES
         2)          .142857            .000000
         3)          .000000           -.006122
         4)          .000000           -.014286
         5)          .102041            .000000

    NO. ITERATIONS=        4
```

SUMMARY

In the previous chapters, models were developed in decision environments where conditions of certainty were assumed. However, in many cases certainty does not exist; instead, risk, uncertainty, or even conflict is present in the decision environment. In such cases, decision theory and the theory of games, the topics presented in this chapter, provide information to aid the decision maker in making efficient decisions. Although real-life applications of decision theory and the theory of games are somewhat rare (or at least rarer than those of many of the other model forms presented in this text), the study of these topics provides the decision maker with insight into the logic of decision making under conditions where certainty does not exist. This includes the types of data that must be gathered and the ways in which these data must be analyzed in order to make well-informed decisions.

REFERENCES

BAUMOL, W. J. *Economic Theory and Operations Analysis,* 4th ed. Englewood Cliffs, New Jersey: Prentice-Hall, 1977.

DORFMAN, R.; SAMUELSON, P. A.; and SOLOW, R. M. *Linear Programming and Economic Analysis.* New York: McGraw-Hill Book Company, 1958.

KWAK, N. K. *Mathematical Programming with Business Applications.* New York: McGraw-Hill Book Company, 1973.

LUCE, R. D., and RAIFFA, H. *Games and Decisions.* New York: John Wiley & Sons, 1957.

NEWMAN, J. W. *Management Applications of Decision Theory,* New York: Harper and Row, 1971.

RAIFFA, H. *Decision Analysis.* Reading, Massachusetts: Addison-Wesley, 1968.

SCHLAIFFER, R. O. *Analysis of Decisions Under Uncertainty.* New York: McGraw-Hill Book Company, 1969.

VON NEUMANN, J., and MORGENSTERN, O. *Theory of Games and Economic Behavior.* 3d ed. Princeton, New Jersey: Princeton University Press, 1953.

WEISS, L. *Statistical Decision Theory.* New

York: McGraw-Hill Book Company, 1961.

WILLIAMS, J. D. *The Compleat Strategyst*, rev. ed. New York: McGraw-Hill Book Company, 1966.

WINKLER, R. L. *Introduction to Bayesian Inference and Decision*. New York: Holt, Rinehart and Winston, 1972.

PROBLEMS

1. A company is going to introduce one of three new products code named X, Y, and Z. The market conditions (favorable, stable, or unfavorable) will determine the profit or loss the company realizes in the first year the new product is introduced as shown in the following payoff table.

	Market Conditions		
Product	Favorable 0.2	Stable 0.7	Unfavorable 0.1
X	$1,200,000	$700,000	$-300,000
Y	600,000	400,000	200,000
Z	350,000	300,000	300,000

a. Compute the expected value of each of the alternatives, and select the best alternative.
b. Develop the opportunity loss table, and compute the expected opportunity loss for each alternative.
c. Determine the expected value of perfect information (EVPI).

2. An investor must decide between two alternative investments, stocks or bonds. The returns for each investment under two possible economic conditions are as follows:

	States of Nature	
Investment Alternatives	$p_1 = .8$ Condition 1	$p_2 = .2$ Condition 2
Stocks	$10,000	$-$4000
Bonds	7000	2000

a. Compute the expected value of each investment alternative, and select the best alternative.
b. What probabilities would have to exist for conditions 1 and 2 before the investor would be indifferent between stocks and bonds?

3. During the summer, a ski shop in Vermont must determine how large its order for skis should be for the coming winter season. The shop manager can make a small, medium, or large order for skis. The demand for skis and subsequent sales will be

a result of the amount of snowfall at the nearby mountain lodges. The following payoff matrix shows the sales for varying amounts of snowfall and order sizes.

	States of Nature		
Order Size	$p_1 = .3$ Light Snowfall	$p_2 = .6$ Average Snowfall	$p_3 = .1$ Heavy Snowfall
Small	$4000	$5700	$ 7200
Medium	2400	8000	10,500
Large	− 1600	4200	12,000

Compute the expected value of each of the alternatives, and select the best alternative.

4. The financial success of a ski resort in the Blue Ridge Mountains is dependent on the amount of snow during the winter months. If the snowfall averages more than 40 inches, the resort will be successful; if the snowfall is between 30 and 40 inches, a moderate return is expected; and if the snowfall averages less than 30 inches, financial losses will accrue. Probabilities for each snowfall amount have been developed by a weather service. The financial return for each snowfall level is

	States of Nature		
	$p_1 = .4$ More than 40 in	$p_2 = .2$ Between 30 and 40 in	$p_3 = .4$ Less than 30 in
Financial return	$120,000	$40,000	− $40,000

A large hotel chain has offered to lease the resort during the winter months for $40,000. Compute the expected value to determine whether the resort should operate or lease. Explain your answer.

5. An oil company owns the offshore drilling rights for oil in a specified area in the Atlantic Ocean off the east coast of Virginia. The company has been offered $20 million for the drilling rights by another oil company. The estimated cost of drilling for oil is $10 million. The preliminary seismographic tests indicate the following probabilities of occurrence for the possible outcomes. The associated oil revenues are in present-value dollars.

Results of Drilling	Oil Revenues $ Value (present value in millions)	Probability of Occurrence
A producing oil well (gusher)	$180	.05
A producing oil well (moderate flow)	70	.20
A producing oil well (marginal)	30	.30
A dry hole	0	.45

a. Develop the payoff matrix for this problem.
b. Compute the expected value for each alternative, and identify the best alternative.
c. Compute the expected value of perfect information.
d. Assume that the oil company is a wildcat operation with limited finances. Discuss the decision-making logic given the potential returns (and losses) and associated probabilities of occurrence. What decision might result?

6. A private investor has come into an inheritance from her grandparents. She is attempting to decide between several investment alternatives. The return after one year is primarily dependent on the interest rate during the next year. The rate is currently 7% and she anticipates it will stay the same or go up or down by at most 2 points. The various investment alternatives plus their returns ($10,000s) given the interest rate changes are shown in the following table.

	Interest Rates				
Investments	$p = .2$ 5%	$p = .3$ 6%	$p = .3$ 7%	$p = .1$ 8%	$p = .1$ 9%
Money market fund	2	3.1	4	4.3	5
Stock growth fund	−3	−2	2.5	4	6
Bond fund	6	5	3	3	2
Government fund	4	3.6	3.2	3	2.8
Risk fund	−9	−4.5	1.2	8.3	14.7
Savings bonds	3	3	3.2	3.4	3.5

Determine the best investment using expected value criterion.

7. A meat market purchases steak from a local meat packinghouse. The meat is purchased on Monday at a price of $2 per pound, and the meat market sells the steak for $3 per pound. Any steak left over at the end of the week is sold to a local zoo for $.50 per pound. The demand for steak and the probabilities of occurrence are as follows:

Demand (lb)	Probability
20	.10
21	.20
22	.30
23	.30
24	.10
	1.00

For this type of problem, the alternative actions are the amounts (between 20 and 24 pounds) to stock, and the states of nature are the demands.

a. Construct the payoff matrix for this problem, and determine the amount that should be stocked.

b. Construct the opportunity loss table, and determine the amount to stock based on the expected opportunity loss of each alternative.

c. Compute the EVPI.

8. A grocer must decide how many cases of milk to stock each week in order to meet demand. The probability distribution of demand is

Demand (cases)	Probability
15	.20
16	.25
17	.40
18	.15
	1.00

Each case costs the grocer $10; the grocer, in turn, sells it for $12. Unsold milk is sold to a local farmer (who mixes it with feed for livestock) for $2 per case. If a shortage exists, the grocer considers the profit of $2 per case to be a cost. In addition, customer ill will costs are $2 per case. Thus, a shortage cost of $4 per case is incurred.

a. Construct the payoff matrix for this problem.

b. Compute the expected value of each alternative amount stocked, and select the best alternative.

c. Construct the opportunity loss table, and determine the best alternative.

d. Compute the expected value of perfect information.

9. The manager of the greeting-card section of a department store is considering her order for a particular line of Christmas cards. The purchase cost is $3 for each box of cards, which will be sold for $5 during the Christmas season. After Christmas, the cards will be sold for $2 a box. The card section manager feels that all leftover cards can be sold at the $2 a box price. The estimated demand during the Christmas season for the line of Christmas cards, with associated probabilities, is as follows:

Demand (boxes)	Probability
25	.10
26	.15
27	.30
28	.20
29	.15
30	.10

a. Develop the payoff matrix for this problem.

b. Compute the expected value for each alternative, and identify the best action.

c. Compute the EVPI.

10. A greenhouse specializes in raising carnations that are sold to florists. Carnations are sold for $3 per dozen and cost $2 per dozen to grow and distribute to the florists.

Unsold carnations left at the end of the day are sold to local restaurants and hotel. for $.75 per dozen. If demand is not met, a customer ill will cost of $1 per dozer is incurred. The daily demand for the carnations (in dozens) is

Daily Demand	Probability
20	.05
22	.10
24	.25
26	.30
28	.20
30	.10
	1.00

a. Develop the payoff matrix for this problem.
b. Compute the expected value for each alternative number of carnations to stock, and select the best alternative.
c. Develop the opportunity cost table for this problem.
d. Compute the EVPI.

11. A private investor is considering the purchase of a beach home on the coast of South Carolina as an investment. She must decide which of three types of mortgage loan to apply for: a fixed rate, a 3-year adjustable rate, or a 5-year adjustable rate. The latter two are determined by the rate on U. S. Treasury Bills at the end of the adjustment period. She plans to sell the house at the end of 15 years and has worked out the present value of the investment given each type of loan and three possible future 15-year trends for treasury bill rates, as shown in the following table.

Mortgage Loan	Treasury Bill Rate Trends		
	Increase	Constant	Decrease
Fixed	90,000	90,000	90,000
3-year	40,000	150,000	205,000
5-year	60,000	110,000	170,000

Determine the best type of loan under conditions of uncertainty using each of the following criteria:

a. LaPlace
b. maximin
c. maximax
d. Hurwicz ($\alpha = .6$)
e. regret (minimax)

12. In problem 6 assume that no probabilities are available for the various interest rates and determine the best investment using each of the following decision criteria.

a. maximax
b. maximin
c. LaPlace

13. In problem 3, now assume that the ski shop cannot estimate the probabilities of snowfall amounts for the winter. Using the same payoff matrix, but now under conditions of uncertainty, determine the appropriate order size by using the criterion of your choice. Explain why you chose the particular criterion you did.

14. A local investor is considering three alternative real estate investments: a motel, a theater, and a restaurant. The motel and theater will be adversely or favorably affected depending on the availability of gasoline, whereas the restaurant will be relatively stable for any condition. The payoff matrix under uncertainty for this decision framework is

	Gasoline Availability		
Investment Alternatives	Shortage	Stable	Surplus
Motel	−$8000	$10,000	$25,000
Theater	−12,000	8000	4000
Restaurant	6000	6000	5000

Determine the best investment under conditions of uncertainty using each of the following criteria:

a. Laplace
b. maximin
c. maximax
d. Hurwicz (α = .4)
e. regret (minimax)

15. A manufacturer is considering several capital investment proposals. The manufacturer can either expand the physical plant, maintain it at its present size, or sell part of the physical plant. Of course, the success of each course of action depends on the future demand for the product. The payoff matrix under conditions of uncertainty for this decision problem is

	Demand		
Investment Alternatives	Increase	Stable	Decrease
Expand	$20,000	$4000	−$10,000
Same	11,000	8000	−2000
Sell	−5000	−2000	15,000

Determine the best investment alternative under conditions of uncertainty using each of the following criteria:

a. Laplace

b. maximin

c. maximax

d. Hurwicz (α = .6)

e. regret (minimax)

16. Compute the payoff matrix for problem 8 assuming conditions of uncertainty (i.e. probabilities for demand are not known). Determine the best amount to stock using each of the following criteria:

a. Laplace

b. maximin

c. maximax

d. Hurwicz (α = .2)

e. regret (minimax)

17. During the summer, a television network is attempting to decide which of the fol lowing three football games to televise on the Saturday following Thanksgiving Day Alabama vs. Auburn, Georgia vs. Georgia Tech, Army vs. Navy. The estimated viewer ratings (millions of homes) of the games differ according to the won-loss records of the six teams, as shown in the following payoff matrix:

	States of Nature		
Game	Both Teams Winning Record	One Team Winning Record, One Team Losing Record	Both Teams Losing Record
Alabama vs. Auburn	10.2	7.3	5.4
Georgia vs. Georgia Tech	9.6	8.1	4.8
Army vs. Navy	12.5	6.5	3.2

Determine the best game to televise under conditions of uncertainty. Use each of the following criteria:

a. Laplace

b. maximin

c. maximax

18. Referring to problem 9, use the following decision criteria to determine the optimal number of cards to stock:

a. maximin

b. maximax

c. Hurwicz (α = .4)

d. regret (minimax)

19. An oil company is considering making a bid on a shale oil development contract to be awarded by the federal government. The company has decided to bid $210 million. It estimates that it has a 70% chance of winning the contract. If the firm wins the contract, management has three alternatives for processing the shale. It can develop a new method for extracting the oil, use the present process, or ship the shale overseas for processing. The development cost of a new process is $30 million.

The outcomes and probabilities associated with developing the new method are as follows:

Event	Probability	Financial Outcome ($ millions)
Extremely successful	.7	$450
Moderately successful	.2	200
Failure	.1	20

The present method costs $7 million, and the outcomes and probabilities for this alternative are given as follows:

Event	Probability	Financial Outcome ($ millions)
Extremely successful	.6	$300
Moderately successful	.2	200
Failure	.2	40

The cost of processing the shale overseas is $5 million. If the shale is shipped overseas, a return of $230 million is guaranteed.

Construct a decision tree for this problem, and determine the optimal decision strategy.

20. The Powhattan Power and Light Company is preparing a rate increase request to present to the state Public Utilities Commission. Key commission staff members have indicated that it is likely that the commission would approve a moderate rate increase that would result in an additional $30 million in revenues during the next three years. The company is also considering a higher rate increase that would result in $80 million in increased revenues for the same period. However, commission staff members have noted that while there is an 80% chance the commission will approve a moderate rate increase, there is only a 30% probability that the higher rate increase will be approved. Further, these staff members have implied that if the higher rate is requested and not approved it might be politically difficult for the commission to approve a moderate increase. The staff members estimate that if the higher rate is rejected and a moderate rate is requested there is a .60 probability that it would be approved, but if the moderate rate is rejected there would be no rate increase at all. Alternatively, if the higher rate is rejected and a low rate is requested there is a .90 probability it would be approved, but if it is rejected no rate increase will be approved. A low rate increase would result in a $10 million increase in revenues. If a moderate increase is requested and rejected, it is certain that a low rate increase would be approved.

Using decision tree analysis, determine the best decision for the company to make.

21. A construction company is being sued as the result of an accident suffered by a participant at a party in a second floor apartment. The plaintiff, along with several

other individuals at the party, was leaning against a balcony railing when it gave way. She was the only one to fall and suffered serious injuries as a result. In her suit, the plaintiff has charged the company with negligence in the design and construction of the balcony and has asked for an award of $2.5 million in damages.

The construction company has an insurance policy to cover this type of liability, and the insurance firm has been advised by its lawyers that there is a 60% chance that the construction company will be found negligent. However, the lawyers have noted that even with a negative verdict, it is uncertain as to what the actual award will be; they estimate that there is a 30% chance the full $2.5 million will be awarded, a 40% chance that it will be around $1 million, and a 30% chance that the award will be only $500,000. The lawyers indicate that if a negative verdict results, there will likely be an opportunity to settle for about $1.2 million before the award is determined by the jury. The lawyers have also informed the insurance firm that they have been approached by the plaintiff's attorney, and they are certain that she would settle out of court for $800,000.

Using the decision tree analysis, determine what the insurance firm should advise their lawyers to do.

22. In problem 21, if the insurance firm was very conservative and decided to ignore the lawyers' probabilistic estimates and instead apply the maximin criterion, what would the decision be?

23. The company in problem 1 is considering contracting with a market research firm to do a survey to determine future market conditions. The results of the survey will indicate either positive or negative market conditions. There is a .60 probability of a positive report given favorable conditions, a .30 probability of a positive report given stable conditions, and a .10 probability of a positive report given unfavorable conditions. There is a .90 probability of a negative report given unfavorable conditions, a .70 probability given stable conditions, and a .40 probability given favorable conditions.

a. Using Bayesian analysis, compute the posterior probabilities for each combination of market condition and report outcomes.

b. Develop a decision tree analysis of the company's decision strategy given that the survey is conducted, and compute the expected value of this strategy.

24. In problem 23, what is the maximum amount the company should pay the marketing firm for the survey report?

25. A professional athlete is negotiating a contract with management. The following two-person, zero-sum game has been developed for the contract negotiations. The different contract strategies and payoffs (in thousands of dollars) are shown below.

		Management strategies		
		x	y	z
Athlete strategies	1	490	220	195
	2	425	350	380

The strategies and payoffs are the result of differences with respect to contract length, deferred payments, bonuses, and so forth. Determine the strategy for each player and the value of the contract.

26. Given the following payoff matrix for a two-person, zero-sum game, solve the game by using the maximin (minimax) principle. Include in your answer: (a) the strategy selection for each player and (b) the value of the game to each player. Does the game have a saddle point?

		Player B strategies			
		w	x	y	z
Player A strategies	1	−10	6	2	40
	2	10	10	8	12
	3	8	−4	0	−10

27. Solve the following two-person, zero-sum game using the maximin (minimax) principle. Determine the pure strategy for each player. What is the value of the game?

		Player B strategies					
		u	v	w	x	y	z
Player A strategies	1	1	1	2	4	5	−5
	2	3	−3	4	3	2	4
	3	6	2	3	5	7	5
	4	2	1	3	4	6	0

28. Show that the payoff matrix of problem 27 can be reduced to either a single row or a single column by using the rule of dominance. Further show that the solution to the game, obtained from the reduced payoff matrix, is the same as was obtained in problem 27.

29. Determine algebraically the mixed strategy for each player, given the following payoff matrix. What is the expected gain for player A and the expected loss for player B?

		Player B strategies	
		x	y
Player A strategies	1	60	50
	2	45	55

30. Consider the following two-person, zero-sum game:

		Player B strategies		
		X	y	z
Player A strategies	1	500	600	300
	2	100	325	250
	3	200	550	450

a. Use the maximin (minimax) principle to determine if pure strategies exist.
b. Identify the cycling path that will result.
c. Using the rule of dominance, reduce the payoff matrix to a 2-by-2 matrix. Discus the payoff cells remaining by referring to the cycling path.
d. Solve algebraically for the mixed-strategy probabilities for players A and B.
e. Determine the expected gain for player A and the expected loss for player B. Discuss the meaning of this solution value.

31. The Army is planning a mock battle between two opposing forces, the blue and the red. The blue force will be the attacking force, and the red force will be on the defensive. Each force has three available strategies. The outcomes of the battles resulting from these strategies are shown in the following payoff matrix in terms of simulated casualties (in thousands of troops).

		Red force strategies		
		X	y	z
Blue force strategies	1	3	6	4
	2	7	−2	5
	3	−4	8	−1

Determine the strategy for each force and the casualties inflicted on one of the forces.

32. Assume that two firms are competing for a market share of the sales for a particular product. Each firm is considering what promotional strategy to employ for the coming sales period. Assume that the following payoff matrix describes the increase in market share for firm A and the decrease in market share for firm B. Determine the optimal strategy for each firm.

a. Which firm would be the winner in terms of market share?
b. Would the solution strategies necessarily maximize profits for either of the firms?
c. What might the two firms do to maximize their joint profits?

	Firm B strategies		
	no promotion	moderate promotion	extensive promotion
Firm A strategies — no promotion	5	0	− 10
moderate promotion	10	6	2
extensive promotion	20	15	10

33. Formulate the following game as a linear programming problem. Solve for the mixed-strategy probabilities for player B, using the simplex method. Show that the mixed-strategy solution for player A is also given by the dual solution in the final simplex tableau.

	Player B strategies	
	x	y
Player A strategies — 1	85	15
2	45	60
3	75	35
4	20	70

34. Formulate the union-management game on pages 409–412 as a linear programming problem. Using the simplex method, solve for managements' mixed-strategy probabilities. Determine the union's mixed-strategy probabilities from the dual solution.

35. Given the following payoff matrix for a two-person, zero-sum game, formulate a linear programming model to solve for the mixed strategy for player A. Solve the linear programming problem, and show that the mixed strategy for player B is also given by the dual solution values for the linear programming problem.

	Player B strategies				
	v	w	x	y	z
Player A strategies — 1	3	2	3	1	6
2	4	4	0	4	3
3	1	5	3	6	4
4	3	2	4	3	2

-9

Markov Analysis

Markov chains, named after the Russian probability theorist A. A. Markov, are a particular class of probabilistic models that are often applicable to decision-making problems in business and industry. Markov chains are a special case of the more general probabilistic models known as **stochastic processes,** in which the current state of a system depends on all previous states. A Markov process is a stochastic process distinguishable by the fact that the current state of the system depends only on the immediately preceding state of the system. For example, an electronic game is constructed so that the dragon moves randomly in and out of the dungeon. The dragon makes a move every two seconds. If the dragon is in the dungeon, there is a .5 probability it will come out after two seconds, and a .5 probability it will stay in the dungeon another two seconds. If the dragon is out of the dungeon, there is a .7 probability it will go back in the dungeon after two seconds, and a .3 probability it will stay out of the dungeon. The machine is electronically wired so that the probability of action on the part of the dragon depends only on its current location at the end of each two-second period of time. Thus, the movement of the dragon from one state to another (in the dungeon or out of the dungeon) is a Markov process, since the outcomes are entirely random and the probabilities of various outcomes depend only on the existing state.

Some problems to which Markov analysis has been applied include consumer brand switching, customer accounts receivable behavior, machine maintenance and operating characteristics, certain classes of inventory and queuing problems, inspection and replacement analysis, and water resource analysis. The properties of Markov analysis and several examples of its application are presented in this chapter. Further information related to Markov chains can be found in Appendixes A and C.

PROPERTIES OF MARKOV PROCESSES

There are two elements that must be determined in the process of constructing a Markov model of a system. These elements are the possible **states** of the system and the probabilities of moving between states (also called **transition probabilities**). A system state is the status of the system at a point in time, such as whether or not a machine is operating, whether an account is paid or not paid, how many customers are using each of several different brands of product, or whether a delivery truck is servicing store A or B. Transition probabilities represent the probability of the system's moving from one state to another during a specified period. These elements and several properties of Markov models will be illustrated in the following example.

Example 9.1   A Machine Operation and Breakdown Problem

In this example, we will consider a single machine in a manufacturing operation. The machine is either in operation or broken and being repaired. Thus, the machine will always be in one of two possible *states:* operation or breakdown. Movement from one of these two states to the other in the next day (time period) is a random process defined by the following probabilities:

$$p(\text{operation}\,|\,\text{operation}) \;\;\; = .60 \qquad p(\text{operation}\,|\,\text{breakdown}) \;\;\; = .80$$
$$p(\text{breakdown}\,|\,\text{operation}) = .40 \qquad p(\text{breakdown}\,|\,\text{breakdown}) = .20$$

For example, $p(\text{operation}\,|\,\text{operation}) = .60$ indicates the probability of moving to the operation state in the next day given that the machine is in operation today. Alternatively, the probability of the machine's breaking down in the next day given that it is in operation today, $p(\text{breakdown}\,|\,\text{operation})$, equals .40. Notice that, if the machine is presently operating, there are only two possible states the machine can be in on the following day— it can continue operating or it can break down. Hence, the sum of the probabilities of those two states' occurring must be 1.0. The reason the probability the machine will go from breakdown to operation is only .8 is that it might take more than one day to repair a broken machine.

These probabilities of moving from one state to another in the next time period (e.g., one day) are the transition probabilities of the Markov model. Because there are a finite number of states that the system can be in at any one time (i.e., the machine is either operating or broken), we can organize the transition probabilities in the form of a table, or matrix, as follows:

	To State	
From State	Operation	Breakdown
Operation	.60	.40
Breakdown	.80	.20

This table is actually a square matrix that indicates the possible state movements of the machine and the transition probabilities. For example, the transition probability of the machine's being in operation today but being broken tomorrow is .40. The Markov process indicated in the preceding table can also be illustrated in a transition probability diagram, as shown in Figure 9.1.

The movement from one state to another according to a predetermined and constant probability, as illustrated in this example, forms the basis of a Markov chain process.

Markov Properties

Example 9.1 illustrated several properties that must exist before a problem can be classified as a Markov process. These properties are summarized in general terms as follows.

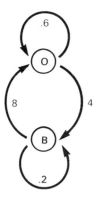

Figure 9.1 Markov Transition Probability Diagram

Property 1 The transition probabilities are dependent only on the current state of the system. In other words, given that the present state is known, the conditional probability of the next state is independent of the states prior to the present state. For example, in our machine breakdown problem, the probability of moving to either state, operation or breakdown, in the next time period is conditional only on the present state of the machine and not on the state of the machine in any prior time period.

Property 2 The transition probabilities are constant over time. For example, in our machine breakdown problem, the probability of going from the operation state to the breakdown state will remain .40 in any future time period.

Property 3 The transition probabilities of moving to alternative states in the next time period, given a state in the current time period, must sum to 1.0. For example, in our machine breakdown problem, the transition probabilities of moving to the states operation and breakdown in the next time period, given that the current state is operation, are .60 and .40, which sum to 1.0.

These properties are quite restrictive and limit the applicability of Markov analysis to real-world problems.

Given that the set of possible states in a Markov chain is finite, a square matrix, P, made up of all p_{ij}'s of the Markov chain can be formed. This table represents the commonly used transition probability matrix. The states *from* which the system moves are listed along the left, and the states *to* which the system moves are listed across the top. The transition probabilities (p_{ij}) of system movement from one of the states on the left, i, to one of the states on the top, j, complete the Markov process description.

$$P = \begin{array}{c} \\ 1 \\ 2 \\ \vdots \\ \vdots \\ \vdots \\ i \\ \vdots \\ \vdots \\ \vdots \\ m \end{array} \begin{array}{cccccc} 1 & 2 & \cdots & j & \cdots & m \\ \left[\begin{array}{cccccc} p_{11} & p_{12} & \cdots & p_{1j} & \cdots & p_{1m} \\ p_{21} & p_{22} & \cdots & p_{2j} & \cdots & p_{2m} \\ \vdots & \vdots & & \vdots & & \vdots \\ \vdots & \vdots & & \vdots & & \vdots \\ \vdots & \vdots & & \vdots & & \vdots \\ p_{i1} & p_{i2} & \cdots & p_{ij} & \cdots & p_{im} \\ \vdots & \vdots & & \vdots & & \vdots \\ \vdots & \vdots & & \vdots & & \vdots \\ \vdots & \vdots & & \vdots & & \vdots \\ p_{m1} & p_{m2} & \cdots & p_{mj} & \cdots & p_{mm} \end{array}\right] \end{array}$$

DEVELOPING THE TRANSITION PROBABILITIES

Understanding the fundamental basis of the transition probability matrix is essential to understanding Markov processes. One of the most popular illustrations of Markov chains is the so-called **brand-switching model.** This general example of Markov processes refers to customers' switching among brands or companies or stores. We will use this process of consumer behavior to demonstrate the development of transition probabilities.

Example 9.2 Customer Brand Switching

Assume that the market under consideration is located in a small, rather isolated town called Westville. Because of the lengthy distance to any other town, virtually all financial and banking business is done in the town. (The reasons for these rather restrictive assumptions will become clear as the example develops.) The town has three banks and 7000 resident customers who have checking accounts at one of the three banks. Since there are only 7000 customers available in the town and each customer will have an account at only one of the three banks, the total customer market for banking must be divided in some way among the three banks. The three banks are the American National Bank, the Bank of Westville, and the Commerce Union Bank.

Now let us assume that an extensive market research study has been conducted on banking services in the town. The study has yielded the number of customers who have had checking accounts at one of the three banks at two different points in time three months apart. The status of bank customers at the two points in time is given in the following table.

Bank	Number of Customers	
	Time 1	Time 2
American National	2000	2100
Bank of Westville	4000	3300
Commerce Union	1000	1600

It would appear that there was a significant shift in customer preference for banks from one point in time to the next. The Commerce Union Bank experienced a net increase of 600 customers, while the American National Bank gained 100 customers and the Bank of Westville lost 700 customers. However, this analysis is superficial. A thorough analysis requires consideration of the underlying features of the customer movement process.

The market research study also yielded the actual gains and losses of customers for each bank. The movement of customers from one bank to another is shown in the table on page 434. For convenience, the banks will now be referred to as A (American National Bank), B (Bank of Westville), and C (Commerce Union Bank).

The table illustrates that although bank B had a net loss of 700 customers, it gained 200 new customers from bank A and 300 new customers from bank C. However, this gain in new customers was offset by losses of 400 customers to A and 800 to C. Note

	From Bank	To Bank		
		2100 A	3300 B	1600 C
2000	A	1600	200	200
4000	B	400	2800	800
1000	C	100	300	600

that for bank B, the retention of old customers is shown at the intersection of row B and column B, and the gain of new customers is shown in the remaining cells of *column* B. The loss of customers is shown in the remaining cells of *row* B. The same format holds for banks A and C. Figure 9.2 illustrates by means of a tree diagram the movement of customers among banks.

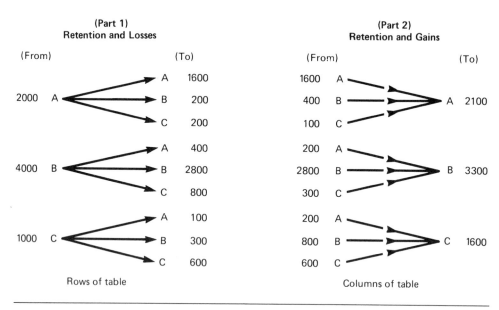

Figure 9.2 *Customer Movement Among Banks*

Note that part 1 of Figure 9.2 relates to the rows of the customer movement matrix, and part 2 relates to the columns. The number of customers who switched from bank A to B, from B to B, and from C to B in part 1 corresponds to the movement of customers *to* bank B in part. 2.

If we assume that the observed movement of customers among banks is *stable* (the same relative movement will continue), we can develop from these figures the probability transition matrix. The probability that bank A will retain current customers is $1600/2000$, or .8. The probability that bank A will lose customers to B is $200/2000$, or .1, and the same for losses to bank C. Interpreting the figures another way, bank B loses $400/4000$, or 10%, of its customers to A; retains $2800/4000$, or 70%; and loses $800/4000$, or 20%, to C. The same approach is used for bank C. The resulting probability transition matrix is given in the following table:

	To Bank		
From Bank	A	B	C
A	.8	.1	.1
B	.1	.7	.2
C	.1	.3	.6

The transition probability matrix is illustrated graphically in Figure 9.3. Note that the transition probability matrix can be reduced to the assumption that only one customer is involved. Thus, if the system is in state A (the customer is a bank A customer), the probability of moving to state A (retaining the customer) is .8, the probability of moving to state B (the customer's becoming a bank B customer) is .1, and so forth. In order to convert states into numbers of customers, we simply multiply the initial number of customers by the resulting transition probabilities. (This will be illustrated in the next section.)

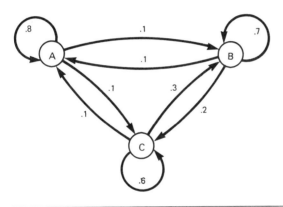

Figure 9.3 *Transition Probabilities Among Banks*

The assumption that the complete flow of customers from each bank to all others is known with certainty is an important consideration in developing the probability transition matrix. For purposes of using such probabilities, it must also be assumed that the same relative flow will continue (the process is stable) and that the transitions will be considered over the same length of time as in the initial study.

Predicting Future States

The value of obtaining the transition probability matrix in a Markov process is that it allows us to predict future states. For the previous example, for instance, we can predict market share of each bank in future time periods. The prediction of future states requires only that the initial state of the system be specified and that the transition probabilities be known. The successive future states of the Markov process are referred to as *chains*— hence the name Markov chains.

Since many systems being analyzed by the Markov method are such that the system is "in" one state and not in any of the remaining states, we will initially assume that there is only one customer in the system and that customer is in one of the states (a customer of one of the three banks). We will then show how this approach is easily expanded to the total population of customers.

Let us label the two points in time used in the marketing research study as time 0 and time 1. We wish to predict the number of customers of each bank at time 2. We will do this by first determining the probability of one customer's being in one of the three states at time 2.

Tree Diagrams

Tree diagrams are a convenient technique by which to illustrate a limited number of transitions of a Markov process. Figures 9.4, 9.5, and 9.6 illustrate the probabilities of the system states for the cases in which the system was initially in states A, B, and C, respectively. An examination of Figure 9.4 indicates that if the system was in state A at time 0, the probabilities of being in states A, B, and C at time 2 are .66, .18, and .16, respectively (as shown in the first row of the transition probability table on p. 438). The derivation of the second and third rows of the transition probability table is illustrated in Figures 9.5 and 9.6, respectively.

The table of probabilities on page 438 relate to the transition over two time periods; thus, they are referred to as two-step transition probabilities.

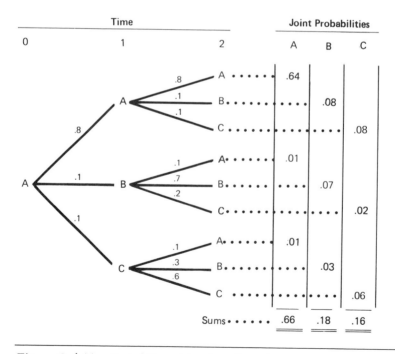

Figure 9.4 Two-Period Transition from State A

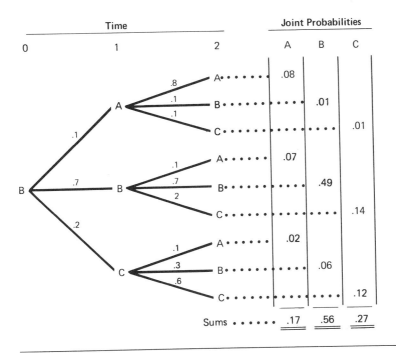

Figure 9.5 *Two-Period Transition from State B*

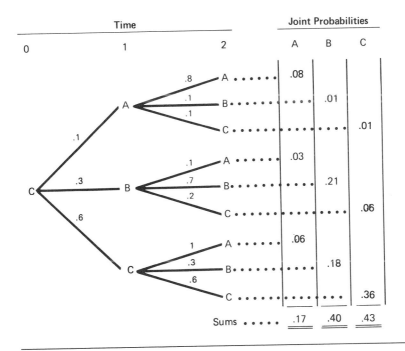

Figure 9.6 *Two-Period Transition from State C*

	From State	To State Time 2 A	B	C
Time 0	A	.66	.18	.16
	B	.17	.56	.27
	C	.17	.40	.43

To convert our one-customer case back to the original example, recall that initially the numbers of customers of each bank were 2000 for A, 4000 for B, and 1000 for C. The predicted number of customers for bank A at time 2 includes retained customers plus customers gained from banks B and C (the column of probabilities under A).

$$2000(.66) + 4000(.17) + 1000(.17) = 1320 + 680 + 170 = 2170$$

Likewise, the numbers of predicted customers for banks B and C at time 2 are

$$2000(.18) + 4000(.56) + 1000(.40) = 3000 \quad \text{(bank B)}$$
$$2000(.16) + 4000(.27) + 1000(.43) = 1830 \quad \text{(bank C)}$$

MATRIX APPROACH

Matrix multiplication provides a convenient vehicle for predicting the state of a Markovian system at some time period beyond a reference time. (See Appendix A for a review of matrix methods.) Given the initial state, matrix multiplication can be used to predict the state of the system at time n.

System State

We first describe the state of the system at time 0 by a one-dimensional matrix called a **vector**. The state of the system at time 0 is given by

$$p(0) = [p_1(0), p_2(0), p_3(0)]$$

where

$p(0)$ = a vector of $p_i(0)$ values
$p_1(0)$ = probability of being in state 1 at time 0
$p_2(0)$ = probability of being in state 2 at time 0
$p_3(0)$ = probability of being in state 3 at time 0

If we assume that the system is in state 1 at time 0, then $p(0) = [1.0, 0, 0]$. Likewise, for states 2 and 3 at time 0, we would have $[0, 1.0, 0]$ and $[0, 0, 1.0]$, respectively.

Transition Probability Matrix

We next describe the transition probability matrix as follows:

P = matrix of transition probabilities

$$
P =
\begin{array}{c}
\text{From State} \\
1 \\
2 \\
3
\end{array}
\;
\begin{array}{ccc}
 & \text{To State} & \\
1 & 2 & 3 \\
\hline
p_{11} & p_{12} & p_{13} \\
p_{21} & p_{22} & p_{23} \\
p_{31} & p_{32} & p_{33}
\end{array}
$$

p_{ij} = probability of going from state i to state j (for example, p_{13} is the probability of going from state 1 to state 3)

Future State Prediction

To compute the probability of being in state j at time 1 (when we are currently at time 0), perform the following operation:

$$p(1) = p(0)P$$

where

$p(1)$ = vector of state probabilities at time 1
$p(0)$ = vector of state probabilities at time 0
P = transition probability matrix

The equation can also be written as

$$
[p_1(1),\, p_2(1),\, p_3(1)] = [p_1(0),\, p_2(0),\, p_3(0)] \cdot
\begin{bmatrix}
p_{11} & p_{12} & p_{13} \\
p_{21} & p_{22} & p_{23} \\
p_{31} & p_{32} & p_{33}
\end{bmatrix}
$$

Returning to Example 9.2, let us assume that we are in state 1 at time 0 (we will now refer to bank A as 1, B as 2, and C as 3). The probabilities of being in each of the three states after one time period (from time 0 to time 1) are given as follows:

$$
[1.0,\, 0,\, 0] \cdot
\begin{bmatrix}
.8 & .1 & .1 \\
.1 & .7 & .2 \\
.1 & .3 & .6
\end{bmatrix}
= [.8,\, .1,\, .1]
$$

If we were in state 2 (bank B) at time 0, we would have for time 1

$$
[0,\, 1.0,\, 0] \cdot
\begin{bmatrix}
.8 & .1 & .1 \\
.1 & .7 & .2 \\
.1 & .3 & .6
\end{bmatrix}
= [.1,\, .7,\, .2]
$$

Finally, if we were in state 3 (bank C) at time 0, we would have

$$
[0,\, 0,\, 1.0] \cdot
\begin{bmatrix}
.8 & .1 & .1 \\
.1 & .7 & .2 \\
.1 & .3 & .6
\end{bmatrix}
= [.1,\, .3,\, .6]
$$

Now, to determine the probabilities of being in the various states at time 2, we simply compute

$$p(2) = p(1)P$$

These probabilities are developed as follows:

$$[.8, .1, .1] \cdot \begin{bmatrix} .8 & .1 & .1 \\ .1 & .7 & .2 \\ .1 & .3 & .6 \end{bmatrix} = [.66, .18, .16]$$

$$[.1, .7, .2] \cdot \begin{bmatrix} .8 & .1 & .1 \\ .1 & .7 & .2 \\ .1 & .3 & .6 \end{bmatrix} = [.17, .56, .27]$$

$$[.1, .3, .6] \cdot \begin{bmatrix} .8 & .1 & .1 \\ .1 & .7 & .2 \\ .1 & .3 & .6 \end{bmatrix} = [.17, .40, .43]$$

Note that these are exactly the same results as were obtained in the tree diagrams in Figures 9.4, 9.5, and 9.6. However, expanding the tree diagrams to one more stage would be tedious indeed. To find the state probabilities for time 3, we compute

$$p(3) = p(2)P$$

$$[.66, .18, .16] \cdot \begin{bmatrix} .8 & .1 & .1 \\ .1 & .7 & .2 \\ .1 & .3 & .6 \end{bmatrix} = [.562, .240, .198]$$

$$[.17, .56, .27] \cdot \begin{bmatrix} .8 & .1 & .1 \\ .1 & .7 & .2 \\ .1 & .3 & .6 \end{bmatrix} = [.219, .490, .291]$$

$$[.17, .40, .43] \cdot \begin{bmatrix} .8 & .1 & .1 \\ .1 & .7 & .2 \\ .1 & .3 & .6 \end{bmatrix} = [.219, .426, .355]$$

Thus, given that we started at time 0 with 2000, 4000, and 1000 customers for each of the respective banks, the prediction of the number of customers using each bank at time 3 is computed as follows:

$$[2000, 4000, 1000] \cdot \begin{bmatrix} .562 & .240 & .198 \\ .219 & .490 & .291 \\ .219 & .426 & .355 \end{bmatrix} = [2219, 2866, 1915]$$

The numbers of customers using each bank after three periods are listed in the following table:

Bank	Number of Customers
1. A	2219
2. B	2866
3. C	1915
Total	7000

Initial State Specification

It should be pointed out that the initial states of the Markov process can be specified in any one of several ways. Because in many Markovian systems the system is in only one of the states, this was the type of problem first illustrated. Since $p_1(0)$ is the probability of being in state 1, $p_2(0)$ is the probability of being in state 2, and $p_3(0)$ is the probability of being in state 3 (at time 0), we represented the possible states in terms of the initial state vector $[p_1(0), p_2(0), p_3(0)]$ as

State	Initial State Probability Vector
1	[1, 0, 0]
2	[0, 1, 0]
3	[0, 0, 1]

However, it does not necessarily have to be the case that the system has a probability of 1.0 of being in one of the possible states (and zero probabilities of being in all other states). Rather, the state of the system might be such that there is some probability that the system will be in each of the states. For example, the initial state vector might be given as [.3, .6, .1], in which case there is a probability of less than 1.0 that the system is in each state (with the probabilities summing to 1.0). Actually, if [.3, .6, .1] is the state vector at time 0, it is simply referred to as the *state* of the system at that time.

The initial state vector need not even be specified in terms of probabilities. For our example, we could have specified the initial state vector in terms of the number of customers of each bank: [2000, 4000, 1000]. Likewise, we could have specified the initial state vector in terms of the fraction of market shares of each bank as [²⁄₇, ⁴⁄₇, ¹⁄₇], or in terms of the decimal portion of market shares of each bank as [.286, .571, .143].

Multiperiod Transition Probabilities

In order to predict the system state at time 1, we multiplied the system state at time 0 by the transition matrix. Then, to get the prediction for time 2, we multiplied the state vector for time 1 by the transition matrix. We repeated this process again to get our prediction for time 3. We can now show that there is a more efficient approach to predicting the state at time n than the previously described successive multiplication.

Note that we got $p(1)$ by computing $p(0)P$, then we got $p(2)$ by multiplying $p(1)$ by P, and, finally, $p(3) = p(2)P$. Now, it can be seen that if $p(1) = p(0)P$ and $p(2) = p(1)P$, then $p(2) = p(0)PP$. Likewise, if $p(3) = p(2)P$, then $p(3) = p(0)PPP$, which is $p(0)P^3$. Thus, in general, $p(n) = p(0)P^n$, where P^n is the nth power of P. In words, the state vector at time n, $p(n)$, is equal to the state vector at time zero, $p(0)$, multiplied by the nth power of the transition matrix, P^n. In terms of the individual elements of the state vector and transition matrix, we can write the following:

$$[p_1(n), p_2(n), \ldots, p_m(n)] = [p_1(0), p_2(0), \ldots, p_m(0)] \cdot \begin{bmatrix} p_{11} & p_{12} & \cdots & p_{1m} \\ p_{21} & p_{22} & \cdots & p_{2m} \\ \vdots & & & \vdots \\ \vdots & & & \vdots \\ \vdots & & & \vdots \\ p_{m1} & p_{m2} & \cdots & p_{mm} \end{bmatrix}^n$$

where

n = number of time periods hence for which a prediction is desired

0 = initial point in time, for which the state is known

m = number of possible states for the system (note that the transition matrix is always $m \times m$)

Thus, to derive the state conditions at time 3 for Example 9.2, we can simply perform the following:

$$[2000, 4000, 1000] \cdot \begin{bmatrix} .8 & .1 & .1 \\ .1 & .7 & .2 \\ .1 & .3 & .6 \end{bmatrix}^3 = [2219, 2866, 1915]$$

STEADY-STATE CONDITIONS

In many cases, the Markov process will converge to a *steady-state,* or *equilibrium, condition.* This is shown for the bank customer example in the following table. The predicted future states are illustrated graphically in Figure 9.7.

Period	Number of Customers		
	A	B	C
0	2000	4000	1000
1	2100	3300	1600
2	2170	3000	1830
3	2219	2866	1915
4	2253	2803	1944
5	2277	2770	1953
6	2294	2753	1953
7	2306	2742	1952
8	2314	2736	1950
9	2320	2731	1949
10	2324	2729	1947
11	2327	2727	1946
12	2329	2725	1946
13	2330	2724	1946
14	2331	2724	1945
15	2332	2723	1945
16	2332	2723	1945

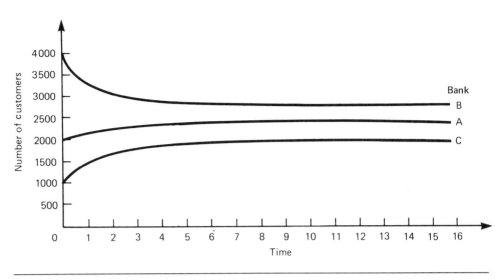

Figure 9.7 *Predicted Markov States for Sixteen Periods*

Notice that the number of customers for each bank converges to a steady state after the fifteenth future period. The steady-state conditions are summarized in terms of numbers of customers and proportions in the following table:

	A	B	C	Total
Number of customers	2332	2723	1945	7000
Proportions	.333	.389	.278	1.000

In general, as n grows larger, the state values tend to stabilize at a steady state. This is a logical occurrence, since the present state tends to lose significance for future states at time periods in the distant future. In other words, if a customer is trading with bank B now, the probability that the customer will be trading with bank A or C will probably be the same for twenty periods from now as for twenty-one periods from now. By the same token, it is logical to presume that the fact that a customer is now trading with bank B holds no significance for determining which bank the customer will be using twenty periods from now. Thus, regardless of which state a system begins in, after a number of periods the probability vectors for A, B, and C will be the same.

Computation of Steady-State Conditions

The steady-state conditions can be computed based on our observation that once a steady state is reached, multiplication of a state condition by the transition probabilities does not change the state condition. That is,

$$p(n) = p(n - 1)P$$

for any value of n after a steady state is reached. For example, if we multiply the state condition of Example 9.2 at the end of period 16 by the transition matrix,

$$[2332, 2723, 1945] \cdot \begin{bmatrix} .8 & .1 & .1 \\ .1 & .7 & .2 \\ .1 & .3 & .6 \end{bmatrix}$$

we obtain the same state values, [2332, 2723, 1945], as we did previously. Thus, a steady state has been reached.

Steady-State Vector

There is an alternative to the methods demonstrated above for determining the steady-state values. The steady-state values can be determined algebraically as follows. We will first represent the state values at steady state by the symbol π. Thus, at steady state the state vector is given, in terms of decimal proportions, as

$$\pi = [\pi_1, \pi_2, \pi_3] = [.333, .389, .278]$$

where

π = vector of state probabilities (relative proportions)
π_1 = value of state condition 1
π_2 = value of state condition 2
π_3 = value of state condition 3

Notice that the time period is not given here since, as steady-state values, these values are independent of time.

Since multiplication of a state condition by the transition matrix yields the same condition at steady state, we can write

$$\pi = \pi \cdot P$$

or

$$[\pi_1, \pi_2, \pi_3] = [\pi_1, \pi_2, \pi_3] \cdot \begin{bmatrix} p_{11} & p_{12} & p_{13} \\ p_{21} & p_{22} & p_{23} \\ p_{31} & p_{32} & p_{33} \end{bmatrix}$$

This assumes that there are three possible state conditions, as there were in the bank switching example. For Example 9.2, we would have

$$[\pi_1, \pi_2, \pi_3] = [\pi_1, \pi_2, \pi_3] \cdot \begin{bmatrix} .8 & .1 & .1 \\ .1 & .7 & .2 \\ .1 & .3 & .6 \end{bmatrix}$$

which yields

$$\pi_1 = .8\pi_1 + .1\pi_2 + .1\pi_3$$
$$\pi_2 = .1\pi_1 + .7\pi_2 + .3\pi_3$$
$$\pi_3 = .1\pi_1 + .2\pi_2 + .6\pi_3$$

We further include the fact that the state probabilities must sum to 1.0.

$$\pi_1 + \pi_2 + \pi_3 = 1.0$$

We now have four equations with three unknowns, which can be solved simultaneously to determine the steady-state values of π_1, π_2, and π_3. Noting that one of the initial three equations is redundant, we can eliminate any one of the three (for example, eliminate the third equation). That is, if we solve for π_1 and π_2, then π_3 is automatically known, since $\pi_1 + \pi_2 + \pi_3 = 1.0$. Therefore, the third equation, which also solves for π_3, is redundant and need not be included. The three remaining equations to be solved simultaneously can be written as

$$-.2\pi_1 + .1\pi_2 + .1\pi_3 = 0$$
$$.1\pi_1 - .3\pi_2 + .3\pi_3 = 0$$
$$1.0\pi_1 + 1.0\pi_2 + 1.0\pi_3 = 1.0$$

Solving these equations simultaneously yields

$$\pi_1 = .333 \qquad \pi_2 = .389 \qquad \pi_3 = .278$$

which are the steady-state conditions.

As noted earlier, as n grows larger, the matrix of transition probabilities to the power n (i.e., P^n) approaches a limiting form in which all rows are identical and equal to the steady-state vector. Thus, for the preceding example, the transition matrix, for a very large value of n, would be

$$P^n = \begin{bmatrix} .333 & .389 & .278 \\ .333 & .389 & .278 \\ .333 & .389 & .278 \end{bmatrix}$$

If we return to the sixteenth period of the table on page 442, we find that we obtain exactly the same values for π_1, π_2, and π_3.

In our simultaneous solution of the equations to obtain π_1, π_2, and π_3, we actually solved for the steady-state *proportions* of market share, or the *probabilities* of one customer's being in any one of the states. To get the *number* of customers for each bank, we simply multiply each of the probabilities, π_1, π_2, π_3, by 7000, which yields

$$\pi_1 = 2332$$
$$\pi_2 = 2723$$
$$\pi_3 = 1945$$

For relatively small problems, such as our bank example, the equations can be solved simultaneously through elementary algebraic substitution. For problems that involve more states, matrix algebra is recommended. Solution of systems of linear equations by matrix algebra is discussed in Appendix A.

Computer Determination of Steady-State Conditions

Most general management science software packages have the capability to perform Markov analysis. In this section we will use the AB:QM software package, demonstrated in previous chapters in this text, to perform on our bank example the steady-state analysis that was accomplished manually in the previous section. Following are the model input data, a summary of the transition matrix, and the steady-state condition results.

```
Program: Markov Analysis

Problem Title : Example 9.2

***** Input Data *****

------------------------------------------------------------
From\To       Value      State 1    State 2    State 3
------------------------------------------------------------
State 1      2000.00      0.800      0.100      0.100
State 2      4000.00      0.100      0.700      0.200
State 3      1000.00      0.100      0.300      0.600
------------------------------------------------------------

***** Program Output *****

<<Steady State>>

-------------------------------------------------
States        Probability          Value
-------------------------------------------------
  1             0.33333           2333.33
  2             0.38889           2722.22
  3             0.27778           1944.44
-------------------------------------------------

***** End of Output *****
```

Example 9.3   A Machine Maintenance Policy

A commercial copy center near a university uses a large photocopy machine that deteriorates rather rapidly, in terms of quality of copies produced, under heavy usage. The machine is examined at the end of each day to determine its status with respect to copy quality. The inspection results are classified as follows:

State	Condition of Copy Machine
1	Excellent
2	Acceptable—some deterioration in quality
3	Marginal—significant deterioration in quality
4	Unacceptable quality—repairs required

Based on past data collected concerning the operation of the machine, the condition of the machine over a period of time has been described by the transition matrix given below.

From State	To State			
	1	2	3	4
1	0	.8	.1	.1
2	0	.6	.2	.2
3	0	0	.5	.5
4	0	0	0	1

The transition probability of 1.0 at the intersection of row 4 and column 4 in the transition matrix shows that when the machine goes to state 4 (yields unacceptable quality and requires repairs), it does not leave this state. However, if the machine is repaired when it is in state 4, it can be assumed that the act of repairing it will return it to state 1 (excellent). Thus, if the machine is repaired each time it reaches state 4, returning it to near perfect condition, the transition matrix can be given as follows:

From State	To State			
	1	2	3	4
1	0	.8	.1	.1
2	0	.6	.2	.2
3	0	0	.5	.5
4	1	0	0	0

The manager of the copy center desires to determine the expected cost associated with a policy of repairing the machine to a like-new condition each time it reaches state 4. She has estimated that the expected costs associated with the various states of the machine are as follows:

State	Condition	Expected Cost per Day
1	Excellent	$ 0
2	Some deterioration in quality	$100 (rerunning copies)
3	Significant deterioration in quality	$400 (refunds to dissatisfied customers)
4	Unacceptable quality—repair required	$800 (repair cost and downtime)

The long-run expected average cost per day can be determined by computing the steady-state conditions for the copy machine, as follows:

$$\pi_1 = \pi_4$$
$$\pi_2 = .8\pi_1 + .6\pi_2$$
$$\pi_3 = .1\pi_1 + .2\pi_2 + .5\pi_3$$
$$\pi_4 = .1\pi_1 + .2\pi_2 + .5\pi_3$$
$$\pi_1 + \pi_2 + \pi_3 + \pi_4 = 1.0$$

The simultaneous solution of the above steady-state equations for the copy center yields the steady-state conditions:

$\pi_1 = .2$ (excellent)

$\pi_2 = .4$ (acceptable)

$\pi_3 = .2$ (marginal)

$\pi_4 = .2$ (repair required)

The long-run expected cost associated with the machine repair policy is given by

$$0\pi_1 + 100\pi_2 + 400\pi_3 + 800\pi_4 = 0(.2) + 100(.4) + 400(.2) + 800(.2)$$
$$= \$280 \text{ per day, on the average}$$

Doubly Stochastic Transition Matrix

It has already been shown that the sum of the transition probabilities in each row of the transition matrix is 1.0. If the *columns* also sum to 1.0, the transition matrix is said to be **doubly stochastic.**

For any doubly stochastic transition matrix in which the number of states is m, the steady-state vector of probabilities is given as

$$\pi_1, \pi_2, \pi_3, \ldots, \pi_m = \frac{1}{m}$$

For example, for the transition matrix

$$P = \begin{bmatrix} \frac{1}{2} & \frac{1}{4} & \frac{1}{4} \\ \frac{1}{4} & \frac{1}{2} & \frac{1}{4} \\ \frac{1}{4} & \frac{1}{4} & \frac{1}{2} \end{bmatrix}$$

where $m = 3$, the steady-state vector is immediately given by

$$\pi = [\pi_1, \pi_2, \pi_3] = \left[\frac{1}{m}, \frac{1}{m}, \frac{1}{m}\right] = \left[\frac{1}{3}, \frac{1}{3}, \frac{1}{3}\right]$$

Existence of Steady-State Conditions

A Markov chain process may not always reach steady state. However, it is possible to determine whether the process will go to steady state. If there is some n for which every element of P^n is greater than zero, then steady-state conditions exist. For example, consider the following transition matrix:

$$P = \begin{bmatrix} 0 & \frac{1}{3} & \frac{2}{3} \\ \frac{2}{3} & 0 & \frac{1}{3} \\ \frac{1}{3} & \frac{1}{3} & \frac{1}{3} \end{bmatrix}$$

Squaring P, we get

$$P^2 = \begin{bmatrix} \frac{4}{9} & \frac{2}{9} & \frac{3}{9} \\ \frac{1}{9} & \frac{3}{9} & \frac{5}{9} \\ \frac{3}{9} & \frac{2}{9} & \frac{4}{9} \end{bmatrix}$$

Since every element of P^n is positive for $n = 2$, we have determined that steady-state conditions do exist. When P^n, for some n, has all positive elements, the matrix is oftentimes referred to as a *regular* transition matrix.

SPECIAL CASES OF MARKOV PROCESSES

Absorbing States

A state is referred to as an **absorbing, or trapping, state** if it is impossible to leave that state. This will occur if any p_{ii} is equal to 1.0—that is, if any transition probability in the retention diagonal, from upper left to lower right, is equal to 1.0.

Further, a Markov chain is said to be absorbing if *any* state is absorbing and it is possible to go from each state to an absorbing state in a finite number of steps. Consider, for example, the following transition probability matrix:

$$P = \begin{array}{c} \\ A \\ B \\ C \end{array} \begin{array}{c} A \quad B \quad C \\ \left[\begin{array}{ccc} 1 & 0 & 0 \\ \frac{1}{2} & \frac{1}{4} & \frac{1}{4} \\ \frac{1}{3} & \frac{1}{3} & \frac{1}{3} \end{array} \right] \end{array}$$

Since $p_{11} = 1.0$, state A is an absorbing state. Also, the probabilities of going from B and C to A in a finite number of steps are positive. Therefore, the Markov chain is absorbing, and the steady-state conditions are $\pi = [1.0, 0, 0]$. Note that the steady-state conditions are not determined by the usual method in the case of the absorbing Markov chain. Rather, $\pi_i = 1.0$ for the i in which there is a trapping state, and $\pi_i = 0$ for all other i. If there is more than one trapping state, then a steady-state condition independent of initial state conditions does not exist.

Example 9.4 The Accounts Receivable Problem

A well-known example of Markov chains with absorbing states is the "accounts receivable" or "bad debt" example, which we will briefly review. In this example, a firm has developed the transition probability matrix given below, where the states are defined as follows:

State	Definition
a	Account paid
1	1 month past due
2	2 months past due
3	3 months past due
b	Bad debt

$$P = \begin{array}{c} \\ a \\ 1 \\ 2 \\ 3 \\ b \end{array} \begin{array}{c} a \quad\; 1 \quad\; 2 \quad\; 3 \quad\; b \\ \left[\begin{array}{ccccc} 1 & 0 & 0 & 0 & 0 \\ .60 & 0 & .40 & 0 & 0 \\ .75 & 0 & 0 & .25 & 0 \\ .50 & 0 & 0 & 0 & .50 \\ 0 & 0 & 0 & 0 & 1 \end{array} \right] \end{array}$$

A bad debt is labeled as such only after three months have passed and the account has not been paid. For example, if an account receivable is in month 2, there is a .75 probability it will be paid off in the next period and .25 probability it will still be unpaid in month 3. Since it is impossible for a bad debt to occur until three months have elapsed, there is a .0 probability of going to state b from the first and second months.

Much useful information can be obtained from this type of matrix configuration through several relatively simple matrix manipulations. (However, these manipulations do require a familiarity with matrix algebra, which is presented in Appendix A.) The first step is to change the matrix into general form as follows:

$$
P = \begin{array}{c} \\ a \\ b \\ 1 \\ 2 \\ 3 \end{array}
\begin{array}{c} \begin{array}{ccccccc} a & b & 1 & 2 & 3 \end{array} \\
\left[\begin{array}{ccc|ccc}
1 & 0 & 0 & 0 & 0 \\
0 & 1 & 0 & 0 & 0 \\
\hline
.60 & 0 & 0 & .40 & 0 \\
.75 & 0 & 0 & 0 & .25 \\
.50 & .50 & 0 & 0 & 0
\end{array} \right]
\end{array}
$$

Now four submatrices exist that are in the following general form:

$$
P = \left[\begin{array}{c|c} I & O \\ \hline R & Q \end{array} \right]
$$

where

I = identity matrix

O = matrix of zeros

R = matrix containing the transition probabilities of being absorbed in the next period

Q = square matrix containing transition probabilities for movement between all nonabsorbing states

The first matrix operation determines the **fundamental matrix, F,** which gives the expected number of times the system will be in any of the nonabsorbing states before absorption occurs (i.e., before the account is paid off or becomes a bad debt). The fundamental matrix is computed by taking the inverse of the difference between the identity matrix and Q,

$$
F = (I - Q)^{-1}
$$

where I is the identity matrix of the same magnitude as Q. For this example,

$$
F = \left(\begin{bmatrix} 1 & 0 & 0 \\ 0 & 1 & 0 \\ 0 & 0 & 1 \end{bmatrix} - \begin{bmatrix} 0 & .40 & 0 \\ 0 & 0 & .25 \\ 0 & 0 & 0 \end{bmatrix} \right)^{-1}
$$

$$
F = \begin{array}{c} \\ 1 \\ 2 \\ 3 \end{array}
\begin{array}{c} \begin{array}{ccc} 1 & 2 & 3 \end{array} \\
\left[\begin{array}{ccc}
1 & .40 & .10 \\
0 & 1 & .25 \\
0 & 0 & 1
\end{array} \right]
\end{array}
$$

Thus, according to the F matrix, if you are in state 1, the expected number of times you will occupy state 2 before the debt is paid off or becomes bad is .4.

The next matrix operation requires the multiplication of F and R.

$$
F \cdot R = \begin{array}{c} \\ 1 \\ 2 \\ 3 \end{array}
\begin{array}{c} \begin{array}{ccc} 1 & 2 & 3 \end{array} \\ \left[\begin{array}{ccc} 1 & .40 & .10 \\ 0 & 1 & .25 \\ 0 & 0 & 1 \end{array} \right] \end{array}
\begin{array}{c} \begin{array}{cc} a & b \end{array} \\ \begin{array}{c} 1 \\ \cdot 2 \\ 3 \end{array} \left[\begin{array}{cc} .60 & 0 \\ .75 & 0 \\ .50 & .50 \end{array} \right] \end{array}
= \begin{array}{c} \\ 1 \\ 2 \\ 3 \end{array}
\begin{array}{c} \begin{array}{cc} a & b \end{array} \\ \left[\begin{array}{cc} .95 & .05 \\ .875 & .125 \\ .50 & .50 \end{array} \right] \end{array}
$$

The $F \cdot R$ matrix reflects the probability of eventually being absorbed, given any starting state. For example, if the account is presently in the second month, there is a .875 probability that it will eventually be paid and a .125 probability that it will result in a bad debt.

If the original P matrix is carried to the second and third power, further information can be obtained.

$$
P^2 = \begin{array}{c} a \\ b \\ 1 \\ 2 \\ 3 \end{array}
\begin{array}{c} \begin{array}{ccccc} a & b & 1 & 2 & 3 \end{array} \\ \left[\begin{array}{ccccc} 1 & 0 & 0 & 0 & 0 \\ 0 & 1 & 0 & 0 & 0 \\ .90 & 0 & 0 & 0 & .10 \\ .875 & .125 & 0 & 0 & 0 \\ .50 & .50 & 0 & 0 & 0 \end{array} \right] \end{array}
, \quad
P^3 = \begin{array}{c} a \\ b \\ 1 \\ 2 \\ 3 \end{array}
\begin{array}{c} \begin{array}{ccccc} a & b & 1 & 2 & 3 \end{array} \\ \left[\begin{array}{ccccc} 1 & 0 & 0 & 0 & 0 \\ 0 & 1 & 0 & 0 & 0 \\ .95 & .05 & 0 & 0 & 0 \\ .875 & .125 & 0 & 0 & 0 \\ .50 & .50 & 0 & 0 & 0 \end{array} \right] \end{array}
$$

Notice that the R matrix changes at each step from P to P^3. This change represents the change in flow of funds from month to month. Thus, the flow of funds (the percentage of paid accounts or of bad debts) in each month can be determined by subtracting the R matrices for each period as follows:

$$
\Delta R_1 = R_1 - R_0 = \left[\begin{array}{cc} .60 & 0 \\ .75 & 0 \\ .50 & .50 \end{array} \right] - \left[\begin{array}{cc} 0 & 0 \\ 0 & 0 \\ 0 & 0 \end{array} \right] = \left[\begin{array}{cc} .60 & 0 \\ .75 & 0 \\ .50 & .50 \end{array} \right]
$$

$$
\Delta R_2 = R_2 - R_1 = \left[\begin{array}{cc} .90 & 0 \\ .875 & .125 \\ .50 & .50 \end{array} \right] - \left[\begin{array}{cc} .60 & 0 \\ .75 & 0 \\ .50 & .50 \end{array} \right] = \left[\begin{array}{cc} .30 & 0 \\ .125 & .125 \\ 0 & 0 \end{array} \right]
$$

$$
\Delta R_3 = R_3 - R_2 = \left[\begin{array}{cc} .95 & .05 \\ .875 & .125 \\ .50 & .50 \end{array} \right] - \left[\begin{array}{cc} .90 & 0 \\ .875 & .125 \\ .50 & .50 \end{array} \right] = \left[\begin{array}{cc} .05 & .05 \\ 0 & 0 \\ 0 & 0 \end{array} \right]
$$

Each of these ΔR matrices represents the change in cash flow from period to period. For example, ΔR_2 indicates that if the account is in month 2, then .125 of the funds will be paid and .125 will become bad debts. Let us assume that the account books show accounts receivable as

One month	$1000
Two months	800
Three months	200

If we transform these data into a **status vector, s,**

$$s = [1000, 800, 200]$$

we can determine that portion of the $2000 total flowing in during each of the three months. This is achieved by multiplying the status vector by each ΔR matrix as follows:

$$s\Delta R_1 = [1000, 800, 200] \cdot \begin{bmatrix} .60 & 0 \\ .75 & 0 \\ .50 & .50 \end{bmatrix} = \begin{matrix} a & b \\ [1300, & 100] \end{matrix}$$

$$s\Delta R_2 = [1000, 800, 200] \cdot \begin{bmatrix} .30 & 0 \\ .125 & .125 \\ 0 & 0 \end{bmatrix} = \begin{matrix} a & b \\ [400, & 100] \end{matrix}$$

$$s\Delta R_3 = [1000, 800, 200] \cdot \begin{bmatrix} .05 & .05 \\ 0 & 0 \\ 0 & 0 \end{bmatrix} = \begin{matrix} a & b \\ [50, & 50] \end{matrix}$$

This information provides an accounts schedule for the three-month period, showing for each period the amount that will be paid and the amount that will become bad debts. For example, of the $2000 total on the books, $1300 will be paid in month 1, while $100 will become a bad debt; $400 will be paid in month 2, while $100 will become a bad debt; and $50 will be paid in month 3, while $50 will become a bad debt.

Transient State

A state is said to be **transient** if it is impossible to move to that state from any other state except itself. For example, in the following transition matrix, state B is a transient state.

$$P = \begin{array}{c} \\ A \\ B \\ C \end{array} \begin{array}{ccc} A & B & C \\ \begin{bmatrix} \frac{3}{4} & 0 & \frac{1}{4} \\ \frac{1}{5} & \frac{3}{5} & \frac{1}{5} \\ \frac{1}{3} & 0 & \frac{2}{3} \end{bmatrix} \end{array}$$

Eventually all movement will be away from state B, and π_2 will equal 0.

For the case in which there is a transient state, the steady-state probabilities can be computed by the usual method, after the zero-value state (i.e., $\pi_2 = 0$ in this case) is first eliminated from consideration. Thus, for the example given, the steady-state probabilities can be computed by simultaneously solving the following equations:

$$\pi_1 = \frac{3}{4}\pi_1 + \frac{1}{3}\pi_3$$
$$\pi_3 = \frac{1}{4}\pi_1 + \frac{2}{3}\pi_3$$
$$\pi_1 + \pi_2 + \pi_3 = 1.0$$

The reader may verify that the steady-state conditions are $\pi = [\frac{4}{7}, 0, \frac{3}{7}]$.

In the accounts receivable example for absorbing states, all nonabsorbing states (i.e., states 1, 2, and 3) are transient states, since eventually all movement will be toward absorption and away from these states.

Cycling Processes

A **cycling**, or **periodic**, Markov process is characterized by all zeros in retention cells (retention cells are in the diagonal from upper left to lower right) and all ones or zeros in nonretention cells of the transition matrix. For example, the following transition matrices exhibit cycling behavior.

$$
P_x = \begin{array}{c} \\ A \\ B \end{array} \begin{array}{c} \begin{array}{cc} A & B \end{array} \\ \begin{bmatrix} 0 & 1 \\ 1 & 0 \end{bmatrix} \end{array}
\qquad
P_y = \begin{array}{c} \\ A \\ B \\ C \end{array} \begin{array}{c} \begin{array}{ccc} A & B & C \end{array} \\ \begin{bmatrix} 0 & 1 & 0 \\ 0 & 0 & 1 \\ 1 & 0 & 0 \end{bmatrix} \end{array}
\qquad
P_z = \begin{array}{c} \\ A \\ B \\ C \\ D \end{array} \begin{array}{c} \begin{array}{cccc} A & B & C & D \end{array} \\ \begin{bmatrix} 0 & 1 & 0 & 0 \\ 0 & 0 & 1 & 0 \\ 0 & 0 & 0 & 1 \\ 1 & 0 & 0 & 0 \end{bmatrix} \end{array}
$$

If we consider P_y, it is apparent that the system will move sequentially from A to B to C to A and so on. Thus, there can be no steady-state conditions for a cycling Markov process.

It is important to note that the process is not cycling unless all nonretention cells of the transition matrix are 1.0 or 0. Stated another way, if any one of the retention cells of the transition matrix is positive, the process is not a cycling process. For example, the following transition matrix is not cycling:

$$
P = \begin{array}{c} \\ A \\ B \\ C \end{array} \begin{array}{c} \begin{array}{ccc} A & B & C \end{array} \\ \begin{bmatrix} 0 & 1 & 0 \\ 0 & 0 & 1 \\ \frac{1}{3} & \frac{1}{3} & \frac{1}{3} \end{bmatrix} \end{array}
$$

Using the standard process, we can determine the steady-state conditions as $\pi = [\frac{1}{6}, \frac{1}{3}, \frac{1}{2}]$.

Recurrent Sets

A Markov chain may trap the process within a *set* of states. The concept is similar to the preceding absorbing state, except that the trap involves more than one state. A recurrent set containing several states is often referred to as a **generalized trapping state**.

Consider the following transition matrix:

$$
P = \begin{array}{c} \\ A \\ B \\ C \\ D \end{array} \begin{array}{c} \begin{array}{cccc} A & B & C & D \end{array} \\ \begin{bmatrix} \frac{3}{4} & \frac{1}{4} & 0 & 0 \\ \frac{1}{2} & \frac{1}{2} & 0 & 0 \\ 0 & 0 & \frac{2}{3} & \frac{1}{3} \\ 0 & 0 & \frac{1}{5} & \frac{4}{5} \end{bmatrix} \end{array}
$$

It is apparent that the system is trapped either in states A and B or in states C and D. Thus, the system has two recurrent sets. Since the long-term behavior of the system is dependent on the starting point, there can be no steady-state solution.

Consider the following system with one recurrent set:

$$
P = \begin{array}{c} \\ A \\ B \\ C \\ D \end{array} \begin{array}{c} \begin{array}{cccc} A & B & C & D \end{array} \\ \begin{bmatrix} \frac{3}{4} & \frac{1}{4} & 0 & 0 \\ \frac{1}{2} & \frac{1}{2} & 0 & 0 \\ 0 & \frac{1}{3} & \frac{1}{3} & \frac{1}{3} \\ 0 & 0 & \frac{1}{5} & \frac{4}{5} \end{bmatrix} \end{array}
$$

Once the system reaches either state A or state B, it remains in one or the other of those states. However, since the system can reach state A or B in a finite number of steps (note that $p_{32} = \frac{1}{3}$), there is only one recurrent set and the steady-state solution can be

An Application of Markov Analysis: Graduate Student Admissions

The Department of Educational Administration at the University of Texas at Austin admitted students to its doctoral program without any enrollment limitations or policy. Enrollment was primarily a function of recruiting success and funds available to support graduate students. However, enrollment trends changed when the department expanded to encompass two new programs and acquired a major foundation grant. In addition, the public school work force appeared to be changing, a factor that could affect student recruiting and shift students away from jobs in public schools and into doctoral programs. Because of these changes, the department wanted to know if the number of students admitted would create an undesirable dissertation load for supervising professors in the future.

A Markov model was developed to help determine the answer to this question. The model consisted of five states, including one absorbing state for graduation. (An absorbing state for forced withdrawal and no return was not

obtained. This is accomplished by observing that in the long run π_3 and π_4 must eventually go to zero. (Note the $\frac{1}{5}$ probability that D will go to C and the $\frac{1}{8}$ probability that C will go to B, from which there is no return to C or D.) Thus, the steady-state conditions are $\pi_1 = \frac{2}{3}$, $\pi_2 = \frac{1}{3}$, $\pi_3 = 0$, and $\pi_4 = 0$, where π_1 and π_2 are computed by the usual method.

As a final example, consider the following transition matrix:

$$P = \begin{array}{c} \\ A \\ B \\ C \end{array} \begin{array}{c} \begin{array}{ccc} A & B & C \end{array} \\ \left[\begin{array}{ccc} 0 & 1 & 0 \\ 1 & 0 & 0 \\ 0 & 0 & 1 \end{array} \right] \end{array}$$

Here we have two recurrent sets, where the system is trapped in A or B or it is trapped in C. Since C is a single absorbing state, the Markov process is an absorbing system. Notice that the recurrent set, which includes A and B, is also a cycling set. Thus, the system outcome is completely dependent on the starting conditions. If the starting condition is state C, the system is trapped in C. If the starting condition is A or B, the system is trapped in A or B and cycles between the two states.

SUMMARY In this chapter, a special class of stochastic processes, called Markov chains, was presented. The fundamental concepts and properties of Markov analysis were discussed, and several examples of the types of problems to which Markov analysis can be applied were presented. The study of Markov models provides valuable insight into the analysis of problems that have several potential outcomes after the passage of periods of time. It should be emphasized that Markov models are *descriptive* models, as opposed to optimization models or methods, and, as such, they are used to predict the system status at future points in time and the expected steady state.

included, since historical data showed a low incidence of this occurrence.) The remaining four states were "enrolled," "withdrawn," "advanced to doctoral candidacy," and "not advanced." Transition probabilities defined the probability of a student's moving from state to state during a semester. The Markov analysis indicated the mean number of semesters that a student in the doctoral program would be in a given state prior to graduation. It was determined that a small increase in student enrollment (i.e., two students) had a significant impact on faculty loads at the dissertation stage. However, the lead time provided by the analysis enabled the department to control the effects of adding students. The analysis further led to a set of decision rules that specified the maximum average number of dissertations per faculty member; the faculty positions required before new programs could be accepted; and the amount of time it would take for imbalances in dissertation load to develop if the number of faculty members decreased.

Source: E. Bessent and A. Bessent, "Student Flow in a University Department: Results of a Markov Analysis," *Interfaces,* 10, no. 2 (April 1980): 52–59.

REFERENCES

BHAT, U. N. *Elements of Applied Stochastic Processes.* 2d ed. New York: John Wiley & Sons, 1984.

CLARK, A. B., and DISNEY, R. L. *Probability and Random Processes for Engineers and Scientists.* New York: John Wiley & Sons, 1970.

FELLER, W. *An Introduction to Probability Theory and Its Applications,* Vol. 1. 3d ed. New York: John Wiley & Sons, 1968.

HOEL, P. G.; PORT, S. C.; and STONE, C. J. *Introduction to Stochastic Processes.* Boston: Houghton Mifflin Company, 1972.

HOWARD, R. A. *Dynamic Programming and Markov Processes.* Cambridge: M.I.T. Press, 1960.

KEMENY, J. G., and SNELL, J. L. *Finite Markov Chains.* Princeton, New Jersey: D. Van Nostrand Company, 1960.

MARTIN, J. J. *Bayesian Decision Problems and Markov Chains.* New York: John Wiley & Sons, 1967.

PARZEN, E. *Stochastic Processes.* San Francisco: Holden-Day, 1962.

SEARLE, S. R., and HAUSMAN, W. H. *Matrix Algebra for Business and Economics.* New York: John Wiley & Sons, 1970.

PROBLEMS

1. Would you classify Markov chain models as deterministic or probabilistic models? Discuss the basis for your answer.

2. A Markov process is dependent on how many previous states?

3. What are the major elements of a Markov process model? Describe each component.

4. A city has two newspapers, the *Morning Herald* and the *Evening Tribune*. At present, each of the two newspapers sell 16,000 of its Sunday edition at newspaper stands around the city. The population of the city is relatively stable, so the newspapers expect the newsstand sales of their Sunday editions to be constant during the next

few years. A market-research study by an independent advertising agency has resulted in the following probability transition matrix for customer purchases of Sunday newspapers from week to week.

	Week $n + 1$	
Week n	Morning Herald	Evening Tribune
Morning Herald	.45	.55
Evening Tribune	.35	.65

Determine the steady-state probabilities and sales of each newspaper.

5. Two firms share the market for a particular product. Firm A is an old and well-established firm, whereas firm B is a new and aggressive competitor. Firm A is alarmed at the progress being made by firm B and has asked its market-research department for a forecast of future market shares for the two firms, assuming that the same market conditions prevail. The current market shares held by the two firms are as follows:

Firm	Market Share
A	80%
B	20%

The market-research department has determined that customers switch between the two firms according to the following probabilities:

	To Firm	
From Firm	A	B
A	.5	.5
B	.6	.4

a. Determine the market-research department's market-share forecast for one period in the future, two periods in the future, and three periods in the future.

b. Based on the results of part a, estimate the equilibrium market share for each firm (rounded to the nearest whole percentage).

c. Illustrate customer switching between the two firms as a Markov transition probability diagram (see Figure 9.1).

6. What is meant by *steady state,* or *equilibrium,* in Markov analysis?

7. Assume that a manufacturing firm wishes to predict the status of machine operations in the future. Through historical records, the firm has determined that if a machine breaks down in a particular week, the probability of breakdown in the following week, after repair, is only .2. However, if a machine has not broken down in a particular week, the probability of breakdown in the following week is .6. The firm has therefore developed the following probability table of machine breakdowns:

Week *n* Status	Week *n* + 1 Status	
	No breakdown	Breakdown
No breakdown	.4	.6
Breakdown	.8	.2

a. Assuming that the machine is not broken down in week *n*, what are the probabilities that the machine will break down in weeks *n* + 1, *n* + 2, *n* + 3, *n* + 4, and *n* + 5?

b. Determine the steady-state condition—that is, forecast the percentage of future weeks in which the machine will break down.

8. A department store is interested in predicting the behavior of customers for which accounts receivable are outstanding. Its credit department has been asked to analyze its records and predict payment probabilities. Historical records have yielded the following payment patterns of credit customers:

Month *n*	Month *n* + 1	
	Paid bill	Did not pay bill
Paid bill	.90	.10
Did not pay bill	.80	.20

Assume that these probabilities are used to predict the behavior of a credit customer with regard to bill payment.

a. If a credit customer did not pay his bill in month *n*, what is the probability he will not pay it in any of the next three months?

b. If a customer did not pay his bill in month *n*, what are the probabilities he will pay his bill in month *n* + 1, in month *n* + 2, and in month *n* + 3? (Note: Assume that monthly bills include purchases made in that month plus any outstanding balance from previously unpaid bills.)

c. Determine the steady-state conditions—that is, the probability the customer will pay a bill or not pay a bill in month *n* + 1, regardless of whether he paid in month *n*.

9. Now assume in problem 4 that the *Morning Herald* is considering a promotional campaign that it estimates will change the transition probability matrix to

Week *n*	Week *n* + 1	
	Morning Herald	*Evening Tribune*
Morning Herald	.60	.40
Evening Tribune	.50	.50

The promotional campaign will cost $300 per week. Each newspaper sold earns the *Morning Herald* $.17 in profit (not including the cost of the promotional campaign). Should the paper promotional campaign be adopted? In other words, will the increase in profit per week offset the weekly promotional cost?

10. Describe and illustrate a state vector of Markov analysis.

11. Describe and illustrate a transition matrix of Markov analysis.

12. Given the following transition matrix for a three-state system, algebraically determine the steady-state conditions.

	1	2	3
1	.6	.2	.2
2	.4	.3	.3
3	.1	.5	.4

13. In a small, rather isolated rural town, virtually all shopping and mercantile business is done in town. The town has one farm and garden center that sells fertilizer to the local farmers and gardeners. The garden center has 9000 customers for fertilizer, and each customer will purchase one of the three available brands of fertilizer: Plant Plus, Crop Extra, and Gro-Fast. An extensive market-research study has determined that customers switch brands of fertilizer according to the following probability transition matrix.

		To	
From	Plant Plus	Crop Extra	Gro-Fast
Plant Plus	.4	.3	.3
Crop Extra	.5	.1	.4
Gro-Fast	.4	.2	.4

Presently, the number of customers who use each brand of fertilizer is

Fertilizer Brand	Customers
Plant Plus	3000
Crop Extra	4000
Gro-Fast	2000

a. Determine the steady-state probabilities for the fertilizer brands.

b. Forecast the customer demand for each brand of fertilizer in the long-run future and the changes in customer demand.

14. Students switch among the various colleges of a university according to the following probability transition matrix.

		To	
From	Engineering	Liberal Arts	Business
Engineering	.5	.3	.2
Liberal Arts	.1	.7	.2
Business	.1	.1	.8

Assume that the number of students in each college of the university at the beginning of the fall quarter is as follows:

Engineering   3000
Liberal
Arts   5000
Business   2000

a. Forecast the number of students in each college after the end of the third quarter, based on a four-quarter system. Determine by first computing P''.
b. Determine the steady-state conditions for the university.

Determine the steady-state conditions.

15. A truck rental firm in the Southeast serves three states—Virginia, North Carolina, and Maryland. The firm has 700 trucks that are rented on a weekly basis; the trucks can be rented and returned in any of the three states. The transition matrix for the movement of rental trucks from state to state is as follows:

| | | Week $n + 1$ | |
Week n	Virginia	North Carolina	Maryland
Virginia	.30	.50	.20
North Carolina	.60	.20	.20
Maryland	.40	.10	.50

Determine the steady-state probabilities and the number of trucks in each state in the long run.

16. Assume that the Commerce Union Bank in Example 9.2 of this chapter is considering an advertising campaign that will alter the probability transition matrix in its favor as follows:

| | To Bank | | |
From Bank	A	B	C
A	.7	.1	.2
B	.1	.5	.4
C	.1	.1	.8

The advertising campaign will cost the bank $15,000 per three-month time period, and every new customer the bank gains will result in a three-month profit of $25. Determine whether or not the advertising campaign should be initiated. Your answer should depend on whether the profit gained per time period will be greater or less than the promotional cost per time period.

17. Describe the meaning of *absorbing*, or *trapping, states* in Markov chains. Give an example.

18. What is meant by *transient states* in Markov chains? Give an example.

19. The company that operates the machine in Example 9.1 has determined that it earns an average of $3000 per day from the production of the machine when the machine is in operation. When the machine is broken down, the company experiences a daily average penalty cost of $2000 because of late deliveries of products and also an average daily repair cost of $1500. Determine the steady-state conditions for the machine problem and the long-run expected average daily return associated with the machine.

20. Refer to Example 9.3, in which repair was performed only when the copy machine reached state 4, unacceptable quality. The result was a long-run expected average daily cost of $280, which included costs of rerunning poor copies, refunds to dissatisfied customers, repair cost, and downtime during repairs. Assume that the owner of the copy center wishes also to consider a policy of performing minor repairs on the machine when it reaches state 3, significant deterioration in quality, so that it returns to state 2, some deterioration in quality. Recall that the major repair conducted when the machine reached state 4 returned the machine to state 1, excellent condition. Thus, the transition matrix for the revised machine repair policy would be as follows:

| | | To State | | |
From State	1	2	3	4
1	0	.8	.1	.1
2	0	.6	.2	.2
3	0	1	0	0
4	1	0	0	0

The expected cost associated with the minor repairs, including labor, parts, and a brief downtime, is $200. Given the expected cost per day for machine states 1, 2, and 4, as previously given in Example 9.2, determine the long-run steady-state conditions and expected long-run average daily costs for the revised policy. Should the copy center owner implement the revised policy or the policy of Example 9.3?

21. Referring to problem 20, assume that the copy center owner wishes to explore the possible policy of performing a complete repair when the machine reaches state 3, which would return the machine to state 1, excellent condition. Thus, the same repair policy would be used for state 3, significant deterioration, as is used for state 4, unacceptable quality. The expected daily costs associated with a state 3 complete repair would be $800, the same as for the state 4 complete repair. Determine the steady-state conditions and compute the long-run expected daily cost of this possible policy. Compare the expected cost of the solution to this problem with that of the solution to problem 20 and the Example 9.3 cost, and indicate the best policy for the owner to follow.

22. Assume that the transition probability matrix for Example 9.2 of this chapter is given by the table on page 461. The steady-state probabilities can be immediately determined. What are they, and why can they be easily determined?

	To Brand		
From Brand	A	B	C
A	.7	.2	.1
B	.1	.5	.4
C	.2	.3	.5

23. Suppose the transition matrix for Example 9.2 is as follows:
    What will happen in this case? What type of process is represented?

	To Brand		
From Brand	A	B	C
A	.8	.1	.1
B	0	1.0	0
C	.1	.3	.6

24. Assume that the transition matrix for Example 9.2 is as follows:
    Determine the steady-state solution. What general type of process is illustrated?

	To Brand		
From Brand	A	B	C
A	.8	.2	0
B	.1	.7	.2
C	.4	.6	0

25. The weather service has determined the following transition probabilities for air pollution movement:

Day *n*	Day *n* + 1		
	Clean	Average	Polluted
Clean	.3	.6	.1
Average	.3	.5	.2
Polluted	.1	.7	.2

    a. Determine the steady-state probabilities for each pollution state.
    b. During a year, how many days will the air be in code state (polluted)?

26. A firm has developed the transition probability matrix given on page 462 for its accounts receivable. The states in this matrix are the months of an outstanding debt. P is a state indicating the debt has been paid, and B is a state indicating the debt has been classified as bad.

	P	1	2	3	B
P	1	0	0	0	0
1	.3	0	.7	0	0
2	.5	0	0	.5	0
3	.6	0	0	0	.4
B	0	0	0	0	1

  a. For each starting state in month 1, determine the probability that a debt will eventually be paid or be classified as bad.

  b. If the firm's books presently have accounts receivable defined by the status vector

$$s = [\$5000, \$3000, \$2000]$$

determine the cash flow for each month.

27. When freshmen at Tech attend orientation, the university's president tells each freshman that one of the two adjacent students will not graduate. The freshmen interpret this as meaning that two-thirds of the entering freshmen will graduate. The following transition probabilities have been developed from data gathered by Tech's registrar. They show the probability of a student moving from one class to the next during an academic year and eventually graduating or dropping out.

	F	So	J	Sr	D	G
F	.10	.70	0	0	.20	0
So	0	.10	.80	0	.10	0
J	0	0	.15	.75	.10	0
Sr	0	0	0	.15	.05	.80
D	0	0	0	0	1	0
G	0	0	0	0	0	1

  a. Is the president's remark during orientation accurate?

  b. What is the probability that a freshman will eventually drop out?

  c. How many years can an entering freshman expect to remain at Tech?

28. Three faculty ranks exist at Tech: assistant professor, associate professor, and full professor. Each year faculty are evaluated and will either stay at their current rank, be promoted to the next rank, or leave. The transition matrix for the movement of faculty on an annual basis is as follows:

	Assistant	Associate	Full	Leave as A/A	Leave as Full
Assistant	.80	.15	0	.05	0
Associate	0	.70	.20	.10	0
Full	0	0	.95	0	.05
Leave as A/A	0	0	0	1	0
Leave as Full	0	0	0	0	1

The transition probabilities reflect the probability of staying at the same rank, or moving from one rank to another, or leaving while still an assistant or associate professor, or leaving as a full professor.

a. What is the probability that a new assistant professor will eventually become a full professor?
b. What is the average length of time that a new assistant professor spends at Tech?
c. What is the average length of time a full professor will remain at Tech as a full professor?

-10

Queuing Theory

Waiting in line is one of the most common occurrences of everyday life. No doubt, you can recall having waited in line during college registration, to check out at a grocery store, to make a deposit or withdrawal at a bank, for service at a hamburger stand, to pay at a toll bridge, for service at a gas station, and in numerous other situations. Waiting lines, often referred to as **queues,** can consist of people, automobiles, equipment, or other units awaiting service. Table 10.1 summarizes several instances of commonly recognized queuing situations.

The study of waiting lines, known as **queuing theory,** is far from new. Queuing theory can be traced back to the classic work of A. K. Erlang, a Danish mathematician, who studied the fluctuating demands on telephone facilities and associated service delays.

Table 10.1 *Commonly Recognized Waiting Line Situations*

Situation	Arrivals	Servers	Service Process
School registration	Students	Registration desk	Course assigned and forms signed
Grocery store	Customers	Checkout counter	Bill computation and payment
Bank	Customers	Teller	Deposit, withdrawal, check cashed
Traffic intersection	Automobiles	Traffic light	Controlled passage through intersection
Doctor's office	Patients	Doctor and staff	Treatment
Machine maintenance	Machine breakdown	Repairpeople	Machine repair
Shipping terminal	Trucks	Docks	Unloading and loading
Assembly line	Product components	Assembly workers	Product assembly
Mail-order store	Mail orders	Mail-order clerks	Processing and mailing products ordered
Telephone exchange	Calls	Electronic switching equipment	Complete connection
Air terminal	Airplanes	Runways	Airplanes landing and taking off
Tool crib	Workers	Tool attendants	Check out or check in of tools

Erlang's work was first published in 1913 under the title *Solution of Some Problems in the Theory of Probabilities of Significance in Automatic Telephone Exchanges*. Thus, waiting line analysis represents one of the oldest of the various topical areas considered in management science.

Waiting lines may exist in the form of observable lines of individuals or objects waiting for service, or they may occur in a more abstract sense, as when machines break down in a factory and must wait for repair. Often customers enter a shoe store or ice cream parlor and take a number, indicating their turn for service, and then browse around the store to inspect the items for sale. This, nevertheless, represents a queuing process.

BASIC COMPONENTS OF A WAITING LINE PROCESS

The basic components of a waiting line process are **arrivals, servers,** and **waiting lines** (queues). These components are illustrated graphically in Figure 10.1.

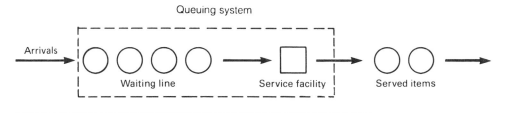

Figure 10.1 *Basic Components of a Waiting Line Process*

Arrivals

Every queuing problem involves the arrival of items, such as customers, equipment, or telephone calls, for service. This element of the queuing process is often referred to as the **input process.** The input process includes the *source* of arrivals, commonly referred to as the **calling population,** and the *manner* in which arrivals occur, which is generally a random process. As you will see later in this chapter, a precise description of the input process is required in order to analyze the overall queuing problem.

Servers

Equally important in the description of a queuing process are the servers, otherwise referred to as the **service mechanism.** The service mechanism may involve one or more servers, or one or more service facilities. For example, a shoe store may have several sales personnel, or a toll road may have several toll gates. The service mechanism may simply consist of a single server in a single facility, such as the ticket sales person selling seats for a movie. In addition to a precise description of the service mechanism in terms of the number and configuration of servers, there must be a description of the manner in which services are completed, which is often a random process.

Queues

The focal point of waiting line analysis is, of course, the waiting line itself. The extent to which queues exist depends primarily on the nature of the arrival and service processes. However, another important determinant of the nature of the waiting line is the **queue discipline.** The queue discipline is the decision rule that prescribes the order in which items in the queue will be served (i.e., first-come, first-served; last-come, first-served; or some other priority rule). Of course, if waiting lines do not exist, this also has important implications for the queuing analysis, since it implies idle servers or excess service capacity.

BASIC STRUCTURES OF WAITING LINE PROCESSES

Waiting line processes are generally categorized into four basic structures, according to the nature of the service facilities: (A) single-channel, single-phase; (B) multiple-channel, single-phase; (C) single-channel, multiple-phase; and (D) multiple-channel, multiple-phase. Each of the four categories of queuing processes is illustrated graphically in Figure 10.2.

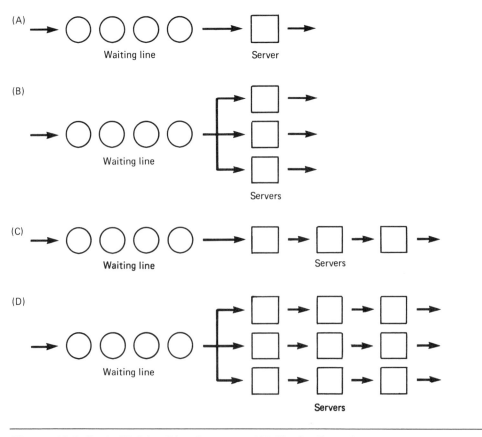

Figure 10.2 Basic Waiting Line Structures: (A) Single-Channel, Single-Phase; (B) Multiple-Channel, Single-Phase; (C) Single-Channel, Multiple-Phase; (D) Multiple-Channel, Multiple-Phase

The number of channels in a queuing process is simply the number of parallel servers for servicing arrivals. The number of phases, on the other hand, denotes the number of sequential servers each customer must go through in order to complete service. An example of a single-channel, single-phase queuing operation would be a post office with only one postal clerk waiting on customers. A post office with several postal clerks waiting on customers would be an example of a multiple-channel, single-phase operation.

When patients go to a doctor for treatment, they often wait in a reception room prior to entering the treatment facility. Then, upon being seated in the treatment room, the patients often receive an initial checkup or treatment from the hygienist, followed by treatment from the doctor. This sort of arrangement constitutes a single-channel, multiple-phase queuing process. If there are several doctors and assistants, the process is multiple-channel, multiple-phase.

The reader may immediately visualize a familiar waiting situation that fits none of the previous categories of waiting line processes. This is expected. The four categories of queuing processes presented are simply the four *basic* categories. Numerous variations can be described. For example, rather than a single queue preceding the multiple-channel, single-phase case, there might be a separate queue preceding each server. This occurs, for example, in grocery stores, banks, and department stores. Also, in the multiple-phase cases, queues may or may not build up prior to each of the secondary server locations, such as the inspection station in a manufacturing job shop operation. In the multiple-channel, multiple-phase case, items might switch back and forth from one channel to the other, between each of the various service phases. It is readily apparent that queuing models can become quite complex. However, the fundamentals of basic queuing theory are relevant to the analysis of all queuing problems, regardless of their complexity. These fundamentals will be the subject of this chapter.

Example 10.1 A Bank's Drive-In Teller

The following example of a waiting line situation is presented to highlight the basic process involved. A bank has one drive-in teller window, at which customers may make deposits, cash checks, and conduct other miscellaneous bank business. The bank opens for service at 9:00 A.M. Customers arrive in their automobiles for service at random intervals. The time required to service each customer is also a random variable. Of course, customers are served on a first-come, first-served basis. The process is reflected in Table 10.2 (p. 468), which describes the first hour of operation at the bank drive-in window.

Table 10.2 indicates that service begins upon each customer's arrival only if no earlier customer is currently being serviced. Otherwise, a waiting line forms and later customers must wait for service. This example suggests some immediate questions for consideration. Is a (worst case) customer waiting time of 11 minutes acceptable? Such an extensive waiting time at a bank drive-in window could result in highly dissatisfied customers and possibly the loss of their business. Is a queue length of up to 4 customers acceptable? The driveway preceding the service window can accommodate only a few automobiles. Customers may balk at seeing a long waiting line and simply refuse to enter the service queue. This also may result in temporarily or permanently lost business. Does the small amount of server idle time imply that the teller is overworked and another drive-in teller is needed, or is the teller simply too slow because of inexperience?

Table 10.2 *Drive-in Teller Waiting Line and Service Process*

Time of Customer Arrival (Random)	Time Service Begins (t_B)	Service Time Required (Random)	Time Service Ends (t_E)	Customer Waiting Time (at t_B)	Server Idle Time (at t_B)	Number of Customers Waiting (at t_E)
9:05 A.M.	9:05 A.M.	4 min.	9:09 A.M.	0 min.	5 min.	2
9:06	9:09	3	9:12	3	0	1
9:08	9:12	5	9:17	4	0	0
9:20	9:20	4	9:24	0	3	2
9:22	9:24	2	9:26	2	0	1
9:23	9:26	1	9:27	3	0	0
9:30	9:30	8	9:38	0	3	3
9:32	9:38	3	9:41	6	0	3
9:33	9:41	4	9:45	8	0	3
9:37	9:45	2	9:47	8	0	4
9:40	9:47	1	9:48	7	0	2
9:41	9:48	7	9:55	7	0	1
9:44	9:55	4	9:59	11	0	0
9:59	9:59	2	10:01	0	0	0
Totals				59	11	22
Averages				4.2 min	18%	1.57 customers

Questions such as the ones presented in the previous paragraph require a formal framework for analysis. The following section presents a general decision framework for waiting line problems.

DECISION FRAMEWORK FOR WAITING LINE PROBLEMS

There is no unified body of knowledge regarding the optimization of waiting line problems, as there is with linear programming or inventory theory. Thus, most texts on queuing theory simply emphasize the development of the queuing system's **operating characteristics.** Operating characteristics describe the performance of the system in the form of such measures as expected customer waiting time and percent server idle time. However, the measures of the system's performance are actually only inputs into a broader conceptual framework, within which most waiting line problems can be analyzed.

Most analyses of waiting line problems eventually reduce to the question of what level of service should be provided—what service capacity should be provided or how many servers are needed. If the decision variable is to be level of service, then the model must formally identify the relationship of level of service to other relevant parameters and variables. The criterion by which this decision model is evaluated is total expected cost.

The general relationship of the decision variable, level of service, to the evaluation criterion, total expected cost, is shown graphically in Figure 10.3. It can be seen that total expected cost is the sum of two separate costs: (1) service cost and (2) waiting cost.

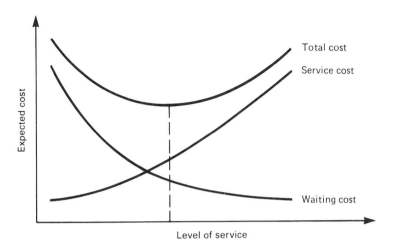

Figure 10.3 *Decision Model for Waiting Line Analysis*

Service Cost

As the level of service is increased, the related service cost will increase. For example, if two dock workers, instead of one, unload trucks at a warehouse depot, cost is increased by the amount of the second worker's wages. The exact shape of the function relating service level to service cost must be determined for each individual case being analyzed.

Another way of including service cost in the analysis of waiting line problems is to include only the cost of server idle time. As the level of service is increased, server idle time is also expected to increase. Either approach to including service-related cost should normally yield the same results. The decision maker might desire to use some value other than the server's wages to measure the unit cost of increased service level. If only server idle time is considered, the opportunity cost of not allocating the server to alternative productive activities can be used, rather than server wages. A case can be made for considering service-related cost in either of the two ways discussed.

Waiting Cost

Although there is generally an inverse relationship between service level and expected customer waiting time, it is difficult to arrive at an explicit statement of waiting cost per unit waiting time. Thus, this question is often ignored in the literature of queuing theory. The system's operating characteristics are simply presented, with the ultimate decision analysis left up to the individual manager. However, since the decision must ultimately rest on relating waiting time to service level, even if no waiting cost is specified, it is implicitly included in the analysis.

Waiting cost can be simply an estimate of the cost of business lost when customers become impatient and leave the place of service because of excessive waiting time. This cost may represent the cost of lost profit on a one-time basis, or it may reflect the long-term cost of permanently losing customers. If the waiting situation occurs internally in an organization, such as when manufacturing workers must wait for parts at a parts department, the cost of waiting should reflect the cost of lost productivity of the worker during the waiting time. Also, the cost of waiting may in some analyses include both the time waiting in a queue and the time being served, i.e., the lost productive time while a worker gets parts at the parts department.

Example 10.2 Decision Analysis of a Tool Crib Operation

The management of a manufacturing firm wishes to determine the best staffing level for its tool crib operation. The plant workers line up in single file at the tool crib to pick up or return tools. The structure of the tool crib process is represented in Figure 10.2 by case A if the tool crib is staffed by one person, and by case B if the tool crib is staffed by two or more employees. The objective is to determine the best staffing level for the tool crib to minimize total service and waiting costs.

The workers arrive at the tool crib randomly at an average rate of 12 per hour (every five minutes on the average). Each employee who works in the tool crib can service the workers (check in or check out tools) in an average of 3.75 minutes (at the mean rate of 16 per hour), but this service time also varies randomly.

The firm can hire employees to staff the tool crib for a wage of $12 per hour. The wage rate for plant workers who line up to check out and return tools at the tool crib is $16 per hour, and the firm uses that amount as a reasonable estimate of the hourly value (opportunity cost) of lost productivity when employees are at the tool crib. Both the time waiting in line and the time at the tool crib picking up or returning tools are included in the employee idle time (i.e., away from work).

The firm has employed queueing theory to determine the average, or expected, number of employees at the tool crib (waiting and in service), for three different tool crib staffing levels; one server, two servers, and three servers. This analysis uses queuing formulas that will be described later in this chapter. This analysis yielded the following results:

Number of Crib Servers	Mean Number of Workers Waiting and Being Served
1	3.0
2	.8727
3	.7647

With the above information, the firm was able to perform the following cost analysis for the different alternatives:

Service Level	Service Cost	Waiting Cost*	Total Cost
1	(12)(1) = 12.00	(16)(3.0) = 48.00	$60.00
2	(12)(2) = 24.00	(16)(.8727) = 13.96	$37.96
3	(12)(3) = 36.00	(16)(.7647) = 12.24	$48.24

*Including time in service.

If the above values for service cost, waiting cost, and total cost were plotted on a graph as a function of service level, the results would be similar to the Figure 10.3 graph. The optimum decision is to staff the tool crib with two servers yielding the minimum sum of service cost plus waiting cost (since this waiting cost includes both the time waiting in line and the time waiting for the server to complete the service, it is generally referred to as "the time in the system," i.e., the queueing "system" as identified in Figure 10.1).

Two issues need to be clarified at this point. First, the time period of the preceding cost analysis is an hour, that is, the cost amounts are per hour of operation. This is not inappropriate since we assume steady state conditions, and therefore the average solution results do not change over time. We could convert the cost analysis to daily figures by multiplying every cost figure by the number of hours of operation per day, but this would not change them in a relative sense. Thus, the total cost per 8-hour day for each staffing alternative would be (1) $480/day, (2) $303.68/day, and (3) $385.92/day, yielding the same decision.

The second question that might be raised concerns why we used the mean *number* in the system (in the queue and in service) rather than the mean *time* in the system for the waiting cost calculation. The answer to this question is that we could have used either measure of system performance and reached the same results. However, if we had used the mean time in the system (waiting and being served) instead of the mean number in the system, we would have needed to also include the mean arrival rate in our calculations. That is, for each hour of operation, the total waiting time by the workers would be the number of arrivals per hour times the mean time waiting for each arrival. For example, let us refer to the alternative of one server. If an average of 12 workers arrived at the queueing system per hour, and each arrival spent an average of ¼ hour in the system, then (12 arrivals/hour) × (¼ hour) = 3 workers, on the average, in the system. If we let λ represent the mean arrival rate, W represent the mean time in the system, and L represent the mean number in the system, then we have stated that $L = \lambda W$. This is an important relationship in queueing theory that we will make reference to again at a later point in the chapter.

Inputs for Decision Analysis of Queuing Systems

Queuing theory provides solution results in the form of operating characteristics, such as the expected number in the system and the expected customer waiting time. As shown in Example 10.2, these queuing theory results can then be used in the decision analysis of a system involving waiting lines. The following discussion of queuing theory will consider the development of these results. Queuing theory provides models (formulas) by which the **operating characteristics,** such as expected waiting time, can be computed under specified assumptions regarding the nature of the queuing process.

As was previously pointed out, because of the wide range of potential approaches to the analysis of queuing problems, queuing theory provides many measures of a waiting line system's performance. The decision maker must select the measures relevant to the problem. For instance, in addition to the two measures of performance discussed in Example 10.2, management might specify that the expected percentage idle time of the server(s) should not exceed 40%.

Alternatively, management might specify that the maximum *number in the system* (the customers waiting plus the customer in service) should never exceed five, with a 90% degree of certainty. By setting up such stipulations, management can add certain desired service conditions to the decision analysis model. Information on whether these conditions are met or violated can be obtained from queuing theory in the form of operating characteristics.

The operating characteristics commonly obtained in the analysis of waiting lines are summarized as follows:

Probability of the service facility being idle
Probability of any specified number in the system
Mean (expected) waiting time per customer
Mean (expected) queue length
Mean time in the system per customer
Mean number of units in the system

QUEUING THEORY ASSUMPTIONS

Queuing theory was developed by making a number of assumptions about the several basic components of a waiting line process. Each change in an assumption leads to a different theoretical model. As has been implied in the previous discussions, an almost infinite variety of waiting line situations exist. Although we will consider only a few of the basic theoretical models here, the overall conceptual basis for queuing analysis should become clear.

Distribution of Arrivals

Queuing models belong to the class of management science models known as probabilistic (stochastic) models. This is because certain elements of the process are included in the model as random variables (as opposed to constant-valued parameters). These random variables are most often described by an associated probability distribution.

Both the arrivals and the service times in a queuing process are generally represented as random variables. For example, the number of customers arriving per unit time (e.g., per hour) at a barber shop may vary randomly but according to some definable probability distribution.

The *number of arrivals* per unit time at a service location may vary randomly according to any one of many probability distributions. However, the distribution most commonly assumed for customer arrivals is the **Poisson distribution.** This assumption about the distribution of arrivals is not without empirical basis. Many statistical studies have resulted in the conclusion that arrivals are Poisson distributed for many queuing processes.

The general model (formula) for the Poisson probability distribution is

$$P(r) = \frac{e^{-\lambda}(\lambda)^r}{r!}$$

where

r = number of arrivals

$$P(r) = \text{probability of } r \text{ arrivals}$$
$$\lambda = \text{mean arrival rate}$$
$$e = 2.71828 \text{ (base of natural logarithms)}$$
$$r! = r(r-1)(r-2)\cdots 3\cdot 2\cdot 1 \quad (r \text{ factorial})$$

The Poisson distribution corresponds to the assumption of random arrivals, since each arrival is assumed to be independent of other arrivals and also independent of the state of the system. One interesting characteristic of a Poisson distribution, which makes it easier to work with than some other distributions, is that the mean is equal to the variance. Thus, by specifying the mean of a Poisson distribution, we define the entire distribution.

The Poisson distribution is a *discrete* probability distribution, since it relates to the *number* of arrivals per unit time. Figure 10.4 (p. 474) portrays the Poisson distribution graphically for several different values of the mean, λ. It can be seen that as the mean becomes larger, the distribution becomes flatter and more symmetrical. For example, if the mean arrival rate (λ) at a barber shop is 2 per hour, the probabilities associated with different numbers of arrivals are as shown in Table 10.3.[1]

Table 10.3 Poisson Distribution of Number of Arrivals Per Hour

r Number of Arrivals	$P(r)$ Probability
0	.1358
1	.2707
2	.2707
3	.1805
4	.0902
5	.0361
6	.0120
7	.0034
8	.0009

An interesting feature of the Poisson process is that if the number of arrivals per unit time is Poisson distributed with a mean rate of λ, then the *time between arrivals (inter-arrival time)* is distributed as a *negative exponential* probability distribution with a mean of $1/\lambda$. Thus, if the mean arrival *rate* per hour is 2, then the mean *time between arrivals* is 30 minutes. This relationship is summarized as follows:

Arrival Rate	Time Between Arrivals
Poisson	Negative exponential
Mean $= \lambda$	Mean $= 1/\lambda$
$\lambda = 2$ arrivals per hr	$1/\lambda = \frac{1}{2}$ hr
	$= 30$ min

[1] A table of Poisson probability values for various values of r and λ is given in Appendix C.

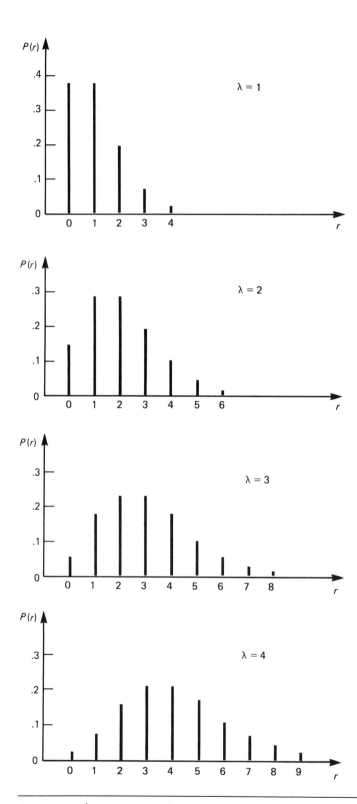

Figure 10.4 *Poisson Distribution*

Distribution of Service Times

Service times in a queuing process may also fit any one of a large number of different probability distributions. The distribution most commonly assumed for service times is the negative exponential distribution. From the preceding discussion of the relationship between the Poisson and negative exponential distributions, if service times follow a negative exponential distribution, the service rate follows a Poisson distribution.

The description of arrivals in terms of arrival *rate* (Poisson) and services in terms of service *time* (negative exponential) is a matter of convention that has evolved in the literature of queuing theory.

Empirical research has shown that the assumption of negative exponentially distributed service times is not valid nearly as often as is the assumption of Poisson-distributed arrivals. Therefore, for actual applications of queuing analysis, this assumption would have to be carefully checked before such a model was used. Other possible distributions of service times will be presented later in this chapter.

The general model (formula) for the negative exponential probability density function is

$$f(t) = \mu e^{-\mu t}$$

where

t = service time

$f(t)$ = probability density associated with t

μ = mean service rate

$1/\mu$ = mean service time

e = 2.71828 . . . (base of natural logarithms)

As in the case of the Poisson arrival rate, the negative exponential service time corresponds to the assumption that service times are completely random. The probability of completing a service for a customer in any subsequent time period after service is begun is independent of how much time has already elapsed on the service for that customer.

The negative exponential distribution is a *continuous* probability distribution, since it relates to time of service. Figure 10.5 illustrates graphically the negative exponential

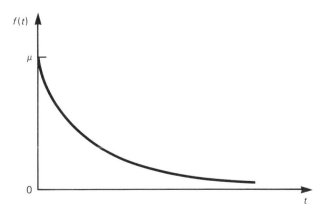

Figure 10.5 *Negative Exponential Probability Density Function*

distribution. It can be seen that short service times have the highest probability of occurrence. As service time increases, the probability function "tails off" (exponentially) toward zero probability. The area under the curve for the negative exponential distribution in Figure 10.5 is determined from its cumulative distribution function, which is computed through integration as follows:

$$F(T) = \int_0^T \mu e^{-\mu t} dt = -e^{-\mu t} \Big]_0^T = -e^{-\mu T} + e^0 = 1 - e^{-\mu T}$$

This may be further described as

$$F(T) = f(t \leqslant T) = 1 - e^{-\mu T}$$

where $F(T)$ is the area under the curve to the left of T. Also,

$$1 - F(T) = f(t \geqslant T) = e^{-\mu T}$$

where $1 - F(T)$ is the area under the curve to the right of T.[2]

For example, if the mean service time $(1/\mu)$ at a theater ticket booth is two minutes, the probabilities that service will take T or more minutes, for various values of T, are as shown in Table 10.4.

Table 10.4 *Probability Ticket Sale Will Take* **T** *or More Minutes*

Service Times of at Least T	Probability $f(t \geqslant T)$
0 min	1.000
1	.607
2	.368
3	.223
4	.135
5	.082
6	.050
7	.030
8	.018
9	.011
10	.007
11	.004
12	.003
13	.002
14	.001

Queue Discipline

As discussed previously, the queue discipline is a decision rule that determines the order in which waiting customers will be selected for service. In queuing theory models, it is

[2] A table of values of e^x and e^{-x} is given in Appendix C.

generally assumed that customers will be serviced on a first-come, first-served basis. If this assumption is not appropriate for the queuing system under study, a different model must be developed.

A feature of customer behavior that can affect the service order is the tendency of customers to become impatient and decide to leave the system before being served. This practice is known in the literature of queuing theory as **reneging.**

Infinite Versus Finite Calling Population

The calling population in queuing theory is the source of arrivals to be serviced. In considering a waiting line situation such as a bank drive-in teller operation, it is reasonable to assume that the calling population is, for all practical purposes, infinite. However, if the source of arrivals for service is a machine shop's ten machines, which must be serviced when they break down, obviously the calling population is finite.

The key consideration in this case is whether the probability of customer arrivals is affected by the removal of one customer from the population (through entry into the service system). The question is analogous to the one that arises in the traditional probability example of drawing balls from a bowl *without replacement*. If there are initially 5 balls in a bowl, the probability of drawing a ball with a certain characteristic is certainly different on the second draw (with 4 balls remaining) than it was on the first draw. However, if there are 500,000 balls in the bowl initially, the probability will be virtually unaffected by the first draw.

Basic queuing theory models generally include the initial assumption of an infinite calling population (source). However, the finite source case is sufficiently abundant in real life that models including this assumption are often developed. Both situations will be presented in this chapter.

Infinite Versus Finite Queue Length

Although queuing theory models generally begin with the assumption that waiting lines could theoretically build up to an unlimited length, this is often not the case in reality. There may be limited space prior to the service facility in which queues can build up. For example, the parking lot at a truck stop can accommodate only a limited number of vehicles, and there may be a law against parking on the adjacent road. Customers may simply refuse to enter a long line, even if space is available. This practice is often referred to as **balking** in the literature of queuing theory. Although the assumption of infinite queues is more attractive from a mathematical solution standpoint, the assumption of queues of a finite length (sometimes referred to as **truncated queues**) is sometimes more realistic.

Steady-State Versus Transient Queuing Systems

A very important assumption of queuing theory concerns whether the system reaches an equilibrium, or steady-state condition. Almost all basic models of queuing theory assume a steady-state condition. That is, it is assumed that operating characteristics, such as queue length and average waiting time, will assume constant average values after the system has been in operation for a period of time. In reality, however, some waiting line systems can never be expected to operate long enough to achieve a steady state. Some advanced queuing theory models have been developed in which the solution depends directly on the elapsed time since the system began operation (transient queuing systems analysis). The emphasis in this chapter, however, will be on steady-state models.

Arrival Rate Versus Service Rate

It is logical to assume that the rate at which services are completed must exceed the arrival rate of customers. If this is not the case, the queues will simply continue to grow, and there will be no steady-state solution. Thus, it is generally assumed that the service rate does exceed the arrival rate.

An interesting relationship among arrival rates, service rates, and expected queue lengths is illustrated in Figure 10.6. If the arrival rate must be less than the service rate, then the ratio of arrival rate to service rate will be less than 1. As that ratio approaches 1, the expected queue length will approach infinity (in the steady-state solution, with certain assumptions).

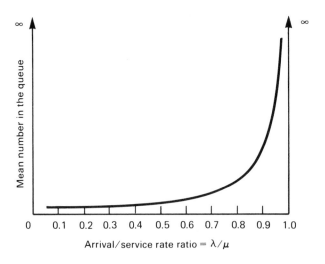

Figure 10.6 *Relationship of Queue Length to Arrival/Service Rate Ratio*

In Figure 10.6, λ represents the mean arrival rate and μ represents the mean service rate. It can be seen that once the ratio of λ to μ exceeds .7, the expected queue length increases very rapidly. This relationship of queue length to arrival rate and service rate assumes infinite (or at least very large) possible queue lengths.

QUEUING SYSTEM NOTATION

Several queuing theory models and their related assumptions will be presented. Each of the different models will be presented in the form of several submodels (equations) that yield the aforementioned operating characteristics for the queuing process. It is common practice in queuing literature to summarize the primary characteristics of a queuing model with certain standard notation. This notation was initially developed by professor D. G. Kendall in 1953, and it was, therefore, referred to as the Kendall notation. The notation was subsequently modified by A. M. Lee in 1966, and, therefore, it is sometimes referred to as the Kendall-Lee notation. The notation generally used follows this format.

$$(a/b/c)\,(d/e/f)$$

where
- a = arrival distribution
- b = service distribution
- c = number of channels (parallel servers)
- d = queue discipline
- e = maximum number in the system
- f = size of calling population

The first and second characteristics represent the probability distributions used to describe the arrival process and the service process. The distributions most frequently assumed for arrivals and services in queuing models are

- M = Poisson distribution
- D = Deterministic, or constant, value
- E_k = Erlang, with parameter k, distribution
- G = General, or undefined, distribution

The distribution represented most often in queuing models is the Poisson distribution. Since the poisson distribution includes the properties of a Markov process, the notation selected by Kendall to denote a poisson distributed process is M (for Markovian). Thus, the M notation for arrivals means that the number of arrivals per unit time is distributed according to a Poisson distribution, and equivalently the times between arrivals (interarrival times) are distributed according to a negative exponential distribution. A similar statement would describe the use of the M for services.

In some cases, the service times are actually constant values (deterministic), as may be the case for mechanical devices. The input process may be deterministic especially if it is the output of some other mechanical device. However, this sort of input process is not considered in this text. The Erlang distribution is a very general distribution, for various values of the parameter k, which often best describes some service facilities. In some cases, the distribution of service times is unknown, but the standard deviation (or variance) is known. Queuing theory results have been obtained for various cases including the deterministic (D), Erlang (E_k) and general (G) cases.

The third characteristic of the Kendall queuing system notation denotes the number of servers in parallel. Thus, an $M/M/1$ system system has one server; an $M/M/2$ has two parallel servers, and so forth.

Often times, the queuing system will be specified by only the first three characteristics, i.e., $(a/b/c)$. This is because it is frequently assumed that the queue discipline is FIFO (first-come, first-served), the maximum number in the system is infinite (unlimited), and the calling population is infinite. Thus, if a queuing system is given by $(M/M/1)$, it is assumed that this is equivalent to $(M/M/1)\,(FIFO/\infty/\infty)$.

SINGLE-CHANNEL, SINGLE-PHASE QUEUING MODELS

A number of single-server queuing models will be presented in this section, including the following:

1. (M/M/1) Poisson arrival rate, exponential service times
2. (M/G/1) Poisson arrival rate, general (or unknown) distribution of service times
3. (M/D/1) Poisson arrival rate, deterministic (or constant) service times
4. (M/E_k/1) Poisson arrival rate, Erlang distribution of service times
5. (M/M/1)(FIFO/Finite Queue/∞) same as first model with a finite queue
6. (M/M/1)(FIFO/∞/Finite Population) same as first model with a finite population

Note that the absence of the (d/e/f) characteristics for the first four models implies the assumption of (FIFO/∞/∞) in each case.

(M/M/1) Model: Poisson Arrivals, Exponential Service Times, One Server

The derivation of the most common case of the single-channel, single-phase queuing process, illustrated in Figure 10.2 (A), will be presented first, followed by several variations. This first model assumes Poisson arrivals and exponential service times and a single server, i.e., the (M/M/1) model.

In all subsequent cases, the following assumptions will be made, unless the specific model discussion states otherwise: (1) first-come, first-served queue discipline, (2) infinite number in the system (i.e., unlimited or nontruncated queue), and (3) infinite calling populations (unlimited arrival source). In addition, we also assume a steady-state solution (equilibrium over time), and the service rate exceeds arrival rate ($\mu > \lambda$).

The purpose of queuing theory is to obtain "solution results" for the various queuing models. The solution results are in the form of operating characteristics that provide measures of the queuing system performance. The measures commonly obtained for queuing models are

L = mean number in the system (number waiting and in service)
L_q = mean number in the queue (mean number waiting)
W = mean time in the system (time waiting and in service)
W_q = mean time in the queue (mean time waiting)
P_0 = probability the system is empty (idle)
P_n = probability of n customers in the system

A detailed presentation of the procedure employed to obtain the solution results will be given for the (M/M/1)(FIFO, ∞, ∞) queuing model. For other queuing models, the solution results will be given without the associated detailed presentation.

Derivation of the Solution Results for the (M/M/1) (FIFO/∞/∞) Model

Several approaches can be used in showing this derivation. The approach taken here emphasizes intuitive understanding rather than elaborate mathematical computations.

Although the intuitive approach is not as attractive from a theoretical point of view, it is hoped that the increase in understandability compensates for this lack of mathematical rigor.

As stated previously, it is assumed that we have steady-state conditions. Therefore, although many queuing probabilities are initially developed as a function of time and then later adjusted to reflect time independence, we shall simply begin our development of the equations with the assumption that the various probabilities considered are not dependent on how long the system has been operating.

The first issue to be considered is the probability of an arrival or an end of service during some increment of time. If the expected number of arrivals per hour (λ) is 1, what is the probability of an arrival during some very short increment of time? First we will assume that we can divide the time period (one hour) into enough increments that no more than one arrival could occur during any one time increment. If we divide the hour into minutes, we have sixty time increments. If no more than one arrival could occur during any one of the sixty time increments and we expect a total of one arrival during the hour, then the probability of one arrival during one time increment is $1/60$. This is determined by multiplying the expected number of arrivals in one hour by the time increment, $1/60$ of an hour. If we expected five arrivals during an hour ($\lambda = 5$), the probability of one arrival during one of the sixty increments would be $5 \times 1/60$ of an hour $= 5/60 = 1/12$. If we drew one ball from a bowl containing sixty balls, of which five were red, the probability of drawing a red ball would be the number of red balls times the probability of drawing any one of the sixty balls: $(5)\,(1/60)$, or $1/12$.

Minutes may not be very small time increments for some systems being considered, such as a queue for a computer system. Certainly more than one arrival could occur in one minute in many systems. To resolve this problem, we simply divide our time period into smaller time increments. Suppose we divided an hour into seconds, so that each time increment was $1/3600$ of an hour. If we expected one arrival in an hour, the probability of an arrival during some time increment would be $1 \times (1/3600) = 1/3600$. If we expected five arrivals in an hour, the probability of one arrival during one time increment would be $5 \times 1/3600 = 5/3600 = 1/720$. We could divide the hour into microseconds and be reasonably sure that no more than one arrival would occur during one time increment.

If we assume that the fraction of an hour is represented by Δt and that the mean (expected) arrival rate per hour is λ, then the probability of one arrival during Δt is equal to $\lambda(\Delta t)$. The same argument holds for the probability of one departure (end of service) during Δt, which is given by $\mu(\Delta t)$, where $\mu =$ mean (expected) service rate. Since we assume that no more than one arrival can occur during Δt and no more than one departure during Δt, we also assume that both an arrival and a departure will not occur simultaneously during Δt. Note that if $\lambda(\Delta t)$ is the probability of an arrival during Δt and $\mu(\Delta t)$ is the probability of a departure, then the joint probability that both will occur simultaneously is $\lambda(\Delta t)\mu(\Delta t) = \lambda\mu(\Delta t)^2$. If Δt is infinitesimally small, then $(\Delta t)^2$ will be virtually zero, and thus $\lambda(\Delta t)\mu(\Delta t) \cong 0$.

There are three possible events during Δt: an addition of one unit in the system, a reduction of one unit in the system, or no change in the system (no arrival and no departure). If $\lambda(\Delta t)$ is the probability of an arrival during Δt, then $1 - \lambda(\Delta t)$ is the probability of no arrival. Likewise, if $\mu(\Delta t)$ is the probability of a departure during Δt, then

$1 - \mu(\Delta t)$ is the probability of no departure from the system. The joint probability of no arrival and no departure is given by the product of the two events.

$$[1 - \lambda(\Delta t)][1 - \mu(\Delta t)] = 1 - \lambda(\Delta t) - \mu(\Delta t) + \lambda\mu(\Delta t)^2$$

The last term is eliminated for the same reason given previously: $(\Delta t)^2 \cong 0$. Thus, we have as the probability of no change $1 - (\lambda\Delta t + \mu\Delta t)$. The states of the system at times t and $t + \Delta t$, with the three possible events during Δt, are shown in Figure 10.7 (where k is the number of units in the system).

Of course, when there are zero units in the system ($k = 0$) at time t, only two events can occur. Either there is no arrival, with probability $1 - \lambda\Delta t$, or there is an arrival, with probability $\lambda\Delta t$. When $k \geq 1$ at time t, all three events can occur, as is shown for the cases where $k = 1$, $k = 2$, and $k = n$ at time t. For example, for the general case where $k = n$ at time t, the probability of moving to $k = n - 1$ at $t + \Delta t$ equals $\mu\Delta t$, the probability of moving to $k = n$ at $t + \Delta t$ equals $1 - (\lambda\Delta t + \mu\Delta t)$, and the probability of moving to $k = n + 1$ at $t + \Delta t$ equals $\lambda\Delta t$.

We will identify P as the probability of the number of units in the system (the state of the system) and denote the number in the system by a subscript, n, to P. Thus, P_n is the probability of n units in the system. Referring to Figure 10.7, we see that there are two ways to have zero in the system at time $t + \Delta t$: when $k = 0$ at time t and no arrival occurs, and when $k = 1$ at time t and one departure occurs. The probability of zero in the system at time $t + \Delta t$ is thus the probability of zero at time t times the probability of no arrival $[P_0(1 - \lambda\Delta t)]$, plus the probability of one at time t times the probability of one departure $[P_1(\mu\Delta t)]$, which yields

$$P_0 = P_0(1 - \lambda\Delta t) + P_1(\mu\Delta t) \tag{10.1}$$

Referring again to Figure 10.7, we can see that there are three ways to have one in the system at time $t + \Delta t$: when $k = 0$ at time t and one arrival occurs during Δt, when $k = 1$ at time t and no arrival or departure occurs, and when $k = 2$ at time t and one departure occurs. Thus, the probability of one unit in the system is given by

$$P_1 = P_0(\lambda\Delta t) + P_1(1 - \lambda\Delta t - \mu\Delta t) + P_2(\mu\Delta t) \tag{10.2}$$

For the general case, the probability of n units in the system at time $t + \Delta t$ is given by

$$P_n = P_{n-1}(\lambda\Delta t) + P_n(1 - \lambda\Delta t - \mu\Delta t) + P_{n+1}(\mu\Delta t) \tag{10.3}$$

We next solve equation (10.1) for P_1 in terms of P_0, as follows:

$$P_0 = P_0(1 - \lambda\Delta t) + P_1(\mu\Delta t)$$
$$(\mu\Delta t)P_1 = P_0 - P_0(1 - \lambda\Delta t)$$
$$(\mu\Delta t)P_1 = P_0[1 - (1 - \lambda\Delta t)]$$
$$(\mu\Delta t)P_1 = P_0(\lambda\Delta t)$$
$$P_1 = P_0\frac{\lambda\Delta t}{\mu\Delta t}$$

The Δt's cancel, and we get

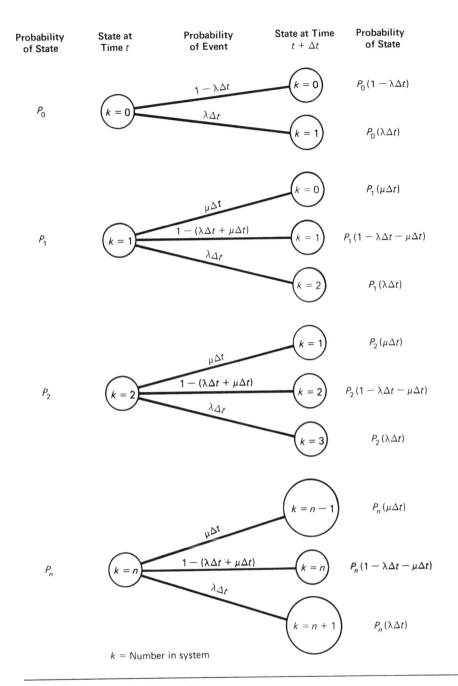

Figure 10.7 Queuing System States

$$P_1 = P_0\left(\frac{\lambda}{\mu}\right) \tag{10.4}$$

We next solve equation (10.3) for P_{n+1} in terms of P_n and P_{n-1}, which yields

$$P_{n+1} = P_n\left(\frac{\lambda + \mu}{\mu}\right) - P_{n-1}\left(\frac{\lambda}{\mu}\right)$$

Substituting the value 1 for n, we get

$$P_2 = P_1 \left(\frac{\lambda + \mu}{\mu} \right) - P_0 \left(\frac{\lambda}{\mu} \right)$$

We can then substitute equation (10.4) for P_1, to yield

$$P_2 = P_0 \left(\frac{\lambda}{\mu} \right) \left(\frac{\lambda + \mu}{\mu} \right) - P_0 \left(\frac{\lambda}{\mu} \right)$$

$$= P_0 \left[\left(\frac{\lambda}{\mu} \right) \left(\frac{\lambda + \mu}{\mu} \right) - \left(\frac{\lambda}{\mu} \right) \right]$$

$$= P_0 \left[\frac{\lambda}{\mu} \left(\frac{\lambda + \mu}{\mu} - 1 \right) \right] \tag{10.5}$$

$$= P_0 \frac{\lambda^2 + \lambda\mu - \lambda\mu}{\mu^2}$$

$$P_2 = P_0 \left(\frac{\lambda}{\mu} \right)^2$$

When we solve for P_3, we find that

$$P_3 = P_0 \left(\frac{\lambda}{\mu} \right)^3 \tag{10.6}$$

Similarly,

$$P_4 = P_0 \left(\frac{\lambda}{\mu} \right)^4 \tag{10.7}$$

Thus, by induction, we can infer that

$$P_n = P_0 \left(\frac{\lambda}{\mu} \right)^n \tag{10.8}$$

From probability theory, we know that the probabilities for all possible outcomes must sum to 1. Thus, we have

$$\sum_{n=0}^{\infty} P_n = 1.0 \tag{10.9}$$

Substituting equation (10.8) for P_n, we have

$$\sum_{n=0}^{\infty} P_0 \left(\frac{\lambda}{\mu} \right)^n = 1.0$$

or

$$P_0 = \frac{1}{\displaystyle\sum_{n=0}^{\infty} \left(\frac{\lambda}{\mu} \right)^n}$$

The denominator of this expression is an infinite geometric series, which converges to

$$\sum_{n=0}^{\infty} \left(\frac{\lambda}{\mu}\right)^n = \frac{1}{1 - \lambda/\mu}$$

Thus, we have

$$P_0 = \frac{1}{\dfrac{1}{1 - \lambda/\mu}} \tag{10.10}$$

$$P_0 = 1 - \frac{\lambda}{\mu}$$

Recalling from equation (10.8) that

$$P_n = P_0 \left(\frac{\lambda}{\mu}\right)^n$$

and substituting equation (10.10) for P_0 in this equation, we get

$$P_n = \left(1 - \frac{\lambda}{\mu}\right)\left(\frac{\lambda}{\mu}\right)^n \tag{10.11}$$

Thus, for steady-state conditions, equation (10.10) yields the probability of no units in the system, and equation (10.11) yields the probability of n units in the system. Notice that equation (10.11) reduces to equation (10.10) when $n = 0$.

The average of some variable X is, by definition,

$$\sum_{\text{all}X} X \cdot P_X$$

Therefore, the average number in the system (denoted by L) is given by

$$L = \sum_{n=0}^{\infty} n \cdot P_n$$

Thus, substituting equation (10.11) for P_n in the previous expression, we get

$$L = \sum_{n=0}^{\infty} n \cdot \left(1 - \frac{\lambda}{\mu}\right)\left(\frac{\lambda}{\mu}\right)^n$$

$$= \left(1 - \frac{\lambda}{\mu}\right)\sum_{n=0}^{\infty} n \cdot \left(\frac{\lambda}{\mu}\right)^n$$

The term $\sum_{n=0}^{\infty} n(\lambda/\mu)^n$ is an infinite geometric series, which converges to

$$\sum_{n=0}^{\infty} n \left(\frac{\lambda}{\mu}\right)^n = \frac{\lambda/\mu}{(1 - \lambda/\mu)^2}$$

and therefore

$$L = \left(1 - \frac{\lambda}{\mu}\right)\left[\frac{\lambda/\mu}{(1 - \lambda/\mu)^2}\right]$$

which reduces to

$$L = \frac{\lambda}{\mu - \lambda} \qquad \text{(mean number in the system)} \qquad (10.12)$$

Our purpose here is to determine several measures of queuing system performance, described as follows:

L = mean number in the system
L_q = mean number in the queue
W = mean time in the system
W_q = mean time waiting in the queue

If we expect λ arrivals per unit time and if each of these arrivals spends an average time in the system of W, then the total time in the system for λ arrivals is λW. For example, if 2 customers arrive and each arrival spends 3 hours in the system, then the total customer hours in the system is 6. This implies that there are 6 ($L = 6$) customers in the system on the average (i.e., customers 1 and 2 in their third hour in the system, customers 3 and 4 in their second hour, and customers 5 and 6 in their first hour). This gives us the relationship

$$L = \lambda W \qquad (10.13)$$

The relationship, $L = \lambda W$, was rigorously proved by J. D. C. Little in 1961 and it is a fundamental relationship that is virtually independent of the number of servers, the arrival distribution, the service distribution, and the queue discipline. This relationship was initially discussed in our Example 10.2—decision analysis of a tool crib operation— where we explained why we could use either L or λW in our cost analysis concerning waiting times. Little also showed through rigorous mathematical proof that $L_q = \lambda W_q$. Thus, we have

$$L_q = \lambda W_q \qquad (10.14)$$

The expected time in the system (W) must be equal to the expected time in the queue (W_q) plus the expected time in the service facility. We already know that the expected time in service is $1/\mu$, so we have

$$W = W_q + \frac{1}{\mu} \qquad (10.15)$$

Therefore, once we have solved for L by equation (10.12),

$$L = \frac{\lambda}{\mu - \lambda} \qquad \text{(mean number in the system)}$$

we then get W from equation (10.13):

$$W = \frac{L}{\lambda} \qquad \text{(mean time in the system)}$$

W_q is given by equation (10.15):

$$W_q = W - \frac{1}{\mu} \qquad \text{(mean waiting time)}$$

Finally, from equation (10.14), L_q is

$$L_q = \lambda W_q \quad \text{(mean number in the queue)}$$

The remaining queuing formulas to be presented for the M/M/1 model, and the queuing equations for the other models presented in this chapter, are in some cases developed by a similar process and in other cases by a much more complex process.

Summary of the (M/M/1) Model Solution Results

The (M/M/1) model variables and relationships are summarized as follows:

λ = mean arrival rate $(1/\lambda$ = mean time between arrivals)

μ = mean service rate $(1/\mu$ = mean service time)

n = number of customers (units) in the system (includes those waiting and in service)

t = time in the system

The Probability of No Units in the System:

$$P_0 = 1 - \frac{\lambda}{\mu}$$

The Probability of n Units in the System:

$$P_n = \left(\frac{\lambda}{\mu}\right)^n \left(1 - \frac{\lambda}{\mu}\right)$$

The Probability of k or More Units in the System:

$$P_{n \geq k} = \left(\frac{\lambda}{\mu}\right)^k$$

Mean (Expected) Number of Units in the System:

$$L = \frac{\lambda}{\mu - \lambda}$$

Mean Number of Units in the Queue:

$$L_q = \frac{\lambda^2}{\mu(\mu - \lambda)}$$

Mean Time in the System:

$$W = \frac{1}{\mu - \lambda}$$

Mean Waiting Time:

$$W_q = \frac{\lambda}{\mu(\mu - \lambda)}$$

Service Facility Utilization Factor (ρ):

$$\rho = \frac{\lambda}{\mu}$$

Proportion Server Idle Time:

$$I = 1 - \frac{\lambda}{\mu}$$

It is also of interest to review the following relationships among the various operating characteristics:

$$P_n = P_0 \left(\frac{\lambda}{\mu} \right)^n$$

$$L_q = L - \frac{\lambda}{\mu} = \lambda W_q$$

$$L = L_q + \frac{\lambda}{\mu} = \lambda W$$

$$W_q = W - \frac{1}{\mu} = \frac{L_q}{\lambda}$$

$$W = W_q + \frac{1}{\mu} = \frac{L}{\lambda}$$

$$I = 1 - \rho = P_0$$

Thus, when any one of the operating characteristics L_q, L, W_q, or W has been obtained, the other three measures of system performance can be determined directly. It should also be noted that the proportion idle time, I, and the probability of zero customers in the system, P_0, are the same.

Example 10.3 Queuing Analysis of a Business FAX Machine

The preceding basic queuing model will be illustrated in the following example problem. The system of interest is a FAX machine in a business firm with a large number of employees who use the machine. Employees arrive randomly to use the FAX machine at an average rate of 20 per hour. This arrival process is approximated by a Poisson distribution. Employees spend an average of 2 minutes using the FAX machine, either transmitting or receiving items. The time spent using the machine (service time) is distributed according to a negative exponential distribution. Employees line up in single file to use the machine and they obtain access to it on a first-come, first-served basis. There is no defined limit to the number who can line up to use the machine.

From this description of the system, we conclude that we can obtain the queuing system's operating characteristics by making use of the solution results obtained for the $(M/M/1)(FIFO/\infty/\infty)$ model presented in the preceding section. The parameters of the arrival and service distributions are as follows:

	Mean Rate	Mean Time
Arrivals	Poisson: $\lambda = 20$/hr	Exponential: $\frac{1}{\lambda} = \frac{1 \text{ hr}}{20} = 3$ min
Services	Poisson: $\mu = 30$/hr	Exponential: $\frac{1}{\mu} = \frac{1 \text{ hr}}{30} = 2$ min

Note that in the following computations, since the parameters λ and μ are used, the time values computed will be in terms of hours.

$$L = \frac{\lambda}{\mu - \lambda} = \frac{20}{30 - 20} = \frac{20}{10} = 2 \text{ persons in the system}$$

There will be an average of 2 persons in the system (waiting and using the FAX machine).

$$L_q = \frac{\lambda^2}{\mu(\mu - \lambda)} = \frac{(20)^2}{30(30 - 20)} = \frac{400}{30(10)} = \frac{400}{300} = 1.33 \text{ persons}$$

There will be an average of 1.33 employees waiting in line to use the FAX machine.

$$W = \frac{1}{\mu - \lambda} = \frac{1}{30 - 20} = \frac{1}{10} \text{ hr } (= 6 \text{ min}) \text{ time in the system}$$

Each employee using the FAX machine will spend an average of 6 minutes in the system (waiting and using the machine).

$$W_q = \frac{\lambda}{\mu(\mu - \lambda)} = \frac{20}{30(30 - 20)} = \frac{20}{30(10)} = \frac{20}{300}$$

$$= \frac{1}{15} \text{ hr } (= 4 \text{ min}) \text{ time waiting}$$

Thus, on the average, each employee using the FAX machine will spend 6 minutes in the process of waiting to use and using the FAX machine, of which 4 minutes will be spent waiting in line. Notice that the difference of 2 minutes, which is spent using the FAX machine, is equal to the value originally specified for $1/\mu$, the mean service time. There will be an average of 2 people in the system and an average of 1.33 people waiting for service. Intuitively, it might seem that if there is an average of 2 people in the system, there should be 1 in service, and the average number waiting will be only 1. However, the expected number in service is actually .67, which is equal to $L - L_q$. Recall that arrivals and service times are *random* over time, so part of the time the service facility (FAX machine) is idle and part of the time more than 1 person is waiting to use it.

An additional operating characteristic, the probability of zero customers in the system, is determined as follows:

$$P_0 = 1 - \frac{\lambda}{\mu}$$

$$= 1 - \frac{20}{30}$$

$$= .33$$

The probability of no customers in the system is .33. Thus, the FAX machine is idle 33% of the time. Of course, the machine is busy 67% of the time, which is the server utilization factor.

$$\rho = \frac{\lambda}{\mu} = .67$$

Probability distributions of the number in the system and of some number (or greater) in the system are computed as shown in Table 10.5. It is of considerable interest

Table 10.5 *Probability Distributions of Number in the System*

n	Probability of n Customers in System $P_n = \left(\dfrac{20}{30}\right)^n \left(1 - \dfrac{20}{30}\right)$	k	Probability of k or More Customers in System $P_{n \geq k} = \left(\dfrac{20}{30}\right)^k$
0	.333	0	1.000
1	.222	1	.667
2	.148	2	.444
3	.099	3	.296
4	.066	4	.198
5	.044	5	.132
6	.029	6	.088
7	.019	7	.058
8	.013	8	.039
9	.009	9	.026
10	.006	10	.017

to note that 13.2% of the time there will be 5 or more people in the system ($P_{n \geq 5} = .132$). Thus, if the room containing the FAX machine has a capacity limit of 4 people, then the FAX room will have sufficient capacity only 87% of the time. Employees will have to line up in the adjacent hall 13% of the time. If we assume that employees cannot line up in the adjacent hall and leave when the FAX room is full, a modified queuing model must be used, assuming a finite possible queue length.

Computerized Analysis of the (M/M/1) Model

First, we will use the AB:QM software package to perform the analysis of Example 10.3. Following that, we will also demonstrate the use of the STORM software package for the same problem.

```
Program: Queuing Theory / M/M/1: STANDARD SINGLE SERVER

Problem Title : Example 10.3

***** Input Data *****

Mean Arrival Rate                                    :      20.000
Mean Service Rate                                    :      30.000


***** Program Output *****

Mean Number of Units in the System          :       2.000
Mean Number of Units in the Queue           :       1.333
Mean Time in the System                     :       0.100
Mean Time In the Queue                       :       0.067
Service Facility Utilization Factor         :       0.667
Probability of No Units in System           :       0.333

***** End of Output *****
```

The STORM computer package provides all the same solution results for the various system operating characteristics. The STORM package also provides the distribution of number in the system (as previously given in Table 10.5) in the form of a histogram. We can see from this histogram that the distribution of number in the system is exponential.

```
                    STORM DATA SET LISTING
                DETAILED PROBLEM DATA LISTING FOR
        Example 10.3 - Queuing Analysis of a Business FAX Machine
                      ROW LABEL   STATION  1


                    # SERVERS            1
                    SOURCE POP         INF
                    ARR RATE           20.
                    SERV DIST          EXP
                    SERV TIME     0.033333
                    SERV STD             .
                    WAIT CAP             .
                    # CUSTMERS           .
                    WAIT COST            .
                    COST/SERV            .
                    LOSTCUST C           .


        Example 10.3 - Queuing Analysis of a Business FAX Machine
                     STATION  1 : M / M / C
                  Q U E U E    S T A T I S T I C S


        Number of identical servers . . . . . . . . .          1
        Mean arrival rate . . . . . . . . . . . . .      20.0000
        Mean service rate per server  . . . . . . .      30.0003

        Mean server utilization (%) . . . . . . . .      66.6660
        Expected number of customers in queue . . . .    1.3333
        Expected number of customers in system   . . .   1.9999
        Probability that a customer must wait . . . .     0.6667
        Expected time in the queue  . . . . . . . . .     0.0667
        Expected time in the system . . . . . . . . .     0.1000


        Example 10.3 - Queuing Analysis of a Business FAX Machine
                     STATION  1 : M / M / C
              PROBABILITY DISTRIBUTION OF NUMBER IN SYSTEM
    Number   Prob  0   0.1  0.2  0.3  0.4  0.5  0.6  0.7  0.8  0.9   1
                  +----+----+----+----+----+----+----+----+----+----+

        0    0.3333I******************                                I
        1    0.2222I***********+-------------------                   I
        2    0.1481I********+-----------------------------------      I
        3    0.0988I*****-----------------------------------------    I
        4    0.0658I***+--------------------------------------------  I
        5    0.0439I**+--------------------------------------------- I
        6    0.0293I*+----------------------------------------------- I
        7    0.0195I*----------------------------------------------- I
        8    0.0130I*-----------------------------------------------I
        9    0.0087I+------------------------------------------------I
       10    0.0058I+------------------------------------------------I
     OVER    0.0116I*------------------------------------------------I
                  +----+----+----+----+----+----+----+----+----+----+
```

Example 10.4 Decision Analysis of Alternative FAX Operations

Suppose the management of the business firm described in Example 10.3 has determined that by assigning an operator to the FAX machine, rather than allowing the employees to operate the machine themselves, it can reduce the average service time from the current 2 minutes to 1.5 minutes. However, the FAX operator's salary is $8 per hour, which must be paid 8 hours per day even if there are no employees wishing to use the FAX machine part of the time. Management has estimated the cost of employee time spent waiting in line and at the FAX machine during service to be $.17 per minute (based on an average salary of $10.20 per hour per employee). Should the firm assign an operator to the FAX machine?

The system operating characteristics required to peform the decision analysis for this problem is L, the mean number in the system. (Remember, this is the same as λW, the mean arrival rate per hour times the mean time in the system per arrival, thus we could also solve for W and then compute λW to reach the same result).

Recall that in the initial problem, the arrival and service parameters were mean arrival rate at $\lambda = 20$/hour and mean service rate at $\mu = 30$/hour. In that case employees operated the FAX machine themselves and the mean number in the system (L) was 2.

In the alternative case, where an operator would operate the FAX machine, the arrival parameter is the same, but the service parameter is mean service time at $1/\mu = 1.5$ minutes, which translates to mean service rate of $\mu = 60/1.5 = 40$/hour. Solving our queuing equation for mean number in the system yields

$$L = \frac{\lambda}{\mu - \lambda} = \frac{20}{40 - 20} = 1 \text{ person in the system}$$

Note that by reducing the mean service time by a half minute, from two minutes to 1.5 minutes, which is a 25% reduction, we have reduced the mean number in the system by 50%, from 2 to 1 employees in the system on the average.

The decision analysis, using the cost figures provided initially, can be summarized as follows:

Alternative	Service Cost/hr	Waiting Cost/hr*	Total Cost/hr
1. No FAX operator	$0	(2)(10.20) = $20.40	$20.40
2. Use FAX operator	$8	(1)(10.20) = $10.20	$18.20

*Waiting cost includes time waiting in line and time waiting at FAX machines.

Note that we have again used cost per hour in our analysis (as we did in Example 10.2). If the number of working hours per day is 8, this analysis can be converted to a daily basis by multiplying all figures by 8, yielding $163.20 per day expected total waiting cost of alternative 1 and $145.60 per day expected total cost of service and waiting for alternative 2. Thus, the firm's management should assign an operator to the FAX machine with an expected annual savings of (163.20 − 145.60) × 250 = $4,400 (assuming a 250 day work year).

A summary of most of the solution results available for the $(M/M/1)$ model are provided and compared for the two alternatives as follows:

Operating Characteristic	Alternative 1 No FAX Operator	Alternative 2 FAX Operator	Differences (Alt. 1 − Alt. 2)
P_0	.33	.50	(.17)
$\rho = \lambda/\mu$	.67	.50	.17
L	2.0	1.0	1.0
L_q	1.33	.50	.83
W	.1 hr (6 min)	.05 hr (3 min)	.05 hr (3 min)
W_q	.0667 hr (4 min)	.025 hr (1.5 min)	.0417 hr (2.5 min)

We have already concluded from our cost analysis that alternative 2 is the best decision and the reduced values of the solution results for L, L_q, W, and W_q all seem to support this conclusion. However, some might be concerned that the FAX operator was idle 50% of the time ($P_0 = .50$) with the second alternative. However, by assigning an operator to the FAX machine, the efficiency of machine utilization (speed of service) was improved by 25% (from 2 minutes to 1.5 minutes), which must be considered, which in turn reduced employee idle time from an average of 6 minutes to 3 minutes, a 50% reduction! We see from the values for W and W_q that the average time waiting was reduced by 2.5 minutes, a 62.5% reduction in mean waiting time. The other half minute reduction in the value of W from alternative 1 to alternative 2 was the reduction in service time, from 2 minutes to 1.5 minutes per service. The decision analysis becomes even more clear if we convert the summary of costs from an hourly basis to a yearly basis, as follows:

	Annual Cost		
Alternative	FAX Operator Service Cost	Employees Using FAX Waiting Cost*	Total Cost
1. No FAX operator	0	$40,800	$40,800
2. Use FAX operator	$16,000	$20,400	$36,400
Cost Increase (Decrease)	$16,000	($20,400)	($4,400)

*Waiting cost includes time waiting in line and time waiting at FAX machine while being serviced.

$(M/G/1)$ Model: Poisson Arrivals, Undefined Service Times, One Server

In many cases, the service time cannot be assumed to fit an exponential distribution. However, if it can be assumed that the service times are independent, with some common probability distribution (*any* general distribution, as long as it is the same for all services) whose mean $(1/\mu)$ and standard deviation (σ) are known, then the following model equations define the system's operating characteristics:

$$\rho = \frac{\lambda}{\mu}$$

$$P_0 = 1 - \frac{\lambda}{\mu}$$

$$L_q = \frac{\lambda^2\sigma^2 + (\lambda/\mu)^2}{2(1 - \lambda/\mu)}$$

$$L = L_q + \frac{\lambda}{\mu}$$

$$W_q = \frac{L_q}{\lambda}$$

$$W = W_q + \frac{1}{\mu}$$

Example 10.5 FAX Machine with Undefined Service Times

For the business FAX machine operation in Example 10.3, service time might be instead some undefined, nonexponential distribution with mean $1/\mu = 2$ minutes $= \frac{1}{30}$ hour and standard deviation $\sigma = 4$ minutes $= \frac{1}{15}$ hour. The following operating characteristics would therefore be obtained:

$$\rho = \frac{20}{30} = 67\% \text{ machine utilization}$$

$$P_0 = 1 - \frac{20}{30} = .33 \text{ probability of no one using the machine}$$

$$L_q = \frac{(20)^2(1/15)^2 + (20/30)^2}{2(1 - 20/30)}$$

$$= \frac{(400)(1/225) + (400/900)}{2/3} = \frac{(3200 + 800)/1800}{2/3}$$

$$= \frac{4000}{1800}\left(\frac{3}{2}\right) = \frac{2000}{600} = 3.33 \text{ employees waiting in line}$$

$$L = 3.33 + \left(\frac{20}{30}\right) = 4.0 \text{ employees in line and using the FAX machine}$$

$$W_q = \frac{3.33}{20} = .1665 \text{ hr} \cong 10 \text{ min waiting in line on the average}$$

$$W = .1665 + \left(\frac{1}{30}\right) = .1665 + .0333$$

$$= .1998 \text{ hr} \cong 12 \text{ min in the system (waiting and using the machine) on the average}$$

It is interesting to compare the results just obtained to those obtained for the exponential service time case presented in Example 10.3. The two sets of solution results are summarized as follows:

	L_q Employees Waiting	L Employees in the System	W_q Minutes Waiting	W Minutes in the System
Exponential service times	1.33	2	4	6
Undefined service times	3.33	4	10	12

Recall from the discussion of the exponential distribution that the standard deviation is equal to the mean. For the case of arbitrary service times, we have doubled the standard deviation from 2 minutes to 4 minutes. Thus, the number in the system and the time in the system have both doubled. The number waiting and the waiting time have both increased by two and a half times. This indicates that, in addition to average service time, the variance of the services has an important effect on the performance of the queuing system.

Computerized Analysis of the (M/G/1) Model

The single-channel, single-phase queuing model with undefined service times (M/G/1) can also be analyzed with the STORM software package previously demonstrated for the (M/M/1) model. Following are the model input and the output analysis for Example 10.5. Notice that the distribution of the service time is input as a "general" distribution with a standard deviation of .06667.

```
                  STORM DATA SET LISTING
              DETAILED PROBLEM DATA LISTING FOR
   Example 10.5 - FAX Machine with Undefined Service Time Dist.
                ROW LABEL        QUEUE 1

                # SERVERS            1
                SOURCE POP         INF
                ARR RATE           20.
                SERV DIST          GEN
                SERV TIME      0.033333
                SERV STD       0.066667
                WAIT CAP            .
                # CUSTMERS          .
                WAIT COST           .
                COST/SERV           .
                LOSTCUST C          .


   Example 10.5 - FAX Machine with Undefined Service Time Dist.
                QUEUE 1 : M / G / C
             Q U E U E    S T A T I S T I C S


      Number of identical servers . . . . . . . .          1
      Mean arrival rate . . . . . . . . . . . .      20.0000
      Mean service rate per server  . . . . . . .    30.0003
      Standard deviation of service time  . . . . .   0.0667
```

```
Mean server utilization (%) . . . . . . . . .    66.6660
Expected number of customers in queue . . . .     3.3333
Expected number of customers in system  . . .     3.9999
Probability that a customer must wait . . . .     0.6667
Expected time in the queue   . . . . . . . .      0.1667
Expected time in the system . . . . . . . . .     0.2000
```

(M/D/1) Model: Poisson Arrivals, Constant Service Times, One Server

Although service time may not be constant for most real situations, it may be the case for mechanically performed operations. For this case, one may simply set $\sigma = 0$ and use the solution results obtained for the preceding (M/G/1) model.

(M/E$_k$/1) Model: Poisson Arrivals, Erlang Service Times, One Server

The Erlang distribution is an important distribution in queuing theory because it can be made to fit most empirically determined service times. The Erlang distribution (density function) is

$$f(t) = \frac{(\mu k)^k}{(k-1)!} t^{k-1} e^{-k\mu t}$$

where μ and k are parameters that determine the dispersion of the distribution. The Erlang distribution is shown, for several values of k, in Figure 10.8. Note that both the

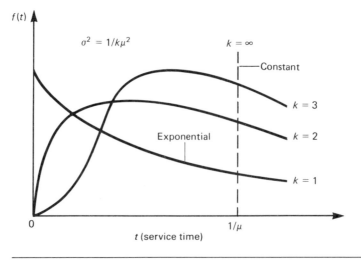

Figure 10.8 *Erlang Distribution for Selected Values of k*

exponential distribution ($k = 1$) and constant times ($k = \infty$) are special cases of the Erlang distribution.

An intuitive interpretation of k can be given as follows. Suppose a single server performs several functions for a customer. If the several respective functions (k) performed have identical exponential distributions with mean $1/k\mu$, then the aggregate service distribution is an Erlang distribution with parameters μ and k. The mean of the Erlang will be $1/\mu$, and the variance σ^2 will be $1/k\mu^2$. However, even if this is not the physical process, the Erlang distribution may fit the service time distribution. It is of interest to note that k is assumed to be an integer value in the Erlang distribution, and the Erlang distribution is therefore simply a special case of the *gamma* distribution, where k can be any real value.

To solve for the operating characteristics for the Erlang (or gamma) service time model, simply set $\sigma^2 = 1/k\mu^2$ and use the solution results for the (M/G/1) undefined service times model.

Example 10.6 Convenience Store Check-out Operation with Erlang Service Times

Assume that the check-out clerk at a convenience store performs two functions ($k = 2$) for each customer (ringing up the sale and bagging the items). The mean times to perform each component of the service are equal and identically distributed with means of one minute. The customer arrival rate is 20 per hour. The operating characteristics are computed for this situation as follows:

$$\rho = \frac{\lambda}{\mu} = \frac{20}{30} = .67$$

$$P_0 = 1 - \frac{2}{3} = .33$$

$$L_q = \frac{\lambda^2\sigma^2 + (\lambda/\mu)^2}{2(1 - \lambda/\mu)}$$

where

$$\sigma^2 = \frac{1}{k\mu^2} = \frac{1}{(2)(30)^2} = \frac{1}{1800}$$

Therefore,

$$L_q = \frac{(400)(1/1800) + (20/30)^2}{2(1 - 20/30)}$$

$$= 1 \text{ customer waiting}$$

$$L = L_q + \frac{\lambda}{\mu}$$

$$= 1 + \frac{2}{3}$$

$$= 1.67 \text{ customers in the system}$$

$$W_q = \frac{L_q}{\lambda} = \frac{1}{20}$$

$$= .05 \text{ hr} = 3 \text{ min waiting}$$

$$W = W_q + \frac{1}{\mu}$$

$$= .05 + \frac{1}{30}$$

$$= .083 \text{ hr} \cong 5 \text{ min in the system}$$

(M/M/1)(FIFO/Finite Queue/∞) Model: Poisson Arrivals, Exponential Service Times, One Server, Finite Queue

In many queuing systems, the length of the queue may be limited by the physical area in which the queue forms; space may permit only a limited number of customers to enter the queue. Such a queue is referred to as a *finite queue* and results in another variation of the single-phase, single-channel queuing model.

The (M/M/1) model must be modified to consider the truncated (finite) queuing system. It should be noted that for this case the service rate does *not* have to exceed the arrival rate ($\mu > \lambda$) in order to obtain steady-state conditions. The resultant operating characteristics, where M is the maximum number in the system, are as follows:

$$P_0 = \frac{1 - \lambda/\mu}{1 - (\lambda/\mu)^{M+1}}$$

$$P_n = (P_0)\left(\frac{\lambda}{\mu}\right)^n \quad \text{for } n \leqslant M$$

$$L = \frac{\lambda/\mu}{1 - \lambda/\mu} - \frac{(M+1)(\lambda/\mu)^{M+1}}{1 - (\lambda/\mu)^{M+1}}$$

Since P_n is the probability of n units in the system, if we define M as the maximum number allowed in the system, then P_M (the value of P_n for $n = M$) is the probability that a customer will not join the system. The remaining equations are

$$L_q = L - \frac{\lambda(1 - P_M)}{\mu}$$

$$W = \frac{L}{\lambda(1 - P_M)}$$

$$W_q = W - \frac{1}{\mu}$$

Example 10.7 Quick Lube Service Facility with a Finite Queue

A one-bay quick lube service facility is located next to a busy highway in a major metropolitan area. The facility only has space for one vehicle in service and three vehicles lined up to wait for service. There is no space for cars to line up on the busy adjacent highway so, if the parking area is full (3 cars), the prospective customers drive on to seek service elsewhere.

The mean time between arrivals for customers seeking lube service is 3 minutes. The mean time required to perform the lube operation is 2 minutes. Both the interarrival times and the service times are exponentially distributed. As stated previously, the maximum number of vehicles in the system is four. The operating characteristics for this system are computed as follows:

$$P_0 = \frac{1 - 20/30}{1 - (20/30)^5} = .38$$

$$P_M = (.38)\left(\frac{20}{30}\right)^4$$

$\cong .076$ probability of $M = 4$ in the system

$$L = \frac{20/30}{1 - 20/30} - \frac{(5)(20/30)^5}{1 - (20/30)^5}$$

$\cong 1.24$ customers in the system

$$L_q = 1.24 - \frac{20(1 - .076)}{30}$$

$\cong .62$ customer waiting

$$W = \frac{1.24}{20(1 - .076)} = .07 \text{ hr}$$

$\cong 4.2$ min in the system

$$W_q = .07 - \frac{1}{30} = .04 \text{ hr}$$

$\cong 2.4$ min waiting

Computerized Analysis of the (M/M/1) Finite Queue Model

This (M/M/1) model with a finite queue also can be analyzed using the STORM software package. Following are the model input and program solution results for Example 10.7. Note that the STORM output also provides a probability distribution of the number in the system which is truncated at $n = 4$, the maximum number in the system. Note also that the STORM output gives the probability of service denials (.0758), which is the same as the P_M value calculated manually above.

```
                    STORM DATA SET LISTING
                DETAILED PROBLEM DATA LISTING FOR
        Example 10.7 - Quick Lube Facility with a Finite Queue
                    ROW LABEL   STATION   1

                        # SERVERS              1
                        SOURCE POP           INF
                        ARR RATE             20.
                        SERV DIST            EXP
                        SERV TIME      0.033333
                        SERV STD              .
                        WAIT CAP              3
                        # CUSTMERS            .
                        WAIT COST             .
                        COST/SERV             .
                        LOSTCUST C            .
```

```
      Example 10.7 - Quick Lube Facility with a Finite Queue
                 STATION  1 : M / M / C / K
                 Q U E U E    S T A T I S T I C S


      Number of identical servers . . . . . . . . . .        1
      Mean arrival rate . . . . . . . . . . . . . . .    20.0000
      Mean service rate per server  . . . . . . . .      30.0003
      Waiting room capacity . . . . . . . . . . . .           3

      Mean server utilization (%) . . . . . . . . .      61.6109
      Expected number of customers in queue . . . .       0.6256
      Expected number of customers in system  . . .       1.2417
      Probability that a customer must wait . . . .       0.6161
      Probability of service denial . . . . . . . .       0.0758



      Example 10.7 - Quick Lube Facility with a Finite Queue
                 STATION  1 : M / M / C / K
         PROBABILITY DISTRIBUTION OF NUMBER IN SYSTEM
  Number  Prob  0   0.1  0.2  0.3  0.4  0.5  0.6  0.7  0.8  0.9   1
              +----+----+----+----+----+----+----+----+----+----+

    0   0.3839|********************+                               |
    1   0.2559|*************-------------------                    |
    2   0.1706|*********-----------------------------------        |
    3   0.1137|******---------------------------------------------  |
    4   0.0759|****-----------------------------------------------|
              +----+----+----+----+----+----+----+----+----+----+
```

(M/M/1)(FIFO/∞/Finite Population) Model: Poisson Arrivals, Exponential Service Times, One Server, Finite Population

For the case of a finite number of machines that must be repaired when they break down, the *infinite* calling population model is not appropriate. As previously stated, this is because the probability of arrivals is affected by the number of arrivals that have already occurred. Recall that previously $1/\lambda$ was defined as the mean time between arrivals. In the case of the finite calling population, however, each machine alternates between being outside the queuing system (i.e., the machine is in operation) and being inside the queuing system (i.e., the machine is being repaired or waiting to be repaired). Thus, $1/\lambda$ is defined as the mean time between breakdowns *of machines in operation*. If the time spent outside the system between failures and the service time are exponentially distributed with means $1/\lambda$ and $1/\mu$, respectively, then the operating characteristics are given as follows:

$$P_0 = \frac{1}{\displaystyle\sum_{n=0}^{N} \frac{N!}{(N-n)!}\left(\frac{\lambda}{\mu}\right)^n}, \quad \text{where } N = \text{population size}$$

$$P_n = \frac{N!}{(N - n)!} \left(\frac{\lambda}{\mu}\right)^n P_0, \quad \text{where } n = 1, 2, \ldots, N$$

$$L_q = N - \frac{\lambda + \mu}{\lambda}(1 - P_0)$$

$$L = L_q + (1 - P_0)$$

$$W_q = \frac{L_q}{(N - L)\lambda}$$

$$W = W_q + \frac{1}{\mu}$$

Example 10.8   Machine Repair in a Job Shop

A company operating a job shop has 30 machines. Due to the type of work performed in the shop, there is a lot of wear and tear on the machines, and they require frequent repair. When a machine breaks down, it is tagged for repair, with the date of breakdown noted. The company has one senior repair person with an assistant who repairs the machines based on an oldest-date-of-breakdown rule (i.e., a FIFO queue discipline). The mean time between machine breakdowns is 60 hours, and the mean repair time is 2.4 hours. Both the breakdown interarrival times and the service times are exponentially distributed. The company would like an analysis performed of machine idle time due to breakdowns.

Computerized Analysis of the (M/M/1) Finite Population Problem

The preceding job shop machine repair problem was analyzed using the STORM package as shown on page 501. It shows that the repair person and assistant are busy 95% of the time repairing machines. Of the 30 machines, an average of 6.3, or 21%, are broken down waiting for repair or under repair. Each broken down machine is idle, (broken down waiting for repair or under repair) an average of 16 hours (two working days, or $2/5 = 40\%$ of a working week). Obviously, this problem needs attention. The company cannot afford to have an average of 21% of their machines idle, with an average idle time of 40% of a working week. Their initial feeling was that with an average of 60 hours between machine breakdowns (one every 7.5 days) and only 2.5 hours to repair a broken down machine, one repair team should be more than adequate. Their intuitive reasoning was not reliable in this case. They will add a second repair team.

A number of additional single-server queuing models have been developed. Examples include systems in which the server works faster as the queue becomes longer and systems in which the arrival rate is reduced as the queue lengthens. Models have also been developed for queue disciplines other than first-come, first-served, such as service in random order or priority discipline models. These and other advanced single-server models are, however, beyond the scope of this book.

```
                    STORM DATA SET LISTING
                DETAILED PROBLEM DATA LISTING FOR
           Example 10.8 - Machine Repair in a Job Shop
                    ROW LABEL        QUEUE 1

                    # SERVERS           1
                    SOURCE POP        FIN
                    ARR RATE     0.016667
                    SERV DIST         EXP
                    SERV TIME         2.4
                    SERV STD            .
                    WAIT CAP            .
                    # CUSTMERS         30
                    WAIT COST           .
                    COST/SERV           .
                    LOSTCUST C          .


              Example 10.8 - Machine Repair in a Job Shop
                   QUEUE 1 : M / M / C / K / K
                   Q U E U E   S T A T I S T I C S


        Number of identical servers . . . . . . . . .          1
        Mean arrival rate per customer  . . . . . .       0.0167
        Mean service rate per server  . . . . . . .       0.4167
        Size of the source population . . . . . . .           30

        Mean server utilization (%) . . . . . . . .      94.7403
        Expected number of customers in queue . . .       5.3680
        Expected number of customers in system  . .       6.3154
        Probability that a customer must wait . . .       0.9474
        Expected time in the queue  . . . . . . . .      13.5984
        Expected time in the system . . . . . . . .      15.9984


              Example 10.8 - Machine Repair in a Job Shop
                   QUEUE 1 : M / M / C / K / K
             PROBABILITY DISTRIBUTION OF NUMBER IN SYSTEM
Number  Prob  0   0.1  0.2  0.3  0.4  0.5  0.6  0.7  0.8  0.9   1
              +----+----+----+----+----+----+----+----+----+----+

    0   0.0526|***                                              |
    1   0.0631|***+--                                           |
    2   0.0732|****-----                                        |
    3   0.0820|****+---------                                   |
    4   0.0886|****+-------------                               |
    5   0.0921|*****------------------                          |
    6   0.0921|*****---------------------                       |
    7   0.0884|*****+--------------------------                 |
    8   0.0814|****+--------------------------------            |
    9   0.0716|****------------------------------------         |
   10   0.0601|***+------------------------------------------   |
   11   0.0481|**+----------------------------------------------|
   12   0.0366|**----------------------------------------------|
   13   0.0263|*+----------------------------------------------|
   14   0.0179|*-----------------------------------------------|
   15   0.0115|*-----------------------------------------------|
   16   0.0069|+-----------------------------------------------|
 OVER   0.0075|+-----------------------------------------------|
              +----+----+----+----+----+----+----+----+----+----+
```

MULTIPLE-CHANNEL, SINGLE-PHASE QUEUING MODELS

Since a large number of real-world queuing systems include multiple servers, an introductory presentation of multiple-channel models will be given. Multiple-channel models, however, can become quite complex, and therefore only a limited case will be considered.

Prior to its presentation, the multiple-channel model should be carefully distinguished from other similar queuing systems. The multiple-channel, single-phase model to be presented assumes that *a single waiting line* forms prior to the service facility. The service facility contains several servers, who serve customers from the single queue as the servers become available. Service is on a first-come, first-served basis. This case was illustrated in Figure 10.2. Such a situation might exist, for example, if there were several postal clerks operating separate stations along the service counter in a post office, with people arriving and waiting in a single line for service from the first available postal clerk.

Another version of this same queuing system configuration is given by the case where customers take a numbered ticket from an automatic dispensing machine upon entry to the post office. Each time a postal employee begins a service he or she presses a button that advances the number shown on the wall by an electronic device. Each time a postal employee finishes a service, he or she glances up at the number shown by the electronic posting device and calls out the next higher number. Thus, the system is in effect a multiple server system with a single queue of customers, being served by a FIFO queue discipline.

This would not be the case for systems such as grocery store checkout counters, where a separate queue forms behind each counter. This type of system would actually represent several single-channel, single-phase facilities operating simultaneously. Since customers do not often move from one line to the other (jockey) in the grocery store example, this system could be studied by applying single-server models to each facility. However, when customers commonly jockey from one queue to another, such as from one teller line to another in a bank, neither the multiple-channel model (for all tellers) nor the single-channel model (for each teller independently) is appropriate for analysis of the system. For more complex queuing processes such as this, simulation can be used.

(M/M/s) Model: Poisson Arrivals, Exponential Service Times, s Servers

The multiple-channel, single-phase model to be presented here assumes Poisson arrivals and exponential service times. Arrivals are assumed to come from an infinite population, and an unlimited (infinite) queue may build up. Service is on a first-come, first-served basis. The mean effective service rate for the overall system is $s \cdot \mu$, where s equals the number of servers and $s \cdot \mu$ exceeds the customer arrival rate (λ). It is further assumed that the service time distribution is the same, regardless of which one of the servers performs the service for a customer.

The steady-state results for the previously described model are given as follows:

$$P_0 = \frac{1}{\left(\displaystyle\sum_{n=0}^{s-1} \frac{(\lambda/\mu)^n}{n!} \right) + \left(\dfrac{(\lambda/\mu)^s}{s!(1 - \lambda/s\mu)} \right)}$$

$$P_n = \begin{cases} \dfrac{(\lambda/\mu)^n}{n!} P_0, & \text{if } n \leqslant s \\[3mm] \dfrac{(\lambda/\mu)^n}{s! s^{n-s}} P_0, & \text{if } n > s \end{cases}$$

$$\rho = \frac{\lambda}{s\mu}$$

$$L_q = \frac{P_0(\lambda/\mu)^s \rho}{s!(1-\rho)^2}$$

$$L = L_q + \frac{\lambda}{\mu}$$

$$W_q = \frac{L_q}{\lambda}$$

$$W = W_q + \frac{1}{\mu}$$

Example 10.9 Truck Arrivals at a Multiple-Channel Shipping Terminal

Trucks arrive at a regional shipping terminal to be unloaded and loaded. The terminal dock has a capacity for three trucks to load or unload simultaneously. As trucks enter the terminal parking lot, the drivers receive numbered cards. When one of the three dock spaces becomes available, the truck with the lowest number backs up to the available dock space. In terms of queuing models, the system can be described as a three-channel, single-phase facility, with first-come, first-served queue discipline.

Further assume that truck arrivals are Poisson distributed and unloading and loading (service) times are exponentially distributed. The terminal grounds are sufficiently large that there is no significant limit to the number of trucks that can be waiting at any one time.

If the average truck arrival rate is 5 per hour and the average service rate per dock space is 2 per hour (30 minutes per truck), the system's steady-state operating characteristics are computed from the following system inputs.

$$\lambda = 5$$
$$\mu = 2$$
$$s = 3$$
$$s\mu = 6$$
$$\rho = \frac{\lambda}{s\mu} = \frac{5}{(3)(2)} = \frac{5}{6} = .8333$$

To determine P_0, first compute the initial term in the denominator of the formula as follows:

$$\sum_{n=0}^{s-1} \frac{(\lambda/\mu)^n}{n!} = \frac{(\lambda/\mu)^0}{0!} + \frac{(\lambda/\mu)^1}{1!} + \frac{(\lambda/\mu)^2}{2!}$$

$$= \frac{(5/2)^0}{0!} + \frac{(5/2)^1}{1!} + \frac{(5/2)^2}{2!}$$

$$= \frac{1}{1} + \frac{2.5}{1} + \frac{6.25}{2}$$
$$= 1 + 2.5 + 3.125$$
$$= 6.625$$

The second term in the denominator of the P_0 formula is

$$\frac{(\lambda/\mu)^s}{s!(1 - \lambda/s\mu)} = \frac{(5/2)^3}{3!(1 - 5/6)} = \frac{125/8}{6(1/6)} = 15.625$$

Therefore,

$$P_0 = \frac{1}{6.625 + 15.625} = \frac{1}{22.25}$$
$$= .0449$$

Since considerable computational effort is involved in calculating the value of P_0, a table of values for P_0 has been provided in Appendix C, Table C.4, for various combinations of $\lambda/\mu s$ (utilization factor) and s (number of channels).

The system's other operating characteristics are as follows:

$$L_q = \frac{P_0(\lambda/\mu)^s \rho}{s!(1 - \rho)^2}$$
$$= \frac{(.0449)(5/2)^3(5/6)}{3!(1 - 5/6)^2} = \frac{(.0449)(125/8)(5/6)}{(6)(1/36)}$$
$$= (.0449)\left(\frac{625}{48}\right)\left(\frac{6}{1}\right) = (.0449)\left(\frac{625}{8}\right)$$
$$\cong 3.5 \text{ trucks waiting}$$

$$L = L_q + \frac{\lambda}{\mu} = 3.5 + \frac{5}{2}$$
$$= 6.0 \text{ trucks in the system}$$

$$W_q = \frac{L_q}{\lambda} = \frac{3.5}{5}$$
$$= .7 \text{ hr} = 42 \text{ min waiting time}$$

$$W = W_q + \frac{1}{\mu} = .7 + \frac{1}{2}$$
$$= 1.2 \text{ hr} = 72 \text{ min in the system}$$

Thus, on the average, there will be 6 trucks in the system, with an average of 3.5 trucks waiting for service. The difference of 2.5 is the average number of trucks in service in the 3 service locations, which reflects the fact that a portion of the time one or more servers will be idle. In fact, the entire system will be idle almost 5% of the time ($P_0 = .0449$). The mean time in the system will be 72 minutes, of which 42 minutes will be spent waiting for a dock space. The difference of 30 minutes is exactly the expected service time, $1/\mu$, originally specified.

It is also of considerable interest to know how many trucks can be expected to be in the system at any one time. Probabilities of various numbers of trucks in the system are given by

$$P_n = \begin{cases} \dfrac{(\lambda/\mu)^n}{n!} \, P_0, \text{ if } n \leqslant s \\ \dfrac{(\lambda/\mu)^n}{s! s^{n-s}} \, P_0, \text{ if } n > s \end{cases}$$

For some particular values of n, the probabilities are as follows.

$$P(n = 1) = \frac{(5/2)^1}{1!} (.0449) = .11225$$

$$P(n = 2) = \frac{(5/2)^2}{2!} (.0449) = .14031$$

$$P(n = 3) = \frac{(5/2)^3}{3!} (.0449) = .11693$$

$$P(n = 4) = \frac{(5/2)^4}{3! 3^{4-3}} (.0049) = .09744$$

$$P(n = 5) = \frac{(5/2)^5}{3! 3^{5-3}} (.0449) = .08120$$

The preceding values are included in a summary of the numbers in the system, along with associated individual probabilities and cumulative probabilities, in the Table 10.6.

This table shows that the probability distribution of the number in the system is rather flat and widely dispersed. Thus, even though the expected (mean) number in the system is 6, management may wish to know the chance of having 10 or more trucks in the system (i.e., the probability that there will be 7 or more trucks waiting to unload and load). The probability of having 10 or more trucks in the system is given by $P(n \geqslant 10) = 1 - P(n \leqslant 9)$, where $P(n \leqslant 9)$ is obtained from the table as .801. Therefore, there is about a 20% chance that there will be 10 or more trucks in the system. In other words, 20% of the time there will be at least 10 trucks in the system.

Table 10.6 *Probability Distribution of Number in the System*

n Number in the System	P_n Probability	N N or Less in the System	$P_n \leqslant N$ Cumulative Probability
0	.045	0	.045
1	.112	1	.157
2	.140	2	.297
3	.117	3	.414
4	.097	4	.511
5	.081	5	.592
6	.068	6	.660
7	.056	7	.716
8	.047	8	.763
9	.038	9	.801
10	.033	10	.834
11	.027	11	.861
12	.023	12	.884
13	.019	13	.903
14	.016	14	.919
15	.013	15	.932

The sample problem raises some interesting questions regarding various methods for changing the service level. Several possibilities exist. Management could consider increasing the number of service positions at the dock (increasing the number of channels). It could also consider trying to increase the service rate with the existing capacity. This might be done by hiring more labor to unload and load trucks, or by installing faster and more efficient equipment. It should be noted that even though several persons might be employed at each individual dock position, the position can still be thought of as one of the several channels, and μ can be varied by adding or subtracting personnel.

Several other multiple-channel, single-phase models have been developed, such as for the cases of truncated queues and finite calling populations. These, however, are beyond the scope of this chapter.

Computerized Analysis of the (M/M/s) Model

The multiple-channel, single-phase queuing model (M/M/3) can be analyzed using the STORM software package demonstrated on several occasions previously in this chapter. Following are the model input and the program output for Example 10.9.

```
                    STORM DATA SET LISTING
                DETAILED PROBLEM DATA LISTING FOR
       Example 10.9 - Multiple-Channel Truck Shipping Terminal
                   ROW LABEL    STATION   1

                   # SERVERS           3
                   SOURCE POP        INF
                   ARR RATE          5.
                   SERV DIST         EXP
                   SERV TIME         0.5
                   SERV STD           .
                   WAIT CAP           .
                   # CUSTMERS         .
                   WAIT COST          .
                   COST/SERV          .
                   LOSTCUST C         .


       Example 10.9 - Multiple-Channel Truck Shipping Terminal
                 STATION   1 : M / M / C
             Q U E U E    S T A T I S T I C S


   Number of identical servers . . . . . . . . .           3
   Mean arrival rate . . . . . . . . . . . . .        5.0000
   Mean service rate per server  . . . . . . .        2.0000

   Mean server utilization (%) . . . . . . . . .     83.3333
   Expected number of customers in queue . . . .      3.5112
   Expected number of customers in system  . . .      6.0112
   Probability that a customer must wait . . . .      0.7022
   Expected time in the queue  . . . . . . . . .      0.7022
   Expected time in the system . . . . . . . . .      1.2022
```

```
        Example 10.9 - Multiple-Channel Truck Shipping Terminal
                      STATION  1 : M / M / C
              PROBABILITY DISTRIBUTION OF NUMBER IN SYSTEM
Number   Prob  0    0.1   0.2   0.3   0.4   0.5   0.6   0.7   0.8   0.9   1
               +----+----+----+----+----+----+----+----+----+----+
    0   0.0449|**+                                                         |
    1   0.1124|******--                                                    |
    2   0.1404|*******+-------                                             |
    3   0.1170|******-------------                                         |
    4   0.0975|*****----------------------                                 |
    5   0.0813|****+-------------------------                              |
    6   0.0677|***+--------------------------------                        |
    7   0.0564|***-------------------------------------                    |
    8   0.0470|**+-----------------------------------------                |
    9   0.0392|**--------------------------------------------              |
   10   0.0327|**------------------------------------------------          |
   11   0.0272|*+---------------------------------------------------       |
   12   0.0227|*+-----------------------------------------------------     |
   13   0.0189|*------------------------------------------------------     |
   14   0.0158|*-------------------------------------------------------    |
   15   0.0131|*--------------------------------------------------------   |
   16   0.0109|*---------------------------------------------------------  |
   17   0.0091|+---------------------------------------------------------- |
   18   0.0076|+---------------------------------------------------------- |
   19   0.0063|+-----------------------------------------------------------|
   20   0.0053|+-----------------------------------------------------------|
 OVER   0.0266|*+----------------------------------------------------------|
               +----+----+----+----+----+----+----+----+----+----+
```

MULTIPLE-PHASE QUEUING MODELS

Multiple-phase queuing models will not be analyzed in detail in this chapter, since they become extremely complex very quickly. However, one case should be discussed. If the multiple-phase system satisfies all the assumptions of Poisson arrivals, exponential service times, infinite calling population, infinite possible queues, and service rate(s) exceeding arrival rate(s), then the multiple-phase system can be analyzed rather easily.

The fundamental point here is that if a service facility has a Poisson input with parameter λ and an exponential service time distribution with parameter μ (where $\mu > \lambda$), then the steady-state *output* of this service facility is also a Poisson process with parameter λ. Thus, each successive facility in a multiple-phase system will have a Poisson input with parameter λ. This condition will hold for the single-channel model and for the multiple-channel model just discussed (if $s\mu > \lambda$).

The individual phases, therefore, may be evaluated independently of one another, and the aggregate operating characteristics can be obtained by summing the corresponding values obtained at the respective facilities. The operating characteristics referred to are total expected waiting time, total expected time in the system, total expected number in queues, and total expected number in the overall system. It is important to note here that the intermediate queues are also assumed to be allowed to build up to any length.

Figure 10.9 illustrates three types of multiple-phase models that can be analyzed by this procedure, if the previously stated assumptions are met. Figure 10.9(A) is simply a single-channel, multiple-phase model. The two phases are evaluated independently, and the individual phase characteristics summed. Figure 10.9(B) represents two stages of a multiple-channel, single-phase process. Thus, each stage is evaluated independently according to the multiple-channel, single-phase equations, and the resulting operating characteristics are summed. Figure 10.9(C) represents a multiple-channel, single-phase stage, followed by a single-channel, single-phase stage for each of the three servers. This system is evaluated by solving the multiple-channel, single-phase equations for the first stage and then solving one of the following stages as a single-channel, single-phase process, with $\lambda_i = \lambda/3$ (where λ_i = mean arrival rate at the second stage for channel i server). Recall that the multiple-channel, single-phase model assumes that the service rate is identical for each server, yielding the assumption that $\lambda_i = \lambda/3$. Since the results are the same for each of the three second-stage servers, only one of these needs to be evaluated.

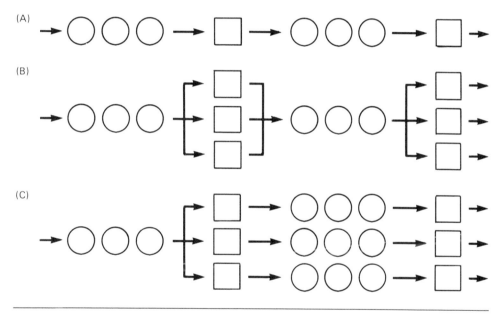

Figure 10.9 *Multiphase Models: (A) Single-Channel, Multiple-Phase; (B) Multiple-Channel, Multiple-Phase (case 1); (C) Multiple-Channel, Multiple-Phase (case 2)*

SIMULATION OF QUEUING SYSTEMS

Although the various queuing models presented in this chapter provide the solution to a wide variety of realistic queuing problems, there are other complex queuing systems to which no specific analytic model is directly applicable. For queuing systems that cannot be solved analytically, simulation provides a viable alternative. Examples of such complex

An Application of Queuing Analysis:
Providing Optimal Telephone Order Service at L.L. Bean

L.L. Bean is a popular retailer of outdoor clothing and equipment with over 65% of its sales in 1989 generated through 800-service telephone orders. Long-term decisions in the telemarketing operation relate to the number of telephone (trunk) lines to install, the number of agent positions, and support equipment, while short-term decisions must be made on daily staff scheduling and queue capacity (i.e., the maximum number of calls waiting). Intermediate decisions include the number of agents that are hired and trained.

While these decisions are normally routine, the situation changes dramatically during the three-week period prior to Christmas at which time 18% of the annual call-order volume is received. At this time, management must make rapid, critical decisions about daily schedules, the number of agents on duty, the number of temporary agents to hire and train, the number of

work stations, the number of telephone trunk lines, and other operational capacity considerations. At the other extreme, following this peak period, the system must gear down to reflect a reduction in call volume.

By 1988 L.L. Bean felt that decisions in this scenario were not optimal and customer service levels had become unacceptable. On sales of $580 million in 1988 the company estimated a loss of $10 million in profit due to the suboptimal allocation of resources and unacceptable customer service. In some time periods, 80% of calls received a busy signal and customers who connected might have waited 10 minutes for an agent. On very busy days the total lost orders because of busy signals and caller abandonment while waiting for an agent approached $500,000 in gross revenues.

To address this problem an economic-optimization model (EOM) was developed based

queuing systems include a network of queues in which the leaving customers from several queuing systems provide the arrivals for succeeding queuing systems. A complex manufacturing system in which the in-process output from several production areas or production lines is the input to subsequent production areas or lines is an example of such a network. For such complex systems, a specific analytical model, such as those presented in this chapter, is not available, and simulation is the only alternative.

The topic of simulation is the subject of Chapter 11 of this text. Several of the examples in Chapter 11 demonstrate, in very general terms, how queuing systems can be modeled and simulated to yield operating characteristics for the queuing system of interest. Also, there are several computer languages (such as Q-GERT and GPSS, referenced in Chapter 11) and textbooks (see, for example, Solomon in the reference list for this chapter) that are specifically directed at the simulation of queuing systems.

SUMMARY Several analytical models of queuing systems have been presented, along with the resulting equations that yield solution results for obtaining measures of each system's perfor-

on queuing analysis. The purpose of the model was to determine the optimal number of telephone trunks for incoming calls, the number of agents scheduled, and the queue capacity (the maximum number of customers who are put on hold to wait for an agent). The model objective was to minimize expected cost rather than simply achieve a specific service level, which is frequently the basis of queuing analysis. In general, the EOM balanced the cost of the resources (i.e., trunk lines and agents) against the sum of queuing costs and the cost of lost orders, at a point where total costs were minimized. Multiple-server and finite queue models were used to estimate operating characteristics for the trunk lines and agents, respectively, which were then used to determine the economic impact of busy signals, customer waiting time, and lost orders. Call arrivals were assumed to be represented by the Poisson distribution and customer service and trunk service lines were assumed to follow the negative exponential distribution.

The model was implemented in 1989, and for the three-week peak holiday season, the number of telephone agents was increased from 500 to 1,275, and the number of telephone trunk lines was increased from 150 to 576. Comparing this three-week period in 1989 (with EOM) and the same period in 1988 (without EOM), showed a 24% increase in calls answered, a 16.7% increase in orders taken, an increase in revenues of 16.3% (approximately $15 million), an 81.3% reduction in the number of callers who abandoned, and a reduction in the average answer speed from 93 seconds to 15 seconds. Annual profits increased by approximately $10 million and the cost savings was estimated at approximately $1.6 million. The model also had the effect of improving agent morale and alleviating customer dissatisfaction due to long waits. The cost for this management science project was $40,000.

Source: P. Quinn et al., "Allocating Telecommunications Resources at L.L. Bean, Inc.," *Interfaces,* 21, no. 1 (January–February 1991): 75–91.

mance. However, the reader can quickly appreciate that the number of conceivable waiting line models is almost infinite.

The purpose of this chapter has been to give you a feel for the analysis of waiting line systems and the methods of obtaining at least rough approximations of the operating characteristics. The techniques of Markov analysis (Chapter 9) and simulation (Chapter 11) can also be employed to analyze queuing systems. The interested reader should explore these techniques with queuing possibilities in mind.

REFERENCES

COOPER, R. B. *Introduction to Queueing Theory,* 2nd ed. New York: North Holland, 1981.

GROSS, D., and HARRIS, C. *Fundamentals of Queueing Theory,* 2nd ed. New York: John Wiley & Sons, 1985.

HILLIER, F. S., and YU, O. S. *Queueing Tables and Graphics.* New York: North-Holland, 1981.

KLEINROCK, L. *Queueing Systems,* Vols. 1 and 2. New York: John Wiley & Sons, 1975.

LEE, A. *Applied Queuing Theory.* New York: St. Martin's Press, 1966.

MORSE, P. M. *Queues, Inventories, and Main-*

tenance. New York: John Wiley & Sons, 1958.

SAATY, T. L. *Elements of Queueing Theory with Applications.* New York: Dover, 1983.

SOLOMON, S. L. *Simulation of Waiting-Line Systems.* Englewood Cliffs, New Jersey: Prentice-Hall, 1983.

WHITE, J. A., SCHMIDT, J. W., and BENNETT, G. K. *Analysis of Queueing Systems.* New York: Academic Press, 1975.

PROBLEMS

1. Consider a service process with the following characteristics:

   Infinite calling population
   Infinite possible queue
   First-come, first-served queue discipline
   Steady-state condition
   Service rate exceeds arrival rate
   Single-channel, single-phase system
   Poisson arrival rate, exponential service times

   Assume that customer arrivals occur at a mean rate of 3 per hour ($\lambda = 3$) and the mean service rate is 5 per hour ($\mu = 5$).

   a. What is the probability of exactly 1 arrival during the first hour? 2 arrivals? 3 arrivals? 4 arrivals? What is the probability there will be 4 or more arrivals during the first hour?
   b. What is the probability that the first arrival will require a service time of at least 6 minutes (.1 hour)? 12 minutes (.2 hour)? 30 minutes (.5 hour)?
   c. What percent of the time will the server be idle?
   d. What is the expected (mean) waiting time per arrival, in hours and in minutes?
   e. What is the mean number of arrivals waiting?
   f. What is the average time in the system (waiting and in service), in hours and in minutes?
   g. What is the average number of arrivals in the system?
   h. What value is the utilization factor?

2. For problem 1, construct a probability distribution for k or more units in the system, for values of k ranging from 0 to 6. Suppose it is highly undesirable to have a waiting line of 3 or more arrivals. What is the probability that this will happen?

3. Refer to problem 1. Compute and prepare a table of the values of λ/μ and L_q for λ values 1, 2, 3, 4, 4.5, and 5. Plot the values of L_q versus values of λ/μ. Describe what happens as the mean arrival rate approaches the mean service rate (i.e., as the ratio of λ/μ approaches 1).

4. A single-server queuing system with an infinite calling population, first-come, first-served queue discipline, Poisson arrival rate, and exponential service time has the following mean arrival and service rates:

   $\lambda = 16$ customers per hour
   $\mu = 24$ customers per hour

   Determine P_0, P_3, L, L_q, W, W_q, and the utilization factor.

5. The ticket booth on a university campus is operated by one person, who sells tickets for a football game on Saturday. The ticket seller can serve 12 customers per hour (exponentially distributed). An average of 10 customers arrive to purchase tickets every hour (Poisson distributed). Determine the average time a ticket buyer must wait in line to buy a ticket and the portion of the time the ticket seller is busy.

   The ticket seller is to be fired for being too slow (and making customers wait too long). The position advertisement stipulates that the person filling this position must serve customers at the average rate of 13 per hour. What will be the percentage reduction in average waiting time per customer with the new ticket seller?

6. A television repair service recieves for repair an average of 6 TV sets per 8-hour day. The service manager would like to be able to tell customers that they can expect to get their repaired TV set back in 4 days. What average repair time per set will have to be achieved by the repair shop to provide a 4-day turn-around on the average? (Assume that both interarrival times and repair times are exponentially distributed). Suppose that the repair shop cannot accommodate (store) more than 30 TV sets at a time. What is the probability that the number of sets on hand (under repair and waiting for repair) will exceed the shop capacity? What is the implication of this solution result?

7. For problem 1, assume that it is possible to control the service rate (e.g., vary the available personnel in the service facility). Assume that the following service rates may be obtained at the associated costs:

Service Rate (μ)	Service Cost per Hour
4 customers/hr	$ 3.00
4.5	6.00
5	9.00
5.5	12.00
6	15.00

   Further assume that the cost of having a customer waiting is estimated to be $10 per hour. Analyze the system over a period of 8 hours. Assume that the system is in a steady state at the beginning of the 8-hour period of analysis.

   a. Determine the optimal service level (service rate) and the associated expected total cost. Prepare a table of values showing your analysis.
   b. Illustrate the decision analysis graphically, showing service cost, customer waiting cost, and total cost for the various service rates considered.

8. Partially completed products arrive at a work station in a manufacturing operation at a mean rate of 40 per hour (Poisson distributed). The processing time at the work station averages 1.2 minutes per unit (exponentially distributed). The manufacturing company estimates that holding each unit of in-process inventory at the work station costs (on the average) $31 per day. At a cost of $52 per day, the company could add extra employees and reduce the service time to .9 minute per unit. Determine whether the company should continue the present operation or add the extra employees.

9. A one-pump country gas station sells only unleaded gasoline pumped by an attendant. The attendant can service a customer in an average of 6 minutes (exponentially
   distributed). Customers arrive at the station at an average rate of 6 per hour (Poisson
   distributed). Determine the average number of customers waiting, the average time
   in the system for a customer, and the average time a customer must wait. If during
   a gasoline shortage the arrival rate increased to 12 customers per hour, what effect
   would this increase have on the average queue length?

10. A manufacturing firm produces a particular product in an assembly line operation.
    One of the machines on the line is a press that has a single line of in-process parts
    feeding into it. Units arrive at the press to be worked on according to a Poisson
    distribution with a mean rate of 8 per hour. Operator processing times are exponen-
    tially distributed with a mean of 6 minutes.

    a. Determine the average number of parts waiting to be worked on, the percentage
       of time the operator is working, and the percentage of time the machine is idle.
    b. The management of the firm has indicated a desire to have operators working
       90% of the time. Determine the mean arrival rate of parts that will allow the
       press operator to meet this criterion. What would be the percentage increase in
       the assembly line operation?

11. A small airport that serves light aircraft has a single runway and one air traffic con-
    troller to land planes. It takes an airplane an average of 12 minutes to land and clear
    the runway (exponentially distributed). Planes arrive at the runway according to a
    Poisson distribution at the rate of 4 per hour. Determine the following:

    a. The number of planes that will stack up (on the average) waiting to land
    b. The average time a plane must circle before it can land
    c. The average time it takes a plane to clear the runway once it notifies the airport
       it wants to land
    d. The FAA has a rule that limits an air traffic controller to landing planes a max-
       imum of 45 minutes, on the average, out of every hour. (The controller must
       have an average of 15 minutes of idle time out of every hour to relieve tension.)
       Does this airport need to hire an extra air traffic controller?

12. All trucks traveling on a particular stretch of interstate highway are required by law
    to stop at a weigh station. Trucks arrive according to a Poisson distribution with a
    mean rate of 200 per 8-hour day. The weigh station can weigh trucks at a mean rate
    of 220 trucks per day (Poisson distributed).

    a. Determine the average number of trucks waiting to be weighed, the average time
       each truck spends at the weigh station, and the average waiting time (before being
       weighed) for each truck.
    b. Given the original conditions in this problem, suppose arriving truck drivers look
       to see how many trucks are at the station. If drivers see 4 or more trucks at the
       weigh station, they will pass the station by and risk being caught and ticketed
       by the state police. What is the probability that a truck will bypass the station?

13. Assume that all conditions of problem 1 are met except that the service distribution
    is unknown. The mean service time is known to be 12 minutes with a standard
    deviation of 6 minutes (in other words, the mean service rate, μ, equals 5 per hour,

and the standard deviation of service times in hours, σ, is equal to .1). Determine the values for the following operating characteristics:

a. Utilization factor   d. L

b. P_0 e. W_q

c. L_q f. W

Prepare a table that summarizes and compares these results with the results obtained in problem 1.

14. In problem 8, suppose that once the manufacturing company adds the extra employees to the work station, it can no longer assume an exponential service time. However, it can assume that service times are independent, and that they have a common probability distribution with a mean of .9 minute and a standard deviation of 1.8 minutes. How will this assumption affect the solution to problem 8?

15. A major seaport on the East Coast has a ship coal loading facility. Coal trucks filled with coal presently arrive at the port facility at the mean rate of 149 per day (Poisson distributed). The facility operates 24 hours a day. The coal trucks are unloaded one-at-a-time on a first-come, first-served basis by automated mechanical equipment that empty the trucks in a constant time of 8 minutes per truck regardless of truck size. The port authority is negotiating with a coal company for an additional 30 trucks per day. However, the coal company will not use this port facility unless the port authority can assure them that their coal trucks will not have to wait to be unloaded at the port facility for more than 12 hours per truck on the average. Can the port authority provide this assurance?

What other observations can you make about this situation?

16. A job shop includes a workstation where items are finished. The finishing operation includes a two-phase process, grinding and buffing (the buffing is done with a wire brush wheel on the side of the grinding machine). Both finishing operations are performed on the same machine by one operator. Items arrive at the finishing workstation randomly from various other workstations in the job shop at an average rate of 50 per hour distributed according to a Poisson distribution. The grinding operation takes an average of .5 minute distributed according to an exponential distribution. This is immediately followed by the buffing operation which takes the same amount of time as the grinding operation, on the average, and is also distributed exponentially.

Determine the average number of items waiting to be finished at the finishing workstation, and the average number in the system (waiting and in the process of being finished). Also, determine the average time the items must wait at the finishing workstation before finishing begins, and the average total time at the finishing workstation (waiting and being finished).

17. Customers arrive at a service facility at the mean rate of 8 per hour. The arrivals are Poisson distributed. Service times are exponentially distributed with a mean of 5 minutes. The calling population is infinitely large; however, the maximum possible queue length is 3 customers. Determine the following:

a. Probability of zero customers in the system

b. Mean number of customers in the system

   c. Mean number of customers waiting

   d. Mean time a customer spends in the system

   e. Mean time a customer spends waiting

   f. Percent of arriving customers lost because of the queue length limitation

18. The associate dean in the College of Business at a major university is in charge of advising business undergraduates. To eliminate some of the congestion in her suite of offices, the associate dean has placed 4 chairs in the outer (secretary's) office and established a rule that if a chair is not vacant, a student cannot wait to see her. The students arrive at a rate of 6 per hour (Poisson distributed), and the average time the associate dean spends advising a student is 15 minutes (exponentially distributed). The associate dean desires to put up a sign on the bulletin board, indicating how long students can expect to be in the office waiting and getting advice so that they can plan not to miss a class. What length of time should be on the sign? What fraction of the students arriving at the dean's outer office will have to leave and come back at another time? In light of your answers to the above two questions, what is your evaluation of the adequacy of this system?

19. A mail-order retail operation employs a bank of 6 telephone operators who process orders using computer terminals. When a terminal breaks down, it must be disconnected and taken to a nearby electronics repair shop, where it is repaired. The mean time between terminal breakdowns is 6 working days, and the mean time required to repair a terminal is 2 working days (both exponentially distributed). As a result of lost sales, it costs the mail-order operation an estimated $50 per day in lost profits each day a terminal is out for repair. The company pays the electronics repair shop $3,000 per year on a service agreement to repair the terminals. The company is considering the possibility of signing a new service agreement with another electronics repair shop that will provide substitute terminals while the broken ones are at the repair shop. However, the new service agreement would cost the mail-order operation $15,000 per year. Assuming that there are 250 working days in a year, determine what the mail-order operation should do.

20. Assume that a firm has 5 machines that periodically break down and require service. The average time between breakdowns is 4 days, distributed according to an exponential distribution. The average time to repair a machine is 1 day, distributed according to an exponential distribution. One mechanic repairs the machines in the order in which they break down.

   a. Determine the probability of the mechanic being idle.

   b. Determine the mean number of machines waiting to be repaired.

   c. Determine the mean time machines wait to be repaired.

   d. Determine the probability that 3 machines are not operating (are being repaired or waiting to be repaired).

21. Assume the conditions given in problem 1 with the following exceptions: mean arrival rate = 8 per hour; mean service rate per server = 5 per hour; and number of servers = 2 (two-channel, single-phase system). Determine the following operating statistics:

   a. Probability of the system's being empty

b. Probability of exactly 4 in the system
c. Utilization factor
d. Mean length of the waiting line
e. Mean time an arrival spends waiting

22. During registration at a university, students in the College of Business must have their course schedules approved by the college advisor. The time it takes for the advisor to approve a schedule is exponentially distributed with a mean of 2 minutes. Students arrive at the advisor's office according to a Poisson distribution with a mean rate of 28 per hour.

    a. Compute L, L_q, W, W_q, and the utilization factor.
    b. The dean of the college has received numerous complaints from students about the length of time they must wait to have their schedules approved. The dean believes an average time of 10 minutes to wait and then get the schedule approved is reasonable. Each graduate assistant the dean assigns to the advisor's office will reduce the average time required for *the advisor* to approve a schedule by .25 minute down to a minimum of 1.0 minute to approve a schedule. How many assistants should the dean assign to the advisor?
    c. The dean is considering adding a second advisor rather than assigning assistants to serve the line of students at the office waiting to have their schedules approved. This new advisor could serve the same number of students per hour as the present advisor. Determine L, L_q, W, and W_q for this altered advisor system.
    d. As a student, would you recommend adding the advisor? Explain your answer.

23. A clinic has 2 general practitioners who see patients daily. Patients arrive at the clinic according to a Poisson distribution with a mean rate of 6 per hour. The time a doctor spends with a patient is exponentially distributed with a mean of 15 minutes. Patients wait in a waiting area until one of the 2 doctors is able to examine them. Since patients typically do not feel well when they come to the clinic, the doctors do not believe it is good practice to have the patients wait longer than an average of 15 minutes. Should this clinic hire a third doctor, and, if so, will this reduce the average waiting time to less than 15 minutes?

24. Assume that an arriving customer must first be serviced in the facility described in problem 1 and then proceed directly to a second facility for a second phase of service. The second facility also meets all the assumptions of problem 1, but with a Poisson distributed service rate with a mean of 4 customers per hour. Thus, the overall system may be described as a single-channel, two-phase process. Determine P_0, L, L_q, W, and W_q for this system.

25. Trucks arrive at a firm's unloading facility according to a Poisson distribution at the mean rate of 20 trucks per day. Only one truck at a time can be unloaded; however, unlimited space is available for trucks to wait for service. Assume an infinite population of trucks. The firm wishes to determine the optimal number of workers to employ to unload the trucks. It is known that each worker can unload trucks at the mean rate of 5 trucks per working day, and that a maximum of 8 workers can be assigned to a truck without diminishing efficiency. The unloading rate varies according to a Poisson distribution. Workers are paid $25 per day, and the estimated cost

of keeping trucks waiting is $50 per day per truck. The firm's management has observed the average number of arriving trucks (20) and the average rate at which workers can unload the trucks (5 per working day) and has concluded that 4 workers ($20/5 = 4$) should be employed. Determine whether the firm has arrived at a good decision. What number of workers would you recommend to management? Illustrate your decision analysis as a graphical decision model to be presented to the management of the firm.

26. In Example 10.9 in this chapter, management of a truck shipping terminal is considering adding extra employees and equipment to improve the average service time per dock to 25 minutes per truck. It would cost the terminal $18,000 a year to achieve this improved service. The terminal estimates that it will increase its profit by $750 per year for each minute it is able to reduce a truck's waiting time. Determine whether or not the management should make the investment to reduce service times.

27. In Example 10.9 in this chapter, management of a truck shipping terminal has decided that the truck waiting time is excessive and desires to reduce the waiting time. Management has determined that there are two alternatives available for reducing the waiting time. It can add a fourth unloading location to the dock, or it can add extra employees and equipment at the existing dock that will reduce the average service time per location from the current 30 minutes per truck to 23 minutes per truck. The present value costs of the two alternatives are approximately equal, so management desires to implement the alternative that will reduce waiting time by the greatest amount. Which alternative should be selected?

28. Referring to problem 4, use an available computer package, such as STORM, to perform a sensitivity analysis on the queuing model solution results for arrival rates ranging from 14 to 18 in increments of one (i.e., $\lambda = 14, 15, 16, 17,$ and 18). Prepare a table summarizing the solution results for the various values of λ.

29. Referring to problem 10, assume that there is a limited capacity for in-process parts preceding the press. No more than 8 parts can be backed up waiting for the press operation. If an arriving part would cause the number waiting to exceed 8, it is placed in a cart and moved to another press operation in the plant. Use an available computer package, such as STORM, to compute the operating characteristics for this revised description of the press system, including the distribution of the number in the system. What is the probability that arriving parts will have to be hauled to the alternate press?

30. Refer to problems 10 and 29. In problem 10 no limitation was assumed on the number of parts that could be backed up waiting at the press. Problem 29 assumed a limit of 8 parts could be waiting at the press (i.e., a finite queue equal to 8). Use an available computer package such as STORM, to solve for the probability distribution of the number in the system for problem 10. Compare this distribution to the distribution obtained in problem 29 solution results. Why are they different? What portion (fraction) of the time is the number in the system in excess of 9 in the problem 10 solution? (Hint: What is the sum of the probabilities for number in the system for $n > 10$?). Why isn't this value the same as the probability of service denial obtained in problem 29?

31. Assume that you have been retained as a consultant to perform a queuing analysis of a large metropolitan post office operation with five stations for service. Customers line up in single file for service on a FIFO basis. The mean arrival rate is 70 per hour, Poisson distributed, and the mean service time per server is 4 minutes, exponentially distributed. Use an available computer package, such as STORM, to compute the operating characteristics for this operation. Does the operation appear to be satisfactory in terms of (a) postal worker's (servers) idle time and (b) customer waiting time and/or the number waiting for service? What percentage of the time can a customer walk in and get served without waiting at all?

·11

Simulation

The subject of this chapter, simulation, represents a divergence from the topics of previous chapters. All chapters thus far have been concerned with the formulation of models that could be solved analytically. Linear programming and transportation problems were solved by using algorithms (theoretically based step-by-step rules). In decision theory and game theory, various alternatives were analytically evaluated by using criteria such as expected value, maximin, and minimax regret. The approach in each case has been to first consider formulation and then develop analytical solutions to the model.

In many cases, the goal has been to determine optimal solutions. However, not all real-world problems lend themselves to mathematical modeling and solution in a manner that results in optimality. Some real-world situations cannot be represented by the concise model forms described in this text because of stochastic relationships or complexity, for instance. For these cases, an alternative form of analysis is **simulation.**

A familiar form of simulation is analogue simulation, in which an original physical system is replaced by an analogous physical system that is easier to manipulate. A typical example is the representation of a mechanical system by an equivalent electrical system. Much of the experimentation in the manned space flight program was conducted using physical simulation that re-created the conditions of space. The focus of this chapter, however, will be computerized mathematical simulation. In this form, simulation can be defined, in general terms, as a means for deriving measures of performance of a complex system by conducting sampling experiments on a mathematical model of the system over periods of time. Presumably, the model of the system includes the relevant components of the system along with their mathematical relationships. The process of simulation normally involves "running" the model on a computer in order to obtain operational information.

The results, or output, of a simulation model are in the form of system **descriptors,** which describe the behavior of the simulated system. For example, the queuing equations in Chapter 10 yielded solutions in the form of descriptors of system performance. (The model results were assumed to be input into a broader framework for the actual decision-making process.)

Since simulation of a model is closely akin to conducting sampling experiments on the real system, the results obtained are sample observations or sample statistics. For example, for a single-channel, single-phase queuing system, the analytically derived queuing equation for the mean number of customers waiting yields a value analogous to a population mean (μ), whereas simulation yields a value analogous to a sample mean ($\bar{x}$). Whether or not the sample mean approximates the steady-state mean of the queuing equation depends on the starting conditions of the simulation, the length of the period simulated, and, of course, the accuracy of the model. In any event, the simulation results do contain sampling variance (error) just as in the case of direct sampling from the population. In cases where the simulation is conducted over time, covariance is included in the results.

Methods for dealing with such output are difficult at best. This points out a factor that should be considered in comparing the simulation models described in this chapter with the analytical models developed previously. Although simulation lends flexibility to analysis, it may do so at the expense of accuracy of results. However, as noted earlier, there may be no practical analytical approach to the problem under analysis, in which case simulation becomes the only alternative.

THE SIMULATION PROCESS

The process of simulating a system consists of several distinct stages, which are summarized in Figure 11.1 (p. 522). The initial stage of the process requires that the problem be identified and formulated for the system (or portion of the system) under analysis. For example, if an inventory system is being simulated, the problem may concern the number of units to order at certain reorder points. This step necessitates the specification of performance criteria, decision rules, and model parameters. Also, system variables must be identified, as well as the relationship between the variables. In an inventory system, this stage might require the identification of cost as the performance criterion, decision rules for when to reorder, and variables such as demand, lead time, and buffer stock.

Once the model components have been identified, the model itself is developed and put into a form that can be analyzed on the computer. In many cases, the model can be written in a specific simulation language that is especially suited for the problem under analysis. When the model has been developed, it must be validated to determine if it realistically represents the system being analyzed and if the results will be reliable. This is a critical area of simulation and usually a difficult task.

The next stage concerns the design of the experiments to be conducted with the simulation model. The ability to experiment on the system is one of the greatest advantages of simulation. Following the preparatory events, the simulation model is run on the computer and the results are obtained, usually in the form of operating statistics, such as the average carrying cost for an inventory system. Once the results have been obtained, it must be determined whether additional experiments are to be conducted. If not, the results are analyzed not only as a problem solution, but in terms of statistical reliability and correctness.

The remainder of this chapter is concerned primarily with the Monte Carlo sampling process and model construction. Many of the stages of the simulation process, such as problem formulation, identification of model components, and analysis of results, are treated only briefly. These important parts of the simulation process are covered in detail in several of the references on simulation at the end of this chapter.

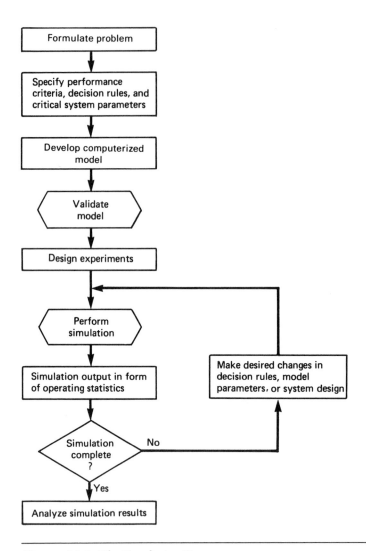

Figure 11.1 The Simulation Process

STOCHASTIC SIMULATION

A characteristic of systems that often results in models too difficult to solve analytically is the presence of certain system components that must be represented as random variables. These random variables are represented in the simulation model by probability distributions, and the model is referred to as probabilistic or stochastic (probabilistic over time). The majority of simulation models based on real-world problems are stochastic models. Because of the popularity of stochastic simulation, it is the primary focus of this chapter.

The Monte Carlo Sampling Process

The term **Monte Carlo sampling** has become synonymous with stochastic simulation in recent years. In reality, however, Monte Carlo sampling can be more narrowly defined as a technique for selecting numbers randomly according to a probability distribution for use in a trial run of a simulation. As such, the Monte Carlo technique is not a simulation study or model in itself but a mathematical-probability technique used within simulation.

The origin of modern stochastic simulation methods and the use of the Monte Carlo technique is attributed to Von Neumann and Ulan, who used the technique as a research tool in the development of the atomic bomb during World War II. Their research involved a direct simulation of the probabilistic problems concerned with random neutron diffusion of fissionable material for nuclear shielding devices. Shortly thereafter, the possibility of applying these same Monte Carlo methods to nonprobabilistic problems was considered by these researchers and by Fermi.

The name *Monte Carlo* is appropriate, since the basic principle behind the technique is the same as the principle underlying many gambling devices such as roulette wheels, dice, and playing cards. Like Monte Carlo methods, these devices produce random samples from well-defined populations.

As previously noted, the primary objective of stochastic simulation is to reproduce realistically the behavior of the system being studied, including the variability of the random variable(s) included in the system. In this section, the development of a random variable generator, also known as a **process generator,** will be discussed.

Example 11.1 Simulating Product Demand

The demand per week for computer terminals at an electronic equipment distributor is a discrete random variable defined by the probability distribution in Table 11.1

Table 11.1 Probability Distribution of Demand

Demand per Week x	Probability of Demand $p(x)$
14	0.2
15	0.4
16	0.2
17	0.1
18	0.1

In the table, $p(x)$ is the probability that demand during any particular week will be x. The purpose of Monte Carlo simulation is to generate the random variable (demand) by "sampling" from the probability distribution. The demand per week could be randomly generated according to the probability distribution, $p(x)$, by spinning a roulette wheel segmented into portions corresponding to the probabilities, $p(x)$, as shown in Figure 11.2 (p. 524).

Given an unbiased spin of the wheel, a quantity for demand per week is generated based on where the wheel stops. Over a period of weeks (many spins of the wheel), the relative frequency with which values are generated will approximate the probability distribution, $p(x)$. This process of generating values of x by randomly selecting from the probability distribution, $p(x)$, in an example of the Monte Carlo sampling method.

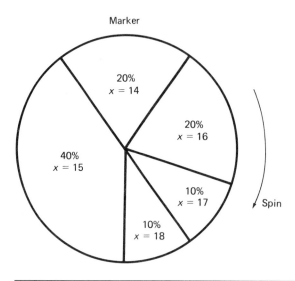

Figure 11.2 *The Monte Carlo Process*

The process of spinning the roulette wheel artificially reconstructs the system of random demand for computer terminals occurring during a given week. In this reconstruction, a lengthy period of *real time* (i.e., a number of weeks) can be represented in a short period of *simulated time* (i.e., numerous spins of the wheel). Obviously, though, it is not generally practical to generate the values of a random variable by spinning a wheel. Alternatively, the process of spinning the roulette wheel can be artificially constructed by using random numbers.

A Random Process Generator

The random process generation technique employs the cumulative distribution function, $F(x)$, of the probability distribution under analysis to generate values of the random variable, x. For our example, the cumulative distribution function, $F(x)$, is shown in Table 11.2.

Table 11.2 *Cumulative Probability Distribution for Demand*

Demand per Week (computer terminals) x	Probability of Demand p(x)	Cumulative Distribution F(x)
14	0.2	0.2
15	0.4	0.6
16	0.2	0.8
17	0.1	0.9
18	0.1	1.0
	1.0	

As shown in the table, the cumulative distribution is defined over the interval (0, 1) and represents the probability that demand will be equal to or less than x (for example, $F(16) = P(x \leqslant 16) = .8$). $F(x)$ is shown graphically in Figure 11.3. Note that the length of the vertical line at each step in Figure 11.3 corresponds exactly to the $p(x)$ probability value for each demand quantity. For example, at the top, the vertical line directly above the value 18 extends from .90 to 1.00. This range corresponds to the probability of a demand for 18 computer terminals, $p(x) = .10$. The same is true for the vertical line above 17, which reflects a probability of .10 (.90 − .80 = .10). Likewise, the probability, $p(x)$, for $x = 16$ is given by the vertical line from .60 to .80, or $p(x) = .20$.

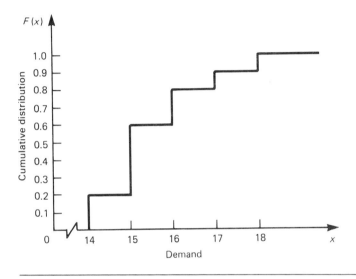

Figure 11.3 *Cumulative Distribution Function*

Thus, the cumulative distribution for x includes a series of ranges in which each range corresponds to a particular demand. If a number, r, between 0 and 1 can be generated randomly, then by determining which range the random number (r) falls in (i.e., the location of the random number along the vertical axis in Figure 11.3), we can find an associated value for demand, x, on the horizontal axis.

For example, a value of $r = .76$ falls on the vertical axis of Figure 11.3, $F(x)$, within the range $.60 \leqslant F(x) \leqslant .80$. This, in turn, corresponds to a demand of 16 units on the horizontal axis of Figure 11.3. Thus, by randomly selecting values of r, we can randomly generate values of x according to the probability distribution for demand.

The process of generating values of the random variable using this Monte Carlo technique can be demonstrated manually, although the process is normally computerized. The first step in the process is to obtain a random number. In a computerized simulation model, subroutines generate **pseudorandom numbers,** a process that will be discussed later in this chapter. However, for the purposes of this manual example, random numbers will be obtained from the table of random numbers in Appendix C. (Appendix C, Table

Table 11.3 Demand Values Associated with Random Numbers

Demand x	Probability of Demand p(x)	Ranges of Cumulative Distribution F(x)	Ranges of Random Numbers* r
14	.2	0.0 → .19	00 → 19
15 ←	4 ←	.20 → .59 ←	20 → 59 ←
16	.2	.60 → .79	60 → 79
17	.1	.80 → .89	80 → 89 r = 39
18	.1	.90 → .99	90 → 99
	1.0		

*Note, for example, that the first range for r includes 20 possible values, from 0 to 19. This range corresponds to the probability of demand for x = 14.

C.5 contains a great number of two-digit numbers ranging from 00 to 99, each of which has been generated in a purely random fashion. Thus, there are 100 possible different two-digit numbers that can be selected on any given random pick from the table. Each two-digit number has an equal likelihood of selection; i.e., the selection probability of each two-digit number is $1/100$.) From Table C.5, the value $r = 39$ is selected. Observing Table 11.3, which is a tabular representation of the $F(x)$ ranges from Figure 11.3, we can see that $r = 39$ corresponds to a demand of 15.

In Table 11.4, the preceding process is repeated 15 times—i.e., for 15 consecutive demand periods (weeks). As before, the random numbers are selected from Table C.5.

These tabular values simulate the weekly demand for computer terminals for 15 weeks. The average demand for the 15 periods is 16 units $(240/15 = 16)$. This simulated average demand can be compared to the expected value of demand computed analytically from the probability distribution.

Table 11.4 Random Generation of Demand for 15 Periods

Demand Period	r	Demand (x)
1	.39	15
2	.73	16
3	.72	16
4	.75	16
5	.37	15
6	.02	14
7	.87	17
8	.98	18
9	.10	14
10	.47	15
11	.93	17
12	.21	15
13	.95	18
14	.97	18
15	.69	16
		$\Sigma = 240$

$$E(x) = \sum_{i=1}^{n} p_i x_i$$

where

$\quad x_i$ = demand i

$\quad p_i$ = probability of demand i

Thus,

$$E(x) = (.2)(14) + (.4)(15) + (.2)(16) + (.1)(17) + (.1)(18)$$
$$= 15.5 \text{ units}$$

The average weekly demand of 16 computer terminals obtained from the simulation is close to the analytical solution, $E(x) = 15.5$ units. The margin of difference between the simulated value and the analytical value is a result of sampling error. Since the Monte Carlo method is actually a probabilistic sampling procedure, the results are subject to the size of the sample taken. Thus, the more periods for which the simulation is conducted, the more accurate the results (i.e., the simulated results approach steady-state conditions). For a more complex model with several stochastic variables, the interaction of the the the random variables might necessitate a great number of simulated periods to approximate steady-state conditions.

Computerized Monte Carlo Simulation

Many general management science software packages include programs with the capability to perform specific types of simulations, such as the simulation of inventory or queuing systems. The AB:QM software package, demonstrated in previous chapters, has the capability to perform general Monte Carlo simulation such as the simulation of product demand in Example 11.1. Following are the program input and simulation output for this example.

```
Program: Simulation / Monte Carlo Simulation

Problem Title : Example 11.1

***** Input Data *****

-----------------------------------
      Value            Probability
-----------------------------------
      14.00               0.200
      15.00               0.400
      16.00               0.200
      17.00               0.100
      18.00               0.100
-----------------------------------

***** Program Output *****
```

```
------------------------------------
                          Cumulative
                 Value    Probability
------------------------------------
Category 1      14.000      0.200
Category 2      15.000      0.600
Category 3      16.000      0.800
Category 4      17.000      0.900
Category 5      18.000      1.000
------------------------------------

Number of Runs          15
Average Value        15.333

***** End of Output *****
```

Note that the average weekly demand of 15.33 units differs from both the manual simulation result of 16.0 obtained in Example 11.1 and the expected value of 15.5 units. However, a simulation of 100 runs, shown below, results in a value approaching the expected value.

```
***** Program Output *****

------------------------------------
                          Cumulative
                 Value    Probability
------------------------------------
Category 1      14.000      0.200
Category 2      15.000      0.600
Category 3      16.000      0.800
Category 4      17.000      0.900
Category 5      18.000      1.000
------------------------------------

Number of Runs         100
Average Value        15.540

***** End of Output *****
```

Example 11.2 Simulation of an Inventory System with Uncertain Demand and Reorder Lead Time

In Example 11.1 we demonstrated how to randomly generate the weekly demand for computer terminals using the Monte Carlo simulation process. However, as was indicated, average product demand could have been determined analytically with little difficulty. Simulation becomes a necessity for inventory analysis when two or more model components are subject to uncertainty, such as product demand *and* reorder lead time. In this example we will consider an expanded version of Example 11.1 in which the probability distribution of the weekly demand for computer terminals, x, is the same as previously given, and the probability or reorder lead time, y, from the computer terminal manufacturer is as shown in Table 11.5.

Table 11.5 *Lead Time Probability Distribution and Associated Random Numbers*

Lead Time (Weeks) y	Probability of Lead Time p(y)	Ranges of Random Numbers r₂
2	.60	00 → 59
3	.30	60 → 89
4	.10	90 → 99
	1.00	

The objective of the electronics distributor is to determine the optimal number of terminals to order from the manufacturer each time an order is placed and when to place an order (that is, the reorder point). The optimal decision is the one that will result in the minimum total inventory cost. The electronics distributor has determined the following cost parameters: order cost, C_o, equals $150 per order; carrying cost, C_c, equals $1 per terminal per week; and shortage cost, C_s, equals $100 per computer terminal per shortage.

Since the objective of the inventory analysis is to determine the optimal size of an order and the best time to place an order, we begin the simulation by testing a selected order size and reorder point. We will start our simulation by selecting an order size, Q, of 40 terminals per order and a reorder point, R, of 30 terminals. Thus, every time 30 or fewer terminals are on-hand in inventory, an order for 40 terminals will be placed. Back ordering will not be allowed when shortages exist. When an order is made to replenish inventory in week n, it will arrive in week $n + y$ (where y = lead time).

In Table 11.6, the simulation experiment is conducted for a 10-week period by hand in tabular form. The random number r_1 relates to the cumulative distribution for weekly demand, and r_2 relates to the lead time cumulative distribution. Random numbers were selected from the last column in Appendix C, Table C.5. Note that the simulation is begun with 20 terminals in inventory, to replicate more closely actual ongoing conditions.

Table 11.6 *Simulation Experiment for Example 11.2 with $Q = 40$ and $R = 30$*

Week	Beginning Inventory	Order Receipt	Inventory Level	r₁	Demand (x)	Ending Inventory	r₂	Lead Time (y)	C_o	+	C_c	+	C_s	=	TC
1	20	0	20	00	14	6	46	2	$150		$ 6		$ 0		$ 156
2	6	0	6	49	15	0	80	3	150		0		900		1050
3	0	40	40	41	15	25	61	3	150		25		0		175
4	25	0	25	94	18	7	89	3	150		7		0		157
5	7	40	47	87	17	30	47	2	150		30		0		180
6	30	40	70	33	15	55					55		0		55
7	55	80	135	67	16	119					119		0		119
8	119	0	119	44	15	104					104		0		104
9	104	0	104	63	16	88					88		0		88
10	88	0	88	25	15	73					73		0		73

Average weekly inventory cost = $215.70

The simulation experiment conducted in Table 11.6 will be briefly described to illustrate the steps of the simulation process. First, note that the simulation begins with an inventory level of 20 terminals, as indicated previously. The following steps occur in the simulation process:

1. A random number, r_1, is selected from the last column in Appendix C, Table C.5. This value is 00. Observing the previously constructed ranges of random numbers for demand, we see that 00 corresponds to a demand of 14 terminals.

2. Subtracting the demanded 14 units from the inventory level value of 20 units yields an ending inventory of 6 units. This is below the reorder point of 30 units, so a new order is placed with the manufacturer.

3. A second random number, r_2, is selected from the last column in Table C.5. This value, 46, corresponds to a lead time of 2 weeks. Thus, the order for 40 terminals will be received from the manufacturer in week 3 (i.e., week $n + y = 1 + 2 = 3$).

4. Since an order was made, there is an order cost of $150; the 6 units of ending inventory results in a carrying cost of $6; and since there were no shortages, there is no shortage cost. Summing these costs yields a total inventory cost for week one of $156.

This same step-by-step process is repeated for the remaining 9 weeks of the simulation experiment. At the completion of the experiment, an average weekly cost of $215.70 is computed.

Although this brief experiment illustrates how a complex inventory system with several random variables is simulated, it is incomplete. Normally a 10-period simulation is much too short to yield a true steady-state result. A 1000-period simulation would be more appropriate. The average weekly inventory cost of $215.70 determined in Table 11.6 is simply one sample value. Further, this particular simulation experiment represents only one part of a larger, more complete experiment. This simulation was conducted for one particular combination of order size (40 units) and reorder point (30 units). In order to complete the simulation experiment, multiple simulation experiments would be required, each with a different combination of Q and R. The combination of Q and R that yields the minimum total cost will indicate the optimal inventory policy.

It is readily apparent that manually performing the simulations necessary to determine all relevant combinations of Q and R in order to obtain the optimal solution would be virtually impossible. Repeating the experiment conducted in Table 11.6 numerous times for 1000 weeks instead of 10 would take days to complete. A true simulation would be conducted on a computer rather than by hand. It would require only a few minutes to complete this entire simulation on a computer.

However, this brief and rather rudimentary example does demonstrate the need for simulation when problem complexities render analytical solutions infeasible. The fact that Q and R are interrelated, so that each must be considered simultaneously to obtain an optimal solution, and the fact that both product demand and reorder lead time are random variables make for a problem that is virtually impossible to analyze by any computational technique other than simulation.

Computerized Inventory System Simulation

The AB:QM software package has a program module to simulate an inventory system similar to that described in Example 11.2 and Table 11.6. In this simulation each combination of Q and R (between a designated set of bounds) is simulated to yield the total inventory cost, which in effect was what was done in Table 11.6 for one set of values of Q and R. Then a search is conducted for all combinations of Q and R to determine a minimum cost solution. For this example, all inventory cost values are the same as in Example 11.2. The bounds on Q are set at 30 and 70 units, respectively, meaning that each value of Q between 30 and 70 units is simulated. Likewise, the bounds for R are set at 30 and 70 units. (Note that these values were determined by trial and error testing using AB:QM). The input data and final program out are as follows.

```
Simulation / Inventory Simulation

***** Input Data *****

Ordering cost         ($/order)      150.00
Holding cost          ($/unit)         1.00
Shortage cost         ($/unit)       100.00
Business days         (/year)        365.00
Min order quantity    (units)         30.00
Max order quantity    (units)         70.00
Min reorder point     (units)         30.00
Max reorder point     (units)         70.00
Initial inventory     (units)         20.00

 --------------------------------------------------------------------------
                           Cumulative                              Cumulative
    Demand    Probability Probability    Lead Time  Probability Probability
 --------------------------------------------------------------------------
     14.00       0.200      0.200           2.00       0.600       0.600
     15.00       0.400      0.600           3.00       0.300       0.900
     16.00       0.200      0.800           4.00       0.100       1.000
     17.00       0.100      0.900
     18.00       0.100      1.000
 --------------------------------------------------------------------------

***** Program Output *****


Mininum Annual Total Inventory Cost  :   51282.500
Mininum Order Quantity               :          67
Mininum Reorder Point                :          36

***** End of Output *****
```

Example 11.3 Simulation of a Queuing System

Queuing systems are often good candidates for simulation analysis, since real systems that include customers waiting for service often do not fit any of the assumptions of the analytic queuing models presented in Chapter 10. The following example illustrates a simulation of a simplified queuing system.

A bank with a drive-in teller window wishes to examine the system with respect to customer waiting time and teller busy time. The time between customer arrivals and the service time are described by the discrete probability distributions in Tables 11.7 and 11.8.

An Application of Simulation:
Fuel Inventory Management in the Electric Utility Industry

The electric utilities industry spends $1.6 billion annually holding oil and coal inventories. However, fuel inventory management is critical not only because of the high costs involved, but also because dramatic fluctuations in fuel demand creates the risk of running out of fuel. In the early 1980s, spurred by a decade-long increase in fuel prices, fuel managers began to doubt the effectiveness of traditional inventory management policies. Traditionally, high levels of inventory were also being questioned both by utility management and regulatory commissions. Prior to 1980 the focus of fuel managers had been on the risk of running out of fuel but in the early 1980s the focus shifted to the cost/risk trade-off involved with high inventories. As a result, in

Table 11.7 Arrival Distribution and Associated Random Numbers

Time Between Arrivals x	Probability $p(x)$	Cumulative Probability $F(x)$	Random Number Range r_1
1	.1	.1	00 → 09
2	.3	.4	10 → 39
3	.3	.7	40 → 69
4	.2	.9	70 → 89
5	.1	1.0	90 → 99

Table 11.8 Service Distribution and Associated Random Numbers

Service Times y	Probability $p(y)$	Cumulative Probability $F(y)$	Random Number Range r_2
2	.4	.4	00 → 39
3	.4	.8	40 → 79
4	.2	1.0	80 → 99

In Table 11.9, the simulation experiment for 20 customer arrivals is conducted by hand in tabular form. The random number streams r_1, for time between arrivals, and r_2, for service times, were obtained from Appendix C, Table C.5 as follows. Values for r_1 were obtained from the sixth column from the left, beginning at the bottom and moving up. Values of r_2 were obtained from the bottom row, beginning at the left and moving to the right.

The following is a brief summary of the manual simulation process employed to generate the values in Table 11.9.

1. A random number, r_1, is selected to generate the time of arrival of the first customer. In this case, the value of r_1 is 28, yielding an associated time until arrival of 2 minutes. Thus, the

1982 the Electric Power Research Institute initiated a fuel inventory project that resulted in the Utility Fuel Inventory Model (UFIM). Overall this model focuses on developing a strategic policy that specifies target inventory levels that are cost effective to guide inventory replenishment orders by a utility. The UFIM includes a Monte Carlo simulation model to probabilistically simulate the dynamic inventory process. The simulation model estimates the expected cost and other inventory related statistics for specific inventory policies. The model is used to test a wide variety of policies based on different types of supply and demand uncertainties, variations in fuel deliveries, and varying fuel burning rates. The UFIM is now used by utilities supplying electricity to about one-third of the country, and since 1984 the accumulated cost savings to the utility industry as a result of the model has been over $125 million.

Source: H. Chao et al., "EPRI Reduces Fuel Inventory Costs in the Electric Utility Industry," *Interfaces,* 19, no. 1 (January–February 1989): 48–67.

Table 11.9 Simulation Experiment for Example 11.3—Simulation of a Queuing System

Customer	Random Number r_1	Time Between Arrivals x	Arrival Clock	Begin Service Clock	Customer Waiting Time	Teller Idle Time	Random Number r_2	Service Time y	Departure Clock	Customer Time in System
1	28	2 min	2	2	0 min	2 min	77	3 min	5	3 min
2	24	2	4	5	1	0	94	4	9	5
3	00	1	5	9	4	0	30	2	11	6
4	92	5	10	11	1	0	05	2	13	3
5	07	1	11	13	2	0	39	2	15	4
6	18	2	13	15	2	0	28	2	17	4
7	93	5	18	18	0	1	10	2	20	2
8	99	5	23	23	0	3	99	4	27	4
9	87	4	27	27	0	0	00	2	29	2
10	33	2	29	29	0	0	27	2	31	2
11	69	3	32	32	0	1	12	2	34	2
12	97	5	37	37	0	3	73	3	40	3
13	28	2	39	40	1	0	73	3	43	4
14	39	2	41	43	2	0	99	4	47	6
15	87	4	45	47	2	0	12	2	49	4
16	06	1	46	49	3	0	49	3	52	6
17	26	2	48	52	4	0	99	4	56	8
18	97	5	53	56	3	0	57	3	59	6
19	79	4	57	59	2	0	94	4	63	6
20	79	4	61	63	2	0	82	4	67	6
					29	10		57		86

first customer arrives at time 2, which is recorded on the arrival clock. The customer enters the service facility immediately, and the begin service clock is also set to time 2. The customer waiting time is recorded as zero, and the teller idle time is recorded as 2 minutes.

2. A random number, 77, is obtained for r_2, which yields an associated service time of 3 minutes. At the end of service, the departure clock is set to the departure time of 5, which is the

time service began, 2, plus the service time, 3. The total time spent in the system is computed and recorded—waiting time, which is zero, plus service time, which is 3, for a total of 3 minutes in the system.

3. This process of obtaining random numbers from Table C.5 and generating associated values of time between arrivals and service time is repeated for all 20 arrivals.

When a customer arrives, if the time of arrival (the value of the arrival clock) is less than the time of departure for the previous customer (the value of the departure clock), the arriving customer must wait to enter service. Service begins at the time of departure for the previous customer, and the customer waiting time is computed accordingly. (For example, customers 2 through 6 all wait for service.)

If the time of arrival for a customer is greater than the time of departure for the previous customer, the arriving customer enters service immediately, and the teller idle time is calculated as the value of the begin service clock for the current customer minus the value of the departure clock for the previous customer. (For example, the teller is idle prior to service for customers 1, 7, 8, 11, and 12.) The total time in the system for a customer is simply the sum of the waiting time and the service time.

All simulation experiments require decisions concerning the *starting* conditions and the *ending* conditions for each simulation run. These conditions can have a significant effect on the overall results and thus are an important part of any simulation. For this example, it was assumed that the system was empty (without any customers waiting or in service) at the beginning of the simulated time. Since the first customer arrived rather quickly, this is probably not a bad starting condition. However, it is generally desirable to begin the system as close as possible to the steady-state condition so that the simulated performance is not biased by start-up conditions.

Likewise, this example includes the ending condition that no arrivals are considered after the twentieth arrival, but customers currently in the system at that time are cleaned out of the system (served) and included as part of the summary results of system performance. For example, customer 19 was in service when customer 20 arrived at time 61; however, the simulation was continued until customer 19 was completed at time 63 and customer 20 was completed at time 67. Some simulation studies, on the other hand, terminate the simulation run at a predefined point in time, and no data or statistics are collected after that point in time. Since both the starting condition and the ending condition tend to distort the overall long-run system performance, it is important to simulate the system for a long enough time to make the effect of those distortions negligible.

Simulation of the bank drive-in teller system for approximately 1 hour (61 minutes to the twentieth arrival, and 67 minutes to the departure of the twentieth customer) is obviously not sufficient to yield valid steady-state results. However, the same process could be continued, via computer simulation, for the entire operating day and repeated for many days' operation to yield accurate estimates of system performance.

Various summary results can be obtained from the simulated results. For example, the average waiting time for any given customer arriving at the drive-in teller operation is 29/20, or 1.45, minutes. However, it is also useful to note that 7 of the 20 customers (35%) do not wait at all, and the 13 customers (65%) who do have to wait for service wait for an average of 29/13, or 2.2, minutes. Furthermore, it is instructive to observe the frequency distribution of waiting times, given in Table 11.10.

Table 11.10 *Distribution of Customer Waiting Times*

Customer Waiting Times	Frequency	Relative Frequency
0	7	35%
1	3	15
2	6	30
3	2	10
4	2	10

From these results, the bank could make probability statements about the expected waiting times, such as 50% of all customers will wait 1 minute or less for service, or only 20% of all customers must wait 3 or more minutes.

The bank is also interested in knowing what fraction of the time the drive-in teller will be busy with drive-in customers, and what fraction of the time the teller can assist with inside bank services. The simulation results indicate that the teller will be busy 57 minutes and idle 10 minutes: 85% busy time versus 15% time available for inside operations.

The average time a customer spends in the system, waiting and being serviced, is 86/20, or 4.3, minutes per customer. However, the 7 customers who do not have to wait to begin service spend an average of only 18/7, or 2.6, minutes in the system (the average service time for the 7 customers). On the other hand, the 13 customers who must wait for service spend an average of 68/13, or 5.2, minutes in the system.

As demonstrated by this example, one of the attractive features of simulation modeling is the capability to derive a wide variety of desired operating statistics concerning the system. Simulation is much more versatile in this respect than most analytic models.

STOCHASTIC SIMULATION WITH CONTINUOUS PROBABILITY FUNCTIONS

The simulation examples presented thus far included discrete probability distributions for the random variables. However, it is often more realistic to use a continuous random variable. The procedure for developing process generators for continuous random variables is different from that for the discrete case.

Example 11.4 Simulating Time Between Machine Breakdowns

A manufacturing company has experienced what it believes to be an excessive number of breakdowns of its machines. Company management wishes to simulate the current behavior of machine operation (and breakdowns) over a long period of time to understand system behavior better. Company staff personnel have determined that the time between machine breakdowns, in weeks, is approximated by the ramp function given below. Fig-

An Application of Simulation: A Queuing Problem at a Security Gate

The Westinghouse Hanford Company is a secured work facility, for which vehicles enter in the morning on a four-lane road and leave in the afternoon on a two-lane road. An average of 7 buses and approximately 285 private vehicles and van pools (vans with 7 to 15 passengers) enter in the morning during a one-hour period at a gate where normally two security guards check vehicles, drivers, and passengers. However, on any given morning there could be as few as one and as many as three guards. The vehicles form a single line for the security check at the gate that extends past the available queue space of 40 vehicles, out onto the highway, which results in a major safety hazard. Buses form a separate line, and since they carry more passengers, they are given priority over the other vehicles for security checks by the guards. When the line becomes too long, private vehicles may leave and continue down the highway to a second gate where another wait might occur. The situation is not only a safety hazard but the waiting time is excessive.

In the afternoon the vehicles exit in one lane and buses in the other, but van pools pick up passengers in the bus lane causing the buses delays while they wait for the van pools to merge into the vehicle lane. The company's objective in the morning was to minimize the queue length while also minimizing the number of security guards. In the afternoon the goal was to move the buses through the gate as early as possible while also minimizing the number of security guards. An analytical queueing model did not fit this particular queuing scenario, so a simulation model was used instead.

The first objective was to validate that the simulation model replicated the actual system.

ure 11.4 is a graphic representation of the continuous probability function, where the random variable x is time in weeks between breakdowns.

$$f(x) = \frac{x}{8}, \qquad 0 \leqslant x \leqslant 4$$

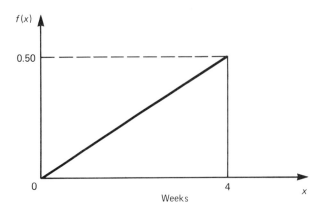

Figure 11.4 *A Continuous Probability Function for Time Between Machine Breakdowns*

Data was collected by observers during a 3-day period in order to determine the arrival rates, nature of the queue, and the service rate. Validation was accomplished by comparing the simulation results to the actual system for the 3-day period. Next, two morning scenarios were tested with the simulation model: first, increasing the number of guards to three while maintaining the single lane of traffic, and second, forming two traffic lines each with a security guard. For the second case, when buses arrived, one guard alternated between lines. The second scenario proved to be an excellent solution at no additional cost. It was implemented and resulted in, for most of the time, less than 5 vehicles waiting in line and a maximum number at any time of 21 vehicles waiting for both lines combined. In addition, the number of vehicles entering the gate increased because vehicles that had been going to the second gate because of the long line now entered the main gate. The new system was able to absorb the added load.

For the afternoon exiting problem, several scenarios were also tested. The best solution assigned one security guard to each of the two exit lanes and had the van pools remain in the bus lane and not change lanes after passenger pickup, which they had done in the past. With this solution buses exited 5–7 minutes earlier than in the original system and a safety problem of passengers crossing traffic lanes to get to van pools was eliminated.

Solutions were achieved for both the morning and afternoon queuing problems by increasing the number of service channels (i.e., entrance and exit lines) and not by increasing the number of servers, which is a typical queuing solution. Thus, since more servers were not used, in both the morning and afternoon cases, effective no-cost solutions were achieved.

Source: E. Landaver and L. Becker, "Reducing Waiting Time at Security Checkpoints," *Interfaces,* 19, no. 5 (September–October 1989): 57–65.

The area under the curve, $f(x) = x/8$ $(0 \leqslant x \leqslant 4)$, represents the probability of the occurrence of the random variable x, time between breakdowns. Therefore, the area under the curve must equal 1.0, since, according to probability theory, the sum of all probabilities of the occurrence of a random variable must equal 1. By computing the area under the curve from 0 to any value of the random variable, x, we can determine the cumulative probability of that value of x. This is demonstrated as follows:

$$F(x) = \int_0^x \frac{x}{8} \, dx = \frac{1}{8} \int_0^x x \, dx = \frac{1}{8} \left(\frac{1}{2} x^2 \right) \Big]_0^x$$

and thus,

$$F(x) = \frac{x^2}{16}$$

Figure 11.5 (p. 538) is a graph of the cumulative distribution function.

It can be seen that the range of values for the random variable x $(0 \leqslant x \leqslant 4)$ coincides with the cumulative probabilities $(0 \leqslant F(x) \leqslant 1.0)$. Thus, for any value $F(x)$ in the interval $(0, 1)$, a corresponding value of x exists. Recall that in the previous discrete random variable case, we associated various values of x with discrete *ranges* of the cumulative distribution for x. In the case of the continuous random variable, however, the

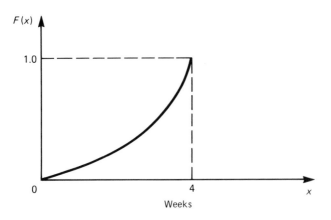

Figure 11.5 *Cumulative Distribution Function for a Value of x*

relationship between x and the cumulative distribution for x is described by a continuous distribution function, $F(x)$. Thus, each cumulative distribution value corresponds to a unique value of x.

Therefore, any value of a random number r (between 0 and 1)[1] can be translated directly into an associated value for x by using the functional relationship for the cumulative distribution, $F(x)$. Since $F(x)$ is defined over the interval (0, 1) and the random number is also defined over the interval (0, 1), we have the relationship

$$r = F(x)$$

and therefore,

$$r = \frac{x^2}{16}$$

Since we wish to obtain a value of the random variable x, given a value for a random number r, we must first solve the preceding equation for x, in terms of r, as follows:

$$x = 4\sqrt{r}$$

Solving for x in terms of r is known as taking the inverse of $F(x)$, denoted by $x = F^{-1}(r)$. Therefore, this approach is referred to as the **inverse transformation technique**.

After a random number r is obtained, a value for x is determined by substituting r into the equation $x = 4\sqrt{r}$. For example, if $r = .25$, $x = 2$. This is also shown on the cumulative distribution function in Figure 11.6.

---

[1] Appendix C, Table C.5 gives all random numbers as two-digit integers. However, computer random number generators typically produce values between 0 and 1, such as .7342382, .1244122, and .4483246. Table C.5 can, therefore, be thought of as random values between 0 and 1, rounded to two digits and multiplied by 100.

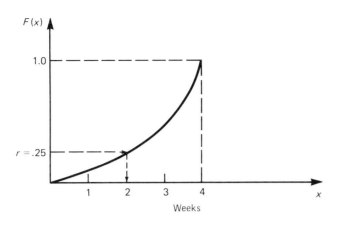

Figure 11.6 *Cumulative Distribution Function for Values of r and x*

The process generator $x = 4\sqrt{r}$ performs the same function as the ranges for r in our previous discrete examples. The values of x are then used in the simulation model in the same manner as in the previous examples.

Returning to our manufacturing example, recall that the continuous random variable x is the time between machine breakdowns in weeks, and management desires to simulate breakdowns for one year. Each of the random numbers in column 5 of Appendix C, Table C.5 is divided by 100 to yield a value between 0 and 1. These values are then used to randomly generate values of x according to the inverse transformation formula, $x = 4\sqrt{r}$. The simulation results are given in Table 11.11 on page 540.

The simulation passes the fifty-second week, and hence one year, after 20 machine breakdowns. Using the same procedure, the company could simulate the machine breakdowns for a lengthy period of time. This particular tabular simulation yields only one sample of breakdowns for a year. A true steady state of the number of annual breakdowns would be obtained by repeating this simulation several hundred times.

Example 11.5 Simulation of a Machine Breakdown and Repair Problem

In this example we will consider an expanded version of Example 11.4. The manufacturing company is attempting to determine whether it should implement, at a cost of $35,000 per year, a plant maintenance program that would reduce the frequency of breakdowns *and* time of machine repair. The continuous probability distribution of time between breakdowns given in Figure 11.4 will be employed again in this example for the existing time between breakdowns. The time in days presently required to repair a machine once a breakdown occurs is defined by the continuous probability function shown in Figure 11.7.

Each time one of the machines breaks down, it costs the company an estimated $800 per day in lost production output.

Table 11.11 *Simulation Experiment for Example 11.4—Time Between Machine Breakdowns*

r	Time Between Breakdowns x weeks $(x = 4 \sqrt{r})$	Cumulative Time (weeks)	Cumulative Breakdowns
.45	2.68	2.68	1
.90	3.80	6.48	2
.84	3.67	10.15	3
.17	1.65	11.80	4
.74	3.44	15.24	5
.94	3.88	19.12	6
.07	1.06	20.18	7
.15	1.55	21.73	8
.04	0.80	22.53	9
.31	2.23	24.76	10
.07	1.06	25.82	11
.99	3.98	29.80	12
.97	3.94	33.74	13
.73	3.42	37.16	14
.13	1.44	38.60	15
.03	0.70	39.30	16
.62	3.15	42.45	17
.47	2.74	45.19	18
.99	3.98	49.17	19
.75	3.46	52.63	20

The task is to develop a process generator to simulate the repair times as given by the probability distribution in Figure 11.7. This distribution is defined by the following continuous functions:

$$f_1(y) = -\frac{4}{5} + \frac{y}{5}, \qquad 4 \leq y \leq 6$$

$$f_2(y) = \frac{6}{5} - \frac{2y}{15}, \qquad 6 \leq y \leq 9$$

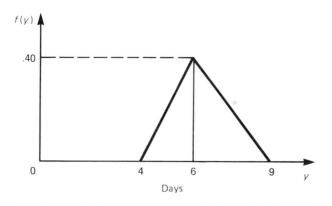

Figure 11.7 *Triangular Distribution for Machine Repair Times*

Together $f_1(y)$ and $f_2(y)$ represent the probability of occurrence of the random variable y. The total area under the curve is 1.00, which represents the total probability. However, 40% of the area under the curve is defined by $f_1(y)$, and 60% of the area under the curve is defined by $f_2(y)$. (To verify those proportions, simply compute the area of the two triangles forming the distribution.)

The first step is to develop the cumulative distribution functions for $f_1(y)$ and $f_2(y)$.

$$F_1(y) = \int_4^y \left(-\frac{4}{5} + \frac{y}{5}\right) dy$$

$$= \frac{y^2}{10} - \frac{4y}{5} + \frac{8}{5}$$

and

$$F_2(y) = \frac{2}{15} + \int_6^y \left(\frac{6}{5} - \frac{2y}{15}\right) dy$$

where $2/5$, in $F_2(y)$, is the area of the first portion of the triangular distribution—that is, the entire area under $F_1(y)$. Thus,

$$F_2(y) = -\frac{y^2}{5} + \frac{6y}{5} - \frac{22}{5}$$

These two functions form the cumulative distribution illustrated in Figure 11.8. Given the cumulative distribution functions $F_1(y)$ and $F_2(y)$, the next step is to set the random number r equal to $F(y)$ and then solve for y in terms of r (i.e., the inverse transformation technique). Setting $F_1(y)$ and $F_2(y)$ equal to r, we obtain

$$r = \frac{y^2}{10} - \frac{4y}{5} + \frac{8}{5}, \qquad 4 \leqslant y \leqslant 6$$

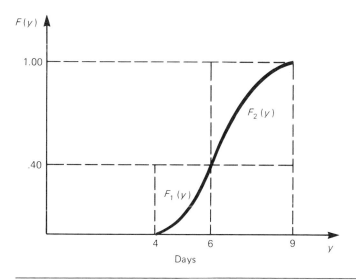

Figure 11.8 *Cumulative Distribution Function for Machine Repair Times*

and

$$r = \frac{-y^2}{15} + \frac{6y}{5} - \frac{22}{5}, \qquad 6 \leqslant y \leqslant 9$$

The next step is to solve the equations for y by using the quadratic formula for an equation of the general form $ay^2 + by + c$:

$$y = \frac{-b \pm \sqrt{b^2 - 4ac}}{2a}$$

Putting the previously developed equations into quadratic form yields

$$0 = \frac{y^2}{10} - \frac{4y}{5} + \frac{8}{5} - r, \qquad 4 \leqslant y \leqslant 6$$

where

$$a = 1/10, b = -4/5, \text{ and } c = 8/5 - r$$

and

$$0 = \frac{y^2}{15} + \frac{6y}{5} - \frac{22}{5} - r, \qquad 6 \leqslant y \leqslant 9$$

where

$$a = -1/15, b = 6/5, \text{ and } c = -22/5 - r$$

Substituting the appropriate values into the quadratic formula yields the inverse functions for y:

$$y = 4 \pm \sqrt{10r}, \qquad 4 \leqslant y \leqslant 6$$

and

$$y = 9 \pm \sqrt{15(1-r)}, \qquad 6 \leqslant y \leqslant 9$$

This results in four values for y. In the first equation, $y = 4 - \sqrt{10r}$ is infeasible because it represents a value of y less than 4 days, and in the second equation, $y = 9 + \sqrt{15(1 - r)}$ is infeasible because it reflects a value greater than 9 days. Thus, the process generators for y are

$$y = 4 + \sqrt{10r} \qquad 0.0 \leqslant r \leqslant .40, \qquad 4 \leqslant y \leqslant 6$$
$$y = 9 - \sqrt{15(1 - r)} \qquad .40 \leqslant r \leqslant 1.00, \qquad 6 \leqslant y \leqslant 9$$

In order to simulate the time of a breakdown, a random number r is selected and substituted into the appropriate equation for y. For example, a random number $r = .30$ falls in the range of $0 \leqslant r \leqslant .40$, so it is substituted into

$$y = 4 + \sqrt{10(.30)}$$
$$= 5.73 \text{ days}$$

This example is demonstrated graphically in Figure 11.9.

Now we have the necessary components to simulate the company's machine breakdowns and repairs and to compute the repair cost for one year. This is accomplished in Table 11.12, where r_1 is the random number stream (from Table C.5) used to determine the time between breakdowns (as shown in Example 11.4) and r_2 is the random number stream used to determine the repair times. The values of r_1 are selected from column 5

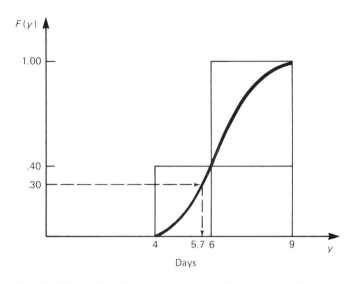

Figure 11.9 *Substitution of a Random Number*

in Table C.5, and the values of r_2 are selected from column 6. Both sets of random numbers have been divided by 100 to yield random values between 0 and 1.

The results of this simulation indicate a total annual machine repair cost of $99,728. However, as we have indicated in our previous examples, this simulation experiment would have to be repeated many times before a steady-state average annual cost could be

Table 11.12 *Simulation Results for Example 11.5—Machine Breakdown and Repair Problem*

r_1	Time Between Breakdowns x weeks	r_2	Repair Time y days	Cost $800y	Cumulative Time Σx
.45	2.68	.19	5.38	$4304	2.68
.90	3.80	.65	6.71	5368	6.48
.84	3.67	.51	6.29	5032	10.15
.17	1.65	.17	5.30	4240	11.80
.74	3.44	.63	6.64	5312	15.24
.94	3.88	.85	7.50	6000	19.12
.07	1.06	.37	5.92	4736	20.18
.15	1.55	.89	7.71	6168	21.73
.04	0.80	.76	7.10	5680	22.53
.31	2.23	.71	6.91	5528	24.76
.07	1.06	.34	5.84	4672	25.82
.99	3.98	.11	5.05	4040	29.80
.97	3.94	.27	5.64	4512	33.74
.73	3.42	.10	5.00	4000	37.16
.13	1.44	.59	6.52	5216	38.60
.03	0.70	.87	7.60	6080	39.30
.62	3.15	.08	4.89	3912	42.45
.47	2.74	.08	4.89	3912	45.19
.99	3.98	.89	7.72	6176	49.17
.75	3.46	.42	6.05	4840	52.63
				$99,728	

determined. Nevertheless, with that reservation in mind, we will use the cost value of $99,728 as a standard against which to compare the reduced costs obtained with the maintenance program simulated in the second part of our example.

As indicated previously, the company is considering the implementation of a maintenance program that would reduce the time between breakdowns, resulting in the following continuous probability distribution of time between breakdowns, x:

$$f(x) = \frac{x}{18}, \quad 0 \leqslant x \leqslant 6$$

Figure 11.10 illustrates this continuous probability function.

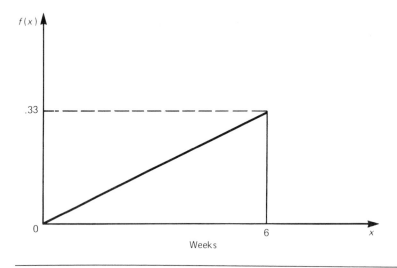

Figure 11.10 *Probability Function for Time Between Machine Breakdowns Under the Maintenance Program*

The maintenance program would also reduce the repair time for machines when they break down, as defined by the following continuous probability distribution function:

$$f_1(y) = -\frac{1}{3} + \frac{y}{6}, \quad 2 \leqslant y \leqslant 4$$

$$f_2(y) = \frac{2}{3} - \frac{y}{12}, \quad 4 \leqslant y \leqslant 8$$

Figure 11.11 illustrates this continuous probability function.

We will now repeat the simulation conducted in the first part of this example, but this time we will employ these new probability functions reflecting the reduced time between breakdowns and reduced repair time resulting from the maintenance program.

First, we must determine the inverse of the function $F(x)$. This results in the following relationship between x, the time between breakdowns, and a random number r:

$$x = 6\sqrt{r}$$

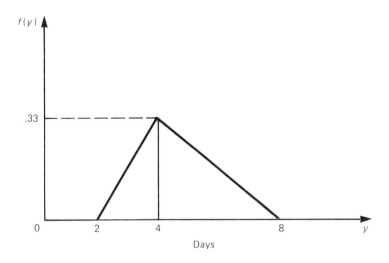

Figure 11.11 *Probability Function for Machine Repair Time Under the Maintenance Program*

Next, by using the inverse transformation technique, we can determine the following relationships between y, the repair time, and a random number r:

$$y = 2 + 6\sqrt{r/3} \qquad 0.0 \leqslant r \leqslant .33, \qquad 2 \leqslant y \leqslant 4$$
$$y = 8 - 2\sqrt{6(1-r)} \qquad .33 \leqslant r \leqslant 1.0, \qquad 4 \leqslant y \leqslant 8$$

Using these newly developed relationships for time between breakdowns and repair time, we can repeat the simulation conducted previously in this example as shown in Table 11.13. To replicate the earlier simulation as closely as possible, we will use the same streams of random numbers from Table C.5 as we used previously.

Table 11.13 *Simulation Results for Example 11.5—The Plant Maintenance Program*

r_1	Time Between Breakdowns x weeks	r_2	Repair Time y days	Cost $\$800y$	Cumulative Time Σx
.45	4.03	.19	3.51	$ 2808	4.03
.90	5.69	.65	5.10	4080	9.72
.84	5.50	.51	4.57	3656	15.22
.17	2.47	.17	3.43	2744	17.69
.74	5.16	.63	5.02	4016	22.85
.94	5.82	.85	6.10	4880	28.67
.07	1.59	.37	4.11	3288	30.29
.15	2.32	.89	6.38	5104	32.58
.04	1.20	.76	5.60	4480	33.78
.31	3.34	.71	5.36	4288	37.12
.07	1.59	.34	4.02	3216	38.71
.99	5.97	.11	3.14	2512	44.68
.97	5.91	.27	3.80	3040	50.59
.73	5.12	.10	3.10	2480	55.71
				$50,592	

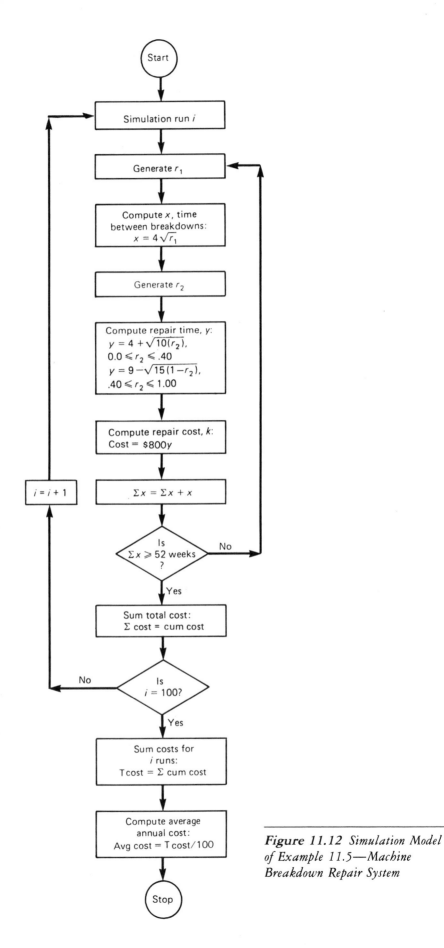

Figure 11.12 Simulation Model
of Example 11.5—Machine
Breakdown Repair System

This simulation results in an annual repair cost of \$50,592, which is \$49,136 less than the annual cost of \$99,728 determined from the first simulation. Since the cost of the new machine maintenance program is only \$35,000, it would seem prudent to implement the maintenance program—if, in fact, we could be reasonably confident that the annual cost as determined in both simulation experiments is accurate. Unfortunately, we cannot display such confidence, since each simulation experiment resulted in only one sample value for annual cost. To be confident of our results, we would have to obtain many samples (i.e., perform many simulations) that could then be used to develop steady-state average costs. The resulting average costs could be employed as a basis of comparison between the present system and the system with the machine maintenance program implemented.

The construction of the first of the two simulation models used in this example is summarized in Figure 11.12.

In an actual simulation experiment, the steps in Figure 11.12 would be re-created in a computer program or a simulation language, and the experiment would be conducted on a computer in several seconds. Notice that this experiment calls for 100 repetitions (or runs) of the experiment. The average annual repair cost as outlined in Figure 11.12 would thus be based on 100 samples of a year's operation.

Computerized Simulation of the Machine Breakdown and Repair Problem

The following computer program, in the BASIC programming language, was written to perform the simulation described in Example 11.5 and illustrated in Figure 11.12. The program was run for 100 repetitions of one year's machine performance, which is equivalent to a sample size of 100. The computer simulation resulted in an average annual maintenance cost of \$100,749.50. There is a \$1,021.50, or 1%, difference between the result determined in our single-sample manual tabular simulation and the result from the complete computer simulation.

```
10   REM **************************************************
20   REM *     BASIC PROGRAM TO SIMULATE EXAMPLE 11.5    *
30   REM *     MACHINE BREAKDOWN AND REPAIR PROBLEM      *
40   REM **************************************************
50   REM
60   REM ****   SET NUMBER OF SIMULATION RUNS TO 100
70   REM ****   AND INITIALIZE VARIABLES
80   REM
90        NUMSIM = 100
100       RANDOMIZE
110       I = 0
120       TCOST = 0
130  REM
140  REM ****   SET SIMULATION RUN TO I
150  REM
160       LET I = I + 1
170       CUMX = 0
180       CUMCST = 0
```

```
190 REM
200 REM ****  SIMULATE TIME BETWEEN MACHINE BREAKDOWNS:
210 REM ****  GENERATE VALUE OF RANDOM VARIABLE, R1
220 REM ****  COMPUTE X, THE TIME BETWEEN BREAKDOWNS
230 REM
240     R1 = RND
250     X = 4*(R1)^.5
260 REM
270 REM ****  SIMULATE REPAIR TIMES:
280 REM ****  GENERATE VALUE OF RANDOM VARIABLE, R2
290 REM ****  COMPUTE Y, THE REPAIR TIME
300 REM
310     R2 = RND
320     IF R2 =< .4 THEN Y = 4 + (10*R2)^.5
330     IF R2 >  .4 THEN Y = 9 - (15*(1-R2))^.5
340 REM
350 REM ****  COMPUTE REPAIR COST
360 REM ****  ACCUMULATE COST OF REPAIRS
370 REM
380     COST = 800*Y
390     CUMCST = CUMCST + COST
400     CUMX = CUMX + X
410 REM
420 REM ****  TEST TO SEE IF SIMULATED TIME HAS BEEN 52 WEKS:
430 REM ****   IF NOT, RETURN TO GENERATE ANOTHER VALUE OF R1
440 REM ****   IF 52 WEKS HAVE BEEN SIMULATED, COMPUTE TOTAL YEAR'S COST
450 REM
460     IF CUMX < 52 THEN GOTO 240
470     TCOST = TCOST + CUMCST
480 REM
490 REM ****  TEST TO SEE IF 100 SIMULATION RUNS HAVE BEEN MADE:
500 REM ****   IF NOT, RETURN TO BEGINNING AND INCREMENT I TO I+1
510 REM ****   IF 100 RUNS HAVE BEEN MADE, COMPUTE TOTAL COST FOR ALL RUNS
520 REM ****   COMPUTE AVERAGE ANNUAL MAINTENANCE COST
530 REM
540     IF I < NUMSIM THEN GOTO 160
550     AVCOST = TCOST / NUMSIM
560 REM
570 REM ****  TERMINATE SIMULATION AND PRINT OUT RESULTS
580 REM
590     PRINT "AVCOST = ",AVCOST," FOR ",NUMSIM," SIMULATION RUNS."
600     END
```

Additional Inverse Transformations

In many problems that are analyzed via stochastic simulation, the random variables of the model are defined by well-known probability distributions. The inverse functions for these distributions can often be developed with little difficulty. Examples of such distributions are the triangular (used in Example 11.5), Weibull, uniform, geometric, and exponential distributions. For example, the exponential distribution, often used in the simulation of queuing systems to generate interarrival times, has the probability function

$$f(x) = \lambda e^{-\lambda x}$$

and the cumulative distribution

$$F(x) = 1 - e^{-\lambda x}$$

Employing the inverse transformation technique yields

$$r = 1 - e^{-\lambda x} \quad \text{and} \quad 1 - r = e^{-\lambda x}$$

Since r is uniformly distributed between $(0, 1)$, $1 - r$ is also uniformly distributed between $(0, 1)$; therefore, r can be substituted for $1 - r$.

$$r = e^{-\lambda x}$$

Solving for x results in the inverse function,

$$x = -\frac{\ln{(r)}}{\lambda}$$

For many distributions, the inverse function does not exist or is so complicated that it cannot be developed. For example, the cumulative function for the normal distribution cannot be developed directly from the probability function. Other distributions such as the often-used beta (employed in PERT analysis) and gamma distributions are complex. In such cases, other methods besides the inverse transformation technique can be used. These include the **rejection method,** the **composition method,** and **approximation techniques.** These techniques, which are useful in dealing with more complex simulation models, are of a specialized nature. Hence, they are best studied in specialized simulation texts (see the references at the end of the chapter).

Random Number Generators

One of the important components of the simulation examples presented in this chapter is the generation of random numbers. Every example model has required random numbers to determine values of random variables. So far, the random numbers we have used have come from the random number table in Appendix C of this text. However, the generation of random numbers is not as simple as it may seem and can have a significant effect on the validity of the model results.

The random numbers in Table C.5 were generated using a numerical technique. Thus, they are not true random numbers but pseudorandom numbers. True random numbers can be produced only by a physical process such as spinning a roulette wheel. However, it is obvious that a physical process cannot be conveniently employed in a simulation model. Thus, the need exists for a numerical technique that can be used to artificially create random numbers.

To truly represent the random variables under analysis in a simulation model, the random numbers must have certain characteristics, as follows.

1. The random numbers should have a uniform distribution. This means that each random number in the interval $(0, 1)$ should have an equal chance of being selected. If this condition is not present (i.e., the values are not uniform), the simulation experiment will be biased and invalid.

2. The generation of the random numbers should be *efficient.* That is, the process for generating the random numbers should be inexpensive and quick, should recycle only after long periods, and should not degenerate into constant values.

3. The sequence of random numbers should be absent of any pattern. For example, although the sequence of numbers 0, 1, 2, 3, 4, 5, 6, 7, 8, 9, 0, 1, 2, 3, 4, 5, 6, 7, 8, 9, 0, 1, 2, 3, 4, 5, 6, 7, 8, 9, 0 is uniform, it is certainly not random.

A number of efficient computer packages now exist that generate random numbers with the above characteristics. These packages are available for almost any computer system and generate random numbers very easily.

OPTIMIZATION IN SIMULATION MODELS

Simulation is a management science tool that does not typically generate an optimal solution to a problem. Instead, a simulation model reflects the operation of a system in a compressed time frame. Although the results of the simulation represent the state of a system, the results should not be considered to be optimal in the same sense as the solution to a linear programming problem is.

However, quasi-optimal solutions can be obtained for simulation models by employing **search techniques.** In other words, a set of different results to a simulation model is "searched" until the best result is found. Optimizing in this manner requires a series of simulation runs, each with predetermined changes made in the decision variables.

As an example, consider the simulation of the inventory system (Example 11.2). Management wishes to determine the optimal combination of order quantity, Q, and reorder point, R. Simulation was shown to be desirable as a mode of analysis because both lead time and demand per week are random variables. The search process requires that predefined values of Q and R be set for each run and the results of the different runs compared. For example, in one particular simulation run (in Table 11.6), the inventory system was simulated with $Q = 40$ and $R = 30$. The results of the run yielded a total average inventory cost of approximately $215. This value reflects one simulation run and is considered as one entry in the following lattice (or grid) of values.

			Q		
	10	20	30	40	50
10					
20					
R 30				$215	
40					

Nineteen other runs are required to complete the lattice for all combinations of R and Q to be considered. The minimum lattice entry is the quasi-optimal solution for the values of Q and R considered. The obvious difficulty with such a search procedure is that for a complex problem with numerous variables, the lattice can become quite large and result in excessive computer time and cost. Also, the values considered for the decision variables may not include the optimal values, as in this example where the Q and R values tested are in increments of 10. The true optimal value may lie between two of the values tested. In such cases, it is usually desirable to determine the values of Q and R in the grid that appear to be optimal and then run another set of simulations in which the values immediately surrounding the optimal grid values are tested to see if a lower cost value exists. This is in effect what was done in the AB:QM computer simulation of Example 11.2.

CONSTRUCTION OF THE SIMULATION MODEL

The essential and probably most difficult aspects of Monte Carlo simulation have been presented. Beyond the generation of the process inputs to the model, constructing the simulation model is a matter of developing the logical relationships for the model of the system. Most of the preceding chapters of this text have dealt with this topic to some extent.

Since simulation models are run on computers, however, the model may consist of mathematically intractable statements or logical relationships that preclude a closed-form analytical solution. The model may consist of submodels or components linked together by a logical relationship. Logical relationships are generally represented by flowcharts or diagrams. We have touched, in general terms, on the construction of a simulation model in our example presentations, especially in Example 11.5. In this section we will discuss the fundamentals of model construction in greater detail.

To demonstrate the development of a complete simulation model, we will consider the following bank drive-in teller window example. The model to be simulated is a single-channel, single-phase queuing system. Times between customer arrivals are randomly generated according to a negative exponential probability distribution with a mean of 3 (minutes). Service times are generated randomly according to a negative exponential probability distribution with a mean of 2 (minutes). The analytical presentation of this queuing example is contained in Chapter 10.

The logic for the model of this system is illustrated in the flow diagram of Figure 11.13. The development of the model can be completed by defining all the system variables and parameters and specifying explicitly the relationships described in each block. For example, if time between arrivals were defined as the variable TBA and arrival time were defined as ARIV, then the relationship of the third block would be $ARIV_n = TBA + ARIV_{n-1}$.

Most of the relationships to be developed for each diagram block are evident. The decision block (diamond) relationship is developed by comparing the customer arrival time to the time the server first becomes available. If the arrival (clock) time is prior to the (clock) time the server becomes available, the program branches to the right. Branching to the left occurs for the reverse time relationship. If the two times are equal, the program can be written to branch either way (the idle time and waiting time are zero).

After the relationships of each block have been developed, the model is converted to computer code (a computer program). An advantage of computer simulation is the ability to include decision blocks (e.g., "Is server available?"). The relationships of each individual diagram block are relatively simple. However, the overall logic of the model may be quite complex when all the relationships are tied together. The individual relationships are tied together by the sequencing of the computer program statements.

Note that even though Figure 11.13 represents a very simple simulation model, it includes the interaction of two probability distributions (time between customer

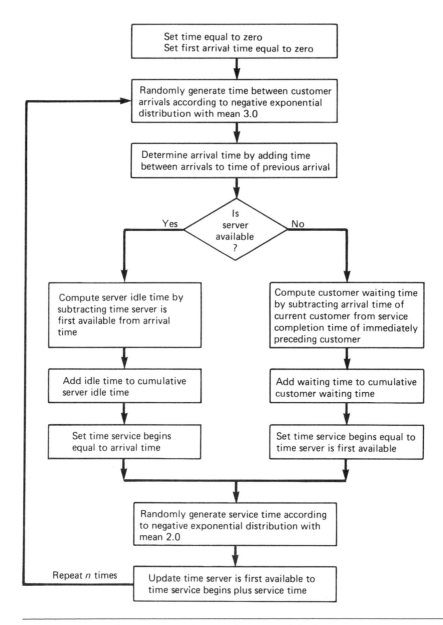

Figure 11.13 Flow Diagram for Simulation Model of Drive-in Bank Problem

arrivals and service time). When random variables are included in any model, regardless of the simplicity of the remaining model, the model becomes quite difficult to solve analytically.

Functions of the Constructed Simulation Model

The simulation model must perform the following functions.

Random Variable Generation

The example shown in Figure 11.13 includes two blocks in which the times between arrivals and the service times are randomly generated. In this case, they are generated from negative exponential probability distributions. The advantage of generating the random variable values from this theoretical probability distribution (rather than an empirical distribution) is that only a single statement is required in the program to perform this function.

Event Control

The flow diagram in Figure 11.13 represents the flow of events. The logic of the program controls the sequence of events. Note that a key variable of the control feature is the time the server is first available. The program compares the arrival time to this control variable to determine the program branching and, thus, the flow of events.

System State Initialization

The status of the system must be defined initially. The first block of the flow diagram performs this function for our example.

System Performance Data Collection

Note that the diagram of Figure 11.13 includes blocks that collect the cumulative server idle time and the cumulative customer waiting time. These are, of course, only two of the system descriptors that might be collected.

Statistical Computations and Report Generation

A final computation of the operational statistics is not shown in Figure 11.13; however, this function occurs after the model has been simulated for the desired length of time (or, alternatively, for the desired number of customer arrivals). At the end of a run of the simulation program, the program branches to the final portion of the program, which computes operating statistics and prints them out. For example, the cumulative idle time can be divided by the total time the system is simulated to yield the percentage server idle time, and the cumulative waiting time can be divided by the total number of customers to yield the mean waiting time per customer. Other statistics relating to system performance can also be collected and printed out, such as the standard deviation, range, median, and frequency distribution for the measured variable. A major advantage of simulation is its capability to collect and provide many different forms of statistical output.

Animation

Animation has become one of the most popular features of modern simulation languages. The animation capability has coincided with the production of microcomputers with powerful graphics capabilities. This feature has resulted in an increased popularity of simulation as a means of analysis. In animation, key elements of the system are shown on the monitor screen as *icons*—images that often appear similar to the elements of the system being simulated. Thus, a system being simulated can be portrayed graphically on the screen and it can change dynamically over time as the simulation progresses. This capability allows a visual observation of the simulation in progress.

Graphics Interface

In addition to animation, another important result of the powerful graphics capabilities of modern computers (especially microcomputers and work stations) is the capability to develop simulation models interactively with little or no coding. This capability allows the user to easily interact with the computer simulation language by simply selecting and moving graphical icons on the screen.

The graphics interface for interactive construction, modification, and execution of simulation models results in an increasingly user friendly environment. The three best known graphics environments are the Apple Macintosh operating system, the IBM OS/2 operating system, and the Microsoft Windows shell environment for DOS machines. Numerous other graphics environments are also available.[2]

Validation of the Model

A major difficulty of simulation is the validation of the model and the model results. The user of a simulation generally wants to be certain that the model is internally correct in a programming sense. Are the various operations performed in a logical and mathematically correct fashion? Does the model actually represent the real-world system being simulated? The old adage "garbage in, garbage out" is especially relevant for simulation. In order to gain some assurances about the validity of a simulation model, several testing procedures have been developed.

First, the model can be run several times for short periods of time or a few operations. This allows the simulation results to be compared with manually derived solutions and discrepancies identified. Another means of testing is to break the model into smaller components and run them separately. This reduces the complexity of seeking out errors in the model. In a similar vein, relationships in the model can be made less complex for testing purposes. For example, stochastic functions can be transformed into deterministic relationships and then tested.

In order to determine whether the model reliably represents the system being simulated, the model results can be compared with real-world data. Several statistical tests exist for performing this type of statistical analysis. However, when a model is developed to simulate a new or unique system, there is no realistic way to ensure that the results reflect the real system.

Other difficulties arising from the validation of simulation models concern the statistical properties of the results. As previously noted, simulation over time can yield output containing covariance. Techniques for analyzing the statistical properties of simulation results containing covariance are quite sophisticated. This highlights the fact that real-world simulation requires not only expertise in model construction but also a considerable degree of competence in statistical analysis.

---

[2] Apple Macintosh operating system is a registered trademark of Apple Computer Inc., IBM OS/2 is a registered trademark of IBM Corporation, and Microsoft Windows is a registered trademark of Microsoft Corporation.

Solutions to several tactical problems also affect whether the simulation model is a valid representation of the system being analyzed. One of these problems relates to starting conditions. Should the simulation start with the system empty (e.g., a queuing facility with no customers in line), or should an attempt be made to establish the simulation so that it will be as close as possible to normal operating conditions at the beginning of a run? Another tactical problem is determining how long the simulation has to be run in order to reach a steady-state condition, if indeed a steady state exists. Studies have shown that simulation often requires a surprisingly long time to reach steady-state conditions. If steady state is not reached, simulation output in the form of averages will not be meaningful.

These factors represent only some of the difficulties that can be encountered in validating a simulation model. In most cases, a standard, foolproof procedure for validation is simply not available. In the long run, the confidence placed in a simulation model often must be based on the insight and experience of the simulation user.

SIMULATION LANGUAGES

The computer programming aspects of simulation can be quite complex. Fortunately, generalized simulation languages have been developed to perform many of the functions of a simulation study. Use of these languages requires only limited knowledge of a scientific or business-oriented programming language. In this section, several of the best known and most readily available simulation languages will be described: GPSS/H, SIMAN IV, SIMSCRIPT II.5, and SLAM II.

GPSS/H

GPSS (general purpose systems simulation) was originally developed in the early 1960s for the IBM Corporation by Geoffrey Gordon. GPSS V was the most recent version developed for running on an IBM mainframe computer. IBM stopped supporting GPSS in 1972, which led to the introduction and support of versions by other vendors. GPSS/H was developed by James Henricksen in 1977 and is marketed by Wolverine Software in both mainframe and PC versions.

GPSS does not require program writing in the usual sense. The system model is constructed via block diagrams, using GPSS-generated block commands that represent operational functions of the system. GPSS is a language oriented to transactions moving in time through a system made up primarily of facilities, queues, and storages. As such, GPSS is highly compatible with queuing and network problems. The use of a GPSS program does not require any previous knowledge of computer programming.

SIMAN IV

SIMAN is a simulation language that can be used for either process-oriented or event-oriented simulation. The SIMAN language was developed by Dennis Pegden in the 1980s, and is marketed by Systems Modeling Corporation. SIMAN was one of the first simulation languages to be available for microcomputers.

Also available is a product called Cinema, which contains all the features of SIMAN and the capability to produce high-quality graphics animation. SIMAN is available for all major classes of computers, including mainframe, mini, work stations, and PC.

SIMSCRIPT II.5

SIMSCRIPT was developed at the RAND Corporation in the early 1960s by Harry Markowitz as a complete programming language. SIMSCRIPT II.5 is a powerful free-form English-like general purpose simulation language. It is not dependent on any predefined coding forms, nor does its implementation depend on any intermediate language, such as FORTRAN or assembler.

SIMSCRIPT defines the system to be simulated in terms of (1) *entities,* which are the components that make up the system; (2) *attributes* of the entities and the system, which are the properties associated with entities; and (3) *sets,* or groups of entities. In SIMSCRIPT, the status of the system is unchanged except at points in time called *event times.* The system is described in terms of two types of events: *exogenous* events (those created outside the simulation framework) and *endogenous* events (those generated internally). Each event incorporated into the simulation model requires the construction of an event subroutine.

The SIMSCRIPT language has been extended to include discrete and continuous model capabilities. SIMSCRIPT II.5 is marketed and supported by the CACI Corporation.

SLAM II

SLAM is an advanced FORTRAN-based language developed by Pritsker that allows simulation models to be developed as (1) network models, (2) discrete event models, (3) continuous models, or (4) any combination of the above.

SLAM is an acronym for simulation language for alternative modeling. By combining network, discrete event, and continuous modeling capabilities, SLAM allows the user to develop models from a process-interaction, next-event, or activity-scanning perspective. The SLAM language is an outgrowth of both the Q-GERT and GASP IV languages developed by Pritsker, which will be described briefly.

Q-GERT, originally referred to as GERT IIIQ, is a network modeling and simulation language especially appropriate for the analysis of queuing systems. Q-GERT was developed by Pritsker during the 1960s. The Q-GERT language is an outgrowth of a previous network modeling and simulation language entitled GERT, also developed by Pritsker. The acronym GERT is for graphical evaluation and review technique. The primary difference between Q-GERT and GERT is that Q-GERT provides the capability to include servers and queues in the network model. Q-GERT also allows the user to keep track of specific entities as they flow through the system. Neither could be done with GERT.

The Q-GERT language is an entirely prewritten and self-contained computer program written in FORTRAN. To make use of the program, the user simply provides the data describing the network model previously formulated.

GASP IV, developed by A. Alan B. Pritsker and Nicholas R. Hurst in 1973, is a successor to the GASP II language, which was entirely a discrete change (next event) language. The GASP II language was an outgrowth of the original work done by Philip J. Kiviat at U.S. Steel Corporation. The primary difference between GASP II and GASP IV is the addition of the capability for continuous simulation to the original discrete capabilities.

Whereas GASP II is a discrete change (next event) language (i.e., the dependent variables of the model change discretely at simulated time points). GASP IV has the capability to perform a combination of both discrete and continuous changes in the same simulation. Thus, GASP IV can be used to simulate not only the more traditional business problems, such as queuing, inventory, and production, but also the Forrester (systems dynamics) type models. This simulation language requires a knowledge of FORTRAN computer programming.

SLAM, which is an outgrowth of the above-described simulation languages, is now available for mainframe, mini, work station, and microcomputers. The microcomputer version of SLAM is called SLAMSYSTEM and it operates under Microsoft Windows. It provides animation, presentation-quality graphics, and a user friendly environment. Animation is also available for mainframe, mini, and work stations using the product called TESS in conjunction with SLAM II.

APPLICATIONS OF SIMULATION

Simulation can be applied to any problem too difficult to be modeled and solved analytically. Some management scientists have noted that any complex real-world problem should first be modeled and solved analytically, even if simplifying assumptions must be introduced, in order to gain an intuitive feel for the model and system and to ensure the validity of the model. This should be followed up by the formulation of a complete simulation model that includes all system complexities, to provide the final basis for analysis and decision making.

Simulation has been applied to an extremely wide range of problems. A few of the more prominent examples in the field of business are discussed in the following paragraphs.

Queuing

A major area of application for simulation has been the analysis of waiting line problems. As indicated in Chapter 10, the assumptions required for analytic solution of queuing problems are quite restrictive. With few exceptions, simulation is the only approach available for considering such problems as multiple-phase queuing systems. Q-GERT, a self-contained computer program, includes the capability to model and simulate virtually any conceivable queuing system with relative ease.

Inventory

Chapter 7 introduced the case in which inventory demand per day, during a constant lead time, was described as a random variable. However, when both demand per day and lead time are random variables, analysis becomes extremely difficult to accomplish by any means other than simulation. In an inventory system, both the number of demands received per day and the size of each demand might be random variables, in which case the random variable demand during lead time would be a function of three random variables. The joint probability distribution created could be analyzed only by simulation.

Networks

In a PERT network, activity times are represented by the beta probability distribution. As has been shown by simulating the network, the analytical PERT solution yields slightly biased results. Also, the PERT approach is limited to the beta probability distribution. If empirical data show that the activity times follow some other distribution, the network could be analyzed with simulation.

In PERT, all activities are assumed to occur with a probability of one. By using simulation languages such as SLAM, you can simulate networks that include not only probabilistic activity times but also probabilistic branching—in other words, the probability that an activity will occur may be less than one. The simulator may also allow other non-PERT features such as looping of activities back to intermediate events and multiple logic concerning event realization. Also, use of simulation languages with network modeling capabilities may provide for special queue nodes that allow the user to analyze networks of queues.

Production

Various problems in production, such as scheduling, sequencing, line balancing, plant layout, and plant location analysis, have been simulated. It is surprising how often production problems can be viewed as queuing processes. The applicability of simulation to queuing problems is one reason a queuing example is generally used to illustrate simulation.

Maintenance

Since machine breakdowns and facility failures typically occur according to some probability distribution, such problems are generally analyzed by simulation. Much analytical work has also been done in this area. Simulation, in conjunction with analytical methods, provides a powerful means for studying such problems.

Finance

Capital budgeting finance problems include estimates of cash flows, which are often composites of many random variables. Simulation has been used to generate values of the various random variables in order to derive estimates of cash flows. A classic article by Hertz in 1964 (see references) illustrated the use of simulation for randomly generating the inputs into a rate of return calculation. The contributing inputs included such random variables as market size, selling price, growth rate, and market share.

Marketing

Marketing problems typically involve a great deal of uncertainty. Simulation gives a marketing strategist the opportunity to experiment with alternative courses of action when faced with a large number of interacting and widely varying random components. In addition, simulation can provide the marketing strategist with insights into the operation of the market under consideration. An example of a possible application of simulation in the marketing environment is contract bidding. Simulation allows the contractor to evaluate various alternative courses of action.

Public Service Operations

Recently the operations of police departments, fire departments, post offices, hospitals, court systems, airports, and other public systems have been analyzed by simulation. Typically, such an operation is so complex that no other technique can be used to successfully analyze the overall system.

Environmental and Resource Conservation

Some of the more recent and innovative applications of simulation have been concerned with the effects of technology on the environment and natural resources. Highly complex models have been developed to ascertain the environmental effects of such projects as nuclear power plants, reservoirs, highways, and dams. In many cases, these simulation models include cost trade-offs to measure the financial feasibility of such projects. Similar models have been developed to simulate air, water, and noise pollution conditions. Other recent developments include the simulation of energy systems to determine the financial and environmental feasibility of capital projects. Such simulation models are important to the business community, since these factors are becoming an increasing part of the business environment.

SUMMARY

Simulation has become an increasingly important tool of analysis in recent years. Numerous surveys have shown simulation to be one of the most widely applied management science tools presently available. Evidence of this popularity is the number of specialized simulation languages that have been developed by industry and academia to deal with specific complex problem areas.

The popularity of simulation is due in large part to the flexibility it offers in analyzing systems, in contrast to more confining analytical methods. In other words, the problem does not have to fit the model or technique; instead, the model is developed to fit the problem. This inherent flexibility of simulation also makes it an excellent tool for experimenting on systems and problems in a laboratory-type atmosphere.

In spite of its versatility, the simulation technique must be used with caution. Validation of the model and its subsequent results can often be tedious or even impossible. Model building and analysis can be expensive and time consuming. This problem has become of such concern that output analysis of simulation results is developing into a new field in itself.

REFERENCES

BANKS, J., and CARSON, J. S. *Discrete-Event System Simulation*. Englewood Cliffs, New Jersey: Prentice-Hall, 1984.

BANKS, J., CARSON, II, J. S., and SY, J. N.

Getting Started with GPSS/H. Annandale, Virginia: Wolverine Software Corp., 1989.

FAYEK, A. M. *Introduction to Combined Dis-*

crete-Continuous Simulation Using PC SIM-SCRIPT II.5. La Jolla, California: CACI Products Co., 1988.

FISHMAN, G. S. *Principles of Discrete Event Simulation*. New York: John Wiley & Sons, 1978.

GORDON, G. *The Application of GPSS V to Discrete System Simulation*. Englewood Cliffs, New Jersey: Prentice Hall, 1975.

GORDON, G. *System Simulation*. 2nd ed. Englewood Cliffs, New Jersey: Prentice Hall, 1978.

HAMMERSLY, J. M., and HANDSCOMB, D. C. *Monte Carlo Methods*. New York: John Wiley & Sons, 1964.

HERTZ, D. B. "Risk Analysis in Capital Investment." *Harvard Business Review* 42 (1964): 95–106.

HOOVER, S. V., and PERRY, R. F. *Simulation: A Problem Solving Approach*. Reading, Massachusetts: Addison-Wesley, 1989.

LAW, A. M., and KELTON, W. D. *Simulation Modeling and Analysis*. 2nd ed. New York: McGraw-Hill Book Company, 1991.

LAW, A. M., and LARMEY, C. S. *Introduction to Simulation Using SIMSCRIPT II.5,* La Jolla, California: CACI Products Co., 1984.

MARKOWITZ, H. M.; KARR, H. W.; and HAUSNER, B. *SIMSCRIPT: A Simulation Programming Language*. Englewood Cliffs, New Jersey: Prentice-Hall, 1963.

MEIER, R. C.; NEWELL, W. T.; and PAZER, H. L. *Simulation in Business and Economics*. Englewood Cliffs, New Jersey: Prentice-Hall, 1969.

MIZE, J., and COX, G. *Essentials of Simulation*. Englewood Cliffs, New Jersey: Prentice-Hall, 1968.

MOORE, L. J., and CLAYTON, E. R. *GERT Modeling and Simulation: Fundamentals and Applications*. New York: Petrocelli/Charter, 1976.

NAYLOR, T. H.; BALINTFY, J. L.; BURDICK, D. S.; and CHU, K. *Computer Simulation Techniques*. New York: John Wiley & Sons, 1966.

PEGDEN, C. D., SHANNON, R. E., and SADOWSKI, R. P. *Introduction to Simulation Using SIMAN*. Sewickley, Pennsylvania: Systems Modeling Corp., 1990.

PRITSKER, A. A. B. *Introduction to Simulation and SLAM II*. 3rd. ed. West Lafayette, Indiana: Systems Publishing Corp., 1986.

PRITSKER, A. A. B., and SIGAL, C. E. *Management Decision Making: A Network Simulation Approach*. Englewood Cliffs, New Jersey: Prentice-Hall, 1983.

RUSSELL, EDWARD C. *Building Simulation Models with SIMSCRIPT II.5*. Los Angeles, California: CACI-Federal, 1983.

SCHRIBER, T. J. *An Introduction to Simulation Using GPSS/H*. New York: John Wiley & Sons, 1991.

SCHRIBER, T. S. *Simulation Using GPSS*. New York: John Wiley & Sons, 1974.

SCHRUBEN, L. *SIGMA: A graphical Simulation System*. San Francisco: The Scientific Press, 1991.

SHANNON, R. E. *Systems Simulation*. Englewood Cliffs, New Jersey: Prentice-Hall, 1975.

TAHA, H. A. *Simulation Modeling and Simnet*. Englewood Cliffs, New Jersey: Prentice-Hall, 1988.

WATSON, H. J. and BLACKSTONE, J. H. *Computer Simulation*. 2nd. ed., New York: John Wiley, 1989.

PROBLEMS

1. Repeat the simulation experiment performed in Example 11.1 in this chapter by generating demand for 15 weeks using the probability distribution of demand shown at the top of page 561.

   Use the third column of random numbers from Table C.5 in Appendix C to perform your experiment. Compute the average weekly demand, compare this result with the analytical result, and explain any difference that may exist.

Demand for Terminals per Week x	Probability of Demand P(x)
14	.10
15	.25
16	.30
17	.20
18	.15
	1.00

2. The time between arrivals at a service station pump is defined by the following probability distribution:

Time Between Arrivals (min)	Probability
1	.15
2	.30
3	.40
4	.15
	1.00

Simulate the arrival of cars at the service station for 20 arrivals. Compute the mean time between arrivals and compare this value with the expected value of the time between arrivals.

3. Repeat the simulation experiment performed in Example 11.2 and Table 11.6 with an order size, Q, of 30 computer terminals, a reorder point, R, of 20 terminals, and a beginning inventory of 30 terminals. Use the tenth column of random numbers from Table C.5 in Appendix C.

4. A retail firm has an inventory policy that requires an order size of 5 units and a reorder point of 3 units. Inventory-related costs include a holding cost of $4 per unit per period, an order cost of $10 per order, and a shortage (or stockout) cost of $40 for an unfilled (i.e., partially filled) order. Units are not backordered. The following frequency distribution for demand was compiled for a 50-week period.

Demand/Week (units)	Frequency
0	2
1	4
2	14
3	20
4	8
5	1
6	1
	50

Lead time (the time until delivery of an order) has the following frequency distribution:

Lead Time (weeks)	Frequency
1	6
2	3
3	1
	10

The firm has a beginning inventory balance of 5 units. All orders are received at the beginning of the week.

a. Develop a simulation experiment to replicate this firm's inventory policy. Simulate for 20 weeks (using the random number table).

b. This simulation experiment reflects one order size and one reorder point. Explain how a simulation model could be designed to determine the optimal (lowest average cost) inventory policy.

5. Repeat the simulation experiment performed in Example 11.3 and Table 11.9 in this chapter with the following probability distributions for arrival intervals and service times:

Arrival Interval x	Probability $p(x)$
1	.10
2	.10
3	.40
4	.20
5	.20

Service Time y	Probability $p(y)$
2	.20
3	.50
4	.30

Use the stream of random numbers from the third column of random numbers employed in Table C.5 for both the arrival interval and service times. Determine the average customer waiting time and the percentage of customers who must wait for service.

6. A bank is attempting to determine whether it should install one or two drive-in teller windows. The following probability distributions for arrival intervals and service times have been developed from historical data:

Time Between Arrivals (min)	Probability
1	.20
2	.60
3	.10
4	.10
	1.00

Service Time (min)	Probability
2	.10
3	.40
4	.20
5	.20
6	.10
	1.00

In the two-server system, assume that a car will always join the shortest queue. When the queues are of equal length, there is a .5 probability the driver will enter either queue.

a. Develop a simulation experiment based on a 30-minute arrival period for both the one- and the two-teller system. Compute the average queue length, waiting time, and percentage utilization of each system.

b. Discuss which is the better system to install.

7. Develop a simulation model to replicate the decision tree analysis in problem 21 in Chapter 8. Simulate for 20 iterations and determine the number of times the insurance firm would choose to settle and not settle the law suit. How would the information provided by the simulation supplement the expected value results provided in problem 21?

8. The time between arrivals of oil tankers at an unloading dock is given by the probability distribution at the top of page 564.

a. Generate randomly the time between arrivals for the first 20 ships.

b. Compute the relative frequency of the times between arrivals in part a. Compare these simulated results with the actual probability distribution. What is the difference between the two a result of?

c. Assume that the time required to unload, clean, and prepare a ship for departure is 5 days. Develop a simulation experiment for the movement of ships to and away from the unloading dock. (Note: Only one ship can be serviced at a time.)

Time Between Ship Arrivals (days)	Probability
1	.05
2	.10
3	.20
4	.30
5	.20
6	.10
7	.05
	1.00

Compute the mean time between arrivals, mean waiting time for unloading, mean number of ships waiting to unload, mean time ships are waiting and unloading, mean number of ships waiting and being unloaded, proportion of arrivals entering an empty system, and the frequency distribution of number of ships waiting.

d. Now assume that the time required to unload, clean, and prepare ships is a random variable defined by the following distribution:

Time to Unload, Clean, Prepare (days)	Probability
3	.10
4	.20
5	.40
6	.30

Repeat part c for this condition.

9. An inventory manager for a firm wants to determine the mean demand for a particular product in stock during the reorder lead time. This information is needed to determine how far in advance of a zero stock level to reorder. Both demand and lead time are random variables, defined by the following probability distributions:

Lead Time (days)	Probability	Demand per Day	Probability
1	.5	1	.1
2	.3	2	.3
3	.2	3	.4
		4	.2

Simulate this problem for 30 reorders to estimate the mean demand during lead time.

10. Given the continuous probability distribution

$$f(x) = \frac{x}{18}, \qquad 0 \leqslant x \leqslant 6$$

develop a process generator by using the inverse transformation technique.

11. Given the following continuous triangular probability distribution, develop a process generator by using the inverse transformation technique.

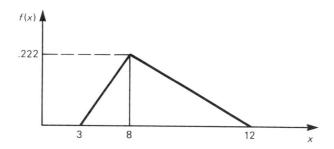

12. Given the following uniform distribution, develop a process generator by using the inverse transformation technique.

13. Repeat the simulation experiment performed in Example 11.4 and Table 11.11 using the following probability function for the time (in weeks) between machine breakdowns:

$$f(x) = \frac{2x}{25}, \qquad 0 \leqslant x \leqslant 5$$

a. Simulate machine breakdowns for one year (i.e., 52 weeks) to determine the number of breakdowns per year. Use the twentieth column of random numbers from Table C.5 in Appendix C.

b. Develop figures similar to those in Figures 11.4 and 11.5 in this chapter to illustrate the probability function for time between machine breakdowns and the cumulative distribution function. Illustrate how the cumulative distribution function works with random number .64.

14. A job shop manager wants to develop a simulation model to schedule jobs through the shop. Part of the simulation model is a process generator for machine time for each job on each machine. The shop manager has estimated that the time for *one particular* job on one machine follows a triangular distribution.

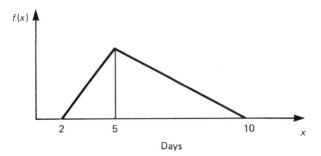

Days

For this machine time, use the inverse transformation technique to develop a process generator that could be used in the simulation model.

15. Suppose in Example 11.5 that the proposed maintenance program encompassed the probability function for time between machine breakdowns given in problem 12, and the following probability functions for machine repair time.

$$f_1(y) = \frac{-1}{6} + \frac{y}{12}, \qquad 2 \le y \le 6$$

$$f_2(y) = \frac{4}{3} - \frac{y}{6}, \qquad 6 \le y \le 8$$

Repeat the simulation performed in Table 11.13 (using the same stream of random numbers from Table C.5), and indicate (based on these admittedly limited results) whether or not the maintenance program should be implemented.

16. A manufacturing firm has determined that its maintenance schedule is reflected by the following probability distribution:

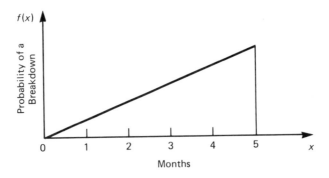

Months

This distribution represents the time between breakdowns (i.e., machine run time). Every time a machine breaks down, it requires repair time, according to the following probability distribution:

Repair Time (days)	Probability
1	.40
2	.30
3	.30
	1.00

Conduct a simulation experiment to replicate the firm's maintenance schedule for 36 months. Compute the average repair time and compare this value with the expected repair time.

17. Interarrival times of customers at a service facility are exponentially distributed with $\lambda = 20$/hour. Develop a process generator for this function and generate ten interarrival times.

18. Develop a flowchart similar to that shown in Figure 11.12 in this chapter for the simulation experiment performed in Example 11.4 and Table 11.11.

19. Discuss how factors related to simulation, such as starting and ending conditions, random number characteristics, duration of the simulation run, and number of simulation runs (i.e., sample size), relate to the validation of simulation model results.

20. Problem 17 in Chapter 9, Markov Analysis, concerns the rental and return of trucks within 3 states on a weekly basis, according to the following probability transition matrix:

| | Week $n + 1$ | | |
Week n	Virginia	North Carolina	Maryland
Virginia	.30	.50	.20
North Carolina	.60	.20	.20
Maryland	.40	.10	.50

Beginning with a truck in Virginia, simulate the rental and location of a truck for a 30-week period. (Use the fourth column of random numbers from Table C.5 in Appendix C.) From the simulation experiment, determine the percentage of time a truck will be in each state (i.e., the probability a truck will be in each of the 3 states during the 30-week period). Discuss the way you might expand this manual simulation experiment so that you could be very confident about the results.

21. The following network is a simplified version of the CPM/PERT project networks presented in Chapter 6 of this text.

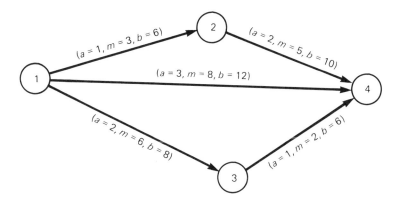

Each branch (i.e., project activity) in the network has a probabilistic time estimate defined by a triangular distribution as follows.

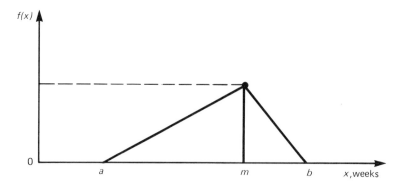

In this distribution a, m, and b are all subjective time estimates (in weeks), where a equals the optimistic time of the project activity, b equals the pessimistic time of the project activity, and m equals the most likely time required for the completion of the project activity.

a. Simulate the completion of this network ten times and compute the average project completion time. (Use the ninth and tenth columns of random numbers from Table C.5.)

b. Determine the percentage of time each of the three different paths in the network was the critical path. What does this indicate to you regarding critical path determination via simulation as compared to the analytical critical path determination presented in Chapter 6?

22. A major international airline has decided to conduct cash planning for the next 3 months, using simulation. Net cash flows (receipts minus disbursements) by month are random variables given by the probability distributions below (where negative values represent net cash outflows and positive values represent net cash inflows).

Net Cash Flows ($000)	Probabilities Month		
	1	2	3
−200	.2	.1	.2
−100	.4	.5	.3
100	.3	.3	.3
200	.1	.1	.2

The airline currently has a cash balance of $200,000 (at the beginning of month 1). The airline's required minimum cash balance, to be kept on hand for future transactions, is $150,000, determined after each month's cash flow reconciliation. Thus, if the month's net cash flow causes the cash balance for the month to be less than $150,000, the airline will borrow sufficient funds to bring the balance up to $150,000. On the other hand, if the resulting balance exceeds the required $150,000, the airline will repay outstanding accumulated borrowings (to the extent possible, given the available cash balance in excess of $150,000 and given the amount of accumulated borrowings outstanding). The airline has no accumulated borrowings currently (at the beginning of month 1).

Given the previous description of the airline's cash flow operation, conduct ten manual simulations of the operation and indicate the results of the simulations in the following table. (Generate the net cash flows for each month by using the first three columns of random number streams in Table C.5, starting on the upper left. That is, start with the random number 39 in the first column and go down the column to generate the ten simulated values of net cash flow for month 1; start at the top of the second column of random numbers to generate the simulated values for month 2; and so forth.)

Simulation Results Table

	Simulation Number									
	1	2	3	4	5	6	7	8	9	10
Month 1										
Beginning cash balance										
Net cash flow										
Resulting cash balance										
Borrowing (repayment)										
Ending cash balance										
Accumulated borrowings										
Month 2										
Beginning cash balance										
Net cash flow										
Resulting cash balance										
Borrowing (repayment)										
Ending cash balance										
Accumulated borrowings										
Month 3										
Beginning cash balance										
Net cash flow										
Resulting cash balance										
Borrowing (repayment)										
Ending cash balance										
Accumulated borrowings										

After entering the results of the manually calculated simulation, answer the following questions. (Assume that the simulation has been conducted a sufficient number of times to yield relative frequency results that approximate probabilities.)

a. What is the probability that borrowing will be required to maintain the airline's desired minimum cash balance in month 1, in month 2, and in month 3?

b. What is the probability distribution (relative frequency distribution) of borrowing for month 3? (Include zero dollars borrowed as part of the distribution, but do not include repayments.)

c. What is the probability that borrowing in the 3-month planning period will exceed $150,000?

d. What is the probability that all accumulated borrowings will be paid off at the end of the planning period?

e. What is the probability (relative frequency) of accumulated borrowings at the end of month 3?

f. What is the average value of accumulated borrowings at the end of month 3?

-12

Dynamic Programming

Most of the chapters in this text describe techniques by which the entire problem is solved with a *single* assault; that is, the variables of the problem are dealt with *simultaneously* or collectively. An exception is decision tree analysis in Chapter 8, in which the branches and nodes of the network tree represent a sequence of decision alternatives, states of nature (with associated probabilities), and expected payoffs associated with the various combinations of decisions and states. **Dynamic programming** is closely akin to decision tree analysis in that problems are subdivided (decomposed) into smaller components (subproblems or stages) where decisions are made sequentially. For this reason, dynamic programming is often referred to as a *multistage* decision process. Dynamic programming considers problems in which the outcome of a decision at one stage affects the results and decision at the next stage. Thus, each subproblem, which may change from stage to stage, is a function of prior stage decisions. Of course, if the stages are independent of one another, each stage can be solved separately and the results aggregated.

The innovator of dynamic programming, and the person primarily responsible for popularizing it, is Richard Bellman. Bellman's work on dynamic programming dates back to the late 1940s and early 1950s, culminating in his classic text, *Dynamic Programming.* Unlike many of the previously presented techniques, dynamic programming does not involve a single problem-solving method (or algorithm), such as the simplex method for linear programming problems. Dynamic programming makes use of many available techniques to solve stage subproblems.

As a concept, dynamic programming is more flexible than most mathematical models and methods in management science. Important applications of dynamic programming have been reported in inventory control, network flows, job shop scheduling, production control, replacement and maintenance, sales planning, work force scheduling, general resource allocation, and numerous other areas. This chapter will present the fundamental concepts of dynamic programming, followed by a number of prototype problems and examples to illustrate model formulation and solution procedures.

FUNDAMENTAL CONCEPTS OF DYNAMIC PROGRAMMING

Dynamic programming includes several interrelated concepts that can be rather confusing when considered simultaneously. However, by studying each of the fundamental concepts individually, one can learn the overall modeling and solution approach to dynamic programming with a minimum of confusion. The purpose of this section is to present and illustrate each of the several concepts separately. It is interesting to note that this approach of studying the concepts of dynamic programming individually reflects the first basic concept of dynamic programming—**decomposition** of the problem into subcomponents for analysis.

Decomposition

The first concept fundamental to the dynamic programming approach to problem modeling and analysis is the subdivision of the problem into a sequence of smaller subproblems. Each subproblem is referred to as a stage or decision point. Because it is based on the principle that a problem can often be evaluated more easily and efficiently by stages, dynamic programming is frequently referred to as a multistage, or sequential, decision process.

The concept of decomposing a problem into a sequence of stages, or subproblems, is illustrated abstractly in Figure 12.1. In this illustration, it is assumed that the given problem can be subdivided into three stages. The basis for determining how to decompose a problem into stages will be presented later in this chapter.

Figure 12.1 *Problem Decomposition into a Sequence of Stages*

Note that (1) the stages are connected by arrows flowing from left to right and (2) the stages are numbered sequentially from right to left. Each of these features is related to separate concepts, to be presented shortly. For our present needs, it is sufficient to know that (1) the arrows are the *linkage,* or *connection,* between problem stages, and they generally represent "information flow" about the current status of the system and (2) the stages are numbered in reverse order to denote *number of remaining decision points.*

Suppose, for example, that a corporation owns plants in Atlanta, Baltimore, and Chicago (plants A, B, and C, respectively). The corporation has budgeted a total of $5 million for plant improvements, to be allocated among the three plants during the coming fiscal year. Decomposition of the problem into three stages is shown in Figure 12.2. The problem is to determine the portion of the $5 million capital to invest at each of the plants in order to maximize returns. Dynamic programming will be used to solve this

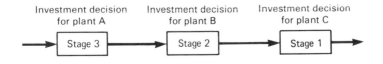

Figure 12.2 *Decomposition of Plant Investment Problem into Three Stages*

problem. The overall problem can be logically broken into three subproblems, or decision points, representing how much to invest in plant A, plant B, and plant C. It should be pointed out that the designation of the investment problem for plant A as stage 3, plant B as stage 2, and plant C as stage 1 is arbitrary and that *any* assignment of the plants to the three stages is acceptable.

Alternatively, suppose that the corporate problem is defined as how much to invest at a single plant over the three-year planning period of 1991, 1992, and 1993. The decomposition of this problem into stages is shown in Figure 12.3. In this problem, the designation of years corresponding to stages should proceed from left to right, corresponding to the direction of the arrows. This is because the arrows represent information regarding the remaining amount of capital available for investment at each decision point (stage). Obviously, the first investment will be in 1991, the second investment in 1992 will depend on how much capital is left from the 1991 decision, and so on. At stage 3, there are three years of investment decisions to be made. At stage 2, only two years of investment decisions remain. At stage 1, the investment decision for the year 1993 is the only remaining decision.

Figure 12.3 *Decomposition of a Single Plant Investment Problem into Three Stages, Based on a Three-Year Planning Period*

Although dynamic programming is often thought of as a technique for analysis over a period of time, this is not *necessarily* the case, as indicated by Figure 12.2. Dynamic programming has, however, been effectively applied to a large number of problems involving decisions over time and is frequently associated with time-dependent problems.

Finally, dynamic programming, like all other management science techniques, employs certain symbolic notation necessary to present the modeling and solution procedure in a concise and generalized fashion. The symbol n is commonly used to denote the stage number. In general, problems that require the application of dynamic programming are decomposed into N stages. The stages range from a maximum of N to 1 (i.e., for the *last* stage, $n = 1$). Thus,

$$n = \text{stage } n, \text{ where } n \in \{N, N - 1, \ldots, n, n - 1, n - 2, \ldots, 2, 1\}$$

The generalized stage numbering approach is illustrated in Figure 12.4, where n represents the number of remaining decision points.

Figure 12.4 *Generalized Illustration of an N-Stage Dynamic Programming Problem*

System Status

The concept of **system status,** or **states,** has already been implicitly introduced in the preceding discussion by the arrows in Figure 12.1 through 12.4. As previously noted, the arrows provide the connection, or linkage, from one subproblem to the next subproblem and generally represent the flow of information about the status of the system from stage n to stage $n - 1$, and so on. It is obvious that this information flow is essential in the problem illustrated in Figure 12.3. Management must know the remaining amount of capital available after the investment decision at stage 3 (1991) to effectively determine the course of action to take at stage 2 (1992). This is equally true for the stage 1 (1993) decision analysis. This concept is illustrated in Figure 12.5.

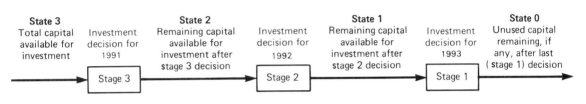

Figure 12.5 *System Status Shown as the Output from Stage n and the Input into the Adjacent Stage n — 1*

Another way of illustrating the concept of input states and stages is shown in Figure 12.6, which shows only two of three stages of a hypothetical problem. It is assumed that 5 units of a particular resource (for example, an inventory of trucks available for shipping) are available initially as input to stage 3. It is further assumed that, given the decision analysis at stage 3, the result will be an increase in the resource by 1 unit, no change, or a decrease in the resource by 1 unit. The resulting input (state) to the stage 2 decision problem will therefore be 6 units of resource, 5 units of resource, or 4 units of resource.

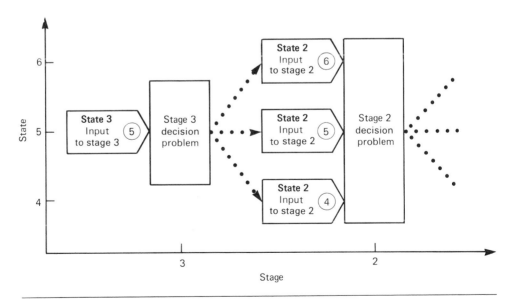

Figure 12.6 *Alternative Inputs to Stage 2 Depend on the Input State to Stage 3 and the Decision at Stage 3*

The decision options available at stage 2 are therefore dependent on (or constrained by) the state input from stage 3 to stage 2, which has resulted from the combination of the state input to stage 3 and the decision at stage 3. For example, there might be a maximum resource capacity of 6 units. If the state input to stage 2 is 6 units, this eliminates the option of increasing the resource by 1 unit at stage 2. If the state input to stage 2 is 5 or 4 units, the decision alternatives are still add 1, no change, or decrease by 1. Similarly, if there were a requirement that no less than 4 units be kept on hand at all times, a state input of 4 units to stage 2 would limit the decision alternatives to no change or add 1 unit.

The illustration in Figure 12.6 demonstrates that the range of possible decision alternatives at a particular stage is a function of the state input to the stage. The state input to a stage is the output from the *previous* (larger number) stage, and the previous stage output is a function of the state input to itself in combination with the decision at that stage. This concept is again illustrated in Figure 12.7.

Figure 12.7 illustrates an additional point of importance—the total information requirements for making a decision at each stage are contained in the stage itself, including the return associated with various alternative decisions and the input to the stage. That is, to perform the decision analysis at stage n, the decision maker needs to know only the values of the stage n input and the decision alternatives and their associated returns at stage n. Thus, the overall problem may be decomposed into N stages, where each stage (subproblem) is evaluated separately, based on the stage input.

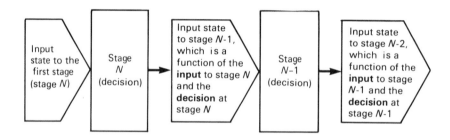

Figure 12.7 *Information Transfer Between Stages Is a Function of the System Status*

The symbol used to denote the state input, which is referred to as the **state variable,** is

$$S_n = \text{state input to stage } n$$

The value of the state variable, S_n, is the status of the system resulting from the previous $(n + 1)$ stage decision.

Decision Variables

The decision variable, which has already been implicitly discussed in the previous section, represents the possible alternative actions and is denoted by

$$D_n = \text{decision variable at stage } n$$

D_n represents the range of alternatives that can be selected from when making a decision at stage n.

The symbolic definitions for stage, input state, and decisions (n, S_n, and D_n) are used in Figure 12.8 to illustrate the general dynamic programming problem. Figure 12.8 completely defines the dynamic programming model of a problem in terms of the concepts presented thus far but does not yet include the return (profit, cost, utility, etc.) associated with the decisions. The return function will be presented shortly. Notice that, in general, each state input variable for stage n is the output of the previous stage, $n + 1$.

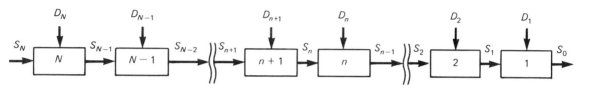

Figure 12.8 *The Dynamic Programming Model Illustrated in Terms of Stages, State Variables, and Decision Variables*

S_0 is a function of S_1 and D_1; S_1 is a function of S_2 and D_2; and, in general, S_n is a function of S_{n+1} and D_{n+1} (except S_N, which is usually given, for an example, as an initial quantity of resource available). Also, S_0 is frequently required to equal zero; that is, the entire quantity of resource should be used.

It was previously pointed out that the possible range of values for D_n is often a function of the input state, S_n. At this point in the discussion of decision variables, it should also be noted that D_n may be further constrained by additional requirements imposed by the *problem structure*. This feature will be illustrated by examples later in the chapter.

Transition Function

Although not specifically identified as such, the concept of a **transition function,** or **transform,** has already been incorporated into our discussion of dynamic programming. This extremely important concept in dynamic programming is discussed in greater detail here.

The transition function describes precisely how the stages of a dynamic programming model are interconnected. It defines, as a functional relationship, the value the state variable will have at each stage. For example, for the example in which a firm plans to invest in three plants (A, B, and C), the transition function is simply $S_{n-1} = S_n - D_n$, or $S_2 = S_3 - D_3$, which denotes that the capital available at stage 2 is equal to the capital available at stage 3 less the amount invested at stage 3. Likewise, $S_1 = S_2 - D_2$ and $S_0 = S_1 - D_1$. If all of the capital is to be invested in the three plants, then $S_0 = 0$ and $D_1 = S_1$, yielding $S_1 - D_1 = 0$.

The transition function for a dynamic programming problem is generally illustrated graphically. An example of a capital investment problem is shown, with the transition function described for each stage, in Figure 12.9.

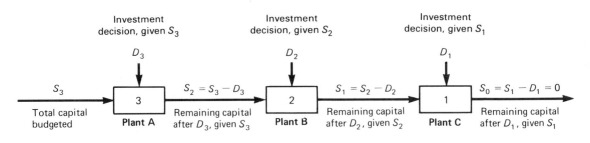

Figure 12.9 *The Transition Function* $S_{n-1} = S_n - D_n$
Describes the Relationship of the Stages in the Capital Investment
Problem

Figure 12.10 further illustrates this concept for two stages by relating it to the same example problem, assuming that $3 million is the amount initially available and that the capital must be invested in $1 million amounts. Note that four alternative decisions are possible at stage N (invest 0, $1, $2, or $3 million), as shown by the branches from ③ (the state input to stage N). Thus, the transition function is shown for each alternative decision as $3 million less the decision amount, yielding the input state (circled amounts) to stage $N - 1$. Further note that the possible decision alternatives at stage $N - 1$ are a function of the value of the input state variable (S_{N-1}). Thus, if the value of $S_N - D_n = S_{N-1}$ is $3 million, the alternatives for D_{N-1} are investments of 0, $1, $2, or $3 million. On the other hand, if the value of the input state is $1 million, the decision values at stage $N - 1$ are limited to 0 or $1 million.

An important element of the model formulation (specification) in dynamic programming is correctly specifying the transition function. The transition function is often described by one of the following forms:

$$S_{n-1} = S_n - D_n$$
$$S_{n-1} = S_n + D_n$$
$$S_{n-1} = S_n \cdot D_n$$
$$S_{n-1} = D_n$$

Correctly specifying a transition function for a given problem may involve incorporating other problem parameters into the function, such as $S_{n-1} = a_n S_n + b_n D_n - c_n$, where a_n, b_n, and c_n are specified parameters of the problem. For example, if S_n is the input inventory level at stage n, D_n is the quantity purchased at stage n, and c_n is the quantity consumed in stage n, then the transition function can be specified as $S_{n-1} = S_n + D_n - c_n$ (i.e., resulting inventory level = beginning inventory + amount purchased − amount consumed), where c_n represents a forecast of monthly consumption of the resource.

The transition function plays a key role in the analysis of any dynamic programming problem. Part of the art of formulating dynamic programming models is to correctly perceive and specify the transition function for the problem being considered.

Stage Returns

The final element in the symbolic representation of a dynamic programming model is the return (profit, cost, utility, etc.) at each stage. The **stage return variable** is denoted by

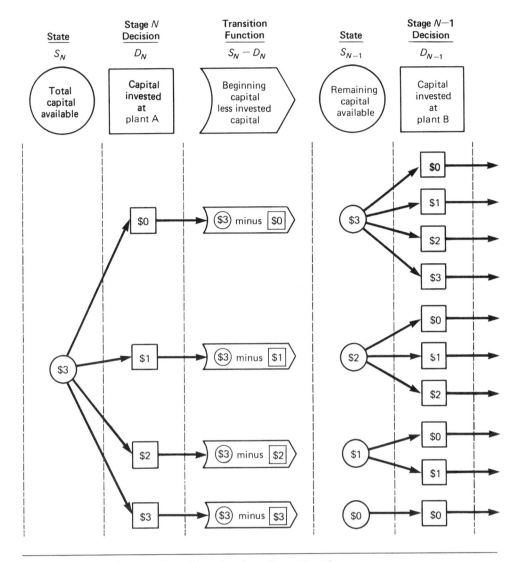

Figure 12.10 *The Transition Function from Stage N to Stage N — 1 for the $3 Million Capital Investment Problem*

R_n = return at stage n

The return at stage n is shown here simply as R_n; a more thorough representation is given by

Return at stage $n = R_n(S_n, D_n)$

where $R_n(S_n, D_n)$ is read as "the return at stage n, which is a function of the state input, S_n, and the decision, D_n." The fact that the return at each stage is a function of both the input status and the stage decision has been stated previously. Henceforth, R_n will be used rather than $R_n(S_n, D_n)$, with the understanding that R_n is a function of both S_n and D_n.

A complete illustration, with all relevant model components, for any stage of a dynamic programming problem is given first in Figure 12.11 and then symbolically in Figure 12.12.

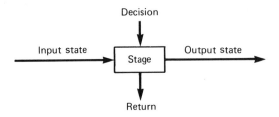

Figure 12.11 *The Model Components for Any Stage of a Dynamic Programming Problem*

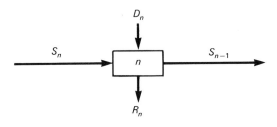

Figure 12.12 *Symbolic Representation of the Model Components for Stage n of a Dynamic Programming Problem*

R_n is also generally given as representative of the stage n return *function*. Since R_n is a function of the state variable, S_n, and the decision variable, D_n, it is properly defined as the return function. Although the precise functional relationship denoted by R_n might be in the form of a mathematical equation such as $R_n = a_n S_n - b_n D_n$, where a_n and b_n are model parameters, the relationship of R_n to S_n and D_n is more frequently described in tabular form. An example for one stage, n, is given as follows:

Stage n

State (S_n)	Decision (D_n)	Return (R_n)
0	0	0
1	0	0
	1	5
2	0	0
	1	5
	2	9

For the example, the input state variable to stage n, S_n, may be one of the integer values 0, 1, or 2 (e.g., a quantity of inventory units available at stage n). The decision variable, D_n, may take on one of the integer values 0, 1, or 2. Thus, the decision alternatives range from 0 to 2 (e.g., the amount of inventory used). However, note that the possible decisions are limited by the amount of inventory available (the input state variable). When $S_n = 0$, D_n is limited to 0. When $S_n = 1$, D_n is limited to 0 or 1. When $S_n = 2$, D_n may be 0, 1, or 2. Thus, the value of D_n is constrained by the input value of S_n. The tabular values for S_n and the corresponding ranges of possible values for D_n give the functional relationship of D_n to S_n.

The values for R_n represent the return (e.g., profit) associated with each possible decision. Of course, the return, R_n, is directly defined by associated values of the decision, D_n. The functional relationship of R_n to D_n for the example is as follows:

If $D_n = 0$, then $R_n = 0$.
If $D_n = 1$, then $R_n = 5$.
If $D_n = 2$, then $R_n = 9$.

Since the values of D_n depend on the value of S_n, and R_n is a function of D_n, R_n is a function of both S_n and D_n. Another way to illustrate this point is

$$R_n = \begin{cases} 9, \text{ if } D_n = 2 \\ 5, \text{ if } D_n = 1 \text{ and if } S_n = 2 \\ 0, \text{ if } D_n = 0 \end{cases}$$

$$R_n = \begin{cases} 5, \text{ if } D_n = 1 \\ 0, \text{ if } D_n = 0 \end{cases} \text{ and if } S_n = 1$$

$$R_n = \{0, \text{ if } D_n = 0 \text{ and if } S_n = 0$$

Refer back to Figure 12.12, which shows that R_n is an output variable of stage n and is a function of the input variables S_n and D_n. It also shows that S_{n-1} is likewise an output variable of stage n as a function of S_n and D_n. Therefore, there are two input variables (S_n and D_n) and two output variables (R_n and S_{n-1}) at each stage of a dynamic programming model.

Figure 12.13 summarizes the relationship among state, decision, and return variables. The term $(D_n \mid S_n = 1) = \{0, 1\}$ is read as "the values that D_n may take on, given that $S_n = 1$, are the values in the set 0, 1." Likewise, the term $(R_n \mid D_n = 1) = 5$ is

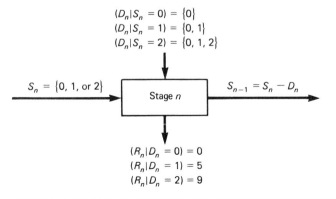

$(D_n \mid S_n = 0) = \{0\}$
$(D_n \mid S_n = 1) = \{0, 1\}$
$(D_n \mid S_n = 2) = \{0, 1, 2\}$

$S_n = \{0, 1, \text{ or } 2\}$ ⟶ | Stage n | ⟶ $S_{n-1} = S_n - D_n$

$(R_n \mid D_n = 0) = 0$
$(R_n \mid D_n = 1) = 5$
$(R_n \mid D_n = 2) = 9$

Figure 12.13 *The Output Variables R_n and S_{n-1} Are a Function of the Input Variables S_n and D_n*

read as "the value of R_n, given that $D_n = 1$, is 5." This discussion further demonstrates why the return function is often written as $R_n(S_n, D_n)$, since R_n is indeed a function of both S_n and D_n.

Stage Optimization

The dynamic programming approach to **stage optimization** is to determine the optimal decision at each stage *for each possible input state value*. Thus, for the previous example, assuming we wish to maximize R_n, the optimal decision for each state value is as follows:

Stage n

State (S_n)	Decision (D_n)	Return (R_n)
0	0*	0*
1	0	0
	1*	5*
2	0	0
	1	5
	2*	9*

The optimal decision at stage *n* for each state value is

Input	*Optimal decision*	*Optimal return*
If $S_n = 0$, then	$D_n^* = 0$,	$R_n^* = 0$.
If $S_n = 1$, then	$D_n^* = 1$,	$R_n^* = 5$.
If $S_n = 2$, then	$D_n^* = 2$,	$R_n^* = 9$.

where D_n^* denotes the optimal value of D_n and R_n^* denotes the associated optimal value of R_n, *for each of the three possible state inputs*. In general, at each stage, the optimal solution must be determined *for each of the possible input values of the state variable*. This concept is illustrated in Figure 12.14. Note that the optimal solution values for D_n and R_n are given for each possible value of input, S_n. As in Figure 12.13, the vertical line between D_n^* and S_n and between R_n^* and S_n denotes the word *given*.

The symbolic notation for the optimal return for each possible state input is defined as follows:

$f_n(S_n, D_n)$ = return at stage *n* for the input value of the state variable, S_n, and the decision, D_n

and

$f_n^*(S_n)$ = *optimal* return at stage *n* for the input value of the state variable, S_n

Actually, the definition of $f_n(S_n, D_n)$ is complete only for the case where $n = 1$; we will develop a more complete definition of $f_n(S_n, D_n)$ later within the framework of

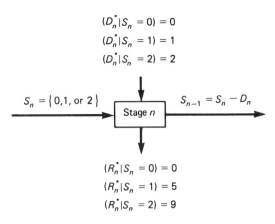

$$(D_n^* | S_n = 0) = 0$$
$$(D_n^* | S_n = 1) = 1$$
$$(D_n^* | S_n = 2) = 2$$

$$S_n = \{0, 1, \text{ or } 2\}$$ Stage n $$S_{n-1} = S_n - D_n$$

$$(R_n^* | S_n = 0) = 0$$
$$(R_n^* | S_n = 1) = 5$$
$$(R_n^* | S_n = 2) = 9$$

Figure 12.14 *The Optimal Values of D_n and R_n, Given the Input Values S_n*

multistage optimization analysis. For the present, using the preceding example, we can say that

$$f_n^*(S_n = 0) = 0 \qquad \text{(the optimal return when } S_n = 0 \text{ is } 0)$$
$$f_n^*(S_n = 1) = 5 \qquad \text{(the optimal return when } S_n = 1 \text{ is } 5)$$
$$f_n^*(S_n = 2) = 9 \qquad \text{(the optimal return when } S_n = 2 \text{ is } 9)$$

In summary, the optimization procedure of dynamic programming requires that, at each stage, the optimal solution be determined for each possible input state value. Furthermore, the optimal return at stage n, for each value of S_n, must be retained (recorded and stored for future use). This value is denoted in general by

$$f_n^*(S_n) = \underset{D_n}{\text{opt}} \{f_n(S_n, D_n)\}, \qquad \text{for each value of } S_n, D_n$$

which is read as "the optimal return *for the value of* S_n equals the optimal value from among the returns associated with each of the possible decision alternatives, D_n, for this particular input state." Thus, for our example, $f_n^*(S_n)$ would be determined three times, for $S_n = 0$, $S_n = 1$, and $S_n = 2$. Given the problem data, this process can be illustrated as follows.

State	Alternative decisions	Associated returns
$S_n = 0$	$D_n = 0$	$f_n(S_n, D_n) = 0$
$S_n = 1$	$D_n = 0$	$f_n(S_n, D_n) = 0$
	$D_n = 1$	$f_n(S_n, D_n) = 5$
$S_n = 2$	$D_n = 0$	$f_n(S_n, D_n) = 0$
	$D_n = 1$	$f_n(S_n, D_n) = 5$
	$D_n = 2$	$f_n(S_n, D_n) = 9$

For $S_n = 0$,

$$f_n^*(S_n) = 0$$

For $S_n = 1$,

$$f_n^*(S_n) = \operatorname*{opt}_{D_n} \left\{ \begin{array}{l} f_n(S_n, D_n) = 0 \\ f_n(S_n, D_n) = 5 \end{array} \right\}$$

Thus,

$$f_n^*(S_n) = 5, \qquad \text{for } S_n = 1$$

For $S_n = 2$,

$$f_n^*(S_n) = \operatorname*{opt}_{D_n} \left\{ \begin{array}{l} f_n(S_n, D_n) = 0 \\ f_n(S_n, D_n) = 5 \\ f_n(S_n, D_n) = 9 \end{array} \right.$$

Thus,

$$f_n^*(S_n) = 9, \qquad \text{for } S_n = 2$$

You will notice two things: (1) we have simply replaced R_n with $f_n(S_n, D_n)$ and (2) the optimal solution procedure is straightforward. However, as previously stated, the definition for $f_n(S_n, D_n)$ is complete only for the case where $n = 1$ (the last stage of the problem). The definition of $f_n(S_n, D_n)$ will have to be significantly expanded for the case in which $n = 2, 3$, etc. This, however, is the next concept to be presented.

Recursion and the Recursive Return Function

The concept of **recursion** is commonly used by computer programmers. For example, a common recursive program statement is

$$X = X + 5$$

This program statement is recursive because, each time it is executed in the program, the current value of X is redefined as the past value of X added to the value 5. In subscript notation, $X_n = X_{n-1} + 5$. If the initial value stored in X_0 were zero and the program looped back through the statement five times, the results would be $X_0 = 0$, $X_1 = 5$, $X_2 = 10$, $X_3 = 15$, $X_4 = 20$, and $X_5 = 25$.

The concept of recursion is extremely useful, since only the value stored in X_{n-1} is necessary to update the value of X_n. Dynamic programming makes use of this concept by using only the return at stage $n - 1$ to update the accumulated return at stage n.

Dynamic programming further reduces information storage requirements by concentrating only on *selected* returns from stage $n - 1$. The returns retained are the *optimal returns* for each possible value of S_{n-1}. For the previous example, the only returns retained (stored) would be $f_n^*(S_n = 0) = 0$, $f_n^*(S_n = 1) = 5$, and $f_n^*(S_n = 2) = 9$. Thus, only three returns would be retained from among the six returns computed (for all possible combinations of S_n and D_n).

In general, we can state the recursive return function of dynamic programming as follows:

$$f_n(S_n, D_n) = R_n + f_{n-1}(S_{n-1}, D_{n-1})$$

which is read as "the total accumulated return at (and including) stage n (given the input state to stage n and the decision at stage n) is equal to the stage n return *plus* the return at stage $n - 1$, given the input state to stage $n - 1$ and the decision at stage $n - 1$." However, as previously stated, it is necessary to retain only the returns associated with the optimal decision at stage $n - 1$ for each possible state input to stage $n - 1$. Thus, the recursive equation, as it is used in dynamic programming, is written as follows:

$$f_n(S_n, D_n) = R_n + f^*_{n-1}(S_{n-1})$$

Returning to the previous example and designating it as the stage 1 subproblem, we have

$$f^*_1(S_1 = 0) = 0$$
$$f^*_1(S_1 = 1) = 5$$
$$f^*_1(S_1 = 2) = 9$$

At stage 2, the decision analysis makes use of not only the return at stage 2 but also the optimal returns from stage 1, to determine the overall two-stage optimal decision. The decision analysis at stage 2 utilizes the recursion equation, which is written as

$$f_2(S_2, D_2) = R_2 + f^*_1(S_1)$$
where
$$f^*_1(S_1 = 0) = 0, f^*_1(S_1 = 1) = 5, \text{ and } f^*_1(S_1 = 2) = 9$$

The recursive return function is similar to the transition function in that it can take on a variety of forms depending on the requirements of the problem structure at hand. Commonly encountered forms for the recursive return function are

$$f_n(S_n, D_n) = R_n + f^*_{n-1}(S_{n-1})$$
$$f_n(S_n, D_n) = R_n - f^*_{n-1}(S_{n-1})$$
$$f_n(S_n, D_n) = R_n \cdot f^*_{n-1}(S_{n-1})$$

As in the case of the transition function, it may be necessary to formulate the recursive return function in a form such as

$$f_n(S_n, D_n) = a_n R_n + b_n f^*_{n-1}(S_{n-1}) - c_n$$

where a_n, b_n, and c_n are specified parameters of the problem.

Example problems, which will be presented later, will illustrate some of the forms required for the return function to correctly represent the problem.

Multistage Sequential Optimization

Multistage sequential optimization could also be called *cumulative optimization analysis*. At a particular stage, multistage optimization includes all previously evaluated stages and incorporates the previously determined optimal solution values into the cumulative return value at the stage under consideration. This concept is illustrated graphically in Figure 12.15.

In general, the optimizing procedure, which makes use of the recursion equation, is given by

$$f^*_n(S_n) = \operatorname*{opt}_{D_n} \{R_n + f^*_{n-1}(S_{n-1})\}$$

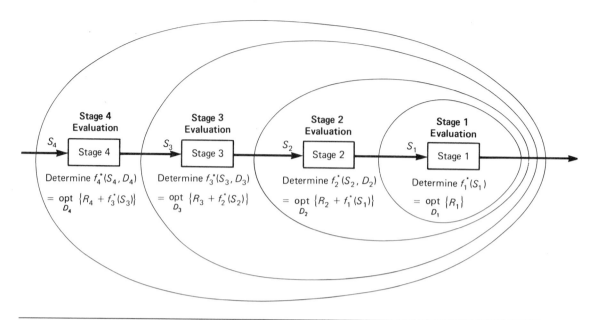

Figure 12.15 *Multistage Sequential Optimization of a*
Dynamic Programming Problem

Recall that S_n in $f_n^*(S_n)$ indicates that the optimal value of D_n must be found for the function contained in brackets, { }, for each possible input state value to stage n. R_n is the set of returns at stage n associated with possible solution values of D_n, and $f_{n-1}^*(S_{n-1})$ is the set of optimal returns for each possible input state to stage $n - 1$.

The only remaining problem in the recursive optimization procedure is specifying the previously determined cumulative optimal return function (at stage $n - 1$) in terms of the input state at stage n, the current stage under evaluation. This is accomplished by making use of the transition function. Recall that the transition function specifies the input to stage $n - 1$ in terms of the input state at stage n and the decision at stage n. We will continue to employ the transition function used in the previous example, $S_{n-1} = S_n - D_n$, where the input resource at stage $n - 1$ is equal to the input resource at stage n minus the amount of resource consumed at stage n.

We can, therefore, restate $f_{n-1}^*(S_{n-1})$ as

$$f_{n-1}^*(S_{n-1}) = f_{n-1}^*(S_n - D_n)$$

Thus, by making use of the transition function, we have specified the previously determined cumulative optimal return function (at stage $n - 1$) in terms of the input state, S_n, and the decision, D_n, at stage n.

The previously given recursive optimizing procedure is now restated in terms of stage n variables, as follows:

$$f_n^*(S_n) = \underset{D_n}{\text{opt}} \{R_n + f_{n-1}^*(S_n - D_n)\}$$

where f_{n-1}^* is the cumulative optimal set of returns determined previously at stage $n - 1$ and $S_n - D_n$ is the transition function describing the output from stage n, which is the input to stage $n - 1$ (in terms of the current stage S_n and D_n variables).

The multistage optimization procedure of dynamic programming begins with evaluation of stage 1, as follows:

Determine $f_1^*(S_1) = \underset{D_1}{\text{opt}} \{R_1\}$, for each S_1 input

The next subproblem solved is at stage 2.

Determine $f_2^*(S_2) = \underset{D_2}{\text{opt}} \{R_2 + f_1^*(S_1)\}$, for each S_2 input

where

$$S_1 = S_2 - D_2$$

Thus,

$$f_2^*(S_2) = \underset{D_2}{\text{opt}} \{R_2 + f_1^*(S_2 - D_2)\}, \text{ for each } S_2 \text{ input}$$

The third-stage decision analysis is given by

Determine $f_3^*(S_3) = \underset{D_3}{\text{opt}} \{R_3 + f_2^*(S_2)\}$

where

$$S_2 = S_3 - D_3$$

Thus,

$$f_3^*(S_3) = \underset{D_3}{\text{opt}} \{R_3 + f_2^*(S_3 - D_3)\}$$

This sequential stage solution procedure is continued through stage N. Notice that in each case the only decision variable under consideration at stage n is D_n. Likewise, notice that at each stage the only return information needed to evaluate the problem is the current stage return and the previous stage set of cumulative optimal returns for all possible values of S_{n-1} (e.g., $S_n - D_n$).

Given the sequential optimization of the recursive return function for three stages, as follows:

Stage 1:
$$f_1^*(S_1) = \underset{D_1}{\text{opt}} \{R_1\}$$

Stage 2:
$$f_2^*(S_2) = \underset{D_2}{\text{opt}} \{R_2 + f_1^*(S_1)\}$$

Stage 3:
$$f_3^*(S_3) = \underset{D_3}{\text{opt}} \{R_3 + f_2^*(S_2)\}$$

where each stage can be optimized individually by making use of the transition function, such as $S_1 = S_2 - D_2$ or $S_2 = S_3 - D_3$, it can be shown that the overall system is optimized at stage 3 by a *sequential imbedded optimization function* of the following form:

$$f_3^*(S_3) = \operatorname*{opt}_{D_3} \left\{ R_3 + \operatorname*{opt}_{D_2} [R_2 + \underbrace{\operatorname*{opt}_{D_1} (R_1)]}_{\text{stage 1}} \right\}$$

stage 2

stage 3

In general, these recursive optimizing functions can be developed by the following steps:

Step A-1 Specify the decision alternatives, D_n (i.e., the alternative values of D_n).

Step A-2 Determine the associated returns, R_n, at stage n for each decision alternative.

Step A-3 Determine the resulting output state, S_{n-1}, for each decision alternative, D_n, considered in step A-1.

Step B Determine the *sum* of the return, R_n, from step A-2 and the cumulative optimal return from the previous stage, $f_{n-1}^*(S_{n-1})$, *given the values of* S_{n-1} from step A-3.

These four steps result in $R_n + f_{n-1}^*(S_{n-1})$ for each possible state (S_n) and decision (D_n).

Step C Finally, *for each value of* S_n, determine

$$\operatorname*{opt}_{D_n} \{R_n + f_{n-1}^*(S_{n-1})\}$$

Step C provides the value of $f_n^*(S_n)$ for each S_n, which will then be used in the next stage $(n + 1)$ evaluation procedure.

Take special note of the fact that each stage involves the computation of the optimal decision for *any* possible input state. It is appropriate, at this point, to quote Bellman's principle of optimality.

> An optimal policy has the property that, whatever the initial state and the initial decision are, the remaining decisions must constitute an optimal policy with regard to the state resulting from the first decision.[1]

Bellman's principle of optimality, which provides the foundation for dynamic programming, ensures that the solution procedure will provide the best course of action for *all future decisions,* regardless of how the current state was arrived at. In terms of stages, given the current state at stage n, the solution procedure provides the optimal solutions for stages $n, n - 1, \ldots, 3, 2, 1$, regardless of whether the decisions made at stages N, $N - 1, \ldots, n + 1$ were optimal.

Figure 12.16 illustrates, by use of a network tree diagram, the principle of optimality and the recursive optimization procedure, beginning at the last stage and solving back sequentially to stage 3. The example in Figure 12.16 assumes that stage 3 offers three alternatives (possible decisions), stage 2 offers two alternatives, and stage 1 offers three alternatives. No attempt is made to explicitly specify the transition function; rather, the tree diagram shows that given that one begins at state 3 in stage 3, the arrows show the

[1] R. E. Bellman and S. E. Dreyfus, *Applied Dynamic Programming* (Princeton, New Jersey: Princeton University Press, 1962), p. 15.

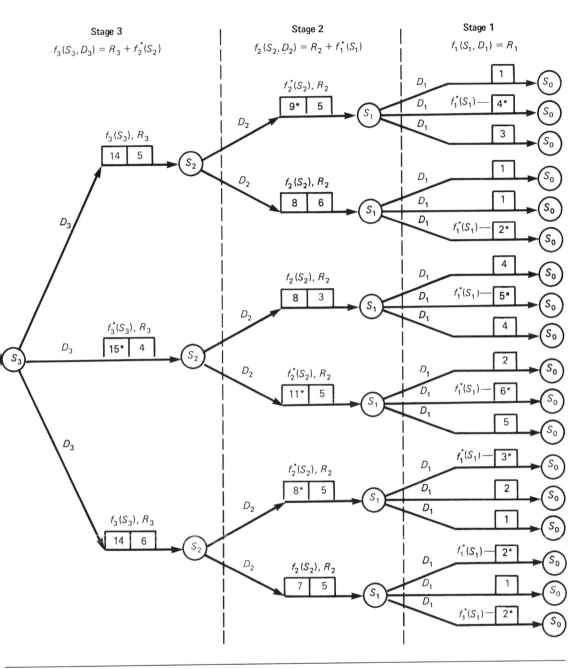

Figure 12.16 *All Possible Decisions, States, and Associated*
Returns for the Sequential Optimization of the Dynamic
Programming Problem, Beginning at Stage 1

resulting movements to the state 2 locations (illustrating different states) for the three
alternative D_3 decisions. Likewise, given the state 2 location, the arrows of the diagram
show the resulting movement to state 1 associated with each possible D_2 action. A similar
explanation is applicable to S_1, D_1, and the resulting S_0 locations.

Thus, Figure 12.16 is an exhaustive enumeration of all possible states and decisions at stage 3, resulting possible states and decisions at stage 2, and possible states and decisions at stage 1. Furthermore, Figure 12.16 portrays the returns associated with each possible alternative decision for each state at each stage (in squares).

Beginning at stage 1, the optimal decision (maximum return) *for each state* (S_1) is indicated by an asterisk. The optimal decision is further denoted by the darkened arrow from each S_1 to one of the three alternative S_0 locations. Thus, for each state we have determined

$$f_1^*(S_1) = \max_{D_1} R_1$$

Moving to stage 2, we determine for each S_2 the optimal decision (maximum cumulative return), where for each S_2 and D_2 the return (R_2) is given in the right-hand box on the arrow from S_2 to S_1. In the left-hand box, on the arrow from S_2 to S_1, is the value

$$f_2(S_2, D_2) = R_2 + f_1^*(S_1)$$

We know the value of $f_1^*(S_1)$ for each alternative because it was retained from the stage 1 analysis for each S_1 value.

We next determine for each S_2 the optimal solution value for D_2,

$$f_2^*(S_2) = \max_{D_2} \{R_2 + f_1^*(S_1)\}$$

In the Figure 12.16 example, the values of $f_2^*(S_2)$ are

$f_2^*(S_2) = 9$
$f_2^*(S_2) = 11$
$f_2^*(S_2) = 8$

Finally, the optimal solution at stage 3 is computed as

$$f_3^*(S_3) = \max_{D_3} \{R_3 + f_2^*(S_2)\}$$
$$f_3^*(S_3) = 15$$

Notice that for each stage in Figure 12.16, after the optimal decision has been determined, it is not necessary to retain information related to other alternatives. For example, after all eighteen alternatives at stage 1 are evaluated, one-third of the returns are retained for the stage 2 analysis. At stage 2, after the six alternatives (three states with two alternative decisions for each state) are evaluated, only one-half of the returns are retained for the stage 3 analysis. Thus, in this simple three-stage example, 67% of the returns are eliminated after the stage 1 analysis and 50% of the returns are eliminated after the stage 2 analysis.

Evaluating every combination of alternatives would require $3 \times 2 \times 3 = 18$ sets of computations, whereas with the dynamic programming approach only 9 sets of computations were required (i.e., observation of the max R_1 for each possible alternative at stage 1 required no computation, stage 2 required 6 sets of computations, and stage 3 required 3 computations).

The savings in computation (and information storage) can be quite dramatic for larger problems. As a general rule of thumb, the number of computations increases exponentially with the number of stages (subproblems) using exhaustive enumeration, but only linearly using dynamic programming. For example, for a problem with 10 decision alternatives at each of N stages, exhaustive enumeration would require 10^N computations. Thus, for a problem with 3 stages the total number of computations would be $10^3 = 1000$, with 5 stages we would have $10^5 = 100,000$, and with 10 stages 10 billion computations. Because of the manner in which dynamic programming discards decision alternatives that are not feasible given the input state variable, it is not possible to predict precisely the number of computations required for any given problem; however, with dynamic programming the computational effort is generally described as increasing at an *additive* rate as the number of stages is increased, whereas with exhaustive enumeration it increases at an exponential rate.

The basic concepts of dynamic programming have been presented. The remainder of the chapter will present prototypes of dynamic programming applications.

DYNAMIC PROGRAMMING APPLICATIONS

This section presents examples of several of the better-known applications of dynamic programming. Each example represents a different modeling structure in terms of the formulation of the recursive return function and/or the transition function of the problem. It should be recognized that each example is a prototype that can be applied to a wide range of problems with similar structures, the only difference being the description of the problem itself. Because of the diversity of potential applications for dynamic programming, however, the examples presented are only some of the most commonly reported types of applications.

Allocation Problem

One of the most common applications of dynamic programming is the allocation of a scarce resource, such as land, work force, investment capital, or space, to several competing activities, such as types of land use, labor projects, or investment projects. The general formulation of this type of problem will be given first, followed by a capital budgeting example.

The problem variables are defined as follows:

K = amount of resource available
N = number of alternative activities (projects)
n = index denoting activity n
D_n = amount of resource allocated to activity n
R_n = return (profit, cost, utility) associated with activity n, given D_n

It is assumed that the problem is such that the solution values for D_n must be integers, and the total return is the sum of the individual returns, R_n. The problem is formulated as

$$\text{Maximize} \sum_{n=1}^{N} R_n = R_1 + R_2 + \cdots + R_N$$

subject to

$$\sum_{n=1}^{N} D_n \leqslant K$$

or

$$D_1 + D_2 + \cdots + D_N \leqslant K$$

where

D_n values are nonnegative integers

(Note that, in general, *maximize* could be replaced by *minimize* for a cost function in the objective function, and the *inequality* could be replaced by an *equality* in the constraint.) The objective here is to maximize the sum of the returns associated with each of the activities, subject to the constraint that the sum of the resource allocations to each of the N activities must be equal to or less than the total amount of resource available, *K*.

Example 12.1 Capital Budgeting Problem

The ABC Company has budgeted $5 million for the coming fiscal year to be allocated among three plants in Atlanta, Baltimore, and Chicago (plants A, B, and C) for capital improvements. The firm has decided to allocate the capital in block amounts of $1 million. Because of the improvements proposed by plant managers, the minimum amount needed at each of plants A and B is $2 million; however, plant C could use as little as $1 million. The maximum investment amounts requested are $4 million at plants A and B and $3 million at plant C. Each of the plant managers has provided the expected return (discounted present value of increase in cash flow) associated with each of the proposed levels of capital investment, as shown in Table 12.1.

Table 12.1 ABC Company Problem Summary

Decision Alternatives	Evaluation Criteria		
Amount Invested (in $ millions)	Return Associated with Investment (in $ millions)		
	Plant A	Plant B	Plant C
1	—	—	4
2	6	5	7
3	8	7	10
4	9	9	—

The company may, of course, decide to invest nothing at one or more of the plants, in which case the return is assumed to be zero. (Note that in some cases a negative return might be associated with investing nothing at a plant.) It is assumed that the ABC Company wants to invest all of the $5 million budgeted for plant improvements. The problem will be formulated and solved as a dynamic programming problem, where the investment decision for each plant is analogous to a stage in the dynamic programming model.

The dynamic programming representation of the plant investment problem is shown in Figure 12.17. Notice that the assignment of plants to stages is, in this case, arbitrary. The problem will be solved sequentially, starting with stage 1 and working backward to stage 3.

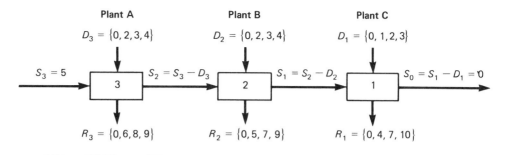

Figure 12.17 *The Dynamic Programming Representation of the Plant Investment Problem*

First, the stage 1 decisions (possible values of D_1) and associated returns are listed for each possible value of the state input variable, S_1. In this problem, S_1 is defined as the capital available for investment at stage 1. For example, if all $5 million were allocated to plants A and B (stages 3 and 2), the input value of S_1 would be zero, making the only possible value for D_1 zero, with an associated return of zero. As the possible values of S_1 increase, the range of alternative values for D_1 and associated returns increase accordingly. The stage 1 subproblem and decision analysis are summarized in Table 12.2.

Table 12.2 Stage 1 (plant C)

Input States S_1	Decisions D_1	Returns R_1	
0	0	0	$f_1^*(S_1 = 0)$
1	0	0	
	1	4	$f_1^*(S_1 = 1)$
2	0	0	
	1	4	
	2	7	$f_1^*(S_1 = 2)$
3	0	0	
	1	4	
	2	7	
	3	10	$f_1^*(S_1 = 3)$
4	0	0	
	1	4	
	2	7	
	3	10	$f_1^*(S_1 = 4)$
5	0	0	
	1	4	
	2	7	
	3	10	$f_1^*(S_1 = 5)$

Notice that the table includes state input values of 4 and 5. For this particular problem this is not actually necessary, because (1) the maximum amount that can be invested at stage 1 (plant C) is $3 million and (2) the firm has initially decided to invest all $5 million available. Therefore, the *maximum* amount of capital that would remain after the plant A and B decisions would be $3 million. However, if the return functions (R_n values associated with D_n values) at plants A and B were characterized by diminishing returns to scale after a point (i.e., a nonlinear return function) and if the firm had not specified that all $5 million would be invested, the state input to stage 1 might exceed the amount that could be invested at plant C. The full range of investment capital available is therefore shown for S_1 to illustrate the general format of the allocation problem.

Notice that the identification of optimal solutions for R_1 and associated D_1 for each possible input state value is trivial. This is true for the stage 1 subproblem in most dynamic programming problems. Oftentimes, the stage 1 optimal solutions can be identified by simple inspection.

The optimal solution values for D_1 and R_1 for each possible input state value (0, 1, 2, 3, 4, and 5) are shaded in the table. Recalling that the solution procedure of dynamic programming requires that we retain the optimal return for each state input, we identify these values in the table as $f^*_1(S_1 = \cdot)$ for each S_1 input. Having completed the stage 1 analysis, we move to the stage 2 analysis.

The values of all variables required for the stage 2 decision analysis are given in Table 12.3.

Table 12.3 Stage 2 (plant B)

(1) Input States S_2	(2) Decisions D_2	(3) Returns R_2	(4) Output States S_1	(5) Optimal Returns, Prior Stages $f^*_1(S_1)$	(6) Total Returns $R_2 + f^*_1(S_1)$	
0	0	0	0	0	0	$f^*_2(S_2 = 0)$
1	0	0	1	4	4	$f^*_2(S_2 = 1)$
2	0	0	2	7	7	$f^*_2(S_2 = 2)$
	2	5	0	0	5	
3	0	0	3	10	10	$f^*_2(S_2 = 3)$
	2	5	1	4	9	
	3	7	0	0	7	
4	0	0	4	10	10	
	2	5	2	7	12	$f^*_2(S_2 = 4)$
	3	7	1	4	11	
	4	9	0	0	9	
5	0	0	5	10	10	
	2	5	3	10	15	$f^*_2(S_2 = 5)$
	3	7	2	7	14	
	4	9	1	4	13	

Transition function: Recursion function:
$$S_1 = S_2 - D_2$$ $$f_2(S_2) = R_2 + f^*_1(S_1)$$

From left to right, each column of values is described as follows:

1. *Input States.* Each possible value of S_2, the input state to stage 2, is given in the first column. For example, if no capital is allocated to plant A (stage 3), the input value to stage 2 will be $5 million. If $4 million is allocated to stage 3, the input to stage 2 will be $1 million, and so on.

2. *Stage 2 Decisions.* In the second column, the range of possible investment decisions at stage 2 is given for each possible input value of S_2. Note that an investment amount of $1 million is not feasible at stage 2 (plant B), as previously stated; thus, if the input value for S_2 is $1 million, the only possible value for D_2 is 0.

3. *Stage 2 Returns.* The plant B returns associated with each possible decision (at stage 2) are given in the third column.

4. *Output States.* The fourth column gives the amount of remaining capital, given the combination of the input state to stage 2 and the investment decision at stage 2. The output state from stage 2 is the input state to stage 1 (i.e., S_1), and it is defined for this problem as $S_2 - D_2 = S_1$.

5. *Optimal Returns for Prior Stages.* The fifth column gives the return for the optimal decision at stage 1, given the state input to stage 1 resulting from the combination of input state and decision at stage 2. Thus, the fourth column gives each possible value of S_1, and the fifth column gives the optimal return at stage 1 associated with that value of S_1. This is why the values of $f_1^*(S_1)$ are retained from the stage 1 analysis.

6. *Total Cumulative Returns.* The final column of values gives, for each combination of S_2 and D_2, the sum of the stage 2 return associated with D_2 (from the third column) and the optimal return at stage 1 associated with the combination of S_2 and D_2 values (from the fifth column). Again, this sum is described functionally for each combination of S_2 and D_2. The total return is

$$f_2(S_2) = R_2 + f_1^*(S_1)$$

where S_1 is defined by the transition function as $S_2 - D_2$. Note that $f_2(S_2)$ is completely defined in terms of the stage 2 state and decision variables, S_2 and D_2, and the return function at stage 2 can also be written as

$$f_2(S_2) = R_2 + f_1^*(S_2 - D_2)$$

The last step of the decision analysis at stage 2 is to identify (by inspection, for this example) the optimal value of the total return for each value of the input state. For each value of S_2, we determine

$$\underset{D_2}{\text{Max}} \{R_2 + f_1^*(S_1)\}$$

and save this information in $f_2^*(S_2)$. The optimal return value for each S_2 value is identified in the table by $f_2^*(S_2 = \cdot)$. The optimal set of values for D_2, R_2, S_1, $f_1^*(S_1)$, and $f_2(S_2)$ for each S_2 input is again shaded. The reason for shading the optimal set of values for each state input will become apparent in the last stage of overall solution analysis.

The third and final stage of the dynamic programming problem is given in Table 12.4. For this stage, there is only one input state value, the $5 million total capital budgeted for investment among the three plants (refer to Figure 12.17). Thus, the solution procedure is relatively simple.

Table 12.4 *Stage 3 (plant A)*

Input States S_3	Decisions D_3	Returns R_3	Output States S_2	Optimal Returns, Prior Stages $f_2^*(S_2)$	Total Returns $R + f_2^*(S_2)$	
5	0	0	5	15	15	
	2	6	3	10	16	$f_3^*(S_3 = 5)$
	3	8	2	7	15	
	4	9	1	4	13	

Transition function:	Recursion function:
$S_2 = S_3 - D_3$	$f_3(S_3) = R_3 + f_2^*(S_2)$

The descriptions of the stage 3 column headings are similar to the descriptions given for stage 2. Again, investment of $1 million at plant A is not a feasible alternative. Total returns are calculated in a manner similar to that used in stage 2, yielding an optimal return of $16 million.

$$f_3^*(S_3) = \operatorname*{Max}_{D_3} \{R_3 + f_2^*(S_2)\}$$

$$= \operatorname*{Max}_{D_3} \{R_3 + f_2^*(S_3 - D_3)\}$$

$$= \operatorname*{Max}_{D_3} \left\{ \begin{array}{c} 0 + 15 \\ 6 + 10 \\ 8 + 7 \\ 9 + 4 \end{array} \right\}$$

$$= \operatorname*{Max}_{D_3} \left\{ \begin{array}{c} 15 \\ 16 \\ 15 \\ 13 \end{array} \right\}$$

$$= 16 \quad \text{(for } D_3 = 2)$$

The overall allocation problem has now been solved, yielding a maximum overall return of $16 million. Note that the optimal value for D_3, from the stage 3 analysis, is an investment of $2 million at plant A (under the column heading D_3, in Table 12.4). The stage 3 analysis shows that the value of S_2 associated with this optimal solution is $3 million. Recall that at stage 2 we determined the optimal solution for each value of S_2. Therefore, returning to stage 2, for an input state value of 3, we find the optimal value of D_2 to be 0, associated with $f_2^*(S_2 = 3)$. Thus, the optimal solution is to invest nothing at plant B.

The value of S_1 associated with $f_2^*(S_2 = 3)$ is 3. We therefore return to the stage 1 decision table and identify the set of shaded values associated with $f_1^*(S_1 = 3)$. The optimal decision at stage 1 is to invest $3 million, with an associated return of $10 million. The overall solution can now be summarized as shown in Table 12.5.

Note that if the problem involved K capital to be allocated among N plants, the same solution procedure would be followed, using dynamic programming for N stages.

Table 12.5 *ABC Company Solution Summary*

Stage	Plant	Optimal Decision D_n^*	Return Associated with Optimal Decision
3	A	2	6
2	B	0	0
1	C	3	10
		Total investment 5	Total return 16

Computerized Solution of the Capital Budgeting Problem

In this section we will demonstrate use of the AB:QM software package for solving dynamic programming problems. Following are the program input data and the solution output for Example 12.1. The computer output stages replicate those depicted in this section.

```
Program: Dynamic Programming / Non-Network

Problem Title : Example 12.1

***** Input Data *****

Problem Type                 :   Maximization
                                 Non-Network

Number of Stages             :   3
Total Resources Available    :   5

Transition Function Type     : 1) S(n-1) = S(n) - D(n)
Recursion Function Type      : 1) f(n) = R(n) + f(n-1)
Return Function Type         : 1) R(n) = Constant


----------------------------------------------
Stage          Maximum Value of Decision
----------------------------------------------
    3                      4
    2                      4
    1                      4
----------------------------------------------


Return Value Table
-----------------------------------------------------
Decision   Stage   3     Stage   2     Stage   1
--------   ---------     ---------     ---------
    0        0.000         0.000         0.000
    1        0.000         0.000         4.000
    2        6.000         5.000         7.000
    3        8.000         7.000        10.000
    4        9.000         9.000         0.000
-----------------------------------------------------
```

```
***** Program Output *****
```

Stage   1

S(1)	D(1)	R(1)	S(0)	f(0)	f(1)
0	0	0.000	0	0.000	0.000
1	0	0.000	0	0.000	0.000
	1	4.000	0	0.000	4.000
2	0	0.000	0	0.000	0.000
	1	4.000	0	0.000	4.000
	2	7.000	0	0.000	7.000
3	0	0.000	0	0.000	0.000
	1	4.000	0	0.000	4.000
	2	7.000	0	0.000	7.000
	3	10.000	0	0.000	10.000
4	0	0.000	0	0.000	0.000
	1	4.000	0	0.000	4.000
	2	7.000	0	0.000	7.000
	3	10.000	0	0.000	10.000
	4	0.000	0	0.000	0.000
5	0	0.000	0	0.000	0.000
	1	4.000	0	0.000	4.000
	2	7.000	0	0.000	7.000
	3	10.000	0	0.000	10.000
	4	0.000	0	0.000	0.000

Stage   2

S(2)	D(2)	R(2)	S(1)	f(1)	f(2)
0	0	0.000	0	0.000	0.000
1	0	0.000	1	4.000	4.000
	1	0.000	0	0.000	0.000
2	0	0.000	2	7.000	7.000
	1	0.000	1	4.000	4.000
	2	5.000	0	0.000	5.000
3	0	0.000	3	10.000	10.000
	1	0.000	2	7.000	7.000
	2	5.000	1	4.000	9.000
	3	7.000	0	0.000	7.000
4	0	0.000	4	10.000	10.000
	1	0.000	3	10.000	10.000
	2	5.000	2	7.000	12.000
	3	7.000	1	4.000	11.000
	4	9.000	0	0.000	9.000
5	0	0.000	5	10.000	10.000
	1	0.000	4	10.000	10.000
	2	5.000	3	10.000	15.000
	3	7.000	2	7.000	14.000
	4	9.000	1	4.000	13.000

```
                            Stage    3
-----------------------------------------------------------------------
S( 3)  D( 3)           R( 3)  S( 2)              f( 2)                f( 3)
-----------------------------------------------------------------------
  5       0            0.000    5               15.000               15.000
          1            0.000    4               12.000               12.000
          2            6.000    3               10.000               16.000
          3            8.000    2                7.000               15.000
          4            9.000    1                4.000               13.000
        ---------------------------------------------------------------


Final Solution
-------------------------------------------------------------
Stage     Optimal Decision        Optimal Return
-------------------------------------------------------------
  3              2                     6.000
  2              0                     0.000
  1              3                    10.000
-------------------------------------------------------------
Total            5                    16.000

***** End of Output *****
```

Sensitivity Analysis

A final and easily performed step in the analysis of the dynamic programming solution is a sensitivity analysis of the solution results for lesser quantities of available capital. For example, suppose the company decided to invest only $4 million, rather than $5 million. It would be necessary to recompute only the stage 3 analysis, since stages 1 and 2 already contain the information needed for a solution to this problem. Table 12.6 shows the new stage 3 analysis for an input state value of $4 million available capital.

Table 12.6 *Stage 3 ($4 million total capital)*

Input States S_3	Decisions D_3	Returns R_3	Output States S_2	Optimal Returns, Prior Stages $f_2^*(S_2)$	Total Returns $R_3 + f_2^*(S_2)$	
4	0	0	4	12	12	
	2	6	2	7	13	$f_3^*(S_3 = 4)$
	3	8	1	4	12	
	4	9	0	0	9	

The maximum return is shown as $13 million for a D_3^* value of 2. The associated S_2 value is 2. Backtracking to stage 2, we find that for $S_2 = 2$ the optimal solution is $D_2 = 0$. The associated S_1 is 2. From stage 1 we find that the optimal solution for $S_1 = 2$ is $D_1 = 2$. Thus, in summary, the optimal solution for total investment capital of $4 million is as shown in Table 12.7.

Table 12.7 *Solution Summary for $4 Million*

Stage	Plant	D_n^*	R_n^*
3	A	2	6
2	B	0	0
1	C	2	7
		4	13

A similar approach can be used to determine the optimal allocation of capital among plants for the case in which only $3 million total capital is available. Table 12.8 gives the new stage 3 analysis.

Table 12.8 *Stage 3 ($3 million total capital)*

Input States S_3	Decisions D_3	Returns R_3	Output States S_2	Optimal Returns, Prior Stages $f_2^*(S_2)$	Total Returns $R_3 + f_2^*(S_2)$	
3	0	0	3	10	10	$f_3^*(S_3 = 4)$
	2	6	1	4	10	$f_3^*(S_3 = 4)$
	3	8	0	0	8	

The stage 3 analysis results in alternative optimal solutions ($D_3^* = 0$ or 2). In order to determine the associated alternative optimal solution values for D_1 and D_2, we simply backtrack for both $S_2 = 3$ and $S_2 = 1$. If $D_3 = 0$, then $S_2 = 3$ and the associated optimal value for D_2 is 0. If $D_3 = 2$, then $S_2 = 1$ and the associated optimal value for D_2 is 0. Using the same approach to backtrack to stage 1, we find the alternative optimal solutions to be as shown in Table 12.9.

Table 12.9 *Solution Summary for $3 Million*

		Alternative 1		Alternative 2	
Stage	Plant	D_n^*	R_n^*	D_n^*	R_n^*
3	A	0	0	2	6
2	B	0	0	0	0
1	C	3	10	1	4
Totals		3	10	3	10

A similar approach can be used to perform sensitivity analysis on the solution results for all available capital amounts, from K down to the smallest amount considered possible. The optimal solutions for $K = 5$ through $K = 1$, in increments of 1, are summarized in Table 12.10.

In summary, note that if the problem had involved N plants, the dynamic programming solution would require evaluation of N stages. Stage 2 in the example problem is a prototype for stages 2, 3, . . . , $N - 1$ of an N stage problem, and stages 1 and N would be similar to those in the example problem.

Table 12.10 *Solution Results for All Available Amounts*

Available Capital K	Optimal Decisions			Total Return
	Plant A D_3^*	Plant B D_2^*	Plant C D_1^*	
5	2	0	3	16
4	2	0	2	13
3	{ 0 2	0 0	3 1 }	10
2	0	0	2	7
1	0	0	1	4

The prototype dynamic programming example presented can be applied to a wide variety of resource allocation problems, as long as the decision variable (and state variable) can be restricted to integer values. The problem might be described, for example, as allocation of workers to projects, machines to jobs, salespeople to territories, floor space to departments, advertising campaign budget to products, and, in general, resources to activities.

Multiplicative Return Function Problem

The following example is actually another version of an allocation problem in which the stage returns are multiplied rather than added; otherwise, it is quite similar to the previous example. The general model is given as follows:

$$\text{Minimize} \prod_{n=1}^{N} R_n = R_1 \cdot R_2 \cdot R_3 \cdot \cdots \cdot R_N$$

subject to

$$\sum_{n=1}^{N} D_n = K$$

where
D_n values are nonnegative integers

The definitions for K, N, n, and D_n are generally the same as in the previous example. The description of R_n will be given in the following example.

Example 12.2 Research Failure Problem

The federal Department of Energy has 4 teams working on 4 energy research projects in a research program. The DOE is concerned with minimizing the probability of failure of the energy research program. The estimated probability of failure for each research team is given as follows:

	Research Team		
1	2	3	4
.60	.80	.45	.75

The overall probability of total failure of the research program is the product of the individual failure probabilities of the projects, or .162.

The DOE has decided that this probability of research failure is too high and has allocated an additional 3 scientists to the research program. The estimated probabilities of failure for each research team for 0, 1, 2, and 3 additional scientists are given in Table 12.11.

Table 12.11 DOE Problem Summary

Number of Additional Scientists	Probability of Failure Research Team			
	1	2	3	4
0	.60	.80	.45	.75
1	.40	.50	.20	.45
2	.20	.30	.15	.30
3	.10	.20	.10	.15

The problem is to determine how many scientists to allocate to which teams. Intuition would seem to indicate allocating additional scientists to the teams that currently have the highest probability of failure, teams 2 and 4. However, the DOE has decided to analyze the problem by dynamic programming. The problem is therefore decomposed into four stages, one for each research team. The four subproblems are to determine how many additional scientists to allocate to team 1, team 2, team 3, and team 4. The stage returns are defined as the probabilities of team failure for particular allocations. Three additional scientists are available, and the objective is to minimize the joint probability of total failure of the research program.

The stage 1 decision analysis is given in Table 12.12, which relates to team 1. Since stage 1 is the last stage of the dynamic programming problem (see Figure 12.17 for an example), it is obvious that the optimal decision at this stage will be to allocate any remaining scientists to team 1. Thus, D_1^* will always equal S_1. Therefore, only the optimal solution for each input state value is given in Table 12.12.

Table 12.12 Stage 1 (team 1)

S_1	D_1^*	R_1	
0	0	.6	$f_1^*(S_1 = 0)$
1	1	.4	$f_1^*(S_1 = 1)$
2	2	.2	$f_1^*(S_1 = 2)$
3	3	.1	$f_1^*(S_1 = 3)$

The stage 2 decision analysis is shown in Table 12.13. The S_2 values are the possible numbers of scientists remaining to be allocated. The D_2 values are the decision alternatives. The R_2 values are the probabilities of failure associated with different allocation decisions for team 2. The value of S_1 is determined as $S_2 - D_2 = S_1$ (the transition function describing the number of scientists remaining after the stage 2 decision). The $f_1^*(S_1)$ values are the optimal decision returns (probabilities of failure) at stage 1, given the value of S_1. The total return for stage 2 is therefore given as the product of $R_2 \cdot f_1^*(S_1)$, which the DOE wishes to minimize. The optimal solution for each value of S_2 is identified in the table by $f_2^*(S_2 = \cdot)$.

Table 12.13 *Stage 2 (team 2)*

S_2	D_2	R_2	S_1	$f_1^*(S_1)$	$R_2 \cdot f_1^*(S_1)$	
0	0	.8	0	.6	.48	$f_2^*(S_2 = 0)$
1	0	.8	1	.4	.32	
	1	.5	0	.6	.30	$f_2^*(S_2 = 1)$
2	0	.8	2	.2	.16	$f_2^*(S_2 = 2)$
	1	.5	1	.4	.20	
	2	.3	0	.6	.18	
3	0	.8	3	.1	.08	$f_2^*(S_2 = 3)$
	1	.5	2	.2	.10	
	2	.3	1	.4	.12	
	3	.2	0	.6	.12	

Stage 3 is given in Table 12.14. The computational procedure is quite similar to that of the stage 2 decision analysis. In this case we must compute, for each value of S_3,

$$f_3^*(S_3) = \underset{D_3}{\text{Min}} \{R_3 \cdot f_2^*(S_2)\}$$

where
$$S_2 = S_3 - D_3$$

Table 12.14 *Stage 3 (team 3)*

S_3	D_3	R_3	S_2	$f_2^*(S_2)$	$R_3 \cdot f_2^*(S_2)$	
0	0	.45	0	.48	.216	$f_3^*(S_3 = 0)$
1	0	.45	1	.30	.135	
	1	.20	0	.48	.096	$f_3^*(S_3 = 1)$
2	0	.45	2	.16	.072	
	1	.20	1	.30	.060	$f_3^*(S_3 = 2)$
	2	.15	0	.48	.072	
3	0	.45	3	.08	.036	
	1	.20	2	.16	.032	$f_3^*(S_3 = 3)$
	2	.15	1	.30	.045	
	3	.10	0	.48	.048	

Stage 4 is given in Table 12.15, which shows that the optimal decision at stage 4 is to allocate zero scientists to team 4 ($D_4^* = 0$). The minimum overall joint probability is shown to be .0240 for the optimal allocation of the 3 additional scientists.

Table 12.15 *Stage 4 (team 4)*

S_4	D_4	R_4	S_3	$f_3^*(S_3)$	$R_4 \cdot f_3^*(S_3)$	
3	0	.75	3	.032	.0240	$f_4^*(S_4 = 3)$
	1	.45	2	.060	.0270	
	2	.30	1	.096	.0288	
	3	.15	0	.216	.0324	

By backtracking, we determine the overall solution as follows. The value of S_3 that is associated with the optimal decision at stage 4 is 3. Returning to stage 3, for an input state value of 3, we find the optimal solution to be $D_3^* = 1$ (for $S_3 = 3$). The S_2 value associated with $f_3^*(S_3 = 3)$ is 2. Returning to the stage 2 table, we find the optimal solution to be $D_2^* = 0$. The S_1 value associated with $f_2^*(S_2 = 2)$ is 2. Returning to stage 1, we see that $D_1^* = 2$ (for $S_1 = 2$).

The optimal solution is summarized in Table 12.16.

Table 12.16 *DOE Solution Summary*

Team (Stage)	Number of Additional Scientists Allocated	Return (Probability of Failure) Associated with Optimal Decisions
1	2	.20
2	0	.80
3	1	.20
4	0	.75
	Sum = 3	Product = .024

An interesting aspect of the solution is that it is contrary to the intuitive solution initially reached prior to solving the problem by dynamic programming, which, you will recall, was to allocate scientists to teams 2 and 4 since they had the highest initial probability of failure.

Computerized Solution of the Research Failure Problem

The solution for Example 12.2 generated using the AB:QM software package is shown on pages 603–604.

Sensitivity Analysis

Sensitivity analysis can be performed on the dynamic programming solution to the research failure problem. To determine the optimal solution for the allocation of only 2 scientists or 1 scientist, we need only reformulate stage 4 for each case.

The stage 4 decision analysis for allocation of only 2 scientists is given in Table 12.17 (p. 605). Reading the optimal decision from stage 4 and backtracking through

```
Program: Dynamic Programming / Non-Network

Problem Title : Example 12.2

***** Input Data *****

Problem Type                        :   Minimization
                                        Non-Network

Number of Stages                    :   4
Total Resources Available           :   3

Transition Function Type            : 1) S(n-1) = S(n) - D(n)
Recursion Function Type             : 3) f(n) = R(n) * f(n-1)
Return Function Type                : 1) R(n) = Constant


-------------------------------------------
Stage           Maximum Value of Decision
-------------------------------------------
   4                         3
   3                         3
   2                         3
   1                         3
-------------------------------------------


Return Value Table
-----------------------------------------------------------------------
Decision    Stage    4      Stage    3     Stage    2     Stage    1
--------    ---------        ---------      ---------      ---------
   0          0.750            0.450          0.800          0.600
   1          0.450            0.200          0.500          0.400
   2          0.300            0.150          0.300          0.200
   3          0.150            0.100          0.200          0.100
-----------------------------------------------------------------------


***** Program Output *****

                                    Stage    1
-----------------------------------------------------------------------
S( 1)  D( 1)            R( 1)  S( 0)              f( 0)          f( 1)
-----------------------------------------------------------------------
   0      0             0.600    0               0.000          0.600
-----------------------------------------------------------------------
   1      0             0.600    0               0.000          0.600
          1             0.400    0               0.000          0.400
-----------------------------------------------------------------------
   2      0             0.600    0               0.000          0.600
          1             0.400    0               0.000          0.400
          2             0.200    0               0.000          0.200
-----------------------------------------------------------------------
   3      0             0.600    0               0.000          0.600
          1             0.400    0               0.000          0.400
          2             0.200    0               0.000          0.200
          3             0.100    0               0.000          0.100
-----------------------------------------------------------------------
```

Stage 2

S(2)	D(2)	R(2)	S(1)	f(1)	f(2)
0	0	0.800	0	0.600	0.480
1	0	0.800	1	0.400	0.320
	1	0.500	0	0.600	0.300
2	0	0.800	2	0.200	0.160
	1	0.500	1	0.400	0.200
	2	0.300	0	0.600	0.180
3	0	0.800	3	0.100	0.080
	1	0.500	2	0.200	0.100
	2	0.300	1	0.400	0.120
	3	0.200	0	0.600	0.120

Stage 3

S(3)	D(3)	R(3)	S(2)	f(2)	f(3)
0	0	0.450	0	0.480	0.216
1	0	0.450	1	0.300	0.135
	1	0.200	0	0.480	0.096
2	0	0.450	2	0.160	0.072
	1	0.200	1	0.300	0.060
	2	0.150	0	0.480	0.072
3	0	0.450	3	0.080	0.036
	1	0.200	2	0.160	0.032
	2	0.150	1	0.300	0.045
	3	0.100	0	0.480	0.048

Stage 4

S(4)	D(4)	R(4)	S(3)	f(3)	f(4)
3	0	0.750	3	0.032	0.024
	1	0.450	2	0.060	0.027
	2	0.300	1	0.096	0.029
	3	0.150	0	0.216	0.032

Final Solution

Stage	Optimal Decision	Optimal Return
4	0	0.750
3	1	0.200
2	0	0.800
1	2	0.200
Total	3	0.024

***** End of Output *****

stages 3, 2, and 1, which were previously optimized for every possible state input, yields the overall optimal allocation of 2 scientists. The optimal decision at stage 4 is $D_4^* = 1$. The value of S_3 associated with the optimal decision at stage 4 is 1. Returning to stage 3, we see that the optimal solution (when $S_3 = 1$) is $D_3^* = 1$. We need not backtrack further, since we have exhausted our supply of scientists ($D_4^* = 1$ and $D_3^* = 1$). Note in stage 3 that the value of S_2 (the output of scientists remaining for stages 2 and 1) is zero for $f_3^*(S_3 = 1)$.

Table 12.17 *Stage 4 (allocation of two additional scientists)*

S_4	D_4	R_4	S_3	$f_3^*(S_3)$	$R_4 \cdot f_3^*(S_3)$	
2	0	.75	2	.060	.0450	
	1	.45	1	.096	.0432	$f_4^*(S_4 = 2)$
	2	.30	0	.216	.0648	

The optimal solution for allocation of only 2 scientists is given in Table 12.18.

Table 12.18 *Optimal Solution for 2 Scientists*

Team	Allocation	Return
1	0	.60
2	0	.80
3	1	.20
4	1	.45
	Sum = 2	Product = .0432

An interesting fact revealed by the sensitivity analysis is that reducing the number of additional scientists from 3 to 2 changes the mix of teams receiving allocations from teams 1 and 3 to teams 3 and 4.

Recomputation of stage 4 for an allocation of only 1 additional scientist reveals that the scientist should be allocated to team 3, with a resulting optimal total return of .0720. The sensitivity of total return (overall joint probability of research failure) to different levels of additional scientists is shown below.

Number of Additional Scientists	Total Return (probability of research failure)	Decisions
0	.1620	No additional scientists
1	.0720	One additional scientist to team 3
2	.0432	One additional scientist to team 3 and one to team 4
3	.0240	Two additional scientists to team 1 and one to team 3

Network Problem

The following example is commonly referred to as the *stagecoach* problem. It is frequently used as a primary illustration of the basic concepts of dynamic programming.

Example 12.3 Routing Problem

This type of problem can be illustrated as a network, as shown in Figure 12.18. A traveler during the 1800s wished to determine the optimal stagecoach route to take from San Francisco to New York. The options were limited in those days. The traveler would have to travel by four different stagecoaches during the overall journey. Initially, at San Francisco, the traveler could choose to travel to three different cities. Upon completion of the first leg of the journey, the traveler could again select from among three different destinations. After completing the second leg of the trip, the traveler was limited in the next destination to two cities. When the third stagecoach ride was completed, the traveler would then travel from that city to the final destination, New York.

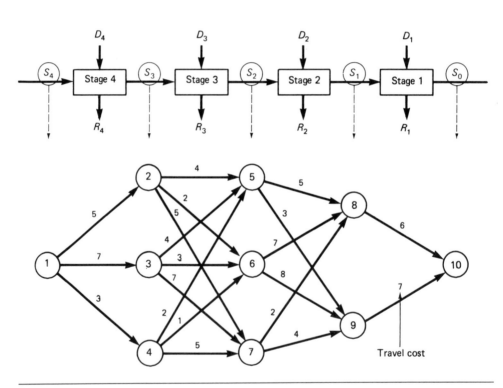

Figure 12.18 *The Network and Dynamic Programming Model of the Stagecoach Routing Problem*

The network diagram in Figure 12.18 illustrates the overall routing problem. San Francisco is denoted by node 1, and New York is denoted by node 10. Nodes 2 through 9 represent intermediate cities. The arrows of the network represent travel options, given that the traveler is at a particular city. The stagecoach fare for each travel option is given by the number along the arrow. The problem is to determine which stagecoach to take on each of the four legs of the journey in order to minimize total travel cost.

The dynamic programming representation of the problem is given at the top of Figure 12.18. The traveler must make four decisions as to which route to follow, prior to each leg of the journey. Thus, the problem is decomposed into four stages where decisions must be made (i.e., which stagecoach to take). Note that in this example the *state* is the *location* of the traveler. Therefore, the stage 4 input state (S_4) is defined as the initial location of the traveler, $S_4 = 1$. After selecting a stagecoach route for the first leg of the journey, the traveler will travel to state 3, which refers to city 2, 3, or 4. Depending on the decision, S_3 will equal 2, 3, or 4. The same explanation follows for the remainder of the journey (and the states of the dynamic programming representation). The traveler will terminate the journey at the destination $S_0 = 10$, city 10.

The problem is solved via dynamic programming by starting with stage 1 (the last leg of the journey) and working backward to the overall optimal solution at stage 4 (the first leg of the journey). The stage 1 decision analysis is indeed trivial, since there is only one option, given that the traveler is at city 8 or city 9. In either case, the traveler selects the stagecoach from that city to New York. The stage 1 decisions and returns are given in Table 12.19. Note that the decisions in Table 12.19 are denoted by $i{\rightarrow}j$, where i is the starting city and j is the destination city.

Table 12.19 *Stage 1*

S_1	D_1^*	R_1	
8	8→10	6	$f_1^*(S_1 = 8)$
9	9→10	7	$f_1^*(S_1 = 9)$

We therefore move to the stage 2 decision analysis given in Table 12.20, where the traveler is assumed to be at city 5, 6, or 7. The traveler must now decide whether to take the stagecoach to city 8 or city 9. Thus, the state 2 values may be $S_2 = 5$, 6, or 7, and the decision alternatives are $D_2 = S_2{\rightarrow}8$ and $S_2{\rightarrow}9$. (In this case, the route $i{\rightarrow}j$ is equally defined by the route $S_2{\rightarrow}j$.)

Table 12.20 *Stage 2*

S_2	D_2	R_2	S_1	$f_1^*(S_1)$	$R_2 + f_1^*(S_1)$	
5	5→8	5	8	6	11	
	5→9	3	9	7	10	$f_2^*(S_2 = 5)$
6	6→8	7	8	6	13	$f_2^*(S_2 = 6)$
	6→9	8	9	7	15	
7	7→8	2	8	6	8	$f_2^*(S_2 = 7)$
	7→9	4	9	7	11	

Note that in stage 2 the decision alternatives $i{\rightarrow}j$ are equivalent to $S_2{\rightarrow}S_1$. In general, the decision alternatives at stage n are represented by $S_n{\rightarrow}S_{n-1}$. S_n is the current city location, and S_{n-1} is the destination for the possible route for one leg of the journey. The stage 2 analysis shows that the optimal route to New York from city 5 is $5 \rightarrow 9 \rightarrow 10$; from city 6, it is $6 \rightarrow 8 \rightarrow 10$; and from city 7, it is $7 \rightarrow 8 \rightarrow 10$.

The stage 3 decision analysis is given in Table 12.21.

Table 12.21 *Stage 3*

S_3	D_3	R_3	S_2	$f_2^*(S_2)$	$R_3 + f_2^*(S_2)$	
2	$2 \rightarrow 5$	4	5	10	14	
	$2 \rightarrow 6$	2	6	13	15	
	$2 \rightarrow 7$	5	7	8	13	$f_3^*(S_3 = 2)$
3	$3 \rightarrow 5$	4	5	10	14	$f_3^*(S_3 = 3)$
	$3 \rightarrow 6$	3	6	13	16	
	$3 \rightarrow 7$	7	7	8	15	
4	$4 \rightarrow 5$	2	5	10	12	$f_3^*(S_3 = 4)$
	$4 \rightarrow 6$	1	6	13	14	
	$4 \rightarrow 7$	5	7	8	13	

In the stage 3 decision analysis, the minimum-cost route to New York from city 2, 3, or 4 is determined by computing the sum of the cost of the upcoming leg of the journey to its termination city (city 5, 6, or 7) and the cost of travel from that termination city to the final destination by the *optimal route*—that is, the cost from city S_3 to S_2 plus the cost of the least-cost route from city S_2 to New York. This cost is given by $R_3 + f_2^*(S_2)$, where R_3 is known for each $S_3 \rightarrow S_2$ route and S_2 is the end point for this leg of the journey. The optimal route for each S_3 location is determined by

$$f_3^*(S_3) = \underset{D_3}{\text{Min}} \{R_3 + f_2^*(S_2)\}$$

Given that the traveler is located at city 2, the optimal route is $2 \rightarrow 7 \rightarrow 8 \rightarrow 10$. If the traveler is at city 3, the least-cost route is $3 \rightarrow 5 \rightarrow 9 \rightarrow 10$, and from city 4, the best combination is $4 \rightarrow 5 \rightarrow 9 \rightarrow 10$. Thus, even if the traveler arbitrarily decided which city to travel to from San Francisco (from city 1 to city 2, 3, or 4), the traveler could be assured of having an optimal route to follow from any one of those cities. The traveler might, for example, decide that the risk of a stagecoach holdup was too great for the routes $1 \rightarrow 2$ and $1 \rightarrow 4$. The stage 3 analysis would then provide the least-cost route from city 3 to New York. This point again illustrates Bellman's principle of optimality, which states that regardless of the initial state and the initial decision, the optimal solution is the one that provides the optimal route from that state to the destination.

The stage 4 decision analysis is given in Table 12.22.

Table 12.22 *Stage 4*

S_4	D_4	R_4	S_3	$f_3^*(S_3)$	$R_4 + f_3^*(S_3)$	
1	$1 \rightarrow 2$	5	2	13	18	
	$1 \rightarrow 3$	7	3	14	21	
	$1 \rightarrow 4$	3	4	12	15	$f_4^*(S_4 = 1)$

Stage 4 shows that the minimum cost for the optimal route from San Francisco to New York is $15. (Travel was cheap in those days.) By backtracking from stage 4 through stage 1, we find the optimal route to be $1 \rightarrow 4 \rightarrow 5 \rightarrow 9 \rightarrow 10$. Note that there is no sensitivity analysis possible for this problem, since the initial input state value (S_4) denotes a location rather than a resource quantity.

A final point should be made regarding the reduction in computational effort brought about by dynamic programming. The number of combinations of different routes that would have to be evaluated to solve this problem by exhaustive enumeration is 18 ($3 \times 3 \times 2 \times 1$). Let us suppose that a particular routing problem involved 3 alternatives from each starting point and the number of starting points was 8 rather than 4, as in the stagecoach example. The evaluation of this problem by exhaustive enumeration would require $3^7 = 2187$ combinations. (This assumes that the final destination is 1 location, and thus the terminal stage offers only 1 alternative, as is the case in the stagecoach example.) Solution by dynamic programming offers a significant computational advantage.

Computerized Solution of the Stagecoach Problem

The solution for Example 12.3, using the AB:QM software package, is shown below.

```
Program: Dynamic Programming / Network

Problem Title : Example 12.3

***** Input Data *****

Problem Type                    :   Minimization
                                    Network

Number of Stages                :  4

Transition Function Type        : S(n-1) = S(n) - D(n)
Recursion Function Type         : f(n) = R(n) + f(n-1)

--------------------------------------
Stage      Number of Decisions
--------------------------------------
  4               3
  3               9
  2               6
  1               2
--------------------------------------
```

Stage	Starting Node	Ending Node	Return Value
4	1	2	5.000
	1	3	7.000
	1	4	3.000
3	2	5	4.000
	2	6	2.000
	2	7	5.000

	3	5	4.000
	3	6	3.000
	3	7	7.000
	4	5	2.000
	4	6	1.000
	4	7	5.000
2	5	8	5.000
	5	9	3.000
	6	8	7.000
	6	9	8.000
	7	8	2.000
	7	9	4.000
1	8	10	6.000
	9	10	7.000

```
----------------------------------------------------------------------
```

***** Program Output *****

Stage   1

S(1)	D(1)	R(1)	S(0)	f(0)	f(1)
9	9 -> 10	7.000	10	0.000	7.000
8	8 -> 10	6.000	10	0.000	6.000

Stage   2

S(2)	D(2)	R(2)	S(1)	f(1)	f(2)
7	7 -> 9	4.000	9	7.000	11.000
	7 -> 8	2.000	8	6.000	8.000
6	6 -> 9	8.000	9	7.000	15.000
	6 -> 8	7.000	8	6.000	13.000
5	5 -> 9	3.000	9	7.000	10.000
	5 -> 8	5.000	8	6.000	11.000

Stage   3

S(3)	D(3)	R(3)	S(2)	f(2)	f(3)
4	4 -> 7	5.000	7	8.000	13.000
	4 -> 6	1.000	6	13.000	14.000
	4 -> 5	2.000	5	10.000	12.000
3	3 -> 7	7.000	7	8.000	15.000
	3 -> 6	3.000	6	13.000	16.000
	3 -> 5	4.000	5	10.000	14.000
2	2 -> 7	5.000	7	8.000	13.000
	2 -> 6	2.000	6	13.000	15.000
	2 -> 5	4.000	5	10.000	14.000

Stage   4

S(4)	D(4)	R(4)	S(3)	f(3)	f(4)
1	1 -> 4	3.000	4	12.000	15.000
	1 -> 3	7.000	3	14.000	21.000
	1 -> 2	5.000	2	13.000	18.000

```
Final Solution
-----------------------------------------------------
Stage      Optimal Decision       Optimal Return
-----------------------------------------------------
  4            1 --> 4                  3.000
  3            4 --> 5                  2.000
  2            5 --> 9                  3.000
  1            9 --> 10                 7.000
-----------------------------------------------------
Total                                 15.000

***** End of Output *****
```

Knapsack Problem

The following prototype is generally referred to as the knapsack problem. The problem is to determine how many of each of several different types of items to put into a knapsack in order to maximize the total value of items packed without exceeding the capacity of the knapsack. Capacity is frequently defined in terms of total weight, and each type of item has a specified weight and value.

The general model formulation for this prototype problem is given as follows:

$$\text{Maximize} \sum_{n=1}^{N} v_n D_n$$

subject to

$$\sum_{n=1}^{N} w_n D_n \leq K$$

where

K = total capacity (i.e., total weight limit)
N = number of different types of items
n = index denoting item type n
D_n = solution value for number of type n items to pack, expressed as a nonnegative integer
v_n = unit value of item type n
w_n = unit weight of item type n

Example 12.4 Cargo Loading Problem

A cargo plane leaving for Alaska has a remaining capacity of 5 tons available for additional cargo. The XZN Corporation wishes to rush several pieces of equipment along on the plane. The weights and values (in hundreds of dollars) for each of 3 types of equipment are given as follows:

Item (n)	Unit Weight (w_n)	Unit Value (v_n)
1	2 tons	$65
2	3	80
3	1	30

The problem is to determine how many of each of the 3 types of equipment to ship on the cargo plane in order to maximize the value of the shipment without exceeding the weight limit of 5 tons. The problem will be solved by dynamic programming, where each stage corresponds to a decision as to the number of units of item n to ship.

The stage 1 decision analysis is presented in Table 12.23. The state input value is the remaining capacity (in terms of weight) for item 1, which may range from a maximum of 5 to 0. The decision variable, D_1, represents the number of type 1 items to load.

Table 12.23 *Stage 1 (item 1)*

S_1	D_1^*	W_1	R_1	
5	2	4	130	$f_1^*(S_1 = 5)$
4	2	4	130	$f_1^*(S_1 = 4)$
3	1	2	65	$f_1^*(S_1 = 3)$
2	1	2	65	$f_1^*(S_1 = 2)$
1	0	0	0	$f_1^*(S_1 = 1)$
0	0	0	0	$f_1^*(S_1 = 0)$
	$W_1 = 2D_1$		$R_1 = 65D_1$	

Note that the value of D_1 is constrained by the input weight capacity available, and, in general, the upper limit for the value of D_1 is given as

$$D_1 \leq \left[\frac{S_1}{w_1} \right]$$

where

$$w_1 = 2$$

$[S_1/w_1]$ is defined as the largest *integer* value that will not violate the capacity constraint—the maximum number of type 1 items that can be multiplied by the unit weight without exceeding the weight capacity S_1. The values given under the column heading W_1 are the total weights for $[S_1/w_1]$, given by $w_1 \cdot D_1$.

Note that only the optimal values for D_1 are given in the stage 1 table, since the firm would completely use any remaining capacity at this stage. The functions defining the values for W_1 and R_1 are given at the bottom of the table ($W_1 = 2D_1$ and $R_1 = 65D_1$).

The stage 2 decision analysis is given in Table 12.24. In each case, the value of D_2 is limited to a maximum integer value of $[S_2/w_2]$, or $[S_2/3]$. The values of R_2 are described by $80D_2$. In general, each value for total return given in the far right-hand column of the table is computed as

Table 12.24 *Stage 2 (item 2)*

S_2	D_2	W_2	R_2	S_1	$f_1^*(S_1)$	$R_2 + f_1^*(S_1)$	
5	1	3	80	2	65	145	$f_2^*(S_2 = 5)$
	0	0	0	5	130	130	
4	1	3	80	1	0	80	
	0	0	0	4	130	130	$f_2^*(S_2 = 4)$
3	1	3	80	0	0	80	$f_2^*(S_2 = 3)$
	0	0	0	3	65	65	
2	0	0	0	2	65	65	$f_2^*(S_2 = 2)$
1	0	0	0	1	0	0	$f_2^*(S_2 = 1)$
0	0	0	0	0	0	0	$f_2^*(S_2 = 0)$
$W_2 = 3D_2$			$R_2 = 80D_2$			$S_1 = S_2 - W_2$	

$$f_2(S_2, D_2) = R_2 + f_1^*(S_1)$$
where
$$R_2 = v_2 D_2 = 80 D_2$$
and
$$S_1 = S_2 - w_2 D_2 = S_2 - 3 D_2$$

The column of values under W_2 summarizes the computations for $w_2 \cdot D_2$. Thus, the return function can be written as

$$f_2(S_2, D_2) = v_2 D_2 + f_1^*(S_2 - w_2 D_2)$$
$$= 80 D_2 + f_1^*(S_2 - 3 D_2)$$

Finally, the optimal decisions for each possible state input value are computed as

$$f_2^*(S_2) = \underset{D_2 \leq [S_2/w_2]}{\text{Max}} \{R_2 + f_1^*(S_1)\}$$
$$= \underset{D_2 \leq [S_2/w_2]}{\text{Max}} \{v_2 D_2 + f_1^*(S_2 - w_2 D_2)\}$$
$$= \underset{D_2 \leq [S_2/3]}{\text{Max}} \{80 D_2 + f_1^*(S_2 - 3 D_2)\}$$

Thus, the recursive return function for the knapsack problem is basically the same as that for the allocation problem presented earlier. However, in this case, the computational procedure for determining the stage n return is

$$R_n = v_n D_n$$

and the transition function is defined as

$$S_{n-1} = S_n - w_n D_n$$

The stage 3 decision analysis is given in Table 12.25. The optimal solution yields a maximum value of 160. The corresponding decision for $f_3^*(S_3 = 5) = 160$ is $D_3^* = 1$. The value of S_2 associated with the optimal solution is 4. Returning to stage 2, for S_2

= 4, we find an optimal decision for D_2 of 0. This optimal solution, $f_2^*(S_2 = 4)$, has a value of 4 for S_1. The optimal value for D_1 associated with $f_1^*(S_1 = 4)$ is $D_1^* = 2$.

Table 12.25 *Stage 3 (item 3)*

S_3	D_3	W_3	R_3	S_2	$f_2^*(S_2)$	$R_3 + f_2^*(S_2)$	
5	5	5	150	0	0	150	
	4	4	120	1	0	120	
	3	3	90	2	65	155	
	2	2	60	3	80	140	
	1	1	30	4	130	160	$f_3^*(S_3 = 5)$
	0	0	0	5	145	145	

$W_3 = 1D_3$	$R_3 = 30D_3$	$S_2 = S_3 - W_3$

The optimal solution is summarized in Table 12.26.

Table 12.26 *Cargo Loading Solution Summary*

Equipment Type	Number of Items	Value (in $100s)	Weight (in Tons)
1	2	130	4
2	0	0	0
3	1	30	1
	3	160	5

Sensitivity analysis can be performed to determine how many of which items would be loaded if the capacity were less than 5 tons. By successively repeating the stage 3 analysis for total inputs (capacities) of 4, 3, 2, and 1, we arrive at the optimal cargo loading solutions in Table 12.27.

Table 12.27 *Solution Summary for Different Capacities*

Available Capacity (S_4)	Number of Items			Total Return
	D_1^*	D_2^*	D_3^*	
5	2	0	1	160
4	2	0	0	130
3	1	0	1	95
2	1	0	0	65
1	0	0	1	30

Scheduling Problem

The following example illustrates a production and inventory scheduling problem. It is not a prototype for scheduling problems per se; however, it does demonstrate several of the features common to scheduling problems.

The basic model formulation for a production and inventory problem will be presented first, followed by an example problem solved by dynamic programming.

The variable definitions for the following production and inventory scheduling problem are given as

S_n = beginning inventory, period n (input variable)
D_n = production quantity, period n (decision variable)
q_n = quantity demanded, period n (specified parameter)
K_n = production capacity, period n (specified parameter)
W_n = warehouse or storage capacity, period n (specified parameter)
R_n = total production and inventory holding cost, period n. For example, if total production cost included a fixed setup cost (FC) plus a variable production cost per unit (VC), and inventory holding cost was a constant cost per unit per period held (HC), then the total production and inventory holding cost would be described by the following return function:

$$R_n = \begin{cases} \text{FC} + \text{VC} \cdot D_n + \text{HC} \cdot (S_n + D_n - q_n), \text{ if } D_n > 0 \\ 0 + \text{HC} \cdot (S_n + D_n - q_n), \text{ if } D_n = 0 \end{cases}$$

Note that quantity demanded, q_n, is to be filled from beginning inventory, S_n, plus production, D_n, in period n, and the inventory holding cost for period n is charged against the period n "ending" inventory, which is defined as

$$S_n + D_n - q_n$$

The basic model formulation for this problem is then given by the following:

Minimize $\sum_{n=1}^{N} R_n$ (where R_n = production and inventory cost function)

subject to

$D_n \leq K_n$, for $n = 1, \ldots, N$ (production capacity)
$S_n + D_n - q_n \leq W_n$, for $n = 1, \ldots, N$ (storage capacity)
$S_n + D_n \geq q_n$, for $n = 1, \ldots, N$ (demand requirement)

where

D_n, S_n are nonnegative integers

The following inventory transition function must hold:

$$S_{n-1} = S_n + D_n - q_n$$

where S_{n-1} is the *ending* inventory for period n and, likewise, the *beginning* inventory for the following period (where $n - 1$ is defined as the period *following* period n). Finally, the beginning inventory for the initial period of the planning horizon (which may be zero) must be specified, and the ending inventory for the last period of the planning horizon may be specified to equal zero or some other desired quantity.

Example 12.5 Production and Inventory Planning Problem

The Apco manufacturing firm produces small quantities of a specialized piece of equipment. It currently has orders for 14 pieces of the equipment, with no expectation of receiving any further orders within the next several months. The firm's customers have requested delivery according to the following schedule:

Delivery Month	Number of Items
January	2
February	5
March	3
April	4

Apco can manufacture a maximum of 5 pieces of equipment per month at a setup cost of $50 plus $20 per unit production cost. It has available storage capacity for a maximum of 4 pieces of equipment; the carrying cost per unit held from one month to the next is estimated to be $4.

The firm wishes to determine the optimal production and inventory holding schedule for the planning period of January through April. It has decided to use dynamic programming to solve the problem. It currently has zero units in inventory, and it wishes to plan for zero ending inventory in April.

The problem will be solved by beginning with the last month, April, as stage 1 and working backward to the first month, January, as stage 4. Since the firm wishes to have zero ending inventory in April, the optimal stage 1 decision is to produce the quantity differential between beginning inventory (S_1) and the amount required to meet demand in that month (4 units).

The stage 1 decision analysis is given in Table 12.28. If the beginning inventory is 4 units (the maximum storage capacity), the firm will produce nothing and fill demand for that month from inventory. If the beginning inventory is zero, the firm will produce 4 units at a cost of $50 + $20 × 4, or $130. The optimal decision for each possible input (beginning inventory level) is given by $f_1^*(S_1 = \cdot)$.

The stage 2 decision analysis is given in Table 12.29. The range of possible values for the input variable, S_2, is from 0 to 4 (where 4 is the maximum inventory storage

Table 12.28 *Stage 1 (April: demand = 4)*

Beginning Inventory S_1	Quantity Produced D_1	Ending Inventory S_0	Production Cost R_1	
4	0	0	0	$f_1^*(S_1 = 4)$
3	1	0	70	$f_1^*(S_1 = 3)$
2	2	0	90	$f_1^*(S_1 = 2)$
1	3	0	110	$f_1^*(S_1 = 1)$
0	4	0	130	$f_1^*(S_1 = 0)$

Beginning inventory = ending inventory from March (stage 2)
Ending inventory = beginning inventory + quantity produced − demand,
  or $S_0 = S_1 + D_1 - 4$
Production cost = setup cost + (production cost)(quantity produced),
  or $R_1 = \begin{cases} 50 + 20D_1, \text{ if } D_1 > 0 \\ 0, \text{ if } D_1 = 0 \end{cases}$

Table 12.29 Stage 2 (March: demand = 3)

Beginning Inventory S_2	Quantity Produced D_2	Ending Inventory S_1	Production Cost $50 + 20D_2$	Inventory Holding Cost $4S_1$	Stage 2 Production and Inventory Cost R_2	Previous Stage Optimal Decision, Given S_1 $f_1^*(S_1)$	Total Return $R_2 + f_1^*(S_1)$	
4	3	4	110	16	126	0	126	
	2	3	90	12	102	70	172	
	1	2	70	8	78	90	168	
	0	1	0	4	4	110	114	$f_2^*(S_2 = 4)$
3	4	4	130	16	146	0	146	
	3	3	110	12	122	70	192	
	2	2	90	8	98	90	188	
	1	1	70	4	74	110	184	
	0	0	0	0	0	130	130	$f_2^*(S_2 = 3)$
2	5	4	150	16	166	0	166	
	4	3	130	12	142	70	212	
	3	2	110	8	118	90	208	
	2	1	90	4	94	110	204	
	1	0	70	0	70	130	200	$f_2^*(S_2 = 2)$
1	5	3	150	12	162	70	232	
	4	2	130	8	138	90	228	
	3	1	110	4	114	110	224	
	2	0	90	0	90	130	220	$f_2^*(S_2 = 1)$
0	5	2	150	8	158	90	248	
	4	1	130	4	134	110	244	
	3	0	110	0	110	130	240	$f_2^*(S_2 = 0)$

Transition function: $S_1 = S_2 + D_2 - 3$

Return function: $f_2(S_2, D_2) = R_2 + f_1^*(S_1)$, where $R_2 = \begin{cases} 50 + 20D_2 + 4S_1, & \text{if } D_2 > 0 \\ 0 + 4S_1, & \text{if } D_2 = 0 \end{cases}$

capacity). The values of D_2 (production quantity in stage 2 for March) are limited by the following constraints:

$$D_2 \leqslant 5 \qquad \text{(production capacity)} \qquad (1)$$
$$S_2 + D_2 - 3 \leqslant 4 \quad \text{(storage capacity for ending inventory)} \qquad (2)$$
$$S_2 + D_2 \geqslant 3 \qquad \text{(demand requirements for March)} \qquad (3)$$

Thus, if beginning inventory S_2 is 4, the maximum production quantity D_2 is 3 because of constraint (2). Likewise, when S_2 is 0, the minimum value for D_2 must be 3 in order to satisfy requirement (3). In any event, the maximum value for D_2 is 5, according to constraint (1).

The transition function links stage 2 to the previously evaluated stage 1 by $S_1 = S_2 + D_2 - 3$ (i.e., March's ending inventory = March's beginning inventory + production - demand). The total return for stage 2 is given by

$$f_2(S_2, D_2) = R_2 + f_1^*(S_1)$$

where

$$R_2 = \begin{cases} 50 + 20D_2 + 4S_1, & \text{if } D_2 > 0 \\ 0 + 4S_1, & \text{if } D_2 = 0 \end{cases}$$

and

$$S_1 = S_2 + D_2 - 3$$

Thus, the total recursive return function can be written, for each combination of S_2 and D_2, as

$$f_2(S_2, D_2) = \begin{cases} 50 + 20D_2 + 4(S_2 + D_2 - 3) + f_1^*(S_2 + D_2 - 3), & \text{if } D_2 > 0 \\ 0 + 4(S_2 + D_2 - 3) + f_1^*(S_2 + D_2 - 3), & \text{if } D_2 = 0 \end{cases}$$

For each value of the input variable S_2, we determine the optimal (minimum) cost as

$$f_2^*(S_2) = \underset{D_2}{\text{Min}} \{R_2 + f_1^*(S_1)\}$$

The optimal solution for each S_2 is denoted by $f_2^*(S_2 = \cdot)$ in the stage 2 table.

The stage 3 (February) decision analysis is given in Table 12.30. The range of possible values for D_3 is determined in a manner similar to that used for stage 2.

$$D_3 \leqslant 5 \qquad \text{(production capacity)} \qquad (4)$$
$$S_3 + D_3 - 5 \leqslant 4 \quad \text{(storage capacity for ending inventory)} \qquad (5)$$
$$S_3 + D_3 \geqslant 5 \qquad \text{(demand requirements for February)} \qquad (6)$$

Note that constraints (5) and (6) can be combined into the following constraint:

$$5 \leqslant S_3 + D_3 \leqslant 9$$

And, in general, for each stage,

$$q_n \leqslant (S_n + D_n) \leqslant (W_n + q_n)$$
$$\text{demand} \leqslant \text{(beginning inventory + production)} \leqslant \text{(storage capacity + demand)}$$

The stage 4 (January) decision analysis is given in Table 12.31. The only value for S_4 is zero, because the firm has no beginning inventory at the beginning of the planning

Table 12.30 Stage 3 (February: demand = 5)

Beginning Inventory S_3	Quantity Produced D_3	Ending Inventory S_2	Production Cost $50 + 20D_3$	Inventory Holding Cost $4S_2$	Stage 3 Production and Inventory Cost R_3	Previous Stage Optimal Decision, Given S_2, $f_2^*(S_2)$	Total Return $R_3 + f_2^*(S_2)$	
4	5	4	150	16	166	114	280	
	4	3	130	12	142	130	272	$f_3^*(S_3 = 4)$
	3	2	110	8	118	166	284	
	2	1	90	4	94	220	314	
	1	0	70	0	70	240	310	
3	5	3	150	12	162	130	292	$f_3^*(S_3 = 3)$
	4	2	130	8	138	166	304	
	3	1	110	4	114	220	334	
	2	0	90	0	90	240	330	
2	5	2	150	8	158	166	324	$f_3^*(S_3 = 2)$
	4	1	130	4	134	220	354	
	3	0	110	0	110	240	350	
1	5	1	150	4	154	220	374	
	4	0	130	0	130	240	370	$f_3^*(S_3 = 1)$
0	5	0	150	0	150	240	390	$f_3^*(S_3 = 0)$

Transition function: $S_2 = S_3 + D_3 - 5$

Return function: $f_3(S_3, D_3) = R_3 + f_2^*(S_2)$, where $R_3 = \begin{cases} 50 + 20D_3 + 4S_2, & \text{if } D_3 > 0 \\ 0 + 4S_2, & \text{if } D_3 = 0 \end{cases}$

619

Table 12.31 Stage 4 (January: demand = 2)

Beginning Inventory S_4	Quantity Produced D_4	Ending Inventory S_3	Production Cost $50 + 20D_4$	Inventory Holding Cost $4S_3$	Stage 4 Production and Inventory Cost R_4	Previous Stage Optimal Decision, Given S_3 $f_3^*(S_3)$	Total Return $R_4 + f_3^*(S_3)$	$f_4^*(S_4 = 0)$
0	5	3	150	12	162	292	454	
	4	2	130	8	138	324	462	
	3	1	110	4	114	370	484	
	2	0	90	0	90	390	480	

Transition function: $S_3 = S_4 + D_4 - 2$

Return function: $f_4(S_4, D_4) = R_4 + f_3^*(S_3)$, where $R_4 = \begin{cases} 50 + 20D_4 + 4S_3, & \text{if } D_4 > 0 \\ 0 + 4S_3, & \text{if } D_4 = 0 \end{cases}$

horizon. Thus, the optimal solution is identified in the stage 4 table by $f_1^*(S_4 = 0) = \$454$ for a production quantity of $D_4^* = 5$. The associated output state value for S_3 is 3 (the ending inventory in January and beginning inventory for February). Backtracking to stage 3, for $S_3 = 3$, we find the optimal decision to be $D_3^* = 5$ with $S_2 = 3$.

For $f_2^*(S_2 = 3)$, the optimal decision is $D_2^* = 0$, with an associated $S_1 = 0$. The optimal production quantity at stage 1, given a beginning inventory of 0, is $D_1^* = 4$.

The overall solution is summarized in Table 12.32.

Table 12.32 *Apco Company Solution Summary*

Stage (n)	Month	Demand (q_n)	Production (D_n^*)	Ending Inventory $(S_n + D_n^* - q_n)$	Production Cost	Inventory Cost	Total Cost
4	January	2	5	3	150	12	162
3	February	5	5	3	150	12	162
2	March	3	0	0	0	0	0
1	April	4	4	0	130	—	130
	Totals	14	14		430	24	454

A form of sensitivity analysis could be performed on this problem by assuming that some beginning inventory was available at the beginning of the planning horizon. Thus, stage 4 could be solved for input values of $S_4 = 1, 2, 3$, and 4, and the optimal strategy identified for each case. Likewise, the problem solution approach need not assume that production and/or warehouse capacities are constant over the planning horizon. A different production and warehouse capacity could be used for each month. Finally, the production cost function could take on a wide variety of forms. For example, production costs might be most appropriately defined by a quadratic or U-shaped cost curve. The basic approach to solution is similar to the one presented in the example.

Forward Versus Backward Recursion

All of the examples presented have employed backward recursion in the problem solution—we began with the last stage (identified as stage 1) and worked backward to the final solution at stage N. Alternatively, it is possible to start at the first stage (stage N) and work *forward* for the solution (i.e., from left to right). This would seem to make sense, especially for problems where the stages represent time periods. For such cases, forward recursion would start with period 1 and work forward to the last period of the planning horizon.

Contrary to intuition, however, the forward computational approach is usually less efficient than the backward recursion approach that has been presented. This is because the state transformation is generally more complex for forward recursion. In the end, both approaches yield equivalent results. Whether forward or backward recursion is used is determined by the individual's preference and the structure of the problem encountered.

Multiple State Variables

The examples presented have included a single state variable, or, more specifically, a one-dimensional state variable. For example, problems have been considered in which the

An Application of Dynamic Programming:
Optimal Flight Overbooking at Scandinavian Airlines

A common practice in the airline industry is to overbook a flight in order to avoid empty seats when passengers do not show up for their flight. In the U.S., no-shows range from 15% to 30% while the range of no-shows in Europe is from 5% to 20%. A major airline will have approximately one-half million empty seats per year on its flights, which translates to a direct annual loss of around $50 million from no-shows. To minimize these losses an airline will overbook, that is, reserve seats in excess of capacity.

Determination of how much a flight should be overbooked is not an easy process and requires that the airline must be able to accurately predict its no-show pattern. Overbooking has traditionally been done by booking control centers in an airline's marketing department. This requires watching and evaluating thousands of daily departures and analyzing huge amounts of historical data. As a result, most major airlines have developed computerized systems for overbooking that collect statistics on no-shows, access air traffic information, and apply no-show policy parameters in order to determine the best overbooking level for each flight.

Scandinavian Airlines (SAS) developed an overbooking system using stochastic dynamic programming as the primarily modeling component. The objective of the model was to

input state to each stage represented the remaining quantity of resource available, the amount of cargo capacity available, the location of a traveler, the work force level, and so forth.

Suppose, however, that a decision maker is faced with the problem of allocating two resources, given mathematically as follows:

$$\text{Maximize } \sum_{n=1}^{N} R_n$$

subject to

$$\sum_{n=1}^{N} D_n^1 \leqslant K$$

and

$$\sum_{n=1}^{N} D_n^2 \leqslant M$$

This example is quite similar to the capital budgeting example presented in Example 12.1. However, in addition to K capital, there is a second resource of total quantity M that also constrains the solution.

Thus, there are two state variables that must be accounted for at each state of the solution procedure. Let us define S_n^1 as the first state variable for the first resource of K quantity, and S_n^2 as the second state variable for the second resource of M quantity. Assuming that we can describe the transition functions by $S_{n-1}^1 = S_n^1 - D_n^1$ and $S_{n-1}^2 = S_n^2 - D_n^2$, the general recursion relation for this problem is given by

determine an optimal booking policy for allocating seats to its two types of passengers, tourist class and first (or Euro class), such that expected losses are minimized. The expected loss is defined as the difference between the maximum profit a flight might generate and the actual profit. At the time of boarding, either class of seats or both classes might be overbooked, which would require that certain class passengers be denied boarding, upgraded, or downgraded, or there may be empty seats. Each event results in a loss or extra cost.

The dynamic programming model (a generalization of the well-known newsboy problem) divides the preflight booking period into daily decision periods. At each time prior to booking, the state of the system is the number of passengers already booked in each class, while the decision variables are the maximum acceptable reservations in each class at a time period. The reservations and cancellations are stochastic variables, and the system changes from state to state over time according to transition probabilities that are functions of the probability distributions of passengers reservations and cancellations. The model result was an overbooking policy for each class seat, tourist and Euro. The model was validated prior to implementation using a simulation program. The new overbooking system resulted in a net annual revenue increase of approximately $2 million (U.S.) dollars over the previously used overbooking system at Scandinavian Airlines.

Source: J. Alstrup et al., "Booking Control Increases Profit at Scandinavian Airlines," *Interfaces,* 19, no. 4 (July–August 1989): 10–19.

$$f_n(S_n^1, S_n^2) = R_n + f_{n-1}^*(S_{n-1}^1, S_{n-1}^2)$$
$$= R_n + f_{n-1}^*(S_n^1 - D_n^1, S_n^2 - D_n^2)$$

Conceptually, the inclusion of multiple states does not present a problem in dynamic programming; however, from a practical point of view it presents significant difficulties. For problems requiring multiple states (or a multidimensional state variable), the solution procedure in dynamic programming becomes considerably more difficult. That is, the number of computations required and the information retention requirements increase dramatically as the number of states is increased. The information storage requirements increase geometrically as the dimension of the state variable increases linearly. For example, if each state variable takes on 20 values, then for two state variables it would be necessary to evaluate $20^2 = 400$ combinations, three state variables would require $20^3 = 8000$ combinations, four state variables would require $20^4 = 160,000$ combinations, and so on. This problem is aptly referred to by Bellman as "the curse of dimensionality." For these reasons, problem analysis by dynamic programming is usually limited to one or, at most, two states.

Finite Versus Infinite Horizons

All of the examples presented have assumed a finite planning horizon, (i.e., a specified number of stages). The intended planning horizon, however, may be infinite. There are several possible approaches to a problem with an infinite planning horizon.

First, many variables exhibit cyclical behavior, such as sales demand over the period of a year. Thus, it might be possible to obtain a solution to the dynamic programming problem whose planning horizon included one full set of fluctuating demands (i.e., one year) and apply this solution indefinitely into the future.

A second approach that has been suggested is to make use of discounting. In the case of cash flows, discounting extends the solution beyond some lengthy point into the future so that the infinite planning horizon becomes insignificant.

Finally, an approach frequently suggested for problems in which the stages represent time periods is to simply update the dynamic programming model and solution at the beginning of each *new* period (or stage). Thus, after each period of "experience," the decision maker would be able to respecify with certainty the input state to the newly defined first stage.

SUMMARY

This chapter presented the fundamental concepts of dynamic programming. Since dynamic programming is an *approach* to problem solving rather than a technique or algorithm, this chapter included a number of concepts that must be grasped prior to the study of specific applications. The first section of the chapter was designed to serve not only as an introduction to dynamic programming but also as a source of reference as you proceed through the second section on applications.

The second section of the chapter presented several of the best-known examples of dynamic programming applications. These include allocation problems, multiplicative return problems, network routing problems, the knapsack problem, and scheduling problems.

These various examples indicate the wide variety of complex problem forms to which dynamic programming can be applied. In fact, many of the more complex problems encountered in topic areas covered by other chapters in this text can also be solved using dynamic programming. However, it should always be remembered that because dynamic programming is a solution approach and not a technique, it often requires a great deal more modeling insight and expertise than some of the other methods presented in this text.

REFERENCES

BECKMAN, M. J. *Dynamic Programming of Economic Decisions*. New York: Springer-Verlag, 1968.

BELLMAN, R. *Dynamic Programming*. Princeton, New Jersey: Princeton University Press, 1957.

BELLMAN, R. E., and DREYFUS, S. E. *Applied Dynamic Programming*. Princeton, New Jersey: Princeton University Press, 1962.

GLUSS, B. *An Elementary Introduction to Dynamic Programming*. Boston: Allyn and Bacon, 1972.

HADLEY, G. *Nonlinear and Dynamic Programming*. Reading, Massachusetts: Addison-Wesley Publishing Company, 1964.

HASTINGS, N. A. J., and MELLO, J. M. C. *Decision Networks*. New York: John Wiley & Sons, 1978.

HILLIER, F. S., and LIEBERMAN, G. J. *Operations Research*. 4th ed. San Francisco: Holden-Day, 1986.

HOWARD, R. A. *Dynamic Programming and Markov Processes*. New York: John Wiley & Sons, 1960.

KAUFMANN, A., and CRUON, R. *Dynamic Programming: Sequential Scientific Management*. New York: Academic Press, 1967.

NEMHAUSER, G. L. *Introduction to Dynamic Programming*. New York: John Wiley & Sons, 1966.

WAGNER, H. M. *Principles of Operations Research*. Englewood Cliffs, New Jersey: Prentice-Hall, 1975.

PROBLEMS

1. An Eastern European diplomat in Washington, D.C. makes several trips per month to his home country to carry classified documents. On each trip the diplomat carries several black market items to sell for a high profit. In order not to arouse suspicion, the diplomat limits the weight of the items to 5 pounds, so that they can be conveniently hidden in a briefcase. The items that the diplomat smuggles are denim jeans, tape cassettes of a rock group, and bourbon. The weight and profit of each item are shown in the following table:

Item	Weight (lb)	Profit($)
1. Denim jeans	2	90
2. Bourbon	3	150
3. Tape cassettes	1	30

Determine the optimal number of each item the diplomat should smuggle in a briefcase to maximize profit. In your dynamic programming formulation, let stage 1 = denim jeans, stage 2 = bourbon, and stage 3 = tape cassettes.

2. Refer to Example 12.1, the capital budgeting problem, in which the ABC Company has budgeted $5 million for capital improvements, to be allocated among 3 plants. The $5 million is to be allocated in $1 million block amounts, with a maximum of $4 million to any one plant. Assume that the capital allocation problem has been modified as follows: Each plant can make use of any amount of capital between 0 and $4 million, in block amounts of $1 million, with the expected returns as given below.

Proposed Levels of Capital Investment (in $ millions)	Discounted Present Value of Increase in Cash Flow (in $ millions)		
	Plant A	Plant B	Plant C
0	0	0	0
1	2	3.5	4
2	6	5	7
3	8	7	10
4	9	9	11

a. Using dynamic programming, determine the optimal allocation of $5 million capital among the 3 plants.
b. Determine the optimal allocation of capital among the 3 plants if only $4 million capital is available for investment.
c. Illustrate the problem graphically as a dynamic programming model, showing stages, decisions, returns, and the transition function.

3. A pharmaceutical company has divided its sales region into 3 areas: north, central, and south. The company has 4 sales representatives whom it desires to allocate to these 3 areas in a manner that will result in the maximum monthly dollar sales. The company will not restrict the number of salespeople that can be assigned to any one area. The sales returns that will be generated in each area from each possible combination of sales representatives are shown in the following table:

Salespeople per Area	Monthly Sales per Area ($1000s)		
	North	Central	South
0	$ 0	$ 0	$ 0
1	22	17	25
2	51	48	45
3	65	71	58
4	82	90	75

Determine the optimal number of salespeople to assign to each area in order to maximize total sales. In the dynamic programming formulation, let stage 1 = north, stage 2 = central, and stage 3 = south.

4. A large manufacturing company has plants in Akron, Buffalo, and Cincinnati. Recently a competing firm went bankrupt, and the company purchased 5 large machines from the bank. The company wants to determine the optimal allocation of the purchased machines among its 3 plants. The expected additional daily product outputs the machines will generate at the plants are shown in the following table:

Machines Allocated	Daily Output per Plant (units)		
	Akron	Buffalo	Cincinnati
0	0	0	0
1	40	35	50
2	65	52	60
3	72	66	70
4	80	92	80
5	105	115	90

Determine the optimal allocation of machines to plants that will maximize the increase in daily output. In the dynamic programming formulation of this problem, let stage 1 = Akron, stage 2 = Buffalo, and stage 3 = Cincinnati.

5. A bus line has purchased 6 additional buses that it plans to use on 3 routes. However, the bus line has not decided how many of the new buses to assign to each of the 3 routes. It has developed estimates of additional profit per week for various alternatives, as shown below.

Number of Buses Assigned	Additional Profit per Week ($)		
	Route A	Route B	Route C
0	0	0	0
1	350	100	225
2	450	250	300
3	500	450	475
4	525	650	600
5	450	700	650
6	400	750	600

a. Use dynamic programming to determine the optimal assignment of buses to each route.
b. Determine the optimal assignment if only 5 buses are available.
c. Illustrate the problem graphically as a dynamic programming model, showing stages, decisions, returns, and the transition function.

6. The city police department must determine the optimal allocation of 12 new police officers to 4 precincts. At least 1 officer must be allocated to each of the 4 precincts, and no more than 4 officers can be allocated to any one precinct. The police department has developed estimates of the number of crimes that can be expected to occur per 8-hour period, given various numbers of allocated officers, as follows:

Number of Allocated Police Officers	Number of Crimes per 8-Hour Period			
	Precinct A	Precinct B	Precinct C	Precinct D
1	40	11	30	20
2	39	8	26	18
3	36	7	23	16
4	32	6	22	14

a. Use dynamic programming to determine the optimal allocation of officers to precincts in order to minimize the total number of crimes per 8-hour period.
b. Assume that only 11 new officers are available to be allocated; determine the optimal allocation of police officers.

Hint: Be sure to carefully define the constraints for the range of values that D_n and S_n can take on at each stage.

7. A manufacturing company has 4 machines on which it can produce 3 products (X, Y, and Z). All 4 machines can be set up to produce all 3 of the products. However, when a machine is set up to produce one of the 3 products, a production run of one

week is always scheduled. Each week the company must determine how many machines to schedule for each of the 3 products, based on sales forecasts for the week. The following table provides a forecast for the 3 products that has been reduced to a forecast of the coming week's profit, given the number of machines scheduled to produce each of the various products.

| | Week's Forecasted Profit ($) | | |
Number of Machines Scheduled	Product X	Product Y	Product Z
0	0	0	0
1	1000	1500	500
2	1900	2500	1600
3	2700	3200	2800
4	3400	3500	4000

Use dynamic programming to determine the optimal number of machines to schedule for production of each of the 3 products for the coming week.

8. Refer to Example 12.2, the research failure problem, in which 3 additional scientists are to be allocated to a research project involving 4 research teams. The objective is to allocate the 3 additional scientists in such a way as to minimize the overall probability of research failure. Assume that the probabilities of failure for various numbers of allocated scientists to each research team have been modified as follows:

| Number of Additional Scientists | Probability of Failure | | | |
	Team 1	Team 2	Team 3	Team 4
0	.6	.7	.45	.75
1	.4	.5	.25	.45
2	.2	.3	.15	.30
3	.1	.2	.10	.15

a. Use dynamic programming to determine the optimal allocation of 3 additional scientists to the 4 research teams, in order to minimize overall probability of project failure.
b. Assume that only 2 additional scientists are available for allocation. Determine the alternative optimal solutions for the number of scientists to allocate to each team.

9. A piece of electronic equipment consists of 4 components (A, B, C, and D) connected in series. If any one of the 4 components fails, the entire piece of equipment will not function. The reliability of each component is described in terms of the probability that the component will *not* fail, and the reliability of the entire piece of equipment is described in terms of the *product* of the component probabilities. The reliability of each component can be improved by installing more than one unit of a component

(i.e., one or more spare backup components). If the original component fails, one of the spare units is automatically switched into the circuit to replace the failed unit. The firm owning the piece of electronic equipment plans to spend up to $600 to add spare backup units to some of the components of the system. However, both the cost and the effect of adding spare units differ for each component, as follows:

Number of Spare Units Installed (x)	Component Reliability (based on the installation of x spare units)			
	A	B	C	D
0	.80	.60	.90	.70
1	.85	.81	.93	.90
2	.90	.99	.95	.98
Cost per spare unit for various components	$100	300	100	200

Given this information, use dynamic programming to determine how many spare units of each component should be installed in order to maximize the probability the piece of equipment will not fail, given a budget allocation of $600. (Hint: The decision variable is the number of spare units to install, whereas the state variable is dollars available for the purchase of spare units. Therefore, if D_n is used to represent the decision variable and c_n is used to represent the cost per spare unit at stage n, then, in general, the state variable transition function can be represented by $S_{n-1} = S_n - c_n D_n$.)

10. A company transports oranges by truck from Los Angeles to Chicago. The possible routes a truck can take and the travel time in hours for the branches of the routes are shown in the following network:

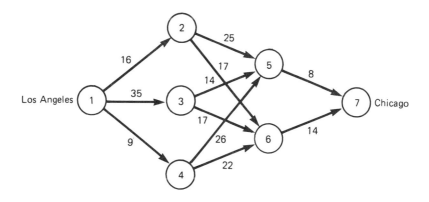

Determine the route from Los Angeles to Chicago that will minimize the total travel time.

11. Assume that the network illustrated in the following figure represents an oil pipeline network, where distances (in hundreds of miles) from node i to node j are shown

along the network branches. Use dynamic programming to determine the shortest route over which to pump the oil from source node 1 to destination node 18.

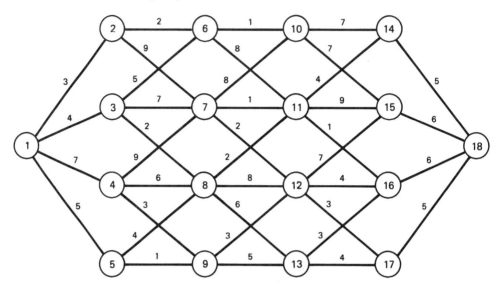

12. Assume that the network illustrated in problem 11 does not represent an existing oil pipeline network but rather the alternative sites for pumping stations (nodes) and associated feasible routes (branches) for pipelines. You may ignore the distance figures shown on the branches of the figure. The costs of constructing pumping stations and the costs of laying pipelines are shown in the following tables.

Construction Costs of Pumping Stations

Station Site (node)	Construction Cost	Station Site (node)	Construction Cost	Station Site (node)	Construction Cost	Station Site (node)	Construction Cost
2	40	6	56	10	45	14	60
3	67	7	55	11	80	15	69
4	53	8	75	12	50	16	58
5	70	9	47	13	65	17	72

Costs of Laying Pipeline

Pipeline Route ($i{\rightarrow}j$)	Cost	Pipeline Route ($i{\rightarrow}j$)	Cost	Pipeline Route ($i{\rightarrow}j$)	Cost	Pipeline Route ($i{\rightarrow}j$)	Cost	Pipeline Route ($i{\rightarrow}j$)	Cost
1→2	20	2→6	10	6→10	47	10→14	30	14→18	10
1→3	47	2→7	29	6→11	15	10→15	49	15→18	35
1→4	39	3→6	23	7→10	31	11→14	37	16→18	26
1→5	36	3→7	48	7→11	20	11→15	41	17→18	50
		3→8	40	7→12	33	11→16	25		
		4→7	34	8→11	21	12→15	43		
		4→8	31	8→12	44	12→16	39		
		4→9	27	8→13	30	12→17	45		
		5→8	46	9→12	21	13→16	47		
		5→9	38	9→13	40	13→17	36		

Use dynamic programming to determine the minimum cost for pumping station sites and associated pipeline routes. Note that the source pumping station at node 1 already exists, and node 18 is the oil tank farm (destination) to which the pipeline must be connected. All costs are given in thousands of dollars.

13. Reconsider Example 12.4, the cargo loading problem, assuming that the plane has a remaining capacity of 11 tons rather than 5 tons. The unit weights and values remain unchanged.

   a. Use dynamic programming to determine how many of each of the 3 types of equipment to ship on the cargo plane in order to maximize the value of the cargo carried.
   b. Assume that 1 unit of item 2 *must* be included on the plane. Show how to obtain the optimal solution, given this constraint, without reworking all three stages of the problem.
   c. Assume that the capacity is 11 tons and constraint b is not applied, but item 3 is revalued at $33 per unit. Determine the optimal number of each unit to ship.

14. Referring to Example 12.5, the production and inventory planning problem in which the Apco manufacturing firm wishes to determine the optimal production and inventory plan for the coming 4 months, assume that the firm can manufacture a maximum of 4 pieces of equipment per month. Given the information provided in the chapter, determine the optimal production and inventory schedule for the 4 months, assuming that all demand must be met.

15. Assume that the Apco firm in Example 12.5 has 3 units in inventory at the end of December. Determine the optimal production and inventory plan for the 4-month planning period.

16. Referring again to Example 12.5, assume that the maximum inventory capacity is 2 units rather than 4 units. Determine the optimal production and inventory plan.

17. A construction firm must use several pieces of specialized earth-moving equipment over the next 5 weeks. Since the firm does not expect to use the equipment on most construction projects, it has decided to rent the equipment from a large equipment rental firm rather than purchase it. The numbers of units of equipment needed for the next 5 weeks are forecasted as follows:

		Week		
1	2	3	4	5
4	6	7	3	5

The rent paid for the equipment will not be considered, since the decision has been made to rent the equipment. However, the costs of obtaining different numbers of units each week and the cost of holding excess units must be considered. A piece of equipment must be rented for a minimum of 1 week. The equipment rental firm charges a fixed fee of $400 for preparation of equipment (regardless of the number of units rented) each time one or more units are rented, plus a delivery charge of

$300 per unit of equipment. The construction firm has estimated the cost of holding excess units of the equipment (over requirements) to be $350 per unit per week. Use dynamic programming to determine the least-cost solution for the number of units of equipment to be delivered and held each week over the 5-week period.

(Hint: Assume that the decision variable, D_n, is defined as the number of units to hold in week n, and r_n is the number of units required in week n. Then, the range of values to be considered for D_n in any n is

$$r_n \leqslant D_n \leqslant 7$$

The state input value for any given week will be the value of the decision variable for the previous week.)

18. Reconsider problem 17 for the case in which the cost of holding excess units of equipment is $450 per unit per week, rather than the previously stipulated $350.

19. Reconsider problem 17 for the case in which the cost of holding excess units of equipment is $550 per unit per week, rather than $350.

20. Reconsider problem 17 for the case in which the cost of holding excess units of equipment is $550 per unit per week, and the cost of returning equipment to the rental firm is $100 per unit returned.

21. The construction firm in problem 17 has concluded that it could get along with 1 unit less than the forecasted need in either or both of weeks 2 and 3, but only by incurring an additional shortage cost (for overtime work) of $300 per unit of shortage. Use dynamic programming to determine the least-cost schedule of rental equipment. (Hint: Note that the lower limit of the range of possible solution values for the decision variable for weeks 2 and 3 must be revised to include 1 unit less than the requirements for those weeks.)

-13

Goal Programming

In Chapter 2, linear programming models were developed within a general framework that encompassed a single objective function. In most cases, the objective was to maximize profit or minimize cost. However, organizations have varied objectives depending on their character, type, function, philosophy of management, and size. Although profit maximization is regarded in classical economic theory as the sole purpose of the business firm and is one of the most widely accepted management objectives, it is not always the only objective. In fact, business firms frequently place higher priorities on noneconomic objectives than on profit maximization. Firms often seek a "satisfactory" level of profit while pursuing such noneconomic objectives as social responsibility, social contributions, public relations, labor relations, and environmental protection. Many public organizations, such as government agencies, have no profit objective at all but rather a myriad of social objectives. In other words, organizations often have multiple objectives.

Management science models are intended to help the decision maker derive better solutions to managerial problems than could be derived without them. Thus, a growing number of studies have appeared that attempt to *describe* the decision-making behavior in organizations. Although some of these descriptive studies have been conceptual in nature, the "satisficing" approach based on the concept of bounded rationality, as suggested by Nobel laureate Herbert A. Simon, has emerged as a pragmatic methodology of decision making. In this approach, a set of tangible, multiple-aspiration criteria replaces an abstract, global optimization criterion. Thus, multiple criteria decision making (MCDM), or multiple objective decision making (MODM), has become fairly well established as a practical approach to seeking a satisfactory solution given the limited information, resources, and cognitive ability of the decision maker.

Goal programming, which reflects Simon's theory of "satisficing," is one of the most powerful and widely applied techniques for modeling modern decision-making problems. It is a powerful tool that draws on the highly developed and tested technique of linear programming but at the same time provides a simultaneous solution to a complex system of competing objectives. A major advantage of goal programming over other techniques in dealing with real-world decision problems is that it reflects the way managers actually make decisions. In other words, goal programming allows the decision maker to incorporate environmental, organizational, and managerial considerations into the model through goal levels and priorities.

Goal programming, originally introduced by A. Charnes and W. W. Cooper and further developed by Y. Ijiri, S. M. Lee, and others, is very similar to the traditional linear programming concept. Implicit within this system is the idea that objectives may be incommensurable (i.e., they may be based on different units of measure). A company's goals of maximizing profit and minimizing pollution can be considered incommensurable objectives because the profit goal is defined in terms of dollars, whereas the pollution goal is defined in terms of tons of chemical wastes. Goal programming can be employed in decision problems with a single goal (objective) and multiple subgoals, as well as in cases having multiple goals and subgoals. Within the goal programming model, goals may be achieved only at the expense of other goals. Although it may not be possible to optimize every goal, goal programming attempts to obtain satisfactory levels of goal attainment that represent the best possible combination of goal achievements. This necessitates the establishment of a weighting system for the goals such that lower-ranked (or weighted) goals are considered only after higher-ranked goals have been satisfied or have reached the point beyond which no further improvement is desirable. These weights can be either ordinal or cardinal.

Since goal programming is a form of linear programming, goal programming models must be formulated under the same limitations, assumptions, and conditions as linear programming models (linearity, divisibility, determinism, etc.). Further, like linear programming problems, goal programming problems can be solved by using the simplex method (in a modified form).

Goal programming has been widely applied to decision problems in business organizations, government agencies, and nonprofit institutions. Example applications include the following:

Academic administration planning	Manpower planning
Accounting analysis	Marketing logistics
Advertising media scheduling	Military strategies
Blood bank logistics	Organizational analysis
Capital budgeting	Personnel administration
Computer resource allocation	Policy analysis
Decision support system planning	Portfolio management
Economic policy analysis	Production scheduling
Educational system planning	Project management
Energy resources planning	Quality control
Environmental protection	Research and development
Facilities layout and location decisions	Transportation logistics
Financial analysis	Urban planning
Health care delivery planning	Water resources planning
Inventory management	

GOAL PROGRAMMING MODEL FORMULATION

To gain some hands-on experience in formulating decision problems with multiple objectives as goal programming models, we will examine several example problems.

Example 13.1 Product Mix Problem

The following production problem was first given as a linear programming example in Chapter 2 (Example 2.1) to illustrate linear programming modeling. In this example, the same general production situation is employed; however, multiple objectives are defined instead of a single objective.

A manufacturing company produces three products, 1, 2, and 3. The three products have resource requirements as follows:

	Resource Requirements		
	Labor (hr/unit)	Materials (lb/unit)	Profit ($/unit)
Product 1	5	4	3
Product 2	2	6	5
Product 3	4	3	2

At present the firm has a normal production capacity of 240 hours of labor available daily and a daily supply of 400 pounds of material.

This problem was originally formulated in Example 2.1 as

Maximize $Z = 3x_1 + 5x_2 + 2x_3$

subject to

$$5x_1 + 2x_2 + 4x_3 \leqslant 240$$
$$4x_1 + 6x_2 + 3x_3 \leqslant 400$$
$$x_1, x_2, x_3 \geqslant 0$$

Notice that this model has a single objective, profit maximization. Now consider the situation where management has developed the following set of multiple goals, arranged in order of their importance to the firm.

1. Because of labor relations difficulties, management desires to avoid underutilization of normal production capacity (i.e., no layoffs of workers).

2. Management has established a satisfactory profit level of $500 per day.

3. Overtime is to be minimized as much as possible.

4. Management wants to minimize the purchase of additional materials because of handling and storage problems.

The firm's management desires to achieve these goals as much as possible. In order to reflect these multiple goals, the previous linear programming model must be reformulated into a goal programming model. First, the goal constraints must be developed.

Labor Utilization

The first goal relates to the labor hours utilized in the production of the three products. Management has decided to avoid underutilization of labor. In order to reflect the possibility of underutilization of labor (as well as overtime), the original linear programming constraint is reformulated as

$$5x_1 + 2x_2 + 4x_3 + d_1^- - d_1^+ = 240$$

The two new variables, d_1^- and d_1^+, are referred to as **deviational variables**. They represent the number of hours less than 240 (d_1^-, underutilization) and the number of hours exceeding 240 (d_1^+, overtime) for the amount of production determined by the values of x_1, x_2, and x_3. For example, if the final solution were $x_1 = 10$, $x_2 = 40$, and $x_3 = 20$, the total labor utilization would be 210 hours. This, in turn, would mean $d_1^+ = 0$ and $d_1^- = 30$ hours. With this level of production, labor capacity would be underutilized by 30 hours. Alternatively, if $x_1 = 20$, $x_2 = 40$, and $x_3 = 50$, the total labor utilization would be 380 hours. This would result in $d_1^+ = 140$ hours and $d_1^- = 0$, or 140 hours of overtime.

Implicit in this analysis is the fact that one of the deviational variables, d_1^- or d_1^+, must always be zero in the solution. In other words, it is not physically possible to have both underutilization and overutilization at the same time. When labor utilization is exactly 240 hours, d_1^- and d_1^+ both equal zero—there is neither overutilization nor underutilization of labor. A constraint in which we attempt to minimize d^-, d^+, or both d^- and d^+ is referred to as a *goal constraint*. One of the fundamental relationships in goal programming is that, in a given goal constraint, one or both of the deviational variables must always be zero.

Now that the labor constraint for production, which reflects the possibility of underutilization or overtime, has been formulated, the goal of avoiding underutilization must be specified. This is accomplished in the objective function as follows:

Minimize $Z = P_1 d_1^-$

P_1 is the preemptive priority designation for this goal. The term $P_1 d_1^-$ reflects the fact that the first priority goal of the firm is to minimize d_1^-, the underutilization of labor. Thus, in solving this problem, the first goal is to minimize d_1^- (drive it as close to zero as possible).

There is also another goal associated with this constraint, the minimization of overtime (d_1^+). The fact that management has ranked this goal third is reflected in the objective function as follows:

Minimize $Z = P_1 d_1^- + P_3 d_1^+$

P_3 designates minimization of d_1^+, overtime, as the third priority goal. Now the objective function reflects management's desire to achieve both of these goals; however, one is more important than the other. It should be noted here that the objective function Z does not represent a unidimensional value such as profit or cost. Instead, Z represents a multidimensional function composed of various priority factors and associated incommensurable objective criteria.

Profit Level

Management's second goal is to achieve the satisfactory profit level of $500. This goal constraint is formulated as

$3x_1 + 5x_2 + 2x_3 + d_2^- - d_2^+ = 500$

where d_2^- is underachievement of the profit goal and d_2^+ is overachievement of the profit goal. The goal is reflected in the objective function by minimizing d_2^-, underachievement of profit, at the second priority level.

Minimize $Z = P_1 d_1^- + P_2 d_2^- + P_3 d_1^+$

In other words, management is perfectly content to allow d_2^+, overachievement, to assume any value possible, as long as the goal of making at least \$500 is achieved by minimizing d_2^-.

Purchase of Materials

Management's final goal is that daily material purchases in excess of 400 pounds be minimized. Formulating the material requirement as a goal constraint results in

$$4x_1 + 6x_2 + 3x_3 + d_3^- - d_3^+ = 400$$

where d_3^- is the underutilization of normal material requirements and d_3^+ is the purchase of extra materials. The goal is reflected in the objective function by minimizing d_3^+ at the fourth priority level.

$$\text{Minimize } Z = P_1 d_1^- + P_2 d_2^- + P_3 d_1^+ + P_4 d_3^+$$

The term $P_4 d_3^+$ reflects management's desire to minimize the purchase of extra materials at a level of priority below those of the other three goals.

The goal programming model for this problem can be summarized as

$$\text{Minimize } Z = P_1 d_1^- + P_2 d_2^- + P_3 d_1^+ + P_4 d_3^+$$

subject to
$$5x_1 + 2x_2 + 4x_3 + d_1^- - d_1^+ = 240$$
$$3x_1 + 5x_2 + 2x_3 + d_2^- - d_2^+ = 500$$
$$4x_1 + 6x_2 + 3x_3 + d_3^- - d_3^+ = 400$$
$$x_1, x_2, x_3, d_1^-, d_1^+, d_2^-, d_2^+, d_3^-, d_3^+ \geq 0$$

Solution of this problem requires that the deviations from the goals specified in the objective function be minimized. The value of the deviational variable (d_1^-) associated with the highest preemptive priority (P_1) must first be minimized to the fullest possible extent. When no further improvement is possible or desired for this goal, the value of the deviational variable (d_2^-) associated with the next highest priority factor, P_2, is minimized, and so on. The solution procedure is a modified simplex approach. It should be pointed out once again that the objective function Z is not a unidimensional but a multidimensional function. In other words, Z represents the sum of unattained portions of each of the goals at different priority levels.

A goal programming model is useful for three types of analysis: (1) determining the input (resource) requirements to achieve a set of goals; (2) determining the degree of attainment of defined goals with given resources; and (3) providing the most satisfactory solution under the varying inputs, aspiration levels, and priority structures. To achieve various goals, we have the following three basic options open in the goal constraint:

Minimize	Goal	If Goal Is Achieved
d_i^-	Minimize underachievement	$d_i^- = 0, d_i^+ \geq 0$
d_i^+	Minimize overachievement	$d_i^- \geq 0, d_i^+ = 0$
$d_i^- + d_i^+$	Minimize both under- and overachievement	$d_i^- = 0, d_i^+ = 0$

Example 13.2 Weighted Goals

This example demonstrates an additional capability of goal programming: the ability to weight goals within the same priority level. Weighting of goals at a given priority level is particularly appropriate, as the measures of achievement are commensurable. For example, sales goals for different products may be weighted according to their relative contribution to profit.

A small manufacturing firm produces washers and dryers. Production of either product requires 1 hour of production time. The plant has a normal production capacity of 40 hours per week. A *maximum* of 24 washers and 30 dryers can be stored per week. The profit margin is $80 for a washer and $40 for a dryer. The manager has established the following goals, arranged in order of their priority.

P_1: Avoid underutilization of normal production capacity.
P_2: Produce as many washers and dryers as possible. However, since the profit margin for a washer is twice that for a dryer, the manager has twice as much desire to achieve the production of washers as to achieve the production of dryers.
P_3: Minimize overtime as much as possible.

Production Capacity

The first goal constraint reflects the production time requirements for both products.

$$x_1 + x_2 + d_1^- - d_1^+ = 40$$

where x_1 and x_2 are the respective number of washers and dryers produced. The deviational variable, d_1^-, reflects underutilization of the normal production capacity of 40 hours per week, while d_1^+ represents overtime. Priority goals 1 and 3 can be reflected as

$$\text{Minimize } Z = P_1 d_1^- + P_3 d_1^+$$

Storage Constraints

The production goal constraints for this problem are

$$x_1 + d_2^- = 24$$
$$x_2 + d_3^- = 30$$

In the first of these goal constraints d_2^- represents the underachievement of the production goal for washers, while in the second goal constraint d_3^- is the underachievement of the production goal for dryers. However, notice that d_2^+ and d_3^+ for the production goals have been eliminated, because these goal levels represent *absolute* maximum values (i.e., storage capacities) not to be exceeded. This demonstrates the capability of goal programming to compensate for those cases in which underachievement or overachievement of goal levels is not possible. This type of constraint is referred to as a *system constraint* because deviation in the positive and/or negative direction is prohibited. In effect, system constraints accomplish the same thing as $\leq$, $=$, or $\geq$ linear programming constraints.

The second priority goal is reflected in the objective function as follows:

$$\text{Minimize } Z = P_1 d_1^- + 2P_2 d_2^- + P_2 d_3^- + P_3 d_1^+$$

These two new terms in the objective function, $2P_2d_2^-$ and $P_2d_3^-$, reflect the second priority goals of minimizing the underachievement of the production goals. However, these goals are *weighted* within the second priority level by the relative profit of the two products. This means that the minimization of d_2^- is twice as important as the minimization of d_3^-. (However, neither of the priority 2 level goals is as important as the priority 1 goal, the minimization of d_1^-.)

The goal programming model for this problem is formulated as

$$\text{Minimize } Z = P_1d_1^- + 2P_2d_2^- + P_2d_3^- + P_3d_1^+$$

subject to

$$x_1 + x_2 + d_1^- - d_1^+ = 40$$
$$x_1 + d_2^- = 24$$
$$x_2 + d_3^- = 30$$
$$x_1, x_2, d_1^-, d_1^+, d_2^-, d_3^- \geqslant 0$$

Example 13.3 Deviational Variable Goal Constraint

Consider Example 13.2, with the added goal that overtime not exceed 10 hours per week, if possible. The priority level of this new goal places it between the old P_1 and P_2 levels. Recall the production requirements goal constraint

$$x_1 + x_2 + d_1^- - d_1^+ = 40$$

In this equation, d_1^+ reflects overtime. Our new goal is that overtime be restricted to 10 hours, which is formulated as

$$d_1^+ + d_4^- - d_4^+ = 10$$

This new equation is in a perfectly acceptable form for goal programming. The deviational variables d_4^- and d_4^+ denote the underachievement and overachievement of the overtime goal level.

Another way to formulate the same goal constraint in terms of decision variables is by adding the allowed overtime of 10 hours to the original production requirement goal as follows:

$$x_1 + x_2 + d_4^- - d_4^+ = 50$$

The new objective function becomes

$$\text{Minimize } Z = P_1d_1^- + P_2d_4^+ + 2P_3d_2^- + P_3d_3^- + P_4d_1^+$$

The new second priority goal specifies that the amount of overtime in excess of 10 hours is to be minimized. This goal is not incompatible with the goal of minimizing overtime. It is quite feasible for management to want to avoid overtime if it can but, if it cannot, to limit overtime to 10 hours. Notice that the positioning of this goal within the priority structure will affect its impact. Placed at the second priority level, it will attempt to hold overtime to 10 hours (or less). Placed last, it would have no effect, as the tighter goal of minimizing overtime to zero would then be at a higher priority level.

The new goal programming model is

$$\text{Minimize } Z = P_1d_1^- + P_2d_4^+ + 2P_3d_2^- + P_3d_3^- + P_4d_1^+$$

subject to

$$x_1 + x_2 + d_1^- - d_1^+ = 40$$
$$x_1 + d_2^- = 24$$
$$x_2 + d_3^- = 30$$
$$d_1^+ + d_4^- - d_4^+ = 10$$
$$x_j, d_i^-, d_i^+ \geq 0$$

Example 13.4 Recreational Facility Funding

A city parks and recreation authority has been given a federal grant of $600,000 to expand its public recreational facilities. Four different types of facilities have been requested by city council members speaking for their constituents: gymnasiums, athletic fields, tennis courts, and swimming pools. The total demand by various neighborhoods has been for 7 gyms, 10 athletic fields, 8 tennis courts, and 12 swimming pools. Each facility costs a certain amount, requires a certain number of acres, and has an expected usage. These parameters are summarized in the following table:

Facility	Cost ($)	Required Acres	Expected Usage (people/week)
Gymnasium	80,000	4	1500
Athletic field	24,000	8	3000
Tennis court	15,000	3	500
Swimming pool	40,000	5	1000

The park authority has located 50 acres of land for construction (although more land could be located if necessary).

The authority has established the following list of prioritized goals:

P_1: The authority must spend the total grant (otherwise the amount not spent will be returned to the federal government).

P_2: The park authority desires that the facilities be used weekly by 20,000 or more people.

P_3: If more land is acquired, the additional amount should be limited to 10 acres.

P_4: The authority would like to meet the demands of the city council members for new facilities. However, this priority should be weighted according to the number of people expected to use each facility.

P_5: The park authority wants to avoid securing land beyond the 50 acres presently available.

Funding Constraint

The cost requirements for the various facilities are shown in the following goal constraint:

$$80,000x_1 + 24,000x_2 + 15,000x_3 + 40,000x_4 + d_1^- = 600,000$$

where $x_1, x_2, x_3,$ and x_4 are the number of facilities of each type to be constructed. The deviational variable d_1^- is the portion of the grant not spent. The deviational variable d_1^+ has been eliminated, since the grant has a specified limit of $600,000 and it is assumed that additional funding is not available. The first priority goal is reflected in the objective function as follows:

Minimize $Z = P_1 d_1^-$

Facilities Use

The expected total weekly usage for all the facilities is formulated as

$$1500x_1 + 3000x_2 + 500x_3 + 1000x_4 + d_2^- - d_2^+ = 20{,}000$$

The deviational variables, d_2^- and d_2^+, are the respective amounts of weekly underutilization or overutilization of the facilities. The priority 2 goal of minimizing underutilization is shown in the objective function as

Minimize $Z = P_1 d_1^- + \boxed{P_2 d_2^-}$

Land Requirements

The land requirements for the various facility types are reflected in the following equation:

$$4x_1 + 8x_2 + 3x_3 + 5x_4 + d_3^- - d_3^+ = 50$$

The deviational variables represent the amount by which the number of acres used is less than 50, d_3^-, and the excess above 50 acres, d_3^+. The park authority desires that the amount of land in excess of 50 acres be limited, if possible, to 10 acres:

$$d_3^+ + d_4^- - d_4^+ = 10$$

This latter goal is reflected in the objective function by the minimization of d_4^+ at the priority 3 level. This goal and the priority 5 goal are shown in the objective function as

Minimize $Z = P_1 d_1^- + P_2 d_2^- + \boxed{P_3 d_4^+ + P_5 d_3^+}$

Facility Demand

The demand for facilities is shown by the following four goal constraints:

$$x_1 + d_5^- - d_5^+ = 7$$
$$x_2 + d_6^- - d_6^+ = 10$$
$$x_3 + d_7^- - d_7^+ = 8$$
$$x_4 + d_8^- - d_8^+ = 12$$

The deviational variables represent the construction of less or more facilities than the number of each type requested. The priority 4 goal of minimizing the negative deviation from the goal levels (i.e., facility demand) is weighted in the objective function by the relative amount of expected usage for each facility. Since the ratios of the expected usage (people/weeks) of the facilities are 3:6:1:2, these weights are assigned to respective deviational variables at the P_4 level.

Minimize $Z = P_1 d_1^- + P_2 d_2^- + P_3 d_4^+ + \boxed{3P_4 d_5^- + 6P_4 d_6^- + P_4 d_7^- + 2P_4 d_8^- + P_5 d_3^+}$

The complete goal programming model for this problem is formulated as follows:

$$\text{Minimize } Z = P_1 d_1^- + P_2 d_2^- + P_3 d_4^+ + 3P_4 d_5^- + 6P_4 d_6^- + P_4 d_7^-$$
$$+ 2P_4 d_8^- + P_5 d_3^+$$

subject to

$$80{,}000x_1 + 24{,}000x_2 + 15{,}000x_3 + 40{,}000x_4 + d_1^- = 600{,}000$$
$$1500x_1 + 3000x_2 + 500x_3 + 1000x_4 + d_2^- - d_2^+ = 20{,}000$$
$$4x_1 + 8x_2 + 3x_3 + 5x_4 + d_3^- - d_3^+ = 50$$
$$d_3^+ + d_4^- - d_4^+ = 10$$
$$x_1 + d_5^- - d_5^+ = 7$$
$$x_2 + d_6^- - d_6^+ = 10$$
$$x_3 + d_7^- - d_7^+ = 8$$
$$x_4 + d_8^- - d_8^+ = 12$$
$$x_j, d_i^-, d_i^+ \geq 0$$

Example 13.5 Multiperiod Investment Problem

In this example, a modified version of the multiperiod investment problem presented in Example 2.7, Chapter 2, will be presented.

An investment firm has $1,000,000 to invest in four alternatives: stocks, bonds, savings certificates, and real estate. The firm wishes to determine the mix of investments that will maximize the cash value at the end of 6 years. Investment opportunities in stocks and bonds are available at the beginning of each of the next 6 years. Each dollar invested in stocks at the beginning of each year will return $1.20 (a profit of $.20) 2 years later, which can be immediately reinvested in any alternative. Each dollar invested in bonds at the beginning of each year will return $1.40 3 years later, which can be reinvested immediately.

Investment opportunities in savings certificates are available only once, at the beginning of the second year. Each dollar invested in certificates at the beginning of the second year will return $1.80 4 years later. Investment opportunities in real estate are available at the beginning of the fifth and sixth years. Each dollar invested in real estate will return $1.10 a year later.

The management of the firm wishes to determine the optimal mix of investments in the various alternatives that will achieve the following goals, listed in the order of their importance.

P_1: In order to minimize risk, the total amount invested in stocks and bonds should be limited to 40% of the total investment.

P_2: The amount invested in savings certificates should be at least 25% of the total investment.

P_3: Real estate is expected to be very attractive in the future. Thus, management would like to invest at least $300,000 in real estate.

P_4: The total cash value by the end of the sixth year should be maximized.

Decision Variables

Figure 13.1 depicts the years in which each type of investment can be made and time to maturity. For example, S_1 represents an investment in stocks at the beginning of year 1.

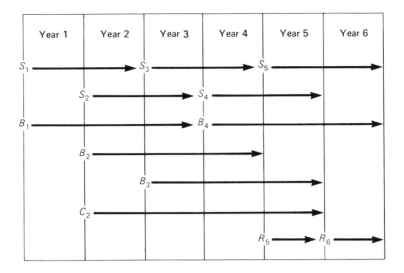

Figure 13.1 *Investment Scheme*

The arrow leading from S_1 goes to the end of year 2, when the return is realized. Using the same notation as in Figure 13.1, the decision variables can be defined as follows:

S_i = amount of money invested in stocks at the beginning of year i; i = 1, 2, 3, 4, 5
B_i = amount of money invested in bonds at the beginning of year i; i = 1, 2, 3, 4
C_2 = amount of money invested in savings certificates in year 2
R_i = amount of money invested in real estate at the beginning of year i; i = 5, 6
I_i = amount of money held idle and not invested during year i; i = 1, 2, 3, 4, 5, 6

System Constraints

In this problem, we have both system constraints and goal constraints. The system constraints define the investment opportunities and cash flows in a given year. For example, at the beginning of the first year, the only investment opportunities available are in stocks and bonds. There is a maximum amount of $1 million available for these two investment alternatives. However, since the minimum time to maturity for the two alternatives is 2 years, if all the $1 million is invested in S_1 and B_1, there will be no funds left for investment at the beginning of the second year. If we denote the amount of money not invested at the beginning of year 1 as I_1, the investment opportunity constraint in the first year is

Year 1: $S_1 + B_1 + I_1 = 1,000,000$

In the second year, the investment opportunities will be S_2, B_2, and C_2. These opportunities plus the amount not invested (I_2) must equal the amount not invested in year 1 (I_1). We can follow the same basic approach for the system constraints of the remaining years (refer to Chapter 2).

Investment Opportunities   *Amounts Available*
Year 2: $S_2 + B_2 + C_2 + I_2 = I_1$
Year 3: $\quad\quad S_3 + B_3 + I_3 = I_2 + 1.2S_1$
Year 4: $\quad\quad S_4 + B_4 + I_4 = I_3 + 1.2S_2 + 1.4B_1$

Year 5: $S_5 + R_5 + I_5 = I_4 + 1.2S_3 + 1.4B_2$

Year 6: $R_6 + I_6 \quad = I_5 + 1.2S_4 + 1.4B_3 + 1.8C_2 + 1.1R_5$

Goal Constraints

We can formulate the four goal constraints as follows:

P_1:   The total amount invested in stocks and bonds, $\sum_{i=1}^{5}S_i + \sum_{i=1}^{4}B_i$, should not exceed 40% of the total investment in all the alternatives, $\sum_{i=1}^{5}S_i + \sum_{i=1}^{4}B_i + C_2 + \sum_{i=5}^{6}R_i$. Thus, we can formulate the following goal constraint:

$$\sum_{i=1}^{5} S_i + \sum_{i=1}^{4} B_i + d_1^- - d_1^+ = .4\left(\sum_{i=1}^{5} S_i + \sum_{i=1}^{4} B_i + C_2 + \sum_{i=5}^{6} R_i\right)$$

Rearranging this constraint, we find the following constraint, where we would minimize d_1^+.

$$.6\sum_{i=1}^{5} S_i + .6\sum_{i=1}^{4} B_i - .4C_2 - .4\sum_{i=5}^{6} R_i + d_1^- - d_1^+ = 0$$

P_2:   Since the amount invested in savings certificates should be at least 25% of the total investment, we should minimize d_2^- from the following goal constraint:

$$-.25\sum_{i=1}^{5} S_i - .25\sum_{i=1}^{4} B_i + .75C_2 - .25\sum_{i=5}^{6} R_i + d_2^- - d_2^+ = 0$$

P_3:   For the real estate investment, we should minimize d_3^- in the following goal constraint:

$$\sum_{i=5}^{6} R_i + d_3^- - d_3^+ = 300{,}000$$

P_4:   Our last goal is to maximize the total cash value by the end of the sixth year. Since we invest any funds available in a given year, except I_i, we can simply try to maximize the investment opportunities that mature by the end of the sixth year and their respective return rates. These investment alternatives are S_5, B_4, and R_6, as shown in Figure 13.1. If we set our cash value goal to an arbitrarily large number M (say \$500,000,000) and minimize d_4^-, in essence we will be maximizing the cash value. Thus, we can formulate

$$1.2S_5 + 1.4B_4 + 1.1R_6 + I_6 + d_4^- = M$$

The complete goal programming model can now be summarized.

Minimize $Z = P_1 d_1^+ + P_2 d_2^- + P_3 d_3^- + P_4 d_4^-$

subject to

$$S_1 + B_1 + I_1 = 1{,}000{,}000$$
$$S_2 + B_2 + C_2 - I_1 + I_2 = 0$$
$$-1.2S_1 + S_3 + B_3 - I_2 + I_3 = 0$$
$$-1.2S_2 + S_4 - 1.4B_1 + B_4 - I_3 + I_4 = 0$$
$$-1.2S_3 + S_5 - 1.4B_2 + R_5 - I_4 + I_5 = 0$$
$$-1.2S_4 - 1.4B_3 - 1.8C_2 - 1.1R_5 + R_6 - I_5 + I_6 = 0$$

$$.6 \sum_{i=1}^{5} S_i + .6 \sum_{i=1}^{4} B_i - .4C_2 - .4 \sum_{i=5}^{6} R_i + d_1^- - d_1^+ = 0$$

$$-.25 \sum_{i=1}^{5} S_i - .25 \sum_{i=1}^{4} B_i + .75C_2 - .25 \sum_{i=5}^{6} R_i + d_2^- - d_2^+ = 0$$

$$\sum_{i=5}^{6} R_i + d_3^- - d_3^+ = 300,000$$

$$1.2S_5 + 1.4B_4 + 1.1R_6 + I_6 + d_4^- = 500,000,000$$

$$S_i, B_i, C_i, R_i, I_i, d_i^-, d_i^+ \geq 0$$

General Goal Programming Model

The previous four examples have demonstrated the general goal programming model formulation, which can be summarized as

$$\text{Minimize } Z = \sum_{k=0}^{K} \sum_{i=1}^{m} P_k(w_{ik}^- d_i^- + w_{ik}^+ d_i^+)$$

subject to

$$\sum_{j=1}^{n} a_{ij}x_j + d_i^- - d_i^+ = b_i \qquad (i = 1, 2, \ldots, m)$$

$$x_j, d_i^-, d_i^+ \geq 0$$

where P_k is the preemptive priority weight ($P_k >>> P_{k+1}$) assigned to goal k ($k = 0$ is reserved for system constraints), w_{ik}^- and w_{ik}^+ are numerical (differential) weights assigned to the deviational variables of goal i at a given priority level k, d_i^- and d_i^+ represent the negative and positive deviations, a_{ij} is the technological coefficient of x_j in goal i, and b_i is the ith goal level.

SOLUTION METHODS OF GOAL PROGRAMMING

Three solution methods of goal programming will be presented in this text: the graphical method, the modified simplex method, and the computer-based solution method. The main purpose of presenting the graphical method is to provide a basic knowledge of the goal programming approach. The graphical method is never used in real-world applications of goal programming. It is a solution method used only for small illustrative problems. The modified simplex method is the general solution method of goal programming. The computer-based solution method of goal programming is based on the modified simplex method.

Graphical Method of Goal Programming

Recall that the objective of goal programming is not the maximization or minimization of a single objective criterion. Instead, the objective is to achieve a set of multiple goals as close to the desired levels as possible. The basic approach we will take is to minimize the deviations between the goals and what we can achieve within the given set of constraints. The deviation from the goal with the highest priority factor will be minimized to the fullest possible extent, the deviation from the second goal will be minimized after considering the first goal, and so on. Thus, in goal programming, the optimum solution is optimum only in the sense that it is the most attractive satisficing solution for multiple objectives. The goal programming model is, therefore, always a minimization problem. To explain graphical solution of goal programming, we will consider Example 13.6.

Example 13.6 Product Mix Problem

An electronics firm produces color television sets. The company has two production lines. The production rate for line 1 is 2 sets per hour, and for line 2 it is 1.5 sets per hour. The regular production capacity is 40 hours a week for each line. The manager of the firm wants to determine the number of hours to operate each line during a week. The following goals have been set for the week; they are ranked according to their priority.

  1. Meet the production goal of 180 sets for the week.

  2. Limit the overtime operation of line 1 to 5 hours.

  3. Avoid underutilization of regular working hours for both lines. Differential weights should be assigned according to the production rate of each line.

  4. Limit the sum of overtime operation for both lines. Again, differential weights should be assigned to each line according to the relative cost of an overtime hour. It is assumed that the cost of operation is identical for the two production lines.

Before the complete model is formulated, there are a few points we should consider. First, the third goal implies that the company has a policy of no involuntary layoffs. Since the productivity of line 1 is 2 sets per hour, as compared to only 1.5 sets for line 2, the manager wishes to avoid the underutilization of regular working hours on line 1 more than on line 2. The productivity goals are weighted accordingly: 2 is assigned to d_2^- and 1.5 to d_3^-. Since it is easier to deal with integers, these values can be doubled to make the ratio 4 to 3. Second, the criterion for determining the differential weights in the fourth goal is the relative cost of overtime. The production rate ratio for the lines is 2 to 1.5. Therefore, the relative cost resulting from an hour of overtime is greater for line 2 than for line 1. The relative cost of overtime ratio for line 1 to line 2 will be 3 to 4. With the experience gained in the model formulation section, we can formulate the following model of the problem.

$$\text{Minimize } Z = P_1 d_1^- + P_2 d_4^+ + 4 P_3 d_2^- + 3 P_3 d_3^- + 3 P_4 d_2^+ + 4 P_4 d_3^+$$

subject to

$$2x_1 + 1.5x_2 + d_1^- - d_1^+ = 180$$
$$x_1 + d_2^- - d_2^+ = 40$$
$$x_2 + d_3^- - d_3^+ = 40$$
$$x_1 + d_4^- - d_4^+ = 45$$

To solve this problem, we will plot one constraint at a time, following the order of the objective function. For example, the most important goal is to meet the production goal of 180 sets. We can plot the production goal constraint and minimize d_1^-, as shown in Figure 13.2A. When we minimize d_1^-, the feasible area becomes the shaded area. Any point in the shaded area and beyond will satisfy the first goal because the total production will be 180 or more.

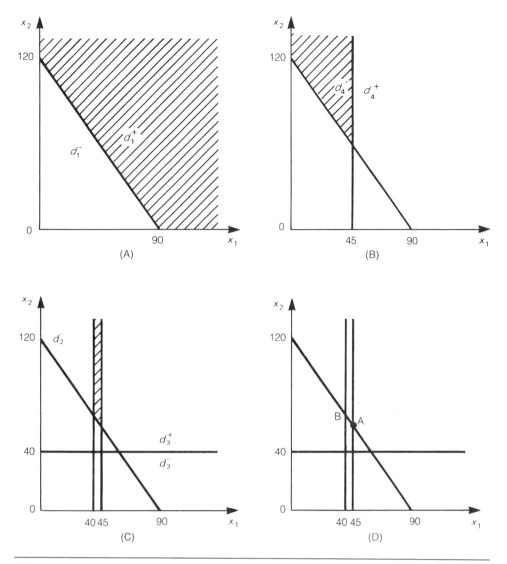

Figure 13.2 *Graphical Solution to Example 13.6: (A)
Achievement of the first goal; (B) Achievement of the first two
goals; (C) Achievement of the first three goals; (D) The optimal
solution*

The second goal is to limit the overtime operation of line 1 to 5 hours. This can be accomplished by minimizing d_4^+ in the fourth constraint. However, this goal must be sought within the feasible area already defined by satisfying the first goal. Thus, the feasible area becomes further reduced, as shown in Figure 13.2B.

The third goal is to avoid the underutilization of regular working hours for each line. This goal would be achieved if we could minimize d_2^- and d_3^-. As can be seen in Figure 13.2C, the third goal is achieved, and the feasible area is now a narrow strip. Within this shaded area, any solution would satisfy the first three most important goals.

The last goal of the problem is to limit the sum of overtime operation for both lines. We must minimize d_2^+ and d_3^+ to achieve the last goal. In the feasible area defined by the first three goals, it is impossible to minimize d_3^+ and d_2^+ all the way to 0. Thus, we must search for the point, within the feasible area, that is closest to $x_2 = 40$ because d_3^+ has a greater numerical weight than does d_2^+ in the objective function. It is obvious that point A is the optimum solution. At point A, we can easily derive the value of x_1 and x_2 by solving the intersecting equalities simultaneously. We obtain $x_1 = 45$ and $x_2 = 60$. By substituting these values in all the goal constraints, we find the following basic variables:

$$x_1 = 45, \quad x_2 = 60, \quad d_2^+ = 5, \quad d_3^+ = 20, \quad \text{and all other variables} = 0$$

Based on the solution values, we can interpret the degree of goal attainment as follows:

P_1:   Attained (production of 180 sets)
P_2:   Attained (5 hours of overtime operation of line 1)
P_3:   Attained (avoid underutilization of both lines)
P_4:   Not attained (5 hours of overtime on line 1 and 20 hours of overtime on line 2)

Modified Simplex Method of Goal Programming

A modified simplex procedure will now be introduced for solving goal programming problems. The simplex method is an algorithmic method that employs an iterative process of obtaining the optimal solution through progressive operations. The simplex solution procedure for goal programming problems is similar to the simplex method of linear programming. However, several distinct differences between the types of models require modification of the simplex process. For this reason, the simplex-based method of goal programming is often referred to as the modified simplex method. Example 13.6 will also serve as our illustration in explaining the modified simplex method of goal programming.

The Initial Tableau

Table 13.1 presents the initial tableau of the goal programming problem. The basic assumption in formulating the initial tableau of goal programming is identical to that of linear programming. We assume that the initial solution is at the origin, where values of all decision variables are zero. In the first constraint, therefore, the total production from the two lines is zero, since $x_1 = x_2 = 0$. Naturally, there cannot be any overachievement of the production goal ($d_1^+ = 0$); therefore, underachievement of the production goal (d_1^-) is 180 units. The variable d_1^- is thus entered into the solution basis, and b_1^* becomes 180. By the same token, d_2^- and d_3^- are also in the solution basis. According to the last constraint ($x_1 + d_4^- - d_4^+ = 45$), since line 1 is not in operation, the overtime operation of the line in excess of 5 hours (d_4^+) must also be zero. Consequently, d_4^- has the b_4^* value of 45, as shown in Table 13.1. In the initial tableau of goal programming, negative deviational variables (d_i^-) always appear in the solution basis.

In goal programming, the purpose of the objective function is to minimize the unattained portions of each of the goals. This is achieved by minimizing the deviational variables through the use of certain preemptive priority factors and differential weights. There is no profit maximization or cost minimization per se in the objective function. Therefore,

Table 13.1 *Initial Tableau*

c_b \ c_j	basis	b_i^*	x_1	x_2	P_1 d_1^-	$4P_3$ d_2^-	$3P_3$ d_3^-	d_4^-	d_1^+	$3P_4$ d_2^+	$4P_4$ d_3^+	P_2 d_4^+
P_1	d_1^-	180	2	3/2	1				-1			
$4P_3$	d_2^-	40	①			1				-1		
$3P_3$	d_3^-	40	1	1			1				-1	
0	d_4^-	45	1					1				-1
	P_4	0								-3	-4	
$z_j - c_j$	P_3	280	4	3						-4	-3	
	P_2	0										-1
	P_1	180	2	3/2					-1			

the preemptive factors and differential weights correspond to the c_j used in linear programming.

The objective function is expressed by assigning priority factors to certain variables. These preemptive priority factors are multidimensional because they are ordinal rather than cardinal values. In other words, priority factors at different levels are not commensurable. This implies that the simplex criterion (z_j or $z_j - c_j$) cannot be expressed by a single row, as is done in linear programming. Rather, the simplex criterion becomes a matrix of $k \times n$ size, where k represents the number of preemptive priority levels and n is the number of variables, including both decision and deviational variables.

Since the simplex criterion is expressed as a matrix rather than a row, we must design a new procedure for identifying the pivot column. The relationship between the preemptive priority factors is $P_k >>> P_{k+1}$, which means that P_k always takes priority over P_{k+1}. It is therefore clear that the procedure for selecting the pivot column must consider the level of priorities.

Now let us examine c_j. In goal programming, c_j is represented by the preemptive priority factors and the differential weights as shown by the goal programming objective function. Most goal programming problems involve a large number of variables. For that reason, in order to make the tableau easier to read, empty spaces are left in the table where zeros should appear.

The simplex criterion ($z_j - c_j$) is a 4×10 matrix, because we have four priority levels and ten variables (2 decision, 8 deviational) in the model. The goal programming procedure first achieves the most important goal to the fullest possible extent, then considers the goal with second priority, and so on. The selection of the pivot column should be based on the per unit contribution rate of each variable in achieving the most important goal. When the first goal has been completely attained, the pivot column selection criterion will be based on the achievement rate for the second goal, and so on. The preemptive priority factors are listed from the lowest to the highest so that the pivot column can be easily identified at the bottom of the tableau. In order to decrease the cumbersome size of the modified simplex tableau, we have omitted the matrix of z_j altogether.

The goal programming problem is a minimization problem. In the minimization problem of linear programming, the z_j value in the right-hand-side (b_i^*) column of the simplex criterion represents the total cost of the solution. By utilizing the same calculation procedure used in linear programming $[z_j(b_i^*) = \Sigma_{i=1}^{k} c_b b_i^*]$, we can obtain the z_j value as

$$z_j(b_i^*) = (P_1 \times 180) + (4P_3 \times 40) + (3P_3 \times 40) + (0 \times 45)$$
$$= 180P_1 + 280P_3$$

The $z_j - c_j$ values ($P_4 = 0$, $P_3 = 280$, $P_2 = 0$, and $P_1 = 180$) in the b_i^* column represent the unattained portion of each goal. For example, in the initial tableau, where the two production lines are not in operation, the second and the fourth goals are already completely attained. How can this be possible? Examining the objective function, we find that the second goal is to minimize the overtime operation of line 1 in excess of 5 hours, and the fourth goal is to minimize the total overtime operation of the two lines. Since we are not operating the lines at this point (at the origin), there can be no overtime operation. Consequently, we have already attained the second and fourth goals. The underachievement of the first goal is 180, because the unfulfilled production goal for television sets is 180 units. For the third goal, the underachievement is 280. Recall that differential weights of 4 and 3 have been assigned to the underutilization of the normal production capacity of 40 hours for each line. Since these two subgoals are commensurable and are at the same preemptive priority level, this procedure is considered appropriate. However, the underachievement of 280 for the third goal is not as easy to interpret as the underachievement of other goals to which no differential weights are assigned.

Now let us examine the calculation of $z_j - c_j$ in Table 13.1. We have already said that c_j (c_b) values represent the priority factors assigned to deviational variables, and that z_j values are products of the sum of c_b times the appropriate variable column coefficients. Thus, the z_j value in the x_1 column is $P_1 \times 2 + 4P_3 \times 1 + 0 \times 1$, or $2P_1 + 4P_3$. The c_j value in the x_1 column is zero, as shown by the blank in the c_j row. Therefore, $z_j - c_j$ for the x_1 column is $2P_1 + 4P_3$. Since P_1 and P_3 are not commensurable, we must list them separately in the P_1 and P_3 rows in the simplex criterion ($z_j - c_j$). Consequently, the $z_j - c_j$ value will be 2 in the P_1 row and 4 in the P_3 row in the x_1 column. By employing the same procedure, we can derive $z_j - c_j$ for the x_2 column ($P_1 \times \frac{3}{2} + 3P_3 \times 1) - 0$, or $\frac{3}{2} P_1 + 3P_3$. For the following three columns in Table 13.1 (d_1^-, d_2^-, and d_3^-), $z_j - c_j$ is zero, since z_j values are identical to the respective c_j values.

For the d_4^- column, $z_j - c_j$ is zero, because z_j and c_j are both zero. For the d_1^+ column, we can calculate the z_j value of $-P_1$ from the tableau. Since the c_j value of the column is zero, $z_j - c_j$ will be $-P_1$. The d_2^+ column has $z_j = -4P_3$ and $c_j = 3P_4$. Thus, $z_j - c_j$ is $-4P_3 - 3P_4$. Now we can calculate $z_j - c_j$ for the d_3^+ and d_4^+ columns as $-3P_3 - 4P_4$ and $-P_2$, respectively (as shown in Table 13.1).

As mentioned earlier, we have combined the calculation procedures for identifying z_j and $z_j - c_j$ values in the modified simplex tableau. The procedure requires more mental calculations, but it makes the tableau somewhat smaller and less cumbersome. This is especially useful if the problem under consideration is a very complex one. For example, if a problem containing 5 preemptive priorities and 25 variables is being analyzed, the 5 $\times$ 25 z_j matrix can be omitted by going directly to the $z_j - c_j$ matrix, which merely involves subtracting c_j as each column's z_j is calculated.

The First Iteration

The criterion used to determine the pivot column is the rate of contribution of each variable in achieving the most important goal (P_1). In other words, the column with the largest positive $z_j - c_j$ value at the P_1 level will be selected as the pivot column. In Table 13.1, there are positive values in the x_1 and x_2 columns. Since there is a larger value in the x_1 column (2 versus $\frac{3}{2}$), x_1 is selected as the pivot column. The pivot row is the row with the minimum nonnegative value, which is arrived at by dividing the b_i^* values by the positive coefficients in the pivot column. The coefficient 1 is circled in Table 13.1 to indicate that it is the pivot element at the intersection of the pivot column and the pivot row. By entering x_1 into the solution base, we affect the underutilization of the regular production capacity of line 1 and the underachievement of the production goal. That is, d_2^- leaves the basis (becomes zero) and d_1^- is reduced from 180 to 100, as described below.

By utilizing the regular simplex procedure, we revise the first tableau to obtain the second tableau, shown in Table 13.2. Production line 1 is in operation for 40 hours and produces 80 television sets. Therefore, the underachievement of the production goal is now 100 sets, as shown by the b_i^* value in the d_1^- row. We have also completely minimized the underutilization of normal production capacity of line 1, and therefore d_2^- has been removed from the solution base. The calculation of new coefficients is usually easier in goal programming than in linear programming, because in goal programming there are many coefficients with the unit value 1 and row elements in the pivot column are often zero.

Table 13.2 Second Tableau

c_j					P_1	$4P_3$	$3P_3$			$3P_4$	$4P_4$	P_2
c_b	basis	b_i^*	x_1	x_2	d_1^-	d_2^-	d_3^-	d_4^-	d_1^+	d_2^+	d_3^+	d_4^+
P_1	d_1^-	100		$\frac{3}{2}$	1	-2			-1	2		
0	x_1	40	1			1				-1		
$3P_3$	d_3^-	40		1			1			-1		
0	d_4^-	5				-1		1	①			-1
	P_4	0							-3	-4		
$z_j - c_j$	P_3	120	3		-4					-3		
	P_2	0										-1
	P_1	100		$\frac{3}{2}$		-2			-1	2		

Let us examine Table 13.2 more closely. The $z_j - c_j$ values in the b_i^* column ($P_4 = 0$, $P_3 = 120$, $P_2 = 0$, $P_1 = 100$) indicate that the unattained portion of the first goal has decreased considerably—by 80, to be exact. This is encouraging, because the goal programming model is a minimization problem and the value of $z_j - c_j$ should decrease at each step toward the optimal point. As our immediate concern is the achievement of the most important goal, we should examine whether $z_j - c_j$ has decreased at the P_1 level at the end of each step. When $z_j - c_j$ at the P_1 level has been completely minimized to zero or there are no more positive $z_j - c_j$ values at the P_1 level, our attention should be focused on the $z_j - c_j$ value at the P_2 level, and so on. In Table 13.2, z_j

— c_j at the P_3 level has decreased by 160, as line 1 is put into operation at its normal capacity of 40 hours.

The Second Iteration

The pivot column is identified as d_2^+ in Table 13.2. The pivot row of d_4^- is determined by the usual procedure. The best way to further achieve the most important goal is by providing overtime operation to line 1. Thus, line 1 will be in operation for a total of 45 hours, as shown in Table 13.3 (the third tableau).

Table 13.3 Third Tableau

C_b	c_j basis	b_i^*	x_1	x_2	P_1 d_1^-	$4P_3$ d_2^-	$3P_3$ d_3^-	d_4^-	d_1^+	$3P_4$ d_2^+	$4P_4$ d_3^+	P_2 d_4^+
P_1	d_1^-	90		$3/2$	1			-2	-1			(2)
0	x_1	45	1					1				-1
$3P_3$	d_3^-	40		1			1				-1	
$3P_4$	d_2^+	5			-1			1		1		-1
	P_4	15			-3			3			-4	-3
$z_j - c_j$	P_3	120	3		-4						-3	
	P_2	0										-1
	P_1	90		$3/2$				-2	-1			2

The above solution indicates that operation of line 1 for 45 hours (i.e., production of 90 television sets) has reduced the underachievement of the production goal by another 10 sets. However, the fourth goal is no longer completely attained, as line 1 has 5 hours of overtime.

The Third Iteration

The pivot column is d_4^+ and the pivot row is d_1^-, as shown in Table 13.3. Table 13.4 presents the fourth simplex tableau. This solution indicates that the production goal is now completely attained. However, production line 1 is in operation for a total of 90 hours (50 hours of overtime), and line 2 is not even in operation yet.

Table 13.4 Fourth Tableau

C_b	c_j basis	b_i^*	x_1	x_2	P_1 d_1^-	$4P_3$ d_2^-	$3P_3$ d_3^-	d_4^-	d_1^+	$3P_4$ d_2^+	$4P_4$ d_3^+	P_2 d_4^+
P_2	d_4^+	45		$3/4$	$1/2$				-1	$-1/2$		1
0	x_1	90	1	$3/4$	$1/2$					$-1/2$		
$3P_3$	d_3^-	40		(1)			1				-1	
$3P_4$	d_2^+	50		$3/4$	$1/2$	-1				$-1/2$	1	
	P_4	150		$9/4$	$3/2$	-3				$-3/2$	-4	
$z_j - c_j$	P_3	120		3		-4					-3	
	P_2	45		$3/4$	$1/2$				-1	$-1/2$		
	P_1	0			-1							

The Fourth Iteration

Because the first priority level goal has been completely achieved, we turn our attention to the second priority level. An additional rule must be invoked at this point: we cannot choose as the pivot column any column with a negative value at a higher priority level. In this case, we could not choose d_1^- as the pivot column, because doing so would decrease the attainment of the top priority goal, as indicated by the -1 at the P_1 level of the $z_j - c_j$ matrix. Taking into account this additional guideline, we can identify x_2 as the pivot column and d_3^- as the pivot row.

The results of the fourth iteration are given in Table 13.5. Production line 2 is in operation for 40 hours. Thus, the operation hours of production line 1 have been reduced from 90 to 60. This solution greatly increases the goal attainment of P_2, P_3, and P_4. As a matter of fact, the third goal (minimization of underutilization of normal operation hours of the two production lines) is now completely attained, as $x_1 = 60$ and $x_2 = 40$.

Table 13.5 *Fifth Tableau*

c_b	basis	b_i^*	x_1	x_2	P_1 d_1^-	$4P_3$ d_2^-	$3P_3$ d_3^-	d_4^-	d_1^+	$3P_4$ d_2^+	$4P_4$ d_3^+	P_2 d_4^+
P_2	d_4^+	15			½		−¾	−1	−½		(¾)	1
0	x_1	60	1		½		−¾		−½		¾	
0	x_2	40		1			1				−1	
$3P_4$	d_2^+	20			½	−1	−¾		−½	1	¾	
	P_4	60			3/2	−3	−9/4		−3/2		−7/4	
$z_j - c_j$	P_3	0				−4	−3					
	P_2	15			½		−¾	−1	−½		¾	
	P_1	0			−1							

The Fifth Iteration

Since P_2 is still not completely attained, the pivot column selection should be made at this level. The largest $z_j - c_j$ is found in the d_3^+ column, which is selected as the pivot column. The pivot row is d_4^+.

The results of the fifth iteration are given in the sixth (and final) tableau, shown in Table 13.6. The solution indicates that line 1 is in operation for 45 hours ($x_1 = 45$) and

Table 13.6 *Sixth Tableau (Optimal Solution)*

c_b	basis	b_i^*	x_1	x_2	P_1 d_1^-	$4P_3$ d_2^-	$3P_3$ d_3^-	d_4^-	d_1^+	$3P_4$ d_2^+	$4P_4$ d_3^+	P_2 d_4^+
$4P_4$	d_3^+	20			2/3		−1	−4/3	−2/3		1	4/3
0	x_1	45	1					1				−1
0	x_2	60		1	2/3			−4/3	−2/3			4/3
$3P_4$	d_2^+	5			−1			1		1	1	−1
	P_4	95			8/3	−3	−4	−7/3	−8/3			7/3
$z_j - c_j$	P_3	0				−4	−3					
	P_2	0										−1
	P_1	0			−1							

line 2 for 60 hours ($x_2 = 60$). Production line 1 has a total overtime operation of 5 hours ($d_2^+ = 5$), and line 2 has 20 hours of overtime ($d_3^+ = 20$). With this solution the first three goals are completely attained, but the fourth goal is not achieved; at P_4, $z_j - c_j = 95$. This result is due to the fact that overtime operations are required in order to achieve the production goal. In other words, the fourth goal is sacrificed in order to achieve the most important goal.

Table 13.6 presents the most satisfactory solution to the problem. It is optimal in the sense that it enables the decision maker to attain the goals as much as possible within the given decision constraints and priority structure. The fourth goal is not completely attained, as shown in Table 13.6, because there is at least one positive $z_j - c_j$ value at the P_4 level while there are no positive $z_j - c_j$ values at the P_1, P_2, and P_3 levels. Two positive values still remain in the $z_j - c_j$ matrix: $\%$ in the d_1^- column and $\%$ in the d_4^+ column. Obviously, we could attain the fourth goal to a greater extent if we introduced d_1^- or d_4^+ into the solution basis. We find, however, a negative value (-1) at the P_1 level in the d_1^- column and a negative value (-1) at the P_2 level in the d_4^+ column. This implies that if we introduced d_1^- into the solution we could improve achievement of the fourth goal at the expense of the first goal. By the same token, introducing d_4^+ would improve the fourth goal at the expense of the second goal. Thus, we cannot introduce either d_1^- or d_4^+ into the solution. A positive $z_j - c_j$ at a given priority level may be used in selecting a pivot column *only* when there is no negative element at a higher priority level.

From an analysis of $z_j - c_j$ values, we can determine where conflict exists among goals. Conflict exists between the first and fourth goals in column d_1^-, and between the second and fourth goals in column d_4^+. Now the decision maker can determine precisely how he or she must rearrange the priority structure if the underachieved goals at the lower levels are to be completely attained. This process gives the decision maker an opportunity to evaluate the soundness of his or her priority structure for the goals. Furthermore, from an analysis of the coefficients in the main body of the tableau, the decision maker can identify the exact trade-offs between goals. For example, in Table 13.6, we can see that if we introduced 30 units of d_1^- into the solution, the fourth goal would be improved by 80. However, this procedure would "undo" the first goal by 30 television sets. The marginal substitution ratio in this case is $\%$ to 1, or 8 to 3. The same type of analysis can also be made for the d_4^+ column. An analysis of the final solution tableau provides a great deal of information about the decision environment and the decision maker's priority structure of goals.

Steps of the Modified Simplex Method of Goal Programming

Now that we have illustrated the modified simplex method, we can summarize the solution steps as follows:

1. Set up the initial tableau for the goal programming model. Assume that the initial solution is at the origin. Therefore, all the negative deviational variables in the model constraints should initially enter the solution basis. List the b_i^* values and the coefficients of all variables in the main body of the table. Also list the preemptive priority factors and differential weights for the appropriate variables by examining the objective function. In the simplex criterion ($z_j - c_j$), list priority levels in the basis column, from the lowest at the top to the highest at the bottom. The z_j values

must be calculated and recorded in the b_i^* column. The last step is to calculate $z_j - c_j$ values for each column, starting with the first decision variable.

2. Determine the new entering variable (pivot column). First, find the highest priority level that has not been completely attained by examining the z_j values in the b_i^* column. When the priority level has been determined, identify the variable column that has the largest positive $z_j - c_j$ value without a negative value at a higher priority level. The variable in that column will enter the solution basis in the next iteration. If there is a tie for the largest positive $z_j - c_j$ value at the highest priority level, check the next lower priority level and select the column that has the greater value at the lower priority level. If the tie cannot be broken, arbitrarily choose a column.

3. Determine which variable will exit from the solution basis. This process is identical to finding the pivot row in the normal simplex procedure. If a tie exists when b_i^* values are divided by the coefficients in the pivot column, find the row that has the variable with the higher priority factor. This procedure enables higher order goals to be attained first and thereby reduces the number of iterations.

4. Determine the new solution. First find the new b_i^* value and coefficients of the pivot row by dividing the previous value by the pivot element (i.e., the element at the intersection of the pivot row and the pivot column). Then find the new values for all other rows by using the calculation procedure,

$$\text{Old value} - \left(\begin{array}{c} \text{intersectional element} \\ \text{of that row} \end{array} \times \begin{array}{c} \text{new value in the pivot row} \\ \text{in the same column} \end{array} \right)$$

Now, complete the table by finding $z_j - c_j$ values for the priority rows.

5. Determine whether the solution is optimal. First, analyze the attainment level of each goal by checking the z_j value for each priority row. If the z_j values are all zero, the solution is the optimal solution. If there exists a positive value of z_j, examine the $z_j - c_j$ coefficients for that row. If there are positive $z_j - c_j$ values in the row, determine whether there are negative $z_j - c_j$ values at a higher priority level in the same column. If there are negative $z_j - c_j$ values at a higher priority level for the positive $z_j - c_j$ values in the row of interest, the most satisfactory solution has been obtained. If there exists a positive $z_j - c_j$ value at a certain priority level and there is no negative $z_j - c_j$ value at a higher priority level in the same column, the most satisfactory solution has not been obtained. Therefore, return to step 2 and continue.

Figure 13.3 illustrates the solution process for goal programming problems.

Some Complications and Their Resolutions

Nonpositive Values

To understand the problem of nonpositive b_i values, consider the following goal constraint:

$$-5x_1 - x_2 + d_1^- - d_1^+ = -25$$

In the initial tableau of simplex goal programming, it is assumed that the solution is at the origin. Therefore, the deviational variable d_1^- takes on the value of -25. However, like the regular simplex method, the modified simplex method requires the non-negativity condition for variables $(x_j, d_i^-, d_i^+ \geq 0)$; thus, $d_1^- = -25$ is not permissible. In order to facilitate the initial solution, multiply both sides by -1. The goal constraint becomes

$$5x_1 + x_2 + d_1^+ - d_1^- = 25$$

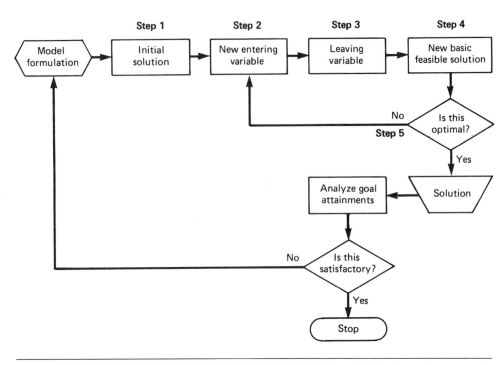

Figure 13.3 *Flowchart of the Solution Process of Goal Programming*

If the goal is to achieve exactly -25 from the original constraint, the goal can easily be achieved by minimizing both d_1^- and d_1^+ at the same priority level. However, if the goal is to make the constraint produce -25 or greater, d_1^- must be minimized in the original equation; in the revised goal constraint, d_1^- should be minimized to achieve the same effect. Similarly, for the constraint to assume a value of -25 or less, d_1^+ must be minimized in the revised equation.

Tie for Entering Variable

During the iterations of any goal programming problem, it is quite possible for two or more columns to have exactly the same positive $z_j - c_j$ value at the highest unattained goal level. As explained previously in this chapter, when such a case occurs, the determination of the pivot column, and consequently the entering basic variable, is based on the $z_j - c_j$ values at the lower priority levels. If the tie cannot be broken, selection between the contending variables can be made arbitrarily. The other variable will generally be introduced into the solution basis in a subsequent iteration.

Tie for Exiting Variable

To determine the variable that will leave the solution basis, divide b_i^* values by the coefficients in the pivot column and determine the row with the minimum nonnegative quotient. If there are two or more rows with identical minimum nonnegative values, the problem of degeneracy arises. This problem should be resolved by determining which row has the variable with the higher priority factor. The solution process can be shortened by selecting the variable with the higher priority factor as the exiting variable, as the higher priority goals will be attained faster.

Unbounded Solution

It is possible that lack of restraints will produce an unrealistic priority structure and, thus, allow one or more variables to increase without limit. In most real-world problems, however, this situation rarely occurs, since goals tend to be set at levels higher than those easily attained within the existing decision environment. If an unbounded solution occurs, it lends insight into an analysis of the decision maker's goal structure. It is often the case when an unbounded solution is obtained that important constraints have been omitted from the problem.

Multiple Optimal Solutions

It is possible for two or more points to provide solutions that produce exactly the same level of goal attainment. Such an occasion never occurs as long as (1) there is only a single deviational variable (single goal) at each preemptive priority level, (2) differential weights are assigned to subgoals at the same priority level, and (3) there exists a conflict among the goals.

Infeasible Solution

A model yields an infeasible solution when *all* system constraints are not satisfied. This result indicates that conflict exists among system constraints. In order to resolve the problem of infeasibility, the system constraints must be carefully analyzed to determine whether or not the conflict can be resolved.

Computer-based Solution of Goal Programming

The modified simplex method of goal programming is the prototype solution technique. Many real-world problems are, however, too complex to be solved by hand using the modified simplex method. To apply goal programming to practical problems, we need a computer-based solution technique. There are several computer programs available, either for a mainframe computer system or for a personal microcomputer, to solve goal programming problems. They are based on the modified simplex method, the revised simplex method, a sequential solution procedure based on an IBM linear programming package (MPSX), or a variation of these techniques.

In this section, we will present a computer-based solution printout of the modified simplex method implemented via AB:QM. The problem we will solve here is the product mix problem presented as Example 13.6. The model is

$$\text{Minimize } Z = P_1 d_1^- + P_2 d_4^+ + 4P_3 d_2^- + 3P_3 d_3^- + 3P_4 d_2^+ + 4P_4 d_3^+$$

subject to

$$2x_1 + 1.5x_2 + d_1^- - d_1^+ = 180$$
$$x_1 + d_2^- - d_2^+ = 40$$
$$x_2 + d_3^- - d_3^+ = 40$$
$$x_1 + d_4^- - d_4^+ = 45$$

Input Procedure

The AB:QM input procedure is presented below. Once the basic model parameters have been specified, the input screen allows the modeler to enter priority and constraint information in the appropriate locations. Movement among the cells of the entry screen is simple, enabling corrections or changes to be made with minor effort.

```
Goal Programming

 ┌──────────────────────────────────────────────────────────────────────┐
 │Problem Title :  Example 13.6 Product Mix                              │
 │Tableau (Yes=1/No=2)          1                                        │
 │Number of Constraints         4          Number of Variables        2 │
 └──────────────────────────────────────────────────────────────────────┘

   ┌──────────────────────────────────────────────────────────────────────┐
   │    W(d+) P(d+) W(d-) P(d-)       X1        X2 T       RHS             │
   │C1            1    1              2       1.5 =       180             │
   │C2     3    4    4    3           1           =        40             │
   │C3     4    4    3    3                     1 =        40             │
   │C4     1    2                     1           =        45             │
   │                                                                      │
   │                                                                      │
   │                                                                      │
   │                                                                      │
   │                                                                      │
   │                                                                      │
   └──────────────────────────────────────────────────────────────────────┘

 ┌──────────────────────────────────────────────────────────────────────┐
 │Help  New  Load  Save  Edit  Run  Print  Install  Directory  Esc      │
 └──────────────────────────────────────────────────────────────────────┘
```

Input Summary

The computer printout at the top of page 659 displays the model input summary. The model is presented in a format similar to that typically used during formulation, enabling rapid comparison of manual and computer models, as well as enhancing intuitive understanding of the model.

Solution Summary

The computer printout on pages 659–661 presents the final simplex solution tableau. The optimal solution was obtained in five iterations. The program output provides an analysis of deviations based on the optimal solution shown in the final tableau, the solution values for the decision variables, the level of goal attainment, and an analysis of conflicts among the goals. The first three goals were completely attained, while the fourth goal was only partially achieved. It is worth noting that attainment of the fourth goal could be improved through a sacrifice in the level of achievement of goals 1 or 2.

```
Program: Goal Programming

Problem Title : Example 13.6 Product Mix

***** Input Data *****

Min Z =        1P1d-1 +      3P4d+2 +      4P3d-2 +      4P4d+3 +      3P3d-3
       +       1P2d+4
Subject to

C1   2x1 + 1.5x2 + d-1 - d+1 = 180
C2   1x1 + d-2 - d+2 = 40
C3   1x2 + d-3 - d+3 = 40
C4   1x1 + d-4 - d+4 = 45
```

***** Program Output *****

Initial Tableau

\Cj Cb\	Basis	Bi	0 x1	0 x2	1P1 d-1	4P3 d-2
1P1	d-1	180.000	2.000	1.500	1.000	0.000
4P3	d-2	40.000	1.000	0.000	0.000	1.000
3P3	d-3	40.000	0.000	1.000	0.000	0.000
0	d-4	45.000	1.000	0.000	0.000	0.000
Zj-Cj	1P4	0.000	0.000	0.000	0.000	0.000
	1P3	280.000	4.000	3.000	0.000	0.000
	1P2	0.000	0.000	0.000	0.000	0.000
	1P1	180.000	2.000	1.500	0.000	0.000

\Cj Cb\	Basis	Bi	3P3 d-3	0 d-4	0 d+1	3P4 d+2
1P1	d-1	180.000	0.000	0.000	-1.000	0.000
4P3	d-2	40.000	0.000	0.000	0.000	-1.000
3P3	d-3	40.000	1.000	0.000	0.000	0.000
0	d-4	45.000	0.000	1.000	0.000	0.000
Zj-Cj	1P4	0.000	0.000	0.000	0.000	-3.000
	1P3	280.000	0.000	0.000	0.000	-4.000
	1P2	0.000	0.000	0.000	0.000	0.000
	1P1	180.000	0.000	0.000	-1.000	0.000

\Cj Cb\	Basis	Bi	4P4 d+3	1P2 d+4
1P1	d-1	180.000	0.000	0.000
4P3	d-2	40.000	0.000	0.000
3P3	d-3	40.000	-1.000	0.000
0	d-4	45.000	0.000	-1.000
Zj-Cj	1P4	0.000	-4.000	0.000
	1P3	280.000	-3.000	0.000
	1P2	0.000	0.000	-1.000
	1P1	180.000	0.000	0.000

Final Solution Tableau at Iteration   5

\Cj Cb\	Basis	Bi	0 x1	0 x2	1P1 d-1	4P3 d-2
4P4	d+3	20.000	0.000	0.000	0.667	0.000
0	x1	45.000	1.000	0.000	0.000	0.000
0	x2	60.000	0.000	1.000	0.667	0.000
3P4	d+2	5.000	0.000	0.000	0.000	-1.000
Zj-Cj	1P4	95.000	0.000	0.000	2.667	-3.000
	1P3	0.000	0.000	0.000	0.000	-4.000
	1P2	0.000	0.000	0.000	0.000	0.000
	1P1	0.000	0.000	0.000	-1.000	0.000

\Cj Cb\	Basis	Bi	3P3 d-3	0 d-4	0 d+1	3P4 d+2
4P4	d+3	20.000	-1.000	-1.333	-0.667	0.000
0	x1	45.000	0.000	1.000	0.000	0.000
0	x2	60.000	0.000	-1.333	-0.667	0.000
3P4	d+2	5.000	0.000	1.000	0.000	1.000
Zj-Cj	1P4	95.000	-4.000	-2.333	-2.667	0.000
	1P3	0.000	-3.000	0.000	0.000	0.000
	1P2	0.000	0.000	0.000	0.000	0.000
	1P1	0.000	0.000	0.000	0.000	0.000

\Cj Cb\	Basis	Bi	4P4 d+3	1P2 d+4
4P4	d+3	20.000	1.000	1.333
0	x1	45.000	0.000	-1.000
0	x2	60.000	0.000	1.333
3P4	d+2	5.000	0.000	-1.000
Zj-Cj	1P4	95.000	0.000	2.333
	1P3	0.000	0.000	0.000
	1P2	0.000	0.000	-1.000
	1P1	0.000	0.000	0.000

```
Analysis of deviations
-----------------------------------------------------------
Constraint  RHS Value         d+           d-
-----------------------------------------------------------
    C1        180.000        0.000        0.000
    C2         40.000        5.000        0.000
    C3         40.000       20.000        0.000
    C4         45.000        0.000        0.000
-----------------------------------------------------------


Analysis of decision variables
-----------------------------------------------------------
Variable            Solution Value
-----------------------------------------------------------
    X1                 45.000
    X2                 60.000
-----------------------------------------------------------


Analysis of the objective function
-----------------------------------------------------------
Priority                  Nonachievement
-----------------------------------------------------------
    P1                        0.000
    P2                        0.000
    P3                        0.000
    P4                       95.000
-----------------------------------------------------------
```

ADVANCED TOPICS IN GOAL PROGRAMMING

Thus far we have discussed the basic concepts, model formulation examples, and solution methods of goal programming. In this section, we will briefly discuss several advanced topics in goal programming.

Sensitivity Analysis

As we saw in linear programming (Chapter 4), an analysis of the effects of parameter changes after the optimal solution has been determined is an important part of any solution process. Since there usually exists some degree of uncertainty concerning the model parameters in real-world problems—for example, priority factors (P_k), goal levels (b_j), and technological coefficients (a_{ij})—sensitivity analysis can provide valuable information in a goal programming solution process. Interested readers should consult the references at the end of this chapter, especially Lee (1972).

There have been several studies published concerning the duality of goal programming. However, the value of duality is not as apparent in goal programming as in linear programming. One important reason is that management goals are not subject to random or irrational changes, as are changes of c_j in linear programming models. In other words, if a decision maker regards a particular goal as the most important goal, he or she most

An Application of Goal Programming:
Inventory Control Model at a Large Chemical Plant

Haifa Chemicals Ltd. (HCL) is one of Israel's largest chemical manufacturing plants. Its annual production volume reaches several hundred thousand tons, valued at more than $130 million (U.S.). HCL produces, stores, and distributes a variety of products, each of which may be produced in several grades and packaged in different ways. HCL's production facilities are located in the Haifa Bay area while its warehouses are spread around the world.

With the ever increasing competition in the world market, HCL management recognized the need to improve its production and inventory planning in several potential problem areas. One of the most difficult problems in managing production and inventory in large chemical plants is the overall evaluation and planning of the

products that are interrelated in their production and transportation process. Another difficulty in inventory control and production management is a systematic trade-off analysis of potential outcomes with respect to the conflicting goals. The conflicting goals HCL recognizes are

> Meeting ordinary demand with certainty and providing higher service level to occasional demand
>
> Keeping inventories at the lowest possible levels so as to minimize inventory costs
>
> Maintaining stable production schedules with similar work loads on the different production facilities

To resolve the complexity of this problem, HCL developed a goal programming (GP) model that

likely will not be interested in a systematic analysis of changes in the optimal solution as the priority 1 goal descends all the way to the least important level. Another reason is that other information obtained from a dual model can be derived easily from the final simplex tableau of the primal solution. For example, the analysis of trade-offs between two conflicting goals can be easily accommodated by the sensitivity analysis without the dual model. In real-world situations, many parameters change simultaneously, so a simple analysis based on certain information derived from a dual model has very little value.

Integer Goal Programming Methods

In many practical decision problems with multiple conflicting objectives, the decision variables make sense only if they assume discrete values. The decision variables in this situation may be people, construction crews, equipment components, assembly lines, indivisible investment alternatives, public works projects, and so forth. Discrete variables can be obtained easily by simply rounding off the values of the decision variables in the solution obtained by the regular goal programming algorithm. However, the procedure of rounding off to the nearest integer frequently yields either an infeasible or a nonoptimal solution, and if the variable values are small numbers, such as those in 0–1 programs, it can produce gross errors. Thus, there is a need to develop efficient integer goal programming techniques.

provided a reliable production/inventory managerial tool.

The model developed at HCL is a multiproduct, multiperiod GP model. The products include a variety of products, their by-products, and raw materials. The periods are chosen as months according to ordinary planning procedures. The objective is to minimize deviations from specified goals so as to keep the inventory system within desired boards by appropriate penalties that reflect the relative importance of the goals. The constraints include the inventory balance, safety stock requirements, by-product requirements, raw materials requirements, and manufacturing facility requirements. Some of the numerical weights in the objective function are derived from real economic costs, while others reflect management

preference with regard to possible outcomes of the model.

The model has resulted in direct savings of a considerable dollar amount, which the company is unwilling to disclose due to reasons concerning the firm's competitive advantage. In addition to financial benefit, the model has provided advantages in less tangible areas such as more systematic procedures, better cooperation between departments, and better monitoring of managerial decisions. It also provided advantages at a strategic level, including mutual effects among products or periods, a tool for tight control on management performance, and a feedback tool. The result of the model is deemed so successful that HCL is planning to extend the model to the entire product line at HCL.

Source: B. Golany, M. Yadin, and O. Learner, "A Goal Programming Inventory Control Model Applied at a Large Chemical Plant," *Production and Inventory Management Journal*, 32, no. 1 (Spring 1991): 16–24.

Interactive Goal Programming

The ordinal solution approach based on the preemptive priorities makes goal programming a powerful decision aid. Yet this very feature also makes it difficult to analyze the trade-offs among the goals. An equally important analysis for managerial decisions is a study of the effects of changes in goal levels (b_i) and technological coefficients (a_{ij}), addition or deletion of constraints, and addition or deletion of decision variables.

Perhaps the best way to analyze simultaneous changes in the model parameters is interactively, with the decision maker and the goal programming model interacting via a computer terminal. The interactive approach can be used to perform an on-line analysis of the effect of changes in model parameters, as well as a complete sensitivity analysis of the optimal solution. The interactive goal programming approach provides a systematic process through which the decision maker seeks the most satisfactory solution. This process allows the decision maker to reformulate the model and systematically compare the solutions in terms of their achievement of multiple objectives.

Decomposition Goal Programming

Decomposition analysis was originally discussed as a computational device for solving large-scale linear programs. Recently, however, decomposition analysis has received increasing attention because of two important characteristics: (1) it can be utilized for resource allocation in a decentralized organization, and (2) it provides management in decentralized organizations with insights into developing organizational structure and information systems.

One of the major deficiencies of previous decomposition methods has been their inability to consider multicriteria decomposition problems due to the decomposition methods' reliance on linear programming formulation. Lee and Rho have developed decomposition goal programming algorithms to facilitate solution of multicriteria decomposition problems. The algorithms are also effective in identifying managerial implications involved in the decomposition process that can be useful in analyzing organizational development and information systems.

Separable Goal Programming

The modified simplex method is effective for solving linear goal programming problems. It is not possible to apply the simplex algorithm to nonlinear problems, however. The optimal solution for nonlinear programs can be either any point along a curved boundary hypersurface of the feasible solution space or any point within the feasible solution space.

Presently, there is no general or universal approach for efficiently solving all general classes of nonlinear programming problems. It appears that the most promising approach to solving nonlinear programming problems is the transformation of the original problem into an acceptable linear approximation that permits the application of the simplex algorithm. The separable programming approach can be adapted to handle multiple objective optimization problems through goal programming.

Chance-Constrained Goal Programming

Chance-constrained goal programming is an effective technique for determining solutions that *satisfice* multiple-criteria decision problems that involve elements of risk and uncertainty associated with technological coefficients (a_{ij}) and levels of resources or goals (b_i). Three basic chance-constrained goal programming approaches have been developed. The first and second approaches present separate derivations that assume that only the technological coefficients (a_{ij}) or resource and/or goal levels (b_i) are random variables. The third approach presents a model that considers the combined effect of random a_{ij} and b_i. With the general chance-constrained goal programming model, an equivalent nonlinear deterministic model can be derived for each of the approaches in a format that is amenable to the separable goal programming model.

SUMMARY

Models developed for managerial decision analysis have often neglected or ignored the unique organizational environment, bureaucratic decision process, and multiple conflicting natures of organizational objectives. In reality, however, these are important factors that greatly influence the decision process. In this chapter, the goal programming approach was presented as a tool that provided for the satisfactory consideration and resolution of multiple objectives, while permitting an explicit consideration of the existing decision environment.

Developing and solving the goal programming model points out where managerial goals cannot be achieved and where trade-offs must be made because of limited resources. Furthermore, this type of model allows the decision maker to review the priority structure critically in view of the solution derived by the model.

REFERENCES

CHARNES, A., and COOPER, W. W. *Management Models and Industrial Applications of Linear Programming*. New York: John Wiley & Sons, 1961.

GIOKAS, D., and VASSILOGLOU, M. "A Goal Programming Model for Bank Assets and Liabilities Management." *European Journal of Operational Research* 50 (1991): 48–60.

GOLANY, B., YADIN, M., and LEARNER, O. "A Goal Programming Inventory Control Model Applied at a Large Chemical Plant." *Production and Inventory Management Journal* 32 (1991): 16–24.

HAIMES, Y. Y. *Hierarchical Multi-Objective Analysis of Large Scale Systems*. New York: Hemisphere Pub. Corp., 1990.

IGNIZIO, J. P. *Linear Programming in Single and Multiple Objective Systems*. Englewood Cliffs, New Jersey: Prentice-Hall, 1982.

IJIRI, Y. *Management Goals and Accounting for Control*. Chicago: Rand-McNally, 1965.

INUIGUCHI, M., and YOSUFUMI, K. "Goal Programming Problems with Interval Coefficients and Target Intervals." *European Journal of Operational Research* 52 (1991): 345–360.

KWAK, N. K., SCHNIEDERJANS, M. J., and WARKENTIN, K. S. "An Application of Linear Goal Programming to the Marketing Distribution Decision." *European Journal of Operational Research* 52 (1991): 334–344.

LEE, S. M. *Goal Programming for Decision Analysis*. Philadelphia: Auerbach Publishers, 1972.

————. *Goal Programming Methods for Multiple Objective Integer Programs*. Atlanta: American Institute of Industrial Engineers, 1979.

————. *Management by Multiple Objectives*. Princeton, New Jersey: Petrocelli Books, 1981.

————. *AB:QM: Allyn & Bacon Quantitative Methods 3.0*. Boston: Allyn and Bacon, 1993.

LEE, S. M., and LUEBBE, R. "A Zero-One Goal Programming Algorithm Using Partitioning and Constraint Aggregation." *Journal of the Operational Research Society* 38 (1987): 633–641.

LEE, S. M., and EOM, H. B. "A Multi-Criteria Approach to Formulating International Project-Financing Strategies." *Journal of the Operational Research Society* 40 (1989): 519–528.

LEE, S. M., SHIM, J., and LEE, C. S. "The Signal Flow Graph Method of Goal Programming." *Computers and Operations Research* 11 (1984): 253–265.

OLSON, D. L. "Comparison of Four Goal Programming Algorithms." *Journal of the Operational Research Society* 35 (1984): 347–354.

RIFAI, A. K. and PECENKA, J. O. "An Application of Goal Programming in Healthcare Planning." *International Journal of Operations & Production Management* 10 (1990): 28–37.

RIOS, I. D. *Sensitivity Analysis in Multi-Objective Decision Making*. New York: Springer-Verlag, 1990.

SCHNIEDERJANS, M. J., and WILSON, R. L. "Using the Analytic Hierarchy Process and

Goal Programming for Information System Project Solution." *Information and Management* 20 (1991): 333–342.

SHIM, J. P., and CHUN, S. G. " Goal Programming: The RPMS Network Approach." *Journal of the Operational Research Society* 42 (1991): 83–93.

STEUR, R. E. *Multiple Criteria Organization.* New York: John Wiley & Sons, 1986.

TABUCANON, M. T. *Multiple Criteria Decision Making in Industry.* New York: Elsevier, 1988.

ZANAKIS, S. H., and GUPTA, S. K. "A Categorized Bibliographic Survey of Goal Programming." *Omega* 13 (1985): 211–222.

ZELENY, M. *Multiple Criteria Decision Making.* New York: McGraw-Hill, 1982.

PROBLEMS

1. Consider the following goal programming graph problem:

$$\text{Minimize } Z = P_1 d_1^+ + P_2 d_2^- + P_2 d_3^- + P_3 d_2^+ + P_3 d_3^+ + P_4 d_4^+$$

subject to

$$3x_1 + 3x_2 + d_1^- - d_1^+ = 120$$
$$x_1 + d_2^- - d_2^+ = 10$$
$$x_2 + d_3^- - d_3^+ = 15$$
$$x_1 + d_4^- - d_4^+ = 5$$

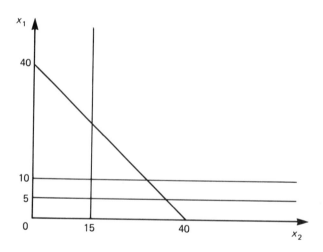

a. Are all the goals satisfied?

b. If not, which goals are not satisfied and by how much?

c. Describe the final solution, listing all the variables in the problem.

2. Set up the initial tableau for problem 1 and complete one iteration (two tableaus) of the modified simplex method.

3. An electronics firm produces two types of radios, AM and FM. Past experience indicates that production of either type of radio requires an average of 1 hour in the plant. The plant has a normal production capacity of 40 hours a week. The marketing department reports that, because of the limited sales force, a maximum of 24 AM and 28 FM radios can be sold per week. The unit profits are $15 per AM radio

and $10 per FM radio. The president of the company has set the following multiple goals, listed in the order of their importance:

1. Avoid any underutilization of normal production capacity.
2. Achieve the sales goals of 24 AM and 28 FM radios. Assign differential weights according to the unit profits.
3. Minimize the overtime operation of the plant as much as possible.

a. If the manager of the firm in this problem had only the single goal of profit maximization within the normal production capacity and sales constraints, how would you set up a goal programming model?
b. Formulate a goal programming model for the problem and solve it by the modified simplex method.

4. A furniture company produces three products: desks, tables, and chairs. All furniture is produced in the central plant. Producing a desk requires 3 hours in the plant, a table takes 2 hours, and a chair requires only 1 hour. The regular plant capacity is 40 hours a week. According to the marketing department, the maximum numbers of desks, tables, and chairs that can be sold per week are 10, 10, and 12, respectively. The president of the firm has established the following goals, in the order of their importance:

1. Avoid any underutilization of production capacity.
2. Meet the order of a retail store for 7 desks and 5 chairs.
3. Avoid overtime operation of the plant beyond 10 hours.
4. Achieve the sales goals of 10 desks, 10 tables, and 12 chairs.
5. Minimize the overtime operation as much as possible.

Solve the problem through two iterations (three tableaus) of the modified simplex method.

5. Tele-Bell Corporation has a scheduling problem. The number of operators needed and their wages are shown in the following table.

	Time Period	Operators Needed	Wages ($/hr)
Morning	Midnight to 4 AM	20	16
	4 AM to 8 AM	40	16
Daytime	8 AM to Noon	200	8
	Noon to 4 PM	160	8
Evening	4 PM to 8 PM	120	12
	8 PM to Midnight	60	16

Operators work 8-hour shifts and begin work at midnight, 4 AM, 8 AM, noon, 4 PM, or 8 PM. The personnel manager has set the following goals in the order of their importance:

1. Secure the required number of operators in the daytime to maintain a 100% service level.

2. Secure at least 80% of the operators needed in the morning and evening.
3. Minimize the labor cost.

Formulate a goal programming model and solve it using AB:QM.

6. A sportswear firm produces two types of bathing suits, regular and bikini. All bathing suits are produced in a modern sewing center. A regular bathing suit requires an average of 5 minutes and a bikini an average of 8 minutes in the sewing center. The two shifts of the sewing center combine to create a normal operation period of 80 hours per week. The unit profits for the bathing suits are $2.00 for regular and $2.50 for bikini. The president of the company wishes to achieve the following goals, which are listed in order of importance:

1. Achieve the profit goal of $2000 for the week.
2. Limit the overtime operation of the sewing center to 8 hours.
3. Meet the sales goal for each type of bathing suit: regular, 500; bikini, 400.
4. Avoid any underutilization of regular operation hours of the sewing center.

a. Formulate a goal programming model for this problem.
b. What will be the change in the objective function if the president decides to achieve the sales goal exactly as stated?
c. Ignoring part b, solve the original problem through one iteration by the modified simplex method.

7. A department store wants to schedule its annual advertising. The total budget is set at $200,000. The store can purchase local radio spots at $100 per spot, local television spots at $500 per spot, and local newspaper advertising at $200 per ad. The payoff from each advertising medium is a function of its audience size and audience characteristics. The generally accepted objective criterion for advertising is audience points. The audience points for the three advertising vehicles are

Radio: 30 points per spot
TV: 150 points per spot
Newspaper: 150 points per ad

The president of the firm has established the following goals for the advertising campaign, in order of their importance:

1. The total budget should not exceed $200,000.
2. The contract with the local television station requires that the firm spend at least $30,000 in television ads. Meet this contract.
3. The corporate advertising policy prohibits annual newspaper ad expenditures in excess of $50,000.
4. The audience points for the advertising campaign should be maximized.

Formulate a goal programming model for this problem.

8. The Midtown City Council is reviewing housing proposals for a new development area. There is some dispute among various interest groups as to what goals should be sought. The zoning committee has recommended three types of housing: one-family houses, deluxe condominiums, and apartments.

The zoning committee has compiled the following data for each type of housing:

	One-Family	Deluxe Condo	Apartment
Land usage, acres per unit	.25	.20	.125
Families housed per unit	1	4	6
Tax base generated per unit	$50,000	$100,000	$150,000
Taxes required for city services	$4000	$8000	$10,000

There are 50 acres available for zoning. The League for Better Housing has conducted a campaign to gain housing for at least 500 families. The Taxpayers' Union has strongly lobbied for an added tax base of $5,000,000. The Gray Panthers have disrupted the city council meetings to demand that taxes for city services be no more than $250,000.

The city council hired a public-opinion survey company to assess the priorities of the citizens. The poll results are as follows:

	Priority		
Goal	1	2	3
Housing for 500 families	55%	35%	10%
Tax base of $5,000,000	40	30	30
Taxes for services, $250,000	15	20	65

Based on this survey, the city council has established the following priorities:

P_1: Provide housing for at least 500 families.
P_2: Establish at least $5,000,000 worth of new tax base.
P_3: Limit taxes for city services to $250,000.
P_4: Reserve at least 5 acres for a neighborhood park area.

a. Formulate this problem as a goal programming model.
b. Go through one iteration by the modified simplex method.

9. Solve the following goal programming problem by the graphical method:

$$\text{Minimize } Z = P_1 d_1^- + P_2 d_4^+ + 3P_3 d_2^- + P_3 d_3^- + P_4 d_2^+ + 3P_4 d_3^+$$

subject to

$$5x_1 + 2x_2 + d_1^- - d_1^+ = 550$$
$$x_1 + d_2^- - d_2^+ = 80$$
$$x_2 + d_3^- - d_3^+ = 32$$
$$x_1 + d_4^- - d_4^+ = 90$$
$$x_j, d_i^-, d_i^+ \geq 0$$

10. A goal programming problem has been solved by the modified simplex method. The final simplex tableau is presented on page 670.

a. Is this solution optimal? Why or why not?
b. Discuss the goal attainment.
c. Are there any goal conflicts? If so, between which goals?
d. What are the trade-offs among the conflicting goals?

c_b \\ c_j	basis	b_i^*	x_1	x_2	P_1 d_1^-	d_2^-	$5P_4$ d_3^-	$6P_4$ d_4^-	d_1^+	P_2 d_2^+	$6P_3$ d_3^+	$5P_3$ d_4^+
$6P_3$	d_3^+	28	0	0	1/5	-6/5	-1	0	-1/5	6/5	1	0
$5P_3$	d_4^+	30	0	0	0	1	0	-1	0	-1	0	1
0	x_1	108	1	0	1/6	-5/6	0	0	-1/6	5/6	0	0
0	x_2	110	0	1	0	1	0	0	0	-1	0	0
$z_j - c_j$	P_4	0	0	0	0	0	-5	-6	0	0	0	0
	P_3	318	0	0	6/5	-11/5	-6	-5	-6/5	11/5	0	0
	P_2	0	0	0	0	0	0	0	0	-1	0	0
	P_1	0	0	0	-1	0	0	0	0	0	0	0

11. Galaxy Microelectronics, Inc. produces three personal computer models: the GMX, GMXL, and GM Portable. The production process involves two fabrication centers. The company has secured 240 worker-hours in fabrication center 1 and 200 worker-hours in fabrication center 2 for the next week's production. Production of the GMX requires 10 minutes in fabrication center 1 and 15 minutes in fabrication center 2; a GMXL requires 5 minutes in fabrication center 1 and 8 minutes in fabrication center 2; and a GM Portable takes 20 minutes in fabrication center 1 and 12 minutes in fabrication center 2.

   Currently, the company has limited technical staff that allows a maximum production of 1500 personal computers per week. The marketing department reports that the estimated sales for the coming week are as follows: GMX, 350; GMXL, 700; and GM Portable, 500. The president of the firm has listed the following goals, in order of priority.

   1. Operate each of the fabrication centers up to the available number of worker-hours for the week.
   2. Limit overtime operation of fabrication center 1 to 10 hours and overtime of fabrication center 2 to 15 hours (no differential weights are required).
   3. Produce a sufficient quantity of each type of personal computer to meet estimated sales levels (no differential weights are necessary).
   4. Minimize overtime operation of the two fabrication centers as much as possible (no differential weights are needed).

   Formulate a goal programming model for the problem.

12. Lambda Corporation is a local upholstery specialist that produces motorcycle seats for Kobayashi Motors, U.S.A. Lambda has two production teams. Team 1 is staffed with relatively new employees and produces an average of 50 seats per hour. Team 2 is staffed with more experienced employees and processes an average of 60 seats per hour.

   Kobayashi Motors has an efficient just-in-time production and inventory system based on the use of kanban cards. Thus, Kobayashi management insists on a daily delivery of 1200 motorcycle seats from Lambda. Currently, the normal operation period for each Lambda team is 8 hours. The production manager of Lambda is trying to determine the best daily operation hours to establish for the two teams in order to achieve the following goals:

P_1: Produce and deliver 1200 motorcycle seats daily to Kobayashi.
P_2: Limit the daily overtime operation hours of team 2 to 3 hours.
P_3: Minimize the daily overtime operation hours of each team as much as possible. Assign differential weights based on the relative cost of overtime.
P_4: Minimize any underutilization of the regular daily operation hours of each team. Assign differential weights based on the relative productivity rate.

a. Formulate a goal programming model for this problem.
b. Solve the problem by using the graphical method.

13. The trust department of the First Federal Bank is attempting to invest $4 million in various investment alternatives. Currently, the department is considering the following alternatives: stock options, real estate (a local shopping center complex), bonds, mutual funds, and gold futures. Real estate, bonds, and mutual funds yield an estimated 17%, 10%, and 8%, respectively. Since stock options and gold futures are speculative, no definite return can be estimated.

The trust department has established the following goals, in order of their importance.

P_1: Minimize the risk by diversifying the investments. No more than 40% of the total investment should be in any one alternative.
P_2: Since there is a rumor that gold will be scarce in the future, try to invest at least 5% of the total investment in gold futures.
P_3: Attempt to earn at least 5% annual return from the total investment.
P_4: Limit the amount invested in speculative ventures (stock options and gold futures) to 30% of the liquid investments (bonds and mutual funds).

Formulate a goal programming model that will determine the amount of money to be invested in each of the various alternatives.

14. A midwestern granary specializes in the sale of wheat. The firm has definite information concerning the cost at which it can buy wheat and the price at which it can sell wheat during the next four months. The amount of wheat that can be sold is restricted by the storage capacity of the firm. The normal capacity of the firm's storage facility is 3000 bushels (overloading of 2000 bushels is allowed in emergencies). The estimated cost, c_i, and the price, p_i, for the next four months are given as follows:

	Months			
	1	2	3	4
Cost (c_i)	$4	4	4	7
Price (p_i)	$6	7	5	6

The quantity of the purchase is assumed to be based entirely on the amount of revenue generated from sales. It is also assumed that sales are made at the beginning of the month, followed by purchases. At the beginning of the first month, there are 2000 bushels of wheat in the warehouse. The president of the firm has the following multiple goals, listed in descending order with respect to what he desires to achieve in the next four months:

1. In the first month, only the normal capacity of the warehouse should be used.
2. The firm should have at least $20,000 for purchases at the beginning of the fourth month.
3. The firm should reserve at least $2000 in each month for emergency purposes.
4. The firm should maximize total profit during the entire four-month period.

Formulate a goal programming model for this problem.

15. A clothing store, which is a branch of a larger store in a nearby city, specializes in sales of men's quality clothing. The store is presently operating with the full-time manager, who works on salary, and 8 part-time salespeople, who earn an hourly wage of $4.20 plus a 20% discount on any clothes they purchase in the store. Among the part-time salespeople, four are experienced in selling men's clothing and the others are new to the job.

Each month the store receives a sales quota. The manager breaks it down into her quota and the quota for the part-time salespeople as a group. For the next month, the store has received a sales quota of $75,000. The manager has allotted $39,000 to herself and $36,000 to the part-time staff. Records of past experience indicate that the manager sells an average of $163.20 worth of clothing per hour. The 4 experienced part-time salespeople sell an average of $96.75 per hour, and the inexperienced salespeople sell an average of $78.75 per hour. The manager has regularly been working 188 hours per month, and each part-time salesperson 50 hours. The manager realizes, however, that she has been putting in many extra hours to meet the monthly quotas. She would like to limit her overtime hours to 44 so that the part-time salespeople get enough hours to meet their quota and to earn sufficient wages.

As an incentive to the manager and other employees, the main store offers bonus and commission plans. The manager receives a 3% bonus on the total sales volume that the store achieves above its sales quota for each month. The manager's objective is to earn an average of $150 per month from this bonus plan. The part-time salespeople receive a 5% commission on all sales that they make over their quota. The bonus is then split equally among the salespeople. The manager feels that if part-time salespeople put forth a determined effort, they should be able to earn about $30 each in additional commission per month. The manager's goals are listed below in order of importance:

1. The store must meet its sales quota of $75,000 for the month.
2. The manager desires to meet her sales quota of $39,000 for the month.
3. The manager would like to limit her overtime for the month to 44 hours.
4. The part-time salespeople must meet their group sales quota of $36,000 for the month.
5. The manager wants the part-time salespeople to work a total of at least 400 hours for the month.
6. The manager would like to earn $150 in bonus and would like to see the part-time salespeople earn a commission of $30 each.

7. If possible, the manager would like to work no more than 188 hours for the month.

8. The manager wants to minimize the total extra hours that part-time salespeople work in the month.

Formulate a goal programming model for this problem.

16. Your grandmother has just won $200,000 in a lottery. Because of her advanced age, you plan to "have fun" investing her winnings for her in the following five alternatives: stock options, real estate, bonds, savings accounts, and diamonds. Real estate and bonds yield an estimated 15% and 10% per year, respectively, while the savings account yields 6%. Since options and diamonds are risky, you cannot assume they will have any yield. You have established the following goals, in order of importance.

1. Minimize the risk by diversifying the investment. No more than 40% of the total investment should be in any one plan.

2. Since diamonds are rumored to be profitable, try to invest at least $50,000 in this plan.

3. Do not invest more in speculative ventures (options and diamonds) than is invested in safer plans.

4. Guarantee that your grandmother will earn an annual yield of at least $25,000 from the investments.

Formulate a goal programming model that will determine the amount of money to be invested in the various plans.

17. Pamela Stein is a dealer of home heating oil in a medium-sized city. She owns a storage tank with a capacity of 10,000 gallons of oil that initially has 4,000 gallons in it. Stein can purchase oil each month either for distribution during the month or for storage for later use. The selling price, purchasing cost, and expected demand during each month are shown in the following table.

	Months		
Home Heating Oil	1	2	3
Selling price (¢/gal)	47	50	52
Purchasing cost (¢/gal)	40	42	45
Expected demand (gal)	6000	8000	7000

Pamela Stein has set the following goals, listed in the order of their importance.

1. Avoid purchasing over 5,000 gallons each month.

2. Meet the demand each month.

3. Maximize total profit during the entire 3-month period.

The oil is assumed to be available for purchase at the beginning of each month, but can be sold throughout the month. Formulate a goal programming model and solve it using AB:QM.

18. The local school district was handed a special order from the state supreme court stating that racial balance must be achieved among the three schools in the district through extensive busing of pupils. The problem is summarized as follows:

Area	School			Pupils
	A	B	C	
1	$ 4	$ 8	$ 8	400 white 200 black
2	16	24	16	300 white 300 black
3	8	16	24	100 white 500 black
Capacity	500	600	400	

The dollar amounts represent the busing cost per pupil from each area to each school. The capacity figures reflect the normal capacity at which the school can provide "quality education." The number of children in each area is divided into two groups, white and black.

The local school district has established the following goals, in order of importance:

1. Busing for more than 30 minutes (at a cost of $20 or more) should be avoided.
2. Every child should be provided a quality education.
3. Racial balance should be achieved among schools.
4. Overcrowding should be equally (proportionally) shared among schools.
5. Total transportation cost should be minimized.

Formulate a goal programming model that will determine the optimal busing schedule for the children in the district.

19. The local zoo has received a donation of $100,000 from the Micheline Penniford Foundation, with several strings attached. In order to receive the funds, the zoo's management must demonstrate compliance with the donor's wishes. The zoo has also established its own priorities, and will consider these once the donation stipulations are met.

The foundation's requirements are as follows:

1. At least 25% of the funds should be used to acquire unusual or attractive animals, preferably from an endangered species.
2. No more than 15% of the funds may be used for administrative costs.
3. Continuing education and training of zoo staff should receive at least $5,000.
4. Facilities for new animals acquired using donation funds should cost no more than the animals themselves.

The zoo's priorities include

1. Provide for ongoing operational needs (current annual shortfall $25,000).
2. Remodel tiger enclosure (up to $15,000).

3. Improve parking lot and provide more access ramps (up to $20,000).

4. Acquire additional animals with appropriate facilities (no real limit).

In order to avoid the issue of allocation of the operating deficit, the zoo has decided that the entire amount will be categorized as administrative costs. An existing ordered wish list of animals will serve to select individual acquisitions, so they need not be considered here. The zoo has a standing policy of buying new animals only if it can provide appropriate facilities, which on average cost 80% of the amount spent on the animals themselves; this policy should take precedence over all other considerations.

Formulate and solve a goal programming model that accurately represents the foundation's requirements and the zoo's priorities. Ensure that all of the funds are allocated.

20. The mergers and acquisitions manager at Great Eastern Bank of San Fernando has received initial approval for creation of an international M&A specialist team. Final approval has been withheld pending a detailed explanation of the composition of the proposed team. Chris, the M&A manager, has chosen to evaluate this problem from a mathematical programming perspective, as numerical results have tended to generate less contention than have subjective opinions.

Chris initially felt an assignment formulation would be appropriate, given the following characteristics of potential team members:

	Characteristic						
Candidate	Target Identity	Target Evaluation	Speed	Accuracy	International Experience	Past Profit	Years with Firm
Albert	poor	excellent	average	good	good	+2.23	6
Bernice	average	good	average	good	poor	+1.10	2
Chris	good	excellent	good	excellent	average	+2.78	12
Davera	average	average	good	average	excellent	−0.43	4
Efraim	good	good	poor	excellent	average	+0.87	8
Francesca	excellent	average	good	good	good	−0.02	5
Gale	average	average	average	average	average	+0.33	2
Hiroshi	excellent	good	poor	excellent	good	+1.43	9
Iskander	poor	good	good	average	excellent	+1.12	5
Javier	good	poor	excellent	good	average	−1.84	1

The characteristics describe each candidate's ability to identify targets and to evaluate targets; the candidate's speed, accuracy, and international experience; and their profit qualifications, using a comparative four-point rating scheme. Chris derived these ratings from considerable contact with these individuals and does not feel they exhibit undue subjective influences. Past profit, as recorded in the table, gives the candidate's past projects' standard deviation from the average profitability of all firm M&A projects over the past five years. The last item represents the candidate's number of years with the firm.

Chris wishes to achieve a balanced team, with an overall goal of optimizing the projects that are identified and pursued. However, profit maximization cannot be achieved directly, as the future performance of each candidate cannot be accurately predicted. Thus, Chris has prepared the following list of objectives, in order of importance.

1. Limit team size to 4 or 5 people (only).
2. Assure that the team's ability to identify and evaluate targets is "excellent" (by inclusion of at least one "excellent" candidate in each characteristic).
3. Assure that the team's speed and accuracy are at least "good" (by inclusion of at least one "good" or "excellent" candidate in each characteristic).
4. Include at least two "good" or "excellent" candidates in terms of international experience.
5. Make the team's combined past average profitability at least one standard deviation higher than the firm's average.
6. Include Chris on the international team.
7. Limit the team to 4 members.

Given the multiple objective nature of this problem, as well as the uncertainty of finding a feasible optimal solution that satisfies all of the objectives simultaneously, Chris decided to use goal programming, but is unsure of how to formulate the model. Your task is to provide Chris with the GP model. If you wish to solve the problem, note that a zero-one solution is required.

21. Given the following final simplex tableau, analyze the solution in terms of the meaning of the solution, goal attainment, goal conflicts, and trade-offs.

c_b	c_j basis	b_i^*	x_1	x_2	P_1 d_1^-	$3P_2$ d_2^-	$2P_2$ d_3^-	P_3 d_1^+	d_2^+	d_3^+
0	x_2	28.0	0	1.0	0	0	1.0	0	0	−1.0
0	x_1	24.0	1.0	0	0	1.0	0	0	−1.0	0
P_3	d_1^+	12.0	0	0	−1.0	1.0	1.0	1.0	−1.0	−1.0
	P_3	12.0	0	0	−1.0	1.0	1.0	0	−1.0	−1.0
$z_j - c_j$	P_2	0	0	0	0	−3.0	−2.0	0	0	0
	P_1	0	0	0	−1.0	0	0	0	0	0

22. Solve the following goal programming problem by using the modified simplex method.

Minimize $Z = P_1 d_2^- + P_2 d_1^- + P_3 d_1^+ + P_4 d_3^-$

subject to

$$x_1 + x_2 + d_1^- - d_1^+ = 80$$
$$x_1 + d_2^- - d_2^+ = 100$$
$$x_2 + d_3^- - d_3^+ = 45$$
$$x_j, d_i^-, d_i^+ \geq 0$$

23. Solve the following goal programming problem by using the modified simplex method.

Minimize $Z = P_1 d_1^- + P_2 d_2^+ + 6P_3 d_3^+ + 5P_3 d_4^+ + 6P_4 d_4^- + 5P_4 d_3^-$

subject to
$$5x_1 + 6x_2 + d_1^- - d_1^+ = 120$$
$$x_2 + d_2^- - d_2^+ = 11$$
$$x_1 + d_3^- - d_3^+ = 8$$
$$x_2 + d_4^- - d_4^+ = 8$$
$$x_j, d_i^-, d_i^+ \geqslant 0$$

24. Solve the following goal programming problem by using the modified simplex method.

Minimize $Z = P_1 d_1^- + P_2 d_3^+ + P_3 d_2^+$

subject to
$$5x_1 + 10x_2 + d_1^- - d_1^+ = 10{,}000$$
$$x_1 + d_2^- - d_2^+ = 700$$
$$x_2 + d_3^- - d_3^+ = 600$$
$$x_j, d_i^-, d_i^+ \geqslant 0$$

25. First West Chemical, Inc. produces two chemical ingredients for pharmaceutical firms: Formula X and Formula Y. Production of each ingredient requires two processes. A unit of Formula X requires 4 hours in process 1 and 3 hours in process 2. A unit of Formula Y requires 2 hours in process 1 and 5 hours in process 2. The maximum available production times for the two processes are as follows: process 1, 70 hours; process 2, 60 hours.

   The production of Formula X results in 1 unit of a by-product XZ for each 4 units of X. The production process for Formula Y yields 5 units of a by-product YK for each unit of Formula Y. The unit profits for Formulas X and Y are $10,000 and $15,000, respectively. By-product XZ yields a $6000 unit profit. By-product YK yields a $3000 unit profit for up to 15 units. Because of the limited market and the danger involved in handling the material, however, any by-product YK in excess of 15 units must be destroyed at a unit cost of $4000.

   The management of First West Chemical has established the following goals, in the order of their importance:

   1. Avoid any underutilization of the normal operation hours of each of the two processes.
   2. Meet the outstanding order for 8 units of Formula X and 7 units of Formula Y.
   3. Limit any overtime operation of each of the two production processes to 10 hours.
   4. Achieve a profit goal of $220,000.
   5. Limit the production of by-product YK to 15 units, if possible.
   6. Minimize the overtime operation of the production processes as much as possible.

   Formulate this problem as a goal programming model.

26. A. J. Fiberglass Company specializes in producing fiberglass canoes. The company supplies this single product to 4 recreation-sports stores at different locations from 3 warehouses also at different locations. The company's new product, Courageous, has received extremely favorable reviews from several sports and consumer group magazines for its balance, durability, and weight. Because of the unexpected but pleasant surge in the popularity of this model, the company will be unable to fill the store

orders. Management has decided that certain store orders must be satisfied, even at the expense of others.

To avoid gross inequity, management would like to balance the proportion of demand satisfied among those stores whose orders could not be fully met. Also, the company's agreement with the local teamsters' union requires that A. J. Fiberglass meet certain minimum transportation levels along certain established routes. Finally, several of the routes over which the product might be shipped are extremely hazardous because of a recent flood and mudslides, so these routes should be avoided.

The A. J. Fiberglass transportation problem is summarized in the following tableau. Decision x_{ij} represents the quantity of Courageous canoes to be transported from the ith warehouse to the jth store.

Warehouse \ Store	1	2	3	4	Supply
1	5 x_{11}	2 x_{12}	6 x_{13}	7 x_{14}	300
2	3 x_{21}	5 x_{22}	4 x_{23}	6 x_{24}	200
3	4 x_{31}	5 x_{32}	2 x_{33}	3 x_{34}	400
Demand	200	100	450	250	1000 / 900

The management of A. J. Fiberglass has set the following goals, in the order of their importance.

1. Fill the order of store 4. A. J. Fiberglass has a guaranteed delivery agreement with this charter customer.
2. Meet the agreement with the teamsters' union by transporting at least 100 canoes over the route from warehouse 3 to store 1.
3. Fill at least 80% of the orders from each store.
4. Keep the total transportation costs to no more than 110% of the budgeted amount of $3245.
5. Avoid the hazardous transportation route from warehouse 2 to store 4.
6. Achieve equity by trying to balance the proportion of orders satisfied between two new customers, stores 1 and 3.
7. Minimize total transportation costs for the problem.

a. If the company were simply trying to minimize total transportation cost, how should it set up a goal programming model?
b. Formulate a goal programming model for the A. J. Fiberglass transportation problem.

27. Advanced Computer Devices, Inc. produces large, expensive computers for government agencies and large business firms. The company has just received notification

that it has been awarded a contract from the U.S. government for 34 new supercom-puters. The contract specifies the required delivery schedule for the computers.

The manufacturing facility is relatively small, and thus it can handle only one production contract at a time. The company, however, has some flexibility. It can operate the manufacturing facility on an overtime basis to achieve a production level beyond its normal production capacity. It can also temporarily lay off, if necessary, some short-tenured regular production workers, down to about 80% of normal capacity. The firm's production capacity and contracted delivery schedule for the next 5 months are as follows:

| Month | Production Capacity | | Delivery Schedule |
	Regular Time	Overtime	
1	7	3	3
2	8	3	8
3	9	3	10
4	10	3	13

The accounting department has analyzed the expected variable, fixed, and over-head costs of producing a computer during each month of the 4-month period. Because of the learning curve effect, the variable cost decreases for units produced on regular time, but this effect is not operative in overtime production. The produc-tion cost per computer for the 4 months (in millions of dollars) is shown below.

| Month | Per Unit Production Cost | |
	Regular Time	Overtime
1	$4.0	$4.6
2	3.9	4.6
3	3.8	4.6
4	3.8	4.6

The government contract calls for a price of $5 million per computer delivered on time. Thus, it is extremely important to meet the delivery schedule by producing on regular production time. The company has the following goals, in the order of their importance:

1. Operate within the limits of production capacity during the 4-month period.
2. Meet the contracted delivery schedule.
3. Operate at or above the 80% level of regular time production capacity.
4. Maximize the total profit from the government contract.

Formulate a goal programming model that will determine the computer production schedule at Advanced Computer Devices, Inc. for the 4-month period.

28. A textile company produces two types of linen materials, a strong upholstery material (x_1) and regular dress material (x_2). The goal programming formulation and an abstract from the output of AB:QM are presented below.

$$\text{Minimize } Z = P_1d_1^- + P_2d_4^+ + (\quad)P_3d_2^- + (\quad)P_3d_3^- + P_4d_1^+$$

subject to:

$$c_1 x_1 + x_2 + d_1^- - d_1^+ = 80 \quad \text{(regular labor hours/week)}$$
$$c_2 x_1 + \qquad d_2^- - d_2^+ = 70 \quad \text{(max sales/week, unit: 1000 yards)}$$
$$c_3 \qquad x_2 + d_3^- - d_3^+ = 45 \quad \text{(max sales/week, unit: 1000 yards)}$$
$$c_4 x_1 + x_2 + d_4^- - d_4^+ = (\quad) \text{(labor hours/week)}$$

Constraint	RHS	d^+	d^-	Variable	Solution	Priority	Nonachievement
C_1	80	10	0	x_2	( )	P_1	( )
C_2	70	0	0	x_1	70	P_2	( )
C_3	45	0	25			P_3	( )
C_4	90	0	0			P_4	( )

According to the accounting department, the approximate profit from a yard of upholstery material is $5.00, while that from a yard of dress material is $3.00. The president of the company feels that overtime operation of the plant of more than 10 hours per week should be avoided because of the accompanying acceleration of costs.

Interpret the priority structure in plain English. (Do not answer in terms of under- or overachievement.)

a. Priority 1:
b. Priority 2:
c. Priority 3:
d. Priority 4:
e. Based on the information above, assign the weights in the objective function.
f. What is the RHS value of the fourth constraint?
g. Fill in the blank spaces of the priority achievement table. If fully achieved, answer 0; otherwise, answer with the under or over achievement amount.
h. How many yards of the regular dress material should be produced per week?
i. Based on the optimal solution, how much would the company obtain in terms of weekly profit?
j. Identify the conflicting goals. Among them, identify the goal achieved by the model.

29. Central Orthopedic Clinic is concerned with the treatment of patients in need of orthopedic care on an outpatient basis. Currently, the clinic has staff personnel as listed in the table on page 681.

The doctors schedule their services so that they can see the majority of their patients at the clinic. However, they are also responsible for filling the orthopedic needs of two hospitals in town, as well as conducting a clinic for the treatment of those unable to pay for private treatment. The doctors' billings are handled through the clinic for all their services and provide the sole income of the business itself.

Personnel Type	Number of Employees
Orthopedic surgeon	6
Full-time nurse	1
Part-time nurse	2
Full-time x-ray technician	1
Part-time x-ray technician	2
Business manager	1
Secretary	6
Receptionist	2
Office staff	4
Maintenance staff	2

The following table gives the employees' average working hours per week and per year, average salaries per hour before and after the 7% salary increase proposed for the next year, and the priority of the salary increase for each personnel type. The physicians receive salaries, but their average hourly salaries are computed based on their hours of work.

*Clinic Personnel, Working Hours, and Wages**

Position	Hours/ Week	Total Hours/ Position/Year	Salary/ Hour	Salary After 7% Increase	Priority for Wage Increase
Orthopedic surgeon	65 ea	20,280	$50.00	$53.50	10th
Full-time nurse	40	2080	10.00	10.70	5th
Part-time nurse	20 ea	2080	9.00	9.63	6th
Full-time x-ray tech	40	2080	8.00	8.56	1st
Part-time x-ray tech	20 ea	2080	8.00	8.56	7th
Business manager	40	2080	20.00	21.40	9th
Secretary	40 ea	12,480	5.00	5.35	2d
Office staff	40 ea	8320	4.50	4.82	4th
Receptionist	40 ea	4160	4.50	4.82	3d
Maintenance staff	14 ea	1456	4.00	4.28	8th

*Salaries are averages of all personnel in each position category.

Information concerning operating revenues, expenses, the number of patients at the clinic, and reserves for other expenses is provided in the table on page 682. For the coming year, all expenses are expected to increase by 5%. However, the proposed average salary increase for personnel is set at 7%.

The Board of Directors of the clinic has established the following goals, in order of priority:

1. Provide job security for all personnel by assigning regular working hours to each personnel type.
2. Provide a 7% salary increase to all personnel (assign differential weights).
3. Provide funds to meet operating expenses (X-ray, medical supplies, and administrative and miscellaneous) on a per patient basis.
4. Provide funds for equipment replacement.

*Patients, Expenses, and Equipment Replacement**

Patients:

Total patients last year	27,850
Expected increase for coming year (5%)	1393
Total expected patients for planning year	29,243
Average charge per patient	$80.00

Expenses:

	Total for the Past Year	Average per Patient	Average per Patient After 5% Increase
X-ray	$ 42,000.00	$ 1.51	$ 1.59
Medical supplies	39,000.00	1.40	1.47
Administrative and miscellaneous	325,000.00	11.67	12.25

Reserves for Other Expenses:

X-ray replacement	$40,000	
Typewriter	4500	
Dictaphone	4000	
Retirement fund	15% of total yearly salaries	
Continuing education of doctors, nurses	16,000	(14,000 last year)

*Figures are based on totals as of December 31 of last year.

5. Provide reserves for the retirement fund.
6. Provide funds for the continuing education fund.
7. Achieve at least a $150,000 profit from the clinic operation.

   Formulate a goal programming model for the next year's operation of Central Orthopedic Clinic by identifying the following: New hourly salary for each personnel type, required expenses, reserves, average number of working hours required per year for each personnel type, and operating expenses per patient.

30. Senator Hobson has hired Scientific Management Consulting, Inc. to advise him on his bid for reelection. After considering the available options and the legal restrictions affecting the reelection campaign, the consultants have prepared a goal programming model with the intention of determining the optimal number of each type of advertisement to purchase. The three options available to Senator Hobson are television ($x1$), radio ($x2$), and newspaper ($x3$) ads. When the output on pages 683–684 was presented to the Senator, he posed a series of questions, which it is your task to answer.

    a. What is the top priority?
    b. What is the second priority supposed to accomplish?
    c. Will this be accomplished?
    d. How much money will be spent?
    e. How many people will be reached?
    f. Why is there no $d+7$ shown?
    g. How many television ads will be placed?
    h. What is the upper limit on the number of radio ads?

```
Program: Goal Programming


Problem Title : Senator Hobson's Reelection Campaign


##### Input Data #####


Min Z = 1P1d+1 + 1P2d-2 + 1P2d-3 + 1P2d-4 + 1P3d+5 + 1P4d+6 + 1P5d-7


Subject to


C1   850x1 + 550x2 + 375x3 + d-1 - d+1 = 100000  ----> total funds available
C2   1x1 + d-2 - d+2 = 30  ------------------------> number of TV ads
C3   1x2 + d-3 - d+3 = 40  ------------------------> number of radio ads
C4   1x3 + d-4 - d+4 = 60  ------------------------> number of newspaper ads
C5   850x1 + 550x2 + 375x3 + d-5 - d+5 = 75000  -----> desired spending level
C6   1x1 + d-6 - d+6 = 75  ------------------------> number of radio ads
C7   9000x1 + 5000x2 + 3750x3 + d-7 - d+7 = 1250000 -> number of people reached


##### Program Output #####

Final Solution Tableau at Iteration   4

------------------------------------------------------------------------------
     \Cj               0        0        0        0       1P2      1P2
     Cb\  Basis    Bi     x1       x2       x3      d-1      d-2      d-3
------------------------------------------------------------------------------
      0   d-1  25000.000  0.000    0.000    0.000    1.000    0.000    0.000
      0   x1      35.882  1.000    0.000    0.000    0.000    0.000   -0.647
      0   x2      40.000  0.000    1.000    0.000    0.000    0.000    1.000
      0   x3      60.000  0.000    0.000    1.000    0.000    0.000    0.000
      0   d+2      5.882  0.000    0.000    0.000    0.000   -1.000   -0.647
      0   d-6     39.118  0.000    0.000    0.000    0.000    0.000    0.647
     1P5   d-7 502058.824 0.000    0.000    0.000    0.000    0.000  823.529
------------------------------------------------------------------------------
     Zj-Cj 1P5 502058.824 0.000    0.000    0.000    0.000    0.000  823.529
           1P4    0.000   0.000    0.000    0.000    0.000    0.000    0.000
           1P3    0.000   0.000    0.000    0.000    0.000    0.000    0.000
           1P2    0.000   0.000    0.000    0.000    0.000   -1.000   -1.000
           1P1    0.000   0.000    0.000    0.000    0.000    0.000    0.000
------------------------------------------------------------------------------


------------------------------------------------------------------------------
     \Cj              1P2       0        0       1P5      1P1       0
     Cb\  Basis    Bi     d-4      d-5      d-6      d-7      d+1      d+2
------------------------------------------------------------------------------
      0   d-1  25000.000  0.000   -1.000    0.000    0.000   -1.000    0.000
      0   x1      35.882 -0.441    0.001    0.000    0.000    0.000    0.000
      0   x2      40.000  0.000    0.000    0.000    0.000    0.000    0.000
      0   x3      60.000  1.000    0.000    0.000    0.000    0.000    0.000
      0   d+2      5.882 -0.441    0.001    0.000    0.000    0.000    1.000
      0   d-6     39.118  0.441   -0.001    1.000    0.000    0.000    0.000
     1P5   d-7 502058.824 220.588 -10.588   0.000    1.000    0.000    0.000
------------------------------------------------------------------------------
     Zj-Cj 1P5 502058.824 220.588 -10.588   0.000    0.000    0.000    0.000
           1P4    0.000   0.000    0.000    0.000    0.000    0.000    0.000
           1P3    0.000   0.000    0.000    0.000    0.000    0.000    0.000
           1P2    0.000  -1.000    0.000    0.000    0.000    0.000    0.000
           1P1    0.000   0.000    0.000    0.000    0.000   -1.000    0.000
------------------------------------------------------------------------------
```

```
  \Cj                        0         0        1P3       1P4        0
  Cb\   Basis    Bi         d+3       d+4       d+5       d+6       d+7
  --------------------------------------------------------------------
    0   d-1  25000.000     0.000     0.000     1.000     0.000     0.000
    0   x1      35.882     0.647     0.441    -0.001     0.000     0.000
    0   x2      40.000    -1.000     0.000     0.000     0.000     0.000
    0   x3      60.000     0.000    -1.000     0.000     0.000     0.000
    0   d+2      5.882     0.647     0.441    -0.001     0.000     0.000
    0   d-6     39.118    -0.647    -0.441     0.001    -1.000     0.000
  1P5   d-7 502058.824  -823.529  -220.588    10.588     0.000    -1.000
  --------------------------------------------------------------------
  Zj-Cj  1P5 502058.824 -823.529  -220.588    10.588     0.000    -1.000
         1P4      0.000     0.000     0.000     0.000    -1.000     0.000
         1P3      0.000     0.000     0.000    -1.000     0.000     0.000
         1P2      0.000     0.000     0.000     0.000     0.000     0.000
         1P1      0.000     0.000     0.000     0.000     0.000     0.000
```

Analysis of deviations
```
----------------------------------------------------
Constraint  RHS Value       d+          d-
----------------------------------------------------
    C1      100000.000     0.000   25000.000
    C2          30.000     5.882       0.000
    C3          40.000     0.000       0.000
    C4          60.000     0.000       0.000
    C5       75000.000     0.000       0.000
    C6          75.000     0.000      39.118
    C7     1250000.000     0.000  502058.824
----------------------------------------------------
```

Analysis of decision variables
```
-----------------------------------
Variable        Solution Value
-----------------------------------
   X1               35.882
   X2               40.000
   X3               60.000
-----------------------------------
```

Analysis of the objective function
```
-----------------------------------
Priority        Nonachievement
-----------------------------------
   P1                0.000
   P2                0.000
   P3                0.000
   P4                0.000
   P5            502058.824
-----------------------------------
```

***** End of Output *****

i. What does the 25,000 in the d− column of the deviations analysis mean?

j. How many people does a radio ad reach?

k. How much does one newspaper ad cost?

l. How much money will be left over?

m. What does the P5 value in the Nonachievement column of the objective function analysis mean?

n. If d−4 equaled 12, how many newspaper ads would be used?

o. If there were more money in the total budget, how many more people could be reached?

p. What do the marginal substitution rates in the goal conflict analysis indicate?

q. If we decided to spend another $25,000, how many more people would be reached? Which ad type(s) and how many additional ads would be purchased? How would the model be rewritten to accommodate this desire?

r. If a proportionality constraint were added, requiring a ratio among the three types of ads, would this decrease the number of people reached?

s. If reaching the entire populace were the top priority and cost minimization were second, how much would be spent? Which ad types and quantities would be used?

31. The local branch of the International Youth Clubs Association is preparing for its annual candy sales drive. Materials for the drive have been donated by local candy stores, which have given the association the option of purchasing additional materials (as described in several questions below). The circumstances of the sale have been described in the form of a goal programming model, resulting in the following computer printout. Three sizes of boxes may be prepared: small (x1), medium (x2), and large (x3).

a. What is the top priority?

b. How many chocolates are in a medium-size box?

```
Program: Goal Programming


Problem Title : Annual Candy Sales Drive


***** Input Data *****


Min Z = 0.09P3d+1 + 0.14P3d+2 + 1P5d-2 + 0.21P3d+3 + 1P6d-4 + 1P1d-5 + 1P4d-6 + 1P2d+7


Subject to

C1    3x1 + 6x2 + 4x3 + d-1 - d+1 = 160   ----------> chocolates available
C2    4x1 + 2x2 + 3x3 + d-2 - d+2 = 300   ----------> cremes available
C3    2x1 + 1x2 + 2x3 + d-3 - d+3 = 70    ----------> fudges available
C4    1.75x1 + 2.5x2 + 3.25x3 + d-4 - d+4 = 99999 -> sales goal
C5    1x1 + d-5 - d+5 = 12                ----------------> advance order
C6    1x3 + d-6 - d+6 = 20                ----------------> advance order
C7    1x1 + 1x2 + 1x3 + d-7 - d+7 = 45    ----------> empty boxes available


***** Program Output *****

Analysis of deviations
-----------------------------------
Constraint  RHS Value      d+        d-
-----------------------------------
   C1        160.000     0.000     8.000
   C2        300.000     0.000   180.000
   C3         70.000     0.000     0.000
   C4      99999.000     0.000 99898.000
   C5         12.000     0.000     0.000
   C6         20.000     0.000     0.000
   C7         45.000     0.000     7.000
-----------------------------------
```

```
Analysis of decision variables
--------------------------------
Variable        Solution Value
--------------------------------
   X1               12.000
   X2                6.000
   X3               20.000
--------------------------------


Analysis of the objective function
----------------------------------
Priority            Nonachievement
----------------------------------
   P1                  0.000
   P2                  0.000
   P3                  0.000
   P4                  0.000
   P5                180.000
   P6              99898.000
----------------------------------

***** End of Output *****
```

c. How many empty boxes will be left over?

d. Will there be any candies left over? If so, which ones, and how many of each?

e. Are there any system constraints in this model? If so, which one(s)?

f. What is the sales goal?

g. What would be the total sales obtained using this solution?

h. Of the four resources, which is the hardest to obtain?

i. What does the third priority attempt to achieve?

j. What is a probable meaning of the three weights in the objective function?

k. What is a reasonable explanation for the fifth priority?

l. What is the meaning of the P6 value in the Nonachievement column of the objective function analysis?

m. If the club were offered a dozen empty boxes at $.50 each, should they buy them? Why or why not?

n. How many of each type of box should be made up?

32. Answer the following questions concerning the computer solution (pp. 687–688) of the multiperiod investment problem presented as Example 13.5.

a. What investment options will be utilized? Specify the types of investments, the periods, and the amounts of the investments.

b. Describe the goal achievement.

c. What will be the total value of the investment at the end of the sixth year?

d. Plot the investment decisions on the available investments scheme (Figure 13.1) by highlighting the optimal decisions.

e. Confirm the adherence of the solution above to the six system constraints.

f. Did the first three goals have any practical impact on the final solution?

g. Would the given solution have been possible if the idle fund variables (I_j) had not been included in the model?

```
Program: Goal Programming

Problem Title : Example 13.5 Multiperiod Investment Problem

##### Input Data #####

Min Z = 1P1d+7 + 1P2d-8 + 1P3d-9 + 1P4d-10

Subject to

C1    1S1 + 1B1 + 1I1 = 1000000
C2    1S2 + 1B2 + 1C2 - 1I1 + 1I2 = 0
C3    -1.2S1 + 1S3 + 1B3 - 1I2 + 1I3 = 0
C4    -1.2S2 + 1S4 - 1.4B1 + 1B4 - 1I3 + 1I4 = 0
C5    -1.2S3 + 1S5 - 1.4B2 + 1R5 - 1I4 + 1I5 = 0
C6    -1.2S4 - 1.4B3 - 1.8C2 - 1.1R5 + 1R6 - 1I5 + 1I6 = 0
C7    .6S1 + .6S2 + .6S3 + .6S4 + .6S5 + .6B1 + .6B2 + .6B3 + .6B4 - .4C2
      - .4R5 - .4R6 + d-7 - d+7 = 0
C8    -.25S1 - .25S2 - .25S3 - .25S4 - .25S5 - .25B1 - .25B2 - .25B3
      - .25B4 + .75C2 - .25R5 - .25R6 + d-8 - d+8 = 0
C9    1R5 + 1R6 + d-9 - d+9 = 300000
C10   1.2S5 + 1.4B4 + 1.1R6 + 1I6 + d-10 - d+10 = 500000000


##### Program Output #####

Analysis of deviations
-------------------------------------------------------
Constraint  RHS Value          d+              d-
-------------------------------------------------------
     C1    1000000.000        0.000           0.000
     C2          0.000        0.000           0.000
     C3          0.000        0.000           0.000
     C4          0.000        0.000           0.000
     C5          0.000        0.000           0.000
     C6          0.000        0.000           0.000
     C7          0.000        0.000      1120000.000
     C8          0.000   300000.000           0.000
     C9     300000.000  1500000.000           0.000
    C10  500000000.000        0.000    498020000.000
-------------------------------------------------------


Analysis of decision variables
-------------------------------------
Variable         Solution Value
-------------------------------------
    S1               0.000
    S2               0.000
    S3               0.000
    S4               0.000
    S5               0.000
    B1               0.000
    B2               0.000
    B3               0.000
    B4               0.000
    C2         1000000.000
    R5               0.000
    R6         1800000.000
    I1         1000000.000
    I2               0.000
    I3               0.000
    I4               0.000
    I5               0.000
    I6               0.000
-------------------------------------
```

```
Analysis of the objective function
-----------------------------------
Priority             Nonachievement
-----------------------------------
   P1                     0.000
   P2                     0.000
   P3                     0.000
   P4              498020000.000
-----------------------------------


##### End of Output #####
```

h. Determine the optimal selection of investments, if the idle fund variables (Ij) were excluded. Use the complete enumeration method (there are only five alternative solution sets). What is the cost of failing to consider the idle fund?

i. Explain the value of each of the four deviational variables present in the final solution.

j. Describe the impact of rearranging the priorities so that the fourth goal (maximization) becomes the first goal.

k. Having considered a model with twelve investment alternatives that resulted in only two selections, describe several potential constraints that could be added to balance the results.

33. The Local Art League Gallery is attempting to allocate its exhibition space for the coming month among six local artists. Substantial past sales data have been used to derive pertinent information. The decision variables represent the square feet of display space allocated to each of the artists.

a. The first two constraints limit the available space to 40% and 30% of the gallery's wall space, respectively. The purpose of these constraints is to maintain

```
Program: Goal Programming

Problem Title : Art Gallery Wall Space Allocation

##### Input Data #####

Min Z = 1P2d+1 + 1P6d+2 + 1P4d-2 + 1P5d+3 + 1P5d-3 + 1P5d+4 + 1P5d-4 + 1P5d+5
      + 1P5d-5 + 1P5d+6 + 1P5d-6 + 1P5d+7 + 1P5d-7 + 1P8d-8 + 1P3d-9 + 1P3d-10 + 1P7d-11

Subject to

C1    1x1 + 1x2 + 1x3 + 1x4 + 1x5 + 1x6 + d-1 - d+1 = 1120  ---------> use 40% of space
C2    1x1 + 1x2 + 1x3 + 1x4 + 1x5 + 1x6 + d-2 - d+2 = 840   ---------> use 30% of space
C3    1x1 - 1x2 + d-3 - d+3 = 0   -------------------------------------+
C4    1x2 - 1x3 + d-4 - d+4 = 0   -------------------------------------\
C5    1x3 - 1x4 + d-5 - d+5 = 0   -------------------------------------> balancing constraint
C6    1x4 - 1x5 + d-6 - d+6 = 0   -------------------------------------/
C7    1x5 - 1x6 + d-7 - d+7 = 0   -------------------------------------+
C8    12x1 + 18x2 + 10x3 + 7x4 + 11x5 + 9x6 + d-8 - d+8 = 10000  -----> monthly expenses
C9    1x4 + d-9 - d+9 = 50   ------------------------------------------> promised space
C10   1x2 + d-10 - d+10 = 150   --------------------------------------> promised space
C11   12x1 + 18x2 + 10x3 + 7x4 + 11x5 + 9x6 + d-11 - d+11 = 1000000 --> maximum profit
```

```
##### Program Output #####

Analysis of deviations
------------------------------------------------
Constraint  RHS Value         d+          d-
------------------------------------------------
   C1       1120.000        0.000     220.000
   C2        840.000       60.000       0.000
   C3          0.000        0.000       0.000
   C4          0.000        0.000       0.000
   C5          0.000        0.000       0.000
   C6          0.000        0.000       0.000
   C7          0.000        0.000       0.000
   C8      10000.000       50.000       0.000
   C9         50.000      100.000       0.000
  C10        150.000        0.000       0.000
  C11    1000000.000        0.000  989950.000
------------------------------------------------


Analysis of decision variables
------------------------------
Variable        Solution Value
------------------------------
   X1             150.000
   X2             150.000
   X3             150.000
   X4             150.000
   X5             150.000
   X6             150.000
------------------------------


Analysis of the objective function
------------------------------------
Priority            Nonachievement
------------------------------------
   P1                    0.000
   P2                    0.000
   P3                    0.000
   P4                    0.000
   P5                    0.000
   P6                   60.000
   P7               989950.000
   P8                    0.000
------------------------------------
```

proper spacing between the paintings. Write the system constraint that is missing from this model.

b. What percentage of the available wall space is utilized in the recommended solution?

c. Constraints 8 and 11 have the same coefficients, but differ in RHS values. Given that the gallery has operating expenses of $10,000 monthly, interpret the relevant priorities.

d. Why is the same amount of space allocated to each of the painters?

e. Why is this amount 150 square feet?

f. One painter is a relative of the gallery administrator; another is far more popular. Both were promised some space. Which is which?

g. What would be the purpose and the result of adding $P8d+9$?

h. Will the gallery be able to cover expenses? Will there be a profit? If so, how much?

i. Convert the balancing priority from a square footage basis to a sales volume basis.

j. Determine the solution if the profit maximization priority were placed before the balancing priority.

k. What would be the effect of raising the RHS of constraint 1 from 40% to 50%?

l. How high would operating expenses have to be before the 40% limit conflicted with the expense coverage goal?

m. Is the 40% space limit a system constraint? Why or why not?

n. How high would operating expenses have to be before the balancing goal was no longer achievable within the 40% limit?

14

Integer and Zero-One Programming

One of the requirements of linear and goal programming techniques is **divisibility.** In other words, each model variable must be able to take on any nonnegative, continuous value in the solution. The divisibility requirement does not present any serious difficulty in most practical problems. For example, it is quite acceptable to use 1.59 hours in machine center A, to put .29 ounce of syrup in a bottle of soft drink, and to produce 1.27 tons of steel.

In certain decision problems, however, the divisibility assumption is totally unrealistic and unacceptable. For example, a solution requiring 2.29 dams on a river system has no practical meaning. In this case, either 2 or 3 dams must be assigned—but *not* 2.29. In a typical production assignment problem, the assignment of people to machines must be made in terms of whole numbers. It is impossible to consider assigning 1.39 people to .75 machine. These types of problems require integer values for the model variables.

In certain problems, costs and/or returns increase or decrease in a stepwise manner. The variables do not move continuously with quantity, but rather move discretely up or down when a certain quantity level is reached. Thus, instead of a continuous function, there is an either-or case for which integer solutions are required.

There are special types of decision problems that restrict variables to values of either zero or one. Capital budgeting, construction scheduling, and assignment problems are good examples of zero-one programming problems. A problem may be set up so that a decision maker must either accept or reject a proposed investment opportunity. Partial acceptance or rejection cannot be considered. In such a case, if the project is accepted the decision variable equals one, and if it is rejected the decision variable equals zero. In like manner, if a construction project is completed by the end of period t, the value of the decision variable is one; if it is not completed at time t, the value of the decision variable is zero.

One method of achieving an integer solution is by rounding off the fractional values of the optimal linear programming solution. This is possible, however, only when the b_i^* value of the constraints can be readily changed. It is not a simple task to round off the fractional values of the basic variables while satisfying the given set of contraints. A special solution technique, referred to as **integer programming,** has been developed for solving this type of problem.

691

The integer programming model requires the following: (1) a linear objective function, (2) a set of linear constraints, (3) nonnegativity constraints for model variables, and (4) integer value constraints for certain variables. When the model requires all integer values for the basic solution variables, it is generally referred to as an all-integer or *pure-integer* problem. When the model requires only certain variables to be integers, it is called a *mixed-integer* problem. When a problem requires only values of zero or one for the decision variables, it is called a *zero-one integer* problem.

Various solution approaches to integer programming problems have been suggested during the past twenty-five years. We shall discuss several of these in this chapter.

INTEGER PROGRAMMING SOLUTION METHODS

A natural, but fallacious, assumption is that the addition of restrictions will simplify solution of a problem. Actually, the introduction of partial restrictions, such as those occurring in integer programming situations, greatly complicates solution. A continuously divisible linear programming model enables the solution technique (e.g., simplex) to focus on corner points alone. Adding an integer restriction effectively increases the number of solutions that must be examined, because the corner points may not all satisfy this new requirement.

Various approaches have been devised to solve integer programming problems. These approaches focus on heuristics, search or enumeration, sequential decomposition, or special aspects of particular situations.

Heuristic approaches range from simply rounding an existing noninteger optimal solution to applying specialized algorithms based on logic unique to a given situation. Although the methodology may be efficient computationally, the solution may not be optimal—and often cannot be proven so. Thus, heuristic approaches are typically employed only when the time or effort required to achieve optimization would outweigh the expected benefits.

Enumeration approaches range from total enumeration to limited search algorithms that focus on selected subsets of the solution space. Total enumeration is unrealistic for all but extremely small problems, as combinatorial explosion rapidly taxes even super-computer capabilities. For example, a 40-variable zero-one model has over 1 trillion solutions; a 10-variable model, in which each variable can range from 0 to 8 in value, also has 1 trillion solutions. Search algorithms include the branch-and-bound method, implicit enumeration (for zero-one models), and the graphical method (for models with only two decision variables).

Sequential decomposition may be used to address integer programming problems through utilization of cutting planes, based on a simplex noninteger solution (the Gomory approach) or, more commonly, through dynamic programming. Every example in Chapter 12 on dynamic programming is, in fact, an integer-solution-only problem.

Special circumstances may permit use of a more efficient specialized algorithm. Among the topics covered in earlier chapters, the transportation, assignment, and network algorithms all address integer requirements more rapidly than do the search methodologies. It is possible, under certain conditions, to combine portions of different algorithms to expedite solution.

Rounding Approach

A simple and sometimes practical approach to solving an integer programming problem is to round off the values of the decision variables derived by the regular linear programming procedure. This approach is certainly easy and practical in terms of effort, time, and cost required to derive an integer solution. The rounding approach may be a very effective technique for large integer programming problems where computational costs are extremely high or for problems where the solution values of decision variables are large. For example, rounding off the solution value for the number of paper clips to be produced from 12,450.2 to 12,450 would probably be acceptable. The major pitfall of this approach is that the solution derived may not be the true optimal integer solution. In other words, the rounded solution may be inferior to the true integer optimal solution, or it may be an infeasible solution. This could be of great consequence if the number of dams to be constructed was rounded to the nearest whole number.

In a maximization problem, the Z value for the optimal integer solution can never be larger than that for the optimal noninteger solution. The relaxed noninteger simplex solution will always yield the maximum Z value, since the solution is on the boundary of the feasible solution space at the extreme corner point. Thus, it is the maximum integer or noninteger solution that can possibly be obtained. This is the reason we can only round down for a maximization problem (and up for a minimization problem). By rounding down, we usually assure that the integer solution will remain in the feasible solution area, although we will always get a lower Z value.

A method similar to the rounding approach is the trial-and-error procedure. Using this method, the decision maker compares each of the integer solutions with the linear programming solution and selects the solution that optimizes the objective function. This method is not very effective when the problem involves a large number of variables and constraints. Furthermore, checking the feasibility of each rounded solution can be very time consuming.

Gomory Approach

Integer programming is a special variant of the standard linear programming approach. Consequently, an optimal integer solution can be derived through the simplex method with some modifications. The modification required for integer programming is the construction of the area of feasible solutions covering all lattice points. This can be accomplished by adding new constraints to the problem and constructing **cutting planes**. This approach was originally proposed by R. E. Gomory.

The Gomory, or cutting plane, algorithm is now primarily of historical interest, because of the availability of more efficient techniques and some undesirable characteristics of the method. The cutting plane approach is very sensitive to such minor matters as the order of the constraints. Unlike the simplex method, with its incremental constantly improving solutions, the Gomory approach provides intermediate feasible solutions only intermittently. Cutting plane solutions may enter phases in which very little improvement is shown through a large number of iterations. Thus, a detailed description of the Gomory approach will not be presented here.

Branch-and-Bound Method

Integer programming problems quite frequently have upper and/or lower bounds for the decision variables. Since the bounded integer programming problem has a finite number of feasible integer solutions, a limited search enumeration procedure serves as a sensible method for determining an optimal solution for this type of problem.

The branch-and-bound method was initially developed by A. H. Land and A. G. Doig, and it was further studied by J. D. C. Little et al. and other researchers. This technique is quite useful in solving integer, mixed-integer, and zero-one integer problems.

The basic steps of the branch-and-bound method (for a maximization problem) can be summarized as follows:

1. The integer programming problem is solved by the standard simplex method with the integer restrictions relaxed.

2. The optimal solution is examined. If the basic variables that have integer requirements are integers, the optimal integer solution has been obtained. If one or more basic variables do not satisfy integer requirements, proceed to step 3.

3. The set of feasible noninteger solution values is branched into subsets (subproblems). The purpose of branching is to eliminate continuous solutions that do not satisfy the integer requirements of the problem. The branching is achieved by introducing mutually exclusive constraints that are necessary to satisfy integer requirements while making sure that no feasible integer solution is excluded.

4. For each subset, the optimal relaxed solution value of the objective function is the upper bound. The best *integer* solution becomes the lower bound. (Initially, this is the rounded-down relaxed solution.) Those subsets having upper bounds that are less than the current lower bound are excluded from further analysis. A feasible integer solution that is as good as or better than the upper bound for any subset is sought. If such a solution exists, it is optimal. If such a solution does not exist, a subset with the best upper bound is selected for branching. Return to step 3.

The steps described above were developed to satisfy the two basic properties of integer linear programs. For a maximization problem, these two properties are as follows: (1) the optimal Z value (the objective function value) for the integer programming problem is always equal to or less than the optimal Z value for the same linear programming problem without integer requirements; and (2) the Z value at each node in the branch-and-bound procedure is the upper bound for the entire branch of descendant nodes. These two properties will be reversed for a minimization problem.

The method used to select an intermediate solution from which to branch (in step 4) will affect the complexity and speed of the solution process. Algorithms may be customized by selecting a branching mechanism suited to the characteristics of the problem. The most popular branching rule is the best-bound rule, demonstrated in this text. Under the best-bound rule, the candidate intermediate solution with the "best" bound is selected as the basis for branching. "Best" is interpreted as *highest* for a maximization problem and *lowest* in a minimization case. This method results in a selective broad search, with any intermediate solution available for branching.

Another branching rule is used to perform depth-first searches. The newest-bound rule calls for selecting the branch with the best bound only from among the intermediate solutions created during the preceding iteration. When a path has been exhausted (through finding either integer or infeasible solutions), branching continues along paths that were considered inferior earlier but now meet the revised bounds. The best-bound rule may be used to select the next intermediate solution from which branching will proceed, again according to the newest-bound rule.

To illustrate the branch-and-bound method, we will consider the problem

Maximize $Z = 3x_1 + 5x_2$

subject to

$$2x_1 + 4x_2 \leqslant 25$$
$$x_1 \leqslant 8$$
$$2x_2 \leqslant 10$$
$$x_1, x_2 = 0 \text{ or nonnegative integers}$$

The optimal relaxed simplex solution to this problem is $x_1 = 8$, $x_2 = 2.25$, and $Z = 35.25$. This solution represents the initial upper bound. The lower bound is the rounded-down solution of $x_1 = 8$, $x_2 = 2$, and $Z = 34$. In the branch-and-bound method, we divide the problem into two parts in order to search for the possible integer solution values for x_1 and x_2. First the variable with the noninteger solution value that has the greatest fractional part is selected. Since in this solution only x_2 has a fractional part, it is selected. Then, in order to eliminate the fractional part of 2.25 (the value of x_2), two new constraints are created. These constraints represent the two new parts to the problem. In this case, the two integer values closest to 2.25 are 2 and 3. By introducing two mutually exclusive constraints, $x_2 \leqslant 2$ and $x_2 \geqslant 3$, we obtain two new problems, which are described in the following as parts A and B. These constraints effectively eliminate all possible fractional values for x_2 between 2 and 3. In effect, they serve to reduce the feasible solution space so that fewer finite integer solutions are evaluated in the problem.

Part A
Maximize $Z = 3x_1 + 5x_2$
subject to
$$2x_1 + 4x_2 \leqslant 25$$
$$x_1 \leqslant 8$$
$$2x_2 \leqslant 10 \text{ (redundant)}$$
$$x_2 \leqslant 2$$
$$x_1, x_2 \geqslant 0$$

Part B
Maximize $Z = 3x_1 + 5x_2$
subject to
$$2x_1 + 4x_2 \leqslant 25$$
$$x_1 \leqslant 8$$
$$2x_2 \leqslant 10$$
$$x_2 \geqslant 3$$
$$x_1, x_2 \geqslant 0$$

Parts A and B are solved by the simplex method, with integer restrictions relaxed. (The graphical solutions for the two parts are shown in Figure 14.1.) The simplex solutions are

Part A: $x_1 = 8$, $x_2 = 2$, $Z = 34$
Part B: $x_1 = 6.5$, $x_2 = 3$, $Z = 34.5$

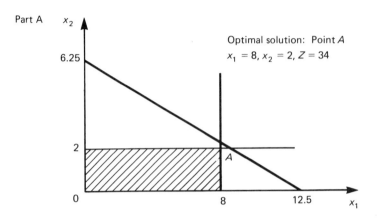

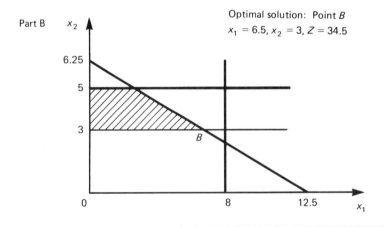

Figure 14.1 *Graphical Solutions of Part A and Part B of the Sample Problem*

Part A yields an all-integer solution. For part A the upper *and* lower bound is now $Z = 34$. The part B noninteger solution warrants a further search, because it has a total profit that is greater than the part A upper bound. It is quite possible that a further search may yield an all-integer solution for which total profit equals or exceeds the part A upper bound of 34.

We branch part B into two subparts, B1 and B2, the first with the constraint $x_1 \leq$ 6 and the other with $x_1 \geq 7$. The two subproblems are stated as follows:

Part B1
Maximize $Z = 3x_1 + 5x_2$
subject to
$$2x_1 + 4x_2 \leq 25$$
$$x_1 \leq 8 \quad \text{(redundant)}$$
$$2x_2 \leq 10$$
$$x_2 \geq 3$$
$$x_1 \leq 6$$
$$x_1, x_2 \geq 0$$

Part B2
Maximize $Z = 3x_1 + 5x_2$
subject to
$$2x_1 + 4x_2 \leq 25$$
$$x_1 \leq 8$$
$$2x_2 \leq 10$$
$$x_2 \geq 3$$
$$x_1 \geq 7$$
$$x_1, x_2 \geq 0$$

The graphical solutions for the two subproblems are shown in Figure 14.2. The simplex solutions are

Part B1: $x_1 = 6, x_2 = 3.25, Z = 34.25$
Part B2:   infeasible

Since part B1 yields a total profit greater than 34 (the previously computed upper bound for part A), it must be further branched into two sub-subproblems, with the constraints $x_2 \leq 3$ and $x_2 \geq 4$. The two sub-subproblems are identified as parts B1a and B1b.

Part B1a
Maximize $Z = 3x_1 + 5x_2$
subject to
$$2x_1 + 4x_2 \leq 25$$
$$2x_2 \leq 10 \quad \text{(redundant)}$$
$$x_2 \geq 3$$
$$x_1 \leq 6$$
$$x_2 \leq 3$$
$$x_1, x_2 \geq 0$$

Part B1b
Maximize $Z = 3x_1 + 5x_2$
subject to
$$2x_1 + 4x_2 \leq 25$$
$$2x_2 \leq 10$$

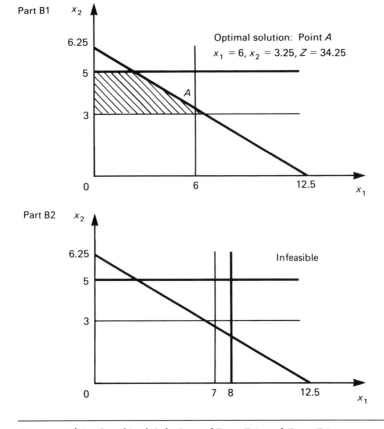

Figure 14.2 *Graphical Solutions of Part B1 and Part B2*

$$x_2 \geqslant 3 \quad \text{(redundant)}$$
$$x_1 \leqslant 6$$
$$x_2 \geqslant 4$$
$$x_1, x_2 \geqslant 0$$

The optimal simplex solutions are

Part B1a: $x_1 = 6, x_2 = 3, Z = 33$
Part B1b: $x_1 = 4.25, x_2 = 4, Z = 33.5$

The two preceding solutions have upper bounds ($Z = 33$ and $Z = 33.5$) that are inferior to the solution value yielded by part A. Therefore, the optimal integer solution is $x_1 = 8, x_2 = 2, Z = 34$, which was yielded by part A.

In the branching and searching procedure, analysis is stopped when (1) a subproblem results in a solution for which the objective function value is inferior to the lower bounds already identified and (2) further branching yields infeasible solutions. However, the characteristics of a given problem may allow incorporation of additional stopping rules. For example, in an all-integer problem in which all contribution coefficients in the objective function are also integers and any one of the potential multiple optimal solutions is acceptable, many iterations can be saved by cutting off branches that cannot *exceed* the current best integer solution. In the sample problem, only three solutions—initial, part

A, and part B—would have been required instead of the seven solutions needed without this stopping rule.

When the search has been completed, the integer solution with the highest objective function value (in a maximization problem) is selected as the optimal solution. The entire branch-and-bound procedure for this problem is shown in Figure 14.3.

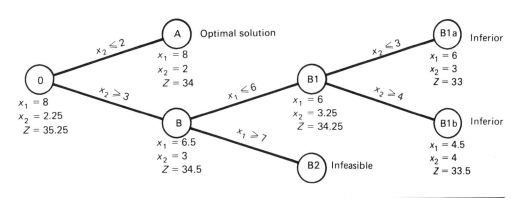

Figure 14.3 *Complete Branch-and-Bound Solution of the Sample Problem*

Example 14.1 Assignment Problem

The assignment problem defined in the following table illustrates an application of the branch-and-bound method to a minimization problem. (Recall, however, that in Chapter 5 we presented an assignment problem solution method that also yields integer solutions.) The objective of the problem is to assign 4 employees to 4 machines in such a manner that the total cost of the work is minimized. This problem consists of a 4 × 4 matrix. Therefore, there are $4! = 24$ feasible solutions.

Employee	Machine			
	A	B	C	D
1	$10	$15	$16	$ 9
2	14	14	8	10
3	11	9	11	18
4	13	13	15	12

To apply the branch-and-bound method, we must establish a tight lower bound on the total cost for all 24 feasible solutions. One way to determine this tight lower bound is by summing the minimum costs of each column, without considering whether or not this amount corresponds to a feasible solution. In this example, the sum of the minimum costs in the respective columns is $10 + 9 + 8 + 9 = 36$.

Since any of the 4 employees can be assigned to machine A, all feasible solutions can initially be branched into 4 subsets. Then, the lower bound is computed for each of the four subsets. If employee 1 is assigned to machine A, there will be 3! = 6 feasible solutions. The lower bound for these six feasible solutions is determined by summing the cost of assigning employee 1 to machine A and the minimum costs of the three remaining columns (columns B, C, and D, without row 1). For example, the lower bound for the subset of assigning employee 1 to machine A will be 10 + (9 + 8 + 10) = 37. This calculation is shown in the following table.

	Machine			
Employee	A	B	C	D
1	⑩			
2		14	⑧	⑩
3		⑨	11	18
4		13	15	12

Similarly, the lower bound for the subset of assigning employee 2 to machine A is 14 + (9 + 11 + 9) = 43, as shown in the next table.

	Machine			
Employee	A	B	C	D
1		15	16	⑨
2	⑭			
3		⑨	⑪	18
4		13	15	12

The lower bounds for the remaining two subsets can be calculated in a similar manner. The lower bounds for the four subsets are listed in the following table.

Subset	Lower Bound	
1A	10 + (9 + 8 + 10) = 37	←lower bound
2A	14 + (9 + 11 + 9) = 43	
3A	11 + (13 + 8 + 9) = 41	
4A	13 + (9 + 8 + 9) = 39	←upper bound

The minimum cost of assignment among the lower bounds of the four subsets is 37, for subset 1A. This amount is selected as the *lower* bound in the first step. The minimum value among the lower bounds of the feasible solutions (if there are any at this step) is selected as the *upper* bound. Subsets 3A and 4A are both feasible solutions. Therefore, the lower bound of subset 4A (39) is chosen as the upper bound. Subsets 2A and 3A have lower bounds greater than the identified upper bound of 39. Consequently, these two subsets are eliminated from further branching.

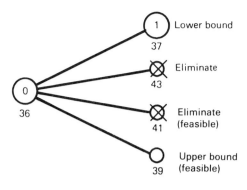

Figure 14.4 *First Step of the Branch-and-Bound Solution*

The analysis of the problem thus far is shown in Figure 14.4. Subset 1A, which has the current lower bound, is selected for further branching. Thus, subset 1A is identified by the circled node 1. Employee 1 has been assigned to machine A. The next step is the assignment of one of the remaining employees (2, 3, and 4) to machine B. If employee 2 is assigned to machine B, the lower bound for this subset is the sum of assignment costs of 1A and 2B and the minimum costs of the remaining two columns, after rows 1 and 2 are deleted. For example, the lower bound for the subset 1A and 2B is $10 + 14 + (11 + 12) = 47$, as shown in the following table.

Employee	Machine			
	A	B	C	D
1	⑩			
2		⑭		
3			⑪	18
4			15	⑫

The lower bounds for the remaining two subsets can be calculated in the same manner, so the bounds of the three subsets are as follows:

Subset	Lower Bound	
1A-2B	$10 + 14 + (11 + 12) = 47$	
1A-3B	$10 + 9 + (8 + 10) = 37$	←lower bound
1A-4B	$10 + 13 + (8 + 10) = 41$	

Among the three lower bounds calculated, the minimum is for subset 1A-3B. Thirty-seven thus remains the lower bound. The lower bounds for the remaining two subsets, 1A-2B and 1A-4B, are greater than the upper bound identified in the first step (39 for subset 4A). Therefore, we can eliminate subsets 1A-2B and 1A-4B from further analysis. The results of the second step of the analysis are shown in Figure 14.5.

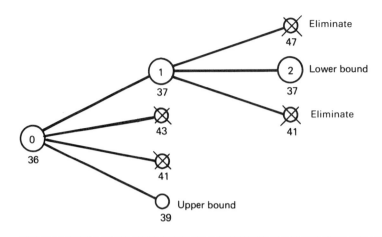

Figure 14.5 *Second Step of the Branch-and-Bound Solution*

Two more employees are still waiting for assignment to machines C and D. The third-step branching must begin from the new lower bound identified by the circled node 2. There are only two possible ways to branch (2! = 2). The two possible assignments are 1A-3B-2C-4D and 1A-3B-2D-4C. If employee 2 is assigned to machine C, the lower bound will be 10 + 9 + 8 + (12) = 39. On the other hand, if employee 4 is assigned to machine C, the lower bound will be 10 + 9 + 15 + (10) = 44. The preceding two subsets are both feasible solutions to the problem. Since the first subset (1A-3B-2C-4D) corresponds to a lower total assignment cost than the second subset (1A-3B-2D-4C), it is selected for comparison with the upper bound (39). The lower bound of subset 1A-3B-2C-4D (39) is not greater than the upper bound (39). Therefore, this subset is an optimal solution. However, since the lower bound is equal to the upper bound, the subset that yielded the upper bound is also an optimal solution. Inspecting the two solutions, we can identify the two optimal solutions shown in the following table.

Assignment 1		Assignment 2	
1 to A	$10	1 to D	$ 9
2 to C	8	2 to C	8
3 to B	9	3 to B	9
4 to D	12	4 to A	13
Total cost	$39	Total cost	$39

The complete branch-and-bound analysis for this problem is shown in Figure 14.6. If the total costs of the final two subsets (1A-3B-2C-4D and 1A-3B-2D-4C) exceeded the upper bound (39), these solutions would be eliminated from further consideration. Then a new node with a minimum lower bound less than the upper bound would be selected for further branching. If no node met this requirement, then the subset that yielded the upper bound would be the optimal solution.

The branch-and-bound method can also be applied to a maximization case of the assignment problem. The procedure is the same as the one just presented, except that the

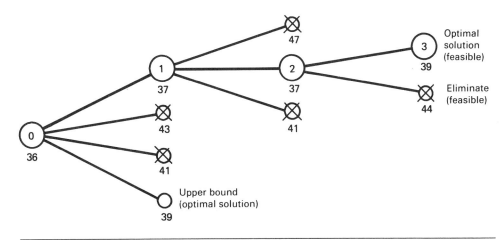

Figure 14.6 *Complete Branch-and-Bound Solution of the Assignment Problem*

calculation process for the upper and lower bounds is the reverse of the process for the minimization case.

ZERO-ONE PROGRAMMING

Many real-world problems require solution values of zero or one only for the decision variables. Assignment, capital budgeting, project scheduling, fixed-cost, location-allocation, and traveling salesperson problems are good examples of this type. Rather than applying the branch-and-bound algorithm, we can use an algorithm that takes advantage of the 0–1 system constraint characteristics.

The zero-one problem can be stated as

$$\text{Minimize } Z = \sum_{j=1}^{n} c_j x_j$$

subject to

$$\sum_{j=1}^{n} a_{ij} x_j \geq b_i \quad (i = 1, 2, \ldots, m)$$

$$x_j = 0 \text{ or } 1$$

Example 14.2 Capital Budgeting Problem

A corporation is considering six possible investment opportunities. The table on page 704 presents pertinent information about the investment projects.

In addition, projects 3 and 4 are mutually exclusive pollution control activities, and project 6 is contingent on the prior acceptance of project 1. The model can be formulated as follows:

$$\text{Maximize } Z = 100x_1 + 190x_2 + 80x_3 + 30x_4 + 220x_5 + 150x_6$$

subject to

$$210x_1 + 340x_2 + 150x_3 + 60x_4 + 540x_5 + 350x_6 \leq 1000$$

Project	Initial Outlay ($000)	New Managerial Staff Need	Average Annual Cash Flow ($000)	Annual Accounting Profit ($000)	Net Present Value ($000)
1	210	3	45	40	100
2	340	5	75	70	190
3	150	2	35	33	80
4	60	1	10	18	30
5	540	8	150	120	220
6	350	3	100	80	150
Requirement or maximum available	Maximum 1000	Maximum 12	Minimum 100	Minimum 100	Maximize

$$3x_1 + 5x_2 + 2x_3 + x_4 + 8x_5 + 3x_6 \leqslant 12$$
$$45x_1 + 75x_2 + 35x_3 + 10x_4 + 150x_5 + 100x_6 \geqslant 100$$
$$40x_1 + 70x_2 + 33x_3 + 18x_4 + 120x_5 + 80x_6 \geqslant 100$$
$$x_3 + x_4 \leqslant 1$$
$$x_6 - x_1 \leqslant 0$$
$$x_j = 0 \text{ or } 1$$

Although the model is not exactly in the desired form (all constraints should be $\leqslant$ for a maximization problem), the general approach to formulating a capital budgeting problem can be clearly seen in this example.

Example 14.3 Either-Or Constraints

A farmer is considering entering one of two possible new markets: dog food or cattle feed. The production processes for the two new products under consideration differ significantly. The farmer has established the following production constraints:

$$2x_1 + 4x_2 + x_3 \leqslant 30 \quad \text{(dog food)} \tag{14.1}$$
$$10x_1 + 8x_2 \leqslant 180 \quad \text{(cattle feed)} \tag{14.2}$$

where
x_1 = bushels of corn
x_2 = bushels of wheat
x_3 = horse meat (100 lb)

Either constraint (14.1) *or* constraint (14.2) is applicable, depending on whether the farmer decides to produce dog food or cattle feed. In order to accommodate the two either-or constraints in the model, we can transform them into the following two constraints:

$$2x_1 + 4x_2 + x_3 \leqslant 30 + yM \tag{14.3}$$
$$10x_1 + 8x_2 \leqslant 180 + (1 - y)M \tag{14.4}$$

where
y = 0 or 1 variable
M = an arbitrarily large value

If the contribution rate (c_j) assigned to y is zero, the either-or constraints are as follows:

1. If $y = 0$, then constraint (14.3) becomes the binding constraint, while constraint (14.4) becomes redundant as its right-hand-side value increases.

2. If $y = 1$, then constraint (14.4) becomes the binding constraint, while constraint (14.3) becomes redundant.

For example, let us assign 10,000 to M.

1. If $y = 0$, we have

$$2x_1 + 4x_2 + x_3 \leq 30 + 0(10,000)$$
$$2x_1 + 4x_2 + x_3 \leq 30 \qquad \text{(a binding constraint)}$$

and

$$10x_1 + 8x_2 \leq 180 + (1 - 0)(10,000)$$
$$10x_1 + 8x_2 \leq 10,180 \qquad \text{(a redundant constraint)}$$

2. If $y = 1$, we have

$$2x_1 + 4x_2 + x_3 \leq 30 + 1(10,000)$$
$$2x_1 + 4x_2 + x_3 \leq 10,030 \quad \text{(a redundant constraint)}$$

and

$$10x_1 + 8x_2 \leq 180 + (1 - 1)(10,000)$$
$$10x_1 + 8x_2 \leq 180 \qquad \text{(a binding constraint)}$$

The procedure described above can be used in many different either-or type situations. Consider the following two cases.

The first case involves inconsistent directions for constraints. It is possible for two mutually exclusive constraints to have different inequality directions, as follows:

$$\sum_{j=1}^{n} a_{1j}x_j \leq b_1 \tag{14.5}$$

$$\sum_{j=1}^{n} a_{2j}x_j \geq b_2 \tag{14.6}$$

Constraint (14.6) can be changed to a $\leq$ constraint by multiplying both sides by -1.

$$\sum_{j=1}^{n} -a_{2j}x_j \leq -b_2 \tag{14.7}$$

Now constraints (14.5) and (14.7) can be transformed into

$$\sum_{j=1}^{n} a_{1j}x_j \leq b_1 + yM$$

$$\sum_{j=1}^{n} -a_{2j}x_j \leq -b_2 + (1 - y)M$$

or

$$\sum_{j=1}^{n} a_{1j}x_j \leq b_1 + yM$$

$$\sum_{j=1}^{n} a_{2j}x_j \geq b_2 - (1 - y)M$$

The second either-or case involves a decision variable that makes sense only when its quantity reaches a certain minimum level L. For example, production of petroleum makes sense only when a well produces at least so many barrels a day; shipment of a certain product to a foreign country is considered only when the order reaches a certain minimum quantity. If the decision variable under consideration is x_k, the situation can be described as

$$x_k = 0 \quad \text{or} \quad x_k \geq L$$

Although the nonnegativity constraint ($x_k \geq 0$) is assumed, for the sake of convenience, we can rewrite the constraints as

$$x_k \leq 0 \quad \text{or} \quad x_k \geq L$$

Then, following the previous procedure,

$$x_k \leq 0 + yM$$
$$x_k \geq L - (1 - y)M$$
$$y = 0 \text{ or } 1$$

Example 14.4 At Least k of r Constraints Must Hold

A major grocery store chain is considering entry into a new market. A total of seven potential sites have been evaluated, with demographic information and cost and sales projections prepared for each. The chain has several criteria it uses to decide whether or not to enter a market; of the five positive indicators, at least three must be present. In addition, because investment funds are limited, the company will not enter an area unless it can initially place a minimum of three stores there. The following model has been developed to describe the situation:

$$\text{Maximize } Z = 450x_1 + 375x_2 + 425x_3 + 550x_4 + 500x_5 + 500x_6 + 450x_7$$

where Z represents the total estimated annual operating profit and $x_1, \ldots, x_7$ represent potential locations, numbered 1 through 7.

Overall Constraints:

$$x_1 + x_2 + x_3 + x_4 + x_5 + x_6 + x_7 \geq 3 \qquad \text{(number of stores)}$$

$$1.2x_1 + .8x_2 + 1.3x_3 + 1.95x_4 + 1.6x_5 + 1.75x_6 + 1.5x_7 \leq 5$$
$$\text{(millions of dollars available for investment)}$$

$$x_i = 0 \text{ or } 1 \qquad (i = 1, 2, \ldots, 7)$$

Criteria Constraints:

$$23x_1 + 15x_2 + 32x_3 + 48x_4 + 34x_5 + 34x_6 + 29x_7 \geq 90$$
$$\text{(thousands of cars driving by per day)}$$

$$450x_1 + 375x_2 + 425x_3 + 550x_4 + 500x_5 + 500x_6 + 450x_7 \geqslant 1400$$

(estimated annual operating profit)

$$.34x_1 + .41x_2 + .27x_3 + .3x_4 + .32x_5 + .26x_6 + .33x_7$$
$$\geqslant .3(x_1 + x_2 + x_3 + x_4 + x_5 + x_6 + x_7)$$

(average ROI)

1. **a.** $2x_1 + 1x_2 + 3x_3 + 0x_4 + 2x_5 + 1x_6 + 3x_7 \leqslant 5$

(competitors within a one-mile radius)

and/or

    b. $21x_1 + 8x_2 + 24x_3 + 45x_4 + 27x_5 + 30x_6 + 22x_7 \geqslant 75$

(thousands of residents within a one-mile radius)

2. **a.** $3x_1 + 2x_2 + 7x_3 + 3x_4 + 6x_5 + 4x_6 + 5x_7 \leqslant 13$

(competitors within a two-mile radius)

and/or

    b. $75x_1 + 21x_2 + 102x_3 + 126x_4 + 74x_5 + 103x_6 + 57x_7 \geqslant 225$

(thousands of residents within a two-mile radius)

Mutually exclusive constraints present a special situation in the case where at least k of r constraints must hold. Suppose these constraints are as follows:

$$\sum_{j=1}^{n} a_{ij}x_j \leqslant b_i \quad (i = 1, 2, \ldots, r)$$

As with the either-or constraints, the 0–1 variable y_i and an arbitrarily large value M can be used to transform the constraints into the following:

$$\sum_{j=1}^{n} a_{ij}x_j \leqslant b_i + y_iM \quad (i = 1, 2, \ldots, r)$$

If $y_i = 0$, then the ith constraint becomes binding as it approaches b_i. If $y_i = 1$, then the ith constraint becomes redundant as its b_i becomes very large ($b_i + M$).

In order to guarantee that at least k of r constraints must hold, we can introduce the following additional constraint:

$$\sum_{i=1}^{r} y_i \leqslant r - k$$

Suppose a model has the following constraints:

$$x_1 + x_2 + x_3 \leqslant 10$$
$$4x_1 + x_2 - x_3 \leqslant 12$$
$$x_2 + 2x_3 \leqslant 8$$
$$3x_1 - x_2 + x_3 \leqslant 9$$

These constraints can be converted to

$$x_1 + x_2 + x_3 \leqslant 10 + y_1M$$
$$4x_1 + x_2 - x_3 \leqslant 12 + y_2M$$
$$x_2 + 2x_3 \leqslant 8 + y_3M$$
$$3x_1 - x_2 + x_3 \leqslant 9 + y_4M$$
$$y_i = 0 \text{ or } 1$$

If only one constraint must hold (all constraints are mutually exclusive), then the following additional constraint is needed:

$$y_1 + y_2 + y_3 + y_4 = 4 - 1 = 3$$

If at least three constraints must hold, then the additional constraint required is

$$y_1 + y_2 + y_3 + y_4 \leq 4 - 3$$

or

$$y_1 + y_2 + y_3 + y_4 \leq 1$$

The transformations necessary for our grocery chain example encompass two types of "at least k of r" constraints: the "at least 3 of 5 criteria" restriction and the two subsidiary either-or ("at least 1 of 2") constraints. Notice that the and/or notation used in the example accurately describes what occurs in an either-or case, as the constraint that becomes redundant may or may not have been simultaneously satisfied. Two alternative formulations of the either-or situation are shown below. Using the 0–1 variables y_1 through y_8, we can integrate the seven criteria-related constraints into the model as follows:

$$23x_1 + 15x_2 + 32x_3 + 48x_4 + 34x_5 + 34x_6 + 29x_7 \geq 90 + y_1 M$$
$$450x_1 + 375x_2 + 425x_3 + 550x_4 + 500x_5 + 500x_6 + 450x_7 \geq 1400 + y_2 M$$
$$.34x_1 + .41x_2 + .27x_3 + .3x_4 + .32x_5 + .26x_6 + .33x_7$$
$$\geq .3(x_1 + x_2 + x_3 + x_4 + x_5 + x_6 + x_7) + y_3 M$$

1. a. $\qquad 2x_1 + 1x_2 + 3x_3 + 0x_4 + 2x_5 + 1x_6 + 3x_7 \leq 5 + y_4 M + y_6 M$
   b. $\qquad 21x_1 + 8x_2 + 24x_3 + 45x_4 + 27x_5 + 30x_6 + 22x_7 \geq 75 - y_4 M - (1 - y_6)M$
2. a. $\qquad 3x_1 + 2x_2 + 7x_3 + 3x_4 + 6x_5 + 4x_6 + 5x_7 \leq 13 + y_5 M + y_7 M$
   b. $75x_1 + 21x_2 + 102x_3 + 126x_4 + 74x_5 + 103x_6 + 57x_7 \geq 225 - y_5 M - y_8 M$

$$y_1 + y_2 + y_3 + y_4 + y_5 \leq 2$$
$$y_7 + y_8 \leq 1$$
$$y_i = 0 \text{ or } 1 \quad (i = 1, 2, \ldots, 8)$$

When two 0–1 adjustment variables are incorporated into the same constraint, no weighting is necessary because the effect of the variables is cumulative rather than counterindicative. Consider the following two constraints with the same sign:

$$10x_1 + 7x_2 \leq 150 + y_1 M + y_2 M$$
$$3x_1 + 5x_2 \leq 100 + y_1 M + (1 - y_2)M$$

In this example, y_1 represents a set of constraints extending beyond these two, while y_2 represents an either-or situation limited to the two constraints shown. If $y_1 = 1$, both constraints are automatically satisfied regardless of the value of y_2. If $y_1 = 0$, indicating that the pair of constraints requires consideration, the value of y_2 will be used to select the constraint that is binding: if $y_2 = 0$, the first constraint is relevant; if $y_2 = 1$, the second constraint is binding. Replacing $(1 - y_2)$ with y_3 would do nothing more than add one variable (y_3) and one constraint ($y_2 + y_3 \leq 1$).

Example 14.5 Fixed-Cost Problem

In undertaking various activities, management commonly incurs fixed costs (fixed-charge, or setup, costs). In such cases, the objective is the minimization of the total cost, which is the sum of variable costs and fixed costs related to a management activity.

Defining x_j as the level of activity j, k_j as the fixed cost of $x_j > 0$, and c_j as the variable cost of activity j, we can determine the total cost as follows:

$$Z = f_1(x_1) + f_2(x_2) + \cdots + f_n(x_n)$$

where

$$f_j(x_j) = \begin{cases} k_j + c_j x_j, & \text{if } x_j > 0 \\ 0, & \text{if } x_j = 0 \\ & x_j \geq 0 \end{cases} \quad \text{for all } j$$

As with the mutually exclusive constraints, the 0–1 variable y_j and a large value M can be utilized in the following fashion to handle fixed charges in a minimization problem:

$$\text{Minimize } Z = \sum_{j=1}^{n} (c_j x_j + k_j y_j)$$

subject to the original constraints and

$$x_j \leq M y_j$$
$$y_j \leq 1$$
$$y_j \geq 0 \text{ and is an integer} \qquad (j = 1, 2, \ldots, n)$$

In this model, the system constraint $x_j \leq M y_j$ can be converted to $x_j - M y_j \leq 0$ for the actual solution process. Some solution methods require the identification of y_j simply as 0–1 variables, whereas others require the explicit formulation $y_j \leq 1$, $y_j \geq 0$, and y_j is an integer for $j = 1, 2, \ldots, n$.

Consider the following production case. A company is considering three different products with the following characteristics:

Product	Fixed Cost	Unit Profit
1	$100 if $x_1 > 0$ $ 0 if $x_1 = 0$	$5
2	$150 if $x_2 > 0$ $ 0 if $x_2 = 0$	$7
3	$ 75 if $x_3 > 0$ $ 0 if $x_3 = 0$	$4

The production constraints are

$$4x_1 + 6x_2 + x_3 \leq 2000$$
$$2x_1 + 2x_2 + 3x_3 \leq 1500$$

The objective of the firm is to maximize profits; thus, fixed costs can be represented as negative profits in the objective function. The problem can now be formulated as

Maximize $Z = 5x_1 - 100y_1 + 7x_2 - 150y_2 + 4x_3 - 75y_3$

subject to

$$4x_1 + 6x_2 + x_3 \leqslant 2000$$
$$2x_1 + 2x_2 + 3x_3 \leqslant 1500$$
$$x_1 - My_1 \leqslant 0$$
$$x_2 - My_2 \leqslant 0$$
$$x_3 - My_3 \leqslant 0$$
$$y_j = 0 \text{ or } 1 \quad \text{for all } j$$
$$x_j \geqslant 0 \quad \text{for all } j$$

Now let us consider a slight modification of the fixed-cost problem. Suppose that a firm is considering producing three different products for the upcoming planning horizon. The pertinent information is given in the following table:

Product	Unit Contribution	Direct Labor Requirement
1	$15	5 hr
2	12	4
3	20	7

The fixed cost of the production facility is based on the amount of labor (number of people working in the production plant and their equipment needs). The industrial engineering department estimates that fixed costs increase in the following steps as a function of the direct labor requirements of the production process:

Fixed Costs	Direct Labor Requirement
$20,000	up to 30,000 hr
30,000	30,000–50,000
40,000	50,000–100,000

The production scheduling model can be formulated as follows:

Maximize $Z = 15x_1 + 12x_2 + 20x_3 - 20,000y_1 - 30,000y_2 - 40,000y_3$

subject to the normal production contraints and

$$5x_1 + 4x_2 + 7x_3 \leqslant 30,000y_1 + 50,000y_2 + 100,000y_3$$
$$y_1 + y_2 + y_3 = 1$$
$$y_j = 0 \text{ or } 1$$

In this model, constraint $y_1 + y_2 + y_3 = 1$ guarantees that only one fixed-cost schedule will be selected, based on the appropriate direct labor requirement.

Example 14.6 Curve Approximation

In the preceding fixed-cost example, a stepwise function was essentially transformed into a form suitable for linear programming solution. Breaks in the function were represented by exclusive 0–1 variables. The same approach can be used to approximate a curve, although there are limits to the accuracy that can be obtained. This technique works best with fairly smooth curves, such as those typically associated with worker learning experience, quantity discounting, or lot sizing. The curve must be broken into segments for which a suitable linear approximation can be established. The segments are then combined in the relevant constraint(s) and incorporated into the objective function, by way of exclusive 0–1 variables.

Consider the manufacture of latex paint base at a paint plant. Costs include both fixed and variable elements, but the elements have proven difficult to separate. From the plant manager's point of view, even the variable costs tend to decrease as the batch size increases. A fairly accurate curve has been fitted to accumulated cost data; this curve is shown in Figure 14.7.

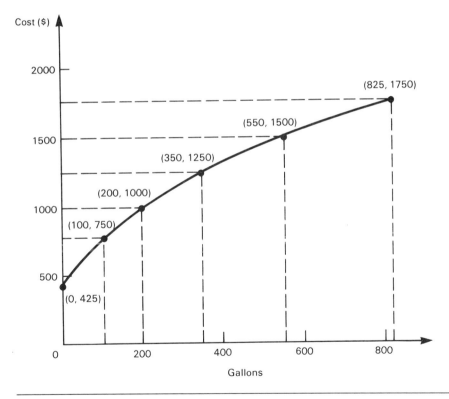

*Figure 14.7 Production Cost Curve Approximation for the
Paint Manufacture Problem*

The points labeled on the graph have been selected as appropriate linearization intervals. Note that the lower end of the curve is open, signifying that a fixed cost of $425 has been recognized and will be incurred only if the paint base is actually produced. We will assume the presence of other decision variables and constraints and will present here only the portions of the model relevant to this example.

$$\text{Maximize } Z = 15x_1 - 425y_1 - 3.5w_1 - 2.5w_2 - 1.667w_3 - 1.25w_4 - .909w_5$$

subject to

$x_1 - My_1 \leqslant 0$	(fixed cost inclusion—redundant)
$x_1 = w_1 + w_2 + w_3 + w_4 + w_5$	(total quantity to produce)
$w_1 \leqslant 100y_1$	(first interval production capacity)
$w_1 \geqslant 100y_2$	(conditional test for full use of first interval)
$w_2 \leqslant 100y_2$	(second interval production capacity)
$w_2 \geqslant 100y_3$	(conditional test for full use of second interval)
$w_3 \leqslant 150y_3$	(third interval production capacity)
$w_3 \geqslant 150y_4$	(conditional test for full use of third interval)
$w_4 \leqslant 200y_4$	(fourth interval production capacity)
$w_4 \geqslant 200y_5$	(conditional test for full use of fourth interval)
$w_5 \leqslant 275y_5$	(fifth interval production capacity)
$x_1 \geqslant 0$	
$w_i \geqslant 0$	
$y_i = 0 \text{ or } 1 \quad (i = 1, \ldots, 5)$	

The variable y_1 will have a value (1) only when x_1 has a value—that is, when some production occurs; the fixed charge will then be deducted in the objective function. The variable y_2 will have a value only when $w_1 = 100$, or all capacity in the first interval has been used, thus allowing production to occur in the second interval. Likewise, y_3 will have a value only when $w_2 = 100$, indicating that all capacity in the second interval (as well as the first) has been used, thus allowing production in the third interval, and so on. The first constraint, representing the fixed cost, is actually redundant, as any production will require a value for y_1, thanks to $w_1 \leqslant 100y_1$. The coefficients of w_1 in the objective function represent the marginal cost of an additional unit of production in the appropriate interval, equal to the slope of the line in the corresponding linear approximation segment.

Let us assume that the model results in an intended production of 475 gallons of latex paint base, or $x_1 = 475$. Resulting variable values are

$$w_1 = 100$$
$$w_2 = 100$$
$$w_3 = 150$$
$$w_4 = 125$$
$$y_1 = y_2 = y_3 = y_4 = 1$$
$$w_5 = y_5 = 0$$

The costs in the objective function total $1431.25 (425 + 350 + 250 + 250 + 156.25). It is readily apparent from the graph that this figure corresponds to the original curve's cost for production of 475 gallons.

Example 14.7 Location-Allocation Problem

Another interesting application of zero-one programming is the location-allocation problem. The problem usually involves multiple market areas (states, warehouses, distribution centers, or other geographical areas), multiple facility locations, known demand at various markets, and known transportation costs from potential facilities to destinations.

For the sake of simplicity, let us assume that each potential facility location is suitable for building only one type of plant to produce one product. The variables for the problem are defined as follows:

x_{ij} = quantity of the product transported from facility i to area j

c_{ij} = transportation cost per unit of product from facility i to area j

K_i = production capacity at facility i

F_i = total fixed cost (amortized construction and operating costs) at facility i

D_j = demand for the product in market area j

y_i = 1 if facility location i is selected, 0 otherwise

The model can be developed as follows:

$$\text{Minimize } Z = \sum_{i=1}^{m} \sum_{j=1}^{n} c_{ij}x_{ij} + \sum_{i=1}^{m} F_i y_i$$

subject to

$$\sum_{j=1}^{n} x_{ij} \le K_i y_i \qquad (i = 1, 2, \ldots, m)$$

$$\sum_{i=1}^{m} x_{ij} \ge D_j \qquad (j = 1, 2, \ldots, n)$$

$$y_j = 0 \text{ or } 1$$

There are many applications of the location-allocation model. Problems involving determining the location of health care facilities (clinics or hospitals), schools, police precincts, fire stations, and computer facilities are good examples. Variations include the so-called set-covering case, in which the addition of new facilities or closing of some existing facilities is evaluated.

Location-allocation formulations are also appropriate for scheduling and personnel assignment problems in which the people are treated as individuals with differentiable skills, rather than as interchangeable workers. Consider the case of a research laboratory with twelve staff scientists. It would be possible to make team selections for a new project using the assignment technique, provided a single criterion could be found. More realistic analysis often leads to either multiple criteria or unrelated restrictions. Suppose there are seven skills required to perform the planned experiments, and no individual researcher has all the necessary skills. The team may contain more than one researcher with any given skill. Set covering is then appropriate in such a situation:

$$x_1 + x_2 + x_4 + x_5 + x_7 + x_9 + x_{10} + x_{11} \ge 1 \qquad \text{(skill 1)}$$
$$x_2 + x_3 + x_4 + x_6 + x_8 \ge 1 \qquad \text{(skill 2)}$$
$$x_1 + x_4 + x_8 + x_{11} + x_{12} \ge 1 \qquad \text{(skill 3)}$$
$$x_2 + x_3 + x_5 + x_9 + x_{10} + x_{12} \ge 1 \qquad \text{(skill 4)}$$

and so on. In this case, zero-one solutions are of course desired. A permutation of the set-covering model is the model in which certain constraints require increased coverage. For instance, there might be a need for two scientists with skill 5, so that constraint might read

$$x_1 + x_3 + x_4 + x_6 + x_7 + x_9 + x_{11} \geq 2 \qquad \text{(skill 5)}$$

Example 14.8 Traveling Salesperson Problem

The traveling salesperson problem is concerned with the minimization of total travel cost (distance, time, expenses, or a combination of these). The decision variable x_{ijk} equals 1 if the journey includes a trip from location i to location j in leg k; otherwise x_{ijk} equals 0.

Consider a simple case in which there are four locations (e.g., cities, states, sales districts, campuses, military installations, factories). Suppose the home location is defined as node 1 and the locations to be visited are numbered 2, 3, and 4, as shown in Figure 14.8.

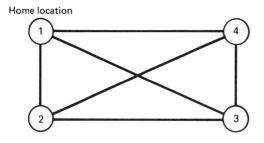

Figure 14.8 *Locations and Routes of the Traveling Salesperson Problem*

There are six possible routes by which the salesperson can visit locations 2, 3, and 4 starting from node 1. The table on page 715 enumerates these routes and identifies the variables that would be assigned values of 1 for each solution.

The travel plan from one location to another is often termed an **arc.**

The problem involves four basic types of constraints. The first set of constraints guarantees that each of the n locations is visited only once, starting from and ending at location (node) 1.

$$\sum_{j=2}^{n} x_{1j1} = 1 \qquad (14.8)$$

$$\sum_{i=2}^{n} \sum_{j=2}^{n} x_{ijk} = 1 \quad (k = 2, 3, \ldots, n-1; i \neq j) \qquad (14.9)$$

$$\sum_{i=2}^{n} x_{i1n} = 1 \qquad (14.10)$$

	Leg			
Travel Plan	1	2	3	4
1	$(1 \rightarrow 2)$	$(2 \rightarrow 3)$	$(3 \rightarrow 4)$	$(4 \rightarrow 1)$
	x_{121}	x_{232}	x_{343}	x_{414}
2	$(1 \rightarrow 2)$	$(2 \rightarrow 4)$	$(4 \rightarrow 3)$	$(3 \rightarrow 1)$
	x_{121}	x_{242}	x_{433}	x_{314}
3	$(1 \rightarrow 3)$	$(3 \rightarrow 2)$	$(2 \rightarrow 4)$	$(4 \rightarrow 1)$
	x_{131}	x_{322}	x_{243}	x_{414}
4	$(1 \rightarrow 3)$	$(3 \rightarrow 4)$	$(4 \rightarrow 2)$	$(2 \rightarrow 1)$
	x_{131}	x_{342}	x_{423}	x_{214}
5	$(1 \rightarrow 4)$	$(4 \rightarrow 2)$	$(2 \rightarrow 3)$	$(3 \rightarrow 1)$
	x_{141}	x_{422}	x_{233}	x_{314}
6	$(1 \rightarrow 4)$	$(4 \rightarrow 3)$	$(3 \rightarrow 2)$	$(2 \rightarrow 1)$
	x_{141}	x_{432}	x_{323}	x_{214}

The second set of constraints assures that there is exactly one departure from each of the n locations.

$$\sum_{j=1}^{n} \sum_{k=2}^{n} x_{ijk} = 1 \quad (i = 2, 3, \ldots, n; i \neq j) \tag{14.11}$$

If $j = 1$, $k = n$; or if $k = n$, $j = 1$

The condition imposed in constraint (14.11) assures that the person will return home on the last leg. In developing a real-world traveling salesperson model, equations of type (14.11) should be written out first and variables that do not satisfy the conditions eliminated. For example, suppose $n = 4$ and $i = 2$; the equation is

$$x_{212} + x_{222} + x_{232} + x_{242} + x_{213} + x_{223} + x_{233}$$
$$+ x_{243} + x_{214} + x_{224} + x_{234} + x_{244} = 1$$

Since $i \neq j$, x_{222}, x_{223}, and x_{224} can be eliminated. The condition "if $j = 1$, $k = n$; or if $k = n$, $j = 1$" further eliminates x_{212}, x_{213}, x_{234}, and x_{244}. Thus, the equation becomes

$$x_{232} + x_{242} + x_{233} + x_{243} + x_{214} = 1$$

The third set of constraints assures that only one leg ends at each of the n locations.

$$\sum_{i=1}^{n} \sum_{k=1}^{n-1} x_{ijk} = 1 \quad (j = 2, 3, \ldots, n; i \neq j) \tag{14.12}$$

If $i = 1$, $k = 1$; or if $k = 1$, $i = 1$

The final set of constraints guarantees that if leg k ends at location j, leg $k + 1$ must start from the same location j.

$$x_{1j1} = \sum_{p=2}^{n} x_{jp2} \quad (j = 2, 3, \ldots, n; i \neq j) \tag{14.13}$$

$$\sum_{i=2}^{n} x_{ijk} = \sum_{p=2}^{n} x_{jpk+1} \quad \begin{pmatrix} j = 2, 3, \ldots, n; i \neq j \\ k = 2, 3, \ldots, n - 2 \end{pmatrix} \tag{14.14}$$

$$\sum_{i=2}^{n} x_{ijn-1} = x_{j1n} \qquad (j = 2, 3, \ldots, n; i \neq j) \qquad (14.15)$$

Constraint (14.13) assures that leg 2 can start from location j only if leg 1 ended at location j. Constraint (14.14) basically does for the other legs what is done for the first leg in (14.13) and the last leg in (14.15); it is just a more general formulation.

The objective function of the model is the minimization of total travel cost, c_{ij}, associated with traveling from location i to location j.

$$\text{Minimize } Z = \sum_{i=1}^{n} \sum_{j=1}^{n} \sum_{k=1}^{n} c_{ij} x_{ijk} \qquad (i \neq j)$$

The traveling salesperson model can be adapted to represent problems involving political campaigns, truck routing, inspection tours, and production scheduling. Although the logic of the model formulation can be easily seen, the actual solution of a real-world traveling salesperson problem is not simple. Usually, such problems are complex, with large numbers of decision variables and constraints. The $(n - 1)!$ explosion of potential solutions in particular hinders large-scale application. A 4-location problem (our example) has $(4 - 1)! = 6$ feasible solutions, a 10-location model has 362,880, and a 16-location model has well over 1 trillion possible combinations. Over the past several years, however, some progress has been made in developing efficient algorithms and computer programs to solve the traveling salesperson problem.

Example 14.9 Knapsack Problem

The knapsack problem is a classic application problem of integer programming. This problem involves filling a knapsack with a given capacity (volume or weight) by selecting certain items from a given number of available articles. Usually, the available quantity of each item is limited to one unit, and each item has certain characteristics in terms of weight, volume, and relative benefits (utilities). The objective of the problem is to determine the optimal combination of items that should be packed in the knapsack to maximize the total benefit within the given knapsack capacity constraints.

Suppose a scout is packing a knapsack for a camping trip. The scout is considering taking 10 different items on the trip. Their values for the trip and weights are shown in the following table:

Item	Value (points)	Weight (lb)
Compass/watch	300	.15
Jar of peanut butter	200	.5
Portable burner	75	4
Canteen	225	2.5
Sleeping bag	250	5
Dried meat	125	2
Fishing gear	75	4
Movie camera	25	1.2
Portable television	10	2
Radio	50	.8

The maximum weight allowed each scout is 15 pounds. Furthermore, there should be at least 1 food item packed in the knapsack and not more than 1 item from among the camera, television, and radio. The model can be formulated in the following manner.

$$\text{Maximize } Z = 300x_1 + 200x_2 + 75x_3 + 225x_4 + 250x_5 + 125x_6$$
$$+ 75x_7 + 25x_8 + 10x_9 + 50x_{10}$$

subject to
$$.15x_1 + .5x_2 + 4x_3 + 2.5x_4 + 5x_5 + 2x_6 + 4x_7 + 1.2x_8 + 2x_9 + .8x_{10} \leq 15$$
$$x_2 + x_6 \geq 1$$
$$x_8 + x_9 + x_{10} \leq 1$$
$$x_j = 0 \text{ or } 1 \text{ for all } j$$

Many variations of the knapsack problem have been developed for real-world applications. The cargo loading problem is a good example of a variation of the knapsack problem. The knapsack problem can be expanded by allowing additional constraints and possible inclusion of more units of item j.

The knapsack problem is computationally challenging, as the total number of possible combinations of n items is 2^n. For example, a problem with 5 items has 32 different combinations, a problem with 10 items has 1024, and a problem with 30 items has over 1 billion possible solution combinations.

Implicit Enumeration Method

You should now be familiar with some of the many real-world problems that require all decision variables to bear values of either zero or one. This section discusses the implicit enumeration method for solving the zero-one problem. Egon Balas developed an algorithm that anlyzes all solutions (feasible and infeasible), although the vast majority of the solutions are enumerated only implicitly. The implicit enumeration method is based on Balas's additive algorithm and Glover's backtracking method, which was applied to the Balas algorithm by Geoffrion.

The technique is to start the solution process with an optimal (actually, even better-than-optimal) but infeasible solution. The procedure then forces the solution toward feasibility while maintaining an optimal solution. The implicit enumeration method is based not on the usual simplex method but on a binary branch-and-bound procedure. The bounding is accomplished by keeping the best feasible solution as the optimality test criterion for new solutions. The branching is performed through the feasibility test and the assignment of the binary value to solution variables.

The contribution rates (c_j) in the objective function should be nonnegative, $c_j \geq 0$. This condition is not actually restrictive, because if $c_j < 0$, x_j can be replaced by $1 - x_j$, where $x_j = 0$ or 1; x_j will then have a positive contribution rate in the objective function. This substitution must be made in the constraints as well.

In order to examine the solution procedure in a systematic manner, we will define the following variables:

A = set of all decision variables

V_j = set of all decision variables that have been assigned a value of either 0 or 1 at the jth iteration

$A - V_j$ = set of free variables (i.e., those that have not entered the solution as yet, after the jth iteration)

I_j = set of free decision variables that could possibly improve the solution at the jth iteration

$\overline{Z}$ = current upper bound value of the objective function

The general solution procedure for the implicit enumeration method is summarized as follows:

Step 1 Make all variables free variables ($V_0 = \emptyset$). They are implicitly equal to zero. If this solution is feasible, the optimal solution has been found. Otherwise, determine the initial upper bound of $\overline{Z}$ when $x_j = 1$ for all j.

Step 2 Find the set of constraints violated when partial solution V_j is implemented. If no constraint is violated, set all free variables equal to zero. This is a feasible solution ($I_j = \emptyset$). If the value of the objective function for this solution is less than the previous $\overline{Z}$, it becomes the new upper bound $\overline{Z}$. Proceed to step 3. If some constraints are still violated, find the value of the objective function for the solution F and set $\overline{Z} - F$ as the objective coefficient limit. Proceed to step 4.

Step 3 When the solution is "fathomed" (that is, cannot be improved any further), initiate the backtracking procedure. The last variable with a value of 1 added to the solution (the rightmost positive element in V_j) is made 0 but left in the solution set (not a free variable). Any elements to the right are dropped. Return to step 2.

Step 4 Find I_j, the set of improving variables, by evaluating each of the free variables on the basis of two criteria: (1) feasibility test 1—it should have a positive coefficient in some violated contraints; (2) the optimality test—the objective function coefficient should be less than the limit $\overline{Z} - F$.

If $I_j = \emptyset$, check all elements in V_j. If they are all negative, terminate the solution. The current upper bound feasible solution, if there is one, is the optimal solution. If all elements in V_j are not negative, return to step 3.

If $I_j \neq \emptyset$, proceed to step 5.

Step 5 Perform feasibility test 2. This test determines whether or not all violated constraints can be made feasible if some or all variables in I_j are made 1 in each of the violated constraints where these variables have positive coefficients.

If so, select the variable in I_j with the greatest coefficient sum and enter it into V_j. Return to step 2.

If not, check all elements in V_j. If they are all negative, terminate the solution. The current upper bound feasible solution, if there is one, is the optimal solution. If all elements in V_j are not negative, return to step 3.

Consider the following example problem:

Minimize $Z = 2x_1 + x_2 + 3x_3 + 2x_4 + 4x_5$

subject to

$$x_1 + 2x_2 + x_3 + x_4 + 2x_5 \geq 4$$
$$7x_1 + x_2 - 3x_4 + 3x_5 \geq 2$$
$$-3x_1 + 3x_2 + 2x_3 - x_5 \geq -1$$
$$x_j = 0 \text{ or } 1 \text{ for all } j$$

The number of possible solution combinations for this problem is $2^5 = 32$. The implicit enumeration method for the problem is applied as follows.

Iteration 0

$$A = (1, 2, 3, 4, 5)$$
$$V_0 = \emptyset$$
$$A - V_0 = (1, 2, 3, 4, 5)$$
$$I_0 = (1, 2, 3, 4, 5)$$
$$\overline{Z} = 12 \text{ (initial upper bound)} \quad \text{infeasible}$$

Since the goal is to minimize the objective function and since all contribution coefficients (c_j) are positive, a good place to start the solution is where all $x_j = 0$. Thus, $A = (1, 2, 3, 4, 5)$ and the V_0 set is empty. $A - V_0$, or the set of free variables, is $(1, 2, 3, 4, 5)$. The initial upper bound $\overline{Z}$ is found by making all $x_j = 1$ in the objective function. This solution ($V_0 = \emptyset$) is, of course, infeasible.

To determine the set of improving variables, I_0, rearrange the constraints in the following manner:

$$\underbrace{x_1 + 2x_2 + x_3 + \quad x_4 + 2x_5 \geq 4}_{f_1} \tag{14.16}$$

$$\underbrace{7x_1 + x_2 \quad\quad\quad -3x_4 + 3x_5 \geq 2}_{f_2} \tag{14.17}$$

$$\underbrace{-3x_1 + 3x_2 + 2x_3 \quad\quad\quad -x_5 \geq -1}_{f_3} \tag{14.18}$$

Then

$$f_1 = -4 + x_1 + 2x_2 + x_3 + x_4 + 2x_5 \geq 0$$
$$f_2 = -2 + 7x_1 + x_2 \quad - 3x_4 + 3x_5 \geq 0$$
$$f_3 = 1 - 3x_1 + 3x_2 + 2x_3 \quad - x_5 \geq 0$$

Since $x_j = 0$ at iteration 0,

$$f_1 = -4 \not\geq 0 \quad \text{(violated constraint)}$$
$$f_2 = -2 \not\geq 0 \quad \text{(violated constraint)}$$
$$f_3 = 1 \geq 0 \quad \text{(unviolated constraint)}$$

The improving variable candidates are those with positive coefficients (feasibility test 1) in the first two constraints.

	x_1	x_2	x_3	x_4	x_5
$f_1 = -4 +$	$1(0) +$	$2(0) +$	$1(0) +$	$1(0) +$	$2(0) \not\geq 0$
$f_2 = -2 +$	$7(0) +$	$1(0)$	$-$	$3(0) +$	$3(0) \not\geq 0$
Sums of coefficients	8	3	1	-2	5

Thus, $I_0 = (1, 2, 3, 4, 5)$. Perform feasibility test 2 by checking whether or not the two violated constraints can be made feasible by making variables in I_0 that have positive coefficients in the first and second constraints equal to 1. The calculations are as follows:

Constraint 1: $f_1 = -4 + 1(1) + 2(1) + 1(1) + 1(1) + 2(1) = 3 \geq 0$
Constraint 2: $f_2 = -2 + 7(1) + 1(1) \quad\quad - 3(0) + 3(1) = 9 \geq 0$

Thus, the partial solution passes the feasibility test. Note that variables with negative coefficients (x_4 in constraint 2) are not assigned a value of 1.

Since the procedure is to add one variable at a time to V_j in search of a feasible solution, the entering variable should be the one that moves the solution closest to feasibility. Because a variable may have positive coefficients in some constraints and negative coefficients in others, its addition to the solution may be "helpful" in some constraints and "harmful" in others. To find an overall measure, determine the sum of the constraint coefficients for each of the free variables in the violated constraints. In the example, x_1 is easily determined to be the most attractive candidate, since the sum of its coefficients is the greatest. The optimality test, or the objective function coefficient test, is not needed here, as a feasible solution has not yet been found.

Iteration 1
$$V_1 = (+1) \qquad \text{(infeasible solution)}$$
$$A - V_1 = (2, 3, 4, 5)$$
$$I_1 = (2, 3, 4, 5)$$

With $x_1 = (+1)$, the solution becomes $x_1 = 1$, $x_2 = x_3 = x_4 = x_5 = 0$. The $+$ sign in front of the 1 indicates that a value of 1 has been assigned to x_1. When a variable has been assigned a value of 0, its subscript will be preceded by a $-$ sign. Once again, perform feasibility test 1 as follows:

	x_1	x_2	x_3	x_4	x_5	
$f_1 =$	$-4 + 1(1) +$	$2(0) +$	$1(0) +$	$1(0) +$	$2(0) =$	$-3 \not\geq 0$
$f_2 =$	$-2 + 7(1) +$	$1(0)$		$-3(0) +$	$3(0) =$	$5 \geq 0$
$f_3 =$	$1 - 3(1) +$	$3(0) +$	$2(0)$	$-1(0) =$		$-2 \not\geq 0$
Sum of coefficients	5	3	1	1		
in constraints 1 and 3						

The first and third constraints are still not satisfied. Thus, the solution is infeasible. Feasibility test 2 of the two violated constraints yields

Constraint 1: $f_1 = -4 + 1(1) + 2(1) + 1(1) + 1(1) + 2(1) = 3 \geq 0$
Constraint 3: $f_3 = 1 - 3(1) + 3(1) + 2(1) \qquad\qquad = 3 \geq 0$

$I_1 = (2, 3, 4, 5)$, and x_2 is the entering variable, as the sum of its coefficients is the greatest. It should again be noted that since the upper bound $\overline{Z}$ is not that of a feasible solution, it is not necessary to perform the optimality test.

Iteration 2
$$V_2 = (+1, +2) \qquad \text{(infeasible solution)}$$
$$A - V_2 = (3, 4, 5)$$
$$I_2 = (3, 4, 5)$$

The result of entering the improving variable x_2 into the solution can be determined as follows:

$$
\begin{array}{ccccc}
x_1 & x_2 & x_3 & x_4 & x_5
\end{array}
$$

$$f_1 = -4 + 1(1) + 2(1) + 1(0) + 1(0) + 2(0) = -1 \not\geq 0$$
$$f_2 = -2 + 7(1) + 1(1) \qquad\quad - 3(0) + 3(0) = \quad 6 \geq 0$$
$$f_3 = \quad 1 - 3(1) + 3(1) + 2(0) \qquad\quad - 1(0) = \quad 1 \geq 0$$

Coefficients in constraint 1   1   1   2

This solution is still not feasible. $I_2 = (3, 4, 5)$, and the entering variable at the next iteration should be x_5.

Iteration 3
$$V_3 = (+1, +2, +5) \qquad \text{(feasible solution)}$$
$$A - V_3 = (3, 4)$$
$$I_3 = \varnothing \qquad\qquad\qquad \text{(fathomed)}$$
$$\overline{Z} = 7$$

The feasibility of the solution can be examined again as follows:

$$
\begin{array}{ccccc}
x_1 & x_2 & x_3 & x_4 & x_5
\end{array}
$$

$$f_1 = -4 + 1(1) + 2(1) + 1(0) + 1(0) + 2(1) = 1 \geq 0$$
$$f_2 = -2 + 7(1) + 1(1) \qquad\quad - 3(0) + 3(1) = 9 \geq 0$$
$$f_3 = \quad 1 - 3(1) + 3(1) + 2(0) \qquad\quad - 1(1) = 0 \geq 0$$

This solution is feasible, as all constraints are satisfied. The solution is $x_1 = 1$, $x_2 = 1$, $x_5 = 1$, $x_3 = 0$, $x_4 = 0$, and $Z = 7$. As this solution is feasible, adding any new variable (making either $x_3 = 1$ or $x_4 = 1$) would only increase the total cost. Thus, $I_3 = \varnothing$ and the solution is fathomed. It should be noted that we have implicitly completed the enumeration of all solutions in which $x_1 = x_2 = x_5 = 1$.

Iteration 4
$$V_4 = (+1, +2, -5) \qquad \text{(infeasible solution)}$$
$$A - V_4 = (3, 4)$$
$$I_4 = (3, 4)$$

Since the solution at iteration 3 was fathomed, the backtracking procedure should be initiated. The rightmost positive element in V_3 (x_5) should be made 0 but left in the solution set, as described in step 3 of the solution procedure. Going back to step 2 of the solution procedure, we analyze the feasibility and optimality of the solution. Of course, this solution is basically the same as the one evaluated at iteration 2. At that iteration, the improving variable set was identified as $I_2 = (3, 4, 5)$. Since x_5 is no longer a free variable, I_4 equals $(3, 4)$. The upper bound has now been derived from a feasible solution, so the improving variables must also pass the optimality test. The objective function coefficients of the improving variables should be less than $\overline{Z} - F$. The value of the objective function for the partial solution $V_2 = (1, 2)$ is 3. Thus, $\overline{Z} - F = 7 - 3 = 4$. Either variable qualifies as an entering variable.

Objective function coefficients
$$
\begin{array}{cc}
x_3 & x_4 \\
\hline
3 & 2
\end{array}
$$

Feasibility test 2 (step 5) must be performed whether or not the violated constraint ($f_1 = -1 \not\geq 0$) can be made feasible, if variables in I_4 are made 1. The test shows that with the solution $(+1, +2, -5, +3, +4)$, $f_1 = 1 \geq 0$. The coefficients of x_3 and x_4 are the same value (1). Thus, we enter x_4, which has a smaller objective function coefficient.

Iteration 5
$$V_5 = (+1, +2, -5, +4) \qquad \text{(feasible solution)}$$
$$A - V_5 = (3)$$
$$I_5 = \emptyset \qquad\qquad\qquad \text{(fathomed)}$$
$$\overline{Z} = 5$$

The feasibility of the solution can be checked as follows:

$$
\begin{array}{ccccc}
x_1 & x_2 & x_3 & x_4 & x_5
\end{array}
$$
$$f_1 = -4 + 1(1) + 2(1) + 1(0) + 1(1) + 2(0) = 0 \geq 0$$
$$f_2 = -2 + 7(1) + 1(1) \qquad\quad - 3(1) + 3(0) = 3 \geq 0$$
$$f_3 = \quad 1 - 3(1) + 3(1) + 2(0) \qquad - 1(0) = 1 \geq 0$$

This solution is also feasible, but the value of the objective function is 2 less than the previous upper bound. Thus, the new upper bound $\overline{Z} = 5$. We have completed implicit enumeration of all solutions with $x_1 = x_2 = x_4 = 1$.

Iteration 6
$$V_6 = (+1, +2, -5, -4) \qquad \text{(infeasible solution)}$$
$$A - V_6 = (3)$$
$$I_6 = \emptyset \qquad\qquad\qquad \text{(fathomed)}$$

The variables in the $A - V_6$ set (only x_3 in this case) should be tested for feasibility and optimality. Constraint 1 is the only constraint violated ($f_1 = -1 \not\geq 0$; see the solution at iteration 2). The x_3 variable easily passes feasibility test 1, as it has a positive coefficient in f_1. The optimality test shows that the objective function coefficient of x_3 ($c_3 = 3$) is greater than $\overline{Z} - F = 2$. Thus, x_3 does not pass the optimality test.

Iteration 7
$$V_7 = (+1, -2) \qquad \text{(infeasible solution)}$$
$$A - V_7 = (3, 4, 5)$$
$$I_7 = (4)$$

The feasibility of this solution was tested at iteration 1. The optimality test should be performed for the three free variables against $\overline{Z} - F = 3$. Only x_4 passes the test.

Iteration 8
$$V_8 = (+1, -2, +4) \qquad \text{(infeasible solution)}$$
$$A - V_8 = (3, 5)$$
$$I_8 = \emptyset \qquad\qquad\qquad \text{(fathomed)}$$

Feasibility test 1 of the solution gives the following:

$$
\begin{array}{ccccc}
x_1\ x_2 & x_3 & x_4 & x_5 &
\end{array}
$$

$f_1 = -4 + 1(1) + 2(0) + 1(0) + 1(1) + 2(0) = -2 \not\geq 0$

$f_2 = -2 + 7(1) + 1(0) \qquad\quad - 3(1) + 3(0) = \quad 2 \geq 0$

$f_3 = \quad 1 - 3(1) + 3(0) + 2(0) \qquad - 1(0) = -2 \not\geq 0$

Sum of coefficients in $\qquad\qquad$ 3 $\qquad\qquad$ 1
constraints 1 and 3

Constraints 1 and 3 are violated. The optimality test is performed for the two free variables that have positive coefficients in the violated constraints: x_3 and x_5. Since $\overline{Z} - F = 5 - 4 = 1$, neither variable passes the test. Thus, $I_8 = \varnothing$.

Iteration 9
$$V_9 = (+1, -2, -4) \qquad \text{(infeasible solution)}$$
$$A - V_9 = (3, 5)$$
$$I_9 = \varnothing$$

We already know from iteration 7 that the variables x_3 and x_5 do not pass the optimality test.

Iteration 10
$$V_{10} = (-1) \qquad \text{(infeasible solution)}$$
$$A - V_{10} = (2, 3, 4, 5)$$
$$I_{10} = (2, 3, 4, 5)$$

This solution is basically the same as the one analyzed at iteration 0. Feasibility test 1 yields

$$
\begin{array}{ccccc}
x_1\ x_2 & x_3 & x_4 & x_5 &
\end{array}
$$

$f_1 = -4 + 1(0) + 2(0) + 1(0) + 1(0) + 2(0) = -4 \not\geq 0$

$f_2 = -2 + 7(0) + 1(0) \qquad\quad - 3(0) + 3(0) = -2 \not\geq 0$

$f_3 = \quad 1 - 3(0) + 3(0) + 2(0) \qquad - 1(0) = \quad 1 \geq 0$

Sum of coefficients $\quad$ 3 $\qquad$ 1 $\qquad$ -2 $\qquad$ 5
in constraints 1 and 2

All the free variables pass the optimality test, $c_j < (\overline{Z} - F) = 5$. Feasibility test 2 shows that

$f_1 = -4 + 1(0) + 2(1) + 1(1) + 1(1) + 2(1) = 1 \geq 0$

$f_2 = -2 + 7(0) + 1(1) \qquad\quad - 3(0) + 3(1) = 2 \geq 0$

Iteration 11
$$V_{11} = (-1, +5) \qquad \text{(infeasible solution)}$$
$$A - V_{11} = (2, 3, 4)$$
$$I_{11} = \varnothing \qquad\qquad \text{(fathomed)}$$

This solution violates only constraint 1, $f_1 = -2 \not\geq 0$. All of the free variables satisfy the feasibility test. However, none passes the optimality test, $c_j < (\overline{Z} - F) = 5 - 4 = 1$. Thus, the solution is fathomed.

Iteration 12

$$V_{12} = (-1, -5) \qquad \text{(infeasible solution)}$$
$$A - V_{12} = (2, 3, 4)$$
$$I_{12} = \emptyset \qquad \qquad \text{(fathomed)}$$

All the free variables pass feasibility test 1 and the optimality test. Feasibility test 2 of the violated constraints indicates the following:

$$f_1 = -4 + 1(0) + 2(1) + 1(1) + 1(1) + 2(0) = \quad 0 \geqslant 0$$
$$f_2 = -2 + 7(0) + 1(1) \qquad \quad - 3(0) + 3(0) = -1 \geqslant 0$$

This solution is therefore fathomed. Since all elements in V_{12} are negative, the solution procedure should be terminated.

The optimal solution is the incumbent solution that has the current upper bound. The optimal solution is therefore $x_1 = x_2 = x_4 = 1$, $x_3 = x_5 = 0$, $Z = 5$, as identified at iteration 5.

As the final step, we check all the solution combinations, as shown in the following table:

Solutions	x_1	x_2	x_3	x_4	x_5	Feasibility	$\overline{Z}$
1	0	0	0	0	0	No	
2	0	0	0	0	1	No	
3	0	0	0	1	0	No	
4	0	0	0	1	1	No	
5	0	0	1	0	0	No	
6	0	0	1	0	1	No	
7	0	0	1	1	0	No	
8	0	0	1	1	1	No	
9	0	1	0	0	0	No	
10	0	1	0	0	1	Yes	5
11	0	1	0	1	0	No	
12	0	1	0	1	1	No	
13	0	1	1	0	0	No	
14	0	1	1	0	1	Yes	8
15	0	1	1	1	0	No	
16	0	1	1	1	1	No	
17	1	0	0	0	0	No	
18	1	0	0	0	1	No	
19	1	0	0	1	0	No	
20	1	0	0	1	1	No	
21	1	0	1	0	0	No	
22	1	0	1	0	1	No	
23	1	0	1	1	0	No	
24	1	0	1	1	1	No	
25	1	1	0	0	0	No	
26	1	1	0	0	1	Yes	7
27	1	1	0	1	0	Yes	5
28	1	1	0	1	1	Yes	9
29	1	1	1	0	0	Yes	6
30	1	1	1	0	1	Yes	10
31	1	1	1	1	0	Yes	8
32	1	1	1	1	1	Yes	12

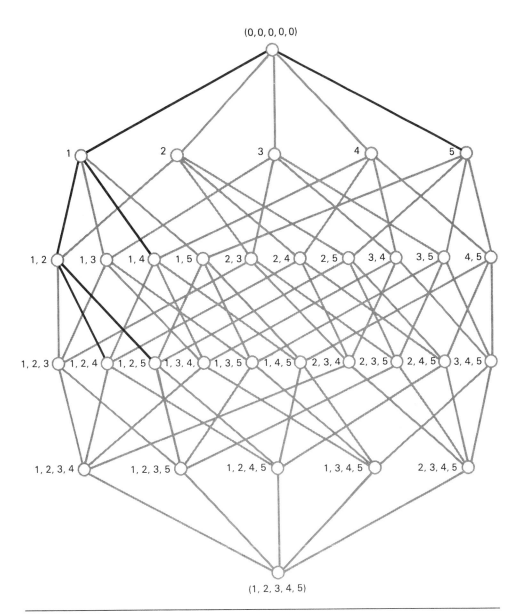

Figure 14.9 *Solution Network of the Sample Problem*

The optimal solution is identified as solution 27. There is also an alternative optimal solution identified as solution 10. If alternative optimal solutions are of interest, the criterion of the optimality test can be modified from $c_j < \overline{Z} - F$ to $c_j \leq \overline{Z} - F$ for the free variables. The complete solution network for the problem is shown in Figure 14.9. The solutions explicitly enumerated are shown by bold lines. Figure 14.10 presents a flow diagram of the implicit enumeration procedure followed in solving the sample problem.

Some Complications of the Zero-One Problem

Because the standard zero-one programming model requires that $c_j \geq 0$ and that all constraints be $\geq$ constraints, special measures must be taken to deal with maximization problems, negative contribution rates, and equality or $\leq$ constraints.

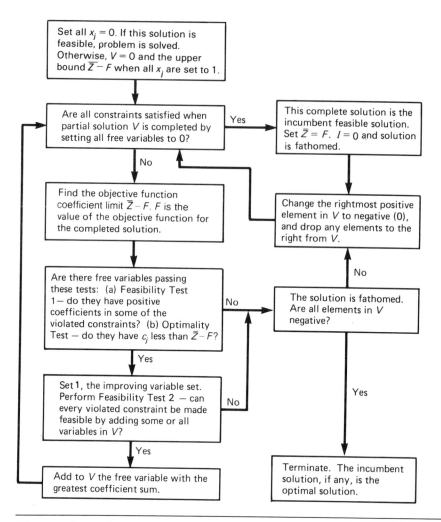

Figure 14.10 Flow Diagram of the Implicit Enumeration Procedure

Maximization Problems

If the problem under consideration is a maximization problem, the objective function can be transformed into a minimization function simply by multiplying it by -1. The solution procedure can then proceed in the usual manner.

Negative Contribution Rates

As discussed earlier, if x_j has a negative objective function coefficient $(-c_j)$, then x_j can be easily replaced by $1 - x_j$. Thus, $-c_j x_j = -c_j(1 - x_j) = -c_j + c_j x_j$, and the objective function coefficient becomes positive.

Equality or $\leqslant$ Constraints

A $\leqslant$ constraint can be easily converted into a $\geqslant$ constraint by multiplying both sides by -1. Any equality constraint can be converted in the following manner: if

$$f_i = b_i$$

Flow diagram text:

Set all $x_j = 0$. If this solution is feasible, problem is solved. Otherwise, $V = 0$ and the upper bound $\overline{Z} - F$ when all x_j are set to 1.

Are all constraints satisfied when partial solution V is completed by setting all free variables to 0?

Yes → This complete solution is the incumbent feasible solution. Set $\overline{Z} = F$. $I = 0$ and solution is fathomed.

No

Find the objective function coefficient limit $\overline{Z} - F$. F is the value of the objective function for the completed solution.

Change the rightmost positive element in V to negative (0), and drop any elements to the right from V.

Are there free variables passing these tests: (a) Feasibility Test 1 – do they have positive coefficients in some of the violated constraints? (b) Optimality Test – do they have c_j less than $\overline{Z} - F$?

No → The solution is fathomed. Are all elements in V negative?

No (from change rightmost box)

Yes

Set 1, the improving variable set. Perform Feasibility Test 2 – can every violated constraint be made feasible by adding some or all variables in V?

No

Yes

Add to V the free variable with the greatest coefficient sum.

Terminate. The incumbent solution, if any, is the optimal solution.

then

$$f_i \leqslant b_i \quad \text{and} \quad f_i \geqslant b_i$$

or

$$f_i \leqslant b_i \quad \text{and} \quad -f_i \leqslant -b_i$$

It should be clear that each equality constraint will be replaced by two inequality constraints. If the problem under consideration has a small number of equality constraints, this procedure is quite satisfactory. If, however, the problem has a large number of equality constraints, this procedure will make the problem very complex. The following is an alternative approach: if

$$f_1 = b_1$$
$$f_2 = b_2$$
$$\cdot$$
$$\cdot$$
$$\cdot$$
$$f_m = b_m$$

then

$$f_1 \geqslant b_1$$
$$f_2 \geqslant b_2$$
$$\cdot$$
$$\cdot$$
$$\cdot$$
$$f_m \geqslant b_m$$

and

$$f_1 + f_2 + \cdots + f_m \leqslant b_1 + b_2 + \cdots + b_m$$

This procedure converts m equality constraints into only $m + 1$ inequality constraints.

Variable Elimination

Variable elimination is a procedure that can be used to make a zero-one problem simpler (and reduce the number of solution combinations) when there is an equality constraint. It eliminates one decision variable from the model (in the objective function and the constraints). Consider the following constraints:

$$x_1 + 2x_2 + 5x_3 = 10$$
$$x_j = 0 \text{ or } 1$$

If

$$x_1 = 10 - 2x_2 - 5x_3$$

then, since $x_1 \geqslant 0$,

$$10 - 2x_2 - 5x_3 \geqslant 0 \quad \text{or} \quad -2x_2 - 5x_3 \geqslant -10$$

and, since $x_1 \leqslant 1$,

$$10 - 2x_2 - 5x_3 \leqslant 1 \quad \text{or} \quad 2x_2 + 5x_3 \geqslant 9$$

An Application of the Branch-and-Bound Technique: Saving Electric Production Costs at Southern Company

The Southern Electric System is one of the largest investor-owned utility systems in the United States. Southern Company operates 239 generating units, representing 33,919 MW in capacity, and serves over three million customers in a 122,000 square-mile area in Georgia, Alabama, Mississippi, and Florida. Southern also has over 3,000 MW of firm sales agreement with utilities in Florida and Texas. With 1989 operating revenues of $7.2 billion and net income of $846 million, Southern Company is considered one of the largest utilities in the United States.

Unlike other forms of energy, electricity cannot be easily stored. A major challenge for

electric utilities is to determine the most economic configuration of generating units to meet the customer loads. Since the system loads fluctuate widely over time, operators face a difficult question: What is the most economic way to mix available generation resources to meet anticipated loads?

The electric utility business has traditionally been very capital intensive. In the last 10 years, however, fuel costs have escalated at a faster rate than all other cost components. To minimize its fuel cost expenditures, Southern Company installed a comprehensive operational-planning software package to forecast system loads,

Computer-Based Solution of Integer Programming

A computer-based solution of Example 14.2, using AB:QM, is presented.

```
Program: Zero One Programming

Problem Title : Example 14.2

***** Input Data *****

Max.   Z =   100x1 + 190x2 + 80x3 + 30x4 + 220x5 + 150x6

Subject to

C1    210x1 + 340x2 + 150x3 + 60x4 + 540x5 + 350x6 <= 1000
C2    3x1 + 5x2 + 2x3 + 1x4 + 8x5 + 3x6 <= 12
C3    45x1 + 75x2 + 35x3 + 10x4 + 150x5 + 100x6 >= 100
C4    40x1 + 70x2 + 33x3 + 18x4 + 120x5 + 80x6 >= 100
C5    1x3 + 1x4 <= 1
C6    -1x1 + 1x6 <= 0

***** Program Output *****

Iteration  1
-----------
Partial solution set :   5

Iteration  2
-----------
Partial solution set :   5   3
```

optimally schedule thermal and hydro units, and estimate future prices of power transactions.

Southern Company Services, Inc. (SCS), the engineering and operating arm of the utility, faces a number of important operating challenges. The control center at SCS is responsible for determining the optimal configuration of thermal units to bring on line to minimize the total production cost. SCS used truncated dynamic programming (DP) with a front-end branch-and-bound (BAB) technique to solve the short-term resource scheduling problem. The branch-and-bound modules use artificial-intelligence rules, which mimic operator judgement, to quickly identify the 30–60 unit combinations to evaluate during any given hour from the thousands of feasible solutions.

The Wescouger optimization program, designed by SCS, saved over $140 million in fuel costs over the past 7 years. Total production cost savings achieved by all Wescouger users are estimated to be around $200 and $300 million per year. In the United States, the program is currently used to schedule around 25% of the nation's generating capacity. Overseas clients who have adopted the Wescouger technology include the Mitsubishi Electric Corporation in Tokyo, Japan, the Korea Electric Power Company in Seoul, Korea, and the National Power Corporation in Swindon, England.

Source: S. R. Erwin et al., "Using an Optimization Software to Lower Overall Electric Production Costs for Southern Company," *Interfaces,* 21, no. 1 (January–February 1991): 27–41.

```
Iteration  3
-----------
Partial solution set :  5  -3

Iteration  4
-----------
Partial solution set : -5

Iteration  5
-----------
Partial solution set : -5   6

Iteration  6
-----------
Partial solution set : -5  -6

Iteration  7
-----------
Partial solution set : -5  -6   2

Iteration  8
-----------
Partial solution set : -5  -6   2   1

Iteration  9
-----------
Partial solution set : -5  -6   2  -1

Iteration 10
-----------
Partial solution set : -5  -6  -2
```

```
Final Optimal Solution at iteration   10

Z =      470.000

---------------------------
Variable         Value
---------------------------
   x 1             1
   x 2             1
   x 3             0
   x 4             1
   x 5             0
   x 6             1
---------------------------

***** End of Output *****
```

SUMMARY

In this chapter we examined various examples of integer programming problems, their model formulations and solution methods. There are many real-world problems that can be formulated as integer programming models. Integer programming problems are intellectually stimulating and interesting to analyze. However, such problems cannot always be solved easily by the solution methods discussed in this chapter. The difficulty lies not in the formulation of the model but in the efficient solution of the problem. The techniques discussed in this chapter work well for problems involving few variables. However, even with the powerful computers available today, many larger integer problems are difficult to solve by integer programming algorithms. When these techniques are applied to large real-world problems, the solution process can be very complex, time consuming, and costly. These solution methods are meant to converge in a finite number of steps. Yet even this finite number of steps has often been found to be prohibitive in terms of computation time or storage requirements. The hope is that, in the future, continued research will produce improved solution methods for integer programming problems.

REFERENCES

BALAS, E. "An Additive Algorithm for Solving Linear Programs with Zero-One Variables." *Operations Research* 13 (1965): 517–546.

BUDNICK, F. S.; MOJENA, R.; and VOLLMAN, T. E. *Principles of Operations*

Research for Management, 2nd ed. Homewood, Illinois: Richard D. Irwin, 1988.

CROWDER, H., JOHNSON, E. L., and PADBERG, M. "Solving Large-Scale Zero-One Linear Programming Problems." *Operations Research,* 31 (1983): 803–834.

DANTZIG, G. B. "On the Significance of Solving Linear Programming Problems with Some Integer Variables." *Econometrica* 28 (1960): 30–44.

ERWIN, S. R. "Using an Optimization Software to Lower Overall Electric Production Costs for Southern Company." *Interfaces,* 21, no. 1 (January–February 1991): 27–41.

GEOFFRION, A. M. "Integer Programming by Implicit Enumeration and Balas' Method." *SIAM Review* 9 (1967): 178–190.

GOMORY, R. E. "An Algorithm for Integer Solutions to Linear Programs." In *Recent Advances in Mathematical Programming,* edited by R. L. Graves and P. Wolfe. New York: McGraw-Hill, 1963.

HILLIER, F. S., and LIEBERMAN, G. J. *Introduction to Operations Research.* 5th ed. New York: McGraw-Hill, 1990.

JOHNSON, E. L., KOSTREVA, M. M., and SUHL, U. H. "Solving 0–1 Integer Programming Problems Arising from Large Scale Planning Models." *Operations Research,* 33 (1985): 803–819.

LAND, A. H., and DOIG, A. G. "An Automati Method of Solving Discrete Programming Problems." *Econometrica* 28 (1960): 497–520.

LEE, S. M. *Introduction to Management Science* 2nd ed. Chicago: The Dryden Press, 1988

LEE, S. M., *AB:QM: Allyn & Bacon Quantita tive Methods 3.0.* Boston: Allyn and Bacon, 1993.

LITTLE, J. D. C. et al. "An Algorithm for the Traveling Salesman Problem." *Operation Research* 11 (1963): 972–989.

MINOUX, M. *Mathematical Programming* New York: John Wiley & Sons, 1986.

NEMHAUSER, G. L., and WOLSEY, L. A. *Integer and Combinatorial Optimization.* New York: John Wiley & Sons, 1988.

SCHRIVER, A. *Theory of Linear and Integer Programming.* New York: John Wiley & Sons, 1986.

TAHA, H. A. *Operations Research: An Introduction.* 4th ed. New York: Macmillan, 1987.

WILLIAMS, H. P. *Model Building in Mathematical Programming,* 2nd ed. New York: John Wiley & Sons, 1985.

PROBLEMS

1. A production manager faces the problem of allocating jobs to two production crews. The production rate is 5 units per hour for crew 1 and is 6 units for crew 2. Each crew normally works 8 hours per day. If the firm requires overtime operations, each crew can work up to 11 hours, according to the union contract. The firm has a special contract with a customer to provide a minimum of 120 units of the product the next day.

   The union contract calls for each crew to work at least 8 hours per day and any overtime not exceeding 3 hours to be in terms of increments of an hour. The operating costs are $200 for crew 1 and $220 for crew 2.

   a. Formulate a linear programming model for this problem.

   b. Solve the problem by the simplex method.

   c. The problem requires an integer solution. Solve the problem by the rounding approach and compare the solution with the graphical solution.

2. The following problem requires an integer solution. Solve it by the branch-and-bound method.

Maximize $Z = \$4x_1 + \$3x_2$

subject to
$$x_1 + x_2 \leqslant 30$$
$$3x_1 + x_2 \leqslant 75$$
$$x_1 + 2x_2 \leqslant 50$$
$$x_1, x_2 = 0 \text{ or nonnegative integers}$$

3. The dietician at the local hospital is planning the breakfast menu for the maternity ward patients. The dietician is planning a special nonfattening diet and has chosen cottage cheese and scrambled eggs for breakfast. The primary concerns in planning the breakfast are the vitamin E and iron requirements of new mothers.

According to the American Medical Association (AMA), new mothers should get at least 12 milligrams of vitamin E and 24 milligrams of iron (fictitious figures) from breakfast. The AMA handbook reports that a scoop of cottage cheese contains 3 milligrams of vitamin E and 3 milligrams of iron. An average scoop of scrambled eggs contains 2 milligrams of vitamin E and 8 milligrams of iron. In accordance with the AMA handbook, the dietician recommends that new mothers eat at least two scoops of cottage cheese for their breakfast. The dietician considers this to be one of the model constraints.

The hospital accounting department estimates that a scoop of cottage cheese and a scoop of scrambled eggs each cost $.05. The dietician is attempting to determine the optimal breakfast menu that will satisfy all the nutritional requirements and minimize total cost. The cook insists that only full scoops of food be served, which necessitates an integer solution. Determine the optimal integer solution to the problem, using the graphical solution technique.

4. Solve the diet problem presented in problem 3 using the branch-and-bound technique.

5. Solve the following integer programming problem by the branch-and-bound technique:

Minimize $Z = 6x_1 + 6x_2$

subject to
$$3x_1 + 2x_2 \geqslant 12$$
$$3x_1 + 8x_2 \geqslant 24$$
$$x_1 \geqslant 2$$
$$x_1, x_2 = 0 \quad \text{or non-negative integers}$$

6. Solve the following mixed-integer programming problem:

Maximize $Z = 2x_1 + 3x_2$

subject to
$$2x_1 + 4x_2 \leqslant 25$$
$$x_1 \leqslant 8$$
$$2x_2 \leqslant 10$$
$$x_1, s_1, s_3 \text{ without integer requirements}$$
$$x_2 \text{ and } s_2 \text{ with integer requirements}$$

7. A central dispatcher for the local police department has just received five calls requesting police investigation. Examining the location map, the dispatcher notes that there are five patrol cars available for investigation. The following table indicates the distances between each patrol car and the trouble spots. The objective of the problem is to minimize total travel time for the patrol cars to respond to the five calls. Solve the problem by the branch-and-bound technique.

	Trouble Spot				
Patrol Car	1	2	3	4	5
A	18	14	10	14	17
B	22	18	8	9	14
C	15	25	12	15	25
D	20	16	16	22	12
E	16	28	10	14	15

8. Your college requires that each student register for at least 13 hours per semester. Tom has narrowed his course selection down to six possible courses. These courses and the minimum study hours required per week are as follows:

Course	Credit Hours	Study Hours
Math 100	5	10
Chemistry 102	4	7
Social Studies 113	3	6
English 108	4	5
Physical Education 134	2	2
Drawing 124	3	1

Tom wishes to meet the college's requirement while having to study as few hours per week as possible. He can register for each class only once, and he cannot register for a partial class. Formulate this problem and solve using AB:QM.

9. A marine transport company has four of its oceangoing freighters scheduled to arrive in port. The ships carry different cargoes from several foreign countries. There are four possible berths at which the vessels can be docked to unload their cargo. Each of the four berths is equipped with different cargo loading and unloading facilities. Given the characteristics of the cargoes and the facilities available at each berth, the manager has estimated the number of hours required to unload each of the ships at each of the four berths. This information is given in the following table:

	Ships			
Berths	1	2	3	4
A	8	14	20	8
B	12	16	16	12
C	16	8	28	12
D	9	12	19	15

a. Formulate a zero-one programming model for the problem.

b. Determine the optimal assignments that will minimize the number of hours.

10. Perry Construction Company is faced with the problem of determining which projects it should undertake over the next 4 years. The following table gives information about each project:

Project	Estimated Present Value	Capital Requirements			
		Year 1	Year 2	Year 3	Year 4
A	180,000	30,000	40,000	40,000	30,000
B	20,000	12,000	8,000	0	4,000
C	72,000	30,000	20,000	20,000	20,000
D	80,000	20,000	40,000	40,000	10,000
Funds available		65,000	80,000	80,000	50,000

a. Formulate a zero-one programming model to maximize the estimated present value.

b. Solve using AB:QM.

11. A chemical company is considering six possible investment opportunities. The following table presents pertinent information about the investment projects.

Project	Initial Outlay ($000)	New Managerial Staff Need	Average Annual Cash Flow ($000)	Annual Accounting Profit ($000)	Net Present Value ($000)
1	700	6	200	160	300
2	1080	16	300	240	440
3	120	2	20	36	60
4	300	4	70	66	160
5	680	10	150	140	380
6	420	6	90	80	200
Requirement or maximum available	Maximum 2000	Maximum 24	Minimum 200	Minimum 200	Maximize

In addition, projects 3 and 4 are mutually exclusive pollution control activities, and project 1 is contingent on the prior acceptance of project 6. Formulate a zero-one programming model for this problem.

12. A scout is trying to pack a knapsack for a forthcoming camping trip. The scout is considering taking ten different items on the trip. Their values for the trip and weights are shown in the following table.

Item	Value for Camping (points)	Weight (lb)
1. Compass/watch	600 points	.15
2. Jar of peanut butter	400	1
3. Portable burner	150	4
4. Canteen	450	5
5. Sleeping bag	500	10
6. Dried meat	250	5
7. Fishing gear	150	7
8. Movie camera	50	4
9. Portable television	20	8
10. Radio	100	2

The maximum weight allowed for each scout is 20 pounds. Furthermore, there should be at least 1 food item packed in the knapsack and not more than 1 item from among the camera, television, and radio. Formulate this problem as a zero-one programming model.

13. Given the following information, formulate a zero-one programming model, and solve the problem using the branch-and-bound technique.

	Machine				
Employee	A	B	C	D	
1	$20	$30	$32	$36	1
2	28	26	32	20	1
3	22	18	16	36	1
4	26	26	22	18	1
	1	1	1	1	

14. A national manufacturing company need to select three new plant locations from five potential cities. Each plant will produce the same product TX2, which will be marketed in four areas. The following table provides the construction cost of the plants in each city and the capacity of each plant, assuming that variable cost ($/unit) is the same for each plant in any given city.

	Construction Costs ($1,000)		
Cities	Plant 1	Plant 2	Plant 3
A1	$20	40	60
A2	20	35	55
A3	15	30	50
A4	30	50	70
A5	40	60	80
Capacity	30,000	50,000	60,000

The table below gives the estimated demand in each of the four market areas and the unit transportation cost from each city to each market area.

To From	B1	B2	B3	B4
A1	$1.50	2.00	2.00	4.00
A2	3.00	1.50	3.00	2.00
A3	3.50	3.50	3.00	1.00
A4	2.00	2.00	1.00	3.00
A5	1.50	1.00	2.00	5.00
Demand	50,000	30,000	40,000	20,000

The management has imposed the restriction that no more than one plant be built in each given city. Formulate an integer programming model to minimize the total cost.

15. Solve the following zero-one problem:

Minimize $Z = 6x_1 + 3x_2 + 9x_3 + 6x_4 + 12x_5$

subject to
$$3x_1 + 6x_2 + 3x_3 + 3x_4 + 6x_5 \geqslant 12$$
$$21x_1 + 3x_2 - 9x_4 + 9x_5 \geqslant 6$$
$$-9x_1 + 9x_2 + 6x_3 - 3x_5 \geqslant -3$$
$$x_j = 0 \text{ or } 1$$

15

Nonlinear Programming

A large portion of this book—in particular, Chapters 2 through 5 and 13—has been devoted to the methods of linear optimization. This is due, in large part, to the development of powerful methods for solution of linear models, including the simplex method and the specialized solution algorithms for transportation and assignment models. Highly efficient computer programs have been designed using specially developed versions of these algorithms, for solution of large-scale, real-world applications.

Extensions and modifications of the linear programming models were treated in Chapters 13 and 14. Chapter 13 considered the fact that a single criterion, or goal, may be inadequate to reflect the real-world requirements of the problem environment. Chapter 14 introduced the case in which treatment of solution variables as continuous values is unacceptable. All of these topics, however, relate to *linear models* in that the assumption of linear relationships first specified in Chapter 2 is still in effect.

The assumption of linear relationships is often appropriate or at least a "good enough" approximation for the range of values considered for the variables of a given problem. For some problems, however, nonlinear relationships (or functions) must be constructed in order to accurately reflect the structure of the problem.

The presentation of inventory models in Chapter 7 included nonlinear relationships. Classical calculus was the basis for solution of these models. Chapter 12 presented the techniques of dynamic programming for solution of nonlinear optimization problems.

The purpose of this chapter is to provide an introduction to the general topic of nonlinear programming. The topic is much too broad and advanced for more than a cursory introduction within the span of one chapter. Much of the theory of nonlinear optimization is directed toward obtaining the necessary and sufficient conditions for an optimal solution. This theory does not, however, exploit the efficiencies provided by computer solution.

Most of the modern-day algorithms for solution of nonlinear programming problems have been developed recently. These algorithms are typically specialized iterative search procedures that do utilize the computer. To adequately cover each type of algorithm would require a book in itself.[1]

This chapter presents a brief overview of the classical theory of nonlinear programming, including most importantly the Karush-Kuhn-Tucker conditions, with the purpose

---

[1] For an excellent in-depth presentation of nonlinear optimization techniques, refer to Luenberger, *Introduction to Linear and Nonlinear Programming*.

of providing some insight into the philosophy of constrained nonlinear optimization. This presentation follows directly the concept of Lagrange multipliers, which is presented in Appendix B.

KARUSH-KUHN-TUCKER CONDITIONS

The general form of the nonlinear maximization problem to be considered is as follows:

Maximize $y = f(x_1, x_2, \ldots, x_n)$

subject to

$$g_i(x_1, x_2, \ldots, x_n) \leq b_i \quad (i = 1, 2, \ldots, m)$$
$$x_j \geq 0 \quad (j = 1, 2, \ldots, n)$$

The problem is to maximize a linear or nonlinear objective function f consisting of n decision variables, subject to m linear or nonlinear constraints $g_i \leq b_i$, and all decision variables x_j, subject to the nonnegativity restriction.

There is no general algorithm available that will solve all problems with this basic structure. However, as previously pointed out, numerous special-purpose algorithms and search procedures have been developed for special cases of the nonlinear programming problem.

The Karush-Kuhn-Tucker conditions provide the basis for recognizing candidates for an optimal solution to a nonlinear programming problem.[2] These conditions are based on the classical calculus methods of solution, which are introduced in Appendix B.

Recall that when y is a function of one variable, x [i.e., $y = f(x)$], in order to determine the value of x for which y is a maximum, $dy/dx = 0$ must be determined. As long as $f(x)$ is differentiable, this yields a candidate for the maximum. If $f(x)$ is a concave function, this yields the maximum. By the same token, when $y = f(x_1, x_2, \ldots, x_n)$, the candidates for the maximum can be determined by computing $\partial y/\partial x_j = 0$ for $j = 1, 2, \ldots, n$ and solving these equations simultaneously for the values of x_j. Again, if $f(x_1, x_2, \ldots, x_n)$ is a concave function, this yields a maximum.[3] Generally, the values of x_j associated with the maximum of y are denoted by x_j^*.

When the nonnegativity restrictions $x_j \geq 0$ ($j = 1, 2, \ldots, n$) are introduced, they may force one or more x_j to become equal to 0. For such cases, the value of $\partial y/\partial x_j$ may be forced to take on a negative value. Thus, in summary, when $f(x_1, x_2, \ldots, x_n)$ is a concave function, the maximum of $y = f(x_1, x_2, \ldots, x_n)$ is obtained where $\partial y/\partial x_j = 0$ if $x_j^* > 0$, or when $\partial y/\partial x_j \leq 0$ if $x_j^* = 0$.

It will become apparent that the conditions set forth by Karush, Kuhn, and Tucker are variations of these classical conditions. Prior to presenting these conditions, we will review the Lagrange multiplier (see also Appendix B).

---

[2] W. Karush, "Minima of Functions of Several Variables with Inequalities as Side Conditions," M.S. thesis, Department of Mathematics, The University of Chicago, 1939; and Kuhn, H. W., and A. W. Tucker, "Nonlinear Programming," in Jerzy Neyman (ed.), *Proceedings of the Second Berkeley Symposium* (Berkeley: University of California Press, 1951), pp. 481–492.

[3] To be more precise, the function must be "strictly" concave, excluding the case where $f(x_1, x_2, \ldots, x_n)$ is a linear function.

The Lagrange multiplier function is formed as follows. Given

$$y = f(x_1, x_2, \ldots, x_n)$$

subject to

$$g_i(x_1, x_2, \ldots, x_n) \leq b_i \qquad (i = 1, 2, \ldots, m)$$
$$x_j \geq 0 \qquad (j = 1, 2, \ldots, n)$$

the Lagrangian expression, denoted by L, is

$$L = f(x_1, x_2, \ldots, x_n) - \sum_{i=1}^{m} \lambda_i[g_i(x_1, x_2, \ldots, x_n) - b_i]$$

Stated more succinctly, given that f and g_i are functions of n decision variables x_j ($j = 1, 2, \ldots, n$), the Lagrange multiplier function is

$$L = f - \sum_{i=1}^{m} \lambda_i(g_i - b_i)$$

where

m = number of constraints ($i = 1, 2, \ldots, m$)
λ_i = Lagrange *multiplier*

The Karush-Kuhn-Tucker conditions assume that the nonlinear problem has been formulated as a Lagrange multiplier expression and differentiated with respect to x_j ($j = 1, 2, \ldots, n$) and λ_i ($i = 1, 2, \ldots, m$). For example, if the general problem includes two decision variables and two constraints, as in

$$y = f(x_1, x_2)$$

subject to

$$g_1(x_1, x_2) \leq b_1$$
$$g_2(x_1, x_2) \leq b_2$$
$$x_1, x_2 \geq 0$$

the Lagrangian expression is

$$L = f(x_1, x_2) - \lambda_1[g_1(x_1, x_2) - b_1] - \lambda_2[g_2(x_1, x_2) - b_2]$$

The classical approach to solution of the Lagrange multiplier expression requires solving the following equations simultaneously:

$$\frac{\partial L}{\partial x_1} = 0, \frac{\partial L}{\partial x_2} = 0, \frac{\partial L}{\partial \lambda_1} = 0, \frac{\partial L}{\partial \lambda_2} = 0$$

Given the preceding discussion, the Karush-Kuhn-Tucker conditions, which must be satisfied to yield candidates for an optimal solution, are as follows. If

$$\frac{\partial L}{\partial x_j} = \frac{\partial f}{\partial x_j} - \sum_{i=1}^{m} \lambda_i \frac{\partial g_i}{\partial x_j} \qquad (j = 1, 2, \ldots, n)$$

then

$$x_j^* \left(\frac{\partial L}{\partial x_j} \right) = 0 \qquad (j = 1, 2, \ldots, n) \qquad \text{(1a)}$$

$$\frac{\partial L}{\partial x_j} \leq 0 \qquad (j = 1, 2, \ldots, n) \tag{1b}$$

$$\lambda_i[g_i(x_1^*, x_2^*, \ldots, x_n^*) - b_i] = 0 \qquad (i = 1, 2, \ldots, m) \tag{2a}$$

$$g_i(x_1^*, x_2^*, \ldots, x_n^*) - b_i \leq 0 \qquad (i = 1, 2, \ldots, m) \tag{2b}$$

$$\text{all } x_j^* \geq 0, \lambda_i \geq 0 \tag{3}$$

Note that (2b) is $\partial L/\partial \lambda_i$.

The preceding conditions are interpreted by the following restatements:

$$\text{If } x_j^* > 0, \text{ then } \frac{\partial L}{\partial x_j} = 0 \qquad (j = 1, 2, \ldots, n) \tag{1a}$$

$$\text{If } x_j^* = 0, \text{ then } \frac{\partial L}{\partial x_j} \leq 0 \qquad (j = 1, 2, \ldots, n) \tag{1b}$$

$$\text{If } \lambda_i > 0, \text{ then } g_i(x_1^*, x_2^*, \ldots, x_n^*) - b_i = 0 \qquad (i = 1, 2, \ldots, m) \tag{2a}$$

$$\text{If } \lambda_i = 0, \text{ then } g_i(x_1^*, x_2^*, \ldots, x_n^*) - b_i \leq 0 \qquad (i = 1, 2, \ldots, m) \tag{2b}$$

$$\text{and all } x_j^* \geq 0, \lambda_i \geq 0 \tag{3}$$

Notice that the requirements for $\partial L/\partial x_j$ are essentially the same as those for $\partial y/\partial x_j$ given previously. Further, notice that when the Lagrange multiplier function is formulated from $g_i \leq b_i$ to $\lambda_i(g_i - b_i)$, it is *assumed* that the inequality may be temporarily stated as an equality. If the solution value of λ_i is positive ($\lambda_i > 0$), this indicates that the solution is bound by constraint i, and therefore the equality assumption is acceptable (see again the discussion of the Lagrange multiplier in Appendix B). However, if $\lambda_i = 0$, the term ($g_i - b_i$) must be allowed to be equal to or less than zero, since the solution is not bound by constraint i (i.e., $g_i < b_i$). Thus, the Karush-Kuhn-Tucker conditions (2a) and (2b) are defined for each constraint i by

Binding Constraint (boundary point optimization)
If $\lambda_i > 0$, then $g_i - b_i = 0$ (that is, $g_i = b_i$) for ($x_1^*, x_2^*, \ldots, x_n^*$)

Nonbinding Constraint (interior point optimization)
If $\lambda_i = 0$, then $g_i - b_i \leq 0$ (that is, $g_i \leq b_i$) for ($x_1^*, x_2^*, \ldots, x_n^*$)

The economic interpretation of λ_i is analogous to that of the dual variables of linear programming, and it is the λ_i that are referred to as the Lagrange *multipliers*. It can be shown that $\partial f^*/\partial b_i = \lambda_i$ (i.e., the "value" associated with relaxing constraint i is given by λ_i).

Satisfaction of the Karush-Kuhn-Tucker conditions, however, yields only the acceptable *candidates* for an optimal solution. The candidates must then be evaluated further to determine the global optimal solution. The situation is analogous to that of the single decision variable case, where solution of $dy/dx = 0$ yields one candidate. The limits of the domain must then be evaluated to determine the global optimal solution, unless $y = f(x)$ is known to be concave, in which case $dy/dx = 0$ yields x^*. This leads to the following extensions of the Karush-Kuhn-Tucker conditions.

If $f(x_1, x_2, \ldots, x_n)$ is a concave function and if $g_i(x_1, x_2, \ldots, x_n)$, for $i = 1, 2,$

..., m, are convex functions, then the results obtained by employing the Lagrangian function will result in an optimal solution if they satisfy the Karush-Kuhn-Tucker conditions. For example, if the objective function is known to be a quadratic cone function, subject to all linear constraints (yielding a convex feasible solution space), then satisfaction of the conditions will yield an optimal solution. This corollary was also presented and proven by Kuhn and Tucker. (See Appendix B for a discussion of concavity and convexity.)

In summary, the Karush-Kuhn-Tucker conditions are necessary but, in general, are not sufficient. Furthermore, these conditions provide only a *test* for optimality and not a procedure for finding a solution.

Example 15.1 Nonlinear Maximization Problem

Consider the following nonlinear maximization problem:

Maximize $y = 8x_1^2 + 2x_2^2$

subject to
$$x_1^2 + x_2^2 \leq 9$$
$$x_1, x_2 \geq 0$$

Forming the Lagrangian expression yields

$$L = 8x_1^2 + 2x_2^2 - \lambda(x_1^2 + x_2^2 - 9)$$

Next we form the Karush-Kuhn-Tucker conditions in the following order: (a) for $x_1^* > 0$; (b) for $x_2^* > 0$; (c) for $\lambda > 0$; (d) for $x_1^* = 0$; (e) for $x_2^* = 0$; and (f) for $\lambda = 0$.

$$\frac{\partial L}{\partial x_1} = 16x_1 - 2\lambda x_1 = 0, \qquad \text{for } x_1^* > 0 \tag{a}$$

$$\frac{\partial L}{\partial x_2} = 4x_2 - 2\lambda x_2 = 0, \qquad \text{for } x_2^* > 0 \tag{b}$$

$$x_1^2 + x_2^2 - 9 = 0, \qquad \text{for } \lambda > 0 \tag{c}$$

$$\frac{\partial L}{\partial x_1} = 16x_1 - 2\lambda x_1 \leq 0, \qquad \text{for } x_1^* = 0 \tag{d}$$

$$\frac{\partial L}{\partial x_2} = 4x_2 - 2\lambda x_2 \leq 0, \qquad \text{for } x_2^* = 0 \tag{e}$$

$$x_1^2 + x_2^2 - 9 \leq 0, \qquad \text{for } \lambda = 0 \tag{f}$$

The previous discussion of the Karush-Kuhn-Tucker conditions distinguished between solution values for x_j in terms of $x_j = 0$ or $x_j > 0$ and for λ_i in terms of $\lambda_i = 0$ or $\lambda_i > 0$. Thus, in general, any Lagrangian formulation of a nonlinear programming problem with n decision variables and m constraints can yield 2^{m+n} possible combinations of solutions (i.e., the n decision variables x_j may be either zero or nonzero, and the m Lagrange multiplier variables λ_j may be either zero or nonzero). Thus, for the problem at hand, there are $2^3 = 8$ combinations of solution values for x_1, x_2, and λ that must be considered. The cases are summarized as follows:

Case	x_1	x_2	λ	Must Satisfy Karush-Kuhn-Tucker Conditions
1	= 0	= 0	= 0	(d), (e), (f)
2	= 0	= 0	> 0	(d), (e), (c)
3	= 0	> 0	= 0	(d), (b), (f)
4	> 0	= 0	= 0	(a), (e), (f)
5	= 0	> 0	> 0	(d), (b), (c)
6	> 0	= 0	> 0	(a), (e), (c)
7	> 0	> 0	= 0	(a), (b), (f)
8	> 0	> 0	> 0	(a), (b), (c)

In order for a solution case to qualify as a candidate for the optimal solution, it must satisfy the Karush-Kuhn-Tucker conditions noted in the right-hand column of the table. The conditions are tested by substituting the case solution values into the relevant condition expressions.

Case 1: $x_1 = 0$, $x_2 = 0$, $\lambda = 0$

Conditions	Test	Result
(d)	$0 \leqslant 0$	OK
(e)	$0 \leqslant 0$	OK
(f)	$-9 \leqslant 0$	OK

None of the required conditions are violated for this case; therefore it is theoretically a candidate for the optimal solution. However, it is clearly not a logical choice for a maximization problem. This case is presented to illustrate the testing of all possible combinations for a solution.

Case 2: $x_1 = 0$, $x_2 = 0$, $\lambda > 0$

Conditions	Test	Result
(d)	$0 \leqslant 0$	OK
(e)	$0 \leqslant 0$	OK
(c)	$-9 = 0$	Not true, therefore a violation

Condition (c) is violated, as $x_1^2 + x_2^2 - 9$, or $(0)^2 + (0)^2 - 9$, clearly does not equal zero. Recall from the previous presentation of Lagrange multipliers that λ takes on a positive value only when the solution is bound by the constraint. Since x_1 and x_2 are zero for this case, the constraint is not binding. Again, this case is given to illustrate the testing of all possible cases. Normally this combination would be discarded by observation without formal testing.

Case 3: $x_1 = 0, x_2 > 0, \lambda = 0$

Note that since $\lambda = 0$, this implies an interior solution for $x_2 > 0$, with $x_1 = 0$. An interior solution for x_2 indicates that the solution is not bound by the constraint. Conditions (d), (b), and (f) must be tested. Starting with condition (d), $16x_1 - 2\lambda x_1 = 0$ (for $x_1 = 0$), which satisfies the requirement $16x_1 - 2\lambda x_1 \leqslant 0$. For condition (b),

$$4x_2 - 2\lambda x_2 = 0 \Rightarrow x_2(4 - 2\lambda) = 0$$

Since $x_2 > 0, 4 - 2\lambda = 0$. This implies that $\lambda = 2$, which violates the case assumption that λ is equal to zero.

For condition (f), $x_1^2 + x_2^2 - 9 \leqslant 0$, or $x_2^2 - 9 \leqslant 0$, or $x_2^2 \leqslant 9$. Since $\lambda > 0$, we have a boundary solution; thus, the solution value of x_2 is 3.

The following is a summary of case 3:

Conditions	Test	Result
(d)	$0 \leqslant 0$	OK
(b)	$\lambda = 2$	Violation of $4x_2 - 2\lambda x_2 = 0$, for $x_2 > 0$
(f)	$(3)^2 - 9 \leqslant 0$	OK

Case 4: $x_1 > 0, x_2 = 0, \lambda = 0$

As in case 3, $\lambda = 0$ implies an interior solution for $x_1 > 0$, with $x_2 = 0$. We also obtain similar results for condition (a).

$$16x_1 - 2\lambda x_1 = 0 \Rightarrow x_1(16 - 2\lambda) = 0$$

Since $x_1 > 0, 16 - 2\lambda = 0$. This implies that $\lambda = 8$, which violates the case assumption that $\lambda = 0$.

Conditions	Test	Result
(a)	$\lambda = 8$	Violation of $16x_1 - 2\lambda x_1 = 0$
(e)	$0 \leqslant 0$	OK
(f)	$(3)^2 - 9 \leqslant 0$	OK

Case 5: $x_1 = 0, x_2 > 0, \lambda > 0$

This case assumes a boundary solution ($\lambda > 0$) for $x_2 > 0$, with $x_1 = 0$. Having tested case 3 for $x_1 = 0$ and $x_2 > 0$, we can easily determine the outcome for this case.

Conditions	Test	Result
(d)	$0 \leqslant 0$	OK
(b)	$\lambda = 2$	OK for $4x_2 - 2\lambda x_2 = 0$ and $x_2 > 0$
(c)	$x_2 = 3$	OK for $x_1^2 + x_2^2 - 9 = 0$; since $\lambda = 2$ and $x_1 = 0, x_2^2 = 9 \Rightarrow x_2 = 3$

Thus, case 5 yields a candidate for the optimal solution.

Case 6: $x_1 > 0, x_2 = 0, \lambda > 0$

Again, we can refer back to the test of case 4, where $x_1 > 0$ and $x_2 = 0$. For condition (a), $16x_1 - 2\lambda x_1 = 0, x_1 > 0$, and $\lambda = 8$. For condition (e), $4x_2 - 2\lambda x_2$ $\Rightarrow 0 \leqslant 0$ (OK). For condition (c), $x_1^2 + x_2^2 - 9 = 0 \Rightarrow x_1^2 - 9 = 0$. Thus, $x_1^2 - 9$ $= 0 \Rightarrow x_1 = 3$.

Conditions	Test	Result
(a)	$\lambda = 8$	OK
(e)	$0 \leqslant 0$	OK
(c)	$x_1 = 3$	OK

Case 6 yields a possible candidate for the optimal solution.

Case 7: $x_1 > 0, x_2 > 0, \lambda = 0$

Conditions (a), (b), and (f) apply for case 7. Testing case (a) yields $16x_1 - 2\lambda x_1$ $= 0 \Rightarrow \lambda = 8$, which is a violation of the assumption $\lambda = 0$. Condition (b) yields $4x_2$ $- 2\lambda x_2 = 0 \Rightarrow \lambda = 2$, which violates the condition $\lambda = 0$. Condition (f), $x_1^2 + x_2^2$ $- 9 = 0$, does not violate the assumption $x_1 > 0$ and $x_2 > 0$.

Conditions	Test	Result
(a)	$\lambda = 8$	Violation of $16x_1 - 2\lambda x_1 = 0$
(b)	$\lambda = 2$	Violation of $4x_2 - 2\lambda x_2 = 0$ (and λ cannot equal 8 and 2)
(f)	$x_1^2 + x_2^2 = 9$	OK

Case 8: $x_1 > 0, x_2 > 0, \lambda > 0$

This case assumes that both x_1 and x_2 are nonzero, with the optimal solution on the boundary created by the constraint, since $\lambda > 0$. Testing yields the following:

Conditions	Test	Result
(a)	$\lambda = 8$	Violation
(b)	$\lambda = 2$	
(c)	$x_1^2 + x_2^2 = 9$	OK

The candidates resulting from testing of the eight combinations of possible solution values for x_1, x_2 and λ can be summarized and evaluated as follows:

Case	(x_1, x_2, λ)	Results of Testing Karush-Kuhn-Tucker Conditions	Value of Solution (y)
1	(0, 0, 0)	OK for $x_1 = 0, x_2 = 0, \lambda = 0$	$y = 0$
2	(0, 0, >0)	Violation	NA*

Case	(x_1, x_2, λ)	Results of Testing Karush-Kuhn-Tucker Conditions	Value of Solution (y)
3	$(0, >0, 0)$	Violation	NA
4	$(>0, 0, 0)$	Violation	NA
5	$(0, >0, >0)$	OK for $x_2 = 3, \lambda = 2, x_1 = 0$	$y = 2(3)^2 = 18$
6	$(>0, 0, >0)$	OK for $x_1 = 3, \lambda = 8, x_2 = 0$	$y = 8(3)^2 = 72$
7	$(>0, >0, 0)$	Violation	NA
8	$(>0, >0, >0)$	Violation	NA

* NA = Not allowed

Therefore, the problem yields three candidates that satisfy the Karush-Kuhn-Tucker conditions (cases 1, 5, and 6), and the optimal solution is given at $x_1^* = 3$, $x_2^* = 0$, $y^* = 72$, with the associated solution value $\lambda = 8$.

The interpretation of λ is $\partial y/\partial b_i$: the rate of improvement in y for incremental relaxation of b_i (the right-hand side of the constraint). For example, if the current constraint $x_1^2 + x_2^2 \leq 9$ were changed to $x_1^2 + x_2^2 \leq 10$, the solution value for x_1^* would be $\sqrt{10}$, since $x_2^* = 0$. Substituting this value into the original equation gives

$$y = 8x_1^2 + 2x_2^2 = 8x_1^2 = 8(\sqrt{10})^2 = 80$$

Notice that this value for y is exactly 8 greater than the previous value. The economic interpretation is analogous to that of the dual variables in linear programming.

For more complex problems (more decision variables or more constraints), it would be extremely difficult and inefficient to obtain the optimal solution directly from the Karush-Kuhn-Tucker conditions, as illustrated in the previous example. These conditions nevertheless provide the necessary information for testing possible solutions for candidacy as an optimal solution. With the aid of modern high-speed computers, more complex problems can be evaluated through partial enumeration procedures. Equally important, the Karush-Kuhn-Tucker conditions provide much of the theoretical insight necessary for development of specialized algorithms for particular nonlinear problems.

Computer Solution of Example 15.1

Nonlinear programming capabilities typically are not available as part of general management science software packages. However, a personal computer software package called GINO[4] solves nonlinear programming problems. Following is the solution for Example 15.1 generated using GINO.

```
   EXAMPLE 15.1  Nonlinear Maximization Problem

MODEL:
    1) MAX= 8 * X1 ^ 2 + 2 * X2 ^ 2 ;
    2) X1 ^ 2 + X2 ^ 2 < 9 ;
END
```

[4] Leon Lasdon, Allan Waren, and LINDO Systems, Inc., *GINO (General Interactive Optimizer)*. See also the associated textbook by Judith Liebman, Leon Lasdon, Linus Schrage, and Allan Waren, *Modeling and Optimization with GINO* (Palo Alto, CA: The Scientific Press, 1986).

```
SOLUTION STATUS:  OPTIMAL TO TOLERANCES.  DUAL CONDITIONS:  SATISFIED.

            OBJECTIVE FUNCTION VALUE

       1)            72.000000

  VARIABLE          VALUE           REDUCED COST
     X1           3.000000             .000000
     X2            .000000             .000000

    ROW    SLACK OR SURPLUS             PRICE
     2)           .000000           8.000000
```

QUADRATIC PROGRAMMING

Problems in which (1) the objective function is a concave quadratic function and (2) the constraints are all linear are a special class of nonlinear programming problems. Formulation of the Karush-Kuhn-Tucker conditions, therefore, results in a set of linear expressions for solution. This set of linear expressions makes solution by the simplex method possible. Preparation of the quadratic programming problem for solution by the simplex method is presented, as well as several modifications in problem formulation required for this special case.

Recall that Karush-Kuhn-Tucker conditions (1a) and (1b) were given as follows:

$$\frac{\partial L}{\partial x_j} = 0, \qquad \text{for } x_j^* > 0 \tag{1a}$$

$$\frac{\partial L}{\partial x_j} \leq 0, \qquad \text{for } x_j^* = 0 \tag{1b}$$

These conditions are now restated simply as

$$\frac{\partial L}{\partial x_j} = 0, \qquad \text{for all } x_j^*$$

However, additional terms are added to the Lagrange multiplier expression to include the nonnegativity requirements ($x_j \geq 0$) and to allow the preceding modification in (1a) and (1b).

Formulation of the Lagrangian expression and the subsequent Karush-Kuhn-Tucker conditions, including the preceding modifications, is illustrated for the general problem with two decision variables (x_1, x_2).

The quadratic programming problem

Maximize $y = f(x_1, x_2)$

subject to

$$g_1(x_1, x_2) \leq b_1$$
$$x_1 \geq 0, x_2 \geq 0 \Rightarrow -x_1 \leq 0, -x_2 \leq 0$$

is restated as

Maximize $y = f(x_1, x_2)$

subject to

$$g_1(x_1, x_2) - b_1 \leqslant 0$$
$$h_1(x_1) \leqslant 0, \qquad \text{where } h_1(x_1) \text{ is } -x_1$$
$$h_2(x_2) \leqslant 0, \qquad \text{where } h_2(x_2) \text{ is } -x_2$$

The Lagrangian expression is given as follows:

$$L = f(x_1, x_2) - \lambda_1[g_1(x_1, x_2) - b_1] - \mu_1[h_1(x_1)] - \mu_2[h_2(x_2)]$$

If we let $f = f(x_1, x_2)$ and $g_1 = g_1(x_1, x_2)$, since $h_1(x_1) = -x_1$ and $h_2(x_2) = -x_2$, the Lagrangian expression can be written as

$$L = f - \lambda_1(g_1 - b_1) + \mu_1 x_1 + \mu_2 x_2$$

where

λ_1 = Lagrange multiplier for g_1 (the original problem constraint)
μ_1 = Lagrange multiplier for h_1 (the nonnegativity requirement for x_1)
μ_2 = Lagrange multiplier for h_2 (the nonnegativity requirement for x_2)

The Karush-Kuhn-Tucker conditions are, therefore, as follows:

$$\frac{\partial L}{\partial x_1} = \frac{\partial f}{\partial x_1} - \lambda_1 \frac{\partial g_1}{\partial x_1} + \mu_1 = 0 \qquad (1)$$

$$\frac{\partial L}{\partial x_2} = \frac{\partial f}{\partial x_2} - \lambda_1 \frac{\partial g_1}{\partial x_2} + \mu_2 = 0 \qquad (2)$$

$$g_1 - b_1 \leqslant 0 \qquad (3)$$

$$\lambda_1(g_1 - b_1) = 0 \qquad (4)$$

$$\mu_1 x_1 = 0 \qquad (5)$$

$$\mu_2 x_2 = 0 \qquad (6)$$

$$x_1, x_2, \lambda_1, \mu_1, \mu_2 \geqslant 0 \qquad (7)$$

Condition (3) is next converted into an equality by introducing a slack variable, s_1, to yield

$$g_1 - b_1 + s_1 = 0 \qquad (3)$$

Since $g_1 - b_1 = -s_1$, condition (4) can be rewritten, by substitution, as $\lambda_1(g_1 - b_1) = \lambda_1(-s_1) = \lambda_1 s_1$:

$$\lambda_1 s_1 = 0 \qquad (4)$$

Thus, in general, the Karush-Kuhn-Tucker conditions for the quadratic programming problem with n decision variables and m constraints are given as

$$\frac{\partial L}{\partial x_j} = \frac{\partial f}{\partial x_j} - \sum_{i=1}^{m} \lambda_i \frac{\partial g_i}{\partial x_j} + \mu_j = 0 \qquad (j = 1, 2, \ldots, n)$$

		from (1) and (2) (a)
$g_i - b_i + s_i = 0$	$(i = 1, 2, \ldots, m)$	from (3) (b)
$\lambda_i s_i = 0$	$(i = 1, 2, \ldots, m)$	from (4) (c)
$\mu_j x_j = 0$	$(j = 1, 2, \ldots, n)$	from (5) and (6) (d)
all $x_j, \lambda_i, \mu_j, s_i \geqslant 0$		from (7) (e)

Conditions (a) and (b) are linear, whereas conditions (c) and (d) are nonlinear. This general problem, however, can be solved using the simplex procedure if the linear equations generated by (a) and (b) are included in the simplex tableau and it is stipulated that both λ_i and s_i (for any i) will never be basic variables at the same time and that both μ_j and x_j (for any j) will never be basic variables at the same time.

The final requirement to form an initial basic solution is to add artificial variables to all linear expressions generated by (a). These equations are then solved in terms of the artificial variables to form the objective function, which is to be minimized (i.e., the objective is to drive the artificial variables out of the basis).

Example 15.2 Quadratic Maximization Problem

The procedure described above will be illustrated for the following quadratic programming problem:

Maximize $y = 4x_1 + 6x_2 - 2x_1^2 - 2x_1x_2 - 2x_2^2$

subject to

$$x_1 + 2x_2 \leq 2$$
$$x_1, x_2 \geq 0$$

The Lagrangian expression is given as

$$L = 4x_1 + 6x_2 - 2x_1^2 - 2x_1x_2 - 2x_2^2 - \lambda_1(x_1 + 2x_2 - 2) + \mu_1x_1 + \mu_2x_2$$

Note: The term $+ \mu_1x_1$ is obtained through the conversion of the non-negativity restriction $x_1 \geq 0$ into the form $-x_1 \leq 0$. Thus, the term $-\mu_1(-x_1)$ becomes $+\mu_1x_1$ and $-\mu_2(-x_2)$ becomes $+\mu_2x_2$.

Thus, the Karush-Kuhn-Tucker conditions for the problem are

$$\frac{\partial L}{\partial x_1} = 4 - 4x_1 - 2x_2 - \lambda_1 + \mu_1 = 0 \tag{a_1}$$

$$\frac{\partial L}{\partial x_2} = 6 - 2x_1 - 4x_2 - 2\lambda_1 + \mu_2 = 0 \tag{a_2}$$

$$x_1 + 2x_2 - 2 + s_1 = 0 \tag{b}$$

$$\lambda_1 s_1 = 0 \tag{c}$$

$$\mu_1 x_1 = 0 \tag{d_1}$$

$$\mu_2 x_2 = 0 \tag{d_2}$$

Equations (a_1), (a_2), and (b) are rewritten with the artificial variables added in (a_1) and (a_2) to yield

$$4x_1 + 2x_2 + \lambda_1 - \mu_1 + A_1 = 4 \tag{a_1}$$
$$2x_1 + 4x_2 + 2\lambda_1 - \mu_2 + A_2 = 6 \tag{a_2}$$
$$x_1 + 2x_2 + s_1 = 2 \tag{b}$$

The problem is now solved via the simplex method with (a_1), (a_2), and (b) as the tableau constraints. The objective function is developed as follows:

Minimize $A_1 + A_2 \equiv$ Maximize $-A_1 - A_2$

where
$$-A_1 = -4 + 4x_1 + 2x_2 + \lambda_1 - \mu_1$$
$$-A_2 = -6 + 2x_1 + 4x_2 + 2\lambda_1 - \mu_2$$

Therefore, the objective function in terms of the decision variables x_j and the Lagrange multiplier variables λ_i is

Maximize $Z = -10 + 6x_1 + 6x_2 + 3\lambda_1 - \mu_1 - \mu_2$

The linear programming problem to be solved via the simplex method is as follows:

Maximize $Z = 6x_1 + 6x_2 + 3\lambda_1 - \mu_1 - \mu_2 + 0A_1 + 0A_2 + 0s_1$

subject to
$$4x_1 + 2x_2 + \lambda_1 - \mu_1 + A_1 = 4$$
$$2x_1 + 4x_2 + 2\lambda_1 - \mu_2 + A_2 = 6$$
$$x_1 + 2x_2 + s_1 = 2$$

$\lambda_1 s_1 = 0$ (i.e., either λ_1 or s_1 must be nonbasic in solution)

$\mu_1 x_1 = 0$ (i.e., either μ_1 or x_1 must be nonbasic in solution)

$\mu_2 x_2 = 0$ (i.e., either μ_2 or x_2 must be nonbasic in solution)

$$x_1, x_2, \lambda_1, \mu_1, \mu_2 \geqslant 0$$

The simplex solution to the formulated problem requires three iterations. The initial simplex tableau is shown in Table 15.1.

Table 15.1 Initial Simplex Tableau

c_b	c_j basis	b_i^*	6 x_1	6 x_2	3 λ_1	-1 μ_1	-1 μ_2	0 A_1	0 A_2	0 s_1
0	A_1	4	4	2	1	-1	0	1	0	0
0	A_2	6	2	4	2	0	-1	0	1	0
0	s_1	2	1	2	2	0	0	0	0	1
	z_j	0	0	0	0	0	0	0	0	0
	$c_j - z_j$		6	6	3	-1	-1	0	0	0

The three iterations of the solution are summarized as follows:

	Basis	
Iteration	Entering Variable	Leaving Variable
1	x_1	A_1
2	x_2	s_1
3	λ_1	A_2

The final simplex tableau is shown in Table 15.2. The final simplex tableau indicates that the nonbasic variables μ_1, μ_2, and s_1 can be entered into the basis without changing the value of z_j. However, μ_1 cannot be entered without removing x_1, because of condition (d_1). The same is true for μ_2 versus x_2, and for s_1 versus λ_1. Notice that in each case the a_{ij} value at the intersection of the subject pair of variables is a negative value (see the

Table 15.2 Final Simplex Tableau

c_b	c_j basis	b_i^*	6 x_1	6 x_2	3 λ_1	−1 μ_1	−1 μ_2	0 A_1	A_2	0 s_1
6	x_1	$\frac{1}{3}$	1	0	0	$-\frac{1}{3}$	$\frac{1}{6}$	$\frac{1}{3}$	$-\frac{1}{6}$	0
3	λ_1	1	0	0	1	0	$-\frac{1}{2}$	0	$\frac{1}{2}$	−1
6	x_2	$\frac{5}{6}$	0	1	0	$\frac{1}{6}$	$-\frac{1}{12}$	$-\frac{1}{6}$	$\frac{1}{12}$	$\frac{1}{2}$
	z_j	10	6	6	3	−1	−1	1	1	0
	$c_j - z_j$		0	0	0	0	0	−1	−1	0

shaded values in Table 15.2). Thus, this solution can proceed no further. Also, notice that the solution value for z_j in the final tableau is 10. Recall that the value of Z, initially calculated as $Z = -A_1 - A_2$, was equal to $-10 + 6x_1 + 6x_2 + 3\lambda_1 - \mu_1 - \mu_2$. Therefore, the solution value for Z is $-10 + z_j$, or $-10 + 10 = 0$. This will always occur, since the only objective is to drive the artificials out of the basic solution. Thus, the solution yielded is

$$x_1^* = \tfrac{1}{3}, \ x_2^* = \tfrac{5}{6}, \ \lambda_1 = 1$$

The value of y^* is calculated as

$$y^* = 4x_1 + 6x_2 - 2x_1^2 - 2x_1x_2 - 2x_2^2 = \tfrac{75}{18} = 4.1667$$

The preceding approach will always yield an optimal solution to a quadratic maximization problem if the quadratic objective function is concave. For a minimization problem, an optimal solution will be obtained if the objective function is convex. The preceding example included a concave objective function, so the solution obtained was optimal. Numerous solution approaches to the quadratic programming problem have been proposed. This approach is only one of several variations.

Computer Solution of Example 15.2

The following solution to the quadratic programming problem of Example 15.2 was generated using the same GINO software package used to solve Example 15.1. Note that the regular nonlinear programming problem is solved rather than the transformed linear formulation derived in the example.

```
EXAMPLE 15.2   Quadratic Maximization problem

MODEL:
    1) MAX= 4 * X1 + 6 * X2 - 2 * X1 ^ 2 - 2 * X1 * X2 - 2 * X2 ^ 2 ;
    2) X1 + 2 * X2 < 2 ;
END


SOLUTION STATUS:   OPTIMAL TO TOLERANCES.   DUAL CONDITIONS:   UNSATISFIED.

          OBJECTIVE FUNCTION VALUE

    1)          4.166667
```

VARIABLE	VALUE	REDUCED COST
X1	.333333	.000010
X2	.833333	.000000

ROW	SLACK OR SURPLUS	PRICE
2)	.000000	.999990

Standard Quadratic Form

Frequently, a quadratic programming problem is reformulated into the *standard quadratic form,* and the Karush-Kuhn-Tucker conditions are derived from this form. The standard quadratic form is

$$\text{Maximize } y = \sum_{j=1}^{n} c_j x_j - \frac{1}{2} \sum_{j=1}^{n} \sum_{k=1}^{n} q_{jk} x_j x_k$$

subject to

$$\sum_{j=1}^{n} a_{ij} x_j \leq b_i \qquad (i = 1, 2, \dots, m)$$

$$x_j \geq 0 \qquad (j = 1, 2, \dots, n)$$

where q_{jk} are given constants such that $q_{jk} = q_{kj}$.

CONVEX PROGRAMMING

Problems in which the objective function is a concave function and all the constraints are convex functions form another special class of nonlinear programming problems. The convexity of the (nonlinear) constraint functions implies that the set of feasible solutions forms a convex set. These conditions greatly simplify the requirements for obtaining the optimal solution to such problems.

One rather well-known technique developed for the solution of convex programming problems is the Sequential Unconstrained Minimization Technique (SUMT). This procedure first formulates the problem into a minimization form, subject to all $\geq$ constraints. It then deals with the objective function and the constraints simultaneously by combining them into a single function (the approach for this formulation procedure is beyond the scope of this text). The solution is then obtained using a gradient search procedure or some similar method.

GRADIENT SEARCH METHODS

As pointed out earlier in this chapter, many of the modern-day solution methods being employed for nonlinear programming problems exploit the efficiencies available from use of the high-speed computer. Basically, these methods make use of the vector of the partial derivatives of the objective function, known as the **gradient.**

These methods can be compared to a mountain climber's successively searching for the peak of the mountain by adopting a policy of going from point A to point B, when

An Application of Nonlinear Programming:
Oil and Gas Production Planning in Australia

SANTOS, Ltd. is a major publicly owned mineral exploration and production company in Australia. The company has contracted sales of dry gas (containing mostly methane) through 2006. The gas is transported through pipelines from the Cooper Basin oil and gas reservoirs located near the center of the eastern half of Australia to Adelaide and Sydney. The Cooper Basin contains approximately 60 small- to medium-sized reservoirs spread out over an area the size of Texas, none of which can supply as much as 10% of the contracted sales.

During the 1970s several oil fields were discovered as well as "wet" gas fields, and because of then high prices of liquid petroleum products, it was decided in 1980 to expand production facilities to recover liquids from the gas, and to build a pipeline to transport the liquids to the southern coast of Australia. The

project was completed in 1984 at a total cost of $1.45 billion (Australian). However, one of the stipulations of the project was that the gas supply to Adelaide and Sydney not be interrupted and service not be compromised. To meet these guarantees, spare capacity was built into the system and it was necessary to balance the dry gas demand requirements with new liquid production. In addition, in order to offset the huge capital costs of the project, it was desired to increase liquid production. Thus, a major issue was how much should production from the dry gas reservoirs be reduced to enable more and sooner production from the "wet" gas wells in order to enhance cash flows. This also impacted on the design of the production facilities. A further complication in this situation was the physical nature of the problem, wherein as more gas was produced, the reservoir pressure declined,

B appears to be the highest point in the neighborhood of *A*. The search is continued until the summit is reached (no more improvement in the objective function can be made).

Of course, difficulties are encountered when more than one peak exists over the domain of the possible solution. Convergence, stopping rules, parameter selection, and computerization all pose problems. Numerous gradient search techniques, however, have been proposed and used. See Luenberger for extensive discussion of these topics.

SUMMARY   This chapter presented an introduction to the topic of nonlinear programming. The basic classical theory underlying nonlinear programming was reviewed, including reformulation of the problem into the Lagrangian expression and testing for optimal solution candidates using the Karush-Kuhn-Tucker conditions. Although the Karush-Kuhn-Tucker conditions do not provide a solution approach for nonlinear programming problems, they do provide considerable insight into the general nature of such problems.

An approach was presented for reformulating a quadratic programming problem and obtaining its solution using the simplex method. This problem, with a concave quadratic objective function subject to all linear constraints, is the simplest of nonlinear programming problems.

Convex programming gradient search methods were discussed briefly. Considerable

thus requiring compressors to be built. In essence, three major questions arose for each reservoir: (1) How many wells should be drilled (at a cost of $1 to $2 million a piece) and when? (2) How much compressor capacity should be installed and when? and (3) At what rate should the gas from each reservoir be produced in order to meet demand over time?

The company developed a nonlinear mathematical programming model to solve this problem called SANTOS Investment Planning System (SIPS). Model constraints included BTUs of gas demanded over time, start up dates for new plant capacity, physical characteristics of the reservoirs and constraints limiting their development, and production rates and schedules. The model determined a production schedule that met physical and logistical constraints while

maximizing the net present value over a 25-year planning horizon. The solution was presented as a decision schedule containing all field, pipeline, and plant investment decisions as well as each reservoir's production schedule. It encompassed answers to the previously posed questions for each reservoir including the number of wells drilled, annual flow rates, spare capacities, compressor capacity, and production rates necessary to meet demand. The model saves SANTOS approximately $3 to $6 million (Australian) annually in investment costs. The model is also used extensively in price negotiations, responding to changes in national energy policy, responding to changes in oil prices (which collapsed in the late 1980s), and coordinating activities among the 11 companies that share the Cooper Basin.

Source: E. Dougherty et al., "Optimizing SANTOS Gas Production and Processing Operations in Central Australia Using the Decomposition Method," *Interfaces,* 17, no. 1, (January–February 1987): 65–93.

progress has been made in this area, and a variety of algorithms and search techniques are available for these cases. Although there is no efficient all-purpose solution method available for nonlinear programming problems, research in this area is actively continuing.

REFERENCES

AOKI, M. *Introduction to Optimization Techniques; Fundamentals and Applications of Nonlinear Programming.* New York: Macmillan, 1971.

BRACKEN, J., and McCORMICK, G. P. *Selected Applications of Nonlinear Programming.* New York: John Wiley & Sons, 1968.

BRADLEY, S. P.; HAX, A. C.; and MAGNANTI, T. L. *Applied Mathematical Programming.* Reading, Massachusetts: Addison-Wesley Publishing Co., 1977.

GOTTFIED, B. S., and WIESEMAN, J. *Intro-*

duction to Optimization Theory. Englewood Cliffs, New Jersey: Prentice-Hall, 1973.

HADLEY, G. *Nonlinear and Dynamic Programming.* Reading, Massachusetts: Addison-Wesley Publishing Co., 1964.

HILLIER, F. S., and LIEBERMAN, G. J. *Operations Research.* 4th ed. San Francisco: Holden-Day, 1986.

HIMMELBLAU, D. *Applied Nonlinear Programming.* New York: McGraw-Hill, 1972.

KUHN, H. W., and TUCKER, A. W. "Nonlinear Programming." In *Proceedings of the*

Second Berkeley Symposium on Mathematical Statistics and Probability, edited by J. Neyman. Berkeley: University of California Press, 1951.

KWAK, N. K., *Mathematical Programming with Business Applications*. New York: McGraw-Hill, 1973.

LOOMBA, N. P., and TURBAN, E. *Applied Programming for Management*. New York: Holt, Rinehart and Winston, 1974.

LUENBERGER, D. G. *Introduction to Linear and Nonlinear Programming*. Reading,

Massachusetts: Addison-Wesley Publishing Co., 1973.

McMILLAN, C., JR. *Mathematical Programming*. 2d ed. New York: John Wiley & Sons, 1975.

TAHA, H. A. *Operations Research, An Introduction*. 5th ed. New York: Macmillan, 1992.

ZANGWILL, W. I. *Nonlinear Programming: A Unified Approach*. Englewood Cliffs, New Jersey: Prentice-Hall, 1969.

PROBLEMS

1. Use the Karush-Kuhn-Tucker conditions to derive the optimal solution to the following nonlinear programming problem:

   Maximize $y = x_1^2 + 2x_2^2 + 11x_1 + 15x_2 + 45$

   subject to

   $$5x_1 + 7x_2 \leq 400$$
   $$x_1 + 3x_2 \leq 120$$
   $$x_1, x_2 \geq 0$$

2. Determine the optimal solution to the following nonlinear programming problem, making use of the Karush-Kuhn-Tucker conditions.

   Maximize $y = -x_1^2 - x_2^2 + 4x_1 + 8x_2$

   subject to

   $$x_1 + x_2 \leq 2$$
   $$x_1, x_2 \geq 0$$

3. Make use of the Karush-Kuhn-Tucker conditions to determine the optimal solution to the following nonlinear programming problem:

   Minimize $y = x_1^2 + 4x_1x_2 + 4x_2^2$

   subject to

   $$x_1 - x_2 \geq 3$$
   $$x_1, x_2 \geq 0$$

4. Determine the optimal solution to the following nonlinear programming problem using the Karush-Kuhn-Tucker conditions:

   Minimize $y = -12x_1 - 15x_2 + 3x_1^2 + .5x_2^2 + 1000$

   subject to

   $$x_1 + x_2 \geq 35$$
   $$x_1, x_2 \geq 0$$

5. Use the Karush-Kuhn-Tucker conditions to derive the optimal solution to the following nonlinear programming problem:

$$\text{Minimize } y = 4(x_1 - 2)^2 + 2(x_2 - 3)^2$$

subject to

$$2x_1 + x_2 \leqslant 6$$
$$x_1 + 3x_2 \leqslant 15$$
$$x_1 + x_2 \geqslant 1$$
$$x_1, x_2 \geqslant 0$$

6. Formulate and solve the following quadratic programming problem using the simplex method:

$$\text{Minimize } y = x_1^2 + 3x_2^2 - x_1 x_2 - 4x_2 + 4$$

subject to

$$x_1 + x_2 \leqslant 1$$
$$x_1, x_2 \geqslant 0$$

7. Formulate and solve the following quadratic programming problem using the simplex method:

$$\text{Maximize } y = -3x_1^2 - 4x_2^2 - 4x_1 x_2 + 3x_1 + 4x_2$$

subject to

$$8x_1 + 6x_2 \leqslant 3$$
$$x_1, x_2 \geqslant 0$$

8. Use the simplex method to determine the solution to the following quadratic programming problem:

$$\text{Minimize } y = 2x_1^2 + 2x_2^2 - 2x_1 x_2 - 6x_1$$

subject to

$$x_1 + x_2 \leqslant 2$$
$$x_1, x_2 \geqslant 0$$

9. Solve the following quadratic programming problem using the simplex method:

$$\text{Maximize } y = -2x_1^2 + 3x_1 + 4x_2$$

subject to

$$x_1 + 2x_2 \leqslant 4$$
$$x_1 + x_2 \leqslant 2$$
$$x_1, x_2 \geqslant 0$$

10. Show the steps for formulation of the initial simplex tableau for the following quadratic programming problem.

$$\text{Minimize } y = 1.5x_1 + 3x_2^2 + x_3^2$$

subject to

$$x_1 + x_2 + 2x_3 \geqslant 20$$
$$x_1 + x_3 \geqslant 10$$
$$x_1, x_2, x_3 \geqslant 0$$

11. Formulate the initial simplex tableau for solution of the following quadratic programming problem via the simplex method.

Maximize
$$y = 3x_1^2 + 2x_2^2 + 2x_3^2 + 2x_1x_2 + 2x_2x_3 - 5x_1 - 3x_2 + x_3$$

subject to
$$x_1 + 2x_2 + 3x_3 \leqslant 6$$
$$x_1 + x_2 + x_3 \geqslant 1$$
$$x_1, x_2, x_3 \geqslant 0$$

16

Implementation of Management Science

Since the end of World War II, a significant number of quantitative techniques have been developed for the practical solution of management problems. In the previous chapters of this text, a broad spectrum of these techniques has been reviewed and some of the more prominent and traditional ones have been analyzed in depth. The successes of these management science techniques have been numerous.[1] In a survey by Gaither, approximately one-half of the 275 firms responding to a questionnaire reported using management science/operations research techniques.[2] Of the firms that applied these techniques, 80% rated the results very good, and 11% rated the results excellent.

In this text, the presentation of the various techniques has emphasized the description and development of the mathematical structures of the techniques. Yet model construction represents only one part of the management science process. In this process, first the system is analyzed and the problem formulated, then the model is constructed and results are achieved and tested, and finally *the model is implemented*. Hence, it would be negligent to conclude this text without providing some insight into this final step of the modeling process, *implementation*.

Implementation is an essential part of the management science process for the simple reason that if the model is not applied to some practical end, the desired results will not be forthcoming. The development of a model is pursued, after all, for the purpose of increasing a system's efficiency as measured by cost reduction, resource utilization, profit, and so forth. If the model does not come to fruition in the form of successful use, then the effort expended in its development is wasted.

Implementation often is a complex and difficult task. In fact, implementation is frequently referred to as the "problem of implementation." The difficulty of implementation has only recently been perceived as a potential problem. Although the new techniques developed during and immediately following World War II showed promise of future success, the evolution of management science was initially slow. It was not until the decade of the sixties that the rapid development of new techniques and applications

[1] Jan H. Huysmans, "Operations Research Implementation and the Practice of Management," in *Implementing Operations Research/Management Science*, ed. R. L. Schultz and D. P. Slevin, p. 273.

[2] Gaither, "The Adoption of Operations Research Techniques by Manufacturing Organizations," pp. 797–813.

of these techniques began to occur. The advancement of computer technology enabled many sophisticated management science techniques to be applied to various operational problems. During this period, many computer firms developed "canned" programs and sophisticated information systems that facilitated the easy, rapid, and economical application of management science techniques.

During the 1960s, a corresponding growth of interest in management science was experienced in academic institutions. Only a few universities entered the decade with formal degree programs encompassing management science–related topics for the business/management student. By the end of the decade, however, numerous schools had developed such programs and, in fact, were emphasizing their development. College graduates armed with management science training and capabilities began moving into the business environment. The influx resulted in an increased appreciation and understanding of the potential of management science among all management personnel. This, in turn, created an atmosphere conducive to further growth of management science within the business community. An understanding of the role, value, and limitations of management science began to emerge. As a result, many firms established their own management science staffs.

Rapid growth is often accompanied by problems, however, and this has been true of the evolution of management science. Both management scientists and managers have begun to question the extent to which these techniques are being applied. A feeling has emerged that the full potential of management science and accompanying computer facilities is not being realized. There is an increased tendency to believe that many models either fail upon implementation or are never implemented at all. Thus, a great deal of attention has been focused on the problem of implementation. (As evidence of this increased attention, Wysocki, in a "bibliography of implementation," identified approximately two-hundred journal articles devoted to the subject of implementation written in a six-year period.[3] This represented almost 75% of the total research output on this topic.)

The purposes of this chapter are first to define implementation in order to provide a framework for the analysis of the variables and factors that have an effect on successful implementation, and then to discuss some of the strategies developed by researchers in the field to ensure successful implementation.

IMPLEMENTATION DEFINED

Implementation has been defined in various ways. We will review several of the more popular and traditional definitions. One definition, provided by Churchman and Shainblatt, holds that implementation is "the manner in which the manager may come to use the results of scientific effort" and that the problem of implementation is "determining what activities of the scientist and manager are most appropriate to bring about an effective relationship."[4] A similar definition by Schultz and Slevin states that implementation

---

[3] Wysocki, "OR/MS Implementation Research: A Bibliography," pp. 37–41.

[4] Churchman and Shainblatt, "The Researcher and the Manager: A Dialectic of Implementation," pp. B69–B87.

"refers to the actual use of operations research/management science output by managers that *influences* their decision processes."[5]

The common thread running through these two definitions is that implementation exists when the model or its results are in use *and* that implementation presupposes some interface or link between the management scientist and the manager. However, it can be assumed with some degree of certainty that the manager does not perceive implementation to have occurred unless some degree of success is achieved in attaining the manager's objectives (i.e., unless the model does what it was intended to do). Conversely, the management scientist may perceive that implementation has been achieved (i.e., the model is successful) if the model is used at all. In other words, some form of perceived success must be present for implementation to have occurred.

A somewhat different and expanded view of implementation suggests that implementation is a *continuous process* encompassing not only the final use of the model, but also problem formulation, model development and construction, and model testing. In this framework, the "experiences" gained from implementation provide feedback to different stages in the management science modeling process. Thus, the model evolves throughout the implementation process. The basic premise of this approach is that successful implementation is dependent on success at each of the various stages of the modeling process. If the problem is not formulated properly, if the model is not constructed correctly, if the results are not valid, then implementation will not be successfully achieved. This framework emphasizes the role of initial management involvement in the management science process in enhancing the possibility of successful implementation.

The notion of implementation's being a continuous, ongoing process is supported by the research of Rubenstein et al.[6] and Markland and Newett.[7] Markland and Newett have proposed that management science projects include six "life phases": prebirth, introduction, transition, maturity, death, and resurrection. These phases represent a life cycle for the project, from its inception to its eventual disuse and rediscovery. These authors demonstrate that various implementation criteria are important at particular phases in the life cycle. The important point to be gained from this research is that eventual successful implementation is dependent on occurrences during each phase of the project.

As can be seen from these various views of implementation, it is difficult to develop a single, specific definition. However, we can surmise that implementation encompasses certain characteristics: (1) it is achieved through successful use of the model, although success is a matter of degree and must be evaluated by the party involved, (2) it is based on an interface between the management scientist and the manager, (3) it must be considered at each phase of the management science process (i.e., life of the project), and (4) it is an ongoing, dynamic process.

---

[5] Schultz and Slevin, "Implementation and Management Innovations," in *Implementing Operations Research/Management Science*, p. 6.

[6] Rubenstein et al., "Some Organizational Factors Related to Effectiveness of Management Science Groups in Industry," pp. B508–B518.

[7] Markland and Newett, "A Subjective Taxonomy for Evaluating the Stages of Management Science Research," pp. 31–39.

THE IMPLEMENTATION PROBLEM

Now that we have developed a working definition of what constitutes implementation, we must turn our thoughts to why, on occasion, it becomes a problem. In other words, it is important to identify those variables, and the relationships among them, that inhibit successful implementation. This, in turn, will facilitate the development of strategies to overcome the problems.

When the problem of implementation was first encountered by managers and management scientists, the causes proposed were somewhat subjective and superficial. Some of the proposed causes included personality and training differences between managers and management scientists, ill-defined problems and improper model formulation, models too sophisticated for the problems they were designed to solve, a lack of understanding of management and decision-making processes by the management scientist, and a lack of understanding of management science techniques by managers.

Grayson suggested five basic reasons management science techniques are not utilized:

1. Shortage of time—techniques are time consuming and decision making often must be made spontaneously.

2. Inaccessibility of data—data is not always available to the manager when and where it is needed.

3. Resistance to change—the organization must often be changed to create an atmosphere for the use of management science techniques.

4. Long response time—management scientists are not geared to working in a manager's time frame. It takes too long to develop models.

5. Invalidating simplifications—management scientists strip away much of the real-world problem with simplifying assumptions.[8]

Several observations can be made regarding the proposed causes of unsuccessful implementation of management science techniques. First, the proposed causes were often opinions based on practical experiences, and as such they tended to be narrow in scope. Although all of these difficulties do occur in individual cases, it is inappropriate to generalize to the problem of implementation as a whole. Second, causes cited were not criticisms of the techniques themselves but rather criticisms of the manner in which the techniques are developed into specific models and applied. This is an underlying characteristic of the analysis of implementation that has been present consistently since the initial recognition that a problem of implementation existed.

As is the case with many forms of problem analysis, attempts to explain the problem of implementation passed quickly from generalization to directed research. One of the earliest examples of a concerted study of the factors related to the success or failure of implementation was conducted by Rubenstein et al. This study resulted in a compilation of ten factors affecting implementation:

1. How much management supports and understands the management science activity.

2. How receptive the recipients of the management science activity are.

[8] Grayson, "Management Science and Business Practice," pp. 41–48.

3. The technical and organizational capabilities of the management science group.

4. At what level the management science group is located in the organization.

5. The amount of influence the management science group has in the organization.

6. The reputation of the management science staff.

7. The amount of resources allocated to management science.

8. How relevant management science is to what the organization needs.

9. The amount of opposition to management science and its level in the organization.

10. How the organization as a whole perceives the success of the management science group.[9]

These factors tend to reflect the relationship of the management science group to the surrounding organization; they describe general conditions that by their nature can positively or negatively influence the success of implementation. Little identified several characteristics that can enhance implementation if they exist *in the model:* simplicity, robustness, ease of control, adaptiveness, completeness, and ease of communication.[10]

Viewing the implementation problem from a practitioner's point of view, Harvey, in a survey of thirty-one companies, identified a set of twenty-three factors that affect the success or failure of implementation.[11] These factors are grouped into three categories of characteristics: those regarding management, the problem, and the management science team and the solution. Factors with regard to management include management's experience with sophisticated quantitative models; the management climate for innovation, change, and conflict; management's use of quantitative criteria for evaluation; and the time frame for decision making. In terms of the problem, factors that relate to the nature of objectives and the manner in which they are stated are considered. Characteristics of the management science team include the sensitivity of the management science group to the organization and the responsibility for implementation, which includes the recognition of the problems implementation can cause.

Harvey noted, however, that the problem of implementation does not consist of any one specific group of characteristics. That is, the problem characteristics vary from organization to organization and from model to model.

Also during the late 1960s, a period devoted to examining the problem of implementation, a somewhat different but insightful view was presented by Churchman and Shainblatt. It had as its emphasis the manager–management scientist interface. In their study, they identified four positions that can be taken on the problem of implementation:

1. Separate function position

2. Communication position

3. Persuasion position

4. Mutual understanding position[12]

---

[9] Rubenstein et al., "Some Organizational Factors Related to Effectiveness of Management Science Groups in Industry," pp. B508–B518.

[10] Little, "Models and Managers: The Concept of a Decision Calculus," pp. B466–B485.

[11] Harvey, "Factors Making for Implementation Success and Failure," pp. B312–B321.

[12] Churchman and Shainblatt, "The Researcher and the Manager: A Dialectic of Implementation," pp. B69–B87.

The essential factor differentiating these four positions is the degree of understanding posited between the manager and the management scientist. The separate function position requires no understanding between manager and management scientist as a precondition for implementation. The second and third positions reflect one party's understanding of the other. The fourth position asserts that a necessary condition for implementation is mutual understanding between manager and management scientist. This last position is the most popular and the one most generally agreed upon as a requirement of implementation.

Recent research on the implementation problem has taken a behavioral approach. An excellent summary of behaviorally oriented research models is presented by Schultz and Slevin in the first text devoted exclusively to implementation.[13] All the behavioral models are similar in that "some measure of implementation, a dependent variable, is explained by a set of so-called independent variables."[14] Twelve different models are presented that encompass, overall, approximately sixty dependent variables related to implementation.

These models highlight the numerous variables and relationships that have been identified as being related to the problem of implementation. They also emphasize the extensive depth and degree of the research now being performed in this area. These models, as well as the other studies identified in this section, demonstrate rather conclusively that there is no set group of reasons for the failure of implementation. Rather, the problem and its causes are, in many cases, unique to a particular firm or business environment. As a result, it is difficult to propose one specific strategy for assuring successful implementation. A strategy must be tailored to fit the specific situation—an effective strategy encompasses characteristics unique to the organization, the particular problem, and the model.

STRATEGIES FOR SUCCESSFUL IMPLEMENTATION

Numerous strategies have been proposed for attaining successful implementation, as might be expected in light of the many variables related to the problem. These strategies are based on a team approach, wherein a number of individuals with different backgrounds and training are drawn into the implementation process to compensate for the different behavioral factors.[15] In addition to the manager and the management scientist, the "team" might include computer scientists, people from the operating area, and nontechnical people (i.e., personnel staff).

Lucas suggests a three-step strategy as follows:

1. The system is designed in conjunction with the proposed uses. In fact, the user takes the lead in development.

---

[13] Schultz and Slevin, eds., *Implementing Operations Research/Management Science.*
[14] Ibid., "Implementation and Management Innovation," pp. 3–20.
[15] Shycon, "All Around the Model," pp. 33–35.

results in a high level of success, whereas low levels of the change process result in low levels of success.

The Lewin theory of change identifies the process by which successful implementation of management science techniques can be achieved. However, the theory of change does not specify how to achieve the change cycle. In other words, no procedure is suggested for achieving unfreezing, change, and refreezing.

As a tool for achieving organizational change, the concept of a *change agent* has been suggested by several researchers. The change agent is usually a neutral individual who mediates between the management scientist and the manager to facilitate change. Often, however, a change agent is a staff or liaison group, since successful implementation is often a result of group effectiveness in producing organizational change. In some cases, the management scientist is identified as the change agent.

Although there is a great deal of uncertainty as to the true identity of a change agent, certainly a change agent of some type must exist. An individual, a group, or some action-based event must be incorporated into the Lewin process to facilitate unfreezing, changing, and refreezing within the organization.

Whatever its identity, the change agent must act as a catalyst in the implementation process by instructing the manager in the new technique and carrying him or her through the implementation process. In order to demonstrate the concept of a change agent within the Lewin change process, a *simulation game* will be presented as the change agent. The simulation game demonstrates how each step of the change process is initiated and successfully achieved.

Simulation Games

Gaming is the use of a computerized simulation model to permit participants to make decisions and observe the behavior of the system as a result of those decisions. A *simulation game* should not be confused with game theory, which was discussed in Chapter 8. A gaming model consists of a simulated environment that mirrors the characteristics of the actual system under analysis. Historically, games have served as a means of studying human behavior, a training device for management personnel, and an instructional aid in university business schools. Simulation games that simulate business environments are often employed at the undergraduate level in finance, management policy, and production and operations management courses.

The simulation game is an on-line computer system well suited to carrying out the steps of the Lewin theory:

1. Unfreezing via game/system introduction
2. Changing via game playing
3. Refreezing via on-line deployment of the system

The initial step of introducing the game occurs in a management training session. The game is employed to demonstrate improved conditions that could result through use of the new technique (i.e., the achievement of newly defined higher objectives or easier achievement of present ones). After what can be accomplished is demonstrated to a manager, the manager usually becomes dissatisfied with the present level of output.

The second step, game playing, involves employing the game model as a teaching device. The game offers an alternative to a manager's previous behavior pattern. By actu-ally playing the game, a manager begins to learn the new technique and ideally becomes more receptive to it. In this step, the unfreezing process continues and may actually mesh with the change step. Old behavior patterns gradually change as new patterns are learned and as the manager becomes more and more dissatisfied with the previous system.

As part of the change process, a manager may be required to develop new objectives. If goals and objectives are successfully displayed as a manager becomes familiar with the game, however, the new goals can be easily learned.

The third step in the gaming procedure is the development of the new technique as an on-line computer system similar to the game used to demonstrate the system. This step enables a manager to continue to use the mode of implementation that was intro-duced in the learning process. In effect, a manager continues to play the game. The value of the on-line system is that it allows a manager to progress through the Lewin steps via one vehicle of learning and implementation. A feeling of continuity is generated that contributes to the success of the implementation process.

A representative framework of the gaming methodology and its relationship to the three-step Lewin change process is depicted in Figure 16.2.

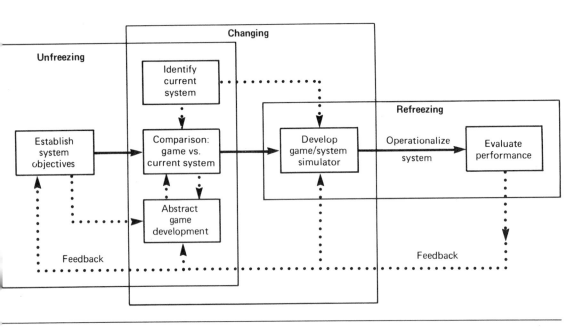

Figure 16.2 The Game/System Simulator

The component parts of this gaming system approach are defined as follows:

1. *Establish system objectives.* System objectives are the goals or results sought from the system to be implemented. Establishing objectives that require a high level of output from a manager's area of responsibility begins the unfreezing step in the change process. A manager becomes dissat-isfied and uncomfortable with his or her current situation.

2. *Abstract game development.* Development of an abstract game is part of a three-step phase that also requires identification of the present system and a comparative analysis of that system and the abstract game. The game is abstract in that it does not necessarily mirror the present system.

Developing the game in this manner enables a management scientist to conceptualize a system without management input and bias.

3. *Identification of the system.* This activity provides a basis for comparative analysis (i.e. comparison of the abstract game and the current system). It further provides the management scientist and the manager with a common point of departure—that is, a basis for discussion.

4. *Comparison of the game and the current system.* By comparing the abstract game with the present system, a manager is able to gain a new perspective. A manager is forced into feeling dissatisfaction with the present system, while being offered an alternative approach. This further enhances the unfreezing step. Taking full advantage of the game environment permits the unfreezing step to be finalized and the change step to be initiated. The structure of the gaming activity is game play followed by critique sessions in which a manager participates via group discussion and/or private questionnaire. The critique sessions have a twofold effect. First, they enable a manager/participant to voice opinions and ask questions, actions that should promote the learning process. Second, the critique sessions offer feedback to the management scientist. This provides input that the management scientist can use to alter the abstract game to reflect a compromised system. By repeating the game playing–critique session cycle several times, a participant begins to learn the fundamentals of the system, while the management scientist refines and develops the system. This process initiates the change step.

5. *Game/system simulator.* In this activity of the gaming framework, a simulation model of the actual system is developed. By employing the model as a game, a manager is in reality learning the actual system that will be operationalized. This activity completes the change step by exposing the new system to the recipient and initiates the refreezing steps by demonstrating the system's effectiveness in achieving results.

6. *Evaluation of performance.* At this stage, the system has reached operationality, and the recipient is involved in its use. However, the management scientist must be careful to remain involved with the implementation process until the manager has completed the refreezing process. This involves evaluating the system to determine whether it meets specifications and achieves desired results. Discrepancies must be corrected through the feedback process before the manager relapses to the previous system. When all problems have been sufficiently resolved, the refreezing step is completed.

This simulation gaming approach has been found to be highly successful in facilitating the implementation of systems. The game-system cycle tends to force the manager through the Lewin steps, thus minimizing the amount of regression from step to step. In effect, the game meshes the unfreezing-changing-refreezing cycle, creating a smooth continuous change process. This points out the fact that the Lewin steps need not be performed distinctly; that is, it is not necessary to complete each step before the next one is started.

The use of a computerized instructional tool like the simulation game model also has other benefits. It involves the manager in the development of the model via the on-line characteristic of the system. The on-line operation encourages the exploration of "what if" questions and the use of computer-generated information. Managers become aware of previously unknown computer capabilities, a situation that can foster an inclination to further experimentation. This is the ultimate accolade for any implementation process—it not only successfully implements the present model but also creates an interest in other management science techniques.

Another important benefit that should be promoted in the implementation process is positive and negative feedback between the manager and the management science

An Application of Implementation:
Successful Implementation of Manufacturing Software

Geisler and Rubenstein conducted a study of manufacturing companies in order to determine factors that might contribute to the successful implementation of manufacturing-related software. Interviews were conducted during a 14-month period in 18 *Fortune* 200 companies that had attempted to implement manufacturing software. The development of such software frequently requires a large capital investment; thus its successful implementation is of particular importance.

The study identified three phenomena associated with software implementation. First, the software application typically occurs as separate achievements with little interaction among other application experiences. Second, vendors tend to be very localized in their interaction with the user, acting independently of other company users. Third, productivity is often measured by outside parties or experts with little knowledge of company strategies, goals, and objectives.

The study revealed that successful implementation is dependent on the degree of group. Managers are often able to discover problems and inconsistencies that the management scientist might not notice. Thus, the implementation process becomes continuous.

Cost of Implementation

An often-overlooked but important aspect of implementation is the cost in time and resources. The financial cost, work force requirements, and computer cost for developing and using a simulation game can be very high. In fact, the costs involved usually make this particular implementation strategy prohibitive for all but the largest firms. Thus, any form of implementation strategy, as well as the management science model, must be carefully analyzed to determine whether the benefits to be gained from implementation will exceed the costs.

The cost of the management science model itself can be a factor in determining whether or not it should be implemented. The easiest costs to determine are the direct work force requirements associated with developing a model (and even these are not always easy to forecast). However, the implementation of management science models often upsets normal operational activities and can result in temporarily decreased output and productivity, lost sales, and disrupted production schedules. These costs are more difficult to forecast and to assign an economic value. The implementation of a model can also disrupt the manager's schedule and consume valuable time that might be spent more profitably elsewhere.

The benefits resulting from a model are obviously measured in terms of increased productivity, profits, and efficiency and reduced cost. It must be determined with some degree of certainty whether the benefits accruing from implementation will exceed the costs. In addition, it must always be considered that failure to implement results in little or no benefit and the waste of the time and money expended for model development and implementation. Previously we have considered the problem of implementation only in regard to the model's not being used, without considering the potential financial losses.

interaction between the software developers and users, on the support from upper management, and on the quality of the planning and objectives related to implementation.

Three implications were developed from the study for improving implementation. First, top management should encourage interaction between the software producers and users (production personnel). Second, management should support the implementation of the software and not be preoccupied exclusively with the productivity of the software. Clear and feasible goals and policies should be set for the software. Third, management should support the (production) user before, during, and after implementation with resources, training, support for risk-taking, and autonomy in making related decisions. In addition, management should encourage manufacturing and other company functions (such as MIS) to work together in the planning process and in the selection and evaluation of software.

Source: E. Geisler and A. H. Rubenstein, "The Successful Implementation of Application Software in New Production Systems," *Interfaces,* 17, no. 3 (May–June 1987): 18–24.

Considered in light of these losses, the problem of implementation can take on new magnitude.

Management Science Within the Organization

One of the variables identified in several of the implementation models is the location of management science within the organization. Such factors as the existence of a management science staff, the location of the management science service within the organizational structure, the size of the management science staff, and the status of the management science group are important in attaining successful implementation.

Many large and medium-size firms have management science departments or staffs concerned exclusively with problem solving and model development. These staffs can be quite large, containing as many as thirty members. Size, however, is not a determining factor; quality is the primary factor in achieving implementation.

The management science staff can exist at numerous locations within the organizational structure. For example, it can be at the top management level, the corporate level, or the operational level. Some firms have management science groups at each of these levels of the organization. The organizational officer to whom the management science staff reports is basically determined by the location of the staff in the organization. There does not appear to be a typical organizational location for management science. The position of the staff in the firm and the political strength of the organizational member in charge of the management science function can be major factors in achieving implementation.

This discussion of the management science staff should not suggest that management science does not exist in those firms where there is no staff or department. In some instances, a member or several members of the management staff perform the management science function. This will become more and more prevalent in the future as a result of increased training in management science techniques at the college level. Both undergraduate business majors and M.B.A. students will be more prepared in the future to develop and implement management science models. Although the manager/management scientist is constrained by lack of time and resources in organizations where a full staff does not exist, he or she has the advantage of being totally involved in the management science process, thus enhancing implementation.

SUMMARY

The purpose of this chapter was to make you aware of and familiar with the problems that can arise in attempting to implement management science models based on the quantitative techniques presented in this text. Implementation was defined, and the various factors that often make it a problem were analyzed.

Although the successes of management science are many and more successes will be forthcoming in the future, there is a need for continued emphasis on and awareness of the problem of implementation. It would be negligent to ignore the full potential of management science because of the obstacles to implementation. This chapter, as well as numerous other sources, indicates that the problem has been recognized, that solutions are being sought, and that research will be continued in the future.

REFERENCES

ACKOFF, R., and RIVETT, P. *A Manager's Guide to Operations Research.* New York: John Wiley & Sons, 1963.

BYRD, J., and MOORE, L. T. *Decision Models for Management.* New York: McGraw-Hill, 1982.

CHURCHMAN, C., and SHAINBLATT, A. A. "The Researcher and the Manager: A Dialectic of Implementation." *Management Science* 11 (1965): B69–B87.

DAVIS, K. R., and TAYLOR, B. W. "Addressing the Implementation Problem: A Gaming Approach." *Decision Sciences* 7 (1976): 677–687.

GAITHER, N. "The Adoption of Operations Research Techniques by Manufacturing Organizations." *Decision Sciences* 6 (1975): 797–813.

GRAYSON, C. J., JR. "Management Science and Business Practice." *Harvard Business Review* 51 (1973): 41–48.

HARVEY, A. "Factors Making for Implementation Success and Failure." *Management Science* 16 (1970): B312–B321.

HUYSMANS, J. H. B. M. *The Implementation of Management Science.* New York: John Wiley & Sons, 1970.

LEWIN, K. "Group Decision and Social Change." In *Readings in Social Psychology,* edited by E. Maccoby, T. M. Newcomb, and E. L. Hartley, pp. 197–211. New York: Holt, Rinehart and Winston, 1947.

LITTLE, J. D. C. "Models and Managers: The Concept of a Decision Calculus." *Management Science* 16 (1970): B466–B485.

MARKLAND, R. E. *Topics in Management Science.* 2d ed. New York: John Wiley & Sons, 1983.

MARKLAND, R. E., and NEWETT, R. J. "A Subjective Taxonomy for Evaluating the Stages of Management Science Research." *Interfaces* 2 (1972): 31–39.

MILLER, D. W., and STARR, M. K. *Executive Decisions and Operations Research.* Englewood Cliffs, New Jersey: Prentice-Hall, 1969.

RUBENSTEIN, A. H.; RADNOR, M.; BAKER, N. R.; HEIMAN, D. K.; and McCOLLY, J. B. "Some Organizational Factors Related to Effectiveness of Management Science Groups in Industry." *Management Science* 13 (1967): B508–B518.

SCHULTZ, R. L., and SLEVIN, D. P., eds. *Implementing Operations Research/Management Science.* New York: Elsevier, 1975.

SHYCON, H. N. "All Around the Model." *Interfaces* 2 (1972): 33–35.

WYSOCKI, R. K. "OR/MS Implementation Research: A Bibliography." *Interfaces* 9 (1979): 37–41.

ZAND, D. E., and SORENSEN, R. E. "Theory of Change and the Effective Use of Management Science." *Administrative Science Quarterly* 20 (1975): 532–545.

PROBLEMS

1. Develop your own definition of *implementation*.

2. Discuss implementation as a continuous process that occurs throughout the life of a management science project.

3. Discuss the reasons why implementation often becomes a problem.

4. List and discuss the various strategies that can be employed to enhance successful implementation.

5. Discuss *change theory* as a framework for achieving successful implementation.

6. Identify some of the specific costs that might accompany management science implementation.

7. Indicate the different levels within the organization at which the management science staff could exist, and discuss the advantages and disadvantages of each.

8. Give your opinion as to the optimal makeup of a management science staff. (What specialties should be encompassed by a management science staff?)

9. Define the four positions that can be taken on the role of the interface between the manager and management scientist in implementation.

10. Discuss the problems that might develop in the implementation of each of the following example models:

    a. Examples 2.2 and 2.3 in Chapter 2
    b. The check-processing network in Chapter 6 (Example 6.4)
    c. Example 12.2 in Chapter 12
    d. Example 13.4 in Chapter 13

11. In Lucas's three-step strategy for achieving successful implementation, the third step is to design a simple and easily understandable model. Is this always a feasible task? Based on your experiences in model development gained from this text, discuss the ways in which this third step might be achieved.

12. Identify the various forms that a change agent can take.

13. Based on the information provided in this chapter, develop your own strategy for attaining successful implementation and devise an example to demonstrate your strategy.

14. Discuss the degree to which you perceive differences in personality and training between managers and management scientists to be a cause of implementation problems. Identify some of these differences.

15. Why is the manager often viewed as more resistant to change than the management scientist?

Introduction to Matrix Methods

A matrix is a rectangular array of numbers arranged into rows and columns. A matrix is usually denoted by enclosing the array of numbers in brackets or parentheses, as follows:

$$\begin{bmatrix} 1 & 3 & 5 \\ 2 & 7 & 6 \end{bmatrix} \quad \text{or} \quad \begin{pmatrix} 1 & 3 & 5 \\ 2 & 7 & 6 \end{pmatrix}$$

The general form of a matrix can be designated by an array of symbols representing entries. These symbols are usually lowercase roman or italic letters with two subscripts, as shown below:

$$\begin{bmatrix} a_{11} & a_{12} & a_{13} & \cdots & a_{1n} \\ a_{21} & a_{22} & a_{23} & \cdots & a_{2n} \\ \cdot & \cdot & \cdot & & \cdot \\ \cdot & \cdot & \cdot & & \cdot \\ \cdot & \cdot & \cdot & & \cdot \\ a_{m1} & a_{m2} & a_{m3} & \cdots & a_{mn} \end{bmatrix}$$

This array is called an m by n matrix because it contains m rows and n columns. In general, each element is denoted by a_{ij}, where $i =$ row location and $j =$ column location.

A matrix is often denoted by a single capital roman or italic letter. For example, the preceding matrix of a_{ij} elements might be denoted by the capital letter A.

A matrix as a whole does not have a numerical value. The values in the matrix, however, can be useful in representing a particular numerical problem. For example, the matrix elements can represent the transition probabilities for a Markov process:

$$P = \begin{bmatrix} p_{11} & p_{12} & p_{13} \\ p_{21} & p_{22} & p_{23} \\ p_{31} & p_{32} & p_{33} \end{bmatrix} = \begin{bmatrix} .6 & .3 & .1 \\ .2 & .5 & .3 \\ .4 & .4 & .2 \end{bmatrix}$$

A matrix with the same number of rows and columns is called a *square matrix*. Such a matrix is referred to as an m by m or n by n matrix. The Markov transition probability matrix in Chapter 9 is such a matrix.

A matrix with only one row is referred to as a **row vector,** and a matrix with only one column is referred to as a **column vector.** The state values of a Markov process are generally given as a row vector, such as

$$S = [s_1, s_2, s_3]$$

MATRIX ADDITION AND SUBTRACTION

Two or more matrices can be added (or subtracted) only if they are of the same dimensions (have the same number of rows and columns). Matrices of equal dimensions are added by adding the corresponding elements of each matrix array. Likewise, subtraction is accomplished by subtracting the elements of one array from the corresponding elements of the other.

Consider, for example, the following 2 by 3 matrices:

$$A = \begin{bmatrix} 2 & 3 & 1 \\ 4 & 7 & 5 \end{bmatrix} \qquad B = \begin{bmatrix} 1 & 2 & 6 \\ 5 & 2 & 3 \end{bmatrix}$$

Determine C, where $C = A + B$. By adding the corresponding elements of each matrix, we obtain

$$\begin{aligned} C &= \begin{bmatrix} 2 & 3 & 1 \\ 4 & 7 & 5 \end{bmatrix} + \begin{bmatrix} 1 & 2 & 6 \\ 5 & 2 & 3 \end{bmatrix} \\ &= \begin{bmatrix} 2+1 & 3+2 & 1+6 \\ 4+5 & 7+2 & 5+3 \end{bmatrix} = \begin{bmatrix} 3 & 5 & 7 \\ 9 & 9 & 8 \end{bmatrix} \end{aligned}$$

As an illustration of matrix subtraction, determine D, where $D = A - B$. By subtracting the elements of matrix B from the corresponding elements of A, we obtain

$$\begin{aligned} D &= \begin{bmatrix} 2 & 3 & 1 \\ 4 & 7 & 5 \end{bmatrix} - \begin{bmatrix} 1 & 2 & 6 \\ 5 & 2 & 3 \end{bmatrix} \\ &= \begin{bmatrix} 2-1 & 3-2 & 1-6 \\ 4-5 & 7-2 & 5-3 \end{bmatrix} = \begin{bmatrix} 1 & 1 & -5 \\ -1 & 5 & 2 \end{bmatrix} \end{aligned}$$

MATRIX MULTIPLICATION

Two matrices can be multiplied only if the number of *columns* of the *first* matrix is equal to the number of *rows* of the *second* matrix. For example, in order for us to determine the product of A and B, the number of columns of matrix A must equal the number of rows of matrix B. In general, the new matrix $A \times B$ is not the same as $B \times A$. Thus,

$$A \times B \neq B \times A \qquad \text{(where} \neq \text{denotes not equal to)}$$

The number of elements in the matrix obtained as the product of the two original matrices is determined by the number of rows in the first matrix and the number of columns in the second matrix.

The requirements for multiplying one matrix by another and the resulting dimensions of the product matrix are summarized below for the multiplication of matrix A

times matrix B to yield matrix C, $C = A \times B$:

1. The number of columns of matrix A must equal the number of rows of matrix B.

Number of columns$_A$ = Number of rows$_B$

2. The dimensions of matrix C are dependent on the number of rows of matrix A and the number of columns of matrix B.

Dimensions: Number of rows$_A$ $\times$ Number of columns$_B$

3. The elements of the new matrix C, formed by multiplying A times B, are given by

$$c_{ij} = \sum_{k=1}^{r} a_{ik} \cdot b_{kj}, \; i = 1, \ldots, m; \, j = 1, \ldots, n$$

where it is assumed that A is an m by r matrix and B is an r by n matrix.

Note that the required condition that the number of columns of A be equal to the number of rows of B is met (the number of columns of A equals r and the number of rows of B equals r). Further note that the resulting product matrix C has m rows and n columns—the number of rows of A and the number of columns of B.

To illustrate the computational procedure for determining the c_{ij} elements of the product matrix, we will determine:

$C = A \times B$
where
$$A = \begin{bmatrix} 2 & 3 & 4 \\ 4 & 2 & 5 \end{bmatrix}$$

$$B = \begin{bmatrix} 1 & 3 \\ 6 & 3 \\ 5 & 1 \end{bmatrix}$$

Note that the number of columns of A is equal to the number of rows of B. The resulting product matrix will be a 2 by 2 matrix (two rows in A and two columns in B) of the general form

$$C = \begin{bmatrix} c_{11} & c_{12} \\ c_{21} & c_{22} \end{bmatrix}$$

The ijth element of C is equal to the sum of the ith row elements of A times the jth column elements of B. Thus the elements of the product matrix are given symbolically by

$$c_{11} = a_{11} \cdot b_{11} + a_{12} \cdot b_{21} + a_{13} \cdot b_{31}$$
$$c_{12} = a_{11} \cdot b_{12} + a_{12} \cdot b_{22} + a_{13} \cdot b_{32}$$
$$c_{21} = a_{21} \cdot b_{11} + a_{22} \cdot b_{21} + a_{23} \cdot b_{31}$$
$$c_{22} = a_{21} \cdot b_{12} + a_{22} \cdot b_{22} + a_{23} \cdot b_{32}$$

The multiplication procedure can be summarized as follows.

$$C = \begin{bmatrix} (\text{1st row of } A \times \text{1st column of } B) & (\text{1st row of } A \times \text{2nd column of } B) \\ (\text{2nd row of } A \times \text{1st column of } B) & (\text{2nd row of } A \times \text{2nd column of } B) \end{bmatrix}$$

Performing the multiplication, we have

$$C = A \times B = \begin{bmatrix} 2 & 3 & 4 \\ 4 & 2 & 5 \end{bmatrix} \cdot \begin{bmatrix} 1 & 3 \\ 6 & 3 \\ 5 & 1 \end{bmatrix}$$

$$= \begin{bmatrix} 2 \cdot 1 + 3 \cdot 6 + 4 \cdot 5 & 2 \cdot 3 + 3 \cdot 3 + 4 \cdot 1 \\ 4 \cdot 1 + 2 \cdot 6 + 5 \cdot 5 & 4 \cdot 3 + 2 \cdot 3 + 5 \cdot 1 \end{bmatrix}$$

$$= \begin{bmatrix} 2 + 18 + 20 & 6 + 9 + 4 \\ 4 + 12 + 25 & 12 + 6 + 5 \end{bmatrix}$$

$$= \begin{bmatrix} 40 & 19 \\ 41 & 23 \end{bmatrix}$$

Consider the following example, in which two 2 by 2 matrices are multiplied, first as $A \times B$ and then as $B \times A$:

$$A = \begin{bmatrix} 2 & 3 \\ 1 & 4 \end{bmatrix} \qquad B = \begin{bmatrix} 5 & 8 \\ 7 & 6 \end{bmatrix}$$

$$A \times B = \begin{bmatrix} 2 & 3 \\ 1 & 4 \end{bmatrix} \cdot \begin{bmatrix} 5 & 8 \\ 7 & 6 \end{bmatrix} = \begin{bmatrix} 10 + 21 & 16 + 18 \\ 5 + 28 & 8 + 24 \end{bmatrix} = \begin{bmatrix} 31 & 34 \\ 33 & 32 \end{bmatrix}$$

$$B \times A = \begin{bmatrix} 5 & 8 \\ 7 & 6 \end{bmatrix} \cdot \begin{bmatrix} 2 & 3 \\ 1 & 4 \end{bmatrix} = \begin{bmatrix} 10 + 8 & 15 + 32 \\ 14 + 6 & 21 + 24 \end{bmatrix} = \begin{bmatrix} 18 & 47 \\ 20 & 45 \end{bmatrix}$$

Although the requirement that the number of columns of the first matrix equal the number of rows of the second matrix is satisfied in each case, the product matrix resulting from $A \times B$ is not the same as that resulting from $B \times A$.

Consider the following case, in which the first matrix is a row vector and the second matrix is a 3 by 3 matrix:

$$A = [100 \ 200 \ 300] \qquad B = \begin{bmatrix} .1 & .7 & .2 \\ .3 & .5 & .2 \\ .8 & .1 & .1 \end{bmatrix}$$

The product of $A \times B$ is computed by the same procedure used above. The number of rows of the product matrix is one (number of rows of A), and the number of columns of the product matrix is three (number of columns of B). Thus, the resulting product matrix is a 1 by 3 row vector.

The product of $A \times B$ is given by

$$A \times B = [100 \ 200 \ 300] \cdot \begin{bmatrix} .1 & .7 & .2 \\ .3 & .5 & .2 \\ .8 & .1 & .1 \end{bmatrix}$$

$$= [10 + 60 + 240 \quad 70 + 100 + 30 \quad 20 + 40 + 30]$$

$$= [310 \ 200 \ 90]$$

This example illustrates a Markov process in which A is the state vector and B is the matrix of transition probabilities. The resulting product matrix (row vector) is the system state vector after one transition period.

SIMULTANEOUS SOLUTION OF A SYSTEM OF LINEAR EQUATIONS

A system of n linear equations with n unknowns can often be more easily solved by using matrix methods. For example, assume we wish to solve the following system of linear equations simultaneously for the values of x_1, x_2, and x_3.

$$x_1 + 3x_2 + 2x_3 = 13$$
$$4x_1 - 2x_2 + 2x_3 = 14$$
$$2x_1 + x_2 + x_3 = 9$$

This set of linear equations can be expressed in matrix form as

$$\begin{bmatrix} 1 & 3 & 2 \\ 4 & -2 & 2 \\ 2 & 1 & 1 \end{bmatrix} \cdot \begin{bmatrix} x_1 \\ x_2 \\ x_3 \end{bmatrix} = \begin{bmatrix} 13 \\ 14 \\ 9 \end{bmatrix}$$

If we define the first matrix of coefficients as A, the second matrix of variables as X, and the third matrix of right-hand-side values as B, we have

$$A \times X = B$$

This can be verified by multiplying matrix A times matrix X (column vector)—the initial set of linear equations is obtained.

We will first consider an intuitive illustration of the matrix solution of a set of simultaneous linear equations. Consider the ordinary algebraic equation

$$2y = 10$$

The solution for y is obtained by multiplying both sides of the equation by the reciprocal of 2,

$$\left(\frac{1}{2}\right) 2y = \left(\frac{1}{2}\right) 10$$

which yields

$$y = 5$$

In general, if we have

$$ay = b$$

then the solution for y is obtained by multiplying by $1/a$:

$$\left(\frac{1}{a}\right) ay = \left(\frac{1}{a}\right) b$$

Note that on the left-hand side of the equation, $(1/a)a$ reduces to 1; this is important for purposes of understanding the following discussion.

When this type of problem is represented in matrix form, as in the case of solving for X where

$$A \times X = B$$

both sides of the equation must be multiplied by a matrix term that reduces A to a matrix form similar to that obtained by multiplying $1/a$ by a.

Identity Matrix

The identity matrix acts in matrix multiplication in the same way as the number 1 acts in the multiplication of ordinary algebra. That is, multiplication of a matrix by an identity matrix leaves the original matrix unchanged, just as $1 \times a = a$ in ordinary algebra. Thus,

$$I \times A = A$$

where the identity matrix is denoted by I.

The identity matrix is always square (the number of rows equals the number of columns) and consists of ones in the diagonal from the upper left to the lower right (the **main diagonal**) and zeros elsewhere. An example of a 3 by 3 identity matrix is

$$I = \begin{bmatrix} 1 & 0 & 0 \\ 0 & 1 & 0 \\ 0 & 0 & 1 \end{bmatrix}$$

The statement that $I \times A = A$ is illustrated by the following. If

$$A = \begin{bmatrix} 3 & 2 \\ 5 & 1 \\ 6 & 4 \end{bmatrix}$$

then

$$I \cdot A = \begin{bmatrix} 1 & 0 & 0 \\ 0 & 1 & 0 \\ 0 & 0 & 1 \end{bmatrix} \cdot \begin{bmatrix} 3 & 2 \\ 5 & 1 \\ 6 & 4 \end{bmatrix}$$

$$= \begin{bmatrix} 3+0+0 & 2+0+0 \\ 0+5+0 & 0+1+0 \\ 0+0+6 & 0+0+4 \end{bmatrix} = \begin{bmatrix} 3 & 2 \\ 5 & 1 \\ 6 & 4 \end{bmatrix} = A$$

Therefore, in order to solve for X in the matrix equation $A \times X = B$, we must multiply both sides of the equation by a term that reduces A to an identity matrix. When A is reduced to an identity, we have $I \times X$, or simply X, remaining on the left side of the equation. This is analogous to multiplying both sides of the equation $ay = b$ by the reciprocal of a in algebra.

Inverse of a Matrix

A method for determining the inverse of a matrix is the Gauss-Jordan elimination method. This method can also be used to solve systems of linear equations and, in fact, is often used as an alternative to the simplex tableau method for solving linear programming problems.

The Gauss-Jordan method is based on the principle that, given a set of linear equations, an equivalent set of equations with the same solution set can be generated by replacing one of the original equations with another equation. The replacement equation is computed by adding to the replaced equation some multiple of one of the other equations in the original set.

Consider the following set of equations:

$$4x_1 + 8x_2 = 160 \tag{1}$$
$$6x_1 + 4x_2 = 120 \tag{2}$$

It is desired to have this set of equations in the general form

$$1x_1 + 0x_2 = A$$
$$0x_1 + 1x_2 = B$$

which is, in effect, the solution of the original set of equations.

In order to achieve this transformation, we must first change the coefficient of x_1 in the first equation to 1 rather than 4. This can be accomplished by dividing equation (1) through by 4, which yields

$$x_1 + 2x_2 = 40 \tag{1a}$$
$$6x_1 + 4x_2 = 120 \tag{2}$$

The next step is to make the coefficient of x_1 in equation (2) zero instead of 6. To achieve this, we multiply equation (1a) by -6 and add the result to equation (2) as follows:

$$-6x_1 - 12x_2 = -240 \qquad \text{(1a)} \times -6$$
$$\underline{6x_1 + 4x_2 = 120} \qquad \text{(2)}$$
$$0x_1 - 8x_2 = -120 \qquad \text{(2a)}$$

Replacing equation (2) in the original system with this sum (2a) yields

$$x_1 + 2x_2 = 40 \tag{1a}$$
$$0x_1 - 8x_2 = -120 \tag{2a}$$

Now we want to transform the x_2 coefficients to 1 and 0, just as we did the x_1 coefficients. First, we divide equation (2a) by -8, which yields the following set of equations:

$$x_1 + 2x_2 = 40 \tag{1a}$$
$$0x_1 + x_2 = 15 \tag{2b}$$

This leaves only the x_2 coefficient in equation (1a) to be changed from 2 to 0. This can be accomplished by multiplying equation (2b) by -2 and adding the result to equation (1a) as follows:

$$x_1 + 2x_2 = 40 \qquad \text{(1a)}$$
$$\underline{0x_1 - 2x_2 = -30} \qquad \text{(2b)} \times -2$$
$$x_1 + 0x_2 = 10 \qquad \text{(1b)}$$

Replacing equation (1a) with this sum (1b) results in the following set of equations:

$$x_1 + 0x_2 = 10 \tag{1b}$$

$$0x_1 + x_2 = 15 \tag{2b}$$

or

$$x_1 = 10, \; x_2 = 15$$

This is the new form we desired, and thus it is the solution set to the original equations.

This same process can be employed to find the inverse of a matrix. First, set up the problem in the following form:

$$\begin{array}{cc} A & I \\ \begin{bmatrix} 4 & 8 \\ 6 & 4 \end{bmatrix} & \begin{bmatrix} 1 & 0 \\ 0 & 1 \end{bmatrix} \end{array}$$

Now perform the Gauss-Jordan steps on both of these matrices simultaneously. First divide the first line by 4.

$$\begin{array}{cc} A & I \\ \begin{bmatrix} 1 & 2 \\ 6 & 4 \end{bmatrix} & \begin{bmatrix} \frac{1}{4} & 0 \\ 0 & 1 \end{bmatrix} \end{array}$$

Now multiply the first line by -6 and add the result to the second line.

$$\begin{array}{cc} A & I \\ \begin{bmatrix} 1 & 2 \\ 0 & -8 \end{bmatrix} & \begin{bmatrix} \frac{1}{4} & 0 \\ -\frac{3}{2} & 1 \end{bmatrix} \end{array}$$

Next divide the second line by -8.

$$\begin{array}{cc} A & I \\ \begin{bmatrix} 1 & 2 \\ 0 & 1 \end{bmatrix} & \begin{bmatrix} \frac{1}{4} & 0 \\ \frac{3}{16} & -\frac{1}{8} \end{bmatrix} \end{array}$$

Finally, multiply the second line by -2 and add the result to the first line.

$$\begin{array}{cc} I & A^{-1} \\ \begin{bmatrix} 1 & 0 \\ 0 & 1 \end{bmatrix} & \begin{bmatrix} -\frac{1}{8} & \frac{1}{4} \\ \frac{3}{16} & -\frac{1}{8} \end{bmatrix} \end{array}$$

The preceding computations result in A^{-1}, the inverse of the original matrix. To check this result using the original set of equations $Ax = B$, where

$$B = \begin{bmatrix} 160 \\ 120 \end{bmatrix}$$

compute the following:

$$x = A^{-1}B$$

$$\begin{bmatrix} x_1 \\ x_2 \end{bmatrix} = \begin{bmatrix} -\frac{1}{8} & \frac{1}{4} \\ \frac{3}{16} & -\frac{1}{8} \end{bmatrix} \begin{bmatrix} 160 \\ 120 \end{bmatrix}$$

$$\begin{bmatrix} x_1 \\ x_2 \end{bmatrix} = \begin{bmatrix} 10 \\ 15 \end{bmatrix}$$

which is the original solution previously computed.

Now let us apply the Gauss-Jordan process to determine the inverse of a 3×3 matrix:

$$\begin{array}{cc} A & I \\ \begin{bmatrix} 1 & 3 & 2 \\ 4 & -2 & 2 \\ 2 & 1 & 1 \end{bmatrix} & \begin{bmatrix} 1 & 0 & 0 \\ 0 & 1 & 0 \\ 0 & 0 & 1 \end{bmatrix} \end{array}$$

Since a_{11} is already 1, the first step is to make $a_{21} = 0$. This is achieved by multiplying the first line by -4 and adding the result to the second line.

$$\begin{array}{cc} A & I \\ \begin{bmatrix} 1 & 3 & 2 \\ 0 & -14 & -6 \\ 2 & 1 & 1 \end{bmatrix} & \begin{bmatrix} 1 & 0 & 0 \\ -4 & 1 & 0 \\ 0 & 0 & 1 \end{bmatrix} \end{array}$$

Now in order to make a_{31} equal to zero, multiply the first line by -2 and add the result to the third line.

$$\begin{array}{cc} A & I \\ \begin{bmatrix} 1 & 3 & 2 \\ 0 & -14 & -6 \\ 0 & -5 & -3 \end{bmatrix} & \begin{bmatrix} 1 & 0 & 0 \\ -4 & 1 & 0 \\ -2 & 0 & 1 \end{bmatrix} \end{array}$$

Next, the a_{i2} values must be transformed to 0, 1, 0. Divide the second line by -14.

$$\begin{array}{cc} A & I \\ \begin{bmatrix} 1 & 3 & 2 \\ 0 & 1 & 3/7 \\ 0 & -5 & -3 \end{bmatrix} & \begin{bmatrix} 1 & 0 & 0 \\ 2/7 & -1/14 & 0 \\ -2 & 0 & 1 \end{bmatrix} \end{array}$$

Next, multiply the second line by -3 and add the result to the first line, and then multiply the second line by 5 and add the result to the third line.

$$\begin{array}{cc} A & I \\ \begin{bmatrix} 1 & 0 & 5/7 \\ 0 & 1 & 3/7 \\ 0 & 0 & -6/7 \end{bmatrix} & \begin{bmatrix} 1/7 & 3/14 & 0 \\ 2/7 & -1/14 & 0 \\ -4/7 & -5/14 & 1 \end{bmatrix} \end{array}$$

Finally, the a_{i3} values must be changed to 0, 0, 1. First divide the third line by $-6/7$.

$$\begin{array}{cc} A & I \\ \begin{bmatrix} 1 & 0 & 5/7 \\ 0 & 1 & 3/7 \\ 0 & 0 & 1 \end{bmatrix} & \begin{bmatrix} 1/7 & 3/14 & 0 \\ 2/7 & -1/14 & 0 \\ 2/3 & 5/12 & -7/6 \end{bmatrix} \end{array}$$

Next, multiply the third line by $-3/7$ and add the result to the second line, and multiply the third line by $-5/7$ and add the result to the first line.

$$\begin{array}{cc} I & A^{-1} \\ \begin{bmatrix} 1 & 0 & 0 \\ 0 & 1 & 0 \\ 0 & 0 & 1 \end{bmatrix} & \begin{bmatrix} -1/3 & -1/12 & 5/6 \\ 0 & -1/4 & 1/2 \\ 2/3 & 5/12 & -7/6 \end{bmatrix} \end{array}$$

Thus, the inverse, A^{-1}, is obtained by the Gauss-Jordan steps.

SOLVING LINEAR PROGRAMMING PROBLEMS BY THE GAUSS-JORDAN METHOD

As noted in Chapter 3, the simplex method is based on the principles of matrix algebra. In fact, the simplex procedure basically follows the steps of the Gauss-Jordan method just presented. In this section the solution of a linear programming problem by the Gauss-Jordan steps will be demonstrated. The linear programming model presented in Chapter 3 and solved via the simplex method in Tables 3.2–3.13 will be used as an example. The formulation for this example is

Maximize $Z = 100x_1 + 80x_2$

subject to
$$2x_1 + 4x_2 \leqslant 80$$
$$3x_1 + x_2 \leqslant 60$$
$$x_1, x_2 \geqslant 0$$

As in the simplex method, the first step is to transform the inequalities into equalities. Also, the objective function must be put into proper form for the Gauss-Jordon solution method by placing all variables on the left side of the equality sign.

$$Z - 100x_1 - 80x_2 = 0 \qquad (0)$$
$$2x_1 + 4x_2 + s_1 = 80 \qquad (1)$$
$$3x_1 + x_2 + s_2 = 60 \qquad (2)$$

We will apply the Gauss-Jordan steps to the problem in equation form instead of transforming the equations into matrix form. This will allow us to more readily observe the similarities between the algebraic approach and the simplex method. It is important to note, however, that the identity matrix is formed by the slack variables s_1 and s_2.

As in the simplex method, the variable that enters the solution must first be identified. By observing the objective function in its original form, we can see that x_1 will contribute the greatest amount, 100, to the achievement of the objective. Therefore, it is selected as the entering variable.

Now that x_1 has been selected as the entering variable, the leaving variable must be selected. This is achieved by solving for x_1 in both constraint equations, while the other variables are assumed to be zero.

$$2x_1 + 4(0) + 0 = 80 \qquad (1)$$
$$3x_1 + 1(0) + 0 = 60 \qquad (2)$$

Therefore,

$x_1 = 40$ in equation (1)
$x_1 = 20$ in equation (2)

This indicates that s_2 should be eliminated. As we move along the x_1 axis in Figure 3.1, s_1 in equation (1) and s_2 in equation (2) are approaching zero (i.e., we are using up those previously unused resources). Since x_1 has a smaller value in equation (2) than in equation (1), s_2 in equation (2) will reach zero first. As in the simplex process, we have determined which constraint is most constraining. Thus, s_2 is the leaving variable.

Now the steps of the Gauss-Jordan process are applied in order to reestablish the identity matrix with x_1 in the basis. This has been achieved when the coefficient for x_1 is zero in equations (0) and (1) and one in equation (2). Recall that equation (2) is selected because s_2 is the leaving variable.

Step 1 Since x_1 must have a coefficient of 1 in equation (2), divide this equation by 3. This results in a new equation, (2a).

$$x_1 + (\tfrac{4}{3})x_2 + (\tfrac{1}{3})s_2 = 20 \tag{2a}$$

Step 2 The variable x_1 must have a coefficient of zero (i.e., x_1 must be eliminated) in equation (1). To achieve this, multiply equation (2a) by 2 and subtract the result from equation (1).

$$
\begin{array}{lrl}
2x_1 + 4x_2 + s_1 & = & 80 \qquad\qquad (1) \\
\underline{-2x_1 - (\tfrac{8}{3})x_2 \qquad\quad - (\tfrac{2}{3})s_2} & = & -40 \qquad\quad (2a) \times 2 \\
(\tfrac{10}{3})x_2 + s_1 - (\tfrac{2}{3})s_2 & = & 40 \qquad\qquad (1a)
\end{array}
$$

Step 3 The variable x_1 must also be eliminated from equation (0). This can be accomplished by multiplying equation (2a) by 100 and adding the result to equation (0).

$$
\begin{array}{lrl}
Z - 100x_1 - 80x_2 & = & 0 \qquad\qquad (0) \\
\underline{100x_1 + (\tfrac{100}{3})x_2 + (\tfrac{100}{3})s_2} & = & 2000 \qquad (2a) \times 100 \\
Z \qquad\qquad - (\tfrac{140}{3})x_2 + (\tfrac{100}{3})s_2 & = & 2000 \qquad (0a)
\end{array}
$$

The new set of equations is

$$Z - (\tfrac{140}{3})x_2 + (\tfrac{100}{3})s_2 = 2000 \tag{0}$$
$$(\tfrac{10}{3})x_2 + s_1 - (\tfrac{2}{3})s_2 = 40 \tag{1}$$
$$x_1 + (\tfrac{4}{3})x_2 + (\tfrac{1}{3})s_2 = 20 \tag{2}$$

Comparing this set of equations with the corresponding simplex tableau (Table A.1) shows that the same relationships exist.

Table A.1 *Completed Second Simplex Tableau*

c_b	c_j basis	b_i^*	100 x_1	80 x_2	0 s_1	0 s_2
0	s_1	40	0	$\tfrac{10}{3}$	1	$-\tfrac{2}{3}$
100	x_1	20	1	$\tfrac{1}{3}$	0	$\tfrac{1}{3}$
	z_j	2000	100	$\tfrac{100}{3}$	0	$\tfrac{100}{3}$
	$c_j - z_j$		0	$\tfrac{140}{3}$	0	$-\tfrac{100}{3}$

Observing the objective function in general form for our new set of equations,

$$Z = (\tfrac{140}{3})x_2 - (\tfrac{100}{3})s_2 + 2000$$

we can see that x_2 is the only remaining variable that has a positive coefficient and, thus, will increase profit.

The leaving variable is selected by solving for x_2 in both equations (1) and (2) and setting all other variables equal to zero.

$$(\tfrac{10}{3})x_2 + 0 - (\tfrac{2}{3})0 = 40 \tag{1}$$
$$0 + (\tfrac{1}{3})x_2 + (\tfrac{1}{3})0 = 20 \tag{2}$$

Therefore,

$$x_2 = 12 \quad \text{in equation (1)}$$
$$x_2 = 60 \quad \text{in equation (2)}$$

Thus, equation (1) is most constrained and s_1 is the leaving variable. The Gauss-Jordan steps are then used to reestablish the identity matrix with x_2 in the solution basis. This has been accomplished when x_2 has a coefficient of one in equation (1) and a coefficient of zero in equations (0) and (2).

Step 1 Since x_2 must have a coefficient of 1 in equation (1), multiply this equation by $\frac{3}{10}$.

$$x_2 + (\tfrac{3}{10})s_1 - (\tfrac{1}{5})s_2 = 12 \tag{1a}$$

Step 2 Eliminate x_2 in equation (2) by multiplying equation (1a) by $\frac{1}{3}$ and subtracting the result from equation (2).

$$x_1 + (\tfrac{1}{3})x_2 \qquad\quad + (\tfrac{1}{3})s_2 = 20 \tag{2}$$
$$\underline{- (\tfrac{1}{3})x_2 - (\tfrac{1}{10})s_1 + (\tfrac{1}{15})s_2 = -4} \tag{(1a) $\times$ ($\tfrac{1}{3}$)}$$
$$x_1 - \qquad (\tfrac{1}{10})s_1 + (\tfrac{2}{5})s_2 = 16 \tag{2a}$$

Step 3 Eliminate x_2 in equation (0) by multiplying equation (1a) by $\frac{140}{3}$ and adding the result to equation (0).

$$Z - (\tfrac{140}{3})x_2 \qquad\quad + (\tfrac{100}{3})s_2 = 2000 \tag{0}$$
$$\underline{(\tfrac{140}{3})x_2 + 14s_1 - (\tfrac{28}{3})s_2 = 560} \tag{(1a) $\times$ ($\tfrac{140}{3}$)}$$
$$Z \qquad\quad + 14s_1 + 24s_2 = 2560 \tag{0a}$$

The new set of equations is

$$Z + 14s_1 + 24s_2 = 2560 \tag{0}$$
$$x_2 + (\tfrac{3}{10})s_1 - (\tfrac{1}{5})s_2 = 12 \tag{1}$$
$$x_1 - (\tfrac{1}{10})s_1 + (\tfrac{2}{5})s_2 = 16 \tag{2}$$

The corresponding simplex tableau is shown in Table A.2.

Table A.2 *Completed Third Simplex Tableau*

	c_j			100	80	0	0
c_b		basis	b_i^*	x_1	x_2	s_1	s_2
80		x_2	12	0	1	$\tfrac{3}{10}$	$-\tfrac{1}{5}$
100		x_1	16	1	0	$-\tfrac{1}{10}$	$\tfrac{2}{5}$
		z_j	2560	100	80	14	24
		$c_j - z_j$		0	0	-14	-24

Again notice the similarity between the simplex tableau and the Gauss Jordan equations.

Analyzing the objective function in regular form,

$$Z = -14s_1 - 24s_2 + 2560$$

we can see that there is no variable that will increase the value of the objective function.

Thus, the optimal solution has been reached.

$$x_1 = 16$$
$$x_2 = 12$$
$$Z = 2560$$

The advantage of employing the simplex procedure is that it is more systematic because it provides distinct steps for each iteration. This, in turn, reduces the chances for error and the necessity of ascertaining the appropriate multiples required to achieve the Gauss-Jordan steps.

-B

Calculus-Based (Classical) Optimization

The essential concept of classical optimization is the slope, or rate of change, of a functional relationship. In the analysis of mathematical models of real-world systems, decision makers are most often interested in determining the optimal values of one or more decision variables. The mathematical model generally consists of the decision variables and their functional relationship to some other dependent variable, such as total output, total profit, or total cost.

In determining the optimal solution, it is necessary to obtain a general equation of the slope of the mathematical function relating the dependent variable to the decision variables. An intuitive understanding of this requirement can be gained by examining the following problem.

Assume that a production process involving one product and one resource input is to be analyzed. The objective is to maximize the dependent variable, output. The problem is to determine the value of the decision variable, resource input, that will maximize output. The functional relationship of productive output to resource input is illustrated in Figure B.1.

Figure B.1 illustrates the standard production function model of economic theory in which productive output increases as resource input increases up to a point, after which diminishing returns are experienced. Production output is maximized at the point where

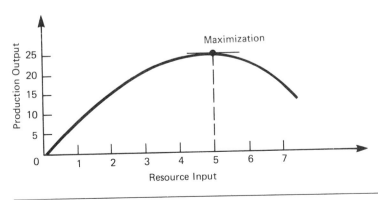

Figure B.1 *Optimal Resource Input and Output*

the curve (the functional relationship of output to input) stops rising and begins to fall. The slope of the curve at the point of maximum output is therefore zero. Thus, if we had a general equation for the slope for all possible values of resource input, we could set the slope equation equal to zero and solve for the input value that maximizes output. This concept is the essence of classical optimization.

MAXIMA AND MINIMA

The purpose of using differential calculus is to determine maximum and minimum values of functions (models). Consider the function illustrated in Figure B.2. Figure B.2 illustrates a function of the variable x. Also illustrated are several terms. The **domain** is the range of values of x. The value of the function for the lower limit of the domain of x is given as A; the value of the function for the upper limit of the domain of x is given as G. These are sometimes referred to as **endpoints**. The domain limits (or endpoints) fall into a general category called **stationary** or **critical points**.

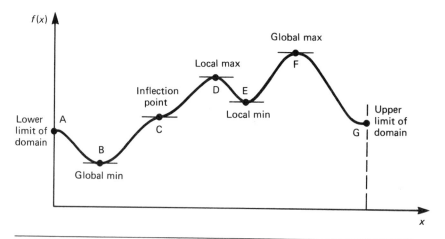

Figure B.2 Maxima and Minima

Some points other than endpoints are also stationary (critical) points. A point (other than an endpoint) on $f(x)$ is considered stationary only if the first derivative of the function is equal to zero at that point—that is, $f'(x) = 0$. All of the points B through F satisfy this condition. Two subsets of the stationary points are **inflection points** and **extreme points**. Extreme points, or extrema, are further identified as either **local** or **global** extrema. In our analysis it is global extrema (or **absolute** extrema) that are of primary interest. Finally, extrema are either maximum or minimum.

In profit maximization we generally attempt to determine the global maximum, whereas in cost minimization the global minimum is of interest. It is important to point out that the global maximum or minimum of a function can be located at the lower or upper limit of the domain of the decision variable. In the illustration, however, this is not the case.

Since a *necessary condition* for a stationary point other than an endpoint is that the first derivative of the function at that point equal zero, we calculate the first derivative of the function, set the first derivative equation equal to zero, and solve for the unknown (in this case, x). As previously pointed out, this is also a necessary condition for determining the extrema of a function. That is,

$$f'(x) = 0 \quad \text{for } x = x^*$$

where x^* is defined as a value of x for which we have an extrema. Determining whether we have a relative maximum, a relative minimum, or a point of inflection requires further differentiation. Note that a relative maximum (minimum) may be either a local or a global maximum (minimum).

The following represents a *sufficient condition* for x^* to be a relative *minimum*:

$$f''(x) > 0 \quad \text{at } x = x^*$$

That is, the second derivative evaluated for the value x^* must be greater than zero. Likewise, a sufficient condition for x^* to be a relative maximum is

$$f''(x) < 0 \text{ at } x = x^*$$

That is, the second derivative evaluated for the value x^* must be less than zero.

In cases where the second derivative is equal to zero, $f''(x) = 0$, x^* is *generally* a point of inflection. It may be necessary to examine higher derivatives, however. The general procedure for this case is as follows. Find the value of the lowest order derivative that is *not zero* evaluated at x^*. If the *order* of the lowest order derivative is even, the second order derivative rules apply. If the order of the lowest order derivative is odd, the critical point is an inflection point.

The preceding discussion is summarized in its simplest form in Figure B.3. (Differentiation will *not* identify these points as extrema; only through comparison with other extrema can they be identified as local or global maxima or minima.) When a function has multiple critical points, it is necessary to compare the value of the function for the various extrema (including the limits of the domain) in order to determine the global (or absolute) maximum and minimum.

In summary, the goal is to determine the absolute (global) maximum and minimum for the function $y = f(x)$ in which the domain of x is given as $a \leqslant x \leqslant b$. The hypothetical function is illustrated in Figure B.4.

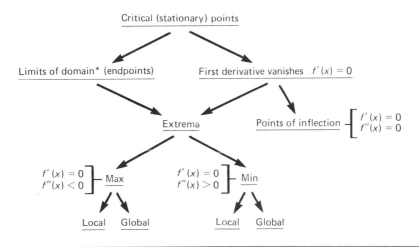

Figure B.3 *Determination of Critical Points*

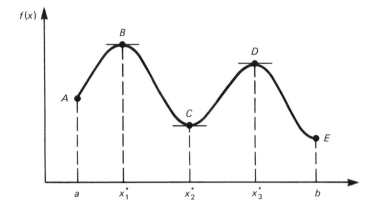

Figure B.4 *Identification of Extrema*

The following is a step-by-step summary of the previous discussion:

1. Necessary Conditions
    a. Calculate the equation for the first derivative. That is, compute $f'(x)$.
    b. Set the first derivative equation equal to zero. That is, set $f'(x) = 0$.
    c. Solve the equation of step 1b for the value of x^*. That is, solve $f'(x) = 0$ for
        $x = x^*$.

2. Sufficient Conditions
    a. Calculate the equation for the second derivative. That is, compute $f''(x)$.
    b. Solve the equation of step 2a for the value of x^* obtained in step 1c. That is, solve
        $f''(x)$ for $x = x^*$.
    c. If $f''(x^*)$ is negative, there is a relative maximum at x^*.
        If $f''(x^*)$ is positive, there is a relative minimum at x^*.
        If $f''(x^*)$ is equal to zero, there is generally a point of inflection at x^*.

3. Determine Global Maximum and Minimum
    a. Substitute the values of x^* into the original equation and determine $f(x^*)$. That is,
        solve for the value of y at $x = x^*$.
    b. Substitute the values of a and b into the original equation and determine $f(a)$ and
        $f(b)$.
    c. Compare all maxima to determine the global maximum.
        Compare all minima to determine the global minimum.

For the function illustrated in Figure B.4, we obtain three values for x^* in step 1c (points
B, C, and D on the function). There are two cases in which step 2c yields a negative
value and one case in which it yields a positive value—$f''(x_1^*) < 0$, $f''(x_3^*) < 0$, f''
$(x_2^*) > 0$. Thus, we have two relative maxima (points B and D) and one relative minimum (point C). By substituting a, x_1^*, x_2^*, x_3^*, and b into $f(x)$ to obtain the values A,
B, C, D, and E, we can determine the global maximum and minimum by inspection.

   Some further discussion of the nature of functions commonly found in business problems is warranted at this point. It is much easier to deal with the problem of determining
maximum or minimum values when the functions are either convex or concave. Both
types of functions are illustrated in Figure B.5.

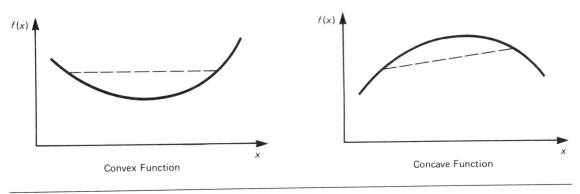

Figure B.5 *Convex and Concave Functions*

A function is said to be convex if a straight line connecting any two points on that function falls entirely above the function. A function is said to be concave if a straight line connecting any two points on that function falls entirely below the function.

If a function is convex, the first derivative set equal to zero must yield at least a local minimum. The limit of the domain may still be the absolute minimum. Likewise, if a function is concave, the first derivative set equal to zero must yield a local maximum.

For many cases in business analysis, the function can be assumed to be either concave or convex. Therefore, the most frequently encountered problem involves computing the first derivative, equating it to zero, and solving for the extrema and then computing the second derivative and evaluating for the value of x^* to determine whether the value is a maximum or a minimum. Although the optimal value generally does not occur at a limit of the domain for unconstrained optimization problems, for constrained optimization problems the optimal value is very likely to occur at the intersection of the objective function and a constraint, which is actually the redefined limit of the domain for the function being optimized.

PARTIAL DIFFERENTIATION

Thus far, we have considered functions of one variable. That is, the dependent variable is a function of only one independent (or decision) variable, $y = f(x)$. We will now consider functions of more than one independent variable, $y = f(x_1, x_2, \ldots, x_n)$.

For example, presume that total sales of a product are a function not only of price but also of advertising.

$S = f(P, A)$

where

S = total sales
P = price
A = advertising

First observe what happens to sales when price varies but advertising is kept at a constant level. Figure B.6 illustrates the relationship of sales to price with advertising held constant.

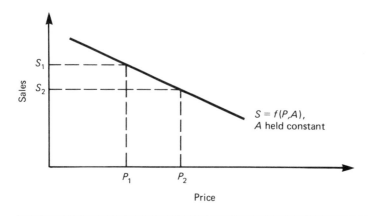

Figure B.6 *Relationship of Sales to Price*

The next step is to hold price constant and observe the behavior of sales as the level of advertising varies. This relationship is illustrated in Figure B.7.

In Figure B.8 the preceding analysis is illustrated on a three-dimensional graph to show the simultaneous relationship of sales to price and advertising. Figure B.8 illustrates sales as a function of two variables, price and advertising.

The dotted line connected to P_1 is a two-dimensional plane illustrating the increase in sales as advertising increases for a constant price (P_1). Likewise, the dotted line connected to A_1 is a two-dimensional plane illustrating the decrease in sales as price increases for a constant level of advertising (A_1). It is apparent from Figure B.8 that maximum sales are obtained at endpoints of the domain for price and advertising, where price equals zero and advertising equals the maximum amount available. It is also obvious that this is not a profit maximizing model since where price equals zero, revenue is also zero. This example does, however, illustrate the analysis of a function of more than one variable.

Recall that if the optimal value for a function is not at an endpoint, the function must be differentiated, set equal to zero, and solved for the optimal value of the independent variable. If there is more than one independent variable, however, **partial dif-**

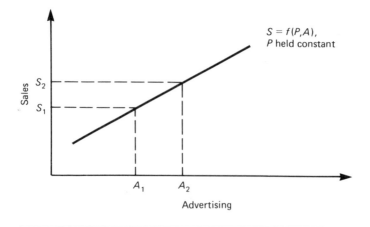

Figure B.7 *Relationship of Sales to Advertising*

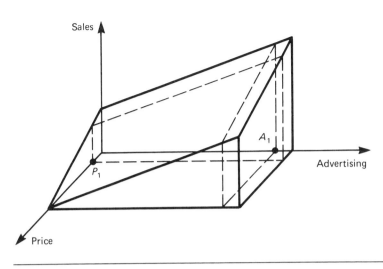

Figure B.8 *Relationship of Sales to Price and Advertising*

ferentiation must be employed. In partial differentiation, all but one of the independent variables are treated as constants; otherwise the process is the same as in ordinary differentiation. The approach is analogous to that of the preceding discussion, where advertising was first held constant in order to observe sales as a function of price and then price was held constant in order to observe sales as a function of advertising.

Partial derivatives provide a general model of the slope of a function relative to one independent variable at a time. The partial derivative of y with respect to x_1 is given as $\partial y / \partial x_1$. Note that we have simply exchanged the lowercase Greek letter delta (∂) for d in the derivative notation. For a graphical illustration of a similar case, see Figure B.9.

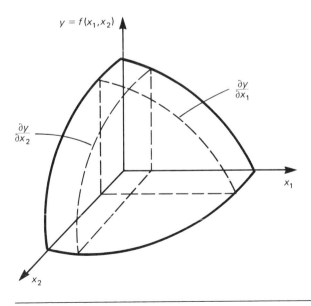

Figure B.9 *Three-dimensional View of $y = f(x_1, x_2)$*

For the equation

$$y = 2x_1^2 + 3x_2^2 - 8x_1 - 12x_2 + 25$$

the partial derivatives are

$$\frac{\partial y}{\partial x_1} = 4x_1 - 8$$

$$\frac{\partial y}{\partial x_2} = 6x_2 - 12$$

In the first case, x_2 is assumed to be a constant. Since the derivative of a constant is 0, the x_2 terms both go to zero. Likewise, in the second case, x_1 is a constant, and it goes to zero when differentiated.

Using the same approach for determining the optimal values of the independent variables as was used previously, set the first derivatives to zero and then solve.

$$4x_1 - 8 = 0$$
$$6x_2 - 12 = 0$$

Thus,

$$4x_1 = 8$$
$$x_1^* = 2$$
$$6x_2 = 12$$
$$x_2^* = 2$$

Therefore, the optimal value of both x_1 and x_2 is 2. Substituting into the original equation, we have

$$
\begin{aligned}
y &= 2x_1^2 + 3x_2^2 - 8x_1 - 12x_2 + 25 \\
&= 2(2)^2 + 3(2)^2 - 8(2) - 12(2) + 25 \\
&= 8 + 12 - 16 - 24 + 25 \\
y^* &= 5
\end{aligned}
$$

Now determine whether this value is a relative maximum or a relative minimum. Determine the second partial derivative of each equation with respect to each independent variable, as follows:

$$\frac{\partial^2 y}{\partial x_1^2} = \frac{\partial(4x_1 - 8)}{\partial x_1} = 4$$

$$\frac{\partial^2 y}{\partial x_2^2} = \frac{\partial(6x_2 - 12)}{\partial x_2} = 6$$

Since each of the second partial derivatives is greater than zero, it is probable that the value is a relative minimum (this is consistent with the rules for the single variable case discussed previously). One additional test must be performed, however, to ensure that it is indeed a relative minimum. The following equation must also be satisfied:

$$\frac{\partial^2 y}{\partial x_1^2} \cdot \frac{\partial^2 y}{\partial x_2^2} - \left[\frac{\partial^2 y}{\partial x_1 \, \partial x_2}\right]^2 > 0$$

The term $\partial^2 y/(\partial x_1 \, \partial x_2)$ is called the **cross partial derivative** and is simply the first partial derivative with respect to x_1 and the partial derivative of that answer with respect to x_2.

$$\frac{\partial^2 y}{\partial x_1 \, \partial x_2} = \frac{\partial \left[\dfrac{\partial y}{\partial x_1} \right]}{\partial x_2}$$

Thus,

$$\frac{\partial y}{\partial x_1} = 4x_1 - 8$$

$$\frac{\partial^2 y}{\partial x_1 \, \partial x_2} = \frac{\partial(4x_1 - 8)}{\partial x_2} = 0$$

Remember that you are differentiating $4x_1 - 8$ with respect to x_2. Therefore treat x_1 as a constant and obtain a second partial derivative, with respect to x_2, of zero. Substituting back into the previous equation, we have

$$\frac{\partial^2 y}{\partial x_1^2} \cdot \frac{\partial^2 y}{\partial x_2^2} - \left[\frac{\partial^2 y}{\partial x_1 \, \partial x_2} \right]^2 = 4 \cdot 6 - (0)$$

$$= 24$$

which satisfies > 0. Since the computation satisfies the equation's requirements, we accept the conclusion that the value is a relative minimum.

In summary, for cases involving more than one independent variable, determine the first partial derivative for each of the independent variables, set each equal to zero, and solve simultaneously for the optimal values. In order to determine whether the value obtained is a relative maximum or a relative minimum, see whether the following rules are satisfied.

Relative Maximum:

$$\frac{\partial^2 y}{\partial x_1^2} < 0, \frac{\partial^2 y}{\partial x_2^2} < 0, \text{ and } \frac{\partial^2 y}{\partial x_1^2} \cdot \frac{\partial^2 y}{\partial x_2^2} - \left[\frac{\partial^2 y}{\partial x_1 \, \partial x_2} \right]^2 > 0$$

Relative Minimum:

$$\frac{\partial^2 y}{\partial x_1^2} > 0, \frac{\partial^2 y}{\partial x_2^2} > 0, \text{ and } \frac{\partial^2 y}{\partial x_1^2} \cdot \frac{\partial^2 y}{\partial x_2^2} - \left[\frac{\partial^2 y}{\partial x_1 \, \partial x_2} \right]^2 > 0$$

If $\dfrac{\partial^2 y}{\partial x_1^2} \cdot \dfrac{\partial^2 y}{\partial x_2^2} - \left[\dfrac{\partial^2 y}{\partial x_1 \, \partial x_2} \right]^2 < 0$, you have what is known as a **saddle point** (neither a max nor a min). It is, for the two independent variable case, analogous to a point of inflection for the one independent variable case. The exploration of this and other possible results is beyond the scope of this appendix.

CONSTRAINED OPTIMIZATION

Thus far, we have considered only optimization of unconstrained functions. That is, we have given no specific attention to restrictions or limitations on the possible values a decision variable can take on.[1] We will now consider the more likely case in which one or more *constraints* (restrictions) must also be satisfied while the stated function is optimized.

A simple example of an inequality constraint is the nonnegativity restriction, as in

Maximize $y = f(x)$
subject to
$x \geqslant 0$

The nonnegativity constraint is illustrated in Figure B.10. This sort of situation can arise when the first derivative is set equal to zero and solved for x, yielding two solutions for x ($-x^*$, $+x^*$). At this point, simply discard $-x^*$ as a possible solution, since it violates the initially specified constraint ($x \geqslant 0$).

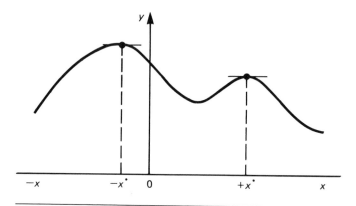

Figure B.10 *Nonnegativity Constraint*

Consider the following maximization example, in which the optimal resource input is determined in order to maximize output:

Maximize $y = 10x - x^2$
where
y = output
x = input

Setting the first derivative, $y' = 10 - 2x$, equal to zero yields $10 - 2x = 0$. Solving for x, we have $x^* = 5$.

Now, suppose there is a maximum of six units of resource input. The problem becomes

Maximize $y = 10x - x^2$
subject to
$x \leqslant 6$

The goal is to maximize the objective function while satisfying the restriction that input be equal to or less than six units. It can be seen from the preceding computations for x^* that the constraint is not violated; therefore, the solution is still $x^* = 5$.

---

[1] This is not completely true since it has been stated that there must be some domain of possible values that x can take on (i.e., $a \leqslant x \leqslant b$), which is, in effect, a restriction.

Consider, however, the following problem:

Maximize $y = 10x - x^2$
subject to
$\quad x \leqslant 4$

This maximization problem is illustrated graphically in Figure B.11.

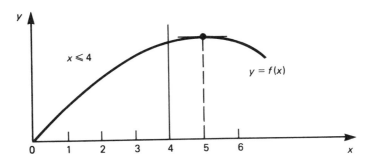

Figure B.11 Optimal Point Bound by a Constraint

It is apparent that the optimal solution obtained by the calculus method, $x^* = 5$, is infeasible; that is, it violates the constraint. It is also apparent from the graphical portrayal of the problem that the optimal solution is at the point $x^* = 4$.

Normally you would proceed to solve for the calculus solution as in the unconstrained case and then check to see if it violates the constraint. If the calculus solution ($x^* = 5$) does violate the constraint, check to see whether the solution occurs at the boundary created by the constraint. This is analogous to checking the limits of the domain discussed previously. Thus $x^* = 4$ is found to be the optimal solution, yielding $y^* = 24$.

The **region of feasible solution** is defined by the following:

Maximize $y = 10x - x^2$
subject to
$\quad x \leqslant 4$
$\quad x \geqslant 0$

The shaded region in Figure B.12 represents the area of feasible solution.

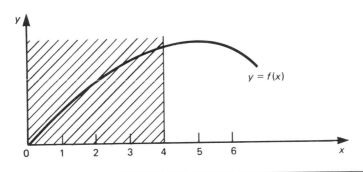

Figure B.12 Area of Feasible Solution

The region of feasible solution points out that when the function $y = 10x - x^2$ is maximized, the conditions $0 \leqslant x \leqslant 4$ must also be satisfied. It does not make sense to assume negative input quantities, and the maximum input quantity available is four units. In fact, it is probably illogical to assume zero input; thus, the constrained domain of x is determined to be $0 < x \leqslant 4$ (the possible values of x do not include zero).

If it is further determined that a minimum of two units of input can be used, up to a maximum of four units, the problem becomes

Maximize $y = 10x - x^2$
subject to
$\quad x \geqslant 2$
$\quad x \leqslant 4$

Recall that the solution $x* = 5$, which was determined by the calculus approach, was discarded because it violated the constraint $x \leqslant 4$. If the feasible solution had not been determined by a graph of the function, the following steps could be performed to arrive at the same feasible solution:

1. Determine the value of y for $x = 2$.

$$y = 10(2) - (2)^2$$
$$y = 16$$

2. Determine the value of y for $x = 4$.

$$y = 10(4) - (4)^2$$
$$y = 24$$

Again the optimal solution is $x* = 4$, which yields $y* = 24$.

Now consider a profit optimization example that is a function of two independent variables,

$$Z = 68x_1 - 3x_1^2 + 52x_2 - 2x_2^2 - 4x_1x_2$$

The partial derivatives with respect to x_1 and x_2 are

$$\frac{\partial Z}{\partial x_1} = 68 - 6x_1 - 4x_2$$

$$\frac{\partial Z}{\partial x_2} = 52 - 4x_2 - 4x_1$$

The partial derivatives are set equal to zero, and the two equations are solved simultaneously.

$$68 - 6x_1 - 4x_2 = 0$$
$$52 - 4x_2 - 4x_1 = 0$$
$$x_1^* = 8$$
$$x_2^* = 5$$

Computation of the second order conditions (second derivative tests) yields

$$\frac{\partial^2 Z}{\partial x_1} = -6 < 0$$

$$\frac{\partial^2 Z}{\partial x_2} = -4 < 0$$

$$\frac{\partial^2 Z}{\partial x_2} \cdot \frac{\partial^2 Z}{\partial x_2} - \left(\frac{\partial^2 Z}{\partial x_1 \partial x_2}\right)^2 = 8 > 0$$

This process ensures that a maximum exists for Z at the points $x_1^* = 8$ and $x_2^* = 5$, yielding $Z^* = 402$.

There is generally an implicit assumption that the decision variables are nonnegative ($x_1 \geq 0$, $x_2 \geq 0$). Now assume that x_1 cannot exceed a value of 6. This is specified as follows:

> Maximize $Z = 68x_1 - 3x_1^2 + 52x_2 - 2x_2^2 - 4x_1x_2$
> subject to
> $x_1 \leq 6$

The solution for x_1 can be determined by examining a two-dimensional graph of Z with respect to x_1, as illustrated in Figure B.13.

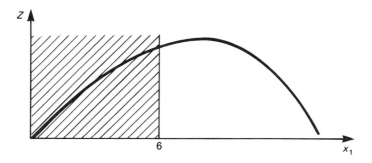

Figure B.13 *Profit with Respect to x_1*

It is apparent that the optimal value of x_1 is 6. But what about x_2? We can also examine a two-dimensional graph of Z with respect to x_2, as illustrated in Figure B.14.

It can be seen that part of the three-dimensional function has been sliced off by the constraint $x_1 \leq 6$. The shaded portion of the two-dimensional curve illustrated in Figure B.14 represents the remaining curve that can be optimized with respect to x_2.

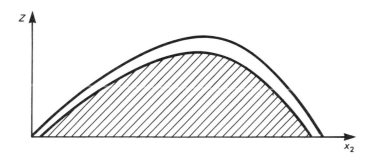

Figure B.14 *Profit with Respect to x_2*

If $x_1^* = 6$ is substituted into the original equation,

$$Z = 68(6) - 3(6)^2 - 52x_2 - 2x_2^2 - 4(6)x_2$$
$$= 300 + 28x_2 - 2x_2^2$$

This equation results in an unconstrained function of one variable that can be solved in the usual manner.

$$\frac{\partial Z}{\partial x_2} = 28 - 4x_2 = 0$$
$$28 - 4x_2 = 0$$
$$x_2^* = 7$$

We have arrived at an optimal solution for the constrained problem of $x_1^* = 6$ and $x_2^* = 7$ (as opposed to $x_1^* = 8$ and $x_2^* = 5$ for the unconstrained case). Substituting into the original profit equation, we have $Z^* = 68(6) - 3(6)^2 + 52(7) - 2(7)^2 - 4(6)(7) = 398$ (as opposed to $Z^* = 402$ previously obtained).

With the aid of graphs, the optimal solution has been determined with relative ease. If the objective function and associated constraint are not graphed, however, it is not apparent whether or not the optimal solution is, in fact, bound by the constraint. For example, consider the following problem:

Maximize $Z = 68x_1 - 3x_1^2 + 52x_2 - 2x_2^2 - 4x_1x_2$
subject to
$x_1 \leq 9$

The problem is illustrated graphically in Figure B.15.

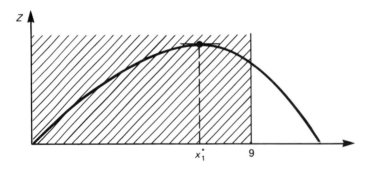

Figure B.15 *Optimal Solution Bound by a Constraint*

It is apparent from the graph that the constraint $x_1 \leq 9$ does not restrict the peak of the profit function. Thus, merely substituting the value $x_1^* = 9$ into the equation and solving for x_2^*, as done previously, yields a less-than-optimal solution.

In this case, the procedure is to determine the values of x_1^* and x_2^* for the unconstrained problem, $x_1^* = 8$ and $x_2^* = 5$, and then observe whether $x_1^* = 9$ (x_2^* retains the value obtained by differentiation) provides a better solution. If it can be assumed that the profit function is concave (which is often the case), it can be seen that if $x_1^* = 8$, then $x_1^* = 9$ is beyond the optimal point. Therefore, $x_1^* = 9$ is discarded. The only other alternative approach is the graphical approach, which can be tedious or even impossible for more than two independent variables.

Thus, it can be seen that investigating the intersection of the objective function and the constraint does not always yield the optimal constrained solution. There is a need for an analytic procedure for determining the optimal value of a function subject to constraints that distinguishes between cases where the constraint is binding and those where it is not binding. The method of Lagrange multipliers is such a technique.

LAGRANGE MULTIPLIERS

The method of Lagrange multipliers enables us to convert an objective function, along with its associated constraints, into a single unconstrained function. The advantage of using this approach is twofold. In the first place, a constrained optimization problem can often be solved more easily using Lagrange multipliers than using the method of substitution previously illustrated. Second, the method of Lagrange multipliers yields an additional solution value that determines whether or not the constraint is binding on the solution. That is, the Lagrange multiplier indicates whether the optimal solution is on the boundary formed by the constraint or at some interior point. Like the calculus solution approach, however, the Lagrange multiplier approach yields only a *candidate* for the optimal solution. It must still be ensured that the global optimal value is not at some critical point not identified by differentiation (i.e., limits of the domain must be investigated, such as the case where $x_1 = 0$, $x_2 = 0$, etc.).

In the first graph in Figure B.16, the global optimal solution is obviously bound by the constraint. The Lagrange multiplier approach yields point B as the candidate for the optimal solution, and it also indicates that a better solution could be obtained (point C) if the constraint did not exist. It does *not,* however, ensure that point B is better than point A. In the second graph in Figure B.16, the Lagrange multiplier approach yields H as the candidate for the (local) optimal solution, but it also indicates that the constraint has no effect on the solution (the solution is not bound by the constraint). We can, therefore, go back and determine the unconstrained optimal value by regular methods of calculus to yield point G. Note, however, that the global optimal value is at point F. Only direct evaluation of the function at its endpoints (for $x = 0$ in this case) is sufficient to identify the global optimal value here.

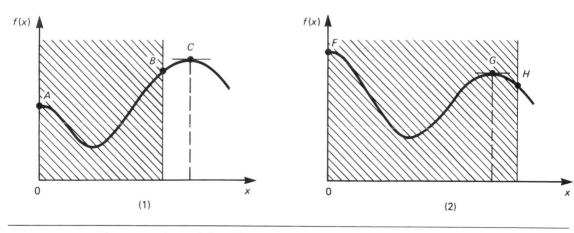

Figure B.16 *Candidates for the Global Optimal Solution*

The Lagrange multiplier approach for converting the objective function and associated constraints into a single unconstrained function is as follows. Given the problem

Maximize $y = f(x_1, x_2)$
subject to
$$g(x_1) = b$$

1. Convert $g(x_1) = b$ to $g(x_1) - b = 0$.
2. Convert to Lagrangian form as follows:

Maximize $L = f(x_1, x_2) - \lambda \cdot [g(x_1) - b]$

In this conversion process, the constraint is first equated to zero and then multiplied by a variable λ, and that product is subtracted from the original objective function. The variable λ is known as the Lagrange multiplier, and it is the solution value of λ that indicates whether or not the solution obtained is bound by the constraint.
Note that $g(x_1) - b = 0$, and thus $\lambda \cdot [g(x_1) - b] = 0$. Therefore, $L = f(x_1, x_2) - 0$, which is the same as the original objective function. If, however, we solve the function $L = f(x_1, x_2) - \lambda \cdot [g(x_1) - b]$ in terms of each of the independent variables, we will have determined a candidate for the optimal solution while satisfying the constraint $g(x_1) = b$.
Consider a problem subject to an equality constraint:

Maximize $y = 5x_1 + 4x_2 + x_1x_2 - x_1^2 - x_2^2 + 10$
subject to
$$x_1 + x_2 = 5$$

First we convert $x_1 + x_2 = 5$ to $x_1 + x_2 - 5 = 0$. The Lagrangian multiplier can then be formulated as

Maximize $L = 5x_1 + 4x_2 + x_1x_2 - x_1^2 - x_2^2 + 10 - \lambda(x_1 + x_2 - 5)$

Next we calculate the partial derivatives with respect to x_1, x_2, and λ, set them equal to zero, and solve the equations simultaneously.

$$\frac{\partial L}{\partial x_1} = 5 + x_2 - 2x_1 - \lambda = 0 \tag{1}$$

$$\frac{\partial L}{\partial x_2} = 4 + x_1 - 2x_2 - \lambda = 0 \tag{2}$$

$$\frac{\partial L}{\partial \lambda} = -(x_1 + x_2 - 5) = 0 \tag{3}$$

Subtracting equation (2) from equation (1), we get

$$1 - 3x_1 + 3x_2 = 0 \tag{4}$$

Multiplying equation (3) by 3 and subtracting from equation (4), we have

$$6x_2 = 14$$

Thus,

$$x_2^* = 2.333$$

Substituting x_2^* into equation (3), we get

$x_1^* = 2.667$

Substituting x_1^* and x_2^* into equation (1) [or equation (2)] yields

$\lambda^* = 2$

Finally, we substitute x_1^* and x_2^* into the original objective function to get

$y^* = 26.33$

The solution is a global optimal value, since the equality constraint *requires* that the sum of x_1 and x_2 equal 5. Thus, there is no need to investigate endpoints.

The interpretation of λ is as follows. If a small amount is added to the right-hand side of the constraint $x_1 + x_2 = 5$, to yield $x_1 + x_2 = 5 + \Delta$, the value of the objective function is increased in the optimal solution by the amount $\lambda \cdot \Delta$. For example, if the constraint is changed to $x_1 + x_2 = 6$ (one unit is added to the right-hand side), we can expect to increase y^* by 2 to yield $y^* = 26.33 + 2.00 = 28.33$.

Lambda (λ) may be interpreted as the marginal opportunity cost associated with constraining the solution. Note in this case that λ is a *positive* value. This indicates that the optimal solution is constrained from achieving its unconstrained optimal value. If λ were *negative,* this would indicate that the constraint was *beyond* the optimal unconstrained solution. For the case of the equality constraint, however, the optimal solution by definition would still be on the constraint boundary. But a negative λ would indicate that the solution was beyond the unconstrained optimal point; therefore, there would be no point in increasing the right-hand-side value.

The preceding problem is illustrated in Figure B.17 on a two-dimensional graph in which x_1 and x_2 are the axes. To yield a third dimension, you must visualize another axis (the y axis) coming straight out of the page toward you.

In Figure B.17, each circular line, known as a **contour line** (or trace line), is successively higher (nearer to you) as it approaches the center point. The center point is the peak of the "hill" and represents the unconstrained optimal solution. The constraint $x_1 + x_2 = 5$ is illustrated by the line connecting $x_1 = 5$ and $x_2 = 5$. The point at which the constraint line touches the contour line (of the objective function) is the constrained optimal solution. Note the values of the axes variables, $x_1^* = 2.66$ and $x_2^* = 2.333$. At their point of intersection, the height of the objective function is equal to $y^* = 26.33$.

If the constraint is changed to $x_1 + x_2 = 12$, the constraint line lies beyond the peak. The solution is still on the constraint line since it is an equality constraint, but the value of λ is negative, indicating that the solution cannot be improved by increasing the value on the right-hand side of the constraint.

Although the Lagrange multiplier method is generally assumed to be used for equality constraints only (for theoretical reasons that are beyond the scope of this chapter), we will illustrate how it can also be used for inequality constraints.

Assume the following problem:

Maximize $y = 5x_1 + 4x_2 + x_1x_2 - x_1^2 - x_2^2 + 10$
subject to

$x_1 + x_2 \leqslant 5$

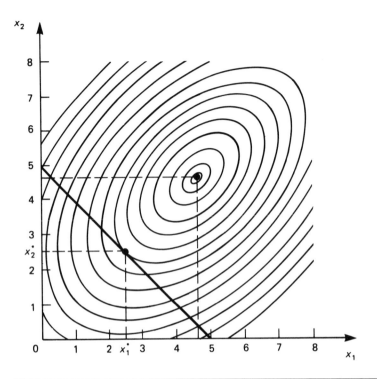

Figure B.17 *Optimal Solution Bound by a Constraint*

A review of Figure B.17 and the previous calculations reveals that the optimal solution is the same as before. The area of feasible solution, however, rather than lying on the constraint line, is now the entire triangle enclosed by the constraint and the two axes. The positive value for λ indicates that the solution could be improved if it were not bound by the constraint; thus, the solution is on the boundary line.

Consider the following problem:

Maximize $y = 5x_1 + 4x_2 + x_1x_2 - x_1^2 - x_2^2 + 10$
subject to
$$x_1 + x_2 \leq 12$$

This problem defines an area of feasible solution that includes the unconstrained optimal solution, as illustrated in Figure B.18.

The problem is solved via the Lagrange multiplier approach by simply setting $x_1 + x_2$ equal to 12 and proceeding as before.

Maximize $L = 5x_1 + 4x_2 + x_1x_2 - x_1^2 - x_2^2 + 10 - \lambda(x_1 + x_2 - 12)$

$$\frac{\partial L}{\partial x_1} = 5 + x_2 - 2x_1 - \lambda = 0$$

$$\frac{\partial L}{\partial x_2} = 4 + x_1 - 2x_2 - \lambda = 0$$

$$\frac{\partial L}{\partial \lambda} = -(x_1 + x_2 - 12) = 0$$

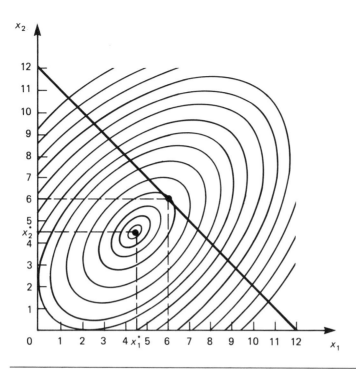

Figure B.18 *Optimal Solution Not Bound by a Constraint*

Solving the equations simultaneously yields

$$x_1^* = 6.167$$
$$x_2^* = 5.833$$
$$y^* = 28.08$$
$$\lambda^* = -1.50$$

It can be seen from the graph that the global optimal value in the area of the feasible solution is not on the boundary of the constraint. Changing the constraint from $x_1 + x_2 \leqslant 12$ to $x_1 + x_2 = 12$ in the formulation of the Lagrangian function will restrict the solution to the boundary. The *negative* solution value of λ, however, indicates that the solution value is beyond the unconstrained optimal solution. Therefore, return to the original objective function and determine the optimal solution, ignoring the constraint, as follows:

$$\text{Maximize } y = 5x_1 + 4x_2 + x_1x_2 - x_1^2 - x_2^2 + 10$$

$$\frac{\partial y}{\partial x_1} = 5 + x_2 - 2x_1 = 0$$

$$\frac{\partial y}{\partial x_2} = 4 + x_1 - 2x_2 = 0$$

Solving the equations simultaneously yields

$$x_1^* = 4.667$$
$$x_2^* = 4.333$$
$$y^* = 30.33$$

In summary, for inequality constraints, proceed as follows:

1. Assume the inequality holds as an equality, and use the Lagrange multiplier approach to determine an initial optimal solution candidate.

2. If λ is positive ($\lambda > 0$), the optimal solution is bound by the constraint and the candidate is a global optimal solution (assuming it is not an endpoint).

3. If λ is negative ($\lambda < 0$), the global optimal solution is not bound by the constraint. Optimize the original objective function, ignoring the constraint.

Take special note of the following. For a maximization problem, if $\lambda > 0$, the constraint binds the solution, and if $\lambda \leq 0$, the optimal solution is an *interior* solution. This refers only to $\leq$ constraints. For $\geq$ constraints, the reverse is true. That is, if $\lambda < 0$, the constraint binds the solution, and if $\lambda \geq 0$, the constraint does not bind the solution. For a minimization problem, the procedure again reverses itself. If the constraint is $\leq b$ and if $\lambda < 0$, the constraint is binding, and if $\lambda \geq 0$, the constraint is not binding. Finally, for minimization, if the constraint is $\geq b$ and if $\lambda > 0$, the constraint is binding, and if $\lambda \leq 0$, the constraint is not binding.

This appendix has considered problems involving only one linear constraint of the equality and inequality types. It is also possible to consider objective functions that are subject to more than one linear constraint and/or nonlinear constraints. Refer to Chapter 15 for a discussion of such problems.

Tables

Table C.1 *Poisson Probability Values*

| | | | | | λ | | | | | |
r	0.10	0.20	0.30	0.40	0.50	0.60	0.70	0.80	0.90	1.00
0	.9048	.8187	.7408	.6703	.6066	.5488	.4966	.4493	.4066	.3679
1	.0905	.1637	.2222	.2681	.3033	.3293	.3476	.3595	.3659	.3679
2	.0045	.0164	.0333	.0536	.0758	.0988	.1217	.1438	.1647	.1839
3	.0002	.0011	.0033	.0072	.0126	.0198	.0284	.0383	.0494	.0613
4	.0000	.0001	.0003	.0007	.0016	.0030	.0050	.0077	.0111	.0153
5	.0000	.0000	.0000	.0001	.0002	.0004	.0007	.0012	.0020	.0031
6	.0000	.0000	.0000	.0000	.0000	.0000	.0001	.0002	.0003	.0005
7	.0000	.0000	.0000	.0000	.0000	.0000	.0000	.0000	.0000	.0001

| | | | | | λ | | | | | |
r	1.10	1.20	1.30	1.40	1.50	1.60	1.70	1.80	1.90	2.00
0	.3329	.3012	.2725	.2466	.2231	.2019	.1827	.1653	.1496	.1353
1	.3662	.3614	.3543	.3452	.3347	.3230	.3106	.2975	.2842	.2707
2	.2014	.2169	.2303	.2417	.2510	.2584	.2640	.2678	.2700	.2707
3	.0738	.0867	.0998	.1128	.1255	.1378	.1496	.1607	.1710	.1804
4	.0203	.0260	.0324	.0395	.0471	.0551	.0636	.0723	.0812	.0902
5	.0045	.0062	.0084	.0111	.0141	.0176	.0216	.0260	.0309	.0361
6	.0008	.0012	.0018	.0026	.0035	.0047	.0061	.0078	.0098	.0120
7	.0001	.0002	.0003	.0005	.0008	.0011	.0015	.0020	.0027	.0034
8	.0000	.0000	.0001	.0001	.0001	.0002	.0003	.0005	.0006	.0009
9	.0000	.0000	.0000	.0000	.0000	.0000	.0001	.0001	.0001	.0002

| | | | | | λ | | | | | |
r	2.10	2.20	2.30	2.40	2.50	2.60	2.70	2.80	2.90	3.00
0	.1225	.1108	.1003	.0907	.0821	.0743	.0672	.0608	.0550	.0498
1	.2572	.2438	.2306	.2177	.2052	.1931	.1815	.1703	.1596	.1494
2	.2700	.2681	.2652	.2613	.2565	.2510	.2450	.2384	.2314	.2240
3	.1890	.1966	.2033	.2090	.2138	.2176	.2205	.2225	.2237	.2240
4	.0992	.1082	.1169	.1254	.1336	.1414	.1488	.1557	.1622	.1680
5	.0417	.0476	.0538	.0602	.0668	.0735	.0804	.0872	.0940	.1008
6	.0146	.0174	.0206	.0241	.0278	.0319	.0362	.0407	.0455	.0504
7	.0044	.0055	.0068	.0083	.0099	.0118	.0139	.0163	.0188	.0216
8	.0011	.0015	.0019	.0025	.0031	.0038	.0047	.0057	.0068	.0081
9	.0003	.0004	.0005	.0007	.0009	.0011	.0014	.0018	.0022	.0027
10	.0001	.0001	.0001	.0002	.0002	.0003	.0004	.0005	.0006	.0008
11	.0000	.0000	.0000	.0000	.0000	.0001	.0001	.0001	.0002	.0002
12	.0000	.0000	.0000	.0000	.0000	.0000	.0000	.0000	.0000	.0001

					λ					
r	3.10	3.20	3.30	3.40	3.50	3.60	3.70	3.80	3.90	4.00
0	.0450	.0408	.0369	.0334	.0302	.0273	.0247	.0224	.0202	.0183
1	.1397	.1304	.1217	.1135	.1057	.0984	.0915	.0850	.0789	.0733
2	.2165	.2087	.2008	.1929	.1850	.1771	.1692	.1615	.1539	.1465
3	.2237	.2226	.2209	.2186	.2158	.2125	.2087	.2046	.2001	.1954
4	.1733	.1781	.1823	.1858	.1888	.1912	.1931	.1944	.1951	.1954
5	.1075	.1140	.1203	.1264	.1322	.1377	.1429	.1477	.1522	.1563
6	.0555	.0608	.0662	.0716	.0771	.0826	.0881	.0936	.0989	.1042
7	.0246	.0278	.0312	.0348	.0385	.0425	.0466	.0508	.0551	.0595
8	.0095	.0111	.0129	.0148	.0169	.0191	.0215	.0241	.0269	.0298
9	.0033	.0040	.0047	.0056	.0066	.0076	.0089	.0102	.0116	.0132
10	.0010	.0013	.0016	.0019	.0023	.0028	.0033	.0039	.0045	.0053
11	.0003	.0004	.0005	.0006	.0007	.0009	.0011	.0013	.0016	.0019
12	.0001	.0001	.0001	.0002	.0002	.0003	.0003	.0004	.0005	.0006
13	.0000	.0000	.0000	.0000	.0001	.0001	.0001	.0001	.0002	.0002
14	.0000	.0000	.0000	.0000	.0000	.0000	.0000	.0000	.0000	.0001

					λ					
r	4.10	4.20	4.30	4.40	4.50	4.60	4.70	4.80	4.90	5.00
0	.0166	.0150	.0136	.0123	.0111	.0101	.0091	.0082	.0074	.0067
1	.0679	.0630	.0583	.0540	.0500	.0462	.0427	.0395	.0365	.0337
2	.1393	.1323	.1254	.1188	.1125	.1063	.1005	.0948	.0894	.0842
3	.1904	.1852	.1798	.1743	.1687	.1631	.1574	.1517	.1460	.1404
4	.1951	.1944	.1933	.1917	.1898	.1875	.1849	.1820	.1789	.1755
5	.1600	.1633	.1662	.1687	.1708	.1725	.1738	.1747	.1753	.1755
6	.1093	.1143	.1191	.1237	.1281	.1323	.1362	.1398	.1432	.1462
7	.0640	.0686	.0732	.0778	.0824	.0869	.0914	.0959	.1002	.1044
8	.0328	.0360	.0393	.0428	.0463	.0500	.0537	.0575	.0614	.0653
9	.0150	.0168	.0188	.0209	.0232	.0255	.0281	.0307	.0334	.0363
10	.0061	.0071	.0081	.0092	.0104	.0118	.0132	.0147	.0164	.0181
11	.0023	.0027	.0032	.0037	.0043	.0049	.0056	.0064	.0073	.0082
12	.0008	.0009	.0011	.0013	.0016	.0019	.0022	.0026	.0030	.0034
13	.0002	.0003	.0004	.0005	.0006	.0007	.0008	.0009	.0011	.0013
14	.0001	.0001	.0001	.0001	.0002	.0002	.0003	.0003	.0004	.0005
15	.0000	.0000	.0000	.0000	.0001	.0001	.0001	.0001	.0001	.0002

Table C.1 *Poisson Probability Values (continued)*

r	5.10	5.20	5.30	5.40	λ 5.50	5.60	5.70	5.80	5.90	6.00
0	.0061	.0055	.0050	.0045	.0041	.0037	.0033	.0030	.0027	.0025
1	.0311	.0287	.0265	.0244	.0225	.0207	.0191	.0176	.0162	.0149
2	.0793	.0746	.0701	.0659	.0618	.0580	.0544	.0509	.0477	.0446
3	.1348	.1293	.1239	.1185	.1133	.1082	.1033	.0985	.0938	.0892
4	.1719	.1681	.1641	.1600	.1558	.1515	.1472	.1428	.1383	.1339
5	.1753	.1748	.1740	.1728	.1714	.1697	.1678	.1656	.1632	.1606
6	.1490	.1515	.1537	.1555	.1571	.1584	.1594	.1601	.1605	.1606
7	.1086	.1125	.1163	.1200	.1234	.1267	.1298	.1326	.1353	.1377
8	.0692	.0731	.0771	.0810	.0849	.0887	.0925	.0962	.0998	.1033
9	.0392	.0423	.0454	.0486	.0519	.0552	.0586	.0620	.0654	.0688
10	.0200	.0220	.0241	.0262	.0285	.0309	.0334	.0359	.0386	.0413
11	.0093	.0104	.0116	.0129	.0143	.0157	.0173	.0190	.0207	.0225
12	.0039	.0045	.0051	.0058	.0065	.0073	.0082	.0092	.0102	.0113
13	.0015	.0018	.0021	.0024	.0028	.0032	.0036	.0041	.0046	.0052
14	.0006	.0007	.0008	.0009	.0011	.0013	.0015	.0017	.0019	.0022
15	.0002	.0002	.0003	.0003	.0004	.0005	.0006	.0007	.0008	.0009
16	.0001	.0001	.0001	.0001	.0001	.0002	.0002	.0002	.0003	.0003
17	.0000	.0000	.0000	.0000	.0000	.0001	.0001	.0001	.0001	.0001

r	6.10	6.20	6.30	6.40	λ 6.50	6.60	6.70	6.80	6.90	7.00
0	.0022	.0020	.0018	.0017	.0015	.0014	.0012	.0011	.0010	.0009
1	.0137	.0126	.0116	.0106	.0098	.0090	.0082	.0076	.0070	.0064
2	.0417	.0390	.0364	.0340	.0318	.0296	.0276	.0258	.0240	.0223
3	.0848	.0806	.0765	.0726	.0688	.0652	.0617	.0584	.0552	.0521
4	.1294	.1249	.1205	.1161	.1118	.1076	.1034	.0992	.0952	.0912
5	.1579	.1549	.1519	.1487	.1454	.1420	.1385	.1349	.1314	.1277
6	.1605	.1601	.1595	.1586	.1575	.1562	.1546	.1529	.1511	.1490
7	.1399	.1418	.1435	.1450	.1462	.1472	.1480	.1486	.1489	.1490
8	.1066	.1099	.1130	.1160	.1188	.1215	.1240	.1263	.1284	.1304
9	.0723	.0757	.0791	.0825	.0858	.0891	.0923	.0954	.0985	.1014
10	.0441	.0469	.0498	.0528	.0558	.0588	.0618	.0649	.0679	.0710
11	.0244	.0265	.0285	.0307	.0330	.0353	.0377	.0401	.0426	.0452
12	.0124	.0137	.0150	.0164	.0179	.0194	.0210	.0227	.0245	.0263
13	.0058	.0065	.0073	.0081	.0089	.0099	.0108	.0119	.0130	.0142
14	.0025	.0029	.0033	.0037	.0041	.0046	.0052	.0058	.0064	.0071
15	.0010	.0012	.0014	.0016	.0018	.0020	.0023	.0026	.0029	.0033
16	.0004	.0005	.0005	.0006	.0007	.0008	.0010	.0011	.0013	.0014
17	.0001	.0002	.0002	.0002	.0003	.0003	.0004	.0004	.0005	.0006
18	.0000	.0001	.0001	.0001	.0001	.0001	.0001	.0002	.0002	.0002
19	.0000	.0000	.0000	.0000	.0000	.0000	.0001	.0001	.0001	.0001

r	7.10	7.20	7.30	7.40	λ 7.50	7.60	7.70	7.80	7.90	8.00
0	.0008	.0007	.0007	.0006	.0006	.0005	.0005	.0004	.0004	.0003
1	.0059	.0054	.0049	.0045	.0041	.0038	.0035	.0032	.0029	.0027
2	.0208	.0194	.0180	.0167	.0156	.0145	.0134	.0125	.0116	.0107
3	.0492	.0464	.0438	.0413	.0389	.0366	.0345	.0324	.0305	.0286
4	.0874	.0836	.0799	.0764	.0729	.0696	.0663	.0632	.0602	.0573
5	.1241	.1204	.1167	.1130	.1094	.1057	.1021	.0986	.0951	.0916
6	.1468	.1445	.1420	.1394	.1367	.1339	.1311	.1282	.1252	.1221
7	.1489	.1486	.1481	.1474	.1465	.1454	.1442	.1428	.1413	.1396
8	.1321	.1337	.1351	.1363	.1373	.1381	.1388	.1392	.1395	.1396
9	.1042	.1070	.1096	.1121	.1144	.1167	.1187	.1207	.1224	.1241
10	.0740	.0770	.0800	.0829	.0858	.0887	.0914	.0941	.0967	.0993
11	.0478	.0504	.0531	.0558	.0585	.0613	.0640	.0667	.0695	.0722
12	.0283	.0303	.0323	.0344	.0366	.0388	.0411	.0434	.0457	.0481
13	.0154	.0168	.0181	.0196	.0211	.0227	.0243	.0260	.0278	.0296
14	.0078	.0086	.0095	.0104	.0113	.0123	.0134	.0145	.0157	.0169
15	.0037	.0041	.0046	.0051	.0057	.0062	.0069	.0075	.0083	.0090
16	.0016	.0019	.0021	.0024	.0026	.0030	.0033	.0037	.0041	.0045
17	.0007	.0008	.0009	.0010	.0012	.0013	.0015	.0017	.0019	.0021
18	.0003	.0003	.0004	.0004	.0005	.0006	.0006	.0007	.0008	.0009
19	.0001	.0001	.0001	.0002	.0002	.0002	.0003	.0003	.0003	.0004
20	.0000	.0000	.0001	.0001	.0001	.0001	.0001	.0001	.0001	.0002
21	.0000	.0000	.0000	.0000	.0000	.0000	.0000	.0000	.0001	.0001

r	8.10	8.20	8.30	8.40	λ 8.50	8.60	8.70	8.80	8.90	9.00
0	.0003	.0003	.0002	.0002	.0002	.0002	.0002	.0002	.0001	.0001
1	.0025	.0023	.0021	.0019	.0017	.0016	.0014	.0013	.0012	.0011
2	.0100	.0092	.0086	.0079	.0074	.0068	.0063	.0058	.0054	.0050
3	.0269	.0252	.0237	.0222	.0208	.0195	.0183	.0171	.0160	.0150
4	.0544	.0517	.0491	.0466	.0443	.0420	.0398	.0377	.0357	.0337
5	.0882	.0849	.0816	.0784	.0752	.0722	.0692	.0663	.0635	.0607
6	.1191	.1160	.1128	.1097	.1066	.1034	.1003	.0972	.0941	.0911
7	.1378	.1358	.1338	.1317	.1294	.1271	.1247	.1222	.1197	.1171
8	.1395	.1392	.1388	.1382	.1375	.1366	.1356	.1344	.1332	.1318
9	.1256	.1269	.1280	.1290	.1299	.1306	.1311	.1315	.1317	.1318
10	.1017	.1040	.1063	.1084	.1104	.1123	.1140	.1157	.1172	.1186
11	.0749	.0776	.0802	.0828	.0853	.0878	.0902	.0925	.0948	.0970
12	.0505	.0530	.0555	.0579	.0604	.0629	.0654	.0679	.0703	.0728
13	.0315	.0334	.0354	.0374	.0395	.0416	.0438	.0459	.0481	.0504
14	.0182	.0196	.0210	.0225	.0240	.0256	.0272	.0289	.0306	.0324
15	.0098	.0107	.0116	.0126	.0136	.0147	.0158	.0169	.0182	.0194
16	.0050	.0055	.0060	.0066	.0072	.0079	.0086	.0093	.0101	.0109
17	.0024	.0026	.0029	.0033	.0036	.0040	.0044	.0048	.0053	.0058
18	.0011	.0012	.0014	.0015	.0017	.0019	.0021	.0024	.0026	.0029
19	.0005	.0005	.0006	.0007	.0008	.0009	.0010	.0011	.0012	.0014
20	.0002	.0002	.0002	.0003	.0003	.0004	.0004	.0005	.0005	.0006
21	.0001	.0001	.0001	.0001	.0001	.0002	.0002	.0002	.0002	.0003
22	.0000	.0000	.0000	.0000	.0001	.0001	.0001	.0001	.0001	.0001

Table C.2 *Values of e^x and e^{-x}*

x	e^x	e^{-x}	x	e^x	e^{-x}
0.00	1.000	1.000	3.00	20.086	0.050
0.10	1.105	0.905	3.10	22.198	0.045
0.20	1.221	0.819	3.20	24.533	0.041
0.30	1.350	0.741	3.30	27.113	0.037
0.40	1.492	0.670	3.40	29.964	0.033
0.50	1.649	0.607	3.50	33.115	0.030
0.60	1.822	0.549	3.60	36.598	0.027
0.70	2.014	0.497	3.70	40.447	0.025
0.80	2.226	0.449	3.80	44.701	0.022
0.90	2.460	0.407	3.90	49.402	0.020
1.00	2.718	0.368	4.00	54.598	0.018
1.10	3.004	0.333	4.10	60.340	0.017
1.20	3.320	0.301	4.20	66.686	0.015
1.30	3.669	0.273	4.30	73.700	0.014
1.40	4.055	0.247	4.40	81.451	0.012
1.50	4.482	0.223	4.50	90.017	0.011
1.60	4.953	0.202	4.60	99.484	0.010
1.70	5.474	0.183	4.70	109.95	0.009
1.80	6.050	0.165	4.80	121.51	0.008
1.90	6.686	0.150	4.90	134.29	0.007
2.00	7.389	0.135	5.00	148.41	0.007
2.10	8.166	0.122	5.10	164.02	0.006
2.20	9.025	0.111	5.20	181.27	0.006
2.30	9.974	0.100	5.30	200.34	0.005
2.40	11.023	0.091	5.40	221.41	0.005
2.50	12.182	0.082	5.50	244.69	0.004
2.60	13.464	0.074	5.60	270.43	0.004
2.70	14.880	0.067	5.70	298.87	0.003
2.80	16.445	0.061	5.80	330.30	0.003
2.90	18.174	0.055	5.90	365.04	0.003
3.00	20.086	0.050	6.00	403.43	0.002

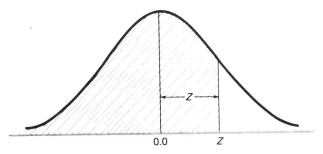

0.0   Z

Table C.3 Normal Probability Values for Values of Z

Z	.00	.01	.02	.03	.04	.05	.06	.07	.08	.09
0.0	.50000	.50399	.50798	.51197	.51595	.51994	.52392	.52790	.53188	.53586
0.1	.53983	.54380	.54776	.55172	.55567	.55962	.56356	.56749	.57142	.57535
0.2	.57926	.58317	.58706	.59095	.59483	.59871	.60257	.60642	.61026	.61409
0.3	.61791	.62172	.62552	.62930	.63307	.63683	.64058	.64431	.64803	.65173
0.4	.65542	.65910	.66276	.66640	.67003	.67364	.67724	.68082	.68439	.68793
0.5	.69146	.69497	.69847	.70194	.70540	.70884	.71226	.71566	.71904	.72240
0.6	.72575	.72907	.73237	.73536	.73891	.74215	.74537	.74857	.75175	.75490
0.7	.75804	.76115	.76424	.76730	.77035	.77337	.77637	.77935	.78230	.78524
0.8	.78814	.79103	.79389	.79673	.79955	.80234	.80511	.80785	.81057	.81327
0.9	.81594	.81859	.82121	.82381	.82639	.82894	.83147	.83398	.83646	.83891
1.0	.84134	.84375	.84614	.84849	.85083	.85314	.85543	.85769	.85993	.86214
1.1	.86433	.86650	.86864	.87076	.87286	.87493	.87698	.87900	.88100	.88298
1.2	.88493	.88686	.88877	.89065	.89251	.89435	.89617	.89796	.89973	.90147
1.3	.90320	.90490	.90658	.90824	.90988	.91149	.91309	.91466	.91621	.91774
1.4	.91924	.92073	.92220	.92364	.92507	.92647	.92785	.92922	.93056	.93189
1.5	.93319	.93448	.93574	.93699	.93822	.93943	.94062	.94179	.94295	.94408
1.6	.94520	.94630	.94738	.94845	.94950	.95053	.95154	.95254	.95352	.95449
1.7	.95543	.95637	.95728	.95818	.95907	.95994	.96080	.96164	.96246	.96327
1.8	.96407	.96485	.96562	.96638	.96712	.96784	.96856	.96926	.96995	.97062
1.9	.97128	.97193	.97257	.97320	.97381	.97441	.97500	.97558	.97615	.97670
2.0	.97725	.97784	.97831	.97882	.97932	.97982	.98030	.98077	.98124	.98169
2.1	.98214	.98257	.98300	.98341	.98382	.98422	.98461	.98500	.98537	.98574
2.2	.98610	.98645	.98679	.98713	.98745	.98778	.98809	.98840	.98870	.98899
2.3	.98928	.98956	.98983	.99010	.99036	.99061	.99086	.99111	.99134	.99158
2.4	.99180	.99202	.99224	.99245	.99266	.99286	.99305	.99324	.99343	.99361
2.5	.99379	.99396	.99413	.99430	.99446	.99461	.99477	.99492	.99506	.99520
2.6	.99534	.99547	.99560	.99573	.99585	.99598	.99609	.99621	.99632	.99643
2.7	.99653	.99664	.99674	.99683	.99693	.99702	.99711	.99720	.99728	.99736
2.8	.99744	.99752	.99760	.99767	.99774	.99781	.99788	.99795	.99801	.99807
2.9	.99813	.99819	.99825	.99831	.99836	.99841	.99846	.99851	.99856	.99861
3.0	.99865	.99869	.99874	.99878	.99882	.99886	.99899	.90893	.99896	.99900
3.1	.99903	.99906	.99910	.99913	.99916	.99918	.99921	.99924	.99926	.99929
3.2	.99931	.99934	.99936	.99938	.99940	.99942	.99944	.99946	.99948	.99950
3.3	.99952	.99953	.99955	.99957	.99958	.99960	.99961	.99962	.99964	.99965
3.4	.99966	.99968	.99969	.99970	.99971	.99972	.99973	.99974	.99975	.99976
3.5	.99977	.99978	.99978	.99979	.99980	.99981	.99981	.99982	.99983	.99983
3.6	.99984	.99985	.99985	.99986	.99986	.99987	.99987	.99988	.99988	.99989
3.7	.99989	.99990	.99990	.99990	.99991	.99991	.99992	.99992	.99992	.99992
3.8	.99993	.99993	.99993	.99994	.99994	.99994	.99994	.99995	.99995	.99995
3.9	.99995	.99995	.99996	.99996	.99996	.99996	.99996	.99996	.99997	.99997

= λ/(Sμ)   Number of Channels: S

R	2	3	4	5	6	7	8	9	10	15
0.02	0.96079	0.94177	0.92312	0.90484	0.88692	0.86936	0.85215	0.83527	0.81873	0.74082
0.04	0.92308	0.88692	0.85215	0.81873	0.78663	0.75578	0.72615	0.69768	0.67032	0.54881
0.06	0.88679	0.83526	0.78663	0.74082	0.69768	0.65705	0.61878	0.58275	0.54881	0.40657
0.08	0.85185	0.78659	0.72615	0.67032	0.61878	0.57121	0.52729	0.48675	0.44983	0.30119
0.10	0.81818	0.74074	0.67031	0.60653	0.54881	0.49659	0.44933	0.40657	0.36788	0.22313
0.12	0.78571	0.69753	0.61876	0.54881	0.48675	0.43171	0.38289	0.33960	0.30119	0.16530
0.14	0.75439	0.65679	0.57116	0.49657	0.43171	0.37531	0.72628	0.28365	0.24660	0.12246
0.16	0.72414	0.61838	0.52720	0.44931	0.38289	0.32628	0.27804	0.23693	0.20190	0.09072
0.18	0.69492	0.58214	0.48660	0.40653	0.33959	0.28365	0.23693	0.19790	0.16530	0.06721
0.20	0.66667	0.54795	0.44910	0.36782	0.30118	0.24659	0.20189	0.16530	0.13534	0.04979
0.22	0.63934	0.51567	0.41445	0.33277	0.26711	0.21437	0.17204	0.13807	0.11080	0.03688
0.24	0.61290	0.48519	0.38244	0.30105	0.23688	0.18636	0.14660	0.11532	0.09072	0.02732
0.26	0.58730	0.45640	0.35284	0.27233	0.21007	0.16200	0.12492	0.09632	0.07427	0.02024
0.28	0.56250	0.42918	0.32548	0.24633	0.18628	0.14082	0.10645	0.08045	0.06081	0.01500
0.30	0.53846	0.40346	0.30017	0.22277	0.16517	0.12241	0.09070	0.06720	0.04978	0.01111
0.32	0.51515	0.37913	0.27676	0.20144	0.14644	0.10639	0.07728	0.05612	0.04076	0.00823
0.34	0.49254	0.35610	0.25510	0.18211	0.12981	0.09247	0.06584	0.04687	0.03337	0.00610
0.36	0.47059	0.33431	0.23505	0.16460	0.11505	0.08035	0.05609	0.03915	0.02732	0.00452
0.38	0.44928	0.31367	0.21649	0.14872	0.10195	0.06981	0.04778	0.03269	0.02236	0.00335
0.40	0.42857	0.29412	0.19929	0.13433	0.09032	0.06065	0.04069	0.02729	0.01830	0.00248
0.42	0.40845	0.27559	0.18336	0.12128	0.07998	0.05267	0.03465	0.02279	0.01498	0.00184
0.44	0.38889	0.25802	0.16860	0.10944	0.07080	0.04573	0.02950	0.01902	0.01225	0.00136
0.46	0.36986	0.24135	0.15491	0.09870	0.06265	0.03968	0.02511	0.01587	0.01003	0.00101
0.48	0.35135	0.22554	0.14221	0.08895	0.05540	0.03442	0.02136	0.01324	0.00826	0.00075
0.50	0.33333	0.21053	0.13043	0.08010	0.04896	0.02984	0.01816	0.01104	0.00671	0.00055
0.52	0.31579	0.19627	0.11951	0.07207	0.04323	0.02586	0.01544	0.00920	0.00548	0.00041
0.54	0.29870	0.18273	0.10936	0.06477	0.03814	0.02239	0.01311	0.00767	0.00448	0.00030
0.56	0.28205	0.16986	0.09994	0.05814	0.03362	0.01936	0.01113	0.00638	0.00366	0.00022
0.58	0.26582	0.15762	0.09119	0.05212	0.02959	0.01673	0.00943	0.00531	0.00298	0.00017
0.60	0.25000	0.14599	0.08306	0.04665	0.02601	0.01443	0.00799	0.00441	0.00243	0.00012
0.62	0.23457	0.13491	0.07550	0.04167	0.02282	0.01243	0.00675	0.00366	0.00198	0.00009
0.64	0.21951	0.12438	0.06847	0.03715	0.01999	0.01069	0.00570	0.00303	0.00161	0.00007
0.66	0.20482	0.11435	0.06194	0.03304	0.01746	0.00918	0.00480	0.00251	0.00131	0.00005
0.68	0.19048	0.10479	0.05587	0.02930	0.01522	0.00786	0.00404	0.00207	0.00106	0.00004
0.70	0.17647	0.09569	0.05021	0.02590	0.01322	0.00670	0.00338	0.00170	0.00085	0.00003
0.72	0.16279	0.08702	0.04495	0.02280	0.01144	0.00570	0.00283	0.00140	0.00069	0.00002
0.74	0.14943	0.07875	0.04006	0.01999	0.00986	0.00483	0.00235	0.00114	0.00055	0.00001
0.76	0.13636	0.07087	0.03550	0.01743	0.00846	0.00407	0.00195	0.00093	0.00044	0.00001
0.78	0.12360	0.06335	0.03125	0.01510	0.00721	0.00341	0.00160	0.00075	0.00035	0.00001
0.80	0.11111	0.05618	0.02730	0.01299	0.00610	0.00284	0.00131	0.00060	0.00028	0.00001
0.82	0.09890	0.04933	0.02362	0.01106	0.00511	0.00234	0.00106	0.00048	0.00022	0.00000
0.84	0.08696	0.04280	0.02019	0.00931	0.00423	0.00190	0.00085	0.00038	0.00017	0.00000
0.86	0.07527	0.03656	0.01700	0.00772	0.00345	0.00153	0.00067	0.00029	0.00013	0.00000
0.88	0.06383	0.03060	0.01403	0.00627	0.00276	0.00120	0.00052	0.00022	0.00010	0.00000
0.90	0.05263	0.02491	0.01126	0.00496	0.00215	0.00092	0.00039	0.00017	0.00007	0.00000
0.92	0.04167	0.01947	0.00867	0.00377	0.00161	0.00068	0.00028	0.00012	0.00005	0.00000
0.94	0.03093	0.01427	0.00627	0.00268	0.00113	0.00047	0.00019	0.00008	0.00003	0.00000
0.96	0.02041	0.00930	0.00403	0.00170	0.00070	0.00029	0.00012	0.00005	0.00002	0.00000
0.98	0.01010	0.00454	0.00194	0.00081	0.00033	0.00013	0.00005	0.00002	0.00001	0.00000

Table C.5 *Random Numbers*

39 65 76 45 45	19 90 69 64 61	20 26 36 31 62	58 24 97 14 97	95 06 70 99 0(
73 71 23 70 90	65 97 60 12 11	31 56 34 19 19	47 83 75 51 33	30 62 38 20 4(
72 20 47 33 84	51 67 47 97 19	98 40 07 17 66	23 05 09 51 80	59 78 11 52 4(
75 17 25 69 17	17 95 21 78 58	24 33 45 77 48	69 81 84 09 29	93 22 70 45 8(
37 48 79 88 74	63 52 06 34 30	01 31 60 10 27	35 07 79 71 53	28 99 52 01 4
02 89 08 16 94	85 53 83 29 95	56 27 09 24 43	21 78 55 09 82	72 61 88 73 6
87 18 15 70 07	37 79 49 12 38	48 13 93 55 96	41 92 45 71 51	09 18 25 58 9
98 83 71 70 15	89 09 39 59 24	00 06 41 41 20	14 36 59 25 47	54 45 17 24 8
10 08 58 07 04	76 62 16 48 68	58 76 17 14 86	59 53 11 52 21	66 04 18 72 8
47 90 56 37 31	71 82 13 50 41	27 55 10 24 92	28 04 67 53 44	95 23 00 84 4
93 05 31 03 07	34 18 04 52 35	74 13 39 35 22	68 95 23 92 35	36 63 70 35 3
21 89 11 47 99	11 20 99 45 18	76 51 94 84 86	13 79 93 37 55	98 16 04 41 6
95 18 94 06 97	27 37 83 28 71	79 57 95 13 91	09 61 87 25 21	56 20 11 32 4
97 08 31 55 73	10 65 81 92 59	77 31 61 95 46	20 44 90 32 64	26 99 76 75 6
69 26 88 86 13	59 71 74 17 32	48 38 75 93 29	73 37 32 04 05	60 82 29 20 2
41 47 10 25 03	87 63 93 95 17	81 83 83 04 49	77 45 85 50 51	79 88 01 97 3
91 94 14 63 62	08 61 74 51 69	92 79 43 89 79	29 18 94 51 23	14 85 11 47 2
80 06 54 18 47	08 52 85 08 40	48 40 35 94 22	72 65 71 08 86	50 03 42 99 3
67 72 77 63 99	89 85 84 46 06	64 71 06 21 66	89 37 20 70 01	61 65 70 22 1
59 40 24 13 75	42 29 72 23 19	06 94 76 10 08	81 30 15 39 14	81 83 17 16 3
63 62 06 34 41	79 53 36 02 95	94 61 09 43 62	20 21 14 68 86	84 95 48 46 4
78 47 23 53 90	79 93 96 38 63	34 85 52 05 09	85 43 01 72 73	14 93 87 81 4
87 68 62 15 43	97 48 72 66 48	53 16 71 13 81	59 97 50 99 52	24 62 20 42 3
47 60 92 10 77	26 97 05 73 51	88 46 38 03 58	72 68 49 29 31	75 70 16 08 2
56 88 87 59 41	06 87 37 78 48	65 88 69 58 39	88 02 84 27 83	85 81 56 39 3
22 17 68 65 84	87 02 22 57 51	68 69 80 95 44	11 29 01 95 80	49 34 35 86 4
19 36 27 59 46	39 77 32 77 09	79 57 92 36 59	89 74 19 82 15	08 58 94 34 7
16 77 23 02 77	28 06 24 25 93	22 45 44 84 11	87 80 61 65 31	09 71 91 74 2
78 43 76 71 61	97 67 63 99 61	80 45 67 93 82	59 73 19 85 23	53 33 65 97 2
03 28 28 26 08	69 30 16 09 05	53 58 47 70 93	66 56 45 65 79	45 56 20 19 4
04 31 17 21 56	33 73 99 19 87	26 72 39 27 67	53 77 57 68 93	60 61 97 22 6
61 06 98 03 91	87 14 77 43 96	43 00 65 98 50	45 60 33 01 07	98 99 46 50 4
23 68 35 26 00	99 53 93 61 28	52 70 05 48 34	56 65 05 61 86	90 92 10 70 8
15 39 25 70 99	93 86 52 77 65	15 33 59 05 28	22 87 26 07 47	86 96 98 29 0
58 71 96 30 24	18 46 23 34 27	85 13 99 24 44	49 18 09 79 49	74 16 32 23 0
93 22 53 64 39	07 10 63 76 35	87 03 04 79 88	08 13 13 85 51	55 34 57 72 6
78 76 58 54 74	92 38 70 96 92	52 06 79 79 45	82 63 18 27 44	69 66 92 19 0
61 81 31 96 82	00 57 25 60 59	46 72 60 18 77	55 66 12 62 11	08 99 55 64 5
42 88 07 10 05	24 98 65 63 21	47 21 61 88 32	27 80 30 21 60	10 92 35 36 1
77 94 30 05 39	28 10 99 00 27	12 73 73 99 12	49 99 57 94 82	96 88 57 17 9

AB:QM Tutorial

AB:QM is a management science software package published by Allyn and Bacon. It has program modules for virtually every topic in this text, and as a result, it is demonstrated in all but a few chapters. It is extremely user friendly, requiring very little instruction to learn how to use. The purpose of this appendix is to provide the first-time user with some help in getting started with AB:QM. With just a little experience, even the most novice computer user will become adept at using AB:QM.

HARDWARE REQUIREMENTS

AB:QM runs on IBM personal computers or a variety of IBM-compatible microcomputers. It requires 256K RAM to run all the program modules. Either a color or monochrome monitor can be used. An IBM, Epson, or compatible printer is recommended. AB:QM can run with a single floppy disk drive, dual disk drives, or a hard disk. It comes in two versions: two 5.25-inch floppy disks or one 3.5-inch disk.

STARTING AB:QM

AB:QM can be started from either a floppy disk system or a hard disk. If it is started from a floppy disk, the following steps should be followed:

1. Insert your DOS diskette in drive A and close the door.

2. Turn the computer on, or if it is on, press simultaneously the ⟨CTRL⟩, ⟨ALT⟩, and ⟨DEL⟩ keys.

3. When the system has "booted up," and A: prompt (A:⟩) should be displayed on your screen.

4. Remove the DOS diskette and insert either one of the 5.25-inch AB:QM disks or the single 3.5-inch AB:QM disk into the A drive, (or, the B drive).

5. Type QM and press the enter (or return) key, (or, if your AB:QM disk is in drive B, type B: and press enter; and then type QM and press enter).

This series of steps should result in the AB:QM menu being displayed on the screen (which will be discussed in a moment).

If a hard disk system is being used, the following steps should be followed:

1. Turn on the computer (making sure nothing is in the A drive and the door is open).

2. Create a directory on the hard disk to store AB:QM (e.g., type MD ABQM).

3. Use the copy *.* command to copy all the files from the AB:QM disk(s) to the hard disk, (e.g., type COPY A:*.*   C:\ABQM).

4. Enter the directory on your hard disk that contains the AB:QM files (using the CD or CHDIR command), (e.g., type CD\ABQM).

5. Type QM and press the enter key.

Again, this will result in the AB:QM menu of programs to be displayed. To run AB:QM in the future, execute steps 4 and 5.

AB:QM MAIN MENU

The AB:QM menu as it would appear on the computer screen is as follows:

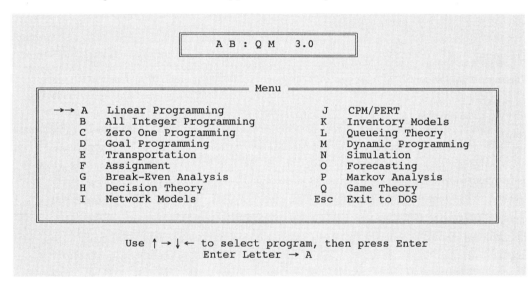

To access any of the program modules type the letter preceding the menu selection, or move the cursor to a module using the arrow keys, and hit the enter key. (However, remember that if the AB:QM version with two 5.25-inch disks is being used, the disk in the A drive might need to be replaced with the other AB:QM disk to access some of the programs.) For example, if the linear programming program module is desired, A is entered. This will result in an almost blank screen with the program title, in this case "Linear Programming," across the top, and the following series of commands in the window across the bottom.

AB:QM COMMANDS AND EDITING FEATURES

The commands allow problems to be entered and solved, the results stored or printed, and provide help if needed. To invoke any of the commands, simply type the first letter. For example, typing H will display the HELP screen that provides a brief, but useful, definition of all the commands as well as descriptions of various editing features. When an AB:QM program is being used and the command words are displayed across the bottom, H can be typed to directly access the HELP screen for assistance. Return to the program can be achieved by hitting ESC.

```
------------------------------------------------------------------
 Key  Command        Description
------------------------------------------------------------------
  N    New            To enter input data.
  L    Load           To load data set from the disk.
  S    Save           To store data set on the disk.
  E    Edit           To correct the input data entered.
  R    Run            To obtain solutions.
  P    Print          To print input and output after running the program.
  I    Install        To specify working disk.
  D    Directory      To get a working disk directory and information.
 Esc   Escape         To exit to the previous stage.
------------------------------------------------------------------


------------------------------------------------------------------
 Key            Description
------------------------------------------------------------------
 Backspace      To delete the character to the left of the cursor.
 Del            To delete character under cursor.
 F7             To insert one row below the cursor.
 F8             To insert one column to the left of the cursor.
 F9             To delete the row containing the cursor.
 F10            To delete the column containing the cursor.
 PgUp           To move the cursor one page up.
 PgDn           To move the cursor one page down.
 Up Arrow       To move the cursor one cell (line) up.
 Down Arrow     To move the cursor one cell (line) down.
 Left Arrow     To move the cursor one cell left.
 Right Arrow    To move the cursor one cell right.
 Home           To move to the first column when you use New or Edit
                   commands.
                To move to the top of the file when you use Run, Help,
                   or Directory commands.
 End            To move to the last column when you use New or Edit
                   commands.
                To move to the bottom of the file when you use Run, Help,
                   or Directory commands.
```

Program Description in HELP

When the HELP command is invoked, it also provides a description of whatever program is being worked in. This description follows the command definitions and editing features on the Help screen. The program description can be accessed by hitting the PG DN key or toggling down with an arrow key. The program description indicates the purpose of the program, defines any program limitations or constraints, and explains how to input the problem data. However, it should be noted that once the chapter material has been read about a particular management science technique, it will probably be very apparent how to input the requested data simply from the text knowledge gained, without having to access the Program Description.

Storing and/or Printing Results

By accessing the PRINT command, problem data can be stored on a separate disk, or printed, or both. When the PRINT command is invoked, AB:QM will ask if it is desired to store output on a disk, or be sent to the printer, or both. If it is to be printed, then a positive response is required; if the output is to be stored on a disk, AB:QM will request a file name and location.

Getting Out of AB:QM

The easiest way to exit AB:QM is to keep pressing the ESC key. This will eventually result in return to the main menu and from there back to DOS.

AN AB:QM EXAMPLE

In order to demonstrate AB:QM, the very simple break-even analysis problem formulated in Chapter 1 on pages 8–10 will be used. In order to solve it, the break-even analysis module is invoked from the AB:QM main menu by typing G. This will result in a blank screen with two empty windows. Next N is typed to enter a ''new'' problem. The following screen will be displayed.

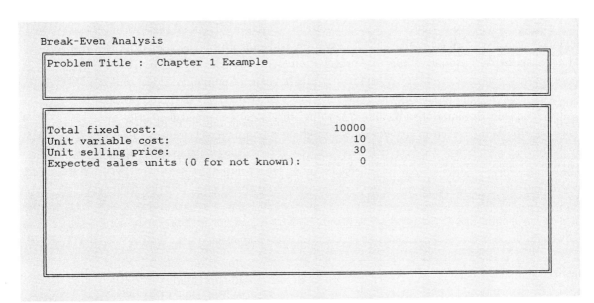

```
Break-Even Analysis
 ┌─────────────────────────────────────────────────────────────────────┐
 │Problem Title :   Chapter 1 Example                                    │
 │                                                                       │
 └─────────────────────────────────────────────────────────────────────┘

 ┌─────────────────────────────────────────────────────────────────────┐
 │Total fixed cost:                            10000                     │
 │Unit variable cost:                             10                     │
 │Unit selling price:                             30                     │
 │Expected sales units (0 for not known):          0                     │
 │                                                                       │
 │                                                                       │
 │                                                                       │
 │                                                                       │
 │                                                                       │
 │                                                                       │
 └─────────────────────────────────────────────────────────────────────┘
```

The headings ''Problem Title,'' ''Total Fixed Cost,'' ''Unit Variable Cost,'' etc., have nothing beside them until items such as ''Chapter 1 Example'' for problem title and

"10000" for total fixed cost are entered. After all those initial inquiries about the problem have been answered and the enter key is pressed, the model is set up in the middle window and the numerical parameters are entered. Following the input of this data, the ESC key is pressed to return to the list of commands, and the RUN command is invoked by pressing R. This results in the following display:

```
Program: Break-Even Analysis

Problem Title : Chapter 1 Example

***** Input Data *****

Total Fixed Cost      :    10000.00
Unit Variable Cost    :       10.00
Unit Selling Price    :       30.00
Expected Sales Units  :        0.00

***** Program Output *****

-----------------------------------------
   Total Fixed Cost      :    10000.00
   Unit Variable Cost    :       10.00
   Unit Selling Price    :       30.00
   Expected Sales Units  :     Unknown
-----------------------------------------

-----------------------------------------
   Break-Even Dollars    :    15000.00
   Break-Even Quantity   :      500.00
-----------------------------------------

***** End of Output *****
```

This computer output includes a summary of the original model plus the solution. Notice that the break-even quantity equals 500 just as we determined on page 10 in Chapter 1. If it is desired to change the problem, return to the command menu (by pressing ESC) and invoke the EDIT command (by pressing E). This will allow any part of the original problem to be changed and then run again. However, the original problem must be stored first if it is desired to save it.

There are several other commands available on the command menu that can be described briefly. Problem data can be saved on a disk by invoking the SAVE command and then telling AB:QM which file to send the data to and the disk location when it asks. To retrieve saved data, the LOAD command is invoked, and AB:QM will ask for the file name and location. The INSTALL command allows a default disk drive location to save your data to be specified. The default disk is normally the working directory, which on a hard disk system is usually the C drive. If you wish data to be saved on disks in the A or B drive instead of C, the INSTALL command is invoked, and the drive location desired typed in. The DIRECTORY command provides a list of all AB:QM files saved in the working directory. The BLOCK command allows you to import or export a block of data.

Solutions to Even-Numbered Problems

Chapter 1   2. See p. 1

4. See pp. 1–2

6. See p. 5

8. See pp. 8–9

10. (a) 500; (b) $12,500; (c) $12,500; (d) $0

12. Profit maximization or cost minimization; decision variables = number of clocks and radios produced; constraints = labor, production cost, materials; and parameters = per unit resource utilization for each product, resource levels, and objective function coefficients.

14. Research and development project, installation of a computer system, plant layout etc.

16. Class registration, grocery counter, traffic light, doctor's office, machine, loading dock, garage, etc.

Chapter 2   2. Max $Z = 40x_1 + 30x_2$

4. Max $Z = 2.25x_1 + 3.10x_2$, s.t. $5.0x_1 + 7.5x_2 \leq 6,500$, $3.0x_1 + 3.2x_2 \leq 3,000$ $x_2 \leq 510$, $x_1 \geq 0$, $x_2 \geq 0$

6. Max $Z = 50x_1 + 40x_2$, s.t. $x_1 + x_2 \leq 350$, $250x_1 + 140x_2 \leq 70,000$, $100x + 30x_2 \leq 27,000$, $x_1 \geq 0$, $x_2 \geq 0$

8. Max $Z = 3.00x_1 + 2.40x_2 + 2.80x_3$, s.t. $x_1 + x_2 + x_3 \leq 27,000$, $4.3x_1 + 3.8x_2 + 3.5x_3 \leq 45,000$, $x_1 \geq 4,000$, $x_3 \geq 4,000$, $x_1 + x_3 \leq 12,000$, $x_1 \geq 0$, $x_2 \geq 0$, $x_3 \geq 0$

10. Max $Z = 1.1x_2 + 1.7x_3 + 1.12x_4 + 1.07s_2$, s.t. $x_1 + x_3 + s_0 = 950,000$, $x + s_1 = .4x_1 + 1.07s_0$, $x_4 + s_2 = x_1 + 3x_2 + 1.07s_1$, $x_1 \geq 0$, $x_2 \geq 0$, $x_3 \geq 0$, $x_4 \geq 0$, $s_0 \geq 0$, $s_1 \geq 0$, $s_2 \geq 0$

12. Max $Z = 150x_1 + 100x_2 + 120x_3 + 115x_4$, s.t. $3x_1 + 5x_2 \leq 200$, $3x_3 + 5x \leq 240$, $3x_1 + 2x_2 \leq 100$, $1.5x_3 + 2.5x_4 \leq 120$, $8x_2 + 8x_4 \leq 1,000$, $200x + 230x_3 \leq 11,000$, $150x_2 + 135x_4 \leq 10,700$, $x_1 \geq 0$, $x_2 \geq 0$, $x_3 \geq 0$, $x_4 \geq 0$

14. $\text{Min} Z = 25x_{1g} + 32x_{11} + 19x_{1p} + 41x_{2g} + 50x_{21} + 38x_{2p} + 17x_{3g} + 23x_{31} + 21x_{3p}$, s.t. $x_{1g} + x_{11} + x_{1p} = 1, x_{2g} + x_{21} + x_{2p} = 1, x_{3g} + x_{31} + x_{3p} = 1, x_{1g} + x_{2g} + x_{3g} = 1, x_{11} + x_{21} + x_{31} = 1, x_{1p} + x_{2p} + x_{3p} = 1, x_{ij} \geq 0$

16. $\text{Max } Z = 315x_1 + 280x_2 + 300x_3$, s.t. $x_1 \leq 25, x_2 \leq 40, x_3 \leq 30, 750x_1 + 350x_2 + 480x_3 \leq 40{,}000, 225x_1 + 250x_2 + 240x_3 \leq 20{,}000, x_1 \geq 0, x_2 \geq 0, x_3 \geq 0$

18. $\text{Min } Z = 20x_{11} + 30x_{12} + 50x_{13} + 25x_{21} + 15x_{22} + 30x_{23} + 45x_{31} + 17x_{32} + 22x_{33}$, s.t. $x_{11} + x_{12} + x_{13} \leq 800, x_{21} + x_{22} + x_{23} \leq 300, x_{31} + x_{32} + x_{33} \leq 600, x_{11} + x_{21} + x_{31} = 400, x_{12} + x_{22} + x_{32} = 700, x_{13} + x_{23} + x_{33} = 500, x_{ij} \geq 0$

20. $\text{Max } Z = 700x_1 + 1{,}000x_2$, s.t. $(x_1/550) + (x_2/300) \leq 1, (x_1/500) + (x_2/400) \leq 1; x_1 \geq 0; x_2 \geq 0$

22. $\text{Max } Z = 130x_{1a} + 150x_{1b} + 90x_{1c} + 275x_{2a} + 300x_{2b} + 100x_{2c} + 180x_{3a} + 225x_{3b} + 140x_{3c} + 200x_{4a} + 120x_{4b} + 160x_{4c}$, s.t. $x_{1a} + x_{1b} + x_{1c} \leq 1, x_{2a} + x_{2b} + x_{2c} \leq 1, x_{3a} + x_{3b} + x_{3c} \leq 1, x_{4a} + x_{4b} + x_{4c} \leq 1, x_{1a} + x_{2a} + x_{3a} + x_{4a} = 1, x_{1b} + x_{2b} + x_{3b} + x_{4b} = 1, x_{1c} + x_{2c} + x_{3c} + x_{4c} = 1, x_{ij} \geq 0$

24. $\text{Max } Z = 9.25x_1 + 8.75x_2 + 9.50x_3$, s.t. $x_1 \leq 175, x_2 \leq 65, x_3 \leq 160, x_1 \geq 87.5, x_2 \geq 32.5, x_3 \geq 80.0, x_3 \leq .4 (x_1 + x_2 + x_3), 3x_1 + 4x_2 + 2x_3 \leq 600, 2x_1 + x_2 + 2x_3 \leq 500, x_1 + 3x_2 + 2x_3 \leq 480, x_1 \geq 0, x_2 \geq 0, x_3 \geq 0$

26. $\text{Max } Z = 17.53x_1 + 10.61x_2$, s.t. $70x_1 + 80x_2 \leq 100, 50x_1 + 40x_2 \leq 80, x_1 \leq 1, x_2 \leq 1, x_1 \geq 0, x_2 \geq 0$

28. $\text{Min } Z = 1x_1 + 4x_2 + 2x_3 + 4x_4 + 2y_1 + 6y_2 + 4y_3 + 6y_4 + 1s_1 + 1s_2 + 1s_3 + 1s_4$, s.t. $x_i \leq 9, y_i \leq 3, x_1 + y_1 - s_1 = 5, x_2 + y_2 + s_1 - s_2 = 6, x_3 + y_3 + s_2 - s_3 = 8, x_4 + y_4 + s_3 = 9, x_i \geq 0, y_i \geq 0, s_i \geq 0$

30. $\text{Min } Z = x_1 + x_2 + x_3 + x_4 + x_5 + x_6$, s.t. $3x_1 + 2x_2 + 2x_3 + x_4 = 700, x_3 + 2x_4 + x_5 = 1{,}200, x_2 + x_5 + 2x_6 = 300, x_i \geq 0$

32. $\text{Max } Z = .7x_{cr} + .6x_{br} + .4x_{pr} + .85x_{ar} + 1.05x_{cb} + .95x_{bb} + .75x_{pb} + 1.20x_{ab} + 1.55x_{cm} + 1.45x_{bm} + 1.25x_{pm} + 1.70x_{am}$, s.t. $x_{cr} + x_{cb} + x_{cm} \leq 200, x_{br} + x_{bb} + x_{bm} \leq 300, x_{pr} + x_{pb} + x_{pm} \leq 150, x_{ar} + x_{ab} + x_{am} \leq 400, .9x_{br} + .9x_{pr} - .1x_{cr} - .1x_{ar} \leq 0, .80x_{cr} - .20x_{br} - .20x_{pr} - .2x_{ar} \geq 0, .25x_{bb} - .75x_{cb} - .75x_{pb} - .75x_{ab} \geq 0, x_{am} = 0, .5x_{bm} + .5x_{pm} - .5x_{cm} - .5x_{am} \leq 0, x_{ij} \geq 0$

34. $\text{Max } Z = 4x_1 + 8x_2 + 6x_3 + 7x_4 - 5y_1 - 6y_2 - 7y_3$, s.t. $x_1 - s_0 \leq 0, x_2 - s_1 \leq 0, x_3 - s_2 \leq 0, x_4 - s_3 \leq 0, s_0 = 2{,}000, s_1 - s_0 + x_1 - y_1 = 0, s_2 - s_1 + x_2 - y_2 = 0, s_3 - s_2 + x_3 - y_3 = 0, s_1 \leq 10{,}000, s_2 \leq 10{,}000, s_3 \leq 10{,}000, x_i \geq 0, y_i \geq 0, s_i \geq 0$

36. $\text{Min } Z = x_1 + x_2 + x_3 + x_4 + x_5 + x_6 + x_7$, s.t. $x_1 + x_4 + x_5 + x_6 + x_7 \geq 30, x_1 + x_2 + x_5 + x_6 + x_7 \geq 45, x_1 + x_2 + x_3 + x_6 + x_7 \geq 43, x_1 + x_2 + x_3 + x_4 + x_7 \geq 40, x_1 + x_2 + x_3 + x_4 + x_5 \geq 50, x_2 + x_3 + x_4 + x_5 + x_6 \geq 55, x_3 + x_4 + x_5 + x_6 + x_7 \geq 60, x_i \geq 0$

38. $\text{Max } Z = x_{AB} + x_{AC}$, s.t. $x_{AB} \leq 7, x_{AC} \leq 6, x_{BE} \leq 2, x_{BD} \leq 5, X_{BC} \leq 10, x_{CD} \leq 3, x_{CF} \leq 9, x_{DE} \leq 4, x_{EF} \leq 3, x_{AB} = x_{BC} + x_{BD} + x_{BE}, x_{AC} + x_{BC} = x_{CD} + x_{CF}, x_{BD} + x_{CD} = x_{DE}, x_{BE} + x_{DE} = x_{EF}, x_{ij} \geq 0$

40. Min $Z = 650(x_1 + x_2 + x_3 + x_4) + 400(y_1 + y_2 + y_3)$, s.t. $160x_1 - 50y_1 \geq 32{,}000$, $160x_2 - 50y_2 \geq 48{,}000$, $160x_3 - 50y_3 \geq 64{,}000$, $160x_4 \geq 48{,}000$, $x_1 = 250$, $x_2 = .85x_1 + y_1$, $x_3 = .85x_2 + y_2$, $x_4 = .85x_3 + y_3$, $x_i \geq 0$, $y_j = 0$

42. Max $Z = y$, s.t. $2y - 5x_1 - 7x_2 - 4x_3 \leq 0$, $4y - 7x_1 - 6x_2 - 8x_3 \leq 0$, $3y - 10x_2 - 8x_2 - 5x_3 \leq 0$, $10x_1 + 14x_2 + 11x_3 \leq 3{,}000$, $18x_1 + 12x_2 + 13x_3 \leq 3{,}800$, $y \geq 0$, $x_1 \geq 0$, $x_2 \geq 0$, $x_3 \geq 0$

44. Max $Z = 150y_1 + 70y_2 + 300y_3 + 900x_4 + 1{,}200x_5 + 600x_6 - 40x_1 - 30x_2 - 60x_3 - 100x_4 - 150x_5 - 120x_6 - 500_{RM}$, s.t. $y_1 \leq 300$, $y_2 \leq 500$, $y_3 \leq 400$, $x_4 \leq 200$, $x_5 \leq 300$, $x_6 \leq 100$, $RM \leq 400$, $x_1 = 2RM$, $x_2 = 3RM$, $x_3 = 1RM$, $x_1 = y_1 + w_1$, $x_2 = y_2 + w_2$, $x_3 = y_3 + w_3$, $x_4 = .8w_1$, $x_5 = .5w_2$, $x_6 = .4w_3$, $x_i \geq 0$, $y_i \geq 0$, $RM \geq 0$

46. $x_1 = 4$, $x_2 = 1$, $Z = 18$

48. $x_1 = 5.3$, $x_2 = 1$, $Z = 49.4$

50. $x_1 = 5$, $x_2 = 3$, $Z = 21$

52. Unbounded

54. Unbounded

56. Infeasible

58. $x_1 = 6$, $x_2 = 1.6$, $Z = 33.6$

60. $x_1 = 4$, $x_2 = 3$, $Z = 57$

62. $x_1 = 456$, $x_2 = 510$, $Z = 2{,}607$

64. $x_1 = 19{,}069.2$, $x_2 = 4{,}784.0$, $Z = 15{,}911.6$

66. $x_1 = 5.5$, $x_2 = 7.0$, $Z = 22{,}200$

68. $x_1 = 1$, $x_2 = .375$, $Z = 21.51$

Chapter 3

2. $x_1 = 40$, $s_1 = 40$, $Z = 2{,}000$

4. $x_3 = 8$, $s_2 = 6$, $Z = 96$

6. $x_1 = 8$, $s_2 = 4$, $Z = 32$

8. $x_1 = 4$, $x_2 = 6$, $s_3 = 12$, $s_4 = 3$, $s_5 = 1$, $Z = 108$

10. $x_1 = 2$, $x_2 = 20$, $x_3 = \frac{45}{8}$, $x_4 = 15$, $Z = 2{,}123.125$

12. $x_1 = 5$, $x_2 = 30$, $s_2 = 15$, $Z = 165$

14. $x_2 = 10$, $x_3 = 1$, $Z = 68$

16. $x_1 = 4$, $x_2 = 2$, $s_2 = 14$, $Z = 22$

18. $x_1 = 2$, $x_2 = 3$, $s_1 = 2$, $Z = 23$

20. Infeasible

22. $x_1 = 6$, $x_2 = 12$, $s_3 = 1$, $s_4 = 0$, $Z = 960$

24. $x_1 = 900$, $x_2 = 400$, $x_3 = 700$, $s_1 = 600$, $s_4 = 440$, $Z = 1{,}740$

26. Multiple optimal solutions: (1) $x_2 = 30$, $x_3 = 10$, $s_1 = 10$, $s_2 = 60$, $Z = 1{,}500$ (2) $x_1 = 20$, $x_2 = 20$, $s_1 = 20$, $s_2 = 20$, $Z = 1{,}500$

28. Multiple optimal solutions: (1) $x_1 = 15$, $x_2 = 10$, $s_3 = 0$, $s_4 = 60$, $Z = 155$; (2) $x_1 = 15$, $x_3 = 10$, $s_3 = 10$, $s_4 = 50$, $Z = 155$

30. Multiple optimal solutions: (1) $x_1 = 10$, $x_2 = 10$, $s_2 = 20$, $Z = 30$; (2) $x_1 = \frac{70}{3}$, $x_2 = \frac{10}{3}$, $s_1 = \frac{80}{3}$, $Z = 30$

32. $x_1 = 7$, $\hat{x} = 1.67$; $Z = 77.33$

34. $x_1 = -\frac{4}{5}$, $x_2 = \frac{12}{5}$, $Z = \frac{184}{5}$

36. Unbounded

38. Multiple optimal solutions: (1) $x_1 = -\frac{52}{5}$, $x_2 = -\frac{46}{5}$, $Z = -60$; (2) $x_1 = -10$, $x_2 = -10$, $Z = -60$

40. $x_1 = 1$, $x_2 = 0$, $x_3 = 2$, $Z = 4$

42. $x_1 = 25$, $x_3 = 13$, $s_1 = 10$, $Z = 37$

44. $x_1 = 4$, $x_2 = \frac{16}{3}$, $x_3 = \frac{4}{3}$, $Z = \frac{52}{3}$

46. $x_1 = 3$, $x_2 = 3$, $s_1 = 5$, $s_2 = 9$, $s_3 = 9$, $s_4 = 1$, $Z = 18$

48. $x_1 = -3$, $x_2 = 6$, $Z = 36$

50. $x_1 = 4$, $x_2 = 3$, $Z = 250$

52. $x_1 = 456$, $x_2 = 510$, $s_1 = 395$, $Z = 2{,}607$

54. $x_1 = 19{,}089.463$, $x_2 = 4{,}773.161$, $s_3 = 3{,}137.376$, $Z = 15{,}907.355$

56. $x_1 = 1$, $x_2 = 3$, $s_3 = 16$, $Z = 680$

58. $x_1 = 1$, $x_2 = .375$, $s_2 = 15$, $s_4 = .625$, $Z = 21.509$

60. $x_1 = 178.571$, $x_3 = 150$, $s_2 = 92.857$, $s_3 = 171.429$, $s_4 = 21.429$, $s_5 = 300$, $Z = 2{,}478.571$

62. $x_1 = 2.4$, $x_2 = .8$, $s_3 = 3.6$, $Z = .224$

64. $x_1 = 400$, $x_4 = 800$, $s_1 = 100$, $s_4 = 6{,}000$, $s_5 = 200$, $s_6 = 0$, $Z = 44{,}000$

66. $x_1 = 11.11$, $x_2 = 33.33$, $x_3 = 38.16$, $x_4 = 25.10$, $s_5 = 532.52$, $s_7 = 2{,}311.30$, $Z = 12{,}466.37$

68. $x_1 = 17.655$, $x_2 = 35.310$, $x_3 = 30$, $s_1 = 7.344$, $s_2 = 4.689$, $Z = 24{,}448.28$

70. $x_1 = 54$, $x_2 = 36$, $x_4 = 10$, $s_2 = 5.999$, $s_3 = 20$, $Z = 9.2$

72. $x_4 = 1$, $x_8 = 1$, $x_{12} = 1$, $Z = 660$

74. $x_1 = 98.461$, $x_2 = 32.5$, $x_3 = 87.307$, $s_1 = 76.538$, $s_2 = 32.5$, $s_3 = 72.692$, $s_4 = 10.961$, $s_6 = 7.307$, $s_9 = 95.961$, $s_{10} = 109.423$, $Z = 2{,}024.567$

76. $x_1 = 9$, $x_3 = 9$, $x_4 = 8$, $y_1 = 2$, $s_1 = 6$, $s_3 = 1$, $Z = 70$

78. $x_2 = 50$, $x_4 = 600$, $x_6 = 125$, $Z = 775$

80. $x_{cr} = 75$, $x_{ar} = 300$, $x_{bb} = 300$, $x_{ab} = 100$, $x_{cm} = 125$, $x_{pm} = 125$, $s_3 = 25$, $s_5 = 37.5$, $Z = 1{,}062.5$

82. $x_2 = 10{,}000$, $x_4 = 10{,}000$, $y_1 = 8{,}000$, $y_2 = 10{,}000$, $s_0 = 2{,}000$, $s_1 = 10{,}000$, $s_2 = 10{,}000$, $s_3 = 10{,}000$, $Z = 50{,}000$

84. $x_2 = 6.667$, $x_3 = 19.667$, $x_4 = 2$, $x_5 = 21.667$, $x_6 = 5$, $x_7 = 11.667$, $Z = 66.667$

86. $x_{AB} = 7$, $x_{AC} = 6$, $x_{BC} = 5$, $x_{BE} = 2$, $x_{CF} = 6$, $x_{EF} = 2$, $Z = 13$

88. $x_1 = 250$, $x_2 = 335.802$, $x_3 = 400$, $x_4 = 340$, $y_1 = 123.302$, $y_2 = 114.567$
$Z = 956,919.8$

90. $x_1 = 537.778$, $x_2 = 44.444$, $x_3 = 4.444$, $x_4 = 226.667$, $Z = 537.778$

92. $y_1 = 300$, $y_2 = 225$, $y_3 = 275$, $x_1 = 550$, $x_2 = 825$, $x_3 = 275$, $x_4 = 200$, $x = 300$, $w_1 = 250$, $w_2 = 600$, RM $= 275$, $Z = 417,500$

Chapter 4

2. Min $Z_d = 120y_1 + 40y_2$, s.t. $2y_1 + y_2 \geq 50$, $4y_1 + y_2 \geq 30$, $y_1 \geq 0$, $y_2 \geq 0$
$y_1 = $ marginal value of labor, $y_2 = $ marginal value of land

4. Min $Z_d = 24y_1 + 30y_2$, s.t. $4y_1 + 2y_2 \geq 6$, $y_1 + 6y_2 \geq 2$, $3y_1 + 3y_2 \geq 12$
$y_1 \geq 0$, $y_2 \geq 0$; $y_1 = $ marginal value of oven-hour, $y_2 = $ marginal value of labor

6. (a) \$.55 is the marginal value of process 1 time, \$.60 is the marginal value of process 2 time; (b) Min $Z_d = 60y_1 + 40y_2$, s.t. $12y_1 + 4y_2 \geq 9$, $4y_1 + 8y_2 \geq 7$, $y_1 \geq 0$, $y_2 \geq 0$; (c) $y_1 = $ marginal value of 1 hour of process 1, $y_2 = $ marginal value of 1 hour of process 2

8. (a) \$.004 is the marginal value of A, \$.014 is the marginal value of B; (b) Max $Z = 12y_1 + 12y_2 + 10y_3$, s.t. $4y_1 + 3y_2 + 5y_3 \leq .06$, $3y_1 + 6y_2 + 2y_3 \leq .10$ $y_1 \geq 0$, $y_2 \geq 0$, $y_3 \geq 0$; (c) $y_1 = $ marginal value of 1 unit of A, $y_2 = $ marginal value of 1 unit of B, $y_3 = $ marginal value of 1 unit of C.

10. (a) \$.10 is the marginal value of carbohydrates; protein and iron have no marginal value; (b) Max $Z_d = 20y_1 + 30y_2 + 12y_3$, s.t. $4y_1 + 12y_2 + 3y_3 \leq .03$, $5y_1 + 3y_2 + 2y_3 \leq .02$, $y_1 \geq 0$, $y_2 \geq 0$, $y_3 \geq 0$; (c) $y_1 = $ marginal value of 1 mg protein, $y_2 = $ marginal value of 1 mg iron, $y_3 = $ marginal value of 1 mg carbohydrates

12. Min $Z_d = 64y_1 + 50y_2 + 120y_3 + 7y_4 + 7y_5$, s.t. $4y_1 + 5y_2 + 15y_3 + y_4 \geq 9$, $8y_1 + 5y_2 + 8y_3 + y_5 \geq 12$, $y_1 \geq 0$, $y_2 \geq 0$, $y_3 \geq 0$, $y_4 \geq 0$, $y_5 \geq 0$

14. Min $Z_d = 400y_1 + 600y_2 + 16,000y_3 + 25,000y_4 + 800y_5 + 900y_6$, s.t. $y + 50y_3 + 2y_5 \geq 25$, $y_1 + 45y_3 + 4y_6 \geq 20$, $y_2 + 40y_4 + 3y_5 \geq 10$, $y_2 + 30y_4 + y_6 \geq 30$, $y_1 \geq 0$, $y_2 \geq 0$, $y_3 \geq 0$, $y_4 \geq 0$, $y_5 \geq 0$, $y_6 \geq 0$

16. Max $Z_d = 6y_1 + y_2$, s.t. $2y_1 + 2y_2 \leq 1$, $-3y_1 - 3y_2 \leq 2$, $y_1 - y_2 = 1$, $y_2 \geq 0$, $y_1 \sim$ unrestricted

18. Max $Z_d = 30y_1 + 40y_2 + 30y_3$, s.t. $y_1 + y_2 - y_3 \leq 2$, $2y_1 + 2y_2 + y_3 \leq 4$ $-3y_1 + y_3 = 3$ $y_1 \geq 0$, $y_2 \geq 0$, $y_3 \geq 0$

20. An increase in c_1 to \$120 does not change the solution point but Z increases to \$880; increasing c_1 to \$200 changes the solution to $x_1 = 6$, $x_2 = 0$, and $Z = \$1,200$

22. $Z > \$80$, $x_1 = 6$, $x_2 = 6$

24. (a) $400/7 \leq b_1 \leq 68$, $45 \leq b_2 \leq 580/11$; (b) $6 \leq c_1 \leq 12$, $9 \leq c_2 \leq 18$

26. (a) $90 \leq b_1 \leq 225$, $108 \leq b_2 \leq 270$; (b) $120 \leq c_1 \leq 300$, $200 \leq c_2 \leq 500$

28. (a) $10 \leq b_1 \leq 22$, $b_2 \geq 13$, $19/2 \leq b_3 \leq 23$; (b) $40 \leq c_1 \leq 160$, $35 \leq c_2 \leq 140$

30. (a) $b_1 \geq 110$, $b_2 \geq 100$, $80 \leq b_3 \leq 160$, $25 \leq b_4 \leq 170/4$; (b) $c_1 \leq 40$, $35 \leq c_2 \leq 45$, $45 \leq c_3 \leq 70$

32. (a) $20 \leq b_1 \leq 120$, $30 \leq b_2 \leq 180$; (b) $\frac{8}{3} \leq c_1 \leq 16$, $5 \leq c_2 \leq 30$; (c) no effect; (d) $x_1 = 20$, $s_1 = 10$, $Z = 200$; (e) no effect

34. (a) $18 \leq b_1 \leq 33$, $b_2 \geq 0$, $b_3 \geq 14$, $17 \leq b_4 \leq 32$; (b) $c_1 \leq 7$, $5 \leq c_2 \leq 8$, $c_3 \geq 7$; (c) $a_{11} \geq \frac{5}{7}$; (d) $x_1 = 6$, $x_3 = 18$, $s_1 = 8$, $s_2 = 14$, $s_3 = 15$, $Z = 174$; (e) no effect

36. (a) $y_2 = 0$, $b_2 \geq 90$; (b) $y_3 = \$2$, $20 \leq b_3 \leq 80$; (c) either, $y_3 = y_4 = \$2$; (d) no; (e) $\geq \$6$; (f) no effect; (g) no effect

38. A reduction in job time to 45 min will change the solution to $x_{13} = 1$, $x_{22} = 1$, $x_{31} = 1$, $Z = 81$; reduction in employee 1 time to 30 min has no effect

40. Yes, a new solution results, $x_{12} = 1$, $x_{21} = 1$, $x_{32} = 1$, $x_{43} = 1$, $Z = 820$

42. Chicken, 225 lbs.

44. Fewer employees would be hired in May and June but the cost reduction is minimal

Chapter 5

2. (a) NW corner = $\$1,710$; least cost = $\$810$; VAM = $\$810$; (b) $x_{13} = 70$, $x_{21} = 30$, $x_{23} = 10$, $x_{32} = 60$, $x_{33} = 10$, $x_{34} = 30$, $Z = \$810$

4. $x_{1A} = 70$, $x_{2B} = 25$, $x_{2C} = 90$, $x_{3A} = 10$, $x_{3B} = 25$, $x_{3D} = 25$, $Z = \$13,200$

6. $x_{12} = 500$, $x_{13} = 300$, $x_{21} = 150$, $x_{23} = 350$, $x_{31} = 600$, $x_{D1} = 300$, $Z = \$28,750$

8. (a) $x_{A2} = 80$, $x_{AD} = 50$, $x_{B2} = 10$, $x_{B3} = 60$, $x_{C1} = 80$, $x_{C2} = 20$, $Z = \$1,530$
(b) Min $Z = 6x_{A1} + 9x_{A2} + Mx_{A3} + 12x_{B1} + 3x_{B2} + 5x_{B3} + 4x_{C1} + 8x_{C2} + 11x_{C3}$, s.t. $x_{A1} + x_{A2} + x_{A3} \leq 130$, $x_{B1} + x_{B2} + x_{B3} \leq 70$, $x_{C1} + x_{C2} + x_{C3} \leq 100$, $x_{A1} + x_{B1} + x_{C1} = 80$, $x_{A2} + x_{B2} + x_{C2} = 110$, $x_{A3} + x_{B3} + x_{C3} = 60$, $x_{ij} \geq 0$

10. $x_{11} = 70$, $x_{13} = 20$, $x_{22} = 10$, $x_{23} = 20$, $x_{32} = 100$, $x_{D3} = 40$, $Z = \$1,240$

12. No effect

14. (a) VAM should be used, $x_{A2} = 70$, $x_{A4} = 80$, $x_{B1} = 50$, $x_{B4} = 160$, $x_{C1} = 80$, $x_{C3} = 180$, $x_{CD} = 60$, $Z = \$8,260$; (b) VAM is optimal; (c) yes, because $C_{C2} = 0$, allocate 70 units to x_{C2}; (d) Min $Z = 14x_{A1} + 9x_{A2} + 16x_{A3} + 18x_{A4} + 11x_{B1} + 8x_{B2} + Mx_{B3} + 16x_{B4} + 16x_{C1} + 12x_{C2} + 10x_{C3} + 22x_{C4}$, s.t. $x_{A1} + x_{A2} + x_{A3} + x_{A4} \leq 150$, $x_{B1} + x_{B2} + x_{B3} + x_{B4} \leq 210$, $x_{C1} + x_{C2} + x_{C3} + x_{C4} \leq 320$, $x_{A1} + x_{B1} + x_{C1} = 130$, $x_{A2} + x_{B2} + x_{C2} = 70$, $x_{A3} + x_{B3} + x_{C3} = 180$, $x_{A4} + x_{B4} + x_{C4} = 240$; $x_{ij} \geq 0$

16. (a) VAM, $Z = \$6,140$; (b) $x_{12} = 10$, $x_{13} = 90$, $x_{22} = 40$, $x_{24} = 140$, $x_{31} = 80$, $x_{32} = 90$, $x_{3D} = 30$, $Z = \$5,960$; (c) no

18. $x_{A1} = 70$, $x_{A3} = 20$, $x_{B3} = 50$, $x_{C2} = 80$, $x_{D2} = 20$, $x_{D3} = 40$, $x_{E1} = 50$, $Z = \$1,410$

20. Select alternative 2, cost = $\$24,930$

22. (a) VAM, degenerate solution, $x_{12} = 120$, $x_{21} = 20$, $x_{23} = 50$, $x_{31} = 180$, $x_{43} = 30$, $Z = \$3,900$ (b) VAM solution optimal with $x_{42} = 0$

24. (a) NW corner = $\$6,050$; least cost = $\$5,800$; VAM = $\$5,000$; (b) $x_{1C} = 300$, $x_{2A} = 150$, $x_{3A} = 50$, $x_{3B} = 300$, $x_{3C} = 50$, $x_{DB} = 100$, $Z = \$5,000$

26. $x_{11} = 30$, $x_{12} = 5$, $x_{14} = 2$, $x_{22} = 20$, $x_{33} = 4$, $x_{44} = 26$, $x_{54} = 10$, $x_{55} = 30$, $x_{64} = 2$, $x_{66} = 20$, $Z = 364$ miles

28. (a) VAM $= \$1,860$; (b) $x_{1C} = 30$, $x_{1D} = 30$, $x_{2C} = 10$, $x_{3A} = 10$, $x_{3B} = 0$, $x_{3D} = 20$, $x_{4A} = 20$, $x_{DB} = 20$, $Z = \$1,680$

30. $x_{11} = 125$, $x_{14} = 25$, $x_{23} = 90$, $x_{32} = 100$, $x_{33} = 30$, $x_{34} = 80$, $Z = \$8,465$

32. $x_{1B} = 60$, $x_{2A} = 45$, $x_{2B} = 25$, $x_{2C} = 35$, $x_{3B} = 5$, $x_{3D} = 65$, $Z = \$1,605$

34. $x_{A2} = 1$, $x_{BD} = 1$, $x_{C1} = 1$, $x_{D1} = 1$, $x_{E3} = 1$, $x_{F3} = 1$, $x_{G2} = 1$, $x_{H1} = 1$, $Z = \$1,070$

36. $x_{11} = 50$, $x_{21} = 50$, $x_{22} = 130$, $x_{32} = 70$, $x_{33} = 180$, $x_{34} = 30$, $x_{44} = 270$, $Z = \$3,375$

38. (a) $x_{AA} = 1,400$, $x_{A2} = 600$, $x_{BB} = 1,300$, $x_{B3} = 400$, $x_{CB} = 100$, $x_{CC} = 1,400$, $x_{C1} = 200$, $x_{C2} = 200$, $x_{11} = 1,400$, $x_{22} = 1,400$, $x_{33} = 1,400$, $Z = \$4,900$

40. (a) $W_1W_1 = 310$, $W_1R_4 = 80$, $W_2R_2 = 20$, $W_2R_3 = 100$, $W_3W_3 = 310$, $W_3R_1 = 50$, $W_3R_2 = 60$, $R_1R_1 = 310$, $R_2R_2 = 310$, $R_3R_3 = 310$, $R_4R_2 = 20$, $R_4R_4 = 290$, $Z = \$2,310$

42. (a) $F_1W_3 = 1,400$, $F_2W_1 = 900$, $F_2W_3 = 100$, $F_3W_2 = 500$, $F_3W_3 = 700$, $DR_1 = 200$, $W_1W_1 = 2,900$, $W_1R_1 = 900$, $W_2W_2 = 3,300$, $W_2R_3 = 500$, $W_3W_3 = 1,600$, $W_3R_2 = 2,200$, $W_4W_4 = 3,800$, $Z = \$31,100$

44. 1B, 2A, 3F, 4D, 5C, 6E, $Z = 36$ nights

46. 1B, 2D, 3A, 4C, 5E, $Z = 51$ days

48. 1C, 2A, 3B, 4D; or 1D, 2A, 3B, 4C; $Z = \$26$

50. A3, B2, C6, D1, E5, F4; or A6, B2, C5, D3, E1, F4; $Z = 14$ miles

52. Official 1 would go to C (instead of A) and official 4 would go to A (instead of C), $Z = 150$ miles

54. 1–1, 2–4, 3–2, 4–5, 5–3; $Z = 78$

56. 1E, 2C, 3D, 4A, 5B; $Z = 290$ units

Chapter 6

2. (a) 3–2 $= 1$, 3–2–1 $= 3$, 3–6 $= 3$, 3–4 $= 4$, 3–6–5 $= 4$, 3–6–5–7 $= 6$; (b) 2 and 1, and 6, 5, and 7

4. 1–4–7–8 $= 17$ hours

6. 1–2–5–4–7–6–9–10 $= 23$ miles

8. 1–4–7–10–11 $= 23$

10. 0–2–4 $= 10$

12. 1–3–4–5–2 $= 12$

14. 1–2–5–4–7–6–9–10–8 and 4–3; 33

16. 4–2–1–3–6–5–9–10 and 6–7–8; 3400 yards

18. 3–2–1–4–7–6–5–9–11, 7 and 10, and 9 and 8; 500

20. 1–2 $= 8$, 1–3 $= 8$, 2–3 $= 1$, 2–4 $= 5$, 2–5 $= 2$, 3–5 $= 0$, 3–6 $= 9$, 5–7 $= 2$, 4–7 $= 5$, 6–7 $= 9$; maximum flow $= 16$

22. 1–2 $= 20$, 1–3 $= 6$, 1–4 $= 5$, 2–3 $= 6$, 2–5 $= 6$, 2–7 $= 8$, 3–4 $= 5$, 3–5

$= 3$, 3–6 $= 4$, 4–6 $= 10$, 4–9 $= 0$, 5–7 $= 6$, 5–8 $= 1$, 5–6 $= 2$, 6–8 $=$ 16, 6–9 $= 0$, 7–8 $= 13$, 7–10 $= 1$, 8–9 $= 10$, 8–10 $= 20$, 9–10 $= 10$; maximum flow $= 31$

24. 1–2 $= 4$, 1–3 $= 4$, 1–4 $= 4$, 2–3 $= 0$, 2–5 $= 4$, 3–4 $= 0$, 3–5 $= 2$, 3–6 $=$ 2, 4–6 $= 4$, 5–6 $= 0$, 5–7 $= 6$, 6–8 $= 6$, 7–8 $= 0$, 7–9 $= 6$, 8–9 $= 6$; maximum flow $= 12{,}000$ cars

26. $x_{12} = 7$, $x_{13} = 5$, $x_{14} = 5$, $x_{25} = 2$, $x_{26} = 5$, $x_{35} = 0$, $x_{36} = 5$, $x_{45} = 5$, x_{57} $= 3$, $x_{58} = 4$, $x_{59} = 0$, $x_{68} = 3$, $x_{69} = 7$, $x_{7,10} = 3$, $x_{8,10} = 7$, $x_{9,10} = 7$, $Z = $ 17

28. 1–2 $= 8$, 1–3 $= 12$, 1–4 $= 10$, 2–3 $= 0$, 2–5 $= 2$, 2–7 $= 6$, 3–4 $= 4$, 3–5 $= 8$, 4–5 $= 5$, 4–7 $= 9$, 5–6 $= 9$, 5–7 $= 5$, 5–8 $= 0$, 6–9 $= 18$, 7–6 $= 9$, 7–8 $= 6$, 7–9 $= 5$, 8–9 $= 7$; maximum flow $= 30$

30. (b) node 1 (0, 0); node 2 (2, 2); node 3 (8, 8); node 4 (8, 8); node 5 (4, 8); node 6 (13, 13); node 7 (15, 15); (c) a (0, 0); b (0, 0); c (2, 2); d (4, 0); D1 (0, 0); D2 (4, 4); e (1, 1); f (0, 0); g (4, 4); h (0, 0); (d) 1–2–3–4–6–7 $= 15$ weeks

32. (a) node 1 (0, 0); node 2 (3, 3); node 3 (10, 13); node 4 (10, 13); node 5 (9, 8); node 6 (10, 14); node 7 (16, 16); node 8 (20, 20); node 9 (23, 23); node 10 (23, 23); node 11 (24, 24); (b) a (0, 0); b (6, 3); c (3, 0); d (0, 0); D1 (3, 0); D2 (4, 0); e (3, 3); f (4, 4); g (5, 1); h (0, 0); i (3, 3); j (0, 0); k (0, 0); l (1, 1); D3 (0, 0); m (0, 0); (c) 1–2–5–7–8–9–10 $= 24$ days; (d) g shares 4 days with f; b and e share 3 days; c shares 3 days with e and f

34. (a) a (2, ⅑); b (7, ²⁵⁄₉); c (4, ⁴⁄₉); d (2.33, ⁴⁄₉); e (5, ¹⁶⁄₉); f (4.5, ²⁵⁄₃₆); g (3, ⁴⁄₉); h (2, 0); (b) node 1 (0, 0); node 2 (2, 2); node 3 (9, 9); node 4 (9, 9.5); node 5 (4.33, 9.5); node 6 (14, 14); node 7 (16, 16); (c) a (0, 0); b (0, 0); c (3.5, 3); d (5.17, 0); D1 (.5, 0); D2 (5.17, 4.67); e (0, 0); f (.5, .5); g (4, 4); h (0, 0); (d) 1–2–3–6–7 $=$ 16 weeks; (e) the critical path changed, e replaced f, the time increased from 15 to 16 weeks; (f) .50; (g) .917; (h) .677

36. (a) node 1 (0, 0); node 2 (4.17, 4.17); node 3 (9.67, 13.84); node 4 (13.17, 13.17); node 5 (17.34, 17.34); node 6 (15.17, 21.84); node 7 (19.84, 19.84); node 8 (26.84, 26.84); (b) a (0, 0); b (8.51, 4.34); c (4.17, 0); d (0, 0); e (3.17, 3.17); f (4.17, 4.17); g (6.67, 0); h (0, 0); i (3.37, 3.37); j (8.67, 8.67); k (0, 0); l (6.67, 6.67); m (0, 0); (c) 1–2–4–5–7–8 $= 26.84$ days; (d) 8.861

38. (a) a (30), b (16), c (10), d (70), e (75), f (40), g (50), h (60); (b) $2,325,000, 22 days; (c) $205,000; (d) 1–2–4–6, 1–2–5–6, 1–3–5–6

40. Max $Z = 4x_{12} + 5x_{14} + 7x_{13} + 8x_{24} + 3x_{34}$, s.t. $x_{12} \le 12$, $x_{14} \le 4$, $x_{13} \le 7$, $x_{24} \le 4$, $x_{34} \le 6$, $T_1 + 20 - x_{12} - T_2 \le 0$, $T_1 + 24 - x_{14} - T_4 \le 0$, $T_1 + 14 - x_{13} - T_3 \le 0$, $T_2 + 10 - x_{24} - T_4 \le 0$, $T_3 + 11 - x_{34} - T_4 \le 0$, $T_4 \le 22$

42. (a) 36 months, $3,630,000; (b) 1–3–4–8, 1–3–4–7–8, 1–3–4–6–8; (c) $3,385,000, 1–3–4–7–8 and 1–3–4–6–8

Chapter 7   2. (a) $Q = 79.705$; (b) $13,549.91; (c) $N = 15.05$; (d) $T_b = 24.177$ days

6. (a) $r = 65.9$ units; (b) $N = 15.056$; (c) no dependent relationship exists; (d) 4.176 days; (e) $r = 15.9$ units

8. (a) 3 orders; (b) no, the average inventory level would increase from 120 to 3(units, and the resulting increase in carrying costs would outweigh the resultir decrease in ordering costs.

10. (a) $Q = 1,200$; (b) \$2,880; (c) $N = 18$; (d) $T_b = 20$ days; (e) 300 tons

12. The solution results are not sensitive to changes in C_o and C_c

14. (a) $Q = 1,224.75$; (b) \$3,265.98; (c) $N = 8.165$; (d) 816.497 units

16. (a) $Q = 1,195$; (b) $N = 4.184$; (c) $t = 62.1$ days; (d) 18.67 days; (e) 78.115 da (f) \$4,183.25

18. $N \cong 6$ runs per year, $T_b \cong 57$ days between runs, length of run $\cong 48$ days: Ja 1—begin; Feb. 18—end, idle; Feb. 27—begin; April 16—end, idle; April 25– begin; June 12—end, idle; June 21—begin

20. (a) $Q = 600$; (b) 3.75 days; (c) 7.5 days; (d) \$9,600; (e) 125 days

22. (a) $Q = 67.13$; (b) 19.365 orders; (c) 18.8 days; (d) 51.64; (e) 15.49; (f) 4.34 day (g) \$393,872.97

24. $V = 70.3$, $S = 20$, $t_1 = .058$ year, $t_2 = .017$ year, $t = .075$ years

26. $Q = 2,560.8$, \$1,347.51

28. For problem 20, TC $= \$9,600$; for this problem TC $= \$6,333.08$; shortag should be allowed

30. Order costs decrease by 50%, carrying costs double, product costs decreased I \$6,375; thus, net savings is \$1,875; the dealer would probably be indifferent

32. $Q < 300$ ($Q = 207$, TC $= \$66,568.76$); $300 \le Q < 500$ ($Q = 300$, TC \$65,384.50); $500 \le Q < 800$ ($Q = 500$, TC $= \$64,704.00$); $800 \le Q$ (Q 800, TC $= \$65,235.00$); select 4% discount

34. Stock 100, $E(100) = \$45.50$

36. Safety stock $= 200$ units

38. $C_o = \$37.50$

40. (a) 840, 52.9; (b) 3,625; (c) 927.3

42. Average weekly cost $= \$146.30$

44. See problem 2

46. (a) $Q = 309.84$; (b) $r = 64.516$; (c) 48 days

48. See problem 10

50. $Q = 371,842.26$, TC $= \$33,465.80$, $N = 13.944$ loans, $r = \$255,000$

52. See problem 16

54. (a) $Q = 500$; (b) \$2,500; (c) 12.5 days; (d) 8.33 days

56. (a) $Q = 310$; (b) \$3,718; (c) $s = 124$ units; (d) problem 3, TC $= \$4,800$

58. $Q = 90.3$, TC $= \$11,960.98$, allow shortages

60. See problem 26

62. Take discount with savings of \$18,325

Chapter 8
2. (a) $E(S) = 7,200$, $E(B) = 6,000$, stocks; (b) $p(I) = .667$, $p(II) = .333$

4. E (operate) $= E$ (lease) $= \$40,000$; lease

6. Bond fund

8. (b) $E(15) = 24$, $E(16) = 27.20$, $E(17) = 26.90$, $E(18) = 21$; stock 16 cases; (c) 16 cases; (d) \$5.80

10. (b) $E(20) = 14.40$, $E(22) = 18.08$, $E(24) = 21.10$, $E(26) = 22.50$, $E(28) = 21.95$, $E(30) = 20.10$; 26 dozen; (c) 26 dozen; (d) \$3.10

12. (a) Risk fund; (b) savings bonds; (c) bond fund

14. (a) Motel; (b) restaurant, (c) motel, (d) theater, (e) motel or restaurant

16. (a) Stock 16; (b) stock 16; (c) stock 18; (d) stock 16; (e) stock 16

18. (a) Stock 25; (b) stock 30; (c) stock 30; (d) stock 28 or 29

20. Request the higher rate increase

22. Settle

24. \$0

26. (a) A selects z, B selects y; (b) 8

28. Row 4 dominates row 1, row 3 dominates row 4, column v dominates all other columns

30. (a) no; (b) (1,z) to (3,z) to (3,x) to (1,x) to (1,z); (c) eliminate row 2 and column y; (d) $p(A1) = .56$, $p(A3) = .44$, $p(Bx) = .33$, $p(Bz) = .67$; (e) $A = B = 366.67$

32. (a) Firm A; (b) no; (c) collude

34. $p_1 = .2$, $p_2 = .8$

Chapter 9
2. Current state only

4. [Morning Herald Evening Tribune] $= [.389\ .611] = [6,244\ 9,776]$

6. The state probabilities eventually become constant, such that, no matter what the starting state, the probability of going to a particular state in the next period will be the same.

8. (a) .008; (b) $p(n + 1) = .8$, $p(n + 2) = .88$, $p(n + 3) = .89$; (c) [.89 .11]

10. Describes the probabilities of moving from a starting state to any of the other system states in the next period

12. [.399 .315 .286]

14. (a) [1772 3906 4322]; (b) [.167 .335 .498], [1,670 3,350 4,980]

16. Initiate campaign

18. It is impossible to move to a transient state from any other state except itself.

20. [$\frac{2}{15}$ $\frac{2}{15}$ $\frac{2}{15}$ $\frac{2}{15}$], \$193.33 per day, implement new policy

22. Doubly stochastic transition matrix, steady state $= 1/m$

24. Transient state, [$\frac{1}{3}$ $\frac{2}{3}$ 0]

26. (a) 1[.86 .14], 2[.80 .20], 3[.60 .40]; (b) month 1: [4,200 800], month 2: [2,6 600], month 3: [1,050 700]

28. (a) .50, (b) 17.5 years, (c) 20 years

Chapter 10

2. $P_{n>4} = .1296$

4. $P_0 = .333$, $P_3 = .099$, $L = 2$, $L_q = 1.33$, $W = .125$, $W_q = .083$, $\rho = .66$

6. 77 minutes, $P_{n>31} = .2821$

8. Add employees; savings of $25.50/day

10. (a) $L_q = 3.2$, $I = .20$; (b) $\lambda = 9/hr$

12. (a) $L_q = 9.09$, $W = .05$ (24 min), $W_q = .0455$ (21.8 min); (b) $P_{n>4} = .318($

14. $L = 2.85$ units

16. $L_q = 3.125$, $W = .0792$ (4.75 min)

18. $W = .9393$ (56.4 min); 36.53%; system appears to be inadequate

20. (a) $P_0 = .2$; (b) $L_q = 1$; (c) $W_q = 1.25$; (d) $P_n = .1825$

22. (a) $L = 14$, $L_q = 13.1$, $W = .5$, $W_q = .47$, $\rho = .93$; (b) 1; (c) $L = 1.19$, $= .26$, $W = .042$ (2.55 min), $W_q = .009$ (.56 min); yes (probably)

24. $L = 4.5$, $L_q = 3.15$, $W = 1.5$, $W_q = 1.05$

26. Implement the improved system

30. $P_{(n \geq 10)} = .1075$

Chapter 11

2. $E(\text{arrivals}) = 2.55$ min

4. (b) Search through the combination of reorder points and order quantities to dete mine the set that results in the minimum cost

6. (a) One teller: average queue length $= 2.2$, average waiting time $= 13.1$ mins; tw tellers: average queue length $= 0, 0$, average waiting time $= .375, .875$ mins; (two tellers seems best

8. (b) Small sample size results in difference in simulated and actual results; (c) mea time between arrivals $= 4.1$ days, mean waiting time $= 5.2$ days, mean shi waiting $= 1$ ship, mean time waiting and being unloaded $= 10.2$ days, mea number waiting and being unloaded $= 2$ ships, proportion of arrivals entering a empty system $= 20\%$, (d) mean time between arrivals $= 4.1$ days, mean waiti time $= 6.25$ days, mean ships waiting $= 1.23$ ships, mean total time $= 11.2$ days, mean total number waiting and being unloaded $= 2.2$ ships, proportion arrivals entering an empty system $= 15\%$

10. $x = 2\sqrt{3r}$

12. $x = 6r$

14. $x_1 = 2 + 12\sqrt{r}/16$, $x_2 = 10 - 2\sqrt{10(1 - r)}$

16. $E(x) = 1.9$ days/breakdown, $n = 2.33$ days/breakdown, difference due to low number of simulations

20. [VA NC MD] = [.47 .47 .06], simulate for longer than 30 weeks

22. (a) $p(1) = .5$, $p(2) = .2$, $p(3) = .4$; (b) [0, 50,000 100,000 150,000 200,000] = [.5 .25 0 .125 .125]; (c) .0667; (d) .40; (e) [0 50 100 150 200 250] = [.4 .3 0 .1 0 .2]; (f) $80,000

Chapter 12

2. (a) A—$2 million, B—$1 million, C—$2 million; (b) multiple optimal solutions: B—$1 million, C—$3 million, or A—$2 million, B—$1 million, C—$1 million

4. Cincinnati—1 machine, Buffalo—2 machines, Akron—2 machines

6. (a) A—4, B—2, C—3, D—3; (b) A—4, B—2, C—3, D-2

8. (a) Team 1—3 scientists; (b) Team 1—2 scientists

10. 1–4–5–7 = 43 hrs

12. Construct pumping stations at 2, 6, 10, and 14; pipeline route = 1–2–6–10–14–18; total cost = $318,000

14. January—3, February—4, March—3, April—4

16. January—2, February—5, March—3, April—4

18. $D_5 = 4$, $D_4 = 6$, $D_3 = 7$, $D_2 = 5$, $D_1 = 5$

20. $D_5 = 4$, $D_4 = 6$, $D_3 = 7$, $D_2 = 5$, $D_1 = 5$

Chapter 13

2. $x_1 = 5$, $d_1^- = 60$, $d_2^- = 5$, $x_2 = 15$

4. Min $Z = P_1 d_1^- + P_2(d_5^- + d_6^-) + P_3 d_{11}^+ + P_4(d_2^- + d_3^- + d_4^-) + P_5 d_1^+$, s.t. $3x_1 + 2x_2 + x_3 + d_1^- - d_1^+ = 40$, $x_1 + d_2^- - d_2^+ = 10$, $x_2 + d_3^- - d_3^+ = 10$, $x_3 + d_4^- - d_4^+ = 12$, $x_1 + d_5^- - d_5^+ = 7$, $x_3 + d_6^- - d_6^+ = 5$, $d_{11}^- + d_1^+ - d_{11}^+ = 10$; $x_1 = 10$, $d_1^- = 10$, $d_5^+ = 3$, $d_3^- = 10$, $d_4^- = 12$, $d_6^- = 5$, $d_{11}^- = 10$; $P_1 = 10$, $P_4 = 22$

6. (a) Min $Z = P_1 d_2^- + P_2 d_5^+ + 4P_3 d_3^- + 5P_3 d_4^- + P_4 d_1^-$, s.t. $5x_1 + 8x_2 + d_1^- - d_1^+ = 4800$, $2x_1 + 2.5x_2 + d_2^- - d_2^+ = 2000$, $5x_1 + 8x_2 + d_5^- - d_5^+ = 5280$, $x_1 + d_3^- - d_3^+ = 500$, $x_2 + d_4^- - d_4^+ = 400$; (b) Min $Z = P_1 d_2^- + P_2 d_5^+ + 4P_3(d_3^- + d_3^+) + 5P_3(d_4^- + d_4^+) + P_4 d_1^-$; (c) $x_2 = 400$, $d_1^- = 1600$, $d_2^- = 1000$, $d_3^- = 500$, $d_5^- = 480$; $P_1 = 1000$, $P_3 = 2000$, $P_4 = 1600$

8. (a) Min $Z = P_1 d_1^- + P_2 d_2^- + P_3 d_3^+ + P_4 d_4^+$, s.t. $x_1 + 4x_2 + 6x_3 + d_1^- - d_1^+ = 500$, $50,000x_1 + 100,000x_2 + 150,000x_3 + d_2^- - d_2^+ = 5,000,000$, $4,000x_1 + 8,000x_2 + 10,000x_3 + d_3^- - d_3^+ = 250,000$, $.25x_1 + .20x_2 + .125x_3 + d_4^- - d_4^+ = 45$, $.25x_1 + .20x_2 + .125x_3 \leq 50$; (b) set d_5^- at P_0; $x_1 = 62.5$, $d_1^- = 437.5$, $d_2^- = 1,875,000$, $d_4^- = 29.375$, $d_5^- = 34.375$; $P_0 = 34.375$, $P_1 = 437.5$, $P_2 = 1,875,000$

10. (a) Yes, unattained P_3 goal cannot be reduced further; (b) $P_1 = $ OK, $P_2 = $ OK, $P_3 \neq $ OK (but unattainable), $P_4 = $ OK; (c) between P_1 and P_3 in d_1^- column, and between P_2 and P_3 in d_2^+ column; (d) d_1^- column — $P_1:P_3 = 1:\%$; d_2^+ column — $P_2:P_3 = 1:^{11}\!/\!\%$

12. Min $Z = P_1d_1^- + P_2d_4^+ + 6P_3d_2^+ + 5P_3d_3^+ + 5P_4d_2^- + 6P_4d_3^-$, s.t. $50x_1$
$60x_2 + d_1^- - d_1^+ = 1200$, $x_1 + d_2^- - d_2^+ = 8$, $x_2 + d_3^- - d_3^+ = 8$, x_2
$d_4^- - d_4^+ = 11$; (b) $x_1 = 10.8$, $x_2 = 11$, $d_2^+ = 2.8$, $d_3^+ = 3$

14. Min $Z = P_1 \sum_{i=1}^{4}d_i^- + P_1\sum_{i=7}^{12}d_i^+ + P_2d_5^+ + P_3d_{17}^- + P_4\sum_{i=13}^{16}d_i^- + P_5d_{18}^-$, s
$y_1 + d_1^- - d_1^+ = 2000$, $y_1 + y_2 - x_1 + d_2^- - d_2^+ = 2000$, $y_1 + y_2 + y_3$
$x_1 - x_2 + d_3^- - d_3^+ = 2000$, $y_1 + y_2 + y_3 + y_4 - x_1 - x_2 - x_3 + d_4^-$
$d_4^+ = 2000$, $- y_1 + x_1 + d_5^- - d_5^+ = 1000$, $- y_1 - y_2 + x_1 + x_2 + $
$- d_6^+ = 3000$, $- y_1 - y_2 - y_3 + x_1 + x_2 + x_3 + d_7^- - d_7^+ = 3000$, $-$
$- y_2 - y_3 - y_4 + x_1 + x_2 + x_3 + x_4 + d_8^- - d_8^+ = 3,000$, $- 6y_1 + 4$
$+ d_9^- - d_9^+ = 0$, $- 6y_1 - 7y_2 + 4x_1 + 4x_2 + d_{10}^- - d_{10}^+ = 0$, $- 6y_1 - 7$
$- 5y_3 + 4x_1 + 4x_2 + 4x_3 + d_{11}^- - d_{11}^+ = 0$, $- 6y_1 - 7y_2 - 5y_3 - 6y_4$
$4x_1 + 4x_2 + 4x_3 + 7x_4 + d_{12}^- - d_{12}^+ = 0$, $6y_1 - 4x_1 + d_{13}^- - d_{13}^+ = 200$
$6y_1 + 7y_2 - 4x_1 - 4x_2 + d_{14}^- - d_{14}^+ = 2000$, $6y_1 + 7y_2 + 5y_3 - 4x_1 - 4$
$- 4x_3 + d_{15}^- - d_{15}^+ = 2000$, $6y_1 + 7y_2 + 5y_3 + 6y_4 - 4x_1 - 4x_2 - 4x_3$
$7x_4 + d_{16}^- - d_{16}^+ = 2000$, $6y_1 + 7y_2 + 5y_3 + 6y_4 - 4x_1 - 4x_2 - 4x_3 - 7$
$+ d_{17}^- - d_{17}^+ = 20,000$, $6y_1 + 7y_2 + 5y_3 + 6y_4 - 4x_1 - 4x_2 - 4x_3 - 7$
$+ d_{18}^- - d_{18}^+ = 100,000$

16. Min $Z = P_1(d_1^- + d_2^+ + d_3^+ + d_4^+ + d_5^+ + d_6^+) + P_2d_7^- + P_3d_8^+ + P_4d$
s.t. $x_1 + x_2 + x_3 + x_4 + x_5 + d_1^- = 200,000$, $x_1 + d_2^- - d_2^+ = 80,000$,
$+ d_3^- - d_3^+ = 80,000$, $x_3 + d_4^- - d_4^+ = 80,000$, $x_4 + d_5^- - d_5^+ = 80,00$
$x_5 + d_6^- - d_6^+ = 80,000$, $x_5 + d_7^- - d_7^+ = 50,000$, $x_1 + x_5 - (x_2 + x_3 - $
$x_4) + d_8^- - d_8^+ = 0$, $.15x_2 + .10x_3 + .06x_4 + d_9^- - d_9^+ = 25,000$

18. Min $Z = P_1\sum_{i=1}^{4}d_i^- + P_2\sum_{i=5}^{10}d_i^- + P_3\sum_{i=1}^{13}(d_i^- + d_i^+) + P_4\sum_{i=14}^{16}(d_i^- + d_i^+) - $
$P_5d_{17}^+$, s.t. $x_{w22} - d_1^+ = 0$, $x_{b22} - d_2^+ = 0$, $x_{w33} - d_3^+ = 0$, $x_{b33} - d_4^+ = $
$\sum_{j=1}^{3}x_{wij} + d_5^- = 400$, $\sum_{j=1}^{3}x_{bij} + d_6^- = 200$, $\sum_{j=1}^{3}x_{wij} + d_7^- = 300$, $\sum_{j=1}^{3}x_{bij} - $
$d_8^- = 300$, $\sum_{j=1}^{3}x_{wij} + d_9^- = 100$, $\sum_{j=1}^{3}x_{bij} + d_{10}^- = 500$, $0.44\sum_{i=1}^{3}x_{wi1} - 0.5$
$\sum_{i=1}^{3}x_{bi1} + d_{11}^- - d_{11}^+ = 0$, $0.44 \sum_{i=1}^{3}x_{wi2} - 0.56 \sum_{i=1}^{3}x_{bi2} + d_{12}^- - d_{12}^+ = $
$0.44 \sum_{i=1}^{3}x_{wi3} - 0.56 \sum_{i=1}^{3}x_{bi3} + d_{13}^- - d_{13}^+ = 0$, $0.67\sum_{i=1}^{3}(x_{bi1} + x_{wi1}) - $
$0.33\sum_{i=1}^{3}\sum_{j=2}^{3}(x_{bij} + x_{wij}) + d_{14}^- - d_{14}^+ = 0$, $0.6\sum_{i=1}^{3}(x_{bi2} + x_{wi2}) - 0.4\sum_{i=1}^{3}\{(x$
$+ x_{wi1}) + (x_{bi3} + x_{wi3}) + d_{15}^- - d_{15}^+ = 0$, $0.73\sum_{i=1}^{3}(x_{bi3} + x_{wi3}) - $
$0.27\sum_{i=1}^{3}\sum_{j=1}^{3}(x_{bij} + x_{wij}) + d_{16}^- - d_{16}^+ = 0$, $\sum_{i=1}^{3}\sum_{j=1}^{3}C_{ij}(x_{bij} + x_{wij}) - d_{17}^+ = $

20. Min $Z = P_1d_1^- + P_1d_2^+ + P_2d_3^- + P_2d_4^- + P_3d_5^- + P_3d_6^- + P_4d_7^- + P_5d_8^- - $
$P_6d_9^- + P_7d_1^+$, s.t. $x_1 + x_2 + x_3 + x_4 + x_5 + x_6 + x_7 + x_8 + x_9 + x_{10} - $
$d_1^- - d_1^+ = 4$, $x_1 + x_2 + x_3 + x_4 + x_5 + x_6 + x_7 + x_8 + x_9 + x_{10} - $
$d_2^- - d_2^+ = 5$, $x_6 + x_8 + d_3^- - d_3^+ = 1$, $x_1 + x_3 + d_4^- - d_4^+ = 1$, $x_3 + x$
$+ x_6 + x_9 + x_{10} + d_5^- - d_5^+ = 1$, $x_1 + x_2 + x_3 + x_5 + x_6 + x_8 + x_{10} - $
$d_6^- - d_6^+ = 1$, $x_1 + x_4 + x_6 + x_8 + x_9 + d_7^- - d_7^+ = 2$, $2.23x_1 + 1.10x$
$+ 2.78x_3 - 0.43x_4 + 0.87x_5 - 0.02x_6 + 0.33x_7 + 1.43x_8 + 1.12x_9 - $
$1.84x_{10} + d_8^- - d_8^+ = x_1 + x_2 + x_3 + x_4 + x_5 + x_6 + x_7 + x_8 + x_9 + $
x_{10}, $x_3 + d_9^- - d_9^+ = 1$

22. $x_1 = 100$, $d_1^+ = 20$, $d_3^- = 45$

24. $x_1 = 800$, $x_2 = 600$, $d_2^+ = 100$

26. (a) Min $Z = P_1d_1^+$, s.t. $x_{11} + x_{12} + x_{13} + x_{14} = 300$, $x_{21} + x_{22} + x_{23} + x$
$= 200$, $x_{31} + x_{32} + x_{33} + x_{34} = 400$, $x_{11} + x_{21} + x_{31} \leq 200$, $x_{12} + x_{22}$

$x_{32} \leq 100$, $x_{13} + x_{23} + x_{33} \leq 450$, $x_{14} + x_{24} + x_{34} \leq 250$, $5x_{11} + 2x_{12} + 6x_{13} + 7x_{14} + 3x_{21} + 5x_{22} + 4x_{23} + 6x_{24} + 4x_{31} + 5x_{32} + 2x_{33} + 3x_{34} + d_1^- - d_1^+ = 0$; (b) Min $Z = P_1 d_1^- + P_2 d_2^- + P_3 \Sigma_{i=3}^6 d_i^- + P_4 d_7^+ + P_5 d_8^+ + P_6(d_9^- + d_9^+) + P_7 d_{10}^+$, s.t. $x_{14} + x_{24} + x_{34} + d_1^- - d_1^+ = 250$, $x_{31} + d_2^- - d_2^+ = 100$, $x_{11} + x_{21} + x_{31} + d_3^- - d_3^+ = 160$, $x_{12} + x_{22} + x_{32} + d_4^- - d_4^+ = 80$, $x_{13} + x_{23} + x_{33} + d_5^- - d_5^+ = 360$, $x_{14} + x_{24} + x_{34} + d_6^- - d_6^+ = 200$, $5x_{11} + 2x_{12} + 6x_{13} + 7x_{14} + 3x_{21} + 5x_{22} + 4x_{23} + 6x_{24} + 4x_{31} + 5x_{32} + 2x_{33} + 3x_{34} + d_7^- - d_7^+ = 3{,}569.50$, $x_{24} + d_8^- - d_8^+ = 0$, $450(x_{11} + x_{21} + x_{31}) - 200(x_{13} + x_{23} + x_{33}) + d_9^- - d_9^+ = 0$, $5x_{11} + 2x_{12} + 6x_{13} + 7x_{14} + 3x_{21} + 5x_{22} + 4x_{23} + 6x_{24} + 4x_{31} + 5x_{32} + 2x_{33} + 3x_{34} + d_{10}^- - d_{10}^+ = 0$

28. (a) Priority 1: Regular labor hours should be at least 80 hours per week. (b) Priority 2: Overtime should be restricted to 10 hours per week. (c) Priority 3: Selling strong upholstery material and regular dress material as much as possible in proportion to their maximum sales per week. (d) Priority 4: Overtime should not be allowed. (e) 5, 3. (f) 90. (g) P1: 0, P2: 0, P3: not attained (underachievement by 25). (h) 20. (i) 410.

30. (a) Do not spend over $100,000. (b) Place at least 30 TV, 40 radio, and 60 newspaper ads. (c) Yes; P2 = 0 in the final solution. (d) $75,000; this may be obtained from constraint C5 (no deviation from 75,000), or from constraint C1 (100,000 − 25,000, the value of $d-1$). (e) 747,941; from constraint C7: 1,250,000 − 502,059 (the value of $d-7$). (f) This item assumed a $\leq$ system constraint, which would have indicated a limited population within the advertising area. No more than the entire population could be reached. (g) 35.882. (h) 75; this is the right-hand-side value of constraint C6, which has its positive deviation (d+6) minimized in the objective function. (i) This represents money that was included in the total funds but was not spent. (j) 5,000; this is the coefficient of radio ads (x2) in constraint C7. (k) $375; this is the coefficient of newspaper ads (x3) in constraints C1 and C5. (l) $25,000; this is the value of d−1. (m) This represents the number of people who were not reached, out of the available population. (n) 48; the current RHS is 60, and d−4 = 12 would indicate falling short of 60 by 12. (o) No one; additional money is currently available (see item 1 above). (p) For every dollar increase in the desired spending level, an additional 10.59 people would be reached. For every unit decrease in the required minimum number of radio ads, an additional 823.53 people would be reached. For every unit decrease in the required minimum number of newspaper ads, an additional 220.59 people would be reached. (q) 264,750; this is the result of multiplying 10.59 (marginal substitution rate for the first goal conflict shown in the Analysis of Goal Conflicts table) by 25,000 additional dollars. Note that 25,000 is within the range limit of 47,416.66 indicated in this table. Reformulation by changing the RHS of constraint C5 from 75,000 to 100,000 provides the answers. Twenty-five units of TV ads will be purchased to increase the number of reached people by 264,750. (r) Most likely, although a ratio stating exactly the current solution's ratio would have no effect. If the ratio were more favorable to television ads than is the current ratio, and if this goal were placed at a higher priority than the minimum number goals, the number of people reached would

increase. (s) The minimum number of radio and newspaper ads would be used, an television ads would make up the rest, matching the current solution. x1 = 91.6₇ x2 = 40; x3 = 60. The cost of this solution would be $122,419.50

32. (a) I1 = 1,000,000; all $1 million will be idle during the first year. C2 = 1,000,000; the $1 million will be invested in savings certificates in the second yea with redemption occurring at the start of the sixth year. R6 = 1,800,000; the $ million plus earned income of $800,000 will be invested in real estate for the sixt year. (b) The first three goals have been fully achieved. The fourth priority goal, t maximize the total cash value at the end of the sixth year, has been achieved "a much as possible," which is in effect maximization. (c) $1,980,000, which may b obtained by multiplying R6 by its return rate of 1.1, or by subtracting d−10 from the RHS of constraint C10. (d) Only C2 and R6 would be highlighted; I1 shoul be added. (e) This may be confirmed by plugging values into the constraints. (f The first three priorities did not have any effect, as they all have slack (d−7, d+8 d+9) in the solution. (g) No, because I1 was utilized to keep funds idle during th first year. No other alternative would have allowed investment in C2. (h)

Solution Set	Return
S1 S3 S5	1,728,000
S1 S3 R5 R6	1,742,400
S1 B3 R6	1,760,000
B1 B4	1,960,000
B1 S4 R6	1,848,000

The cost of failing to consider the idle fund is the difference between the curren solution and the best no-idle-fund solution of (B1 B4), or $20,000 (i) d-7 indicate that $1,120,000 more than required to hold the total investment in stocks an bonds below 40% was invested in other alternatives. The total investment in all th alternatives was $2,800,000; 40% of this is $1,120,000. d+8 indicates tha $300,000 more than required to raise savings certificates above 25% of total invest ment was invested in them. Savings certificates constituted 1/2.8000 or 35.71% o the total investment. Investing $700,000 (from $1,000,000 − 300,000) woul have meant savings certificates would have constituted .7/2.8 or 25% of total inves ment. d + 9 indicates that the minimum desired level of real estate investmen ($300,000) was exceeded by $1,500,000. d−10 indicates underachievement of th (artificially large) return goal. As any very large number could have been used, th actual value here is irrelevant. (j) As the first three priorities had no impact (see iter f above), there will be no change. (k) Minimum and maximum investment require ments, and minimum and maximum ratios among investments, which are mor restrictive. (It would also help if there were more alternatives available. The numbe of available alternatives range from 1 to 3 per year, with an average of only 2.)

Chapter 14

2. $x_1 = 22$, $x_2 = 8$, $Z = 112$

4. $x_1 = 2$, $x_2 = 3$, $Z = 25$

6. $x_1 = 8$, $x_2 = 2$, $Z = 22$, or, $x_1 = 6.5$, $x_2 = 3$, $Z = 22$

8. $x_2 = 1$, $x_4 = 1$, $x_5 = 1$, $x_6 = 1$, $Z = 15$

10. $x_1 = 1$, $x_4 = 1$, $Z = 260{,}000$

12. Max $Z = 600x_1 + 400x_2 + 150x_3 + 450x_4 + 500x_5 + 250x_6 + 150x_7 + 50x_8 + 20x_9 + 100x_{10}$, s.t. $.15x_1 + x_2 + 4x_3 + 5x_4 + 10x_5 + 5x_6 + 7x_7 + 4x_8 + 8x_9 + 2x_{10} \leq 20$, $x_2 + x_6 \geq 1$, $x_8 + x_9 + x_{10} \leq 1$, $x_i = 0$ or 1

14. Min $Z = 1.5x_{11} + 2x_{12} + 2x_{13} + 4x_{14} + 3x_{21} + 1.5x_{22} + 3x_{23} + 2x_{24} + 3.5x_{31} + 3.5x_{32} + 3x_{33} + x_{34} + 2x_{41} + 2x_{42} + x_{43} + 3x_{44} + 1.5x_{51} + x_{52} + 2x_{53} + 5x_{54} + 1{,}000 \times (20y_{11} + 40y_{12} + 60y_{13} + 20y_{21} + 35y_{22} + 55y_{23} + 15y_{31} + 30y_{32} + 50y_{33} + 30y_{41} + 50y_{42} + 70y_{43} + 40y_{51} + 60y_{52} + 80y_{53})$, s.t. $\sum_{j=1}^{4} x_{ij} \leq 30{,}000y_{i1} + 50{,}000y_{i2} + 60{,}000y_{i3}$, $\sum_{k=1}^{3} y_{ik} \leq 1$, $\sum_{i=1}^{5}\sum_{k=1}^{3} y_{ik} = 3$, $\sum_{i=1}^{5} x_{i1} \geq 50{,}000$, $\sum_{i=1}^{5} x_{i2} \geq 30{,}000$, $\sum_{i=1}^{5} x_{i3} \geq 40{,}000$, $\sum_{i=1}^{5} x_{i4} \geq 20{,}000$, $x_{ij} \geq 0$ and integer $y_{ik} = 0$ or 1; $i = 1, 2, 3, 4, 5$; $j = 1, 2, 3, 4$; $k = 1, 2, 3$

hapter 15

2. $x_1 = 0$, $x_2 = 2$, $y = 12$, $\lambda = 4$

4. $x_1 = 4.57$, $x_2 = 30.43$, $\lambda = 15.43$, $y = 1014.35$

6. $x_1 = .3$, $x_2 = .7$, $\lambda_1 = .1$, $y = 2.55$

8. $x_1 = 1.5$, $x_2 = .5$, $\lambda = 1$, $y = -5.5$

10. Max $Z = -1.5 + 0x_1 - 6x_2 - 2x_3 + 4\lambda_1 + 2\lambda_2 + M_1 + M_2 + M_3 + 0s_1 + 0s_2 + 0A_1 + 0A_2 - MA_4 - MA_5$, s.t. $\lambda_1 + \lambda_2 + M_1 + A_1 = 1.5$, $-6x_2 + \lambda_1 + M_2 + A_2 = 0$, $-2x_3 + 2\lambda_1 + \lambda_2 + M_3 + A_3 = 0$, $x_1 + x_2 + 2x_3 - s_1 + A_4 = 20$, $x_1 + x_3 - s_2 + A_5 = 10$, and the following condition must hold, $\lambda_1 s_1 = 0$, $\lambda_2 s_2 = 0$, $\mu_1 x_1 = 0$, $\mu_2 x_2 = 0$, $\mu_3 x_3 = 0$

hapter 16

2. See p. 759

4. See p. 762

6. For example, computer costs, production costs, consultation costs, equipment costs, hiring and training costs, plant redesign costs, etc; see p. 841

8. Management science specialists, computer scientists, mathematicians, economists, industrial and system engineers, etc.

12. See p. 765

14. Differences could include personality, technical training, age, managerial experience, level of authority, political astuteness, etc.

Glossary

absorbing state—a state in a transition matrix for a Markov process that is impossibl to leave

activity—project operations or tasks to be conducted in a CPM/PERT network

adjacent set—the nodes in a shortest route network problem directly connected to node in the permanent set for which the shortest routes have not yet been determined

arrival—the units, items, or customers coming into a queuing system for service

artificial variable—a temporary variable added to an = or > linear programmin constraint to facilitate solution when the initial basic solution is outside the solution spac

assignment method—a solution method for solving the assignment problem in whicl unique assignments equal to the rows or columns are sought in an iterative process

assignment problem—a variation of the transportation problem in which the suppl and demand at all sources and destinations equal one

balking—customers refusing to enter a waiting line

balanced transportation problem—a transportation problem in which total suppl from all sources exactly equals total demand at all destinations

basic feasible solution—the variables that have (nonzero) values at a solution poin as defined in a simplex tableau of a linear programming problem

Bayes's law—a formula for computing the posterior probability given marginal an conditional probabilities

beta distribution—a probability distribution used frequently in CPM/PERT analysi to describe activity times

bill of materials—a compilation of information on all raw materials, components, an subassemblies required for each end item in an MRP system

branch—a line in a network that connects pairs of nodes

branch and bound—an approach for solving integer programming problems in whicl the basic variables for the relaxed simplex solution are bounded with integer values an solved as subproblems

break-even analysis—a mathematical model resulting in a volume level that equate revenue and cost

calling population—the source of arrivals in a queuing system

carrying cost—costs associated with holding a certain stock of inventory on hand

chain—a sequence of connecting branches between two nodes in a network

chance-constrained goal programming—a technique for determining solutions that satisfice multiple criteria decision problems that involve elements of uncertainty for model parameters

channels—the number of parallel servers available for servicing arrivals in a queuing system

complementary slackness—a linear programming property that holds that for a positive basic value in the primal, the corresponding dual variable will equal zero

conditional probability—the probability of an event that is conditional on the occurrence of a prior event

conflict—a decision situation wherein the interests of two or more decision makers are in competition

conservation of flow—in a maximal flow network problem, the assumption that total flow into a node must exactly equal the total flow out of the node

constraint—a mathematical function that defines specific limitations or scarce resources in a management science problem

continuous variable—a variable that can have a fractional, noninteger value

convex programming—an approach for solving nonlinear programming problems in which the objective function and all constraints are convex functions

corner point—in linear programming, a possible solution point formed by the intersection of two constraints

crashing—the shortening of a CPM/PERT network by rushing one or more critical path activities to completion in less than normal time by devoting more resources to the activities

crash-time cost—the cost associated with crashing an activity in a CPM/PERT network

criterion variable—a mathematical symbol representing a measure for evaluating solutions, such as profit or cost

critical activities—activities along the critical path in a CPM/PERT network

critical path—the longest path through a CPM/PERT network

critical path method (CPM)—a network technique used for planning and scheduling of projects in which activities must be completed according to a precedence relationship

critical points—the endpoints of the domain of a variable

cutting plane approach—a technique for solving integer programming problems in which additional constraints are sequentially added to the optimal (relaxed) simplex solution until a feasible integer solution results

cycle—a sequence of connecting branches in a network that connects a single node to itself

cycling Markov process—a Markov transition matrix characterized by all zeroes in retention cells and all ones in nonretention cells

decision tree—a schematic diagram of a sequence of alternative decisions and the resul‌ of these decisions

decision variable—a mathematical symbol that represents the solution to a probler‌ in terms of a decision

decomposition—breaking down a dynamic programming problem into a sequence ‌ smaller subproblems or stages

degeneracy—(1) a condition in a linear programming problem created by a tie for th‌ pivot column, in which a series of solutions with the same objective function value ca‌ result; (2) a condition in a transportation problem in which the number of occupied cel‌ in a tableau must equal the number of rows plus the number of columns minus one ‌ a solution is not possible

descriptors—results that describe the behavior of a simulated system

deterministic—models developed under conditions of assumed certainty‌ nonprobabilistic

deviational variable—a variable representing the overachievement or underachieve‌ ment of a goal level in goal programming

directed branch—a branch in a network with a specified direction, commonly indicate‌ by a line with an arrow

discrete variable—a variable that can only equal whole, nonfractional, values

divisibility—a mathematical property that allows values to be fractional

domain—the range of values of a variable

dominance—when a particular strategy would be selected by one player in a gam‌ regardless of the strategy the other player selected

dual—an alternative form of a primal linear programming model that provides an ecc‌ nomic interpretation of the model resource parameters

dummy activity—an activity used in a CPM/PERT network to show a precedenc‌ relationship among activities but does not consume time or resources

dummy column—a column added to balance a transportation or assignment tablea‌ when supply exceeds demand

dummy row—a row added to balance a transportation or assignment tableau whe‌ demand exceeds supply

dynamic programming—a solution approach in which problems are subdivided int‌ smaller subproblems where decisions are made sequentially

earliest time—the point in time in a CPM/PERT network at which all activities leac‌ ing to a node have been completed

economic order quantity (EOQ) model—a classic, deterministic inventory model i‌ which the optimal order quantity is determined as a function of carrying, ordering, an‌ shortage costs

entering nonbasic variable—the variable that enters the basis in a simplex tablea‌ iteration

enumeration—successively evaluating all feasible solutions to a problem until the optimal solution is found

event—project milestones in a CPM/PERT network that occur at points in time typically signifying the beginning and/or end of project activities

exogenous variable—a variable that derives its value from outside the system being modeled and that typically is not controlled by the decision maker

expected opportunity loss—a decision-making criterion in which the expected regret experienced because of the selection of a decision alternative is minimized

expected value—the weighted average payoff for a given course of action in a decision situation computed by summing the payoffs for each action multiplied by the probabilities associated with each state of nature

expected value of perfect information—the maximum amount a decision maker might pay to obtain perfect information, computed by subtracting the expected return without perfect information from the expected return with perfect information

feasible solution—a solution that does not violate any of the model constraints

feasible solution space—a region bounded by the model constraints within which none of the solution values violate the constraints

finite queue—a queue that can accommodate only a limited number of arrivals

float—the amount of time an activity can be delayed in a CPM/PERT network without lengthening the critical path duration

free slack—the amount of time by which an activity in a CPM/PERT network can be delayed without causing any delay to its immediate successor activities

fundamental matrix—in Markov analysis, a matrix that gives the expected number of times a system will be in any nonabsorbing state before absorption occurs

fundamental primal-dual relationship—in a linear programming problem, the value of the primal objective function is bounded by the corresponding value of the dual objective function

game theory—a decision situation in which a decision maker is competing with other rational, goal seeking opponents

Gauss-Jordan method—an approach for solving a set of linear equations in which an equivalent set of equations to an original set with the same solution can be generated by replacing one of the original equations with another equation

goal constraint—a constraint in a goal programming model for which positive or negative deviation from a goal level is allowed

goal programming—a variation of linear programming in which there are multiple objectives instead of a single objective

gradient search methods—procedures for solving nonlinear programming problems in which a vector of the partial derivatives of the objective function are used to search for the maximum (or minimum) solution value along a nonlinear surface

Hurwicz criterion—a decision making criterion in which the decision maker multiplies the maximum payoff of each decision alternative by a coefficient of optimism, reflecting the decision maker's optimism, multiplying the minimum payoffs by one minus this value, and selecting the highest weighted total

identity matrix—a square matrix consisting of ones along the main diagonal and zeroes elsewhere

implementation—the practical use of a management science model

implicit enumeration—a method for solving zero-one integer programming problems in which a branch-and-bound procedure is used to force an infeasible but optimal solution to feasibility with solution values of zero and one

infeasible problem—a linear programming model for which there is no solution that simultaneously satisfies all system constraints

integer—values that are whole numbers and are not fractional

integer programming—a form of linear, mathematical programming in which solutions for the model variables are restricted to integer values

inverse transformation technique—a mathematical process for solving a function in terms of one of the variables, for use in a simulation

just-in-time—an inventory system developed by the Japanese in which a stage in a production system demands and withdraws in-process units from a preceding stage only at the rate and time the items are consumed, thus minimizing in-process inventory

kanban—the Japanese word for card, two of which control the stage-to-stage authorization for the release of in-process inventory in a just-in-time production process

Karush-Kuhn-Tucker conditions—conditions that provide the basis for recognizing candidates for an optimal solution to a nonlinear programming problem, based on calculus methods of solution

Kendall notation—standard notation summarizing the primary characteristics of a queuing model

Lagrange multipliers—a method for solving nonlinear problems in which the objective function and constraints are converted into a single unconstrained function

Laplace criterion—a decision-making criterion in which it is assumed that all states of nature are equally likely to occur and expected values for each outcome are computed accordingly

large M method—a procedure in linear programming in which an artificial variable is given a coefficient of positive or negative M, representing a large value, in the objective function so that the artificial variable will not be included in the optimal solution

latest time—the latest time an event in a CPM/PERT network can occur without delaying the completion of the project beyond the critical path time

lead time—a lag from the time an order is placed until it is received

least cost method—a method for determining the initial solution to a transportation problem by successively allocating to cells in the tableau with the lowest cost

leaving basic variable—the variable in the basis of the simplex tableau that is leaving the basic solution during an iteration

LINDO—a computer software package for solving linear programming problems

linear—mathematical relationships that are directly proportional, having a constant rate of change or slope

linear programming—a mathematical modelling technique for allocating scarce resources among one or more activities in order to maximize or minimize an objective, in which all the mathematical relationships are linear

management science—the applications of the methods and techniques of science and mathematics to problems of managerial decision making

marginal value—the maximum amount a decision maker might pay for the one additional unit of a resource in a linear programming problem

Markov chains—the successive future states of a Markov process

Markov process—a stochastic process for which the current stae of the system depends only on the immediately preceding state of the system

master production schedule—an outline of the production plans for all end items in an MRP system

materials requirement planning (MRP)—a computer-based production and inventory planning and control system employed primarily for products that are assemblies of component parts

matrix—a rectangular array of numbers arranged into rows and columns and enclosed within brackets

maximal flow problem—allocating flows in a capacitated network in order to maximize the total flow through the network from a source to a destination

maximax criterion—an optimistic decision-making criterion wherein the decision maker selects the alternative that represents the maximum of the maximum payoffs

maximin criterion—a conservative decision-making criterion wherein the minimum return for each decision alternative are compared and the alternative that yields the maximum of the minimum returns is selected

maximization problem—a linear programming model in which the objective function is being maximized

minimal spanning-tree problem—determining the route of connections between all points of a network, such that the total length of the connections is minimized

minimization problem—a linear programming model in which the objective function is being minimized

mixed integer problem—a linear programming model for which some of the variables are restricted to integer solution values and other values can have continuous values

mixed strategies—in a game each player will attempt to formulate a strategy that is indifferent to the opponent's strategy by randomly selecting among strategies according to a predefined plan in which each strategy is selected a percentage of the time

model—a mathematical representation of a problem

modified distribution method (MODI)—a procedure for determining the solution to a transportation problem that is a mathematical alternative to the stepping-stone method

modified simplex method—a solution method for goal programming problems similar to the simplex method

Monte Carlo sampling—a technique for selecting numbers randomly according to probability distribution for use in a trial run of a simulation

multiple criteria decision making—approaches to problems which seek the satisfactory achievement of several objectives instead of optimizing a single objective

multiple optimal—a problem for which there is more than one set of solution values that result in the same optimal objective function value

multistage sequential optimization—all previously determined optimal solution values at all previously evaluated stages incorporated into the cumulative return value at the stage under consideration

negative exponential distribution—a continuous probability distribution commonly used to describe service time in a queuing system

network—a diagram made up of nodes and branches that represent a precedence relationship among activities or routes and paths in a system

node—one of a set of junction points in a network, commonly denoted by a circle

noninstantaneous receipt model—a variation of the EOQ model in which inventory is replenished in a constant stream over time

nonlinear programming—mathematical programming problems in which some or all of the mathematical relationships are not linear

normal distribution—a probability distribution that approximates a bell-shaped curve in shape

northwest corner method—a method for determining the initial solution to a transportation problem in which an initial allocation is made to the cell in the upper left hand corner of the tableau and subsequent allocations are to adjacent cells

objective function—a mathematical relationship defining the objective of a problem

operations research—the application of scientific and mathematical methods to operational problems

operating characteristics—measures describing the performance of a queuing system

ordering costs—costs associated with replenishing the stock of inventory on hand

parameter—generally constant numerical values included in the formulation of the relationship among variables

partial differentiation—a form of differentiation in which all but one of the independent variables are treated as constants

path—a sequence of connecting branches between two nodes in a network in which direction along the path is specified

payoff matrix—a table showing the payoffs for a player that result from all combinations of strategies from each player in a game

penalty cost—in VAM, the difference between the lowest cost and the next highest cost in a row or column of a transportation tableau defined as the penalty for making an allocation that does not have the lowest cost

permanent set—a set of nodes in a shortest route problem for which the shortest routes have been determined

phases—the number of sequential service steps each arrival must go through in a queuing system

pivot column—the column in the simplex tableau that corresponds to the entering nonbasic variable

pivot row—the row in the simplex tableau that corresponds to the leaving basic variable

Poisson distribution—a discrete probability distribution commonly used to define arrivals in a queuing system

posterior probability—the marginal probability of an event altered by additional information

postoptimality analysis—the analysis of parameter changes and their effect on linear programming solutions; also known as sensitivity analysis

preemptive priority—the ranking of goals according to the preference of the decision maker in goal programming

primal—the original form of a linear programming model

probabilistic—models developed under conditions of uncertainty

product structure record—a compilation of information on all raw materials, components, and subassemblies required for each end item in an MRP system; also called a bill of materials

prohibited assignment—an assignment in an assignment problem that cannot be made, and as such, is assigned a large cost, M

prohibited route—a route in a transportation problem over which it is not possible to ship items

proportionality—the rate of change, or slope, of a functional relationship that is constant

pseudorandom numbers—random numbers generated using a numerical technique instead of a physical process

pull system—a production process in which a stage demands and withdraws in-process units from the preceding stage only at the rate and time the stage consumes the items, typical of Japanese just-in-time systems

pure strategy—a strategy that neither player would risk changing in a game

push system—a production process in which a forecast of demand sets inventory levels at each stage in the process

quadratic programming—nonlinear programming problems in which the objective function is a concave quadratic function and the constraints are linear, thus allowing solution by the simplex method when the Karush-Kuhn-Tucker conditions are applied

quantity discount model—a variation of the EOQ model in which there is a price discount for goods purchased to replenish inventory, if they are purchased in sufficient quantity

queue—a line of items, units, or customers waiting for service

queue discipline—the decision rule that prescribes the order in which items in a queue will be served

random process generator—a process for generating values of a random variable using the Monte Carlo technique in a simulation

recurrent sets—a Markov chain in which the process may be trapped within a set of states; also known as a generalized trapping state

recursive return function—the total accumulated return at a stage in a dynamic programming problem, computed as the stage return plus the return at the previous stage given the input state and decision at the previous stage

regret criterion—a decision-making criterion in which the decision maker attempts to minimize the regret resulting from a wrong decision, where regret is computed by subtracting the alternative payoffs for each state of nature from the maximum payoff for that state, and selecting the alternative that minimizes the maximum regrets

relaxed solution—the simplex solution values with no integer restrictions in an integer programming problem

reorder point—the inventory level at which an order is placed to replenish the inventory stock

right-hand-side value—the value to the right of an equality or inequality sign in a linear programming constraint

risk—a condition that exists in a decision situation when perfect information is not available, but the probabilities that certain outcomes will occur can be estimated

saddle point—a point of equilibrium in a game wherein neither player will risk changing their strategy

safety stock—extra inventory kept on hand to avoid inventory shortages when the demand during lead time is not known with certainty

satisficing—seeking a satisfactory level of achievement for several goals as opposed to maximizing a single objective

scientific method—a methodology for the analysis of problems that includes observation, problem definition, model construction, model validation, problem solution, and implementation

search technique—a procedure for searching through a set of different simulation results until the best result is found

sensitivity analysis—the analysis of parameter changes and their effect on linear programming solutions; also known as postoptimality analysis

server—the individual or mechanism that serves a customer in a queuing system

service level—a specified percentage of total customers whose orders are met on a regular basis

shadow prices—the solution values for the dual in a linear programming problem indicating the marginal value of resources

shared slack—slack shared among several concurrent activities in a CPM/PERT network

shortage costs—costs that occur when demand exceeds the supply of inventory on hand and customer orders cannot be met

shortest route problem—a problem in which the objective is to find the shortest route from an origin to one or more destinations through a network of alternative routes

simplex method—a set of mathematical steps based on matrix algebra for solving a linear programming problem

simplex tableau—a table in which the steps of the simplex method are carried out

simulation—a means for deriving measures of performance of a complex system by conducting sampling experiments on a mathematical model of the system over time

simulation game—the use of a computerized simulation model to permit participants to make decisions and observe the behavior of the system as a result of those decisions

sink node—the final destination, or end, of a network

slack—the amount of time an activity can be delayed in a CPM/PERT network without lengthening the critical path duration

slack variable—a variable added to the left-hand side of a $\leq$ constraint in order to convert it to an equation in a linear programming model

source node—the origin of a network

stage optimization—determining the optimal decision at each stage of a dynamic programming model for each possible input state value

stages—the decomposed subproblems of a dynamic programming problem

state variable—the status of the system resulting from the previous stage decision in a dynamic programming problem

steady state—(1) the state values that a Markov system tends to stabilize at as the number of repetitions grows larger; (2) constant, average values that the operating characteristics of a queuing system will assume after the system has been in operation for a period of time

stepping-stone method—a method for determining the solution to a transportation problem that reflects the steps of the simplex method

stochastic process—a probabilistic model in which the current state of a system depends on all previous states

subjective probability—a measure of one's degree of belief in future outcomes

surplus variable—a variable subtracted from the left-hand side of a $\geq$ constraint in order to convert it to an equation in a linear programming model

system constraint—a constraint in a goal programming model for which positive and negative deviation is prohibited

system state—the status of a probabilistic system at a point in time

total slack—the maximum amount of time available to schedule an activity in a CPM/PERT network minus the estimated duration of the activity

transient state—a state i is a transient state if there exists a state j that is reachable from state i, but the reverse is not true (state i is not reachable from state j)

transition function—a function that describes precisely how the stages of a dynamic programming model are interconnected

transition matrix—a matrix of transition probabilities for a Markov process

transition probability—the probability of moving between states in a Markov process

transportation problem—a linear programming problem in which items are transported from a number of sources, with limited supplies, to a number of destinations with specific demands, at the minimum cost

transportation tableau—a table format for the solution of a transportation problem

transshipment problem—a variation of the transportation problem in which items can be shipped from sources to intermediate points before they are shipped to their ultimate destinations

trapping state—a state in a Markov transition matrix that is impossible to leave; also known as an absorbing state

traveling salesman problem—a network problem for which the objective is to determine the sequence in which all nodes are visited once at the minimum travel distance

truncated queue—a queue of finite length

unbalanced problem—a transportation or assignment problem in which supply and demand are not equal

unbounded problem—a model in which the objective function can increase indefinitely without reaching a constraint boundary

undirected branch—a branch in a network in which items may flow or travel in either direction

unrestricted variable—a decision variable in a linear programming model that can take on negative as well as positive values

utility—a measure of an individual decision maker's preference for monetary return as opposed to avoiding risk

utility curve—a graph that relates utility values to dollar values

utilization factor—the proportion of time a server is busy in a queuing system

value of a game—one player's gain and another player's loss in a game

variable—a mathematical symbol in a model or function that can vary over a range of values

variable elimination—a procedure for making a zero-one integer programming problem simpler by eliminating one decision variable from the problem if there is an equality constraint

vector—in a Markov process, a one-dimensional matrix

Vogel's approximation method (VAM)—a method for determining the initial solution to a transportation problem in which allocations are made in a manner that minimizes the penalty cost for selecting a wrong tableau cell for allocation

weighted goals—a method for ranking goals within the same priority level of a goal programming model

zero-one integer problem—a linear programming problem in which the variable solution values are restricted to zero or one

zero-sum game—in a game situation the sum of one player's positive payoff and the other player's negative loss is zero